Integrated Marketing Communications

Visit the *Integrated Marketing Communications, 2nd ed.* Companion Website at **www.booksites.net/pickton** to find valuable learning material including:

For students
- PowerPoint presentation offering a summary outline of the text
- Expanded case study material with questions
- Quiz words: crossword style quiz concerning IMC concepts
- Revision route map: indicates where principle IMC topics are covered in the text
- Links to relevant sites on the web
- List of useful addresses and organisations
- Internet resource finder
- An online glossary to explain key terms

For lecturers
- PowerPoint slides that can be downloaded and used as OHTs
- Expanded case study material from main text with questions
- Additional case studies
- Contents comparison of the 1st edition and 2nd edition of the text
- Additional assessment questions, tutorial assignments and current issues projects
- Solutions to student quiz words
- Chapter by chapter overviews
- Details of CD
- Topic route map: indicates where principle IMC topics are covered in the text

Second Edition

Integrated Marketing Communications

David Pickton ● Amanda Broderick

FT Prentice Hall
FINANCIAL TIMES

An imprint of **Pearson Education**
Harlow, England • London • New York • Boston • San Francisco • Toronto
Sydney • Tokyo • Singapore • Hong Kong • Seoul • Taipei • New Delhi
Cape Town • Madrid • Mexico City • Amsterdam • Munich • Paris • Milan

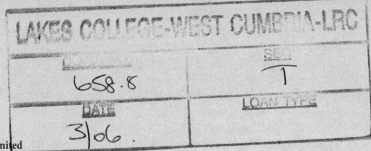
Pearson Education Limited

Edinburgh Gate
Harlow
Essex CM20 2JE
England

and Associated Companies around the world

Visit us on the World Wide Web at:
www.pearsoned.co.uk

_____

First published 2001
Second edition published 2005

ISBN 0 273 67645 8

British Library Cataloguing-in-Publication Data
A catalogue record for this book is available from the British Library

Library of Congress Cataloging-in-Publication Data

Pickton, David.
    Integrated marketing communications / David Pickton, Amanda Broderick.--2nd ed.
        p. cm
    Includes bibliographical references and index.
    ISBN 0-273-67645-8
    1. Communication in marketing. I. Broderick, Amanda. II. Title.

    HF5415.123.P53 2004
    658.8'02--dc22   20044047715

10 9 8 7 6 5 4 3 2 1
09 08 07 06 05

Typeset in 10/12 pt Minion by 30.
Printed and bound by Ashford Colour Press, Gosport, Hants.

The publishers' policy is to use paper manufactured from sustainable forests.

Short contents

Contents

Contents

The field of integrated marketing communications (IMC)

Integrated marketing communications recognises the need to plan and build-up all relevant marketing communications so that they work together in harmony to greatest effect and with greatest efficiency. *Integrated Marketing Communications*, 2nd edition does just this – describes the scope of marketing communications by providing a comprehensive coverage of the topic in a unique 'integrated' format.

Target audience

Geared toward both undergraduate and post-graduate students studying marketing communications as part of a core degree programme, this book is ideal for courses on marketing communications, advertising, public relations, sales promotions, and direct marketing. The structure allows instructors to use the book flexibly to suit their individual teaching requirements.

Book structure

Chapters 1 and 2 set the scene in describing the scope of marketing communications and what is meant by *integrated* marketing communications. **Part 1** delves into the marketing communications process and shows how this process flows from sender to receiver. **Part 2** focuses on the management aspects of marketing communications. Topics covered include planning and plans; organisational implications; agency operations; research and analysis; audiences; budgets, objectives, strategies and tactics; creative, media, and production implementation; and control and evaluation. **Part 3** explores the actual integrated marketing communications mix – the mix of ingredients that work together to create successful and effective marketing. This includes coverage of public relations, sponsorship, advertising, direct marketing communications, sales promotions, merchandising, point of sale, packaging, exhibitions, trade shows, personal selling and sales management. The authors provide a conceptual framework for each part as indicated. Visual models open each part to help reinforce the key segments that are vital in integrated marketing communications.

Key features and pedagogy

● An **Integrated Marketing Communications Framework** consists of three IMC Models and is used throughout the book. Each part of the book features a model and each chapter explains an aspect of the model. The models, therefore, provide graphic outlines of integrated marketing communications, highlight significant aspects of IMC and, collectively, describe all relevant aspects of IMC.

- **Professional perspectives** offer insight into the viewpoints and experiences of actual practitioners. Companies featured include Royal Mail, Experian, Icon Brand Navigation, Sinclair Marketing Services, BMP, O&M and others.
- **NEW! Integrated real-world case studies** illustrate marketing communication issues that face the marketing manager. Integrated into each part of the book, these include Concern, Škoda and Pampers. Further exploration of each case can be found on the CD which accompanies this book.
- **In-View** boxes provide specific examples or highlight specific problems or issues that further illustrate issues that marketing professionals face on a daily basis.
- **NEW! Warning flashes**, placed in the margin, help clarify complex issues and help reinforce key points.
- **NEW! Need to know checkpoints** drive home important details that nurture good decision-making.
- **Margin definitions** provide handy definitions of key terms.
- **Strong End-of-Chapter Pedagogy** clinches all the key issues that are presented in each chapter. These include Self-review questions, Projects, Comprehensive references, and Selected further reading.
- **Full glossary** serves as an additional resource for students.

CD

Ground-breaking CD!

Unique and innovative, *Integrated Marketing Communications, 2e,* now comes with a CD with robust and visually tantalising materials to enhance learning.

CD resources

1 Presentation to provide students with an overview of the book and introduce them to the key models and principles of Integrated Marketing Communications (IMC). This slide show alerts students to the interactive component of the text and serves as a useful revision aid.

2 Three integrating case studies relevant to each of the three parts of the book. Within each case study section are:

- Powerpoint presentation providing an overview of the cases
- Extended version of each 'part' case study (Pampers, Škoda and Concern)
- Creative material including tv, poster and radio advertisements
- Summary of chapter questions relating to each part of the book
- Further information including references, articles and directions to further material

3 Further resources, this section includes:

- Internet Resource Locator – a list of web addresses indexed by topic
- Revision Route Map which identifies where to find the key issues in the text
- Glossary from the main text

About the authors

David Pickton is Head of the Marketing Department at De Montfort University. He is on the editorial board of the *Journal of Marketing Communications* and *Marketing Intelligence and Planning*. He is also a fellow of the Chartered Institute of Marketing and of the RSA. He has many years experience of lecturing and business consultancy.

Amanda Broderick is Senior Lecturer in Marketing and Head of Research in the Marketing Group at Aston Business School. She has been awarded numerous research excellence prizes from benefactors including the European Marketing Academy, the Chartered Institute of Marketing and the Academy of Marketing; and has over 30 articles in journals, books and conference proceedings. Her teaching and research focuses on marketing psychology, and consultancy and management development clients include Procter & Gamble, Tesco, the NEC Group, Carillion and Promodes (France).

This book is dedicated to our loves:
Miggie, Anna, Michael, Paul, Harry and Edward
And to others we hold dear

To our readers:
Knowledge is as a fine wine.
May you drink, and having drunk,
may your thirst be quenched ... until tomorrow

Acknowledgements

We are indebted to many people and grateful for their support for both editions. We thank the following for their contributions to specific chapters:

Jim Blythe, Chapters 3 and 30
John Gammon, Chapter 28
Phil Garton, Chapter 4
Bob Hartley, Chapter 12
David Hudson and Kit Jackson, Chapter 15
Chris Vaughn-Jones, Chapters 16 and 23
Mike Pedley, Chapter 18
Tony Proctor, Chapter 20
Trevor Slack and John Amis, Chapter 25
Michael Starkey and Tracy Harwood, Chapter 31
Alan Tapp, Chapter 27
Ray Wright, Chapter 26

We would also like to thank those who contributed to Professional Perspectives and those who assisted us in preparing the integrative case study material in the book and on the CD.

Matti Alderson, ex-ASA
Steve Almond, Barclaycard
James Best BMP DDB
David Bond, ex-Royal Mail
Professor Leslie de Chernatony, Birmingham
    University
Barry Clarke, Clarke Hooper
Barry Cleverdon, The NEC Group
Will Collin, Naked Communications
Professor Susan Douglas, New York Stern University
Professor Gordon Foxall, Cardiff University
Harriet Frost, OMP
Robert Heath, Icon Brand Navigation
Adrian Hitchen, SRI
Paul Kilminster, Northcliffe Press Ltd
Bob Lawrence, West Midland Safari and Leisure Park
Dr Nick Lee, Aston University
Colin McDonald, McDonald Research
Graeme McCorkell, IDM

Peter McKenna, Smurfit Communications
Derek Morris, Unity
Steve Paterson, Hamilton Wright
Mark Patron, Claritas (Europe)
Ian Ramsden, The Hothouse
Professor John Saunders, Aston University
Professor Don Schultz, Northwestern University
Andrew Sinclair, Sinclair Marketing Services
Keith Slater, Ingersoll Rand
David Thomas, Thomas Douglas
Adrian Vickers, Abbott Mead Vickers BBDO
Richard Webber, Experian

We also thank the following for their valuable comments in pre-revision reviews:

Conor Carroll – University of Limerick
Janine Dermody – University of Gloucestershire
Aul Hewer – University of Stirling
Hana Hjalmerson – Stockholm School of Economics
Kathleen Hughes – Dublin Institute of Technology
Tore Kristensen – Copenhagen Business School
Caroline Oates – Sheffield Hallam University
Peeter Verlegh – Erasmus University
Ray Wright – Anglia Polytechnic

We finally thank our editors, production staff and all those involved in bringing this 2nd edition to fruition. These include: Thomas Sigel, Senior Acquisitions Editor; Janey Webb, Development Editor; Nicola Chilvers, Senior Desk Editor; Peter Hooper, Editorial Assistant; Colin Reed, Senior Designer; Adam Renvoize, Senior Designer and Amanda Thomas, Project Control Team Leader. To these understanding folk go our apologies alongside our thanks. Only we and the publishers know the trials and tribulations involved. Patience is a wonderful gift. Publishers appear to hold it in good measure. It was certainly needed.

David Pickton and Amanda Broderick
Spring 2004

Publisher's acknowledgements

We are grateful to the following for permission to reproduce copyright material:

In View 1.1 *Strand Cigarette Advertisement*, reproduced by kind permission of The History of Advertising Trust Archive; Ch1 Project *Virgin Atlantic logo*, reproduced by kind permission of Virgin Atlantic Airways, Copyright © Virgin Atlantic Airways 2003; Exhibit 2.3 from table from *Integrated Marketing Communications*, Butterworth Heinemann Ltd., (Linton, L., and Morley, K., 1995), reproduced by kind permission of Butterworth Heinemann Publishers, a division of Reed Educational & Professional Publishing Ltd.; Ch3 Cadbury Pack Shots image reproduced courtesy of Cadbury Trebor Bassett; In View 3.2 *Michelin logo*, reproduced by kind permission of Michelin Tyre plc; Exhibit 3.4 from table from '*An information processing model of advertising effectiveness*', by McGuire, W.J., in *Behavioral and Management Science in Marketing*, Davis, H.L. and Silk, A.J., eds., Ronald Press, (1978), Copyright © John Wiley & Sons, Inc. 1978. This material is reproduced by permission of John Wiley & Sons, Inc.; Exhibit 3.5 from table on pp. 39 to 52 from '*Construction and Validation of a scale to measure celebrity endorser's perceived expertise, trustworthiness and attractiveness*', in *Journal of Advertising, 19 (3), 1990*, CtC Press (1990), reprinted with permission, CtC Press 2000. All Rights Reserved; In View 3.5 *AA logo*, reproduced by kind permission of The AA; Exhibit 3.7 adapted from table from *Social Learning Theory*, Prentice-Hall, (Pearson Education, Inc.), (Bandura, A., 1977); Exhibits 4.3 and 16.1 adapted from a table and a figure from Sally Dibb, Lyndon Simkin, William Pride and O.C. Ferrall, *Marketing: Concepts and strategies, Third European Edition*, Copyright © 1997 by Houghton Mifflin Company. Used with permission; Exhibit 4.8 from figure from *Attention and Effort*, Prentice-Hall, (Kahneman, D., 1973); Exhibit 5.4 figure *The New PHD*, The New PHD Agency, Copyright © 1999 The New PHD Agency; Exhibit 5.5 from table from *The Fundamentals of Advertising*, Butterworth Heinemann Ltd., (Wilmshurst, J., 1985), reproduced by kind permission of Butterworth Heinemann Publishers, a division of Reed Educational & Professional Publishing Ltd.; Exhibit 8.2 adapted from information from *Mintel's European Marketing Intelligence, Country Special Report: France, Country Special Report: Germany, Country Special Report: UK, Country Special Report: Italy, and Country Special Report: Spain*, Mintel International Group Ltd., (1994); Exhibit 8.5 adapted from table from Cateora, P., *International Marketing, 10th Edition*, Irwin, (1997), reproduced with the permission of The McGraw-Hill Companies; Exhibit 8.6 from table from *Global Marketing Management, 6th Edition*, Prentice-Hall, (Pearson Education, Inc.), (Keegan, W.J., 1999); Exhibit 11.3 adapted from figure from '*Mirror, mirror on the wall*', in *Market Research Society Survey Magazine, 1 June 1983*, The Market Research Society (MORI), (Worcester, R., and Lewis, S., 1983); In View 11.3 adapted from table and text from '*Total Research Equitrend Survey*', in *Marketing*, 12 February 1998, p. 24, Reproduced from *Marketing* magazine with the permission of the copyright owner, Haymarket Business Publications Limited; Exhibit 11.4 adapted from pp. 17–50 from '*European Retailing: Convergences, Differences and Perspectives*', in *International Retailing: Trends and Strategies*, Pitman, (Tordjman, A.; eds., McGoldrick, P.J., and Davies, G., 1995), reprinted with the permission of Pearson Education; In View 11.4 from text and figures *Maluma* and *Taketa* on p. 11 from *Communication and Design*, by Pilditch, J.G.C., The McGraw-Hill Publishing Company Limited, (1970), reproduced with the kind permission of the McGraw-Hill Publishing Company; Exhibit 11.5 adapted from a table from '*The Perception Question*', in *Marketing*, 12 February 1998, p. 24–25, Reproduced from *Marketing* magazine with the permission of the copyright owner, Haymarket Business Publications Limited; In View 11.5 from a table from '*Brand of the Year*', in *Marketing*, 11 December 1997, p. 27, Reproduced from *Marketing* magazine with the permission of the copyright owner, Haymarket Business Publications Limited; Exhibit 11.7 adapted from table and text from '*How superbrands score over rivals*', in *Marketing*, 8 October 1998, p. 9, Reproduced from *Marketing* magazine with the permission of the copyright owner, Haymarket Business Publications Limited; Exhibit 12.1 from figure from *The Management of Sales and Customer Relations: book of readings*, Thomson International Press, (Hartley, R., and Starkey, M.W. (eds.), 1996), reproduced by permission of Thomson Publishing Services; Exhibit 12.2 from figure from Abberton Associates/CPM International, Thame, UK, *Balancing the Selling Equation*, 1997; Exhibits 13.2, 13.4, 13.8, 13.11 from adaptations of figures and tables on p. 168 from *How to Plan Advertising*, Cassell, in association with the Account Planning Group, (Cooper, A. (ed.), 1997), reproduced by permission of Thomson Publishing Services; In View 13.5 from Butterfield, L. (1997), *Excellence in Advertising*, The Institute of Practitioners in Advertising, Butterworth Heinemann; Exhibit 15.7 adapted from a table from '*We can work it out*', in *Marketing*, 23 January 1997, pp. 22–24, (Dye, P., 1997), Reproduced from *Marketing* magazine with the permission of the copyright owner, Haymarket Business Publications Limited; Exhibit 16.3 adapted from table on p. 43 from *Survey of Market Research*, American Marketing Association, (Kinnear, T.C. and Root, A.R., 1988); Exhibit 17.3 from table from *Competitive Positioning: Key to Market Strategy*, (Hooley, G.J., and Saunders, J.A., 1993), reprinted with the permission of Pearson Education; Exhibit 17.4 from table from Bartos, R. (1976), quoted in *Behavioural Aspects of Marketing*, Butterworth-Heinemann, (Williams, K.C., 1981); Exhibit 17.5 from table on p. 34 from '*The concept and application of life style segmentation*', in *Journal of Marketing*, Vol. 38, January 1974, American Marketing Association, (Plummer, J.T., 1974); Exhibit 17.9 from table on p. 12 from '*Cooperate to Accumulate*', in *New Perspectives*, June 1997, Adams Business Media, (Ward, M., 1997); Exhibit 17.10 *The ACORN Classification System*, from CACI Information Services, Copyright © 1999 CACI Limited, All rights reserved. ACORN and CACI are registered trademarks of CACI Limited; Exhibit 17.11 from table on p. 33 from '*Profile for Profits*', in *New Perspectives, July 1996a*, Adams Business Media, (Ward, M., 1996); Exhibit 17.12 *Prizm*, promotional leaflet, (1997), reproduced by kind permission of Claritas; In View 17.5 from CACI Information Services, Copyright © 1999 CACI Limited, All rights reserved. LifestylesUK and CACI are registered trademarks of CACI Limited; Exhibit 17.13 from figure from *The Multimedia Guide to Mosaic*, Experian, (1998); Exhibit 19.3 adapted from table from *Integrated Marketing Communications: Pulling it Together and Making it Work*, NTC Business Books, (Schultz, D., Tannenbaum, S.I., and Lauterborn, R.F., 1994); Exhibit 19.6 from figure from Colley, R. (1961), *Defining Goals for Measured Advertising Results*, Copyright © 1999 Association of National advertisers, Inc. All rights reserved. Reprinted by permission. The ANA book *Defining Goals for Measured Advertising Results* from which this exhibit is taken may be purchased online at www.ana.net; Exhibit 19.7 from figure from Belch, G. and Belch, M.A. (1998), *Advertising and Promotion: an Integrated Marketing Communications Perspective, 4th Edition*, McGraw-Hill, reproduced with permission of The McGraw-Hill Companies; Exhibit 19.8 from table from Rossiter, J., and Percy, L. (1997), *Advertising Communications and Promotion Management, 2nd Edition*, McGraw-Hill, reproduced with permission of The McGraw-Hill Companies; Table 21A.1, Figures 21A.1, 21A.2, 21A.3 from table and graphs from RAJAR 1995 and RAJAR W 196 by permission of RAJAR Ltd.; Exhibit 21.9 adapted from figure from *Marketing Management, 10th Edition*, Prentice-Hall, (Pearson Education, Inc.), (Kotler, P., 2000); Exhibit 22.13 from figure from Speirs, H.M. (1992), *Introduction to Printing Technology*, British Printing Industries Federation, reproduced by kind permission of H.M. Speirs, author of *Introduction to Printing Technology*, 1992,

Acknowledgements

BPIF, London; Exhibit 23.4 adapted from figure from *Marketing Communications Strategy*, BPP Publishing Ltd., (Betts, P., Huntingdon, S., Pulford, A., and Warnaby, G., 1995), Copyright © BPP Publishing Ltd. 1995; Exhibit 24.2 adapted from figure from '*Marketing and Public Relations*', in *Journal of Marketing*, Vol. 42, No.4, 1978, pp. 13–20, American Marketing Association, (Kotler, P. and Mindak, W., 1978); Exhibit 30.3 adapted from table from *Assessing trade show functions and performance: an exploratory study*, in *Journal of Marketing*, Vol. 51, 1987, pp. 87–94, American Marketing Association, (Kerin, R.A., and Cron, W.L., 1987); Exhibit 31.2 from figure from *Negotiation Skills Trainer Manual*, Huthwaite International, Copyright © 1998 Huthwaite Research Group Limited; Exhibit 31.4 adapted from figure from *Making Major Sales*, Gower Press, (Rackham, N., 1990), Copyright © 1990 Huthwaite Research Group Limited, SPIN® is a registered trademark of Huthwaite Research Group Limited; National Statistics, National Statistics website: www.statistics.gov.uk, © 2001 Crown Copyright, Crown copyright material is reproduced with the permission of the Controller of HMSO; Exhibits 31.6 and 31.7 from figures on pp. 9–21, from '*From Key account Selling to Key Account Management*', in *Journal of Marketing Practice: Applied Marketing Science, Vol. 1, No. 1,* MCB University Press Limited, (Millman, T., and Wilson, K., 1995); Plate 1 *Tony Blair Speech: F/L at Podium*, Picture NO. 272812–85, reproduced by kind permission of the Press Association Photo Library; Plate 2 *St Michael at Marks and Spencer logo*, Copyright © Marks and Spencer plc.; Amazon.com is a registered trademark of Amazon.com, Inc. in the U.S. and/or other countries. Copyright © 2000 Amazon.com, Inc. All rights reserved; Plate 5 Häagen Dazs advertisement, supplied by the Advertising Archive Ltd., Copyright © The Pillsbury Company; Plate 6 from screen shot of Amazon.com® web-site, Copyright © 2000 Amazon.com, Inc. Amazon.com is a registered trademark of Amazon.com, Inc. in the U.S. and/or other countries. Copyright © 2000 Amazon.com, Inc. All rights reserved; Plate 8 *BT 1998 World Cup* advertisement, British Telecommunications plc and Craik Jones Watson Mitchell Voelkel Ltd.; Plates 9 and 10 Benetton advertisements, Modus Publicity, on behalf of Benetton; Plate 11 *ASA advertisement*, reproduced by kind permission of the Advertising Standards Authority; Plate 13 *Respect for Animals advertisement*, reproduced by kind permission of Respect for Animals, Copyright © www.respectforanimals.com; Plate 14 *Pretty Polly 'Legs' advertisement*, reproduced by kind permission of Pretty Polly Ltd and Sara Lee; Plate 15 from Playtex Wonderbra 'Hello Boys' advertisement, Copyright © 2000 Playtex Limited, reproduced by kind permission of Sara Lee Intimates UK Limited; Plates 17 and 18 *MOSAIC Clever Capitalists* and *MOSAIC Profiling of Leicester*, Experian Ltd; Plate 19 photographs of Fosters Ice 'street art' campaign reproduced by kind permission of Pd3 Tully and Co.; Plate 20 *British Airways Image* reproduced by kind permission of British Airways; Plate 21 *Tango*, Britvic Soft Drinks Ltd. We are grateful to The Advertising Archive for supplying the following advertisements: French Connection; Häagen-Dazs; Pretty Polly and Wonderbra.

Adams Business Media for the following articles: 'Using lifestyle information for cross-selling' and 'Using segmentation products for retail location' published in *New Perspectives* July 1996; American Marketing Association for the article 'Maybe we should start all over with an IMC organization' published in *Marketing News* 25th October 1993; BUPA and The Chartered Institute of Marketing for the article 'Strong Vital Signs' published in *Marketing Business* September 2002; Butterworth-Heinemann Ltd for the articles 'Positioning a new car model as value for money' by I Linton and K Morely 1995 and 'Clerical Medical' from *Excellence in Advertising* by L Butterfield 1997; Centaur Communications for an extract concerning envelope design by P Farrow published in *Precision Marketing* 12th October 1998; The Chartered Institute of Marketing for the following articles: 'editorial', 'Latin Spirit', 'Selling Responsibility', 'Terminology Confusion' and 'Your cheque is in the (e)mail' published in *Marketing Business* June 2002; 'Getting away from it all' published in Marketing Business July/August 2002; 'Top 10 Advertising Agencies in the World' published in *Marketing Business* September 2002; 'Building Brand Image', '10 million tick electoral roll opt-out box' and 'Corporate Colours should be registered' published in *Marketing Business* February 2003; 'Put your website on the map' published in *Marketing Business* March 2003; 'Eat, drink and be healthy' by R Gray published in *Marketing Business* May 2003; 'Shock Value' by I Schlater published in *Marketing Business* July/August 2003 and 'Keeping Promises' by P Bartram published in *Marketing Business* October 2003; Concern for information about their charitable company 2003; The Economist Newspaper Limited for the articles 'The Internet improves on direct mail' published in *The Economist* 27th April 1996 and 'A survey of the software industry' published in *The Economist* 25th May 1996; Elsevier Limited for extracts adapted from *Public Relations Techniques* by T Hunt and J Grunig 1994; *Excellence in Advertising: The IPA Guide to Best Practice* edited by L Butterfield 1997 and 'Telemarketing at Simon Jersey' from *CIM Handbook* by Michael Starkey 1997; Experian for the article 'How Insurance companies can use segmentation products' published in *Social Climbers or Mobile Networkers: Customer classification systems designed to detect fraudulent or inflated claims* by S Hall 1998; Michael Finn for the article 'He knows a man who can' by M Finn published as 'Integration once again rears its not so ugly head' *Marketing Magazine* June 1994; Haymarket Business Publications Limited for the following articles: 'The Art of Planning' published in *Promotions and Incentives* by Crawford April 1994; 'Award winning exhibitor – The Marketing Exhibition Effectiveness Awards' published in *Marketing* 1996; 'Coke can get in shape to battle copycat brands' by Marshall published in *Marketing Magazine* 1st August 1996; 'Toyota launch New Year sponsorship deal with ITV' by Cook published in *Campaign* 19th December 1997; 'Pointing the way to PR' by R Cobb published in *Marketing Magazine* 12th March 1998 and 'Integrated Tunisia' published in *Marketing Magazine* 10th September 1998; Hewlett-Packard Limited for the article 'Computer-Aided sales support at Hewlett-Packard' published in *HP World* March 1988; Institute of Practitioners in Advertising for an article from *Success of Advertising* by IPA; Marketing Week for an extract from 'Check out in-store tools' published in *Marketing Week* 3rd July 1997 36–37; McGraw-Hill Publishing Company for the articles 'Customer Contact Management at RS Components' published in *The Business and Marketing Environment* by Palmer and Hartley and an extract from *A Preface to Marketing Management* 7th edition by J Peter and J Donnolley 1997; Media Week for the articles 'Foster's Ice – Cool!' published in 'The Media Week Awards 1996-The Finalists', *Media Week* 1996b and 'Pepsi turn blue as they see themselves in the mirror' published in 'Media Coup of the Year', *Media Week* 1997; NTC/Contemporary Publishing Group for the article 'Social norms and De Beers advertising campaign' from *Integrated Marketing Communications* by Don Schultz © 1993; Origin Publishing for the article 'Customer information and service at Post and Telekom Austria' adapted from 'PTA installs Brite's IVR to improve Customer Service' published in *Focus Magazine* Autumn 1997; Public Relations Institute of New Zealand for the PRINZ Code of Ethics published on www.prinz.org.nz; Quantum Publishing for the article 'Eight options for programme sponsorship' by S Armstrong published in *Media Week* March 1996; and Thomson Learning for an extract from an advertising campaign for Kit Kat by Shelbourne and Baskin as published in *How to Plan Advertising* edited by A Cooper.

We are grateful to the Financial Times Limited for permission to reprint the following material:

In View 6.1 New ways to sell cars, © *Financial Times*, 7 June 1995; In View 11.1 Marketing emotional branding, © *Financial Times*, 18 February 2000; In View 15.3 Dream teams define relationships, © *Financial Times*, 7 April 1997.

In some instances we have been unable to trace the owners of copyright material, and we would appreciate any information that would enable us to do so.

An Introduction to Integrated Marketing Communications

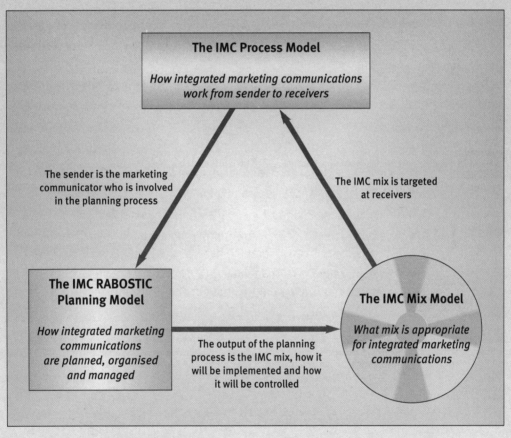

The IMC Process Model

How integrated marketing communications work from sender to receivers

The sender is the marketing communicator who is involved in the planning process

The IMC mix is targeted at receivers

The IMC RABOSTIC Planning Model

How integrated marketing communications are planned, organised and managed

The output of the planning process is the IMC mix, how it will be implemented and how it will be controlled

The IMC Mix Model

What mix is appropriate for integrated marketing communications

The Integrated Marketing Communications (IMC) Framework

Chapter 1

What is marketing communications?

Objectives

- To introduce the concept and meaning of marketing communications
- To identify the various components of marketing communications
- To highlight the importance of understanding target audiences
- To present the IMC Framework and the three models of marketing communications which form the basis of the three parts of this book
- To provide 'signposts' to identify where key aspects of marketing communications appear throughout the book

Professional perspective

David Pickton and Amanda Broderick

Marketing communications bridges the gap between an organisation and its many stakeholders. It is the 'face' of the organisation that its audiences learn to know and respect. Marketing communications is pervasive. It occurs formally and informally, internally and externally to the organisation, at all contact points, wherever and whenever people interact with the organisation.

Marketing communications is one of the most exciting and creative areas within marketing. Offering many career opportunities in this growing multi-billion pound/euro industry, it is continually innovating and requires progressive managers who must demonstrate initiative and dynamism if they are to meet the ongoing challenges. One such challenge facing the industry today is that of integration – to ensure the cohesion of the many activities involved in marketing communications, from advertising and public relations to exhibitions, packaging and sales management. These are all covered comprehensively within the book, alongside the strategic and planning issues necessary to integrate the activities effectively.

David Pickton

Amanda Broderick

The Integrated Marketing Communications Framework

The title of this book is *Integrated Marketing Communications*, which suggests that there is something more to marketing communications than a loose set of activities. It is a concept under which a company integrates and co-ordinates its many communications channels to deliver a clear and consistent message about the organisation and its products. Kotler (2003) defines integrated marketing communications as:

> **a way of looking at the whole marketing process from the viewpoint of the customer.**
>
> (p. 563)

Integration is something with which the marketing communications industry at large is increasingly concerned and which they are actively trying to achieve (albeit with mixed success). In practice, it is very difficult to ensure that marketing communications are integrated but such difficulty should not prevent people from trying, as the rewards of synergy and coherence are significant. The book is structured around three parts based on three models of Integrated Marketing Communications (IMC), and summarised in the IMC Framework on page 1:

- The IMC Process Model
- The IMC RABOSTIC Planning Model
- The IMC Mix Model

Before we can discuss integrated marketing communications, however, an overview of what is meant by marketing communications is necessary. Chapter 1 achieves this by setting the context for the three IMC models around which the book is based by introducing the concept and terminology of marketing communications.

What is marketing communications?

Advertising

The use of paid mass media, by an identified sponsor, to deliver marketing communications to target audiences.

Promotions

Term used interchangeably with marketing communications. Traditionally identified as one of the four key components of marketing.

Marketing communications

Communications with target audiences on all matters that affect marketing performance.

Target audience

Those individuals or groups that are identified as having a direct or indirect effect on business performance, and are selected to receive marketing communications.

Corporate communications

Marketing and other business communications about the organisation to selected target audiences.

In the past, you have probably come across marketing communications under some other commonly used names such as '**advertising**' or '**promotions**'. Over recent years '**marketing communications**' has become the favoured term among academics and some practitioners to describe

> all the promotional elements of the marketing mix which involve the communications between an organisation and its target audiences on all matters that affect marketing performance.

It is important to recognise that we are talking about market*ing* communications not just market communications. Market*ing* involves more parties than just those defined by market members. For market*ing* to be successful many people have to be involved in the communication process both within the organisation and outside it. It is for this reason, that the description of marketing communications given above does not say target 'markets', it says **target 'audiences'**. This is one of the most important concepts identified in this book and will be discussed in more detail later.

Another term that has also become fashionable is '**corporate communications**', but some distinctions between this and marketing communications will be identified in a moment. The variation in the use of terminology is very confusing but not unexpected when we consider that so many people are involved in the whole arena of communications, each with their own interests, biases and predispositions. It is inevitable that some will use one term or description in preference to another. This simply has to be understood and accepted. It is important, however, that some of the distinctions between these terms are considered here.

Marketing communications and advertising

Probably the most common area of confusion is to think of marketing communications as another word for advertising. Advertising has been around for a long time and is used extensively by the general public to mean all sorts of things. Everybody knows something about advertising because it is seen and heard every day. Important though it is, advertising is only a *part* of marketing communications and is not an alternative term to it. Chapter 26 discusses advertising in length.

Marketing communications, the marketing mix and the 4Ps

Marketing mix

Range of marketing activities/tools that an organisation combines and implements to generate a response from the target audience.

Marketing communications is a *part* of marketing just as advertising is a *part* of marketing communications. When asked, 'What is marketing?' it is usual to talk about the '**marketing mix**' and the most typical way of describing this is as the '4Ps' – Product, Price, Place and Promotion. While we do not want to enter the debate as to whether or not this is the best way to define the marketing mix, what is important is that promotional activities are a fundamental part of marketing.

Marketing communications and promotions

It is more difficult to differentiate 'promotions' from marketing communications, so much so that it is wise to consider it as a term that can be used interchangeably with it and we do so at various times within this book. In particular, the concept of the

Marketing communications mix

The range of activities/tools available to an organisation to communicate with its target audiences on all matters that affect marketing performance.

'marketing communications mix' is commonly called the 'promotions mix' or the 'promotional mix'; indeed, Crosier (1990) clearly states that the terms have exactly the same meaning in the context of the '4Ps'. Although it can be easily argued that marketing communications is a broader concept than promotions, in the context of this book there is no intended difference in their general meaning or use.

Why use the term 'marketing communications' at all?

You may be wondering at this point why should we even want to confuse or replace the perfectly acceptable word 'promotions' with a rather more cumbersome phrase, 'marketing communications'? The answer, first, is that this is a term which is gaining in popularity. Second, the word 'promotions' is also used as a shortened version of 'sales promotions' which is actually only a part of the bigger promotions picture that marketing communications represents (see Chapter 28). Third, as recognised by DeLozier (1976), all the marketing mix elements have a marketing communications impact. Therefore, in a sense, marketing communications is a slightly wider concept than promotions.

> **The promotional mix has long been viewed as the company's sole communications link with the consumer. However, this kind of provincialism can often lead to sub-optimization of the firm's total communications effort. Because if viewed in isolation, promotion can actually work against other elements in the marketing communications mix.**
>
> (DeLozier 1990, p. 165)

Marketing communications and corporate communications

What about marketing communications and corporate communications: how are these differentiated? One way of considering the problem is to suggest that the generic term ought to be corporate communications of which marketing communications is a part. In this way, it can be said that corporate communications includes marketing communications *and* some other forms of communications as well, that is, communications which are not related to marketing activities. So, perhaps, it can be argued that communications with employees or shareholders or other stakeholders that are not on marketing matters would be examples of corporate communications but not marketing communications. In this way, the distinction between the two is only one of *content* of communication, not of *methods* of communication.

Blauw (1994) defines corporate communication as 'the integrated approach to all communication produced by an organisation directed at all relevant target groups' and van Riel (1995) makes the distinction that corporate communication consists of three main forms; marketing communication, organisational communication and management communication. Management communication is perceived by van Riel as the most important of the three, and comprises communications by managers with internal and external target groups. Organisational communication he defines as a heterogeneous group of communications activities which include internal communication, corporate advertising, public relations and other communications at the corporate level. In this grouping he includes much of what we include in marketing communications (which we see as a natural extension of product promotions to include any corporate promotion that impacts on marketing performance). Marketing communications, which van Riel states takes the largest share of the corporate communication budget, consists primarily of those forms of communication that support sales of particular goods and services; as such he presumably restricts marketing communications to the product level only.

FOOD FOR THOUGHT

An internal memo from a department head to her team, communicating the launch of a new appraisal and training system, is an example of a management communication – one element of corporate communications.

To clarify, what the reader of this book should recognise is that marketing communications have to cover not only promotions of goods and services but also corporate promotions as well. This is because images and impressions of the organisation have profound effects on the success or otherwise of individual goods and services. Indeed, this notion can be extended still further if we also consider the promotion of individuals as well. Certainly this applies to political marketing in which members of political parties are promoted as heavily (if not more so) than the policies they represent (Plate 1).

In the commercial world, Richard Branson is a good example of the figurehead of the Virgin empire who has been promoted with good effect to the benefit of all the organisations he represents. The Virgin brand transcends all the businesses and products within its portfolio. In a similar way, Cadbury and Nestlé have both associated the company name and company values very closely with all of their products.

The marketing communications process and the IMC Process Model

Fundamental to the understanding of marketing communications is an understanding of the marketing communications process, i.e. how marketing communications work from the sender of the communication to the receiver of it. This, structured around the IMC Process Model, forms the basis for the first part of the book. Schramm (1960) is frequently attributed with originally modelling the communications process as involving four key components. These are shown in Exhibit 1.1:

● The sender is the originator or source of the message. In practice, agents or consultants may actually do the work on behalf of the sender.
● The message is the actual information and impressions that the sender wishes to communicate.
● The media are the 'vehicles' or 'channels' used to communicate the message without which there can be no communication. Media can take many different forms.
● The receivers are the people who receive the message.

NEED TO KNOW

☑ *The challenge of marketing communications is to communicate the right message, in the right way, to the right people, in the right place, at the right time!*

The skill is in ensuring that this whole process is carried out successfully, that the right messages are received by the right people in the right way. But things do go wrong!

Schramm's (1960) concept of the communications process is the foundation of our understanding of marketing communications, and the four elements provide a basic structure. The IMC Process Model, however, provides a much more comprehensive framework for understanding how

Exhibit 1.1 The communication process

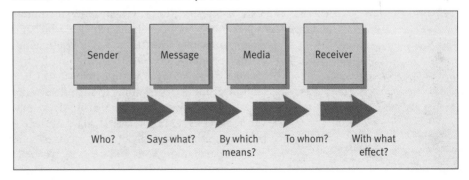

Exhibit 1.2 The IMC Process Model

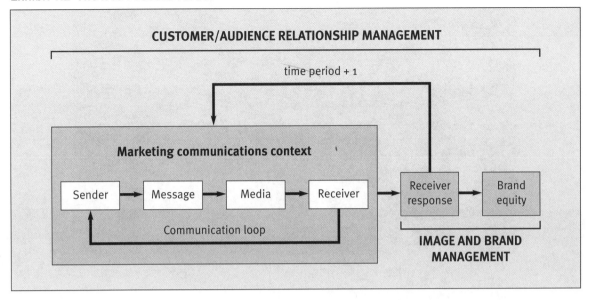

marketing communications work. This is presented in Exhibit 1.2 and is used to guide readers through Part 1 of this book.

There are more key elements in our model of the marketing communications process, compared to Schramm's. Four of the elements are in common with Schramm's model: sender, message, media and receiver. The receiver box, however, is expanded to identify that either they may be members of the target audience or non-members – marketing communications are frequently seen and heard by others than those an organisation has targeted. Receivers may subsequently take no action or a variety of different actions which include purchase, consumption and word-of-mouth communication with others. The IMC Process Model recognises that marketing communications may fall short and not be received by all or only a limited number of receivers.

IN VIEW 1.1

Communications that have gone wrong!

There are some humorous examples of where messages have gone wrong, such as the case of the army soldiers, who were told to pass back the message, 'Send reinforcements, we are going to advance'. By the time it was finally communicated it had become, 'Send three and four pence, we're going to a dance'. Or messages with unintended meanings like the one of the young priest who was heard to say to his congregation, 'Anyone wishing to become a mother, please see me in the vestry after the service'. Or the old lady who wrote to complain about the way her neighbours parked their cars in front of her house, 'They've all got back passages, let them park their cars up there'.

Strand cigarettes

The most notorious example of marketing communications going wrong is the Strand cigarette case. Strand was a popular brand of cigarette until a new advertising campaign

Source: Reproduced by kind permission of The History of Advertising Trust Archive

was launched. Far from creating more sales, the advertising ultimately resulted in the brand being removed from the market. If anybody needs an example that advertising *does* work, the Strand cigarette example stands head and shoulders above the rest. Unfortunately, the effect was negative, not positive, which is why you will never hear of it being offered as an example of advertising effectiveness.

Strand's new advertising, when launched, showed the cigarette being smoked by a man in a trilby hat and trench coat with collar raised up around his neck standing on a street corner by a lamp post or on a bridge. The man was always alone. The image was always black and white – colour was not available then. The image was cold and bleak. The headline read, 'You're never alone with a Strand'.

There seemed to be nothing to create offence. The intention was to suggest that whatever you were doing or wherever you might be, Strand cigarettes would not let you down. Strand was a cigarette you could always rely on. When sales plummeted, executives needed to find out what went wrong. Research told them that people were given the impression that if they smoked Strand cigarettes they would not have any friends. The only one they would be left with is their Strand cigarette. They would be consigned to a very lonely existence.

What was intended and what was actually conveyed were two totally different things. The effect was so bad for the company that they decided their only course of action was to remove the brand entirely from the market.

Apart from illustrating that things can go wrong, this example also emphasises the need to pretest marketing communications *before* they are used in a campaign to help eliminate any misconceptions that might be caused. Strand learned their painful lesson well. The old adage, sometimes known as Murphy's Law, often applies: 'If it can go wrong, it will'.

Marketing communications context

The macro- and micro-environment in which marketing communications take place.

Communications loop

The two-way nature of communications from sender to receiver and back again.

One-way communication

Communication from a sender to a receiver with no feedback or dialogue.

Two-way asymmetric communication

Communication from a sender to a receiver with little or delayed feedback, producing a non-direct dialogue.

Two-way symmetric communication

Direct dialogue between a sender and receiver of communications.

t + 1

Simply refers to the change that takes place from one period of time (t) to the next period of time (t + 1).

Customer/audience relationship management

The strategic and tactical tasks involved in the management of positive, personal and continuing communication between an organisation and its audiences overtime; recognising that this should be complementary to image and brand management.

Image and brand management

The strategic and tactical tasks involved in the management of positive, 'non-personal' communication between an organisation and its audiences; recognising this should be complementary to customer/audience relationship management.

A number of additional elements are included in Exhibit 1.2. The first, the **marketing communications context**, is the macro- and micro-environment in which communications take place. This context can profoundly affect the nature and meaning of marketing communications. The second element is the **communications loop**, which recognises the two-way nature of communications and the problems of encoding, decoding and 'noise'. Grunig and Hunt (1984) have referred to the communications loop as involving one-way, two-way asymmetric and two-way symmetric communications. They see advertising, some public relations and other promotional activities as typifying one-way communications. **One-way communication** is from a sender to a target audience with no feedback or dialogue. Traditionally this may have been the case although some feedback is always possible through research. This would then be described as **two-way asymmetric communication** in that there is some communication flow between sender and audience and back again but the feedback or response is delayed and, therefore, not in the form of direct dialogue.

In **two-way symmetric communication** (which can be described as the 'richest' form of communication) there is a direct dialogue between the sender and audience. Traditionally, this has been a major benefit of personnel selling activities, but changing technology is now creating new opportunities for interactivity and near-immediate response. It is increasingly possible for near two-way symmetric communication to be used in traditional mass media promotions. There has been a huge growth in interactive and direct response TV, the Internet and telephone call centres. Importantly, greater symmetric two-way communications enhances the marketing communications process and limits the potentially negative effects of noise, encoding, and decoding misinterpretations in the communications loop through direct dialogue.

A third additional element of the model is the receiver responses to the marketing communications process. These may include attitudes, associations and behaviours to the communications such as perceived quality and loyalty. These receiver responses create the brand equity. Brand equity has been defined as:

> the strength, currency and value of the brand ... the description, and assessment of the appeal, of a brand to all the target audiences who interact with it
>
> (Cooper and Simons 1997, pp. 1–2)

In sum, it is the value of the company's names and symbols. The valuation of brands (the financial expression of brand equity) as assets on the balance sheet has become recognised as an important indication of organisational performance.

The **t+1** element of the IMC Process Model recognises that brand equity is built and changes over time and past exposure/response to a marketing communication can impact on the subsequent process and output of a communication in time period +1.

'Customer/audience relationship management' and 'image and brand management' are highlighted at the outside of the IMC Process Model. These are the two key strategic tasks facing those responsible for integrated marketing communications and the management of the IMC process. The planned activities of marketing communications and all the unintended or uncontrolled communications between an organisation and its audiences collectively affect the outcome of these two core and overlapping management tasks.

Broadly speaking, customer/audeince relationship management recognises the lifetime value of customers; that is the potential repeat and increased purchase behaviour of customers if an exchange relationship is established, maintained and enhanced. It is strongly associated with one-to-one communications. Image and brand management tends to be associated with communication 'at a distance' with many target audiences. It is frequently seen as the primary function of advertising and public relations which can be supported with elements of sales promotion. It is strongly associated with one-to-many communications. Both these concepts are covered in more detail in Chapters 11 and 12.

Target audiences defined

Identifying target audiences is fundamental to good marketing communications. It is common practice in marketing to emphasise the importance of the target market but this has to be taken further in marketing communications. Target markets describe *customers* – the people who buy goods and services. They also describe *consumers* – the people who literally use or consume the goods and services. Sometimes customers and consumers are the same people but often they are not. In family consumable purchases and industrial purchases, for example, the users of products are not necessarily the same as the buyers. It makes sense in marketing communications to consider communicating with both *buyers* and *users* if the communications effort is to be most successful. For example, in promoting toys, the marketing communications effort may be focused at parents *and* children and they may do so in very different ways. A marketing communications plan focused in this way may be more like two plans integrated together.

But we need to go still further! We need to go beyond the target market in determining our target audiences. We need to consider who else may be involved in the purchase decision or who else might influence it. If we are able to influence the *influencers* then there is greater likelihood that our communications will be successful. For this reason, target audiences can include members of the trade, opinion leaders, members of the media, employees, clubs and associations, aunts and uncles and anybody else who is relevant. In the public relations profession they refer to all these possible groups as '**publics**'. This is not to say that everybody is actually selected as part of the target audience group. These people or publics form our marketing communications '**segments**' (just as in market segmentation) from among whom our chosen targets must be selected.

Exhibit 1.3 illustrates one way we can highlight the audience segments from which we can select the targets for our marketing communications. As can be easily seen, the target market members highlighted in bolder lines represent only a part of the total picture. Opinion leaders and innovators (who may be influential especially in new product launches or re-launches), only some of whom may be part of the target market, may be singled out for particular communications. Other target audience groups will be selected on the basis of their value to the company in favourably influencing the target market members. The DMU term shown in Exhibit 1.3 refers to the **Decision-Making Unit**. This is a concept that is covered in Chapter 4. The DMU, also known as the decision-making group, recognises that there can be a number of people or players who will directly influence the buying decision. These players include the users (who may be different people to the purchasers), the deciders, the influencers and the purchasers themselves. The group may be formally organised, such as in a business-to-business purchase context, but more frequently is an unorganised group who influence the decision to buy. The example given in In View 1.2, on children's influences on consumer purchase decisions, is a good illustration of the financial impact that members of the DMU can have.

Once the target audiences have been determined as part of an integrated marketing communications effort, it is then possible to make decisions about how each of the targets will be treated. Decisions will be made as to which marketing communication tools will be used and which media should be selected.

Publics

Term favoured by the public relations profession, referring to the many target audiences that communications may be focused towards.

Segment

Group of individuals who are expected to respond in a similar way to an organisation's marketing activity.

Decision-Making Unit (DMU)

This concept recognises the involvement of a range of people in the decision-making process. The DMU comprises a number of 'players' that may have an effect on the purchase outcome e.g. influencers, gatekeeper, specifier, decider, buyer and user.

Exhibit 1.3 Selecting multiple target audience members

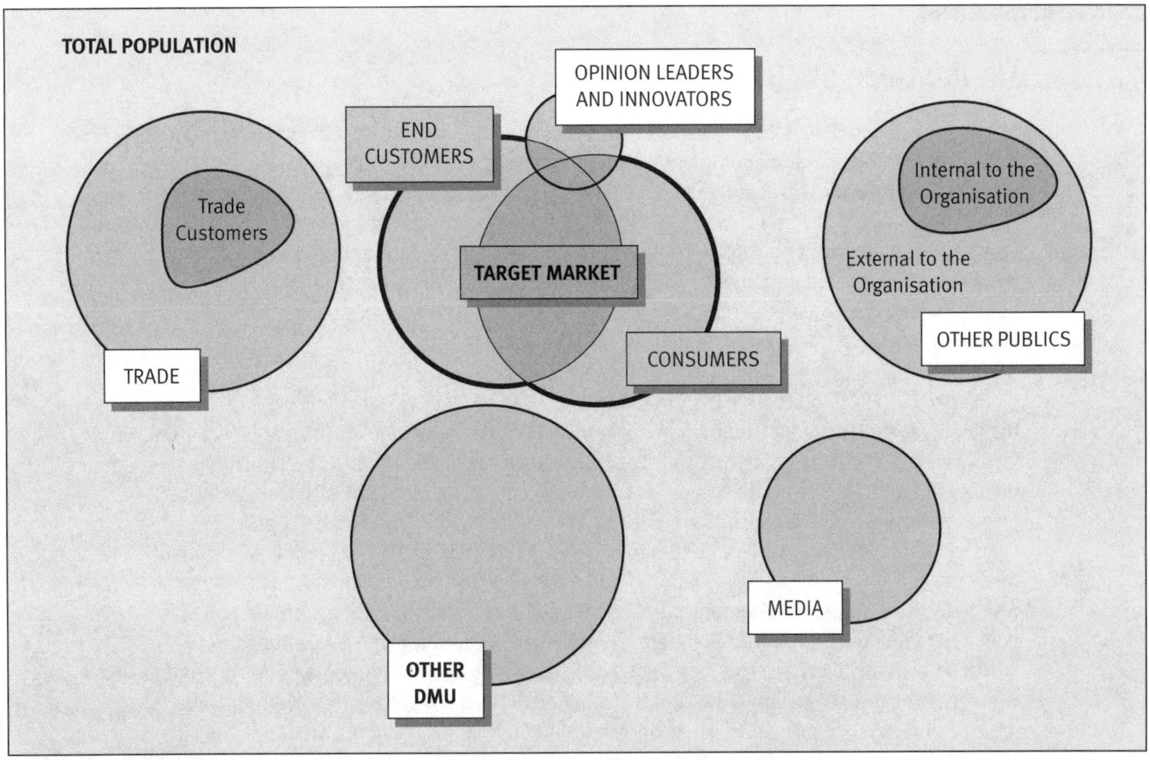

TOTAL POPULATION

OPINION LEADERS AND INNOVATORS

END CUSTOMERS

Trade Customers

TARGET MARKET

Internal to the Organisation

External to the Organisation

OTHER PUBLICS

CONSUMERS

TRADE

MEDIA

OTHER DMU

IN VIEW 1.2

Children's influence on consumer purchases

Housewives were asked if their children up to the age of 15 influenced the purchase of a range of family products. The results are shown below. The percentage figures represent housewives who agreed that their children exert an influence. The equivalent value represents the amount of family spending affected.

	Equivalent value	Children's influence
Day-to-day meals	£13bn	54%
House	£6.3bn	22%
Holidays	£3.3bn	44%
Children's clothes	£1.9bn	70%
Car	£1.6bn	17%
Computers	£1.6bn	33%
Soft drinks	£1.5bn	60%
Restaurants	£1.0bn	30%
Toys	£512m	73%
Breakfast cereals	£291m	73%
TV/HiFi	£58m	22%
TOTAL	£31bn	

Source: adapted from Hotline (1997) based on Saatchi and Saatchi data

IN VIEW 1.3

Chubb Security Systems

Chubb, an organisation noted for its locks and security systems, developed a security product particularly suited to manufacturing organisations based in small factory units. Market research identified the specific target market for the product and the buying behaviour of that target.

A campaign was developed which focused on the decision-making unit (DMU). The DMU concept recognises that buying decisions are often the result of decisions affected by many people and not just the purchaser. The DMU is the group of people (or players) who are most influential and involved in the purchase and use of the product. Four key players are commonly identified: the *buyer*, the *user*, the *specifier* and the *decider* (although the DMU can be described in various other ways – see Chapters 4 and 17).

Research told Chubb that for their market there were, in fact, two key DMU players. One was the financial director who acted both in the capacity of decider and buyer. The other was the factory manager who acted in the capacity of specifier and user. In other words, the financial director would make the final decision about which security system to buy, then actually be responsible for the purchase contract. The factory manager would influence the purchase by specifying the type of system required and be responsible for its use. The *combined* efforts of these two players would dictate whether a purchase would be made and, if so, which systems would be shortlisted and eventually purchased. Marketing communications targeted on only one or the other of the players would represent missed opportunities to maximise sales.

The industrial sales force has long known the value of identifying multiple points of contact within customer organisations. Users of the other elements of the marketing communications mix sometimes fail to do so. Chubb recognised the potential. They did not send a single, general communication to their potential organisation customers. Chubb's campaign focused on two people within each organisation. And it did so in an interesting and creative way. Small metal moneyboxes were purchased into which were put coins and information leaflets. Each moneybox had a lid, a lock and a key. A locked moneybox and covering letter was sent to the finance director of each of the potential customer organisations. At the same time, a letter with a key was sent to the factory manager of each organisation. In all cases, research had identified the names of each recipient so that the mailing was carefully targeted and personalised.

The covering letters, which gave no details of the product being promoted, requested that each finance director should contact the factory manager and that each factory manager should contact the finance director. In this novel way, members of the DMU were invited to get together to discuss what their mailings were about. Only after coming together were they able to discover the contents of the moneybox and the Chubb security system being offered. Why were coins put into the moneyboxes? Simply to ensure that the moneyboxes rattled. In this way they were more intriguing.

The campaign was a success – it was an award winner. To the delight of the company, sales targets were not only met, they were exceeded.

The award-winning Chubb Security Systems campaign illustrated in In View 1.3 is a good example of target audience identification. It was based on Chubb's sound understanding of the role performed by different members of the Decision-Making Unit. The campaign featured the use of direct mail as this was the most cost-efficient and effective way of contacting Chubb's target audience. There would, of course, have been other elements involved in the total campaign, a campaign that proved to be very effective indeed because it did not rely just on a single player in the DMU, but *all* key players, and took advantage of a novel approach to create impact. Other marketing communication activities available to Chubb include:

- personal selling via the telephone and face-to-face;
- the use of exhibition stands;
- leaflets and promotional giveaways; and
- advertising in business and industrial magazines.

Industrial media (another target audience group) may have been targeted with press releases to encourage editorial coverage. The trade (yet another target audience group) may have been offered sales promotion incentives. Crime prevention officers and insurance companies (still more target audience groups) may have been sent leaflets and information bulletins to generate a favourable impression of Chubb security systems. They may, in turn, have recommended the systems and offered lower insurance premiums to those companies who have them installed, and so on. All these approaches are possible once a sound appreciation of target audiences has been gained. In fact, this sort of understanding actually facilitates the creative process by opening up new creative possibilities. And this is what much of the marketing communications business is about.

In summary, Part 1 is structured around the IMC Process Model and the concepts are signposted in Exhibit 1.4.

Exhibit 1.4 Signposts for Part 1

Key elements of the marketing communications process	Where found in Part 1
Sender or source of communication	Chapter 3
Message or content of the communication	Chapter 3
The communications loop – the communications loop recognises that marketing communications is a two-way process involving feedback. It also recognises that things can go wrong in both giving and receiving information	Chapter 3
Receiver – the receiver part of the marketing communications process extends the simple notion of a receiver by recognising that messages are received by both target and non-target audience members no matter how well targeted our communications might be. There will also be others whom we would have wished to receive our communications but who do not do so. In addition, the receivers will either then do nothing about the communication or will undertake some form of action that could include purchase, consumption or communicating with others. Other forms of action may involve filling in a coupon, asking for more information, attending an event that has been promoted, etc.	Chapters 3–4
Media – the carrier of marketing communications	Chapters 5–6
The marketing communications context – this is the environment in which the marketing communications take place	Chapters 7–10
Receiver response – attitudes, associations and behaviours to the marketing communications	Chapter 4
Brand equity – the value of the company's names, symbols and images to all the target audiences who interact with it	Chapter 11
Image and brand management – the strategic and tactical tasks involved in the management of positive, 'non-personal' communication between an organisation and its audiences	Chapter 11
Customer / audience relationship management – the strategic and tactical tasks involved in the management of positive, personal and continuing communication between an organisation and its audiences	Chapter 12

The marketing communications planning process and the IMC RABOSTIC Planning Model

Just as Part 1 of this book is based on a model, so too is Part 2. The model this time focuses on the management aspects of marketing communications. It focuses on the tasks and decisions that have to be considered and made when planning and, ultimately, implementing marketing communications. Exhibit 1.5 details the IMC RABOSTIC Planning Model. The bottom of the model highlights that *all* elements of the model must be considered for effective planning, organisation and management of integrated marketing communications.

Planning cycle

The sequence of decisions and activities involved in putting together a marketing communications plan.

On the left-hand side of the model is shown the **planning cycle** which firstly involves research and analysis of the situation and feedback from previous marketing communications campaigns and activities. What follows is a set of decisions that must be put together to form the final marketing communications plan(s). If integration is to take place, a whole series of plans will have to be formulated. Often, however, plans are considered in relative isolation of one another. The process, nevertheless, is the same. Although there may be some argument about the sequence in which the decisions should take place, the decision areas are basically common to all general business and marketing planning (see, for example, Wilson and Gilligan 1998; Kotler 2003;

Exhibit 1.5 The IMC RABOSTIC Planning Model

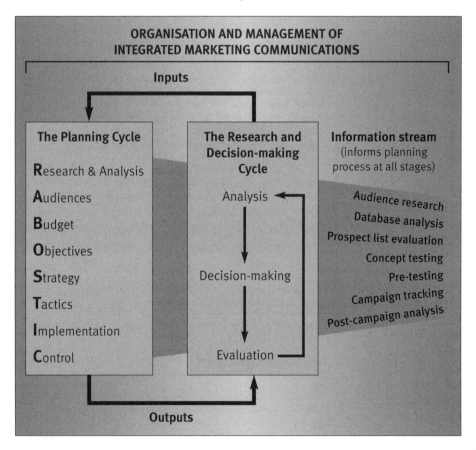

McDonald 1995). Where business and marketing plans refer to target markets, the marketing communications plan should refer to target audiences for reasons already described. The areas of the planning cycle form the acronym RABOSTIC.

On the right-hand side of the model is shown the **information stream** which illustrates the flow of information that is used in the planning process to aid the formulation of integrated marketing communications plans. In the centre of the model, the **research and decision-making cycle** shows analysis being used to inform decision-making. Evaluation takes place when plans are put into action. The insights gained are then cycled back into the analysis for the further development of the next planning phase. The information stream is constantly tapped into, both to input and to extract information, throughout the planning process. It is important to realise that it is not used simply at the beginning and the end, but throughout the planning process.

Whatever else the planning process seeks to do, it aims to result in plans which are, in essence, *decisions* about what we want to achieve and how we are going to achieve them. Plans should be actionable! The IMC RABOSTIC Planning Model is covered in Part 2 and each stage of the model can be found in the chapters outlined in Exhibit 1.6.

Information stream
The flow of information used in the marketing communications planning process.

Research and decision-making cycle
The circular process of analysing, deciding and evaluating marketing communication plans and actions.

Exhibit 1.6 Signposts for Part 2

Elements of the integrated marketing communications planning process	Where found in Part 2
The planning, research and decision-making process	Chapter 13
Organisation and management of IMC	Chapters 14–15
Research	Chapter 16
Audiences	Chapter 17
Budget	Chapter 18
Objectives	Chapter 19
Strategy and tactics	Chapter 19
Implementation	Chapters 20–22
Control	Chapter 23

The marketing communications mix and the IMC Mix Model

The marketing mix is one of the foundation stones of marketing just as the marketing communications mix lies at the foundation of marketing communications. For ease of reference, the marketing mix has become known as the 4Ps, a term and classification devised by E. Jerome McCarthy and first used in his basic marketing text. The term 'marketing mix', however, was first coined by Neil Borden of Harvard Business School in 1948. It gained in popularity after his address to the American Marketing Association in 1953 (Gould 1979). The marketing mix represented, to Borden, a range of 'ingredients' which, rather like a recipe, would create a product capable of satisfying customer and consumer requirements if 'mixed' properly. Borden's original set of ingredients consisted of twelve elements: product planning, pricing, branding, advertising, promotions, packaging, display, personal selling,

WARNING

❗ *Marketing communications, advertising, promotions and corporate communications are often used interchangeably by practitioners and academics. Be aware of the different definitions to reduce confusion!*

15

channels of distribution, physical handling, servicing and fact-finding/analysis. As a means of simplifying the list, McCarthy shortened it to four: Product, Pricing, Place and Promotion. The Place element, of course, relates to Borden's distribution elements of physical handling and channels of distribution. These were referred to as *place* (getting the products to the marketplace) rather than *distribution* because '3Ps and a D' does not have the same ring to it as 4Ps!

It is important to note that half of Borden's original list of twelve elements has been shortened into the *promotion* 'P' – branding, advertising, promotions, packaging, display and personal selling. In some respects, this hardly seems to do it justice. Indeed, despite its popularity, many authors have criticised the limitations of the 4Ps classification of the mix (for example, see Kent 1986; van Waterschoot and van den Bulte 1990; Jefkins 1991; Pickton and Wright 1995).

We can see from this brief history of marketing why the general term for this area of marketing has become known as promotion and why there has been a need to refer to a promotions mix to give recognition to the variety of activities that fall into this category. However, it is also clear that the list provided by Borden fails to make reference to other forms of promotion (such as public relations) which have an equal right to be included in the mix. Successive researchers and authors on the subject have attempted to remedy this.

As explained earlier, another term, 'marketing communications', is becoming widely used as an alternative descriptor to 'promotion' as there is really no need to link it directly to the 4Ps of the marketing mix. Many people favour it, as it seems more appropriate in describing a range of communications activities. For our purposes in this book, we do not make a distinction between the two, but where 'sales promotions' as a term is used, it represents a sub-group within the promotions or marketing communications mix.

Despite whatever drawbacks it may have, probably the simplest way of classifying the marketing communications mix is as the four elements basically proposed by numerous authors such as DeLozier (1976) and Kotler et al. (1999) (or in slightly modified form by other authors such as Crosier 1990; Shimp 1997; and Belch and Belch 1995). This four-way split of the promotional mix is shown in Exhibit 1.7.

Exhibit 1.7 A simple classification of the marketing communications mix

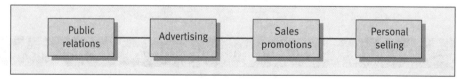

If, for the sake of simplicity, this approach is adopted, it follows that all the various marketing communications activities would have to fit into one or other category if it is to have any true value as a classification. Unfortunately, this cannot be done in any satisfactory way because there are activities that could legitimately be placed into more than one box, e.g. direct response advertising, sponsorship, exhibitions and merchandising. The categories are actually overlapping and it would be better to illustrate them as in Exhibit 1.8.

By adopting this basic arrangement it is possible to develop a new concept to represent the marketing communications mix. This concept, forming the basis for Part 3 of the text, is the Integrated Marketing Communications (IMC) Mix Model and is presented in Exhibit 1.9. While illustrating that there is a wide range of marketing

Exhibit 1.8 Overlapping categories of the marketing communications mix

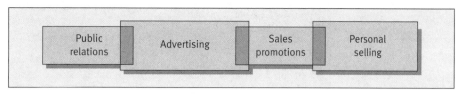

Exhibit 1.9 The IMC Mix Model

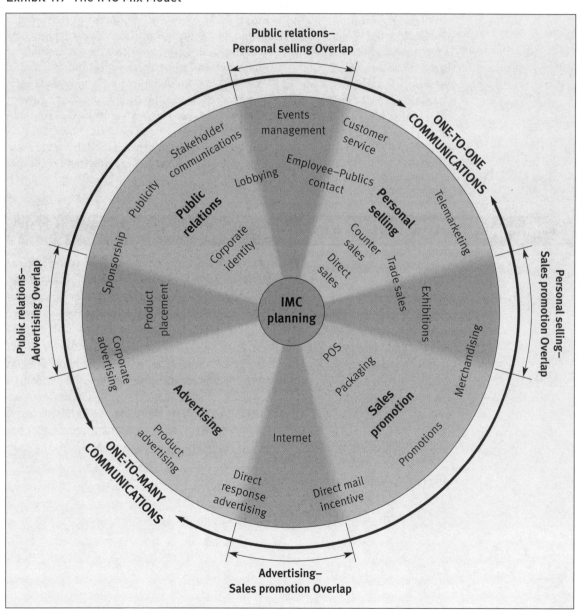

Exhibit 1.10 Signposts for Part 3

Elements of the integrated marketing communications mix	Where found in Part 3
Public relations	Chapters 24–25
Advertising	Chapter 26
Direct marketing communications	Chapter 27
Sales promotions	Chapters 28–30
Personal selling	Chapters 30–31

communications activities, the IMC Mix Model recognises that many of these activities overlap; there are marketing communications elements that may be categorised as both Public Relations and Advertising (for example, corporate advertising), both Advertising and Sales Promotion (for example, direct mail), both Sales Promotion and Personal Selling (for example, exhibitions) and both Personal Selling and Public Relations (for example, lobbying). The IMC Mix Model does not try to include every possibility but does identify the major areas of marketing communications listed by most writers on the subject. Part 3 of this book devotes eight chapters to covering various aspects of the marketing communications mix in detail. The chapter headings have been chosen to represent the most common and popular areas of the mix and are outlined in Exhibit 1.10. These chapters should be read for a deeper understanding of each of the marketing communications activities.

Summary

Chapter 1 has raised questions about how marketing communications is defined and how it relates to, and is often used interchangeably with, other commonly used terms such as advertising, promotions and corporate communications. Emphasis has been placed on recognising that marketing communications need to be focused towards a range of target audiences and not just customers. Three models, outlined in the Integrated Marketing Communications Framework, have been introduced. These models are used as the basis and as 'maps' for the three parts of the book. The IMC Process Model explains how marketing communications work and the IMC RABOSTIC Planning Model helps identify the key issues that surround integrated marketing communications planning and management. The IMC Mix Model has been introduced to help understand the wide range of elements that form the communications mix, and why it is important to consider them as integrated, overlapping activities. Exhibits 1.4, 1.6 and 1.10 provide further 'signposts' so that readers can see at a glance in which chapters key aspects of marketing communications appear.

Self-review questions

1 What does the promotions mix consist of?

2 Describe the importance of target audiences and how they differ from target markets.

4 What does a decision-making unit comprise?

5 What is the difference between one-way, two-way asymmetric and two-way symmetric communications?

6 What is the marketing communications planning process?

Project

virgin atlantic

You are a marketing consultant briefed with the task of evaluating the potential target audiences of Virgin Atlantic. Prepare a 10-minute presentation outlining recommendations identifying with whom and why Virgin Atlantic should be communicating.

Visit **http://www.virgin.co.uk** for further information.

References

Belch, G.E. and Belch, M.A. (1995), *Introduction to Advertising and Promotion. An Integrated Marketing Communications Perspective* 3rd edn. Chicago: Irwin.

Blauw, E. (1994), *Het Corporate Image, vierde geheel herziene druk* 4th edn. Amsterdam: De Viergang.

Cooper, A. and Simons, P. (1997), *Brand Equity Lifestage. An Entrepreneurial Revolution.* TBWA, Simons Palmer, September.

Crosier, K. (1990), *Dictionary of Marketing and Advertising.* In: M. Baker, 2nd edn, Macmillan Press.

DeLozier, M.W. (1976), *The Marketing Communications Process.* McGraw-Hill.

Fletcher, K., Wheeler, C. and Wright, J. (1992), Success in database marketing: some crucial factors. *Marketing Intelligence and Planning*, 10 (6), 18–23.

Fletcher, K., Wheeler, C. and Wright, J. (1994), Strategic implementation of database marketing: problems and pitfalls. *Long Range Planning*, 27 (1), 133–141.

Gould, J.S. (1979), *Marketing Anthology.* West.

Grunig, J.E. and Hunt T.T. (1984), *Managing Public Relations.* Holt Rinehart and Winston.

Jefkins, F. (1991), *Modern Marketing Communications.* Blackie.

Kent, R.A. (1986), Faith in the 4Ps. *Journal of Marketing Management*, 2 (2), 145–154.

Kotler, P. (2003), *Marketing Management – Analysis, Planning, Implementation and Control* 11th edn. Prentice Hall.

Kotler, P., Armstrong, G., Saunders, J. and Wong, V. (1999), *Principles of Marketing* 2nd European edn. Prentice Hall Europe.

McDonald, M. (1995), *Marketing Plans – How to Prepare Them: How to Use Them* 3rd edn. Butterworth-Heinemann.

Murphy, J. (1998), What is branding? In *Brands: The New Wealth Creators* (S. Hart and J. Murphy, eds). Macmillan.

Pickton, D.W. and Wright, S. (1995), Marketing – a case of myth-taken identity. *Proceedings of the Dissent in Management Thought Conference*, London, September.

Pilditch, J. (1970), *Communication by Design*. McGraw-Hill.

van Riel, C.B.M. (1995), *Principles of Corporate Communication*. Prentice Hall.

Schramm, W. (1960), *Mass Communications*. The University of Illinois Press.

Shimp, T.A. (1997), *Advertising, Promotion, and Supplemental Aspects of Integrated Marketing Communications* 4th edn. Fort Worth: The Dryden Press.

Schultz, D.E. (1993), The customer and the database are the integrating forces. *Marketing News*, 27 (24), 14.

Schultz, D.E. (1997), Integrating information sources to develop strategies. *Marketing News*, 31 (2), 10.

van Waterschoot, W. and van den Bulte, C. (1990), The classification of the marketing mix revisited. *Journal of Marketing*, 56 (1), 1–8.

Wilson, R.M.S. and Gilligan, C. (1998), *Strategic Marketing Management* 2nd edn. Butterworth-Heinemann.

Selected further reading

Hart, S. and Murphy, J. (1998), *Brands: The New Wealth Creators*. Macmillan.

Schultz, D.E., Tannenbaum, S.I. and Lauterborn, R.F. (1994), *Integrated Marketing Communications: Pulling It Together and Making It Work*. NTC Business Books.

Chapter 2

What is integrated marketing communications?

Professional perspective

Professor Don E. Schultz Northwestern University

Integrated marketing communications (IMC) seemed to be a rather simple concept at first, that is, aligning and co-ordinating a marketer's messages and incentives and directing them to customers and prospects. Yet, in retrospect, it has proven to be one of the major marketing innovations of the past decade. While the marketing concept has supposedly always focused on consumer needs, the practice of IMC has truly provided the first major effort to really put the customer in the centre of the firm's marketing activities.

The attempt to integrate, align and co-ordinate marketing communication programmes challenges many of the traditional organisational structures that have grown out of the industrial age. Indeed, in implementing an IMC programme, many organisations have found that they literally have to turn the organisation upside-down, starting with customers and prospects, not products and services and combining efforts from the view of the customer rather than from the view of the organisation. IMC may be obvious to managers but it is not easy to implement.

The rise of electronic commerce and communication, i.e. the Internet and World Wide Web revolution, has provided an even more pressing need for integration. Indeed, it is these very technologies that have not only made IMC possible, but they have created the demand for integration in all areas of the firm. Where once we spoke of 'one sight, one sound' for external communication as being the goal of IMC, today we speak of organisational integration and the management of brand contacts, in other words, every place and every way in which the organisation touches its customers, employees, shareholders and stakeholders. Thus, IMC has moved from being simply a method of co-ordinating and aligning external messages the firm wanted to send to relevant populations towards a more holistic view of communication as the backbone of not just the marketing function but the entire business enterprise as well.

In this chapter, you will find a comprehensive definition of integrated marketing communications and some of the major features of an IMC approach. One thing you should keep in mind as you read, however, is that IMC is not a task or a tool or even a function that is to be mastered and implemented. Instead, IMC is a 'work in progress' for as communication changes and evolves so must IMC. Learn what is here for that will provide the basis for your understanding of what is likely to come.

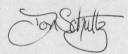

What is *integrated* marketing communications?

Chapter 1 introduced the concept of marketing communications and emphasised that it covered a range of promotional activity targeted towards one or more specified audiences. It follows that the greatest marketing communications impact will be achieved if all the elements involved are *integrated* into a unified whole. By integrating the range of promotional mix elements so that they work in harmony or **synergy** with each other, opportunities are created to improve the effectiveness of the total marketing communications effort.

The notion of integrated marketing communications is not a new idea although it has become much more popular in recent years. Intellectually there is a lot to commend integration but it is not easy to achieve for reasons explained later in this chapter.

Synergy

The effect of bringing together marketing communication elements in a mutually supportive and enhancing way so that the resulting whole is greater than the sum of its parts.

Public relations (PR)
The planned and sustained effort to establish and maintain goodwill and mutual understanding between an organisation and its publics.

Target audiences
Those individuals or groups that are identified as having a direct or indirect effect on business performance, and are selected to receive marketing communications.

Advertising
The use of paid mass media, by an identified sponsor, to deliver communications to target audiences.

Some would argue that **public relations** organisations have, since their very inception, recognised the value of integrated promotions not least because they recognised, at an early stage, the importance of the variety and variability of their **target audiences**, or 'publics', with whom they have had to communicate. To some extent this may be true but in many ways integration has only been taken seriously in the marketing communications industry at large since the early 1980s when advertising agencies such as Ogilvy & Mather and Young & Rubicam started conceiving of integrative concepts (which were variously termed 'Orchestration', 'Whole Egg', 'New Advertising' and 'Seamless Communication') and attempted to recognise more formally the need to bring a variety of other promotional tools together with **advertising** which had been their traditional focus.

IN VIEW 2.1

Advertising's place in the marketing communications mix

Many people consider advertising as the most important element of the marketing communications mix. This is, in part, due to the way some people use 'advertising' to describe any and all forms of promotion or communication (readers of this text will understand already that this is an inappropriate way to define advertising). Even those who distinguish between the elements of the mix still persist in believing that advertising accounts for the biggest promotional spend and is the most important form of promotion. This is not a valid view! Undoubtedly, advertising is an important promotional tool but so are the other tools in the mix. Estimates of sales promotion expenditures are dogged by difficulties of what to include and what not to include in estimates. There are also difficulties in obtaining data, similarly with PR. Some estimates of expenditure suggest both individual areas exceed that of advertising which in real terms has somewhat flattened out over the years. It should be recognised that sales promotions involve trade and consumer communications, point of sale, merchandising and discounting such as price offers. It is an area of marketing communications that covers a vast array of activities. It should not be surprising, therefore, that some people think that sales promotions significantly outweigh advertising.

Actual sums spent on marketing communications vary from country to country as industry structures, previous experiences and media landscapes (balance and predominance of different media) vary. For example, around 60% of Denmark's advertising is spent in newspapers compared with just 16% in Portugal. The favoured advertising medium in Italy and Greece is TV. It falls into second place in the UK and third place in Switzerland and the Netherlands to newspapers and magazines. Posters play a more important role in France than in most other European countries and, though accounting for only a small proportion of advertising expenditure, cinema advertising in Belgium represents a higher proportion of expenditure than in any other European country. Direct marketing communications expenditure in Germany outspends the UK by almost 100%. Per head of population, direct mail expenditure is highest in the Netherlands and Portugal is among the lowest by a very significant margin. More details of these expenditures can be found in *The European Marketing Pocket Book* published by NTC.

IN VIEW 2.2

The Institute of Practitioners in Advertising look for integration

When judging their Advertising Effectiveness Awards, the Institute of Practitioners in Advertising (IPA) have looked for evidence of integration in the form of what they have called 'joined-up thinking'. In their awards during the mid-1990s they gave special prizes to those entries that displayed the best examples of integration. In introducing the 1996 awards, the Convenor of the judging panel described integration as '... one of the leading strands of marketing thinking in the '90s' (Duckworth 1997, p. xiv).

In those awards, the IPA described their judging criteria (in which integration, innovation and impact all played major roles) in the following way:

- Joined-up thinking
- Strategic impact
- Creative excellence
- Media ingenuity
- Campaign leverage
- Consistency and innovation

Joined-up thinking is the term they used to describe the extent to which a common 'thread' or consistency could be seen running throughout a campaign from early information analysis to final ideas and executions across many promotional elements. It is from 'joined-up thinking' or integration that the other benefits such as creative excellence, strategic impact, campaign leverage and consistency flowed. Although the IPA previously emphasised the role of integration, it is fair to say that their 1998 and 2000 awards were more concerned with identifying the particular significance of advertising, which is understandable given their focus. Despite this, they nevertheless highlighted the learning achieved from their 1998 awards as the effect advertising has across multiple internal and external target audiences – a key element of integrated marketing communications. They also highlighted what they termed 'advertising's magnifier effect on other communications' and the key issue being a 'common brand understanding and common brand passion not standardised message' (Kendall 1999, pp. xix–xx). In the 2002 awards (published in 2003), they have not just focused on advertising but have recognised the impact of other promotional tools integrated with advertising such as sponsorship, PR, direct marketing, and sales promotions. All these facets are addressed in this book.

Sales promotion
A myriad of promotional activities, sales promotion is associated with free offers, price deals, premium offers, merchandising, point-of-sale displays, leaflets and product literature.

Direct mail
The use of postal services to deliver marketing communications materials. It may be considered an aspect of advertising in that it is used as a mass medium even though it can be used for individually targeted messages.

The impetus for this change of heart probably had more to do with the problems being faced by the advertising industry at large rather than any particular desire to seek improvement. Advertising was seen at the time (and is probably considered still to be the case by many) as the senior or 'elder statesman' of the marketing communications business. It has only been with a high degree of reluctance (which continues to be displayed) that members of the advertising profession have accepted the equal role played by the other areas of the promotional mix. Indeed, elitist attitudes are commonplace with each marketing communications specialism claiming greater significance over the others. Of course, for particular situations, a case can be made that more emphasis should put on one element of the promotions mix in relation to the others, but it would be false to claim that, say, advertising is better than public relations or that **sales promotions** are better than **direct mail**, etc. Each promotional element has its place.

Institute of Practitioners in Advertising

One of a number of professional advertising industry bodies based in the UK.

Advertising Effectiveness Awards

These are given to campaigns judged to have proven their effectiveness. They represent examples of excellent marketing communications practice.

There is increasing talk of the importance of integration of the marketing communications mix and the **Institute of Practitioners in Advertising** (IPA), who are responsible for the prestigious **Advertising Effectiveness Awards**, have looked for evidence of 'joined-up thinking' in their assessment of effective award-winning campaigns. Despite such initiatives, there remains limited practical evidence of the adoption of integrated marketing communications. This is partly due to ignorance, unwillingness and inertia, and partly due to the sheer difficulties of achieving true integration.

Definition and key features of integrated marketing communications

Put in its simplest form, integrated marketing communications (IMC) is the bringing together of all marketing communications activities. To many, IMC has become recognised as *the process of integrating all the elements of the promotional mix*. While this may be considered an adequate working definition, it fails to highlight a number of significant features which IMC should embrace. A range of definitions is presented in Exhibit 2.1.

Exhibit 2.1 Definitions of IMC

Authors	Definition
Duncan, 2002	IMC is a process for managing the customer relationships that drive brand value. More specifically, it is a cross-functional process for creating and nourishing profitable relationships with customers and stakeholders by strategically controlling or influencing all messages sent to these groups and encouraging data-driven, purposeful dialogue with them.
Shimp, 2000	An organisation's unified, coordinated effort to promote a brand concept through the use of multiple communications tools that 'speak with a single voice'.
Kotler et al., 1999	IMC is the concept under which a company carefully integrates and coordinates its many communications channels to deliver a clear, consistent and compelling message about the organisation and its products.
Betts et al.,1995	IMC is the strategic choice of elements of marketing communications which will effectively and economically influence transactions between an organisation and its existing and potential customers, clients and consumers.
Reported in **Schultz**, 1993	IMC is a concept of marketing communications planning that recognises the added value of a comprehensive plan that evaluates the strategic roles of a variety of communication disciplines – for example, general advertising, direct response, sales promotion, and PR – and combines these disciplines to provide clarity, consistency, and maximum communications impact (American Association of Advertising Agencies).

These definitions vary considerably in terms of their complexity and, to some extent, their emphases. Although a comprehensive definition may be cumbersome, it should be able to better capture the essence and completeness of integrated marketing communications. With this in mind, a complete definition should attempt to elucidate the features identified in Exhibit 2.2. Achievement of all features is a very tall order indeed; even award-winning integrated campaigns will invariably fall short of the ideal.

Exhibit 2.2 Features of integrated marketing communications

- *Clearly identified marketing communications objectives* which are consistent with other organisational objectives.
- *Planned approach* which covers the full extent of marketing communications activities in a coherent and synergistic way.
- *Range of target audiences* – not confined just to customers or prospects nor just to imply end customers but include all selected target audience groups. These may be any specified 'public' or group of 'publics' – stakeholders (e.g. employees, shareholders, suppliers), consumers, customers and influencers of customers and consumers, both trade and domestic.
- *Management of all forms of contact* which may form the basis of marketing communications activity. This involves any relevant communication arising from contact within the organisation and between the organisation and its publics.
- *Effective management and integration of all promotional activities and people involved.*
- Incorporate all *product/brand ('unitised') and 'corporate' marketing communications* efforts.
- *Range of promotional tools* – all elements of the promotional mix including personal and non-personal communications.
- *Range of messages* – brand (corporate and products) propositions should be derived from a single consistent strategy. This does *not* imply a single, standardised message. The integrated marketing communications effort should ensure that all messages are determined in such a way as to work to each other's mutual benefit or at least minimise incongruity.
- *Range of media* – any 'vehicle' able to transmit marketing communication messages and not just mass media.

The following definition incorporates the salient features of IMC. It is a more extensive definition than is typically given in most descriptions because it seeks to emphasise the variety of complex aspects of integration identified by many authors. Importantly, it emphasises that integrated marketing communications is much more than the integration of promotional or marketing communications mix elements.

Definition of integrated marketing communications

Agents

Term used here to describe all individuals and organisations involved in the marketing communications process within and external to the organisation.

Contacts

Any personal or non-personal communication between selected target audience members and the organisation.

Product

Refers to brands, goods, services and any specific object of promotion, and can include, for example, events and personalities.

Integrated marketing communications is a process which involves the management and organisation of all '**agents**' in the analysis, planning, implementation and control of all marketing communications **contacts**, media, messages and promotional tools focused at selected target audiences in such a way as to derive the greatest enhancement and coherence of marketing communications effort in achieving predetermined **product** and corporate marketing communications objectives.

In its simplest form, IMC can be defined as the management process of integrating all marketing communications activities across relevant audience points to achieve greater brand coherence.

The search for integration should not be taken to imply a uniformity of communications which many authors seem to suggest. While creative treatments and messages should be mutually consistent, this is not necessarily to prescribe a single treatment, message or approach. A single, common theme has much to commend it but it is perfectly feasible to consider the integration of disparate approaches and messages targeted at a variety of groups. What needs to be said to shareholders may well be different to messages targeted at employees, which may well be different to the trade, which may well be different to customer group A, which may well be different to customer group B. And the images accompanying these messages may also need to be different. Indeed, it may be argued that under such circumstances there is greater need for integration and management of that integration if confusion is to be avoided.

Having said this, it should be noted that it is typical, good practice to distil the 'essence' of a product or corporation as a brand by the selection of a few choice words and single proposition which all involved with that brand can recognise and to which they can respond. These are factors that have to be considered when developing marketing communications. The selection of one or more messages is a management decision that should be considered in the light of prevailing circumstances and objectives. It is not something that should be prescribed universally. The issue is one of the benefits of a standardised message versus different but mutually consistent messages.

Benefits of integrated marketing communications

The principal benefit derived from the integration of marketing communications is *synergy*. Synergy has been described as the 2 + 2 = 5 phenomenon. By bringing together the various facets of marketing communications in a mutually supportive and enhancing way then the resulting 'whole' is more than the simple sum of its parts. This can be seen when, for example, images and messages used in television advertising are carried through poster and magazine advertisements and are also presented at point-of-sale display, on packaging, sales promotion and merchandising and in other promotional activities. Each element enhances and supports the others in a consistent fashion. For example in BUPA's campaign, highlighting online purchasing in the advertising generated a 400% increase in website hits (Marketing Business 2002). Research has confirmed the link between increased integrated marketing communications and increased sales, share and profit (Marketing Week 2002a).

Exhibit 2.3 lists Linton and Morley's (1995) ten potential benefits of integrated marketing communications. While such benefits may be sought, they are not always achieved because of difficulties of implementation. Some benefits, such as unbiased marketing recommendations, greater marketing precision and high calibre consistent service, have as much to do with the quality and ability of the personnel involved as they have to do with benefits of integration.

Exhibit 2.3 Benefits of integrated marketing communications

● Creative integrity	● Operational efficiency
● Consistent messages	● Cost savings
● Unbiased marketing recommendations	● High-calibre consistent service
● Better use of media	● Easier working relations
● Greater marketing precision	● Greater agency accountability

Source: Linton and Morley (1995)

IN VIEW 2.3

Integration strengthens BUPA's vital signs

BUPA

BUPA's recent marketing strategy repositioned its brand and integrated its offering. The core brand proposition – 'BUPA the Personal Health Service' – was promoted on TV, in press and radio advertising, through direct marketing, sponsorship, PR and internal communications. The website – **www.bupa.co.uk** – plays an important role in BUPA's integrated marketing activities, featuring all communications and offering online quotations and customer service support. BUPA's prompted awareness of the brand currently stands at 97% with Simon Sheard, Group Marketing Director stating that 'we have succeeded in positioning BUPA as the only dedicated independent healthcare specialist in the UK.'

Source: Adapted from *Marketing Business* 2002, p. 41

Negative synergy

Term used to represent the negative effects of not achieving synergy between integrated marketing communications elements. Lack of integration may not merely result in no synergistic benefits, but may actually result in detrimental consequences that could be caused through confusion, lack of effectiveness and efficiency, or misunderstanding.

Not only should the positive benefits of integration be considered, but so too should the consequences of not achieving integration – and it should not be assumed that a lack of integration simply results in a neutral situation. The problem of '**negative synergy**' or dysfunction should be recognised. A lack of integration of marketing communications elements not only means that various promotional tools have to perform independently of the other elements but also that, collectively, the total effort can be counter-productive. Negative effects can be produced. For example, sales promotion activities can portray a cheap or value-for-money product with money-off coupons and discount offers whereas distribution and merchandising activity may attempt to show the product in a status or prestige context with a high value image. The ensuing confusion may result in reduced sales. Duplication of effort and wasted effort can also result in higher costs. It has to be understood that there is a price to pay for *not* achieving integration. These factors are considered further in Chapter 23, Control and Evaluation of Integrated Marketing Communications.

WARNING

Where integration is not applied, there are potential dangers of marketing communication dysfunction in which the activities and effort become counter-productive.

The 4Es and 4Cs of integrated marketing communications

Integration is not easy to achieve but when it is achieved, the 4Es and 4Cs of IMC create the synergistic benefits of integration.

The 4Es of integrated marketing communications are:

- *Enhancing* – improve; augment; intensify.
- *Economical* – least cost in the use of financial and other resources; not wasteful.
- *Efficient* – doing things right; competent; not wasteful.
- *Effective* – doing the right things; producing the outcome required; not wasteful.

The 4Cs of integrated marketing communications are:

- *Coherence* – logically connected; firmly stuck together.
- *Consistency* – not self-contradictory; in agreement, harmony, accord.

- *Continuity* – connected and consistent over time.
- *Complementary communications* – producing a balanced whole; supportive communications.

Confusion is caused between the use of 'efficiency' and 'effectiveness' but distinguishing between them is important. Like 'economical', they are both to do with *not* being wasteful, but it is possible to be very efficient in terms of doing *things right*, but unless you are being 'effective' you may not be doing *the right things* – the task may be wrongly defined. It is, therefore, possible to be efficient without being effective and vice versa. The issue is one of managing integrated marketing communications efficiently and economically but also ensuring that the right marketing communications tasks are selected in the first place.

As suggested earlier, it is common to believe that integrated marketing communications can only be achieved by adopting a standardised message. Or, to put it in the terms used above, enhancing and coherent communications can only be achieved by developing a single message/image throughout. This is a basic misconception although it does carry an element of truth and good practice depending upon the 'level' of integration to which it is applied (see Chapter 23, Control and Evaluation of Integrated Marketing Communications). In developing a campaign or part of a campaign targeted at a specific audience, a single proposition is less likely to confuse and is more likely to create impact. However, to the extent that integrated marketing communications may be targeted at many different audiences with multiple objectives, it is more likely that not one but multiple messages may be used. What is significant is that those messages should be coherent, consistent and complementary. They may be different but should not be contradictory and in so doing, the brand's (corporate and product) proposition should not be compromised. In the words used in In View 2.2, it is more important to achieve a 'common brand understanding and common brand passion, not standardised message' (Kendall 1999).

Impetus for integrated marketing communications

To integrate or separate marketing communications is a major issue. As Duncan and Everett (1993) observe, in practice promotional mix elements have been operated as discrete communications functions. This segregation is reflected in the fragmented structure of the marketing communications industry with specialist agencies operating in relative isolation of each other. Advertising agencies' previous inability to embrace the new emphases being placed on marketing communications has encouraged new agency development in areas such as communications strategy, PR, corporate identity, branding and brand naming, packaging, media sales, the new media, direct mail, sales promotions, direct response TV, telemarketing and sponsorship. Still more recently has seen the growth of Internet agencies such as Doubleclick which now operates offices throughout the world specialising in providing advertising solutions specifically for the Internet.

As the degree of specialisation increases, the increasing separation of promotions may seem a natural development from the point of view of the service providers. However, while the execution of specialist functions may be channelled through separate service providers, clients have a need for an integrated, strategic view. The great irony is that increased segregation has occurred at a time when the call for integration has never been greater. Spurred on by the perceived competitive edge and financial benefits derived from offering more integrated services, it is only recently that the marketing communications industry has started to come to terms with the challenges of integration (see Chapters 14 and 15, Organisational Implications of Integrated Marketing Communications and Agency Operations).

IN VIEW 2.4

Agency perspectives on and activities in integration

- In August 2002, WPP-owned J Walter Thompson (JWT) recognised the importance of IMC by setting up the agency's first integrated creative team to create ideas that work across many customer contact points.

  KLP Euro RSCG achieved the number one position for the second time running in 2002 in the *Marketing Week* Promotional Marketing Agencies Reputations survey. Phil Bourne, chief executive, stated 'I hope our position is the result of awareness of our ability to deliver an integrated solution. There is a trend among clients to want this sort of facility'. Another top scorer, Tequila's chief executive Paul Biggens commented: 'The industry has been talking about integration for 10 to 15 years. Our position is now media neutral. We have specialist skills in a number of different disciplines – events, direct marketing, sales promotion, sponsorship, and digital. A typical scenario for us is to have clients working across most of those'.

- Charles Grant-Salmon of UK's Hobbs Marketing states, 'We recognised seven years ago the need to integrate the service with other areas of the cycle to enable us to offer a more total solution to enable our customers to have tighter control and a better and more complete return from their investment (*Marketing Week* 2002b).'

- Rainey Kelly Campbell Roalfe's approach to handling client marketing communications business led it to attracting blue chip clients such as Virgin Atlantic, Scottish Courage, Smith and Nephew, Allied Domecq, The Times, The Sunday Times and Ionica. The agency saw its approach to integrative thinking as a competitive advantage and as a value-added service to its clients. Importantly, the founding members saw integration as a *mindset* not a *skillset* with the real challenge expressed as finding the 'big idea' around which to integrate. Creativity is critical, but creativity is seen as a team approach that extends across all media applications – 'it is broader and more conceptual with a focus on ideas'. They described 'ideas before advertising, and ideas beyond advertising'. Significantly, the client is seen as a valued team member in the process.

Source: Rainey (1997).

In comparison:

- BMP DDB chairman, Chris Powell, is realistic about agencies' ability to create integrated campaigns. He says, 'It's probably true to say all agencies are struggling. It's hard enough to do a traditional campaign. We haven't got good enough at developing integrated campaigns … there is a much greater acceptance of media neutrality, but agencies are also having to cut corners to create campaigns because of tighter margins' (*Marketing Week*, 2002c).

- While recognising and accepting the benefits of integration, Winston Fletcher, chairman of the Bozell UK Group, warned that advertising agencies should 'stick to their core business'. He is 'committed to the view that most clients require, and rightly demand, a plethora of different marketing communications services, working in harmony and singing the same tune', but he does not believe that it needs to be achieved by having a single, 'through-the-line', all-singing, all-dancing agency. The Bozell UK Group includes one of the world's leading website agencies and major agencies operating in public relations, sponsorship, direct marketing and sales promotions as well as advertising. Indeed, Fletcher believes that his Group offers a more comprehensive range of marketing communications than any other group in the UK. He believes that interests are best served by letting advertising agencies do what they are best at doing – advertising. As he points out, it is estimated that £151.5 bn ($250 bn) is spent on above-the-line advertising worldwide. 'If advertising were a country it would be the world's 14th biggest'. 'Happily, marketing communications is a vast and growing pool, and there is plenty of room for us all to swim in it without jostling each others' lanes' (Fletcher 1997).

● A recent Institute of Practitioners in Advertising workshop highlighted that to be effective integrated marketing communications should actively reinforce agreed brand values in any dialogue with the market and should be measured by its short- and long-term effects. David Iddiols of HPI suggests, therefore, that 'the "Brand Soul" should be omnipresent in thought, word and deed. This is quite straight forward in theory ... in practice, however, attempts to implement an integrated plan often flounder.' As Richard Jeans has put it, 'Finding an idea which will work on TV, in PR, as a direct marketing approach, on exhibition stands and on bus tracks inevitably leads you to the lowest common denominator communications.' However, Iddiols research indicates integration is both possible and desirable and where it is achieved, he refers to this as 'Marketing Superglue' (Iddiols 2000; Jeans 1998).

Marketing database technology

The use of accurate customer and prospect customer information, competitor information, market information and internal company information stored on a computer database to focus marketing activities towards targets.

Segregation of marketing activities can also be seen within the structures of client organisations. It is common for the various marketing communications functions to be the responsibility of different managers and departments which operate autonomously of each other. Eisenhart (1989) has identified a move to rectify this situation and claims there is a trend for organisations which seek to adopt an integrated marketing communications philosophy to physically integrate into one department the people responsible for various marketing communications functions. While this may be a trend, one would have to comment on the limited evidence that this, in any way, represents anything more than a minor foray into a new management approach. The vast majority of organisations still cling on to their old prejudices. Developments in **marketing database technology** will increasingly encourage greater integration but, as Fletcher et al. (1994) have discovered, there are major organisational barriers which can arise when a company attempts to integrate itself as it moves into database marketing in any significant way.

Undoubtedly, changes occurring in the large, influential advertising agencies and agency groups are providing a significant impetus for integration and change within the industry at large. This movement has occurred slowly but with growing momentum and the reasons for these changes are numerous. A few are specified below, together with other factors that have encouraged the adoption of favourable attitudes towards integration. A summary of factors encouraging integrated marketing communications is shown in Exhibit 2.4 followed by an explanation of each.

Exhibit 2.4 Summary of factors encouraging integrated marketing communications

- Lack of real growth in advertising expenditure
- Shrinking employee base
- New promotional agencies setting up in competition with traditional advertising agencies
- Growth in media independents
- Clients moving to management consultants for strategic advice and planning
- Increasing sophistication of client managers
- Perceived competitive advantage and financial benefits of offering integrated services
- Growth in international communications
- Locus of retail power
- Recognition of the need for a strategic view of marketing communications – growth in acceptance of relationship marketing and recognition of internal audiences
- Technological advances especially in database technology
- Integrated marketing communications perceived to provide extra benefits

Media inflation

The rise in media prices year on year.

Public relations (PR)

The planned and sustained effort to establish and maintain goodwill and mutual understanding between an organisation and its publics.

Sales promotion

Widely used term covering a myriad of promotional activities, excluding advertising, PR and personal selling. Sales promotion is associated with free offers, price deals, premium offers, and other promotions including merchandising, point-of-sale displays, leaflets and product literature.

Direct mail

The use of postal services to deliver marketing communications materials. It may be considered an aspect of advertising in that it is used as a mass medium even though it can be used for individually targeted messages. It should not be confused with direct marketing, which is a much broader concept.

Advertising

The use of paid mass media, by an identified sponsor, to deliver communications to target audiences.

Lack of real growth in advertising expenditure

While year-on-year expenditure on advertising has increased, it has fundamentally not done so in real terms. It has basically kept pace with **media inflation**. This has been the general pattern in the UK and is reflected in many places around the world. A notable exception to this is China. It is also fair to note that as the UK economy has grown since the mid-1990s, advertising has experienced some growth compared to that in other countries moving from 5.1% of global adspend to 6.3% by 2000. However, this can be contrasted with the greater growth that has been experienced in other promotional areas such as **public relations**, **sales promotions** and, particularly, in **direct mail** (which enables more highly targeted communications) and the use of Internet promotions.

From the marketer's perspective, **advertising** (which, as a form of marketing communications uses mass media and mass communications methods – see Chapter 26) is increasingly being questioned as the best or most appropriate form of communication to achieve certain promotional objectives. Undoubtedly, advertising has a role to play but this role is being re-evaluated as just one of many communication approaches. This is particularly so as greater emphasis is placed on value-for-money and return on investment. Direct mail and money-off sales promotions, for example, are much better able to demonstrate direct responses and sales effects. If these are the effects sought, if more targeted efforts are required and if short-term response is the objective, then advertising may be allocated proportionally lower spends. Niall Fitzgerald, chairman of Unilever, was reported as complaining, 'I do not find today's advertising agencies being much of a match for tomorrow's marketing opportunities' (Bainbridge 1997, p. 21).

This situation has had a profound effect on advertising agency income and has given rise to a change in the balance of 'power' away from traditional advertising in favour of other marketing communications elements. Advertising agencies have been forced to respond to this situation with many claiming a more 'all-embracing' attitude towards all forms of promotional activity (some are referring to this as 'media neutral planning') and the integration of specialist agencies within agency groups who collectively can offer a more comprehensive service. None of these comments are intended in any way to denigrate advertising – it is a powerful form of promotional activity – but, so too, are other promotional tools and these are becoming more widely recognised.

Shrinking employee base

This is very much related to the point above. Advertising agencies, in particular, have suffered markedly in the downsizing of their staffing levels as clients and agencies have all sought greater operating efficiencies. This has provided an even greater spur to advertising agencies to widen their outlook and services provided. Some agencies and agency groups refer to themselves as 'one-stop shops' and 'media neutral agencies', and claim to provide all the services needed to integrate the various elements of the promotional mix.

New promotional agencies setting up in competition with traditional advertising agencies

A changing balance of emphasis of promotional mix spend to areas other than advertising has led to a significant growth in the development of new promotional agencies specialising in particular areas of the promotional mix. These include direct marketing/mail, merchandising, web advertising and design, conferences and exhibitions, incentives, sales promotions, public relations and others. A particular example of this trend can be seen in the start-up of new agencies specialising in the 'new' media and offering Internet and new technology services. While on the one hand this creates an even more fragmented environment in the communications industry it also provides a greater impetus to the need for integration. This is certainly a role perceived by many of the large and influential agencies.

Growth in media independents

Media independents

Companies specialising in planning and buying media. They buy space and time (e.g. time spots on television) from media owners, and sell to agencies and advertisers. They, themselves, are not media owners.

Traditionally, advertising agencies have been responsible for the purchase of media time and space on behalf of their clients. For this, they received commission from the media. This, in fact, has been the conventional form of payment for advertising agencies and a major source of their income. Increasingly, **media independents** have taken on the role of media purchase; this has left advertising agencies seeking other forms of income generation. Increasing reliance has been placed on the charging of fees for services (see Chapter 15 for details of agency payment systems) and a more integrative service being offered.

Clients moving to management consultants for strategic advice and planning

Many of the top advertising agencies have lost the initiative and corresponding income in providing marketing communications strategic planning and development services to major clients who have increasingly turned to management consultancies for what they might consider to be more independent strategic advice (Proctor 1996). Because these management consultancies have no allegiances to any particular marketing communications approach, clients argue that they are in a better position to adopt a more integrative and less biased attitude.

Increasing sophistication of client managers

Clients are becoming increasingly sophisticated in their use of promotional activities, and in what they expect from those activities and how they should organise themselves and their agencies to achieve the best outcomes. Whilst it may be true to say that the degree of such sophistication varies significantly, more client organisations appreciate the importance and interrelatedness of marketing communication activities and expect them to be 'orchestrated' together. To some extent these clients are reorganising themselves internally to achieve better integration and they expect their agencies to do likewise. While some managers are becoming more sophisticated this is also coming at a time when some companies are reducing their marketing staffing and resources. This can create a greater reliance on agencies to provide an integrated service.

Perceived competitive advantage and financial benefits of offering integrated services

NEED TO KNOW

☑ *Channel-neutral planning – also termed media neutral planning – is the complete communications strategy in which customers are reached through a tailored mix of media, based on customers' individual relationship with the brand and the channel. It incorporates direct marketing, PR and point-of-purchase, as well as traditional media formats such as TV and radio, is based on the concept of IMC, and has risen to the top of the agenda in the communications industry* (Marketing Business *2003*; Marketing Week *2002d*).

If it is the case that clients are becoming more sophisticated and that they are organising themselves to benefit from integrated marketing communications activities, there will be a need for agencies of whatever persuasion either to offer fully integrated services 'in-house' or show their ability to work with a range of specialist agencies in an integrated fashion. While the impetus for change within some agencies may be to avoid some of the negative effects of the changes already taking place, other promotional agencies are being spurred on by the more positive side of change. They perceive that a competitive edge and financial rewards may be derived from offering services to clients that are more integrated.

Growth in international communications

One of the factors that has had a significant effect on the recognition for integration is the increase in international marketing activities. As companies have faced the challenge of marketing in many countries they have had to face up to the need for internationally recognised brands that have been capable of transcending national borders and cultural boundaries. This has required a strong sense of integration of marketing communications with corresponding consideration of internationally acceptable brand names and creative treatments. Sometimes this has led to standardised treatments. Sometimes treatments are developed that vary from country to country but do so within a single international strategy.

Locus of retail power

Stakeholders

Term used to describe the many and various groups of people who have an interest or involvement with an organisation. Stakeholders include suppliers, customers, consumers, investors, employees and distributors.

Relationship marketing

View that emphasises the importance of the relationships developed between an organisation and other parties including customers, partners, suppliers and the trade.

Especially for fast moving consumer goods (FMCG) manufacturers, the increased power and control held by retailers is forcing change. Retailers expect and demand integrated trade and consumer marketing communication strategies.

Recognition of the need for a strategic view of marketing communications – growth in acceptance of relationship marketing and recognition of internal audiences

Commonly, the whole field of marketing has concerned itself with external audiences – namely end customers and consumers. Over the years, however, the importance of internal audiences, strategic partners, members of the distribution chain, and all other **stakeholders** have become increasingly recognised for the important roles they play in the total marketing process. This has led to an increased emphasis on what has been called '**relationship marketing**' and a heightened recognition that marketing communications must embrace many more audiences than just end customers and consumers (important though they are). To undertake this 'new' role, specification of target audiences and the integration of the full range of marketing communications need to be reappraised. In many respects, this is not new at all. Trade marketing has always involved promotions to groups other than end customers. PR agencies have placed, for a great number of years, importance on all groups of internal and external audiences, or 'publics' as they tend to be called. But the acceptance of 'relationship marketing' concepts have, more than ever before, created a climate in which emphasis on integrated marketing communications, targeted at numerous audiences, can flourish.

Technological advances especially in database technology

There have been many major technological advances in the world of marketing communications; some of these have gone largely unappreciated. There have been advances in printing inks and printing technology which, for example, have led to full-colour daily newspapers in recent years and an explosion in sales promotion and merchandising activity. There have been major developments in mailing technology and mail delivery services. New media have sprung up seemingly from nowhere, such as the Internet. Among the technological innovations that have really taken the industry by storm are in database technology and systems. The growth in computing sophistication, which has revolutionised data collection, storage, retrieval and analysis, has been truly phenomenal. So much more information can be manipulated about every aspect of business. This includes information about customers and consumers and their buying and media habits. The opportunities for integrated marketing communications and the need for them to enhance customer contact management have never been greater.

NEED TO KNOW

☑ *Integrated marketing communications requires that a much broader perspective is taken (than has typically been the case in the past) of the range of target audiences with whom to communicate and the range of marketing communications activities that can be applied.*

Integrated marketing communications perceived to provide extra benefits

The benefits of integrated marketing communications were identified earlier in the chapter. As more clients and agencies recognise these benefits, the incidence of integrated marketing activities will increase.

Barriers to integrated marketing communications

The concept of integration is warmly embraced by some while others are more reserved in their views. Some consider it inevitable while others consider it undesirable. What is indisputable is the fact that the whole communications industry is going through a period of change that is having a significant impact upon working practices and philosophies. Whether the dissenters to integration like it or not, the industry is adopting practices of integration urged on by many of the large players – clients, promotion agencies and media owners.

The changes that have occurred over recent years have held up to view the inadequacy of many existing marketing communications practices. There is a need for industry change if the challenges of the future are to be met. The impetus for this change has probably been strongest in organisations such as the large fast moving consumer goods (FMCG) companies operating globally in their search for international integration of their promotions. This imperative has forced a major review of the structure and operations of these companies and the advertising and promotions agencies that handle their international accounts.

Integration is not easily achieved and while the problems of integration are not insurmountable, they are significant for a variety of reasons. These are summarised in Exhibit 2.5 and explained below.

Exhibit 2.5 Summary of factors discouraging integrated marketing communications

- Mind-set
- Taxonomy and language
- Structure of organisations
- Elitism
- Magnitude of task
- Adequacy of budgets
- Manager ability
- Agency remuneration systems
- Dimensions of integration

Mind-set

Mind-set

Particular way of thinking or view held.

The **mind-set** built up over many years of practice has rewarded specialisation and overlooked the need for, and benefits of, integration. Gonring (1994) has identified the fear of change and loss of control felt by individuals associated with the industry. Robbs and Taubler (1996) have highlighted agency creatives' aversion to integration and their lack of willingness to work across the media and promotional mix tools. Schultz (1993) has commented on the cult of specialisation and the history, tradition and experience of companies as limiting factors to the fulfilment of integration. Thus, we find that members of the marketing communications industry are not necessarily favourably disposed towards the concept of integration because their thinking and attitudes are already set against it.

Moreover, there is the question of what it is that we wish to integrate. For many, their thinking is limited and may extend only to the integration of various elements within a single campaign rather than the full array of communication targets and activities. Many client organisations relegate promotional activities to the tactical level and fail to appreciate their strategic significance. It is as though they are concerned with 'single battles rather than the whole war'. True integration has to take the widest view.

Taxonomy and language

The very taxonomy and language which is used to describe the promotional (or marketing communications) mix has a detrimental effect on the integrative process. The result is that we perceive and encourage the use of promotional activities as discrete activities i.e. advertising is separated from corporate identity which is separated from merchandising which is separated from personal selling, etc.

The mix taxonomy (albeit it in simplified form), can be identified as personal selling, advertising, sales promotion and public relations (see Chapter 1) or, as Shimp (2000) identified, personal selling, advertising, sales promotions, sponsorship, publicity and point-of-purchase communication. These forms of categorisation are increasingly inadequate in expressing the range of activities they seek to describe and present major classification difficulties. It is difficult, for example, to know where to place, within the categories of the mix, such varied activities as direct mail, product placement and endorsement, exhibitions, internal forms of communications, etc. These issues have been addressed initially in Chapter 1 where the IMC Mix Model was introduced to overcome some of the criticisms of the promotional mix taxonomy. It should be recognised, though, that the IMC Mix Model itself is a classification approach and, so too, suffers from similar criticisms.

Despite the shortcomings of the promotional or marketing communications mix, we shall continue to make reference to it throughout this book. There is nothing inherently wrong with the terminology; the difficulties lie in how to classify the marketing communications elements for ease of use. Chapters 24 to 31 are devoted to identifying the promotional mix elements in turn. While the promotional mix taxonomy may be a limiting concept, it is also one that forms the basis to identify and appreciate the many forms of marketing communications in practice. By taking each element in turn, it also facilitates a growth in understanding each and their relationship to each other (and thus their integration). It is adopted here, recognising its limitations as well as its advantages.

NEED TO KNOW

☑ *The promotional mix and marketing communications mix are terms that are typically used interchangeably throughout this book. Should there be any occasion when a distinction is drawn, this will be clearly identified.*

Vertical communications

Internal communications between different hierarchical levels of employees, e.g. between managers and their subordinates.

Turf battles

Discussions and disagreements between groups of employees from different parts of an organisation, each favouring their own points of view. This is associated with power struggles within organisations between individuals and sections.

Functional silos

The barriers erected between functions and departments that tend to cause separation between functional groups.

Structure of organisations

The structure of organisations may make it difficult to co-ordinate and manage disparate specialisms as one entity. Organisations have typically subdivided their tasks into sub-units (departments) in order to cope with the magnitude of operations. Management's response when faced with large, many-faceted tasks has been to disaggregate them and give them to specialists. This has certainly been true of marketing communications. To do otherwise presents tasks of co-ordinating and communicating with many organisations composed of many disparate individuals. While project teams and cross-functional assignments can help to break down organisational barriers there still remain problems of hierarchical structures, **vertical communications**, 'turf battles', power struggles and 'functional silos' (Gonring 1994; Schultz 1993) in which individuals and groups are protective of their own specialisations and interests. Significantly, the increasing use of marketing database technology and systems offer new structural mechanisms for facilitating organisational integration. On a more negative note, some organisations are scaling down their marketing departments in the belief that marketing has not lived up to its promise.

Elitism

Not only do organisational structures encourage separatism, there is a sense of perceived elitism exhibited by individuals within each promotional mix specialism. PR specialists extol their superiority over advertising specialists who likewise extol their virtues over PR, direct mail and sales promotion, etc. While such views are held, it is unlikely that specialists will come to the 'promotional discussion table' as equals to determine what is best for the total marketing communications effort.

FOOD FOR THOUGHT

It is interesting to note that the total level of expenditure on marketing communications is unlikely to be monitored by companies. Budgets are so disaggregated as to make it difficult to assess the full cost of marketing communications as they range from stationery and livery to advertising and corporate hospitality. The sales department and its activities, so much a critical part of the total marketing communications effort, will invariably hold its budgets completely separate from other budgets. This comment is not intended as a criticism of budgeting activities, rather as an observation of them.

Magnitude of task

It is very difficult to conceptualise the 'Big Picture' and to muster all the organisational influences needed to achieve integration. A survey carried out in 1993 by the OmniTech Consulting Group for the journal *Advertising Age* discovered that nearly 60% of respondents believed that the need to have a broad perspective was the biggest obstacle to IMC. Just over 50% cited insufficient budgets as the number two impediment (Fawcett 1993). While this example is now a decade old, there is little evidence that the magnitude of the task has diminished in many organisations.

There are many dimensions and levels of integration (as identified below and in Chapter 14) which all pose their individual and collective difficulties. To be implemented, integrated marketing communications requires the involvement of the whole organisation and its agents from the chief executive downwards.

Adequacy of budgets

Too frequently, organisations fail to fully appreciate the more strategic and longer-term values of marketing communications. Expenditure on them is rarely considered an investment, although with the growth in the recognition of the value of brands (the **brand equity**) this situation is slowly changing. Budgets are often set with the short term in mind rather than the long term and as a cost rather than an investment. The result may be that budgets are lower than those needed for the full integration of marketing communications. Many companies, for example, fail to invest adequately in the development and maintenance of an appropriate database.

Brand equity

The value of the brand's name, symbols, associations and reputation to all target audiences who interact with it.

Manager ability

Cross-disciplinary skills create a barrier to IMC. The skills required are wide with few possessing the ability to master them.

Agency remuneration systems

This particularly applies to advertising agencies whose income has traditionally come from **media commission** (see Chapter 15 for details). There has, therefore, been a strong incentive for advertising agencies to favour advertising activities above other forms of marketing communications. The systems of agency payment are now changing and, to some extent, they now overcome the disincentive to integrate.

Media commission

The financial commission given to advertising agencies and media independents by media owners when they buy advertising space or time.

Dimensions of integration

There are many dimensions of integration. If integration of marketing communications is to be achieved the problem must be addressed in each dimension. It is common to think of integration as being almost exclusively about the integration of the promotional mix elements. This is a gross oversimplification of the problem. Other dimensions include the integration of creative elements, intra- and inter-organisational factors, integration of the promotional mix with other marketing mix factors, information and database systems, integration of communications targeted towards multiple audiences – internal and external, corporate and **'unitised' communications**, and geographical integration.

Some authors (e.g. Smith, Berry and Pulford 1997) have preferred to use the term 'levels of integration' in this context. It is felt that 'levels' applied to this concept is misleading in that it implies a degree of hierarchy or priority. 'Dimensions' is preferred, here, to suggest a simple listing without implied order, priority or hierarchy although the actual impact each dimension may have is likely to differ depending upon circumstances. Each dimension is described in more detail in Chapter 23, Control and Evaluation of Integrated Marketing Communications. The term 'levels of integrated marketing communications' will be used in Chapter 23 to refer to strategic versus tactical perspectives of integration.

'Unitised' communications

This is an uncommon term, used here to distinguish between marketing communications that promote the organisation as a whole (corporate communications) and those that promote parts or 'units' of the organisation, such as its goods, services, brands, individuals or sections of the organisation.

Summary

Integration of marketing communications is essential if the full benefits and impact of marketing communications are to be achieved. Although integration is not a new concept, it is one that is increasingly being recognised and valued. Many people emphasise integration as the 'pulling together' of the elements of the promotional mix. While this is an important aspect of integration, it is just one of many possible considerations which have been identified in this chapter as 'features' of integrated marketing communications.

In practice it is difficult to achieve integration in its widest sense but failure to do so may not only result in lack of synergy but, more negatively, in counter-productive communications. An important part of integrated marketing communications is its management and organisation.

Having provided a comprehensive definition of integrated marketing communications, this chapter identified some of the benefits of integration and proposed the 4Es and 4Cs of integrated marketing communications.

Integrated marketing communications as a concept and as a practice has become increasingly popular over recent years. Many academics advocate integration and many members of the communications industry proclaim the need for greater integration. While recognising the call for greater integration, this chapter has identified a range of factors that either encourage integration or present barriers to its achievement. Interestingly, many of the reasons encouraging the growth of integrated marketing communications are externally driven – they are factors outside the control of organisations, clients and agencies. Factors inhibiting integration are frequently internally, organisationally driven which are typically within the control of management to overcome if there is a will to do so.

Self-review questions

1 List at least five benefits of integrated marketing communications. Are there other benefits you can identify that are not included in Linton and Morley's list?

2 What do you think Linton and Morley meant in their list of benefits when they referred to 'unbiased marketing recommendations'?

3 Nine features of integrated marketing communications have been identified in this chapter, only one of which refers to the integration of promotional tools. Name and describe the other eight.

4 What do you understand by the terms 'dysfunctional' or 'counter-productive' marketing communications?

5 What is the difference between 'efficient' and 'effective' marketing communications?

6 'For marketing communications to be successfully integrated, a single message should always be used'. Do you agree with this statement? If not, what are the arguments for using multiple messages? Try to think of examples, either real or hypothetical, to illustrate your case.

➔

7 Why should such factors as limited or lack of real growth in advertising expenditure and shrinking advertising agency employee base encourage the growth of integrated marketing communications?

8 Identify the technological advances that have helped provide an impetus for integrated marketing communications.

9 There are a number of management and organisational issues that tend to act as barriers to integrated marketing communications. Identify what these are and comment on the difficulty you think organisations face in overcoming them.

10 Do you consider integration of marketing communications to be a desirable thing? Given the difficulties in achieving integrated marketing communications, would it be better not to try?

Project

You are a newly appointed marketing executive and your marketing director has asked you to produce a report that she can present at the next board meeting. In your report, you should succinctly highlight the issues the company might have to face when first attempting to improve the integration of their marketing communications effort. Within your report, you should outline why companies are moving towards integration and identify the main reasons for and against integration.

References

Bainbridge, J. (1997), It was a bad year for … . *Marketing*, 18 December, 21.

Betts, P., Huntington, A., Pulford, A. and Warnaby, G. (1995), *Marketing Communications Strategy* 2nd edn. BPP Publishing.

Bird, D. (1992), Five ways to integrate marketing. *Marketing*, 9 January, 10.

Brand Strategy (2002), Skoda's velvet revolution, 22 April.

Duckworth, G. (ed.) (1997), *Advertising Works 9: IPA Advertising Effectiveness Awards 1996*. NTC Publications.

Duncan, T.R. and Everett, S.E. (1993), Client perceptions of integrated marketing communications. *Journal of Advertising Research*, May/June, 30–39.

Eisenhart, T. (1989), Playing together: marketing and communications catch the team spirit. *Business Marketing*, July.

Fawcett, A.W. (1993), Integrated marketing door open for experts. *Advertising Age*, 8 November, Special Report, S2.

Fletcher, W. (1997), Ad world is alive and well despite the obituaries. *Marketing*, 23 October, 6.

Fletcher, K., Wheeler, C. and Wright, J. (1994), Strategic implementation of database marketing: problems and pitfalls. *Long Range Planning*, 27 (1), 133–141.

Gonring, M.P. (1994), Putting integrated marketing communications to work today. *Public Relations Quarterly*, Fall, 39 (3), 45–48.

Hume, S. (1993), Integrated marketing: who's in charge here? *Advertising Age*, 22 March, 64 (12), 3/52.

Iddiols, D. (2000), Marketing superglue, *ADMAP*, May.

Jeans, R. (1998), Integrating marketing communications, *ADMAP*, December.

Kendall, N. (ed.) (1999), *Advertising Works 10: IPA Advertising Effectiveness Awards 1998*. NTC Publications.

Kotler, P., Armstrong, G., Saunders, J. and Wong, V. (1999), *Principles of Marketing* 2nd European edn. Prentice Hall.

Linton, I. and Morley, K. (1995), *Integrated Marketing Communications*. Oxford: Butterworth-Heinemann.

Marketing Business (2003), Disregarding bias, February, 14.

Marketing Business (2002), Strong Vital Signs, September, 41.

Marketing Week (2002a), Everyone wins in integration game, 18 April.

Marketing Week (2002b), The right formula, 26 September.

Marketing Week (2002c), Integrated message pulling industry apart, 28 March.

Marketing Week (2002d), Shift the media-neutral concept up a few gears, 13 June.

Proctor, D. (1996), Presentation to the *IPA Advertising and Academia Seminar*, London, September.

Rainey, M.T. (1997), Presentation to the *IPA Advertising and Academia Seminar*, London, September.

Robbs, B. and Taubler, D. (1996), Will creatives prevent agencies from adopting integrated marketing? *Marketing News*, 23 September, 30 (20), 4.

Schultz, D.E. (1993), Integrated marketing communications: maybe definition is in the point of view. *Marketing News*, 18 January.

Shimp, T. (2000), *Advertising, Promotion, and Supplemental Aspects of Integrated Marketing Communications* 5th edn. New York: Dryden Press.

Smith, P., Berry, C and Pulford, A. (1997), *Strategic Marketing Communications*. London: Kogan Page.

Selected further reading

Advertising Works IPA Advertising Effectiveness Awards Series 1–12 (1980–2003). NTC Publications.

Duncan, T.R. (1994), Is your marketing communications integrated? *Advertising Age*, 24 January, 26.

Duncan, T. and Everett, S.E. (1993), Client perceptions of integrated marketing communications. *Journal of Advertising Research*, May/June, 30–39.

Schultz, D. and Schultz, H. (2004), *IMC: The New Generation*. McGraw-Hill.

Schultz, D.E., Tannenbaum, S.I. and Lauterborn, R.F. (1994), *Integrated Marketing Communications: Pulling It Together and Making It Work*. NTC Business Books.

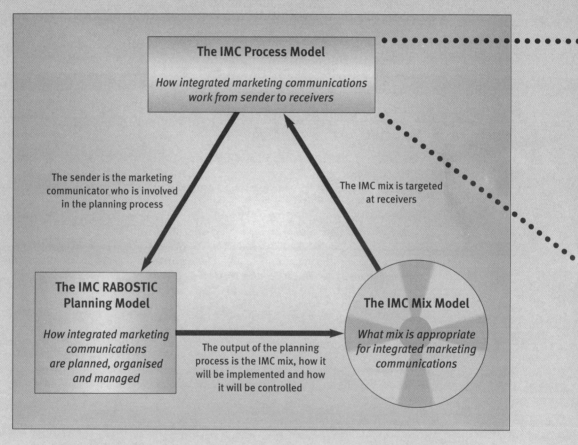

The IMC Process Model

*How integrated marketing communications
work from sender to receivers*

The sender is the marketing
communicator who is involved
in the planning process

The IMC mix is targeted
at receivers

**The IMC RABOSTIC
Planning Model**

*How integrated marketing
communications
are planned, organised
and managed*

The output of the planning
process is the IMC mix, how it
will be implemented and how
it will be controlled

The IMC Mix Model

*What mix is appropriate
for integrated marketing
communications*

The Integrated Marketing Communications (IMC) Framework

Part 1

The Integrated Marketing Communications Process

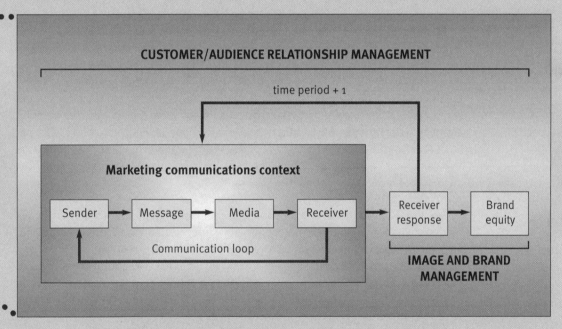

The Integrated Marketing Communications (IMC) Process Model

Concern

Concern, an international relief and development charity, has divisions in the US, Ireland, Northern Ireland, England and Wales, and Scotland. In the mid-1990s, Concern was experiencing a fall in revenue and facing challenging market conditions coupled with a historic lack of investment in marketing.  An integrated marketing communications strategy turned around the fortunes of the organisation so much so that at the height of the emergency in Afghanistan, 300,000 people were surviving on aid being delivered by Concern.

The strategy started with merging databases to enable the marketing approach to be properly integrated. Four marketing databases were combined into a new marketing information system. To make the most of the new information system, new procedures were also introduced to ensure donation and standing order processing could cope with new volumes. This attention to procedures paid dividends when responses started to come in better than anyone could have imagined. At one point standing orders numbered 11,000 in one month, from previous volumes of 200 per year! A comprehensive Donor Lifetime Value model was developed. This model was used to forecast and manage future lifetime value by evaluating donors recruited from each source. Information about the best donor sources was fed back into the donor recruitment strategy.

The new marketing team developed a fresh approach to donor recruitment. A rich mix of media was used and the campaign was fully integrated across the UK and Ireland. Each medium had a target return on investment from recruited donors of 1:1 in the first year (indicating that the costs of the campaign would at least be covered by revenues), rising to 4:1 by the fifth year. The packs, inserts and advertisements featured topical and hard-hitting messages coupled with a clear response device. A consistent message appeared across all media during the generic fundraising campaigns.

Direct mail packs were developed for specific emergency appeals. The Afghanistan campaign featured packs for high and normal value donors. The packs updated donors about the situation in Afghanistan using a letter, a clever email-like insert, a programme update memo and photographs of individual families to bring the appeal to life. A simple donation slip and reply paid envelope completed the pack. The appeal pack imparted emotive information in a straightforward way. The appeal for money was kept reasonably low key as the news spoke for itself. The letter's opening paragraph acknowledged the donor's status as a supporter and interested party. The simplicity of the pack, using cheap, typed inserts, was in keeping with the charity's image. The non-donor or normal donor pack used cheaper materials, fewer inserts and solicited a direct debit. The letter was slightly stronger in tone.

Appeal response capability was honed, allowing Concern's appeal advertisements to achieve first appearance in the UK press and DRTV before other charities. Use of

DRTV was refined to the point where Concern could air appeals within 48 hours of a disaster occurring. Two generic adverts were developed that could be adapted to fit each circumstance, one for immediate disaster relief and the other for the recruitment of regular donors. DRTV was also considered to have had a major impact on brand awareness, following its use integrated with press and direct mail.

Sometimes taking advantage of increased public awareness needs a brave decision. Concern's courage reaped dividends when they timed an appeal showing the plight of Afghanistan's people soon after the American disaster of 11 September 2001. Fourteen press ads, four TV ads and several direct mail packs were rapidly produced to target key market segments. The appeal raised £4 million to counteract the effect of war and avert famine.

Email's potential for rapid response was recognised and capitalised on, with emails despatched within two hours of a disaster occurring. Recipients were encouraged to pass the email on to a friend, exploiting the viral potential of email. Up to the minute news about the unfolding disaster was conveyed to a growing email list, accompanied by further requests for donations. Special donation response websites were developed for each campaign.

The plan has now been running for two years. Impressively, all financial targets for the five-year plan, ending 2004, were achieved by end 2001. All investment has paid back within the first year. The charity has regained its leadership of the Republic of Ireland market and doubled its donor market share in the highly competitive UK market. Following the encouraging performance of early campaigns, donor recruitment targets have been increased for 2002. Concern are now able to roll out new creative approaches targeting specific age groups with much greater confidence. The team now have detailed knowledge of which media perform best and will potentially return the best lifetime value.

CD

More details of this case study can be found on the CD.

Chapter 3

Creating shared meaning in marketing communications – from sender to receiver

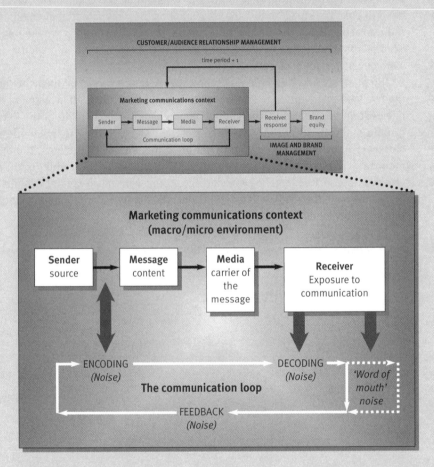

The IMC Process Model

CD

A key objective in Concern's campaign was to position themselves in the British marketplace. As you read Chapter 3 and refer to Case Study 1 on the CD, consider how Concern's credibility is created through their marketing communications activities. Is there any evidence of the organisation modifying marketing communications as a result of audience feedback?

Chapter outline

- An introduction to the communications loop
- The use of signs in encoding and decoding
- How meaning is created
- Sender credibility
- Likeability of a communication
- Modelling in marketing communications

Objectives

- To outline the four main elements of how communications work: encoding, decoding, noise and feedback
- To detail how meaning is conveyed through signs
- To review the mechanisms by which people perceive and categorise the world around them
- To demonstrate how credibility is created, and what can be done to improve the credibility of communications
- To outline the significance of likeability in communications
- To explain the role of modelling in marketing communications

Professional perspective

Ian Ramsden Managing Director, The HotHouse

We receive information via our five senses and, although we use them all, individually, we have a preference for one. To understand this, go shopping with a female and see how touch and sight are the most used senses, whilst with a man it's auditory (what he's told!). People don't buy on price alone. They perceive the world in their own unique way and we must always try and understand what people prefer to be communicated with and so match their preferences.

Being able to communicate on as level a playing field as possible is the goal of all marketers so that messages can be understood.

Remember the original 'Next' Directory and its inclusion of fabric swatches? Or the 'talking envelope' from IBM France in 1980? Two superb examples of enlightened thinking that both communicated at a personal level and positioned the companies as innovators in their fields.

Those companies created messages that were well targeted, easily understood and easy to respond to. Yet, all too often, we limit ourselves to the cheapest method of communication possible rather than trying to understand *what* the customer will respond to. We consider the words, the visuals, the layout, involvement and response devices, but rarely do we consider the feel of our communication and its quality.

→

As communications work on several levels, we should try and understand which level is most appropriate. If we don't then we may fall into one of several traps including inappropriate language, poor production values and bad use of a particular medium, to name just three.

In short, 'It's not what you say, it's the way that you say it' that can say so much about the company, the products and the service the customer should expect.

A case of *Caveat Emptor* perhaps?

An introduction to the communications loop

Communications loop

The two-way nature of communications from sender to receiver and back again.

IMC Process Model

Description of the principal elements involved in the process of communication between sender and receiver.

Communication

Transactional process between two or more parties whereby meaning is exchanged through the intentional use of signs and symbols.

The **communications loop**, outlined in the **IMC Process Model**, recognises the two-way nature of communications between senders and receivers and the issues of message encoding and decoding, feedback and 'noise' (refer to Chapter 1). These issues involve the psychology of **communication**, specifically:

- the ways in which messages are created;
- the elements which make up the message;
- the ways in which messages are interpreted by the recipient so that meaning is extracted from them;
- the areas where messages are misinterpreted, where the meaning of part of the message is different for one person than for another, and where elements of the message become obliterated. Communication does not take place if the receiver does not receive the message, or if the message becomes so distorted that it changes its meaning.

Communication has been defined as a transactional process between two or more parties whereby meaning is exchanged through the intentional use of symbols (Engel et al. 1994). The key elements here are that the communication is intentional (a deliberate effort is made to bring about a response), it is a transaction (the participants are all involved in the process), and it is symbolic (words, pictures, music, and other sensory stimulants are used to convey thoughts). Since human beings are not telepathic, all communication requires that the original concepts be translated into symbols that convey the required meaning. This means that the individual or firm issuing the communication must first **encode**, or reduce the concepts to a set of symbols which can be passed on to the recipient of the message; the recipient must **decode** the symbols to understand the original message. This means that the participants in the process must share a common view of what the symbols involved actually mean; the parties must share a common field of experience. This is illustrated in Exhibit 3.1 and In View 3.1, The Marlboro man.

Encoding

The process of creating intended meaning in a message.

Decoding

The process of converting a message into meaning.

The sender's field of experience and the receiver's field of experience must overlap, at least to the extent of having a common language. The overlap is likely to be much more complex and subtle in most marketing communications; advertisements typically use references from TV shows, from proverbs and common sayings, and will often make puns or use half-statements which the audience is able to complete because they are aware of the cultural referents involved. This is why foreign TV adverts often seem unintentionally humorous, or even incomprehensible.

Exhibit 3.1 Model of the communication process

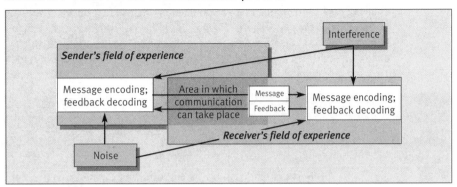

→

IN VIEW 3.1

The Marlboro man

The lean, rugged cowboy used on the Marlboro cigarette billboards was first commissioned in 1954 by Philip Morris, the US tobacco company, to reposition Marlboro cigarettes into a male market. Until then, Marlboro had been promoted as a cigarette for women, with red filter-tips and the slogan 'To match your lips and finger-tips'. A change of advertising agency (to Leo Burnett) generated the change in approach; macho images were prescribed, and cowboys, pilots, deep-sea divers and successful businessmen were all used to symbolise the product until finally the cowboy became predominant. Since 1962 all advertisements for Marlboro have featured the cowboy.

Of course, the company is not implying that Marlboro is only for cowboys; the cowboy has a worldwide recognition as symbolising freedom, independence, masculinity, adventure and the outdoors life. Worldwide screenings of Westerns have ensured that the image is universal, so the message implied in the image comes across to people of all cultures. The cowboy image also has an irresistible appeal to many men; it is easy for the average office-working wage slave to escape into a fantasy of riding the range and fighting the bad guys.

Philip Morris have laid down strict international guidelines for the creation of the advertisements, to ensure that all parties understand the concept and keep to the 'party line'. These are as follows:

1 The cowboy is the hero, he controls the world around him.
2 The cowboy must be credible; the authenticity of every detail must never be questioned.
3 Marlboro pictures are candid; they should never be artificial or mannered.
4 Marlboro advertisements must be executed to the highest standards to ensure optimum impact.
5 There must be great variety in Marlboro advertisements with regard to both subject and layout; there is still so much to discover in 'Marlboro country'.
6 Marlboro country is grand; the beauty of its scenery and its impressive size should always be emphasised.

→

Philip Morris spend approximately $300m per annum in Europe on advertising, of which Marlboro takes the major share. The success of the cowboy has been such that, despite European bans on cigarette advertising, and despite legal restrictions which preclude almost all the verbal content of cigarette advertisements, Marlboro is still Philip Morris's most important brand, and one of the biggest-selling products in a difficult market.

The cowboy's rugged image says nothing about the characteristics of the product; the advertising works by providing a simple way for the consumer to decode the brand and remember it.

Noise

Distortions created in the encoding or decoding process that can result in inaccurate interpretation of meaning.

Interference

Like noise, interference creates message distortion. A distinction can be made between the two by suggesting that interference is deliberately generated noise.

Feedback

This occurs when there is two-way communication, so that communications flow between sender and audience and back again.

Two-way asymmetric communications

Communications from a sender to a receiver with little or delayed feedback, producing a non-direct dialogue.

Two-way symmetric communications

Direct dialogue between a sender and receiver of communications.

Word of mouth

Communication not originated by the sender that is passed on to others after the original marketing communications messages have been transmitted.

Noise is made up of the surrounding distractions present during the communications process, and varies from children playing during the commercial break through to arresting headlines in a magazine. **Interference** is a deliberate attempt to distract the audience's attention. For example, a car driver may be distracted away from a radio ad by another car cutting in (noise) or by seeing an interesting billboard (interference).

Feedback takes place when there is two-way communication; there is some communication flow between sender and audience and *back again*. Two-way communication may be **asymmetric** – the feedback or response is delayed and, therefore, not in the form of direct dialogue – or **symmetric** – there is a direct dialogue between the sender and audience (Grunig and Hunt 1984). See Chapter 24 for more details. Feedback will always increase the potential for more accurate communication, which is one reason why personal selling is such a powerful communications tool; it allows the customer to ask questions and the sales person to respond directly and, frequently, immediately. Feedback helps to ensure redundancy in the communication; that is to say, unnecessary repetition of the basic message while allowing greater opportunity to ensure the message has been received and understood. It should be appreciated that the different marketing communications tools facilitate varying degrees and timing of feedback.

In looking again at our IMC Process Model which can be seen at the beginning of the chapter, the communications loop is shown as extending beyond the original sender to the receivers to illustrate another important aspect of the total communications process. Marketing communications are not only disseminated by the original sender, they are received and passed on by the receivers to others through a process that is commonly referred to as **word of mouth**. This 'extra' communication can be very powerful indeed but can result in miscommunication because the original message has now gone through a process of encoding, decoding, more encoding as it is passed on and yet more decoding as it is received by others. Sometimes, the messages can be enhanced in this process and sometimes diminished and distorted. Noise and interference can once again disrupt the communications activity and word of mouth can be carried out by targeted and non-targeted audience members. Importantly, word of mouth is very difficult to control and, in many ways, this is illustrative of the complexity of the marketing communications process that any student and practitioner of the subject would be advised to understand.

The use of signs in encoding and decoding

The use of signs in encoding and decoding

Sign

A sign is anything that signifies something.

Semiotics

The scientific discipline of studying the meanings associated with signs, symbols and brands.

A **sign** is 'anything that stands for something (its object) to somebody (its interpreter) in some respect (its context)' (Pierce 1986). Meaning is always conveyed through signs, which are used in both encoding and decoding processes. Marketers transfer cultural meanings into products through the use of signs in their advertisements (McCracken 1986). **Semiotics**, the study of signs and meaning, has classified signs into three categories, outlined in Exhibit 3.2.

Exhibit 3.2 Categorising signs

Type of sign	Definition	Example
Icon	A sign that looks like the object, or represents it visually in a way that most people would relate to	A drawing of someone relaxing on a beach would signify a holiday to most people
Index	A sign that relates to the object by a causal connection	A sweaty athlete coming into a locker room relates to a drink; most people are familiar with the idea of being thirsty after playing sport, even though the drink itself is not shown
Symbol	An artificial sign which has been created for the purpose of providing meaning	Most people are familiar with the intertwined arrows used to denote recyclable materials. This conveys an image of 'greenness' to the products it appears on

Denotative meaning

A meaning that is the same for everybody.

Connotative meaning

A meaning that is not shared.

The most obvious symbols are, of course, words. Words only have meanings as they are interpreted by people – and over long periods of time, even words change their meanings. For example, 'nice' has come to mean polite, pleasant or enjoyable, yet a hundred and fifty years ago it meant 'precise'. Meanings of words can be **denotative**, i.e. having the same meaning for everybody, or **connotative**, i.e. having a meaning which is unique to the individual. Although everybody knows what 'strawberries' are (denotative) some individuals are allergic to them and might associate the word with the allergy (connotative). Because connotative meanings vary among individuals, marketers need to develop empathy with their target audiences. This is easiest when the marketer and the audience are as similar as possible in terms of background and outlook.

Semiotics is concerned with the study of the role of symbols and signs in communications; syntactics is about the structure of communications; and semantics is the study of the meaning of words. All three fields of study help to ensure that the correct meanings are ascribed to the symbols and words; the meaning conveyed by a word is not always the dictionary definition, any more than the meaning conveyed by a picture is solely in the image itself.

Communication is carried out in many other ways than the verbal or written word. Only 30% of communication uses words; people communicate by pictures, non-verbal sounds, smell, touch, numbers, artefacts, time and kinetics. Many of these elements are used by marketers – for example, women's magazines sometimes have scratch-and-sniff cards which contain new fragrances, and charities sometimes send out free pens to prospective donors so that they can more easily fill in direct-debit contribution forms. Exhibit 3.3 demonstrates some of the ways these silent communication methods are used by marketers. In View 3.2 illustrates the use of an icon and In View 11.4 in Chapter 11, which revisits the theme of images, indicates the often-hidden power of even apparently meaningless symbols and pictures.

Exhibit 3.3 Silent communication methods

Medium	Example
Numbers	The Porsche 911 is an example; there is an implication that the car is the latest in a long series (although Americans might associate 911 with the emergency telephone number)
Space	An image of a man and a woman standing close together implies that they are lovers; likewise an image of wide open spaces implies freedom
Artefacts	Images of what people own imply their social status. Also, small gifts and free samples convey a small obligation to the recipient
Time	Images of people in a hurry might imply success and energy to Northern Europeans and Americans; to an African it would imply somebody who has no time for other people and is arrogant
Kinetics	People who are walking (or running) imply a fit and active lifestyle; those who are gesticulating with their hands imply intellectual discussion, or argument

IN VIEW 3.2

The Michelin Man

www.michelin.co.uk

The Michelin Man (real name *Bibendum*) is composed entirely of tyres and was invented to promote the benefits of using the French tyre company's products.

Probably the best-known symbol of any European tyre company, the Michelin Man appears on the company's advertisements, has been used as a three-dimensional model on the company's delivery vehicles and even on toys. He is instantly recognisable and has secured an indelible place in the English language.

As Michelin's icon, he denotes friendliness and long-term reliability; as a cultural icon, he connotes rotundness (though in a humorous and positive way).

Are signs culturally universal?

The main problem with silent languages is that they are not culturally universal. Most body language does not transfer well to other cultures, even when the cultures are otherwise close. Well-known examples are the two-fingers sign which is highly insulting to British people but which can denote merely 'two' in the rest of Europe; the thumb and index finger circle which denotes 'OK' to Americans but which denotes 'money' to the Japanese (Ferrieux 1989); and showing the soles of the feet to Thai people, which again is insulting (Glover 1990). Other examples are more subtle. Japanese people tend to show their emotions less in public than do Americans, Indians tend to regard shabby or torn clothes as denoting poverty whereas North Europeans often associate this with independence and freedom, and numbers which are considered lucky in some cultures are neutral in others (Costa and Pavia 1992). An interesting populist book covering these and other issues is Desmond Morris's *Manwatching: A Field Guide to Human Behaviour* (1978).

Ethnocentrism

The practice of assuming that others think and believe as we do.

Communication problems can arise because of **ethnocentrism**, as detailed in Chapter 8. Ethnocentrism is the practice of assuming that others think and believe as we do. Ethnocentrism is one of the few features of human behaviour that belongs to all cultures; the tendency is for people to believe that their own culture is the 'right' one and everybody else's is at best a poor copy (Shimp and Sharma 1987). This easily leads to misunderstandings and outright rejection of the communication, and is remarkably common.

Using simile, metaphor and allegory to create meaning

Simile

Comparison of one thing with another using the words 'like' or 'as': e.g. 'He fought like a lion in battle.'

Metaphor

Association of one thing with another suggesting that the two are the same: e.g. 'He was a lion in battle.'

Simile links one meaning to another by the use of comparative terms (Stern 1987). For example, Murphy's Irish Stout uses the slogan, 'Like the Murphy's I'm not bitter', linking the laidback approach of the Irish actor to the smoothness of the beer. **Metaphor** takes this a stage further by omitting the comparative term. Wedgwood china uses the slogan 'The other side of English elegance' to promote their crockery, linking the product to elegance. Metaphors create an image in consumers' minds, building on a shared perception of the qualities of the object and extending these to the product. Metaphor is often used in car advertising; the Jaguar XJ-S is claimed to be 'the stuff of legends'; the Renault Laguna claims that 'Evolution favours the strong, the smart, the lean, the swift' and shows the car next to a picture of a wolf. Metaphors are not necessarily verbal; many are created by the juxtaposition of images.

Allegory

Message that is used to symbolise a deeper meaning.

Allegory is a form of extended metaphor in which the product is linked to a meaning which is outside the narrative itself. For example, products are sometimes given a personification (e.g. Mr Muscle, the cleaner 'who loves the jobs you hate'). Caffrey's Irish Ale plays heavily on an Irish personality, showing the Irish expatriate (possibly in New York) drinking the beer and being 'transported' back to a misty green landscape. The brand is thus linked to a probably mythical view of Ireland and the Irish; the observer relates instantly to the imagery, yet the commercial could just as easily have been shot in a Dublin bar, with the drinker being transported to a New England landscape.

IN VIEW 3.3

Goodfella's pizza

Although pizza has its origins in Italy, it is often seen as being quintessentially American. So when Goodfella's was launched, the brand was given a distinctly American theme. Apart from the brand name (taken from the gangster movie of the same name), the commercials were shot in an idealised New York pizza parlour, with various customers doing 'American' things: cops arguing over baseball games, women discussing their love lives, and a waiter with a strong New York accent delivering the pizza.

The ingredients, prices and pack sizes of the pizza are never mentioned; availability is limited to a statement that it comes 'from the freezer compartment' (it is, in fact, a frozen product available from supermarkets). The allegorical content of the advertisement is such that the image comes across; the pizzas are perceived as being typically American, of a very high quality (Goodfella's is a premium brand) and as being of pizza-house standard. The latter is important, since the product is being positioned as substituting for a delivery pizza, which has implications for pricing. The net result of the campaign is that Goodfella's has, within the space of three years, become established as the market leader in premium-price frozen pizzas.

For all its American image, most Americans would not have heard of the brand; the pizzas are actually manufactured in Ireland, by an Irish-based company!

How meaning is created

Information processing

Information processing

The stages of thought that the individual goes through to convert incoming stimuli into useful knowledge.

Meaning is about translating the content of communications into relevant concepts within the individual's experience. **Information processing** describes the stages of thought that the individual goes through in order to convert incoming stimuli into useful knowledge. There are several models of information processing. McGuire's model (1976) is outlined in Exhibit 3.4.

Exhibit 3.4 McGuire's information processing model (1976)

Stage	Explanation
Exposure	The consumer must have proximity to the message
Attention	The consumer must be aware of the message and must allocate information-processing capacity to it
Comprehension	The consumer must understand the message, interpreting it to get the meaning that the sender intends it to have
Acceptance	The message must be absorbed into the consumer's existing set of beliefs and knowledge. If existing attitudes and beliefs are changed during this process then persuasion has also occurred
Retention	The message becomes part of the individual's long-term memory

Source: Reproduced from table from '*An information processing model of advertising effectiveness*', by McGuire, W.J., in *Behavioural and Management Science in Marketing*, Davis, H.L. and Silk, A.J. eds., Ronald Press, (1978), Copyright © John Wiley & Sons, Inc. 1978. This material is reproduced by permission of John Wiley & Sons, Inc.

Marketing communications clearly involves much more than merely placing as many adverts as possible in as many places as possible. The message must key in to the consumer's existing thought patterns and patterns of belief. This has major implications for strategy; is it more important to spend more money creating the right message than on buying media space to expose the message to the public? There are many examples of high-impact communications that have been achieved with small media expenditure – the Benetton series of billboard advertisements being one of them. Benetton has used controversial, even offensive, images in its advertising to create maximum impact, and has also gained considerable press exposure as the advertisements themselves create controversy which is reported as news. Such examples of high-impact communications carry with them corresponding risks. Benetton has found these to be both to their benefit and to their cost. The use of 'shock tactics' in marketing communications messages is considered in Chapter 10, Marketing Communications Ethics. These may be contrasted with other approaches identified in this chapter which emphasise the importance of the likeability of the communication.

Perception

Perception

The process of synthesising information to make sense of the world. People's perceptions of the same stimuli can vary.

Perception is the process by which individuals select information from the surrounding environment and synthesise it into a world-view. Because there is so much going on around us at any one time, we usually select only that which is most immediate or interesting, depending on our level of involvement. Inevitably this means that there are gaps in each individual's view of the world, and these gaps are usually filled in by using previous experience, or analogies drawn from elsewhere. Each individual's world map differs from every other individual's because it is, in part, a construct of the imagination.

Part of the function of marketing communications is to ensure that the product occupies the right place in the consumer's world-view. If the product is a high-quality, high-priced product then it needs to be mapped next to other premium products; this affects the type and style of the communications. If, on the other hand, the product is a cheap, serviceable version then it needs to be mapped next to other everyday products. In this connection, individuals often use surrogates to judge quality – for example, price is often used as an indicator of quality in circumstances where other clues are not available.

Apart from the basic five senses (touch, taste, smell, sight, hearing) there are senses of temperature, of balance, of internal well-being (or otherwise) and so forth. Each sense is feeding information to the brain constantly, so the amount of information being collected would seriously overload the system if the brain did not select from the environment around the individual and cut out the extraneous noise. In effect, the brain makes automatic decisions as to what is relevant and what is not; experiments have shown that some information is filtered out by the optic nerve even before it gets to the brain. People quickly learn to ignore extraneous noises; for example, as a visitor to someone else's home you may be sharply aware of a loudly ticking clock, whereas your host may be entirely used to it and unaware of it except when making a conscious effort to check that the clock is still running.

Therefore the information entering the brain does not provide a complete view of the world. Construction of a world-view involves assembling the remaining information to map what's happening in the outside world. Any gaps will be filled in with imagination and experience. The cognitive map is therefore not a 'photograph'; it is a construct of the imagination, affected by the following factors:

1 *Subjectivity*. Each individual has a unique world-view to which the new information is added.
2 *Categorisation*. This is the 'pigeonholing' of information, and the prejudging of events and products. This can happen through the process of chunking whereby the individual organises information into chunks of related items (Miller 1956). For example, a picture seen while a particular piece of music is playing might be chunked as one item in the memory, so that sight of the picture evokes the music and vice versa.
3 *Selectivity* is the degree to which the brain is selecting from the environment. It is a function of how much is going on around the individual, and also of how selective (concentrated) the individual is on the current task. Selectivity is also subjective; some people are a great deal more selective than others.
4 *Expectations* lead individuals to interpret later information in a specific way. For example, look at this series of letters and numbers:

$\mathcal{A}$ $\mathit{13}$ C $\mathcal{D}$ $\mathcal{E}$ $\mathcal{F}$ G $\mathcal{B}$ $\mathcal{J}$

10 11 12 13 14 15 16

The number 13 appears in both series, but in the first series it would be interpreted as a B because that is what the brain is being led to expect. (The B in Matura MT Script looks like this: $\mathcal{B}$.)
5 *Past experience* leads us to interpret current experience in the light of what we already know. Sometimes sights, smells or sounds from our past will trigger off inappropriate responses; the smell of bread baking may recall a village bakery from twenty years ago, but in fact the smell could have been artificially generated by an aerosol spray near the supermarket bread counter.

Sender credibility

Credibility
The degree to which communications are believed.

Corporate umbrella branding
The organisation and all its products are branded under the same corporate name, for example Heinz.

Family umbrella branding
The organisation has a corporate brand and a separate brand for its products, for example Marks & Spencer's St Michael brand.

Celebrity endorsement
The use of a well-known person to promote a company or product brand.

Credibility is the degree to which the company's communications are believed. The effectiveness of a message will depend on the receiver's perception of credibility on the part of the sender (Hovland et al. 1953). Credibility may be achieved in many ways. It may be generated through associations built up over time with the brand itself. A brand may be first tentatively tried and then repurchased if found satisfactory. A level of trust may be engendered after numerous use and repurchase cycles. Credibility may be achieved through association with the producer or provider because other brands have been found satisfactory. This is one benefit of **corporate umbrella** and **family umbrella branding** (see Chapter 11) in which the brand is associated with other brands. Cadbury and Sony are examples of two companies that pursue this approach. Credibility may also be achieved through the recommendation of others – friends, relations, associates, etc.

Celebrity endorsement of products is of particular interest to the marketing communicator and is used quite extensively. The credibility of the celebrity is important to create a believable link between the meaning(s) associated with the celebrity and the product. McCracken's Meaning Transfer Model states that distinctions of class, status, gender, age, personality and lifestyle types are all part of what the celebrity endorser transfers to the product (McCracken 1989). Products have personalities, too, and if the personality of the celebrity endorser is close to that of the product the endorsement will be more effective (Fortini-Campbell 1992).

Cadbury uses corporate umbrella branding across its chocolate products
Source: Courtesy of Cadbury Trebor Bassetts.

IN VIEW 3.4

Celebrity endorsement is big business

In 2001, Anna Kournikova earned around £7 million, only £220,000 of which was for playing tennis. Footballer David Beckham can expect to earn over £1 million for each endorsement he agrees to do. In the USA, 20% of all TV advertisements contain celebrities. In India, a company is expected to hire a Bollywood star or cricketer (preferably both) if it wants to appear reliable. But the country that has truly embraced the concept of fame and materialism is Japan. Many famous faces will only advertise over there on condition that none of the adverts will be shown outside the country – partly because the products they are endorsing are not ones which they would wish to be associated with back home. But, when the sums involved usually stretch into the millions, they are prepared to make exceptions. So Sean Connery, who refuses any endorsement deals in the West, can be seen drinking a certain brand of scotch; Silvester Stallone extols the virtues of ham; and Pierce Brosnan (James Bond) endorses women's cosmetics.

The award-winning campaign for the supermarket, Sainsbury, features TV chef Jamie Oliver on TV, in PR and in sales promotions. Sainsbury's research has indicated that one quarter of their profits in 2001 were attributable to this celebrity involvement. The supermarket continued to use Jamie Oliver throughout 2002 and extended his contract, reported to be worth £1m per year, into 2003.

Source: Adapted from Losowsky (2002/3), Blackstock (2002)

Credibility has been perceived as comprising three components (Ohanian 1990):

- attractiveness
- trustworthiness
- expertise.

Exhibit 3.5 Ohanian's celebrity endorser credibility scale

Attractiveness	Trustworthiness	Expertise
Attractive–Unattractive	Trustworthy–Untrustworthy	Expert–Not Expert
Classy–Not Classy	Dependable–Undependable	Experienced–Inexperienced
Beautiful–Ugly	Honest–Dishonest	Knowledgeable–Unknowledgeable
Elegant–Plain	Reliable–Unreliable	Qualified–Unqualified
Sexy–Not Sexy	Sincere–Insincere	Skilled–Unskilled

Source: Ohanian (1990)

Attractiveness

Attractiveness is an important component of credibility, but it is interesting to note that gender also plays a role in purchase intentions resulting from celebrity endorsement. Attractive female celebrity endorsers and models generate more positive attitudes among both male and female observers (Debevec and Kernan 1984), but male observers are more likely to buy from male endorsers and female observers are more likely to buy from female endorsers (Caballero et al. 1989).

Although liking a celebrity endorser (and therefore liking the advertisement) are usually closely linked to subsequent purchase behaviour, it is quite possible to find the endorser attractive yet still not buy the product. The **product match-up hypothesis** (Forkan 1980) states that the celebrity endorser's image should match as closely as possible with the product's characteristics if the advertisement is to be credible. A close match also leads to better recall and more positive brand effects (Misra and Beatty 1990).

Product match-up hypothesis

Hypothesis stating that a celebrity endorser's image should match as closely as possible to a product's characteristics if the promotion is to be credible.

Trust

There are two key bases of trust: trust based on a legal or contractual relationship, and trust based on the characteristics of the individual. Trust in the individual also appears to have two components: characteristic-based trust and process-based trust (Zucker 1986). Exhibit 3.6 presents examples of these components of trust. Celebrity endorsers, and indeed the sponsoring company, must be perceived as trustworthy to engender credibility.

Expertise

Expertise is composed of aptitude, training and experience, and is domain-specific in that receivers of a message will only trust an endorser within specific areas of expertise. While trustworthiness appears to be more important to the receiver than expertise (Friedman et al. 1976), expertise tends to improve the persuasion element of the message and thus can lead to product purchase (Aaker and Myers 1987).

Exhibit 3.6 Components of trust

Component	Explanation and examples
Institutional trust	Based on the rule of law, this type of trust is acquired through contracts and legal obligations. For example, in the UK consumers are able to trust retailers because the law states that retailers must give refunds if goods are unfit for use – so shoddy merchandise can be returned
Characteristic-based trust	This pertains only to individuals, and is a major factor in personal selling. The buyer believes that the salesperson is someone who can be trusted, and often comes about because there is a social similarity between the buyer and the salesperson
Process-based trust	Exchanges requiring trust will ultimately lead to long-term relationships (Good 1988). Trust of this type does not appear early in relationships, so the parties are likely to rely on contracts and the rule of law much more

IN VIEW 3.5

The 4th Emergency Service Campaign (1993 – 2002)

The AA operates the largest breakdown service in the UK, with over 13 million members (more than a third of all UK licence holders). Although the AA provides many other services for its members, including car, home and travel insurance, pre-purchase inspections of second hand cars, car servicing, tyre fitting and indeed every conceivable assistance to motorists, it is the breakdown service, which attracts the bulk of the membership to join.

However, the AA is not the only breakdown service. It faces strong competition from arch-rivals the RAC (Royal Automobile Club) and others such as Green Flag and Direct Line. These days even the large supermarket chains are selling breakdown assistance.

In the late 80's and early 90's the AA's advertising emphasised the friendliness of its services; rescued motorists were shown saying 'He's a very nice man'. The range of services was highlighted by the 'I know a man who can' slogan. This campaign was very successful in the day, but there was a need to address a more aggressive competitive marketplace, which was making huge inroads into the fleet and company car business.

The cheaper breakdown services operated by using the local garage network rather than have their own patrols on stand by like the AA. AA patrols were dedicated to fixing members cars and had no interest in anything other than solving the member's problem in the most effective way. The AA decided they needed an ad campaign that would differentiate in the breakdown market by emphasising the professionalism of the service whilst maintaining the friendly image.

Research showed the AA was seen as having friendly people who helped out in emergencies. The previous campaign had focused on the former attribute; the new one would focus on the latter. Adverts showed the AA's similarities with the other emergency services (the police, the fire brigade and the ambulance service) in how it operated and provided service to it's members. It had a 24-hour, highly skilled work force dealing with real-life breakdown emergencies. The AA was thus positioned alongside other professional rescuers as 'to our members we're the 4th Emergency Service'. The ads ended with the statements 'in fact the AA gets someone out of trouble every 8 seconds' and 'we're proud to be Number 4 – to our members we're the 4th Emergency Service'.

This advertising positioned the AA above its competitors, and, consequently, membership increased too. Linking the service to other professionals had paid off – and the new image supported by revised vehicle livery and patrol uniforms paid off where it counted, in increased membership. The success of the campaign also had an excellent spin-off – a marked improvement in staff motivation and pride in their work.

Likeability of a communication

Likeability is clearly an important aspect of marketing communications (although it can be contrasted with the use of 'shock tactics' covered in Chapter 10). Some research has shown that it appears to be the single best predictor of sales effectiveness with likeability scales predicting 97% of sales successes (Biel 1989); interest clearly relates to likeability (Stapel 1991), and enjoyment appears to be a good indicator in advertising pretests (Brown 1991).

TV adverts are often seen as entertainment; many are produced to very high standards, and are interesting in their own right. When tobacco advertising was banned on British TV, a long-running series of adverts for Hamlet cigars was released on video; audiences actually bought the advertisements as entertainment.

There is a clear relationship between liking an advert (and other promotions) and subsequent sales, but it is not necessarily a positive relationship. Liking the advert seems to be related to whether the product is meaningful and relevant to the consumer at the time (Biel 1990); there seems to be some evidence that food and beverage adverts are more likely to be liked than are non-food adverts (Biel and Bridgwater 1990). Liking is usually linked to a positive view of the product, and this could lead to an increase in sales (Biel 1990; Stapel 1991).

The situation may reverse when dealing with many financial services products, however. Wells (1980) postulated that products could be placed on an approach–avoidance continuum, with products such as pensions and life insurance at the avoidance end of the scale. This is because such products are only bought in order to avoid bad outcomes, and most people prefer not to think about ageing and death (Mintel 1993). Because the adverts must necessarily deal with unpleasant matters, the more unpleasant the message is, the more likely it is to result in a purchase. It may be difficult to untangle all the factors involved, since an unpleasant advert is likely to be ignored, and the viewer is therefore less motivated to process the information cognitively. The elaboration likelihood model (see Chapter 4 for more details) implies that such viewers would only process the information peripherally, and that therefore adverts for financial services work best as image-builders (Petty and Cacioppo 1983), as they are likely to do for many other product categories. This may be true of TV advertising generally, since relatively few of the audience will be involved with the given product category just at the time the advert goes out, and will therefore not give the advert their close attention. Interestingly, there is some US evidence that commercials which are zapped (the viewer switches channels using the remote control) are more likely to have a positive effect on brand purchase than those which are not zapped. This is because the viewer has to be attentive to the advert and process its content to know that it is a candidate for zapping (Zufryden et al. 1993).

Humour and warmth are often used in promotions to make them more likeable (Weinberger and Spotts 1989). Humour makes the observer pay more attention (Lammers 1991), but there is no evidence to show that humour has a positive effect on brand likeability (Zhang and Zinkhan 1991). In other words, humour may make the marketing communications more likeable, but does not necessarily make the brand itself more likely to be bought. Humour may enhance persuasion effects, however (Scott et al. 1990). Warmth shows a positive correlation with purchase intention (Aaker et al. 1986), and also leads to lower levels of irritation. Humour and warmth both lead to higher levels of recall (Speck 1991).

This area of marketing communications effectiveness is difficult to research, because showing the respondents promotional material in a laboratory situation predisposes them to pay particular attention ('we will be asking questions later' is a well-known way of making someone be more attentive). The situation is therefore not realistic compared with the usual viewing environment where there are many distractions and tempting diversions to draw away the viewer's attention. For this reason, different researchers often report different findings.

Modelling in marketing communications

Modelling

Attempt to realistically represent the processes involved in marketing communications.

Modelling in this context is the use of actors in promotions to show the product in use, or to suggest how the product will improve the lifestyle of its purchasers. Models can either be people with whom the observer can identify (a typical housewife, motorist, homeowner, etc.) or people whose lifestyle the observer aspires to (air hostess, racing driver, business executive).

Marketers can use the concept of pain avoidance in motivating consumers by modelling the negative consequences of not using a product. For example, the London Underground ran a series of advertisements showing commuters who had been prosecuted for fare-dodging, complete with a detailed account of the consequences of the action ('It was the embarrassment of having to stand up in court and admit fiddling a £1.30 fare. And I lost my job.'). Another example might be a housewife whose washing powder 'Can't shift those greasy stains'. In each case, the consumer is invited to see the possible negative consequences of fiddling the fare, or using the wrong washing powder; credibility is generated by using models that the observer can relate to, and meaning is generated by showing consequences that the consumer might wish to avoid.

The effectiveness of the role model in modelling behaviour will depend on the personal characteristics of the role model. Attractive models will usually be imitated more than unattractive ones, successful-looking models are given more credence than unsuccessful-looking ones, and a model who is perceived as being similar to the observer is also more likely to be emulated (Baker and Churchill 1977). Interestingly, when models are demonstrating some difficult task, it appears that they are more effective if they are seen to initially have some difficulty with the task, but finally overcome the difficulty, as opposed to models who perform the task easily first time. This may be because the observer identifies more easily with the model in those circumstances, even though in other, non-threatening circumstances the competent model gives an ideal to be aimed at (Manz and Sims 1981). For example, a weekend jogger may make a better model for a healthy breakfast cereal than a professional athlete, whereas the professional may make a better model for a pair of running shoes. This is due to the perceived similarity of the amateur to the observer. What is relevant here is the *degree* of personal identification or association with the model. As commented on

Product placement

The process of arranging for a company's products to be seen or referred to in the media such as during television and radio programmes, videos, video games and cinema films.

earlier, celebrities are used extensively in this context to help create positive associations and credibility. Most obviously, this involves the use of recognised actors, sports people, musicians, etc. in advertisements and sales promotions, but similar associations can be achieved through **product placement** where the product is seen, for example, within a TV programme or movie (see Chapter 25).

There are several theories regarding the way modelling works. First of these is the category accessibility theory, which suggests the process of observing the modelled behaviour activates an interpretive process that makes the information in the modelling more accessible. If the interpretive process is closely related to information that helps to specify the appropriate behaviour, the information itself becomes more accessible so that the behaviour is more likely to be imitated (Bandura 1977). For example, a consumer observing a TV advert in which a housewife is making a meal may begin the same thought process that he or she goes through when making a meal. This makes the actual information in the advert (which may be about how to make a meal using a particular stock cube) more accessible since the observer can more easily imagine using the cube when making a meal.

The characteristics of the observers also play a part in the effectiveness of modelling. Individual differences in cognitive processing and in the ability to perform the modelled behaviour affect the process. Some people are lacking in imagination and are unable to visualise themselves carrying out the modelled behaviour, especially if (for example) the modelling is being described on the radio rather than shown on TV, or is being shown via a static medium such as a billboard, item of direct mail, brochure or press advert. Consumers who are dependent, lack confidence and self-esteem, and have been frequently rewarded for imitative behaviour are more likely to copy successful-looking models (Froming and Chambers 1983).

A second theory that helps explain modelling is expectancy theory. Here the models influence the observers' expectations, firstly concerning their ability to perform the

IN VIEW 3.6

Tango

Tango is an orange-flavoured drink with a tangy flavour that appeals to children and adults alike; it is aimed at a predominantly young market, however. During the late 1980s and early 1990s, the product's UK advertising used the slogan 'You know when you've been Tangoed' to emphasise the sharp impact the product has on the taste buds.

The first group of advertisements featured a round, fat, orange-coloured individual who would appear out of nowhere and slap the face of the Tango drinker in the advertisement. The intention was to convey the shock value of the product on the drinker; instead, the message picked up by many observers (especially children) was that it was OK to slap anyone drinking Tango in the face. Needless to say, this was not the message the advertisers wanted to convey.

In effect, observers had identified with the wrong model. Instead of identifying with the Tango drinker, they had identified with the fat, orange-painted individual (who perhaps seemed to be having a more interesting life). The face-slapping advertisements were fairly quickly withdrawn. Although Tango continues to be advertised in a startlingly original way, face-slapping is no longer on the agenda.

task, secondly about the possibility of benefiting from the outcome of the behaviour. For example, an advert showing a before-and-after shot of a person who has lost weight may make other overweight people more confident of their own ability to do so (self-efficacy expectations). A further shot of the now-slim person enjoying a better social life or getting more attention from people of the opposite sex may arouse an expectation that this is a natural consequence of losing weight (outcome expectations) (Manz and Sims 1981). These expectations may or may not be realistic, and sometimes promotions have been criticised for raising unwarranted expectations.

The process of observing and integrating modelling behaviour can be further broken down. Bandura (1977) describes four sub-processes that intervene in modelling, as detailed in Exhibit 3.7. These processes occur below the conscious level, and over a very short period of time; the observer goes through the processes while watching the modelled behaviour, and will usually accept or reject the message contained therein within seconds.

Exhibit 3.7 Processes which influence modelling

Process	Description and explanation
Attentional process	The ways in which observers observe, and extract information from the modelling. These are influenced by the characteristics of both model and modelled behaviour
Retention processes	The effect of the model on the observer's perception. Also, the degree to which the modelled behaviour is remembered
Production processes	Converting symbolic representation into appropriate behaviour. This is to do with the observer's cognitive process, in terms of extracting the right message from the modelled behaviour. This requires the modelling to be unambiguous; given the non-verbal nature of most modelling, this presents considerable difficulties
Motivational processes	The degree to which the outcomes of the modelled behaviour are seen to be rewarding, or undesirable as appropriate. If the observer of a slimming advert would prefer not to lose weight, or is indifferent to the idea, the modelling will have no effect

Source: Adapted from Bandura (1977, p. 89)

Summary

This chapter has detailed the encoding, decoding, noise and feedback elements of the communications loop which is a fundamental part of the process of sending messages from sender to receivers in the marketing communications process model. Further details concerning the 'message' are covered in Chapter 20, Creative Implementation, and 'feedback' in Chapters 23 and 24, Evaluation and Control of Integrated Marketing Communications and Public Relations respectively, which can all be read in conjunction with this chapter. Meaning is encoded and decoded through the use of symbols. In order for an encoded message to be decoded correctly, the senders and receivers must share a common field of experience. As each individual has their own view of reality, marketing communications have a major role in positioning brands correctly in the customers', consumers' and other target audience members' 'world-maps'.

The factors that influence the perception of a credible message have been outlined, specifically: the degree of attractiveness of the sender (either the company or endorsing celebrity), the level of trust achieved and the expertise perceived by the receiver.

The chapter has also been concerned with the affective responses of people towards marketing communications. The likeability of advertising is generally a good indicator of its communications value; people tend to pay attention to messages they like, whether the likeability is generated by such things as humour, or by celebrity endorsement, or by the attractiveness of the models used. Much of the pleasurable feelings associated with marketing communications come from the promotions themselves, but of course the effect is subjective; an individual may not like the particular celebrity used to endorse the product, or may not get the joke in the humorous advertisement. Equally, some people respond better to models who are ordinary people, or who are like themselves in some way, whereas others respond better to models who are more attractive and more successful than themselves, since this is how they aspire to be.

Self-review questions

1 What is the difference between decoding and encoding?

2 Explain how meaning is captured in symbols and icons.

3 What is the difference between denotative and connotative meaning?

4 If ideas can be transmitted through symbols, why are there so many cases of misunderstood communications?

5 What is kinetics?

6 How are similes, metaphors and allegories used to create meaning?

7 What are the three components that comprise a credible communication?

8 What is modelling in marketing communications?

9 What effects do the characteristics of the observer have on modelling effectiveness?

Project

Using Ohanian's celebrity endorser credibility scale, explain the success (or otherwise) of an advertisement or other piece of promotion of your choice. Prepare a short presentation outlining which celebrity would be the most appropriate for the advertisement and why.

References

Aaker, D.A., Stayman, D.M. and Hagerty, M.R. (1986), Warmth in advertising: measurement, impact and sequence effects. *Journal of Consumer Research*, 12, 365–381.

Aaker, D.A. and Myers, J.G. (1987), *Advertising Management* 3rd edn. Englewood Cliffs NJ: Prentice Hall.

Baker, M.J. and Churchill, G.A. Jr (1977), The impact of physically attractive models on advertising evaluations. *Journal of Marketing Research*, 14 (November), 538–555.

Bandura, A. (1977), *Social Learning Theory*. Englewood Cliffs NJ: Prentice Hall, p. 89.

Biel, A.L. (1989), Love the advertisement, buy the product? *ADMAP*, October.

Biel, A.L. (1990), Love the ad. Buy the product? *ADMAP*, September, 21–25.

Biel, A.L. and Bridgwater, C.A. (1990), Attributes of likeable television commercials. *Journal of Advertising Research*, 30(3), 38–44.

Blackstock, C. (2002), Pukka! TV chef serves tasty profit. *The Guardian*, 4 December.

Brown, G. (1991), Modelling advertising awareness, *ADMAP*, April.

Caballero, M., Lumpkin, J.R. and Madden, C.S. (1989), Using physical attractiveness as an advertising tool: an empirical test of attraction phenomenon. *Journal of Advertising*, 29 (August–September), 16–22.

Costa, J.A. and Pavia, T.M. (1992), What it all adds up to: culture and alpha-numeric brand names. In *Advances in Consumer Research*, vol. 19 (J.F. Sherry Jr and B. Sternthal, eds). Provo, Utah: Association for Consumer Research, p. 40.

Debevec, K. and Kernan, J.B. (1984), More evidence on the effects of a presenter's physical attractiveness: some cognitive, affective and behavioural consequences. In *Advances in Consumer Research*, vol. 11 (Thomas C. Kinnear, ed.). Provo, Utah: Association for Consumer Research, pp. 127–132.

Engel, J.F., Warshaw, M.R. and Kinnear, T.C. (1994), *Promotional Strategy*. Chicago: Irwin.

Ferrieux, E. (1989), Hidden messages. *World Press Review*, July.

Forkan, J. (1980), Product matchup key to effective star presentations. *Advertising Age*, 51, 42.

Fortini-Campbell, L. (1992), *Hitting the Sweet Spot*. Chicago, IL: The Copy Work Shop.

Friedman, H.H., Termini, S. and Washington, R. (1976), The effectiveness of advertisements using four types of endorsers. *Journal of Advertising*, 6 (Summer), 22–24.

Froming, W.J. and Chambers, W. (1983), Modelling: an analysis in terms of category accessibility. *Journal of Experimental Social Psychology*, September, 403–421.

Glover, K. (1990), Dos and taboos: cultural aspects of international business. *Business America*, 13 August.

Good, D. (1988), Individuals, interpersonal relations and trust. In *Trust: Making and Breaking Co-Operative Relations*, (D. Gambetta, ed.). New York: Basil Blackwell.

Grunig, J.E. and Hunt T.T. (1984), *Managing Public Relations*. Holt Rinehart and Winston.

Hovland, C.I., Janis, I.L. and Kelley, H.H. (1953), *Communication and Persuasion*. New Haven, CT: Yale University Press.

Lammers, H.B. (1991), Moderating influence of self-monitoring and gender on responses to humorous advertising. *Journal of Social Psychology*, 131, 57–69.

Losowsky, A. (2002/3), Because they're worth it. *Hotline*, Winter, 46–48.

Manz, C.C. and Sims, H.P. (1981), Vicarious learning: the influence of modelling on organisational behaviour. *Academy of Management Review*, January, 105–113.

McCracken, G. (1986), Culture and consumption: a theoretical account of the structure and movement of the cultural meaning of consumer goods. *Journal of Consumer Research*, 13 (June), 71–81.

McCracken, G. (1989), Who is the celebrity endorser? Cultural foundation of the endorsement process. *Journal of Consumer Research*, 16 (December), 310–321.

McGuire, W.J. (1976), An information processing model of advertising effectiveness. In *Behavioral Management Sciences in Marketing* (H.L. Davis and A.J. Silk, eds). New York: Ronald Press.

Miller, G.A. (1956), The magical number seven, plus or minus two: some limits on our capacity for processing information. *Psychological Review*, March, 81–97.

Mintel (1993), Advertising financial services. *Personal Financial Intelligence*, 1, 1–48.

Misra, S. and Beatty, A. (1990), Celebrity spokesperson and brand congruence: an assessment of recall and affect. *Journal of Business Research*, 21 (September), 159–173.

Morris, D. (1978), *Manwatching: A Field Guide to Human Behaviour*. St Albans, Herts: Triad Panther.

Ohanian, R. (1990), Construction and validation of a scale to measure celebrity endorser's perceived expertise, trustworthiness and attractiveness. *Journal of Advertising*, 19 (3), 39–52.

Petty, R.E. and Cacioppo, J.T. (1983), Central and peripheral routes to persuasion: application to advertising. In *Advertising and Consumer Psychology* (L. Percy and A.G. Woodside, eds). Lexington, MA: Lexington Books.

Pierce, C.S., quoted in Mick, D.G. (1986), Consumer research and semiotics: exploring the morphology of signs, symbols and significance. *Journal of Consumer Research*, 13 (September), 196–213.

Scott, C., Klein, D.M. and Bryant, J. (1990), Consumer response to humor in advertising: a series of field studies using behavioural observation. *Journal of Consumer Research*, 16, 498–501.

Shimp, T. and Sharma, S. (1987), Consumer ethnocentrism: construction and validation of CETSCALE. *Journal of Marketing Research*, August, 280–289.

Speck, P.S. (1991), The humorous message taxonomy: a framework for the study of humorous ads. *Current Issues and Research in Advertising*, 1–44.

Stapel, J. (1991), Like the advertisement but does it interest me? *ADMAP*, April.

Stern, B.B. (1987), Figurative language in services advertising: the nature and uses of imagery. In *Advances in Consumer Research* vol. 15 (Michael J. Houston, ed.). Provo, Utah: Association for Consumer Research.

Weinberger, M.G. and Spotts, H. (1989), Humor in US versus UK television advertising. *Journal of Advertising*, 18 (2), 39–44.

Wells, W.D. (1980), Liking and sales effectiveness: a hypothesis. *Topline*, 2 (1).

Zhang, Y. and Zinkhan, G.M. (1991), Humor in television advertising – the effect of repetition and social setting. *Advances in Consumer Research*, 18, 813–818.

Zucker, L.G. (1986), Production of trust: institutional sources of economic structure. In *Research in Organisational Behaviour,* vol. 8 (H.C. Staw and W. Cummings, eds), 53–111.

Zufryden, F.S., Pedrick, J.H. and Sankaralingam, A. (1993), Zapping and its impact on brand purchase behaviour. *Journal of Advertising Research*, 33 (January/February), 58–66.

Selected further reading

Blythe, J. (1997), *The Essence of Consumer Behaviour*. Hemel Hempstead: Prentice Hall.

Gambetta, D. (1988), *Trust: Making and Breaking Co-Operative Relations*. New York: Basil Blackwell.

Morris, D. (1978), *Manwatching: A Field Guide to Human Behaviour*. St Albans, Herts: Triad Panther.

Percy, L. and Woodside, A.G. (eds) (1983), *Advertising and Consumer Psychology*. Lexington, MA: Lexington Books.

Umiker-Seboek, J. (1987), *Marketing and Semiotics: New Directions in the Study of Signs for Sale*. Amsterdam: Mouton de Gruyter.

Chapter 4

Marketing communications psychology

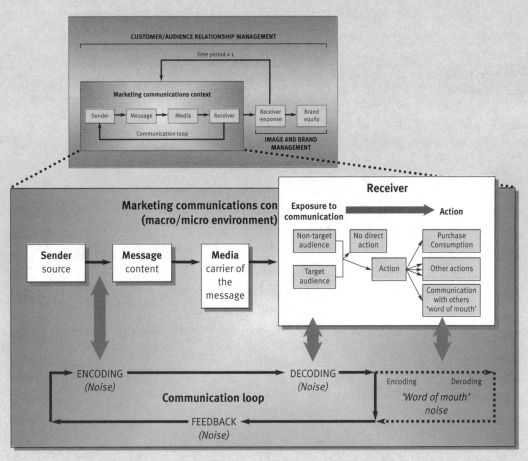

The IMC Process Model

CD

Using Exhibit 4.3 in Chapter 4 and Case Study 1 on the CD, identify the relevant influences on charity gift-giving decisions. Do you think Concern's current marketing communications address these influences? Would you recommend any changes?

Chapter outline

- Alternative paradigms of buyer behaviour
- Stages in decision-making
- Pre-purchase and purchase
- Post-purchase evaluation
- Product disposal
- The role of marketing communications in buyer behaviour
- Theories of marketing communication
- Psychological influences on buyer behaviour
- Experience, learning and the role of memory
- Attitude formation, change and its effects on behaviour

Objectives

- To distinguish between cognitive and behavioural models of decision-making
- To identify the key stages in the decision-making process
- To outline the social influences on decision-making
- To outline the personal influences on decision-making
- To discuss the concept of cognitive dissonance
- To demonstrate the alternative hierarchy of effects models in marketing communications
- To outline how individuals process information
- To explain the concept of attention
- To identify the influences on the interpretation of messages
- To outline the three key types of learning
- To demonstrate the importance of attitudes in the decision-making process

Professional perspective

Gordon Foxall Distinguished Research Professor, Cardiff University

One of the most frequently cited contributions to the study of persuasion is the Yale University Communications Research Program (see, for instance, Hovland, Janis and Kelley 1953). Most writers on advertising and other forms of persuasive communication draw on its conclusions without giving much attention to its theoretical sources. But the program's conclusions cannot be fully appreciated shorn of their conceptual context, and an understanding of the theoretical concerns of the day can be a spur to continued investigation now. In fact the program drew on a range of theoretical positions from psychoanalysis to learning theory, from field theory to reference group analysis. (An excellent overview is provided by Eagly and Chaiken 1993.) The common theme was controlled laboratory study of communications effects: source credibility, one-sided versus two-sided appeals, primacy versus recency of opposing messages, and so on. An important reason for reconsidering the Yale program lies in its recurrent theoretical theme that draws on reinforcement theory, especially as it was presented by Hull. The aim was to understand better how the source (Who?), message structure and content (Says what?) and audience characteristics (To whom?) influence the effectiveness of a persuasive message.

Their adaptation of reinforcement theory was based on the finding that a response that is rewarded (or reinforced) will be performed more often. Hence beliefs and attitudes are verbal responses that are likely to become habitual if they are followed by positive arguments or reasons for holding them. A message (Popcorn is nutritious because ...) is a stimulus; the extent to which the individual accepts the arguments given for the advertiser's claim denotes his or her beliefs and attitudes, and these are reinforced by the current or *anticipated* rewards of holding them. But the theoretical range adopted by the Yale group ruled out any narrow adherence to a strict behaviourism: it was the anticipated incentives promised by a communication whose advocacy was accepted in the form of beliefs and attitudes that mattered. Such incentives included social and personal benefits such as approval and esteem as well as the tangible benefits provided by product attributes. From this stemmed a range of hypotheses with regard to such matters as the persuasive nature of credible sources.

The theoretical basis of the Yale program remains influential; for example, learning theory is a vital component of models of persuasion found in Rossiter and Percy's (1997) advertising model, and in consumer situation theory (Foxall 1997).

Gordon R. Foxall

This chapter is split into two areas of marketing psychology:

1 Theories of buyer behaviour and marketing communications with particular application to the social and personal influences on buyer behaviour.
2 The psychological influences on buyer behaviour.

Alternative paradigms of buyer behaviour

We will first consider the application of theories of buyer behaviour[*] to the integrated marketing communications process. The theoretical aspects of behaviour are presented so as to enable the student to consider the impact of buying theory on marketing communications practice.

Theories of decision-making behaviour generally fall into one of two schools of thought.

- the cognitive paradigm
- the behavioural paradigm.

The cognitive paradigm

Decision-making

The process the decision-maker goes through in arriving at a final decision. Decision-making can involve the use of thoughts and feelings, and can be affected by others and previous behaviour.

This perspective of **decision-making** activity is so called because it focuses on the individual's thought processes when making a decision. The cognitive paradigm sees consumer choice as a problem-solving and decision-making sequence of activities, the outcome of which is determined principally by the buyer's intellectual functioning, and rational, goal-directed processing of information (Assael 1995). This implies that the buyer is an intelligent, rational, thinking, and problem-solving organism, who stores and evaluates sensory inputs to make a reasoned decision (Markin and Narayana 1975). Observed action, therefore, is attributed to intra-personal information processing. Buyers compare and evaluate alternative brands in relation to the buyer's purposes and aims. Buyers do not have perfect knowledge of all alternative products (the **total set**), they are only aware of a proportion of the products available (the **awareness set**) and they reduce what they know to a smaller manageable set before making a decision (the **evoked set**). The implication for management is that one key objective must be to get products into the buyer's evoked set (some people call this the 'consideration set'). Achieving awareness, while of itself important, is an insufficient base on which to found successful marketing communications management.

Total set

The complete set of alternative choices in a decision.

Awareness set

A proportion of possible choices in a decision.

Evoked set

Limited selection of choices brought to mind and from among which a final selection may be made.

Models of behaviour from the cognitive paradigm generally present behaviour as a process. They are most frequently represented by diagrams that look like flowcharts with many lines and arrows indicating the direction of the sequence of activities. These models have evolved over many years since the earliest forms of the 1950s. In the most current form they have many components, as in the latest version of the Engel, Blackwell and Miniard model (2000) shown in Exhibit 4.1.

---

[*] While reading this chapter, it should be noted that researchers and authors in this general field tend to use the terms 'customers', 'buyers' and 'consumers' rather interchangeably. Elsewhere in this text, we have been at pains to emphasise distinctions between customers whom we define as buyers and consumers whom we define as users. A customer may also be the consumer, but this need not necessarily be the case, and our discussion of the Decision-Making Unit later in this chapter makes this clear. As a consequence, 'consuming' behaviour may be described in very different terms to 'buying' behaviour. However, it remains the case that this general area of study is frequently referred to as 'consumer' behaviour by which it is most likely to address buying processes. While this may seem a little strange, it should be appreciated that there is clearly a lot of overlap between the two and that the consuming process is ultimately a principal driver of buyer behaviour. Throughout the chapter we shall be referring to the research and writings of others and need to adopt the same conventions as they have used and are popularised in much published work. Generally, therefore, we shall use buyer behaviour and consumer behaviour interchangeably with no intention in the context of this chapter to suggest any distinction. Where we do wish to distinguish between the two, this will be clearly identified.

Exhibit 4.1 Engel, Blackwell and Miniard Model of Consumer Behaviour, 2000

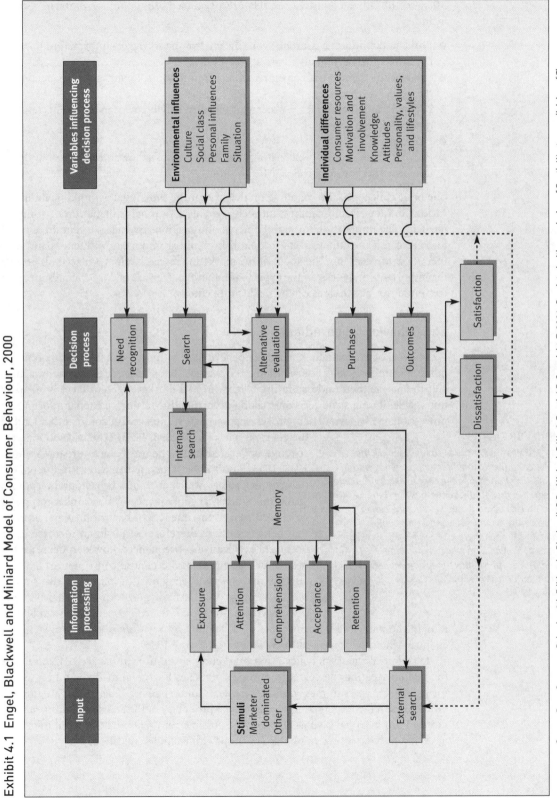

Source: From *Consumer Behavior*, 9th Edition, by Blackwell, R.D., Miniard, P.W., & Engel, J.F. Copyright © 2001. Reprinted with permission of South-Western, a division of Thomson Learning: www.thomsonrights.com Fax: +1 800 730–2215

Most of the other cognitive models are organised along similar patterns. Stages include:

● Problem definition: a stimulus from the environment triggers information processing from which a consumer perceives a need.
● Information search: the consumer collects information to aid in the satisfaction of the need.
● Evaluation of alternatives: a process of problem solving, which will be affected by a range of influences.
● Purchase.
● Post-purchase evaluation: consumption will be followed by an evaluation to determine whether the need was satisfied or not.

The basic concept of the cognitive models is that the individual is thinking about the various influences and can, if requested, provide a rational explanation of a buying incident. The implication for marketing communications managers is that there needs to be research into the process to establish the most important influences and how they affect the decision. The focus of the marketing research effort is placed on finding the important influences, in the expectation that the later use of corporate resources in communications activities can be made more efficient.

The behavioural paradigm

Proponents of this paradigm generally believe that to find out what is going on in the mind of an individual is not achievable. They argue that if individual behaviour is difficult to analyse then understanding behaviour at a market segment level is virtually impossible. Rather than decision-making occurring due to intra-personal information processing, the behaviourist approach suggests that stimuli are predominantly found in the environment (Foxall 1990, 1993). The behavioural perspective is derived from operant behaviourism (Skinner 1938, 1953; Foxall 1993). Operant behaviourism is a philosophy of psychology which attributes behavioural responses to the environmental consequences which similar responses have produced. Consequences of behaviour may reinforce that behaviour and, therefore, result in an increase in its occurrence. Negative consequences, however, decrease the behaviour's occurrence, and neutral consequences have no effect at all. Operant behaviourism maintains two fundamental assumptions: the frequency with which behaviour is performed is a function of the consequences of such behaviour in the past, and determinants of behaviour must, therefore, be sought in the environment rather than within the individual (Foxall 1993).

FOOD FOR THOUGHT

There are far more texts focused on the cognitive school than on the behavioural school. This is because the cognitivist approach to research is essentially quantitative and the academic community has historically leaned significantly toward concepts which can be 'measured'. Thus there is a large body of research material available on which to base the development of cognitive theories. More recently this imbalance is being addressed (e.g. Foxall 1990, 1993).

Behavioural theorists believe that marketing communications activity should be focused on creating the correct environmental cues for the individual and on monitoring the responses to these cues as a guide to future activity. This means attention is on the benefits to be gained from choosing a product, e.g. the access to a lump sum of money from personal savings plans, or the possible pain that might be felt if the product is not purchased, e.g. not being able to pay for a child's education.

Types of problem solving

Cognitive models appear to be more relevant where the individual perceives there to be a high risk associated with the product (these are sometimes referred to as high involvement products). This risk may take the form of:

- a financial commitment, e.g. car, house, pension plan, etc.;
- a social risk, e.g. gift giving, clothing, cosmetics, etc.; or,
- an added risk of personal disappointment, e.g. interior decorations.

Elaboration Likelihood Model

Describes the amount of thoughtful consideration, or elaboration, a receiver gives to a communication.

Petty and Cacioppo's (1983) **Elaboration Likelihood Model** recognizes that individuals are sometimes willing to think very carefully about a piece of marketing communication and sometimes hardly think about it at all. The degree of amount of thoughtful consideration in these circumstances is called *elaboration*. It represents the amount of effort the recipients are willing to put in for themselves and, in this way, add to the communication by bringing in their own thoughts, attitudes, feelings and experiences. Simply, it is about the relationship receivers have with a piece of communication and how they embellish or elaborate on it. The nature and amount of elaboration will have an impact on the persuasiveness of the communication. Elaboration can take many forms and involve searching for more information, consulting with others, exploring feelings, thinking and so on.

Research has indicated that the levels of motivation, ability and predisposition to enter into elaboration vary between people and will be affected by the nature of the communication. There are two principal routes in the elaboration likelihood process. The first, a 'central' route, is typified by 'a person's careful and thoughtful consideration of the true merits of the information presented in support of an advocacy' (Petty and Cacioppo 1986). The second, a 'peripheral' route, is where there is little elaboration. In this case, the persuasiveness of the message relies on peripheral cues such as the perceived credibility of the sender, familiarity with the message or product, how much the communication is liked and the reactions of others to the communication.

Extensive problem solving

Part of the decision-making process in which the decision is extended owing to the perceived complexity of the final decision.

Extensive problem solving is the name given to the decision-making process when the individuals take longer to arrive at the decision point because of the perceived complexity of the decision outcomes (Engel et al. 2000).

Most product choices do not require extensive problem solving. In these cases the cognitive models are generally over-complex and past behaviour begins to have a more significant part to play in reducing the time spent on decision-making. At the other extreme end of the cognitive school is **routine problem solving,** which is often characterised by habit, in which there is little if any thought given to the range of alternatives and buying behaviour largely replicates past satisfactory purchases.

Routine problem solving

Characterised by habit, this form of decision-making involves little consideration of alternatives.

If we consider the vast diversity of buying behaviour for even a short time it is clear that individuals rarely spend a great deal of time engaging in decision-making. The majority of purchases are relatively routine and the buying activity is minimised. Ehrenberg and Goodhart (1979) suggest that the greater part of buying activity is rooted in past experiences and that for many products the buying process is relatively habitual, that is to say there is little variation from purchase to purchase.

ATR model

Three-stage process of behaviour involving the movement from Awareness to Trial to Repeat behaviour.

They suggest that a three-stage model is more appropriate for predicting the aggregate activity within a given market. The stages are Awareness, Trial and Repeat (or reinforcement) (hence it is known as the **ATR model** – Exhibit 4.2). At this aggregate level the focus is not on the individual but on the clusters that constitute market segments for a particular product. In the ATR type of model the switching behaviour of individuals is less important than knowing the brand share for the particular product.

Exhibit 4.2 The ATR model

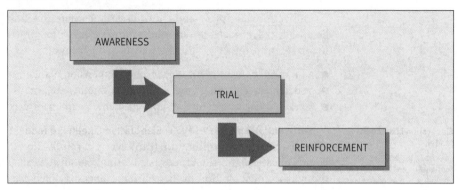

Source: Adapted from ATR model awareness diagram from *Essays on Understanding Buyer Behavior*, J. Walter Thompson and the Market Research Corporation of America, (Ehrenberg, A.S.C. and Goodhart, G.J., 1979). Reproduced with permission.

Generally, larger brands will perform significantly better than smaller brands because they will gain proportionately more from the switching away from secondary brands than vice versa.

There is a strong connection between the ATR model and the concept of the evoked set. In both concepts it is possible for the buyers to know of the existence of many more brands (Awareness) and products but not to choose them. As with other cognitive models, it is vitally important to move consumers from simple awareness of the product to a point at which some consumption is undertaken (Trial). Only after this initial buying act can consumers engage in evaluation of the behaviour. Did they buy the right thing? Did it meet/exceed expectations? Would they buy again (Repeat) or would they revert to previous patterns? It is quite normal for 'brand loyal' customers to shop around in this way as they are checking that their consumption pattern brings the best results. The objective for management is to establish a pattern of buying focused on their product as the most frequently purchased rather than the only one purchased. Allowing the consumer to learn from experience that your product is best is of more value than any amount of advertising stating that your product is best.

Buying without deciding?

Let us conclude this section by looking at 'buying without deciding'. At first this phrase looks incomprehensible but if you consider the growing market for services, in both business and consumer markets, then you can see that many decisions are being made on behalf of the 'real' buyer but without the person, or company, ever having to consider the full complexity of the decision. For example, if you are investing in a personal pension plan then you simply hand over a sum of money, the plan manager decides which stocks and shares to invest in and manages your funds to achieve a return. You are allowing a specialist to make decisions about your future on your behalf. The same is true when a company hands over carriage of its goods to a third-party contractor. The company is deciding to allow the carrier to choose the vehicles, etc. that are necessary to move the goods from place to place. This form of conducting business is increasingly common as specialist skills are expensive to develop and companies offering to remove the problem are relatively welcome.

Another form of buying without deciding is becoming increasingly common. This could be labelled '*automatic buying*'. At present it is most common in business-to-business activities. Companies are increasingly using computer-controlled systems for ordering components and reducing stock levels. These systems are capable of placing orders with suppliers without any human intervention. The role of the humans in such systems is in defining the scope and scale of the automation. One example would be General Motors which has supply links which can generate orders for components, such as bumper units (from a choice of hundreds of potential patterns), to be delivered within hours of the orders being placed. This enables the most efficient use of GM's capital and offers customers short delivery times. Most large grocery companies operate very similar resupply systems using a standard **electronic data interchange (EDI)** network. International Stock Exchanges conduct billions of pounds worth of transactions using automated processes, as do most other important financial centres, without any human intervention. The future implication for marketers is that the links between companies will become increasingly sophisticated and that it is important to be aware of developments in technology which create new communications opportunities.

Electronic data interchange (EDI)

Method of transferring data from computer to computer.

From a consumer perspective automatic buying has been around for centuries. Many households operate using shopping lists as their stock control process. If the item is on the list then it is bought; if it is not then the shopper does not look for it. Marketers have struggled with the problem of how to get their products on shoppers' lists since the idea of retailing first began. The future of this particular problem is likely to become increasingly complex. Consider what would happen if shoppers automated their lists using a computer. They could then enter a shopping service search engine on the Internet and seek out the best value package from a range of grocery companies without ever coming into contact with a single store. This would lead to a significant reduction in the number of opportunities to influence the decision and make the marketer's life much more difficult. Access to the customer's communications network would take on a vital importance. Tesco's online shopping service 'ties-in' its shoppers by allowing them to develop their own favoured electronic list to simplify the repeat ordering process. Strategically, computers will probably play the largest part in changing consumer buying patterns into the twenty-first century and marketers will have to be alert to all of the possibilities for change in communications structures and methods.

Stages in decision-making

Whether cognitive or behavioural models of behaviour are adopted, there are four stages in the decision-making process:

- pre-purchase
- purchase
- post-purchase evaluation
- product disposal.

The behaviours and related issues of each of these stages are detailed below.

Pre-purchase and purchase

Exhibit 4.3 outlines the main influences on pre-purchase and purchase decision-making. The second half of this chapter discusses the psychological influences in detail. The social and personal influences are presented first.

Exhibit 4.3 The influences on decision-making

Social influences	Personal influences	Psychological influences
● Reference groups	● Demographic	● Perception
● Culture and subcultures	● Situational	● Personality
	● Involvement	● Experience, knowledge and ability
		● Attitudes

Source: Adapted from Dibb et al. (1997)

Social influences on decision-making: the decision-making unit and reference groups

In the real world individuals do not go about their daily lives as if they were the only beings on the planet. They have families, friends and neighbours. They generally have a work environment and a social environment that are different from each other. These different groups all have an impact on the buying decisions that individuals make. Many of the goods and services consumed by these groups have a display function that is used to communicate status or achievement in some way. One of the more obvious examples of this function may be shown by the car parked outside the house. This can communicate wealth, or business success, and it thus becomes a symbol for others to recognise the achievement of the owner without the owner having to say anything.

The car example demonstrates that the outcomes of the buying process may have an impact on significant others. The most obvious example of the impact of buying behaviour on other people is in the behaviour associated with gift giving which usually involves careful consideration of the impact on the intended receiver (Belk 1979). It is not unexpected that individuals other than the buyer may have an influence on the choice of product. For example, when a family with two teenage children is deciding where to go for its holiday there may be much discussion between family members as to the merits, or otherwise, of the individual product offers (Corfman and Lehman 1987). It then becomes difficult to measure just who is the decision-maker in such a context. The concept of the **Decision-Making Unit** recognises that there can be a number of people or players who will directly influence the buying decision. If we extend this concept to business-to-business marketing then we can see that 'group decision-making behaviour' is commonly utilised rather than individuals going off into isolation and doing what they think is best. Most large organisations have buying committees involving users as well as technical specialists so that the 'optimum' decision can be made.

Any source of social influence can be considered as a potential audience for marketing communications. These sources of influence are usually called '**reference groups**' (Sprott 1958).

Influencers and deciders

The way that an individual's culture plays a part in how marketing communications are perceived is considered in Chapter 8. It is important for marketers to take this factor into account when constructing the messages within the communications strategy. The individual can also belong to several sub-cultures that reflect certain opinions and preferences. For example, a person's religion and age group could affect a wide range of different topics. You are likely to hold similar opinions to many of your friends. As a result you will also value their opinions more highly when making

Decision-Making Unit (DMU)

Also known as the Decision-Making Group, the DMU concept recognises the involvement of a range of people in the decision-making process. The group may be formally organised, such as in a business-to-business purchase context, but more frequently is an unorganised group which influences the decision to buy. The DMU comprises a number of 'players' that may be described in slightly different terms by different authors, e.g. influencers, gatekeeper, specifier, decider, buyer and user.

Reference group

Group of people to whom an individual relates such that her/his behaviour is potentially influenced by that of others in the group. There are many possible groups that may act as a reference group: family, peers, work colleagues, professional bodies, social groups, etc.

IN VIEW 4.1

Influencers

Ask yourself about the sources of information on fashion clothing and two major sources are likely to appear in your list. One source is the television, the other is magazines. The editors, reviewers and presenters working in these media have a significant filtering role in selecting the pieces of information that reach our decision environment. For example, magazines such as *Vogue* have been considered as essential reading for those wishing to keep up to date with one aspect of the fashion scene.

Similarly the contact that the individual has with salespeople will have an influence on the decision to buy or not to buy. Why should the salesperson in an electrical goods shop offer a Sony TV in preference to a Panasonic? How the marketer communicates the benefits to the salesperson will ultimately affect the attitudes of the salesperson and their willingness to promote your product in preference to competitors' products.

For marketers the implication is that there are a range of influencers and decision-makers and that all of them offer potential as target audiences when constructing communications strategies.

decisions. Some of these associations can be very strong while others are relatively weak. For example, people living in the south of Italy do not share the same view of the country as people living in the north. Their views, while different, will have little impact on most decisions. However, where the issue of food is concerned there will be considerable differences. This aspect of regionality can be seen in most countries across the world. It is not the intention here to engage in a comprehensive review of the effects of culture and sub-culture but it is important that market communicators recognise the need for sensitivity across groups.

As stated earlier, close friends and relatives of the individual will often play a part in the decision process. The specific part will depend on what is being bought, when and for what purpose. As a general tool for analysing these influences we can use the concept of roles. Within each decision there are several roles to be fulfilled in the Decision-Making Unit (Exhibit 4.4). These are usually described as *influencers* (providers of information and direction); *gatekeeper* (filtering information to the

Exhibit 4.4 The Decision-Making Unit

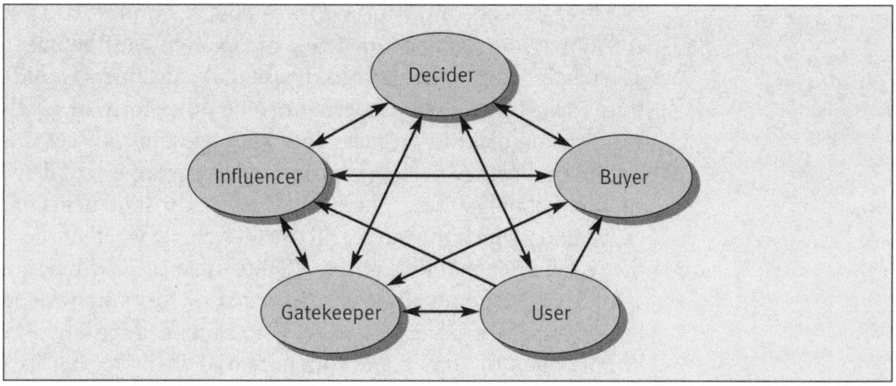

decider); *decider* (the person that makes the choice); *buyer* (the person who pays for the choice); and *users* (those who consume the choice). You should note that these roles may be taken by groups rather than by an identifiable individual.

Taking the example of a holiday for a family with two teenage children we could expect to find that all family members will state their preferences for the type of holiday (influencers). If the mother takes responsibility for collecting brochures for the family to look at then she will be taking on the gatekeeper role. Then another round of discussions is likely before some criteria for making a decision can be identified. It may be the mother who offers certain places as being 'acceptable' to all members (again a gatekeeping role). The family may then decide collectively or the decision may be taken by the parents. In a typical family the cost would be shared by the wage earners (who may be one or more of the family members) and all family members would take the holiday (as users).

Other influencers include the views of other family and friends. There may indeed be some social pressure to conform to a wider group norm for the type of holiday taken. What about the travel agent and the brochures? These sources will also impact on the information environment in which the decision is taken. This example demonstrates the potential complexity of group decision-making. As marketers it is necessary to consider the whole system of relationships when constructing a marketing communications strategy.

Business-to-business decision-making units

In business-to-business communications the personal element of the contact between buyer and salesperson may be the most influential aspect of the decision-making process. Vast amounts of goods and services are sold as a result of salespeople visiting potential customers with the aim of bringing away an order. The majority of these deals will be for a few hundred pounds whilst others will be multi-million pound contracts, for example when negotiating for construction projects. The more money is involved then the more people are likely to be involved in the decision process. At the highest level this can even involve government officials acting on behalf of the business organisation, for example by setting up trade missions to open up new foreign markets.

Although potentially much more complex in terms of the system within which the decisions are made we should not forget that the people involved are not so very different from the ordinary consumers that we were looking at earlier. The decision still has an information environment and it is still taken by an identifiable set of people. In these respects there are opportunities for marketing communications to be used to influence the outcome of the decision.

Three aspects of business-to-business communication serve to set it apart from consumer communication. These are explicit contractual specification, negotiation and relationships. The most likely use that consumers would have for an explicit contract is when they buy property or some other form of long-term commitment, such as a pension plan. In business dealings a specific contract is far more common. Many important business buying decisions have a great deal of detail specified in the form of contractual obligations. There are usually clear statements of quality and performance expectation which the buyer will use to evaluate whether the seller has successfully met the requirements of the contract. Quite often there will be a requirement to provide a sample of the goods to be made so that quality might be tested before production begins or before delivery is made. For example, a stationery company might provide a sample ream of copy paper to a potential client so that its suitability for use in the client's copiers can be assured. Quite simply, businesses tend to be inherently conservative, thus are less likely to take risks and will seek to ensure that satisfactory performance will be guaranteed.

In consumer markets in developed economies, the opportunity to negotiate prices is strictly limited although more opportunity exists in less developed economies. In business-to-business deals it is still normal to engage in negotiation as to price, quality, delivery, payment terms and a range of other contractual matters. In a consumer situation the choice is often to take the deal or leave and start again elsewhere. In a business situation there is likely to be a challenge to the original offer with the aim of achieving a better offer. Marketing communications in such situations can create an environment for the discussion; a deal may be won through the abilities and efforts of the sales team.

In many business-to-business situations there will be a relationship between members of the buying group and the selling team. More often than not this will be a one-to-one relationship in which the people have known each other for some time and have engaged in several previous transactions. This feature of organisational buying offers marketers a significant opportunity to affect the buyer's decisions.

There are opportunities for direct contact with the influencers as well as the decider and there are opportunities to build loyalty based on beneficial mutual exchange of information. In fact there are so many opportunities that the relationships between buyer and seller often resemble the relationships between old friends (Weitz 1978). The selection and training of the sales team thus becomes a much more important feature of business-to-business communications. At this level there is potential for the salesperson to become one of the major influences on the buyer's decision. The interpersonal skills of the salesperson and their authority to negotiate a deal that the buyer will find acceptable, at least on face value, are critical factors in closing the sale.

The three elements of specification, negotiation and relationships are not the only differences when considering marketing communications in a business-to-business setting. They do, however, form a core around which most business decisions will be made but the essential marketing skills of research, targeting and communication remain as important in business-to-business marketing as they are in consumer marketing.

Personal influences on decision-making

The Decision-Making Unit identifies that consumers draw from people within their various environments when making decisions about a product. In addition to the players in the Decision-Making Unit, there are other influences that can affect the pattern of buying and consumption. This section looks at the impact that some of these other factors can have on the decision-making process. The key factors include:

- ideals and aspirations
- demographics and psychographics
- the purchase situation
- the amount of time given to buying
- the level of consumer involvement.

Ideals and aspirations

An individual with little money has little opportunity to express their desire for high-priced luxury goods. This desire remains latent until the economic circumstances of the individual change. For many consumers this means that the desire will go unmet.

One assumption underpinning the study of economics is that society as a whole has unlimited desires that are only constrained by a lack of resources needed to fulfil them. In terms of many luxury products this assumption is generally valid; not everybody can afford a large house with several cars. Consumers have ideals that they generally aspire to and their activities are focused on partial achievement of the ideal rather than full achievement (Mitchell 1986). The success of lottery games across the world indicates the general desire for an improvement in circumstances. The financial implications of consumption are a significant constraint on buying activity and are reflected in the growth of credit financing of current consumption.

Demographics and psychographics

Any individual's history to date will have created a relatively unique set of circumstances surrounding that individual. Information about this set of circumstances is called demographics and includes details of age, gender, income, occupation and education. When gathering data, research companies often seek to establish facts such as disposable income and buying patterns. The income of the individual is only a part of this data gathering. There will be considerations about the area in which the individual lives and type of accommodation. Psychographic factors which relate to lifestyle within both work and social groups are also major considerations. The education of the individual may also affect the capability to decipher the messages from the various environments. The influences are enduring in that they exist whether or not the individual is engaging in buying activity (Dahl 1992). See Chapter 17 for more details about these aspects.

Purchase situation

There are other influences that are rooted in the purchase situation itself. Particularly important in this regard is the importance of the communications made with the individual at the point of sale (Iyer 1989). Customers may be attracted by price-based offers, e.g. three for the price of two packs, or they may value the information provided by a member of the retailer's staff before making a decision as to which product best suits the need. The point of sale (POS), or point of purchase (POP) as it is also known, is an immensely rich opportunity for marketing communications management to influence the outcome of the decision-making activity; it is an important area within the marketing communications mix.

Time available

A final key influence on the decision is the amount of time available. The growth of supermarkets has been aided by the consumers' desire to spend less time on shopping. As with all other resources, time is relatively constrained thus time spent engaging in information search and shopping is time that could be spent on other activities. The amount of time that an individual is prepared to spend on the decision is usually dependent upon the perceived importance of the decision outcome. When the individual has learnt about shopping, for most types of goods, then there is an increasing desire to reduce the time it takes up (East et al. 1994). Convenience of access and product range width become essential features of successful businesses. If consumers perceive little value in the products as symbols then they are less likely to spend time on the decision-making activity.

Consumer involvement

The degree to which consumers are involved in different aspects of the consumption process, such as products, advertisements and the act of purchasing, has grown to be regarded as one of the central determinants of consumer behaviour (Broderick and Mueller 1999; Laaksonen 1994). The main reason for this lies in the potential of **involvement** to account for the differences in the degree of both the mental and the physical effort a consumer is willing to devote to consumption-related activities. Most writers present the individual buyer as having either a high involvement level or a low involvement level. The specific state depends upon a range of factors such as the perception of the benefits to be gained, the perceived costs and the perceived risk of poor performance (Mittal 1989). For every factor there are both resource implications and personal esteem implications and this adds to the complexity of the concept. For example, the purchase of a can of tomatoes, or a carton of milk, should be regarded as relatively low involvement because it has little financial or social risk attached to it. By comparison, the purchase of a car or a holiday is highly involving. The potential benefits from success could be very high but the personal costs of failing could also be very high. In addition to the product itself being more or less involving, individuals themselves can have different levels of involvement. For example, while frozen ready-made meals tend to be less involving as a product category, UK consumers are more involved with the purchase of them than Italian consumers (Broderick 1997). Issues of involvement are also significant in business-to-business situations as well as business-to-consumer.

Hierarchy-of-effects models describe the step-wise process through which individuals move when exposed to marketing communications; this includes the cognitive (thinking), affective (feeling) and conative (doing) steps. There are a number of hierarchy-of-effects models, three of which are detailed later in this chapter. What emerges from the study of involvement is a method of organising the hierarchy-of-effects models. For products that usually have a high level of buyer involvement the

Consumer involvement

The degree to which consumers involve themselves in the whole consumption process. Although it is commonly referred to as 'consumer' involvement, it is best thought of as 'customer' involvement, and relates to the level of involvement with which the customer engages in the purchase decision. Involvement can vary significantly, depending upon product category and the customer's level of interest or predisposition. Levels of involvement can vary from high (e.g. purchase of a car) to low (e.g. purchase of a chocolate bar).

Hierarchy-of-effects models

Models that describe the stages individuals are said to progress through in moving from initial unawareness to final action such as purchase and consumption. A range of models or ways of describing the stages in the process exist.

Exhibit 4.5 Levels of consumer involvement in food across the EU

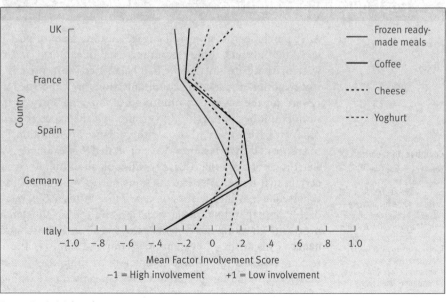

Source: Broderick (1997)

IN VIEW 4.2

The impact of involvement on hierarchy-of-effect models

High involvement products: e.g. washing machine

THINK – consider a range of different products.

FEEL – establish a priority ranking between the alternatives based on attitudes toward the different product attributes.

DO – buy the top ranking product from the list.

Low involvement products: e.g. bar of chocolate

DO – buy your favourite chocolate bar.

FEEL – satisfied after eating it.

THINK – satisfaction comes from that kind of chocolate so choose that one next time.

hierarchy appears to follow a Think-Feel-Do pattern. Buyers consider the various aspects of the problem to be solved then they work out a preferred way of solving the problem and finally they carry out any necessary activity. By comparison, buyers of low involvement goods display a Do-Feel-Think pattern. They recognise the problem, buy the product to address the problem then they reflect on the experience. This latter pattern fits well with the routines that most of us exhibit when buying groceries and also applies to any other products for which we have a great deal of experience.

Post-purchase evaluation

Cognitive dissonance

Term coined by Leon Festinger to describe a psychological state in which there is some incongruity (dissonance) between two or more thoughts. The resulting inconsistency encourages individuals to modify their thoughts to be more compatible or harmonious. Dissonance when recognised is an unstable state of mind.

After purchase, the buyer will engage in some form of post-purchase evaluation. It is usual that we seek some reassurance that our efforts, and resources, have not been wasted. That is to say that we had been effective in gaining the rewards sought. The vast majority of marketing communications are concerned with the idea of a positive reward for the act of consumption. As consumers expect benefit to flow from consumption it becomes critical to ensure that the expected benefits are delivered. Most products have associated costs, either financial or emotional, and consumers will seek to ensure that their resources are not wasted. For example, a woman buying an expensive dress for a special occasion will look at all the other women so that she can be certain that no one else has the same outfit. When she compares herself against the others, she may also wish to appear more fashionable, more wealthy, or even more desirable (depending on the occasion and the circumstances). The outcome of the process of checking the benefits gained against the costs is known as **cognitive dissonance**. This form of evaluation is not the same as the marketing management techniques used to evaluate campaigns. Techniques for that kind of evaluation are described in Chapter 23. Rather we are concerned here with the individual evaluations of specific purchase decisions.

The evaluation process will generally include a search for information that confirms the buying act as 'good'. Where the information conflicts with our desired outcome then cognitive dissonance results. For the most part we anticipate that our expectations will be met. When they are we feel justified in our decisions. When our expectations are unmet the range of consequences can be very wide. For example, if you buy a coffee in a local coffee shop and it is not to your taste you may simply leave it and note not to use that coffee shop again. If you have just purchased a computer and it will not start then the problem is more serious. You will have to engage in future activity to redress the situation. It is important for marketers to minimise the level of dissonance or there can be serious consequences. The response of the company to your new demands will be critical to the resolution of your problem. In extreme cases, it is possible that you would have to resort to legal action to resolve such an issue. Obviously, you would be unlikely to recommend such a company to anyone else.

It is important to meet the buyer's expectations. This may not generate much positive feedback. If you can exceed buyer's expectations then you may get a small boost from the positive word-of-mouth communications that follow. If you fail to meet expectations then negative word-of-mouth communications rapidly follow. The extent of the damage is essentially dependent on the initial expectation gap and your subsequent response to requests for redress. In this respect 'expectation gap' avoidance is a better strategy than subsequent damage limitation. Strategies to inform buyers' expectations thus have an important part to play in creating the setting for the evaluation stage of the decision process.

If the expected level of benefits is delivered then it is unlikely that consumers will do much more than register their satisfaction in positive memories. If the level of benefit exceeds the expected level then it is possible that consumers will spread the good news among a limited group of their immediate family, friends and workmates. This form of **word-of-mouth communication** is uncontrollable. Marketers delivering very high levels of product quality, value and service can offer opportunities for consumers to feel that their expectations have been exceeded. It is mostly at these higher levels that positive word-of-mouth communication takes place. Occasionally there will be examples of 'downmarket' companies generating word-of-mouth based largely on one of the three variables. An example of this would be Aldi's entry into the UK grocery market which was based on the value proposition using edge-of-town locations, secondary product brands and low prices as its key strategies. The positive communication developed out of customers learning that secondary brands were of an acceptable quality standard and that the overall pricing structure led to significant value benefits. Aldi's launch proved successful in gaining market share after just a few years of operation.

Unfortunately for marketers there is much more word-of-mouth communication from dissatisfied customers. When benefits do not meet expectations then there is a problem. At the minimum end of dissatisfaction, the experience will challenge the consumer's attitudes toward the product and the brand. This negative view may also spread to the attitudes about the retailer and the manufacturer. At the most damaging end of dissatisfaction, the experience may result in legal action which hits the headlines and thus negatively influences thousands of potential customers. The level of damage is usually confined to the immediate group of family, friends and workmates but the strength of the communication is usually such that it does directly influence the receivers' views. Can you think of a good experience and a poor experience that you have had? What did you do about them? How many people did you tell? If you are a typical consumer you will have told more people about the negative experience than

Word-of-mouth communications

Literally, verbal communication between individuals. Word-of-mouth is typically a part of the total process of marketing communications in which messages are transmitted from the sender to many receivers. Word-of-mouth communications are the conversations held between the receivers, whether or not all members received the original marketing communication. Opinion leaders and other reference group members may have a strong influence on the effectiveness of the original intended message.

you did about the good experience. In this way bad news travels faster than good news. At the most extreme end of our scale the news will be spread by other media agencies and the negative influence can be widespread within a matter of hours.

Product disposal

The last stage in the consumption process is the disposal of the product. Very few of the products of a modern society are thoroughly consumable. There will be the retailer's bag and the manufacturer's packaging to dispose of shortly after buying. Later on there is likely to be a carton, or some similar inner container, to be disposed of. In many societies the amount of waste created by the mass consumption of goods is seen to be an increasing problem. There is consumer pressure to reduce the level of packaging and also to eliminate unnecessary costs. Ultimately, this can lead to government intervention to reduce the impact of waste on the environment. In Germany, for example, the law requires that most packaging is recovered through the distribution channel and that as much as possible is made from recyclable materials. Consumers are actively encouraged to recycle paper and containers so as to reduce waste. Manufacturers and retailers have responded by creating new messages which stress the 'environmental friendliness' of their products. A good example of this is the Body Shop which has built a global business on basis of ethical trading and a management philosophy which suggests that concern for the environment is a central component of its trading strategy.

As the amount of products consumed worldwide increases so we should expect consumers' concern for their environment and the implications of mass consumption to have an increasing influence on the decision process. Those companies that are visibly attempting to improve the consumers' environment will be perceived positively. Those companies which are perceived to be degrading the environment may be perceived negatively and potentially have reduced market shares as a consequence.

The role of marketing communications in buyer behaviour

One main role of marketing communications is to have an impact on individual decision-making. Another important function is to influence the influencers so that they provide positive direction to the decision-makers. As the different types of models suggest, these impacts could be made at a number of stages within the decision-making process. Some secondary roles of marketing communications are to assure the decision-makers, and influencers, that the right choice has been made and to provide reinforcement to these groups so that they may repeat the desired behaviour at the next opportunity. The various methods of communication each have advantages and disadvantages in terms of their use at each stage. Careful selection of the alternative methods is required if resources are to be used in the most effective, economical and efficient manner.

For companies engaged in marketing communications there will probably be a varied range of business objectives. Individual consumers' views of corporate image are inextricably linked with the performance of the products at the same time as being affected by the perception of the company in its wider setting of business and society. For example, oil companies such as Exxon and Shell have had to work very hard to improve a corporate image tarnished by accusations of lack of concern for the protection of the environment. This example illustrates the lack of control that companies have over the total information environment.

There are three elements to the timing of marketing communications. These can be identified as before the sale, at the point of sale, and after the sale. In the planning process the management team has to pay attention to all three time elements. Whether you are a committed cognitivist or a behaviourist is probably of little importance in managing the creation of pre-sale communications. The cognitivists might argue that attention should be given to forming positive attitudes toward the company and its products (getting the products into the evoked set), while the behaviourists might argue that it is important to provide the environmental cues that suggest that consumption of the product will bring positive rewards (reinforcing the behaviour). It could be argued that providing information that implies satisfactory product performance will achieve the objectives of both schools of thought. The vast majority of pre-sale communications are scene setting for the act of purchasing and as such they are likely to achieve both behaviourist and cognitivist objectives. The objective for the communication would need to be much more explicitly stated before any significant choice between approaches becomes necessary.

At the point of sale the differences between the two paradigms are much more marked. The cognitive paradigm struggles with the idea that buyers spend little time in considering their purchases. The emphasis on thinking is potentially reduced as the stimuli from the immediate environment take prominence in affecting decisions. For example, the buyers in the supermarket, buying food on a monthly basis, are usually faced with a massive variety of alternatives which will meet their needs. The information processing effort required to evaluate all of these alternatives is too time-consuming and so buyers look for decision rules that cut down this cost (Thaler 1985). Examples of such 'rules of thumb' (more accurately defined by academic works as **heuristics**) are brand loyalty; buying on price; bargain hunting; buying on past experience; and buying on visual impact (packaging has a major role to play at this stage of decision-making). At the point of sale the behaviourist school has a significant edge in explaining behaviour but not in every case. Even in the supermarket example there will be occasions when the buyer stops to consider the specific purchase and shifts to a more cognitive mode, e.g. when buying a gift or when selecting the wine for a dinner party.

After-sales communications have grown in importance over the last 20 years. They were relatively limited, usually to account holders in large department stores and car owners, but more recently there has been an explosion in the number of potential after-sales contact opportunities. Every major store chain now operates a loyalty card scheme that captures data on the purchases of individuals. Manufacturers now gather much more data on their warranty cards and market research companies can offer lists of names and addresses when asked for tailored profiles of consumers of specific types of goods. The aim of all of this activity is to retain contact with the buyer. At this stage the theoretical approach will depend upon the objective for the contact. Behaviourists would be aiming to provide shorter-term impact, e.g. coupons for next purchase or invitations to special in-store events, while cognitivists will probably be seeking a longer-term objective, e.g. collecting reward points such as air miles or offering new services to existing customers at preferential rates. Once again there is no right way of going about communicating with the potential market. The selection of message, media and timing will depend on the objectives sought by the company.

Simultaneously, the company has to consider the impact of the wider environment on its communications. It is not only competitors that are striving to influence the buyers. Consumer groups and media commentators should be considered as alternative

Heuristics
Problem-solving rules.

sources of information to the buyers and their output needs to be considered when forming objectives and implementation plans. In this respect, the evaluation process should take into account not only the activities of the company but also those outside influences that are believed to have had an impact on the implementation of the plan.

This section demonstrates that communications, both marketer controlled and from other sources, are inextricably linked with behaviour at all stages of decision-making. This linkage has been shown to have significant implications for the planning, control and evaluation of the management process.

Theories of marketing communication

As identified earlier, the hierarchy of effects models describe the step-wise process through which individuals move when exposed to marketing communications. There are many theories as to how marketing communications may be applied to affect buyer behaviour. Three hierarchy of effects models are outlined in Exhibit 4.6 to illustrate the diversity of perspectives.

Exhibit 4.6 Hierarchy of effects models

AIDA model	DAGMAR model	ATR model
Awareness	Awareness	Awareness
Interest	Comprehension	Trial
Desire	Conviction	Reinforcement
Action	Action	

One of the earliest models for the management of marketing communications was the Awareness–Interest–Desire–Action structure proposed in the nineteenth century by Elmo Lewis (usually known by its acronym as the AIDA model). Lewis's model proposes that buyers move from one state to the next on the way to consumption. It is the sequence of states that gives this type of model its form and many later models adopt the idea of a sequence of states. They largely vary in the number of states and their description of those states. For example, Lavidge and Steiner suggested that the sequence should be Awareness–Knowledge–Liking–Preference–Conviction–Purchase. The link to Lewis's model is obvious. In all of the sequential models there are difficulties in researching the levels of awareness needed to proceed to the next stage, whatever its label, and it is a well-established fact that positive preferences do not automatically lead to consumption.

Colley provides an improvement on the sequential model by relating it to the objective to be achieved (1961). Colley's model has four stages which are essentially similar to those in the traditional sequential models (Awareness–Comprehension–Conviction–Action). The difference between Colley's approach and that of the sequential models is that Colley suggests that any stage could provide the objective for marketing communications independent of the rest. This model is usually known by the acronym DAGMAR (Defining Advertising Goals for Measured Advertising Results). By associating the sequence with management objectives and an indication that results could be measured, Colley took a step forward in the application of marketing communications theory.

The sequential models are rooted in the cognitive tradition and require the buyer to think about the communication in order to be able to comprehend the marketer's message. If we consider the market situation when these models were formed we can see that this is a logical conclusion. They were formed when there were relatively low levels of marketing activity and when buyers lacked access to comprehensive product offerings. The models can be seen to be most relevant in a new product, or unknown product, scenario in which the buyer needs to be given information before arriving at a decision. In today's marketing environment there is a vast array of information available and for the majority of products buyers have at least some experience of consumption.

Ehrenberg's Awareness–Trial–Reinforcement model approaches the question of communications effects from a behaviourist perspective (Ehrenberg 1974). Like the sequential models this model is usually known by its acronym as the ATR model. The main focus of Ehrenberg's work has been in the fast moving consumer goods sector and thus may be less generally applicable than the sequential models. Unlike the sequential models Ehrenberg argues that buyers are generally very aware of the range of alternative products and brands available. He argues that buyers have considerable buying experience and that they follow relatively stable buying patterns. The communications emphasis is thus shifted to the reinforcement of benefits gained from previous consumption. This focus addresses the learning process with the aim of improving the prospects for the development of brand loyalty and future consumption.

The assertion that communications are being used to 'reward' the buyer for a successful decision is appropriate if linked to the work of Batra and Ray (1983). These researchers discovered that for low involvement goods the main effect of advertising was to improve the buyer's perceptions of the brands purchased. They found little impact on the overall attitudes held by the buyers (which is in contrast to the traditional sequential models). Batra and Ray found that for such low involvement products, attitudes were usually formed after consumption had taken place.

Psychological influences on buyer behaviour

The first half of this chapter focused on the players within the Decision-Making Unit and the wider social environment. We will now move onto the intra-personal factors in the decision-making process, specifically addressing:

- How do individuals make sense of the vast numbers of stimuli in the world around them?
- How do individuals sort out the communications they want to receive from those that they do not?

Perception

Information processing

The stages of thought that the individual goes through to convert incoming stimuli into useful knowledge.

Information processing describes the stages of thought that the individual goes through in order to convert incoming stimuli into useful knowledge (refer to Chapter 3). The first indication that most individuals get of any marketing activity is likely to be visual. The next most important sense is hearing and between these two senses we would probably cover 90% of all management-controlled stimuli received. Just think of how many shopfronts you pass on your journey to work each day. Each one would have contained several messages. Add to this the number of posters on billboards, walls, bus stops, buses and vans. How many do you give your attention to? While you may 'perceive' them you probably do not pay attention to many of them.

Exhibit 4.7 demonstrates that comprehension starts with a stimulus which is attended, that is to say that it has already been perceived and selected from all other stimuli in the individual's environment. It is important to recognise this starting point because it is only after the stimulus has been given attention that we have the opportunity to affect the individual's information processing, understanding, response and recollection of the message.

Exhibit 4.7 The AILA framework

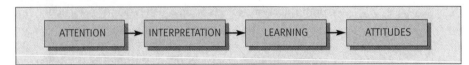

Perception

The process of synthesising information to make sense of the world. People's perceptions of the same stimuli can vary.

Perceptual filter

The means by which an individual reduces the multitude of stimuli to those to which attention can be paid. This is a largely involuntary action.

Adaptation

The process of acclimatisation to messages in which changes in the perceptual filtering process take place over time.

Perception is the process by which information is acquired through the five senses (Wade and Tavis 1990). As the information processing capacity in humans has limited resources, researchers have suggested that we have a '**perceptual filter**' which allows us to select one stimuli from a multitude to give our attention to. We cannot attend to all stimuli; the Capacity Model of Attention (Exhibit 4.8) demonstrates how our limited information processing resources may be allocated (Kahneman 1973).

When managing marketing communications, it is often extremely difficult to measure the influence of attention and interpretation on the final comprehension of the message. Similarly it is impossible to model the cognitive processing of the message. This leaves the most frequent judgement about a communication's impact to the measurement of its impact on the recipient's memory.

Buyers are being continuously subjected to an increasing number of ever more attention-seeking messages. They do not wish to attend to all of these messages, so attention declines (Alsop 1984). Doubling the number of messages sent out does not double the number of messages attended to. This is known as **adaptation**. Consider the case of advertising during the Olympic Games. Numerous companies sponsor the

Exhibit 4.8 Capacity model of attention

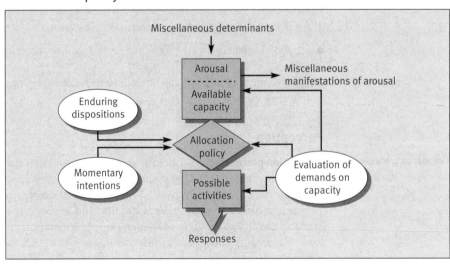

Source: Kahneman (1973)

IN VIEW 4.3

Attention-generating devices in marketing communications

Animals	Fear	Novelty
Babies	Humour	Position
Colour	Intensity	Sex
Contrast	Movement	Size
Design	Needs	Celebrities

Coca-Cola's trademark red is more effective than Pepsi's blue, according to a survey conducted by legal firm Marks & Clerk which specializes in trademark and patent law. The research revealed that Coca-Cola's red, BP's green and yellow and easyJet's orange were thought highly valuable by business people. Only 37% of British businesses have registered their corporate colours as trademarks, despite the fact that 80% of business people say corporate colours are important to the success of the business. 'The trademark can only protect a very specific colour,' said Clarke Graham, partner at Marks & Clerk, 'But the colour of a brand creates a very obvious form of recognition which helps a consumer make purchasing decisions.'

Source: Marketing Business 2003, p. 7

FOOD FOR THOUGHT

All of the attention-generating methods outlined in In View 4.3 can be combined to create more sophisticated messages. Indeed in today's communications environment it is relatively unusual to find a communication that simply relies on one method to attract the attention of the buyer. Even in the simple case of a supermarket selling cans of beans there are elements of position (aisle within the store), size (amount of space given to the display), colour (on pack design) and possibly an attempt to influence the buyer's motivation (in any promotional materials supporting the sale). See Chapters 28 and 29.

Ad-wearout

The impact of an advertisement (or as may apply to any other form of marketing communications) as it declines when it is repeated.

Games and produce advertising targeted at this event, yet how many of these companies can you remember seeing? Which brand names do you associate with the Games? You probably could not recite an exhaustive list, yet more and more companies are adding their sponsorship to future Games. Adaptation suggests a finite attention level even when number of messages to attend to increase.

Another phenomenon closely linked to adaptation is **ad-wearout**. The impact of an initially stimulating communication gradually declines as it is repeated. This is mostly due to buyers having learned the content from earlier exposures to the message. Each time the message is received, the buyer gives it less and less attention (Calder and Sternthal 1980). Eventually the buyer simply ignores the message. In some cases the constant repetition of the message becomes an irritation for the buyer. Radio advertising is particularly susceptible to the latter response since it depends much more on intensity as its attention-grabbing device. The fact that the buyer cannot easily turn away from the message becomes an aggravating factor leading to a decline in the buyer's image of the company. Such repetitive advertisements can thus have a damaging impact on buyers' attitudes toward the company rather than providing the manager's desired improvement in the product's image. Banner advertising on the Web can create similar aggravation.

IN VIEW 4.4

Perception – are the birds flying left or right?

Personality

Psychologists have provided a rich source of studies of personality over the past century. Notable names are Freud, Jung, Horney, Mischel, Kelly, and so on. Each author has a particular perspective on the construction of personality and how it impacts on an individual's actions. The difficulty from a management point of view is in the selection of a perspective that can provide an accurate prediction of behaviour. In selecting a perspective the main questions have to be, 'How much of the behaviour observed can be explained by the use of this theory?' and 'How consistent is this theory in predicting future behaviour?' In the simplest terms, the nature of the individual's personality does affect the interpretation of the message. The problem for marketing management is that markets consist of all personality types and it is virtually impossible to construct messages that have the same meaning to all individuals within the

Exhibit 4.9 Product adopter 'types' and their relationship to the product life cycle

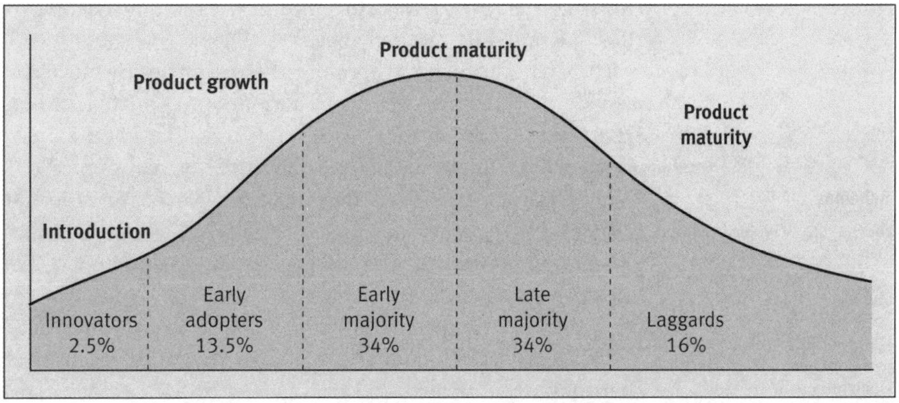

audience. Within a specific target group, however, it may be possible to use the concept of personality to enhance the precision of the message interpretation.

One example of personality types, described in terms of risk assessment, are those that adopt products at different stages in its life cycle: innovators, early adopters, early majority, late majority and laggards (Exhibit 4.9). In a given market, there tend to be types of customer who are described as innovators. The innovators are people who tend to be risk takers and like to take the lead with new products and experiences. In comparison, the laggards exhibit a different personality type and tend to be conservative in their behaviour and are risk averse.

Experience, learning and the role of memory

The individual gathers, over a lifetime, a considerable store of experiences. The memories of many of these experiences are combined to provide frames of reference against which future activities and information can be judged. How do you know what is good behaviour and what is bad? How do you know whether something is fashionable or laughable? Your experiences have been learning events, most of them small but occasionally significant. Each individual has a complex set of memory relationships which are drawn upon to provide explanations for current situations. From these relationships and explanations come your attitudes toward the situation.

The majority of our normal day-in day-out buying activity takes place without a great deal of thought taking place. Why is this? Surely if we are spending our money then we want to know that we have spent it wisely? The answer is of course we want to know we are spending our money well but it does not mean that we have to calculate each and every buying event. Many of the events are simple repetitions of past behaviour. For example, buying a newspaper on the way to work. In this example you would be likely to visit the same shop each day at approximately the same time and to buy the same newspaper as you did the day before and the day before that and so on. You do not need to evaluate every single act. The purchase has become a habit and positive outcomes are expected. Only if something external interferes with this pattern would you change your choice of shop or newspaper. This is an example of a **script**, so called because each and every time it is played out it has the same actions and outcomes just like a play on the stage. We have experienced a wide range of buying situations by the

Script

Repetition of previous behaviour.

time we reach adulthood and these experiences have built our store of memories as to what kind of decision-making is necessary in a particular situation (Smith and Houston 1985). It is this store of knowledge that enables us to reduce the time and effort taken to buy our daily needs.

The way in which we organise the memories of our experiences, so that they can provide us with these guides to action, is to construct linkages between the various experiences. These linkages will enable us to see when a situation is similar to one that has happened in the past, what difficulties it might entail and how they may be overcome. The patterns that these linkages form are called **schemas** (Einspruch and Forman 1985). Schemas can be considered as our foundations for understanding. Other writers may call the linkages frames of reference. The label may vary but the function is essentially the same (Crocker et al. 1984). The linkages enable us to identify similar experiences and to determine what our future actions should be.

So we may conclude that effective use of stored memory is critical to efficient decision-making. The next question is how do we decide what to store in the memory? The answer to this lies in investigating the role of learning.

Types of learning

There are three main types of learning. There is **experiential learning**, called 'behavioural learning' in some texts, by which memories are created from direct experience of the buying, or consuming, act. For example, we all know that chocolate gives us a chemical buzz, which makes us feel a little better, so that is the positive aspect that we store in memory. We also know that really high-quality chocolate costs a large amount of money and that is a negative aspect to be stored in memory. For the most part then we buy medium-quality chocolate so that we still get the buzz but not the economic pain. For every situation that we experience the memories that we store will be both good (rewarding) and bad (punishing). When we consider new situations we will tend to act toward what we think will be positive rewarding outcomes while attempting to avoid any potentially negative outcomes (Lapersonne et al. 1995). Experiential learning is probably the most important form of learning as far as most consumer products are concerned because of its focus on our own positive consuming experiences.

The second form of learning is based on the experiences of others. This is **vicarious learning**. Its name stems from the Latin word for substitute and it means that we are taking on our interpretation of the direct experience of others as if it were our own experience. For example, if you watch someone put their hand in a fire and get burned, then from that you learn the negative memory that pain comes from putting your hand in the fire. Thus for future reference you are not likely to put your hand in the fire. At this point you are probably thinking what has this got to do with marketing communications? Think about all those advertisements that show the product enhancing the image of the user in some way. It may be a female perfume ad in which men fall at the girl's feet after she uses the product or it might be an ad for a holiday in which the family shown does not argue because there is so much to do in the resort. In both cases the outcome shown is positive thus desirable and the expectation is that you will remember the user's rewards and think of the product in a positive way (Bandura 1977). The idea is to always show the product giving the user a reward for its use. The objective is to get others to copy the behaviour of the actor in the ad.

Finally, there is problem-solving learning. This is normally called **cognitive learning** and usually requires some degree of insight to arrive at a solution to the perceived problem. In cognitive learning there is a sequence of activity which is similar to that of

Schemas

Foundations of understanding. Schemas are remembrances of experiences that allow us to make sense of our environment and determine suitable courses of action, by recognising linkages and similarities with previous experience.

Experiential learning

Learning through behaviour and experience. Learning by doing.

Vicarious learning

Learning from the experiences of others, not by one's own direct experience.

Cognitive learning

Learning by thinking through a problem or task.

the cognitive models described earlier in this chapter. Initially we have to define the problem together with any constraints on our resources. Then we have to find a range of solutions, evaluate them and choose one (possibly more) to act upon. Finally, we have to evaluate our actions for memory purposes (Wright and Rip 1980). This form of learning is thus most likely to be used in situations that are either infrequent, unexpected or very important in some way.

A good example would be buying a house. For most people, wherever in the world they may live, the purchase of a house would be the largest single buying act that they undertake in their lifetime. It has financial importance and it is usually an infrequent activity (perhaps undertaken once in a decade). Let us examine how cognitive learning can be applied in this situation. Let us assume that we are considering a couple thinking about getting married and looking for a home. They do not have any children at present and both are working. Stage one: the property must be within the financial constraints set by savings and any mortgage considerations; in this case that will probably mean that it will also enable the couple to continue working (i.e. it must be within reasonable travelling distance from the workplace). Stage two: is it a flat, a house, a bungalow, an apartment? Which area should it be in? What state of repair should it be in? These factors will influence the choice of properties that can be considered as meeting the initial need. Stage three: visit the potential solutions; obtain surveyors reports as necessary; discuss with mortgage lenders the possibility of funding any specific purchase. Stage four: buy the chosen property and arrange to move in (bearing in mind that moving house rates highly on the list of stressful life events!). Stage five: live in the house; get to know the neighbours; consider the outcomes of moving.

By now our couple will have an enormous amount of memories to work with. What they save and what they reject will depend on how important the memory is

IN VIEW 4.5

The Co-op goes interactive

The Co-operative Society is one of the UK's largest grocery providers with millions of customers using its stores. As with most UK grocers the trade in wines and spirits is becoming increasingly important. Here was the root of the problem. The organisation identified that many of its customers had little confidence when it came to selecting wine. Customers had clear definitions of the consumption situations but little idea of products that would satisfy their requirements. As a result they tended to stick with low-cost, well-known varieties. This meant that increasing the range on offer was not delivering increased revenues.

It was decided to provide an interactive, touch-screen 'wine selector' based on PC technology to help inform customers of the suitability of the wider range. The system offers a range of different choice criteria for the customer to start the search. The computer then displays a range of wines at varying prices which will satisfy the buyer.

Success! 27,000 contacts were made with the trial system in its first 14 months of operation. Customers felt little embarrassment in using the system and felt that they had learned about the product without the risk of wasting money on unsatisfactory purchases. This example shows how helping the customer to learn the information that you want them to learn is far more effective than hoping that they will learn from continued experience. Not only did the Co-op increase its revenues but the provision of the system was viewed as a positive benefit to the customers.

perceived to be. Much of the information regarding rejected properties is likely to be forgotten fairly quickly, unless rejected for some outstanding reason. The problems associated with the financial arrangements are much less likely to be forgotten especially since there are likely to be continual payments to the lender to remind the couple of their obligations. These memories will stay with the couple for their lifetimes and will provide the schema for their next house purchase.

In conclusion, we can see that the three different forms of learning have an impact on the way in which we generate memories. The ability to store these memories, in a meaningful way, and to retrieve them when needed is critical to the effective and efficient operation of the individual's decision-making process.

Attitude formation, change and its effects on behaviour

We should consider the implications of learning for marketing communications. Retained memories fit together to form schema relating to groups of products, brands, categories and markets. These schema provide one foundation for the development of attitudes toward this set of groups.

An attitude comprises three components:

- Cognitive – thinking
- Affective – feeling
- Conative – doing.

Attitude

A consistent, cognitive, affective and conotive response to some form of internal or external stimulus.

Attitudes may be considered as a relatively consistent response to some form of stimulus, either internal or external. For example, most Western societies believe that democracy is an important part of their life and most people possess attitudes which are favourable toward the idea of political and social representation. As a converse, these same societies generally believe that destroying the natural environment is a bad thing and attitudes are generally negative toward any activities which imply harm to the environment. At an individual level this could translate to 'This group of people are really good' (positive) or 'This product is absolutely useless' (negative). From this simple look at attitudes we can see that they possess *direction*. They will guide our actions toward positive outcomes (remember behavioural learning) and against negative outcomes (Sheppard et al. 1988). This leads to the potential for conflict between something that is both desirable and undesirable at the same time! For example, cigarettes are seen by some as very desirable products, perhaps from both an image and a physiological perspective. Yet these consumers are also aware of the long-term damage that smoking may do to their health. How might these individuals resolve this inner conflict?

The answer lies in another dimension of attitudes. Attitudes possess direction and they also possess *strength*. There are issues about which you hold very strong attitudes and issues about which you could be convinced of the merits of a different view. Consider the views of orthodox Jews; they are clearly very passionate about their religion and they will not buy food products that do not conform to a kosher specification. By comparison think about the notepaper that you are using. What influences you most, the practices of the manufacturing company or the price in the store? How flexible is your approach to this product? The chances are that price is significantly more influential. Obviously some attitudes affect a great deal of our activities while the majority of our attitudes are only weakly held. The more important attitudes are commonly

NEED TO KNOW

☑ *Attitudes comprise cognitive, affective and conative components that possess both direction and strength.*

called *beliefs*. They form the core of our relationships with the rest of the world. They contain our views on religion, ethics, morality and are a major source of direction.

One common way of investigating the influence of attitudes is to look at the functions that they perform for the individual. Katz (1960) outlines four functions for attitudes:

- utilitarian function
- value expressive function
- knowledge function
- ego-defence function.

Katz (1960) suggests that people act so as to maximise their rewards and minimise their 'punishments' (the *utilitarian function*). This fits with the behavioural learning example given above. The second function is to provide an opportunity for the individual to express their feelings. Using this dimension we can see that the purchase of Nike trainers may be to link the individual with the sporting stars in the Nike ads. Alternatively people may buy items to display affiliation with a particular group. Political causes are an obvious example but so too would be the purchase of a red Aids ribbon (the *value expressive function*). When we buy products we frequently use the attitudes stored in memory as a guide. Similarly when we process communications we use our attitudes to evaluate the perceived messages. In this respect our attitudes serve as a frame of reference (the *knowledge function*). Finally, most people consider that what they believe is right and that information to the contrary must be solidly proved correct before it may be accepted as true. We feel positive toward those messages which appear to improve our own self-image but we feel negative toward messages that appear to threaten our self-image. For example, most male fragrance products suggest enhanced attraction to females. By comparison, many insurance adverts suggest that if you do not take out sufficient cover then there may be unfavourable results (the *ego-defence function*).

In the example of cigarettes we can see these functions at work. First, there is the physiological stimulus that smoking provides. This is clearly positive in its direction (utilitarian). There may also be a social aspect to the behaviour which provides further positive direction toward smoking. Smoking may also be positively viewed if the individual feels that the act enhances their image in the eyes of others. For example, does smoking show a challenge to the establishment, in effect an expression of individuality? (value expressive). Most smokers know the risks associated with smoking but perceive the risk to be far off in time and the benefits to be near in time so the effect of the risk is discounted (knowledge). However, they choose to believe that the immediate social and physiological benefits outweigh the potential longer-term health risks (ego-defence). Hence they continue to smoke even though they know it could be damaging.

Personal experience is not the only source of attitudes. We saw how there are different forms of learning and these can have an impact on the formation of our attitudes. So far we have concentrated on the experiential learning route. If we consider the vicarious learning route we can see that the attitudes of our parents and other members of the family can influence our views. In the initial stages of personal development we are relatively dependent upon our parents' views and many people continue to hold these views into later life. Similarly we learn what others view as good and what is not from the people in our social and working environments. We can then choose to accept or reject their views.

When there is a problem with relatively unknown characteristics we have to engage in a search for important information. We use this information in evaluating possible solutions to the problem. In this cognitive learning process we develop attitudes to the pieces of information that we find and link them to the existing schema that we possess. For example, when buying a used car we may know that the Consumers' Association produces a guide to used cars. We may value this as a source of impartial evidence against which we can measure those cars that we like in the showroom. We may have to learn about the insurance charges on each car and potential running costs. All of these items will have a positive or a negative direction. Eventually we will combine these views to arrive at a decision.

Manufacturers usually provide us with information that positions a product against competing products or offers a particular image. The objective in either case is to ensure that the direction of the attitude is positive and that the strength of the attitude is maximised.

A great deal of effort is expended on market research by manufacturers who want to know whether or not their product is viewed positively and what buyers think of the competing products within the marketplace. This activity is important because it provides a reflection on the success, or otherwise, of past marketing actions and also an indication of future actions that need to be undertaken to improve the product's performance. With slightly different research techniques it is also possible to test potential reactions to new product proposals and thus reduce the risks of product failure (Chapters 16 and 23).

Attitude change

What do manufacturers do if the attitudes are not as favourable as they might wish? The answer is that it depends on the importance of the particular attributes of the product in question. Buyers do not value all attributes of a product equally; some are clearly more important than others. If the product is poorly rated on the most important attribute(s) then there is a significant problem for the manufacturer. It has been suggested that to gain advantage over its competitors the product should have a distinct advantage in one, or preferably more, attributes that the buyer views as important. It follows that the primary focus for attempts to change attitudes should be on these *salient attributes*. If the manufacturer cannot achieve an advantage in these attributes then the main alternative lies in distracting the buyer's attention by focusing on other attributes and attempting to convince the buyer that these attributes should be seen as important. In other words, change the buyer's set of salient attributes. Marketing communications are the obvious means for achieving such attitude changes (Wilkie and Pessemier 1983).

There are other forces which are beyond the control of manufacturers and marketing communications systems. The main change agent is experience. The buyer has thousands of experiences every week. These provide cues for the slow adjustment of attitudes. For example, in the 1960s the cleanliness of supermarkets was considered to be a major factor in choosing where to shop. By the 1990s everyone assumes that the shop will be clean and the focus is on other aspects of the shopping trip. Similarly, buyers become accustomed to the increasing improvement in service levels and product ranges and what was the leading edge of service standards soon becomes the norm and the advantage gained is only temporary. The focus of the marketing communications effort is to show the buyer that you currently have an advantage and to gain the largest share of the new market opportunities that the advantage may bring. For example, the first companies to offer telephone banking have secured the largest shares and the widest recognition by being first. The buyers' experiences of normal banking were not strongly positive and thousands of customers changed in the expectation of improvement. Telephone banking was so successful in the UK that all of the major banks now provide the service as part of their business.

Technological change is a major force in peoples' lives. Computers and communications have revolutionised the world for most people without the significance of the change being noticed. Now your video recorder will have a small chip controlling its actions; you can see major sporting events live from the other side of the world. Companies' computers can 'talk' to one another by dedicated telephone lines, exchange orders and payment data without any human intervention. Consider the impact of computers on global financial transactions. What impact has this had on your country's economy? No country stands in isolation from this process of change and none can hold back the tide of change. Marketing communications serve to show this new world to the buyers. The objective is to gain the buyers' attention and to show them that change offers improvement.

With respect to salient attributes and environmental change, marketing management has to maintain a close watch on the wider world and not become too closely focused on its own, or even its competitors' products. In order to be able to communicate with buyers there is a need for marketing management to understand the world in which those buyers live. The Honda company understood this very well when they researched the US motorcycle market in the 1960s and found a gap in what was offered by the US manufacturers. Their launch of a new category of small bikes focused on the identified needs and lifestyles of the potential market and it proved to be the beginning of the end for the US motorcycle industry.

The link between attitudes and behaviour

Attitudes are clearly important to buyers, however they do not always translate directly into behaviour. A positive attitude may be limited by other factors. For example, you like that yellow jumper but your partner thinks that it is awful. You may choose to buy a different item in order to maintain the relationship. You may like BMW cars but you may not have the money to buy one. You might like to get drunk on occasions but not when you are out with the boss at an important meeting. There are a wide range of circumstances under which a positive attitude does not bring about a purchase.

Similarly a negative attitude does not automatically stop a purchase. We saw this in the example of cigarette smoking. If there are sufficiently strong attitudes to overcome the negative aspects then the behaviour may still take place. The importance of attitudes is also moderated by the importance of the purchase. We could say that if the purchase is important then generally the attitudes toward the product will be important. If the purchase is routine or part of a habit then there is less chance that attitudes will have an influence on the buying process.

Summary

This chapter has introduced the concept of buyer decision-making and looked at how it may be modelled from a cognitive and behavioural perspective. The four common stages of decision-making have been identified and the influences and critical issues within each stage discussed:

1 Pre-purchase
2 Purchase
3 Post-purchase evaluation
4 Product disposal.

Marketing communications must have an impact on buyer behaviour if it is to be seen to be effective. Exhibit 4.3 outlined the main influences on decision-making. Attention to the core themes in this chapter should help to create a firm foundation for developing communications activities.

This chapter has focused on the method by which individuals process information from the environment. The interpretation of the encoded messages is dependent upon a range of factors which may, or may not, lead to an accurate understanding of the message intended.

We have seen that lifelong learning takes place and have identified a range of different methods by which learning can take place. This aspect of the individual allows marketers to vary the message delivery for specific target audiences. If you look closely at the world around you then you will see examples of each of the learning styles being used.

Attitude studies are, perhaps, the most common form of market research output. They inform much of the management of the communications process. In this section we have looked at the role that attitudes play in decision-making, how they are formed and how they might be changed. We have also seen that positive attitudes do not always lead to sales, for a number of reasons. Nonetheless attitude studies provide management with the essential data for structuring their activities.

Self-review questions

1 What are the main differences between the cognitive and behavioural paradigms?

2 What are the five stages of cognitive decision-making?

3 What is routine problem solving?

4 Why is it important to understand the individual in a wider context?

5 What are the individual roles in the Decision-Making Unit?

6 How does involvement affect the decision-making process?

7 What is the management value in the hierarchy models of communications effects?

8 What are the key stages of information processing?

9 Identify the four main psychological influences on the interpretation of messages.

10 Contrast the three main types of learning.

11 How can marketers use the concept of vicarious learning in the construction of communications messages?

12 Describe some of the actions management can take if consumers' attitudes toward the product are not as positive as desired.

13 What is the impact of attitudes on behaviour?

Project

Select a product or service and identify all of the Decision-Making Unit roles that may be involved in the purchase of it. How could a marketing communicator have an effect on each of these roles?

Select two or three examples of TV and magazine advertisements that you think are trying to appeal to people's aspirations. Identify the aspirational appeals they are using and comment on their appropriateness. Do you consider the use of aspirational images and messages common? If so, why do you think their use is so widespread?

References

Alsop, R. (1984), Study of Olympic ads casts doubt on value of campaigns. *The Wall Street Journal*, 6 December, B33.

Assael, H. (1995), *Consumer behaviour and marketing action* 5th edn. Ohio: South Western College Publishing.

Bandura, A. (1977), *Social Learning Theory*. Englewood Clifffs NJ: Prentice Hall.

Batra, R. and Ray, M. (1983), Advertising situations: the implications of differential involvement and accompanying affect responses. In *Information Processing Research in Advertising* (R., Harris, ed.). Lawrence Erlbaum Associates, pp. 127–151.

Belk, R. (1979), Gift-giving behaviour. In *Research in Marketing*, vol. 2 (J. Sheth, ed.). Greenwich, CT: JAI Press.

Brandweek (1996), Marketers are always looking for good pitchers. 26 February, p. 27.

Broderick, A.J. (1997), Cross-national consumer behaviour in the European food retail environment: the strategic impact of culture on consumer involvement with food. Unpublished doctoral thesis, Leicester: De Montfort University.

Broderick, A.J. and Mueller, R.D. (1999), A theoretical and empirical exegesis of the consumer involvement construct: the psychology of the food shopper. *Journal of Marketing Theory and Practice*, 7 (4), 97–108.

Calder, R. and Sternthal, B. (1980), Television commercial wearout: an information processing view. *Journal of Marketing Research*, 17, 173–186.

Capon, N. and Burke, M. (1980), Individual, product class, and task-related factors in consumer information processing. *Journal of Consumer Research*, 7, 314–326.

Capon, N. and Davis, R. (1984), Basic cognitive ability measures as predictors of consumer information processing strategies. *Journal of Consumer Research*, 11, 551–563.

Childers, T.L., Houston, M.J. and Heckler, S.E. (1985), Measurement of individual differences in visual versus verbal information processing. *Journal of Consumer Research*, 12, 125–134.

Crocker, J., Fiske, S. and Taylor, S. (1984), Schematic bases of belief change. In *Attitudinal Judgement* (J. Eiser, ed.). New York: Springer-Verlag.

Colley, R. (1961), *Defining Advertising Goals and Measuring Advertising Results*. New York: Association of National Advertisers.

Corfman, K. and Lehman, R. (1987), Models of co-operative group decision-making and relative influence: An experimental investigation of family purchase decisions. *Journal of Consumer Research*, 14.

Dahl, J. (1992), Travel styles of the rich are immune to recession. *Wall Street Journal*, 4 March, B1.

Dibb, S., Simkin, L., Pride, W.M. and Ferrell, O.C. (1997), *Marketing Concepts and Strategies*, 3rd European edn. Houghton Mifflin.

Dowd, E.T. and Pety, J. (1982), Effects of counsellor predicate matching on perceived social influence and client satisfaction. *Journal of Counselling Psychology*, 29 (2), 206–209.

Eagly, A. H. and Chaiken, S. (1993), *The Psychology of Attitudes*. Fort Worth, TX: Harcourt Brace Jovanovich.

East, R., Lomax, W., Willson, G. and Harris, P. (1994), Decision making and habit in shopping times. *European Journal of Marketing*, 28 (4), 56–71.

Ehrenberg, A. (1974), Repetitive advertising and the consumer. *Journal of Advertising Research*, 14, 25–34.

Ehrenberg, A. and Goodhart, G. (1979), *Essays on Understanding Buyer Behaviour*. JW Thompson and the Market Research Corporation of America.

Einspruch, E.L. and Forman, B.D. (1985), Observations concerning research literature on neurolinguistic programming. *Journal of Counselling Psychology*, 32, 589–596.

Engel, J., Blackwell, R. and Miniard, P. (2000), *Consumer Behaviour*. Texas: Dryden.

Foxall, G. R. (1997), *Marketing Psychology*. London: Macmillan.

Foxall, G.R. (1990), *Consumer Psychology in Behavioural Perspective*. London: Routledge.

Foxall, G.R. (1993), Situated consumer behaviour: a behavioural interpretation of purchase and consumption. In *Research in Consumer Behaviour*, 5 (R.W. Belk, ed.). Greenwich, CT: JAI Press.

Gardner, M. (1981), An information processing approach to examining advertising effects. Unpublished doctoral dissertation, Graduate School of Industrial Administration, Pittsburgh, PA: Carnegie-Mellon University.

Hovland, C.L., Janis, I.L. and Kelley, H.H. (1953), *Communication and Persuasion*. New Haven, CT: Yale University Press.

Iyer, E. (1989), Unplanned purchasing: knowledge of the shopping environment and time pressure. *Journal of Retailing*, 65, 30–40.

Kahneman, D. (1973), *Attention and Effort*. Englewood Cliffs, NJ: Prentice Hall.

Kassarjian, H.H. (1981), Low involvement: a second look. *Advances in Consumer Research*, vol. 8, pp. 31–34.

Katz, D. (1960), The functional approach to the study of attitudes. *Public Opinion Quarterly*, 24, 163–204.

Laaksonen, P. (1994), *Consumer Involvement: Concepts and Research*. London: Routledge.

Lapersonne, E., Laurent, G. and Le Goff, J-J. (1995), Consideration sets of size one: an empirical investigation of automobile purchases. *International Journal of Research in Marketing*, 12, 55–66.

Marketing Business (2003), Corporate colours should be registered. February, p. 7.

Markin, R.J. and Narayana, C. (1975), Behaviour control: are consumers beyond freedom and dignity? In A*dvances in Consumer Research*, vol. 3 (B.B. Anderson, ed.). Ann Arbor, MI: Association for Consumer Research, pp. 222–228.

Mitchell, R. (1986), How Pontiac pulled away from the pack. *Business Week*, 25 August, pp. 56–57.

Mitchell, A. (1989), Involvement: a potentially important mediator of consumer behavior. *Advances in Consumer Research*, vol. 6, pp. 191–196.

Mittal, B. (1989), Must consumer involvement always imply more information search? In *Advances in Consumer Research*, vol. 16 (T. Srull, ed.). Utah: Association for Consumer Research, pp. 167–172.

Petty, R.E. and Cacioppo, J.T (1983) Central and peripheral routes to persuasion: application to advertising, in L. Percy and A. Woodside (eds), *Advertising and Consumer Psychology*, Lexington Books, pp. 3–23.

Petty, R.E. and Cacioppo, J.T. (1986), *Communication and Persuasion: Central and Peripheral Routes to Attitude Change*. Springer-Verlag.

Sheppard, B., Hartwick, J. and Warshaw, P. (1988), The theory of reasoned action: a meta-analysis of past research with recommendations for modifications and future research. *Journal of Consumer Research*, 15, 325–343.

Skinner, B.F. (1938), *The Behaviour of Organisms*. New York: Century.

Skinner, B.F. (1953), *Science and Human Behaviour*. New York: Macmillan.

Smith, R. and Houston, M. (1985), A psychometric assessment of measures of scripts in consumer memory. *Journal of Consumer Research*, 12, 214–224.

Sprott, W. (1958), *Human Groups*. Harmondsworth: Penguin.

Sujan, H. (1986), Smarter versus harder: An exploratory attributional analysis of salespeople's motivations. *Journal of Marketing Research*, 23, 41–49.

Richardson, J.T.E. (1977), Mental imagery and memory: Coding ability or coding preference? *Journal of Mental Imagery*, 2, 101–115.

Rossiter, J. and Percy, L. (1997) *Advertising Communications and Promotion Management* 2nd edn. Boston, MA: Irwin McGraw-Hill.

Thaler, R. (1985), Mental accounting and consumer choice. *Marketing Science*, 4, 199–214.

Wade, C. and Tavis, C. (1990), *Psychology*. New York: Harper & Rowe.

Weitz, B. (1978), Relationship between salesperson performance and understanding customer decision making. *Journal of Marketing Research*, 15.

Wilkie, W. and Pessemier, E. (1983), Issues in marketing's use of multi-attribute models. *Journal of Marketing Research*, 10, 428–441.

Wright, P. and Rip, P. (1980), Product class advertising effects on first-time buyers' decision strategies. *Journal of Consumer Research*, 7, 151–175.

Selected further reading

Bloch, P.H., Sherrell, D.L. and Ridgway, N.M. (1986), Consumer search: an extended framework. *Journal of Consumer Research*, 13 (June), 119–124.

Burns, A.C., Biswas, A. and Babin, L.A. (1993), The operation of visual imagery as a mediator of advertising effects. *Journal of Advertising*, 22, 71–85.

Cohen, J.B. and Chakravarti, D. (1990), Consumer psychology. *Annual Review of Psychology*, 41, 243–288.

Feldman, L.P. and Hornik, J. (1981), The use of time: an integrated conceptual model. *Journal of Consumer Research*, 7 (March), 407–419.

Foxall, G.R. (1992), The behavioural perspective model of purchase and consumption: from consumer theory to marketing practice. *Journal of the Academy of Marketing Science*, 20 (2), 189–198.

Foxall, G.R. (1993), A behaviourist perspective on purchase and consumption. *European Journal of Marketing*, 27 (8), 7–16.

Gazzaniga, M.S. (ed.) (1988), *Perspectives in Memory Research*. Cambridge, MA: MIT Press, pp. 245–273.

Schiffman, L.G. and Kanuk, L.L. (1997), *Consumer Behavior* 6th edn. Upper Saddle River, NJ: Prentice Hall.

Stone, R.N. (1984), The marketing characteristics of involvement. In *Advances in Consumer Research*, vol. 11 (T.C. Kinnear, ed.). Provo, UT: Association for Consumer Research, pp. 210–215.

Unnava, H.R. and Burnkrant, R.E. (1991), An imagery-processing view of the role of pictures in print advertisements. *Journal of Marketing Research*, 28, 226–231.

Vaughn, R. (1986), How advertising works: a planning model revisited. *Journal of Advertising Research*, 27 (February–March), 57–66.

Zaichkowsky, J.L. (1985), Measuring the involvement construct. *Journal of Consumer Research*, 12 (December), 341–352.

Zaltman, G. (1997), Rethinking market research: Putting people back in. *Journal of Marketing Research*, 34, 424–437.

Chapter 5

Media – the carriers of the message

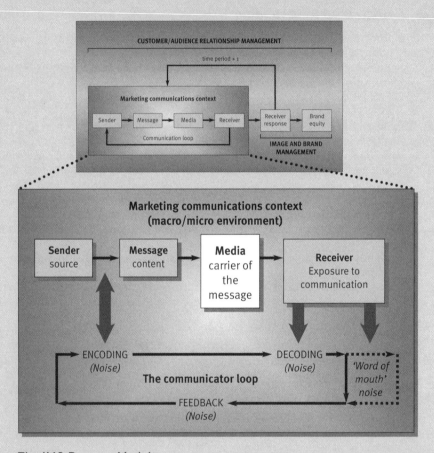

The IMC Process Model

Case Study 1 on the CD outlines that Concern's marketing communications uses consistent messages across media. On reading Chapter 5, identify the range of media used by Concern. Are there other media you would recommend? Evaluate the role of word-of-mouth communication in Concern's marketing communication campaign.

Chapter outline

- Media – what is it? Extending the popular view
- Central role of the media
- The media and the promotional mix
- A few words about 'word of mouth'
- Media classes and media vehicles
- The marketing mix as marketing communications
- Characteristics of the media
- Media growth
- Media effect – the media as relationship builders
- Integration of the media

Objectives

- To define media in its widest sense as carriers of marketing communications messages to embrace *all* media opportunities
- To encourage a creative view of media possibilities
- To emphasise the pervasive nature of word of mouth
- To recognise that the whole of the marketing mix plays a role in marketing communications
- To identify the characteristics of the main media and encourage consideration of the strengths and weaknesses of other media types
- To introduce the concept that media effects can enhance and detract from marketing communications messages

Professional perspective

David Bond Head of Telesales, Royal Mail

When thinking of media I am continually surprised by the ever expanding choices and creativity available to advertisers. Is your message best carried by taxi, on an underground train, a poster, a cyclist toiling up a mountain in the Tour de France, by mail or a banner on someone's Internet site? The marketplace is becoming more diverse and consumers themselves experience new channels to the marketplace. The major challenge has to be how can we get the attention of the individual in a way that creates action and positive perception. I remember Peter Dix comparing media options to a battlefield. He said 'a combination of ground, air and sea attack is always better than one approach that potentially fails'. I guess that combinations and synergy of the media will be the winner at the end of the day. But which ones?

David Bond

Media – what is it? Extending the popular view

This chapter is one of three chapters that specifically focus on the media and the reader may wish to read all of these in conjunction with one another: Chapter 5, Chapter 6, E-media, and Chapter 21, Media Implementation. The last of these chapters appears later in the book as it emphasises elements of planning and using the media which are most relevant to Part 2 of this book.

David Bond's professional prespective usefully highlights two important aspects of media that are particulary significant to our understanding of integrated marketing communications. The first is that media opportunities abound. The second is that to take advantage of these, media choices should be integrated to achieve greatest effect.

When many people think about the media, they think about mass media. That is, they tend to think about the media most associated with advertising, particularly television and press. From an integrated marketing communications perspective this would be an exceptionally narrow view of media because media can be described as all 'vehicles' or 'channels' that can carry or transmit messages. They can be very many different things and it is useful to define them as such.

NEED TO KNOW

☑ *Marketing communications media are all forms of media that can transmit marketing communications messages whether focused at a mass audience or at an individual.*

A definition of marketing communications media

A marketing communications medium (singular of media) **is anything that is capable of carrying or transmitting a marketing communications message to one or more people.**

Marketing communications media are all forms of media through which marketing communications messages are conveyed. They take very many different forms from television broadcasts to a key ring carrying a company logo.

Marketing communications medium

In its widest sense, *anything* that is capable of carrying or transmitting marketing communications messages.

Ambient media

'Ambient advertising', according to Concord – the specialist outdoor agency that claims to have first defined it – 'is non-traditional out-of-home advertising' (Phillips 1998, p. 16). In our terminology, it would be better to use the term ambient promotions because by their very nature they use unusual media, not the mass media associated with advertising. They also tend to be particularly transient in nature. If they are so short-lived, why are they used? Quite simply because they attempt to generate huge amounts of publicity. They represent some very unusual and different media opportunities. One example is a 600 ft Beck's beer bottle that was sown into a 30-acre field. Other examples are the 'Sega Saturn' logo that was projected onto the side of the Houses of Parliament and Adidas who projected an image of their sponsored football players onto the White Cliffs of Dover. But **ambient media** do not have to be about huge displays. At the Atlanta Olympics, Lynford Christie wore contact lenses sporting the Puma logo. The Welsh Tourist Board extolled cleaner Welsh air by writing messages on the backs of dirty Birmingham and London vans and Nike, sponsors of the orange-kitted Dutch team, put their 'swoosh' on amber traffic lights around Amsterdam for a night. Nor do ambient promotions have to be confined to the visual senses. Unilever put the scent of Radion washing powder onto transport tickets and there are examples of scents being used in theatres and supermarkets.

Ambient media

Less usual, transient, external media, such as laser projections, or the use of fields into which messages are cut.

FOOD FOR THOUGHT

The identification and choice of media is probably only as limited as our imaginations.

Exhibit 5.1 provides a list of some of the more obvious media available for marketing communications messages. The list is not exhaustive. The identification of media is probably only as limited as our imaginations allow.

Exhibit 5.1 Table of marketing communications media possibilities

Press
Newspapers – daily, weekly, local, regional, national
Magazines – weekly, monthly, quarterly, annual, general interest, special interest, consumer, trade, association, in-house, company, club
Directories

Television (analogue and digital)
Local, regional, national, international
Terrestrial
Satellite
Cable
Video, home and in-store
Teletext

Cinema
Local, regional, national

Posters
Transport – on buses, taxis, trains, boats, poster vans, adtrailers
Outdoor – on poster site hoardings (billboards), bins, posts, benches, 'fly-posting' on walls, aerial banners, sports grounds sites
Indoor – at point of sale and at exhibitions: on windows, shopping trolleys, counters, shelves, hanging signs; on stands and displays, on notice boards, in public toilets

Radio (analogue and digital)
Local, regional, national, international

The Internet
WWW
email
Global

Direct mail
Leaflets and letters delivered through the post or by hand

People/word of mouth
Sales staff
Other employees
Customers/consumers
Members of the media
Members of the trade
Other 'publics'

Leaflets and brochures
All sorts from annual financial report brochures and catalogues to special event leaflets, special offer flyers and press releases

Stationery
Business cards, letterheads, memos, fax invoices, receipts, envelopes, pencils and pens, paperclips, etc.

Packaging
All forms of packaging can carry promotional messages

Merchandise Items
Calendars, diaries, giftware, greetings cards, labels, bookmarks, all forms of clothing items, nameplates, badges, cups, sports equipment, and a great deal more

Point-of-sale displays (POS)
Shelf displays, dump-bins, carousels, tent cards, posters, videos, exhibition boards and stands

Livery and signage
Signage on and in shops, offices, buildings
Vehicle signage – cars, vans, lorries, trains, planes
Uniforms/working clothes
Sign posts, illuminated signs, 'A' frames, etc.
Display signs

Others
Ambient media
Postal services
Telephone – land, mobile
Product items themselves
Beer mats
Drip mats
Floor mats
Balloons
Hot air balloons/'blimps'
Golf tees and golf holes
Back of car park tickets and other tickets
Stickers
Milk bottle tops
Bags
Flags
PR stunts/events
Electronic media – computer and video games, CD-ROMs, DVDs etc., etc.

IN VIEW 5.1

Pepsi turn blue as they see themselves in the Mirror

Pepsi turned many of its contemporaries green with envy when it managed to colour the Concorde and the *Daily Mirror* blue for the day. It was heralded as the media coup of the year as Pepsi was re-launched in a new blue can on 12 April 1996 as part of a £200 million global campaign.

Abbott Mead Vickers BBDO, Pepsi's agency, arranged for the *Daily Mirror* to appear in pale blue newsprint with a Pepsi-blue masthead as Cindy Crawford and Claudia Schiffer unveiled a blue Concorde replete with Pepsi logo. Posters featured images such as a blue bottle of tomato ketchup and blue strawberries with the strap line 'Change the Script'. André Agassi, Claudia Schiffer and Cindy Crawford appeared in TV advertising.

The whole re-launch involved hundreds of events and promotional activities staged around the world to ensure massive publicity media coverage. This was one re-launch that was not going to go unnoticed.

Source: Adapted from *Media Week* (1997)

Central role of the media

NEED TO KNOW

☑ *The selection of the right media is fundamental and vital to the success of marketing communications.*

In our marketing communications process model we can see the important central role media plays in carrying marketing communications messages from the sender to the receiver. When carefully selected, the media carry our messages to our chosen receivers (target audiences) without undue wastage. If the media is badly selected it can result in our messages achieving little impact, or being received by too few or the wrong people. In a crowded marketplace, messages can go unnoticed. Media, carefully controlled and utilised, can make all the difference as indicated in In View 5.2.

Selection of the right media is fundamental to the success of marketing communications. For integrated marketing communications a range of media should be selected and used jointly for best effect. It is the case, however, that no matter how well selected, there is always the potential for messages to be received by non-target audience members. As such, there is always likely to be a degree of wastage. It is the task of media planners and buyers to reach the right audiences with minimum wastage but with maximum effect. This task is considered in much more detail later in Chapter 21, Media Implementation. What is not always appreciated is the creativity that can be employed in media selection and use. Foster's Ice and Millers are good examples of the unusual or unexpected use of media (In View 5.3 and Plate 19).

IN VIEW 5.2

Shockingly long legs

Pretty Polly maximised the effect of its poster by arranging for a 'special build' poster site to be constructed. No one can doubt the extra effect created (Plate 14).

Foster's Ice – cool!

Foster's Ice agency, Paul Tulley and Co., made use of a 'street art' poster campaign to promote the product. Nine of the most influential artists were invited to encompass the spirit of Foster's Ice with one-off street artworks (Plate 19). The campaign was supported by PR and press competitions, a website that featured all the billboards created, and paint spraying events. The artwork was used for double-page spreads and a visual package to be run on club screens. The campaign crossed into the realms of technology, music, cinema art and point of sale material.

Millers TV

By way of a different approach, The Media Centre and Rainey Kelly Cambell Roalfe created a series of 'adfomercials' for their client's Miller Pilsner brand. A three-minute advertisement that appeared like a 'mini-programme', *Miller Time*, was used to relaunch the product. This type of format had been used elsewhere with success, particularly in the USA. The television campaign was started seven weeks before Christmas and ran for six 'shows'. It was supported by 96- and 48-sheet posters and national press advertising within television listing sections. Although television media frequency was low, the audience was assured of high awareness levels through the support media and the publicity that accompanied the campaign.

Source: Adapted from *Media Week* (1996b)

What is important to recognise is that without media – the carrier of the marketing communications message – there can be no marketing communications. An understanding, therefore, of the basic range and characteristics of the media is an important prerequisite for using media well.

The media and the promotional mix

The marketing communications or promotional mix, however it may be named, is an attempt to classify all the possibilities available for marketing communications activities. It follows that if the media have to be used to transmit marketing communications messages, there should be a close link between the media possibilities and the promotional mix. This is, indeed, the case.

The mix has been described in Chapter 1 and in its simple form, which most people recognise as one way to classify it, it comprises four elements: personal selling, advertising, public relations and sales promotions. These four elements are represented in the Integrated Marketing Communications Mix Model also introduced in Chapter 1 and expanded in Part 3.

Personal selling extensively, but not exclusively, makes use of the spoken word whether this be face-to-face or at a distance. Of course many other media are used to support selling activities in the form of other marketing communications some of which sales staff can use in their day-to-day activities such as leaflets, brochures, price lists, audio-visual aids and so on. Chapter 31 covers this area in more detail.

NEED TO KNOW

☑ *A task of media planners is to reach the right audiences with minimum wastage but with maximum effect.*

Advertising makes use of mass media which have traditionally included press, TV, cinema, posters and radio. Nowadays, it can also be said to make use of video releases and, significantly, direct mail which is increasingly being recognised as a mass medium, too, given the numbers of people that can be reached through the mail. *Reader's Digest* has extensively used direct mail as a primary medium for many years and does so to reach millions of people. Another medium increasingly recognised as a mass medium used for advertising is the Internet. Although very 'young' as a medium at this stage, the Internet has the potential to become the largest of the mass media with no geographical boundaries and the ability to reach target audiences on a global scale at low cost. The mass media are typically referred to as the 'above-the-line' or 'advertising media'. Please see Chapter 26 for more details.

Public relations also makes use of the same mass media as well as using a range of other media to further its aims. Chapter 24 covers PR in greater detail.

FOOD FOR THOUGHT

The Internet has the potential to become the largest mass medium with no geographical boundaries and with the ability to reach target audiences on a global scale at low cost.

The other media possibilities shown in Exhibit 5.1 (i.e. the non-mass media) generally come under the heading of 'sales promotions' which is often used as a 'miscellaneous' heading within the simple promotional mix classifications. In a sense, in this classification system they have nowhere else to be categorised. Using sales promotions as a 'dump-bin' category tends to undermine the vital role it plays and, as can be seen from Exhibit 5.1, it can count for a huge number of media opportunities.

However, many people are uncomfortable with leaving sales promotions as a miscellaneous category, believing that it should not be left as the 'Cinderella' of the mix. They would prefer to at least consider corporate communications and packaging as separate categories. Corporate communications, which some subsume under public relations, makes use of any and all media as necessary. Stationery, livery and signage come under the purview of corporate communications. Chapters 24 and 25 on public relations, corporate promotions and sponsorship take these issues further.

FOOD FOR THOUGHT

Packaging should not be underestimated in terms of its marketing communications impact.

Packaging is, typically, an under-estimated medium insofar as it tends to be taken somewhat for granted. However, just a moment's thought allows us to appreciate how ubiquitous, significant and powerful a medium it is. Packaging is considered at length in Chapter 29.

IN VIEW 5.4

Carling Black Label – a premier pack design

Design Consultancy, Tutssels, suggested that Bass, owners of the Carling Black Label beer brand, should make more of its sponsorship of the Carling Football Premiership. The result was a new special edition pack only made available for around a 10-week period. Importantly, the new can design made its impact by gaining strong displays in major retail outlets. During a period when the market only increased by 18.2%, sales of Carling Black Label rose by 33% while the special edition can was on sale.

Packaging counts

Although packaging is often considered as relatively incidental, this really should not be the case. Packaging is a multi-million pound industry in its own right. When Pimms, an alcoholic drink, was being re-launched, the advertising creatives took their inspiration from the newly designed bottle. The labelling inspired the development of a television campaign that reflected a 1930s 'feel' and a slow and easy lifestyle which could be readily associated with the Pimms drink. Packaging and advertising were integrated and worked in harmony to create the benefits of promotional synergy.

A few words about 'word of mouth'

Word of mouth

Communication not originated by the sender that is passed on to others after the original marketing communications messages have been transmitted.

Word of mouth (WOM) represents a very powerful medium but one which is very difficult to control. It is, perhaps, not considered a marketing communication medium in any conventional sense, yet it should be because of its sheer force and impact. WOM can just about involve anybody and everybody from customers and consumers to employees and journalists.

Personal selling is an important part of the total marketing communications armoury and, of course, makes extensive use of verbal communications. Members of the sales force are, undoubtedly, significant players in the marketing communications process. This applies whether it is the manufacturer's sales force, the service provider's sales force or any intermediary within the trade. However, insofar as the originator's own sales force is considered part of the original marketing communications, this is not usually classified as 'word-of-mouth' communication even though in a literal sense it typically is. WOM tends to be reserved to describe the communications that take place 'beyond' the originator's communication in whatever form this may have occurred. For our purposes, this distinction may be considered as 'splitting hairs'. What is important to recognise is the powerful impact that communications can have between the many and various members of the marketplace. Therefore, anybody who talks about an organisation or its products is taking part in word of mouth. We should also include here an extension to the term to include all those who write about companies and their products. Many journalists act as opinion leaders on behalf of their readers and listeners. This brings into focus all forms of editorial coverage, the control of which is an important function within the public relations field.

NEED TO KNOW

☑ *Word of mouth is the process by which messages are communicated from one person to another after the sender has sent out his/her original messages. It is difficult for the marketing communicator to control but it has the potential to be very powerful.*

We should not forget the role played by all employees of an organisation whether or not they formally meet customers or other external publics. Those that are 'customer-facing' are particularly important as the direct contact they have with customers influences customer perceptions of the organisation.

Significantly, there is the word-of-mouth role played by the customers, consumers and other members of the public themselves. They can exert an immense influence on the marketing communications process. The roles of consumer innovators and opinion leaders are particularly

NEED TO KNOW

☑ *Anybody who talks (and writes) about an organisation or its products is engaging in the word-of-mouth process.*

NEED TO KNOW

☑ *Even though word of mouth may not be identified formally within an integrated marketing communications plan, the IMC planner has to recognise its importance and include in the plan activities which may favourably influence word of mouth.*

important in this context as are the various roles played by the members of the decision-making unit. See Chapter 4 for more discussion on buyer behaviour and consumer behaviour issues.

Even though WOM may not be identified formally within an integrated marketing communications plan, the IMC planner has to recognise its influence and include in the plan activities which may favourably influence the main 'influencers' (target audience) and not just consider the members of the target market – customers and consumers.

IN VIEW 5.6

Market mavens

We probably all know at least one person who is a market maven. A maven is a person who appears to be knowledgeable about everyday things, an expert on day-to-day matters. Market mavens are people who know where to shop, who know all about different products and brands, what are the latest promotions. They are sought after as major sources of advice. Their views are valued and they receive prestige and satisfaction from supplying information to friends and others. They are shapers and formers, they are market opinion leaders (Feick and Price 1987) whose word of mouth can play a significant role in buyer and consumer behaviour.

Media classes and media vehicles

Inter-media decisions

Choices made between media classes.

Intra-media decisions

Choices made between different media vehicles.

Media class

Refers to the media as a main category, such as television, radio, cinema, posters, press, direct mail, the Internet, etc.

Media vehicles

The actual media within a media class. For example, *The Times, Cosmopolitan, Time magazine, Readers Digest* and so on are media within the 'Press' media class.

Media implementation is considered in Chapter 21 in Part 2 of this book. In that chapter it is emphasised that both **inter-media** and **intra-media** decisions have to be made. Inter-media decisions are ones about which **media classes** to use and having done this, intra-media decisions are about choosing the right **media vehicles**. Media classes are the main categories of media. They are most closely associated with the advertising media but can include all major forms – press, posters, TV, radio, cinema, direct mail, Internet, packaging, point-of-sale display, etc.

Once the main media classes have been selected it is then necessary to decide which specific media vehicles to use – which specific magazines or newspapers, which form of packaging, which sort of display items, which poster sites, which TV or radio stations and at what times, which cinemas and so on. Although this chapter is primarily about media in general terms and, therefore, mainly about media classes, it should not be forgotten that there are significant variations between the media vehicles even in a single media class. This can easily be seen by looking at the vast array of magazines on display on newsagents' shelves (Exhibit 5.2).

Exhibit 5.2 Example of media vehicles within a media class

Media class	Media vehicles	
Magazines	**Examples**	
Consumer	General interest	*Reader's Digest* *Punch*
	Computing	*PC Format* *.net*
	TV and entertainment guides	*The Radio Times* *Time Out*
	Food and health	*Good Food* *Good Health* *Slimming*
	Hobbies and leisure	*Practical Photographer* *Woodworking*
	Home and garden	*Amateur Gardener* *Good Housekeeping*
	Men's	*Esquire* *FHM*
	Women's	*Cosmopolitan* *Hello*
	Cars and motoring	*Auto Trader* *Motoring and Leisure*
	Music	*NME* *Melody Maker*
	Sport	*The Sporting Life* *Football Italia*
Business	Aeronautical	*Aerospace International* *Flight*
	Agriculture	*Farmers Weekly* *International Agricultural Development*
	Architecture and building	*The Architect's Journal* *Building Design*
	Business and management	*The Economist* *Newsweek*
	Chemical Industry	*Pharmaceutical Marketing* *Asian Plastics*
	Retailing	*The Grocer* *Drapers Record*
	Finance	*The Banker* *Financial Advisor*
	Manufacturing	*European Process Engineer* *World Pumps*
	Medicine	*MIMS Africa* *Medicine Digest*
	Property	*Estates Gazette* *Facilities Management Journal*

The marketing mix as marketing communications

Wayne DeLozier (1976) was one of the first authors to strongly feature the role played by all the elements in the marketing mix in the marketing communications process. We all recognise in marketing the interrelatedness of all the marketing mix elements that are frequently (if rather narrowly) defined as the 4Ps: Promotion, Product, Place and Price. DeLozier correctly identified as part of this interconnectedness, that each of the 4Ps carries with it marketing communication values. This is equally true whatever marketing mix classification is used e.g 7Ps. It is as though the mix elements act as media vehicles in their own right. This view has also been adopted by Rossiter and Percy (1997) who write of a new marketing mix which collectively contribute towards integrated marketing communications.

The *promotional* element of the mix is obvious. This is the element we recognise as the marketing communications element.

The *product* DeLozier defined in both physical characteristics and in packaging terms. The product speaks volumes. Its size, colour, shape, the material from which it is constructed, the type of packaging in which it is contained all influence buying decisions because of what these features say to customers. The use of metallic finishes convey solidity, precious metals and their colours convey expense and quality. The perfume industry has long capitalised on the power of packaging. The cigarette industry has made use of longer lengths and menthol flavourings to communicate different product impressions. Little blue grains in soap powders have been used to convey cleaning power. Fragrances are added to detergents to create the impression of freshness.

Place refers to channels and physical distribution. In this context, store image and atmosphere, location and layout, and point-of-sale displays can profoundly affect the impressions created in the minds of customers. The very type of outlet communicates with the market – discount store, department store, chain store, exclusive outlet. And, of course, retailers make extensive use of marketing communications tools to convey their own messages. Channel strategy, whether intensive, selective or exclusive, also engenders impressions about the product in the minds of customers and consumers.

Finally, we can highlight the marketing communications influence of price. High prices relative to competing products convey impressions of quality. Low prices can convey cheapness and poor quality. From time immemorial, retailers have recognised the value of offering sales and the use of psychological pricing. Sales promotion money-off offers represent value for money and not-to-be beaten deals. Setting prices at £9.95, £49.99, £7890 are all examples of charm pricing designed to make the price seem less.

Characteristics of the media

Given the vast array of media, it is not possible to review each medium. What follows is intended to give a flavour of the variety of characteristics of the media. The reader is encouraged to consider the issues at greater length by thinking about the list provided in Exhibit 5.3 and other non-mass media that might be added. Consideration should be given to their relative strengths and weaknesses and their ability to undertake such multifarious marketing communications tasks as:

- Reaching a mass market
- Reaching a highly defined niche
- Creating impact

- Creating awareness
- Attracting and holding attention
- Create associations with certain values

- Developing a strong image
- Suitability for enhancing the brand
- Encouraging direct action
- Enhancing credibility/prestige
- Conveying detailed information
- Use as a reference source
- Appealing to many senses

- Creating favourable trade reaction
- Being flexible in its use as a marketing communications media vehicle
- Suitability as a primary medium
- Availability
- Longevity
- and so on.

Exhibit 5.3 Media characteristics

Medium	Principal characteristics		Sources of audience research information
	Advantages	Disadvantages	
BROADCAST Analogue/digital	Reaches large and mass audience Increasingly able to target selected audience groups	High airtime cost Production costs can be high Transient message (fleeting exposure)	BARB TGI
TV Terrestrial/satellite/cable Local/regional/ national/international	Highly visible High impact Low cost per exposure High creative flexibility/appeals to multiple senses – sight, sound, colour, movement Can generate excitement and involvement Perceived as having high credibility/ prestige Ability to demonstrate product Can create strong image-branding Good for generating high levels of awareness Content synergy possible with programmes being broadcast Effective with sales force and trade Sponsorship and product placement opportunities Direct response can be facilitated	May not offer sufficient target audience selectivity Viewers' attention not always focused on TV Can take a long time to produce Zapping/channel hopping easy Information content limited Typically long lead times and difficult to change message at short notice (careful management can overcome these)	
Radio Local/regional/ national/international	Low airtime cost Low production cost Can be produced and aired quickly Message can be changed quickly Message can be topical Sponsorship opportunities Direct response can be facilitated Some audience selectivity by airtime Geographic selectivity/local coverage High acceptance of repeated messages	Only uses audio message Transient message (fleeting exposure) Listeners' attention often distracted while doing other things Creative treatment and quality often very mixed/poor Information content limited Perceived as lacking in persuasiveness by many Audience passive receivers of information	RAJAR

➜

Exhibit 5.3 continued

| Medium | Principal characteristics | | Sources of audience research information |
	Advantages	Disadvantages	
Internet World Wide Web (WWW) Web page email	Message can be changed quickly and easily Interactivity possible Can create own pages cheaply Can advertise on others' web pages Very low cost possible Very large audience potential Direct sales possible High information content possible on own Web pages	Limited visual presentation Audience not guaranteed 'Hits' may not represent interest – casual browsers Relies on browsers finding page Can create irritation Large number of target groups may not use the Internet yet Creative limitations	ABC//electronic BPA interactive II/PRO I
PRESS	Selective Production costs can be very low	Impact limited to visual sense Short life	JICNARS NRS
Newspapers Local/regional/ national/international Daily/weekly/ weekday/weekend	Short lead time Frequent publication Advertorials possible Geographical selectivity possible Newspapers are actively read Classified sections actively searched High information content possible Broad acceptance/believability Some creative flexibility Direct response facilitated	Mediocre reproduction quality Micro-environment often crowded with advertisements	JICREG ABC VFD TGI
Magazines Local/regional/ national/international Weekly/monthly/annual Consumer/business/trade Technical/professional General/special interest Men's/women's Controlled circulation Association/club/ company/house magazine	Highly selective Production costs can be low High information content possible Short lead time Frequent publication available for many titles Content synergy possible with editorial and magazine image Can have extended life (pass-along audience) Magazines are actively read Classified sections are actively searched Some titles have high prestige and credibility Creative flexibility (visual and olfactory possible (scratch patch)) Good quality reproduction (full colour) Direct response facilitated Product placement possible Inserts and advertorials possible Direct response facilitated	Impact limited to visual sense (although olfactory sense possible) Micro-environment often crowded with advertisements Limited geographic options in key titles Long lead time for some titles	JICNARS NRS ABC TGI
Directories Local/regional/ national/international periodically/annual/ intermittent Consumer/business/ trade	Long life Directories are actively searched and read Synergy with content and editorial where available Low production cost High selectivity possible High information content possible	Can have very long lead times Low impact Very limited creative flexibility in most titles Limited visual presentation	ABC

Exhibit 5.3 continued

Medium	Principal characteristics		Sources of audience research information
	Advantages	Disadvantages	
POSTERS **Outdoor – boards** Local/regional/ national Roadside (billboards) Stations (rail, underground, bus, ports, airports) Shopping areas Venues (e.g. sports grounds) Specialised (e.g. aerial, benches, bins) **Outdoor – transport** Buses Taxis Poster vans **Inside** Shopping centres Buses Taxis Underground trains Public toilets	Reaches broad, diverse audience High repeat exposure (frequency) High attention-getting possible with good design Prominent brand identification possible Relatively low cost Can create strong impact of simple message Message can be placed close to point of sale High geographic selectivity Visible throughout the day	Creative limitations Short exposure time Message must be simple Limited audience selectivity Seldom attracts readers' full attention Posters areas are highly variable many may not have high impact	POSTAR
CINEMA Local/regional/national	High quality production possible Limited audience size and profile can be appropriate for some products (reduced wastage) 'Captive' audience Extended length advertising is possible and acceptable High selectivity through film, certificate and cinema choice Product placement in film available High creative flexibility/appeals to multiple senses – sight, sound, colour, movement	Cost of production can be high (but not necessarily so) Limited audience size and profile	CAVIAR CAA NRS
DIRECT MAIL Letters Catalogues/price lists Brochures/leaflets/ booklets Circulars Newsletters Cards Samples etc.	Highly audience selectivity Can be personalised Circulation is controlled by advertiser, wasted circulation can be avoided Circulation can be limited to what is affordable Can be used to encourage action/direct response/sales Aspects of its performance can be easily measured e.g. responses High information content possible	Can be associated with 'junk mail' Each exposure is expensive	

IN VIEW 5.7

How long does it last?

Television commercials only last as long as they are broadcast unless caught on home-recorded videotape. Cinema commercials only last for the length of time they are screened. Posters stick around until the end of their campaign period.

If you have ever had to wait in a doctor's or dentist's waiting room you will have a good idea of the longevity of certain media vehicles. Magazines left lying on tabletops date back months and even years. Copies of women's magazines, car magazines, lifestyle magazines, house and cooking magazines and the ubiquitous *Reader's Digest* adorn the waiting rooms. Whereas directories may be used for years, a promotional light projection used as an ambient medium may last for only a few minutes.

How long do ads last in people's minds? Well, good campaigns can create such enduring images and messages that they can last for years after the campaign has ended. Sometimes longer than the originators would wish as they try to upgrade their images and relaunch their products.

Watney's Red Barrel beer branding was incredibly successful for many years. A whole variety of media was used to both develop and maintain the brand image – advertising media, merchandising items, livery and corporate identity, packaging, etc. Even the pubs themselves became extensions to the brand. The brand truly adopted a multimedia portfolio that was used to make this an exceptionally popular international product.

Unfortunately for Watney's, CAMRA, the Campaign for Real Ale, became a strong environmental force in the industry as it campaigned against what it identified as unsatisfactory, not 'real' beers. Red Barrel became a focus of attention. The tide turned away from Watney's who became associated with beers not up to the standards of 'real ale'. Sales fell and Watney's had to change their image. Easier said than done. The very success of the previous years had resulted in brand images that would not go away. The Red Barrel was removed from the market but the stigma remained. For over a decade after its withdrawal, memories of Watney's Red Barrel remained.

What quickly becomes apparent from any assessment of the media is that no one medium can be or do all things. To make a realistic assessment of each medium it is necessary to think about the nature of the product being promoted and the marketing objectives that need to be met. A few words of caution are, therefore, appropriate. The details presented in Exhibit 5.3 are generalised comments that could be misleading if taken to apply in every situation. The performance of specific media vehicles may not match all the strengths identified for the media class of which it would be part. Equally, some media vehicles can overcome some of the weaknesses, particularly if used creatively. For example, posters and radio are often perceived as relatively weak media but they can be highly effective. With the restrictions placed on cigarette advertising, posters have been very effective for the Benson and Hedges and Marlboro brands. The advantage of integrated marketing communications is that media are selected to complement each other as recognised in David Bond's professional perspective at the beginning of this chapter.

WARNING

! *Care has to be exercised when evaluating media. Although a particular media class may have certain strengths and weaknesses in general, specific media vehicles should be considered as their strengths and weaknesses may differ from those typical of the class.*

Media growth

The media scene is one that is changing. Chapter 7 on the changing marketing communications environment highlights media fragmentation as one such change, in which media vehicles are proliferating. This is coinciding with improved technology giving rise to new and exciting media such as the Internet and other electronic media, which is the subject of the next chapter. The light projections referred to in the section on ambient media have only been possible in recent years with the advent of laser technology, providing a media experience that had previously never before been seen. In this way, new media classes are being invented.

In 1997 the New PHD agency in the UK predicted that by the year 2005 there will be 200 TV channels (there were only four in 1985), that nearly two-thirds of households will be multi-set TV homes, that the number of poster sites will have more than doubled their 1985 figures, that there will be as many as 350 (seven times as many as there were in 1985) independent national and local radio stations (INR and ILR stations), that cinema screens will have nearly doubled their 1985 figures, that consumer magazine titles will have increased to 3500 and that the Internet will be used in 35% of

Exhibit 5.4 The media and the future

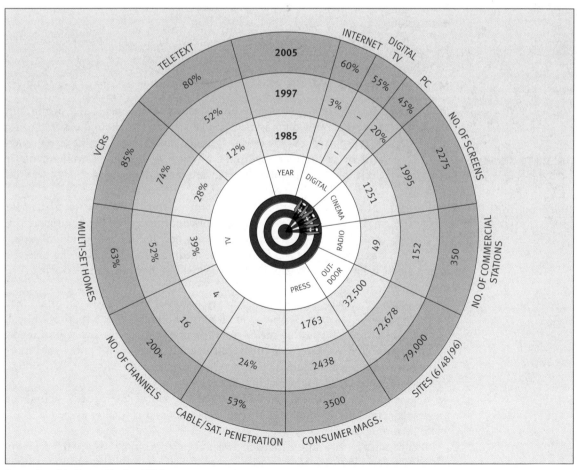

Source: Copyright © 1999 The New PHD Agency

homes. Their figures are shown in Exhibit 5.4. These figures today appear conservative. Media opportunities are growing worldwide through technological, social, cultural, economic and political change.

Media effect – the media as relationship builders

Media produce relationships with the receiver that may be weak or strong, important or incidental. Whatever they are, the media have an impact on the nature of them. Viewing an advertisement on the back of a bus while driving to work generates a different relationship and sort of response than watching a commercial in the cinema sitting next to your partner prior to the start of a film you are eager to see, which is different again to experiencing media in a supermarket or exhibition hall, or sitting through a powerpoint sales presentation in a company office.

One approach to identifying the differences between the media and our responses to them is to use the following classification:

● mode of transmission
● timing
● context
● format
● reception

Each of these variables represents differences in opportunity and use.

Mode of transmission

Mode of transmission represents the 'technical' aspects of the media and significantly affects the way in which a medium is made available to us. It is about the way in which the message is transported and the sensory mix the media uses. It is the effect generated by virtue of a medium's physical properties. Developments in electronic and optical technology are revolutionising media use with the Internet, digital television and interactive television.

NEED TO KNOW

☑ *Differences in the characteristics of the media may be classified by considering their mode of transmission, timing, context, format and reception.*

The mode of transmission has a major impact on how we 'participate' in the media. This has been recognised for many years (e.g. Wright 1973) and Marshall McLuhan, a well-renowned and influential media expert, has developed his own concept of media as transmitters of messages. So strong did he believe the impact of media to be that he coined the famous saying, 'The medium *is* the message!'

McLuhan (1964) has described media as extensions of man, no less important than hand, eye or ear, and having profound implications on his actions, responses and cultural organisations. But not all media are the same. McLuhan's concept of media differentiates between electronic media such as TV, cinema and radio (and more recently we would have to add the Internet) and mechanical media such as the press. It is the advent of electronic media that has resulted in what McLuhan has called the development of the 'global village'. He would argue that the Internet is a natural and inevitable extension of what began with telegraphy and is further evidence of the world becoming 'smaller'.

McLuhan has further differentiated between the media on the basis of the degree of our participation in them. Media that, because of their modes of transmission require us to 'work' at understanding and interpreting them, he has called 'cool' media. Media that present us with less 'work' and, thereby less participation, he has called 'hot' media. Of the main mass media, only television is truly 'cool' (not 'hot' as we might intuitively think). Television presents us with data that has to be interpreted from an abstract mosaic of dots or lines of information. The picture has to be 'reconstructed'. In a technical sense, McLuhan would describe TV as 'low definition' which requires much information to be filled in by the viewer. Hot media such as cinema that is transmitted in a totally different form is 'high definition'. The picture does not have to be 'reconstructed'. It is presented as a whole. Movement is conveyed through the passage of around 25 such pictures per second. While interpretation and participation is required, it is at a much lower level than television. The notion of 'hot' and 'cool' are relative terms. Radio and press he has classified as hot media whereas posters vary according to their mode of transmission – printed or electronic.

Is it important for us to understand these distinctions? Well, they are presented here very briefly only to emphasise the point that our relationship with the media varies from one medium to another and because of this, the marketing communications message is affected. Although McLuhan has not supported his contentions with experimental evidence, Wright (1973) has shown that modality (mode of transmission) does affect the response of a perceiver and the receiver's attitudes towards the transmission. This has been further supported by the work of Herbert Krugman, some details of which are presented later.

Timing

Timing refers to the time of day at which the media (and so the marketing communication) can be seen or heard. This is closely related to 'context' as we shall see in a moment. Increasingly, the media are available to us 24 hours of the day although they may be used by different target audience groups. By way of example of the significance of timing, breakfast TV tends to generate a different relationship with the audience than that generated by afternoon or evening TV. The type of programmes transmitted reflect this. A morning newspaper may be read in bed, over breakfast, while travelling to work, etc., and the state of mind, mood, responsiveness and attentiveness, in short the relationship induced, is likely to differ at these different times. Weekend newspapers are often considered to be read at a more relaxed pace and in a more relaxed atmosphere. Direct mail delivered in the morning post is likely to be read in a different mood to that read more casually later in the day. Text messages sent by companies on mobile phones may be received at any time of day and at times that can be very disruptive. As this form of communication becomes more popular it could become more irritating and the messages viewed negatively.

Context

Media context is referred to in Chapter 7, The Changing Marketing Communications Environment, as the micro-environment in which marketing communications occur. Studies which date back to the early 1960s and 1970s, for example Crane (1964) and Kennedy (1971), have clearly shown the impact of editorial climate on marketing communications. Psychological studies on perception and memory bear this out. The work in this area is not new and is widely accepted.

Context can relate to 'media context' which is primarily the editorial and advertising climate in which any marketing communications take place. Media vehicles develop their own 'atmosphere' conveyed by the editorial tone they adopt. Some media vehicles are recognised for their prestige (*The Tatler*), some for their expertise (*Scientific American*), some for their humour and irreverence (*Punch*), some for their impartiality (*Which?* guides). Some media contain very little advertising, some contain a great deal or may be devoted entirely to advertising. An advertisement seen on a page with many others may create a different effect to a direct mailing that arrives with the morning post.

Context can also refer to the physical and social surroundings in which the media are available. On this point the media classes vary significantly. Physical differences can be illustrated by contrasting the viewing of an outdoor poster with sitting in a cinema or reading a direct mail leaflet in the office or seeing an indoor poster placed on the wall of a public toilet. While TV may be watched relaxing at home, posters may be viewed in a more hectic environment driving to work or travelling on the tube during the rush hour. Social contexts can be illustrated by reference to the summary list of social contexts provided by The Media Circle in Exhibit 5.5. Although this exhibit refers to the mass media, the importance of context is equally relevant to the non-mass media as well. A good example of this is the use of sales promotions at point of sale within retail outlets.

Exhibit 5.5 Social contexts of the media

Medium	Social context
Television	Family/individual
Press	Individual
Posters	Community
Cinema	Couple/family/kids
Radio	Individual
Direct mail	Individual
Internet	Individual

Source: Adapted from *The Media Circle* (Wilmshurst 1985, pp. 256–264)

Format

Format relates to the marketing communications flexibility each of the media facilitate – layout, size, use of colour, graphics, design, typography and general style of the marketing communications. Each of the media create more or less flexibility in the formats they allow; 'super site' posters can transmit images many feet high. Whereas 'mode of transmission' dictates what is possible, 'format' is ultimately how well this is used in the creation of marketing communications.

Television and cinema offer sound, sight, movement and colour. They are exciting media and offer lots of creative opportunities. The Internet uses the TV screen but in a very different way. Movement is very restricted but this will change as technological advances improve its transmission and reception through developments such as broadband. Significantly, the Internet permits interactivity although increasingly this will also be possible with TV. Radio is a much less invasive medium. It relies on sound as its only sensory input. Nevertheless, the apparent paucity of sensory input can be compensated by its ability to appeal to the imagination. Press and direct mail offer creatives many opportunities but have traditionally had to rely on the single sense of sight. Print technology has made colour available to newspapers in recent years but the quality is limited. Magazines and leaflets, on the other hand, are usually printed on high-quality papers with high-quality reproduction. The technology of recreating fragrances has introduced a second sensory input to print with various forms of 'scratch patches' and the use of a range of print materials have now introduced the dimension of 'touch'. Posters also have to make use of print with its inherent limitations but can do so with 'larger than life' effect.

Reception

While mode of transmission is related to the medium itself as a physical entity, 'reception' is related to the audience who receive the messages via the media. Ultimately, it is their response to the media and the messages they contain that we are concerned about and their response is affected both by the media and the receiver's predisposition at the time of reception. Hence the reason why timing, context and format are important; it is the cumulative effect that induces a relationship between the marketing communications media and message, and their audiences.

Herbert Krugman's (1962, 1965, 1966, 1970, 1971) experiments, as long ago as the 1960s and 1970s, shed some interesting light on how we receive and process communications. This helps to explain from a psycho-biological perspective some of McLuhan's contentions that we do react differently to different media.

Krugman measured brainwaves and determined that our brainwave patterns were affected while viewing media. He concluded from his studies that we show different degrees of involvement with the media (media involvement) that may be measured as active or passive involvement. The notion of involvement was later taken up by Ray (1973) and Robertson (1976) who used the concept to describe the degree of involvement we have towards products (product involvement) which could be either high or low involvement.

Television and cinema would be defined as passive, whereas print – newspapers, magazines and posters – are more active. Passive, low involvement media significantly enhance learning compared with active, high involvement media. Why this should be so has been suggested in numerous psychological studies (for example, Festinger and Maccoby 1964; James 1890), explanations for which have been found in distraction theory, dissonance theory, selective perception theory, memory theory and differential responses to both animate and inanimate stimuli. The relaxed, low level of involvement in television (even though it may be a medium which calls for our attention) from a mental processing point of view allows passive and incidental learning. Our critical and 'perceptual defences' so much more strongly present in active high involvement media are dampened and our acceptance of what we see is generally heightened. Passive learning, 'what is caught rather than what is taught', which is mobilised through passive media is typically effortless, responsive to animate stimuli, amenable to relaxation and is characterised by an absence of resistance to what is learned (Krugman and Hartley 1970). Reading a newspaper is so much harder work.

By contrast, if we are actively searching for information, the printed media can perform so much better. This is perhaps why the small and insignificant classified lineage advertisements that we see in every newspaper and magazine can be so effective – we are actually wanting information and will take the trouble to seek it out. We are predisposed to active media and as active learners we select active media for our investigations. The Internet, while primarily an active medium, also permits a degree of passivity depending on what we are using it for. Interestingly, recent research indicates that there are clear and significant differences in the way we process Internet advertisements depending on whether the product being advertised is high or low involvement (Anon 2004).

What all the foregoing discussions represent is that in developing marketing communications we need to think very carefully about the impact that the media themselves will have on our messages. If used wisely, media can enhance marketing communications not only through their ability to reach our target audiences but also through their inherent properties as carriers of our messages.

FOOD FOR THOUGHT

Much of the work on the assessment of the physiological effects of the media was carried out in the 1960s and 1970s. The results are still valid today but little interest has been shown in these issues over the last two decades.

Although much of the research work on which the preceding comments were based was carried out some years ago, the findings are still relevant today. To some extent the interest in media effects which was popular in the 1960s and 1970s has not been carried forward into the 1980s and 1990s (and now the new millennium), with few researchers focusing on this aspect of marketing communications. This is a great pity as there are many questions still left unanswered and new questions still to be posed – all the more so when we consider the developments in communication technology that have brought about new opportunities especially in electronic media.

Integration of the media

As a final word on the media, it is important to emphasise the benefits of using a range of media in integrated marketing communications. Too great a reliance on a single medium or unnecessarily limiting the media selected can reduce the effectiveness of individual campaigns and the total IMC impact. It is perfectly reasonable to select particular media for special emphasis and it is quite usual to choose a primary medium to be enhanced by a range of secondary or support media. Synergy is achieved through a range of media as emphasised in the professional perspective at the beginning of this chapter.

Summary

The media are the carriers of marketing communications messages. They are a fundamental part of the marketing communications process. Even the other elements of the marketing mix have been identified as purveyors of marketing communications messages. Media come in all shapes and sizes, each medium with its own characteristics. These characteristics can be used by media planners to improve the effectiveness of marketing communications by ensuring that messages are received by the right audiences and by creating synergy between the messages and the media used to convey those messages. Distinctions between the media can be made by classifying the media vehicles in terms of their modality, timing, context, format and reception.

When considering the media, most people immediately think about the mass media used in advertising, in particular television, press, radio, posters and cinema. This is a very narrow way of considering media. More creatively, media opportunities exist everywhere a marketing communications message can be displayed. Recently, there has been a growth in the use of ambient media, which has taken advantage of unusual, but striking, media opportunities.

Word of mouth has been described in this chapter as a medium because of its potential for both stimulating and distorting marketing communications messages. Unfortunately, for the marketing communicator, it is a medium that cannot easily be controlled but, nevertheless, its power should not be underestimated.

What is ultimately important is how target audience members receive marketing communications messages which typically come from a variety of media in succession. Research has indicated that we all, as receivers, respond to different media in different ways. From an integrated perspective this can be harnessed to increase the synergy of marketing communications.

Self-review questions

1 Exhibit 5.1 provides a list of possible media choices. Are there any other specific examples that you can identify that can be added to the list?

2 In the context of integrated marketing communications, why do you think that it is important not to define the range of media too narrowly, especially not to define it only as mass media?

3 What is meant by 'ambient media'?

4 When considering media effects, it was suggested that the characteristics of the media could be classified into five categories. What are these categories and what does each represent?

5 What is meant by 'low' and 'high' definition media?

6 Is it likely that an advertisement for a new personal pension scheme appearing in the financial press will be perceived differently to the same advertisement appearing in a sports magazine? If so, what might the different perceptions be and what has caused them?

7 In the professional perspective at the beginning of this chapter, Peter Dix is quoted as saying, with regard to media options, 'a combination of ground, air and sea attack is always better than one approach that potentially fails'. What do you think he really meant by this analogy?

Projects

Review Exhibit 5.3 and expand the list of advantages and disadvantages listed for each medium. Select three new examples of media e.g. packaging, mobile phones for text messaging and video releases. Using the list provided in the section on the Characteristics of the Media and any other factors you consider relevant, identify the strengths and weaknesses of each medium you have chosen.

You are a media planner faced with the task of selecting the primary and a small selection of secondary media for the launch of a new restaurant in a major city. Which media do you think would be best? Bare in mind the sort of considerations identified above, and consider the need to create impact by choosing media that will differentiate the new restaurant from its competitors in the city.

→

Consider the Internet as a medium and the way banner advertising is used. Think carefully about the points raised in the section on Reception. What are the implications of passive and active media use applied to advertising on the Internet?

References

Anon (2004) The study of the perception of meanings in web ads versus print ads. Review of paper to appear in the *Journal of Marketing Communications.*

Crane, L.E. (1964), How product, appeal and program affect attitudes towards commercials. *Journal of Advertising Research*, 4 (1).

DeLozier, M.W. (1976), *The Marketing Communications Process.* McGraw-Hill.

Feick, L.F. and Price, L.L. (1987), The Market Maven: a diffuser of marketplace information. *Journal of Marketing* 51 (January), 83–97.

Festinger, L. and Maccoby, N. (1964), On resistance to persuasive communications. *Journal of Abnormal Pyschology*, 68 (4).

James, W. (1890), *Principles of Psychology.* New York: Dover Publications.

Kennedy, J.R. (1971), How program environment affects TV commercials. *Journal of Advertising Research*, 11 (1).

Krugman, H.E. (1962), An application of learning theory to TV copy testing. *Public Opinion Quarterly*, 26.

Krugman, H.E. (1965), The impact of TV advertising. *Public Opinion Quarterly*, 29 (3).

Krugman, H.E. (1966), The measurement of advertising involvement. *Public Opinion Quarterly*, 30 (4).

Krugman, H.E. and Hartley, E.L. (1970), Passive learning for television. *Public Opinion Quarterly*, 34 (2).

Krugman, H.E. (1971), Brainwave measures of media involvement. *Journal of Advertising Research*, 11 (1).

McLuhan, M. (1964), *Understanding Media.* Routledge and Kegan Paul.

Media Week (1996a), The Media Week Awards 1996 – The Winners. *Media Week.*

Media Week (1996b), The Media Week Awards 1996 – The Finalists. *Media Week.*

Media Week (1997), Media coup of the year. *Media Week* pp. 14–15.

Pandya, N. (1998), Sales promotions: it's all about the image. *The Guardian*, 20 June.

Phillips, S. (1998), Space invaders. *Hot Line*, Issue 5 (Winter) 16–19.

Ray, M.L. (1973), Marketing communication and the hierarchy of effects. Working Paper, Marketing Science Institute, November.

Robertson, T.S. (1976), Low commitment consumer behaviour. *Journal of Advertising Research*, 16 (2).

Rossiter, J.R. and Percy, L. (1997), *Advertising Communications and Promotion Management* 2nd edn. McGraw-Hill.

Wilmshurst, J. (1985), *The Fundamentals of Advertising* Heinemann.

Wright, P. (1973), The cognitive processes mediating acceptance of advertising. *Journal of Marketing Research*, 10 (February).

Selected further reading

Each of the main industry publications contain useful information about the media, for example, *Media Week, Campaign, PR Week* and *Marketing Week.*

Chapter 6

E-media

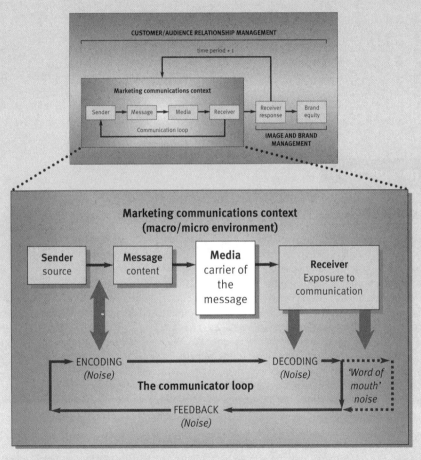

The IMC Process Model

CD

Having identified the range of media Concern uses in Chapter 5, what role and value does e-media play in Concern's marketing communication strategy? Refer to Case Study 1 on the CD.

Chapter outline

- What are 'e-media'?
- Cybermarketing
- The use of multimedia in marketing communications
- The Internet and the World Wide Web
- Marketing communications on the Internet and the World Wide Web
- Digital and interactive television
- CD-ROM/DVD
- Permission marketing

Objectives

- To highlight the major e-media opportunities
- To relate e-media to 'cybermarketing'
- To recognise some of the benefits and limitations of the Internet
- To describe some of the multiple promotional uses of e-media

Professional perspective

Will Collin Partner, Naked Communications

What are e-media? Setting aside the literal meaning, the common understanding of this phrase is any digital, interactive or online communications platform; ranging from the Internet and interactive kiosks and CD-ROMs, to digital TV and radio, and emerging multimedia wireless devices.

Why does this hotch-potch of technologies merit a chapter of its own? The reason is that these new media are creating fundamental changes in marketing communications, in three principal areas: the way people 'consume' media; the role of media in marketing communications; and the commercial basis of media companies themselves.

Firstly, we are seeing the erosion of mass media in favour of many more niche or narrowly focused media. Digital TV channels or websites can profitably cater to minority audiences, as production costs are lower. Consumers will still come together for mass media experiences like *Coronation Street,* but will increasingly fragment into smaller communities of interest for more and more of their media consumption.

Secondly, media are becoming more than just an outlet for advertising. Through interactive services (such as the Web or *Open* on digital satellite TV), media are evolving from being simply a supplier of audiences for ads into commercial partners providing a channel for sales and customer service. Media used to be the place where people 'looked at' your brand; now they can also examine it, buy it and use it.

Finally, these changes will fundamentally alter the economics of the media industry. Media companies' income will increasingly come from the transactions they host rather than just the ads they run. At the same time, some revenues – notably from classified newspaper ads – will diminish as consumers use new media alternatives.

In all, this offers a wealth of opportunity for marketers who embrace the new environment. For media companies, the ultimate prize is to become true commercial partners at the heart of the customer relationship.

What are e-media?

E-media

Any digital, interactive or on-line communication platform such as the Internet, inter-active TV and electronic multimedia.

CD-ROM and DVD

Compact Disc Read-Only Memory and Digital Video Disk. These are laser-read disks containing huge quantities of digital information.

FOOD FOR THOUGHT

E-media offer not just marketing communications benefits but also new ways of interacting with business and with one another.

Chapter 5 introduced the concept and importance of media. Without the media, marketing communications messages cannot be transmitted to their target audiences. Although the term 'media' strictly refers to anything that is capable of transmitting messages, traditionally (as was identified in the previous chapter) they tend to be thought of in a much narrower sense and are most closely associated with the mass media.

Developments in telecommunications, electronics and computing are now ushering in a new era and have opened up new avenues for marketing communications. The term '**e-media**' has been coined to reflect these new avenues and is associated with such high-tech developments as digital and interactive TV, teletext and videotext, the World Wide Web and the Internet, **CD-ROM and DVD**, video and multimedia. Significantly and increasingly, the technology associated with e-media permits:

- interactivity
- shorter response times
- more direct communications, and
- more sophisticated communications.

Such is the power of e-media that not only is it revolutionising marketing and marketing communications but it is also influencing our very behaviour. There have been many outlandish claims for the growth and impact of e-media based on early usage trends. These should be treated with caution. Their impact, however, should not be under-estimated even if their adoption rates are of more modest proportions.

Exhibit 5.4 in the previous chapter gave estimates of media usage into the year 2005, proposed by New PHD, an agency specialising in new media. Their forecast compares the growth of selected e-media with the more traditional forms of mass media. Their picture is very much one of increasing use and availability of media in general but with a significant role to be played by e-media in particular.

Cybermarketing

Cybermarketing

Term used to describe marketing activities using e-media.

Cybermarketing (Keeler 1995) is a relatively new term which has been used to describe marketing activities using the media of computers and telecommunications, in other words, it is a term used to describe marketing using e-media.

A brief list of the methods used in cybermarketing includes:

- multimedia, computer animation and virtual reality
- the Internet and the World Wide Web
- digital and interactive television
- CD-ROM/DVD

A number of benefits are claimed for the use of cybermarketing over more traditional marketing activities (Keeler 1995). These benefits are the direct result of the advantages obtained from the use of e-media.

- Saves money and helps stretch the marketing communications budget.
- Saves time and cuts the steps in the marketing process (e.g. creates more direct access to customers).

- Gives customers another way to buy while enabling them to take control of the purchasing process (e.g. no sales people pressurising you to buy, easier to compare prices between competing products, can buy from home or office, products can be delivered rather than collected).
- Offers 'rich' information and is interactive.
- Communication can be real time, **online** or **offline**.
- Offers instant reach; local, national and international.
- Lowers barriers to entry and offers the opportunity for equal access for all businesses.
- Can be continuously available.

Online

Use of a computer while linked via telephone modem to other computers.

Offline

Use of an e-medium computer disconnected from a modem.

It is clear to see, even from this brief list of benefits, the power of e-media and cyber-marketing activities, and why they are being considered by many as a revolution in marketing communications and in business practices.

The sections that follow now consider each of the areas of cybermarketing in turn.

The use of multimedia in marketing communications

Multimedia

The use of many media forms; usually most associated with electronic media.

Multimedia can be defined as the combination of different formats, including text, pictures, animation, narrative, video and music into a single medium. Multimedia applications can be made on numerous different media including television and cinema, but it is the growing development of specific hardware and dedicated multimedia applications that is of particular interest here. These applications are increasingly likely to be interactive allowing viewers to do things, control where they want to go and to skip backwards and forwards according to their wishes. Information can be presented in much more entertaining ways. Viewers are attracted to using multimedia because it is a more active, multi-sensory medium; they can move at their own pace, they can experiment and they can receive immediate feedback on their progress. Because of these features, multimedia applications tend to be more effective in terms of holding interest and improving retention of information (Ryan 1995). On the downside, a disadvantage can be the cost, time and expertise required to develop them if they are to be most effective. However, these are more than outweighed by their benefits judging by the increasing number of companies that make use of them.

IN VIEW 6.1

New way to sell cars

The increasingly competitive motor car industry is always looking for new ways to sell its products. It is no surprise, therefore, that manufacturers should turn to advanced technology as a means to gain an edge over their competitors. Multimedia point-of-sale kiosks are an obvious choice. The glamorous nature of the product lends itself to multimedia presentations and interactive features can let prospective customers 'configure' their own model. The Rover Group claims to have the most advanced system of its type. Under the name Discus, the system has been rolled out to the manufacturer's 500-strong dealer network. What makes Discus different to most multimedia 'kiosk' applications is its connection to other information technology systems. Not only does it link through Rover's manufacturing systems – so orders can be processed quickly – it also links into the dealer's own systems. 'As far as I am aware, Rover is the only manufacturer that is integrating with the dealer's own systems. Modern cars are so complex that customers can easily be bombarded with facts. You could give them a telephone directory and tell them to study the options. But with Discus they don't have to drink from a fire hose – they can sip from a glass,' says Mr Stubbs, Rover's product manager for Discus. 'It also helps the sales staff. It is so hard to keep up with the changes. This system makes sure they give the right answers to customers,' he adds.

Source: P. Manchester, © *Financial Times* (7 June 1995)

Although initially developed for education and learning, many of the early commercial uses of multimedia were in the financial services industry. NatWest Bank, for example, launched a multimedia videoconference link for its customers as long ago as July 1994. And not only can customers be targeted, multimedia applications can be targeted towards employees for staff training and internal communications.

Some examples of the use of multimedia for marketing communications are:

- *Promotional material*. Multimedia applications can communicate information on a company and its products. They can be used to bring presentations to life. Products can be demonstrated. Company annual reports can be made more interesting and understandable. Information can be presented in much more exciting forms than can be achieved with simple brochures and leaflets. If stored on a CD-ROM, they can be used on viewers' own PCs, otherwise they require significant hardware to be displayed.
- *Customer interaction*. Daewoo's launch into the British car market relied heavily on its sales approach within its manufacturer's own showrooms. A hands-off approach was adopted so that prospective customers would not feel pressured by sales people. Multimedia stations were used within showrooms that were accessed directly by customers who could 'interrogate' and interact with the stations, view models from various angles, 'design' their own cars from the options available and have their questions answered.

IN VIEW 6.2

Video link with stockbrokers

Barclays Bank operate an interactive stock dealing and information service called BarclayZone. A two-way video link is provided between customers and Barclays Stockbrokers' head office in Glasgow. One of the specific aims of the service is to allow customers to take charge of the process. The facility was designed to show videos that provided general information on the stock market. When customers felt they had enough information to make a purchase, they could make a deal or begin a videoconference with a stockbroker. BarclayZone was developed by Barclays Multimedia, an in-house development unit, and featured images from Star Trek which were designed to make the use of the service less daunting and more entertaining.

- *Staff training.* Multimedia lends itself to staff training applications because of its ease of use, cost savings and effectiveness. Once developed, their use is cheaper than bringing staff to a central location and providing instructors. Staff can learn at their own pace at their own places of work. Modules most relevant to their needs can be selected and the software can provide feedback on progress by including self-evaluation questions, scoring of answers and correction of mistakes.
- *Online and offline help for employees.* Multimedia can be used as an interactive data source of information for employees. This can be updated regularly and can be extremely useful in ensuring that customers are provided with correct information.
- *Internal communications.* Organisations can face extreme difficulties in ensuring adequate internal communications. Multimedia is another weapon in the communications armoury. It can be very effective in communicating organisational change and new product launches.
- *Online and offline help to external customers.* Multimedia applications can be used to assist customers in just the same way as they can be used for employees although the design of the application is likely to be different. They might explain ordering procedures, use of a software product or the construction of complex pieces of machinery in industrial marketing situations.

Computer animation and virtual reality

Computer animation is a type of multimedia that has become popular for promotional purposes. The techniques and technologies that have been used in movies such as *Jurassic Park* and *The Matrix* are now being employed in the promotion industry. The characters that used to be drawn by hand are now being generated by computer, and animation sequences that would have taken weeks or months to produce can now be created using a PC or workstation in a matter of hours or days. The application of such animation is being used in TV, cinema, video and CD-ROM/DVD for many different promotional uses. Its use also extends to marketing research and product development.

Virtual reality (VR) is, perhaps, the ultimate in multimedia technology. It is not the same as animation. No matter how realistic the latest animations may appear, you will always see the same scenes from the same viewpoints and perspectives. Virtual reality

---

IN VIEW 6.3

Using video streaming and webcasting

A recent survey conducted by the Chartered Institute of Marketing shows that 47% of marketers are planning to stream video on their website. An overwhelming 93% of respondents believe that intranets facilitate innovation even though 40% do not understand what 'streaming' means and 25% do not understand the concept of webcasting. While many marketers realise the potential of using video online and many are planning to do so – 48% for training courses on their intranets for example – there are important perceived barriers. Cost is a problem for 59% whilst 54% think users experience difficulty playing the video.

Source: Marketing Business, June 2002d, p. 8

is a 'place' you can enter and walk through. Your eye-line, positioning, direction of view dictates what you see just as it would in real life. This is achieved with the use of very powerful computing and software which can identify your position in virtual space, determine which objects should be visible from this viewpoint, read their coordinates from the VR 3-D database and transform them into perspective. It does this in 'real time' as though everything is happening 'now'. That is, it reacts and regenerates images as and when you move as a constant flow – between 10 and 30 times a second, or around 50 milliseconds per frame. In contrast, animation is a fixed sequence of pre-rendered images, rendered offline and not in 'real time'. They do not react to the viewer and every time they are shown exactly the same sequence is presented. These images produce the illusion of movement at around 25 frames per second.

There are two types of virtual reality, *immersive* and *non-immersive* (Exhibit 6.1).

Exhibit 6.1 Virtual Reality

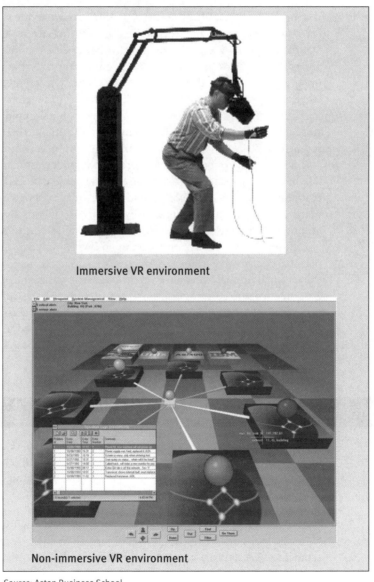

Immersive VR environment

Non-immersive VR environment

Source: Aston Business School

Immersive VR, often employing the use of headset and gloves wired up to a computer, gives the user the illusion of being 'immersed' in a 3-D virtual world. Non-immersive VR involves the creation of a 3-D world inside a computer, but viewed in 2-D on a screen. This is sometimes referred to as 3-D modelling and is used in computer-aided design (CAD).

Online and offline applications

Multimedia kiosks

Free-standing kiosks where computer access is facilitated either using CD-ROMs/DVDs or linked to other computers. These may be kiosks provided in retail stores, for example.

In understanding multimedia, it is important to differentiate between the content of an application and the way in which it is delivered. Once an application has been developed it can be delivered to the end-user in a number of ways including CD-ROM/DVD, **multimedia kiosks** and the Internet. The choice of the delivery mechanism depends on the volume of information to be communicated, the target audience, the objectives of the application and the way it is to be used. CD-ROM/DVD, for example, is appropriate for applications that use interactivity, video images and audio tracks because large amounts of information can be stored and accessed speedily.

Broadly speaking, e-media can be classified as either online or offline. Online media are accessed in 'real time'. They are dynamic and are able to provide continuously updated information if the provider so wishes. Online media include the Internet, teletext and videotext which are available through the television (and telephone lines in the case of videotext which can provide electronic shopping by viewing products on screen and ordering via a telephone link) and many financial services which use sophisticated telecommunications links.

Teletext is an application that is frequently under-estimated. Although its creative flexibility is extremely limited, its use is extensive. Van Oosterom estimated in 1996 that in the UK alone, some 17 million viewers made over 14 million requests for information each week. New PHD (1998), the new media agency, has predicted that around 80% of households will have teletext facilities by the year 2005.

Offline new media are best explained by reference to CD-ROMs/DVDs, which may be transmitted remotely or given to users to use on their own hardware. Educational applications have made extensive use of offline multimedia. They are designed as self-contained items that include all the information the provider intends the user to have access to. Once produced, the information it contains is fixed for the life of that CD-ROM and can become dated unless physically replaced. Multimedia kiosks or stations would typically be offline facilities although they could be linked to online services.

The Internet and the World Wide Web

Internet

Collection of globally interrelated computer networks that facilitate computer communications.

The **Internet** holds many exciting prospects for marketers to assist in marketing applications, from marketing communications and research to relationship marketing with customers and other stakeholder groups. It is the marketing communications aspects with which we are most concerned here.

The Internet is a computer network or, more accurately, a collection of interrelated networks which span the globe and which allow users with the appropriate hardware and software to communicate with each other. It was conceived as a US government research project in 1969, primarily to allow scientists, engineers and military researchers to communicate with each other. It remained the domain of government, government agencies, universities and libraries until 1991 when a ban on its use for commercial purposes in the US was lifted. However, it was not until 1993 that public interest in the Internet really took off, mainly because a newer multimedia version of the Internet, called the **World Wide Web**, was invented. When people talk about the Internet nowadays, they are invariably referring to the facilities available through the World Wide Web.

World Wide Web
Huge collection of documents and files available through the Internet.

The current interest in the Internet is phenomenal. The actual number of people across the world who use the Internet on a regular basis is several million, although the total number who have more casual access is very much higher, possibly around 50 million. Estimates of the number of users vary significantly but whatever they may be, they are growing all the time.

FOOD FOR THOUGHT

The interest in and the growth of the Internet is astounding. As a medium, it is set to have a profound impact on business and daily life. It can be anticipated that this impact will increase significantly over the next decade.

As a marketing and marketing communication tool, the Internet, and in particular the World Wide Web, offers tremendous opportunities and some forward-thinking organisations have already moved to seize them. Many more organisations are still trying to come to grips with the new technology. Importantly, the Internet is no respecter of size of organisation. The opportunities it affords are open equally to small and large organisations alike. There are no high costs of entry to preclude all but the market leaders so all organisations can take advantage. Indeed, some have suggested that it 'levels the field of play' so that it is easier for smaller companies or even individuals to compete with larger operators.

NEED TO KNOW

☑ *The Internet offers tremendous new opportunities to businesses whatever their size. As a medium, it is equally accessible to large and small operators alike. Their marketplace, far from being local, can be anywhere in the world.*

How the Internet is constructed

To enable computers connected to the Internet to communicate and understand information exchanged between them, they all use the same standard Internet Protocol (IP). All the information that can be accessed on the Internet is held on computers known as 'servers' that are attached to the giant Internet network at points called 'nodes'. These servers are owned either by companies who want to distribute information on the network or by organisations that charge people for access to the network and for supporting services (**ISPs** – Internet Service Providers). One count puts the number of servers attached to the Internet worldwide at approximately 80,000 (Faughan 1996). That was a few years ago and, given the rate of growth of the Internet, today's number is likely to be significantly more. Most individuals and businesses access the Internet via a PC and standard telephone connection to an ISP. The ISP's computer is attached to, and is part of, the Internet. The ISP can provide a range of services from an account or address on its computer and the access software which allows access to the Internet, through to provision of websites, dedicated high-speed telephone lines and other services. But the status quo in cyberspace is changing fast. Battles are being waged between ISPs, the traditional phone companies and international VANs (Value Added Networks) to offer improved global Internet services. The battle will eventually determine who controls the Internet and whether telephone companies are a dominant force in this new medium, or whether they are relegated to being a commodity supplier of bandwidth to other organisations. One of the more recent developments is the coming together of Netscape and AOL in America creating one of the most powerful forces on the Internet as we move into the twenty-first century.

ISPs
Internet service providers – organisations that provide access to the Internet.

IN VIEW 6.4

Virtual Bacardi

In July 2001, Bacardi Breezer, available in over 25 countries, invested £500,000 in a major re-launch of its website. The interactive site includes a high-tech, but simple-to-use virtual desktop jukebox and several topical sections. 'Lifestyle' is split into four click-throughs – style, music, screen and out there. 'What's New' gives information on the latest promotions, while 'Fun Stuff' includes branded screen savers. 'E-marketing is going to play an increasingly important role in helping us fulfill our marketing objectives,' says Marketing Director Maurice Doyle. 'Interactivity is key in helping us to create a deep and regular dialogue with consumers, which we need in order to maintain profitable life cycle of the brand.'

Source: Marketing Business, June 2002b, p. 11

Although, in the USA, telephone usage for the Internet is free (the Internet uses local telephone charges which in the USA are free), in much of the rest of the world competition is going to force ISP providers and telephone companies to review their operations to bring down the cost of the Internet. This will, of course, result in making the Internet even more popular. A recent example is the spate of free ISP offers (no connection charges) from retailer ISPs such as Dixons, Tesco, WH Smith, Virgin, BT, etc. In one case, Tempo (screeming.net), has joined forces with a telephone provider to offer free weekend telephone connection to, and use of, the Internet. The prediction is that in the not too distant future, the Internet will be free throughout Europe.

In addition to ISP services, there are several specialist online service organisations that provide both commercial online services and access to the Internet. AOL (America Online) and CompuServe are two such organisations that provide the Internet 'surfer' with some useful landmarks and signposts (Green 1996). Such 'signposts', 'landmarks' and 'maps' are vital if the Internet is to continue its growth, as finding your way around can be very difficult. Organisations such as Yahoo! provide valuable services in indexing and cataloguing websites and acting as **'search engines'** to help surfers find their way efficiently around the World Wide Web. See In View 6.5.

The World Wide Web (WWW or Web for short) may be described as the multimedia version of the Internet and consists of hundreds of thousands of pages (known as 'websites', 'web pages', or 'home pages') which are rich in graphics and photographs mixed with text. It is based on a protocol (an agreed standard) called Hyper Text Transfer Protocol (HTTP) and it is this mechanism which allows Web information to be transferred over the Internet.

It was the recent invention of the 'browser' which has really encouraged the phenomenal growth in the use of the Internet. It has allowed companies to add colour, graphics,

FOOD FOR THOUGHT

At present, people in the USA are able to use the Internet at no charge other than that levied by service providers. There are no telephone costs. This has facilitated growth in the usage of the Internet in the States. Telephone charges have tended to limit the use of the Internet in Europe and elsewhere in the world. It is highly likely that this situation will not continue. Many people involved with the Internet would like to see costs reduced and even withdrawn completely.

Search engine

Website that maintains an index of other web pages and sites that may be searched using keywords. Access to other sites is facilitated by hypertext links – links that may be simply clicked on to move from one web page to another.

NEED TO KNOW

One of the major advantages of browser software technology is that through the use of hypertext links (highlighted words and icons), it is possible to move from one web page to another at the simple click of the mouse.

IN VIEW 6.5

Directories and engines: the key difference

There is a key difference between a search engine and a directory. Two of the best-known names in the search business, Yahoo and Google, fall into these two distinct camps.

Yahoo, a directory, is compiled by humans who also create a short description shown alongside its address when it is required. Directories list only websites, as opposed to individual pages, and categorise them in a way that a search engine does not. Because a directory does not use crawlers, you must submit your website for inclusion.

Google, a search engine, compiles its index of over three billion web pages using a 'crawler' (a piece of software) which trawls the Web in search of new pages. If the sites meet its criteria, the crawler adds them to its index, whether they have been submitted for inclusion or not. The basis for inclusion depends on a number of factors.

Source: Marketing Business, March 2003b, p. 23

video and multimedia capabilities to the messages that they leave on the Internet and for users to view and jump between web pages with ease. Merely by clicking on any word that is highlighted on the page, the browser jumps to another page using links known as 'hypertext' links. As users jump from page to page on the Web, they are said to 'surf' the Internet. As a result, the Internet has evolved from being primarily a messaging service to a place for advertising, marketing and selling products and services, and the terms 'Internet' and the 'Web' are now invariably used interchangeably.

Whilst we usually think about accessing the Internet through a computer, and indeed there are over 500 million users through computers, it is important to view the electronic marketplace in a wider context. Over 150 million Internet users access it through direct response television (DRTV) and over 1 billion through mobile media, e.g. web-enabled personal digital assistant, mobile telephone. Indeed in Japan, 51% of the population now access the Internet via mobile phone in comparison to 49% by computer.

IN VIEW 6.6

Browsers

'The boffins in Switzerland who invented the World Wide Web in 1991 did not see fit to include such frivolities as clickable pictures or sound. It was a tool for scientists, who after all could read. Text was quite good enough, and would avoid wasting the Internet's scarce transmission capacity with graphic files simply for decoration.

'It took a 23 year-old programmer at the University of Illinois called Marc Andreessen to cast a vote for the common man. In 1993, he developed Mosaic, a multimedia Web "browser" that made it easy to view documents on the Web and jump between them. It was the first piece of Internet software to recognise that the network's future lay not with scientists but with ordinary people, who liked their information dressed up in multimedia frills. A year later Mr Andreessen joined up with Jim Clark, a wealthy computer industry entrepreneur, to launch Netscape and jump-start the Internet industry software market.'

Source: © The Economist, London (25 May 1996)

Marketing communications on the Internet and the World Wide Web

Keeler (1995) has suggested that the marketing uses of the Internet are fivefold:

Sending messages (email)

One of the primary functions of the Internet is to act as a worldwide exchange or clearing house for electronic mail, or email. The Internet itself does not offer email functionality but acts rather like a post office service for delivering email from one part of the world to another. Email is the most basic and widely used facility on the Internet and allows not only communication on a one-to-one basis but also messages to be sent to myriad addresses at the touch of a keypad. As an added valuable resource, mailing list services are available which compile the email addresses of those who have subscribed to particular interest groups. An email can then simply be sent to the mailing list service and the message is then sent automatically to all the subscribers. This acts rather like direct mail. A list of mailing lists can be located at: http://catalog.com/vivian/interest-group-search.html.

Transferring files

Using programs based on the File Transfer Protocol (FTP), computer files can be transferred from one computer to another across the Internet. This can be a valuable feature for connecting parts of the same organisation, or for linking companies to suppliers or customers.

Monitoring news and opinions

The Internet is used for online discussion and interaction through Bulletin Board Services (BBS) and other discussion groups. Again, this can be a valuable feature in communicating with a variety of marketing communication target audiences. Newsgroups are user groups placed into subject and interest categories. Unlike email, messages are added to the Internet which have to be read via 'newsreader' software. Discussion and

IN VIEW 6.7

Mobile email

Accessing email remotely (away from your desk) is increasingly becoming important to the marketer. With a notebook computer and a GPRS (General Packet Radio Service) mobile phone, you can surf the Internet and access your email wirelessly from anywhere your mobile can get a signal at speeds similar to those on a standard 56k modem. Some devices combine the functionality of a mobile phone and palmtop computer in one unit, like Nokia's 9210 Communicator or the Handspring Treo, both of which allow users to surf the web and access email, while also functioning as a regular mobile phone and personal organizer. For larger companies, the Blackberry is a device designed to allow multiple users to access corporate email accounts.

Source: Marketing Business, July/August 2002f, p. 37

chat rooms facilitate the ability for consumers to communicate with each other online (referred to as '*word-of-mouse*'). This is the equivalent of the verbal word-of-mouth phenomenon discussed in traditional marketing communication models.

Searching and browsing

A very large amount of digitised information ranging from books, periodicals, reference works and government publications is available through the Internet. It is only with the ongoing development of searching protocols that the vastness of the Internet can be appreciated. One of the criticisms has been the difficulty some people have in finding the information they require in an efficient manner.

Posting, hosting and presenting information

Company reports, marketing communication messages and information can be posted to a named site on the Internet for others to view.

Keeler's original five uses can be expanded and made more specific when including the World Wide Web elements of the Internet which have grown so strongly since his original publication.

Advertising

Advertising can take a number of forms on the Internet and these are described in Chapter 26. The multimedia capabilities of the Web allow advertisers to use colour, graphics, movement, video and sound. Advertising can also be carried out, somewhat strangely, via radio on the Web. For example, Virgin's website allows users to listen to Virgin Radio, the first European radio station to broadcast live on the Internet (Vadon 1996). Limitations tend to be technical ones to avoid slow response times but this is becoming much less of a problem. The colours often used tend to be garish, again for technical reasons, but advances in technology will overcome these limitations too. The Web can be a cheap means of getting an advertising message across to a large number of people whether on your own website or through advertising on others' sites. Small

IN VIEW 6.8

Business use of WWW

A European survey of 5000 retailers, banks and commercial organisations revealed that 'information gathering' was the most significant use of the Web. This emphasises the way in which the Web is proactively used for searching for information. This feature highlights one major benefit of using the Internet as a marketing communications medium – Internet users actively seek out information that is relevant to their needs and interests. While the survey was specifically of business users, it is likely that a similar situation pertains to domestic, consumer users.

The second largest use was cited as collaborating with other organisations. Marketing, customer service, information publishing, selling products and services and purchasing products and services were the other major categories cited. Not surprisingly, marketing ranked highly with just under half suggesting that this was its most significant purpose.

IN VIEW 6.9

The Internet improves on direct mail

Much advertising is said to be wasted. Many years ago, Lord Leverhume was quoted as commenting that as much as half his advertising was a waste; the problem was, he did not know which half. Likewise, some direct mail has been criticised as being junk mail, not reaching the right people with the information and the offers that are of interest to them.

Companies are now turning to the Internet as a means of combining elements of both advertising and direct mail. They claim it is more relevant to the viewer through improved targeting and is more cost effective than traditional direct mail.

'Juno Online ... is offering free email access to anybody in America with a personal computer and a modem. In exchange, subscribers part with their demographic details – and put up with advertisements in the corner of their computer screens. Because subscribers know that they will receive advertising anyway, they have a strong interest in describing themselves to Juno as accurately as possible. Unlike direct mail, which may go unopened and unread, advertising on Juno is paid for only when the recipient gets it. And there is a cost saving: Juno, and FreeMark Communications, which launches a rival free email service on May 6th, both reckon they will be around eight times cheaper than direct mail, while offering advertising that consumers are likely to respond to.'

Source: © *The Economist*, London (27 April 1996)

businesses, for example, can advertise to a potential market of millions for less than the cost of a single-page advertisement in most magazines (Kehoe 1995). The World Wide Web does not permit targeting as such, other than through the selection of which websites to use for advertising purposes. It is the users' self-selection of sites that creates the targeting process – Internet users will view those sites that are of interest to them as they 'surf the Net'.

Public relations and sponsorship

The Web is being used more and more for a variety of public relations functions such as the posting of notices on new products, company reports, financial and performance data, monitoring newsgroups for coverage and opinions on companies and brands, and the distribution of press releases. Most companies who distribute press releases on the Web will archive these releases and other promotional articles so that users can access them easily again. Web 'press kits' can be provided, packed with material for use by journalists and for distributor promotions. For example, this was done successfully by the film company, Buena Vista, when first releasing their film, 'Starship Trouper'. Other organisations sponsor web pages and use the Web for sponsoring conferences, industry and sporting events and publications.

Sales promotions

Sales promotion devices such as competitions and couponing are being used in web pages to aid sales and encourage involvement and repeated access (i.e. increase page traffic). Company and brand literature, advertising and packaging frequently include web addresses and invite users to visit and use websites as an extension of the company's marketing communications. Many sites invite users to leave their names and addresses perhaps as part of a competition entry. These can then be used for database development, targeted promotions and special offers.

Direct sales

Despite lingering concerns about security, the Web is being used more and more for distributing product information and online ordering. For example, Allied Dunbar became the first UK insurance company to put interactive quotations on the Internet in 1995 (Kelly 1996). Computer hardware and software, books, music and vacation/travel-related items are the biggest sellers on the Web. Amazon has become an extremely large and profitable company by selling books on a global scale over the Internet. It is possible to use the Internet to compare products and prices and select the best. There are even software programs known as 'intelligent agents' that can be used to search for the best deals. While this is potentially good for the customer, it may commoditise the market for sellers.

NEED TO KNOW

☑ *The interactive nature of the Internet creates opportunities for data to be gathered on Internet users. This data can be used for further promotional and marketing activities.*

Exhibitions

Although this application of the Internet may not be the most obvious, virtual exhibitions are an interesting development. They bring together customers, suppliers and competitors without the necessity of leaving the office or home and may, of course, be viewed at times most convenient to the user. Many industries rely very heavily on exhibitions as part of their promotional activity. The Internet creates the virtual exhibition at a fraction of the cost to all involved. It would not be wise to abandon traditional exhibitions at this stage, but the Internet provides a beneficial addition.

Marketing research

One of the more recent uses of the Web is for market research in the form of customer opinion surveys, product interest and reaction surveys, as well as experimental discussion or focus group activities. Some companies ask customers who visit their site for

IN VIEW 6.10

Online purchasing by the grey market

The 'grey' market (variously defined as 45+ and 50+) are at the heart of the increase in online travel purchases. The 50+ segment is the fastest-growing group on the Web and is predicted to be the largest by 2005 in the UK. (They are already the largest user group in Sweden.) Marketers can take advantage of the unique niche marketing capabilities of the Internet. Says one travel operator, 'Marketing in an environment where the other groups won't see the message is an ideal situation'. Observers of the so-called 'silver surfer' market have noted that older users, with fewer time constraints, surf more frequently and spend longer online. As a result, they enter a phase which Forrester Research has called 'hyper-speed learning'. This can enable users to master online activities – like booking travel – three times faster than the average user.

Source: Marketing Business, February 2003a, p. 26

personal details which can then be used for profiling purposes, direct marketing and for polling customer opinion.

Developing closer links with customers and other target groups

The Web can allow companies to gather better information about their customers and other target groups and to strengthen their relationship with them. This is particularly possible with the introduction of intranet facilities (see below). Holiday Inn allows direct booking for its hotels and VISA provides information to help their card customers find the nearest ATM cash machine. General Motors allows customers to design their own cars on the Internet and Guinness received an extraordinary **hit-rate** on its website by allowing visitors to download a PC screensaver that was based on its very successful television advertising campaign. Other companies such as SAP and Microsoft are using the Web as a means of providing online customer service and helpdesk support. For example, SAP has a free online database of past problems with its software and solutions which customers can search to see if they can find a match with their own problems.

Intranets and extranets

Intra- and extranets are particular uses of the Internet which take advantage of the Internet's international linking of computers and network. They are closed user groups or private networks to which only specific users can gain access. An organisation may set up one or more **intranets** essentially as an internal facility to improve communications among staff locally, nationally and internationally. Information of all types can be shared from internal telephone directories to details of the latest product launch with the added advantage that it can be updated continuously and can facilitate interactive, two-way communication.

The so-called **extranet** is a particular application of the intranet that includes nominated users outside the organisation while still preventing open access to all Internet users. An organisation might set up one or more extranets to include current and potential suppliers, shareholders and customers. Access to the information can be limited and focused to suit the specific user group. In this way, it becomes an extremely powerful communication medium that greatly enhances the organisation's relationships with its stakeholder groups. It is even possible to create 'virtual commu-

Hit rate

Term used to describe the number of times a web page or site is visited.

Intranet

Closed or private network on the Internet to which only specific users. internal to an organisation, can gain access.

Extranet

Application of an intranet that permits access to specific users outside an organisation's normal intranet while still preventing access by the general public.

IN VIEW 6.11

Pinpoint the parcel

In the brief annals of doing business on the Internet, Federal Express's customer website has become a legendary success story. The package delivery giant, which moves 2.4 million pieces every day, put up a server in 1994 on the World Wide Web that gave customers a direct window into FedEx's package-tracking database. By letting 12,000 customers a day click their way through web pages to pinpoint their parcels – instead of asking a human operator to do it for them – FedEx was soon saving up to $2 million a year by some estimates.

Source: Business Week (26 February 1996)

nities' by allowing users of an extranet to communicate directly with each other. Successful examples include pop group and soccer fan clubs, and business software customer groups.

Potential pitfalls of the net and the Web

Despite their undoubted potential, marketers should also be aware of the pitfalls of the Internet and the World Wide Web as a marketing communication medium. While these are potential disadvantages, many of them can be overcome with good planning and management. These include:

Poor targeting capabilities

The potential audience may be large but the customer has to search out the company's website. As more and more companies and individuals advertise on the Internet, the problem of standing out amid the clutter will pose major challenges to organisations. However, as has already been identified earlier, the fact that the user is proactively surfing the Internet can be a positive advantage.

Cost

While web pages can be extremely cost efficient and effective, the actual cost of developing a home page that is kept updated and that offers good design, good functionality and which will stand out from among the tens of thousands of others can be high. The content needs to be appropriate and well presented and the search engine and database structure needs to be flexible and intuitive to make its access quick and easy to use. Research by Hamlin Harkins for the WebSite Internet Consultancy suggested that UK companies are spending an average of nearly £23,000 a year on their sites and that this is likely to increase to around £56,000 a year (Oldroyd 1996).

Just as PR is considered, incorrectly, by many as free, so too, the use of the Web for marketing communications should not be considered free.

Cost can also be an issue to users. The more time spent on the Internet, the more cost is incurred in telephone charges. However, this may not be a problem for much longer as it is predicted that telephone charges will be reduced and probably dropped altogether.

Incompatible marketing messages

Websites are often created by the IT departments rather than the marketing departments. Poor internal communications can lead to inconsistent messages being put out by the different parts of the organisation. Provided that the marketing communications are integrated this would not be a problem.

Immaturity of the Internet medium

The Internet and, in particular, the Web, has undoubted marketing potential, but it will not become a mature, reliable and secure medium for some years to come. At present, it is surfed by a large number of early adopters across the world, but until the speed and the reliability of the service and the penetration of the medium are improved, it will not be embraced by the mass market (Hewson 1996).

Conservative nature of customers

This applies not so much to the viewing of the Internet as to its use for completing financial transactions. Research indicates that worries over security are a major stumbling block.

Communications speed

Limitations in communications speed are technical considerations that will lessen in impact over time. Realistically, multimedia communications need a bandwidth of at least two million bits per second (Manchester 1995) yet current modem technology falls well short of this. This has a significant impact on the design of web pages and their speed of use. More sophisticated multimedia elements can make for very effective pages but can slow down their use to such an extent that users will not want to visit them. BT and cable companies are addressing this problem and in 1999 started offering services that they claimed could speed up the process more than 100 times compared to typical modems.

Search difficulties

Especially for casual users, searching for particular information or web pages can be difficult, time-consuming and frustrating.

Digital and interactive television

Television as we generally tend to know it has relied on analogue transmission and is not interactive. Digital transmission, which is being introduced around the world, is opening up new possibilities and a significantly increased number of channels. The marketing communications potential is enormous and represents a television technological revolution that the general population seems to be taking in its stride. The new digital transmissions can be received by satellite or through existing aerials and can be received either by new digital televisions or by adding a special decoder to existing sets.

But the television is basically a 'dumb' machine that is only capable of receiving information, not transmitting information. Interactive television is a very different concept as it allows the viewer to send signals back to the service provider. Interactivity on a mass market scale is being facilitated through the technological developments of satellite, cable, optical fibres and digital transmissions. Just as the opening up of the Internet has resulted in a major shift in the use of PCs for communications, so, too, the advent of interactive TV is predicted to have an enormous impact, particularly for services such as:

● video-on-demand
● home shopping services and
● home banking services.

The likely impact is considered to be so great because the market penetration is so much higher for televisions than it is for PCs. Although the availability of interactive TV is still limited, this is set to change in the not-too-distant future with the increased introduction of digital channels and the coming together of computing, television and telecommunication technologies. This will result in a blurring of the distinctions between the PC, the TV and (through modems) telephone communication.

Video-on-demand is an interactive facility that would provide customers with instantaneous access to a particular movie (and the advertising that would accompany it). Despite numerous trials around the world, video-on-demand is unlikely to become a reality in Europe for many years yet. A cheaper and easier service to deliver is 'near video-on-demand' which has already been adopted by some satellite television companies. Near video-on-demand will play the same movie on different channels, but starting 15 or 30 minutes apart.

Most people are already familiar with the concept of *home shopping* through the shopping channels that are available from some cable television services. However, the home shopping service that is currently offered is very inflexible. The viewer can only react to a particular advertisement or offer by phoning a number displayed on the screen. Home shopping through interactive TV offers greater opportunities for the viewer and for the marketer. For example, by scrolling through online catalogues, interactive TV will allow viewers to choose the products they are interested in and request more detailed information if so wished. It allows many more products to be offered and for viewers only to select those of relevance. Technologists are already experimenting with virtual shops that shoppers can visually 'walk around'.

According to a MORI poll in 1994, one in five people would use *home banking* (Whitmore and Jones 1994) although most commentators believe this figure will rise as facilities become available and people become more used to the technology. Denmark's Lan & Spar Bank became Scandinavia's first financial services company to offer home banking to its customers in 1994. Within two years, 10% of its customer base were using the service. There are now few financial service providers who do not use some form of telecommunication banking facility. Some, such as Abbey National which made an announcement in mid-1999, are actively trying to discourage customers from using traditional high street services by charging fees for some over-the-counter transactions.

Interactive television is the subject of massive investment by the major telecommunications and entertainment companies. To date, only a few countries have moved

IN VIEW 6.12

Your cheque is in the (e)mail

Financial services provider Egg has launched 'Egg Pay' which allows customers to digitally transfer money, up to the value of £200, via email to any of the UK's 110 million bank accounts. Latest research from Egg and MORI shows that a third of all British adults – some 14 million people – say they are interested in digital payment services. Email usage has increased exponentially since the 1990s with some 20 million British adults now using email, whilst cheque usage has seen a 34% decline since 1990.

Money can be sent to anyone with an email address and a UK bank account. There is no need to register for Egg Pay to receive a payment. 'British people's love of the cheque-book has failed in recent years. Consumers seem to be finding more convenient methods of payment, which fit into their busy lifestyles', comments Patrick Muir, Director of Marketing, Egg UK.

Source: *Marketing Business*, June 2002c, p. 7

interactive TV beyond the trial stage and it is likely to take more time for these technologies to mature than many people originally thought (*The Economist* 1995).

The UK is believed to be as advanced as any other country. NatWest Bank and BT started the UK's move into interactive television in 1995 when it rolled out a trial home banking service to 250 homes in the Cambridge area in conjunction with local cable television companies. Other services provided in the Cambridge trial included home shopping and video-on-demand (Andersen Consulting 1996).

Similar trials have been conducted all over Europe. In the Netherlands, a joint-venture organisation has been set up between Philips and KPN that has already finished trials of an interactive television service. Deutsche Telecom, which has a near monopoly of the German cable market, has a range of trials underway in Berlin, Hamburg, Cologne, Nuremberg, Leipzig and Stuttgart. Elsewhere, Hong Kong Telecom and Singapore Telecom are involved in similar ventures in the Far East, while Telcom Australia and News Corporation are testing various services in Canberra. In Belgium, the national operator, Belgacom, is running a video-on-demand trial.

The main issue for companies to address is whether to access homes via telephone or cable. Many companies have an optical-fibre network linking into customers' homes. The amount of data and the breadth of services that they can deliver is so much greater than the service available across a telephone network. However, in the UK for example, BT's telephone network covers the entire country, whereas a home shopping service via cable would require the agreement of many cable companies.

CD-ROM/DVD

CD-ROM stands for computer disk-read only memory. Like DVD (digital video disk), it is a thin plastic disk covered with a coating onto which digital data has been encoded. It is sometimes referred to as an optical storage medium, because it uses a laser beam of light to pick up the digital information from a track that has been etched into the disk. A single CD-ROM can hold 540 megabytes of data, which is roughly equivalent to all 20 volumes of the *Oxford English Dictionary* or half a million pages of text, making it a very efficient means of storing data. The latest technology that is now available uses DVD drives and disks; these are able to store and retrieve even more data so that it is possible to view an entire feature-length movie from disk. Also available in the high street are read-write CDs and DVDs and hardware so that it is now possible to record your own information on CDs and DVDs.

Permission marketing

Permission marketing

Any marketing communications that offer opt-in or opt-out opportunities to recipients so that further marketing communications are only received by those who wish to receive future emails.

Much of the e-media that have been described above is based on the concept of **permission marketing.** That is the use of a respondent 'opt-in' clause as opposed to 'opt-out' at the point of data collection. This technique establishes a relationship between the marketer and the recipient of the marketing communication by empowering consumers in the sense they will only receive communications they have actively requested. Permission-based email marketing, for example, includes an unsubscribe option with every email whereby the recipient can easily turn unwanted emails off. This is particularly pertinent in light of electoral roll results where 24.3% of UK adults have opted out of having their data used for commercial purposes (*Marketing Business*

2003a). Opt-in is compulsory for SMS (short messaging service) text marketing as outlined in EU regulations. Interactive campaigns that recipients have opted into have had a positive response. In research of 705 respondents in the UK, Italy and Germany, 43% of respondents said they felt that the campaigns they received via SMS have a positive impact on the advertised brand, with only 7% having a negative opinion; 68% of respondents would most likely or definitely recommend that friends receive such messages and 43% said they would be likely to respond by viewing an ad or visiting the website (*Marketing Business* 2002a, p. 35).

Summary

E-media includes any digital, interactive or online communications such as digital and interactive TV (and radio), the Internet, teletext and videotext, the use of CD-ROMs/DVDs and multimedia applications. E-media are being heralded as a media revolution facilitated by advances in technology and the increasing acceptance of that technology by businesses and the market. The use of the e-media for marketing and marketing communications purposes is frequently referred to as cybermarketing. Cybermarketing can take advantage of much greater direct communications with customers and direct marketing opportunities.

The Internet is a significant part of the new media revolution and is growing at a phenomenal rate. The prediction has to be that it will increasingly become part of all our daily lives and will have a huge impact on our very behaviour. It offers many opportunities, not just advertising, for marketing communicators. The digitisation of telecommunication transmissions for television, in particular, is resulting in larger numbers of channels and interactivity. As with the Internet, these developments are having a substantial effect on marketing communications. Over time, it is likely that many of these developments will merge so that the distinction between them will blur. The television will also be a computer and a communications centre. Information and communications will be accessible online and with CD-ROMs and DVDs, offline. The ability to compact and store vast amounts of digitised data will facilitate multimedia applications that will bring marketing communications to 'life'.

Self-review questions

1 What are the advantages of marketing products on the Internet and the World Wide Web (a) to business, (b) to customers?

2 What is meant by cybermarketing?

3 What is meant by multimedia?

4 What is the benefit of the use of hypertext links?

5 Identify some of the main uses of the Internet for marketing communication purposes.

6 What are intranets and extranets and why might these be particularly useful for marketing communications?

7 What are the main pitfalls or limitations of the Internet and the World Wide Web for marketing communications? Do you think these limitations will continue to be as restrictive in the future?

8 Describe the impact of digital television for marketing and marketing communications.

Project

Spend some time surfing the Internet and the World Wide Web. As you do so, pay particular attention to the way in which different web pages are designed and how well they make use of hypertext links and page layout. Contrast the websites of different organisations and assess their communications impact. What features seem to work best and which seem to hinder their use from a user's perspective? Identify the use of advertising within the pages and how the advertisements make use of hypertext links to move around the Web. What is the quality of their content and graphics? Consider the limitations imposed on the presentation of the advertising by the current technology.

If you have access to an intranet or an extranet (perhaps as a customer of a retailer operating on the Internet), assess how the net is used, what information it contains and the opportunities it affords for marketing communications purposes.

References

Andersen Consulting (1996), *List of Interactive Trials in the World*. Andersen Consulting.

Cane, A. (1996), Barclays unveils share dealing by video link. *Financial Times*, 4 January.

Client Focus Systems (1996), *Interactive Dealing Service Set Up*. Client Focus Systems, February.

The Economist (1995), Multimedia's no-man's land. *The Economist*, 22 July.

The Economist (1996), The internet improves on direct mail. *The Economist*, 27 April.

The Economist (1996), A survey of the software industry. *The Economist*, 25 May.

Faughan, L. (1996), And now the Internet. *Business and Finance*, 26 May.

Gareiss, R. (1995), The Online Corporation: choosing the right internet service provider. *Data Communications*, 21 November.

Green, H. (1996), AOL in line for on-line service monopoly. *Sunday Business*, 2 June.

Hewson, D. (1996), You'll drop before you shop on the Net. *Sunday Times*, 16 June.

Keeler, L. (1995), *Cybermarketing*. New York: Amacom.

Kehoe, L. (1995), Internet brings global network to the home office. *Financial Times*, 6 December.

Kelly, S. (1996), Ringing in the changes. *Computer Weekly*, 30 May.

Lambeth, J. (1996), Business fails to make net profit. *Computer Weekly*, 18 July, 8.

Manchester, P. (1995), New way to sell cars. *Financial Times*, 7 June.

Marketing Business (2002a) RU ready to buy? June, 35.

Marketing Business (2002b) Latin spirit. June, p. 11.

Marketing Business (2002c) Your cheque is in the (e)mail. June, 7.

Marketing Business (2002d) Terminology confusion. June, 8.

Marketing Business (2002e) Wish you were here. July/August, 26–27.

Marketing Business (2002f) Getting away from it all. July/August, 37.

Marketing Business (2003a) 10 million tick electoral roll opt-out box. February, 6.

Marketing Business (2003b) Put your website on the map. March, 21–25.

New PHD (1998), The competitive media environment. Presentation given to the *IPA Academia Workshop*, September.

Oldroyd, R. (1996), Web entrants getting little return on outlay. *Sunday Business Computer Age*, 12 May.

Ryan, M. (1995), *The Power of Multimedia in Financial Services*. Newsletter Andersen Consulting, Dublin, Summer.

Vadon, R. (1996), A radio renaissance worldwide. *Financial Times*, 8 July.

van Oosterom, J. (1996), A helicopter view of the new media. *ADMAP*, February, 32–35.

Whitmore, A. and Jones, L. (1994), *Consumers' Attitudes to Home Finance and Technology*. ICL Financial Services and MORI, July.

Selected further reading

Brock, T. (1999), Cybersense. *Washington Business Journal*, 2 May.

Ellesworth, J.H. and Ellesworth, M.V. (1995), *Marketing on the Internet*. Wiley.

Hoffman, D. and Novak, T. (1996), 'Marketing in hypermedia computer-mediated environments: conceptual foundations. *Journal of Marketing*, 60 (July), 50–68.

Peters, L. (1998), The new interactive media: one-to-one but to whom? *Marketing Intelligence and Planning*, 16 (1), 22–30.

Whitehorn, A. (ed.) (1996), *Multimedia: The Complete Guide*. Dorling Kindersley.

Chapter 7

The changing marketing communications environment

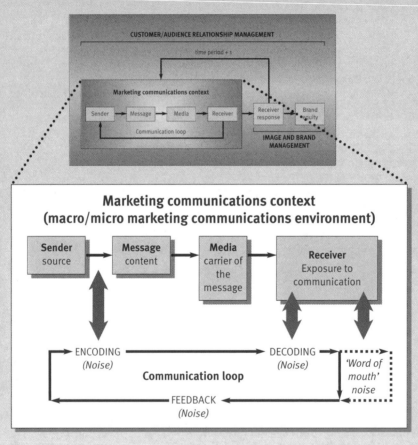

The IMC Process Model

CD

Use PRESTCOM to analyse Concern's environment. What do you consider to be the most critical environmental factors for Concern? Who would you define as Concern's competitors? How would you describe the market that Concern is operating in?

Professional perspective

Derek Morris Managing Partner, Unity

The world is changing as new technology completely transforms the way that people are connected. 'Communications' is no longer a part of the economy, it *is* the economy. Its impact will change the way we live and act at a fundamental level; and it will certainly change the way that the marketing communications industry will have to behave.

There are more media, consumed in more ways, by more people than ever before. There are more brands, doing more things, in more places than ever before. There is the same amount of money, in the same pockets, to be spent in the same time as before. The net result of this is that the paradigms of business will be fundamentally rewritten. The life cycles of companies and the way they behave will be drastically altered.

The new e-economy will herald a fundamental change in the power of the consumer. In the past, consumers had little media choice and little control over their media: it was a matter of chance if one's marketing communications hit roughly the right people. The media planner's job was to find ways that

➜

slightly improved the chance that such a hit would be made. But in the very close future this will all change. The viewers will be in control; they will be able to choose if they want to see your marketing communication and at what level they wish to engage with it. So, instead of us beaming ads at them, they will be in charge of calling down information.

It is easy to see that the e-revolution will elevate the role of marketing to a new level within companies. New technology will put the consumer right in your face. It will force a new kind of transparency to company offerings. This will demand a big attitudinal shift in the marketing profession. An understanding of the environmental factors affecting this New World, such as those described in this chapter, and their impact on the marketing communications of the twenty-first century, will be a necessary starting point for all those embarking on a career in the marketing communications industry.

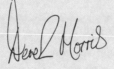

The macro- and micro-environment – the context of marketing communications

Organisations need to adapt constantly in response to never-ending environmental change. The investigation and analysis of the environment is fundamental to organisational well-being because of the way every part of the organisation's operations are affected.

We can see from our integrated marketing communications process model, which forms the basis for this section of the book, that the environment provides the *context* in which *all* marketing communications (and business activities in general) take place. It is this environment which has shaped the marketing communications industry and its operations as we know them today.

Most marketing textbooks emphasise the environment in its widest sense – that is, at its *macro* level. However, for our purposes in marketing communications, we need to recognise not only **macro-environmental** factors but also those which function at the *micro* marketing communications level. This then provides the *total* context in which marketing communications occur. At the marketing communications macro level there are both *internal* and *external* factors to be considered. The distinction between the two is self-explanatory. Internal factors are those related to internal organisational, operational, managerial and resource issues; external factors are those outside the boundary of the organisation and are not usually subject to its direct control (although organisations may seek to influence some of them through indirect means).

Macro-environment

The marketing communications macro-environment is the wider environment in which the organisation operates. It includes both internal and external factors that affect the organisation.

To avoid unnecessary confusion, readers should be aware that the terms 'macro-environment' and 'micro-environment' in the context of marketing communications are similar, but not identical to the use of these terms in a wider business and marketing context. Economists, in particular, use both terms to represent a business's external environment. The reason for this is that the unit of analysis is the whole business. In the

Micro-environment

The marketing communications micro-environment is the immediate environment or surroundings in which marketing communications occur.

PRESTCOM

An extended environmental and organisational analysis framework representing the Political environment, the Regulatory environment, the Economic environment, the Social environment, the Technological environment, the Competitive environment, the Organisational environment, and the Market environment.

SWOT

Organisational analysis framework representing organisational Strengths, Weaknesses, Opportunities and Threats.

case of marketing communications, the units of analysis are very much more specific: they are the items of communications themselves. Macro-environmental factors are, thus, all those outside the immediate context of the marketing communications themselves in just the same way that economists view the business macro-environment as those factors outside the immediate context of the business.

In the context of marketing communications, **micro-environmental** factors relate to the media context in which any form of promotion appears; they are those elements which 'surround' the piece of promotion. In a similar way, economists view the micro-environment of a business as those factors that immediately surround the business. The micro-environment of a piece of promotion may be the editorial content of a newspaper, other pieces of mail which arrive at the same time as a leaflet drop, other products placed next to a shelf display in a supermarket, other stands at an exhibition, programmes which come before and after the commercial break on television, and many other examples. The micro-environment has a major impact upon the effectiveness of marketing communications and is considered later in this chapter.

Looking at the macro-environment first, Exhibit 7.1 illustrates an overview of the external *and* internal groups that affect the organisation's marketing communications. As shown, there are many groups that can have an impact and these can be both domestic and international. External to the organisation there are groups from within the 'competitive and market environment' and these include the obvious ones such as customers and competitors. There are other interest groups such as shareholders and the City and these are referred to in the figure as 'other publics and external stakeholders'. And there are those related to the operations of the 'marketing communications industry' itself which act as facilitators and regulators of marketing communications activities. Internal to the organisation are all the staff who run the operations and manage the organisation in all of its various departments. As individuals and groups they are the internal stakeholders.

An understanding of the workings of the macro-environment can be undertaken through **PRESTCOM** and **SWOT** analysis, which are briefly described below. This analysis (or at least those elements which impact upon marketing communications) forms part of the first tasks in the Integrated Marketing Communications RABOSTIC Planning Model, which is covered in detail in Part 2 of this book.

Analysis of the macro-environment

PEST

Environmental analysis framework representing the Political environment, the Economic environment, the Social environment, and the Technological environment.

Many authors recommend the use of a **PEST** analysis as a means of breaking down the macro-environment into its component parts. The letters are an acronym for **P**olitical, **R**egulatory, **E**conomic, **S**ocial and **T**echnological environmental factors. Most general marketing textbooks cover these areas in some detail and further recommend that SWOT (Strengths, Weaknesses, Opportunities and Threats) analysis is carried out to improve the analytical process by developing a deeper understanding of the environmental impact upon the organisation. Strengths and weaknesses relate to internal

Exhibit 7.1 The marketing communications *macro*-environment

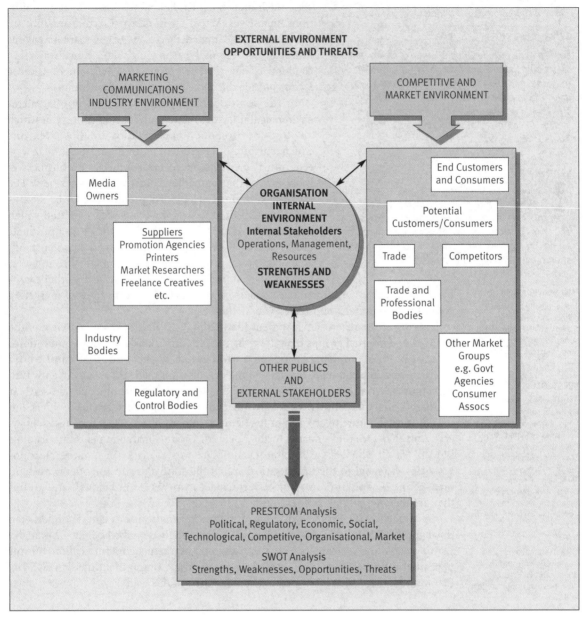

factors and opportunities and threats relate to external factors. References such as Greenley (1989), McDonald (1991), Johnson and Scholes (2002), Brassington and Pettitt (2003), Wilson and Gilligan (1997), Kotler et al. (1999) and many others provide further descriptions of these aspects and are recommended for further reading. A critical commentary of SWOT analysis can be found in Pickton and Wright (1998).

An area that is often less well reported is that of legal or **R**egulatory control. This is a significant 'environmental area' in marketing communications and includes both legislation and self-regulation issues. To make the macro-environmental analysis complete, other areas that should also be highlighted for inclusion are analyses of the

Exhibit 7.2 The relationship between PEST, PRESTCOM and SWOT

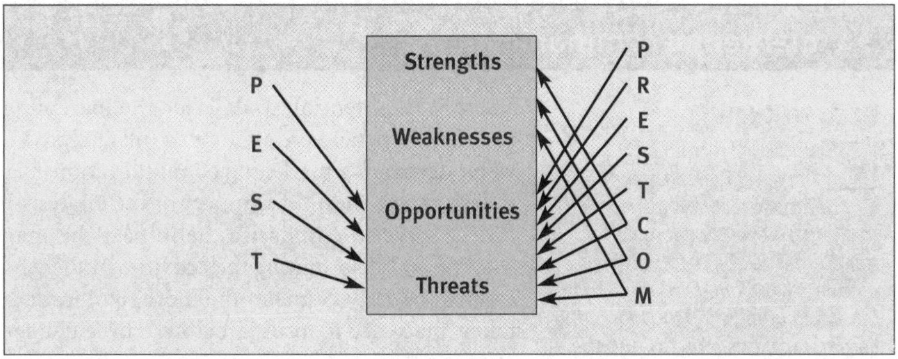

Competition, the **O**rganisation itself, and the **M**arket. By adding these we can create a new acronym 'PRESTCOM' to identify the full array of macro-environmental factors which should be analysed when developing marketing communication plans.

Competition is clearly an important area to consider in any business planning activity. Identifying competitors and their brands, and understanding (and predicting) their behaviour should be high on any list of priorities. The organisation's own strengths and weaknesses should be assessed in relation to those of the competition. Analysis of the **O**rganisation should include any and all factors that are likely to influence marketing communications efforts and effectiveness. This should include the people involved throughout the organisation and the systems and structures it uses to facilitate marketing communications. The Gas-Co case in Chapter 19 is a good illustration of what can go wrong within the organisation if internal communications are not integrated. The PEST acronym does not include an evaluation of the organisation and, as such, overlooks the dimension of organisational strengths and weaknesses. **M**arket, as the final category within PRESTCOM, concerns analysis of customers, consumers, intermediaries, suppliers, and any other relevant market influencers. Again, this analysis can be related back to the organisation's own strengths and weaknesses, as Exhibit 7.2 illustrates. What details to include within a comprehensive PRESTCOM analysis is something that is improved with experience. The challenge is to identify all relevant details without overburdening the analysis with irrelevant or insignificant issues. This analysis and the SWOT analysis that follows will be different for every company, even those operating in the same marketplace. The importance of this process cannot be overstated and companies may carry out these activities in a variety of ways. The particular staff involved, their range of responsibilities, whether outside agencies are included in the process, the level of detailed information that is included, the use of internal databases and commissioned external research, etc., are all factors that will vary. The challenge is to identify all influential issues affecting marketing communications, predicting future outcomes and producing integrated plans that when implemented will meet the organisation's marketing communications objectives. Any reader uncertain of PEST/PRESTCOM and SWOT analysis is encouraged to study these areas further.

Overview of selected macro-environmental changes affecting marketing communications

There is no intention to describe the marketing communications environment in detail here although a full analysis of the environment is vital when developing marketing communications plans in which very specific investigation should form part of the analysis process. The details that follow serve to emphasise the impact the macro-environment has in shaping and determining the activities of the whole marketing communications industry. Some of the more significant general changes that have taken place are identified below. These changes have had a profound effect on business, marketing and marketing communications practices. They will continue to shape the relationships between organisations and their markets well into the future.

Computer technology – storage, analysis, retrieval, databases

There have been tremendous advances made in the development of computer technology. The pace of change in the computing industry has been increasing at an exponential rate. The impact this has had on business, education, leisure and home life is revolutionising our day-to-day living and working. Technological change has irrevocably changed the very fabric of society.

We have access to our money through high street automatic cash machines; we pass through supermarket checkouts with the flash of bar codes; we play sophisticated interactive games on our home computers; we can practically carry our office around in a laptop computer; holidays and flights can be booked at the touch of a button anywhere in the world; we can shop from the comfort of our armchairs; manufacturing processes have been 'robotised'; communications have been digitised. Advances in computing hardware and software have made all this and many more things possible.

In particular, huge strides have been made in the storage, analysis, and retrieval of vast amounts of data. This has led to the growth of database technology that is increasingly being used to collate information on customers and their buying behaviour. Armed with this information much more carefully targeted communications and improved customer relationships are possible. The growth and popularity of **geodemographic** systems based on whole population census data such as **MOSAIC** and **ACORN** (see Chapter 17) are good examples of what is now possible through the use of computers which, not many years ago, would have been unthinkable in commercial settings.

Geodemographic segmentation

Method of segmenting the market based on the classification of small geographic areas (enumeration districts) according to the characteristics of their inhabitants – principally house types and house locations.

MOSAIC and ACORN

Two commercially available geodemographic systems.

Not only has there been a growth in information providers such as Experian, Claritas, Carat, CACI and very many more, but increasing computing power at decreasing cost has permitted individual companies to develop their own marketing information and database systems. Increasingly, these systems are not stand-alone but are being networked to deliver even more powerful marketing information.

Communications technology – international telecommunications, satellite, cable, Internet/new media

Communications technology has developed alongside increases in computing power. Satellite dishes can be seen from rooftops while cable companies dig up roads and pavements as they lay new optic fibre two-way communications cables. Telephone

Broadcast

Widely and publicly available radio and television transmissions.

Narrowcast

Restricted radio, television, video and audio transmission.

Internet

Collection of globally interrelated computer networks that facilitate computer communications.

World Wide Web

Huge collection of documents and files available through the Internet.

Banner advertisement

Type of advertisement often appearing as a banner across the whole or part of the width of a web page.

Web pages

A web page is like a file available through the World Wide Web, typically containing text, images and links to other pages. An organisation's website is likely to contain a collection of web pages, each with its own file reference (html address).

Viral marketing

Email promotion that encourages recipients to pass on what they have received to others who they think will be interested.

Permission marketing

Narrowly, email promotions that offer opt-in or opt-out opportunities to recipients so that further marketing communications are only received by those who wish to receive future emails. More broadly, it relates to any marketing communications (e.g. direct mail) that offer opt-in and opt-out options.

Spam emails

Emails containing general information sent to a wider audience who have not requested the email (typically based on an email list, perhaps bought from a list broker or another company).

Ambient media

Less usual external media, such as laser projections, or the use of fields into which messages are cut.

companies, mobile and fixed, proliferate their international communications coverage. Phenomenal growth can be seen in terrestrial, cable and satellite **broadcast** and **narrowcast** transmission.

The Internet is a remarkable innovation that is revolutionising personal and business communications. It is a new and exciting medium for marketing communications developed out of new technology. The boundaries of the **Internet** and the **World Wide Web** are constantly being pushed forward as companies experiment with this new communications and marketing channel. Any individual, small business or organisation can transmit and receive messages on the Internet. It can be used for information, promotion and sales. Many businesses have extended their marketing communications by developing their own Internet sites. Guinness, for example, extended its 'Anticipation' campaign by including a downloadable screensaver featuring footage from its advertisement on its World Wide Web site.

Many other companies produce **'banner' advertising** on other companies' **web pages**. Yet others run special competitions to encourage greater involvement with their viewers while at the same time promoting their products. Some use it as their only means of promotion and sales; successes have been reported in the sales of books and records in just this way.

Melita have launched 'Web Contact', which facilitates connection of a company's website to its telephone call centre. Customers visiting the web page may simply point and click buttons requesting either an instantaneous call back or a scheduled call back at a time determined by the customer. The customer simply fills in some basic information on the computer screen and clicks on 'send'. When the call centre returns contact by telephone, the telesales agent's computer screen will automatically display the customer's details.

Growth in the use of email has created some interesting developments in marketing communications opportunities. Email may be described as electronic direct mail and may be delivered on a variety of devices such as the PC, iTV, WAP and the PDA. This has given rise to the development of **'viral marketing'** – email that is passed on from one recipient to another – and **'permission marketing'** – recipients agreeing to opt in to receive email promotions. Permission marketing seeks to reduce **spam emailing**. More information about e-media is given in Chapter 6.

Fragmentation of media

Not only is there a proliferation of new media such as the Internet and **ambient media** which increase media choice, but a significant fragmentation of traditional media is also occurring. Terrestrial television stations have increased in number. New technology, satellite and cable, now make it possible to receive tens of stations. In the future, it is predicted that we shall receive hundreds of stations each carrying their own advertising. Independent local and national radio stations have increased in number as their audiences increase and demand their own types of broadcast.

Press media have undergone major changes. New magazines and newspapers, both trade and consumer, come and go, each targeted towards its own specialist audience. Newsagent and supermarket shelves sag under the weight of new titles. Companies produce their own customer titles – in-flight, on-train, by store. *The M&S Magazine*, Sainsbury's *The Magazine*, *A Taste of Safeway* and *The Somerfield Magazine* now have among the highest levels of readership of all magazines in the UK and technology permits each issue of these magazines to be produced in many different versions to appeal to particular target sub-groups.

Cinema is once again becoming more popular. New themed and multipurpose cinema complexes are being developed to cater for a wider range of entertainment. As audience numbers increase so do the opportunities for advertising and merchandising.

Significantly, the media are appealing to more highly targeted segments of the market – particular age groups, lifestyles and hobbies, trade specialisms, special interest groups. Mass media, even TV, is giving way to targeted media. Fragmentation of the media, new and old, creates new opportunities and challenges for media planners.

Social change – demographics, lifestyles, attitudes, values, spending, expectations

The only thing certain about change is change itself. It will continue. But where should we start in documenting social change? It is such a huge topic. The social impact of changes in economics, politics, technology, sciences, medicines, etc. are so far-reaching that it is almost impossible to comprehend. And as people (and their relationships) change, so do the means and approaches used to communicate with them.

Demographic changes

Changes in basic population characteristics such as occur over time in social class constitution and age ranges.

Demographic changes (population restructuring) mean that we are seeing a rise in the importance of both younger markets *and* older markets. Younger people are exerting more of an influence on purchase behaviour at an earlier age and have more spending power than before. They are expressing their individuality in what they buy and which brands they support. More people are living to an older age. Their purchasing power has led to the identification of new target groups. Insurance companies, for example, now feature specific policies for the over-50s in their promotions.

Changing family units and a reappraisal of male and female roles have had a significant impact on family and personal life. This is being reflected in advertising featuring more men doing household chores and looking after babies while more women are portrayed in executive and 'high-powered' occupations outside the home. Values are being questioned. Attitudes and lifestyles are changing. In responding to change, society is creating and encouraging more change. It becomes a spiral that feeds on itself. Some would argue that change is for the better, some would take the opposite stance. What all this means for the marketing communications industry is a major challenge in keeping pace with the new realities, in maintaining credible communications with audiences who are talking 'new languages', and in generating new marketing communications priorities.

IN VIEW 7.1

Celebrating the grey market

The 'grey' market is a growing and increasingly profitable market area. Well known and lesser celebrities have all been used to promote and endorse products to the over-50s. Holidays, stair lifts, health and life insurance are all examples of products receiving the celebrity treatment. As people live longer and expect an improved quality of life we can expect more and more promotions focused towards the over-50s.

IN VIEW 7.2

The effect of environmental changes on Nike

Nike has been heralded as a major success story. First set up in 1972, by 1979 they had captured 50% of the US market for running shoes. By 1984, Nike's worldwide turnover had reached US $919.8 million (€852 million). By the late 1990s, revenues were at US $2 billion (€1.85 billion).

Nike traded on fashion trends for trainers. They developed their brand originally to appeal to young opinion leaders and then to the wider market. Over the years, they have appealed to older age groups. They were the brand with 'street credibility', the brand to be seen in, the brand that distinguished their wearers. It seemed as though they could not put a foot wrong. Nike went from strength to strength. Other brands attempted to follow in Nike's footsteps and many have been successful too, cashing in on a growing market developed out of an item of footwear which moved from practical sports shoe to fashion accessory and statement. As the market fragmented, so did Nike and the other companies. Trainers are now made for every occasion, sports and otherwise, each season bringing new styles and colours.

However, in 1998 the bubble burst, society and its markets moved on. Customers turned their interests elsewhere, sales dropped. Customers' growing concerns over Nike's use of labour in low-cost countries did not help. These issues together with internal problems led Nike to lay off thousands of workers as their output and profits declined. The business reality is that Nike flourished as they took advantage of market change and now they are forced to rethink as the markets change again.

Increased understanding and emphasis on market segmentation and targeting

At the same time that technological developments have made possible the ability to store and collate masses of consumer and customer information, companies have increasingly recognised the benefits of segmenting and targeting customers and users in order to undertake more direct and personal communication. In this regard, technology has favoured increased marketing development and sophistication. Mass marketing is giving way to more 'customised' marketing approaches even on international and global levels. The use of databases has facilitated target marketing activities and has resulted in a change of emphasis in the use of specific promotions/marketing communications elements. Mass marketing communications will still continue but may increasingly be used to support other more targeted efforts.

Changing role and expectations of marketing – relationship marketing; loyalty marketing; database marketing; greater marketing accountability; internal marketing

Internal organisational changes have had a profound effect on marketing activities in general. Structures have become flatter and many organisations have improved their customer focus. Although many textbooks on marketing tend to create the impression that marketing and its management are generally accepted as indispensable parts of

Relationship marketing

View that emphasises the importance of the relationships developed between an organisation and other parties including customers, partners, suppliers and the trade.

Loyalty marketing

Marketing activities intended to encourage customers to continue purchasing a particular product or purchasing from a particular supplier.

Database marketing

The use of accurate customer and prospect customer information, competitor information, market information and internal company information stored on a computer database to focus marketing activities towards targets.

Locus of power

The place where most power in a structure or system resides.

Push promotional strategy

The focusing of promotional effort by manufacturers or suppliers of goods and services to encourage the trade channel members to stock, promote and sell products.

Pull promotional strategy

The focusing of promotional effort to encourage end customers and consumers to demand goods and services.

Gross national product

Measure of a nation's output and wealth.

business life, vital to the well-being of the organisation, this view is not universally maintained or agreed in entirety. Many question the role of marketing within their organisations and criticise what some describe as marketing failures. The result has been to reorganise marketing effort with many of what some would say are indispensable marketing functions falling outside the remit of the marketing department. Customer services activities would be a good example of this. From a marketing communications point of view this can lead to a fragmentation of effort, a lack of integration and control and, in turn, less effective communications. Perhaps if marketing managers had recognised earlier the importance of internal audiences as part of their total marketing communications activities, if they had recognised the need to market themselves better internally, then their positions may well have been stronger.

Other changes, resulting from external pressures, have placed greater emphasis on the need to develop relationships and customer loyalty. **Relationship marketing** and **loyalty marketing** have become widely accepted terms in the marketing vocabulary. This change of focus has created new challenges for promotions and communications and, with the advent of **database marketing**, a new breed of marketing professionals are coming to the fore.

Industry structures – power of the retailer

The whole structure of industry is having a profound effect on organisational and marketing activity. Communications, computing and physical distribution technology are facilitating major changes in channels of distribution. Retailers, particularly in consumer goods areas, are experiencing a shift in the **locus of power** in their favour to the detriment of manufacturers. The retailers now 'call the shots'. This may be argued as a natural consequence of heightened customer power in which retailers are closer to the final customers and are, therefore, in a better position to meet their needs. At the same time, partially as a response to the shift in power and partly as technological developments allow, manufacturers are themselves 'getting closer to the customer' and choosing to do business direct. They are, in effect, becoming retailers. These represent important changes to the way in which marketing communications are being undertaken. They are having a significant impact on the relative emphasis placed on the elements of the marketing communications mix and the use of **push and pull promotional strategies** (see Chapter 19). These strategies refer to the way in which marketing communications are targeted at the trade as well as to customers and consumers.

Growth of service sector

Throughout the developed world the proportion of **gross national product** accounted for by manufacturing industry is declining. Emphasis is being placed in service sectors such as finance, insurance, tourism and leisure. The marketing of services compared with the marketing of goods create some very different challenges to marketing communications activities.

Manufacturing systems technology – mass production to mass customisation

New manufacturing systems and production techniques have revolutionised the mass production approach so favoured by Henry Ford who set the tone for manufacturing technology in the early part of the twentieth century. As we move into the twenty-first century, it is now possible to achieve economic production without the need for large-scale production runs. Again, this has been helped by computer technology and 'robotisation'. The result is a more varied product mix meeting the particular needs of more numerous target markets. As more organisations focus their efforts on more targets, marketing communications tasks correspondingly become more focused and demanding.

Changing national and international economies

This is a well-reported area on national and local news daily. Changes in the economic climate and economic performance result in major shifts in business activity and social welfare. The well-being of nation states is inextricably mixed with international economies. Taxes rise and fall. Disposable incomes vary. At times of boom, people spend on luxury items. At times of bust, the 'belt has to be tightened'. With international trade, the fortunes of all trading nations are affected. A strong currency leads to cheaper imports but can have catastrophic effects on local manufacture, employment and spending power as exports become too expensive for overseas markets.

As the sort of demographic changes identified earlier take effect, such as a growing elderly population, changes in the use of **disposable and discretionary income** can be observed. For example, greater amounts have to be set aside for such items as pensions and health care.

Shifts in economic activity can have unexpected effects. It appears that increasing numbers of higher earners, for example, are switching towards discount grocery retailers in order to release more of their money to spend on luxury items.

Disposable and discretionary incomes

The sums of money available to people to spend after other committed expenditure (e.g. mortgage and tax payments) has been paid.

International competition and markets – global brands

One of the major forces of economic and market activity over the last few decades has been the internationalisation of business and the increasing development of global brands. The marketing strategies of global brands have had a profound effect on marketing communications activities. These are discussed in greater detail in Chapter 8.

Marketing communications industry structures, organisation and management, payment systems, client/agency relationships

In response to the many environmental changes taking place, the relationships between clients and their agencies have changed. These changes include the way in which both agencies and clients structure themselves to achieve greater integration of marketing communications. Chapter 14 looks at some of the organisational implications of integrated marketing communications.

IN VIEW 7.3

Brands renamed

Many companies believe that the benefits of developing global brands are so great that they are even willing to 'sacrifice' successful national brand names to create them.

Nationally famous brands such as Marathon and Opal Fruits, Immac and Ulay disappeared as their names were changed to be the same as those already available in other markets around the world. Marathon became Snickers, Opal Fruits became Starburst, Immac became Veet and Ulay became Olay.

Over recent years the relative priorities given to different promotional agencies have been changing. PR, direct marketing, sales promotion and 'new media' agencies have become relatively stronger as the client's promotional money is spent **below-the-line** and as clients look for measurable returns on their expenditure. This has placed advertising agencies in a different competitive environment requiring fundamental adjustments to their operations. For example, the **commission-earning system**, so much a part of the advertising industry, has been giving way to new **fee-based remuneration** approaches which are necessary if advertising agencies are to attract and keep client business. Chapter 15 describes agency operations in more detail.

Marketing communications production technology e.g. inks, printing, mailing

Although overshadowed by technological developments in other areas, marketing communication production technology has led to new and improved opportunities. Improvements in ink technology, for example, has given rise to full colour printing in national and regional newspapers – this has been a relatively recent innovation to processes which previously could only have coped with **monochrome**. 'Electronic inks' and '**electronic paper**' are currently being developed that will allow text and images (even moving images) to change on the page triggered by an electronic signal (e.g. Peterson 1998 and Jacobson 1997). Fragrance capture is allowing readers to sample perfumes as they read magazines.

Machinery dealing with the personalised printing, sorting, stuffing and despatching of mail items has, along with other developments, allowed direct mailing to come to the fore, increasing mailout volume to their millions while reducing their costs substantially. Once again, computers have had a major role to play in revolutionising print, press, mail, video, TV and cinema production.

Marketing communications industry regulation

The laws and codes of practice regulating the marketing communications industry are constantly being reviewed. The amount and balance of legal control versus **self-regulation** varies from country to country and with the growth of the powers attributed to the European Community there is concern over the harmonisation of those controls. The advent of international broadcast communication has caused some difficulties in 'policing' situations where communications originate in one country and are broadcast in another. Codes of practice for the marketing communications

---

Below-the-line communications

Marketing communications that make use of the non-commission-paying media in all their forms, i.e. all forms of promotions other than advertising. Sometimes, incorrectly, it is referred to as below-the-line advertising. Although it remains a popular term, its usefulness is limited as it encompasses such a broad range of promotional activity.

Commission-earning system

System of payment in which advertising agencies are paid commission for booking media on behalf of clients.

Fee-based remuneration

A method of charging a client for work rendered based on a set agreed sum of money (a fee).

Monochrome

Single colour or black and white.

Electronic inks and electronic paper

Mechanism of producing text and images by using small electronic impulses on special 'paper' that changes colour in response to electrical charges.

Self-regulation

Voluntary control of acceptable marketing communications agreed by the marketing communications industry itself.

IN VIEW 7.4

Girl power shocks regulators

Marketing communications are regulated by law and by voluntary industry self-controls. Inevitably, there are examples where promotions break the law or infringe industry regulations. Sometimes the infringements are unintentional, on other occasions promotions are specifically designed to shock or offend. The difficulty is invariably one of determining whether such examples are acceptable or whether they should be banned.

The Nissan Micra car was promoted as a car for young women. A press advertisement featured a man holding his crotch as if in pain. The caption read, 'Ask before you borrow it', the implication being that his girlfriend had hit him because he had used her Micra without being given permission to do so (Plate 7).

Another ad showed a woman wearing a stiletto heeled boot resting on the buttocks of a naked man. The caption read, 'Put the boot in'.

One point-of-sale promotion that was banned was an on-pack sales promotion for a bottled beer. At point of sale, attached to the bottles was a free special edition of 'Loaded' magazine. This particular magazine typically contains offensive material and the special on-pack edition was no exception. Complainants considered the material to be pornographic and obscene with exceptionally rude quotes from famous people.

industry attempt to follow good professional practice and adhere to the principles of legal, decent, honest and truthful communications. It is in the area of decency that most difficulties arise as society changes its boundaries of what it defines and accepts as ethics, morals and decency. Chapters 9 and 10 are devoted to the regulation and ethics of marketing communications.

Players in the marketing communications industry

Simon Broadbent and Brian Jacobs describe in their book, *Spending Advertising Money* (1984), the marketing communications industry as a game for four players: the consumer, the advertiser, the agency and the media owner. Of course, in reality, each 'player' is a group made up of many individuals and organisations, which complicate the total scene, but the four-player model is a useful simplification of those involved. Exhibit 7.3 shows an adaptation of their four-player model extended to include consideration of marketing communications in a wider sense.

Exhibit 7.3 Players in the marketing communications industry

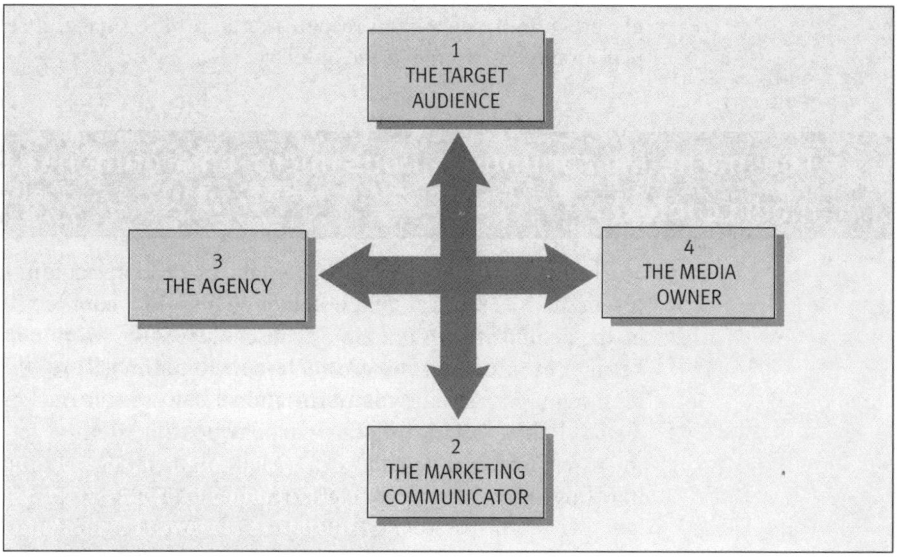

1 *The target audience.* This 'player' represents all the recipients of marketing communications messages. They are the many groups of people towards whom marketing communications may be focused. The famous economist Adam Smith has been attributed with popularising the view that 'consumption is the sole end and purpose of production' and this places the consumer in a major role. But for marketing communications not only is the consumer important, so are all those involved in the purchase process and those that influence the process whether for services or goods, or for consumer or industrial products, or whether they are internal audiences or external audiences.

2 *The marketing communicator.* The marketing communicator is the sender of the message, the business wishing to sell its products, the organisation or individual wishing to communicate with its target audiences. Because marketing communications can be very complex with large budgets being allocated to their development and delivery, it is usual that assistance is sought from outside agencies.

3 *The agency.* The agency or, frequently, agencies are the intermediaries who help to create and produce marketing communications messages. An agency's work may include market research, media sales, production, advertising, PR, sales promotion, packaging and all the other elements of the marketing communications mix. Increasingly, agencies have specialised in certain areas of promotion although they have also had to address the problems of working together or otherwise attempting to ensure integration of effort. Some agencies have attempted to provide their myriad services 'under one roof', others have formed **agency groups** in order to provide more comprehensive services, still others have remained specialists.

Agency group

Network of agencies working together.

4 *The media owner.* The media owner is the organisation that provides the medium which carries the message. The most obvious and renowned media owners are those associated with the advertising (mass) media – TV, cinema, radio, press, and posters. But marketing communications media is a term that can be applied to anything which can carry marketing communications messages: video, merchandise items, promotional giftware, shopping trolleys, direct mail leaflets, point-of-sale display, bins, park benches and many other items. See Chapter 5 for a fuller discussion of the media.

These, then, may be described as the principal players within the marketing communications industry in a simplified form. Exhibit 7.4 attempts to illustrate the industry players in more detail and recognises the professional and regulatory bodies that also play an important role in the industry.

The marketing communications micro-environment – the media context

Marketing communications do not take place in a vacuum. Every item of promotion is sensed – seen, heard, felt, tasted or smelt – in a context. Something else will always be happening at the same time. This context is the *micro*-environment in which marketing communications are received. Sometimes, the context acts as a positive, reinforcing force to the communications. The context and communications are synergistic. Public relations activities frequently attempt to take advantage of the micro-environment to add extra 'weight' to their communications. A good example of how this can be used to good effect is shown in In View 7.5.

Exhibit 7.4 Illustration of the range of players in the marketing communications industry

Agencies, consultancies, professional bodies, trade bodies	Marketing communications target audiences
PR agencies	Consumers
Sales promotion agencies	Customers
Ad agencies	Trade and channel members
Media independents	Employees
Direct mail agencies	Stakeholders
Corporate identity specialists	Media
Retail designers	Central and local government
Printers	Consumer associations
Freelance designers	Special interest groups
Production companies	Decision Making Unit members
Merchandisers	Others
Product placement companies	
Brand name companies	
Internet/Web/e-marketing agencies	
Marketing researchers	**Media owners**
Pack designers and specialists	TV companies
New media agencies	Radio companies
Exhibition and conference organisers	Poster companies
Pioneer sales forces	Newspaper publishers
Telesales specialists	Magazines publishers
Mailing houses	Directory publishers
Mailing lists specialists	Cinema companies
Professional bodies	Video companies
Regulatory bodies	Internet companies/ISPs
Media sales agencies	Others
Management consultants	
Sponsorship specialists	
Celebrity managers	
Modelling agencies	**Marketing communicators**
Exhibition centres	Anybody
Call centre operators	Everybody
Others	

IN VIEW 7.5

Virgin Atlantic criticise 'Twittish Airways'

Media coup

The ability to attract extensive media coverage (publicity) through a staged event, activity or news story.

Knocking copy

Text that offers negative or disparaging comments about someone or something else.

Virgin Atlantic achieved something of a **media coup** when it was able to place an advertisement along the bottom of the front page of *The Sunday Times*. The advertisement featured '**knocking copy**' that took advantage of the criticisms British Airways was receiving over its new 'ethnic art' corporate identity. To add insult to British Airways injury, the Virgin Atlantic advertisement appeared directly below an article entitled 'BA to kill off £60m ethnic art tailfins', which featured the problems BA was having over its brightly decorated aircraft designs. In so doing, the advertisement, based on a headline used in *The Sun* newspaper the week before, was made more relevant and generated more impact than the advertisement could possibly have done if it appeared on its own.

Sometimes the context reduces the impact or value of the communications effort. It may even have a negative effect. Some years ago, it was suggested that an offer of a season ticket for a famous orchestra should be included with a local authority mailing. The orchestra was sponsored by, and closely associated with, the local authority. There would be obvious synergy between the two. Savings could also be made as there would be only one mailing cost. Fortunately, it was realised in time that the mailing, which included a request for payment of local authority charges, would not be a suitable context in which to ask for extra payment for a season ticket to see an orchestra, even an internationally recognised one. Moreover, the mailing would have been indiscriminate, being sent to many people who would have had no interest in the offer. The idea was abandoned.

Another example of an inappropriate context is a mismatch between the medium and the message. A local restaurant owner decided (or was persuaded) that it would be a good idea to advertise on the side of bin bags. The bags were distributed by refuse collectors as they collected household rubbish. Promoting good eating on the side of rubbish bags is not one that readily springs to mind as a good idea.

At the other extreme, examples of promotions that have gained benefit from their media context include a government anti-smoking campaign featuring arch-enemy 'Nic-o-tine'. Television advertisements were screened during a Superman film. The story line of the advertisement and the film were consistent and both would be seen by the target age group at a time when the viewers would be most sympathetic to the fight of good over evil; health, vitality and strength over ill-health.

The 1998 World Cup football tournament in France was an obvious time for advertisers to make the most of high television audience ratings and relate their products to footballing. McDonald's, Mastercard and Budweiser sponsored the tournament as well as placing advertisements during commercial breaks. Vauxhall cars sponsored the

IN VIEW 7.6

Campaign gets the red card

Even the best laid plans go astray. Adidas sportswear were set to cash in on David Beckham's popularity. They had signed Beckham to a sponsorship deal and for weeks the England star had stared out from posters and television ads that featured him taking a free kick and growing from a young boy into a 'mature' football player, all part of a multi-million pound promotion timed to coincide with the 1998 Football World Cup.

Adidas was well pleased – until Beckham became the third player in the tournament to be sent off. England was then defeated in the tournament. The campaign was withdrawn.

This was not the least of Adidas's problems. The campaign to promote their Predator Accelerator boot also featured Holland and AC Milan striker, Patrick Kluivert, who was sent off for elbowing a Belgian defender; the France and Juventus midfielder, Zinedine Zidane, who was shown the red card for stamping on a Saudi player; and the Italy and Juventus striker, Alessandro del Piero, who was injured before the World Cup and lost his place in the starting line-up.

Adidas's experience was something of a repeat of the problems faced by Nike during the Barcelona 1992 Olympics. On that occasion, Nike had sponsored Sergei Bubka, the Ukrainian pole-vaulter; Michael Johnson, the American 200-metre sprinter; and Noureddine Morceli, the Algerian middle-distance runner. All failed dismally in their individual events.

Channel 3 football coverage and Boddingtons beer sponsored the Fantasy World Cup programme. Numerous advertisements were produced featuring football themes, fans and players. Products ranged from Pringles and Walkers Crisps, to Ariel and Bold washing powders, to Adidas, Umbro and Nike sportswear, to BT (Plate 8) and One2One communications, to foodstuffs from Sainsbury's, Kelloggs Frosties, Coca-Cola and Snickers. Even Customs and Excise took the opportunity to promote their crackdown on drug abuse and BBC Education advertised their French language pack.

Summary

The marketing communications environment provides the context in which marketing communications take place. It is dynamic and constantly changing. Under the heading of macro-environment, some of the more interesting developments were referred to here. Two analytical frameworks that are used in corporate and marketing planning, as well as for marketing communications planning, were introduced: PRESTCOM and SWOT. The macro-environment was described as being composed of factors both internal and external to the organisation. This view is, perhaps, at odds with conventional descriptions of the macro-environment which usually only emphasise factors external to the organisation. However, it was pointed out that we have been addressing the macro-environment for *marketing communications* specifically and not the macro-environment of the organisation. For marketing communications to be integrated, its activities have to embrace internal audiences as well as extend to external audiences. Organisational, managerial, operational and resource issues all impact on the quality of marketing communications. There are, thus, dimensions both internal and external to the organisation that must be considered.

The various bodies involved in the marketing communications industry were briefly introduced as 'players' within the industry. All of these form a complex interweaving of activity that ultimately results in the world of promotions, advertising and marketing communications as we know it today.

The final part of this chapter emphasised the micro-environment which has a meaning peculiar to marketing communications. The micro-environment is the media context which surrounds any form of marketing communications. This context has an impact on the meaning and reception of marketing communications as part of the decoding process that was introduced in Chapter 3.

Self-review questions

1 What do the PRESTCOM and SWOT acronyms mean?

2 Search through two or three national newspapers and identify the advertisements targeted at the over-50s age group. Analyse these advertisements to identify how the images and messages have been developed to appeal specifically to this group.

3 What do you consider to be the impact, and the advantages and disadvantages for marketing communications, of ever-increasing numbers of TV channels?

4 What are relationship marketing and loyalty marketing? What examples of marketing communications activities will assist these types of marketing effort?

5 What is meant by the marketing communications micro-environment? Why is it important to understand the significance of this when developing marketing communications?

Project

Find three examples where the micro-environment appears to work to the benefit of a piece of promotion. Find three examples where the opposite appears to be true, in which the micro-environment seems to detract from the promotion. Try to find your examples across a range of promotional elements, for example PR, sales promotion, point of sale, advertising, exhibitions, direct mail, personal selling. Write a summary report identifying how and why the micro-environment can produce a positive and negative impact on marketing communications.

References

Brassington, F. and Pettitt, S. (2003), *Principles of Marketing* 3rd edn. Financial Times Prentice Hall.

Broadbent, S. and Jacobs, B. (1984), *Spending Advertising Money* 4th edn. Business Books.

Greenley, G. (1989), *The Strategic and Operational Planning of Marketing*. McGraw-Hill.

Jacobson, J. (1997), *Electronic Paper*. http://www.media.mit.edu/micromedia/elecpaper.html

Johnson, G. and Scholes, K. (2002), *Exploring Corporate Strategy* 6th edn. Financial Times Prentice Hall.

Kotler, P., Armstrong, G., Saunders, J. and Wong, V. (2001), *Principles of Marketing* 3rd European edn. Prentice Hall.

McDonald, M.H.B. (1991), *The Marketing Audit*. Heinemann.

Peterson, I. (1998), Rethinking Ink. *Science News Online*, 20 June. http://www.sciencenews.org/sn

Pickton, D.W. and Wright, S. (1998), What's SWOT in strategic analysis. *Strategic Change*, 7 (2), 101–109.

Wilson, R.M.S. and Gilligan, C. (1997), *Strategic Marketing Management* 2nd edn. Butterworth-Heinemann.

Selected further reading

O'Connor, J. and Galvin, E. (1997), *Marketing and Information Technology*. Financial Times Pitman Publishing.

Kotler, P., Armstrong, G., Saunders, J. and Wong, V. (2001), *Principles of Marketing* 3rd European edn. Prentice Hall.

Pickton, D.W. and Wright, S. (1998), What's SWOT in strategic analysis. *Strategic Change*, 7 (2), 101–109.

Chapter 8

The international context of marketing communications

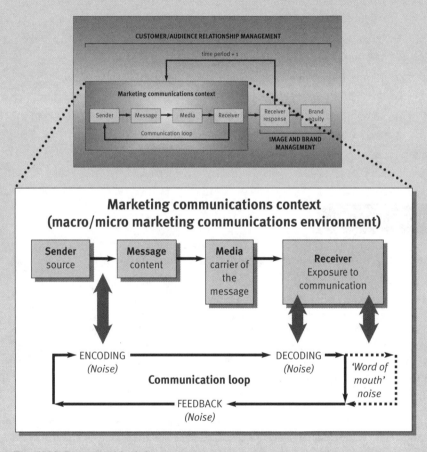

The IMC Process Model

CD

Concern targets the US, Eire, Northern Ireland, England and Wales, and Scotland. Does Concern pursue a customisation or standardisation marketing communication strategy for the countries/regions in which they operate? Why do you think they have gone about it in this way?

Chapter outline

- The importance of international marketing
- The international dimensions of the marketing communications environment
- Standardisation versus adaptation of marketing communications
- Strategic responses to the standardisation question
- The impact of the international context on marketing communications

Objectives

- To identify the motivations to internationalise
- To present the international extensions of the PRESTCOM analysis framework
- To outline the standardisation versus adaptation debate and its impact on the marketing communications mix
- To provide an overview of the marketing strategies available to the internationalising organisation
- To summarise the key components of the international context of the marketing communications mix

Professional perspective

Professor Susan Douglas Professor of Marketing and International Business, **New York Stern University**

Powerful forces are transforming global markets and dramatically changing ways of doing business. Increased movement of people, goods and organisations across borders have resulted in the emergence of global market segments and the growth of globally integrated markets. Advances in communications and information systems technology continue to shrink distances, linking markets through flows of information, image and ideas. These trends create inexorable forces toward market integration and mean that managers need to adapt and rethink communication strategies to respond to increasing globalisation.

In international markets, communication with a target audience is more complex than in domestic markets, because communication takes place across multiple cultural contexts, which differ in terms of language, literacy and other cultural factors. A verbal message has to be translated so that it is clearly understood by target audiences in all contexts. Even use of visual symbols contains pitfalls due to differences in colour association or interpretation of symbols. Appeals to humour, sex, etc. also need to be treated with care due to differences in cultural context and taboos. In interpersonal communications, rules relating to punctuality, distance between speakers and other conventions need to be respected. As a result, marketing communications often need to be adapted to avoid misinterpretation or miscommunication.

International marketing communications can also be an important force integrating people in cultures across the world. Messages using universal symbols and slogans are disseminated and establish a common mode of communication among target audiences in different parts of the world. Advertising images such as the Colours of Benetton campaign incorporating peoples of different nations and diverse cultural backgrounds reinforce cultural pluralism and multicultural values. The growth of global media, such as Star TV or MTV, which target global audiences worldwide, strengthen links between markets throughout the world. Consequently, while on the one hand international marketing communications can be viewed as a colonising force propagating Western values and mores, they are also an important force integrating societies and establishing common bonds, universal symbols and culture of consumption among peoples in disparate corners of the globe.

The importance of international marketing

With the trend to a global economy, many organisations perceive their market to be unrestricted by national boundaries. Organisations have increasingly been expanding their operations outside their domestic market in order to take advantages of growth and profit opportunities. Numerous empirical studies have identified the motivations to internationalise (e.g. Burt 1991; Laulajainen 1991; Dawson 1994). These include:

- domestic market saturation, making it more expensive to gain market share;
- limits placed on domestic growth in the home country by public policy limiting further growth in market share of an organisation;
- identification of growth or niche opportunities in the international marketplace;
- recognition of higher profits in the international marketplace because of differences in competitive and/or cost structures;
- risk distribution across the international marketplace, so that the organisation is not as susceptible to national economic cycles;
- opportunities of buying power consolidation within the organisation or through joint-buying arrangements.

When the organisation internationalises, the marketing activities take place within a complex environment. Marketing communications are the most visible and the most culture-bound of an organisation's marketing functions, and as such are particularly influenced by the international context. Although all of the environmental considerations of marketing communications outlined in Chapter 7 are pertinent in the international marketplace, there are further, specific influences on the marketing communications mix when it operates internationally.

The international dimensions of the marketing communications environment

Exhibit 8.1 identifies key environmental influences both general and specific to the international marketplace.

Exhibit 8.1 PRESTCOM environmental analysis

PRESTCOM	Dimensions	International dimensions
Political	<ul><li>Government policies</li><li>Political stability</li><li>Taxation</li></ul>	<ul><li>Attitudes towards overseas multinationals</li></ul>
Regulatory	<ul><li>Legislation</li><li>Self-regulation</li></ul>	<ul><li>Cross-border trade regulation</li><li>Disparity in media laws and regulation between countries</li></ul>
Economic	<ul><li>Customers' resources</li><li>Economic development</li><li>Economic infrastructure</li><li>Currency stability</li></ul>	<ul><li>Financial structures</li><li>Penetration of media</li><li>Exchange rates</li></ul>
Social	<ul><li>Sub-cultures</li><li>Values</li><li>Lifestyles</li><li>Norms and customs</li><li>Ethics and moral standards</li><li>Taboos</li></ul>	<ul><li>Culture</li><li>Language</li><li>Ethnocentrism</li><li>Xenophilia</li></ul>
Technological	<ul><li>Telecommunications</li><li>Computing technology</li></ul>	<ul><li>Availability of overseas technological expertise</li></ul>
Competitive	<ul><li>Competitive intensity and diversity</li></ul>	<ul><li>Access to personnel</li><li>Competitive/cost structure disparities</li></ul>
Organisational	<ul><li>Strengths and weaknesses</li><li>Planning</li><li>Structure</li></ul>	<ul><li>Headquarters/subsidiary relationship</li><li>Corporate orientation</li><li>Degree of centralisation</li></ul>
Market	<ul><li>Raw materials costs</li><li>Demand</li><li>Market value</li><li>Stage in category life cycle</li><li>Product usage</li><li>Market demographics</li></ul>	<ul><li>Economies of scale</li><li>Channels of distribution/chain of supply</li><li>Global media</li><li>Variability in market expectations</li></ul>

Political and regulatory environment

Different countries have different ethical ideas and legislation on what type of products may be advertised. For example, in Germany the term 'diet' attached to a product is strictly regulated, so that The Coca-Cola Company's 'Diet Coke', as advertised in the UK, has to be adapted to 'Coca-Cola light' for Germany[1].

The content of the creative approach is also affected by the political and regulatory environment. For example, the US is much less tolerant of nudity in advertising than France. Benetton's 'Black Mama' poster advertisement featuring the bare breasts of a black woman nursing a white child was banned in the US because it contravened regulations regarding nudity (Plate 9).

In addition to national disparities in legislation, regional differences are also evident. For example, the regions in Spain are very distinct from each other, historically, geographically and culturally. This strong regionality is reflected in the political

[1]Chapter 8 'diet Coke' logo 'Coca-Cola', 'Coke', 'diet Coke', 'diet Coca-Cola' and the 'Dynamic Ribbon' are registered trade marks of The Coca-Cola Company and are reproduced with kind permission from The Coca-Cola Company

system. Each of the 17 communities has its own parliament and executive with the power to issue laws that are applicable only to that particular region.

The political and regulatory environment also has an impact on the following:

● the media that marketing communicators are permitted to employ;
● the use of foreign language in marketing communications;
● the use of advertising material prepared outside the country;
● the use of local versus international advertising agencies;
● the specific taxes that may be levied against marketing communications.

Economic environment

Disparities in channel networks and infrastructures occur cross-nationally. The structure of financial institutions and the methods of payment available can have an impact not only on business transactions, but also on the degree of standardisation of the marketing communications. The sophistication and penetration of media channels also differ substantially across the world. For example, TV ownership and the penetration of personal computers with Internet access are much lower in Central Europe than in Northern Europe.

Customer's resources, in terms of total household income and disposable income, have a significant effect on the product categories and types of brands purchased. For example, negative income elasticity for food products is common across the EU (Bareham 1995). As household income increases, the percentage of the total spent on food decreases. Nevertheless, although France has a higher level of total household income than Spain and Italy, food expenditure as a percentage of total household expenditure is significantly higher in France, reflecting the importance of food to the consumer (Exhibit 8.2).

Italy spends a relatively high proportion of total household expenditure on food (18% in 1992) in comparison to other EU countries (European Marketing Intelligence 1994d). The average monthly expenditure of households, however, shows enormous disparities across the different areas of Italy. In 1991, monthly expenditure in the north of Italy was 35.7% higher than that of the south, Sicily and Sardinia, and 8.3% higher than the central area of Italy. These disparities reflect the economic division between northern and southern Italy. This economic division is also reflected in consumption habits. Northern Italians generally consume more frozen and processed foods than elsewhere in Italy. This is because the lifestyle of the northern Italian is

Exhibit 8.2 EU expenditure on food as a percentage of total expenditure

Highest average household income				Lowest average household income
Germany	**UK**	**France**	**Spain**	**Italy**
14%	11%	19%	17%	18%

Source: Adapted from *European Marketing Intelligence* (1994 a, b, c, d, e)

suited to convenience shopping and eating habits. In the south, tradition and lower incomes mean less processed food is consumed. Additionally, the rural nature of the south means that fresh foods are more readily available. It is also the tradition of southern families for the wife to remain at home to prepare meals for the family.

Social environment

Culture

Culture influences every aspect of marketing: the products people buy, the attributes they value and the principles they accept are all culturally based choices. For example, different levels of awareness, knowledge and familiarity with products in general, and specific brands may result in differential attitudes towards similar products (Jain 1989). To produce compelling marketing communication programmes in one or many social settings requires a special sensitivity towards the group(s) for whom the message is intended.

According to Henessey (1992) and Cateora (1993), culture is the integrated sum total of learned behaviour traits that are shared by members of a society. Hollensen (1998) defines culture as:

> **the accumulation of shared meanings, rituals, norms and traditions among the members of an organisation or society. It is what defines a human community, its individuals, its social organisations as well as its economic and political system. It includes both abstract ideas such as values and ethics, as well as material objects and services such as clothing, food, art and sports that are produced or valued by a group of people.**

It is important to have an understanding of the dimensions of a target country's cultural characteristics, namely language, religion, education, attitudes and values, social organisation, political life and aesthetics (design, music, colour and brand names). Advocating the purchase of a product whose use is inconsistent with a local culture will result in failure even if the communication appeal chosen did not violate the culture *per se.* Sensitivity to national *business* culture is also important in international marketing. For example, time and space have different meanings to business people in different environments. With respect to time, a person may wait two hours or more after the pre-designated time for an appointment to take place in a Latin American country. In Germany, it is wise to make an appointment well in advance. In the USA, a deadline signifies the degree of urgency, but in the Middle East, an attempt to impose a deadline may be cause for cessation of work (Cateora 1993).

NEED TO KNOW

☑ *Culture and society are distinct concepts, although they are often used interchangeably. Society is made up of people; their culture is the way they behave.*

The terms 'culture' and 'society' are frequently used interchangeably, but may be perceived as distinct. In simplest form, society is made up of people; their culture is the way they behave (Brown 1963). In other words, a society is not a culture; it has a culture. Although each society has a culture, it does not follow that there are not cultural differences within a given society or that several different societies may not share, at least to a large extent, a common culture. As a geopolitical unit, for example, the US constitutes one society, yet, even if groups like the Native Americans or the foreign born are excluded, there is still considerable variation in cultural patterns within continental USA. On the other hand, it has been argued that the UK shares, to a large extent, a common culture with the US, yet it is a separate, well-defined society that forms an independent political unit (Usunier 1996).

Sub-culture

Sub-cultural divisions are based on a variety of socio-cultural and demographic variables, such as religion, geographic locality, race, age, sex, even working status. Schiffman and Kanuk (1999) define sub-culture as:

> a distinct cultural group that exists as an identifiable segment within a larger, more complex society.

The members of a specific sub-culture possess beliefs, values and customs that set them apart from other members of the same society. Although they adhere to most of the dominant cultural beliefs, values and behavioural patterns differ for the larger and more complex societies, for example, the Welsh, the Scottish, the Catholic Northern Irish and the Protestant Northern Irish in the United Kingdom.

Country of origin influences, ethnocentrism and xenophilia

Country of origin image is the sum beliefs, ideas and impressions that a person holds of products of a specific country and directly affect where a certain product is positioned in consumers' minds (Martin and Eroglu 1993). Country of origin serves as an extrinsic product cue like brand name, warranty, and price (Bilkey and Nes 1982). Together with other cues, country of origin has been shown to influence buying intentions and behaviour. In practice, country of origin cues take five forms:

1 'Product originating in ...' or 'made in ...': a product made within a territory.
2 Geographical indicator or appellation of origin: a region or locality of a territory, where a given quality, reputation or other characteristic of a product is essentially attributable to its geographical origin.
3 Traditional expression: a traditionally used name referring, in particular, to the method of production or quality of a product for the purpose of the description and presentation of a product originating in the territory.
4 Description: names used on labelling, commercial documents (e.g. invoices) and advertising.
5 Labelling: all descriptions and other references, signs, designs or trade.

Among other things, country of origin influences appear to be product dependent (Cordell 1992). In certain industries, it is argued, the unique character of a product derives from the physical and human environment in which it is produced. A few industries already have geographical trademark protection (which date back hundreds of years) including Scotch Whisky, Champagne and Stilton, Cheshire and Leicester cheeses. Indeed, interest in setting up geographical trademarks has grown; more and more groups of producers are independently taking action to protect the commercial value of their geographical designations (Freedman 1994).

In 1987, Shimp and Sharma applied Sumner's (1906) concept of ethnocentrism to consumer behaviour. In their studies, Shimp and Sharma (1987) defined **consumer ethnocentrism** as being related to consumer beliefs about the appropriateness and morality of buying foreign products. Marketing researchers have found that people view their own country as the reference against which all other country groups are judged. Furthermore, there is a tendency to view one's own group as superior to other groups. This has led to a traceable distinction between in-group countries and out-group countries; consumers view products from their own country more favourably (Bannister and Saunders 1978; Kaynak and Cavusgil 1989). In the US, for example, labelling restrictions have been imposed on imports since the late 1800s, specifically to give the consumer the right to be ethnocentric in their purchasing. The wording of Section 304 of the Tariff Act (19 USC 1304) makes clear this intention: 'imported articles are required to be marked in a conspicuous place so that the ultimate purchaser in the US will be aware of their origin and can choose between buying a foreign or domestic good'. In addition, following its defeat in the First World War, German products were required to carry the 'Made in Germany' labelling, in English, as both a punishment and to warn European consumers (Morello 1984). These early examples of legislation demonstrate that manufacturers and policymakers have been aware of consumer ethnocentric tendencies for years.

Xenophilia

An affinity or liking for things foreign.

Conversely, purchases and buying intentions can be influenced by **xenophilia** tendencies, i.e. an affinity for things foreign. To date consumer xenophilia has not received as much attention as has consumer ethnocentrism. Nevertheless, some interesting examples have emerged from literature reviews. In particular researchers have noted that if a country is not well developed, domestic consumers might prefer products made in developed countries (Bilkey and Nes 1982; Cordell 1992). This has been particularly true in the former communist countries where decades of producing low-quality goods have made consumers wary of domestically produced products (Mueller and Gajdusek 1996). The purchase and consumption of foreign (mostly Western) brands may also be used to make a political statement by consumers (Raju 1995). Xenophilia tendencies, however, can also transcend traditional chauvinistic biases; British consumers, for example, have been found to prefer imported goods over domestic even though domestic goods consistently get high-quality ratings (Smith 1996). Other countries that have a healthy self-image but are import receptive include Mexico, India and Chile (Labarre 1994). One researcher has suggested that the interest in exotic foreign products is a reaction against cultural homogeneity (Gitelson 1992).

Ethnocentrism (and xenophilia by extension) is generally held to be not a 'fact of human nature' but a result of particular conditions. Consumer ethnocentric tendencies are reduced, for example, when consumers achieve a higher level of education, higher income level, and have greater opportunities to travel abroad (Usunier 1996). Research has also shown those less educated and politically conservative, and workers who are patriotic and/or feel threatened by imports either personally or generally (Shimp and Sharma 1987 and Shimp et al. 1995) are more likely to exhibit consumer ethnocentric tendencies.

A fundamental flaw of much country-of-origin research is that it assumes consumers are aware of a product's country of origin. An examination of country-of-origin literature shows, however, that there is much ambiguity in country-of-origin cues. Frequently, manufacturers purposely hide or mislead the consumer about the geographical origin of a product, but sometimes country of origin is just simply too difficult to confine to one country. The ambiguous, misleading or deceptive use of country-of-origin product cues have been termed '**captious cues**' (Mueller and Broderick 1999). The country-of-origin literature is replete with examples of captious cue marketing strategies.

Captious cues

The ambiguous, misleading or deceptive use of country of origin product identifiers (cues).

Manufacturers in the Czech Republic, for example, have placed English or German labels on their products (both domestic and exports) in an attempt to confuse consumers about the products' real geographical origin (Green 1995). In China, approximately 36% of all Chinese-produced consumer products use a variety of methods to produce a Western 'feel' to the brand (Gilley 1996). These methods include using blonde models, English language packaging, and foreign-sounding brand and company names. Western companies too have been cited for using captious cues. The original Häagen Dazs ice-cream manufacturer, though a New York firm, tried to project a Danish origin by coming up with a foreign-sounding brand name. Western electronics manufacturers are also notorious for producing Japanese-sounding brand names for domestically produced products. Other examples can be found at the legal offices of the Scotch Whisky Federation and French champagne industries. The Scotch Whisky Federation has four full-time lawyers devoted to protecting its geographical trademark while the champagne industry has had at least 60 actions since the 1960s (Freedman 1994).

An equal number of recent examples of captious cue strategies are used not to mislead the final consumer but are used to circumvent quota and visa restrictions. A number of examples cite the trans-shipment of Chinese-produced goods through Macau or Hong Kong for country of origin re-labelling (Menendez 1996). Trans-shipping is done to capitalise on Chinese wages which are 20% of Hong Kong's (Biers 1996). Other country of origin re-labelling includes Israeli products, which enjoy a special status in the United States. As long as Asian-produced products are returned to Israel and then shipped as 'product(s) of Israel' to the US, they can be labelled as such (Mottley 1996).

Not all captious cue strategies are used to purposely mislead or hide country of origin. The continued need to be internationally competitive means that companies must take a global view of sourcing, manufacturing and operations (Cordell 1992). A result of cross-country operations is that verification is not as easy as it sounds (Crain 1994). Indeed, multi-country processing in an increasingly global economy means that more and more products involve multi-country processing. Wholesalers which accumulate products from a number of foreign countries also cite difficulties in labelling products. In practice, international sourcing has become especially crucial in industries where margins are small, e.g. textile and apparel. Not surprisingly, it is in these industries that many of the captious cues are found.

Technological and competitive environment

Internationalising organisations may be able to capitalise on overseas technological expertise to enhance their product characteristics and have access to more sophisticated media channels. Cost structure disparities between countries may enable an organisation to take advantage of greater economies of scale or higher profit margins.

Organisational environment

A key influence on international marketing communications is the extent to which managerial decision-making is centralised at a head office in the home country or is delegated to host country operations. This has a direct influence on the likely marketing communication strategy an organisation will adopt: standardised marketing communications which are virtually the same from country to country, or a strategy which reflects the regional and national society in which they operate.

Market environment

Variability in market expectations is a key environmental force. Differing expectations can have an impact on the types of products and services that are acceptable to a market, the appeals used in marketing communications and the distribution outlets the consumers are likely to buy from. Market expectations can differ more within a country than across countries. Some organisations have been able to capitalise on the existence of these global market niches. For example, Pepsi Max is targeted at the teenage youth market with its interest in music, sports and fashion.

Patterns of demand may also differ in an international context. For example, food consumption differs noticeably in northern and southern Europe. Consumption of potatoes and fatty products are higher in the north, while in the south, consumption of cereals and vegetable oil are higher. The French consume more kilograms per inhabitant of red meat than Spain, Italy, Germany or the UK. In contrast, Italy and the UK consume below the regional average of 62.6 kilograms per inhabitant. The consumption of frozen foods exhibits particular disparities, with Italy consuming the least, and the UK the most. Both differing lifestyles and differing penetration levels of frozen products may explain the discrepancy in demand (i.e. the demand for convenience food is greater in the UK as there are more working women and frozen products have both greater availability and sophistication).

Standardisation versus adaptation of marketing communications

Standardisation strategy

The use of similar or identical marketing communications across countries.

Adaptation strategy

Marketing communications messages and media that are changed from country to country to better suit the particular requirements of individual markets.

One important strategic decision an international marketer has to make, is whether to standardise the communication mix worldwide or adapt it to the environment of each country or cultural group. The **standardisation** versus **adaptation** debate rose to preeminence in the classic globalisation debate of the 1980s (Levitt 1983; Quelch and Hoff 1986; Wind 1986; Kotler 1988). On the one hand, there is evidence of the globalisation of economies through the transfer of capital, products, technology and know-how, and the convergence of consumer tastes and preferences worldwide. According to the standardisation argument, because people everywhere want the same products for the same reasons, companies can achieve economies of scale by unifying marketing communications around the globe.

> The global corporation operates with resolute constancy – at low relative cost – as if the entire world (or major regions of it) were a single entity; it sells the same things in the same way everywhere.
>
> (Levitt 1983)

The proponents of globalisation maintain that in a rapidly internationalising world, the key component of success is the development of globally recognised products and brand images. For example, Gillette used a global advertising campaign to launch the Sensory shaving system. Companies such as Coca-Cola and McDonald's have also carried out this philosophy of efficiency successfully.

On the other hand, there is the increase in the presence of ethnic minorities and nationalism which is tending to differentiate economies and cultures and suggests the need for differentiated communications. The idea of globalisation has been strongly challenged; for example, Wind (1986) states it is the 'myth of globalisation'. Wind (1986) argues against globalisation on the basis of three factors:

- standardised products are over-designed for some countries and under-designed for others;
- already existing company country networks can be undermined; and
- the standardisation activity dampens the entrepreneurial spirit.

The choice between standardisation and adaptation is an issue of strategic and financial importance since excessive adaptation imposes loss of control and extra costs while rigid standardisation threatens local customer appeal and global market share. The debate is far from simple. Little empirical evidence has been found for the world-

IN VIEW 8.1

Standardisation versus adaptation viewpoints

Different cultural preferences, national tastes and standards, and different business institutions are vestiges of the past ... The world's needs and desires have been irrevocably homogenised. This makes the multinational corporation obsolete and the global corporation absolute ... Instead of adapting to superficial and even entrenched differences within and between nations, the global corporation will seek sensibly to force suitably standardised products and practices on the entire globe. (Levitt 1983)

Is Ted Levitt right about the globalisation of markets? Yes. Does that mean that you standardise and homogenise the way you perform marketing in every country in the world throughout the marketing mix? Of course not. (Porter 1992)

When it comes to product strategy, managing in a borderless world doesn't mean managing by averages. It doesn't mean that all tastes run together into one amorphous mass of universal appeal. And it doesn't mean that the appeal of operating globally removes the obligation to localise products. The lure of a universal product is a false allure. The truth is more subtle ... Managing effectively in this new borderless environment means paying attention to delivering value to customer – and to developing an equidistant view of who they are and what they want. Before anything else comes the need to see your customers clearly. They – and only they – can provide legitimate reasons for thinking global. (Ohmae 1989)

Being a truly global company means being an insider in the major markets around the world. (J. Krielen, Commercial Director, Nestlé, reported in De Jonquieres 1991)

Unilever in most of its product groups still adheres to the adage 'think global, act local'. Of course, we are re-evaluating our current portfolio with a view towards harmonisation. And we feel that our core brands should all have an international dimension. But, to enable a flexible response to market trends, still a lot has to be done locally. Unilever still uses the local market as its power base. For products with international potential, we have central guidelines as to how they should be marketed. However, local managers can still make modifications if they are consumer-relevant. (J.W. Eenhoorn, Group Executive, Unilever, reported in De Jonquieres 1991)

For GFT, globalisation is not about standardisation, it's about a quantum increase in complexity. The more the company has penetrated global markets, the more sustaining its growth depends on responding to the myriad of local differences in its key markets around the world. To be global means to recognise differences and be flexible enough to adapt to them. (Marco Rivetti, Chairman, Gruppo GFT, reported in Howard 1991)

wide homogenisation of tastes and the preferences of a 'world consumer'. Those interested in the influence of culture on consumer behaviour and the implementation of marketing (e.g. Dubois 1987) have found arguments in favour of cultural resistance to the globalisation process. Many have questioned the Levitt thesis, maintaining that a localising strategy is superior. Localising implies differentiation of products depending

Exhibit 8.3 Advantages and disadvantages of standardised marketing communications

Advantages	Disadvantages
• Economies of scale in production and distribution	• Few products lend themselves to global marketing communications
• Lower costs as a result of reduction in planning and control	• Differences in culture, market, economic development; consumer needs and usage patterns; media availabilities; legal restrictions; language, traditions, values, beliefs, lifestyle, music, etc.
• Abilities to exploit good ideas on a worldwide basis and introduce products quickly into various world markets	
• A consistent international brand and/or company image	• Increasing cultural diversity
• Simplification of coordination and control of marketing communications programmes	• Potential of alienating consumers

on the idiosyncrasies of major identifiable world market segments. Based upon the general concept of polycentrism (Wind et al. 1973), the localisation philosophy maintains that the needs of international markets are too culturally diverse to be standardised. Each market must be dealt with according to its own peculiarities, making international differentiation of products necessary. In View 8.2 provides an example of a localised advertising strategy employed by Nescafé.

Proponents of an adaptation strategy acknowledge that the diverse needs of international markets can be satisfied more successfully by flexible international businesses. On the other hand, due to economies of scale with standardisation, the price can be made so attractive that efficiency can prevail over effectiveness (Porter 1986). Even if both strategies are theoretically viable, these points of view appear to be too extreme to be useful to the majority of marketers. There exists, in reality, a continuum between the extremes of one global identity and a locally tailored identity. A compromise position would call for international companies to design global products and to market them in a modified manner according to the different needs of international markets.

IN VIEW 8.2

Adapting Nescafé instant coffee

In Norway, the coffee drinking tradition was for ground coffee brewed and kept hot on the stove all day. In order for Nescafé to move consumers away from ground coffee to instant, its advertising communicated the welcoming, homely associations previously attached to ground coffee.

In comparison, Japan, a largely tea-drinking nation, needed an advert where the refined tea-drinking traditions were clearly communicated to move consumers to consider instant coffee as an acceptable alternative to tea.

In other words, 'be global, act local' (e.g. Wind 1986; Huszagh et al. 1986). Consider the different market-perceived needs for a camera. In the USA, excellent pictures with easy, foolproof operation are expected by most of the markets; in Germany and in Japan, a camera must take excellent pictures but the camera must also be of state-of-the-art design. In Africa, where penetration of cameras is less than 20% of the households, the concept of picture-taking must be sold. In all three markets, excellent pictures are expected but the additional utility or satisfaction derived from a camera differs among cultures.

IN VIEW 8.3

When is standardisation appropriate?

- Brands that can be adapted for a visual appeal, avoiding the problems of trying to translate words into dozens of languages.

- Brands that are promoted with image campaigns that play to universal appeals such as sex or wealth.

- High-tech products and new products coming to the world for the first time, not steeped in the cultural heritage of the country.

- Products with nationalistic flavour if the country has a reputation in the field.

- Products that appeal to a market segment with universally similar tastes, interests, needs and values.

Strategic responses to the standardisation question

Centripetal forces

Internal organisational forces (e.g. policy, structure, culture, economies of scale) 'pulling' an organisation to standardise marketing programmes.

Centrifugal forces

Country-level forces external to an organisation 'pushing' it to adapt marketing programmes.

Global strategy

Strategy that is based on taking advantage of cultural similarities to produce standardised, global marketing communications.

Global niche strategy

Strategy for standardised marketing communications that focus on similar niche groups across countries.

The PRESTCOM environment produces both **centripetal** and **centrifugal forces** impacting on the organisation's decision to standardise its products and marketing communications (Melewar and Saunders 1998). Company-level centripetal forces of the need for organisational control and simplicity, the centralisation of operations and economies of scale pull an organisation to standardise marketing programmes. In the opposite direction are centrifugal country-level forces that push an organisation to adapt marketing programmes. The country-level variables include values, language, nationalism, customs and traditions, and create a varying degree of cultural distance between the domestic and target countries. Thus, strong centripetal forces (greater cultural distance) will decrease marketing mix standardisation.

Organisations have used one of four key strategies when operating internationally, the choice of which depends on the outcome of the environmental analysis specific to the organisation, brand and market. Exhibit 8.4 presents the four strategies available:

- A **global strategy** is based on cultural similarities instead of differences. This strategy is adopted if there is a high degree of homogeneity both within a culture and between cultures.
- A **global niche strategy** is based on the identification of a similar group or groups of people across countries. For example, students in the UK are perceived to be more similar to students in France, Germany and Greece, in terms of lifestyle and values, than they are to the rest of the UK population.

Exhibit 8.4 The cross-cultural marketing strategy framework (CroCMas)

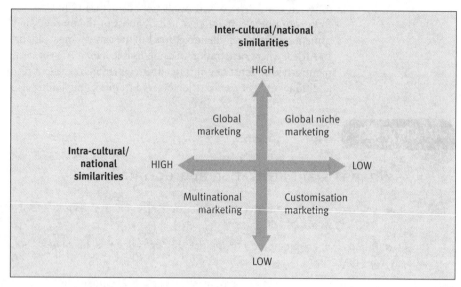

Source: Broderick et al. (1998)

Multinational strategy

Strategy recognising cultural diversity to develop marketing communications adapted to suit different countries.

Customisation strategy

The development of individual marketing communications specifically designed for each country.

● A **multinational strategy** is based on the premise of cross-cultural differences and is guided by the belief that each foreign market requires its own culturally adapted marketing communication strategy.

● A **customisation strategy** recognises the differences in consumers both within and between cultures and, therefore, communicates on an individualised basis.

If consumer differences are recognised and an adaptation strategy is selected, a further decision to make is the degree of adaptation. Exhibit 8.5 presents a framework that focuses on four marketing mix strategies available to an organisation. An organisation can standardise or localise both product and marketing communication programmes. All four cells may represent growth opportunities for the organisation. To determine which cell represents the organisation's best strategy, the marketer must conduct cross-cultural consumer analysis to obtain consumer reactions to alternative promotion executions.

Exhibit 8.5 International marketing communications strategies

Product	Communication strategy	
	Standardised	*Localised*
Standardised product	Same product: use current communications strategy	Use same product: adapt communications
Localised product	Adapt product: use current communications strategy	Total adaptation: new product and new communications strategy

Source: Adapted from table from Cateora, P., *International Marketing, 10th Edition*, Irwin, (1997), reproduced with the permission of The McGraw-Hill Companies.

IN VIEW 8.4

Global brands

RoperASW is optimistic about the future of global brands in the global marketplace. Based on interviews with 31,000 consumers in Europe, the Middle East, Asia and the Americas, the global research company concluded that 80% of consumers expect there to be more global brands and 60% say that is a good thing. However, consumers prefer a brand that is positioned in a way that makes it locally relevant. They are also concerned about honesty and integrity in a global company.

The one negative finding is that 41% of interviewees are wary of 'Americanisation'. Apart from in the US itself, consumers dislike American TV and feel Americanisation is bad for the world.

For more information log on to **www.roperasw.com**.

Source: Marketing Business, September 2002, p. 6

The impact of the international context on marketing communications

Marketing communication and symbols

Symbols

Things that represent, stand for, or are associated with something else.

Communication, whether inter or intra-cultural, can only take place when the participants in the process share a set of meaningful symbols. **Symbols** work as a powerful means of association or suggestion. For example, a fox may represent cunning, and an owl, wisdom. This association may or may not be made, as not every culture builds the same associations. The whole range of symbols used in communication, from language to non-verbal cues and ideological principles, beliefs, values and norms, are attributed meaning on the basis of experience. The more divergent the experiences of individuals, the more difficult it is for effective communication to take place.

Meaning symbols are principally conveyed through brand names, packaging and advertising. As symbolic interpretations can differ across cultures, the marketing communicator must be aware of the symbols utilised in an international context. For example, meanings associated with colours differ cross-culturally. In many Asian countries, white is associated with death and grief compared with birth and happiness connotations in Western countries.

IN VIEW 8.5

Cross-cultural colour symbolism

The colour green suggests freshness and good health in the UK, but is often associated with disease in countries with dense green jungles; it is a favourite colour among Arabs but forbidden in portions of Indonesia.

The universal symbol for mourning is not black. In many Asian countries it is white; in Brazil it is purple, yellow in Mexico and dark red in the Ivory Coast.

Americans think of blue as more masculine, but red is more manly in the UK and France. While pink is the most feminine colour in the UK, yellow is more feminine in most of the world.

Source: Adapted from Copeland and Griggs (1986), p. 63

Marketing communication and language

Understanding the use of language is fundamental to the international marketing communicator. When internationalising communications, part of the message, which is culturally unique, can be lost in the translation. A particular linguistic/cultural group expresses a 'world view' (Usunier 1996) and a slogan or advertising copy that is effective in one language may mean something completely different in another language. Translation errors are one of the major difficulties of internationalising marketing communications. Consider the following examples: General Motors, translating its slogan 'Body for Fischer' into Flemish for its Belgium campaign, found out belatedly that the meaning was equivalent to 'Corpse for Fischer'. General Motors' Vauxhall Nova was translated in Spanish markets as 'No Go'. The Jolly Green Giant brand was translated as the 'Intimidating Green Ogre' in Iraq and the Farsi translation of Kentucky Fried Chicken's logo 'Finger Lickin' Good became 'It's so good you will eat your fingers' in Iran. In Italy, 'Schweppes Tonic Water' had to be reduced to 'Schweppes Tonica' because 'il water' turned out to be an idiom for a bathroom (Henessey 1992).

The language input in marketing communications, directly relevant in terms of designing advertising copy, is also indirectly relevant in terms of understanding consumer moods and emotions. For example, life insurance advertising implies the evocation of death, which may be taboo in certain cultures, or subject to the use of a particular vocabulary and subdued style (Usunier 1996).

High-context communications

Most of the information of the communication relies on factors external to the communication itself; it relies on contextual cues to give it meaning. It requires a high level of interpretation by the receiver.

Low-context communications

The communication is largely self-contained, and does not rely on contextual cues to convey its meaning.

An important distinction in communication is whether or not the messages being sent by the speaker are in a high or low context. 'A **high-context communication** or message is one on which most of the information is either in the physical context or internalised in the person, while very little is in the coded, explicit, transmitted part of the message. A **low-context communication** is just the opposite; i.e. the mass of the information is vested in the explicit code' (Hall 1976). In low context cultures, messages are explicit and words carry most of the information in communication. In a high context culture, less information is contained in the verbal part of a message. For example, in a low context culture, one gets down to business very quickly, but in a high context culture, it takes considerably longer to conduct business because of the need to know more about a business person before a relationship develops. Context influences communication by bringing together the cultural interpretative mechanisms that allow a message to be explained. For example, the cultural assumptions between age and credibility may be positive, negative or neutral, so that such unspoken questions as, 'does this young speaker deserve trust?' are established within the context of the communication. Exhibit 8.6 outlines the contextual differences in the cultures around the world.

Marketing communication and cultural values

The values evident in a particular culture will have an impact on the type of communication appeals that are appropriate. For example, German advertising appeals tend to be more effective if they are rational and cognitive, French if they are emotional and hedonic, and British if they are self-critical and humorous. Korean advertisements include significantly more elderly persons than in the US, UK and France as wisdom is highly valued in Far Eastern cultures (Cutler et al. 1992). An advertising appeal that states 'our company has been in business for over 20 years' would be more successful in Japan than 'act today … and save money on this new model', as Japanese values encompass a respect for longevity, reliability and the concept that there is a right time for everything.

Exhibit 8.6 High and low context cultures

Factors/dimensions	High context	Low context
A person's word	Is his or her bond	Is not to be relied on; get it in writing
Responsibility for organisational error	Taken at highest level	Pushed to lowest level
Space	People breathe on each other	People maintain a bubble of private space and resent intrusion
Time	Polychronic – everything in life must be dealt with in its own time	Monochronic – time is money Linear – one thing at a time
Negotiations	Are lengthy – a major purpose is to get the parties to know each other	Proceed quickly
Competitive bidding	Infrequent	Common
Country/regional	Japan/Middle East	USA, Northern Europe

Source: Keegan (1993)

Cultural values are also expressed in social norms. For example, within Europe, 70% of UK couples currently buy diamond engagement rings whereas in Germany, there is no engagement ring tradition; couples simply get married. Social norms have an impact on what appeals a brand should communicate (In View 8.6).

IN VIEW 8.6

Social norms and De Beers advertising campaign

De Beers' challenge to advertise diamonds to the world was to identify a single powerful consumer motivation out of a turmoil of national differences, among markets as culturally, religiously, historically and economically diverse as Europe and Asia, the Gulf and the USA, Australia and South America. The central advertising objective was to strengthen diamond jewellery's position as the ultimate gift of love in a single approach, unifying all the important mature and developing countries, yet flexible enough to recognise local needs.

A few examples of the diversity in social norms affecting the marketing of diamond jewellery include:

● In Islamic circles, bridal sets (comprising necklace, earrings, bracelet and ring) symbolise parental care and are given by both sets of parents as a nest egg for the bride.
● US traditions include the 'Sweet Sixteen' diamond for fathers to give their daughters in recognition of their transition to womanhood. The birth of a child is often commemorated with diamond jewellery.
● Japan has historically had a pearl-based jewel tradition. There was no Japanese word for diamond until the 1960s.
■ In Eastern cultures, from Turkey to the Far East, everything revolves around gold as a form of security or portable wealth.

Source: Adapted from Duckworth (1996)

Hofstede (1980) conducted seminal research on work-related cultural values. He investigated the evidence of cultural values in 40 countries along four main dimensions. The dimensions include:

- *Power distance* – the extent to which a society and its individual members tolerate an unequal distribution of power in organisations and in society as a whole.
- *Uncertainty avoidance* – the extent to which people in a society tend to feel threatened by uncertain, ambiguous, risky or undefined situations.
- *Femininity/masculinity* – masculine-dominant value systems favour assertiveness, earning money, showing off possessions and caring little about others. Feminine societies favour nurturing roles, interdependence between people and caring for others.
- *Individualism/collectivism* – individualism is based on the principle of asserting one's independence and individuality and society has a responsibility to maximise individual freedom. Collectivism views the group as the basic resource and therefore group values are favoured (loyalty, sense of belonging, sense of personal sacrifice for the community) (Usunier 1996).

Value systems are ordered along these dimensions and affect human thinking, organisations and institutions in predictable ways. All have implications for the behaviour of individuals in organisations. Problems can arise, for example, when multinational companies try to unify the remuneration systems of local sales staff and when they attempt to apply standardised incentive systems linked to the parent company's culture to local sales representatives. While in the UK, emphasis is placed on precise and individualised sales targets and fostering competition within the sales force, Hill et al. (1991) emphasise a very different philosophy in the collectivist, Japanese, culture:

> **Tradition is an important determinant of Japanese compensation plans. Because their social system is based on hereditary and seniority criteria, salary raises, even for sales forces, are based on longevity with the company. Similarly, commission systems are tied to the combined efforts of the entire sales force, fostering the Japanese team ethic, and downplaying the economic aspirations of individuals.**
>
> (Hill et al. 1991, p. 23)

Organising for international marketing communications

A further international marketing communications issue companies face is whether to use advertising agencies from the local market, on a global basis or combine both. For example, Colgate acquired Kolynos' line of oral-care products in Latin America for which McCann-Erickson World Wide is responsible. Young & Rubicam advertising agency, however, has the bulk of Colgate business elsewhere (Beatty 1995). Global advertising agencies have their own set of strengths and weaknesses as outlined here.

Certainly there are pros and cons to working with a global advertising agency. On the whole, global agencies have good experience of different markets and are keen to take on global campaigns. They tend to adopt a consistent approach and possess a high degree of creativity. On the negative side, they can lack sufficient local market knowledge leading to poor differentiation. Their sheer size can result in too many administrative layers, inflexibility and predilection for 'big budget' prices.

According to Keegan (1993), in selecting an advertising agency for international marketing communications, the following issues should be considered:

1 Company organisation: companies that are decentralised internationally may want to leave the marketing communications decisions to a local subsidiary. Highly centralised companies may use one advertising agency for global communications.

2 National responsiveness: is the global agency familiar with the local culture and buying habits in a particular country, or should a local selection be made?
3 Area coverage: does the agency cover all relevant markets?
4 Buyer perception: what kind of brand awareness does the company want to project? If the product needs a strong local identification, it would be best to select a national agency. (Adapted from Keegan 1993.)

Exhibit 8.7 presents the world's top 10 advertising agencies and their expenditure. From the Exhibit, it can be seen that 5% of the world's top 20 advertising agencies account for 35% of total world advertising spend of $250 billion. These agency groups have a large number of overseas offices. For example, Leo Burnett has over 80 overseas offices with about a quarter located in the USA. Many of the agencies are also transnational in ownership. Much of the pressure for the internationalisation of agency networks has come from the big marketers who, in pursuit of their global markets, have driven the expansion of their agencies.

Exhibit 8.7 Top 10 advertising agencies in the world

Rank	Organisation	Headquarters	Volume ($bn)
1	WPP Group	London	27.7
2	Omnicom Group	New York	23.4
3	Interpublic Group	New York	20.1
4	Dentsui	Tokyo	14.1
5	Young & Rubicam	New York	12.0
6	Cordiant	London	9.8
7	Havas Advertising	L-Perret, France	7.3
8	True North Comm.	Chicago	7.0
9	MacManus Group	New York	6.8
10	Hakuhodo	Tokyo	6.7

Source: Advertising Age (21 April 1997)

Summary

As organisations increasingly expand overseas, it is crucial to understand the forces within the international environment. This chapter provides an extension to the PRESTCOM framework, as presented in Chapter 7, and outlines key environmental forces pertinent in an international context. Whether to standardise or adapt marketing communications when internationalising is a debate that has been ongoing since the 1980s. The arguments for and against the two philosophies are presented. Four alternative international marketing communications strategies are outlined: Global, Global Niche, Multinational and Customisation, the choice of which depends on the degree of intra- versus inter-cultural variation. Finally, the impact of the international context on four key components of marketing communications is discussed.

Self-review questions

1 Identify the main reasons why organisations are increasingly internationalising.

2 What does PRESTCOM stand for and why should an organisation use this analysis framework?

3 What are the environmental factors that are particularly pertinent in the international marketplace?

4 What are the three main reasons for an organisation's use of a 'captious cues' strategy?

5 Outline the advantages and disadvantages of an adaptation strategy for marketing communications.

6 When should an organisation use a multinational marketing communications strategy?

7 What is the significance of symbols in international marketing communications?

8 How is a low-context culture likely to affect marketing communications?

9 How do individualism and collectivism values affect marketing communications?

10 What are the advantages and disadvantages of using a global advertising agency?

Project

Select a foreign country and analyse it from an international marketing communications environment perspective. Your analysis should follow a PRESTCOM framework. Discuss the implications of your analysis for a company developing an integrated marketing communications programme for that country. What specific problems or limitations might a company face in the development and implementation of an IMC programme in areas such as advertising and other promotional mix elements?

References

Advertising Age (1997), Top 10 advertising agencies in the world. *Advertising Age*, 21 April.

Bannister, J. and Saunders, J. (1978), UK consumers' attitude towards imports: the measurement of national stereotype image. *European Journal of Marketing*, 12 (8), 562–570.

Bareham, J. (1995), *Consumer Behaviour in the Food Industry: A European Perspective*. Oxford: Butterworth-Heinemann.

Beatty, S.G. (1995), Is only one for Colgate. *The Wall Street Journal*, 1 December.

Biers, D. (1996), US bid to check export origins of Hong Kong garment makers. *The Wall Street Journal*, 23 July, A19.

Bilkey, W. and Nes, E. (1982), Country of origin effects on product evaluations. *Journal of International Business Studies*, 8, 89–99.

Broderick, A.J., Greenley, G.E. and Mueller, R.D. (1998), Utilising consumer involvement for international decision-making in the food retail market. *Proceedings of the EMAC Conference*, May, Stockholm, pp. 481–500.

Brown, I.C. (1963), *Understanding Other Cultures*. Englewood Cliffs, NJ: Prentice Hall.

Burt, S.L. (1991), Trends in the internationalisation of grocery retailing: the European experience. *International Review of Retail Distribution and Consumer Research*, 1 (4), 487–515.

Cateora, P. (1993), *International Marketing* 6th edn. Irwin.

Copeland, L. and Griggs, L. (1986), Going International. New York: Plume Books/New American Library.

Cordell, V. (1992), Effects of consumer preferences for foreign sourced products. *Journal of International Business Studies*, 2nd quarter, 251–269.

Crain, R. (1994), Why verification isn't as easy as it sounds. *Global Trade and Transportation*, August, 12.

Cutler, R.D., Javalgi, R.G. and Erramilli, M.K. (1992), The visual component of print advertising: a five-country cross-cultural analysis. *European Journal of Marketing*, 26 (4), 7–20.

Dawson, J.A. (1994), Internationalisation of retailing operations. *Journal of Marketing Management*, 10, 267–282.

De Jonquieres, G. (1991), Unilever's food operations. *Financial Times*, 28 October.

Dubois, B. (1987), Culture et marketing. *Recherche et Applications en Marketing*, 2 (3), 37–64.

Duckworth, G. (ed.) (1996), Advertising Works 9: Advertising effectiveness awards. *Institute of Practitioners in Advertising*, NTC Publications, pp. 307–320.

European Marketing Intelligence (1994a), *Country Special Report: France*. Mintel International Group Ltd.

European Marketing Intelligence (1994b), *Country Special Report: Germany*. Mintel International Group Ltd.

European Marketing Intelligence (1994c), *Country Special Report: UK*. Mintel International Group Ltd.

European Marketing Intelligence (1994d), *Country Special Report: Italy*. Mintel International Group Ltd.

European Marketing Intelligence (1994e), *Country Special Report: Spain*. Mintel International Group Ltd.

Freedman, P. (1994), Boundaries of Good Taste. *Geographical Magazine*, April, 66 (4), 12–14.

Gilley, B. (1996), Lure of the West. *Far Eastern Economic Review*, 15 August, 70.

Gitelson, J. (1992), Populux: the suburban cuisine of the 1950s. *Journal of American Culture*, 15 (3), Fall, 73–78.

Green, J. (1995), Culture clash. *The Prague Post*, 14–20 June, 10–11a.

Hall, E.T. (1976), *Beyond Culture*. New York: Doubleday.

Henessey, J. (1992), *Global Marketing* 2nd edn. Houghton Mifflin Company.

Hill, J.S., Still, R.R. and Boya, U.O. (1991), Managing the multinational sales force. *International Marketing Review*, 8 (1), 84–87.

Hofstede, G. (1980), *Culture's Consequences: International Differences in Work-Related Values*. Beverly Hills, CA: Sage.

Hollensen, S. (1998), *Global Marketing*. Prentice Hall.

Howard, R. (1991), The designer organisation: Italy's GFT goes global. *Harvard Business Review*, September–October.

Huszagh, S.M., Fox, R.J. and Day, E. (1986), Global marketing: an empirical investigation. *Columbia Journal of World Business*, 20 (4), 31–43.

Jain, S.C. (1989), Standardisation of international marketing strategy: some research hypotheses. *Journal of Marketing*, 53, January, 70–79.

Kaynak, E. and Cavusgil, T. (1989), Consumer attitudes towards products of foreign origin: do they vary across product classes? *International Journal of Advertising*, 2, April–June, 157–167.

Keegan, W. (1993), *Global Marketing Management* 6th edn. Prentice Hall.

Kotler, P. (1988), *Marketing Management, Analysis, Planning, Implementation and Control*. Prentice Hall.

Labarre, P. (1994), Quality's silent partner. *Industry Week*, 243, 18 April, 47–48.

Laulajainen, R. (1991), International expansion of an apparel retailer: Hennes and Mauritz of Sweden. *Zeitschrift fur Wirschaftsgeographie*, 35 (1), 1–15.

Levitt, T. (1983), The globalisation of markets. *Harvard Business Review*, April/May, 92–107.

M&M Europe (1995), *M&M Poll of Advertisers*. July, pp. iv–vii.

Marketing Business (2002) Overseas update. September, 6.

Martin, I. and Eroglu, A. (1993), Measuring a multi-dimensional construct: country image. *Journal of Business Research*, 28, 191–210.

Melewar, T.C. and Saunders, J. (1998), Global corporate visual identity systems: standardisation, control and benefits. *International Marketing Review*, 15 (4), 291–308.

Menendez, G. (1996), Made in Macau – or China. *American Shipper*, August, 26–27.

Morello, G. (1984), The 'Made in' issue: a comparative research on the image of domestic and foreign products. *European Research*, 12, January, 5–21.

Mottley, R. (1996), How Israel offers virtual NAFTA status. *American Shipper*, 38, May, 68–69.

Mueller, R.D. and Broderick, A.J. (1999) Utilising captious cues for international marketing strategy. *Proceedings of the Association of International Business Conference*, Charleston.

Mueller, R. and Gajdusek, P. (1996), Czech made – Czech quality: the promotion of Czech country of origin. *Journal of East West Business*, 2 (3/4), 143–156.

Ohmae, K. (1989), Managing in a borderless world. *Harvard Business Review*, May–June.

Porter, M. (1992), The strategic role of international marketing. In *Global Marketing Management. Cases and Readings*. Boston, MA: Harvard Business School.

Porter, M.E. (1986), Changing patterns of international competition. *California Management Review*, 28 (2), 9–39.

Quelch, J.A. and Hoff, E.J. (1986), Customising global marketing. *Harvard Business Review*, 64, May–June, 59–68.

Raju, P.S. (1995), Consumer behaviour in global markets: the ABCD paradigm and its application to Eastern Europe and the Third World. *Journal of Consumer Marketing*, 12 (5), 37–56.

Schiffman, L. and Kanuk, L.L. (1999), *Consumer Behaviour*. Prentice Hall.

Shimp, T. and Sharma, S. (1987), Consumer ethnocentrism: construction and validation of the CETSCALES. *Journal of Marketing Research*, 26, August, 280–289.

Shimp, T., Sharma, S. and Shin, J. (1995), Consumer ethnocentrism: a test of antecedents and moderators. *Journal of the Academy of Marketing Science*, 23 (1), 26–37.

Smith, D. (1996), A deficit of consumer loyalty. *Management Today*, July, 22.

Sumner, W.G. (1906), *Folkways: A Study of the Sociological Importance of Usage. Manners, Customs Mores, and Morals*. Boston: Ginn.

Usunier, Jean-Claude (1996), *Marketing Across Cultures*. Prentice Hall.

Wind, Y. (1986), The myth of globalisation. *Journal of Consumer Marketing*, 3, Spring, 23–26.

Wind, Y., Douglas, S.P. and Perlmutter, H.V. (1973), Guidelines for developing international marketing strategies. *Journal of Marketing*, 37, April, 14–23.

 ## Selected further reading

Anholt, S. (1995), Global message, pan European advertising. *Grocer* 217, 22, April, 35–40.

Kanso, Ali (1992), International advertising strategies: global commitment to local vision. *Journal of Advertising Research*, January–February.

Li, W., Leung, K. and Weyer, R. (1993), The roles of country of origin information on buyers' product evaluations: signal or attribute? *Advances in Consumer Research*, 20, 684–689.

Maheswaren, D. (1994), Country of origin as a stereotype: effects of consumer expertise and attribute strength on product evaluations. *Journal of Consumer Research*, 21, September, 354–365.

Rodwell, T. (1996), Local flavour for a global message is common sense. *Marketing*, 19, December, 16.

Schramm, T. (1955), *The Process and Effects of Mass Communication*. University of Illinois Press.

Simango, C. (1999), *International Marketing Communications*. Blackwell.

Chapter 9

Regulation and legal controls

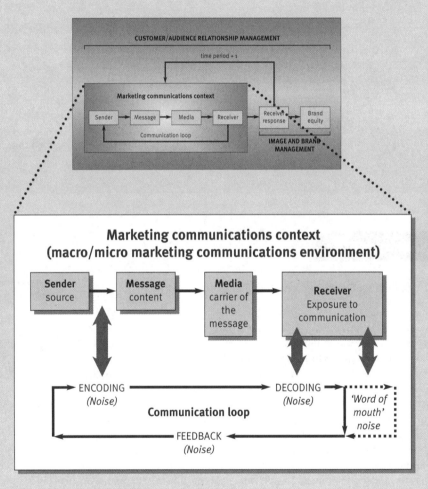

The IMC Process Model

CD

For each marketing communication medium identified in Chapter 5 that Concern uses, identify the relevant regulatory body. Of the regulations imposed by these bodies, which elements are of particular relevance for Concern?

Chapter outline

- Need for regulation and control
- Forms of regulation and control
- Legal regulation and control
- Self-regulation and control
- An international comparison of approaches to self-regulation

Objectives

- To address the arguments for regulation and control of marketing communications
- To identify the two main forms of regulation; legal and self-regulation
- To provide an overview of the variety of legal regulations affecting marketing communications
- To provide an overview of the system of self-regulation in an international context but with particular reference to the British system as an exemplar of good practice
- To emphasise the difference between broadcast and non-broadcast regulations

Professional perspective

Matti Alderson Ex-Director General, Advertising Standards Authority

If it were possible – or desirable – to contrive a completely *tidy* marketing environment, self-regulation would be supplanted by strictly enforced legislation. The law would impinge on every nuance and claim in every medium. Competition, comparisons, even humour, would be regimented with infuriating precision.

But consumers aren't tidy thinkers, and they would balk at such bullying; tastes and choices, even in advertisements, are personal and often illogical.

The fact is that the two extremes, of law alone or of pure self-regulation, are equally flawed. Clogged courts hearing minor issues at one end of the spectrum versus fraudulent advertising with no criminal remedy at the other wouldn't benefit consumers or reputable companies. Even television and radio, which both have direct statutory backing, subscribe to a regime where self-imposed rules are the daily currency.

The solution for non-broadcast advertising is the ASA. Non-statutory, non-industry, non-government, the Authority supervises an independent process that works successfully within framework legislation.

Self-regulation is enlightened self-interest: companies earn credibility with consumers by following strict, self-imposed rules and sanctions. Legislation then bites where sharp teeth are needed to discourage or punish serious miscreants. The two are not in competition. On the contrary, the synergy between them is crucial to producing in the UK the world's highest advertising standards.

The UK's mature system and codes are used as a model around the world, fostering regular ASA contact internationally. And as a founding member of the European Advertising Standards Alliance in Brussels the

ASA communicates regularly with legislators and opinion formers around the EU. This ever-broadening plurality of influence and its legislative consequences have a direct bearing on advertising regulation which is pivotal to safeguarding consumers and advertising freedoms.

Legislation, self-regulation, consumer protection and ethical practice are interdependent. For the future, the evolution of the Internet and other media will diminish external control on the messages consumers see and increase the importance of self-regulation. And as an industry practitioner, it will be your turn to play your own part in the continued success of our widely exported UK system. This text will provide a sound beginning, and I commend it to you.

Martin Anderson

Need for regulation and control

What do you think about the account executive's ideas for advertising the slimming product in In View 9.1? Do you think that this would be an acceptable advertisement?

The example features sexual material broadcast during peak viewing periods when young children could be watching and some of the stills from the TV ad are intended to be used on posters and in magazines. Some viewers might consider the advertisement to be acceptable but the visual treatment could cause widespread offence to others.

IN VIEW 9.1

Slim and sexy

'Picture this,' enthused the over-zealous account executive, 'It will be multi-cast on satellite, cable and terrestrial TV – Prime Time – and ably supported by some "hot" poster and magazine graphics, some of the more interesting shots. The slogan – "This Could Be You. Live Your Dreams". Sales will go cosmic.' The clients looked on enthralled. They were hooked.

The account executive continued. 'The scene ... a Caribbean island. On the horizon, a golden setting sun rests on a rippling azure sea. Background music – slow, easy and *sexy*. Palm trees sway seductively over whispering sands. Long shadows caress the contours of naked bathers. I mean these are your beautiful people. The camera focuses tight and pans slowly, provocatively over the legs, hips, waist and bust of one of the rich tanned beauties and then slowly, very slowly over the bronzed Adonis lying next to her. Their bodies, slim and lithe, writhe. They are having some serious fun in the sun.'

The voice-over: '*This Is You. Live Your Dreams. Be slim and sexy with "Slim and Sexy", a slimming product that really does work. It is your guaranteed passport to paradise. You know you want it, you deserve it, now you can have it.*'

The clients were stunned. The account exec's voice broke the momentary silence, 'What do you think?'

What about the advertisement's explicit claim that the product guarantees a slimmer and sexier 'you', and its implicit claims of sexual promiscuity? Could such a product support such assertions? Would you allow the advertisement to be broadcast and displayed? Should advertising and other promotions be regulated in some way? Should there be rules and controls to curb promoters' actions? If so, how might this be achieved?

This hypothetical example illustrates the reason why some form of regulation and control is needed. Without rules, and the enforcement of those rules, it would be possible to create promotions that use language and images which many people would consider to be unacceptable, perhaps for many different reasons. Even with such rules, there are no guarantees that all will be perfect, but by having controls, misdemeanours are restricted. Yet caution also has to be exercised. An over-burdensome system of regulations and controls would stifle business activity and be difficult to maintain.

Social acceptability and ethics

There would be few who would argue against the need for marketing communications to be seen as socially acceptable, but the issues of acceptability and responsibility are, in part, socially determined ethical ones (Chapter 10 considers ethical issues in greater depth). There can be extreme difficulty in defining what is, and what is not, ethical especially when the notion of social acceptability changes over time and varies from one culture or country to another. Not all individuals can even agree on what might create offence. The Sally Lines example in In View 9.2 section illustrates this. What is acceptable to one person may be deemed unacceptable to another. For this reason, regulations are concerned about what might cause *widespread*, rather than individual, offence.

Some viewers are offended by nudity whereas others cannot see what the fuss is all about. The highly controversial Benetton advertising of the mid-1990s provides a good example of this. The 'Black Mama' poster campaign which featured a white baby at the naked breast of a black woman gave rise to numerous complaints throughout Europe but was generally considered not to cause significant or widespread offence. In other words, it was seen as being socially acceptable in today's society. This was not the case in the USA where the posters were never seen. Regulations in the USA prohibit such public nudity in poster advertising. The advertising was, however, published in American magazines where it

NEED TO KNOW

☑ *The regulatory system cannot ensure that offence is never caused. What regulators attempt to do is to avoid offence being serious or widespread.*

WARNING

❗ *It is extremely difficult to ensure that marketing communications are equally acceptable in all international countries. Direct mail, international television broadcasts and the Internet are areas where particular attention has to be paid.*

IN VIEW 9.2

Sally crosses the line

The ferry company 'Sally Lines' used a headline in one of their advertisements, 'Only Sally Goes All The Way For £40'. On seeing the advertisement, a lady whose name also was Sally, took offence. Having originally complained to the company and received no satisfaction, she complained to the Advertising Standards Authority (ASA). On investigating the complaint, while the ASA respected that Sally had been offended, they ruled that the advertisement was acceptable in that it was not likely to cause grave or widespread offence.

did cause offence to many, not on the grounds of nudity, but because of racial concern. Another Benetton example is shown in Plate 10.

In the increasingly **global 'village'** in which we live, where technology facilitates worldwide communications, the issues of social acceptance become more and more complex to determine and to police. This is particularly so for the international broadcast media of television, radio and the Internet because people in different countries hold different views of what they consider to be ethical and acceptable. In particular, issues of taste and decency can create extreme difficulties.

Where a piece of promotion is clearly telling lies or is deliberately misleading, the ethics are somewhat more clearcut. We expect promoters to tell the truth. We do not wish ourselves or others to be misled. Not only are there voluntary, self-regulation codes governing truthfulness but there are also many legal regulations that protect the unwary from the unscrupulous. Too burdensome a system of regulatory control, however, would not be satisfactory. For many, greater control represents a lessening of freedom.

Global village

Term coined by Marshall McLuhan to describe the way in which communications appear to be making the world seem smaller and interactions more immediate.

NEED TO KNOW

☑ *Acceptance of images and messages vary widely across the world. Perfectly acceptable marketing communications in one country would be banned in another.*

Freedom of choice and information

Marketing communications provide information that facilitates freedom of choice between competing goods and services. Some have argued that advertising and promotions are:

> an essential part of any real democracy, which is always based on *freedom of choice*. Democracy recognises and respects the ability of each individual person to assimilate information and make well-informed choices. Advertising is also the voice of free enterprise.

> (Roger Neill 1990, reported in Boddewyn 1992, p. 145)

'But of course,' argued Sir Gordon Borrie, Director General of the Office of Fair Trading,

> While competition requires that people be free to advertise, misleading statements will distort competition. An efficient and truly competitive market depends upon the ready availability of truthful information and the suppression of misleading information and deception. And a great paradox of competition is that those who are not succeeding in competition, those who are failing to compete on legitimate grounds, may often resort to misleading the public. Obviously, this is to the detriment of consumers but it is also to the disadvantage of their competitors. This is why certain rules and regulations are required ... regulation is essential to give advertising the credibility and the reputation that are necessary for it to fulfil its marketing function. How can advertising effectively perform its task if lies are the norm or hyperbole is simply unrestrained?
> (Borrie 1990, p. 1)

NEED TO KNOW

☑ *The principles of the self-regulation system are based on a sense of fair play to all. Marketing communicators should be socially responsible and encourage fair competition. They should undertake marketing communications that are legal, decent, honest and truthful.*

The challenge for all parties involved in promotions – those in the industry, the government and consumer representatives – is knowing how much freedom and how much control should be allowed and, having decided this, who should enforce any restraints that are imposed.

Regulations and restrictions may be imposed for reasons other than to avoid offending somebody or simply to ensure truthfulness. For example, restrictions are placed on cigarette, alcohol and drugs promotions because their consumption is deemed to be dangerous.

Comparative advertising

Advertising in which competing products are compared.

Comparative advertising is constrained to avoid unfair trading practices, and rules are applied to product description and labelling to encourage accurate information and comparisons between competing brands. It has been suggested that marketing communications should be constrained to purely factual information and should avoid any reference to emotional and persuasive appeals. Yet freedom of information is not only freedom to convey facts. Even a cursory look around at packaging, public relations, sales promotions, direct marketing communications, television, press and poster advertising will reveal that there is very little promotional effort put into purely informative promotions. Rather, a great deal of effort goes into what the French advertisers call, 'Faire rêver, faire sourire' – to make people dream and to make people smile. Indeed, it is difficult to conceive of a world of marketing communications without its emotional and entertainment dimensions. Research into people's attitudes to promotions reveals that they welcome promotions that they find entertaining.

Scale of the problem

FOOD FOR THOUGHT

The number of items that receive complaints is only a very tiny fraction of all forms of marketing communications. Of this, still fewer complaints are actually upheld.

Marketing communications is the most visible of all marketing activities and it is subject to constant inquiry by competitors, regulators, consumers and consumer groups. Each year there are literally millions of advertisements and millions of other forms of promotions – printed, distributed, displayed and broadcast all around the world. In reality, it is only a few of them that are offensive, misleading, unfair or false. Of course, when such marketing communications are brought to the public's attention there are understandable and grave concerns. But the extent of such misconduct needs to be put into context.

Self-regulation

Voluntary control of acceptable marketing communications agreed by the marketing communications industry itself.

The British system of **self-regulation**, which has been called the most developed and effective self-regulatory system in the world, results in about 12,000 cases a year being investigated. Of these, about 1000 promotions have to be withdrawn or modified. In the US, the combined actions of the Federal Trade Commission (FTC), the National Advertising Division (NAD), the National Advertising Review Board (NARB) and the Federal Courts result in less than 300 adjudicated cases.

Clearly, some will argue that these may only represent the tip of an iceberg. But given the scale of all promotions, those that are unacceptable (legally and by the measures of self-regulation) must represent only a tiny fraction. Nevertheless, this tiny amount should still be considered as unacceptable as they reduce the credibility of the remaining vast majority.

Forms of regulation and control

Marketing communications throughout Europe and elsewhere are subject to constraints. Some are specified in law and others are self-imposed by the marketing communications industry itself. The extent of these constraints varies significantly from country to country although attempts are being made to exert a degree of standardised control throughout the European Community. Indeed, this is an increasingly important issue as the 'barriers' between countries are diminishing and the new telecommunications technology is making access throughout the world so much easier.

Marketing communications activities are regulated by an interplay of rules laid down by law and by a process of self-regulation. How well the combination of regulations work, however, varies significantly from country to country. Whereas legal rules are set and administered by the state, self-regulation is a process of commercial and industry practice in, first, determining the rules to be applied and second, in imposing mechanisms for monitoring and enforcing those rules. Self-regulation means that the rules are drawn up and enforced by the marketing communications industry itself, are developed within the context of a legal framework, and complement any laws which may be in existence. As circumstances and laws change, so should the self-imposed, voluntary regulations.

The case for legal controls

Statutory regulation and control restricts marketing communications by the use of government rules and penalties that are enforced through the courts of law. This approach basically emphasises that the public interest is best served through mandatory regulation because business cannot be trusted to regulate itself. It also assumes that consumers and competitors left to their own devices are not otherwise able to counteract or challenge bad practice.

FOOD FOR THOUGHT

If there were no legal controls, would organisations feel free to undertake unethical practices?

Some argue that unless clear legal guidelines are imposed, companies will always try to promote their goods and services in whatever way they feel fit to do so. Unless there are statutory curbs, they will not feel duty bound to abide by practices that are in the best interests of the customer and society at large. Competitive pressures will lead to less acceptable conduct than would be desirable.

Such arguments clearly represent views that highlight the 'dark side' of human and organisational behaviour. These views seem to have some justification. Even when legal controls are imposed some organisations still persist in flaunting those controls. How much more so if no regulation existed at all? Over recent years, there has been a growth in occurrences of promotions deliberately featuring shock tactics. The result of these has been extensive media coverage bringing the items being promoted to the attention of the public at no extra cost to the promoter, so 'extending' their marketing communications budget.

The major advantage of legal control lies in its universal applicability – the laws apply to all and should apply fairly to all – which a laissez-faire or self-regulatory system may not be able to achieve. Conversely, the drawing up and enforcing of statutes, and the application of case law, is not a straightforward process. Legal controls have been accused of being oppressive, time-consuming, rigid, ineffective and, in many instances, costly.

IN VIEW 9.3

Sweden's system of regulation

It is notable that before 1970, Sweden used a system of self-regulation similar to that which operates in Britain today. However, in the 1970s, the self-regulatory system almost completely disappeared to be replaced by strong legal and government intervention. Since that time, only a limited self-regulatory system has been reintroduced to complement the legal controls.

The case for self-regulation

Self-regulation codes of practice are set by the bodies representing the marketing communications industry both as general codes of practice and as professional codes of conduct which each body specifies and seeks to maintain. Some codes apply across the industry, professional codes of conduct apply to specific interest groups (such as public relations, sales promotions, direct marketing, point of sale, merchandising, advertising and others, which have their own professional associations), some apply to specific media and some apply to specific products. For example, in Finland (as with other Nordic countries there is strong emphasis on legal controls), commercial television regulates itself. It **pre-vets** all television commercials and follows its own code of practice based on the International Chamber of Commerce (ICC) International Code of Advertising Practice.

Pre-vetting

The process of checking and approving advertisements before they are released.

The principal advantages of self-regulation controls over legal controls are that they are much more flexible, they are easier to administer and can be changed relatively easily and quickly to take account of changing circumstances and public interest. Given the volume of work handled by self-regulatory bodies each year, if disputed in court, the work would be extremely slow and prohibitively expensive. The European Advertising Standards Alliance maintains that 'the law and self-regulation working independently but in harmony provide the swiftest and most comprehensive protection for consumers' (EASA, p. 1). Importantly, adoption of self-regulatory controls shows the promotions industry in a favourable light and, if working effectively, encourages the respect of the public. If self-regulation is seen not to be working, however, the opposite can easily result and a lack of trust can be engendered in the public.

Exhibit 9.1 Pros and cons of self-regulation

Pros of self-regulation	Cons of self-regulation
• Usually faster and less expensive, more flexible and up-to-date. Responsive	• Business competition and innovation are impaired because of restrictions, e.g. comparative advertising is restricted
• Does not require 'injury' be proven as in law. Burden of proof lies not with complainant but with promotor to prove claim to be correct	• Voluntary regulations may only impose minimum standards and enforcement may be lax
• Assists and complements statutory regulation. Goes beyond minimum prescribed by law	• May be hampered by 'anti-trust' and similar laws that preclude compulsory membership and adoption (some may be able to opt-out)
• Generates greater moral cohesion than the law. They are voluntarily and willingly imposed by the industry to reflect current values and norms to the benefit of all	• Lacks effective judicial and sanction tools
• The system helps minimise friction between businesses and consumers. Statutory regulation tends to encourage clashes	• May have too little financing to be effective
• The media – the intermediaries and carriers of the message – are willing participants in enforcement of self-regulation. The media as a third party between the promoter and the market adds a further layer of scrutiny and enforcement	• System may lack too few 'lay' people and involve too many industry representatives with the potential of over-indulgent self-interest

Source: Adapted from *Global Perspectives on Advertising Self-Regulation: Principles and Practices in Thirty-eight Countries*, 1st Edition. Boddewyn, J.J., Quorum Books, Copyright © 1992 Boddewyn, J.J. Reproduced with permission of Greenwood Publishing Group, Inc., Westport, CT

It is, therefore, in the interests of the marketing communications industry to 'police' itself and be seen enforcing its own rules.

Legal regulation and control

There are over 270 statutes and regulations that affect UK marketing communications (Kolah 2002). Some of these are identified in Appendix 9.1 at the end of this chapter. Despite the impression that this long list might create, the UK tends to favour a broadly voluntary code of practice because of the many advantages this has over legal controls. Many of the Acts affect very specific areas of business and are not necessarily applicable to everybody. Other countries have their own legal constraints on top of which, European countries have many directives imposed by the European Community. The degree of legal control varies significantly from one country to another with some countries preferring to emphasise legal controls above the self-imposed, voluntary alternative. Some countries, however, have very little regulation whether legal or voluntary.

A brief selected list of British statutes and some of the areas they cover is given in Exhibit 9.2.

Exhibit 9.2 Example of legislation

Legislation	Coverage
Sex Discrimination Acts (1975 and 1986) Race Relations Act (1976)	Marketing communications should not discriminate on grounds of sex, marital status, colour, race or ethnic origin
Trades Description Act (1968) Sale of Goods Act (1979)	False impressions should not be created, goods offered for sale should match their description, statements should be accurate and true, products supplied should be fit for the purpose described, companies and individuals may not represent themselves or their products as those of others
Indecent Advertisements (Amendment) Act (1970) Obscene Publications Act (1959 and 1964)	It is an offence to publish or exhibit any picture or written material that is of an obscene or indecent nature
Unsolicited Goods and Services Acts (1971, 1975 and Amendments (1975)	The distribution of material that has not been specifically requested, such as may be sent via direct mail, is regulated under these controls
Food Labelling Regulations (1984)	Packaging details are affected by this statute
The Fair Trading Act (1973) The Control of Misleading Advertisements Regulations (1988)	Powers are given to the Office of Fair Trading (OFT) requiring adherence OFT approved codes. OFT has the power to prosecute those whose marketing communications are deemed to mislead
The Competition Act (1980)	Regulates the form competitions may take
Price Indications (Methods of Payment) Regulations (1991) Price Marking Order (1991) Price Marking (Amendment) Order 1994	The statutes regulate pricing activities, their setting and marking
Pyramid Selling Schemes Regulations (1989 and Amendment 1990)	Types of sales structures are controlled under these regulations
Tobacco Advertising and Promotions Act 2002	Bans tobacco advertising and other forms of tobacco promotions

IN VIEW 9.4

Law stubs out tobacco promotions

Tobacco advertising, sales promotions and sponsorship became unlawful in the UK at 00.01 on Friday 14 February 2003. The ITC's Code already prohibited UK TV advertising of all tobacco products and the European Directive, *Television Without Frontiers (89/552/EEC)*, banned it throughout the European Union. The Tobacco Advertising and Promotions Act (2002) simply extended this to other media – print, billboards, Internet and direct mail as well as broadcast. The Act also bans sales promotions, free gifts, coupons and sponsorship.

The legislation comes after a long period of political lobbying by tobacco companies and consumer groups alike and will be fully implemented by 31 July 2005 when a ban on tobacco sponsorship of international sports such as Formula One and world snooker will come into force. Particular regulations concerning 'point of sale' and 'brand stretching' (brand sharing) form part of the legal changes which are further supplemented by an EU Directive agreed in December 2002 which deals with four types of cross-border promotions – Internet, radio, printed publications and international sponsorships.

Within the Act and accompanying regulations there is some latitude (although European and other international restrictions may apply). Advertising can still take place within the tobacco trade and in publications not intended for the UK (even if originated in the UK). Point of sale could be permitted in outlets, on vending machines and on specialist Internet sites where the majority of their sales are for tobacco-related products.

Corrective advertising

Corrective advertising

The requirement for advertisers to produce promotional material to correct any previous advertising considered to be misleading or incorrect.

Although not used extensively, there is a legal control used in the USA which has been considered for use in Europe. This is the use of **corrective advertising**. In America, the Federal Trade Commission (FTC) has the power to require an advertiser to do more than simply remove a piece of promotion that it considers to be unfair or deceptive. On the grounds that the claims made in such promotions are likely to still be remembered, the FTC can order the advertiser to cease its offending promotions and produce *extra promotional material* to rectify any deception or misinformation previously given.

Probably the most famous case is the first one ordered by the FTC in the 1970s. It involved Warner-Lambert, the manufacturer of Listerine mouthwash. Warner-Lambert took the FTC to court to challenge its ruling but they lost the case. For over 50 years Listerine had been promoted with the claim that gargling with it would help to prevent colds and sore throats. The company could not substantiate its claim and the FTC ordered Warner-Lambert to run $10 million worth of corrective advertising over a period of 16 months stating that Listerine did not help to prevent colds or sore throats.

Self-regulation and control

The self-regulation system of control of marketing communications is essentially a voluntary one although *provision* for self-regulation is a stated requirement in the legal regulations of many countries. This particularly applies to the regulation of broadcast media (television and radio) which have generally been considered as more invasive and persuasive. As the approach adopted to self-regulation differs between

Above-the-line communications

Term used to generally describe advertising promotions: that is, promotions that make use of commission-paying mass media – television, press, cinema, radio and posters. Also called above-the-line promotions and above-the-line advertising.

Below-the-line communications

Marketing communications that make use of the non-commission-paying media in all their forms, i.e. all forms of promotions other than advertising. Sometimes, incorrectly, it is referred to as below-the-line advertising. Although it remains a popular term, its usefulness is limited as it encompasses such a broad range of promotional activity.

the **above-the-line** and **below-the-line** media, this section of the chapter is broken down into two main areas, 'non-broadcast' and 'broadcast' self-regulation and control, and is preceded by a brief description of the general principles of self-regulation.

General principles of voluntary self-regulation and control

A simple phrase is used which captures the essence of what these regulations are trying to maintain and can be found in the documents of the leading regulatory bodies. All forms of marketing communications should be: *legal, decent, honest and truthful.*

The restrictions, regulations and controls that are imposed in the industry are all seeking the attainment of these ideals, ideals that marketing communicators need to recognise and seek to work towards within their daily practices. Codes of practice are set which are expected to be applied in both the 'spirit' and the 'letter'. By this it is meant that marketing communicators should adhere to the 'intentions' of the codes as well as the actual words used. It is also expected that all promotions should be produced with:

- a sense of responsibility to consumers and society
- acceptance of the principles of fair competition and business practice.

Legal

No promotion should omit anything which is required by law nor contain anything that breaks the law or incites anyone to break it. The specific details of the law varies from country to country but the broad intentions remain fairly common.

WARNING

> ! Marketing communications should be legal, decent, honest and truthful. They should be produced with a sense of responsibility to consumers and society. They should show acceptance of the principles of fair competition and business practice.

Decent

Promotions should not contain anything that is likely to cause *widespread* offence, fear or distress. Shocking claims or images should avoid being used for the sake of creating attention. If they are used, a valid and acceptable reason will need to be given. It would be impossible to ensure that promotional activity never causes offence although it is generally in the best interests of the promoter to work within the parameters of common decency. This is of particular concern in the context of those groups who are more sensitive, susceptible or disadvantaged such as children, the disabled and racial groups. However, the definition of decency is not a clear one and the prevailing standards have varied over the years and in different places around the world. In Britain, there are a number of laws which relate to the issues of offensiveness and decency such as the Obscene Publications Acts of 1959 and 1964, and the Indecent Advertisements (Amendment) Act (1970). Marketing communicators should always consider public sensitivities before using potentially offensive material as part of their ethical practices. It is not uncommon to find, however, that in each generation there are organisations that choose to test the limits of ethics and public taste.

Honest and truthful

Promotions should not exploit inexperience or lack of knowledge and no claims should be made which are inaccurate, ambiguous or intend to mislead whether through explicit statement or through omission. Promoters have the primary responsibility for ensuring that their promotions conform to the law of the land (and this needs to be applied to all countries in which the promotions are made available given that each country's laws are likely to differ). Interestingly, the British Code of Advertising, Sales Promotion and Direct Marketing, which is described below, does allow for *obvious* untruths or exaggerations that are *unlikely* to mislead because the audience would consider them as acceptable exaggerations.

Advertisers and promoters are allowed to express opinions provided that it is clear that they are opinions and not made to look like fact. Where there are differences of informed opinion about any claims that are made in promotional material, the promotions should *not* attempt to portray such claims as universally agreed. Before submitting a piece of promotion for publication or broadcast, promoters should hold documentary evidence to prove all claims made, whether direct or implied, and should be able to provide this evidence if requested so to do. The Independent Television Commission (ITC), the Radio Authority (RA) and the Advertising Standards Authority (the industry's primary self-regulatory bodies) are always available for consultation by anyone who wishes advice over the acceptability of any material being used. *All* broadcast advertising is required to be **pre-vetted** before transmission but problems can arise in the case of satellite transmissions to and from countries beyond the jurisdiction of the ITC and RA. Non-broadcast marketing communications do not need to be pre-vetted under normal circumstances although there are special cases where this does not apply.

Pre-vetting

The process of checking and approving advertisements before they are released.

Non-broadcast self-regulation and control

In Britain, *non-broadcast* promotions are regulated by the Committee of Advertising Practice (CAP) and the Advertising Standards Authority (ASA). Despite the emphasis on 'advertising' in its name, the work of the ASA actually embraces sales promotion, direct marketing communications and electronic promotions (e.g. email, text transmissions, banner and pop-up advertisements) activities as well. Its remit also covers cinema and video commercials. Professional standards in these and other areas of marketing communications are also maintained through the professional bodies which represent those interests: bodies such as the Institute of Practitioners in Advertising (IPA), the Advertising Association (AA), the Incorporated Society of British Advertisers (ISBA), the Institute of Sales Promotion (ISP), the Institute of Direct Marketing, the Direct Marketing Association (DMA) and the Institute of Public Relations (IPR), to name but a very few. Each professional body maintains its own codes of conduct and ethics and these are expected to be adhered to by all individual members.

History and development of British Advertising and Promotion Standards

In 1937 the International Chamber of Commerce (ICC) first issued their International Code of Advertising Practice. This was revised in later years to keep pace with changing circumstances and practices. The declared aim of the ICC was, and still is, 'to promote high standards of ethics in marketing by self-regulation against a background of national and international law'.

The ICC define the term 'advertising' in its broadest sense to embrace other forms of promotion irrespective of the medium used, including advertising claims on packs, labels and point of sale. Their four guiding principles (legal, decent, honest and truthful) have been followed ever since by numerous regulatory bodies throughout the world and are identified in their *General principles of voluntary self-regulation and control*. How well they are maintained, however, is a somewhat different issue.

When British television broadcast its first commercials in 1955, the television companies were obliged to conform to a single code of practice. It was at this time that it was first fully recognised that a similar code of practice for non-broadcast promotions would be sensible. The development of this code enabled a harmonisation of the existing voluntary codes into a unitary whole.

The Advertising Association initiated the task of compiling a code for non-broadcast promotions and, consisting of representatives from all sectors of the industry, the Committee of Advertising Practice (CAP) was formed. In 1961 the first edition of the British Code of Advertising Practice (BCAP) was published. It used, as a model, the International Code of Advertising Practice developed by the ICC. In the following year (1962), the Advertising Standards Authority (ASA) was set up to monitor and ensure that non-broadcast promotions met the clauses set out in the Code and that they adhered to those same familiar basic tenets adopted by the international community; advertising should be legal, decent, honest and truthful.

Over the years, the ASA have ensured that the Codes have evolved in line with changing public attitudes and legislation. The latest edition (11th), published in March 2003, emphasises the ASA's ever-increasing responsibilities by adopting the title 'British Code of Advertising, Sales Promotion and Direct Marketing'. Since 1995, they have included non-broadcast electronic media within their scope. Exhibit 9.3 charts some of the milestones leading to the system of self-regulation as it exists today within Britain.

Exhibit 9.3 Key dates in the development of British self-regulation

1937	Publication of the International Chamber of Commerce (ICC), International Code of Advertising Practice
1955	Recognition that a unified code of practice is needed to cover non-broadcast advertising in Britain
1961	First edition of the British Code of Advertising Practice produced by the Committee of Advertising Practice (CAP)
1962	The Advertising Standards Authority (ASA) is formed
1963	ASA first report issued
1972	The outcome of complaints first published by ASA ASA sets up Copy Advice Department
1974	Funding for ASA and CAP changed to a system of surcharge on advertising expenditure
1974	Labour Government threatens stronger legal controls. ASA respond with tougher Codes and an improved system
1974	The Sales Promotion Code is first introduced
1978	The Office of Fair Trading supports the ASA but calls for legal controls to back-up the self-regulatory system
1984	EC Directive issued on misleading advertising
1988	Legislation is introduced in the form of the Control of Misleading Advertising Regulations
1989	Courts declare that the ASA 'clearly exercise a public law function'. They subject its procedures to judicial review and find them 'perfectly proper and satisfactory'
1992	The ASA extends its scope to regulate the use of personal data for direct marketing purposes as well as the content of mailings
1995	Non-broadcast electronic media (e.g. the Internet, computer and video games, CD-ROMS) included in ASA's scope
2003	Latest Code of Advertising, Sales Promotion and Direct Marketing (11th edition) published

The British Code of Advertising, Sales Promotion and Direct Marketing

The Advertising Standards Authority (ASA) is the independent body responsible for ensuring that the voluntary, self-regulatory system of control of non-broadcast advertising and promotion works in the interests of both the public and the marketing communications industry alike. In practice, this actually means that their work includes above-the-line media except TV and radio (which have their own regulatory system), as well as below-the-line promotions which include sales promotions, the Internet and some direct marketing activities. Classified advertising, however, is excluded. Appendices 9.2 and 9.3 show the terms of reference and coverage of the Codes for which the ASA are responsible. The codes cover both consumer and trade promotions but it can be seen that the ASA do not directly involve themselves in many of the promotional areas associated with personal selling, packaging and public relations. The Codes themselves are devised by the Committee of Advertising Practice (CAP), the members of which include organisations that represent the advertising, sales promotion and media businesses. They are enforced through the ASA. More details are available from their websites **www.asa.org.uk** and **www.cap.org.uk**.

Relationship between the codes and the law

Unlike the law, self-regulation places the burden of proof on the promoters; it is they who have to prove their claims, it is not the job of the complainants to disprove them.

NEED TO KNOW

☑ *The Codes of Advertising and Sales Promotion are intended to be interpreted in their 'spirit' and not just the 'letter'.*

The Codes can also be interpreted in their 'spirit' and not just the 'letter' – this clearly emphasises that promotions should adhere to the sense and purpose of the Codes not only to their precise wording.

Self-regulatory bodies are not law enforcement agencies and some cases can only be satisfactorily resolved through legal action. In some areas of promotional activity local authority trading standards officers and environmental health officers have significant roles to play, for example in certain aspects of product packaging, weights and measures, point-of-sale displays, sale offers, and the safety of products.

To strengthen the legal controls of advertising, the 1988 Control of Misleading Advertisements Regulations were introduced. These regulations met the requirements of EC Directives (85/50 and 97/55 EC) without compromising the Codes of Practice and the work of the ASA. The Regulations preserved the benefits of the self-regulatory system while providing statutory powers to the Office of Fair Trading (OFT) to seek injunctions in court in those exceptional circumstances where it was felt that the self-regulatory controls had failed. Very few cases have ever been taken to court.

How the self-regulation system works

The British system relies on the co-operation of all parties involved in commissioning, producing and publishing marketing communications. This includes the marketing communicators, their agencies, the media and trade and professional organisations. The system works well as a complementary part of the legal system.

The strength of the system

> ... depends on the long-term commitment of all those involved in commercial communications. Practitioners in every sphere share an interest in seeing that advertisements and promotions are welcomed and trusted by their audience; unless they are accepted and believed they cannot succeed. If they are offensive or misleading they discredit everyone associated with them and the industry as a whole.

(CAP 1995, p. 79)

The Committee of Advertising Practice (CAP)

The Committee of Advertising Practice draws up the Code of Advertising, Sales Promotion and Direct Marketing and these are regularly reviewed and modified in line with legal changes and changing social norms – at least as far as the Committee view them. Its membership represents a range of marketing communications bodies, around 20 in all. The latest version of the Codes was published as an 11th edition in March 2003.

For the most part, there is *no* requirement for marketing communications under the remit of the Codes to be 'pre-vetted', unlike the requirement for broadcast advertising. Pre-vetting, were it needed, would involve a process of giving clearance to promotional material before it is published. The only exceptions to this are where CAP has determined this to be necessary as in the case of persistent offenders.

As might be appreciated with such a large committee, there is the need for the more detailed work to be conducted by sub-groups of the CAP. This is done by two standing review panels which meet on a regular basis and by a number of working groups which are convened over limited periods to look at specific issues concerning self-regulation as they arise. The Sales Promotion and Direct Response Panel is responsible for sales promotions, direct marketing and mail order. The General Media Panel focuses on advertising, mass media and issues not covered by the other panel. Both review panels appoint industry experts and a member of the ASA Council who help the ASA and the CAP in producing advice to the industry and in interpreting the Codes both in individual cases and on broad issues.

The Advertising Standards Authority (ASA)

The ASA is a limited company set up in 1962 to act independently of the Government and the promotions business to promote high standards in advertising, and monitor and enforce the self-regulatory system. In this instance 'advertising' is defined by the terms of reference of the Codes as shown in Appendix 9.2 at the end of the chapter and, as can be seen, incorporates activities other than advertising. The ASA publicises its work through advertising, seminars, speeches, leaflets and briefing notes, articles and editorials. Through its copy advice services it also provides free, confidential pre-publication advice to promoters, agencies and the media on the suitability of promotions. If there is any doubt, the copy advice team will advise on whether or not a piece of promotion is likely to contravene the Codes. Other important areas of the work of the ASA are the publication of Advice Notes and 'Ad Alerts' to the promotions industry and the co-ordination of sanctions operated by its members.

The ASA's task is to ensure, as far as it is able, that all advertising and sales promotion (as defined by its terms of reference) adhere to the Codes determined by the Committee of Advertising Practice. It is a task which involves a great deal of interpretation as the problems are often questions of social acceptability and on this point there is no clearcut answer. For this reason there are numerous occasions when the ASA is called in to investigate complaints and issue a judgement on its findings.

The ASA, unlike many of its counterparts throughout the world, actively encourages the public to notify it in cases of concern or complaint (Plate 11). In fact, it handles around 12,000 complaints each year. It also conducts its own research in which it assesses levels of compliance with the Codes, identifies trends and anticipates areas for action and guidance.

The Council of the ASA comprises a chairman and 12 members, two-thirds of whom are people unconnected with the promotions business and who are selected to reflect a range of backgrounds and experience. At monthly meetings, the Council considers and makes judgement about the items of marketing communications brought before it. It then informs the interested parties – the promoter, their agent and, where relevant, the complainant of their adjudication. The Council can give the promotion a clean bill of health where it is of the opinion that there is no evidence of a contravention of the Codes. Alternatively, where an advertisement is deemed to be contrary to the Codes, everyone responsible for commissioning, preparing, placing and publishing it will be asked to act promptly to amend or withdraw it.

It is clear that the workings of the CAP and ASA are closely intertwined. In fact, they share a joint Secretariat that carries out the day-to-day functions of the two bodies. Through the Secretariat, the ASA not only investigates the complaints it receives but also gives equal emphasis to carrying out its own research and monitoring activities which, at any one time, might be focused towards particular media and product categories. It falls to the Secretariat to make recommendations to the ASA Council for their final adjudication. The ASA's rulings are published weekly on their website (**www.asa.org.uk**). Ad Alerts are issued electronically immediately any contravention is identified.

When applying the codes, the ASA Council's interpretation and judgement is considered final although advertisers and promoters may be asked to furnish further information or substantiation before a decision is made. In making their decision, conformity to the Codes is assessed based not just on the details of the content of the promotion but also on the general impression and probable impact created, taken in the context in which it appears. The ASA's decision will thus be affected by such things as the audience (intended and actual), the medium and the product as well as the promotional material itself. Promoters are expected to conform to all the appropriate rules even though they may not be legally enforceable.

Despite these high ideals, however, there are miscreants in the industry. Some might be flaunting the law or at least 'sailing very close to the wind'. If this is the case, legal proceedings could be started. Local government trading standards officers could be asked to investigate product claims and bring criminal proceedings if appropriate. The OFT can place an injunction in more extreme cases. Some promotions may be considered quite offensive in their style, use of visuals and messages even though they may not contravene the law.

If the self-regulation system works, how could such promotional material ever be accepted by the media? The answer is not an easy one. First, promoters may genuinely be unaware of possible problems or concerns as indicated in In View 9.5.

IN VIEW 9.5

Have you been Tango'd?

When Tango first released its humorous 'Have You Been Tango'd' series of advertisements featuring its orange Tango man, one ad in the series showed a Tango drinker being hit around the head by the orange-gloved Tango man. This action was being repeated by children emulating the 'Tango experience'. As a consequence, some children suffered damaged and burst eardrums. Tango immediately and voluntarily removed the offending advertisement from the series as soon as they were told of the problems.

Second, the promotional material may be in a 'grey area' in which it is not certain that the material will cause offence (although in such circumstances the promoter, the agency or the media can ask for early advice through the ASA's copy advice team). However, one suspects that chances are taken and sometimes material published even if complaints are likely to be received.

Third, there are suspicions and accusations that certain promoters and their agencies deliberately produce material which they know is against the regulations but do so because they are more concerned with appealing to their targets rather than worrying about other members of the public or the concerns of other members of the industry. More cynically, there are concerns that promoters are deliberately being contentious in order to court publicity through which they receive far more media exposure than they would ever have paid for. This is one accusation levelled at organisations like Benetton, Club 18–30, Campaign for Racial Equality and Talk Radio, and is particularly compelling when they are seen to repeat their behaviour on numerous occasions. It is not untypical in these cases to find that by the time the ASA have investigated and come to a decision, the campaign, or at least the part that is causing offence, has already come to an end.

Criticism in these cases has not only to be levelled at the advertiser but also at their agency(ies) and the media for accepting the promotions. Again, the cynical, if practical response, is to recognise the difficult position the media are placed in when offered business worth a great deal of money. How can they afford to turn it down? It is with these issues in mind that the ASA and the poster industry (as many of the offending promotions have used the poster medium) have agreed a new sanction to help prevent recurrent misdemeanours (see the section on Sanctions, below).

Complaints procedures

The ASA encourage complaints from the marketing communications industry and from members of the public. Complaints about TV and radio advertisements and promotions which fall outside the remit of the Codes are not investigated, nor are any complaints which are subject to legal dispute – these are referred to the appropriate bodies such as the Independent Television Commission, the Broadcasting Standards Council, the Radio Authority, Trading Standards Officers and the Office of Fair Trading.

IN VIEW 9.6

Club 18–30 drop their posters

In the case of Club 18–30, sexual references were featured in their poster advertising. Although complaints were received and the advertisements banned, it was not Club 18–30's target audiences who were offended. As an added bonus, as often may be the case in such circumstances, the publicity generated benefited the advertiser considerably. It is worthy to note that this is an interesting example of where the content of advertising material caused widespread offence because of its placing on poster sites. This medium was viewed by the general public and not just members of Club 18–30's target market. No request to remove the advertisements was issued where they appeared in specialist consumer media. This issue of acceptability of promotional material is, therefore, one not just of its content but a combination of its content and the context or media in which it appears.

Complaints received by the ASA are investigated free of charge but they must be in writing, accompanied by a description or copy of the offending promotion and a note of where and when it appeared. The identity of complainants from the general public are considered confidential but industry members such as competitors are published.

The ASA Secretariat on behalf of the Council undertake the investigation and present recommendations to the Council. Where appropriate, the Secretariat will seek expert advice.

Complaints fall into one of five broad categories:

1 Promotions which obviously conflict with the Codes (these are given priority).
2 Complaints where there is a well-founded case for investigation.
3 Promotions where the promoter is likely to need to make only minor modifications.
4 Complaints where the complainant's interpretation of either the promotion or the Codes does not correspond with the ASA's.
5 Promotions which are outside the scope of the Codes.

All complaints are taken seriously and are given equal weight whatever their source. The ASA will undertake investigations even if only a single complaint is received. Where necessary, they will request further substantiation of claims from the promoter in coming to a decision. The Codes, in fact, require that promoters should have documentary evidence to prove all claims before submitting any promotion for publication. Therefore, should the ASA request evidence or proof of claims, they expect an immediate response. Exhibit 9.4 shows the complaints procedure diagrammatically.

NEED TO KNOW

✓ *The ASA (and the broadcast media regulatory bodies) only require one complaint to trigger an investigation.*

Sanctions

The ASA have no legal powers and are not a law enforcement body. The sanctions open to the ASA to enforce their decisions are indirect. Yet, for the vast majority of instances, their actions are effective. The ASA rely on consensus and persuasion in the industry and an effective network of sanctions.

At one level, through the work of the ASA in upholding the Codes and publicising good practice, it is expected that the promotions industry will voluntarily maintain the high standards expected of them. Advertisers, promoters and their agencies should employ professional conduct such that they do not knowingly produce material which would contravene the Codes and their knowledge of the Codes should be such that mistakes through ignorance should not occur. However, particularly in the areas of taste and decency, the decision about what is acceptable is not always clearcut.

A number of sanctions exist where an advertisement or promotion is in conflict with the Codes.

- *Refusal of space*: the media can refuse to accept the advertisement. This is not an option for some sales promotions, direct mail material and the Internet.
- *Adverse publicity*: adverse publicity may result from the rulings published by the ASA and further publicised in the media. Such negative publicity would not be in the interests of the promoter or their agency. The ASA believe this exerts effective industry and peer pressure to comply.
- *Trade sanctions*: trading sanctions may be imposed or recognition revoked by the promoter's or agency's professional association.
- *Removal of trade incentives*: financial and other incentives provided by trade, professional or media organisations may be withdrawn.

Exhibit 9.4 ASA complaints procedure

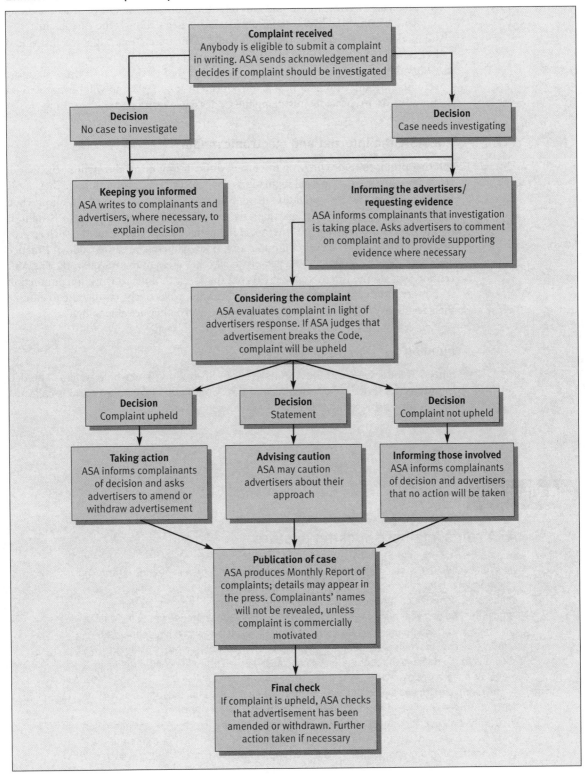

Complaint received
Anybody is eligible to submit a complaint in writing. ASA sends acknowledgement and decides if complaint should be investigated

Decision
No case to investigate

Decision
Case needs investigating

Keeping you informed
ASA writes to complainants and advertisers, where necessary, to explain decision

Informing the advertisers/ requesting evidence
ASA informs complainants that investigation is taking place. Asks advertisers to comment on complaint and to provide supporting evidence where necessary

Considering the complaint
ASA evaluates complaint in light of advertisers response. If ASA judges that advertisement breaks the Code, complaint will be upheld

Decision
Complaint upheld

Decision
Statement

Decision
Complaint not upheld

Taking action
ASA informs complainants of decision and asks advertisers to amend or withdraw advertisement

Advising caution
ASA may caution advertisers about their approach

Informing those involved
ASA informs complainants of decision and advertisers that no action will be taken

Publication of case
ASA produces Monthly Report of complaints; details may appear in the press. Complainants' names will not be revealed, unless complaint is commercially motivated

Final check
If complaint is upheld, ASA checks that advertisement has been amended or withdrawn. Further action taken if necessary

- *Legal action*: if a misleading advertisement or promotion continues to appear after the ASA has ruled against it, the ASA can refer the matter to the Office of Fair Trading (under the Control of Misleading Advertisements Regulations) who can obtain a legal injunction to prevent its further appearance. If the injunction is ignored this would be deemed to be in contempt of court and legal action would proceed.
- *Mandatory poster pre-vetting (usually for a period of two years)*: this, the most recently introduced sanction, was introduced in June 1998 and will be imposed on any advertiser repeatedly infringing the Codes when using poster advertising.

The ASA, the Internet and electronic media

Internet promotions are proving to be very difficult to control throughout the world. Of course, all the existing legal regulations apply to Internet promotions as they apply to any medium, but interpretation of such controls are open to some question when applied to this new medium, particularly given its global distribution. In Britain, it falls to the ASA to regulate the Internet along with other electronic media such as promotions on CD-ROMs, and computer and video games. The same Code of Practice applies to these new media as they apply to all other areas of the ASA's work. The ASA cannot regulate the Internet globally. What they seek to do is to work in conjunction with other international self-regulatory bodies who, collectively, co-operate to enforce their regulatory influences. Time will tell how effective they are able to be.

Funding

Since 1974, the CAP and the ASA have been self-funding. The whole system is funded by surcharges levied on advertising and direct marketing expenditure and is collected by the Advertising Standards Board of Finance.

IN VIEW 9.7

ASA rules against shocking posters

On 1 June 1998, the poster industry and the Committee of Advertising Practice introduced a new deterrent. Its aim, to crack down on those organisations that appeared to be deliberately adopting controversial, shocking poster campaigns. Their ruling, the imposition of a two-year mandatory pre-vetting period, was in response to the increasing incidence of such campaigns. As stated by the ASA, the 'trick was to run a deliberately controversial poster campaign and then bask in the afterglow of free press coverage oblivious to the damage that bad publicity can cause to the credibility of advertising as a whole' (www.asa.org.uk).

The Campaign for Racial Equality was the first organisation to fall foul of the new sanction. The second was Talk Radio. Any posters produced for or by both organisations were pre-vetted over a period of two years after the infringements. The ASA are particularly concerned to crack down on those who 'have deliberately flouted the Code with the intention of generating complaints, PR and subsequent notoriety' (CAP 2003, p. 94).

IN VIEW 9.8

Media prerogative

If media owners receive promotional material that they believe fails to conform to the Codes, they can refuse to accept it for publication. This is known as 'media prerogative'. They are under no obligation to publish every advertisement offered to them.

The more cynical, however, will be aware of the dilemma this can pose for media owners particularly if large sums of money are involved. Any decision to refuse advertising can result in significant losses of revenue for the media owner.

Media owners may prefer to rely on the complaints system rather than making a decision of their own or even refer advertisers to the ASA's Copy Advice team who would advise them of the appropriateness of the promotion. In this way, the media owners can still place the advertising and receive their monies in the knowledge that if a complaint is made by a company or member of the public the ASA can still give a ruling. If the ASA's decision is that the promotion should be withdrawn, then the media owner can simply comply with these instructions.

The still more cynical will recognise that where this happens, the time delay for such instructions to be issued can mean that the campaign has already come to the end of its course. Any instruction to withdraw the offending promotion may, therefore, be ineffective.

Broadcast self-regulation and control

In many respects, broadcast advertising is as much legally regulated as self-regulated. It appears under the main heading of self-regulation and control in that its day-to-day operations are not undertaken through the legal system. The fact that such operations have to be maintained, however, is a legal requirement.

Independent television started in Britain in 1955 and at that time the control of advertising was left to the individual independent television (ITV) companies themselves rather than through the over-arching body of the Independent Television Authority (ITA) (later to become the Independent Broadcasting Authority (IBA) and currently the Independent Television Commission (ITC)). The ITV companies vetted commercials through their own central Copy Clearance Secretariat.

In 1962, the Pilkington Committee reported its concern over what it considered to be sloppy standards and it was at that time that the ITA appointed its first Head of Advertising Control. Although the ITV companies still carried on their vetting work, no commercial was approved for broadcast until the ITA had given clearance.

The Broadcasting Act 1990 had a major impact on the television and radio broadcasting industry in Britain recognising, as it did, significant changes and developments in the broadcasting environment and technology. The Act made it a statutory duty of the newly formed Independent Television Commission (ITC) and the Radio Authority (RA) to draw up, review and enforce their own codes of standards and practice in television and radio advertising and sponsorship. The RA has no involvement with BBC radio broadcasts and the ITC, likewise, has no involvement with BBC television services. It was at this time that the process came full circle with the responsibility for the clearance of commercials reverting back once again to the television and radio companies. However, as statutory bodies in their own right, the ITC and the RA maintain an executive overview of both advertising and programming and the licensing of broadcast companies to ensure that all services and regulatory activities are being properly and fully implemented. It falls to them to carry out the role of investigating complaints and monitoring compliance with their Codes. In the near future, these bodies will be incorporated into a single regulatory body called OFCOM.

Both the ITC and RA publish their own Codes of Advertising Standards and Practice and supplementary publications covering Programme Sponsorship and Scheduling. In common with the Advertising Standards Authority which is responsible for non-broadcast advertising and promotions, all the Codes are developed to assert the same general principles. In drawing up the Codes, the ITC and the RA both took into account the Broadcasting Standards Council's (BSC) own Codes of Practice, indeed they were required to do so under the terms of the Broadcasting Act 1990. The BSC had come into being in May 1988 as a pre-statutory body set up by the Government. It issued its first set of Codes in 1989 although it was not until the 1990 Broadcasting Act that it became a statutory body (along with the RA and the ITC) on 1 January 1991. The BSC was established because of public and government concerns over issues of violence, language and sexual conduct portrayed particularly on the television screen. Unlike the RA and ITC, the BSC covers not only independent television and radio but also BBC broadcasts. Their remit covers both programmes and advertising.

Pre-vetting and the role of the Broadcast Advertising Clearance Centre (BACC) and the Radio Authority Copy Clearance Centre (RACC)

Unlike the work of the Advertising Standards Authority which covers non-broadcast promotions, all television and radio advertising is required to be pre-vetted prior to broadcast. In practice, for particular categories of radio commercials (some will be handled by the radio stations themselves) and TV commercials, this takes the form of the advertising script and planned scheduling (and any supplementary evidence to support claims) being sent to Broadcast Advertising Clearance Centre (BACC) or the Radio Authority Copy Clearance Centre (RACC) for approval. The independent local and national radio stations and the television companies themselves are, however, ultimately responsible for the approval and broadcast of commercials which they may refuse to broadcast if they feel that the advertising fails to comply with the Codes in any way. It is hoped that by vetting scripts prior to production, any relevant changes to material can be made without incurring the costs of re-shooting and re-recording which would otherwise be necessary if the advertising was only checked at completed production stage. The fact that a commercial may be accepted at an early pre-vetting stage does not guarantee that it will be accepted for broadcast as it is only after it is fully produced that the radio or TV company will give it final clearance. Penalties can be imposed on the radio and television companies if they fail to discharge these duties which are formally required as part of their broadcast licensee contracts.

The Broadcasting Standards Council (BSC), the Independent Television Commission (ITC) and the Radio Authority (RA) Codes

The RA and ITC Codes, which cover aspects of advertising, sponsorship and scheduling of advertisements, have been drawn up with due regard to the Broadcasting Standards Council Code of Practice and requirements relating to television advertising in the EC Directive on Television Broadcasting (1989) and the Council of Europe European Convention on Transfrontier Television 1989 which came into force on

1 May 1993. Appendix 9.3 at the end of this chapter gives a fuller description of the coverage of these Codes.

The Codes are comprehensive and relate to what the ITC, RA and the law consider acceptable. They cover product and service areas not accepted for broadcast or which may only be broadcast under particular conditions; matters of taste and offence; the use of children and animals; technical and reproduction considerations; price claims; testimonials; comparisons; and discrimination. See Appendix 9.5 for details of particular product areas that may not be advertised on British television and radio. Some advertisements, like programmes, may only be aired after the 9pm or 10pm '**watershed**'.

Watershed

The time up to which television advertising and programming are rigorously restricted. After the watershed, more adult material is considered acceptable.

Programme sponsorship and product placement

Sponsorship of television and radio programmes is handled somewhat differently to advertising. In the case of radio, the RA does not require sponsorship proposals to be cleared in advance but the radio station must ensure that its sponsored programmes do comply to the RA's Codes.

For television, the ITC and the BBC have developed their own codes covering both sponsorship and product placement. Both of these promotional tools are growing areas in marketing communications and the television stations have to be ever vigilant in maintaining their standards and compliance with regulations. In particular, product placement is an insidious form of promotion which, although perfectly acceptable, can be less obvious and more difficult to control.

Complaints procedures

Complaints may emanate from any source and they are all treated with equal regard. As part of their own monitoring procedures, complaints may be issued by staff of the ITC, RA and BSC themselves. Irrespective of how many complaints are received for any particular advertisement, an investigation will be made. Complaints may be made to the ITC or the RA for television and radio advertising respectively. Complaints can also be made to the Broadcasting Standards Council on any form of broadcast advertising. All bodies produce their own Complaints Reports as does the European Advertising Standards Alliance on cross-border complaints (for broadcast and non-broadcast advertising alike).

Unlike non-broadcast advertising, all broadcast advertisements will have already been pre-vetted and, as such, the first stage of investigation invariably involves checking with the Broadcast Advertising Clearance Centre, the Radio Authority Copy Clearance or the broadcast companies themselves. Because of the obligations placed by the RA and ITC on licensees to vet copy before accepting it and then, before broadcast, satisfying themselves that the final production does not infringe the Codes of Practice, it is often possible for them to provide satisfactory answers without the need to take matters further. However, where an infringement is still suspected, further investigations are made and a decision reached either to uphold the complaint or not.

Sanctions

Once an initial decision to uphold a complaint has been made, even if the advertisement is still the subject of further confirmatory investigations or subject to appeal, broadcast of it should cease pending resolution of any points of dispute. Should a complaint be upheld, the advertisement cannot be subsequently broadcast without appropriate modification to bring it in line with the Codes.

Where an advertisement is considered to be misleading and evidence to the contrary is not provided, legal proceedings may ensue under the Control of Misleading Advertisements Regulations 1988 (as amended by the Broadcasting Act 1990). It would be rare for such a situation to occur given the stringent checking and pre-vetting process to which all broadcast advertising is subjected. Any misleading claims may be made either explicitly or through inference and are more likely to be of a minor nature that may result in the cautioning of advertiser and agency.

Funding

The RA's and ITC's costs are met principally from the licence fees it charges the independent radio and television companies (the licensees). These fees cover all the work of the RA and the ITC, not just their work in connection with the Codes of Advertising Standards and Practice and Programme Sponsorship. The work of the Broadcast Advertising Clearance Centre (BACC) and the Radio Authority Copy Clearance (RACC) which act as the principal pre-vetting agencies for both television and radio advertisements is funded by the television and radio companies themselves.

An international comparison of approaches to self-regulation

Most self-regulation systems have been initiated from the 1970s onwards, probably as a consequence of the rise of consumerism as a major force during that decade, and the parallel development of consumer protection legislation in many countries. The British system is one of the earliest and strongest. Although the first British Code of Practice was published in 1961, and had its antecedents even before that, its self-regulation system developed substantially in the 1970s in response to the prospect of government legislation. Significantly, countries that have developed self-regulation systems have all either adopted or adapted the International Chamber of Commerce (ICC) Code of Practice or have at least accepted the same guiding principles.

The International Advertising Association (IAA) has conducted four main surveys of advertising self-regulation (ASR) bodies throughout the world and updated them on a regular basis. Of the more recent updates, Boddewyn (1992) surveyed 37 countries from among which he identified some 20 countries having well-developed and centralised self-regulatory systems.

In other countries he found less developed systems where only certain parts of the advertising industry or particular industries (e.g. alcohol, pharmaceuticals and tobacco) had issued rules and applied them without the benefit of a central ASR body. This applied to 12 of the countries he surveyed.

Where self-regulation was limited or non-existent, a number of countries had strong legal regulation instead. At the time of the survey, four countries, Denmark, Finland, Luxembourg and Sweden, had no self-regulation systems as such although Sweden had adopted a 'responsible advertiser' scheme in which a person nominated in each advertising agency gives 'expert' judgement on all advertisements prior to publication or release to a client. While the advertising sector in Luxembourg was little structured with no professional body, the emphasis in Denmark, Finland, Norway and Sweden was on the use of a state-employed consumer ombudsman to ensure that advertisements met the legal controls set.

Even in the countries with centralised advertising self-regulation, actual practices vary greatly. While they all accept complaints as a means of monitoring activity, only

Brazil, France, Italy, Spain, the UK and the USA maintain a system of regular monitoring of their own. Most ASR systems seem to define their role as an intermediary between advertiser and complainant rather than as a watchdog for the industry. The number of ASR caseloads differs significantly also. In France, Japan, South Africa and the UK, thousands of complaints and enquiries are handled each year from consumers and competitors. The actual number of cases settled ranges from little more than a handful of complaints in Spain and Japan to over 3000 in the UK. These differences reflect different ASR policies: some ASR bodies actively solicit complaints and monitor ads while others do not, some isolate important cases only, some handle national ads but not local ones, and some deal with all the media while others handle only some of them. Permanent ASR staff are usually small in number and range from only one or two in Germany to 14 or so in Japan and the USA, to over 50 in the UK. Whereas all systems handle complaints about false and misleading ads (although in Germany they are passed on to a separate body) not all of them concern themselves about cases of 'unfairness', 'taste, decency and opinion'.

Thus it is evident that in all countries surveyed by Boddewyn (1992) some approach was adopted to the checking of advertisements but the degree of this checking varied enormously. In some countries a range of promotional activity was included in the term 'advertising' whereas, in others, the scope of coverage was limited. A further report on the self-regulation practices in 22 European countries is available from the European Advertising Standards Alliance (EASA) (see **www.easa-alliance.org**).

The European Advertising Tripartite (EAT), a body that represents and furthers the interests of the European promotions industry, published its report in 1992 on Advertising and Self-Regulation. They described the survey on which it was based as 'a major new analysis of self-regulatory systems and their codes of advertising practice throughout the EC and in five EFTA countries'. It covered 17 countries in all. They concluded that:

> **It is heartening to see the extensive and robust nature of many of the existing schemes. More importantly, this study has confirmed our view that a regime based on self-regulation works.**
>
> (Coronel 1992, p. 4)

IN VIEW 9.9

Regulation systems

Countries with centralised self-regulation

Argentina, Australia, Austria, Belgium, Brazil, Canada, France, Germany, India, Ireland, Italy, Japan, Netherlands, Philippines, Singapore, South Africa, Spain, Switzerland, United Kingdom and United States

Countries with strong legal controls

Denmark, Finland, Norway, Sweden

Source: Boddewyn (1992)

The European Advertising Standards Alliance

The growth of advertising and other promotions, such as direct mail, across national boundaries has spurred on increasing concern over the difficulty of regulating those promotions across international borders. Even if a piece of promotional material meets the regulations in the originating country, it is perfectly possible that it may contravene the regulations in another country receiving the promotion. With the advent of satellite broadcasts, for example, a television advertisement made in Sweden featuring frontal nudity may cause no problem for the Swedes but would not be acceptable in the UK. National self-regulatory bodies cannot control promotions that appear in other countries' media.

To counter this problem, the European Advertising Standards Alliance (EASA) was set up. It is supported by the self-regulatory organisations from a range of European Community and European Free Trade Association countries with the aim of facilitating the control of promotions throughout Europe. EASA takes advantage of the fact that although the customs, tastes, cultures and traditions in each of the European countries differ, they are all linked by their common desire to ensure that advertising and promotions are legal, decent, honest and truthful and have self-regulatory systems to prevent, or otherwise limit, any transgressions of these principles. With its secretariat based in Brussels, EASA initiates and supervises investigation of cross-border complaints, co-ordinates policy among its members, encourages common action where appropriate and acts as a forum for discussion between legislators, regulators, consumer bodies and the advertising industry in Europe. EASA does not have, nor does it encourage, the development of a single, pan-European Code of Practice which its members believe would neither be practical nor in their best interests. Such an approach would not be able to respond flexibly and fairly to the varied needs of consumers and businesses in the different countries represented.

IN VIEW 9.10

The European Advertising Standards Alliance (EASA)

The 26 countries represented in the European Advertising Standards Alliance and their National Self-Regulatory Organisations

From November 2001, the Alliance membership consisted of 28 Self-Regulatory Organisations (SROs) from 22 European countries and 4 non-European countries and a range of industry organisations supportive of self-regulation.

Austria	Österreichischer Weberat (ÖWR)
Belgium	Jury d'Ethique Publicitaire/Jury voor Ethische Praktijken Inzake Reclame (JEP)
Czech Republic	Rada Pro Reklamu (CRPR)
Denmark	Reklame Forum (RF)
Finland	Liiketapalautakunta (LTL)
France	Bureau de Vérification de la Publicité (BVP)

Germany	Deutscher Werberat (DW)
	Zentrale zur Bekämpfung unlauteren Wettbewerbs e. V (ZEN)
Greece	Enossi Etairion Diafimisis-Epikoinonias (EDEE) (pending the establishment of a new SRO
Hungary	Önszabályozó Reklám Testület (ÖRT)
Ireland	Advertising Standards Authority for Ireland (ASAI)
Italy	Instituto dell'Autodisciplina Publicitaria (IAP)
Luxembourg	Commission Luxembourgeoise pour l'Ethique en Publicité (CLEP)
Netherlands	Stichting Reclame Code (SRC)
Portugal	Instituto Civil da Autodisciplina da Publicidade (ICAP)
Russia	Reklamny Sovet Rossii (RSR)
Slovak Republic	Rada Pre Reklamu (SRPR)
Slovenia	Slovenska Oglaševalska Zbornica (SOZ)
Spain	Asociación para la Autorregulación de la Comunicación Comercial (Autocontrol)
Sweden	MarknadsEtiska Rådet (MER)
Switzerland	Commission Suisse pour la Loyauté (CSL)
Turkey	Reklam Özdenetim Kurulu (RÖK)
United Kingdom	Advertising Standards Authority (ASA)
	Broadcast Advertising Clearance Centre (BACC)
Canada	Advertising Standards Canada (ASC)
New Zealand	Advertising Standards Authority (ASANZ)
South Africa	Advertising Standards Authority of South Africa (ASASA)
USA	Advertising Review Council (ARC)

Industry Associations among EASA membership include: World Federation of Advertisers, European Association of Communications Agencies, Association of Commercial Television in Europe, European Newspaper Publisher's Association, European Publishers Council, Association Européenne des Radios, European Association of Directory and Database Publishers, European Federation of Magazine Publishers, Interactive Advertising Bureau Europe, European Group of Television Advertising, Advertising Information Group and International Advertising Association.

EASA responds to complaints received from businesses and members of the public. A letter of complaint concerning a cross-border promotion is simply sent to the usual national regulatory body, such as the ASA or ITC in the case of the UK, the Deutscher Werberat in the case of Germany or the Bureau de Vérification de la Publicité in the case of France, which will do the rest. They will ensure that the complaint is passed on to the appropriate self-regulatory organisation which will then carry out its own investigations. The members of EASA recognise the importance of self-regulation and the need for adequate controls if the promotion industry at large is to remain credible. It is their interest to do all in their power to prevent unacceptable promotions; however, their powers have yet to be put to the test in handling a major international, cross-border case. Additional information on EASA's objectives, activities, publications, members and alerts is available on their website **www.easa-alliance.org**.

Summary

Regulation of marketing communications is a fundamental part of marketing communications practice. No one should operate in the industry without some awareness and understanding of the details although it is, ultimately, a complex field.

Regulations fall, broadly, into two categories: legal regulation and self-regulation. The extent to which any one country relies on one or the other or a balance between the two varies significantly. There are advantages and disadvantages of each. In Britain, there is a well-developed system of self-regulation imposed, enforced and funded by the marketing communications industry itself.

There are a variety of legal statutes – acts, regulations, orders and amendments – covering the myriad applications of marketing communications topics from recruitment advertising to door-to-door selling, from competitions and lotteries to price offers and sales. The laws influence and control the use of claims, designs, logos, trade marks and many other features that could be used in marketing communications. They affect promotions using and targeted at children and various sectors of the community. They influence all forms of business practices and marketing communications is no less affected.

Self-regulation follows the same tenets as legal controls and covers areas that would be difficult to police through legal enforcement. Various Codes of Practice and professional codes of conduct are produced that all members of the marketing communications industry are expected to abide by. Unfortunately some do not, but these represent the very small minority. By and large, the self-regulation system is said to work very efficiently in Britain and in many other countries around the world. Much of the difficulty in determining good practice revolves around the determination of ethical practices recognising that standards of decency and social acceptance differ from place to place and from time to time.

The approaches to regulating broadcast and non-broadcast marketing communications vary, broadcast media being more heavily influenced by legal controls. TV and radio promotions are pre-vetted before they are broadcast, whereas this does not apply to non-broadcast media. The principal bodies involved in self-regulation in Britain are the ITC and RA (to be combined as OFCOM), BSC, BACC, RACC, ASA and CAP. International bodies such as EAT and EASA exist to promote ethical practices within and across national boundaries.

Self-review questions

1 Produce a list of the major advantages and disadvantages of self-regulation and legal regulation.

2 What are the four basic principles underlying most international self-regulation systems?

3 For which areas of marketing communications self-regulation is the ASA responsible?

4 Why are broadcast advertisements pre-vetted when non-broadcast marketing communications are not?

5 What sanctions and controls can be imposed under the self-regulation system in Britain?

6 Identify the main bodies involved in self-regulation (broadcast and non-broadcast) within Britain.

Project

Carefully consider the legal and self-regulation frameworks. Identify current examples of marketing communications you suspect might contravene the regulations. Using these as examples, prepare a presentation giving a balanced case for regulatory control while maintaining freedom of speech and information.

References

ASA website **www.asa.org.uk**.

Boddewyn, J.J. (1986), *Advertising Self-Regulation: 16 Advanced Systems*. International Advertising Association.

Boddewyn, J.J. (1992), *Global Perspectives on Advertising Self-Regulation*. Quorum Books.

Borrie, G. (1990), *The role of advertising and the need for regulation*. In *Advertising in the 1990s: the Case for Advertising in the Single Market of the 1990s*. The Advertising Association.

CAP (2003), *The British Code of Advertising, Sales Promotion and Direct Marketing* 11th edn. Committee of Advertising Practice.

Christy, R. (1999), Ethics in marketing communications. In *Marketing Communications: Contexts, Contents and Strategies* 2nd edn (C. Fill, ed.). Prentice Hall Europe.

Coronel, M. (1992), *Advertising Self-Regulation*. European Advertising Tripartite.

EASA (undated), *The European Standards Alliance: Promoting Effective pan-European Self-Regulation*.

Kolah, A. (2002), *Essential Law for Marketers*. Butterworth-Heinemann.

Neelankavil, J.P. and Stridsberg, A.B. (1980), *Advertising Self-Regulation: A Global Perspective*. Communications Arts Books.

Neill, R. (1990), This House believes that the European Parliament should not control advertising. Speech given by Roger Neill, International Advertising Association World President, at the House of Commons, London, 22 October, reported in J.J. Boddewyn (1992), *Global Perspectives on Advertising Self-Regulation*, Quorum Books.

Stridsberg, A.B. (1974), *Effective Advertising Self-Regulation*. International Advertising Association.

Selected further reading

www.asa.org.uk

www.cap.org.uk

www.easa-alliance.org

Botan, C. (1997), Ethics in strategic communication campaigns: the case for a new approach to public relations. *Journal of Business Communication*, 34 (2), 188–202.

Harker, D. (1998), Achieving acceptable advertising: an analysis of advertising regulation in five countries. *International Marketing Review*, 15 (2), 101–118.

Ritsema, H. and Piest, B. (1990), Telemarketing: the case for (self) regulation? *European Management Journal*, 8 (1), 63–66.

Saunders, D. (1996), *Sex in Advertising – Best Ads*. Batsford Design Books.

Saunders, D. (1996), *Shock in Advertising – Best Ads*. Batsford Design Books.

Appendix 9.1 Statutes affecting marketing communications

Betting Gaming and Lotteries Acts 1963–1985
Broadcast Act 1990
Children and Young Persons Acts 1933 and 1963
Competition Act 1980
Consumer Credit (Advertisements) Regulations 1989
Consumer Credit (Exempt Advertisements) Order 1985
Consumer Protection Act 1987 and the Code of Practice for Traders on Price Indications
Control of Misleading Advertisements Regulations 1988
Copyright, Designs and Patents Act 1988
Data Protection Act 1984
European Communities Act 1972
Fair Trading Act 1973
Financial Services Act 1986 and Investment Advertisement Exemption Orders
Food Labelling Regulations 1984
Indecent Advertisements (Amendment) Act 1970
Insurance Companies (Advertisements)(Amendments) No. 2 Regulations 1983
Lotteries and Amusements Act 1976 and Amendments
Mail Order Transaction (Information) Order 1976
Malicious Communications Act 1988
Medicines (Advertising) Regulations 1994
Medicines (Monitoring of Advertising) Regulations 1994
Misrepresentation Act 1976
National Lottery Act 1993 and National Lottery Regulations 1994
Obscene Publications Acts 1959 and 1964
Price Indications (Method of Payment) Regulations 1991
Price Marking Order 1991
Price Marking (Amendment) Order 1994
Property Misdescriptions Act 1991
Pyramid Selling Schemes Regulations 1989 and Amendment 1990
Race Relations Act 1976
Restrictive Trade Practices Acts 1976 and 1977
Sales of Goods Act 1979
Sex Discrimination Acts 1975 and 1986
Sunday Trading Act 1994
Supply of Goods and Services Act 1982
Telecommunications Apparatus (Advertisements) Order 1985
Telecommunications Apparatus (Marketing and Labelling) Order 1985
Timeshare Act 1992
Tobacco Advertising and Promotions Act 2002
Trade Descriptions Act 1968
Trade Marks Act 1994
Trading Stamps Act 1964
Unfair Contract Terms Act 1977
Unsolicited Goods and Services Acts 1971, 1975 and (Amendment) Act 1975

Plate 1: Marketing communications covers the promotion of goods, services, the corporation and even individuals. In political marketing, the promotion of Tony Blair is key to the New Labour campaign. (*Marketing communications and corporate communications, p.6*)

MARKS & SPENCER

StMichael

Plate 2: Marks & Spencer uses both corporate umbrella and family umbrella branding strategies.
(*Branding strategies, p. 246*). Copyright © Marks & Spencer plc.

Plate 3: Coca-Cola is one of the world's most famous brand names. In 2003, the Business Week and Interbrand Survey named Coke 'leading global brand' recognising that it represents significant emotional advantages over its competitors, which consumers want, recognise and are willing to pay for. (*Brand name, p. 251*) Plate 3 'Coca-Cola' bottle 'Coca-Cola', 'Coke', 'diet Coke', 'diet Coca-Cola' and the 'Dynamic Ribbon' are registered trade marks of The Coca-Cola Company and are reproduced with kind permission from The Coca-Cola Company.

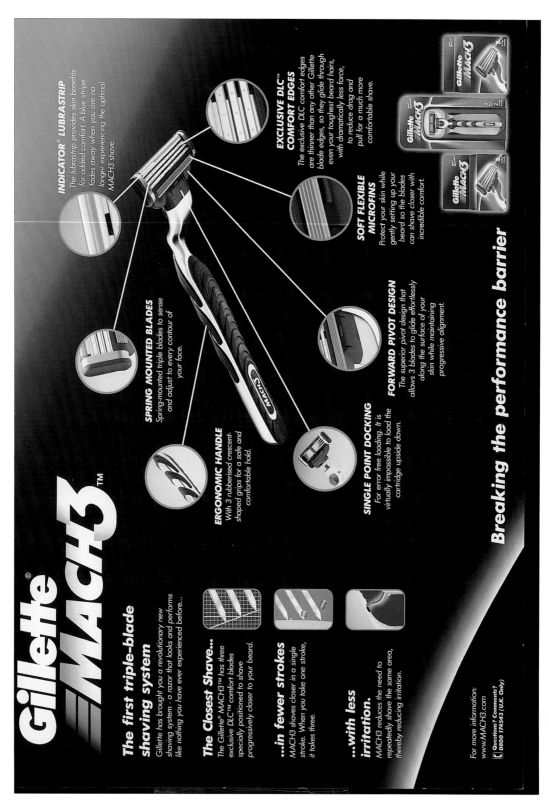

Plate 4: The Gillette Mach3 advertisement utilises a functional appeal; it communicates the brand's specific attributes capable of solving consumers' consumption-related problems. (*Brand values, p.257*)

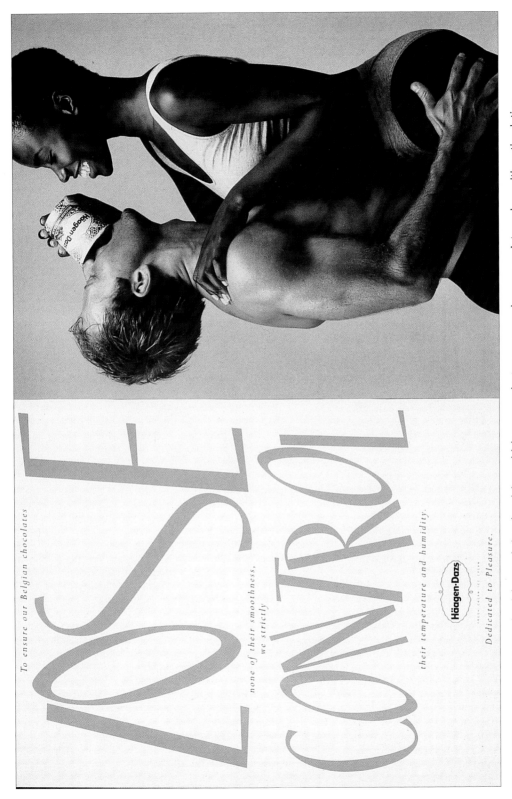

Plate 5: Häagen Dazs uses experiential appeals in advertising, which communicates sensory pleasure, variety and cognitive stimulation. (*Brand values, p.257*). Copyright © The Pillsbury Company.

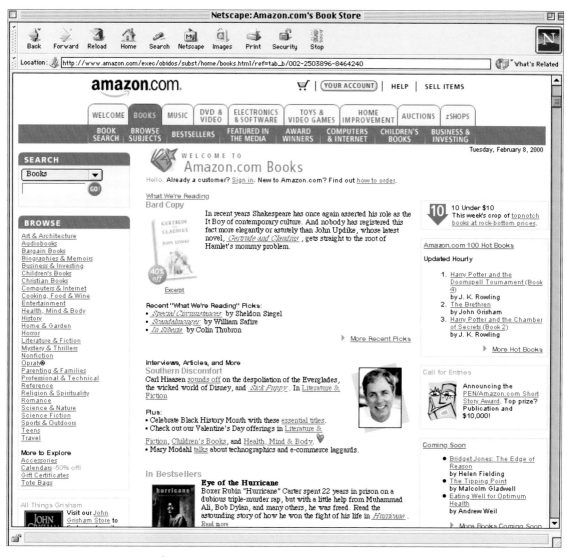

Source: Screenshot of Amazon.com® web site. Amazon.com is a registered trademark of Amazon.com, Inc. in the U.S. and/or other countries. Copyright © 2000 Amazon.com, Inc. All rights reserved.

Plate 6: Amazon.com is one of a number of companies that have used new media channels to successfully sell an old product in a creative new way. (*In View 12.4, p.274*)

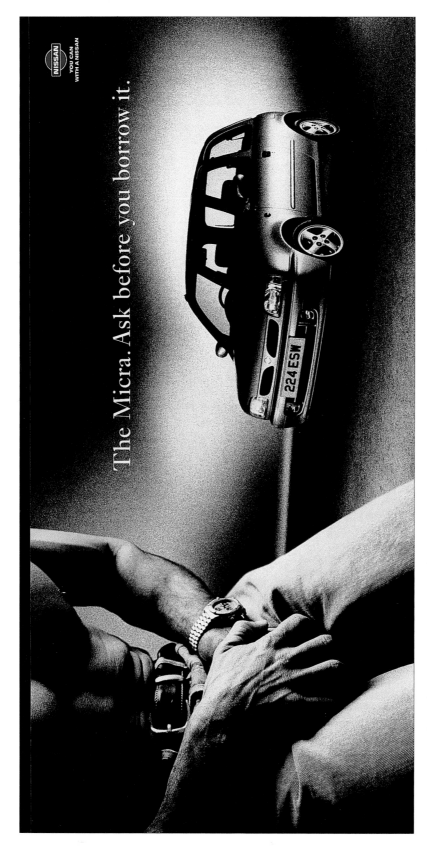

Plate 7: In View 7.4 *(p.161) describes how 'girl power' advertisements such as this one shocked some viewers.*

BT's line up for the World Cup.

USA from 12p

France from 13p

Cameroon from 56p

Japan from 31p

Italy from 15p

Austria from 19p

Colombia from 68p

Brazil from 56p

Germany from 13p

South Africa from 38p

Tunisia from 31p

Cut the cost of phoning footie fans abroad with BT.

For just £1 per country per month, BT's Country Calling Plans give you 25% off calls to that country.

Add PremierLine and Friends & Family and the saving is 43% on up to six nominated numbers. That's day and night.

You can choose up to five countries from 100. So don't stand on the sidelines, give us a shout.

BT

See how much you can cut off your BT phone bill – with BT.
Free*fone* **0800 001 800.**

Plate 8: BT take advantage of the 1998 World Cup football tournament to make their advertising more relevant. (*p.165*)

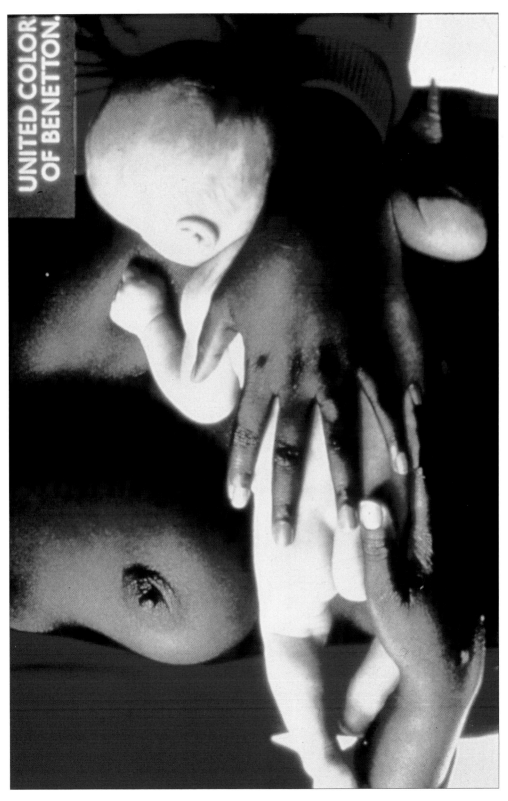

Plate 9: The 'Black Mama' poster campaign caused widespread offence in various countries. Cultural taboos are expressed in the political and regulatory environment, the ad being excluded from poster sites in the US where they are much less tolerant of public nudity. *(Political and regulatory environment, p.170)*

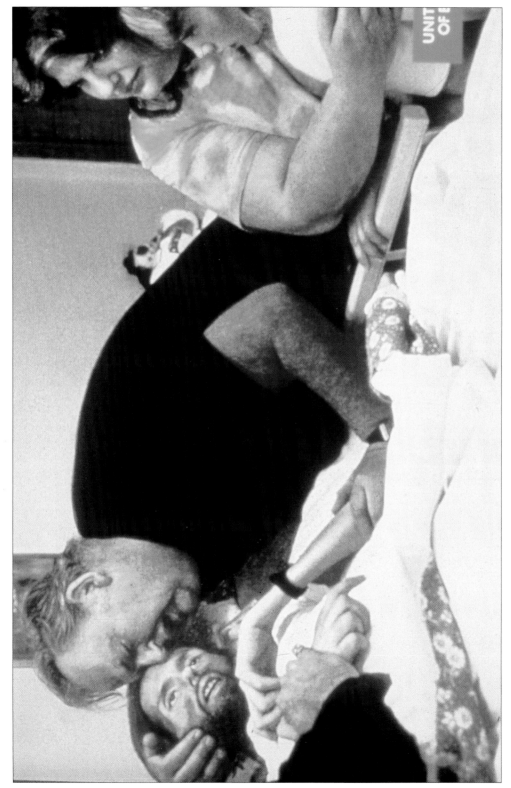

Plate 10: Benetton court controversy again with this poster advertisement. (*Social acceptability and ethics, p.193*)

Appendix 9.2 Terms of reference for the British Codes of Advertising and Sales Promotion (applies to trade and consumer markets)

The Codes apply to:

a) advertisements in newspapers, magazines, brochures, leaflets, circulars, mailings, emails, text transmissions, fax transmissions, catalogues, follow-up literature and other electronic and printed material
b) posters and other promotional media in public places, including moving images
c) cinema and video commercials
d) advertisements in non-broadcast electronic media, including online advertisements in paid-for space (e.g. banner and pop-up advertisements)
e) viewdata services
f) marketing databases containing consumers' personal information
g) sales promotions
h) advertisement promotions

The Codes do not apply to:

a) broadcast commercials, which are the responsibility of the Independent Television Commission or the Radio Authority (soon to be incorporated into OFCOM)
b) the contents of premium rate services which are the responsibility of the Independent Committee for the Supervision of Standards of Telephone Information Services (ICSTIS); marketing communications that promote these services are subject to ICSTIS regulation and to the CAP Code
c) marketing communications in foreign media (there are some exceptions and EASA co-ordinates cross-border complaints)
d) health-related claims in marketing communications addressed only to the medical, dental, veterinary and allied professions
e) classified private advertisements including those appearing online
f) statutory, public, police and other official notices
g) works of art exhibited in public or private
h) private correspondence
i) oral communications, including telephone calls
j) press releases and other public relations material
k) editorial content, for example of the media and of books
l) regular competitions such as crosswords
m) flyposting (most of which is illegal)
n) packages, wrappers, labels and tickets, timetables and price lists unless they advertise another product, a sales promotion or are visible in a marketing communication
o) point-of-sale displays except for those covered by the sales promotion rules
p) political advertisements
q) website content, except sales promotions and advertisements in paid-for space
r) sponsorship, marketing communications that refer to sponsorship are covered by the Code
s) customer charters and codes of practice

Appendix 9.3 General coverage of the British Codes of Advertising and Sales Promotion

The Codes contain sections on the following specifics:

General rules
Principles
Substantiation
Legality
Decency
Honesty
Truthfulness
Matters of opinion
Fear and distress
Safety
Violence and anti-social behaviour
Political advertising
Protection of privacy
Testimonials and endorsements
Prices
Availability of products
Guarantees
Comparisons with identified competitors and/or their products
Other comparisons
Denigration and unfair advantage
Imitation
Recognising marketing communications and identifying marketers
Advertisement features
Free offers

Sales promotion rules
Sales promotion rules are designed primarily to protect the public but they also apply to trade promotions and incentive schemes and to the promotional elements of sponsorships

Protection of consumers, safety and suitability
Children
Availability
Administration
Free offers and free trials
Prize promotions
Significant conditions for promotions
Other rules for prize promotions
Front page flashes
Charity-linked promotions
Trade incentives

Direct marketing rules
Distance selling
Database practice

Specific rules – apply to
Alcoholic drinks
Children
Motoring
Environmental claims
Health and beauty products and therapies
 General
 Medicines
 Vitamins, minerals and other food supplements
 Cosmetics
 Hair and scalp
Weight control
Employment and business opportunities
Financial products
Betting and gaming
Tobacco, rolling papers and filters

Appendix 9.4 Coverage of RA and ITC codes of advertising and sponsorship

Presentational issues

Separation of advertisements and
    programmes
Scheduling of advertisements
Use of presenters and programme
    performers
Sound effects, noise and stridency
Discrimination
Product placement
Reproduction techniques
Subliminal advertising
Captions and superimposed text

Treatment of content

Taste and offence
Appeals to fear and superstition
Protection of privacy and exploitation
Protection of the environment
Animals (use of in advertisements)
Children (advertising directed towards
    and use of children in advertisements)
Health and safety
Motor cars and driving
Misleadingness
Price claims
Comparisons
Denigration of other products, services,
    advertisers and advertisements

Testimonials
Guarantees
Use of the word 'free'
Competitions
Inertia selling

Products and services

Unacceptable products and services
Politics, industrial and public
    controversy
Religion
Charities
Matrimonial and introduction agencies
Alcoholic drink
Financial advertising
Medicines, treatments, health claims,
    nutrition and dietary supplements
Lotteries and pools
Homework schemes
Instructional courses'
Home shopping features
Premium rate telephone services

Miscellaneous

Mail order and direct response
    advertising
Advertising on ancillary services
Pan-European and non-UK advertising

Appendix 9.5 Examples of RA and ITC unacceptable product categories

Breath-testing devices and products which claim to mask the effects of alcohol
The occult
Betting tips
Betting and gambling (except those granted special permission such as football pools
    and particular lotteries)
All tobacco products
Private investigation agencies
Commercial services offering advice on personal or consumer problems (except
    solicitors and other specific professional services designated by the ITC)
Guns and gun clubs
Pornography

Chapter 10

Marketing communications ethics

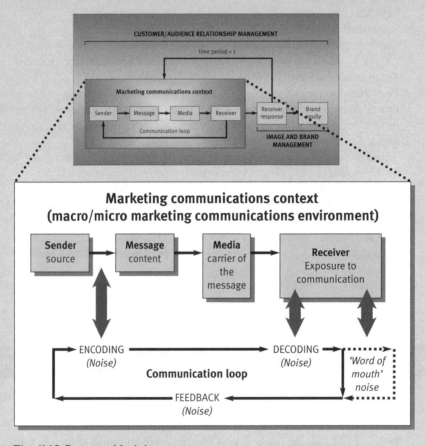

The IMC Process Model

CD

Case Study 1 on the CD outlines the charity Concern's marketing communication stategy. Select a range of Concern's competitors, and evaluate the competing images utilised. To what extent do these charities use shock tactics? Consider the pros and cons of shock tactics for the Concern campaign, in terms of ethical decision-making.

Objectives

- To define marketing ethics
- To outline alternative perspectives of ethical decision-making
- To demonstrate the importance of ethical decision-making for integrated marketing communications
- To outline the purpose of corporate social responsibility programmes and cause-related marketing
- To identify and discuss the key ethical concerns in integrated marketing communications

Professional perspective

Dr. Nick Lee Aston Business School

Marketing communications are now ubiquitous cultural artefacts, and also financially vital to the success of most organisations. Thus, almost everyone nowadays has an opinion regarding the ethics (or, more likely, the lack thereof) of marketing communications. However, beginning to understand the ethics of marketing communications is about more than simply having an opinion, and shouting louder than everyone else. The real key is in the interplay of different ethical frameworks and philosophies in relation to any situation.

Take the concepts of deontology (the idea that there are absolute moral rights and wrongs) versus teleology (the idea that morally right actions benefit the greatest number of people). For example, if a given advertisement uses an offensive image to sell a product, then many people would consider that unethical. However consider the possibility that if the advertisement does not air, then products may not sell, ultimately causing factory shutdowns and job losses. Perhaps the ethical argument is not quite so cut and dry. Or from another angle, is it ethical to use offensive images to encourage charity donations, or reduce drink-driving?

Furthermore, the idea of ethical relativism is also crucial. In other words, should we impose our own ethical standards onto others? This could be as simple as considering whether an advertisement is morally wrong simply because I think it plays 'fast and loose' with the truth, or as complex as considering whether my international salesforce should practice bribery in countries where it is the norm – even though my home culture considers it unethical.

→

These and other ethical concepts are not simply dusty relics from the academic 'ivory tower', they fundamentally inform how we deal with ethical dilemmas – whether we realise it or not. In particular, as practitioners you should understand that being an ethical communicator is about more than just adhering to the 'letter' of regulations or standards, it's also about upholding the 'spirit', and without a grasp of ethical philosophy this can be an elusive goal.

Introduction

Marketing ethics

The systematic consideration of marketing and marketing morality related to 4P issues (product, price, place, promotion).

Marketing has been described as an 'ethically neutral system or management tool serving as an unequivocal market good' (Beardshaw and Palfreman 1990). However, other perspectives of marketing suggest it is profoundly value laden (e.g. 2nd Laczniak 1983; Smith 1995), manipulates the consumer in anything but an innocent way, and contributes to the destructive and wasteful side of consumerist society (Fineman 1999). The function within business firms most often charged with ethical abuse is marketing (Murphy and Laczniak 1981). It is this debate that has given rise to the consideration of societal marketing and **marketing ethics**. Prior to the 1960s, marketers either displayed disinterest in issues related to their social responsibilities or deliberately ignored them (Sheth et al 1988). In recent years there has been a much higher profile of consumer activists protesting about the shortcomings of marketing tactics: for example, protest groups such as Greenpeace, Friends of the Earth or the UK Consumer Association, and boycott websites such as **www.saigon.com/nike** and **www.mcspotlight.org**.

As Chapter 9 identifies, the self-regulation of marketing and media communications operates within a broader legal framework. Professional and regulatory bodies such as the Market Research Society, the Advertising Standards Authority and Chartered Institute of Marketing set ethical guidelines applying to certain issues. Whilst specific ethical guidelines are in evidence, in particular with regard to the marketing and advertising of food, medical and alcohol products (for example alcohol drunk in UK TV advertisements must be sipped rather than gulped), the industry guidelines emphasise general requirements of decency, legality and honesty concerning the truthfulness of advertising claims and the means by which these claims are presented. These requirements are not defined in any great detail. Thus, from a managerial point of view, the boundaries of what might be claims are nebulous (Hackley and Kitchen 1999).

Any credible company would like to consider its business practice ethical. Most organisations do not intend to behave unethically, as purely from an economic perspective customers who feel they have been unfairly treated will not re-purchase from that particular company (Carrigan and Attalla 2001). But there are certain potential pitfalls organisations should be aware of which could damage the credibility of the company and in particular the way it presents itself to the external market environment. This chapter outlines the concept of marketing ethics and identifies the ethical considerations in marketing communications decision-making. The main ethical issues in integrated marketing communications are outlined in Exhibit 10.1.

Exhibit 10.1 Ethical issues in integrated marketing communications

Marketing communication tool	Ethical issues
Personal selling	● Questionable/psychological sales techniques (e.g. high-pressure selling) ● Overselling (e.g. overestimating customer's problems, over-promising product performance, over-specifying product requirement) ● Misrepresentation (i.e. beyond permissible puffery, including by omission) ● Conflicts of interest (e.g. incentives to push products not best suited to customer
Advertising	● Deceptive/misleading advertising (including puffery that amount to 'soft core deception') ● Advertising that 'manipulates' behaviour (i.e. advertising as 'hidden persuader' that creates 'false' needs leading to unnecessary/harmful demand) ● Advertising to children
Sales promotion	● Deceptive/misleading sales promotions
Direct marketing	● Misrepresentation of products (i.e. misleading advertising via direct mail, etc.) ● Violations of consumer privacy (e.g. unauthorised use of mailing lists) ● No intention of fulfilling orders (i.e. fraudulent practices)

Source: From '*Marketing strategies for the ethics era*', in *Sloan Management Review*, Vol. 36, No. 4, 1995, pp. 85–98, (Smith, N.C., 1995). Reproduced with permission.

What are ethics?

> 'Ethics' most often refers to a domain of inquiry, a discipline, in which matters of right and wrong, good and evil, virtue and vice, are systematically examined. 'Morality', by contrast is most often used to refer not to a discipline but to patterns of thought and action that are actually operative in everyday life. In this sense, morality is what the discipline of ethics is about. And so business morality is what business ethics is about. (Goodpaster 1992, p. 111)

Ethics are issues of what is right and wrong. Marketing ethics examines systematically marketing and marketing morality, related to 4P-issues such as product safety and liability, advertising truthfulness and honesty, fairness in pricing, power within the channels of distribution, privacy in Internet and database marketing, and forthrightness in selling (Smith and Quelch 1993). As Christy (1999) writes in the context of marketing communications, concerns expressed by society include

> misleading or false advertising; shocking, tasteless or indecent material in marketing communications; high pressure sales techniques, particularly when applied to vulnerable groups; telesales calls that seem to intrude on personal privacy; PR communications that seem to distract or obfuscate, rather than inform; payment of bribes to win business. (p. 48)

While truthfulness and honesty remain unassailable requirements of socially acceptable marketing communications, what constitute facts can be challenged and phraseology, while not untruthful, may mislead through false impressions, either deliberately or unintentionally. It is, however, in the areas of taste and decency that most difficulty arises in defining ethical marketing communications. Among other aspects, criticism has been levelled at the portrayal of men and women; sexist promotions; marketing communications to children; the portrayal of green and environmental issues; the portrayal of sexual images and reference to sexual innuendo; intrusion of privacy; images designed to shock (see Plate 13); use of bribery and incentives; the promotion of socially unacceptable products; false claims; bad and offensive language and imagery (see Plate 12). These are, of course, the very issues that the law and the self-regulation system are designed to monitor and control.

Ethical practices

There are many marketers who seek to establish acceptable ethical guidelines and practice, and disseminate these within the industry (Hunt and Vitell 1992; Laczniak, 1993; Smith 1995). Legislation has played a part in raising consumer expectations of marketing behaviour, and regulation has also helped move us from the 'caveat emptor' position of the 1960s to a more socially responsible era in marketing (Smith 1995). Most major multinational firms have published codes of conduct to demonstrate their commitment to better business behaviour (e.g. Levi Strauss, The Body Shop), as have professional marketing organisations such as the Market Research Society or the American Marketing Association. Globally, there have been hundreds of organisations and institutes established to research and promote ethical business behaviour (e.g. European Business Ethics Network, Hong Kong Ethics Development Centre). Examples of ethical practice include AmEx as one of the first US-based companies in compliance with the strict EU Directive on Privacy because its cardholder lists are never sold to third parties. In 2000, the company launched a major print advertising campaign using the familiar tag line, 'do you know me?' The company promises anonymity online (Binkley 2000). Other firms from controversial industries have taken steps recently to engage in responsible marketing, for example, Harrah's chain of casinos recently introduced a Code of Commitment dealing with marketing and advertising activities that will forbid advertising in media aimed at teenagers and avoid messages that stipulate that gambling is a rite of passage (Binkley 2000). Exhibit 10.2 outlines ethical guidelines as identified by a variety of authors.

Smith (1995) suggests a marketing ethics continuum upon which there are different positions to evaluate marketing decisions. In summary the positions include,

- *Caveat emptor* – ethical business is defined as profit maximisation within the law.
- *Ethics code* – corporate codes of ethics or the codes of industries or professional bodies representing standards by which industries, firms, individual managers judge their performance or, at least, standards to which they aspire.
- *Consumer sovereignty* – marketing ethics are determined by the three criteria of the consumer sovereignty test: consumer capability, information and choice (see Exhibit 10.2).
- *Caveat venditor* – the maximisation of consumer satisfaction (or well-being).

Exhibit 10.2 Ethical guidelines

Topic	Guidelines
Issues in advertising (Brinkmann 2002)	● Don't exploit fear or superstition ● Do not further violence or discrimination ● Don't plagiarise ● Don't misuse quotations, statistics, research ● Be careful with children and minors
Four basic principles in public relations (Brinkmann 2002) See Appendix 10.1	● Openness ● Loyalty ● Integrity ● Credibility
Marketing practice guidelines (Smith 1995)	● Do unto others as you would have them do unto you ● Would I be embarrassed in front of colleagues/family/friends if the media publicised my decision? ● Are there any payments that could not be fully disclosed in company accounts? ● Good ethics is in the firm's long-term best interests ● Would an objective panel of professional colleagues view this action as proper? ● When in doubt, don't
Marketing communicator's rules of behaviour (Laczniak and Murphy 1991)	● The Golden Rule – act in a way that you would expect others to act towards you ● The Professional Rule – take only actions which would be viewed as proper by a panel of your professional peers ● Kant's Categorical Imperative – act in a way such that the action taken under the circumstances would be acceptable behaviour for everyone facing those same circumstances ● The TV Test – act in a way that you would feel comfortable explaining to the general public
Consumer sovereignty test (Smith 1995)	● Consumer capability – is the target market vulnerable in ways that limit consumer decision making? (vulnerability factors – age, education, income, etc.) ● Information – availability and quality. Are consumer expectations at purchase likely to be realised? Do consumers have sufficient information to judge? ● Choice – opportunity to switch. Can consumers go elsewhere? Would they incur substantial costs or inconvenience in transferring their loyalty?
Ethical judgement of advertising (Nwachukwu et al. 1997)	● Individual autonomy – the ability of the individual to recognise the manipulative power of advertising ● Consumer sovereignty – the level of knowledge and sophistication of the target audience (e.g. the marketing of infant formula in less developed countries illustrates low consumer sovereignty) ● Harmfulness of product – the nature of the product (advertising cigarettes can be deemed unethical as the product is detrimental to people's health)
American Marketing Association Code of Ethics	● The marketer's professional conduct must be guided by the adherence to all applicable laws and regulations ● Being honest in serving consumers, clients, employees, suppliers, distributors and the public ● Participants in the marketing exchange process should be able to expect that products and services offered are safe and fit for their intended uses ● All parties intend to discharge their obligations, financial and otherwise, in good faith ● Rejection of high-pressure manipulations, or misleading sales tactics ● Not manipulating the availability of a product for purpose of exploitation ● Meet obligations and responsibilities in contracts and mutual agreements in a timely manner ● Avoid manipulation to take advantage of situations to maximise personal welfare in a way that unfairly deprives or damages the organisation or others

The business case for ethical practice

Marketers are encouraged to behave in an ethical manner because information about a firm's ethical behaviours is thought to influence product sales and consumers' image of the company (Mascarenhas 1995). There is conflicting evidence, however, as to whether this proposition holds true. Exhibit 10.3 summarises some key consumer results, with a clear picture emerging that although ethical organisations are valued by consumers, they often have insufficient information and do not seek out this information to determine whether the companies are ethical.

However, the communication of ethical business practices has become a very valuable advertising appeal. Ethical actions often start as, or rapidly become, content for advertising, sales promotion or PR campaigns. There is also evidence that companies suffer commercially from boycotts; Shell were estimated to have lost between 20% and 50% of their sales during the Brent Spar boycott (Klein 2000), and the Nestlé boycott is said to have cost the firm $40 million (Nelson-Horchler 1984). Gelb (1995) argues the power of consumer boycotts is increasing, with more buyers re-fusing to buy a branded product or a class of products to achieve some socially responsible outcome. In Exhibit 10.4, Carrigan and Attalla (2001) summarise the main consumer attitudes to ethical purchasing. The US-based Business for Social Responsibility organisation cites various surveys that respectively demonstrate that an ethics code will:

- Strengthen financial performance
- Improve sales, brand image and reputation

Exhibit 10.3 Consumer responses to ethical organisations

Positive behaviour	
Forte and Lamont (1998)	Consumers making purchases on the basis of a firm's role in society
Simon (1995)	85% of respondents had a more positive image of a company that supported something they cared about. 15% would be more likely to pay more for a product or service associated with a cause important to them
Creyer and Ross (1997)	A company's level of ethical behaviour is an important consideration during the purchase decision. US consumers are willing to pay higher prices and reward ethical behaviour. Consumers would buy products from unethical firms, but only at a lower price
Mason (2000)	One-third of consumers are seriously concerned with ethical issues. 44% UK public have boycotted a product for ethical reasons in 2000
Skowronski and Carlston (1987)	Consumers punish unethical behaviour
Negative behaviour	
Dragon International study (1991)	Only 26% of respondents could name any socially responsible firms, and only 18% could name a least socially responsible firm
Folkes and Kamins (1999)	Consumers do not necessarily reward ethical behaviour
Boulstridge and Carrigan (2000)	Consumers lacked information to distinguish whether a company had or had not behaved ethically

Exhibit 10.4 A categorisation of consumer attitudes to ethical purchasing

		Ethical awareness	
		High	Low
Ethical purchase intention	High	Caring and ethical	Confused and uncertain
	Low	Cynical and disinterested	Oblivious

Source: From '*The myth of the ethical consumer – do ethics matter in purchase behaviour*', in *Journal of Consumer Marketing*, Vol. 18, No. 7, 2001, pp. 560–577, Emerald Group Publishing Limited, (Carrigan, M. and Attalla, A., 2001). Reproduced with permission.

- Strengthen employee loyalty and commitment
- Limit vulnerability to activist pressure and boycotts
- Avoid fines and court-imposed remedies
- Avoid loss of business (e.g. in 1999 the Japanese government revoked Credit Suisse's business licence in Japan for 'misleading and inappropriate' financial accounting practices).
- Enable greater access to capital (e.g. billions of pounds in assets are managed in portfolios that screen for ethical, environmental and other socially responsible practices) (*Marketing Business* 2002a).

Corporate social responsibility (CSR) programmes and cause-related marketing

Corporate social responsibility

A business philoshpy that recognizes the social, cultural and environmental consequences of business pactices and subsequently demonstrates actions that appear to further some social good, beyond the interests of the firm and that which is required by law.

Corporate social responsibility (CSR) and sustainability are ethical choices that a company will make about the way it will go about is business. CSR programmes demonstrate actions that appear to further some social good, beyond the interests of the firm and that which is required by law. CSR investment may entail embodying the product with socially responsible attributes, such as pesticide-free or non-animal-tested ingredients. It may also involve the use of signals, such as the union label in clothing, that convey to the consumer that the company is concerned about certain social issues. This results in the belief that, by using these products, consumers are indirectly supporting a cause and rewarding firms that devote resources to CSR (Gauzente and Ranchhod 2001).

Cause-related marketing

A commercial activity by which business and charities or causes form a partnership with each other to market an image, product or service for mutual benefit.

Cause-related marketing, an aspect of CSR, is a commercial activity by which businesses and charities or causes form a partnership with each other to market an image, product or service for mutual benefit. According to studies commissioned from Research International, 88% of consumers are aware of a cause-related marketing programme and participating companies are perceived as being more trustworthy and more innovative. Another finding is that 76% of consumers have taken part in such programmes, of whom 77% were positively influenced at the point of purchase or decision-making (*Marketing Business* 2002b).

IN VIEW 10.1

CSR programmes in action

British Gas's CSR programme is branded 'Here to Help'. Jon Kimber, a senior marketing manager at the company, explains that the programme grew out of its work on energy efficiency. 'One of the things that struck us was that, as we help people with energy efficiency, there's an opportunity for us to help them in a number of other areas,' says Kimber. The result is a broad-based programme in which British Gas works with local authorities and seven charities, reaching out in particular to people living in deprived areas. Kimber explains, 'We send a trained assessor to the individual's property and they conduct a home assessment. We take a holistic approach to people's needs.' The home assessment enables them to identify benefits and charitable funds that people could be eligible for. Those helped by the programme have so far received over £2 million of previously unclaimed government benefits. 'The potential is even greater as we roll this programme out across the country,' says Kimber. British Gas is targeting 500,000 households and expects to invest £75 million in the programme. But it is also helping to position British Gas as a socially responsible corporate citizen – no bad thing for a company that's had more than its fair share of negative headlines.

Source: Bartram 2003, *Marketing Business*, October

IN VIEW 10.2

Cause-related campaigns

A Tesco promotion offers customers a 'Computers for Schools' voucher for every £10 spent in-store or on petrol. Customers collect and donate the vouchers to schools for redemption for computers and related equipment. This has been run by Tesco since 1992 and over £70 million worth of computers and equipment has been provided. The benefits to Tesco are improved customer loyalty, recognition as an innovative retailer and enhanced corporate profile in the community.

Similarly, the Avon Breast Cancer Crusade has been running for ten years, raising over £8 million. The programme has now been exported and is running in 30 countries, from which Avon hopes to raise $250 million by the end of this year. The commercial benefit, confirmed by research, is high awareness of this activity among Avon staff and customers, communicating Avon's commitment to women.

HSBC has announced a US $50 million 'eco-partnership' with Earthwatch, Botanic Gardens Conservation International and WWF. Ambitious projects including cleaning up three of the world's major rivers for the benefit of 50 million people who depend upon them and saving 20,000 rare plant species from extinction. In addition 2,000 HSBC staff will take part in fieldwork and become environmental champions within the group. The reason given for this investment by HSBC chairman Sir John Bond is: 'Companies as well as individuals have a responsibility for the stewardship of this planet, which we hold in trust for the future.' Doubtless, there has also been consideration of the likely improvement of perceptions of HSBC, at a time when banks are criticised for uncaring attitudes.

Source: Marketing Business, June, 2002a

IN VIEW 10.3

Implementing CSR

1 Founding values

Entrepreneurs start a company and imbue it with their own values and attitudes. Richard Branson and Body Shop's Anita Roddick are good examples of business people who brought a passionate set of values to their companies.

2 Leading by example

As the company grows, employees take on the founders' values. 'New people joining quickly see what is expected of them,' says Goyder.

3 External relations

The company spreads its values through its relationships with suppliers, customer, communities and shareholders. These relationships are critical to creating value. 'You're only as successful as the quality of these relationships,' declares Goyder.

4 A clear message

'You cannot have successful relationships unless you have a clear purpose and clear values,' says Goyder. 'The first role of the leader is to ensure that there is a clear and consistent idea of why the company exists and what it stands for.'

5 Honesty

Leadership is key to ensuring that the company's message is consistent. You can't say one thing to your employees and another to the shareholders. So a company must not be two-faced, but speak with one voice.

6 Being responsible

Recognise that responsible business practice is as important an ingredient of business success as the corporate strategy, the quality of products or marketing effectiveness.

7 The pay-off

Adopting a tick-box attitude to CSR is not a predictor of business success. 'Effective leadership, based on clear purpose and values which permeate an organisation and its relationships, is,' says Goyder. 'A close examination of a company's relationships is essential to the assessment of its leadership, and therefore of its future ability to generate economic value.'

Source: Goyder 2003 in Bartram 2003, *Marketing Business*, October

Ethical concerns in integrated marketing communications

Misleading advertising

The use of misleading, exaggerated or confusing claims in advertising is a key issue in marketing communication ethics. Positioning a product using these claims not only can be ethically unsound but creates customer confusion, negative publicity and can result in legal and/or regulatory censure. For example in the use of health claims, under UK food law, brand owners are not allowed to talk about any positive effects consumption of their product might have on a disease. They can, however, highlight positive effects on indicators of a disease (*Marketing Business* 2003). Brands must be able to back up a health proposition with hard evidence.

IN VIEW 10.4

Misleading advertising: cautionary tales of 'health' positioning

In 2000, Ribena Toothkind found itself in hot water with the Advertising Standards Authority (ASA) for press and poster advertising showing bottles of Ribena Toothkind as bristles on a toothbrush and the line 'There is only one soft drink accredited by the British Dental Association', which was deemed to be misleading as it implied oral health benefits. Procter & Gamble has also been accused of presenting a product – in this case its Sunny Delight drink – in a far healthier light than its contents justify.

In 2002, Tetley Tea was slammed by ASA for making exaggerated and misleading poster advertising claims that the anti-oxidants it contains can keep hearts healthy – one of the offending ads even carried a 10-foot high flashing plastic heart.

Also in 2002, Australian wine brand BRL Hardy's drew flak for a cause-related marketing campaign in which it paid more then £50,000 in sponsorship fees to the Breast Cancer Campaign in return for using the charity's logo on its bottles. Scientists attacked the partnership, complaining that studies have shown a link between alcohol consumption and breast cancer. Tom Sanders, professor of nutrition and dietetics at King's College London and a government adviser on food and diet, compared the initiative to putting an ad for a lung disease charity on cigarette packets. 'It is extremely ill-advised of the breast cancer charity to get involved with a wine company, which is, after all, trying to promote the consumption of alcohol. It sends out a confusing message to women about the risks they run,' Professor Sanders said. Pamela Goldberg, chief executive of Breast Cancer Campaign, replied: 'The link between alcohol and breast cancer is not a causal link. It's a slight increase in risk.' Whether a link between breast cancer and alcohol is definitively established or not, the Breast Cancer Campaign's reputation has been damaged as a result of this partnership.

Source: Gray 2003, *Marketing Business*, May

Taste and decency

Issues of taste and decency are of concern to the regulatory bodies in the marketing communications industry. For example, the Advertising Standards Authority commissions regular consumer surveys into perceptions of taste and decency. These findings help the ASA reach decisions when adjudicating on cases of possible infringement of their codes.

The use of shock tactics in advertising is nothing new, yet are the main contributors to protests about issues of taste and decency. Shocking campaigns often generate a surge of spin-off publicity – effectively, free advertising – which money could not buy. Among the first companies to court controversy with their advertising was the Italian clothing company Benetton, which has highlighted social issues with provocative imagery, from a man dying of AIDS and a soldier holding a human thigh bone to an Arab and Israeli holding a globe and a newborn baby still attached to the umbilical cord. Benetton's advertising director Paolo Landi explains:

> A company that emphasises value is no longer communicating with the consumer but with the individual, meaning the sum total of his or her essence, personality and needs. By entering the universe of values, the brand frees the product from the world of merchandise and manufacturing and makes it a social being of its own. By addressing an individual rather than a customer, the brand can identify its

IN VIEW 10.5

Bad language

Findings from ASA's research into consumer reactions to bad language in advertisements and promotions revealed their top six concerns. The words found to be most unacceptable were:

Fcuk, F**k, Buck Off, Bullsheet, Feck and Peace Off.

Source: ASA web page **www.asa.org.uk** (12 February 1999)

IN VIEW 10.6

Shocking advertising

The winner of Campaign Magazine's 2003 Press Awards was the Discovery Channel's ad for its programme Age of Terror, showing a plane apparently headed for a tower block with the tagline 'Terrorism has changed the way we view the world'. The first runner-up was a Barnardos ad which was part of the charity's 'Abuse through prostitution' campaign showing a young girl with a grotesquely aged face sitting on a bed with a man asleep beside her, while the other commendation went to Schweppes for its long-lens, paparazzi-style shot through a bedroom window of Sven Joran Eriksson and Ulrika Jonsson look-alikes apparently being interrupted mid-strip by the unexpected arrival of the football manager's Italian girlfriend.

Source: Sclater 2003, *Marketing Business*, July/August

target on the basis not of age or income, but of a shared vision of what is important, starting from a set of common values. (*Marketing Business*, 2003)

Shocking images are used to enhance ad recall and are often used by charities and public-service organisations where the subject matter is inherently shocking and/or the organisations have small budgets with which to compete, e.g. the Department of Transport's teen road safety film in which the main character is seen at home, with friends and walking to school. It is only when he rushes across a main road to catch up with his girl-friend, and an approaching car passes through him, that we realise he is dead and the person we can see is his ghost. The chilling message is that traffic is the biggest single killer of 12 to 16-year-olds (*Marketing Business* 2003).

FOOD FOR THOUGHT

Shock tactics are the use of shocking (unusual, provocative, controversial, intrusive) images in advertising for the purpose of attracting attention and debate and often generate free publicity.

Finally, In Views 10.7 and 10.8 provide examples of intrusive and controversial marketing communications.

IN VIEW 10.7

Intrusive advertising: the most annoying company in Canada

Infolink Communications Ltd, begun in 1994 by George Teodore and Cesar Correia, has grown into a bustling business by sending thousands of unsolicited advertisements by fax. Armed with 800 phone lines and state-of-the-art fax technology, the company can transmit up to 40,000 pages of advertisements, press releases and corporate-disclosure documents to targeted audiences in an hour. Over the past three years, the company has grown by 300%, and in 1998 it is expected to generate more than $5 million in revenue.

Source: Harris 1997

IN VIEW 10.8

Controversial marketing communications

In 2001 retail operator Midland Mainline sent out fake London parking tickets to 50,000 customers. The small print said the ticket was a promotional leaflet and added that customers could either 'explode with rage or take the train'. Unfortunately, many customers exploded with rage on receiving the tickets, and were even more angry when they realised it was a publicity stunt. Some rail travellers's wives were also furious, believing their husbands had made secret trips by car to London.

Source: Marketing Business 2002b, Marketing Business, June

Summary

This chapter has outlined the concept of marketing ethics and identifies the main considerations in ethical marketing communications decision-making. Marketing ethics examines systematically marketing and marketing morality related to 4P issues. Exhibit 10.1 outlines the major ethical issues in integrated marketing communications and the two main ethical concerns, misleading advertising and issues of taste and decency are considered in more detail at the end of the chapter. A number of ethical guidelines are discussed, as identified by a variety of authors and these are summarised in Exhibit 10.2. From this, it is clear that there are a number of different positions from which to evaluate marketing communications decisions and Smith (1995) delineates the continuum upon which they can be perceived.

The Business Case of practicing ethical marketing communications is given, detailing that marketers are encouraged to behave in an ethical manner because information about a firm's ethical behaviours is thought to influence product sales and consumers' image of the company (Mascarenhas 1995). However, as there is conflicting evidence of consumer response to ethical marketing communications practices, Exhibit 10.3 elaborates the pros and cons. Finally, corporate social responsibility (CSR) and cause-related marketing are considered as strategies. CSR programmes demonstrate actions that appear to further some social good, beyond the interests of the firm and that which is required by law. Cause-related marketing, an aspect of CSR, is a commercial activity by which businesses and charities or causes form a partnership with each other to market an image, product or service for mutual benefit.

Self-review questions

1 What are the main ethical issues in integrated marketing communications?

2 How do the ethical positions of Caveat emptor and Caveat venditor differ?

3 Laczniak and Murphy (1991) proposed some rules of ethical conduct. Do you think that businesses could follow these rules consistently?

4 What are the implications for business of not practising ethical decision-making?

5 How does cause-related marketing differ from CSR?

6 Why do marketing communicators use shocking appeals?

Project

'In 2001 Philip Morris became the latest in a growing stable of beleaguered blue-chip multinationals to put ethics at the heart of its corporate communication, bringing on Doner Cardwell Hawkins to handle an international advertising brief stressing its social responsibility. The strategy has its pitfalls. While companies such as BP and Shell have moved away from their image as gas-pump pariahs by emphasising their social and environmental stewardship, it has backfired for others, like Monsanto and Exxon, reinvigorating hostile pressure groups and inviting ridicule. Such a misstep could prove disastrous for Philip Morris' (*Marketing Business* 2001).

Evaluate the ethical considerations of the above mini-case and develop a business case for Philip Morris's CSR programme.

References

Arnold, M. (2001), Walking the ethical tightrope. *Marketing*, 12 July, 17.

Bartram, P. (2003), Keeping promises. *Marketing Business*, October, 29–33.

Beardshaw, J. and Palfreman, D. (1990), *The Organisation in Its Environment*. London: Pitman.

Beauchamp, T.L. and Bowie, N.E. (2001), *Ethical theory and business*. Upper Saddle River, NJ: Prentice Hall, Inc.

Binkley, C. (2000), Harrah's new code to restrict marketing. *The Wall Street Journal*, 19 October, B16.

Bishop, J.D. (2000), Is self-identity image advertising ethical? *Business Ethics Quarterly*, 10, 371–398.

Bishop, L. (2002), Ethical dilemma. *Marketing Business*, June, 32–33.

Bloom, P.N. and Gundlach, G.T. (eds), *Handbook of Marketing and Society*. Thousand Oaks, CA: Sage Publications.

Boatright, J.R. (2000), *Ethics and the Conduct of Business*. Upper Saddle River, NJ: Prentice Hall, Inc.

Botan, C. (1997), Ethics in strategic communication campaigns: The case for a new approach to public relations. *The Journal of Business Communication*, April, 34 (2), 188–202.

Boulstridge, E. and Carrigan, M. (2000), Do consumers really care about corporate responsibility? Highlighting the attitude-behaviour gap. *Journal of Communication Management*, 4 (4), 355–368.

Boylan, M. (2001), *Business Ethics*. Upper Saddle River, NJ: Prentice Hall, Inc.

Brinkmann, J. (2002), Business and marketing ethics as professional ethics. *Journal of Business Ethics*, November/December, 14 (112), 159–177.

Carrigan, M. and Attalla, A. (2001), The myth of the ethical consumer – do ethics matter in purchase behaviour? *Journal of Consumer Marketing*, 18 (7), 560–575.

Caudill, E.M. and Murphy, P.E. (2000), Consumer online privacy: legal and ethical issues. *Journal of Public Policy and Marketing*, 19, 7–19.

Coleman, L.G. (1991), Marketing and medicine can mix and still be ethical. *Marketing News*, 25 (10), 16.

Creyer, E.H. and Ross, W.T. (1997), The influence of firm behaviour on purchase intention: do consumers really care about business ethics? *Journal of Consumer Marketing*, 14 (6), 421–433.

Dornoff, R.J. and Tankersley, C.B. (1975), AMA Code Ethics. *Journal of Consumer Affairs*, Summer, 97–103.

Dragon International (1991), *Corporate reputation: Does the consumer care?* London: Dragon International.

Drumwright, M.E. and Murphy, P.E. (2001), Corporate societal marketing. In Bloom, *Handbook of Marketing and Society*, 162–183.

Dunfee, T.W., Smith, N.C. and Ross, W.T. Jr. (1999), Social contracts and marketing ethics. *Journal of Marketing*, July, 63 (3), 14–32.

Fineman, S. (1999), Marketing ethics: commentary. In *Rethinking Marketing*, Sage, London, pp. 183–185.

Foley, J.P. (1999), Misplaced marketing commentary ethics in advertising: a report from the Pontifical Council for Social Communication. *The Journal of Consumer Marketing*, 16 (3), 220–221.

Folkes, V.S. and Kamins, M.A. (1999), Effects of information about firms' ethical and unethical actions on consumer attitudes. *Journal of Consumer Psychology*, 8 (3), 243–259.

Forte, M. and Lamont, B.T. (1998), The bottom line effects of greening: implications of environmental awareness. *Academy of Management*, 12 (1), 89–90.

Garrett, D.E. (1987), The effectiveness of marketing policy boycotts: environmental opposition to marketing. *Journal of Marketing*, 51 (April), 46–57.

Gaski, J.F. (1999), Does marketing ethics really have anything to say? – A critical inventory of the literature. *Journal of Business Ethics*, 18 (3), 315–334.

Gauzente, C. and Ranchhod, A. (2001), Ethical marketing for competitive advantage on the internet. *Academy of Marketing Science Review*, 10, 1–6.

Gelb, B.D. (1995), More boycotts ahead? Some implications. *Business Horizons*, 38 (2), 70–77.

Goodpaster, K.E. (1992), Business Ethics. *Encyclopaedia of Ethics*, 111–115.

Goyder, M. (2003), *Redefining CSR*, Tomorrow's Company, 19 Buckingham Street, London.

Gray, R. (2003), Eat, drink and be healthy. *Marketing Business*, May, 36–38.

Hackley, C.E. and Kitchen, P.J. (1999), Ethical perspectives on the postmodern communications Leviathan. *Journal of Business Ethics*, May, 20 (1), 15–26.

Haddow, I. (2001), Brazil in UK AIDS drugs row. **www.news.bbc.co.uk**, 3 February.

Harris, J. (1997), The most annoying company in Canada. *Canadian Business*, 70 (18), 137–138.

Hunt, S.D. and Vitell, S. (1992), The General Theory of Marketing Ethics: A Retrospective and Revision. In *Ethics in Marketing* (Craig Smith and John A. Quelch, eds).

Kelly, E.P. (2000), Ethical and online privacy in electronic commerce. *Business Horizons*, May/June, 43 (3), 3.

Klein, N. (2000), *No Logo*. London: Harper Collins.

Laczniak, G.R. (1983), Framework for analysing marketing ethics. *Journal of Macromarketing*, 1, 7–18.

Laczniak, G.R. and Murphy, P.E. (1993), *Ethical marketing decisions: The higher road.*

McWilliams, A. and Siegel, D. (2001). Corporate social responsibility: A theory of the firm perspective. *The Academy of Management Review*, January, 26 (1), 117–127.

Marketing Business (2001), A tale of two campaigns. *Marketing Business*, November/December, 6.

Marketing Business (2002a), Selling responsibility. *Marketing Business*, June, 25–27.

Marketing Business (2002b), Editorial. *Marketing Business*, June, 1.

Mascarenhas, O.A.J. (1995), Exonerating unethical marketing behaviors: a diagnostic framework. *Journal of Marketing*, 59, 43–57.

Mason, T. (2000), The importance of being ethical. *Marketing*, 26 October, 27.

Mortensen, R.A., Smith, J.E. and Cavanagh, G.F. (1989), The importance of ethics to job performance: An empirical investigation of managers perceptions. *Journal of Business Ethics*, April, 8 (4), 253–259.

Murphy, P.E. and Laczniak, G.R. (1981), Marketing ethics: A review with implications for managers, educators and researches. *Review of Marketing*, 251–266.

Murphy, P.E. and Laczniak, G.R. (1981), The function within business firms most often charged with ethical abuse is marketing. *Review of Marketing*, 251.

Murphy, P.E. (2002), Marketing ethics at the millennium: Review reflections and recommendations. *Blackwell Guide to Business Ethics*.

Murphy, P.E. (2000), Corporate ethics statements: An update. *Global Codes of Conduct*, 295–304.

Nelson-Horchler, J. (1984), Fighting a boycott: image rebuilding, Swiss style. *Industry Week*, 220, 54–56.

Nwachukwu, S.L.S., Vitell, S.J., Gilbert, F.W. and Barnes, J.H. (1997), Ethics and Social Responsibility in Marketing: An Examination of Ethical Evaluation of Advertising Strategies. *Journal of Business Research*, 39, 107–118.

O'Donahoe, S. and Tynan, C. (1998), Beyond sophistication: dimensions of advertising literacy. *International Journal of Advertising*, 1, November, 467–478.

Peterson, K.I. (1995), The influence of the researcher and his procedure on the validity of group sessions, *Combined Proceedings*, American Marketing Association, Chicago, Il, pp. 146–148.

Pires, G.D. and Stanton, J. (2002). Ethnic marketing ethics. *Journal of Business Ethics*, March, 36, 111–118.

Randall, V.M. (1999/2000), Dysfunctional marketing fails. *Communication World*, Dec/Jan, 17(1), 5.

Reed, M. (1999), Wide open to the web warriors. *Marketing*, 4 February, 18–20.

Rogers, D. (1998), Ethical tactics arouse public doubt. *Marketing*, 6 August, 12–14.

Ross, W.T. and Robertson, D.C. (2000), Lying: the impact of decision context. *Business Ethics Quarterly*, 10, 409–440.

Scheibal, W.J. and Gladstone, J.A. (2000), Privacy on the net: Europe changes the rules. *Business Horizons*, May–June, 13–18.

Schlegelmilch, B. (1998), *Marketing ethics: An international perspective*. London, UK: International Thomson Business Press.

Sclater, I. (2003), Shock value. *Marketing Business*, July/August, 16–18.

Sheth, J.N., Gardner, D.M. and Garrett, D.E. (1988), *Marketing Theory: Evolution and Evaluation*. New York, NY: John Wiley & Sons.

Simon, F.L. (1995), Global corporate philanthropy: a strategic framework. *International Marketing Review*, 12 (4), 20–37.

Singhapakdi, A. (1999), Perceived importance of ethics and ethical decision in marketing. *Journal of Business Research*, 45 (1), 89–99.

Singhapakdi, A. and Vitell, S.J. (1993), Personal and professional values underlying the ethical judgements of marketers. *Journal of Business Ethics*, July, 12 (7), 525–532.

Skowronski, J.J. and Carlston, D.E. (1987), Social judgment and social memory: the role of cue diagnosticity in negativity, positivity and extremity biases. *Journal of Personality and Social Psychology*, 52, 689–699.

Smith, N.C. (2001), Changes in corporate practices in response to public interest advocacy and actions. *Handbook of Marketing and Society*, pp. 140–161.

Smith, N. C. (1995), Marketing strategies for the ethics era. *Sloan Management Review*, 36 (4), 85–98.

Smith, N.C. and Quelch, J.A. (1993), *Ethics in Marketing*.

Smith, N.C. and Quelch, J.A. (1996), *Ethics in Marketing*, Boston, MA: Irwin.

Sparks, J.R. and Hunt, S.D. (1998), Marketing research ethical sensitivity: Conceptualisation, measurement, and exploratory investigation. *Journal of Marketing*, 62, 92–109.

Szymanski, D.M. and Hise, R.T. (2000), E-satisfaction: An initial examination. *Journal of Retailing*, 73 (3), 309–322.

Ulrich, P. and Sarasin, C. (1995), *Facing public interest: The ethical challenge to business policy and corporate communications*. London: Kluwer Academic Publications.

 ## Suggested further reading

Centrum Public Relations code of ethics: www.centrumpr.co.n2/code-of-ethics.

Dunfee, T.W., Smith, N.C. and Ross, W.T. Jr (1999), Social contracts and marketing ethics. *Journal of Marketing*, 63 (3), 14–32.

McWilliams, A. and Siegel, D. (2001), Corporate social responsibility: A theory of the firm perspective. *Journal of Business Ethics*, 26 (1), 117–127.

Pires, G.D. and Stanton, J. (2002), Ethnic marketing ethics. *Journal of Business Ethics*, 36, 111–118.

World Association of Internet Marketing code of ethics: www.waim.org.

Appendix 10.1 PRINZ Code of Ethics

The primary obligation of membership of the Public Relations Institute of New Zealand is the ethical practice of public relations. This Code sets out the principles and standards that guide PR decisions and actions.

1. Advocacy and Honesty

A member shall:
i.   Provide independent, objective counsel for clients or employers
ii. Promote the ethical, well-founded views of clients or employers
iii. Be honest and accurate in all communications – and act promptly to correct erroneous communications
iv. Avoid deceptive practices

2. Balancing Openness and Privacy

A member shall:
i.   Promote open communication in the public interest wherever possible
ii. Respect the rights of others to have their say
iii. Be prepared to name clients or employers represented and the sponsors for causes and interests represented
iv. Safeguard the confidences and privacy rights of present, former and prospective clients and employers

3. Conflicts of Interest

A member shall:
i.   Disclose promptly any existing or potential conflict of interest to affected clients or organisations
ii. Disclose any client or business interest in published or broadcast editorial work

4. Law Abiding

A member shall:
i.   Abide by the laws affecting the practice of public relations and the laws and regulations affecting the client

5. Professionalism

A member shall:
i.   Actively pursue personal professional development
ii. Explain realistically what public relations activities can accomplish
iii. Counsel colleagues on ethical decision-making
iv. Decline representation of clients or organisations that urge or require actions contrary to this code
v.   Not engage in irrelevant or unsubstantiated personal criticism

(**www.centrumpr.co.nz**, 2002)

Chapter 11

Image and brand management

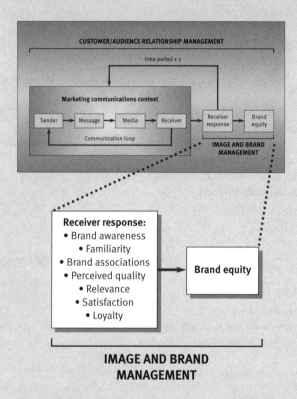

The IMC Process Model

Using the material in Case Study 1, describe Concern's brand image and its position in comparison to other similar charities. Do you think this is a distinctive position? In particular you may wish to consider whether or not the brand name helps or hinders the brand proposition.

Chapter outline

- What is image and brand management?
- Branding and brands
- Corporate, product and own-label branding
- The components of a brand
- The benefits of branding
- Brand equity
- Managing the brand

Objectives

- To introduce the concept of image and brand management
- To differentiate between corporate, product and own-label branding
- To introduce the distinctions between brand image, personality and identity
- To outline the components of branding
- To demonstrate the benefits of branding to the consumer and brand owner
- To introduce the measurement of brand equity

Professional perspective

Professor Leslie de Chernatony University of Birmingham

The wealth of an organisation is, to a not insignificant extent, judged by the strength of its brands – be it in consumer or business-to-business markets, with brands that have either a high product or high services component. Those organisations that have thriving brands have a coherent, company-wide understanding of the unique benefits of their brand. The difference between a brand and its 'equivalent' commodity form is that the brand has added values. These values can be broadly categorised as functional, nationally based values and emotional, psychosocial values. To thrive, managers need to ensure that the cluster of values they offer to consumers must be relevant, superior to competitors and sustainable.

The challenge is not just finding a unique, superior cluster of values and communicating these externally to consumers, but it is also about developing internal value delivery systems and communicating to staff their roles in enacting these brand values. The internal communication challenge is to facilitate understanding of the brand values, and then to gain the commitment from all staff to act in a way that supports these values.

Brands start their lives in brand planning documents, but ultimately they reside in consumers' minds (rationally) and in consumers' hearts (emotionally). Brand evaluation is therefore based on appreciating what consumers *think* about the brand and how they *feel* about it. It is more difficult to sustain the rationally based functional values of a brand than the emotionally based values.

When consumers evaluate brands they rely on many informational cues, of which memory is a key consideration. While the organisation strives to portray a highly desirable identity for the brands, because of consumers' perceptual processes and their brand experiences, plus interactions with other groups, the image they hold of the brand may well differ from the projected identity. The wider the gap between the brand identity and brand image, the more likely this is to trigger managerial action. However, there can be a tendency amongst managers to play down such discrepancies, since this is challenging the dominant shared cognitive mind-set about the nature of brands. Ignoring consumer feedback about the brand's image can lead to a weaker brand. Responding to an identity-image brand enhances the likelihood of a more viable brand.

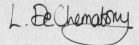

What is image and brand management?

Customer/audience relationship management

The strategic and tactical tasks involved in the management of positive, 'personal' and continuing communication between an organisation and its audiences overtime; recognising this should be complementary to image and brand management.

Image and brand management

The strategic and tactical tasks involved in the management of positive, 'non-personal' communication between an organisation and its audiences; recognising this should be complementary to customer audience relationship management.

The Integrated Marketing Communications Process Model identifies two key strategic tasks for those responsible for integrated marketing communications – '**customer/ audience relationship management**' and '**image and brand management**'. Chapter 12 discusses the importance of recognising marketing communications from a customer relationship perspective. This chapter outlines the significance of branding to an organisation and the activities involved in image management. Image and brand management tends to be associated with communication 'at a distance' with many **target audiences**. It is frequently seen as the primary function of advertising and public relations that can be supported by elements of sales promotion. It is strongly associated with one-to-many communications. Image and brand management comprises four key objectives:

- to understand what the organisation's brand(s) comprises;
- to communicate the brand(s) to channel intermediaries, consumers and other target audiences;
- to manage brands through their life cycles, and
- to enhance brand equity.

Branding and brands

Target audience

Those individuals or groups that are identified as having a direct or indirect effect on business performance, and are selected to receive marketing communications.

Branding

Strategy to differentiate products and companies, and to build economic value for both the consumer and the brand owner.

Brand

The totality of what the consumer takes into consideration before making a purchase decision.

Branding and **brands** are identified in the IMC Process Model as an output of the marketing communications process and as the broad, over-arching task of image and brand management. Branding describes the values generated in the minds of people as a consequence of the sum total of marketing communications effort. There is greater likelihood of producing better brands through *integrated* marketing communications.

As a marketing tool, branding is not just a case of placing a symbol or name onto products to identify the manufacturer, a brand is a set of attributes, that have a meaning, an image and produce associations with the product when a person is considering that brand of product. As Runkel and Brymer (1997) explain:

> Harley-Davidson is not just a corporate name of a motorcycle manufacturer – for hundreds and thousands of people, Harley-Davidson is a way of life rich in imagery, attitude, meaning and distinctive expressive and central values. (p. 6)

Exhibit 11.1 summarises a number of key definitions of a brand. A brand has been viewed as the totality of what the consumer takes into consideration before making a purchase decision (e.g. Riezebos 1994; Ambler and Styles 1995). Brands represent a long-term strategy around which economic value for both customer and the brand owner can be built.

Exhibit 11.1 Defining branding

Definition	Source
A bundle of intrinsic and extrinsic offerings blending both functional and psychological benefits.	Gardner and Levy 1955
A successful brand is an identifiable product, service, person or place, augmented in such a way that the buyer or user perceives relevant unique added values which match their needs most closely. Furthermore, its success results from being able to sustain these added values in the face of competition.	de Chernatony and McDonald 1998
A name, term, design, symbol or any other feature that identifies one seller's goods from those of other sellers.	Dibb et al. 1994
A brand is a distinguishing name and/or symbol (such as a logo, trademark, or pack design) intended to identify the goods and services of either one seller or a group of sellers, and to differentiate those goods or services from those of competitors.	Aaker 1991
Designed to enable customers to identify products or services which promise specific benefits.	Wilson et al. 1995

The real growth of branding occurred after the Civil War in America with the growth of national firms and national advertising media (Kotler 1994). Picture the scene, the American Wild West many years ago. Vast areas of open countryside. Cattle roaming the land. No fences or partitions separating one ranch from another. The cattle owners had a problem: their major assets all looked alike and were free to mingle. How could they be told apart? To solve the problem, each rancher developed his own simple symbol to signify his ranch. With a hot branding iron the symbol was placed on the side of each animal. The cattle were 'branded'. Cattle which were inherently the same were differentiated by a single point of difference – the distinguishing feature of a brand mark – the brand. Used in this way, the brand denotes ownership or origin. It tells you where the brand has come from. Branding was also used by the Romans and the Greeks to denote purpose. A shoemaker would have the sign of a boot over his shop and a butcher the signs of meat. Historians of marketing refer to Bass Triangle, registered as the first trade mark in England in 1876, as the first British brand and which is still going strong today (Cowley 1991).

Today, though, we use signs or brand markings to do more than signify use or merely distinguish between products. The aim of branding is to create impressions that differentiate products and companies by saying that one is not just different from the rest, but in some respect, it is better than the rest.

IN VIEW 11.1

Marketing emotional branding

A courageous stand on an important social issue, or a cynical attempt to exploit people's emotions? Yet again, a Benetton advertising campaign is provoking controversy – this time with its disturbing portraits of American prisoners on death row.

Oliviero Toscani, creative director, insists that Benetton is an example of that all too rare phenomenon: a caring company. Outside its headquarters in Treviso, Italy, he says, 'we have even got little boxes on the trees for the birds'.

But some consider the campaign outrageous. In Britain, more than 70 people have asked the Advertising Standards Authority, an industry body, to ban the advertisements, accusing the company of crassness and insensitivity in using images of the condemned to sell its knitwear.

A brand used to be merely the name on the side of a box that told you what was inside it. But as the Benetton campaign shows, brands are being laden with ever-heavier layers of meaning as marketers try to plug into people's innermost emotions, values, perceptions and beliefs.

Brands such as Body Shop, Virgin, and Nike have become as well known for their outlook on life as for their products – Body Shop for its environmental awareness, Virgin for its 'us against them' approach and Nike for its 'just do it' attitude.

Some older brands are trying to make the transition, too. Diageo, the world's largest drinks group, is running a global advertising campaign for Johnnie Walker whisky featuring true stories of personal courage, such as Harvey Keitel's battle with stage fright. The whisky itself is nowhere to be seen.

Things were different a generation ago. In the postwar decades, a period of rapid innovation in consumer goods, companies strove to make new products such as detergents that washed whiter or cars that went faster, then sold them by advertising the product's advantages.

Advertisers now look back on that era as the golden age of marketing.

Today, they lament, the spread of sophisticated manufacturing technology means so many companies are making roughly the same products at roughly the same price that there is little point in advertising a product's attributes.

'Since the 1960s we have entered into a period of parity manufacturing and parity marketing, meaning that there are almost no categories in which you can have an exclusive advantage any more,' says John Grace, New York-based executive director of Interbrand, the branding consultancy.

'The result is you have to look for other dimensions with which to attract consumers: not the functional aspects of products, because you don't own those any more, but the emotional aspects, which is really what branding is about.'

The Henley Centre, a London-based forecasting group, points to another dimension to emotional branding, too. 'As we have become better off, the simple acquisition of goods is not half as exciting or satisfying as it used to be, and we are increasingly looking for higher-order needs to be satisfied,' says Martin Hayward, director of consumer consultancy.

'When you are starving, you don't care what you eat: you'll just take food. But we are now at the stage where we're worried whether we are going to the right sushi bar, whether it's trendy or not, and whether it says the right thing about us.'

Benetton says its controversial advertising campaigns – previous examples of which have included images of dying Aids victims and a black stallion mounting a white mare –

are intended to provoke discussion of global issues, not to sell clothes. But Mr Toscani acknowledges a link between the two.

'Today, any product is made of two things: a percentage of material and a percentage of image. And the part of the product that is made of image is getting bigger,' he says.

'Products are all so similar that there isn't much difference between one brand and another. So what's left? There is the possibility of making a brand very well known, so that when you think of Benetton your first thought is not a sweater, not something to wear, but a brand that's got a certain kind of courage.'

Will all brands end up trying to connect with people's emotions? In a sense, they already do. Marlboro, with its 'Marlboro Country' theme, taps into the idea of the frontier spirit, and Coca-Cola's 'real thing' theme appeals to our desire for authenticity. Even something as mundane as Procter & Gamble's Sunny Delight juice drink packs in the emotions associated with sunshine and delight.

Robert Jones, a London-based director of Wolff Olins, the branding consultancy, says these products lie at one end of a spectrum, while at the other lie relatively few products and services that have 'almost a kind of high concept attached to them', such as humanity for Benetton, fun for Disney, usability for Apple or democracy for Ikea.

'There are probably no more than 100 of these around the world at the moment, and I think they've got there because of the passion and commitment of the people behind them rather than because anybody sat down and thought that, in a particular sector at a particular stage of the maturity of the market, it was necessary to go for a high concept,' he says.

Still, taking the moral high ground has gained a greater sense of urgency as global brands are targeted by environmentalists, anti-globalisation campaigners and other protest groups, raising the possibility that more companies will try to crowd into Benetton's patch.

Branding experts say this could turn out to be a mistake if consumers interpret it as hypocrisy. 'It only really works if everything you do supports the thing that you're standing for,' says Mr Jones. 'For me, there's a huge dissonance between what Benetton's posters say and their pullovers. They're two different worlds, really.'

Mr Toscani, however, is unrepentant. 'When you put a product on a top model and you advertise that as an image, isn't that even worse?' he asks. 'I mean, will you look like that when you put on the product that is advertised that way?'

'I think it's much more cynical to do what other people do than what I do. At least I'm not pushing any product. I'm just showing you something we should be talking about.'

Source: © The Financial Times Limited (18 February 2000)

Corporate, product and own-label branding

In common with other elements of this book, because we are ultimately concerned with *integrated* marketing communications, it is important that we take a broad view of branding. It is usual for books on the subject to relate the process of branding to goods and services only, although the image of the organisation as a whole exerts a strong influence on the brand image of the product. It tends, however, to be left to corporate identity specialists to talk about the 'branding' of companies. It is unfortunate to separate the two because they are inextricably mixed. The branding of a company is no less a branding exercise, and certainly no less important, than the branding of a product. This is clearly emphasised by Simon Mottram, a director of Interbrand, who calls this 'corporate branding' (Mottram 1998).

Branding strategies

A brand can identify one item, a family of items or the seller. There are typically four main branding strategies:

1 *Corporate umbrella branding* – the organisation and all its products are branded under the same corporate name, for example Heinz.
2 *Family umbrella branding* – the organisation has a corporate brand and a separate brand for its products, for example Marks & Spencer's St Michael brand (Plate 2).
3 *Range branding* – a number of related products are grouped together under one brand name, for example Lean Cuisine's range of low calorie foods.
4 *Individual branding* – each product is branded separately, for example the brand Penguin is reserved for chocolate biscuits, even though there may be a range of different packaging options.

There has been a significant move away from individual line branding towards corporate branding in the last ten years. The costs of creating and supporting individual brands has become prohibitive. It is estimated that it would now cost, on average, more than £1 billion to develop a new brand across Europe, the US and the Far East. This cost restriction, together with increased retailer power, is making it difficult for stand-alone brands to compete in some markets and explains the focus on corporate brand management (Mottram 1998). Indeed, King (1994) sees the corporate brand as becoming a major discriminator in consumer choice, rather than the functional attributes of objects made by the company.

The corporate brand, as with product brands, can be seen to comprise three discrete but overlapping concepts: personality, identity and image (Bernstein 1984). Recognising the distinctions between these concepts goes a long way towards understanding the elements that lie under direct management control and which, therefore, may be manipulated for corporate and marketing communications purposes.

Corporate personality

The composite organisational traits, characteristics and spirit.

● **Corporate personality** is a term used in a similar way to a person's personality. It is, essentially, who the organisation is. 'It is the soul, the persona, the spirit, the culture of the organisation manifested in some way' (Olins 1990). It is the composite of its traits, the sum total of its characteristics that can be both intellectual and behavioural. Corporate personality is relatively enduring although it can undergo transformation through merger, acquisition, or where there is a change of chief executive and senior management. Mission statements often try to capture a sense of corporate personality provided that they truly try to reflect the organisation rather than being a smart piece of rhetoric. Corporate *personality* is the 'raw' material of corporate *identity*.

Corporate identity

The basis upon which the organisation is known and understood, and the means by which corporate personality is expressed.

● **Corporate identity** is the means by which corporate personality is projected, transmitted or communicated. Identity is conveyed by physical 'cues' or features, or what Olins (1990), one of the leading practitioners in corporate identity work, calls *outward signs*. Corporate identity is the basis on which the organisation is known and understood (whether or not this is deliberate and planned, intentional or unintentional, managed well or badly). As Bernstein (1984) has described it, 'it is the clothes and mannerisms of the organisation. Everything the organisation does transmits a message'. The outward signs of corporate identity have to be consistent; if not, they can lead to ambiguity and confusion.

Corporate image

The impression of an organisation, created by the corporate identity, as perceived by the target audiences.

- **Corporate image** is the impression created by the corporate identity. It is the perception held of the organisation by its audiences. 'Identity means the sum of all the ways a company chooses to identify itself to all its publics. Image on the other hand is the perception of the company by these publics' (Margulies 1977). Corporate image is a representation in the audiences' minds and *hearts* because *feelings* become associated with thoughts. Corporate image is what is *felt* and *thought* about an organisation.

There is no doubt about the value of a positive corporate image to all target audiences. It works on behalf of the organisation as a whole and all the product brands with which it is associated. Corporate image is, in fact, the outcome of many communications activities and organisational actions. It is the image perceived by an organisation's audiences and is the consequence of its interactions with those audiences.

In reality, an organisation will have many images, not just one, because each target audience is affected by its own interests and contacts. The local community may hold different perceptions of the organisation to financial investors who, in turn, see the organisation in a different light to employees who perceive the organisation in a different way to customers and consumers. Although there may be differences in the message to different audiences, the underlying image should be consistent; the

---

IN VIEW 11.2

Building corporate image

An example of the factors involved in establishing a corporate brand image virtually from scratch is that of Seeboard Energy. This was formed in the UK from an existing electricity utility during deregulation of the power industry. From being a monopoly supplier to two million customers in a particular region, it found itself in a battle for electricity and gas customers against national giants and a range of new companies.

With competitors claiming to offer cheaper solutions and employing door-to-door selling, customers were haemorrhaging at a rate that reached 10,000 a week during 2001. The first step was research. This found 'a radically different view of the organisation internally and externally,' says John Ingall, managing partner of Archibald Ingall Stretton, the agency bought in to produce a customer retention programme.

'There was enthusiasm and passion internally but none of this was being communicated to customers, whose perceptions were that it was slow, old-fashioned and traditional.' All touchpoints between customers and company were mapped.

'We investigated how we could present Seeboard's proposition at all these different touchpoints. You then have to go internally into the organisation and transform it, so that the people who are making these touchpoints actually deliver', says Ingall.

An integrated programme encompassed training, advertising, exhibitions, direct marketing, call centres and internal communications. This was on the theme of the company's creative passion for helping customers, making the staff and their culture the 'heroes'. This culture genuinely existed, Ingall insists. 'The essence of the solution was based on a fundamental truth of the brand. That is why it worked.'

While there is still switching of energy suppliers by consumers and businesses, Seeboard is now making net gains. Further, the internal transformation reduced staff churn to an all-time low, resulting in savings on recruitment and training costs that could be diverted to the marketing budget.

Source: Marketing Business, February, 2003, p.15

differences between images should be ones of emphasis rather than nature. It is best to think of *the* corporate image as a single entity with, perhaps, variations on the theme to suit particular audience groups. The management of these images is an imprecise 'science' and is affected by factors within and outside management's control.

An image, which may be good, bad or confused, is a reality. It is the reality constructed by an organisation's audiences. An organisation is only as good as our impression of it. It is, therefore, a major management task to ensure that its corporate identity is managed to achieve a desired image in whatever way it chooses to define it. The *identity* should match the *personality* so that the *image* formed is a reasonable facsimile of the organisation. Any attempt to 'hype' the organisation by encouraging inaccurate perceptions becomes transparent and only succeeds in reducing credibility, and aggravating distrust and cynicism in the longer term. The corporate identity should be 'the outward sign of the inward commitment' (Olins 1990). Corporate image should be consistent with corporate behaviour.

Corporate identity programmes

A credible corporate identity programme needs to be built on a true understanding of the organisation and its situation. It is, essentially, about building the corporate brand. Factors affecting the development of corporate identity are modelled in Exhibit 11.2.

Exhibit 11.2 Developing corporate identity programmes

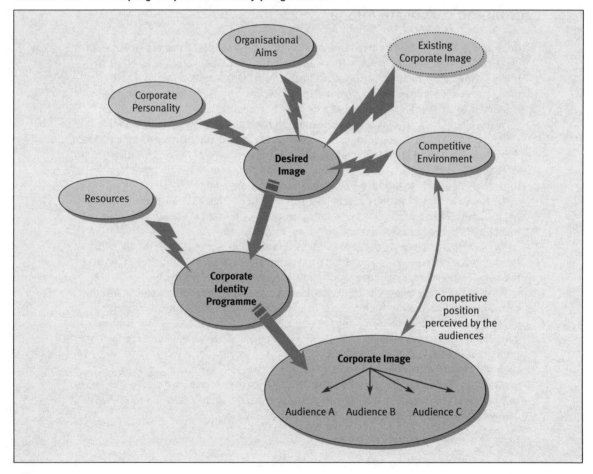

While there are opportunities to develop a corporate identity from scratch, most corporate identity work is for organisations that wish to enhance their image or create a change of impression. Under these circumstances, a new corporate identity programme has to be developed recognising the existence of a currently held image. The corporate identity task is, therefore, not so much one of *creating* a corporate identity but, rather, one of *re-creating* it by taking into account what has gone before and the current perceptions held by the organisation's publics.

Some organisations attempt to make major shifts in their identity programmes, perhaps necessitated by environmental events, while others prefer to make incremental, almost imperceptible steps. Worcester and Lewis (1983) suggested that one way of measuring the effectiveness of a new identity campaign is to track levels of awareness of the campaign and the degree of shift in public attitudes. Exhibit 11.3 is a modification to their original proposals. In identifying any change, it is important that sufficient time is allowed to elapse before starting any measurement in order that effects may be noticed and have an impact.

Exhibit 11.3's box A represents a corporate brand's poor performance with low awareness of the campaign and very little attitude shift. Box B also represents a poor performance. The campaign receives high levels of awareness but with little corresponding change in attitudes. Both boxes A and B represent poor campaign effectiveness and a probable waste of resources. Box C represents an effective campaign in that awareness levels are high and attitudes are shifting to the desired position. Box D is probably the ideal position. Attitudes have shifted to the desired position and, therefore, the result is achieved. Levels of awareness of the campaign are low. This suggests that the means used to create the new position have been less obvious so that there will be little danger of the audiences' feeling that they have been manipulated.

FOOD FOR THOUGHT

 People power

In 1998, a survey conducted by MORI/MCA investigated levels of company commitment and understanding in UK employees. They found:

- *Only 5% of staff strongly agree that their view and participation are valued by their organisation.*
- *16% believe strongly in their organisation's vision for the future.*
- *37% say their level of understanding and commitment to organisational goals are high. Consider how this lack of commitment, understanding and confidence translates into the personality your people give to your organisation. Imagine how it influences the way your people relate to external target audiences.*

Exhibit 11.3 Measuring corporate identity campaign effectiveness

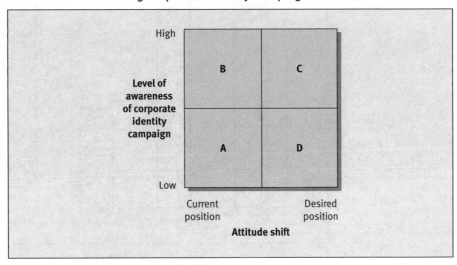

Source: Adapted from Worcester and Lewis (1983)

Branding and customer relationship management

A corporate brand can be built on people's skills, attitudes, behaviour, style and responsiveness. The discriminating variable becomes the company's culture, the staff within the company become a main brand builder and an important medium of communication. Inadequate communication of the corporation's values, and individuals' roles in delivering them, can result in inconsistencies between the brand's espoused values and the values perceived by stakeholders when dealing with staff (de Chernatony 1999). Chapter 12 discusses the importance of the customer experience, both formal and informal, between a supplying organisation and a potential or actual customer over time. For example, consider a supermarket business that advertises an image of high-quality service and friendliness. The customer, exposed to the advertising message, expects this friendliness but once inside the supermarket has to deal with a surly checkout operator. The gap between expectations and perceptions will cause dissatisfaction with the service that will in turn have a negative effect on the brand's image.

Own-label branding

Own-label brand

Product that carries the name of the resellers – wholesalers or retailers – rather than the manufacturers, and is sold exclusively through the resellers' outlets.

Since the 1980s, the competitive balance of power has gradually shifted from manufacturers to retailers. This is particularly evident in the grocery sector where the top five companies dominate the marketplace (Exhibit 11.4). Retailers are now using proprietary 'own-label' brands as strategic weapons against any number of competitors. Own-label brands carry the name of the resellers – wholesalers or retailers – rather than the manufacturer and are sold exclusively through the resellers' outlets. This means that the resellers exercise total marketing control and can, therefore, generate higher gross margins. With own brands generating higher profit margins and providing retailers with the opportunity to develop a distinct corporate identity and differentiated product offering, the scope of own branded ranges has substantially widened.

Exhibit 11.4 Food market share of top five retailers (%)

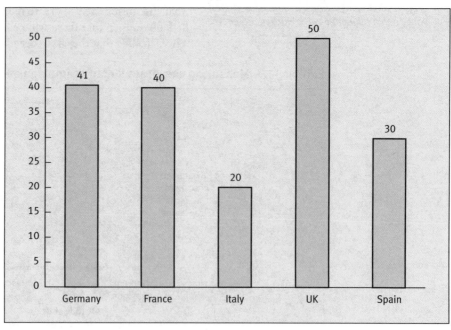

Source: Adapted from Tordjman (1995). Copyright © 1995 Pitman, (Tordjman, A.; eds.: McGoldrick, P.J., and Davies, G.), reprinted with the permission of Pearson Education

Retailers have responded in a variety of different ways to the opportunities of own-branding. All the major six (Tesco, Sainsbury, Safeway, Waitrose, Marks & Spencer and Asda/Wal-Mart) have some kind of commitment to own-brands. Marks & Spencer is renowned for its St Michael brand name, that for a long time has been synonymous with good quality and reasonable prices. Recently they have collaborated with designers to produce a range of designer-produced M&S fashion lines. Similarly to M&S, Sainsbury's has a reputation for high-quality own-label products sold at premium prices. Fresh food and 40% of non-perishables are own-label. Waitrose too has a history of commitment to own-label strategy. The other three have all introduced own-label ranges in response to competition from discount stores such as Aldi. Asda launched its own-label range in 1985 and now carries over 8000 product lines. Tesco introduced the Value range in 1994 and now has over 12,000 own-label products as well as sub-brands including Nature's Choice. In 1994, Safeway introduced its budget brand, Savers.

Euromonitor (1986) has defined six main types of own-label branding:

- Own-label using a different name, which may become as well known as the reseller itself, for example St Michael at Marks & Spencer.
- Own-label using the reseller's own name.
- 'Super' own-labels like Sainsbury's Novon detergent range.
- 'Exclusive' own-labels which tend to be introduced temporarily as a promotional strategy but do not use the retailer's brand name.
- Generics, which is a plain-label variant, for example Tesco's Value range.
- Surrogate own-labels, which are manufacturer's brands that are exclusive to a chain of stores.

The components of a brand

Although many textbooks on branding raise the question about whether or not to brand, in some sense it is possible to argue that everything is branded in some way. This may be a simple mark that conveys very little or it might be very much more sophisticated. Even apparent commodity-type products such as metal tubing or screws are branded through packaging, labelling and logos. All it takes is the placing of a name, logo, a consistent form of packaging, use of colour, shapes, typography or a short description as in a strap line and brands are being created. The brand name and brand logo are two crucial components in the creation of brand identity.

Brand name

The brand name is the part of the brand that can be spoken which can include letters, words and numbers such as Coca-Cola (Plate 3) and Pentium III. This may be separate from the trade name, which is the full and legal name of an organisation. The full trade name of National Westminster Bank Plc is typically branded as NatWest Bank.

Brand logo

The logo is the element of the brand that is frequently not words, including symbols and pictures. The logo can also be termed a brand mark, for example the baby symbol on Procter & Gamble's Fairy Liquid. Exhibit 11.5 presents the findings from a survey of 300 people, conducted by Infratest Burke, to identify 12 visual brand logos (*Marketing*, February 1998). The high percentage of logos correctly identified indicates the enduring nature of the images created by the logos.

Exhibit 11.5 Brand logos

Visual brand logo	Brand name	% correctly identified
Golden arches	McDonald's	90%
Crossed fingers	National Lottery	83%
Piper	BT	82%
Badge logo	BMW	73%
Tyre man	Michelin	76%

Source: *Marketing* 12 February 1998, p. 24). Reproduced from *Marketing* magazine with the permission of the copyright owner, Haymarket Business Publications Limited

Brand identity manual

Many organisations have a brand or corporate identity manual that clearly specifies how the elements of identity should be used. This is to ensure consistency throughout the entire organisation. Not only will the manual show identity designs; it will specify the precise use of colours (by reference to Pantone colour numbers or similar reference codes); it will specify typefaces, type styles and acceptable type sizes; it will specify positioning of logos and similar design features. The brand identity manual is a reference book that should be used when considering the design and production of any new material including signs, livery, letterheads, business cards, packaging and leaflets etc. It is the rulebook that indicates how the identity should be used in all forms of visual communications. The key elements of an identity programme are listed below:

Design elements: e.g. logo, graphics, type style – typeface, type sizes, layout/format, use of colours

Statements: e.g. copy style, slogans

Applications: e.g. corporate advertising, stationery (letterheads, business cards, complement slips, envelopes, etc.), signage (factory/office/shop fronts and interiors), livery (cars, uniforms, furnishings, etc.), merchandising, packaging

The benefits of branding

Exhibit 11.6 summarises the key benefits of branding to both the consumer and the brand owner. From a consumer perspective, branding helps to identify a product. It acts as a shorthand and time-saving device to facilitate the purchase of items that satisfy consumer needs (Dibb et al. 1994). As James Lenahan, Head of Consumer Drugs, Johnson and Johnson explains,

> **If you have a brand you know and trust, it helps you make choices faster, more easily.**   (Fortune 1996)

The brand also represents a credible guarantee of quality and satisfaction to the consumer. This guarantee of satisfaction is often important enough to the consumer that they are willing to pay an abnormal price (Murphy 1990). This is certainly the case with 'superbrands'. Superbrands are brands which offer significant emotional and/or

Exhibit 11.6 Consumer and brand owner brand benefits

	Key benefit	*Components*
Consumer	Identification	Simplifies decision-making process
	Risk assessment	A guarantee of consistent quality
	Representation	Embodies what the individual stands for.
		Hedonistic needs, social status etc.
Brand owner	Price premium	Increase profit margins
	Brand loyalty	Reduced threat of price war
	Growth	New product development
	Barriers to entry	Competitors find it harder to take market share
	Legal device	Protection from counterfeiting and 'me-too' entries

physical advantages over their competitors which (consciously or subconsciously) consumers want, recognise and are willing to pay for and are recognised with bi-annual awards. Interbrand's 2002 league table of the world's 100 most valuable brands saw Coca-Cola again taking number one spot, followed by Microsoft and IBM. The brand is 'super' not just because of customer recognition: Exhibit 11.7 identifies that in a survey conducted by Infratest Burke, over 50% of customers who buy superbrand products would not buy an own-label version even if the price were substantially lower.

From a brand owner's perspective, branding can be a powerful defence against competitive incursions and new launches. Strong brand loyalty for an organisation's products deters competition from entering the market. To survive, a new competitor would have to turn the leading brands' loyal customers into brand switchers by what Light (1997) calls bribery. But as Light points out, those customers will not become loyal to the brand as they will only become '**deal loyalists**', who are likely to revert back to the original brand should the deal end.

Deal loyalists

Customers who purchase a brand only when it is on special promotion, and switch between brands to purchase those on 'deal'.

Branding also provides a springboard for brand extension, not simply brand growth. A diversification or product extension by an organisation will often be enhanced by the use of an existing brand name with positive associations. A previous brand relationship will reassure customers by suggesting that the positive associations gained from the original product will have been passed onto the new product through the brand name.

The danger of using a brand this way is that if the attributes of the new product do not conform to the associations of the brand, the brand value may be damaged resulting

Exhibit 11.7 Own-label price reduction required to switch from superbrand

	Häagen Dazs	Heinz beans	McVities	Perrier	Walkers	Kit Kat
Wouldn't switch at any price (%)	41%	60%	41%	32%	42%	34%
Typical own-label price (pence)	200	23	55	59	19	20
Price drop required for switch to own-label (pence)	77	14	27	37	13	11

Source: *Marketing* (8 October 1998, p. 9). Reproduced from *Marketing* magazine with the permission of the copyright owner, Haymarket Business Publications Limited

in the potential failure of the new product and damage to the original. Despite the inherent danger in using a brand name for very diverse products, an example of success is Yamaha, which has used its corporate brand name on products as diverse as motorcycles, musical instruments and canned tuna fish, or Virgin with planes, cola and music retailers.

● Brand equity

Brand equity

The value of the brand's name, symbols, associations and reputation to all target audiences who interact with it.

Brand value

The financial expression of brand equity.

Until recently, the principle of **brand equity** was little understood or used by most brand owners. However, in the last few years the concept has become recognised as a major dynamic in the business world. Companies reason that the importance of brands extends beyond their simple role as a sales and marketing tool. Paul Polman, of Procter & Gamble, recently asserted that the difference between his company's market value (c. £37 billion) and the accountants' estimate of its asset value (c. £8 billion) is largely made up by the **value** of its brands (Cooper and Simons 1997).

Brand equity has been defined as:

> the strength, currency and value of the brand … the description, and assessment of the appeal, of a brand to all the target audiences who interact with it.
>
> (Cooper and Simons 1997, pp. 1–2)

In sum, it is the value of the company's names and symbols. The valuation of brands (the financial expression of brand equity) as assets on the balance sheet has become recognised as an important recognition of organisational performance.

> Companies which base their businesses on brands have outperfomed the stock-market in the last 15 years … analysis comparing the share price of a group of 68 companies dependent on brands with the performance of the FTSE 350 index found that the branded group did consistently better.   (Smith 1997)

Measuring brand equity

The financial community is now recognising brand equity in their financial assessment of company performance. To do this, however, a measurement of brand equity must be taken. There is not one single and consistent framework proposed by the marketing industry. Several approaches have been proposed to evaluate brand equity which differ in the number and type of criteria used. Examples of some of the principal approaches are presented in Exhibit 11.8.

Through the management of the brand description, brand strength and brand future, brand equity assets can be developed and enhanced. The links between these four key components from the various measurement approaches are highlighted in Exhibit 11.9 (page 256) and discussed in detail below.

NEED TO KNOW

☑ *The key components that create brand equity include brand description, brand strength and brand future.*

Brand description

The first major component of brand equity is brand description. This is what the brand represents, depending on the associations, values and beliefs the customer has about the brand. It includes the brand's distinctiveness, its perceived quality and the esteem with which it is held in the eyes of the consumer. These should be viewed in the light of the important customer purchase motivations in that product category.

Exhibit 11.8 Different approaches to measuring brand equity

Proposer	Factors measured	Comment
David Aaker	• Awareness • Brand associations/differentiations (e.g. personality, perceived value) • Perceived quality and market leadership • Loyalty • Market behaviour measures (e.g. share, distribution)	A series of guidelines rather than a fixed model
Millward Brown Brand Dynamic	• Presence (e.g. familiarity) • Relevance to consumer needs • Product performance • Competitive advantage • Bonding (e.g. endorsement on key attributes)	Identifies brand's strengths and weaknesses across some key consumer factors
Total Research Equitrend	• Salience • Perceived quality • User satisfaction	Measures combined to produce an absolute brand equity score
Young & Rubicam Brand Asset valuator	• Differentiation + Relevance = Strength • Esteem and Knowledge = Stature	Each pair of measures are multiplied together to produce 'strength' and 'stature' scores
Cooper & Simons TBWA Simons Palmer	• Brand quality reflects the distinctiveness and relevance of its brand associations, its esteem and perceived popularity and leadership • Brand quantity covers awareness, penetration, loyalty, satisfaction ratings, sales shares (consumer measures) • Brand future reflects its potential for organic growth (e.g. potential to boost trial distribution), its 'fitness' for the changing marketplace (e.g. new legislation, technologies, consumer patterns and trade structures) and brand extendibility (e.g. new launches)	This incorporates a measure of its future potential. A brand's performance on these dimensions should be 'scored' in the context of the competition
Interbrand	• brand weight • brand breadth • brand depth • brand length	Measures include a brand's relative market share within its category, how broad an appeal the brand has across customer groupings, customer loyalty to the brand and potential and actual extensions to the brand

Source: Adapted from Cooper and Simons (1997, p. 8)

Brand associations

If a brand symbol does not create meaning or association it can be argued that a brand exists in name only and does not have any brand equity (Krishnan 1996). It is, therefore, no more than a trademark. Through the process of association, brands have value. It is the task of the marketing communicator to create a sense of difference, a sense of value and a competitive advantage. In many product categories there is little tangible differentiation. For example, despite technological sophistication, products

Exhibit 11.9 Managing brand equity

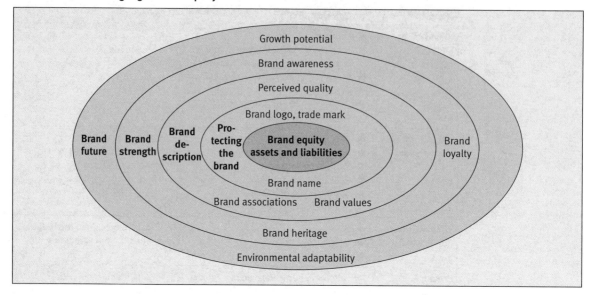

such as televisions and personal computers have become commodities with much similarity between brands (Kohli and Thakor 1997). When faced with little difference in products within a category, a customer will tend to choose one brand that produces the most positive associations.

Once a customer has built an overall association for a brand this becomes an expectation for the brand. Positive brand associations act as a promise from the brand owner to the customer (Light 1997). If the promise is not met in subsequent customer encounters with the brand, marketing money is wasted as the customer will have negative associations that may be hard to reverse without expensive persuasion for retrial of the product (Zhivago 1994). When customers have good associations with a brand, the brand is likely to be purchased at a higher price than that of a competitor's brand, with which they have poor or merely less favourable associations.

Over time consumers can build up many associations with a great number of brands, for example, the brand Nike may produce the following associations (Krishnan 1996):

- athletic shoe
- durable
- Michael Jordan
- the swoosh symbol
- comfort.

Some of these associations may be brand attributes (functional or perceptual), while others may be gained from usage experience (comfort). Whatever the source of the associations they combine to create an overall association with the brand Nike. The sum of a consumer's brand associations is the meaning given to the brand by the consumer.

Perceived quality

Perceived quality is being recognised as one of the most important aspects of brand equity, and has been shown to have a direct impact on sales performance, a brand's ability to sustain a price premium and a firm's overall financial performance.

> Among all brand associations, perceived quality has been shown to drive financial performance. It is often a major strategic thrust of business.
>
> (Professor David Aaker, University of California, in *Marketing*, 12 February 1998, p. 24)

Brand values

The specific meaning of the brand is created by appealing to any of three basic consumer needs:

Functional appeal

The communication of the brand's specific attributes or benefits capable of solving consumers' current consumption-related problems

Symbolic appeal

The brand communications' appeal to consumers' desire for self-enhancement, group membership, affiliation and belongingness.

Experiential appeal

The brand's appeal to the consumers' desire for sensory pleasure, variety and cognitive stimulation.

- **Functional appeal** – the communication of the brand's specific attributes or benefits capable of solving consumers' current consumption-related problem(s). For example, Gillette Mach3 communicates its three progressively aligned blades, which give the closest shave ever, in fewer strokes with less irritation (Plate 4).
- **Symbolic appeal** – the brand's appeal to consumers' desire for self-enhancement, role position, group membership, affiliation and belongingness.
- **Experiential appeal** – the brand's appeal to the consumers' desire for sensory pleasure, variety and cognitive stimulation (Shimp 1997). For example, Häagen Dazs communicates the physical sensations of eating their ice-cream (Plate 5).

A growing recent trend is the arrival of brands that can be considered 'entrepreneurial revolutionaries' (Cooper and Simons 1997). In a particular product category, these brands can be seen as risk takers by identifying completely different brand values that are or become important customer motivations to purchase the brand. By recognising that customers have, or can be, changed, these brands can reposition the current category leaders and undermine their brand equity. Brands such as Virgin, First Direct, Daewoo and Microsoft have all used marketing communications to build brand equity rather than simply increase their sales share. Indeed, in several instances, these progressive brands are essentially parity products (or have only small differences). The

IN VIEW 11.3

Perceived quality of male and female top five brands

The Equitrend brand equity survey, conducted by Total Research, investigates the perception of 120 major brands in 23 categories. Interviews were conducted with 1002 nationally representative consumers who were asked to evaluate the quality of each brand on an 11-point scale, where 11 is outstanding and 0 is unacceptably poor.

Rank	Male top five brands	Perceived quality	Female top five brands	Perceived quality
1	Mercedes-Benz	9.05	Mercedes-Benz	8.55
2	BMW	8.75	Fisher-Price	8.32
3	Duracell	8.22	BMW	8.23
4	Sony Televisions	8.17	Disney World Florida	8.14
5	Bosch Power Tools	8.01	Cadbury's Dairy Milk	8.13

Source: research from Total Research Equitrend Survey (*Marketing*, 12 February 1998, p. 24). Reproduced from *Marketing* magazine with the permission of the copyright owner, Haymarket Business Publications Limited.

Exhibit 11.10 How some entrepreneurial revolutionaries are reframing sector values

Sector	Brand	Sector value shift
Airlines	Virgin Atlantic	● Reframing business flight values from status to enjoyment of the experience
Banking	First Direct	● Raising importance of practical accessibility over (hollow) 'friendly' approachability
Breakdown services	AA	● Breakdown services solve personal emergencies, not just make your car go again
Cars	Daewoo	● Shifting debate from product benefit or driver experience to the practicalities of purchase and ownership
Credit cards	Goldfish	● Fun and emotional response is a discriminator not simply functional performance
Personal computing	Microsoft	● The debate has shifted from hardware to software: from 'what can you do with it' to 'what can it do for you'

Source: Cooper and Simons (1997)

marketing communications are used to re-frame the product category expectations and lift their brand apart from the others (Exhibit 11.10).

How customers learn meanings associated with products and brands is investigated through semiotics. **Semiotics** is the science of signs and symbols and seeks to understand the process of communication that create values and meanings such as those used in branding. In View 11.4 demonstrates the often subconscious meanings we can give to signs, symbols and brands.

Semiotics

The scientific discipline of studying the meanings associated with signs, symbols and brands.

IN VIEW 11.4

Branding and semiotics

In 1970, James Pilditch, founder and Chairman of Allied International Designers, one of Europe's largest design groups of the time, produced a book, *Communication by Design*, in which he included a very powerful example of the effect of symbols. He suggests that even abstract sounds and shapes, which intrinsically have no meaning in themselves, convey meaning to us.

Two shapes are shown below. One is called 'Maluma', the other is called 'Taketa'. Which shape, do you think, is which?

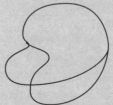 

The chances are that you have called the shape on the left, which has smooth curves, Maluma, and the one on the right with its sharp angles, Taketa. Why? Neither the words nor the shapes have any meaning yet we are able to make these connections. We have learned how to make associations between things and we use this learning to help us understand our world – to create meaning for ourselves. Marketing communicators are able to put an understanding of such things to good use in developing brand and corporate identity.

Source: Reproduced from Communication and Design, by Pilditch, J.G.C., (1970), reproduced with the kind permission of the McGraw-Hill Publishing Company.

Brand strength

The second major component of brand equity is brand strength. This indicates the prominence and relative dominance of a brand. Levels of awareness, brand history and loyalty are important elements within this component.

Brand awareness

Generating awareness of a brand is the first step in any communications campaign. Awareness needs to be created before interest, desire and action can be initiated. There are two main levels of awareness:

- *Prompted awareness* – once a brand name is suggested to a consumer, the consumer recalls being aware of it already.
- *Unprompted awareness* – the brand name is 'top-of-the-mind' when a product category is suggested. Unprompted awareness is considered more valuable because customers are more likely to think first about those brands at the top-of-their-mind when making a purchase decision.

IN VIEW 11.5

Brand recall

Adwatch produces league tables of brands' positive recall responses. The table outlined below details the best brand recall in any single week in 1996 and 1997.

1997	1996	Brand	Score (% recall)	Budget £m
1	1	BT	94	158.6
2	2=	National Lottery	89	10.6
3	6=	Walkers Crisps	86	3.1
4=	–	Orange Tango	84	3.0
4=	11=	Asda	84	24.0
6=	9=	Safeway	83	27.3
6=	–	Halifax plc	83	17.4
6=	11=	Andrex	83	9.3

Source: *Marketing* (11 December 1997, p. 27). Reproduced from Marketing magazine with the permission of the copyright owner, Haymarket Business Publications Limited.

Brand heritage

Brand heritage is the corporate experience and reputation that a brand has acquired over time including its origins and advertising development (Abimbola et al. 1999). A long-standing reputation for quality and consistency, for example, signals a specific kind of trust in the brand owner.

Brand loyalty

The core component of brand loyalty is the customer's willingness to repeat purchase. A customer's willingness to buy other brands of the brand owner (cross-selling strategy) and to buy higher value brands (up-selling strategy) are also important components. A customer may move up the loyalty ladder (Exhibit 11.11) from trial purchase, brand preference (repeat purchase) through to brand insistence where the customer will not buy any other brand in that product category even if their preferred brand is not available in a particular outlet. A customer that insists on a brand is also one that is likely to provide positive word-of-mouth communication.

> While marketers have long viewed brands as assets, the real asset is brand loyalty. A brand is not an asset. Brand loyalty is the asset. Without the loyalty of its customers, a brand is merely a trademark, an ownable, identifiable symbol with little value. With the loyalty of its customers, a brand is more than a trademark. A trademark identifies a product, a service, a corporation. A brand identifies a promise. A strong brand is a trustworthy, relevant, distinctive promise. It is more than a trademark. It is a trustmark of enormous value. Creating and increasing brand loyalty results in a corresponding increase in the value of the trustmark.
>
> (Light and Morgan 1994, p. 11)

Brand future

The third major component of brand equity is brand future. This reflects a brand's ability to survive future changes in legislation, technology, retail structure and consumer patterns and it also indicates its growth potential, e.g. niche to mainstream, from local to global (Cooper and Simons 1997).

Exhibit 11.11 The loyalty ladder

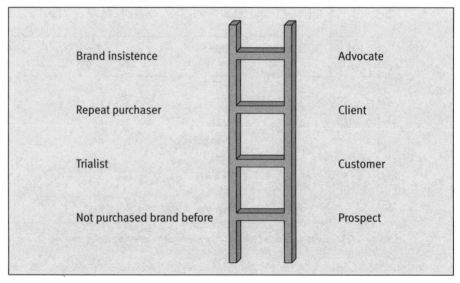

Managing the brand

At the beginning of this chapter four key objectives were outlined in image and brand management:

● to understand what the organisation's brand(s) comprises;
● to communicate the brand(s) to channel intermediaries and consumers;
● to manage brands through their life cycles, and
● to enhance brand equity.

In order to accomplish these objectives three planning activities are necessary:

Competitive positioning

The communication of how a brand is different from the competition in terms of key consumer choice criteria.

1 Firstly, a group of core and peripheral brand values must be identified. An understanding of the distinct capabilities that distinguish the brand from competition is necessary to ensure effective positioning. Competitive positioning is a shorthand mechanism that helps audiences to appreciate what the brand can do for them and how it is different from the competition.

2 Secondly, to ensure that those brand values which have been identified as important and motivating to the target audience are communicated effectively and efficiently. These communications should bear in mind that different target audiences have different points of contact with the organisation and as such there is potential for mixed messages.

3 The third activity is to be able to manage the brand values over a period of time so that a clear vision of the brand's direction can be perceived over at least a five-year period (In View 11.6).

IN VIEW 11.6

A brand equity lifestage model

Cooper and Simons (1997) have developed a brand equity lifestage model with three phases and two further scenarios that can describe the equity lifestage of a particular brand.

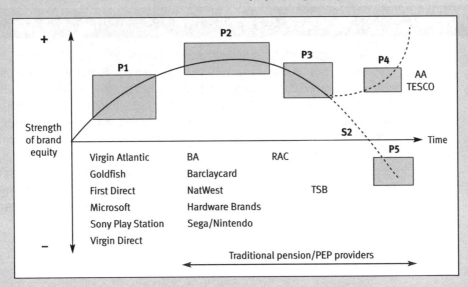

- P1 is the rapidly rising brand equity strength of a relatively new brand. The entrepreneurial brands will be found here, although not all new, growing brands can be classed as such. First Direct, for example, has been a catalyst for change in consumer banking, whereas in its sector, Chicken Tonight is simply taking share without making consumers rethink their requirements from an evening meal.
- P2 is the mature brand that is more concerned with brand maintenance and defence. Brands can either take pro-active steps to manage their brand equity in the face of competition (e.g. Mercedes and BMW) or more reactively respond to market developments (e.g. NatWest and Barclays).
- P3 is the waning brand that is experiencing an erosion of its equity, and, hence, losing its reputation and appeal. Among these brands, some will almost be household names (e.g. TSB and Woolworths) while others will have faded into the background (e.g. Smedley's and Harp lager). A continuous erosion is not inevitable. Indeed, once the danger signals become apparent the brand owner should take positive steps to avoid further erosion. However, some companies may choose to manage the brand's decline recognising that corporate resources are better focused elsewhere.
- P4 is a formerly declining brand that is either experiencing a, or engineering its own, resurgence. In the sports market Adidas's and Umbro's brand equities are reviving. Both were triggered by outside factors, the recent fashion trend for canvas trainers from the 1970s and England's success at Euro '96 respectively.
- P5 is a brand whose equity is continuing to decline despite, or without, efforts to strengthen itself. Hi-Tec and LA Gear have fast declining brand equities, which have not benefited from any of the forward waves of the sports or youth fashion markets. The lifestage model introduces the concept of negative brand equity at S2. Negative equity happens when, despite product and price parity with the competition, a product's branding has a detrimental impact on product purchase intention.

Source: Cooper and Simons (1997)

Summary

Chapter 11 has outlined one of the two key strategic tasks identified in the IMC Process Model, that of *image and brand management*. For greatest marketing communications synergy, this concept should be related to, and integrated with, the second strategic task, *customer/audience relationship management*. Types of branding strategies have been presented including an overview of the development of corporate branding. The benefits of branding to the brand owner and consumer are discussed together with an understanding of which elements of branding are under direct management control and which are not. The components and measurement of brand equity have been outlined and the importance of brand equity to performance and company valuation has been stressed. Four key objectives in image and brand management are presented together with the planning activities necessary to achieve them.

Self-review questions

1 Identify and explain each of the four main branding strategies and give at least two examples for each strategy.

2 Evaluate the similarities and differences between corporate and product branding.

3 Why has there been an increase in own-label branding?

4 What are the benefits of branding to the brand owner and the consumer?

5 Why is brand equity important to an organisation?

6 What are the main objectives and planning activities of image and brand management?

Project

Select a brand and try to measure its brand equity. Conduct a small consumer survey investigating brand awareness, perceived quality and brand loyalty. Write a 1000-word summary report presenting the survey findings together with your analysis of the brand's associations, values communicated in its advertising, heritage and future. Collect together the similar reports of your class members and map the measurements on the brand equity life cycle. In comparison to the other brands, where does your brand fit on the life cycle? What would be an appropriate strategy to manage the brand into the future?

References

Aaker, D.A. (1991), *Managing Brand Equity*. New York: The Free Press.

Abimbola, T., Saunders, J. and Broderick, A.J. (1999), Brand intangible assets evaluation: a conceptual framework. *Proceedings of the Chartered Institute of Marketing Research Seminar: Assessing Marketing Performance*, Cookham, pp. 1–18.

Ambler, T. and Styles, C. (1995), Brand equity: towards measures that matter. *Pan'agra Working Paper*, No. 95–902, London, Centre for Marketing, London Business School.

Bernstein, D. (1984), *Company Image and Reality: A Critique of Corporate Communications*. Holt, Rinehart and Winston.

Cooper, A. and Simons, P. (1997), *Brand Equity Lifestage. An Entrepreneurial Revolution*. TBWA Simons Palmer, September.

de Chernatony, L. (1999). People Power. *Marketing Business*, May, 54.

de Chernatony, L. and McDonald, M. (1998), *Creating Powerful Brands in Consumer, Service and Industrial Markets*. Oxford: Butterworth-Heinemann.

Dibb, S., Simkin, L., Pride, W. and Ferrel, O.L. (1994), *Marketing – Concepts and Strategies*. Houghton Mifflin Company.

Euromonitor (1986), *Own Brands*.

Fortune (1996), *Brand Attributes*. pp. 6–12.

Gardner, B.B. and Levy, S.J. (1955), The product and the brand. *Harvard Business Review*, 33 (March–April), 33–39.

King, S. (1994), Brand building and market research. In *Advances in Consumer Marketing* (M. Jenkins and S. Knox, eds). London: Kogan Page, pp. 119–135.

Kohli, C. and Thakor, M. (1997), Branding consumer goods: insights from theory and practice. *Journal of Consumer Marketing*, 14 (2–3), Spring, 206–220.

Kotler, P. (1994), *Marketing Management, Analysis, Planning, Implementation and Control.* Prentice Hall.

Krishnan, H. (1996), Characteristics of memory association: A consumer based brand equity perspective. *Journal of Consumer Marketing*, 14 (4), October, 389–405.

Light, L. (1997), Brand loyalty management: the basis for profitable growth. *Direct Marketing*, 59 (11), March, 36–44.

Light, L. and Morgan, R. (1994), *The Fourth Wave: Brand Loyalty Marketing.* New York: Coalition for Brand Loyalty.

MAPS Strategic Intelligence Report (1994).

Margulies, W.P. (1977), Make the most of your corporate identity. *Harvard Business Review* (July–August).

Marketing (1997), Can Guinness keep ahead? 20 November, 19.

Marketing (1997), Brand of the year. 11 December, 27.

Marketing (1998), The perception question. 12 February, 24–25.

Marketing (1998), How superbrands score over rivals. 8 October, 9.

Marketing Business (1998), Career watch. December.

Marketing Business (2003), Case study: building brand image. February, 15.

Mottram, S. (1998), Branding the corporation. In *Brands: The New Wealth Creators* (S. Hart and J. Murphy, eds). Macmillan Press, pp. 1–12.

Murphy, J.M. (1990), *Brand Strategy.* Cambridge: Director Books.

Olins, W. (1990), *The Corporate Personality.* London: The Design Council.

Pilditch, J. (1970), *Communication by Design: A Study in Corporate Identity.* McGraw-Hill.

Riezebos, H.J. (1994), *Brand Added Value: Theory and Empirical Research about the Value of Brands to Consumers.* The Netherlands: Eburon Publishers.

Runkel, K. and Brymer, C. (1997), Brand valuation (the nature of brands). *Premier*, 2nd edn, p. 6.

Shimp, T. (1997), *Advertising, Promotion, and Supplemental Aspects of Integrated Marketing Communications.* Fort Worth: The Dryden Press.

Smith, A. (1997), Brand builders perceive pattern. *Financial Times*, 23 June.

Tordjman, A. (1995), European retailing: convergences, differences and perspectives. In *International Retailing: Trends and Strategies* (P.J. McGoldrick and G. Davies, eds). London: Pitman Publishing, pp. 17–50.

Wilson, R.M.S., Gilligan, C. and Pearson, D.J. (1995), *Strategic Marketing Management.* Butterworth-Heinemann.

Worcester, R. and Lewis, S. (1983), Mirror mirror on the wall. *Market Research Society Survey Magazine*, 1 June.

Zhivago, K. (1994), Branding: keep your promises. *America's Network*, 98 (16), 82.

Selected further reading

de Chernatony, L. (1988), Own label – an adjunct to brands. *Journal of Retailing and Distribution Management*, 16 (4), 18–21.

Feldwick, P. (1996), What is brand equity anyway, and how do you measure it? *Journal of the Market Research Society*, 38 (2), April, 85–105.

Harrington, S. (1997), Virgin birth. *In-Store Marketing*, November, 22–23.

Lannon, J. (1994), Mosaics of meaning: anthropology and marketing. *The Journal of Brand Management*, 2 (3), December, 155–168.

Levitt, T. (1981), Marketing intangible products and product intangibles. *Harvard Business Review*, 59 (May/June), 94–102.

Park, C.W., Jaworski, B.J. and MacInnis, D.J. (1986). Strategic brand-concept image management. *Journal of Marketing*, 50 (October), 135–145.

Pearson, S. (1996), *Building Brands Directly.* Macmillan Press Ltd.

Walgren, C., Ruble, C. and Donthu, N. (1995), Brand equity, brand preference and purchase intent. *Journal of Advertising*, 24 (3), Fall, 25–41.

Chapter 12

Customer/audience relationship management

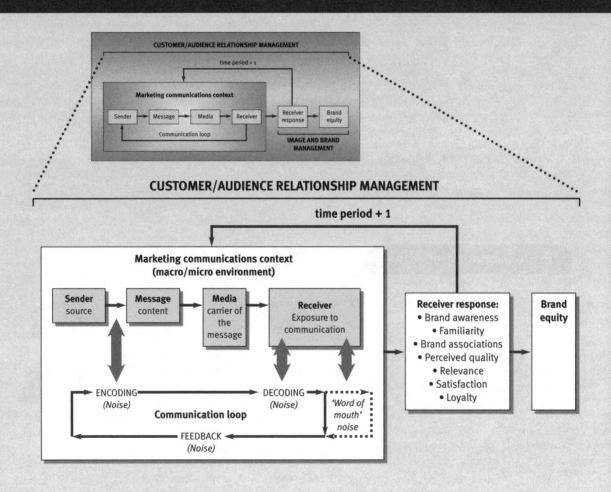

The IMC Process Model

CD

Consider carefully the issues of relationship building in the Concern case. What value does building long-term customer relationships have for Concern? Which other audiences should Concern focus on for building relationships? What marketing communications tools should Concern use to help build relationships? What are the management implications of CARM for Concern, for example, in relation to database management?

Chapter outline

- What are customer/audience relationship management and customer contact management?
- Database marketing
- Electronic marketing and telemarketing
- Strategic implications of customer contact management

Objectives

- To introduce customer and audience relationship management and show its relevance to integrated marketing communications
- To emphasise the importance of recognising the marketing communications implications inherent in managing customer and audience contact
- To provide an outline of the component activities of customer contact management
- To demonstrate the benefits of an integrated approach to customer contact management
- To identify strategic issues related to customer contact management

Professional perspective

Steve Almond Senior Manager, Electronic Commerce Barclaycard

Today, you can log onto the Internet, call up any number of stores, browse the goods on display and pay online using your credit card. With a further click of the mouse button you can log onto your credit card website, enter a password and check your outstanding credit card balance, view details of your most recent purchases and pay any outstanding bills. If you are away from your office, or home, you can access your credit card account by inserting your Barclaycard in your mobile phone and reading the information displayed on the phone screen. Early in 1999, Barclays Bank announced its free Internet access service to support its recently launched Internet banking service for personal and business customers. For those customers who choose not to use the Internet, Barclays provides a telephone banking service in addition to its traditional 'bricks and mortar' branch service. Even when the 'bricks and mortar' service is closed its customers can use the ATM (automated teller machine) to withdraw cash, check their balance or access additional banking services. These examples highlight how major UK banks have recognised the need to make services available to customers through an ever widening range of access channels. The result is increased but complex customer contact opportunities. New technology has made a profound impact on how products and services can be delivered to customers. Equally, customers are becoming increasingly demanding in how they expect to access the products and services available from their suppliers.

Certainly in the service industries, more customers want access to their services from anywhere in the world and at any time of the day or night. From the suppliers' perspective, the ability to provide 'any time, anywhere' access to their services is an evolving major competitive issue – and certainly not one which is limited to the banking industry. Of paramount importance today for businesses is the ability to understand which access channels the customer wishes to use; to know which channels have been used and to be aware of the 'transactions' undertaken by those customers across any, or all, of those channels. Each and every time a customer makes contact with the business, the 'transaction' must be recorded and information about it is made available – or reflected – at the next point of contact. Only through effective capture, archiving and 'on-demand' retrieval of customer contact information is it possible to maintain any continuity of relationship with a customer. Without the tools to enable such continuity of relationship it becomes difficult to make available new products or services, or complete additional sales, with no duplication, omission or wasted effort on the part of the business (or frustration on the part of the customer). Effective customer contact management is a necessity today for many businesses but as the relentless march of technology makes available more sales and contact channels to the customer, so customer contact management becomes an extremely powerful marketing tool and an increasingly critical element of success for all businesses.

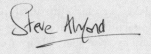

What are customer/audience relationship management and customer contact management?

Transactional marketing

Marketing in which the emphasis is placed on each individual purchase situation in contrast to relationship marketing.

Relationship marketing

View that emphasises the importance of the relationships developed between an organisation and other parties including customers, partners, suppliers and the trade.

Customer loyalty

This concept is usually taken to mean the degree of loyalty a customer has towards a brand or an organisation. It is something that companies endeavour to encourage but given the competitive environment frequently find that customers are not so loyal to a single brand or organisation. An alternative perspective is to reverse the consideration and think about the degree of loyalty a company has towards its customers.

Customer relationship management, also frequently referred to as customer relationship marketing, both shortened to CRM, has become a popular focus in marketing and business in general over recent years. So much so, that the majority of readers of this text will undoubtedly have come across the terms previously. Its popularity has spread to such an extent that it is considered a new business 'phenomenon' by many. This has been driven in no small way by the fact that customer acquisition and retention have become top management priorities and that the trend towards e-business and the increasing importance of the Internet as a customer care and sales channel have brought a feeling of uncertainty to companies (Stone and Woodcock 2001). Although this may be the case, in essence, CRM has always been at the very heart of the marketing concept since its inception. Both extol the importance of customers to the business. What has, perhaps, become more evident with the advent of CRM is the emphasis on the need to view customers in the long term in developing relationships rather than consigning customers to short-term transactions. This has given rise to the so-called shift from **transactional marketing** to **relationship marketing** as such issues as **customer loyalty**, brand loyalty and **customer lifetime value** have become key to marketing planning and strategy. Put simply, organisations have increasingly realised the importance and value of investing in and creating customer satisfaction and, having done so, endeavouring to keep those customers in preference to continually replacing old customers with new ones. As long ago as the late 1980s and early 1990s, it was recognised that in some industries, cutting the customer defection rate by around as little as 10% could double profits (Reichheld and Sasser 1990).

Brand loyalty
The degree of loyalty a customer has towards a brand in favouring it over other alternatives. It is something that companies endeavour to encourage but given the competitive environment frequently find that customers are not so loyal to a single brand.

Customer lifetime value
The total estimated revenue that a customer is expected to be worth to a company usually expressed as Net Present Value (NPV) i.e. after discounting for inflation.

FOOD FOR THOUGHT

Customer loyalty is often thought of as the customer's loyalty to the company. Consider the reverse, what is the company's loyalty to the customer?

CARM
This extends the CRM concept to a wider range of audience groups than just customers, a range that integrated marketing communications need to address. It involves the strategic and tactical management tasks to achieve positive ongoing communications and long-term relationships between an organisation and its audiences.

Customer contact management
The strategic and tactical tasks involved in the management of positive, 'personal' communication between an organisation and its customers; recognising this should be complementary to image and brand management.

Image and brand management
The strategic and tactical tasks involved in the management of positive, 'non-personal' communication between an organisation and its audiences; recognising this should be complementary to customer/audience relationship.

Non-personal marketing communications
One-way (asymmetric) communication (at a distance) with prospects and customers.

A variety of authors have made claims as to the relative costs and returns of keeping existing customers compared with the greater cost of recruiting new ones. Some have reported it can range from being between 2 to 20 times as expensive to gain a new customer as it is to retain an existing one (Goodman et al. 2000) but the range can be even greater in some specialist industries. Organisations will seek a balance of maintaining repeat purchasers (previous customers coming back for more) and new purchasers (attracting new customers). Clearly, this balance will vary from situation to situation. In the case study on Škoda which starts Part 2 of this book, Škoda had to focus significant effort on attracting new customers if they were to increase sales; they could not simply rely on their loyal but small band of previous customers. Changing perceptions and attracting the interest of new customers had to become major marketing communications objectives for their campaigns. In contrast, for Concern, the case that kicked off Part 1 of the book, while they had to look for new donations they, as does every other charity, sought increased contribution from those who were already charitable givers (existing 'customers').

CRM, like marketing itself, has many different definitions as authors and practitioners place their own 'spin' on the area. In some respects, we will do likewise later, when we extend CRM into **CARM** – customer/audience relationship management – which we do because of the particular emphasis we must place on a variety of audiences when considering the full implications of integrated marketing communications. The Gartner Group (2000) describes CRM as a 'management discipline – even a philosophy – that requires business to recognise and nurture their relationship with customers', and define it in terms resonant of the marketing concept. Others are quick to criticise that there can be too much emphasis placed on the 'relationship', recognising that some customers simply want a transaction and not an ongoing relationship and that this would frequently depend upon the product or service offered (Szmigin and Bourne 1998). These authors tend to prefer the term 'customer management' (Woodcock et al. 2000). McCann (1999) sensibly offers the view of a relationship continuum from low (transactional) to high (relational).

By way of offering some definition of CRM, Andersen Consulting (1998) suggest it is,

'The practice of identifying, attracting and retaining the most valuable customer to generate profitable growth. It is the process by which companies manage relationships with their existing customers and new prospects'.

Stone and Woodcock (2001) highlight the way in which modern technology lies at the heart of much of CRM which they define as

'A term for methodologies, technologies and e-commerce capabilities used by companies to manage customer relationships'.

What other descriptions of CRM have in common is the explicit or implicit implication of recognising the significance of *all* customer contact points in that these are the bases upon which customers experience the organisation and develop their relationships. The Hewson Consulting Group (2000) emphasises that CRM embraces all sales partners up and down the supply chain and all channels and media from the Internet to field sales. The Gartner Group (2000) highlight the importance and relevance of everyone in the business working at the customer interface. For these reasons, another alternative term used in place of CRM by some is that of **customer contact management**, which we define in such a way as to differentiate it from **image and brand management** which involves **non-personal marketing communications** such as television advertising (see later).

These customer contacts have also been called 'moments of truth', so named by Jan Carlzon (of SAS airlines) to identify all occasions when customers interact with a firm whatever the medium of contact – face-to-face, on the telephone, through POS, literature, direct mail, the Internet, etc.

These issues have profound implications for integrated marketing communications, not least because CRM, or (better still) CARM, highlights the importance of communications at all points of contact in building relationships with customers and other targeted groups. Whilst in most of the literature on CRM the constant reference point is the 'customer', for integrated marketing communications it is vital to widen this customer perspective to include consumers *and* other audiences. The implications of customer relationship management and customer contact management are so important to a full understanding of IMC that to leave them out would be a serious omission and this is why this chapter is devoted to the subject. Throughout the chapter, to avoid unnecessary complications, we shall confine our reference to customers but we invite readers to constantly reflect on the issues of CRM and customer contact management applied to other audience groups and the communications implications that are created. Examples of other relevant audiences would include the internal audiences of employees and external audiences such as investors/shareholders/'the City', media personnel (e.g. journalists), and government ministers and officers (who are often the focus for political lobbying). In all these examples, critical areas of the marketing communications mix include PR, media relations, corporate communications, etc. Another important audience group is that of intermediaries. When utilising promotional push strategies in which marketing communications are targeted towards the trade and channels of distribution (as opposed to end customers), managing these relationships have an enormous impact on the success of IMC campaigns.

Much of marketing communication theory is focused on increasing awareness and influencing behaviour as in the classical **AIDA model**, for example (see Chapter 4). However, the experience of the potential and actual customer in dealing with an organisation is likely to have a lasting impression on individuals. If the contact experience meets the customer's expectations then the experience will have anything from a neutral to a positive effect on the individual. However, if the organisation is difficult to deal with, individuals will soon form a negative attitude to the organisation. How do customers feel when they cannot make contact on the phone? How do they feel when the customer service line is constantly engaged; or when the technical support number turns out to be an automated response call handler; or when they wish to place an order but the selling organisation procedures make it difficult to do so? For large organisations there is little point in spending £10 million on advertising if the organisation is impossible to deal with, just as a small, one-person business is wasting time and money on door-to-door flyers if there is no means of handling the telephone enquiries they might generate. We live in a world where people expect an immediate response. The intensity of competition means if your company cannot respond to the customers' needs right away someone else probably will. Picking up this theme, McKenna (1997) focuses on the speed of information dissemination and communication. Customers expect the right information and marketing communications at the right time (as defined by them, not the companies) and become dissatisfied if this is not achieved. Stone et al. (2001) query the extent to which 'marketers today are ready to do this'.

One way of viewing the broad strategic tasks of integrated marketing communications is to view them as involving the combination of two strategic imperatives, those

AIDA model

A marketing communications concept that models the stages through which marketing communications should move a potential customer: Awareness, Interest, Desire and Action. It is one of a number of hierarchy-of-effects models.

FOOD FOR THOUGHT

Dissatisfied customers will tell nine times more people about negative brand experiences than satisfied customers about positive experiences.

of 'image and brand management' (Chapter 11) and 'customer contact management'. These can be perceived as falling along a continuum from 'non-personal communications' to 'personal communications'. Personal communication involves a two-way dialogue (face-to-face or at a distance) with prospects and customers. Managing this activity is referred to as customer contact management, which may be described in the following way:

> Customer contact management requires the coordination and management of all activities involving personal communication between an organisation and its customers and prospects. This personal communication may be in person, by mail, telephone, fax, email, Internet or other approaches such as video-conferencing.

This chapter considers marketing communications that facilitate direct two-way dialogue between the supplying organisation and the potential or actual customer. Links between sales, customer service, database marketing, telemarketing and direct response marketing are identified.

The activities of customer contact management usually come under the control of different functions within the organisational structure and this makes it difficult to ensure integration. Typically field sales, direct response marketing and customer services are likely to be separate functions in large organisations, each with their own executive head. Exhibitions, trade shows, telemarketing and Internet services may all be handled by different personnel. The consequence of this is that customer contact management is likely to be fragmented and difficult to co-ordinate. The possible outcome is that customers will become confused, frustrated and disappointed. These issues are of concern in all marketing situations whether it is the marketing of consumer goods and services, industrial products or in business-to-business marketing.

Customer contact management in business-to-business marketing communications

Much of marketing and, hence, marketing communications, theory has tended to focus on consumer goods, particularly fast moving consumer goods (FMCGs). Many people fail to recognise, however, the vast amount of business-to-business marketing communications that is conducted even by the big FMCG manufacturers whose primary contact is with the trade (their real customers), not the consumers. Although huge sums of money are spent in promoting to 'end' customers and consumers by such companies, their 'first-line' customer contact is with trade customers. Managing trade contacts (e.g. wholesalers and retailers) is very different from the sort of contact that may be made with consumers. Volumes and values of transactions are high and typically involve multiple products. Pricing, promotional deals, shelf space, stock control and delivery all need to be agreed. It is a little too simplistic to say that these issues are sorted out by sales representatives. A sales representative from a major manufacturer no longer visits every retail branch. Negotiations for key accounts are conducted at a senior level; once a contract is set up much of the daily contact is via computer-to-computer (**Electronic data interchange – EDI**) and telephone. Customer contact management involves the co-ordination of many communications activities; negotiations, pricing, discounts, promotional deals, inventory, logistics and shelf space, all of which are unique to each major customer. And this takes place at many levels, at many locations and via many means, face-to-face, telephone, fax, letters, EDI, email, Internet and video links.

Electronic data interchange (EDI)

Method of transferring data from computer to computer.

IN VIEW 12.1

Customer contact management at RS Components

RS Components is the UK's largest distributor of electronic and electrical components. Its products are sold via a catalogue and telesales operation to industrial, educational, research and public sector organisations. The computer-controlled call centre has a capacity of 20 operators employed in-house who regularly handle up to 7500 calls per day. The customer calls with their customer number, order number, part numbers from the catalogue, and quantity. Calls should be answered within three rings. The order is typed directly into the computer. On completion the picking document is printed in the warehouse with a bar code. The bar code helps guide a bin along a conveyor system through the warehouse to the correct stock bays. The order is picked and shipped the same day it is received and the invoice is despatched at the same time. Express delivery companies are used to ensure next day delivery. The company has now expanded into other European markets and offering its services via the Internet.

Source: Adapted from Palmer and Hartley, *The Business and Marketing Environment* (1996), McGraw Hill.

Database marketing

The use of accurate customer and prospect customer information, competitor information, market information and internal company information stored on a computer database to focus marketing activities towards targets.

The more non-routine and expensive the purchase, the greater the degree of inter-action between seller and the potential buyer. With major sales the interactions between supplying and buying organisations may be many and varied with many potential contact points. The supplying organisation may initiate contact with the customer via a number of means, such as field sales, telesales, direct mail, customer service, finance office, order processing and delivery. The customer may initiate contact from a number of different points and levels in their own organisation; from goods inward, invoice payments, buying department, stores, user department, technical services, design, quality control and maintenance. The customer's own knowledge about their purchasing behaviour and about the supplying company may be fragmented. The supplying organisation needs to be able to manage pre-purchase, transaction, and post-purchase situations in order to build relationships. The need for customer contact management then becomes apparent. Without recognition of the important role marketing communications plays in customer contact management, it is likely that even the most imaginative consumer promotions are destined to fail. From an integrated marketing communications perspective, it thus becomes vital to appreciate the implications of customer contact management and seek to build these into any marketing communications programme.

Database marketing

Fundamental to the management of customer contacts (trade, end customers and consumers) is the development of **database marketing**. In many respects, database marketing is the driving force within much of the new thinking behind integrated marketing communications and, as all [authors] agree, better information is fundamental in moving transactional marketing to CRM, increasing loyalty, keeping the right customers, and resulting in better profits and lower costs (Stone et al. 2001). According to Schultz (1997),

> 'As you integrate communications you must integrate marketing activities. To integrate marketing you must integrate sales and selling, and to integrate those functions, you must integrate the entire organisation ... The goal is to align the organisation to serve consumers and customers. Databases are rapidly becoming the primary management tool that drives the organisation's business strategy'.

The speed of technological change throughout the 1990s in the fields of database management, network computing and telecommunications was startling. The merging technologies of computing and telecommunications have opened up new frontiers in personal communications that allow companies a two-way dialogue with thousands of customers without geographic limits. The Internet, super-highways, and satellites may be the glamour end of the new technology, but without the database, companies would not be able to store and handle large volumes of customer information on which many marketing communications are based. Database marketing has been defined as:

> an interactive approach to customer contact management relying on the maintenance of accurate customer and prospect customer information, competitor information, and internal company information. The database is used to provide information for computer-aided sales support, direct response marketing, and to support customer information and service systems.
>
> Hartley and Starkey (1996)

NEED TO KNOW

☑ *The key components of database marketing include computer-aided sales support, direct response marketing and customer information and service.*

This definition attempts to embrace the potential applications and user groups of marketing databases. The three components of database marketing – computer-aided sales support, direct response marketing, and customer information and service – may be described as follows.

Computer-aided sales support (CASS)

Computer-aided sales support

The electronic systems for direct access to customer and product data by the sales team.

Computer-aided sales support (CASS) requires the field sales team, sales support team, and telemarketing team to have direct access to the database via PCs or notebook computers whether office based, mobile or located in outstations. In addition to access to records, the system should support electronic communication such as fax and email, and personal tools such as diary/organiser, word processing, spreadsheet, and proposal generation.

Direct response marketing

Marketing system based on individual customer records held on a database. These records are the basis for marketing analysis, planning, implementation of programmes, and control of all this activity. This system ensures a focus on marketing to customers rather than on the marketing of products.

Direct response marketing (DRM)

Direct response marketing (DRM) involves the use of the database for campaigns using addressable communications (such as direct mail, mail order, telemarketing, email and text messaging) targeted at existing or potential customers and for fulfilment of direct response advertising campaigns including press and DRTV (direct response television advertising).

Customer information and service

The systems in place to allow customers to contact the organisation quickly and easily.

Customer information and service (CIS)

Customer information and service (CIS) allows customers to contact the organisation quickly and easily, possibly using a freephone or local number, using email or over the Internet. The reasons for the contact may include; bill query, warranty claim, technical problem, product/service information, or servicing required.

IN VIEW 12.2

Computer-aided sales support at Hewlett Packard

Hewlett Packard (HP) have developed a strategy for enhancing customer service and improving sales force performance which utilises improved database and communication systems. Large companies such as HP receive up to and over 1 million enquiries annually by phone, mail and email. Much of the internal and field sales personnel's time was taken up sorting and handling these queries. The time taken to process such enquiries may mean that customers' first impressions are not necessarily favourable. HP's CASS project involved the enhancement of the company's databases and communication systems and equipping of the field sales force with lap top computers and modems so they could connect to the company's systems from home. This resulted in the field sales force spending more time with the customer; up from 26% to 35% of their available time. This was partly because qualification of sales leads by internal sales personnel (including telesales) resulted in only 5% of these leads being passed to field sales. The quality of these leads is much higher and the speed at which they are acted on is much faster. Other benefits are that customer, product, stock, and order status information is accessible by the field sales representatives and also that marketing is better able to analyse promotional activity and customer response.

Source: HP World (March 1988) and described in Palmer and Hartley (1996)

IN VIEW 12.3

Customer information and service at Post and Telekom Austria

As part of a concerted drive to retain its dominant position in the market, PTA (Post and Telekom Austria) opened a new call centre that is served by an IVR (interactive voice response) platform. With the increasing liberalisation of telecommunications, PTA knew that customer service will become more important than ever before.

In the late 1990s PTA had around 4 million customers and received in the region of 20,000 enquiries by telephone each day. The new call centre was opened with 430 agents, a figure that increased almost fourfold by 2000. 'Customer service is of paramount importance to us at PTA', said Mr. Gerhard Hagenauer, the Call Centre Project Manager of PTA.

'The IVR solution enables us to handle our customer enquiries more efficiently and effectively than ever before.' This system gathers and routes information on all incoming calls according to the service required and origin of the caller. This information is forwarded via CTI (computer / telephony integration) to the Aspect call centre system which then completes the call transfer to the appropriate agent.

Source: Platt (1993)

Provision of customer service by telephone is not new; however, the use of the telephone has been extended into new product and service categories during the last ten years. Technical help lines have been available for many years for users of industrial products and services. Consumer durable manufacturers (especially of electrical products) have also provided help lines, usually direct to their service companies. The result of this direct enquiry may be to bypass the local agent or retailer who traditionally were the first stop for a customer with a problem. The Careline Report (1995) published by the L&R Group define carelines as 'telephone numbers printed on-pack which the customer can ring for advice or information about a product, often free of charge'. According to research conducted by L&R, 81% of products in the USA carried a careline, 22% in the UK. The average response time in the USA was 1.4 seconds with a range from 1 second to 10 seconds. In the UK the average response time was 2.7 seconds with a range from 1 second to 20 seconds. To the traditional medium of the telephone, other electronic communications opportunities are virtually revolutionising the way businesses manage their customer contact and communication. This is the subject of the next section.

Electronic marketing and telemarketing

Electronic marketing

The utilisation of the Internet to transact business; also known as e-commerce.

Three components of database marketing have been identified, computer-aided sales support, direct response marketing, and customer information and service. **Electronic marketing** and telemarketing are now playing an increasingly important role in the integrated management in all three of these components. Electronic marketing, or electronic commerce (e-commerce) as it is becoming widely known, embraces all the developments of the Internet and wireless communications which are so rapidly being accepted as second nature to us all as part of the general business environment, the impact of which on all marketing and marketing communications activities cannot be overestimated.

Telemarketing has been described as:

the planned and controlled use of telephone communication to build profitable transactions and relationships with customer groups (actual and potential) who impact on an organisation's success.

IN VIEW 12.4

E-commerce: the case of Amazon.com bookstore

Some companies have used new media channels to 'make a splash' by selling an old product in a creative new way. Amazon.com, for example, opened for business on the Internet in June 1996, selling one of the oldest, lowest-tech products – books – via a new medium. Opening a bookstore is not normally front-page news, but Amazon.com's combination of buy-from-home convenience, huge selection (2.5 million titles) and low prices has gained people's attention. Also getting some attention is the fact that Amazon.com's Internet-based bookstore has gone from strength to strength in a world where not all dot com companies have survived. See Plate 6.

The use of the telephone as a sales tool dates from the 1950s when it was used in the USA for selling newspaper advertising space. During the 1960s, Ford in the USA were using it extensively to identify potential customers and offer test drives (The Henley Centre 1994), a campaign that notched up a staggering 22 million telephone calls. The Direct Marketing Association estimates suggest that in 2000 there were 90,000 registered lines with BT for freephone and local call numbers which is more than double the number for 1996. The usage continues to rise and is mirrored in other parts of the world. However, the Henley Centre's 'Teleculture 2000' report provides a sobering reminder to those organisations that fail to focus on customer service 68% of people would prefer not to deal with an organisation again if a single call is badly handled.

Facilitating the use of telephone as a major medium of marketing communication is the development of **call centres**, which may be described as the hub of any telemarketing operation. It may be a single room with only a few operators or it may be a number of linked sites with thousands of operators. Modern call centres usually provide a mix of automated and personal service features via an **automated call distributor**. That is when the customer is asked to press a number on the phone to select the service. Once through, and depending on the service selected, you may be connected to a customer service agent who can pull your details onto the computer screen with a few keystrokes; this may be your account number or post code.

A call centre is a complex mix of telephone exchange, automated call distributors, computers and software for handling calls, links to databases and other computer applications and people. It is a highly specialised activity and many specialist companies have developed to provide agency services for their clients. Call centres can be located anywhere in the world. Being labour intensive (even with automation) new call centres are appearing in countries with low labour costs. Organisations may develop their own in-house operations and expertise or use the services of the agencies. However, flexibility is important depending on the nature of the service required and the campaigns running at any one time. Organisations with in-house facilities may at times require the extra capacity an agency can provide.

Call centre

Central resource that groups personnel together for telemarketing, both outbound (sales calls to customers and potential customers, or relationship marketing activities) and inbound (customers, responding to direct response advertising, customers requiring service).

Automated call distributor

Electronic system by which telephone calls can be routed to appropriate departments or contacts without the need for direct human contact.

IN VIEW 12.5

Telemarketing at Simon Jersey

Simon Jersey is an excellent example of a company having switched to telesales. The company is a leading supplier of uniforms to businesses, especially the hotel and catering industries. From a manufacturing plant in Accrington (UK) the company distributes to 22 countries via offices in London and Strasbourg. Due to the rising costs of traditional marketing and distribution activities, especially of the field sales force, the company reorganised around a 'fully integrated telemarketing system handling both inbound and outbound calls staffed by a range of telemarketing agents'. The telesales screens are served by a database so that the sales agent can satisfy most needs directly over the telephone including: catalogue requests, order enquiries, stock availability, entering orders, arranging 24-hour delivery, invoice and account queries. The database is also used for managing and tracking new leads.

Source: Starkey (1997)

Strategic implications of customer contact management

There are a number of strategic implications associated with effective customer contact management. Among them include the implications of integration, reducing cost of sales and communication, coverage and penetration, customer retention/relationship marketing, and extended marketing communication options.

Integration

Many have argued the strategic value of database marketing, customer service, relationship marketing and integrated marketing communications. Technology in the form of marketing databases, networked computer systems and modern digital telecommunications now provide reliable solutions in improving and profiting from enhanced customer contact management. The technical interfaces between computing and telecommunications are being harmonised, providing better integration and bringing cheaper, speedier and more reliable systems. Traditional marketing and sales structures have been largely based on functions such as field sales management, sales administration, advertising and promotion and customer service. In more recent times, organisations have set up separate direct mail, telemarketing and Internet operations. Unfortunately, traditionally structured marketing departments tend to have difficulty in coping with these changes.

The challenge for marketing managers is in deciding how best to organise for marketing in terms of structure, systems and budgets so as to achieve integration of the marketing functions, avoid duplication, share expenses and control activities. From the customer's point of view the organisation should appear seamless. Exhibit 12.1 illustrates the tools and activities used in customer contact management. The 'tools' consist of the hardware and software required to run the systems. The database is most likely to sit within a networked computer system and may be connected to a call centre. The 'activities' are the support activities such as database building, campaign management and evaluation, research and analysis on customer and campaign records. The 'functions' are the user departments that rely on the database and networked communications for their day-to-day activities. Note that the call centre does not usually belong to one user department. Sales may use the call centre to verify and qualify sales leads prior to sending an expensive representative to call. Direct response marketing is likely to include a response option via website and telephone as well as mail and will require the use of the call centre. Customer information and service is likely to receive more enquiries by telephone than letter although the use of email is becoming more widely used. At times, all these activities may revolve around a major event such as a trade show or promotional campaign, which will cause a peak in Internet and telephone activity and database usage as all functions pitch in.

Unfortunately, and as is the nature of things, computer and telecom communication systems in most organisations will have been installed piecemeal over time; upgrades, add-ons, adaptations etc. are the norm. Few organisations are lucky enough to have predicted all their needs in advance and ordered or developed a complete integrated system. Stone and Woodcock (2001) report 'that few companies have successfully leveraged fully the relevant new technologies'. In many organisations, customer contact management will not be found in one system but in a number of different systems that have been installed over the years. These separate systems rarely fit together well and give rise to problems of integration. The Hewson Group estimated

Exhibit 12.1 Tools and activities for customer contact management

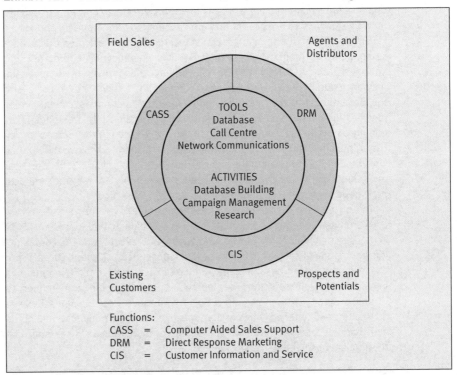

Source: Hartley and Starkey (1996)

that in 2000 there was a 70% growth in the European market for CRM software applications and services direct from software vendors including e-commerce to US$1.3 billion (Stone and Woodcock 2001). It is, of course, virtually impossible for most companies to keep up to date with technological change even if they wanted to, as new developments take place so quickly and continuously. The process of dealing with an organisation needs to match or exceed customer expectations. Vast amounts spent on corporate image and brand building will be wasted if intermediaries, final customers and other key audiences find that the organisation cannot meet their expectations.

IN VIEW 12.6

To integrate or not to integrate?

The limitations of integration are illustrated by this example from the world of insurance. The name of the company is disguised. Alpine Insurance is a large European general insurance company who has been operating successfully for many years. Policies have traditionally been sold via a network of insurance brokers. Alpine Insurance have recently taken over a small insurer who specialised in selling insurance direct to members of affinity groups such as trade unions, professional bodies and public sector organisations. This business operated traditionally by either including promotional flyers in the

→

organisation's mail-outs or by mailing members directly. Members are usually offered an incentive such as 15% discount and are encouraged to respond by phone.

On taking over this smaller specialist insurer, Alpine rebranded the business with the corporate name 'Alpine'. Indeed, this is what we might expect corporate communication specialists to advise. Now imagine that you have a policy with the original Alpine Insurance purchased via your insurance broker, and that you now receive a mail-shot from the direct marketing division (now named Alpine Municipal) as a member of a professional organisation offering you 15% discount. When you call via the free phone number to enquire as to whether you can claim a further 15% discount on your policy you are advised that 'Alpine Insurance' and 'Alpine Municipal' are operated as two different companies even though they are part of the same group. 'Alpine Municipal', the direct marketing operation, is happy to give you a new quotation but this will have no connection to the present policy purchased from 'Alpine Insurance' via a broker.

This raises a number of issues. From the customer's perspective there may be some confusion and a feeling of dissatisfaction. In particular, what does the '15% off' mean if it is not 'off' the regular premium you are paying at present? From the company's perspective it is attempting to sell a commodity product, possibly at different prices, via different channels, but using the same name; difficult to achieve. From the intermediary's perspective (the brokers) they may feel their business is being undermined as the insurance company promotes direct business under the same name. These issues cut right across the traditional activities of branding, corporate communications, product offers, and channels to market. True integration means more than a simple name change and *all* the implications need to be considered.

With so many ways to engage in personal communications, organisations are in danger of losing control. A management without a clear vision of what is possible, what they desire and what their customers desire, may find that costs run out of control. According to Friedman and Goodrich (1998), the end result of this lack of control is 'a sprawling mix of sales reps, call centres, re-sellers and, perhaps, a website or two'. Under the heading, 'multiple channels as a customer alignment strategy', they discuss the relationship between changing buyer behaviour and the emergence of multiple sales channels. They argue that many individual and corporate customers are migrating away from face-to-face encounters with sales representatives, not only to save money, but also to take greater control of the buying process.

Reducing cost of sales and communications

Estimates are regularly made as to the cost of employing sales representatives. For example, CPM International commissioned research from Abberton Associates who concluded in 1997 that in the UK more than 470,000 people were employed in the selling function (excluding retail staff) at a cost of £19.3 billion and this was estimated to be more than double that spent on advertising. A typical sales person costs £49,400 to employ but was only paid £21,400 in salary and commission. The remainder was spent on overheads and expenses such as head office expenses, management and systems, communications, car, meals and accommodation. This survey also concluded that the average time the sales person spent selling in front of the customer was only 6%. The typical cost of a sales call was calculated at between £27 for consumer goods and £210 for capital goods (Exhibit 12.2).

Exhibit 12.2 Typical sales call costs

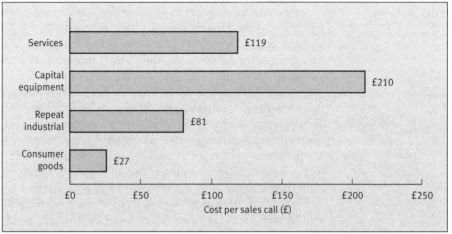

Source: Abberton Associates (1997)

Thus, any strategies that can reduce these costs or increase efficiency are well worth exploring. Oxford Associates and Rowland Moriarty calculated the cost of sales by channel for a US based high technology company (Friedman and Goodrich 1998). From Exhibit 12.3 it can be seen that tremendous cost savings can be achieved by trading customer contact down from field sales representatives to distributors or telesales. Even though the figures in Exhibits 12.2 and 12.3 are now somewhat dated, the points they make are perfectly valid and apply to sales and marketing practices throughout the world.

Exhibit 12.3 Transaction cost by channel: US-based high-tech company

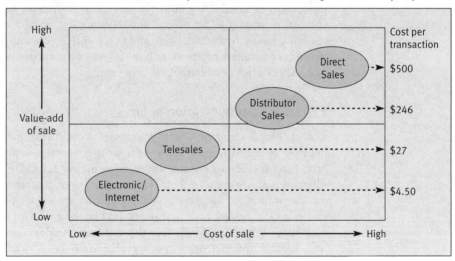

Source: From chart from '*Sales strategy in a multiple channel environment*', in '*Journal of Selling and Major Account Management*', Vol. 1, No. 1, pp. 38–48, 1998, The Sales Research Trust Ltd., (Friedman, L.G., and Goodrich, G., 1998). Reproduced with permission.

Coverage and penetration

Serving existing customers in the most appropriate and cost-effective way is only one part of the jigsaw. Finding new customers in a cost-effective way is another. In addition to the direct field sales force (the most expensive method) it is possible to use distributors, contracted sales agents, direct mail, telesales, and the Internet to find new customers. However, rather than seeing sales as one activity, Abberton Associates (1997) suggest deconstruction of the activity into its constituent parts, for example, lead generation, re-seller development, negotiation, administration etc. are separate functions. Thus, differing activities may be served via a different means at different times. A multi-channel coverage strategy is therefore needed. Some customer groups are also difficult to reach. For example, small to medium-sized enterprises (SMEs) are sometimes difficult to reach by traditional methods due to the cost of employing a direct sales force. Alternative channels such as telesales or a web page may provide a solution.

Rather than allow multi-channels to develop haphazardly, careful consideration should be given to the need, the cost and the margins expected. Some organisations have already switched their total operations to new channels, whereas others are new entrants taking advantage of the new low-cost channels to serve traditional markets. Some organisations are developing a mixed approach with different functions handled by different means. Some financial service companies have set up direct customer carelines which may bypass the local branch or agent. For example, even when your car insurance is purchased via a local agent any claim may now be handled centrally direct via a customer careline. Some financial and insurance companies are now conducting their entire operation via the telephone; for example, First Direct Bank and Direct Line Insurance have cut the cost of selling financial services by more than half.

Customer retention/relationship marketing

New technology enables organisational and individual customers to exercise their preferences for conducting business. More information for the customer, new market entrants providing wider choice, and development of new channels means that the customer has more control. Companies that work on old and tired assumptions about how their customers prefer to do business may be surprised at how quickly customers desert them when new alternatives come along.

Extended communication options

The traditional and generalist approach to sales and customer management comprising field sales force, distributors (for smaller accounts), and sales office for order processing and administration seems inappropriate for today's business environment. Allowing customers more choice over the means of contact and improving customer service, while at the same time reducing the contact and transaction costs for both the supplying and buying organisation, should be the goal. Opportunities exist that now make this goal attainable whether this is a one-off sales transaction such as buying a book over the Internet, or an ongoing relationship between a buyer and seller.

Exhibit 12.4 shows the disaggregated sales activities and the possible means of contact. The aim is, of course, to trade the customer contact down to lower cost options while improving the service offered. The exact mix of activities and means of contact depend on the type of sales situation. However, the following questions are helpful in deciding how to organise for customer contact management:

Exhibit 12.4 Sales activity and means of contact

Means of contact	Cost of contact	Sales activity							
		Lead generation	Lead qualification	Establishing need	Negotiation	Account development	Problem solving	Ordering/ logistics	Queries
Key account manager	HIGH			X	X	X	X		
Field sales executive			X	X	X	X	X		
Technical specialist						X	X		X
Distributor/agent		X	X	X	X	X	X	X	X
Direct mail		X						X	
Telesales/ call centre		X	X	X		X	X	X	X
Fax								X	X
EDI								X	X
Internet	LOW	X						X	X

1 What are the customers' preferences and are they homogeneous or varied?
2 What are the activities needed? i.e. lead generation and qualification, negotiation, account development, order taking, enquiries, problems/technical support, fulfilment, logistics, etc.
3 What are the present/estimated costs of contact and transaction?
4 Which means/channels best match the interaction of (1), (2) and (3)?
5 Have customers been categorised e.g. by lifetime value, buyer behaviour (FRAP – frequency of purchase, recency of last purchase, amount bought, product category bought) loyalty, etc.?
6 How should customer contact be organised?
  – which means/channels should be offered?
  – who should be responsible for customer contact management?
  – should customer contact activities be organised in-house or should third-party agents for sales, database management, telemarketing etc. be used?
  – should the pricing strategy be adjusted to reflect the means and cost of customer contact and order transaction, or be uniform across channels?

Summary

The growth in emphasis on customer relationship management (CRM) has increased our understanding of valuing customer relationships and lifetime values rather than limiting our perception to customer transactions. Whereas CRM appears to focus on end customers to the exclusion of intermediate customers, consumers and other key audience groups, integrated marketing communications requires that all relevant audiences are duly considered (CARM).

Relationships are the aggregation of multiple transactions and these are themselves the accumulation of points of customer contact or 'moments of truth'. Customer contact management requires the management of all activities where the organisation interfaces with its customers and prospects. This includes all types of selling and communication activity, and customer service – face-to-face, trade fairs, direct response marketing, telemarketing, and electronic marketing.

For an integrated approach to customer contact management the tools required are likely to include the database, call centre and networked communications. Ideally these are likely to be financed and managed as an organisational resource rather than that of a functional department. The user functions may be described as computer-aided sales support, direct response marketing, and customer information and service. To support these tools and functions the organisation needs to engage in activities such as database building, telemarketing, campaign management and research.

The strategic issues of CRM involve the paradox of achieving cost reduction while at the same time improving the coverage and penetration of markets, and the enhancement of customer service, which are all necessary to retain existing customers and attract new ones. By recognizing that not all customers are worth the same and that appropriate customer contact can be maintained at lower cost for some customer groups compared with others, this apparent paradox can be resolved.

Self-review questions

1 What is CARM?

2 What is meant by 'moments of truth'?

3 What have been suggested in this chapter as the two broad strategic tasks of integrated marketing communications?

4 Why is database marketing considered to be so important to CRM/CARM and customer contact management?

5 What are the components of a modern customer contact management system?

6 What factors have led to the rapid development of integrated customer contact management systems?

7 Identify the benefits of an integrated customer contact management system.

8 Summarise the strategic issues that should be considered when reviewing existing customer contact activities.

Project

Discuss the impact on the organisation (structure, jobs, investment, etc.) of a move from a traditional sales and customer service system of branch offices, field sales representatives, agents and distributors, to a more centralised telemarketing and Internet operation. Use either a manufacturing company or a financial services company as the basis for your answer.

References

Abberton Associates (1997), *Balancing the Selling Equation: Revisited*. Thame, UK: CPM International Ltd.

Andersen Consulting (1998), *Customer Relationship Management in the Automotive Industry: Profiting from Improved Customer Focus*. Andersen Consulting.

Friedman, L.G. and Goodrich, G. (1998), Sales strategy in a multiple channel environment. *The Journal of Selling and Major Account Management*, 1 (1), 38–48.

Gartner Group (2000), *Putting Customer Relationship Management to Work*. Gartner Group.

Goodman, J., O'Brien, P. and Segal, E. (2000), Selling quality to the CFO. *Quality Progress*, March.

Hartley, B. and Starkey, M.W. (eds) (1996), *Management of Sales and Customer Relations*. London: Thomson International Press.

The Henley Centre (1994), *Teleculture 2000*. UK: The Henley Centre.

Hewson Consulting Group (2000), *CRM Handbook* 3rd edn. Hewson Consulting Group.

The L&R Group (1995), *Careline Report*. L&R.

McCann, D. (1999), The Customer Continuum. *Management Accounting*, January, 38–39.

McKenna, R. (1997), *Real Time*. Boston, MA: Harvard Business Press.

Palmer, A.J. and Hartley, B. (1996), *The Business and Marketing Environment* 2nd edn. London: McGraw-Hill.

Platt, G. (1993), Database programs help build business. *Business Marketing*, November, 60.

Reicheld, F.F. and Sasser, W.E. (1990), Zero defections: quality comes to services. *Harvard Business Review*, Sept–Oct.

Schultz, D.E. (1997), Integrating information sources to develop strategies. *Marketing News*, 20 January, 31 (2), 10.

Starkey, M.W. (1997), Telemarketing. In Jobber, D. (ed.), *Selling and Sales Strategy*. London: Butterworth-Heinemann.

Stone, M. and Woodcock, N. (2001) Defining CRM and assessing its quality, in Foss, B. and Stone, M., *Successful Customer Relationship Marketing: New Thinking, New Strategies, New Tools for Getting Closer to Your Customers*. London: Kogan Page.

Stone, M., Abbott, J. and Buttle, F. (2001), Integrating customer data into CRM strategy, in Foss, B. and Stone, M., *Successful Customer Relationship Marketing: New Thinking, New Strategies, New Tools for Getting Closer to Your Customers*. London: Kogan Page.

Szmigin, I. and Bourne, H. (1998), Consumer equity in relationship marketing. *Journal of Consumer Marketing*, 15 (6), 544–557.

Woodcock, N. Starkey, M.W. and Stone, M. (2000), *The Customer Management Scorecard: State of the Nation – A Strategic Framework for Benchmarking Performance against Best Practice*. London: Business Intelligence.

Selected further reading

Foss, B. and Stone, M. (2001), *Successful Customer Relationship Marketing: new thinking, new strategies, new tool for getting closer to your customers*. London: Kogan Page.

Gummesson, E. (1999), *Total Relationship Marketing: Rethinking Marketing Management from the 4Ps to the 30Rs*. Oxford: Butterworth-Heinemann.

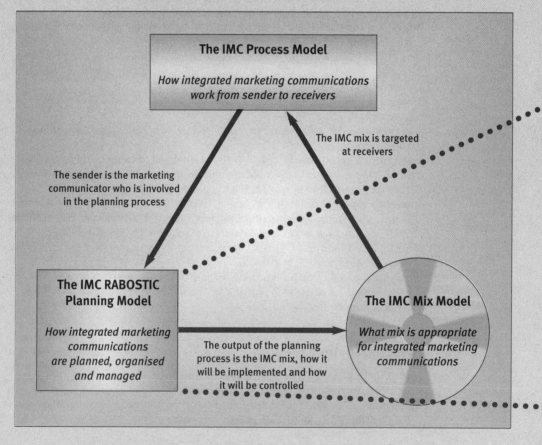

The IMC Process Model

How integrated marketing communications work from sender to receivers

The IMC mix is targeted at receivers

The sender is the marketing communicator who is involved in the planning process

The IMC RABOSTIC Planning Model

How integrated marketing communications are planned, organised and managed

The output of the planning process is the IMC mix, how it will be implemented and how it will be controlled

The IMC Mix Model

What mix is appropriate for integrated marketing communications

The Integrated Marketing Communications (IMC) Framework

Part 2

Managing Integrated Marketing Communications Planning

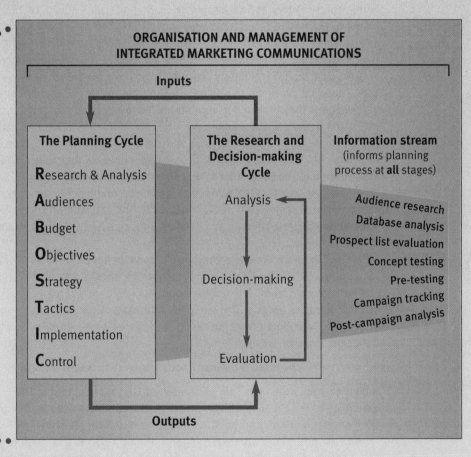

ORGANISATION AND MANAGEMENT OF
INTEGRATED MARKETING COMMUNICATIONS

Inputs

The Planning Cycle

Research & Analysis
Audiences
Budget
Objectives
Strategy
Tactics
Implementation
Control

The Research and Decision-making Cycle

Analysis

Decision-making

Evaluation

Information stream
(informs planning process at **all** stages)

Audience research
Database analysis
Prospect list evaluation
Concept testing
Pre-testing
Campaign tracking
Post-campaign analysis

Outputs

The Integrated Marketing Communications (IMC)
RABOSTIC Planning Model

Škoda

A man walked into a garage, 'Can you let me have a pair of windscreen wipers for a Škoda?' The garage owner replied, 'Yes, that seems like a fair swap!'

Since coming under the wing of the Volkswagen Group, Škoda cars have been a marketing success story and an integrated marketing communications triumph. Škoda's image in the mid to late 1920s was very different to their image in the 1980s and 1990s. Once a highly respected manufacturer, Škoda, the third oldest car manufacturer in the world, had become the butt of many jokes, but the tide is turning.

1995 was Škoda's centenary year which also saw the launch of the Felicia range of cars – the first products to leave the Škoda factory developed in conjunction with Volkswagen. They received acclaim from the industry as the 'best budget buys'. In 1996, the Octavia was launched into the international market and this took Škoda into a completely new market sector, the mid-size range, which broadened the appeal of Škoda cars from private family buyers to commercial fleet users. The Octavia was introduced into the UK in June 1998 to widespread acclaim but sales only reached a little over 2,500 units. With an advertising launch budget of £10m, this represented a staggering advertising cost of £4,000 per car. The stigma attached to Škoda's image appeared to be little affected and Škoda's appeal, such as it was, remained restricted to brand loyalists.

VW had to turn around the fortunes of Škoda. In the UK, their cars were award winners but the Škoda *brand* still had far to go. The stigma attached to owning a Škoda still had not gone away. The turning point was the launch of the Fabia in 2000 amid a flurry of industry awards. The company addressed the credibility problem head-on instead of pretending it was not there. The creative proposition agreed by Škoda and their agency, Falon, was,

The Fabia is a car so good, you won't believe it's a Škoda

Advertising spend on the Fabia was around £4.5m compared to the Toyota Yaris at around £9m and the Renault Clio at £17m. The company used an integrated marketing communications campaign to create a much larger share of voice than the relative spends would otherwise suggest. Primary advertising media were TV, press and posters. Škoda worked very closely with all of its agencies as they developed and pursued their above and below the line push and pull strategies. Consumer PR played a critical role and was handled by Sputnik who, in particular, targeted opinion forming journalists to increase media coverage. Direct marketing communications were handled by Archibald, Ingall, Stretton who immediately set about gaining a better understanding of the changing customer profile, developing a customer database and understanding what attitudes made someone a Škoda 'acceptor' or 'rejector'. Their direct marketing (DM) communications supported a range of other promotions used in the campaign and built on the multiplier effect that advertising has on DM response.

Other notable marketing communications activities involved the development of a website which soon passed an average hit rate of 34,000 visits per month. Exposure marketing, as Škoda termed it, involved taking the cars and display materials to county shows, shopping centres, supermarkets and events such as the Crufts show. These and other similar activities were frequently jointly arranged with Škoda's independent franchised retailers (around 180 outlets) through which all sales were channelled. At all times, close communications were maintained between Škoda's internal employees and retailer employees as part of the total integrated marketing communications effort. Sales promotion merchandise and point-of-sale materials which mirrored images found on the website were provided for the retailer network. These included stationery, literature, clothing, workwear, pens, gifts and displays. A review of the retailer network was an important part of the process as was the training of retailer staff. Financial incentives were also part of the 'package' to the retailers as was an upgrading of their retailer premises and showrooms. Joint advertising promotions were undertaken with the retailers based on a wide selection of specially developed advertisements that could be personalised for the retailer's local market. These were provided digitally on CD-ROM so they could be sent direct to local papers.

Research and evaluation were important components of the whole integrated marketing communications campaign. Research that took place *before* the campaign helped shape Škoda's marketing communications objectives and strategy and resulted in the development of their agency briefs. Promotional concepts were pretested to be sure that the creative treatment would be accepted. Tracking studies were used to monitor sales, market share, performance and competitor activity as the campaign proceeded. At year end, campaign outcomes were evaluated against the objectives set (recognising that the marketing communications effort would still be carried forward in some modified form). Although the campaign featured the Fabia, the marketing communications were expected to have an impact on the whole Škoda range and would extend their cumulative effect over subsequent years. This proved to be the case. All evaluations revealed an outstanding marketing communications success story. Škoda car sales for 2005 are now projected to be 50,000 units representing a 2% share of the total UK market.

Not only did Škoda's cars receive awards, so did their marketing communications. *Marketing Week* and the Chartered Institute of Marketing declared the Fabia promotions as the Grand Prix winners in their 'Effectiveness Awards 2000'. They were also Gold and Best Change of Direction winners of the 2002 Institute of Practitioners in Advertising awards. *Campaign* listed Škoda in their 10 best direct mail campaigns.

More details of this case study can be found on the CD.

CD

Chapter 13

Marketing communications planning and plans

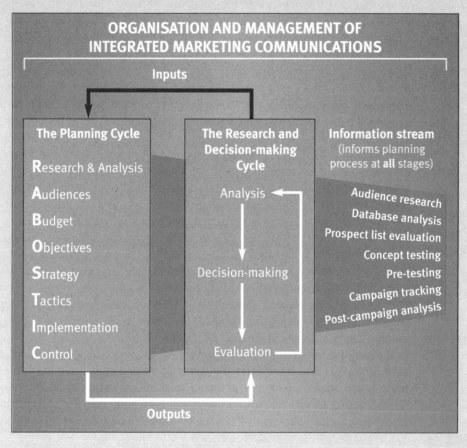

The IMC RABOSTIC Planning Model

CD

From the Part 2 integrative Škoda case and the additional detail on the CD, identify the critical aspects/issues from the case that correspond to each stage in the RABOSTIC planning model. Prepare a summary table detailing your findings.

Objectives

- To introduce the IMC RABOSTIC Planning Model
- To demonstrate the interrelated process of integrated marketing communications planning
- To outline the planning process
- To detail the eight key stages in a marketing communications plan
- To present the key issues in campaign management

Professional perspective

Steve Paterson Planning Director, Hamilton Wright

Integrated promotions and marketing solutions
The need to make the marketing pound work harder in an increasingly noisy marketplace means that all parts of the campaign must work together – above the line, below the line; TV and PR. You can no longer guarantee that a mass audience will be reached by a single medium, and so every element needs to work together. Someone has to co-ordinate this, and the planner who sets the objectives and strategy and works out the tactics of the campaign is ideally placed to do this.

Third party/employee buy-in
The sales chain often incorporates third parties, and will always incorporate own staff, be it retail outlets, sales forces or telephone call centres. Anticipating customer response in the forms of briefing the telephone call handlers, in branch literature for retail staff, or making the third parties part of the selling process can often mean the difference between success and failure of a promotional campaign.

The planner as champion of the customer
Reaching the right target audience with the right message is critical to achieving a successful campaign. Databases of customers provide transactional behaviour that can be very powerful when added to qualitative and quantitative market research. The planner is best placed to be able to interpret both, and to marry them up to produce insights into what would appeal to customers both rationally and emotionally. As customer segmentation is understood better, and media becomes evermore discrete and diverse, the planner can identify propositions that will appeal to different segments of the target audience, and then guide towards the best media to reach these segments.

The IMC RABOSTIC Planning Model

Planning cycle

The sequence of decisions and activities involved in putting together a marketing communications plan.

Part 1 of this book was based on the IMC Process Model and each of the chapters in Part 1 discussed the various aspects of that model. The same approach is now taken in Part 2 of the book which covers Chapters 13 through to 23. The model featured is the IMC RABOSTIC Planning Model.

On the left-hand side of the model is shown the **planning cycle** which firstly involves research and analysis of the situation and feedback from previous marketing communications campaigns and activities. What follows is a set of decisions that must be put together to form the final marketing communications plan(s). If integration is to take place, a whole series of plans will have to be formulated. Often, however, plans are considered in relative isolation of one another. The process, nevertheless, is the same for each. Although there may be some argument about the sequence in which the decisions should take place, the decision areas are basically common to all general business and marketing planning (see, for example, McDonald 1995; Wilson and Gilligan 1998; Kotler 2003). Whereas business and marketing plans refer to target markets, marketing communications plans should refer to target audiences for reasons that should now be obvious to readers. For a quick review, see Chapter 1. The areas of the planning cycle form the acronym RABOSTIC.

Information stream

The flow of information used in the marketing communications planning process.

Research and decision-making cycle

The circular process of analysing, deciding and evaluating marketing communication plans and actions.

On the right-hand side of the model is shown the **information stream** which illustrates the flow of information that is used in the planning process to aid the formulation of integrated marketing communications plans. In the centre of the model, the **research and decision-making cycle** shows analysis being used to inform decision-making. Evaluation takes place when plans are put into action. The insights gained are then cycled back into the analysis for the purposes of controlling the process and for further development of the next planning phase. The information stream is constantly tapped into, both to input and to extract information, throughout the planning process. It is important to realise that it is not used simply at the beginning and the end, but throughout the planning process.

Whatever else the planning process seeks to do, it aims to result in plans which are, in essence, *decisions* about what we want to achieve and how we are going to achieve them. Plans should be actionable! Each of the chapters in Part 2 looks at particular aspects of the RABOSTIC Model in turn and Exhibit 13.1 highlights these.

Exhibit 13.1 Chapter coverage of the IMC RABOSTIC Planning Model in Part 2 of the book

Elements of the integrated marketing communications planning process	Where found in Part 2
The planning, research and decision-making process	Chapter 13
Organisation and management of IMC	Chapters 14 and 15
Research	Chapter 16
Audiences	Chapter 17
Budget	Chapter 18
Objectives	Chapter 19
Strategy and tactics	Chapter 19
Implementation	Chapters 20–22
Control	Chapter 23

While RABOSTIC, in common with other planning models (see Exhibit 13.3), appears as a very sequential range of activities, in practice these are overlapping and iterative. Much of the information gathering, processing and decision-making take place on a regular or even continuous basis. Reviews may be undertaken at any time and modifications made. Hence the importance of recognising the information stream in the RABOSTIC model. For example, Budgets may be determined before or after Objectives are set and modified or broken down into sub-elements of allocations as strategies and tactics are decided upon. Readers should not presume that *any* planning process is totally fixed. The RABOSTIC acronym is used to help us to remember the various planning stages but each stage is not isolated from the others. They are interrelated and mutually dependent. Decisions in one area will affect decisions in another and planning practices vary from organisation to organisation. The adaptation from Cooper's planning cycle presented in Exhibit 13.4 illustrates the way in which the planning process is 'circular' and not entirely sequential. Aspects covered in this chapter and in Chapter 19 are particularly relevant to each other and readers are advised that there is some benefit in reading both chapters together.

Planning for integrated marketing communications

The coordination and integration of all marketing communication activities to achieve interrelated objectives has been advocated in this book. This is necessary to enable companies to compete in an increasingly sophisticated marketplace. With this growing sophistication, firms need to be able to anticipate problems and forecast demand. Planned activities are one way to help meet exigencies of the marketplace. Plans provide directions for all those involved in the marketing and marketing communications effort.

Chapter 23 uses a military analogy to describe the levels of integrated marketing communications and an understanding of these helps to evaluate the quality of integration achieved. This analogy can also be used to help understand the integrated communications planning process. Three levels can be identified using the military analogy: level 1, the overall war; level 2, battles within the war; and level 3, skirmishes. All activities within a war need to be integrated to achieve common goals as all points of customer contact need to be integrated and planned (Exhibit 13.2). Thus, a **marketing communications campaign** can be broadly defined as the performance and integration of all promotional activities into a programme designed to achieve interrelated goals (Parente et al. 1996). The overall marketing communications campaign is analogous to a war. The many battles within the campaign are the communications mix elements or geographical areas targeted. For example, the advertising campaign is a series of advertisements, and the activities that help produce them, which are designed to achieve interrelated goals. Skirmishes are localised, relatively short-lived tactical battles, which can be perceived as short-term 'changes on the road', to fight competitive activities. The effect of all promotional elements should be synergistic, that is, each individual or unit's activity should be co-ordinated so that the combined effect of all contributions is greater than the sum of its parts.

Like most business plans, the integrated **marketing communications plan** begins with an overview of the activity. This is particularly important for integrated planning as the priorities in the planning process must be identified as should the key tasks across the programme (see In View 13.1). Each communication tool, as identified in Exhibit 13.2, should not be seen as a separate activity that might each produce incremental

Marketing communications campaign

The performance and integration of all promotional marketing communications activities into a programme designed to achieve interrelated goals.

Marketing communications plan

Document that summarises the main issues and details of marketing communications activities, including relevant background information and marketing communications decisions.

Exhibit 13.2 Marketing communications is a conversation between a brand and its audience

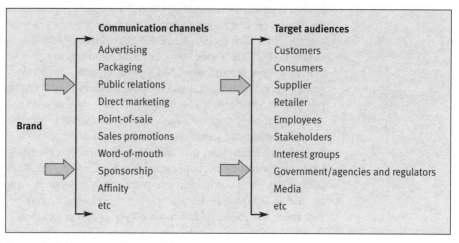

Source: Adapted from Cooper (1997, p. 168)

results, but rather as a series of interrelated marketing communications tools that support each other. Readers should recognise that each communications element may have its own plan, but is also a building block in an integrated plan. Each building block should be related and cross-referenced to other blocks to produce synergy and a consistent value message. Advertising, PR, sponsorship, direct marketing, telemarketing, press information, internal communications, sales promotions, exhibitions, salesforce communications, distributor communications, retail support, point-of-sale, product and technical information, corporate identity, corporate communications, relationship marketing, etc. can be used to complement each other and strengthen the overall impact of a campaign.

IN VIEW 13.1

Positioning a new car model as value for money

This model from a volume car manufacturer competes in the small family saloon class. In terms of price, performance and features, it is competitive with other models in the sector. However, to differentiate it from competitors, the key proposition to consumers is low cost of ownership. The manufacturer markets through a national network of franchised dealerships. The campaign must therefore concentrate on marketing the concept to dealerships as well as the consumer. Failure to achieve dealership commitment could ruin the impact of a consumer campaign at the point-of-sale.

Consumer advertising

Consumer advertising in national and regional press and television stresses the concept of value for money by highlighting low cost of ownership benefits such as fuel economy, longer service intervals, simplicity of servicing and repair, and the availability of low-cost finance. Consumers are invited to call a freephone number to request a brochure or ask for further information.

Dealer customer direct marketing

Existing dealership customers who fit the consumer profile for the new model are mailed with an information pack and video which explain the concept of value for money. As an incentive to take a test drive, they are offered a choice of free motoring accessories, further reinforcing the concept of value for money.

Dealership launch material

To ensure that the network is fully committed to the new programme each dealership receives a detailed product briefing and launch pack at a series of regional business meetings. The launch pack explains how to communicate the concept to customers and prospects and describes the launch support material available. The pack contains support material for sales, service and parts departments who will all be involved in marketing the concept to consumers. A guide for the sales team explains the different value for money features and describes how to present those features to prospects.

Dealership promotional material

Posters, display modules and other point-of-sale material reinforce the messages of the consumer advertising campaign within the dealership. An audio tape describing how dealership service helps to maintain low cost of ownership through scheduled servicing and competitive parts and repair costs is given to every consumer who buys a new car.

Aftersales service

A series of direct marketing programmes is used to maintain contact with customers and reinforce the concept of value for money after the sale. The campaign includes low-cost servicing vouchers to encourage customers to use the dealership service operations, do-it-yourself workshops to encourage customers to carry out routine service tasks themselves and guidelines on economical motoring.

Summary

The campaign ensures that there are no weak links in communication between the manufacturer and the customer. The impact of the consumer campaign could have been wasted if it had not been followed up effectively at dealership level.

Source: Linton and Morley (1995)

The planning process

Planning is the process by which one establishes a series of major decisions relating to audiences, budgets, objectives, strategy and tactics. As with all plans, the marketing communications plan is inevitably hierarchy. For example, the objectives first detail where the organisation intends to go, the strategy outlines how the organisation intends to get there and finally, the tactics present the precise route to be taken.

Numerous planning formats have been developed by academics and practitioners providing varying levels of detail (Exhibit 13.3). All the chapters in this part of the book provide an in-depth examination of each of the stages outlined in Exhibit 13.3 together with two chapters (Chapters 14 and 15) that consider some of the organisation and management implications. This chapter provides an introduction and framework

Exhibit 13.3 A summary of typical planning formats

All plans	Cooper	Smith et al. SOSTAC	J. Walter Thompson advertising agency	RABOSTIC	Typical response
Situation	Familiarise	Situational analysis	Where are we? Why are we here?	Research and analysis	Develop a situational analysis Understand the market and its influencers Understand competitors Identify problems Identify opportunities
Targets	Who are we talking to?			Audience(s) identification	Determine who should be targeted for marketing communications
Resources				Budgets and allocations	Decide how much resource is needed
Objectives	What are we trying to achieve?	Objectives	Where could we be?	Objectives	Set what needs to be achieved
Strategy	How do we expect to achieve it?	Strategy	How could we get there?	Strategy	Develop message, media and marketing communications strategy
Tactics		Tactics		Tactics	Develop message, media and marketing communications tactics Schedule activities including plans to evaluate progress
Implementation		Action		Implementation	Put the plan(s) into action
Evaluation and control		Control	Are we getting there?	Control	Measure and track the effectiveness of the marketing communications

in which to view the marketing communications plan as a whole. Each section within this chapter presents an overview of the key planning issues and summarises them into easy-to-remember headings.

Marketing communications planning can be considered a continuous cycle that consists of a number of activities. Before presenting details of the RABOSTIC model, an overview of Cooper's planning cycle (1997) usefully emphasises the 'circular' nature of the planning process (Exhibit 13.4) and its relationship to the development and implementation of marketing communications plans.

The key stages within Cooper's planning cycle are:

1 *Familiarise:* The first stage in the planning cycle involves the study of the brief from the client and the analysis of existing data, which might consist of published market reports, distribution data like Nielsen, usage and attitude surveys, awareness tracking studies and marketing communications research.

2 *Hypothesise:* Stage two entails the commissioning of more research if necessary in order to define the strategy. There might be several strategic options open for development that need to be identified and which concept research can help to finalise.

Exhibit 13.4 The marketing communications development process and research inputs

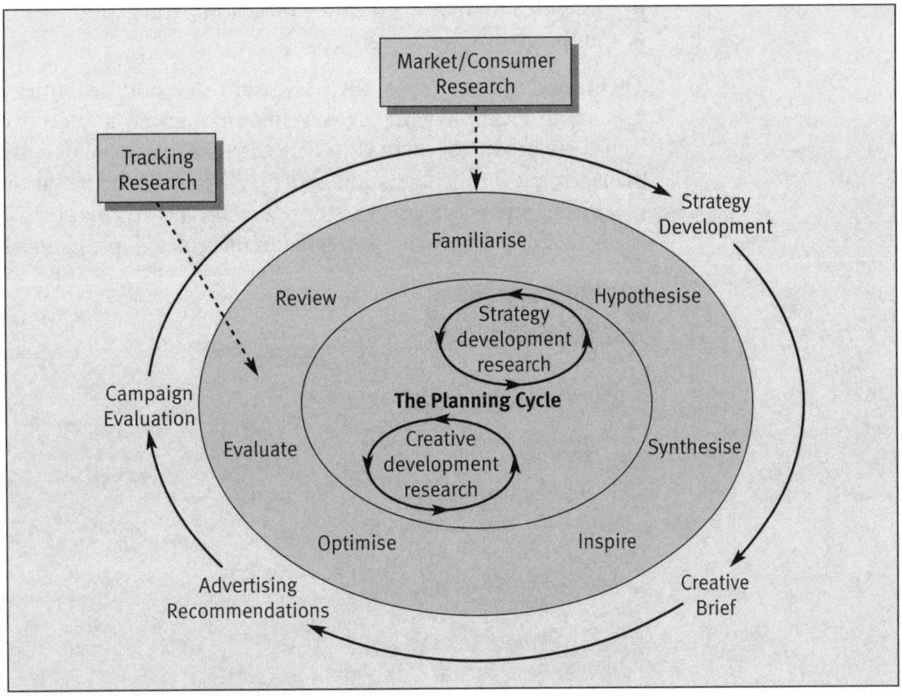

Source: Adapted from Cooper (1997)

3 *Synthesise and inspire:* The third stage includes the briefing of the creative team for the task, having had the client's input and agreed the strategic course for the brand.

4 *Optimise:* The fourth stage involves the commissioning/doing of diagnostic research on initial creative ideas, to determine what effect the promotions will have on attitudes to the brand, and how individual elements will work; discussing implications with the creative team in terms of how any weak aspects in communication or desired effect can be dealt with in this stage.

5 *Evaluate:* Stage five involves the supervision of any pre-testing to ensure that branding and message recall are at satisfactory levels.

6 *Review:* The sixth and final stage in the planning cycle entails the tracking of the results of the marketing communications in terms of sales, awareness and image so that modifications can be made to subsequent campaigns.

The marketing communications plan

The process of planning has been outlined above. Understanding the elements within the process is necessary in order to write your own plans. As an example, In View 13.2 details a complete outline of a plan and the following sections provide an overview:

● Situational analysis: Research and analysis
● Determine marketing communications targets: Audiences
● Setting budget allocations, making resources available: Budgets
● Setting objectives: Objectives

- Strategic decision-making: Strategy
- Operational decision-making: Tactics
- Campaign management: Implementation and action
- Campaign evaluation: Control.

These sections detail the RABOSTIC eight-step outline framework for planning marketing communications campaigns. While an overview of objectives, strategic decisions and tactics are provided, these issues are discussed in more detail in Chapter 19. Campaign management (implementation issues) is discussed further at the end of this chapter and specific elements are covered more extensively in Chapters 20, 21 and 22. Campaign evaluation and control is considered in more detail in Chapter 23.

IN VIEW 13.2

An outline plan

1 Executive summary

2 Situation analysis
  2.1 Company analysis
  2.2 Competitor analysis
  2.3 Consumer analysis
  2.4 Market analysis
  2.5 Product analysis
  2.6 Problems and opportunities

3 Target market profile

4 Objectives
  4.1 Marketing objectives
  4.2 Communication objectives
  4.3 Advertising objectives

5 Marketing communication strategy
  5.1 Advertising strategy
    5.1.1 Creative strategy and execution
      5.1.1.1 Objectives
      5.1.1.2 Strategy
      5.1.1.3 Tactics or executions (in appendix)
    5.1.2 Media strategy
      5.1.2.1 Objectives
      5.1.2.2 Strategy
      5.1.2.3 Tactics or vehicles
      5.1.2.4 Cost estimates
      5.1.2.5 Continuity schedule
  5.2 Sales promotion strategy
  5.3 Public relations strategy
  5.4 Direct marketing strategy
  5.5 Other (such as Event marketing)

6 Campaign evaluation

7 Budget

8 Appendices

Source: Adapted from Parente et al. (1996)

1 Situation analysis: research – 'where are we now?'

The starting point of a plan is an analysis of where the company/brand is now. This analysis of background information is the research foundation that provides the basis for identifying the audience, budgets, objectives, strategy and tactics. The planner needs to have a thorough understanding of market economics, competitor activities, the consumers' relationship with the product category, the consumers' relationship with the individual brands, and the consumers' relationship with the promotions. Chapter 7 presented the **PRESTCOM** framework which can be used for analysing the situation and Exhibit 13.5 gives a flavour of some of the main questions that need to be answered.

PRESTCOM

An extended environmental and organisational analysis framework representing the Political environment, the Regulatory environment, the Economic environment, the Social environment, the Technological environment, the Competitive environment, the Organisational environment, and the Market environment.

Exhibit 13.5 The situation analysis

Structure	*Example content*
Organisational analysis	● What are the company's sales and profits?
	● What is the company's mission and objectives in general and for its various products and services?
	● What financial, technological and managerial resources are available?
	● What have been the results of previous campaigns? How effective have they been and why?
Competitor analysis	● Who are direct and indirect competitors of the brand?
	● What resources do they have?
	● What are the real and perceived distinctions between brands?
	● What have been the competitors' marketing communications in the past? What impact have they had?
	● What do we expect our competitors to do in the future?
Consumer analysis	● Who are the customers and consumers? What are our customer profiles?
	● What motivates them to buy and consume? What are their buying and use habits? How do they respond to our/our competitors' offerings? What are their buying and consumption patterns?
	● What do they look for in the brand? What are their brand perceptions (brand maps)?
Market analysis	● What is the sales distribution pattern?
	● What geographic areas warrant specific attention?
	● What population segment(s) are most likely to respond to the company?
	● What are the market opportunities?
	● What significant changes are taking place with regard to political, regulatory, economic, social and technological forces?
Product analysis	● Does the product have the ability to give consumers what they want?
	● Does the product's total offering promise to deliver or address what consumers want?
	● Does the delivery of the product match consumers' expectations?
	● Are there production and distribution issues affecting the availability of the product?

2 Determine marketing communications targets: audiences – 'who are we talking to?'

Choosing who should be targeted for marketing communications is an early and absolutely vital step in the planning process. It is self-evident that customers or potential customers should be a focus of attention but, sometimes, this blinds us to the fact that very many more audiences may need to be selected. Chapter 1 first identified the distinctions between customers and consumers and highlighted the need to consider other publics or audience groups for our marketing communications attention. Many groups such as the media, friends, colleagues, opinion leaders may be strong influencers in purchase decisions and it may be wise for any marketing communications plan to attempt to favourably influence the influencers. Decision-making groups (or units – DMUs) have also previously been highlighted as important and these may need to be considered as part of the targeting effort. Chapter 17 is devoted to consideration of audiences. Chapters 3 and 4 from Part 1 of the book are also relevant.

3 Setting budget allocations, making resources available: budgets – 'what resources do we need?'

Although identified as the third stage in the RABOSTIC Planning Model, budget setting can occur at various stages. Some companies may specify a budget that the objectives, strategies and tactics have to be tailored to fit. Other companies may permit flexibility in the budget according to what objectives are set. As well as the total financial budget, specific budgets need to be allocated to the various elements of a campaign and this can only satisfactorily be done after the objectives and strategies have been determined.

But budget setting has implications beyond the financial and extends into the broader consideration of resource allocation. Smith et al. (1997) have usefully summarised the relevant issues as the **3Ms**, that is:

3Ms model

Summary of the resource requirement for campaign management including Men (personnel requirements), Money (financial requirements), and Minutes (timing requirements).

● Men (men and women required to carry out the marketing communications tasks)
● Money (budgets) and
● Minutes (time-scale)

While Chapter 18 is devoted to approaches in determining overall financial budgets, as the 3Ms model clarifies, other resources will need to be considered in terms of staffing, expertise and time-scales. Typically, organisations employ outside agencies that specialise in marketing communications activities to support the company's efforts and skills. Chapter 15 features agency operations.

4 Objective setting: objectives – 'what are we trying to achieve?'

An objective is 'the goal or aim or end result that one is seeking to achieve' (Butterfield 1997). Objectives are necessary for planning operations at all levels of the business. There may be corporate objectives, financial objectives, marketing objectives, and broad marketing communications objectives as well as objectives for each element of the marketing communications mix. Objectives are hierarchically related with corporate objectives at the 'top', but they should be interrelated for integrated planning to be successful.

AIDA model

Marketing communications concept that models the stages through which marketing communications should move a potential customer: Awareness, Interest, Desire and Action. It is one of a number of hierarchy-of-effects models.

Marketing communications objectives typically refer to sales and/or to the goals the marketing communications have in affecting the mind of the target audience. **AIDA** (attention, interest, desire, action) is one model that identifies the various stages a buyer goes through before buying and objectives may be related to these. For example,

Wonderbra's 'Hello Boys' advertisement has attention-generation as a clear objective (Plate 15). This and other hierarchy of response models have been discussed in Chapter 4.

It is argued that objectives should be SMARRTT: specific, measurable, achievable, realistic, relevant, targeted and timed (Exhibit 13.6) because of the benefits this creates. **SMARRTT objectives** ensure a planner has clear and precise goals to build the strategy and against which to evaluate the campaign. In practice, there are many examples where objectives 'fail' the SMARRTT test as they are frequently ambiguous and badly worded. There may be many reasons for this, some of which may be justified. But as a rule of thumb, it is wise to try to make objectives as SMARRTT as possible unless there is a good reason not to.

SMARRTT objectives

Acronym that represents the level of detail that objectives should aim to achieve. It is a development from 'SMART' objectives that are referred to by some other authors. SMARRTT objectives are Specific, Measurable, Achievable, Realistic, Relevant, Targeted and Timed.

Exhibit 13.6 SMARRTT objectives

Objectives	Why?
Specific	Objectives should be clear, precise and directional about what is to be achieved
Measurable	Objectives should possess a quantified measurement statement (e.g. a percentage or absolute amount to be achieved) to enable precise evaluation of the campaign
Achievable	Objectives should be capable of being reached, in that the company/department/ suppliers have the resources to achieve the objectives set
Realistic	Objectives set should be realistic. For example, large brand adoption percentages of a new product in short time-scales are unrealistic. Unrealistic objectives are demoralising when the goals are not met and are subject to poor evaluation
Relevant	Objectives should be appropriate for the task at hand. Once a problem or task is identified, the specific objectives should address that problem
Targeted	All objectives should be related to the target audience(s) that are to be reached. If there is more than one target audience group in the campaign, objectives will be needed for each
Timed	Objectives should have a clearly stated time frame to indicate by which time they are expected to be achieved. This enables the scheduling of the campaign to be monitored and indicates when the results can be evaluated

5 Strategic decision-making: strategy – 'how could we get there?'

Strategy provides the direction for all those involved in the campaign to follow. It provides the framework within which they should operate. It is the means by which marketing communications are intended to achieve the objectives stated.

Marketing communications strategy should recognise who the campaign is talking to (the target audiences), what the campaign wants the target(s) to do, and what the campaign can tell the targets to influence them. By way of example, Exhibit 13.7 outlines four strategic decisions that may be taken at this stage of the planning process.

The actual nature of the strategy will vary according to the objectives set, the budget available and the nature of the marketing communications intended. The strategies shown in Exhibit 13.7 emphasise the focus on the brand but in the wider context of marketing communications other issues may come into play. Public relations activities, for example, may have a different target audience than the brand's customers and may have somewhat different objectives to fulfil.

Exhibit 13.7 Strategic decisions

Four key strategic decision areas	Decision-making goals
Brand values	The identification and choice between those consumer motivations and perceptions that can be represented in the brand and by which marketing communications is able to create or influence
Unique selling proposition	The concept by which the brand can be perceived to meet the needs of the target audience uniquely
Competitive positioning	How the brand's values and USP are communicated to the target audience in a way that maximises the brand's differential advantage over competition
Competitive activity	How the competitive advantage can be maintained against erosion in the marketplace over time

IN VIEW 13.3

Clerical Medical

Clerical Medical appointed Butterfield Day Devito Hockney (BDDH) to help them develop a campaign in the, what was then, newly deregulated financial services market. The problems Clerical Medical faced were legion: small share, distributed indirectly (through IFAs) at a time when the market was increasingly moving towards direct contact, disparate product ranges (pensions, investments and life assurance), no clear brand positioning or history of advertising and a name that was not only dull but also misleading (they don't do medical insurance!). In fact Clerical Medical had been set up in 1824 to look after the financial needs of clerics (the clergy) and doctors – two of the leading professions of that era.

Early exploratory qualitative research (at the time of the pitch) had been set up by the agency to examine the general attributes of companies in the sector. One of the techniques used in the research was that most basic of all: an adjective card sort exercise. As the cards, bearing single words like 'upmarket', 'friendly', 'secure', 'modern' etc., were being spread around the floor of the venue, one respondent leant forward and plucked a card bearing the word 'professional' from the array.

'That's interesting,' he said, 'I've never thought of one of these companies catering for professionals.' (In fact, ironically, the card had originally been written to describe a company's approach, not its audience.) Nevertheless, this was indeed the 'blinding flash' – the groups that followed merely served to confirm the power of a strategic and creative route based on the idea of 'professional'.

All the pieces suddenly slotted into place: 'Professional' explained Clerical Medical's name and origins, it flattered and motivated the professional IFA intermediaries, and it (accurately) reflected the more upmarket bias of the company's product range and current customer base. More important still, interpreted in an inclusive way, it formed the basis of a campaign based on the line 'The Choice of the Professional' that in turn was powerful and effective in bringing in new customers – particularly from the wealthier ABC 1 segment.

Source: Butterfield (1997)

6 Operational decision-making: tactics – 'what specific activities do we need to do to get there?'

The tactics section of the planning process details the specific activities and events that are going to be undertaken to address the objectives. They follow on from the strategy formulation. The most convenient way to think about tactics is to think about them as the elements of the marketing communications mix. This is not entirely accurate, though, as each of the elements can also be considered at a more strategic level too, so one can talk both in terms of PR or sales promotions strategies as well as PR and sales promotions tactics.

7 Campaign management: implementation and action

Although implementation is clearly the ultimate expression of the campaign plan, it is not so much part of the plan as the putting of the plan into action. Until this is done, plans are only a paper exercise. Implementation is, thus, the day-to-day running or operationalisation of what the plan intended to do when put into action. This requires campaign management to ensure a smooth operation as many things can go wrong or situations change during the campaign period. Plans may have to be re-written. All resources have to be managed in terms of people, money and time schedules as the campaign progresses. Many agencies may be involved in the implementation process from direct marketing agencies and fulfilment houses to packaging specialists and printers. For the purposes of this text, three chapters are included in the context of implementation, Chapter 20 – Creative Implementation, Chapter 21 – Media Implementation, and Chapter 22 – Production Implementation. These three chapters contain the more detailed aspects of creative, media and production executions. Stage 8, the continuous monitoring of progress, is important throughout the implementation period as well as at its end.

8 Campaign evaluation: control – 'are we getting there?'

Marketing communication campaigns need to be evaluated primarily in terms of:

1 their efficiency – how productive is the campaign in terms of providing value for money, and
2 their effectiveness – how productive is the campaign in terms of achieving what it is supposed to be achieving.

While a campaign should clearly be evaluated against the SMARRTT objectives set, there is often no single, simple and reliable way in which to measure all marketing communications effects. A good approach is to measure more than one level of effect in order to build an overall picture of how customers and other targeted audiences are responding to the campaign (Exhibit 13.8).

When evaluating a campaign, the planner should address the following questions:

● What was expected to happen?
● What did happen?
● What was the effect of each of the marketing communications elements as well as their collective effect? Can these effects be separated from other factors?
● What were the reasons for success or failure?
● What was learnt from the campaign?
● What should happen next? What does this tell us that we can learn for the next planning period?

Exhibit 13.8 Common measures of marketing communications effects

Type of effect	Relevant research
Retail sales	Retail audit Consumer audit
Direct sales	% response to direct communications % conversion to sales
Consumer buying behaviour	Panel data Own transactional data
Claimed consumer behaviour	Survey research
Attitude to brand	Survey/qualitative research
Perceptions/image of brand	Survey/qualitative research
Awareness of brand	Survey research
Attitudes to/communication of advertising	Survey/qualitative research
Recall of advertising	Survey research
Exposure to advertising	Media research

Source: Adapted from Cooper (1997)

Campaign management

Campaign management has numerous implications for the planning process, and it is useful to consider these in more detail. The management of campaigns should address the questions detailed on the left side of Exhibit 13.9 and organise the activities detailed on the right.

As the 3Ms model presented earlier in the chapter, i.e. Money, Minutes and Men, provides a useful framework, this section will cover these three areas together with creative, media and production planning issues.

Money

The financial justification of the marketing communications effort needs to be presented as a business case in terms of costings and forecasts. The forecasts may be based on the 'baseline' (what has happened in previous promotions), industry averages, industry 'best in class', consultative or expert input and sales force input.

Exhibit 13.9 The processes of effective campaign management

● What are the functions to be performed, whose responsibilities?	**Campaign flow**
● Do we need internal or external resource?	**Resource management**
● What do we need from our internal/external suppliers?	**Briefing**
● How long does it take, what should be the sequencing?	**Scheduling**
● What does it cost, are we being cost efficient and effective?	**Budgetary control**

Money plans are often presented in a campaign schedule. This details the tactical activities and events planned, the dates of these events, the projected expenses and revenues, and the contingency plans. The contingency plan may include a monetary reserve in case of unexpected costs and any clashes in the schedule caused by media or production bottlenecks.

IN VIEW 13.4

Integrated calendar of events

Months	1	2	3	4	5	6
Sales force integration	■	■	■	■	■	■
Print advertising	■	■	■			
Direct mail	Event	ETA				
Outbound telemarketing	■	■				
Follow-up mailings		■		■		
Confirmation calls		■		■		■
Events/ appointments		■		■		■
Follow-up mail/phone			■		■	
Ongoing communication		■		■		■
Lead generation	■	■	■	■	■	■

Minutes

A detailed sequence of timed tactical activities are often presented in an activity schedule and graphically illustrated in a calendar of events. The activity schedule details what is to be done, the interdependence of actions, the critical pathways (identification of potential bottlenecks), the status of the project, slippage and revised timings. In View 13.4 could be very much more detailed and the actual elements identified would be a function of the elements used in the campaign plan. The time periods could be expressed in days or weeks rather than months if TV or daily newspapers are used as part of the media schedule. Media plans, as will be seen in Chapter 21, typically are shown as schedules of this type. Exhibit 13.10 outlines common campaign status reporting language used on plans.

Exhibit 13.10 Campaign status reporting

Terminology	Explanation
'Provisional'	Task, decision or resource has been identified but formal approval has not yet been sought
'Submitted'	Awaiting approval
'Approved'	Approval provided with timings
'Budgeted'	Budgetary approval provided
'Development'	Suppliers have been briefed and the 'meter is ticking'
'Live'	Campaign hits the marketplace
'Completed'	No further activity necessary
'Closed'	Analysed/documented

Men

The project file includes the campaign plan, team members and responsibilities, briefing forms, timetables, materials descriptions, events descriptions, authorisations and forecasts. When thinking about the personnel issues in planning it is important to identify the internal and external resources required, and who is responsible for which tasks. The following three subsections detail the marketing resources that need to be planned:

- in-house versus outsourcing personnel (the choice of using company-owned or marketing communications agency resources),
- the creative brief (detailing the interaction between internal and external resources), and
- the media planning process.

In-house versus outsourcing personnel

A marketing communications plan is frequently developed by a marketing director and her or his staff, but one or more marketing communications agencies may also be involved in its preparation. If outsourcing is selected, the client company works alongside its agency(ies) to interpret its brand to its target audience in terms of a marketing communications campaign (the execution of the marketing communications plan).

As discussed in Chapter 15, typical roles in a client–agency relationship include:

- the client marketing manager
- the agency account director
- the agency creative team
- the agency planner.

The account manager or director is the key contact that mediates between the specialists in the agency and the client's marketing (brand) manager or director. Account managers orchestrate the whole marketing communications development process, and have ultimate responsibility for the strategy and creative brief.

The creative team produce the marketing communications themselves and an account planner, where used, ensures that an understanding of consumer attitudes and reactions is brought to bear at every stage of the development of a campaign. The planner brings a consumer and market perspective to strategy development, creative development, pre-testing of marketing communications and tracking of the brand's progress. The planner uses market and research data to guide this process. Most good creative teams want to know the consumer beyond a mere demographic definition. They want to know about the kind of attitudes held – to the product category, to the brand, to promotions in this market. They want to know what the consumer wants, rather than what the client wants. The good planner brings this sharply into focus – like an expressive photograph.

The account planner works with other members of the agency team, the client's research department and research suppliers. The planner implements a disciplined and systematic approach to the creation of marketing communications. As an overview, the planner will be concerned with the relevance of the marketing communications to the target audience, and its effectiveness in the market. This is done by bringing a consumer perspective to the marketing communications in order that the brand and the consumer (in particular and other audiences in general) are drawn together. Put a little simplistically but in a way that makes the point:

Client says: 'My product'.

Account director says: 'My client'.

Creative director says: 'My ad'.

Planner says: 'My consumer'.

In the strategy development stage the planner will collect and synthesise data to guide strategic development. This is done by understanding attitudes and behaviour of people; by gaining insight into the consumer relationship with the brand and the marketing communications; by understanding the competitive situation and the market forces and conditions. Then the planner will help define the positioning and relevant proposition that encapsulates the rational and emotional appeals of the brand. Of course, the marketing personnel of the client company itself should be well versed in these issues, too, and where an account planner is not used, the brand manager or her equivalent will have to be responsible for providing these insights.

In the creative development stage, the planner will commission diagnostic research on creative mock-ups to check whether the marketing communications is achieving the desired responses. Feedback will be gained on how the marketing communications is working and what effect it is having. Marketing communications responses will be interpreted with sensitivity in order to stimulate the creative process further but not all creatives agree as to the benefits of such research on their creative decisions.

In the approval stage, the planner will help to provide reassurance on how and why the particular piece of marketing communications will work for the brand. In the post-campaign stage, the planner will commission and use research to track the progress of the brand.

The creative brief

The creative process starts with the strategy development which produces the creative brief (or briefs), which leads to the initial creative work produced typically by one or more marketing communications agencies.

Creative briefing is pivotal because it represents the stage in the marketing communications process where the strategic understanding developed by company personnel reaches the external specialists whose jobs it is to really solve the creative problem (Butterfield 1997). In View 13.5 outlines a typical creative brief used by Bartle, Bogle and Hegarty advertising agency. More details are provided in Chapter 20.

IN VIEW 13.5

A creative brief form

Client	
The product is:	
The brand is:	
The role of advertising: a. What do we want people to do as a result of seeing this advertising? b. How do we believe the advertising will work to achieve this?	
Who are we talking to?	
What is the single most important thing this advertising should convey? a. Why should people believe this? b. What practical considerations are there?	
Date Job no. 1st review Final sign-off Creative director Team leader Budget estimate £ Media	

Source: adapted from Butterfield (1997)

The media planning process

The media plan comprises audiences, objectives, strategy and tactical decisions on media selection. The functions of media planning can be summarised as **AMBA**: Audience, Media, Buying and Assessment.

AMBA model

Media planning process model that includes Audience, Media, Buying and Assessment.

● Audience: the target audience must be assessed in media terms; what are the types of media the target audience consumes?
● Medium/media choice: the media available needs to be evaluated and the considerations of intra-media choice made (Exhibit 13.11).
● Buying media efficiently: research needs to be conducted to enable the media buyer to get the best rates from the medium and achieve a competitive rate for the target audience reach.
● Assessment: the efficiency of the media plan pre- and post-activity must be analysed.

Further details on the media can be found in Chapters 5 and 6 and more information on media planning are given in Chapter 21.

Exhibit 13.11 Differences in media

	TV	Cinema	Radio	Press and magazines	Outdoor	Internet
Budget issues	High cost entry	Expensive	Cheap	Variable costs but easy to buy	Expensive	Cheap to try
Media planning issues	Dramatic Important, influential Difficult for small targets	Even more dramatic than TV Slow coverage build	Can catch people 'in situ' (e.g. driving) Limited coverage Station demographics differ widely	Personal medium Regional variation Low impact	'Loud' Quick Research limited so far	'Trendy' Conversational in tone Small penetration

Source: Adapted from Cooper (1997)

Production

Chapter 22 looks at the area of production specifically. Basically, unless marketing communications items are produced, there are no marketing communications (except for personal communications by word of mouth). TV ads have to be produced, radio commercials have to be produced, any form of print such as advertising or leaflets and brochures have to be produced. Exhibition displays have to be produced, sales promotion items and promotional giveaways have to be produced. Signage and packaging have to be produced. Yet this whole area of production is simply not addressed in so many textbooks. Indeed, it is an aspect of marketing communications that many will have no direct experience of, even though it is frequently the specialists in marketing communications agencies who take responsibility for such output. Yet production is such an important aspect of the marketing communications business. Because production involves so many aspects, not all can be covered here in this text, but Chapter 22 does focus on print production as it is a part of a vast amount of promotional activity.

Summary

This chapter has outlined the communications planning process and marketing communications plans. It has provided an important framework, the IMC RABOSTIC Planning Model, that can be used for the eight stages in the marketing communications planning process in determining subsequent plans:

1 Situational analysis: Research and analysis
2 Determine marketing communications targets: Audiences
3 Setting budget allocations, making resources available: Budgets
4 Setting objectives: Objectives
5 Strategic decision-making: Strategy
6 Operational decision-making: Tactics
7 Campaign management: Implementation and action
8 Campaign evaluation: Control

The IMC RABOSTIC Planning Model also identifies the Research and Decision-making Cycle and the Information Stream as integral parts of the planning process. The chapter also highlighted that each of the chapters in Part 2 of this book take the RABOSTIC elements in turn and present them in greater detail.

The final part of this chapter addressed issues of campaign management and emphasised their importance to the successful implementation of marketing communications activities.

Self-review questions

1 Describe the differences between objectives, strategy and tactics.

2 What are the six key stages in Cooper's planning cycle?

3 Outline the eight stages of the IMC RABOSTIC Planning Model and how they are used in developing marketing communications plans.

4 Explain the value of SMARRTT objectives.

5 What does the 3Ms model say about campaign management?

6 What is the account planner's role in a marketing communications agency?

7 Describe the functions of media planning outlined by the AMBA model.

Project

As part of its subsidiary business activity a major airline is about to launch a new executive wine and leisure club called 'Life's Great Pleasures'. The club is aimed at upmarket business executives aged between 25 and 54. The club will offer cases of the world's finest wines at discount rates, together with a range of food/wine/travel-related offers such as tasting evenings, 'gourmet' weekends and visits to famous wine-growing regions around the world.

As well as providing an added-value service to existing business travel customers, the new club would hopefully provide a rich source of new business travel prospects.

A number of profitability models had been developed to assess the viability of the new club and a margin of £30 per new club member was agreed upon to assist promotional costs. The budget is €200,000 to launch the product.

As a member of the marketing team your task is to identify the target audiences at whom your campaign will be aimed and a comprehensive set of SMARRTT marketing communications objectives around which the product launch will be designed. Produce a 10-minute presentation to the marketing director with your output.

(*Source*: Adapted from The Institute of Direct Marketing diploma, 1999)

References

Butterfield, L. (1997), *Excellence in Advertising*. The Institute of Practitioners in Advertising, Oxford: Butterworth-Heinemann.

Cooper, A. (1997), *How to Plan Advertising*. The Account Planning Group, London: Cassell.

Kotler, P. (2003), *Marketing Management – Analysis, Planning, Implementation and Control* 11th edn. Prentice Hall.

Linton, I. and Morley, K. (1995), *Integrated Marketing Communications*. The Chartered Institute of Marketing, Oxford: Butterworth-Heinemann.

McDonald, M. (1995), *Marketing Plans – How to Prepare Them: How to Use Them* 3rd edn. Butterworth-Heinemann.

Parente, D., Vanden Bergh, B., Barban, A. and Marra, J. (1996), *Advertising Campaign Strategy*. Orlando: The Dryden Press.

Smith, P., Berry, C. and Pulford, A. (1997), *Strategic Marketing Communications*. London: Kogan Page.

Wilson, R.M.S. and Gilligan, C. (1998), *Strategic Marketing Management* 2nd edn. Butterworth-Heinemann.

Selected further reading

Burnett, J. (1993), *Promotion Management*. Boston: Houghton Mifflin.

Dacey, J.S. (1989), *Fundamentals of Creative Thinking*. Lexington Books.

Forsth, L. and Nordvik, B. (1995), Building a vision – a practical guide. *Creativity and Innovation Management*, 4 (4), 251–257.

Mintzberg, H., Quinn, J.B. and Ghoshal, S. (1995), *The Strategy Process* European edn. Prentice Hall.

Ries, A. and Trout, J. (1982), *Positioning: the Battle for Your Mind*. New York: Warner Books.

Chapter 14

Organisational implications of integrated marketing communications

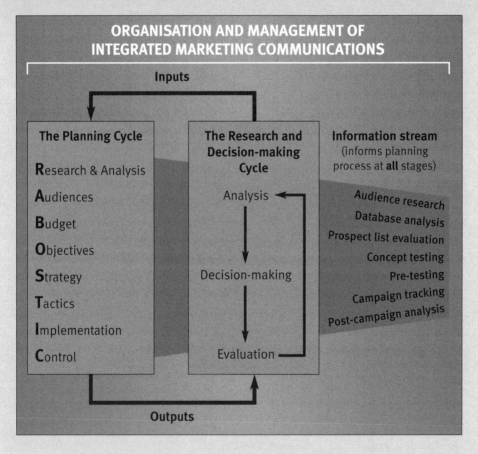

ORGANISATION AND MANAGEMENT OF INTEGRATED MARKETING COMMUNICATIONS

Inputs

The Planning Cycle

Research & Analysis

Audiences

Budget

Objectives

Strategy

Tactics

Implementation

Control

The Research and Decision-making Cycle

Analysis

Decision-making

Evaluation

Information stream
(informs planning process at **all** stages)

Audience research
Database analysis
Prospect list evaluation
Concept testing
Pre-testing
Campaign tracking
Post-campaign analysis

Outputs

The IMC RABOSTIC Planning Model

CD

Using the information in Case Study 2 on the CD and your own research, identify the range of agencies used by Škoda in developing its integrated marketing communications campaign for the Fabia. Referring to Exhibits 14.2 to 14.6, which of these structures do you believe best illustrates that used by Škoda? Critically evaluate to what extent marketing communications integration has been achieved using this organisational structure. What impact on the overall campaign outcome did Škoda's internal communications and communications with its retailers have?

Chapter outline
- The organisation and management task
- Marketing communications are fragmented!
- Organisation of what?
- Who should be organised for integrated marketing communications – client or agency?
- Organisational barriers to integration
- Organising for integrated marketing communications
- The role and importance of the database in integrated marketing communications

Objectives
- To generate an appreciation of the issues and difficulties involved in organising for integrated marketing communications
- To emphasise the fragmented nature of marketing communications
- To identify the major barriers to organisational integration of marketing communications
- To offer some outline suggestions of ways in which integrated marketing communications may be organised
- To emphasise the importance of database management within the organisational structure for today's integrated marketing communications

Professional perspective

Adrian Vickers Founder, Abbott Mead Vickers BBDO

The marketing communications industry is a large and distinctive industry represented by many diverse groups whose interests are frequently focused towards particular aspects of the profession – advertising, media buying, sales promotions, account planning, creative development, direct mail, corporate identity, the new media, public relations, print buying, brand naming, film production, packaging and so the list goes on. Each group brings to the party its own perspective, specialism and expertise.

As agencies and their clients seek to improve the integration of their marketing communications, the task of organising and managing the many people involved becomes increasingly problematical. Yet this is a challenge that must be faced in partnership. Occasionally, it is a challenge faced with conflicting interests.

Client response to this challenge is mixed – so are the solutions provided by agencies. Some have formed groups of marketing communications specialists who are used to co-operating if that is what the client brief requires. But the industry seems likely to remain significantly fragmented, not just because of vested interests, but also because the skills brought to bear within each specialism are unique and precious. While there may be no single solution, there are many factors that have a bearing on the 'how to organise?' and 'how to manage?' questions. This chapter and other parts of the book should be read to gain insight into these.

The solution to the challenge set by integrated marketing communications will develop to match client needs. Many agencies who are specialists today may encourage the development of more generalist skills in some of their people. The marketing communications industry thrives on diversity. Clients and agencies alike will seek and find their own solutions to the task of integration. This has been true over all the years I have been in advertising. And the success of the industry speaks for itself. It has spawned a vast, thriving, dynamic, creative, and very enjoyable world in which to work.

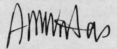

The organisation and management task

FOOD FOR THOUGHT

One of the greatest challenges facing the marketing communications industry is the achievement of integrated marketing communications.

Chapter 2 highlighted a range of features, dimensions and levels of integrated marketing communications (IMC) and identified a number of barriers to it being achieved. These issues are picked up again in Chapter 23 which considers the evaluation and control of IMC. Among those barriers was the structure of organisations. Unless IMC is managed and organised appropriately, it will not succeed. This is probably the greatest challenge facing IMC and the marketing communications industry.

The momentum has begun. Integration is now a fundamental and growing part of the marketing communications business. The question no longer is 'should we integrate?' but, rather, 'how can we integrate?' Integration is taking place, it is merely done better by some than others and there is no single best approach, it is a question of managerial choice. The task, however, becomes more complex under certain circumstances. Six factors can be identified.

- *Size of business.* Theoretically, smaller businesses should have less difficulty in ensuring integration of their marketing communications activities than large companies. They often do not because of other issues such as ignorance of the problem, lack of expertise and fewer resources. The larger the company, the more operating divisions, the greater the number of brands, the more people involved, the more complex the integration problem becomes and the more necessary it becomes, too.

NEED TO KNOW

There is no one, single, best approach to how marketing communications should be organised to achieve integration. It is for managers to decide the most suitable approach to adopt in the light of prevailing circumstances affecting the organisation.

- *Number of stakeholders and audiences.* As the number of stakeholder and audience groups increase (people with vested interests in the company including shareholders, suppliers, employees, consumer rights groups, the media, lobbyists, customers and consumers) so does the marketing communications task and the problems associated with its organisation.
- *Type of business.* An industrial capital goods supplier will have very different marketing communications needs and processes than **FMCG** companies. There will be a very different customer base, a different means of operating the business and a very different emphasis in the use of the promotional mix.

FMCG

Fast-Moving Consumer Goods – typified, for example, by such products as soap powders, cosmetics, sweets and crisps.

- *Diversity of marketing communications.* This is very much related to the above points. The greater the diversity of marketing communications activities, the greater the complexity of task. This diversity may be somewhat dictated by the size and nature of the business as well as its aims and objectives.

- *Locus of business activity – local, national or global.* The more international or global business operations become, the more emphasis that has to be put on the means of integrating marketing communications. Some argue that it is the globalisation of companies that has provided one of the strongest forces for integration and the impetus for client companies and their agencies to operate in a much more integrated fashion. For example, McCann-Erickson Worldwide is an early example of an agency going international to serve Exxon, a major client, and to follow Coca-Cola as it penetrated world markets (Griffin 1993).

- *Distribution system(s) operated.* Companies choosing to distribute their goods and services directly to end customers and users face a very different marketing communications task than those who operate through intermediaries such as agents, wholesalers and retailers. The longer the distribution chain becomes and the greater the number of distribution systems used, the more challenging the marketing communications effort becomes and the more complex becomes the organisational task.

NEED TO KNOW

☑ *The longer the distribution chain and the greater number of distribution systems used, the more complex the organisational task becomes to control integrated marketing communications. The integration of marketing communications for a direct marketing operation is very different to the integration of marketing communications for an operation using intermediaries.*

Organisational implications arise directly from the features of IMC listed in Chapter 2 and the problems of both planning and implementation. The fundamental need is to realign marketing communications to look at it the way the customers and other stakeholders and audiences see it – that is as a flow of information from indistinguishable sources (Schultz et al. 1994) or as Schultz has also phrased it, it requires an '**outside-in approach**' (Schultz 1993). Moriarty (1994) has put the problem succinctly,

Outside-in approach to integrated marketing communications

Way of looking at marketing communications by adopting a perspective that starts by first looking outside the organisation for direction and understanding of the task required, and then determines marketing communications by secondly considering the organisation itself. It is a perspective determined by playing the role of an outsider looking into the organisation.

A totally integrated communications program accounts for all types of messages delivered by an organisation at every point where a stakeholder comes into contact with the company. (p. 38)

Ogilvy and Mather have referred to the process of integration as '**orchestration**'. This is particularly appropriate from the point of view of managing and organising integration. We can use the analogy of an orchestra to illustrate different ways of achieving integration. The writer of marketing communications plans is like a composer. It is then the job of the conductor to interpret those 'plans' and act as a leader and controller of the orchestra; setting the pace, tempo and co-ordination. The members of the orchestra are the specialists, just as we find specialists in each area of the promotional mix. They implement the plan and work together as a team. Without the musical score and conductor (the plan and the controller), their contributions would result in chaos.

Orchestration

Graphic way of referring to the process of integrating marketing communications.

A similar but different approach can be seen in a jazz, rather than classical, orchestra. It becomes a different way of managing the task. There is still the need for an overall 'plan' but rather than having a single 'supreme' leader, the musicians work together by agreement and previously determined rules. They will all 'integrate' on the basis of the piece being played but will be allowed much greater freedom than with classical music. They will be allowed to improvise around agreed musical themes and will shift the emphasis from one instrument to another around those themes, one musician leading at one point in time, then another. It is much more an 'organic' rather than 'mechanistic' approach. So too with marketing communications – its managers work as a team. While working to an overall strategic IMC plan they may be allowed freedom to 'improvise' within that plan, different elements of the promotional mix being given emphasis at different times depending upon prevailing needs.

FOOD FOR THOUGHT

Integration requires strategic planning at the highest level and excellent internal communications throughout the organisation.

Whatever the way selected for integration, strategic planning at the highest level is necessary together with excellent communication between all those involved. Management must decide how this is to be achieved.

McKinsey's 7S approach to management

One very popular and useful way to conceptualise the management task is to consider the 7S model developed by the consultants, McKinsey. Their model highlights the seven variables critical to successful implementation. All of the variables are interrelated and rely on each other for organisational success. The 7S model applies very well to integrated marketing communications.

- *Structure* – organisational and management structure. Defined responsibilities and reporting hierarchies. Who is responsible for what and for whom.
- *Strategy* – direction and means.
- *Skills* – organisational capabilities and competencies.
- *Staffing* – people, their development, deployment, management and working relationships.
- *Style* – leadership approach, management style.
- *Systems* – practices and procedures.
- *Shared values* – internal communication, beliefs, attitudes, culture, shared understanding.

Marketing communications are fragmented!

Whether we like it or not, all the various elements of marketing communications are fragmented and are likely to stay so because of the need for specialists. In reality, it is impossible to conceive of a situation in which one person or organisation is able to

IN VIEW 14.1

Outside-in not inside-out

Marketing principles have long extolled the virtues of starting with the customer and working back to the organisation. Some have criticised marketing communications for failing to do this. Emphasis has been on the organisation first and the customer second. Don Shultz, a leading exponent of IMC, calls for an 'outside-in' approach rather than an 'inside-out' approach.

'Start with the customer or prospect and work back to the brand or organisation. That's the outside-in approach. Most organisations are structured to deliver inside-out communications. That is, they're set up to send out messages when they want to send them, to people they want to send them to, in the form they want to use, at the time they want to send them, and so on. Much of this approach is dictated by the budget cycle or when money is available. Unfortunately, customers and prospects don't necessarily need or want communications when the organisation wants to communicate. They need and want communication when it is right for them.'

Source: Schultz (1993)

FOOD FOR THOUGHT

The nature of marketing communications is fundamentally fragmented.

master all the various aspects of the marketing communications function, the task is too diverse. Michael Finn in In View 14.2 quotes the view expressed by one marketing director on the subject.

Throughout the industry we see specialists in every aspect of marketing communications from corporate identity work to mailing houses. Given the nature of marketing communications, integrated or not, it is difficult to conceive of situations where one organisation attempts to carry out all the work 'in-house'. It is possible, but not usually practical. Even the smallest of businesses go to printers for help in designing and producing stationery and leaflets, even if they do not use any other 'agent'.

In Chapter 7, The Changing Marketing Communications Environment, the large number of 'players' in the industry were identified. These ranged from clients, agencies and media owners to professional and regulatory bodies. With so many 'specialists' involved it is not hard to appreciate why it can be so difficult to integrate every aspect of marketing communications and why, until more recently, it has not even really been tried. But it should be emphasised that IMC is *not* about one organisation trying to do everything itself. It is about orchestrating the many specialists who each form part of the total marketing communications effort. It should also be recognised that the fragmentation of marketing communications is not confined to the range of specialist agencies and bodies external to client companies. The internal structures of the clients' own organisations also encourage fragmentation. 'Marketing' is separated from 'personnel', which is separated from 'accounts', etc. Even those activities we associate with marketing are fragmented so 'sales' becomes separated from 'advertising' which is separated from 'corporate communications' which is separated from 'customer service' and so on. They are separated to enhance the expertise of specialists, but in doing so make it difficult to ensure the achievement of the 4Es and 4Cs of IMC identified in Chapter 2. In that chapter, it was suggested that integrated marketing communications should be Economical, Efficient, Effective, and Enhancing; and that they should be Coherent, Consistent, Complementary and maintain Continuity.

FOOD FOR THOUGHT

It is unlikely that marketing communications will be successfully integrated unless the internal organisation within client organisations is first addressed. Departments within organisations exist to enhance specialism yet they also tend to discourage integration.

IN VIEW 14.2

He knows a man who can

Michael Finn, Managing Director of Duckworth Finn Grubb Waters, tells of a conversation he had with a marketing director of a large FMCG company. When asking about that company's policy towards integration he was told that their criteria was to buy the best. 'Likely to get it all in one place?' he asked. 'Unlikely,' was the reply. 'John Hegarty of Bartle Bogle Hegarty will create a great enduring advertising campaign for you, but for the fulfilment pack, he knows a man who can. In theory, it would be wonderful to get all your specialised requirements in one place. I just don't believe it is possible to be specialist at everything – witness the demise of department stores, quite good at a lot of things, but not good enough at most of them.'

Source: Finn (1994)

Some suggest that the best way to organise IMC is by putting all the specialisations together within one internal division and with one all-embracing agency. Eisenhart's research in America as long ago as 1989 revealed what he called a trend for organisations to physically integrate into one department the people responsible for the various marketing communications functions (Eisenhart 1989). Many client organisations, however, which have tried to structure themselves for integration have not chosen this route, favouring instead to encourage greater communications and joint working practices between different parts of the organisation, sometimes under the leadership of a senior management coordinator. General Motors, for example, set up a 'Communication Council' of 41 communicators and directors throughout the corporation. Collectively, they agreed and prioritised tasks and appointed 'Stakeholder Communication Teams', composed of a 'champion', a lead coordinator and other departmental representatives, to carry them out (Prescott 1991).

Organisation of what?

Chapter 23 makes it explicit that the integration of marketing communications is something that exists to varying extents. It can take place at different *levels* from strategic to tactical, from corporate to local promotions. It can take place to different *degrees* from total integration to very little integration, which can lead to dysfunctional communications and suffer from negative effects. It can be seen to operate in different *dimensions*, involving integration of a whole variety of aspects, not just integration of the promotional mix. *All* these various 'parts' which come together to make IMC need to be organised both *within* the client organisation and *outside* it, bringing together all the relevant agencies that need to be involved. The organisational task is one that is determined by managerial preferences, resources and the scale of integration sought. The task of achieving integration, however, should not be under-estimated. It requires a great deal of planning and managerial effort.

Who should be organised for integrated marketing communications – client or agency?

The answer is that both clients and agencies, *and all other parties involved*, need to be appropriately organised to achieve integrated marketing communications. To the extent that a client organisation may be willing to accept less than full integration, this may be reflected in a less than fully integrated organisational setting.

Michael Finn, quoted earlier, gave the example of an FMCG marketing director who was happy to select his agencies on the basis of their individual expertise. His company, as client, provided the integrating force. Finn (1994), however, also hold the view that one of the driving forces of integration is the reduction in size of marketing departments. With limited resources available at their disposal, they look for an 'integrated' agency to do the work for them. Apparently, here are two opposing standpoints – should it be the client or the agency who integrates marketing communications? In essence, they are merely two ways of trying to achieve the same aim. The best outcome is for them both to be involved in, and organised for, integration.

NEED TO KNOW

☑ *Integration requires that all parties involved in the marketing communications effort should be organised to achieve greatest effect.*

IN VIEW 14.3

Views differ about the management of integrated marketing communications

Gary Moss, a senior executive at Campbell Soup and formally an executive at J. Walter Thompson, USA, is a firm believer in IMC, but equally strongly believes that integration should be the client's, not the agency's responsibility. The client must reserve the right to choose whatever agency is needed, carry out work in-house where necessary and not depend on one agency.

Conversely, Mark Goldstein, president of Earle Palmer Brown Advertising, believes that agencies are capable of coordinating IMC programmes and that they, not the client's ever-changing brand management staff, should control it. Goldstein sees the biggest barrier to IMC as the client's short-term emphasis on sales targets, but he emphasises too that in order for agencies to do the job they must reorganise themselves.

Rob Nolan, vice-chairman of Creative Services, Leo Burnett, points out it does not matter who controls IMC as long as somebody does – it is a question of getting on with the job of implementing it.

Source: Hume (1992)

Organisational barriers to integration

Integrated marketing communications basically does not fit easily into the organisational structure adopted by most firms. Integration will not happen without substantial effort and resource. Exhibit 14.1 provides a brief overview of some of the more obvious barriers to integration.

Organising for integrated marketing communications

It is now obvious that there is no one best way to organise for IMC any more than there is a best way to organise any aspect of business. It is, however, possible to consider a range of options. The questions are, 'How should the client be organised?', 'How should its agency(ies) be organised?' and 'How should the relationships between the client and its agency(ies) be organised?'

NEED TO KNOW

☑ *Three important questions arise when organising for integrated marketing communications: how should the client be organised? how should its agency(ies) be organised? how should the relationships between the client and its agency(ies) be organised?*

Linton and Morley (1995) are quite categorical in their recommendations: 'In integrated marketing all marketing programmes are channelled through a central co-ordinator and handled by a single agency' (p. 1). This view is generally not supported by research in the USA (e.g. Duncan and Everett 1993 and Caywood et al. 1991) and is not countenanced by many organisations. It is one approach, and one which could be adopted by some, but it is not the only approach.

RHM's Bisto brand has been handled by the client producing an annual plan that is presented to, and discussed by, a meeting of all the Bisto promotional agencies which go away and develop their own plans.

Exhibit 14.1 Organisational barriers to integrated marketing communications

- **Lack of horizontal communication**
  Management – planning, reporting and implementation tend to be established in vertical hierarchies. For IMC to work, communication needs to be facilitated horizontally *across* functional disciplines. Even within the function of marketing, organisational structuring can result in a separation of corporate communications, sales management, brand/product management, trade sales, advertising, merchandising, etc.

- **Functional specialisation**
  Marketing communications is a fragmented arena. Functional specialists tend to strongly defend their 'territories'.

- **Decentralisation**
  The current trend to 'empower' the workforce by decentralising decision-making could be a force that discourages integration unless such decentralisation is 'orchestrated'.

- **Lack of corporate direction and communication**
  Some organisations have been accused of having too little corporate focus. Even where organisations have clear missions, aims and strategies they may not adequately communicate them.

- **Lack of IMC planning and expertise**
  The skills required to manage IMC need to span across functional specialisation. Few people and organisations have acquired the necessary abilities to achieve high levels of IMC. Research on marketers reported by Cleland (1995) identified lack of expertise as the most significant reason given as to why companies were not yet implementing IMC.

- **Lack of budget**
  This was the second most significant reason for not implementing IMC given by marketers (Cleland 1995).

- **Lack of database**
  Databases are vital to successful IMC. More will be said on this important aspect in the last section of this chapter.

- **Fear of change**
  Fear is an often cited area of concern whenever there are changes taking place. The unknown and ambiguity associated with change can be traumatic.

This is followed up by an 'away-day', when the agencies challenge each other's proposals before arriving at a final plan to which they all subscribe, having worked on it as equal partners (Mitchell 1994).

Gillette have used the international network of Omnicom agencies for its 'Best a man can get' campaigns. Two executives from BBDO, the 'lead' agency based in New York, did nothing else but travel the world policing all campaigns for consistency and continuity. If something was not working to his satisfaction, Brian Cleverly, general manager for Gillette Northern Europe, would be able to call New York, which would put resources behind solving the problem (Mitchell 1994).

It is neither possible nor appropriate in a book of this nature to pursue all the issues, politics, power struggles and management approaches to organisation.

One-stop shop/through-the-line agency

Terms used to describe agencies that claim to offer complete marketing communications solutions. Full service agency is an associated term.

Management texts proliferate on these subjects. However, by way of an overview, Exhibits 14.2 to 14.6 illustrate some broad options available for structuring client and agency relationships to facilitate IMC. Although multiple agencies are shown, the client may choose a single **'one-stop shop'** or **'through-the-line'** agency (see Chapter 15 about agency operations for more details).

Exhibit 14.2 Anarchic structure

No integration of marketing communication activities within the client organisation nor between the agencies. This has typified much of the marketing communications effort until recent years.

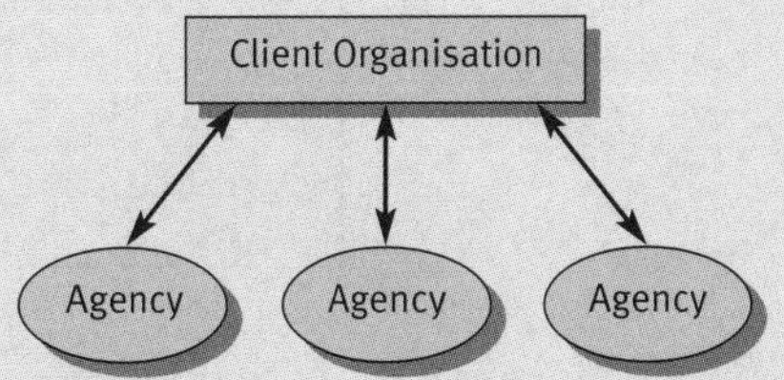

Client Organisation

Agency   Agency   Agency

Exhibit 14.3 Client-centred integration structure

Integration of marketing communication activities within the client organisation but no integration between the agencies. Client takes on sole responsibility to ensure integration. Locus of planning and control lies with the client.

The Client Marketing Communications Division may be physically organised as a single department or may be numerous departments and individuals organised to facilitate communication and teamwork on marketing communications tasks.

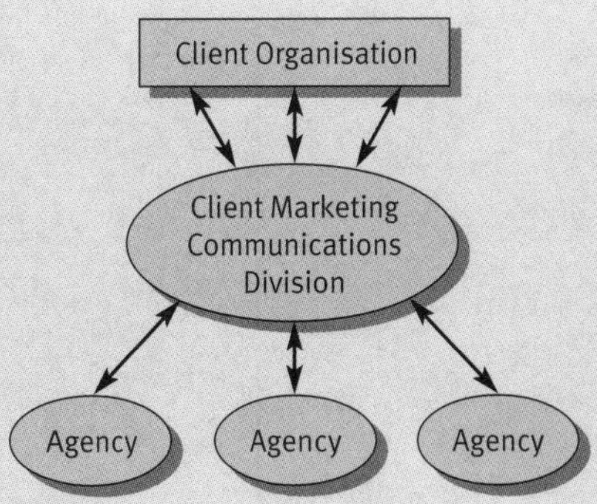

Client Organisation

Client Marketing Communications Division

Agency   Agency   Agency

Exhibit 14.4 Federal integration structure

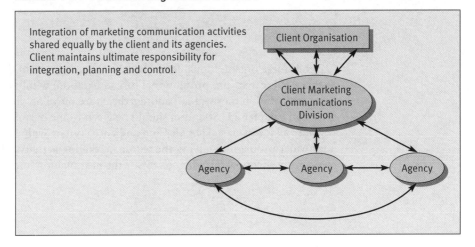

Integration of marketing communication activities shared equally by the client and its agencies. Client maintains ultimate responsibility for integration, planning and control.

Client Organisation

Client Marketing Communications Division

Agency   Agency   Agency

Exhibit 14.5 Agency-centred integration structure

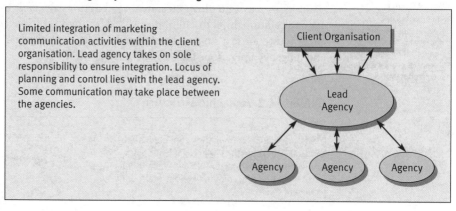

Limited integration of marketing communication activities within the client organisation. Lead agency takes on sole responsibility to ensure integration. Locus of planning and control lies with the lead agency. Some communication may take place between the agencies.

Exhibit 14.6 Centralised client and lead agency integration structure

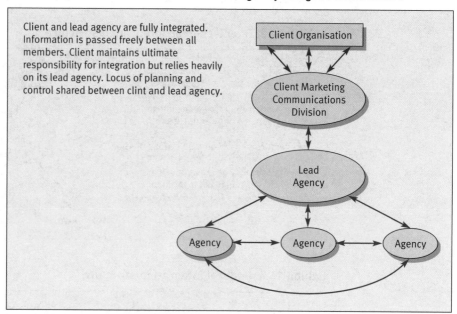

Client and lead agency are fully integrated. Information is passed freely between all members. Client maintains ultimate responsibility for integration but relies heavily on its lead agency. Locus of planning and control shared between clint and lead agency.

While these organisational forms begin to address some of the IMC problems, such as those of creative and promotional mix integration, without considerable management intervention they will not address the entire range of 'dimensions of integration' shown in Chapter 23. Attention should be given to the overall IMC task that needs to consider all forms of stakeholder and audience contact with the client. This is, in fact, a far wider problem involving the whole marketing activity. This is one reason why some people are now referring to IMC as the next major 'philosophy' of marketing.

The role and importance of the database in integrated marketing communications

Database

Collection of information, usually on computer, stored to provide useful, convenient and interactive access to information.

One of the barriers to achieving IMC identified in Exhibit 14.1 was the lack of a **database**. Further reference is made of the significance of the management of databases in Chapter 12 in which it was recognised that much of the growth and improvement in customer and audience relationship management is dependent upon the maintenance of databases. It is vital, therefore, to build one or more interlinked databases into the organisational structure if there is to be any real chance of integrating marketing communications activities targeted towards the organisation's many different audiences.

Schultz (1997) maintains that 'Databases no longer are just the basis for tactical activities a company wishes to execute. They are rapidly becoming the primary management tool that drives the organisation's business strategy' (p. 10). Information is needed to make sound management decisions. A well-managed database is where much of that information is stored. As the number of specifically targeted contacts and audiences proliferate while at the same time the ability to gather ever more detailed information on those targets increases, it is the computer and the database which provides the technological solution to manage this information 'revolution'.

FOOD FOR THOUGHT

There is increasing debate about issues of privacy of information versus freedom of information. The collection of increasing amounts of data about individuals, their habits, behaviour and personal details is causing grave concern to many, particularly when these details are being collected for commercial gain. There are fears that such information may be used for unscrupulous purposes and that information may not always be fair and accurate, unnecessarily prejudicing members of the public. Such concerns have been expressed, for example, with regard to credit ratings.

One major marketing growth area has been that of direct marketing and this has been encouraged by the technical ability to capture and utilise data in huge quantities. All types of organisations have been encouraged to develop databases, not least the major retailers. Especially with the increasing emphasis on customer loyalty and life time values, the amount of information being collected on customers and their individual buying behaviour has grown enormously. Retailers, for example, know who you are, where you live and what type of house you live in; what you buy, when you buy and where you buy; your favourite brands, how frequently you purchase them and whether you are influenced by promotional offers. This is not to suggest, however, that capture and manipulation of such information is always a good thing. There is growing public concern about how much personal information is held by organisations and the extent to which this is detrimental to an individual's interests.

Historically the database has been focused on the end-user but, today, it is being used as a major integrating force impacting on all aspects of customer and audience relationship management which includes consumers, end customers and trade customers as well as other stakeholder groups. Technology has created a role for databases such that they are an increasingly integral part of business management in general and marketing management in particular. Unfortunately, there are also significant organisational barriers which limit their use by many companies (Fletcher et al. 1994). While the use of databases is not a straightforward business, more and more organisations are reorganising to take advantage of their benefits.

Database marketing

The use of accurate customer and prospect customer information, competitor information, market information and internal company information stored on a computer database to focus marketing activities towards targets.

The term '**database marketing**' has been used to represent this new ability to manipulate information for marketing purposes and is described as 'an interactive approach to customer contact management relying on the maintenance of accurate customer and prospect information, competitor information and internal company information' (Hartley and Starkey 1996, p. 158). The database now provides the basic information on which to develop strategy and integrate all marketing activities. Those organisations failing to take advantage of the database revolution are exposing themselves to unnecessary competitive risk and are limiting their marketing potential.

IN VIEW 14.4

The man from Del Monte says 'Yes' to new database

Del Monte created a central database that sought to hold information, for example, about all of its thousands of retail customers. The database analysed buying patterns at each store and produced profiles of the stores' customer purchases. These were matched against local geodemographic data.

Based on those profiles, Del Monte was able to identify whether each store was reaching its expected target. Del Monte management were then able to direct their marketing effort with accuracy, from product launch, distribution and stocking decisions to marketing communications plans involving targeted sales force effort, in-store promotions, direct mail and advertising.

The process created value-added information that Del Monte shared with all its trading partners to assist their efforts. Sales rose through closer partnership with distribution chain members and through better targeted marketing communications.

Source: Yarborough (1996)

Summary

Integrated marketing communications cannot be achieved unless considerable effort is put into structuring the client organisation and its external agencies to achieve integration. Numerous organisational barriers exist which may prevent integration from happening and these are presented in Exhibit 14.1. One barrier in particular, that of the lack of a database, is highlighted in the final section of this chapter which discusses the growing importance of databases to marketing communications activities and to the whole management process of modern organisations.

Marketing communications is, by its very nature, fragmented, requiring specialists to undertake its many different aspects. This adds to the difficulty in achieving integration. Many would argue that it is primarily the task of the client organisation to ensure that integration is achieved. Increasingly, however, marketing communications agencies are taking on the role of assisting the client in this task, if only for their own self-preservation in seeking competitive advantage over those agencies not offering integrative services.

This chapter has suggested that there is no single best way to organise for integrated marketing communications and that management has to determine the best approach for them according to prevailing circumstances. Five broad organisational structures are proposed, each permitting varying amounts of integration: anarchic, client-centred integration, federal integration, agency-centred integration, and centralised client and lead agency integration.

1 Identify the six factors suggested that make the task of integration more complex.

2 The process of integration has been referred to as 'orchestration'. What does this mean?

3 What does Schultz mean when he refers to an 'outside-in' approach to marketing communications integration?

4 There are numerous organisational barriers that prevent or detract from integration. Identify and describe, in your own words, each of these.

5 Why is database management considered to be an important aspect of integrated marketing communications? Refer also to Chapters 2 and 12 to answer this question.

Project

A range of options which might facilitate the organisation of integrated marketing communications have been illustrated in this chapter in Exhibits 14.2 to 14.6. Identify the relative strengths and weaknesses of each. Are there any other structures that could be identified? In general, which form of organisational structure do you think is better at facilitating IMC and why?

References

Caywood, C., Schultz, D. and Wang, P. (1991), Integrated marketing communications: a survey of national consumer goods advertisers. *Northwestern University Report*, June.

Cleland, K. (1995), Few wed marketing communications. *Advertising Age*, 27 February, 66 (9), 10.

Duncan, T.R. and Everett, S.E. (1993), Client perceptions of integrated marketing communications. *Journal of Advertising Research*, May/June, 30–39.

Eisenhart, T. (1989), Playing together: marketing and communications catch the team spirit. *Business Marketing*, July.

Finn, M. (1994), Integration once again rears its not so ugly head. *Marketing*, 6 June, 10.

Fletcher, K., Wheeler, C. and Wright, J. (1994), Strategic implementation of database marketing: problems and pitfalls. *Long Range Planning*, 27 (1), 133–141.

Griffin, T. (1993), *International Marketing Communications*. Oxford: Butterworth-Heinemann.

Hartley, B. and Starkey, M.W. (eds) (1996), *The Management of Sales and Customer Relations*. London: International Thomson Press.

Hume, S. (1992), Execs debate: who rules in integrated marketing area? *Advertising Age*, 63 (47), 3 and 42.

Linton, I. and Morley, K. (1995), *Integrated Marketing Communications*. Oxford: Butterworth-Heinemann.

Mitchell, A. (1994), A Clear Message. *Marketing*, 17 February, 175–185.

Moriarty, S.E. (1994), PR and IMC: the benefits of integration. *Public Relations Quarterly*, 39 (3), 38–45.

Prescott, D. (1991), Public Relations at General Motors: An Integrated Marketing Communications Approach. Masters Thesis, University of Colorado, School of Journalism and Mass Communication.

Schultz, D.E. (1993), Maybe we should start all over with an IMC organisation. *Marketing News*, 25 October, 27 (22), 8.

Schultz, D.E. (1997), Integrating information resources to develop strategies. *Marketing News*, 20 January, 31 (2), 10.

Schultz, D.E., Tannenbaum, S.I. and Lauterborn, R.F. (1994), *Integrated Marketing Communications: Pulling It Together and Making It Work*. NTC Business Books.

Yarborough, J. (1996), Putting the pieces together. *Sales and Marketing Management*, 148 (9), 68–74.

 ## Selected further reading

Meudell, K., Callen, T. and Lussey, H. (1999), *Management and Organisational Behaviour: A Student Workbook* revised edn. Financial Times Pitman Publishing.

Mullins, L.J. (1999), *Management and Organisational Behaviour* 5th edn. Financial Times Pitman Publishing.

Chapter 15

Agency operations

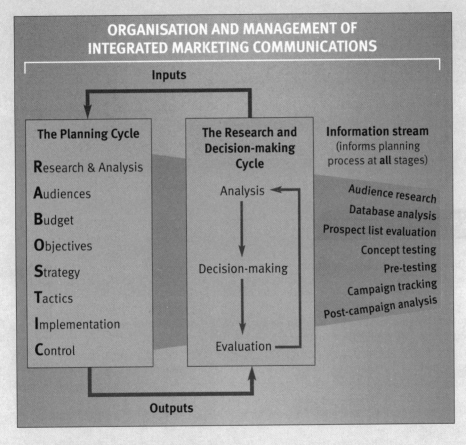

ORGANISATION AND MANAGEMENT OF INTEGRATED MARKETING COMMUNICATIONS

Inputs

The Planning Cycle

Research & Analysis
Audiences
Budget
Objectives
Strategy
Tactics
Implementation
Control

The Research and Decision-making Cycle

Analysis

Decision-making

Evaluation

Information stream
(informs planning process at **all** stages)

Audience research
Database analysis
Prospect list evaluation
Concept testing
Pre-testing
Campaign tracking
Post-campaign analysis

Outputs

The IMC RABOSTIC Planning Model

CD

Using the Internet as your primary information source, research each of the agencies Škoda has used as featured in Case Study 2. For each agency, try to identify its mission and creative approach. How consistent are these with each other and with Škoda's brand values? How important do you believe such consistency is in integrated marketing communication planning?

Chapter outline

- The changing situation
- The need for agencies
- Agency roles
- Types of agencies
- The international dimension
- The agency selection process
- Agency remuneration
- Managing the client–agency relationship

Objectives

- To explain the general operations of agencies and why they are needed
- To identify different types of agencies
- To propose a process for selecting agencies
- To describe and comment on different agency payment systems
- To identify factors affecting client–agency relationships

Professional perspective

James Best Group Chairman, BMP DDB

Ad agencies, like other businesses, succeed by offering their clients what they want. Which, for most clients most of the time, is advertising: broadly targeted communications in paid-for media, which stimulate or reinforce consumer behaviour to the benefit of the advertisers and satisfaction of their customers.

To do this job well, agencies have evolved to be multi-disciplinary groups of specialists – writers, art directors, strategic thinkers, researchers, media planners and buyers, print and TV production experts, etc. etc. – whose skills are orchestrated by the project and relationship managers we call account people. So you could say that the 'traditional' ad agency is by definition 'integrated', but with the efforts of all its specialists focused on the creation and production of advertising, rather than other communications.

This focus has proved effective over the years. Substantial international businesses have grown up on the basis of cost-effective, business-building campaigns. Such campaigns are hard to create and maintain, highly prized by clients and absorb all the work of the talented specialists agencies employ.

So to build more broadly 'integrated' communications capabilities presents ad agencies with some considerable challenges. They may see the desirability of better integrating the different disciplines of commercial communications, but most of their clients don't look to them to do it. Large, experienced clients possess the skill and resources to pick 'the best' in each and any field of communications they feel they need and to integrate their efforts themselves. Indeed, it's a core marketing client skill and satisfying for them as professionals to do. They find generalists tend not to demonstrate the highest skills in any one communications area, so marketing managers recognise the need for top-level talent to address their top-level challenges in specific creative disciplines.

By the same token, the best people in the different disciplines tend to favour devoting their talents to their own chosen area. Peer-group recognition and other rewards tend to follow outstanding achievement in any one of the recognised communications skills, be it advertising or PR or direct marketing. The concept of the agency 'supergeneralist', versed in all communication disciplines and able to perform them all together for his clients, is sadly unrealistic. So the 'one-stop shop' has died as a serious contender for big budget business in most sectors and agencies of all types remain specialists.

However, ad agencies are neither stupid nor blind. They appreciate the value of better integration of their clients' communications programme. They want to participate in the process – indeed, their resources and position often mean they are best placed to lead it. Their solution has generally been to build, buy or bond with chosen counterparts in the specialist disciplines relevant to their clients. Rather than trying to do it all themselves, they do it with really good people they can work with. It is seldom easy, but it works and clients can receive the best service and best advice without compromising their agencies' focus or culture.

IN VIEW 15.1

HHCL and Mazda

If you had left an agency in the fifties and gone to Mars and returned today, you would still recognise the place. If you walk out today and come back in ten years, you will either not recognise the place, or be stepping into a museum.

(Rupert Howell, HHCL managing partner)

At Howell Henry Chaldecott Lury which has invested heavily in integration, project teams are made up of experts, present at every client meeting, all with the same brief. HHCL is paid on a fee basis, which means there is no incentive to propose an above-the-line solution because they will not make any extra money from the media spends anyway. The agency have established their credentials with aggressive statements on integration such as, 'We don't espouse integrated marketing, we live it'. As they are a company working in project teams they expect and hope that they will break the boundaries of a brief. They estimate their time project by project and charge fees accordingly. This means they do not have to recover remuneration further downstream on production, processing or other bought-in items and services.

Given the lean staffing and non-hierarchical structure at the agency, some below-the-line practitioners acknowledge Howell Henry's creative acumen but challenge the agency about its ability to implement a multi-layered promotional campaign. HHCL claim to have the skills to take ideas through to advertising, direct marketing and sales promotions. They do not offer corporate PR or sponsorship skills.

Mazda marketing director Jan Smith is a long-time advocate of integrated marketing and HHCL's presence of through-the-line capabilities was a convincing factor when she appointed HHCL to the manufacturer's £6 million account. Mazda is one of the more forward-thinking clients in terms of integrating its marketing agencies. Jan Smith says, 'Every element of marketing should come together like the segments of an orange'. Mazda set up regular brainstorming meetings involving its marketing department, its advertising agency (HHCL) and its PR consultancy, the Quentin Bell Organisation. In these situations the usual boundaries between advertising and PR are broken down and the respective parties 'bat' around creative ideas.

In the Howell Henry model of an agency, the client deals directly with a team made up of every department, from creative planning to account handling. The integration issue is met by including in that team experts in direct marketing, sales promotion or whatever marketing communications mix is deemed appropriate. It is a one-stop shop charging on a fee basis. In theory, this approach means that the agency has no interest in promoting one marketing communications technique over another.

Source: developed from Gray (1994), Marshall (1994), Watkins (1994)

The changing situation

Since agencies, by their very nature, are centres for the generation of creative thinking in one of its most applied forms, and with the ultimate in critical sponsors and audiences, it is hardly surprising that such hot beds of invention and creation should continually change, regroup and reinvent themselves in new forms with new aims, desires and ways of working.

This is even more understandable when set against the established industry ethos of continuously pushing back the boundaries of what is acceptable and possible combined with that which is practical and most effective, especially in a rapidly changing world constantly seeking new ideas, challenges and ways of doing things.

A state of flux exists which, in most other commercial settings, would be considered as at best untidy and at worst utterly unmanageable, and yet agencies thrive in this atmosphere and the personalities within the industry continue to move forward, the same names appearing either in different combinations, or rising Phoenix-like, from yet another reorganisation.

However, there is order in this apparent chaos, and there are certain discernible common threads running throughout the industry.

- Agencies are establishing much closer internal relationships between disciplines, and are much more conscious of the value of integrated planning.
- Much greater international co-operation is also now evident, with agencies establishing linkages on an international basis to work together exploiting each other's strengths and specialities.
- There is a clear pattern emerging of a greater flexibility in agency remuneration methods.

Of course, these may all have been forced on them by the explosive growth in communications. Or they may have sought to maximise the benefits for themselves and for their clients thereby ensuring their very existence, since they must create and supply services which satisfy the needs of their clients. To do this they have recognised the need to be proactive, reactive, inventive, derivative, commercial, artistic, egotistic, practical, effective and efficient, and above all believe in themselves and their ability to improve the lot of their clients.

The need for agencies

In practice there are three ways in which a company may choose to handle its marketing communications. The marketing department might consider using in-house capabilities, or engage the services of an agency (full service or specialist), or a combination of both. The latter is now perhaps the most common choice rather than one or other exclusively, especially since few companies are in a position to provide the necessary management and creative skills to develop and maintain all the activities associated with an integrated communications campaign without the need for outside expertise. This is reflected in the approaches to organisational structure presented in Chapter 14.

In the widest sense, the term 'agencies' can be applied to any outside advisors and can range from consultancies to print and fulfilment specialists. In its earliest form, it was used to refer to advertising agencies that primarily earned their income through the commission they were paid by the media for buying advertising space on behalf of their clients. They truly operated in an 'agency' capacity. As the range of marketing communications activity widened, a host of specialists have set up to assist their clients in all forms of promotional and marketing communications work. The details that follow have deliberately been kept broad to give a flavour of the way in which agencies operate. They do not cover the detailed workings of specific agencies. It should also be recognised that some emphasis has been placed on reflecting the workings of advertising agencies in particular as a basis of much of the description given. This should be borne in mind as the workings of agencies operating in the fields of, say, PR or product placement or sales promotion or corporate identity may differ significantly.

NEED TO KNOW

☑ *Three options are available to organisations in the use of agencies: (a) not to use them and do all the work in-house, (b) engage the services of one or more agencies, or, most likely, (c) a combination of both, use agencies and carry out some work in-house.*

Agencies as a general rule replace the need for setting up and maintaining creative, production, media buying, process control and other very specialised functions as an integrated subdivision within an organisation's own control. Having made the decision to make use of the services of an agency a company must adopt an appropriate approach to the management of its activities at the interface in order to ensure maximum effectiveness in its marketing communications campaigns. First, the company must clearly identify the specific aspects of marketing communications which it wants to address and to organise itself internally to raise, discuss and clarify those areas and subjects. Second, the company must use the information so obtained to identify the appropriate external agencies or consultants who can contribute successfully to the specific aspects of marketing communications it has identified. The task of integrating all the internal and external activities was the subject of the previous chapter.

Agency roles

Exhibit 15.1 shows the typical services that a client may contract from an agency either on a full service or an individual basis. The specific duties of each function will obviously vary according to the marketing communications discipline (PR, sales promotion, direct mail, advertising, etc.).

Exhibit 15.1 Agency roles

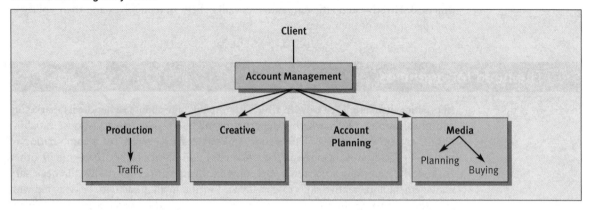

Account management

Account managers

Also called account handlers, account executives and account directors. People who work within agencies and whose primary role is to interface between the client and the agency.

Often called account handlers, executives or directors, **account managers** carry out a number of interrelated functions. They are primarily responsible for the management and administration of the client's account. The account manager will be the first level of client contact with the agency and is responsible for 'driving' the account. Account managers in effect wear two hats as they are at the interface between the client and the agency. On the one hand they represent the clients' needs and aspirations. On the other, they represent the agency's point of view. The account manager will communicate to the client what the agency is capable of doing and will also communicate to the agency team the client's requirements. It is the account manager who is responsible for making sure that the agency team e.g. creatives, media planners and production, work closely to the client's brief. They may work in tandem with account planners and the client in developing an understanding of the client's market and determining the final brief with which the agency will then work. They are also responsible for co-ordinating the agency's efforts to meet the deadlines set. The account manager often has the role of minimising the culture clash between the client and the agency often termed the clash between art and commercialism. In many below-the-line agencies account managers also do planning as an integral part of the whole job (Crawford 1994).

NEED TO KNOW

☑ *Account managers go under a variety of titles: account executives, account handlers, account managers, account directors.*

Planning

Account planners

Agency people responsible for developing a clear understanding of the market situation in which marketing communications will take place. Involves research and knowledge of the market, relevant buying processes and the client's position. Account planners will use this knowledge to assist in planning for marketing communications.

Not all agencies maintain the account planning function, preferring it to be dispersed among other staff as a more collective activity. Where **account planners** are employed, they are primarily responsible for handling the research in the communications planning process. Whereas the account manager is said to represent the client in the agency, the account planner represents the client's market – the customers and consumers. They are responsible for the marketing communications strategy, assisting in the development of the creative brief, customer/consumer research and the evaluation of the campaign at all stages of the process. They are responsible for analysing data at the situational analysis stage of the planning process. They will have to interpret market research reports for inclusion in the creative brief. Their strategic analysis is crucial at the objective and target audience identification stages of the planning process. They will be responsible for orchestrating the testing of any of the creative work and will also be responsible for evaluating the effectiveness of the campaign via tracking studies, etc. The responsibilities of the planning function within an agency may vary according to the discipline (see In View 15.2).

Creative

Creatives are responsible for writing and designing the message and the image to communicate to the target audiences. Creatives will work to a brief that has been set by the client and the account management team. Creative teams will often work in pairs and this is particularly so within advertising agencies. **Copywriters** are responsible for the words that will be used in an advertisement and **art directors** are responsible for the visuals. The actual completion of finished artwork and production is likely to be further contracted out via the production department to other specialists such as commercial artists, computer animators, film directors, photographers and printers. Within a PR agency the creative work will typically be handled by a copywriter but many staff may have multiple responsibilities of which copywriting will be but one.

Production and traffic

Production is typically handled as a specialist function within the agency and may be further subdivided into specialisms such as radio, print and TV/cinema/video depending upon the work of the agency. It is the responsibility of the production department working with other members of the agency to ensure completion of the final piece of work in whatever form in appropriate quantities and to appropriate quality standards.

Traffic is a project control function that ensures that work in all its various stages is completed on time so that it is passed forward within the agency to meet its final deadline. The traffic controller will be responsible for chasing agency staff to complete their work in sufficient time for it to be passed on to others to complete their tasks and finally onto production after client approval. The use of client contact reports, job numbers and deadline dates generated by account managers is a mechanism used by agency staff to facilitate the trafficking process.

Creatives

General term for art directors, designers and copywriters. Responsible for developing creative and design solutions.

Copywriters

Those responsible for producing creative ideas and marketing communications text or 'copy'. Typically work in partnership with art directors.

Art directors

Those responsible for producing creative ideas and visual designs. Typically work in partnership with copywriters.

Production

The department or agency section responsible for arranging for all work to be produced based on original concepts provided by the creatives.

Traffic

Describes the function that ensures that the development and production of agency work is completed to deadline through all the various stages from initial brief, through creative solutions, to final production. It is a crucial part of agency operations.

IN VIEW 15.2

Planning function at IMP direct marketing agency

Beth Baldwin, planning director at IMP direct marketing agency, argues that below-the-line planners have a much larger remit than planners in above-the-line agencies and gives the following insight into the planning function. 'The first requirement of planners is that they are well rounded and experienced marketing people. But on top of that they must have the expertise in market analysis, thorough knowledge of what information exists, consumer motivations, creative development, guarding the brand, tracking and monitoring, loyalty programme construction and media planning in the widest sense. This includes list buying, test construction, targeting, segmentation, computer modelling and response analysis. They must also possess an appreciation for what advertising, direct marketing, sales promotion, sponsorship and PR can be expected to contribute.'

Source: Crawford (1994)

Media planning/buying

This function is particularly relevant to advertising agencies and in PR companies it is represented by media relations and responsibility for identifying the most appropriate media to generate maximum favourable publicity for their clients. Direct mail specialists would have no need for this activity as such. Instead, the production and mailing functions, for example, are of greater importance including the identification of appropriate geodemographic neighbourhoods to target as well as buying in mailing lists. In a sales promotions agency the equivalent function would be responsible for deciding on the most appropriate promotional vehicle and negotiating a favourable rate with any third parties to be involved.

Although media has been described earlier in a wide context (Chapter 5) as anything capable of carrying marketing communications messages, in this context, it has almost universally been accepted as the planning and buying of the mass media. This view, however, is slowly changing as agencies embark on what is coming to be called **media neutral planning** which is where integrated marketing communications is being more readily accepted.

Media planners are responsible for deciding which media to choose for a particular campaign. The **media buyers** are responsible for buying the space or time in the media. Much of the skill in media buying lies in negotiating rates with media owners seeking to achieve cost savings over quoted rate cards. Any savings achieved are seen as a cost efficiency. The media buyer is also responsible for ensuring that all the relevant 'paperwork' is completed and confirming details to other members of the agency. Much of the groundwork used by media planners is presented in Chapter 21 in which issues such as media selection, frequency, reach and impact are considered.

NEED TO KNOW

☑ *In the context of media planning and media buying, the term 'media' is used principally to refer to the mass media.*

Media neutral planning

Planners recognise the value of all media within a campaign and do not seek to presume a bias of one medium over another – each is chosen as the best fit for the job.

Media planners

Usually best applied to those responsible for planning the selection, scheduling and use of marketing communications mass media in advertising agencies and media independents.

Media buyers

Those responsible for buying media time and space in the mass media.

Types of agencies

Agency types can, in essence, be categorised along two dimensions: the disciplines offered and the services offered, and can be plotted on a chart such as that in Exhibit 15.2.

Agencies are present in all shapes and sizes and range from the **à la carte/specialist** concentrating, for example, on creative, media or planning services for a specific marketing communications discipline, to the full service agency with an integrated multi-discipline approach. **Multi- or full-service agencies** aim to offer their clients a

A la carte/specialist agency

Agency offering limited, specialist services in a specific area of marketing communications.

Multi- or full-service agency

In contrast to an 'à la carte' agency, the full-service agency offers a complete and integrated range of marketing communications services. One-stop shop and though-the-line agency are associated terms.

Exhibit 15.2 Agency types

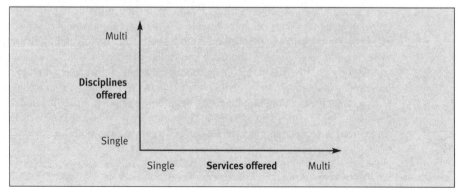

complete range of services including account management, planning, creative and media across the major (if not all) marketing communications elements. As a consequence, such agencies offer **above-** and **below-the-line** solutions, thereby moving toward an integrated marketing communications package. These agencies have been termed **through-the-line** agencies because of this feature. However, doubts are frequently raised within the industry about the wisdom and, indeed, the economy of using so-called *full-service* agencies. Often their services do not strictly encompass the full range of marketing communications activities. Those agencies that claim to offer full-service solutions will typically do so by being a part of a larger group of agencies either through direct ownership or through some form of partnership arrangement. Exhibit 15.3 shows the advantages and disadvantages of managing the marketing communications effort in-house as opposed to hiring a specialist agency or a multi-service/multi-discipline agency.

Integrated agencies

As we approached the millennium with the increased pace of developments in knowledge transfer and information technology, interest in the ethos of integration intensifyed among marketers. Many have said that integrated marketing communications will define the relationship between marketing managers and their chosen agencies. In the context of agency operations, integrated marketing communications

Above-the-line communications

Term used to generally describe advertising promotions: that is, promotions that make use of commission-paying mass media – television, press, cinema, radio and posters. Also called above-the-line promotions and above-the-line advertising.

Below-the-line communications

Marketing communications that make use of the non-commission-paying media in all their forms, i.e. all forms of promotions other than advertising. Sometimes, incorrectly, it is referred to as below-the-line advertising. Although it remains a popular term, its usefulness is limited as it encompasses such a broad range of promotional activity.

Through-the-line communications

Marketing communications that span both above- and below-the-line activities.

Exhibit 15.3 Marketing communications management options

Management issues	In-house	Specialist	Multi-service/disciplined
Viewpoint	Understand your own problems. Views may be limited, not objective	Objective viewpoint, fresh ideas	Objective viewpoint, fresh ideas
Media solutions neutrality strength	Unlikely to be any bias toward particular discipline	You decide on disciplines to be used	Tend to be partial to agency's original e.g. advertising
Knowledge and expertise	Limited to internal resources. Unlikely to have specialists in all areas	Experts in their fields. You can pick specialists in each area	May lack expertise in all areas
Management and control	Total control but increased pressure of workload	Needs careful coordination and control and careful briefing	Easier to manage a one-stop shop
Confidentiality/ security	Low risk as all in-house	Higher risk if a number of agencies working on account	Minimal risk as only one agency briefed
Speed/timing	Should be faster	Can be slow due to coordination	May be faster
Cost	May be cheaper although do not benefit from buying power in certain areas e.g.	Fewer overheads. Are able to shop around	Can be expensive to use

is the result of the amalgamation of all the marketing communications skills where each discipline has an equal say in the devising of strategy (Slingsby 1994). The result of this is to offer a clear, planned, coherent communication to target audiences, eliminating much of the 'clutter' previously apparent in non-integrated campaigns.

With an increasing number of clients expecting more integrated services from agencies, through-the-line solutions are becoming more the rule than the exception. For example, Abbot Mead Vickers, who owned 20 other communications agencies at the time, reported in 1997 that 60% of their new business enquiries were for marketing communications briefs rather than advertising briefs (IPA 1998). There is, therefore, a considerable move toward agencies gearing themselves up to provide a wide range of promotional tools alongside their existing disciplines. These agencies are in a position to offer, directly or indirectly, a comprehensive range of marketing communications services which can be made available to their clients through one shop, via subsidiary companies or through network alliances, the latter having grown over recent years.

Increasingly, agencies of every size, type and description are advising their clients on total marketing communications packages, and in many cases their ability to offer integrated services belies both their size and origins. One of the key issues at this time is the emerging blueprint for the restructured advertising agency capable of creating campaigns for increasingly fragmented or finely segmented audiences through the many and various media. This is apparent among some of the largest advertising agencies in the world who have expanded their operations into other areas of marketing communications other than advertising with, it must be said, varying degrees of success.

The emergence of the one-stop shop

There was evidence in the early 1980s of a growing realisation among some of the biggest agencies such as WPP and Saatchi and Saatchi, that there were advantages to be had from bringing together all the disciplines in a wholly or majority-owned structure and offering a '**one-stop shop**' approach, thereby giving the client a complete, holistic approach to solving their problems (Green 1991).

One-stop shop

Term used to describe agencies that claim to offer complete marketing communications solutions. Through-the-line and full service agency are associated terms.

This appeared to be a sound concept and one to which most observers and practitioners subscribed. However, as in most things, time proved to be a great leveller. While the benefits of the concept still stand, the practice has proven to be difficult for many. A closer examination of the actual implementation of the concept reveals that many companies which claimed 'one-stop shop' status were not really offering integrated services, but rather were delivering advertising with incidental add-ons. Below-the-line service divisions were rarely represented at board level, and each discipline was often made a separate profit centre. This served to accentuate the internal divide preventing, or at the very least erecting partial barriers to, the actuality of providing an integrated package (Direct Response 1995). Direct marketing agencies have always tended to be the 'poorer cousins' and have suffered from the greater political clout and board level access which has been available to advertising agencies in attaining lead agency status (Reed 1994).

The new generation of integrated agencies

More than ten years on and having learned some painful lessons, the new generation of marketers are moving into the highest levels of the industry, opening up what some believe to be a more harmonious future for a properly integrated style of account management (Direct Response 1995). The new companies on the whole realise that they need to meet the challenge of creating truly integrated communications and not following the old 'one-stop shop' principle of separate entities roughly forced together and reluctantly displaying a corporate logo, paying lip service to corporate togetherness while conducting internecine warfare behind closed doors.

Marketing communications neutrality

It is fair to argue that the new 'one-stop shop' practice will never work while any part of the whole, e.g. direct marketing or sales promotion, is regarded as a second-class citizen and not allowed to be fully represented as an integral part of the whole. Unfortunately, there is still anecdotal evidence leading to the belief that certain agencies that claim full integration are not offering this in reality, since they maintain, for example, a direct marketing or PR division as optional extras and, therefore, the account handlers do not fully represent all the communications disciplines. Even now it is interesting to note that some advertising agencies often have a member on the boards of below-the-line consultancies but that these organisations have no main board representation themselves (Direct Response 1995).

The Lowe Howard Spink advertising agency has maintained a long association with its direct marketing subsidiary, the Brompton Agency, due to the fact that their clients are demanding an integrated solution with the ready availability of a wide diversity of skills. On the strength of this they will very often include the direct marketing agency in their pitches, not as an add-on but as a part of the whole offering (Direct Response 1995). Similarly many advertising agencies such as McCann-Erikson have found it worthwhile to bring public relations consultancies on board on an ad hoc basis when pitching for new business (Gray 1994). However, there is a concern that in such situations, the disparity in size between the budgets of the two agencies results in the advertising agency becoming the lead player, subsuming the voice of its smaller 'partner' to its own vision of the end result.

Structural implications for integration

In truly integrated agencies there is only one company, one profit centre, one voice and one persona. To such an organisation the existence and encouragement of departmentalism is an anathema, and the existence of informally erected 'Chinese Walls' is not tolerated (Slingsby 1994). These have been referred to previously as 'functional silos' in Chapter 2. Departmental or discipline self-aggrandisement is diametrically opposed to pure objectivity in satisfying the client's need. Any vestige of separateness or superiority between one discipline and any of the others induces a competitive battle to secure larger shares of budgets. The aim of maintaining absolute objectivity in the search for the best solution in these situations is then lost.

The common experience is that skills not available in-house are bought in as required by the agencies in an attempt to demonstrate fully integrated services. This approach, of an advertising agency with a whole series of 'bolted on' below-the-line companies, in general fails to convince. Divisions of opinion as to methods, systems and approach, both creatively and commercially, are still evident. Potentially they produce a messy situation and image both internally as well as externally. There are some clients who believe that many advertising agencies do not really understand how to work through-the-line and that agencies still have a long way to go before being able to provide a real contribution to the clients' businesses beyond the production of effective advertising.

The failure of advertising agencies to adapt to clients' integrated needs in the 1990s has resulted in many of their 'traditional' accounts being won by below-the-line agencies and branding and management consultancies who are able to provide a wide range of solutions to the clients' problems (Smith 1997). For example, in 1997 Cable & Wireless Communications appointed below-the-line agency Rapier Stead & Bowden to manage its £45m integrated launch campaign. In the same year Wolff Olins, best known for its corporate design work, but who are now marketing themselves as a brand consultancy, was handed the £10m account for the re-launch of Freepages along with a role in the launch of Channel 5 (Curtis 1997). In response to this many of the bigger advertising agencies are looking at ways to restructure their business in order to make them more flexible, efficient and accountable.

A la carte/specialist agencies

It must be acknowledged that the 1990s have seen clients becoming much more knowledgeable and experienced in the area of marketing communications (Smith 1997). With clients becoming more sophisticated in their marketing communications requirements, they are more likely to question a given solution. Marketing managers in certain organisations feel more comfortable dealing with a number of specialist suppliers. Naturally this, in turn, has led to the explosion in the marketplace of the number and type of specialists offering their services. The client has the choice of a number of discipline-specific promotions agencies as well as those offering specialist services within or across disciplines, e.g. creative, production, media and planning.

Although many clients believe in the concept of through-the-line marketing communications in a general and corporate sense, many take the position that it is the role of the brand manager to provide the 'glue' to create the harmonious whole. Indeed many clients and agencies will argue strongly that you do not have to use a single agency grouping to achieve integrated communications. Therefore at the same time as clients are using integrated agencies there is a trend toward the use of the à la carte solution with clients handpicking highly specialised players to play particular solo instruments, orchestrated by the client as conductor into a symphony of communication (Robertson 1995). For example, for their 1995 European advertising account alone, Nike were using both independent agencies Wielden and Kennedy and Simons Palmer for their creative requirements, CIA Medianetwork for media buying and McCann Erikson's international network for work in Asia (Reed 1995).

However, clients such as Royal Mail Streamline have found that one of the problems associated with using a number of disparate agencies is that co-ordination can be a real problem (Reed 1994). They try to overcome this by having regular joint planning meetings. But getting agencies together has significant cost and overhead implications that are generally reflected in the fees charged. On top of this there is the perpetual dispute over who owns the business, which is generally determined by which agency gets the biggest slice of the budget.

Integrated communications initiative

It is true to say that while some agencies have demonstrated that they can work successfully with agencies from other disciplines there are many examples where the same combinations mix as well as oil and water, there being no meeting of minds, style or understanding. This is such an overt problem that in February 1994 the Public Relations Consultants Association convened a meeting together with the Institute of Practitioners of Advertising and the Sales Promotions Consultants Association with the stated aim of improving understanding by each other of their respective disciplines. The result of this 'summit' meeting was the establishment of the Integrated Marketing Communications Initiative (Gray 1994).

'Virtual' agencies

Virtual agencies

Term used to describe the selection of specialist individuals from different agencies or from within an agency group to work together as though they were members of the same agency.

One recent development has seen the emergence of 'virtual agencies' whereby the client handpicks a number of specialists, either from different agencies or a large communications group, to produce a 'dream team' (see In View 15.3). Many clients argue that this then allows them to take control of the brand and operate a more holistic team approach thus avoiding the communications, cost and delivery problems often associated with the traditional sequential approach to campaign planning (Richards 1997).

IN VIEW 15.3

Virtual agency – Channel 5's 'dream team'

Channel 5, the television network, was launched in the UK in May 1997. Its £5 million multimedia campaign was created by a 'dream team', cherry-picked by marketing and communications director, David Brook, who tailored his own 'virtual' advertising agency, known collectively as 'Team 5'. 'The idea was to get the best people in each discipline. The days of the full service agency supplying everything are long past', explained Brook. The Channel 5 campaign was developed by Brook with advertising company Mother which in turn worked with a Dutch creative operation called KesslesKramer, media independent TMD Carat, media strategists Michaelides & Bednash and design company Wolff Olins.

Posters and radio were part of a creative media strategy that introduced Channel 5 branding to the fifth column of TV listings pages before its launch. A branded magazine and a TV listings pull-out were distributed via *The Sunday Times* and *The Sun*. PR and promotional work with the Spice Girls included a specially commissioned single and the band also featured in on-air promotions and editorial. Channel 5's research one month after the launch showed that 91% of consumers were aware of the launch and 88% had seen some of the marketing.

Brookes argues that 'close integration between client and the "dream team" can only be achieved if the client structures are open and flexible ... but the logistical problems are not as great as they might at first appear'. As clients clamour for greater accountability and tighter control over how their money is spent, however, 'dream teams' are one viable solution. Brook says, 'As clients get more knowledgeable about the different parts of the marketing process, they [dream teams] will become a more common approach.'

Source: Carter, M., Dream Teams Define Relationships, © *Financial Times*, 7 April 1997

Media specialists

The increasing fragmentation of the media has led to the growing importance of media planning and buying. The evidence is that this growing media fragmentation is leaving many clients confused and unsure of the most effective way of getting their message across. Heavyweights Procter & Gamble, for instance, decided to farm out media buying to Saatchi and Saatchi and LeoBurnett as long ago as April 1994 as they had come to the conclusion that the media had become too fragmented for them to continue an in-house buying function (Tylee 1994).

There is a growing belief in the industry that the term 'full service' advertising agency is becoming largely redundant. Large advertising agencies such as Abbot Mead Vickers and Lowe Howard Spink, past proponents of the full service concept, have hived off their media services to media specialists within their groups. According to the Incorporated Society of British Advertisers (ISBA) there are now very few advertisers of any size that are not using media specialists for at least part of their business.

The change in media and the shift away from established patterns of purchase and planning has generated intense competition between full service advertising agencies and media independents. The fragmentation of the media has resulted in the increased complexity of media buying which in turn has led to the need for greater expertise in the buying and planning functions. Media independents specialise in media planning and buying. Because of this added specialism, and the increasing usage by clients of such specialists, media independents have increasingly been able to negotiate substantial price reductions through their buying power, a power derived through acting for many clients and agencies. Media independents are particularly well established in Western Europe where they handle the large majority of media purchases.

The international dimension

The agency selection process becomes more complex for those organisations operating in several international markets. Not only do they need to consider whether or not to use agencies offering specialist or multi-disciplines and services, but also whether to choose multinational agencies who have a presence in several international markets or to choose their international agencies à la carte. International differences in regulations, social and cultural values, economic and market structures, and media opportunities can increase the complexity of marketing communications planning decisions.

Changes in Europe resulting in the single European Market and the accessibility of new Eastern Europe markets have dramatically altered the business environment in which marketing communications agencies now operate. Many clients are now looking for international communications solutions and expect agencies to offer suitable structures to meet their demands. In response to these changing needs many communications agencies are expanding internationally either through acquisition of local agencies or by setting up satellite offices in the host countries. In 1994, IBM replaced 40 advertising agencies around the world with just one multinational agency, Ogilvy & Mather Worldwide. This was followed in 1998 with the announcement that they were reducing their international direct marketing agency roster of thirty to just four (Campbell 1998).

Strategic alliances

To compete with the global presence and buying power of the multinational agency giants, many local agencies are joining independent agency networks such as the Alliance International Group and Dialogue International. Over the last few years the industry has also seen a number of instances where agencies have formed strategic alliances to satisfy client needs. An example of this working on an international level was the appointment by Sony in 1995 of UK independent agency Simons Palmer Denton Clemmon & Johnson as lead agency on the £48 million-plus launch of its Playstation video game equipment in Europe. This is of special interest in that Simons Palmer pitched for the account in partnership with rival agency Ogilvy & Mather. By working in partnership with Ogilvy & Mather, the agency was able to snatch the $48m-plus European launch of Sony's Playstation away from the likes of Grey, BMP DDB Needham and Lowe Howard Spink (Reed 1995).

Another development in the industry has been the emergence of 'virtual agencies', which are made up of specialist teams from several agencies. In 1998 British Airways and their global alliance partners, American Airlines, Cathay Pacific and Qantas, launched their 'One World' umbrella brand using a virtual agency made up from agency staff from the UK and the US.

Standardisation or adaptation

One of the major decisions brand managers need to make relates to the creative strategy. In practice managers can choose to standardise or adapt their communications message. Dibb et al. (1994) have suggested that managers can choose to promote an international brand along a continuum running from one extreme which involves using the same standardised campaigns everywhere, to the other extreme where entirely different campaigns are adapted for localised use. They argue that the challenge for managers is to produce campaigns which make sufficient concessions to local needs, while avoiding the lowest common denominator trap of blandness i.e. think globally act locally. This theme is considered in greater detail in Chapter 8.

In an M&M survey of European multinational advertisers, consistency of message was considered to be a key benefit of standardising advertising internationally (Taylor and Ross 1995). Sega, Sony and Philips are just three blue-chip client names that took steps in 1995 to harmonise their brand image. There are also cost savings to be gained from a standardised approach which can include reduced production costs, i.e. making one commercial rather than several, and transferring best practice in planning and media buying. For example, a British Airways television advertisement in 1995 cost approximately £1.4 million to produce. However, this commercial was shown across 28 different countries to one billion people thus spreading the costs to the company (Summers 1995).

BBH chairman John Hegarty's famous dictum 'Big ideas cross borders' is one

Creative hot shops

Agencies specialising in creative ideas and solutions, other aspects of campaigns being handled by other agencies.

reason local **creative hot shops** such as his own have been able to attract major international advertisers such as Levis, Coca-Cola, Heineken, Polaroid and Electrolux (Reed 1995). The criticism is that such methods lead to metropolis-oriented advertising. But BBH believe that early product categories to tap into 'attitudinal boundaries' were youth, luxury goods and business, where customers in different countries are looking for identical values (Kemp 1995). The long-running relationship between Levis and BBH is evidence that international advertising can be run from an independent shop rather than a major league agency network. Hegarty argues that international networks are not as capable of creating mould-breaking work (Watkins 1995). This is supported by the fact that Cannes advertising creative award winners are frequently independent agencies.

The agency selection process

There is a well-defined and logical process of agency selection which, when followed, enables both clients and agencies to identify those areas which require clarification in the joint relationship and serves to establish the ground rules for both parties:

- Define requirements
- Develop pool list
- Select shortlist through a 'credentials pitch'
- Issue brief
- The pitch
- Final evaluation and choice.

Each year industry magazines such as *Campaign, Marketing Week* and *Marketing* conduct surveys on choosing and working with the various marketing communications agencies/consultancies (advertising, sales promotion, direct mail, packaging design, event management/conferences, PR, sponsorship and so on). The following selection criteria have been identified through this research and these are presented in Exhibit 15.4.

Exhibit 15.4 Agency selection criteria

Pre-pitch:	Example questions
Services offered	– Planning, creative, research, integrated, international?
Agency size	– How many clients, is it part of a group, will I be a major client?
Quality of work	– Past and present, creativity/effectiveness awards?
Relevant experience	– In market sector, promotional discipline?
Competing accounts	– Are there any clashes/conflicts of interests?
Cost	– What is the likely cost, method of remuneration?
Location	– Is the agency conveniently located?
Reputation	– Track record, working relationships, success?
The pitch:	**Example questions**
Presence of senior staff	– Will the pitch team be actually working on the account? Who will work on the account?
Human chemistry	– Is there good chemistry/culture fit between both parties? Can relationships be formed?
Strategic awareness	– Understanding of the brief, quality of thinking and research, ability to question and provide solutions?
Quality of proposals	– Creative, media, joined-up thinking, orchestration? Do the solutions answer the brief, do they excite?
Integration skills	– Does the agency demonstrate an understanding of the issues of integration and have means to achieve integration?
Value for money	– Are the proposals cost-efficient? Are they likely to be cost-effective?

The selection criteria outlined will be used by the client throughout the process from pool-listing and credentials presentation through to the pitch, evaluation and final choice. Clients are increasingly turning for support in this process to agency assessment consultancies which help make rational informed judgements about selection and methods and level of remuneration.

Defining requirements and developing a pool list

Having decided on their principal marketing communications requirements emanating from their overall marketing strategy, the first stage for the client in the agency selection process is to define the agency requirements, that is, what does the client company want from its marketing communications agency(ies)? Does it want above-, below- or through-the-line solutions, does it want strategic planning services or just creative and so on? Once the client has defined its agency requirements, the next step is to develop a pool list of suitable agencies. This can be quite a daunting task simply due to the number of agencies in operation. For example, there are approximately 1500 public relations agencies alone in the UK. There are, however, a wide range of sources of information and advice available to marketing communications managers. The various marketing communications disciplines all have industry bodies (a selection is shown in Exhibit 15.5) that represent both the agencies and their clients. These organisations can provide useful help and guidance during this difficult and yet vital part of the selection process. Most have information centres, registers of agencies/consultants, award-winning case material and other useful data.

Added to this is the wealth of information provided in the various trade magazines and publications. Magazines such as *Campaign* and *PR Week* regularly carry news of client accounts and campaigns together with commentary and criticism. Each year they also publish a listing of the top agencies in their field and the type of business they handle. For example, *Campaign Portfolio* provides a listing of advertising agencies, the work they do and their addresses and contact numbers. Industry directories are another useful source of information. Clients looking for a public relations agency, for example, can turn to directories such as *Contact* and *Hollis UK Press and Public Relations Annual.*

Most agencies will provide a selection of their work on request, indeed many agencies have Internet home pages containing case studies, examples of their work and background information about their organisation. Clients can also contact an agency's current clients for comments. The Advertising Agency Register Group (AAR) holds on file details of a large number of agencies, both above- and below-the-line, and for a fee they will provide a list of candidate agencies and a selection of their work.

Exhibit 15.5 Industry organisations

- The Institute of Practitioners of Advertising
- Incorporated Society of British Advertisers
- The Institute of Sale Promotions
- Sales Promotions Consultants Association
- Direct Marketing Association
- Institute of Direct Marketing
- Mail Order Traders Association
- The Institute of Public Relations
- The Public Relations Consultants Association
- European Sponsorship Consultants Association
- Institute of Sports Sponsorship

Credentials shortlist and the brief

Credentials presentation

An opportunity for selected agencies to present details of their backgrounds, history and achievements in order to convince a potential client to include them on its agency selection shortlist.

Client brief

Usually a written document, but could be presented verbally, outlining relevant background information and the principal marketing communications task to be undertaken.

The agencies selected are often invited to a '**credentials presentation**' and the pool list is then whittled down to a shortlist of usually three or four agencies who, once they have signed a confidentiality agreement, are invited to a briefing meeting. The detail of a **brief** will vary from situation to situation but a good brief should contain the following elements as a minimum:

- company and product/brand history and background
- marketing objectives
- marketing communications objectives
- target markets/audiences
- product/service specifications
- distribution strategy
- pricing strategy
- budget
- timing.

The pitch

Agency pitch

Short for agency sales pitch, the pitch is an opportunity for an agency to present itself, its ideas and proposed solutions to a client's brief, usually in competition with other shortlisted agencies for the chance of winning the client's business.

The **pitch** presentation is in essence a microcosm of the whole communications campaign where the agency presents to the client a 'snapshot' of the campaign as defined by the brief. A pitch presentation is often preceded by several meetings or discussions between the client and the agency (see In View 15.4). For some clients, a set-piece pitch presentation is often replaced in favour of a series of informal meetings and discussions at both the company and the agency. In 1988, the Head of Marketing in Coopers and Lybrand's corporate finance division held as many 40 meetings with a shortlist of four PR agencies before making the final agency choice (Cobb 1998).

Agencies generally have around four to six weeks to prepare for a pitch. The cost of a major pitch can vary significantly depending on the nature of the brief. Bearing in mind that the agency may not win the account, it has to be acknowledged that they will have expended considerable resources in researching and developing a presentation well enough for there to be a reasonable chance of success with the client. To this end, there is a substantial debate as to whether or not the agency should be partially or fully reimbursed for a pitch. The current situation in the UK is that clients and agencies are miles apart over this question, yet this 'won't pay' stance is unique to the UK. In France or Germany, for instance, agencies receive an agreed contribution toward the cost of the pitch. Some agencies will only carry out pitches if they can claim some of their expenses back again from the prospective client; this also helps discourage clients who are simply 'fishing' for creative ideas. Other agencies, such as BBH, will only carry out an ideas pitch as opposed to presenting fully developed creative work. Some industry members see pitches as inefficient for both agencies and clients and, although many agencies believe that clients should contribute toward the cost of pitches, this feeling has never been translated into a collective policy. At the end of the day, agencies have to be prepared to do a pitch for free in order to be shortlisted and have a chance at being awarded the business.

IN VIEW 15.4

Racing for the pitch – Simons Palmer and Sony Playstation

Phil Harrison, communications director for Sony computer Entertainment Europe, says the Simons Palmer (SP) agency was clearly set for the shortlist, based on its credentials presentation. 'But one of the reservations we had was the fact that it was not a full-service network agency and we were doing a European launch. We wanted to make sure it could take its obvious strengths in the UK and make sure they were implemented in Europe.'

Beginning – February

After an informal telephone conversation between a Sony representative and SP Managing Director, the agency was invited to a meeting to present their thoughts on youth marketing. The presentation was good enough to get the agency on the pitch list despite the fact that the brief was for a pan-European campaign and the agency was solely UK based. SP was up against some big Euro-hitters – BMP DDB Needham, Grey and Lowe Howard Spink.

Phil Harrison, the European communications director on the Playstation, wasn't just after an agency that could deliver excellent strategy and creative input. He wanted a relationship that could help improve the work. 'For six months we were going to be living in each other's pockets. We were looking for quality, but also for the personality of the agency – what made it tick.'

Before the first of the three meetings SP had with Sony, the agency team had a meeting to have their customary 'why won't we win this business?' discussion. They identified Europe as the key weakness the potential client might worry about. The solution was to approach Ogilvy & Mather Europe who, SP felt, has one of the best international networks. The proposition was that SP effectively commission Ogilvy & Mather to act on its and Sony's behalf throughout Europe. SP had made advertising history: on one piece of business they would be simultaneously agency and client. With the European solution in place, SP went through a series of pre-pitch meetings with Sony. In three meetings, SP responded to the brief; gave a preliminary view of the advertising strategy; and revealed to the client some of the advertising routes under consideration. The agency's intention is that 'by the time a client walks into a pitch they're very receptive'.

The pitch – 11 April

The critical decision the agency had to face was what kind of creative work the client was prepared to buy. There were some clues; Phil Harrison put a 21-year-old games designer on the Sony pitch team – probably 'hipper' and more aware of the scene than most agency creatives. So SP decided to push the boat out and present with one very bold creative idea. The pitch itself was conducted in the agency. SP presented the strategy in its basement boardroom and then, for a break, moved the client into another room where kids were playing on the Playstation and its competitors. After the break, client and agency went up the stairs and were confronted by the actor-comedian, Hugh Dennis, from the TV series Punt and Dennis, who started to shout abuse at them in the style of the American evangelical, bible-thumping character from the mooted campaign. Harrison says he found the idea instantly amusing; 'it was a fantastic way of articulating the work', he said.

Harrison describes the pitching process as 'very intense for a client, because it's such an important decision, but it's also a very interesting psychological exercise'. What was abundantly clear was the very narrow margin between victory and defeat for an agency. 'It was between two agencies, and we went with SP on gut feeling', Harrison remembers.

Source: developed from Reed (1995), Tylee (1994), Batstone (1995a)

Agency remuneration

In practice clients can remunerate agencies by using four different methods, either singularly or in combination. These methods are:

- media commission
- fees
- mark-ups
- performance related.

Not all methods are equally appropriate for all types of agency. Media commission is a traditional method of payment for advertising agencies and is a method of payment relevant for media independents – in other words, those agencies that base their primary work on the use of mass media for which media space or time has to be purchased.

Methods used in practice

The results of the 1996 annual survey of advertising agency remuneration by the specialist accountancy firm Willot Kingston Smith showed that clients and agencies use a wider range of methods than ever before (Owen 1996). Exhibit 15.6 shows that commission is estimated to account for the largest slice of advertising agency income (43%); this is closely followed by the fee system (41%). What is interesting is that although performance-related payments only account for less than 2% of advertising agency billings, they had increased three-fold since the previous year. Also significant is the fact that performance-related payments are now responsible for at least a portion of income at 41% of the agencies surveyed, up from a figure of 31% in 1995 (in 1993 this figure was just 13%); 93% of advertising agencies continue to use mark-ups and media commission. They all use fees. It is clear from this that on many accounts different methods might be used, for example a media agency might charge a fee for the planning and charge commission for the buying. While the actual proportions may have changed over recent years, it still remains the case that agencies and clients prefer a mixture of approaches which are best determined by the nature of the work undertaken.

> **FOOD FOR THOUGHT**
>
> *From a client's perspective, there is a lot to commend performance-related payment by results remuneration. It emphasises the need for agencies to produce work that meets objectives and that is measured against some form of criteria to show that it has been effective.*

Exhibit 15.6 Advertising agency gross income

	1996	1995
Media commission	42.8%	45.9%
Fee	41.0%	39.4%
Mark-up	14.5%	14.1%
Performance-related	1.7%	0.6%

Source: From table from '*The state of pay*', in *Campaign*, August 1996, pp. 18–19, Reproduced from *Campaign* magazine with the permission of the copyright owner, Haymarket Business Publications Limited, (Owen, J., 1996)

The fact that the Willot Report reveals swings in popularity for each remuneration system year on year, indicates how little agreement exists on the ideal system. The truth is that no ideal system can exist; each method has its weaknesses, and each is suited to different types of client accounts and is subject to different negotiating stances and ploys.

Media commission

It was a radio comedian called Fred Allen who once irreverently said 'Advertising agency – eighty-five per cent confusion and fifteen per cent commission'. David Abbott, joint chairman and creative director of Abbott Mead Vickers BBDO told *Campaign* magazine that this joke 'is showing its age – most advertising people can't remember a 15% commission'. Commission is now increasingly being replaced by time charges and performance-related bonuses (Batstone 1995b).

Advertising agencies have traditionally received between 12.5% and 15% off rate card prices as commission from the mass media owners (plus any other discounts they may have been able to negotiate). The growing power of clients has seen pressure being exerted on agencies to pass on some of their commission to clients. This is known as **commission rebating**. In practice, therefore, the commission remuneration system can adopt many guises – for example, as a sliding scale, or differential rates for different media using the traditional 15% as the benchmark from which to negotiate.

Commission rebating

Arrangement between a client and its advertising agency (or media independent) whereby some of the media commission the agency receives is passed on to the client by way of a discount on media costs.

The growth of media specialists, coupled with the fact that many of the traditional full-service advertising agencies have hived off their media planning and buying has seen commission-only based remuneration systems all but disappear. Also with the increasing fragmentation of the media, it is more and more difficult to remunerate an agency's input to a campaign on commission alone as the complications and variability present in today's market include so many media opportunities that, essentially, do not offer commission.

The impact commission can have on an agency's finances, of course, depends on the total sums involved and the prime problem revolves round the unpredictability of expenditure levels making it difficult, if not impossible, for agencies to plan their finances based on a commission-only system. It is difficult for agencies to make accurate economic forecasts or manage cash flows and overheads efficiently when its income can be affected by last-minute cuts in a client's media budget. A graphic example of this was the Air New Zealand account where the Mattingly agency lost the account just as a new and expensive branding television commercial was coming to air. After a brief break the commercial reappeared, though the account had been taken on by Saatchi & Saatchi. Another problem with the commission system is that when agencies are being paid a percentage of the mass media spend, the client cannot be sure of the agency's objectivity. It will be naturally in the agency's interest to recommend increased above-the-line media spends.

NEED TO KNOW

☑ *If payment is made by commission on mass media spend, there is the obvious potential for agencies to recommend those marketing communication activities that generate commission, namely, advertising. With a fixed total marketing communications budget, this could lead to advertising solutions being proposed in favour of other marketing communications mix activities such as sales promotions, PR, etc.*

Nevertheless, the commission system has remained remarkably robust in spite of all the criticism from both sides of the industry principally through the underpinning given it by powerful clients such as Procter & Gamble and Unilever. It is unlikely that in practice such companies are not taking into account factors such as workload and creative requirements. It could be argued that remuneration based on commission is very often merely a simple way for the client to approximate the required resource level. Clients can measure commission against the actual resources deployed, demanding detailed explanations from their agencies to form a commercial view as to value received.

Mark-ups

Mark-up

Percentage or actual sum of money added to the fee charged to an agency by a supplier (e.g. printer). The marked-up total is then charged to the client.

Agencies will contract out work to third-party suppliers, for example, print, radio and video production, research and commercial artwork. If the agency is compensated in some other way for the costs of handling work with third parties then they may pass on the costs to the client without a **mark-up**. Alternatively, and most typically, agencies will look to receive part of their remuneration from an agreed mark-up charged on the cost of purchases from third-party suppliers; the rate of mark-ups can vary significantly depending upon the nature of the work undertaken and the degree of agency involvement. Mark-ups between 10% and 15% would not be unusual but can vary significantly.

Fees

Fee-based remuneration

A method of charging a client for work rendered based on a set agreed sum of money (a fee).

A **fee-based remuneration** may involve an agreement based on the time required to develop the work or, in some instances, may be based on an agreement as to the cost involved. An agreed amount, perhaps as a percentage, will be added on for the agency. Such a resource-based approach to remuneration is far more acceptable to those above-the-line agencies who have developed better internal management systems to evaluate workloads and determine work done. In practice, forecasting work is not an easy task. A fee arrangement is most likely where below-the-line promotional activity is involved and advertising accounts where there is no (or limited) media buying involved.

Retainer

Fee paid by the client to its agency, usually on a regular basis, to retain the services of the agency. The fee is calculated to recompense the agency fairly for work it anticipates carrying out.

Fees are normally based on the workload anticipated by the agency and is arrived at by a calculation of the total hours forecast, multiplied by charges set by the agency. The specific charges are likely to vary according to the staff employed on a client's account. It is usual for agencies to work on an agreed monthly or quarterly fee or **retainer**. Payment by fees, of course, gives greater financial stability to agencies allowing them far better control over their cash flow. From the perspective of the client, a fee system also ensures that the advice they receive on how much to spend, where and with which media, is objective and not coloured by the suspicion of other motives.

However, one of the problems with time-based fees is that great creative ideas can be the result of a flash of insight or the result of weeks and possibly months of grind and many would accept that to pay for such ideas by the hour is illogical and unlikely to satisfy either party. For example, it took the creatives at BBH just 45 minutes to create 'Launderette' for Levis. This was a commercial that transformed the fortunes of the company in Europe (Owen 1996). A trend seen over the last few years has been the move away from retainer-based fees to **project-by-project billing**, the drawback to the client being that they risk losing a dedicated team if they move off a retainer payment system.

Project-by-project billing

System whereby the agency charges the client for each individual project it undertakes.

Performance related

The trend toward payment by way of fees appears to be irreversible but there is an increasing willingness to experiment with remuneration systems that provide agencies with rewards for campaign effectiveness.

For example, Walkers Snack Foods have given bonuses to their agencies tied into traditional measures of advertising effectiveness; a particular example of this being used in practice is BMP DDB's campaign for Walkers Crisps starring Gary Lineker.

Performance-related payment by results

System whereby agency remuneration is linked to agreed performance criteria.

One of the results of using **performance-related measures** is that it encourages both the client and the agency to concentrate on the objectives of the marketing communications campaign. These may be in terms of business results such as sales or market share, they may be results expressed in terms of consumer behaviour such as trials, telephone response or showroom traffic, or they may be expressed in the form of a change in brand awareness levels, customer perceptions, or declared buying intentions. The use of such a system thus makes the objective-setting stage of the campaign all the more important for both the agency and the client.

However, the major difficulty for the industry is to come up with a formula that can assess the effectiveness of a particular campaign without penalising the agency for factors beyond its control. The perennial problem for agencies and clients alike is that of isolating the effect of a particular promotional campaign from other influencing factors such as other marketing mix and promotional activity. However, the various industry effectiveness awards have demonstrated that it is not impossible to make marketing communications campaigns accountable. The area of measurement and evaluation is advancing rapidly with better models coupled with improved computer capability in terms of hardware, software and the imaginative use of such capability.

Another argument made against performance-related systems is the uncertainty and instability that it creates for agencies. This is often overcome by considering it as an 'override' and combining it with fee- or commission-based remuneration.

Managing the client–agency relationship

A 1996 research report by the Marketing Forum, ISBA and the IPA on client–agency relationships likened it to a marriage where often 'there is little commitment and divorce is painful but easy' (Dye 1997). Examples of long-running relationships can be found, such as J. Walter Thompson's partnership with Unilever, which has lasted for over half a century. However, for every long-running marriage there are several ill-fated affairs.

Research by Durden et al. (1997) has shown that there are a common set of variables which appear responsible for the break-ups of agency–client relationships over time and between countries. Dissatisfaction with agency performance and changes in agency management were common. Another highly rated variable suggests that clients perceive their ex-agencies as being generally unable to manage their side of the relationship effectively. Research from the 1996 Marketing Forum conference (Dye 1997) identified a number of factors likely to result in a breakdown of relationships with suppliers of marketing services (see Exhibit 15.7).

Although coming some way down the list, concerns over budgets and charges have consistently been reported as causing client concern. These concerns were given substance by the work carried out by Advertising Research Marketing (ARM) looking into the cost effectiveness of agencies. They discovered a number of abuses to which clients were subjected, abuses which came to light after clients had approached ARM to carry out an evaluation. Interestingly, in recent years, media consultants and auditors have been exerting a growing influence on the media marketplace as clients seek greater accountability from their agencies in the areas of media planning and buying.

The ISBA say that now clients are much more knowledgeable about how agencies work than they were previously, they are much more prepared to question and challenge. Since they themselves have had to become more accountable, they are demanding greater accountability from their agencies. At the same time research has shown that agencies have had similar concerns about client accountability as well as 'gripes' about inadequate briefings, pitch costs, vague targets and objectives, lack of reasonable lead times, lack of research and tracking, indecision, inexperienced brand managers and late payments.

Exhibit 15.7 Factors likely to result in a breakdown of relationships with suppliers

Marketing forum conference 1996

Breakdown factors	Delegates %
Lack of personal chemistry	47
Unreliable delivery	44
Poor creative performance	38
Lack of proactive thinking	30
Poor communication	23
Lack of strategic input	22
Poor business results	19
Inability to learn from experience	18
Going over budget	17
Overpriced production	13
Short-term project approach	8
Withholding information	8
Uncompetitive media buying	5
No regular appraisals	5
Other	2

Source: Dye (1997). Reproduced from *Marketing* magazine with the permission of the copyright owner, Haymarket Business Publications Limited.

In response to these concerns the various industry bodies such as the IPA, the ISBA and the DMA have drawn up joint 'best practice' guidelines for future client–agency relations. For example, the ISBA publishes 'Best Practice', the purpose of which is to advise clients how to work successfully with their advertising agencies. It contains sections on agency selection, the contract, agency remuneration, day-to-day relationship and creative and media issues. The ISBA, the IPA and the Direct Marketing Association have also published best-practice pitch guidelines in an effort to improve client–agency relationships.

Since the mid-1990s there has been a drive from both sides of the industry for improved client–agency relations. Many in the industry believe that the way forward for both the client and the agency is to develop joint agreements based on the principle of partnership sourcing, something which is common in other industries, where both parties aim to improve the quality and efficiency of each other's operations (Summers 1995).

Summary

The 1990s saw considerable change in terms of agency dynamics with agencies reorganising their operations to meet the clients' increasing demands for efficiency and effectiveness. Clients are demanding more flexible agency offerings which has resulted in the emergence of a wider range of agency types such as integrated agencies, media specialists, creative hot shops and virtual agencies. Agencies are establishing much closer internal relationships between disciplines and are increasing their international presence either through expansion or the formation of alliances.

When developing a communications campaign an organisation may require a number of specific skills such as creative design, market research, media planning/buying, production or general campaign management. Many companies, therefore, find themselves, at some stage or other, considering the services of a marketing communications agency. There are various types of agencies ranging from those that offer a specialist discipline and/or service to agencies that offer a full range of disciplines and services. There are several management issues, all with advantages and disadvantages, that need to be considered when selecting the type of agency to hire.

There is a well-defined and logical process in selecting agencies, which involves defining client requirements, developing an agency pool list, reviewing credentials, shortlisting, issuing the brief, pitch evaluation and final choice. Throughout this process a range of selection criteria may be considered. Clients can remunerate agencies by using several different payment methods, all of which have advantages and disadvantages. In practice, more flexible remuneration methods are being used with the fee method becoming increasingly popular at the expense of the commission method. Performance-related remuneration is also gaining in popularity.

Self-review questions

1. What are the key issues an organisation should consider when deciding whether to use an agency or manage their marketing communications in-house?

2. Evaluate the alternative agency types available to a client wishing to develop an integrated through-the-line campaign.

3. What should be included in a briefing document to an agency?

4. What criteria should a client use to shortlist and appoint an agency?

5. What are the pros and cons of the alternative remuneration systems from both client and agency perspectives? Include in your considerations the major advantage and major difficulty in applying performance-related payment by results and why it is said that a fee-based system of agency remuneration leads to more objective agency advice.

6. Why might a media commission-based system of payment be inappropriate for a PR agency?

7. What are the key elements to maintaining a healthy client–agency relationship?

Project

Look through the previous six months' issues of industry magazines such as *Admap*, *Campaign*, *Direct Response*, *Marketing*, *Marketing Direct*, *Marketing Week*, *Media Week*, *PR Week*, *Revolution*, etc. and identify articles on agency operations, remuneration, pitches and new accounts. Write a short report on some of the more significant changes taking place and the opinions expressed by industry commentators.

References

Batstone, M. (1995a), How the account was won. *Campaign Report*, 15 September, 3–7.

Batstone, M. (1995b), Do they mean us? *Campaign*, 25 August, 26–27.

Campbell, L. (1998), IBM slashes DM roster to core. *Marketing*, 12 February, 9.

Carter, M. (1997), Dream teams define relationships. *Financial Times*, 7 April, 17.

Cobb, R. (1998), Pointing the way to PR. *Marketing*, 12 March, 29.

Crawford, M. (1994), The art of planning. *Promotions and Incentives*, April, 34–38.

Curtis, J. (1997), Is the ad agency all washed up? *Marketing*, 23 October, 30–31.

Dibb, S., Simkin, L. and Yuen, R. (1994), Pan-European Advertising: think Europe – act local. *International Journal of Advertising*, 13, 125–136.

Direct Response (1995), Direct marketing through the eyes of mainstream advertising Executives. *Direct Response*, May, 25–29.

Durden, G., Orsman, T. and Michell, P.C.N. (1997), Commonalities in the reasons for switching advertising agencies: corroboratory evidence from New Zealand. *International Journal of Advertising*, February, 16 (1), 62–69.

Dye, P. (1997), We can work it out. *Marketing*, 23 January, 22–24.

Gray, R. (1994), Ads pack more punch with PR. *Campaign Report*, 6 May, 33–38.

Green, A. (1991), Death of the full-service ad agency? *Admap*, January, 21–24.

Hunt, A. (1994), Cutting a deal to suit the client's purse. *Ad/Media*, August, 47–48.

IPA (1998), IPA Advertising and Academia Seminar. 17 September, Abbot Mead Vickers BBDO, London.

Kemp, G. (1995), Top European agencies: success of the standalone agencies. *Campaign Report*, 14 July, 10.

Marshall. C. (1994), Gratuity not included. *Marketing*, 3 August, 18–19.

Michell, P. and Saunders, N. (1995), Loyalty in agency–client relations: the impact of the organisational context. *Journal of Advertising Research*, March/April, 9–22.

Owen, J. (1996), The state of pay. *Campaign*, 23 August, 18–19.

Reed, D. (1994), All set to integrate? *Campaign Report*, 1 July, 2–3.

Reed, D. (1995), Advertising agencies à la carte. *M&M Europe*, June, 22–24.

Reid, A. (1994), Is it time to write a consultancy code of honour? *Campaign*, 19 August, 15.

Richards, R.D. (1997), Are agency costs out of hand? *Marketing*, 15 May, 26–27.

Robertson, A. (1995), The keys to agency success. *Admap*, January, 17–19.

Slingsby, H. (1994), Integration circuit. *Marketing Week*, 18 February, 32–35.

Smith, S. (1997), How will agencies adapt to clients' changing needs? *Admap*, January, 28–29.

Summers, D. (1995), Pitch battle. *Financial Times*, 6 April, 20.

Taylor, T. and Ross, L. (1995), Agencies with impact. *M&M Europe*, July, 1–7, 34–35.

Tylee, J. (1994), The relationship crisis. *Campaign*, 13 May, 30–32.

Watkins, S. (1994), Re-engineering: what does it mean? *Campaign*, 1 July, 34–35.

Watkins, S. (1995), The world's top agencies. *Campaign*, 16 June, 28–29.

Selected further reading

Account Planning Special Issue (2003), *Marketing Intelligence and Planning*, 21 (7).

ISBA (1995), *Best Practice: Managing the Advertiser/Agency Business Relationship*. ISBA.

Chapter 16

Research and analysis for integrated marketing communications decision-making

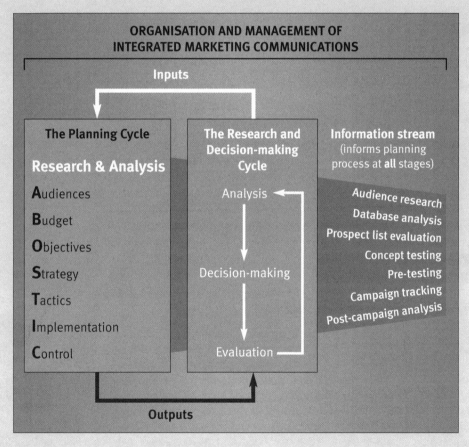

ORGANISATION AND MANAGEMENT OF
INTEGRATED MARKETING COMMUNICATIONS

Inputs

The Planning Cycle

Research & Analysis

Audiences
Budget
Objectives
Strategy
Tactics
Implementation
Control

The Research and Decision-making Cycle

Analysis

Decision-making

Evaluation

Information stream
(informs planning process at **all** stages)

Audience research
Database analysis
Prospect list evaluation
Concept testing
Pre-testing
Campaign tracking
Post-campaign analysis

Outputs

The IMC RABOSTIC Planning Model

CD

If you were developing a new campaign plan for Škoda in Case Study 2, what information would you wish to have and how would you go about collecting it? In addition to reading Chapter 16, it may be helpful to review Chapter 7, The Changing Marketing Communications Environment.

Objectives

- To define the role of market research in marketing communications planning, in terms of rationale, relationships, procedures and responsibilities
- To establish the main types of research available
- To explain a number of important, subsidiary issues in relation to methods of data collection
- To provide a review of the sources available to marketers for understanding markets, and to relate these to marketing communications

Professional perspective

Richard Webber Managing Director, Experian

Working as an analyst within a marketing communications function is definitely not a job for those who want to engage only a narrow aspect of their intelligence. At one moment you may be using evaluative skills to assess the commercial implications of a recently completed qualitative survey. Next you may be employing sharp statistical skills to build a model to maximise response to a forthcoming mailshot. Later in the day the intuitive side of the brain will be called on to assess how best to structure masses of existing customer data so that answers to tomorrow's business issues can be rapidly and reliably given.

In the past the domains of the market researcher and of the direct mail analyst were foreign to each other and neither got involved in issues to do with individual customer profitability which belonged within the domain of operations or customer service departments. Today life is very different. Companies have learned that investment in client retention and in cross-selling new products to loyal customers is a less expensive method of improving market share than concentrating exclusively on recruiting new customers, as many used to do.

Analysts therefore are required to take a broader view of the business. The segmentation systems they develop have to be strategic rather than operational in and applied across all stages of the customer cycle from recruitment to development. They must monitor the cost and profitability of servicing different types of customer, not just recruiting them. They must consider how best to vary the manner in which different types of customer are treated whatever their point of contact, branch, call centre, fulfilment operation or Internet and what products to promote to each segment, what benefits to stress, what incentives to offer, what terms to offer.

Whereas marketing communications analysts once focused on understanding consumers' behaviour, now they have to take responsibility for designing the data flows that can deliver relevant segmentation data to the point of contact with the customer and in a form which can be understood by customer-facing staff. As brands are increasingly defined by the consumer as the service experience that is provided by the supplier, the communications analyst cannot escape becoming involved in the debate over what that experience should be and how it should be customised to meet the needs of individual customer groups.

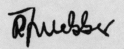

The role of research in integrated marketing communications

The rationale

Marketing/market research

The information-gathering and analysis part of the marketing function that provides relevant information on which marketing decisions may be based and evaluated. Market research is that part of marketing research directed towards market information.

The marketing concept holds that it is good basic business sense to put in front of consumers a product designed as far as possible to appeal to them, and possessing the attributes that they want. This assumes that those marketing products and managing marketing communications know in some detail what consumers actually prefer. **Market research** meets this need, as it is the means of providing accurate, impartial information to marketing decision-makers. This can apply just as much to the evaluation of actual marketing communications, as to the goods they seek to promote on behalf of clients. Knowing what the consumer wants gives marketers an important advantage. Not only should such information facilitate rational decision-making, but it should also help in risk reduction. In a commercial world in which resources are always finite, this latter point can be vital.

There are two key ways of collecting information about the marketplace detailed in Exhibit 16.1:

● the marketing information system
● marketing research projects.

It is important that an organisation has an ongoing system of data collection to aid marketing decision-makers in the integration of activities. Chapter 23 specifically deals with how the quality of marketing communications integration can be evaluated. This chapter focuses on market research projects as applied to the analysis and evaluation of marketing communication campaigns. However, both chapters are concerned with the flow of information that is referred to as the *Information Stream* in our IMC RABOSTIC Planning Model. Research and analysis is typically seen as the starting point to planning with evaluation and control as its end point. This can be a misleading way of looking at the process which is, in reality, a continuous activity. Chapters

Exhibit 16.1 Data for decision-making

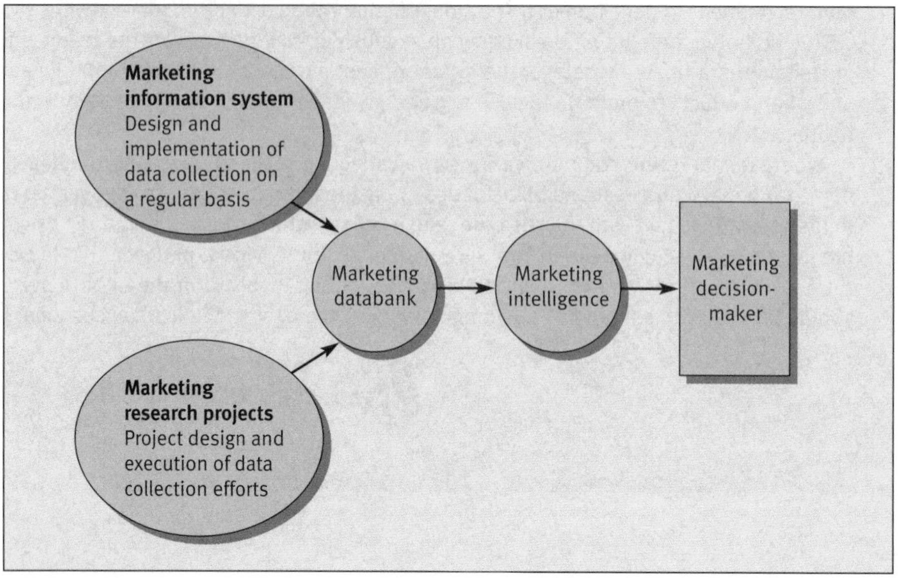

Source: Dibb et al. (1994)

16 and 23 should be considered together and readers may wish to read them in conjunction to achieve a more rounded perspective of the use of information in the total (RABOSTIC) process.

Market research is defined as the:

> Function which links the consumer, customer, and public to the marketer through information – information used to identify and define marketing opportunities and problems; generate, refine, and evaluate marketing actions; monitor marketing performance; and improve understanding of marketing as a process. Marketing research specifies the information required to address these issues; designs the method for collecting information; manages and implements the data collection process; analyses the results; and communicates the findings and their implications.

(Bennett 1988, pp. 117–118)

Personnel in market research

In terms of personnel, it is worth considering the relationships between the various 'players' involved in the evaluation of marketing communications using market research. Fundamental to the whole process is the client company whose goods need promoting. There might be a marketing research manager in a larger, client company, who would liaise internally with marketing personnel, such as brand or product managers. Externally, the product/brand manager would normally liaise mainly with the account executive at the communications agency (Chapter 15). Similarly, the marketing research manager (or other designated person) at the client company would liaise mainly with executives at the chosen market research agency.

All this assumes that both the communications agency and the market research agency are being employed directly by the client company. This often is the case, though not invariably so. Sometimes, the communications agency will employ the market research agency directly, or even employ its own researchers on a full-time basis. This is because it provides the opportunity to trial or pretest ideas for an important campaign, before they are shown at all to the client.

In situations where both types of agency are employed directly by the client company, then a delicate relationship is likely to exist between creative staff at the communications agency and the market researchers involved. It is, of course, the client's prerogative to pretest the ideas of the communications agency, and not to do so would be unwise for reasons already stated. However, it becomes an act of faith on the part of any creative team to hand over their work for evaluation to a researcher whom they may not even have met before.

In short, they need to be able to rely on the expertise and impartiality of the researcher without undue concern. Equally, it behoves the researcher to reassure the creative team that everything possible will be done to evaluate their work fairly and impartially with respondents. The creative team are more likely then to commit themselves to participating in the research process and taking note of the results, whatever those might be. After all, much time, effort, prestige and potential business might be affected by the results of the market research, and the best possible quality of information is crucial. Even then, it is not unknown for the 'creatives' to disregard research findings, if they do not 'feel right'. However, for present purposes, it has to be assumed that all parties are attempting to act as rational decision-makers.

Roles and responsibilities of personnel

Whether employed by a communications agency directly or the client of such an agency, the way in which a market research agency becomes involved in a project is broadly the same. Initially, the need for research would become apparent, and the 'problem', as it might be termed, would have been defined to a greater or lesser extent. At that point, the research agency would be briefed. The scope of the proposed research project would be explained (i.e. a whole campaign or just specific aspects of it). Also, the stage of the project: pretest, post-test, any artwork or other stimulus material for evaluation, would be inspected and any helpful market data might be passed on as background illumination. There would usually be an opportunity for the researcher to clarify any vital points, such as budgetary or time constraints. However, it should be noted that a briefing might also be relatively informal, even to the extent of only being over the telephone for smaller jobs or where speed was of the essence (as is frequently the case!).

Market research brief

Document or verbal instruction outlining the market research problem and task.

Market research proposal

Document outlining proposals designed to fulfil the research brief.

Normally, the researcher would respond to a **brief** with a document called a '**proposal**'. This would be a discussive document, setting out the ideas of the research agency for a solution to the problem. As it is quite usual for more than one research agency to be briefed about any given job, it also has to be a selling document. The research agency would seek to impress the client with its grasp of the problem, its past experience at handling similar work, its proposed solution and value-for-money costing. Defining specific marketing research objectives in the proposal is very important indeed to give the project direction, and provide criteria for judging its ultimate success. Research design would cover such issues as methodology and sampling, plus comment on the implications of any constraints.

If the client was sufficiently impressed with the proposal, and had faith in the agency and the allotted research executive, then the work would be awarded. Again, this process is sometimes 'short-circuited' if the researcher is known and trusted, or if the work is very urgent. Often, a given communications agency or client company will

Exhibit 16.2 Roles and responsibilities of client and agency personnel

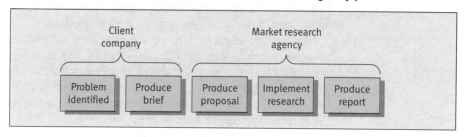

have a favoured research agency at a point in time. In essence, this might well be as simple as certain people liking each other, working well together and trusting each other's abilities.

Other factors that might affect the outcome include the perceived ability of the research agency to protect confidential data (from computer hackers, for instance), or membership of the Market Research Society Interviewer Quality Control Scheme. This registers bona fide interviewers in the UK and provides them with an ID card (including a photograph). This tends to reassure respondents.

In Britain, the market research industry in general is regulated by a body called the Market Research Society (MRS). This is a highly respected body, both in the UK and abroad. Apart from running training courses and offering professional qualifications, it has the Code of Practice of the Market Research Society. This is a voluntary code (it has no force of law) concerned with correct professional behaviour and 'best practice'. This is updated as necessary to take account of changing times and circumstances. However, one of the reasons that British market research is generally well regarded is because of the almost universal adherence among UK professionals to the MRS Code of Practice. Client companies from all walks of commercial life (including marketing

IN VIEW 16.1

An outline of a typical research proposal

1 Project title

2 Statement of marketing problem
   - General description of problem
   - Outlines prior discussions between client and agency

3 Purpose and scope of project
   - Project's objectives
   - Justification for project
   - Limitations of project

4 Data sources and research methodology

5 Estimate of time and personnel requirements

6 Cost estimates

Source: Peter, J. and Donnelly, J. (1994), *A Preface to Marketing Management*, 7th edn, Irwin, pp. 50–51, reproduced with permission of The McGraw-Hill Companies

communications) can, therefore, be assured of more or less uniform standards of ethical behaviour and high levels of expertise from UK market research agencies. The scheme mentioned above for registering interviewers is just one facet of MRS activities.

The use of research in integrated marketing communications

Each element within the marketing communications mix can be evaluated in terms of:

- *Efficiency*: doing things right,
- *Effectiveness*: doing the right things,
- *Economy*: doing things within a specified budget.

For direct marketing communications, for example, effectiveness can be measured by the percentage response received and efficiency by the cost of that response. Chapter 25 provides examples of the evaluation criteria of public relations. Chapter 23 details the evaluation stages in a marketing communications campaign as a whole.

This evaluation process can be used for a number of different purposes in integrated marketing communications. Exhibit 16.3 details some of the most common uses.

Message research is used for pretesting and post-testing all aspects of creative messages, while **media research** looks at the effectiveness of different media as vehicles for the message. Chapter 23 looks at these in more detail. There are specific techniques for other elements of the communications mix, such as company representative 'detail' testing (evaluating what should and should not be said by the representatives of a client company about a product). Another example might be the post-evaluation of particularly strong publicity achieved during a PR campaign, or after some unforeseen event. Whatever use the research is initiated for, it encompasses the following seven stages:

Message research

Part of marketing research focused on testing all aspects of creative messages.

Media research

Part of marketing research focused on researching media selection and use.

1 Problem formulation.
2 Determine research design.
3 Data collection method design.
4 Sample design.
5 Data collection.
6 Analysis and interpretation of data.
7 Prepare research report.

Exhibit 16.3 Research activities of 587 companies

Research type	% of companies
Motivation research	37
Media research	57
Copy research	50
Advertising effectiveness	65
Competitive advertising studies	47
Public image studies	60
Sales force compensation studies	30
Sales force quota studies	26
Sales force territory structure	31
Studies of sales promotions (premiums, coupons, deals, etc.)	36

Source: Adapted from Kinnear and Root (1988, p. 43)

Types of market research

An overview of the types of market research available for marketing communications is provided in Exhibit 16.4. The remaining sections of the chapter will discuss each type of research in more detail and the related issues surrounding these market research methods.

Secondary research

Secondary research is often known as 'desk research'. It is essentially exploratory in nature, and is frequently used to uncover basic facts about a market and the products that compete in it (e.g. total market size by value and volume, products by value, volume and percentage market share). This may be a 'one-off' requirement, perhaps to provide background material to help brief a marketing communications agency. Alternatively, it might be a routine exercise within a client company to monitor the progress of its own products and to look for new opportunities. So, secondary sources often contribute significantly to an understanding of what is happening in the marketplace.

A key characteristic of secondary research is that the user always gathers it from existing, published sources (i.e. 'second-hand' or secondary material). There are many such sources in the UK, ranging from those as easily accessible as Yellow Pages to government statistical publications of various kinds (e.g. *Business Monitor*). Numerous trade associations can also provide helpful literature on occasion. Secondary data can be purchased from specialist companies, such as Mintel, either as 'off-the-shelf', syndicated reports or as regular, market data (e.g. retail and other audits such as Nielsen). These would all be examples of sources external to the eventual user, but there can also be internal sources of secondary data, such as those generated by accounting and ex-factory sales. They would, of course, be specific to a particular company.

The Internet has recently become an important external source, and other technological developments, such as CD-ROMs and email, have assisted in the storage, retrieval and transmission of secondary data. There are also various online services

Exhibit 16.4 Categorising market research data

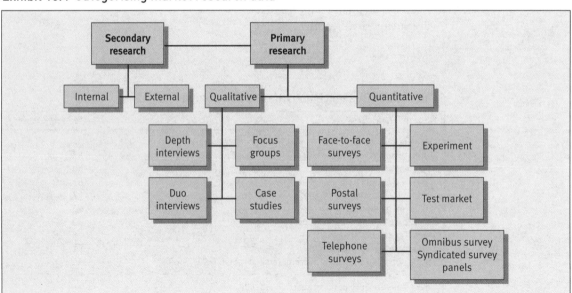

from which data can be obtained, some of which are interactive. Of course, all these can interlock very effectively with modern computer-based management information systems or less broad marketing information systems.

While potentially very useful, secondary data is not always the 'gold mine' opportunity that it might appear to be at first sight. Because it was almost invariably produced originally for a purpose not specific to the needs of the current user, it seldom meets exact requirements. Of course, determined 'detective work' can help minimise that problem. However, secondary data is sometimes fairly old (especially that obtained at no cost), and often there is no way of checking its accuracy. The secondary user may, therefore, be inadvertently perpetuating previous mistakes. Having said that, secondary research can save time and money, and even if ad hoc work (custom designed primary research) is still ultimately necessary, the secondary research carried out can help define objectives and suggest possible avenues for research design.

Primary research

In contrast, primary research always gathers data at first hand. It is customised to suit the research problem in hand for a specific client. It can be exploratory in nature, or it may have conclusive measurement of some sort as the deliberate aim (see 'qualitative' and 'quantitative' research in the next section).

Qualitative research

Qualitative research is an in-depth, investigative approach with an in-built discretion on the part of the interviewer to 'dig and delve' into the interviewees' responses as necessary in any direction that might seem productive. This type of research can be described as 'exploratory'. Such work is usually tape-recorded for subsequent ease of analysis, and requires considerable skill and experience on the part of the interviewer. There are four methods of data collection commonly employed in qualitative research which are summarised in Exhibit 16.5.

Exhibit 16.5 Types of qualitative data collection methods

Depth interviews	Face-to-face interviews on a one-to-one basis are used whenever individual clarification with the respondent is essential (e.g. company representative detail testing) or a sensitive topic needs investigating (e.g. it may not be appropriate to discuss personal health or sexual habits in a group).
'Duos' interviews	Interviews with a pair of respondents, to introduce a discussive element that can be especially helpful with experts in certain technical areas (e.g. pharmacists and a new pack design for a cold remedy).
Focus groups	A group discussion technique which demands the most skill from the interviewer (called a moderator in this context), and much ground can be covered rapidly and productively. It is appropriate for any situation in which all group members are equally able or qualified to make a contribution, without the need for extensive one-to-one clarification. Provides a social context and a synergistic 'brainstorming' effect.
Case histories (case studies)	Intensive investigation of situations which are relevant to the problem situation. A detailed description of the case is formulated (e.g. retail stores, sales territories, markets) in order to obtain a better understanding. Especially suitable for complex situations where numerous variables interact to produce a problem or opportunity.

The aim of qualitative research is to find out what 'relevant others' think (e.g. target consumers about aspects of a possible TV advertisement), and to uncover whatever issues are important in the situation. Such an approach is only feasible on a relatively small sample, and there is deliberately no intention to measure anything, except in broad, relative terms. So, findings from such research are illustrated with 'flavoursome' quotes, rather than percentages.

Quantitative research

Quantitative research is designed to explain what is happening and the frequency of occurrence. It is an approach that has measurement as its main aim, and reported findings are usually illustrated with percentages. Of necessity, samples are relatively large in size, with the intention of creating statistical validity. To enhance this objective, questionnaires are designed so that all respondents are replying to consistently the same questions. For many people in Britain, street interviewers in the high street with their clipboards are a familiar sight. This type of interviewing uses a highly structured, 'tick boxes' style of questionnaire. However, it can be difficult to measure people's views unless a set of relevant issues has been established and defined by some prior, investigative procedure. That is why quantification classically follows secondary research, qualitative research or both.

There are a number of approaches to quantitative data collection. Exhibit 16.6 summarises the key methods.

Issues in data collection

Having looked at various methods of market research, it is important to highlight ancillary issues of data collection. For instance, it was mentioned earlier that qualitative research was small sample research, but relatively large samples were used for quantitative surveys. This is in accord with the quite different intended purpose of the two types of research, namely investigation and measurement, respectively. That being the case, how respondents in a sample are selected together with sources of market research error are presented.

Sampling methods

There are two quite different approaches to sampling, each with strengths and weaknesses:

Probability sampling

Sampling methods in which all elements of a given population have an equal chance of being selected.

Non-probability sampling

Sampling methods in which elements of a given population do not have an equal chance of being selected.

- **Probability sampling:** each population element has a known, non-zero chance of being included in the sample and is known as random sampling.
- **Non-probability sampling:** this is a non-random method, which relies on personal judgement and, therefore, prohibits estimating the probability that any population element will be included in the study.

The proposition of the basic form of probability sampling (known as simple random sampling) is identical to a prize draw, in which the number and identity of all the participants is known, and each has just one ticket. The probability of any one person's

Exhibit 16.6 Types of qualitative data collection methods

Face-to-face surveys	
Street interviews	Interviewers stand in a strategic town centre location (called 'mall intercept' in the USA) and recruit to a pre-determined quota (by age, sex, product usage etc.).
Hall tests	Respondents are still recruited on the street, but are interviewed nearby indoors. There they can more easily be shown product-related materials (e.g. taste tests, new pack designs).
Cold calling	Interviewers go door-to-door, without a prior appointment. Usually they work to a quota or have been directed there via a random sampling technique. Time consuming, expensive and even potentially dangerous for interviewers.
By appointment	Interviewers go door-to-door, with a prior appointment. Less time consuming, and much more appropriate for business-to-business research.
Telephone surveys	Personal interviewing, like those above, but not face-to-face. Quick and cheap, with possible easier access to hard-to-reach respondents, but time-constrained by 'respondent fatigue'. Works well with quick, highly structured questionnaires, but any stimulus material has to be sent in advance.
Postal surveys	Large samples relatively cheaply is the attraction, but not suitable for use with stimulus material. Classically short, very clear questionnaires. However, respondents are pre-recruited for some large questionnaires (e.g. 90 pages for lifestyle surveys). Typically low response rates with uneven geographical spread. Useful for smaller, specialist 'populations' (e.g. the medical profession).
Continuous research	Consists of omnibus surveys and panels. The former run at regular intervals, and allow a few questions at a time to be put to special interest groups (e.g. young mums) cheaply by several clients on the same questionnaire. Each only receives the results to their own questions. Panels are pre-recruited, and common uses include special interest groups, consumer panels and media measurement (e.g. TV viewing figures and readership surveys).
Syndicated surveys	One-off surveys on a subject of wide potential interest, which can be sold 'off-the-shelf' to anyone (e.g. Mintel Reports). They become secondary sources to the buyer, although obvious potential buyers might be asked for areas of interest before the survey is carried out.
Experiment	Conducted with one or more independent variables which are consciously manipulated or controlled and their effect on a dependent variable is measured.
Test market	'A controlled experiment, done in a limited but carefully selected part of the marketplace, whose aim is to predict sales or profit consequences, either in absolute or relative terms, of one or more marketing actions' (Achenbaum 1974).

ticket being drawn from the 'hat' can easily be calculated (hence, 'probability' sampling), and in this example, all will have an equal chance of selection. Other types of probability and non-probability sampling are summarised in Exhibit 16.7.

Market research samples can be drawn in this way, but only if you are lucky enough to have a complete and accurate list, or sampling frame as it is called, of the 'population' of interest (e.g. all golfers in the UK). This approach only has any point in

Exhibit 16.7 An overview of sampling methods

Probability sampling	
Simple random sample	Each person in a population has a known and equal chance of being selected.
Stratified sample	Samples are divided into mutually exclusive and exhaustive sub-sets, strata or separate sub-populations, e.g. people who live in high, medium and low income areas. Simple random samples are then taken from each strata.
Cluster sample	A number of clustering units, usually geographically-based, are selected from mutually exclusive and exhaustive sub-sets. Either all the people in a unit are selected or a random sample from the sub-set is selected, e.g. school children's attitudes towards exams, select certain schools.
Non-probability sampling	
Convenience sample	Respondents selected on the basis of the convenience of the researcher; respondents just happen to be where the information for the study is being collected.
Quota sample	Respondents are selected to represent the population on some pre-specified control characteristics.
Judgement or purposive sample	Respondents selected because they can best serve the research purpose, from an expert judge's opinion.

relation to quantitative research. It is expensive and time-consuming, and selected respondents cannot easily be substituted. For this reason, it is seldom used in commercial market research.

A much more common approach is non-random (or non-probability) sampling. All qualitative research falls into this category, as it uses small samples, with no intention of creating statistical validity. Convenience sampling is used in this situation (e.g. any eight cat owners to discuss cat foods). The version of non-random sampling that is associated with quantitative research is called quota sampling. The overall composition of the sample is designed to suit the purpose in hand, and individual interviewers are allotted quotas to fill that are defined by relevant variables. For instance, one interviewer might have a quota requiring interviews with 20 non-smokers, made up of 10 males and 10 females and all spread across four age ranges.

Sample size, random error and sampling error

In practice, the estimation of an ideal sample size for any given quantitative research project is usually mostly on the basis of past experience. Sampling theory, however, provides a formula for the statistical calculation of sample size, see Kinnear and Taylor (1991) for details.

However the sample size is chosen, it has to be large enough to support statistical validity. In other words, it has to be adequate to allow the researcher to draw inferences from the sample, which can then be generalised onto the larger population of interest. The term validity essentially means accuracy; it has been defined as the extent to which differences in scores on a measurement instrument reflect true differences among respondents or are due to random error or chance (Churchill 1995). Research must also be reliable. That means that if any given survey was repeated in identical circumstances, then the results should be more or less the same from one sample to the next (assuming that time had not intervened to bring about significant change).

NEED TO KNOW

☑ *Reliability is concerned with the consistency and predictability of the research findings. Validity is concerned with the question: are we measuring what we think we are measuring?*

Sampling error

Inaccuracy caused through selecting a sample rather than the population as a whole.

This automatically introduces yet another important consideration, known as **sampling error**. If a number of samples were taken from the same population, then, as mentioned above, the results from these identical surveys should be approximately the same. However, the fact that you would be sampling each time, and not carrying out a census of the whole population, would be the cause of slight differences. If, and only if, a random sampling process had selected the sample, then this difference in relation to any given sample could be calculated as an actual percentage error. This is called sampling error, and can be defined as the extent to which the average situation in a sample (in relation to some statistic) varies from the actual average situation in the population of interest.

There is nothing that can be done to eliminate sampling error; it is simply a fact of life. Having more rather than fewer respondents will tend to reduce it, but there is an obvious trade-off here against increasing costs. Of course, sampling error exists for non-random quota samples too, but it is just that it cannot be calculated. Sometimes it is possible to form a reasonably accurate estimate, if similar past surveys have been sampled using both methods. For this reason, some would say that quota sampling is an 'act of faith', but there is plenty of accumulated evidence to show that it works.

Non-sampling error

Errors or inaccuracy caused through the research process that can be attributed to factors other than sampling errors.

There is also **non-sampling error**, just to complete the picture, which can be actively combated only by careful training, planning and monitoring procedures (quality control) (Lipstein 1975). This comprises all the things that can go wrong or can vary when carrying out a survey. It includes bias on the part of the interviewer, which might involve minute differences in the administration of the questionnaire from one interview to the next, or from one interviewer to another. Non-response (i.e. refusal to be interviewed) is another possible cause, as there is no way of telling if those agreeing to be interviewed are in some subtle way different, or atypical, from those who refuse. Non-sampling error is likely to affect both the validity and reliability of the survey data.

Next, a point about how improved technology can be used to minimise interviewer bias. The advent of personal computers has paved the way for the use of on-screen questionnaires, and the direct input of responses by interviewers. As the routing through the questionnaire is automatic depending on the previous answer, scope for human error is considerably reduced.

CAPI

Computer Assisted Personal Interviewing.

This assists quantitative data collection in two main ways. Firstly, when cold-calling or interviewing by appointment, a laptop computer can be used in a process known as Computer Assisted Personal Interviewing (**CAPI**). The results of the day's work can then be downloaded by telephone to head office. Secondly, computerised workstations are arranged as banked units to facilitate telephone interviewing. Such a facility is likely to be centrally located, and to be the property of a specific market research agency. The equipment offers great flexibility and effectiveness, and the opportunity to process the data very rapidly indeed. The catchphrase for this is Computer Assisted Telephone Interviewing (**CATI**).

CATI

Computer Assisted Telephone Interviewing.

Market monitoring: continuous research and syndicated surveys

Even before marketing communications can be developed for a product, or before the need to evaluate them becomes apparent, there is a basic and fundamental need to understand what is happening in the marketplace. It is not just a case of trying to learn about the needs of the consumer (though that is also crucial).

The client company needs to understand the structure of the market, the relative importance and position of competing companies; their products, their marketing communications, their pricing structures and indeed learning everything possible about that market, as well as understanding the needs of customers and consumers. It also means developing strategies based on this understanding to launch or sustain products, which of course, includes platforms for marketing communications. The point is that from the perspective of a large, modern company, market analysis is a necessary ongoing process, and not just an occasional or intermittent activity.

Market monitoring is the term that could be applied to this ongoing and comprehensive process of market analysis. Data is obtained from a variety of sources, both primary and secondary. Generally speaking, secondary sources (often as regular services) supply much of the data, with primary research being used to fill the gaps, or to evaluate new ideas. In effect, the market research manager of a large, modern company has a 'tool kit' at her disposal, and needs to be able to select the right tool for any specific task.

Audits

Audit data is the 'bread and butter' of most routine market monitoring. It is gathered by a variety of means and offered as a number of unique services by specialist agencies. It is available both for traditional retail markets (e.g. Nielsen) and for a variety of the specialised markets (e.g. the Medical Data Index from Medical Intercontinental Statistics). Each industry client pays a subscription, and receives the latest data at regular fortnightly, or perhaps monthly, intervals. It can usually be obtained in a variety of formats, such as hard copy (largely outdated), online (sometimes interactive) and CD-ROM.

It is basic market data in the sense that it permits analysis of a market or part of a market in terms of sales by value and volume. It also allows the progress of individual companies, products, product variations and even prices to be monitored in some detail over time. As such, it is an invaluable aid and a constant source of reference. It is also of use when attempting to locate gaps in the market for a possible new product. It should be noted, however, that a number of organisations, including Boots and Marks & Spencer, refuse to provide data for such purposes.

Modern technology, and particularly the personal computer, has made a great deal of difference to the way in which audit data can be handled inside the client company to answer queries. Technology has also made a considerable difference to the way in which data is now gathered. At one time, virtually all audit data was gathered using panels, and this approach is still important (e.g. The Taylor-Nelson/AGB Superpanel which collects purchase information from 8500 respondents repeatedly over time). The hand-held bar-code scanner is a technological development that enables participants to scan all their grocery purchases. The data from such respondents can be sent via a modem down the telephone line to the head office collection point. Previous technology would have necessitated a 'pantry audit' (or even dustbin audit!) by an interviewer at the respondent's home.

EPOS
Electronic Point of Sale.

Particularly in the grocery sector, **EPOS** (electronic point of sale) scanning in supermarkets has taken over from panel research to some extent. It holds out the valuable possibility of an eventual census of product purchase (Scantrack currently claims to cover 60% or more of the grocery trade). Store loyalty card schemes from the major supermarket companies (also clothes stores) are maturing to the point at which product purchase can be directly linked to demographics such as age, sex and other variables. However, not everyone co-operates with these schemes.

WARNING

⚠ *The reader should not become confused between audit data and the term 'marketing audit'. A marketing audit is a far-reaching and periodic review within a company of its entire marketing effort. It has little direct connection with audit data, other than that it might utilise it as a source of information.*

IN VIEW 16.2

Book bar codes

ISBN 0-273-62513-6

9 780273 625131 >

EAN 13 prefix | 4 digits identify publisher | 5 digits identify book title | Check digit

The target group index (TGI)

TGI is another very widely used data facility in the UK but it is a specific service offered by the British Market Research Bureau (BMRB). It has run continuously since 1968, and gathers data from approximately 24,000 adult respondents per year using an extensive self-completion questionnaire. It updates its figures on a six-monthly basis, with an annual report running to over 30 volumes. It covers a vast range of products and services from alcohol to spot creams, which is one of the reasons why it is so useful.

Apart from its very wide coverage of products, it also collects product usage data by brand and extent of usage (heavy, medium, light and non-use). This data is cross-tabulated by demographic profiles (age, sex, income, etc.), media consumption and a series of attitudinal, 'lifestyle' statements. Thus, if some sort of marketing communication were to be aimed at heavy or light users of a product, then it would be fairly simple to find out 'what made them tick'. It would then be possible to reflect their interests in some appropriate way in the promotion. Not only that, but knowing the pattern of media consumption would allow rational decisions to be made about how the marketing communication should be conveyed to the target consumers.

The TGI Index is a very powerful marketing tool. A caveat, however, is that for some of the more esoteric cross-referencing opportunities (e.g. *Sun* readers who holiday in the Bahamas), data in individual cells might fall to levels at which care might need to be exercised about statistical validity.

Geodemographic and psychographic data

Geodemographic data classifies small geographical areas according to the characteristics of their inhabitants. It links demographic data, such as age, gender, income, social class and marital status to location, and segments customers according to where and how they live. **Psychographic segmentation** differentiates and aggregates consumers in terms of psychological dimensions, such as values, lifestyles, attitudes, interests and opinions (Mullen and Johnson 1990).

Commercial products capturing this kind of information are available throughout Europe. For instance, they allow the researcher to look at specific regions or even cities, towns and villages and to specify which variables they want to see as a distribution on

Geodemographic segmentation

Method of segmenting the market based on the classification of small geographic areas (enumeration districts) according to the characteristics of their inhabitants – principally house types and house locations.

Psychographic segmentation

Segmentation based on psychological dimensions such as values, lifestyles, attitudes, interests and opinions.

the map. For example, you could see how the population of London is distributed in terms of social class or age, right down to postcode level and type of house or neighbourhood. Clearly, such information could be useful to marketers. Chapter 17 details the commercial availability of geodemographic and lifestyle data products. Specific, branded services include ACORN, MOSAIC, PINPOINT, CAMEO and SUPERPROFILES. All of these can be cross-referenced to TGI data to bring in the element of product purchase. While care is needed in interpreting such data, its potential power is obvious.

Syndicated research and market reports

This possible data source was touched upon earlier in relation to methods of quantitative data collection. Syndicated research is available to all 'off-the-peg', and for that reason can be relatively inexpensive to purchase. Certain agency providers tend to specialise in this type of research. What can be obtained might vary from an entirely survey-based report for half-a-dozen clients, to a briefer and more basic mixture of secondary data and some primary data sold to hundreds of firms. Of course, this also affects the cost, which in the latter case might be less than £200. Mintel, Keynote and Frost & Sullivan are all well-known names in this context. Such reports tend to fill gaps in the regular data provision set up by a company. It might be, for instance, that a completely new market or product opportunity needs to be looked at, initially at very little cost. However, it should not be forgotten that a surprising amount of free access to survey results exists, and consulting a copy of the Directory of Published Market Research can reap rewards.

Omnibus surveys

An omnibus survey is a form of continuous research. These surveys are the unique products of certain agencies, and an intending user has to take out a subscription to that service. Each omnibus survey covers a particular special interest group. For instance, MAS runs a monthly telephone omnibus survey called Business Line that targets 2000 small businesses. Some similar services are available that address special interest groups using panels (e.g. the Martin-Hamblin monthly telephone panel of 500 GPs). However, a defining feature of an omnibus survey is that a fresh sample is recruited every time it runs.

The major usefulness of such a service is that the company researcher has a means of asking just a few questions at a time, as the need arises. The subscription usually generates a credit balance of a certain number of points. These are then used up over time, with more complex questions requiring more points. Clearly this is highly cost-effective compared with ad hoc research. Of course, it does mean questions from several clients being on the same questionnaire, but each only receives his or her own results. It does give rise, though, to debates about respondent fatigue, and viewing order effect.

Media measurement

As identified earlier, while there are numerous uses for market research, the most common uses for marketing communications are message research and media research. Message research, used for pretesting and post-testing all aspects of creative messages, is usually conducted through ad hoc methods. Media research looks at the effectiveness of different media as vehicles for the message. Existing media research data can often be bought commercially. The services that fall under the media research heading have a very important function in the whole context of marketing communications. Respectively, they measure quantitatively the readership of major publications, radio listening and TV audience viewing figures.

In the UK, the National Readership Survey uses one of the few remaining random samples in commercial market research (currently Research Services Ltd). It also uses CAPI and aided recall (i.e. prompt cards) to record the readership of approximately 230 publications as accurately as possible from 36,000 households per annum. This includes all national newspapers, as well as a considerable number of special interest publications (e.g. *Exchange and Mart, Racing Post*, etc.). The results are released monthly and half-yearly, split by extent of readership, region and demographic factors. They are clearly very helpful to anyone involved in placing advertising in print media.

The Broadcasters Audience Research Board (BARB) oversees the Electronic Audience Measurement Service in relation to TV viewing figures. It allocates two contracts: one to collect the data and one to maintain the panel from which it is gathered. Basically, there are nine regional panels (in accord with designated TV regions), each composed of 500 households, and making a grand total of 4500. Each is equipped with an electronic 'people meter' (developed by A.C. Nielsen), that rests on top of the TV set, and records who is in the room and what they watch. The data can then be sent down the telephone line via a modem to the main computer facility at head office.

FOOD FOR THOUGHT

Detailed information on TV viewing habits could be amalgamated with other survey data, such as that on lifestyles and product usage from the TGI (data fusion). This would create virtual consumers, whose lives would be mapped in incredible detail, but they would not be actual respondents. It would then be possible, theoretically, to select the period of airtime that was best for a particular product type, or even specific brand.

The BARB panel is of particular importance, as viewing figures generate ratings points for TV programmes, and even parts of programmes. These have become the currency by which the cost or desirability of any given period of airtime can be judged for advertising purposes. The service, therefore, is much in demand by media schedulers at marketing communications agencies.

In addition to these two important services, there is the Radio Joint Audience Research (RAJAR), which does the same for radio broadcasts. Also, the Poster Audience Research (POSTAR), uses statistical modelling to assess stationary, roadside poster sites.

Test marketing

As identified earlier in the chapter, a market test is a controlled experiment in which one or more proposed marketing actions are trialed in a limited section of the marketplace (Brennan 1990). Test marketing assesses the viability of a new product before embarking on a full launch programme. By implication, it is bound to involve some means of exposing the product to the consumer that is more limited than a full, national launch. Also, it does tend to be more appropriate for consumer goods that are intended for the general public.

There are two main ways of achieving this limited degree of product exposure. The first is the area, or standard test market. This involves choosing a geographical area that is likely to be representative of the rest of the country in respect of that product. After all, if the test is expected to be predictive, then this factor is of importance. In the UK, areas selected for test marketing tend to coincide with designated TV regions. This makes it possible to deliver TV advertising and other promotion during the test in a fairly precise way. The period of the test is likely to be for either six months or one year, as sufficient time is required for audit data to demonstrate a firm trend in sales (perhaps despite some seasonality). Unfortunately, it is also long enough for competitors to become aware of the situation. Then, they might attempt to copy the idea, sabotage the results or both.

A variation on this theme can make the process more discreet, depending on the type of product. If it is one that would normally be sold mainly through large stores, then the product could be released through a number of different branches of the same chain store; this is called controlled test marketing. However, that would also make it difficult to advertise on TV, and so it would tend to suit products that relied mainly on point-of-sale display material. The store company would also need to be already included in the data collection programme for an appropriate retail audit, so that the outcome to the test could be assessed. For details on other types of test markets, for example electronic, simulated, mini and calibrated, see Churchill (1995).

IN VIEW 16.3

Test marketing misfires

When Campbell Soup first test marketed Prego spaghetti sauce, Campbell marketers say they noticed a flurry of new Ragu ads and pence-off deals that they believe were designed to induce shoppers to load up on Ragu and skew Prego's test results. They also claim that Ragu copied Prego when it developed Ragu Homestyle spaghetti sauce, which was thick, red, flecked with oregano and basil, and which Ragu moved into national distribution before Prego.

Source: Morris (1982), p. 31

Perceptual mapping

Perceptual mapping adds another dimension to the analysis of markets and marketing information. The basic proposition is that if it were possible to obtain the views of consumers on different dimensions of a product, couched in comparative terms, then spatial maps could be drawn up. These could show the relative distance between different products of the same general type in terms of these dimensions. Thus, an assessment using two dimensions would produce a flat, two-dimensional map and so on. Of course, maps utilising more than three dimensions can only exist in cyber space, and so the technique can quickly leap to the limits of the human imagination. That might actually make them less easy to appreciate as a marketing tool, though no less useful as an aid to generating relevant marketing communications.

Exhibit 16.8 demonstrates a typical two-dimensional perceptual or market map. It is a hypothetical example based on consumer perceptions of different makes of car. Input data in a real exercise would be gathered from consumers using primary research, and probably some sort of attitude measurement technique. Statistical tools such as factor analysis, cluster analysis and discriminant analysis are used to analyse the data (see Hauser and Koppelman 1979). Crucially, it can be assumed that the brands close together on the map were perceived as similar in terms of cost and quality. Also, the distribution forms little groups or clusters, which could be given names and seen as different segments of the same, overall market. Clearly, the make of car in

Exhibit 16.8 Example of a perceptual map

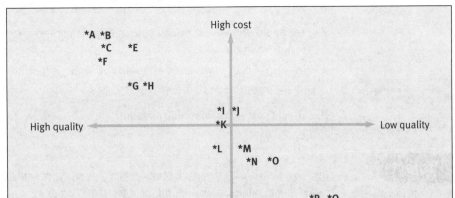

the group including *S is likely to appeal to very different consumers in terms of demographics and lifestyle than, say, the group containing *B. So, appropriate but different marketing communications could be devised for these two market segments.

Summary

This chapter has outlined the importance of market and consumer analysis for integrated marketing communications decision-making. Market research is the means of providing accurate, impartial information to marketing decision-makers, and is necessary for the development and evaluation of marketing communications.

The main uses of market research in marketing communications were identified and the variety of data collection methods discussed. A comprehensive review of possible data sources for understanding markets was presented. This information should be cross-referenced with Chapter 7, The Changing Marketing Communications Environment, which outlines the macro- and micro-environmental analyses necessary in marketing communications planning.

Self-review questions

1 What sort of a document is a research proposal, and what purpose does it serve?

2 What is the difference between primary and secondary research?

3 How does a group discussion (or focus group) differ from other possible qualitative research methodologies?

4 Explain what you understand by 'cold calling' in relation to quantitative research methodology.

5 Why is sampling error a 'fact of life'?

6 What difference has the advent of EPOS made to audit data services?

7 Find and outline one particular point of care that needs to be exercised in relation to the TGI.

8 What does the abbreviation 'BARB' mean, and what is its function in the area of media measurement?

9 What is perceptual mapping used for?

Project

Britango wants to launch a new carbonated soft drink. Your marketing manager has asked you to put together a report identifying data sources to aid in the development of the marketing communications campaign. Your marketing manager particularly wants to know what information is available to plan the introduction of the product into the supermarkets and to develop the TV and radio advertising.

References

Achenbaum, A.R. (1974), Market testing: Using the marketplace as a laboratory. In *Handbook of Marketing Research* (R. Ferber, ed.). New York: McGraw-Hill.

Bennett, P.D. (1988), *Dictionary of Marketing Terms*. American Marketing Association.

Brennan, L. (1990), Meeting the Test. *Sales and Marketing Management*, 142 (March), 57–65.

Churchill, G.A. (1995), *Marketing Research Methodological Foundations*. The Dryden Press.

Dibb, S., Simkin, L., Pride, W. and Ferrel, O.L. (1994), *Marketing – Concepts and Strategies*. Houghton Mifflin Company.

Hauser, J.R. and Koppelman, F.S. (1979), Alternative perceptual mapping techniques: relative accuracy and usefulness. *Journal of Marketing Research*, 16 (November), 495–506.

Kinnear, T.C. and Root, A.R. (1988), *Survey of Market Research*. Chicago, IL: American Marketing Association.

Kinnear, T.C. and Taylor, J.R. (1991), *Marketing Research: An Applied Approach*. McGraw-Hill.

Lipstein, B. (1975), In Defense of Small Samples. *Journal of Advertising Research*, 15 (February), 35.

Morris, B. (1982), New Campbell entry sets off a big spaghetti sauce battle. *The Wall Street Journal*, 2 December, 31.

Mullen, L. and Johnson, S. (1990), Quoted in McGoldrick, P.J., *Retail Marketing*. McGraw-Hill Book Company Europe.

Peter, J.P. and Donnelly, J.H. (1994), *A Preface to Marketing Management* 6th edn. Homewood, IL: Irwin.

Selected further reading

Chisnall, P.M. (1997), *Marketing Research*. McGraw-Hill.

Crimp, M. and Wright, L.T. (1995), *The Marketing Research Process*. Prentice Hall.

Dickson, J.P. and MacLachlan, P. (1992), Fax surveys? *Marketing Research: A Magazine of Management and Applications*, 4 (September), 26–30.

Fern, E.F. (1982), The use of focus groups for idea generation. *Journal of Marketing Research*, 19 (February), 10–13.

Stewart, D.W. (1984), *Secondary Research: Information Sources and Methods*. Sage Publications.

Sykes, W. (1990), Validity and reliability in qualitative market research: a review of the literature. *Journal of the Market Research Society*, 32 (July), 289–328.

Tyebjee, T.T. (1979), Telephone survey methods: the state of the art. *Journal of Marketing*, 43 (Summer), 68–78.

Chapter 17

Identifying target audiences and profiling target markets

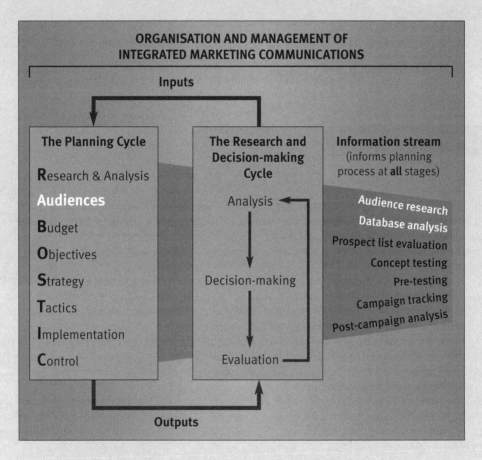

ORGANISATION AND MANAGEMENT OF INTEGRATED MARKETING COMMUNICATIONS

Inputs

The Planning Cycle

Research & Analysis
Audiences
Budget
Objectives
Strategy
Tactics
Implementation
Control

The Research and Decision-making Cycle

Analysis

Decision-making

Evaluation

Information stream
(informs planning process at **all** stages)

Audience research
Database analysis
Prospect list evaluation
Concept testing
Pre-testing
Campaign tracking
Post-campaign analysis

Outputs

The IMC RABOSTIC Planning Model

CD

Referring to Chapter 17 and Case Study 2 on the CD, in addition to your own research, profile Škoda's target audiences. Provide a rationale for the segmentation criteria utilised. Refer to Exhibit 17.2 to structure your profile.

Chapter outline

- The decline of mass marketing
- Market segmentation
- Types of segmentation
- Commercially available segmentation classifications
- Using segmentation for marketing communications

Objectives

- To introduce the context in which targeted marketing is taking place
- To outline the concept and uses of market segmentation
- To present the five key types of market segmentation
- To discuss the main segmentation products commercially available
- To demonstrate the applications of segmentation and profiling

Professional perspective

Mark Patron Executive Vice President, Claritas (Europe) BV

Today it is a thousand times cheaper to hold a customer's details on a computer than it was 20 years ago. Media and markets are fragmenting. Marketing budgets continue to be squeezed. The ability for advertisers to identify key customers and prospects is no longer a 'nice to have' but a necessity. This is achieved through the use of databases for segmentation and targeting.

Over the last ten years companies have embraced database marketing and now know who are their best customers. Over the next ten years leading companies will move to one-to-one marketing by developing customer relationship management (CRM) capabilities so that they can give the right offer, to the right person, at the right time and through the right channel.

One-to-one marketing requires changing business focus from share of market to share of customer. However, few companies measure share of customer at the individual customer level. Another barrier to one-to-one marketing is that it can be administratively too complex for marketing departments to get their arms around and offer customers complete customisation.

Computer costs halve every 18 months, but companies' IT spends remain constant. Companies must therefore be processing twice as much data every 18 months. As a result marketing departments are becoming data rich but information poor. A good segmentation strategy can help everyone in the organisation sort and understand that data.

One-to-one marketing promises to make marketing more efficient. CRM and a good segmentation strategy, particularly if it is based on share of customer, can make one-to-one marketing technically and administratively more practical and achievable.

The decline of mass marketing

> One of the most profound realisations to strike any marketer is that there is a great diversity among customers.   (Louden and Della Bitta 1993, p. 30)

Consumer markets are increasingly fragmented and turbulent as customers are becoming more knowledgeable, discerning and demanding. Media channels have also narrowed and increased in number. Rather than being limited to terrestrial TV channels, consumers have access to cable, satellite and digital TV. There has been a similar explosion of highly targeted radio stations and consumer magazines. And the Internet provides a whole new medium altogether.

It is within this environment that marketers are moving away from broad mass marketing to a more targeted approach. Kotler and Armstrong (1997) identify a trend towards targeted marketing which allows sellers to better identify their marketing opportunities – relevant offers to the right customers at the right time. This is having a profound impact on the mix and media used in marketing communications. Essentially this involves focusing marketing communications on targets that provide the greatest opportunity while attempting to minimise messages aimed at the wrong targets. The targeted marketer operates by answering four fundamental questions:

- Who exactly are the consumers most likely to become users of a brand?
- Where are they located?
- How can they be reached most efficiently with marketing communications tools?
- When is the best time in the consumer's life to apply the tools?

Marketers are recognising that customers are not all alike – that they differ in terms of demographics, attitudes, needs, location and social affiliations. This is also reflected in the significant shift in promotional spend from mass media, such as television or national press, towards more targetable means of communications such as direct mail, telemarketing and other direct response media (Chapter 27). These micro-marketing media, if they are to be used effectively, require detailed information about individual consumers and the local marketplaces in which they live. Chapter 1 gave details about the importance of defining target customers *and* target audiences. This chapter concentrates on the means by which we can begin to identify these groups by describing the principal methods of market segmentation.

Market segmentation

Market segmentation

The process of dividing a market into homogeneous segments using one or a range of possible alternative segmentation methods, each segment being composed of customers or consumers sharing similar characteristics.

Marketers can approach a market through either market aggregation or **market segmentation**. Market aggregation (or mass marketing) is where there is little or no application of subdivision of the market. Even though there is diversity between consumers, they are seen to be sufficiently alike to approach as a homogeneous group when marketing a particular product. Alternatively, market segmentation can be implemented. 'Market segmentation is the process of splitting customers into different groups, or segments, within which customers with similar characteristics have similar needs. By doing this, each one can be targeted and reached with a distinct marketing mix' (McDonald and Dunbar 1995, p. 10). This definition has three key tasks for the marketer:

Targeting

The selection of one or more market segments.

Positioning

The relative perceptual position of one brand compared with competing brands.

- to define the market and find segments within it (segmentation);
- to select the most profitable segments that can be served the most effectively and efficiently by the company's resources **(targeting)**; and
- to communicate to that segment to appeal to their specific wants and needs better than competitors **(positioning)**.

Segmentation is used when the differences between consumers are seen to be substantial enough so that, to effectively market a product, customers are put into groups. By dividing a larger market into smaller segments with different preferences and subsequently adjusting the product (or service) to the preferences of the individual segments, the overall distance between what the company is offering to the market and what the market requires is reduced (Hansen 1972).

It is becoming increasingly evident that most markets are not homogeneous, but are made up of different individual customers, sub-markets or segments. The practice of mass marketing, where there are significant differences, leaves an organisation vulnerable to more clearly targeted competitors. Marketing is concerned with identifying and satisfying user needs. Offering one product for all segments means the needs of some users are not wholly satisfied, and is therefore wasteful on resources. Taken to extremes, of course, every user is a unique market segment, for everyone has slightly different needs. However, few companies have the resources to be all things to all people, and this implies that a choice needs to be made concerning which segments to serve, thus taking up a position somewhere between the two extremes (Exhibit 17.1).

Exhibit 17.1 Alternative marketing approaches

Mass marketing (Undifferentiated marketing)	Target the whole market with one marketing mix
Target marketing	Target one or more segments within a market with different marketing mixes
– Niche and concentrated marketing	Target one segment within a market with one marketing mix
– Differentiated marketing	Target multiple segments with different marketing mixes
Mass customisation marketing	Target all segments in the market with different marketing mixes

Consumers, and the neighbourhoods in which they live, vary greatly in terms of the brands, advertising campaigns and promotions to which they will respond. An in-depth understanding of the typical customer of a brand is required to plan and implement effective and efficient marketing communications. Segmentation and targeting of customers allows marketing communicators to more precisely position and deliver their messages and prevent wasted coverage to people falling outside the target market.

Types of segmentation

Every product or service has a particular customer profile, which can be expressed in terms of likely age, occupation, sex, income, location, among many other variables. By targeting media to specific groups of consumers based on these purchasing profiles,

Exhibit 17.2 Bases for segmentation

Types of segmentation	Demographics	Geographics	Geodemographics	Psychographics	Behavioural
Variables	• Age • Sex • Lifestage • Type of residence • Income • Occupation • Education • Religion • Ethnic origin • Nationality	• Postcode • City, town, village or rural • Coastal or inland • County • Region (often based on television regions) • Economic or political union/association • Country or continent • Population • Climate	• The segmentation of consumers where they live – using demographic data to classify neighbourhoods	• Values, attitudes, motivations • Interest, opinions, hobbies (lifestyle)	• Benefits sought • Purchase occasion • Purchase behaviour • Usage • Perceptions and beliefs

marketing communicators can sell more productively and profitably. Exhibit 17.2 presents an overview of the key types of segmentation bases.

Demographic segmentation

Demographics are general customer and consumer characteristics, e.g. age, income, education and gender. Segmentation of the market may be based on the variables outlined in Exhibit 17.2 or there may be segmentation on a multi-demographic basis, that is, a combination of any number of these variables.

Demographic segmentation

Segmentation based on general population characteristics.

Demographic segmentation is the most common method of dividing the overall market (Gunter and Furnham 1992, p. 4). Their popularity is based on the ease with which they can be measured, their association with the sale of many products and services, and the fact that they are useful for the targeting of advertising material through related media. Croft (1994, p. 25) notes, however, that using a demographic base alone 'rarely provides a complete understanding of user differences'. In particular, Croft highlights the problems of segmenting by age alone and gives the examples of those consumers who are 'young at heart' or 'mature beyond their years'. These consumers would not necessarily behave according to their age norms. In fact, changes in population demographics such as the ageing of baby boomers (those born from 1946 to the 1960s) also questions the stability of demographic information. In one study of lifestyle it was indicated that the majority of people 55 and over said they look, act and feel at least 10 years younger than they are. This indicates that, in the case of age, there is a widening gap between chronological age and psychological age. This effect could, therefore, have influence on consumers' purchasing behaviour.

Socio-economic segmentation

The classification of consumers on the basis of education, income and occupation.

Education, income and occupation together form a **socio-economic segmentation** basis. In the UK, the ABC1 socio-economic system is popular with many advertising agencies. Consumers are divided into six classes (i.e. A, B, C1, C2, D and E) based on the occupation of the head of the household. So for example, consumers in social grade A have higher managerial, administrative or professional occupations and are of upper middle class. Consumers in social grade C2 are skilled manual workers and belong to the skilled working class. However, with increased social mobility and the blurring of class divisions, this socio-economic segmentation system is not as accurate as it used to be.

Lifestage

Segmentation based on the different stages of life that people go through, incorporating such factors as age, marital status and family size. The Family Life Cycle (FLC) is an example of lifestage segmentation.

Lifestage is another composite socio-demographic variable that incorporates age, marital status and family size. As lifestage is dynamic in that it incorporates changes that an individual is likely to experience throughout life. Thus, this type of segmentation is not only a major predictor of consumer needs, but indicates when the consumer will be attracted to a particular product field. This is particularly useful for consumer durables. The lifestage segmentation tool was first developed by Wells and Gubar (1966). In View 17.1 illustrates the application of lifestage to financial products and Exhibit 17.3 highlights the nine lifestages in the family life cycle (FLC).

Geographic segmentation

Segmentation based on location measures.

Geographic segmentation

Geographic segmentation involves dividing a market using one or more of the variables outlined in Exhibit 17.2. This data must be regularly monitored due to population shifts.

Geodemographic segmentation

Method of segmenting the market based on the classification of small geographic areas (enumeration districts) according to the characteristics of their inhabitants.

Geodemographic segmentation

Geodemographic segmentation is the classification of small geographical areas according to the characteristics of their inhabitants. It links demographic data to location and segments customers according to where and how they live.

Enumeration districts

Small collections of households or properties based on census data collection.

Geodemographic datasets are built around postal sectors, **enumeration districts**, postcodes, retail centres, grid squares, media and administrative regions or local authorities. These areas and neighbourhoods tend to exhibit common demographic

---

IN VIEW 17.1

Lifestage segmentation for financial products

Under 16		16 – 24	24 – 45	Beyond 45 and high net worth
	STUDENTS			
Young savers schemes				
Plastic cards services; ATMs, credit cards, charge cards and new debit cards				
		Home loans and home related services		
		Consumer finance		
		Insurance		
			Investment services	
			Pensions	

Exhibit 17.3 Stages of the family life cycle (lifestage segmentation)

Stage	Financial circumstances and purchasing characteristics
Bachelor stage Young, single, not living at parental home	Few financial burdens, recreation oriented, holidays, entertainments outside home
Newly wed Young couples, no children	Better off financially, two incomes, purchase Home, some consumer durables
Full nest 1 Youngest child under 6	Home purchasing peak; increasing financial pressures, may have only one income earner; purchase of household 'necessities'
Full nest 2 Youngest child over 6	Financial position better still improving; some working spouses
Full nest 3 Older married couples with dependent children	Financial position better still; update household products and furnishings
Empty nest 1 Older married couples, no children at home	Home ownership peak; renewed interest in travel and leisure activities; buy luxuries
Empty nest 2 Older married couples, no children at home, retired	Drastic cut in income; medical services bought
Solitary survivor Still in labour force	Income good but likely to sell home
Solitary survivor Retired	Special needs for medical care, affection and security

Source: Hooley and Saunders (1993, p. 144). Copyright © 1993 (Hooley, G.J., and Saunders, J.A.), reprinted with the permission of Pearson Education

and lifestyle characteristics, which can be used to distinguish purchasing patterns and responses to advertising campaigns.

Behavioural segmentation

Behavioural segmentation

Segmentation based on behavioural characteristics towards particular goods or service categories.

Consumers can be segmented by their behaviour towards a particular product or service, including the variables outlined in Exhibit 17.2. Transactional information on existing customers can be used to derive **behavioural segments** that produce information on current behaviour. For example, customers may be segmented according to their frequency of purchase or the different benefits they seek when selecting a product or service such as convenience, status and performance.

Psychographic segmentation

Psychographic segmentation

Segmentation based on psychological dimensions such as values, lifestyles, attitudes, interests and opinions.

Psychographic segmentation differentiates and aggregates consumers in terms of psychological dimensions, such as values, lifestyles, attitudes, interests and opinions (Mullen and Johnson 1990). Such segmentation is generally used when purchasing behaviour is correlated with the personality or lifestyle of consumers (Jobber 1995). In this case, consumers with different personalities or lifestyles have varying product or service preferences and may respond differently to marketing mix offerings.

IN VIEW 17.2

Linking lifestage and geographical segmentation – nest eggs

Once the children have left home, parents tend to find out exactly how much they have been spending on them all these years. This can be a pleasant surprise and the surplus cash can be used to enjoy those years leading up to retirement and beyond. These 'empty nesters' are prime prospects for products like gardening equipment, DIY, holidays of all kinds and small but fully equipped cars.

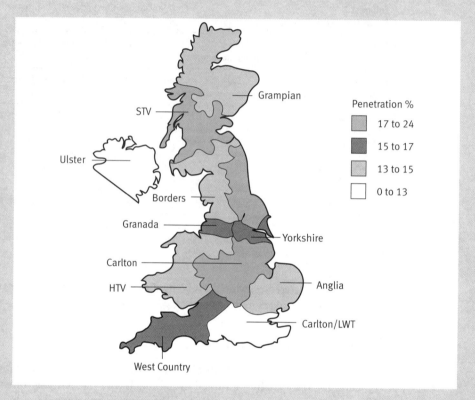

Source: *New Perspectives* (1997a); data courtesy of Equifax UK

There was a flux of academic interest in psychographic research in the 1970s when the method emerged (e.g. Plummer 1974; Wells 1975; Wind 1978). Market researchers at the time were looking for new methods to segment markets. Up until this time, demographics and socio-economic factors were the main segmentation tools used in industry. There was recognition that important demographic distinctions simply do not exist in many product categories and even when they do, one cannot intelligently decide how to attract any particular market segment unless one knows why the distinctions exist (Gunter and Furnham 1992). This prompted the search for a new segmentation base. Psychographics offered a solution with its richer data on consumers than demographics previously offered.

Demand for commercial psychographic classification systems followed academic research. Lesser (1988, p. 36) described exactly why organisations are so interested in this method of segmentation, 'Psychographic research has provided corporate planners with detailed, precisely focused information about why consumers buy their products.' Understandably, there was a great deal of interest in the methods. Indeed in 1977, a survey by the American Marketing Association found that 37.9% of marketing firms frequently used psychographic research methods (Lesser and Hughs 1986).

While demographics identify who is purchasing a particular product or service and associated details about where and how they live (geodemographics), psychographics look at why they buy. Although demographics are essential for marketers for identifying life patterns for most people, they, as Gunter and Furnham (1992, p. 64) describe, 'don't go far enough'. Psychographics add value and richness to demographic data when describing consumer behaviour for segmentation purposes. Exhibit 17.4 highlights the contrasting results of profiling from demographic data compared with psychographic data (Bartos 1976).

Demby (1974) was one of the first to investigate the topic of 'psychographics' and provided a three-level definition:

Generally, psychographics may be viewed as the practical application of the behavioural and social sciences to marketing research.

More specifically, psychographics is a quantitative research procedure that is indicated when demographic, socio-economic and user/non-user analyses are not sufficient to explain and predict consumer behaviour.

More specifically, psychographics seeks to describe the human characteristics of consumers that may have bearing on their response to products, packaging, advertising and public relations efforts. Such variables may span a spectrum from self-concept and lifestyle to attitudes, interests and opinions, as well as perceptions of product attributes.   (Gunter and Furnham 1992, pp. 64–65)

Exhibit 17.4 Differing profiles for four categories of women in the USA

Category	Profiles	
	Demographics	**Psychographics**
Stay-at-home housewife	Older, least affluent, least educated, has fewer children at home	Sees herself as tense, refined, low on ego and humour
Housewife who plans to work	Younger, more affluent, much better education, has younger children at home	Sees herself as tense, awkward, stubborn, affectionate, creative, kind, sociable, trustworthy, not egocentric
The working woman who says 'it's just a job'	Works in a clerical or other category, better educated than 'stay-at-home' but less than 'plans to work'; income on par with 'plans to work'	Sees herself as awkward, tense, affectionate, not very intelligent or creative
The working woman who believes her work is a career	The most affluent, best education, slightly younger than 'just a job' but older than 'plans to work'	Has very strong self-image, is amiable, affectionate, efficient, broad-minded, refined, trustworthy, sociable and creative

Source: Bartos 1976 in Williams (1981, p. 92)

There are many differing definitions of psychographics in the literature that have caused some confusion in the subject. Some authors cite psychographics as the analysis of personality traits and cognitive behaviour alone, while others put emphasis on consumer lifestyles as a basis for psychographic segmentation. Thus, the terms lifestyles and psychographics are often used interchangeably.

The heart of many psychographic measurement instruments are AIO statements. These statements measure Attitudes (or activities), Interests and Opinions and can be either general statements or product/behaviour-specific. Such statements are presented to consumers in **AIO inventories** and the measuring tools are in the form of Likert scales. The final results are constructed through factor analysis to determine underlying themes or factors. Plummer (1974) identified four areas that AIO rating statements measure in relation to people's activities; these are shown in Exhibit 17.5.

AIO inventory

Collection of Attitudes, Interests and Opinion statements used to assess respondents' views.

Psychographics can be used to segment markets or be used to develop customer profiles. Mehotra and Wells (1977) outlined four different examples of the kind of studies for which psychographics can be useful. These are general or product-specific segmentation analyses, and general or product-specific profiling analyses. General segmentation classifies respondents into relatively homogeneous groups to form a typology. Product-specific segmentation asks product-specific questions in order to form groups of product users. General profiling is achieved through large questionnaires, variables (e.g. media usage) are identified as determinants of a type of consumer behaviour. Finally, product-specific profiling initially identifies a target group of consumers, then profiles them according to a set of product-relevant variables (Heath 1995).

NEED TO KNOW

☑ *A Likert scale is a market research tool to capture attitudes quantitatively. It is a summated scale consisting of a series of statements to which the subject responds. The respondent indicates agreement or disagreement with each statement on an intensity scale. For example,*

The future looks very black.

Strongly agree (5) agree (4) undecided (3) disagree (2) strongly disagree (1)

Most people can be trusted.

Strongly agree (5) agree (4) undecided (3) disagree (2) strongly disagree (1)

There has been great interest from consumer researchers who have used psychographics to identify the following groups:

- opinion leaders;
- store-loyal consumers;
- consumer activism (Hufstad and Pessemier 1973);
- social class.

All these, among many other studies mostly carried out in the mid-1970s, have related psychographics to recurring topics in consumer research in order to develop profiles. They are mostly related to consumer behaviour in general. Others such as Plummer (1970, 1974) used psychographics to segment product-specific markets. In Plummer's

Exhibit 17.5 Variables in AIO statements

Lifestyle dimensions			
Activities	*Interests*	*Opinions*	*Demographics*
Work, hobbies, social events, vacation, entertainment club membership, community, shopping, sports	Family, home, job, community, recreation, fashion, food, media, achievements	Themselves, social issues, politics, business, economics, education, products, future, culture	Age, education, income occupation, family size, dwelling, geography, city size stage in life cycle

Source: Plummer (1974, p. 34)

case, the analysis of credit card users resulted in profits that are more specific. These studies have provided new and special segmentations of consumers, along with aiding the development of psychographic profiles and trend data.

Psychographic profiles can be used to develop consumer typologies. The Needham, Harper and Steers advertising agency (1975) developed a number of general typologies. The study aimed to classify the consumer population into groups, so that consumers within the groups had similar lifestyles (Mehotra and Wells 1977). Therefore, rather than identifying segments within particular product-specific markets or identifying consumer behaviour, this general study segmented the whole consumer market. Rather than searching for what particular consumers have in common, this study admitted the possibility that users of a product might fall into several quite different segments (Wells 1975). The examples above give a flavour of the early work in the area of psychographic measurement. This burgeoning interest has been carried forward and more recent uses of psychographics include:

- pharmaceutical manufacturers using emotions to motivate consumers to ask their doctors about drugs (Morgan and Levy 1998);
- agricultural companies looking at what drives farmers' buying decisions (Bernick 1996);
- car manufacturers looking at why consumers buy specific cars (Morgan and Levy 1997) and their attitudes to particular cars (VW/Audi 2002).

In View 17.3 illustrates some of the typologies identified concerning shopping types based on psychographic and behavioural studies. With the extraordinary growth in databases, companies can make extensive use of their own transactional and research data to segment their existing customers to create their own customer profiles. Marks and Spencer Financial Services (2003) have done this to create a composite customer profile composed of behavioural, geodemographic and psychographic components. They have segmented their customers into five macro-segments and 27 micro-segments. The Royal Bank of Canada segments its customers into discrete segments based on attitude, behaviour, current and potential profitability, expected purchasing behaviour, vulnerabilities and channel preferences. Tesco uses seven key segmentation

IN VIEW 17.3

Shopping typologies developed from psychographics

- The convenience shopper
- The recreational shopper
- The price-bargain shopper
- The store-loyal shopper (McGoldrick 1990; Stephenson and Willett 1969)
- Traditionalist ('*I have some old fashioned tastes and habits*')
- Outgoing/individualistic ('*I would rather fix something myself than take it to an expert*')
- Quality service ('*I will go out of my way to find a bank with good service*')
- Socially conscious ('*If my clothes are not in fashion it really bothers me*')
- Other-directed ('*I usually ask for help from other people in making decisions*')

Marks and Spencer macro-segments include: Hard Core Revolvers; Revolvers; Transactors; Inactives; and Dormant. Their micro-segments include: Family Focused Mums; Complementary Casuals; Shop Arounds; Immaculate Greys; Couples Next Door; Traditional Brigade; and Everyday Office Attire.

systems based on lifestage, profitability, channel, shopping habits, promotional promiscuity, brand advocacy and basket typology.

The most commonly cited American psychographic segmentation system is SRI Consulting Business Intelligence's VALS™. This system, originally developed by cultural anthropologist, Arnold Mitchell in the late 1970s, classified consumers into groups based on their attitudes to social values such as military spending and abortion rights. Mitchell found a correlation between social values and consumer purchase patterns. (The original VALS framework is shown in Exhibit 17.6.) Over about a ten-year period the social values began to diffuse in society. In 1989, a team of experts from SRI International, Stanford University, and University of California, Berkeley undertook a research effort to refresh VALS. They found an explicit link between certain enduring psychological attributes and purchase behaviour. The link was stronger than the link between attitudes to social values and purchase behaviour. It was also less likely to change over time since many psychological attributes tend to be fairly constant through a person's life. The VALS framework was redesigned based on these research findings and for a short time was called VALS2™. Over the years other minor modifications have been made to VALS including reverting back to its original name VALS, which is used today. The current VALS system, (shown in Exhibit 17.7) however, continues to classify individual consumers into one of eight groups based on key psychological attributes and several demographics. The current system also incorporates two important concepts into its framework: primary motivation (represented in the horizontal dimension of the framework) and resources (represented in the vertical dimension). VALS recognises three primary consumer motivations: ideals, achievement and self-expression. The extent to which consumer's wishes may be turned to reality is fostered or restricted by their resources which include but are not limited to HH income, education, self-confidence, and willingness to try new products. The VALS system applies specifically to the US English-speaking population aged 18 years or older and somewhat more generally to Western society. The basic eight US VALS types are described below. There is also a United Kingdom VALS and a JapanVALS™. JapanVALS divides society on the basis of two key consumer concepts: life orientation (which is similar to the US primary motivations) and attitudes to social change. JapanVALS identifies four primary life orientations: Traditional Ways, Occupations, Innovation, and Self-Expression. The ten Japanese consumer segments are also described below for interest.

Exhibit 17.6 Orginal VALS psychographic framework

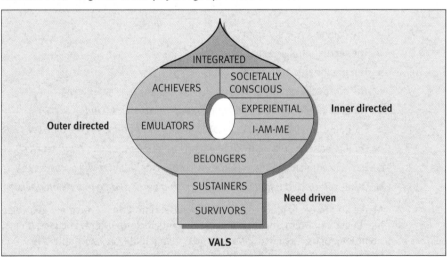

Exhibit 17.7 Current VALS framework

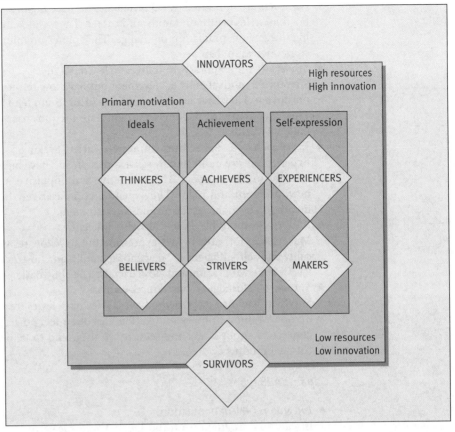

Source: From figure of current VALS™ framework from www.sric-bi.com/VALS, reproduced by kind permission of SRI Consulting Business Intelligence, (2003)

Western VALS types

- *Innovators* – Take charge. Sophisticated. Curious.
  Innovators are successful and sophisticated with high self-esteem. They have abundant resources and exhibit all three primary motivations in varying degrees. They are willing to take charge and are change leaders. They are the most receptive to new ideas and technologies. Their purchases reflect cultivated tastes for upmarket, niche goods and services.
- *Thinkers* – Reflective. Informed. Content.
  Thinkers are motivated by ideals. They have high resources. They are mature, satisfied and reflective. They tend to be well educated and actively seek out information seekers in the decision-making process. They favour durability, functionality and value in products.
- *Believers* – Literal. Loyal. Moralistic.
  Believers are motivated by ideals but have low resources. They are strongly traditional and respect rules and authority. They are fundamentally conservative, slow to change and are technology averse. They choose familiar goods and services and established brands.

- *Achievers* – Goal Orientated. Brand Conscious. Conventional.
  Achievers are motivated by achievement and have high resources. Their goal-orientated lifestyles centre on family and career. They avoid situations that encourage a high degree of stimulation or change. They prefer premium products that demonstrate success to their peers.
- *Strivers* – Contemporary. Imitative. Style Conscious.
  Strivers are motivated by achievement but have low resources. They are trendy and fun-loving. They have little discretionary income and tend to have narrow interests. They favour stylish products that emulate the purchases of people with greater material wealth.
- *Experiencers* – Trend Setting. Impulsive. Variety Seeking.
  Experiencers are motivated by self-expression and have high resources. They appreciate the unconventional. They are active and impulsive, and stimulation from the new, different and risky. They spend a comparatively high proportion of their income on fashion, socalising and entertainment.
- *Makers* – Responsible. Practical. Self-sufficient.
  Makers are motivated by self-expression but have low resources. They value practicality and self-sufficiency. They choose hands-on constructive activities and spend leisure time with family and close friends. They buy basic products.
- *Survivors* – Nostalgic. Constrained. Cautious.
  Survivors lead narrowly focused lives. They have fewest resources of all types. They do not exhibit a primary motivation and often feel powerless. They are primarily concerned about safety and security so they tend to be brand loyal and buy discounted products.

Japan-VALS types

- *Integrators* (4% of population)
  Integrators are highest on the Japan VALS measure of Innovation. These consumers are active, inquisitive, informed, affluent and lead trends. They travel frequently and consume a wide range of print and broadcast media including niche and foreign media.
- *Self-Innovators and Self-Adapters* (7% and 11% of population)
  Both these groups score high on Self-Expression. These consumers desire personal experience, fashionable, display, social activities and graphic entertainment.
- *Ryoshiki Innovators and Ryoshiki Adapters* (6% and 10% of population)
  Both these groups score highest on Occupations. Education, career achievement and professional knowledge are of personal concern but home, family and social status are guiding factors.
- *Tradition Innovators and Tradition Adapters* (6% and 10% of population)
  Both these groups score highest on the measure of Traditional Ways. These consumers adhere to traditional religions and customs, prefer long-familiar home furnishings and dress, and hold conservative social opinions.
- *High Pragmatics and Low Pragmatics* (14% and 17% of population)
  Neither of these groups score highly on any orientation dimension. They are not very active and not well-informed. They have few interests and seem flexible or even uncommitted in their lifestyle choices.
- *Sustainers* (15% of population)
  Sustainers score the lowest on the Innovation and Self-Expression dimensions. Lacking money, youth and high education, these consumers dislike change and are typically orientated to sustaining the past.

The ability to predict consumer behaviour tends to be higher for psychographic studies than for demographic studies. Although psychographics may be poor predictors of individual behaviour, they do provide sharper contrasts between groups than do demographics. Individual level prediction results from psychographics are on par with personality research. Wells (1975) summarised the prediction results:

> When there is an absence of good reason that the psychographic construct would be closely related to the specific consumer behaviour being studied, correlations run between +0.20 and –0.20, with many close to zero. When the psychographic constructs have been shown to be clearly relevant to the behaviour being studied, individual correlations have been in the 0.20's and 0.30's. When relevant dimensions have been linked together in multiple regression, multiple correlations have been in the 0.50's and 0.60's. (p. 206)

Psychographic variables do not, therefore, account for a large portion of the variance in many of these studies. However, there is some accounting for differences amongst groups. Bass et al. (1968) argue it is this identification of differences in groups which is more important than explaining variance for individual behaviour.

Commercially available segmentation classifications

Successful marketing campaigns are dependent on accurate answers to the following questions:

1 Who are my customers?
2 What are they like?
3 What do they buy?
4 Where can I find them?
5 How can I reach them?

The answers to these questions may be found from in-house customer data, data from primary research sources such as the Target Group Index, MORI Financial Services and AGB Superpanel, or from other data providers (Chapter 16).

WARNING

> *While academics have spilt behavioural and psychographic segmentation into two types (see Exhibit 17.2), commercially available products have grouped behavioural segmentation and interests, opinions and hobbies as a lifestyle product, and values, attitudes and motivations as a psychographic product.*

Three key types of segmentation products have become commercially available from data providers in Europe: geodemographics, lifestyle systems and psychographics. Exhibit 17.8 gives some examples of each type. Psychographic products typically include data on values, attitudes and motivations, while lifestyle products are a combination of interests, opinions, hobbies and behavioural variables. There is, however, considerable overlap between the types of data products available. So, for example, a number of lifestyle products have been combined with geographical information. While the major data providers are mainly American or British-owned, data are available across Europe and most of the rest of the world.

In the UK, geodemographic consumer classification was made commercially available with the launch by CACI of ACORN in 1979. Lifestyle data appeared in the mid-1980s, and has been particularly useful for direct mail. Psychographic products are the most recent and are being increasingly used in advertising campaign development.

Geodemographic products are easy to understand and to use. As they are postcode-based systems, they are easily applied to a customer database and a wide range of other postcoded databases, from customer files to market research panels or external prospect lists. These products support a wide range of marketing applications, including

Exhibit 17.8 Commercial segmentation products

Types of segmentation	Demographics	Geographics	Geodemographics	Psychographics	Behavioural
Variables	<ul><li>Age</li><li>Sex</li><li>Lifestage</li><li>Type of residence</li><li>Income</li><li>Occupation</li><li>Education</li><li>Religion</li><li>Ethnic origin</li><li>Nationality</li></ul>	<ul><li>Postcode</li><li>City, town, village or rural</li><li>Coastal or inland</li><li>County</li><li>Region (often based on television regions)</li><li>Economic or political union/ association</li><li>Country or continent</li><li>Population</li><li>Climate</li></ul>	<ul><li>The segmentation of consumers where they live – using demographic data to classify neighbourhoods</li></ul>	1 Values, attitudes, motivations 2 Interest, opinions, hobbies (lifestyle)	<ul><li>Benefits sought</li><li>Purchase occasion</li><li>Purchase behaviour</li><li>Usage</li><li>Perceptions and beliefs</li></ul>

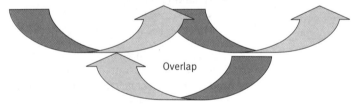

Geodemographics	Lifestyle	Psychographics
MOSAIC	Prizm	Neighbourhood RISC
ACORN	Chorus	Social Value Groups
	LifestylesUK	Monitor
	Dimensions	

Overlap

direct mail and leafleting, local market modelling, store performance evaluation, site location and media planning. Typically, however, geodemographics are not available at an individual consumer level as they are based on census data. The data is, therefore, based at household, postcode or enumeration district level. An enumeration district is a collection of approximately 150 households in which census data is grouped. Postcoded data is information specific to, on average, 15 households (Plate 18).

Lifestyle data *does* provide information about specific consumers as data is collected from individual consumer surveys or questionnaires on guarantee cards. Lifestyle products contain verifiable customer information like income, product usage and consumer interests. It is current and can be collected continuously unlike census-based geodemographics. Lifestyle surveys, however, cover a sample of the national population, so total individual coverage on a variety of variables is not available as data from the surveys is modelled onto the rest of the population. Thus, important customer groups may be under-represented. Geodemographic data contain information on everyone but only in an aggregated form; lifestyle data contains detailed information on some of us but nothing at all on the rest (Exhibit 17.9).

Exhibit 17.9 Postcode (geodemographic) versus individual (lifestyle) data

Postcode level	Individual level
Comprehensive coverage	Sporadic coverage
Only a postal match required	Full name and address required for match
Less discriminatory	Highly discriminatory
Limited descriptive powers	Greater predictive potential

Source: New Perspectives (June 1997)

Geodemographic products

Geodemographic products are based on the reduction of the innate complexity of the many variables which can describe neighbourhoods to a single 'neighbourhood' type for each distinctly different sort of neighbourhood that can be identified. The most commonly used geodemographic products are Experian's MOSAIC and CACI's ACORN systems.

MOSAIC is available in 16 countries in which 779 million people are classified. Additionally, the product GlobalMOSAIC can analyse consumers across national markets to support the development of international strategies. MOSAIC (UK) allocates every one of the 1.6 million postcodes in the UK into one of 12 broad groups and 52 detailed types, based on the types of consumers living there. For example, Clever Capitalists are typically wealthy people involved in business, particularly in the setting up and financial management of companies and in broking, commercial trading, importing and exporting. This group is characterised by company directors living in large detached houses, though not necessarily with extensive grounds, in well-established residential areas within reasonable reach of city centres. Children are typically of secondary school age or students and there is a higher proportion of foreigners than in the more suburban clusters within group one. Golders Green, Finchley and Hendon are areas of London where this target group is particularly over-represented (Plate 17).

MOSAIC uses a wide range of detailed information from sources such as the Census, the electoral roll, credit, company director, retail and Royal Mail data to find small areas sharing common housing, population and socio-economic characteristics. By linking customer addresses or market research surveys to MOSAIC via the postcode, it becomes possible to model virtually any aspect of customer behaviour on a geographical basis right down to postcode level.

CACI's geodemographic classification system 'ACORN', consists of 6 categories, 17 groups and 54 types (Exhibit 17.10). ACORN has also been subdivided into a number of industry-specific products (Exhibit 17.11).

Lifestyle products

Historically the main reason for building large lifestyle databases has been for direct mail. Names and addresses of consumers are selected by matching them with the characteristics of a promotional campaign's target market. There are four key players in the lifestyle market: Claritas with the Prizm product, Experian's Chorus, CACI's Lifestyles and Equifax's Dimensions. While lifestyle data typically includes interests, hobbies and purchase history, there is considerable fusion with geodemographic data. For example, Prizm has analysed lifestyle interests, lifestage and income into 19 groups and 72 distinct

Exhibit 17.10 The ACORN classification system

ACORN Categories	ACORN Groups
A Thriving	1 Wealthy Achievers, Suburban Areas 2 Affluent Greys, Rural Communities 3 Prosperous Pensioners, Retirement Areas
B Expanding	4 Affluent Executives, Family Areas 5 Well-off Workers, Family Areas
C Rising	6 Affluent Urbanities, Town and Grey Areas 7 Prosperous Professionals, Metropolitan Areas 8 Better-off Executives, Inner City Areas
D Settling	9 Comfortable Middle Agers, Mature Home Owning Areas 10 Skilled Workers, Home Owning Areas
E Aspiring	11 New Home Owners, Mature Communities 12 White Collar Workers, Better-off Multi-ethnic Areas
F Striving	13 Older People, Less Prosperous Areas 14 Council Estate Residents, Better-off Homes 15 Council Estate Residents, High Unemployment 16 Council Estate Residents, Greatest Hardship 17 People in Multi-ethnic, Low-income Areas

Source: CACI (1997). Reproduced from *The ACORN Classification System*, from CACI Information Services, Copyright © 1999 CACI Limited, All rights reserved. ACORN and CACI are registered trademarks of CACI Limited.

Exhibit 17.11 Industry-specific ACORN

Change ACORN	Targeting neighbourhoods by the changing demographics of consumers
Household ACORN	Target individual households by socio-economic type, age (MONICA), and family composition
Investor ACORN	Target neighbourhoods by their likelihood to spend on high value products
Scottish ACORN	Target Scottish neighbourhoods by socio-economic type
Financial ACORN	Target small areas in terms of their financial activity
Customer ACORN	Target neighbourhoods using client's own data

Source: *New Perspectives*

IN VIEW 17.4

MOSAIC and social class

Old ideas about class behaviour are confirmed by research into the leisure habits of different groups of people. Those who visit the theatre most come from MOSAIC groups like 'Stylish Singles' and 'High Income Families'. Around 7% and 3% of each respective group visits the theatre at least once a month. The profiles of bingo players are in direct contrast to this with the 'Council Flats' and 'Low Rise Council' groups having the highest numbers of players.

Source: Data courtesy of Experian; *New Perspectives* (July 1996)

clusters. This has been overlaid onto postcodes (Exhibit 17.12). Prizm works from the individual upwards to group level, using individual data at a household level to provide segmentation. This is the reverse of traditional census-based geodemographics which work down from the entire population to create the smallest groups possible. Claritas operates in 20 countries worldwide covering 1.5 billion consumers and operates the largest lifestyle databases in the UK, France and the Netherlands.

Exhibit 17.12 Example prizm segment

D2 (58) Bungalows and Bunkers 0.64% of total UK households

This segment typically owns their own detached house or bungalow in provincial areas. They enjoy gardening, grandchildren, charities and voluntary work, golf, religious activities, walking, The National Trust and motoring. There are high levels of car ownership in this segment. They take a variety of holidays, particularly coaching holidays. They have savings, stocks and shares and unit trusts. They are typically long-term residents and are quality and middle market newspaper readers.

Source: Claritas, 1997

IN VIEW 17.5

BAA uses CACI's LifestylesUK

British Airports Authority (BAA) supplied CACI with a file from their BonusPoints loyalty scheme members. BonusPoints are awarded for spend in retail outlets at BAA terminals. BonusPoints customers were split into two categories – high and low value. These high and low value definitions had been previously identified by BAA's direct marketing communications agency, Barraclough Hall Woolston Grey, by assessing profit contribution per customer. The objective of this analysis was to gauge how well CACI's LifestylesUK (database with 44 million individuals each one selectable by 300 different lifestyle attributes) discriminated between high and low value customers. LifestylesUK was applied to all records on the client's file and profiles of high and low value customers produced. The profile was then applied to the entire LifestylesUK database and recommendations made both for tagging the existing database with additional information and for prospecting high-value new customers.

High value BAA BonusPoints members tend to live in expensive houses, have high incomes and are frequent business flyers. Additionally they take many personal holidays, with skiing and short breaks to the Continent being particular favourites. They are wine lovers and read The *Daily Telegraph*. High-value customers do not read the *Daily Star*, watch lots of TV, play bingo or make weekly contributions to a Christmas hamper fund.

BAA's profile was applied to the whole of the LifestylesUK database. This allowed BAA to target likely high-value prospects with a specific accuracy index. Either every potential

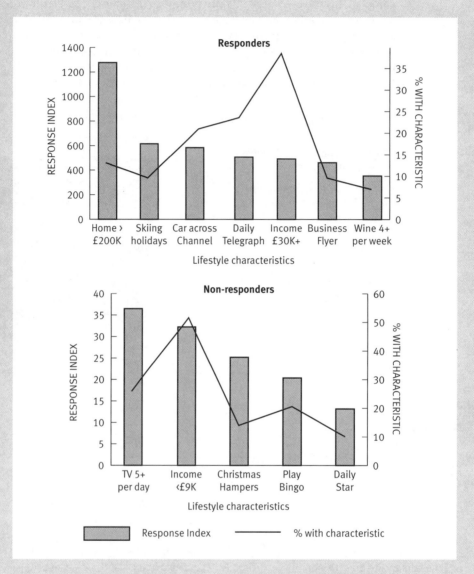

high-value customer could be targeted or BAA could select LifestylesUK variables featured in the profile like drinking or skiing, in order to send the customers offers which would be more relevant to their lifestyle and purchasing patterns.

By tagging new BonusPoints customer records with LifestylesUK, BAA has the ability to recognise which of these new customers will become high-value customers before they have even made any transactions. This means that BAA can allocate their marketing communications budget more effectively by relating it to the potential of their customers.

Source: from CACI Information Services, Copyright © 1999 CACI Limited, ALl rights reserved. Lifestyles UK and CACI are registered trademarks of CACI Limited.

IN VIEW 17.6

Using lifestyle information for cross-selling

ICD Marketing Services, now part of Experian, provide lifestyle profiles of individuals who are considering buying various types of health insurance (specifically health, temporary disability, permanent disability, accident or fatal illness). The results show the sheer volume of individual data and how a preference for one particular type of product or service can give a valuable indication of which other goods the customer is likely to buy. There is an equal balance of interest between men and women, with those keenest to know in the 25–44 age bracket. The majority (60%) are married. Three-quarters of them own their own homes – most typically flats, maisonettes or semi-detached houses, with the proportion of flat-dwellers running ahead of the national average profile. Most of these properties have been bought relatively recently and more than a third have lived in their homes for less than seven years. One in three considering taking out health insurance has a personal pension plan and a significant number also have instigated some sort of savings plan for their children. Two out of five say they are interested in seeking financial advice. Prime holiday destinations are UK (72%), Europe (63%) or the USA and Canada (21%); they are not big business travellers. Two in every five give regularly to charity and this group are above average in their pursuit of listening to music, watching videos and going to the pub. They are regular readers of popular newspapers such as *News of the World*, *Sun* and *Mirror*, they are more likely to subscribe to magazines, eat out on family occasions and spend up to three hours a day watching TV. More than half of them make use of mail order to buy fashion and sports leisurewear, shoes, music, books and videos.

Source: *New Perspectives*, July 1996, pp. 34–35

Psychographic products

Psychographics is a method of consumer segmentation by attitudes and beliefs. Psychographic segmentation has long been used in creative development by advertising agencies, because of the powerful insights it can give into the motivations and lifestyles of the target audience. Creative messages can be devised that are most relevant to the target segment or different messages can be targeted at different segments, if media flexibility is up to the job. Some major agency networks have their own proprietary systems. The heroine of the Gold Blend coffee campaign was a 'lively lady' in the McCann's classification (*New Perspectives*, December 1997). There are three key psychographic products: Social Value Groups, Monitor and Neighbourhood RISC.

Experian has recently formed an alliance with the Paris-based Research Institute for Social Change (RISC) to develop a new customer classification system called Neighbourhood RISC. Neighbourhood RISC combines psychographics and geo-demographics to provide an insight into why particular brands are attractive to particular consumer groups and how best to design promotional campaigns that appeal to prospective purchasers. The product targets customers or prospects by socio-cultural type rather than by demographics – it targets by attitudes rather than behaviour. It is currently available in the UK, France, Sweden and the US.

Neighbourhood RISC subdivides consumers into ten socio-cultural types: Explorers, Pleasure Seekers, Mobile Networkers, Avid Consumers, Social Climbers,

Exhibit 17.13 The neighbourhood RISC axes (Europe)

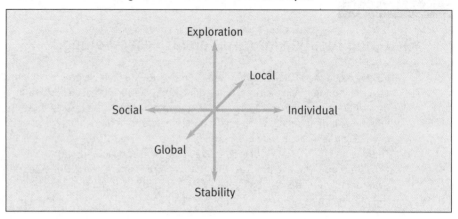

Source: Experian (1998)

Care Givers, Moral Guides, Traditionalists, Guardians and Survivors. In simple terms, the RISC system divides human personality into three key motivational axes:

● from self-focused to socially conscious,
● from conservative to explorative,
● from locally focused to globally aware (Exhibit 17.13).

Each of the ten Neighbourhood RISC types represents a combination of the matrix. For example, a typical Social Climber is a short-term thinker, consumption-driven, price-oriented, fashion-focused, easygoing and focused on his self-image. The product predicts how many residents within each postcode unit fall into each of the ten RISC categories. Thus, Neighbourhood RISC allows companies to achieve a deeper understanding of the driving forces of consumers which operate at a postcode or small area level.

Neighbourhood RISC focuses not so much on what people say and do, as on the values which will lead them to feel affinity with individual brands (Exhibit 17.14). Its empirical research explores the socio-cultural overlay to an organisation's customer database, and helps marketers recognise the likely response of different market segments to different styles of promotion. The data provides a very useful framework for all aspects of a company's marketing communications. For example, an insurance company knows the postcodes associated with the claims it receives, and thus can build a MOSAIC profile. By using Neighbourhood RISC, claimants can be analysed, for example, by their attitude towards change, by their propensity to identify with messages emphasising individuals or social norms or by their local/global orientation.

Exhibit 17.14 Sample of neighbourhood RISC socio-cultural trends

● Enjoyment of consumption	● Achievement
● Blurring of the sexes	● Personal appearance
● Taste for risks	● Demand for law and leaders
● Pleasure	● Networking
● Integrity	● Social fairness

Source: International Research Institute for Social Change (1997)

IN VIEW 17.7

Psychographic segmentation for Bird's Eye

Synergy Consulting's psychographic product, The Social Value Group, allocates consumers to one of seven groups on a two-dimensional values trend map, with three main segments: sustenance-driven, outer-directed and inner-directed.

On the values trend map, Bird's Eye MenuMaster occupied the sustenance-driven segment, which was in rapid decline as society moved into other segments. The obvious route would have been to reposition MenuMaster in the outer-directed segment, where values such as looking beautiful for others, looking healthy, having good things and flaunting them are important; but Lean Cuisine got there first, and occupied the territory. To counter this strategy, Bird's Eye repositioned MenuMaster in the inner-directed segment (with its leading-edge values). Unfortunately this was not credible for such consumers because the brand's historical positioning had not been relevant to them. Bird's Eye solution to the problem was to reverse MenuMaster into its original positioning and launch a completely new brand – Healthy Option – aimed at the inner-directed segment. Healthy Option was built to appeal to the value systems of this segment and became a success, giving Bird's Eye two brands within the market and a strategic position difficult for Lean Cuisine to attack.

Neighbourhood RISC dimensions will be particularly predictive where companies sell on the basis of image and identification.

Using Neighbourhood RISC, marketers can identify the marketing messages which are most likely to be successful within any local area and identify the local market areas which are most responsive to promotions which stress any particular aspect of the brand's image.

Only in exceptional circumstances should psychographic segmentation be used in isolation. The true value of Neighbourhood RISC, is as a supplementary overlay and as a segmentation tool to vary the content or copy of a communication.

Using segmentation for marketing communications

Data drives the communication strategy in terms of who to target, what to offer them and how to talk to them. By analysing and understanding the preferences and buying habits of customers you can determine which segments of your customer base have the best future potential. You can then create communication programmes targeted at specific consumers to sell the right products and services to the right customers at the right time. The key uses for segmenting and profiling a target market are:

- to find the best fit between target profile locations and media catchment areas to optimise spend on TV, radio, press, cinema and posters;
- to drive the targeting of direct marketing activity, particularly through postal sector rankings for door-to-door campaigns;
- to understand the facts about your customers;
- to identify new target markets previously undiscovered;

- to point you towards sources of likely sales prospects for a particular product or for a whole range of products;
- to select the most effective media;
- to develop more pertinent marketing communications targeted at the correct type of individuals;
- to choose the most appealing prizes and incentives for dealer events, competitions and promotions;
- to indicate the areas where sales pushes would be most effective;
- to set prices and indicate the type of extra products and services you could offer;
- to add substance to creative briefings and strategic planning of marketing communications;
- to spot similarities and differences between buyer groups, for example, model, price, gender and age;
- to maximise cross-selling opportunities among existing customers;
- to evaluate the risk of the likelihood of future financial loss when targeting new customers;
- to plan media buys;
- to select direct mail lists;
- to map product usage v. potential;
- to evaluate site locations and trade areas;
- to match the right audience to the right message;
- to position promotions.

(Adapted from *New Perspectives*, July 1996)

IN VIEW 17.8

Using segmentation products to tailor communications

General Cable wanted to build a high-value customer base for its cable business (1.3 million homes in its franchise areas): two main products – cable TV (with all Sky programmes plus cable-exclusive channels as well as the terrestrial services) and a telephone service (Telco). MOSAIC and Financial MOSAIC codes were appended to General Cable's database by matching on postcode. Additionally, individual family, lifestyle and financial information from Claritas was obtained and matched to specific customers by name and address. This process will usually yield a match rate of 30–40%, that is, the percentage of the company's customers that will be found on the Claritas database. The combination of census and lifestyle data enabled precise sub-groups to be more clearly defined. For example, one niche group of Telco customers fitted into the category of 'grannies at home' – single, over 50 years old and usually female, they made a lot of phone calls to keep in touch with their families. Although they didn't generate a lot of revenue, they were loyal customers. Marketers were able to use the information to tailor their offering to the customer more precisely.

Source: New Perspectives, June 1997, p.14

IN VIEW 17.9

Using segmentation products for retail location

Kindercare Learning Centres is an international toddler-to-teenager child care concept with purpose-built centres in a number of cities. In broad terms, Kindercare defines its target market as large new housing developments with a high proportion of dual income families. 90% customers live within a three-mile radius of the child care centres, so geodemographic analysis is valuable in two respects: to define exactly where a centre should be located and to pinpoint potential customers by postcode for direct mail campaigns. Experian's MOSAIC geodemographic targeting system was able to evaluate locations in terms of population, age groups, income levels, households with children, major residential development, local employment trends, inward relocation potential, child care provision and economically active females. Geodemographic segmentation and targeting, therefore, aided retail network site selection, planning and promotion.

Source: New Perspectives, July 1996, pp. 18–19

IN VIEW 17.10

How insurance companies can use segmentation products

The power of differentiation is everything when determining good and bad risk on an insurance portfolio. Effective customer segmentation means more profit for insurers and lower premiums for customers. In today's fiercely competitive market, a good customer segmentation system can make all the difference between profit and loss on an insurance ledger.

Customer classification systems are being used by insurers to identify patterns of claiming on portfolios. With systems like MOSAIC, the UK's 25 million addresses are divided into 52 separate classifications with names such as Clever Capitalists, Affluent Blue Collar, Graffitied Ghettos, Bohemian Melting Pot and Chattering Classes. Unlike existing insurance rating systems which operate at postcode sector level (e.g. NG10 5), MOSAIC works at full seven-digit postcode level so that every postcode in the UK – an average of 15 households each – falls into one of the 52 MOSAIC types. By using such classification systems, insurers can begin to make geographical and socio-economic sense of the pattern of claims on their portfolios. In other words, they can extrapolate from existing claims information and qualify the likelihood with which a person in any one of the country's 1.5 million postcodes will make a claim. The information is based on statistical modelling. It is not saying, for example, that all people living within the postcode NG1 5HF are fraudsters. But it can tell us that, based on previous claims data, inhabitants of this postcode have a higher or lower propensity to claim. From this, one can establish where clusters of claimants originate, which MOSAIC types are more likely to claim and the magnitude of the claim. Within each MOSAIC classification, one can further discriminate by age group, income, sex and so on. Analysing the insurance market using Neighbourbood RISC, of the ten RISC types, Social Climbers and Mobile Networkers are significantly more likely to claim for whatever they feel they can get. Social Climbers also are more than twice as likely to claim fraudulently as the average customer. These people see insurance as an empowerment ladder that enables them to get what they want. In other words, it gratifies their materialism through the purchase of the latest hi-tech items. Social Climbers and Mobile Networkers are:

- risk-takers who want products to help them take risks,
- experimenters whose objectives are essentially personally orientated,
- often spontaneous and interested in novelty and sensation,
- often influenced by others,
- short-termists, who dislike long-term commitment,
- fashion conscious and consumption-driven,
- often attracted by innovative marketing and promotions.

At the opposite end of the moral spectrum, Care Givers are much less likely to make claims. In fact, statistics reveal that Social Climbers are over four times more likely to make a fraudulent claim than the Care Giver. Care Givers see insurance as part of their normal responsible behaviour. Care Givers' main characteristics are:

- sharing and family orientation, with an emphasis on solidarity,
- authenticity and risk avoidance,
- socially committed and supportive of cooperative concepts,
- well-informed, long-term thinkers interested in long-term commitment,
- interested in the company behind the brand,
- expect assistance and service.

This customer segmentation system will also prove useful geographically to help to set premiums and to estimate possible numbers of fraudulent claims and liabilities when incidents such as the recent storms occur. For example, Social Climbers are over-represented in areas such as Leicestershire, Bedfordshire, Northamptonshire, the West Midlands, Buckinghamshire, Derbyshire and Staffordshire. At the other end of the moral spectrum, Care Givers are over-represented in areas such as East Sussex, Dorset, West Sussex, Isle of Wight, Tyne and Wear, West Glamorgan and Essex. Clearly, this is taking a very high geographic level and is purely statistical, but at a micro-market level, specific streets or clusters of streets can be identified as representing higher or lower insurance risk.

Source: Hall (1998)

Summary

Within the context of the decline in mass marketing, segmentation, targeting and positioning has been introduced. This chapter outlines the main types of market segmentation and the variables measured within each type: demographic, geographic, geodemographic, behavioural and psychographic. The leading commercially available products are introduced and a framework is presented that links the commercially available products to the segmentation type the product captures. Finally, the main applications of segmentation are discussed.

Self-review questions

1 What is mass marketing?

2 What is mass customisation marketing?

3 Explain the rationale behind geodemographic segmentation.

4 How can lifestage segmentation be used for marketing communications?

5 What is behavioural segmentation?

6 Differentiate between the two main definitions of psychographics.

7 Why should marketing communicators use psychographic segmentation?

8 What are the main differences between geodemographic and lifestyle data?

Project

Select a product or service and determine what segmentation tools you could use to help with the development of its marketing communications. Prepare a ten-minute presentation with your recommendations.

References

Bartos, R. (1976), quoted in Williams, K.C. (1981), *Behavioural Aspects of Marketing*. William Heinemann Ltd.

Bass, F.M., Tigert, D.J. and Longsdale, R.T. (1968), Market segmentation: group versus individual behavior. *Journal of Marketing Research*, 5 (August), 264–270.

Bernick, K. (1996), Psychographics: hype or hard-hitting strategy? *Agri Marketing*, 34 (6), 34–36.

CACI (1997), *The Acorn Classification System*. Promotional leaflet.

Claritas (1997), *Prizm*. Promotional leaflet.

Croft, M.J. (1994), *Market Segmentation: A Step-by-Step Guide to Profitable New Business*. Routledge.

Demby, E. (1974), Psychographics and from whence it came. In *Life Style and Psychographics* (W.D. Wells ed.). American Marketing Association.

Experian (1998), *The Multimedia Guide to Mosaic*. Nottingham.

Gunter, B. and Furnham, A. (1992), *Consumer Profiles: An Introduction to Psychographics*. Routledge.

Hall, S. (1998), *Social Climbers or Mobile Networkers: Customer Classification Systems Designed to Detect Fraudulent or Inflated Claims*. Nottingham: Experian.

Hansen, F. (1972), Backwards segmentation using hierarchical clustering and q-factor analysis. ESOMAR Seminar, May.

Heath, R.P. (1995), Psychographics: Q'est-ce que c'est? *American Demographics*, 74–81.

Hooley, G.J. and Saunders, J. (1993), *Competitive Positioning. The Key to Market Success*. Hemel Hempstead: Prentice Hall.

Hufstad, T.P. and Pessemier, E.A. (1973), The development and application of psychographic life style and associated activity and attitude measures. In *Life Style and Psychographics* (W.D. Wells, ed.). American Marketing Association.

International Research Institute for Social Change (1997), RISC: *We Scan the World. Venue de Villiers,* 75017 Paris, France.

Jobber, D. (1995), *Principles and Practice of Marketing.* McGraw-Hill Book Company Europe.

Kotler, P. and Armstrong, G. (1997), *Marketing: An Introduction* 4th edn. Prentice Hall International.

Lesser, J.A. (1988), How to conduct an $80,000 market study for pocket change. *Management Review,* June.

Lesser, J.A. and Hughs, M.A. (1986), The Generalizability of Psychographic Market Segmentation Across Geographic Location. *Journal of Marketing,* 50 (1).

Louden, D.L. and Della Bitta, A.J. (1993), *Consumer Behavior* 4th edn. McGraw-Hill Inc.

Marks and Spencer Financial Services (2003), Presentation at IDM Workshop, Leeds University.

McDonald, M. and Dunbar, I. (1995), *Market Segmentation.* Macmillan Press.

McGoldrick, P.J. (1990), *Retail Marketing.* McGraw-Hill Book Company Europe.

Mehotra, S. and Wells, W.D. (1977), Psychographics and buyer behaviour: theory and recent empirical findings. In *Consumer and Industrial Buying Behavior* (A.G. Woodside, J. Sheth and P.D. Bennett, eds). New York: North Holland.

Morgan, C. and Levy, D. (1997), Why we kick the tires. *Brandweek,* 38, 36.

Morgan, C. and Levy, D. (1998), To their health. *Brandweek,* 39, 3.

Mullen, L. and Johnson, S. (1990), In *Retail Marketing* (P.J. McGoldrick, ed.). McGraw-Hill Book Company Europe.

New Perspectives (1996a) Profile for profit. Issue 1 (July), 33.

New Perspectives (1996b), The only way is up. Issue 1 (July), 10–14.

New Perspectives (1997a), Ripe for the picking. Issue 1 (July), 34–35.

New Perspectives (1997b), Play ground? Issue 1 (July), 18–19.

New Perspectives (1997), International outlook. Issue 11 (December), 6.

Plummer, J.T. (1970), Applications of life style research to the creation of advertising campaigns. In *Life Style and Psychographics* (W.D. Wells, ed.). American Marketing Association.

Plummer, J.T. (1974), The concept and application of life style segmentation. *Journal of Marketing,* 38 (January).

Riche, M.F. (1989), Psychographics for the 1990s. *American Demographics,* 11(7), 24–29.

SRI Consulting Business Intelligence (2003) www.sric-bi.com/VALS

VW/Audi (2002), Internal company report.

Wells, W.D. (1975), Psychographics: a critical review. *Journal of Marketing Research,* 12.

Wells, W.D. and Gubar, G. (1966), Life cycle concepts in marketing research. *Journal of Marketing Research,* 3 (4), 355–363.

Williams, K.C. (1981), *Behaviour Aspects of Marketing.* William Heinemann Ltd.

With particular thanks to Experian, Claritas, CACI and Equifax.

Selected further reading

Dickenson, N. (1998), The brave new world of segmentation. *Campaign,* 6 February, 36–37.

Kahle, L.R. and Kennedy, P. (1989), Using the list of Values (LOV) to understand consumers. *Journal of Consumer Marketing,* Summer, 6 (3), 5–13.

Leventhal, B. (1997), An approach to fusing market research with database marketing. *Journal of the Market Research Society,* October, 39 (4), 545–558.

Peltier, J.W. and Schribrowsky, J.A. (1997), The use of need-based segmentation for developing segment-specific direct marketing strategies. *Journal of Direct Marketing,* Autumn, 11 (4), 53–62.

Sleight, P. (1995), Explaining geodemographics. *ADMAP,* January, 27–29.

Wells, W.D. (1981), Psychographics: a critical review. In *Perspectives in Consumer Behaviour* 3rd edn (H.H. Kassarjian and T.S. Robertson, ed.). Scott Foresman and Company.

Chapter 18

Setting budgets and allocating resources

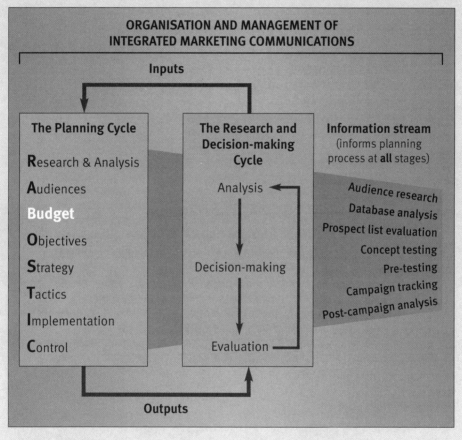

The IMC RABOSTIC Planning Model

Utilising the information in Case Study 2 on the CD and your own research, undertake a competitive analysis of the relative advertising budgets that you have been able to identify. Comment on the return on investment each car manufacturer has achieved (compare and contrast advertising spend with sales).

Chapter outline

- Budgets, the resource and the constraint
- Setting the budget
- Marketing communications expenditure and sales effects
- Budgeting in practice
- Organisational characteristics

Objectives

- To clarify the need for budgeting and emphasise budgets as an investment
- To establish methods that can be utilised to set budgets and review those methods
- To suggest that there is no single best budgeting approach
- To indicate that budgeting is far from being an exact science and that negotiation forms a part of the process

Professional perspective

Andrew Sinclair Managing Director, Sinclair Marketing Services Ltd

Budgeting, once the sole domain of the Finance Department, is now a key marketing issue. The accountability of direct marketing has brought about two major changes in enlightened companies.

Firstly, budgets are no longer imposed by top management, but are driven by the Marketing Department's ability to maximise return on investment. In the past many profitable marketing campaigns have been deemed to be complete when 'the budget' has been spent, even where continued investment would have brought significant returns.

Secondly, ROI budgeting is being applied to individual campaigns removing the need for guesswork or 'gut' feeling. For instance, continuous testing has shown that in the theatre the eighth mailing to a list of previous ticket bookers will bring a better ROI than a mailing to a cold list.

In short, marketers should welcome accountability and use considered budgeting as the cornerstone for their successful marketing campaigns.

Budgets, the resource and the constraint

The irony about budgets is that while they provide the basic resource for marketing communications, they tend to be thought of as a constraint on what can be done. A constraint set by financial managers on marketing managers. It tends to be felt that budgets are always too small. This, of course, is probably a simple human reaction (although in some cases, the budgets are too small to achieve the marketing communications objectives set). Some budgets can be measured in their millions whereas others, admittedly, are more modest. What should always be borne in mind is that marketing communications activities are an expense to the organisation. Better still, they should be thought of as an investment but, as with any investment, the organisation rightly expects there to be a return. Spending money on marketing communications is an opportunity to spend money in order to make money. Until recently, the view of marketing communications as a cost has tended to predominate. Nowadays, with increased emphasis on brand values and accounting practices devel-

NEED TO KNOW

☑ *Marketing communications expenditures should be thought of as investments not just expenses.*

oping approaches to assess brand assets, marketing communications are increasingly recognised as investments in brands. This has particularly applied to advertising, which has been associated more closely with brand image but, of course, all marketing communications activities have a bearing on this. The fact that organisations still tend to perceive advertising and other promotions as an expense rather than an investment is underlined in the cutting of promotional budgets in times of reducing sales and recessions when, in fact, they should be reviewed as investments.

One of the difficulties that arises out of the process of budgeting is the difficulty of budgeting for the whole of the marketing communications activity, not just advertising. Whilst integration of marketing communications activities have been encouraged as the way forward in producing campaigns that really count, organisations are not typically set up to deal with marketing communications in an integrated way. Consequently, organisations do not set budgets for the whole array of marketing communications activities as though they are a single investment. Budgets tend to be set for various parts as though they are individual aspects, although the actual practice in

NEED TO KNOW

☑ *What is included in marketing communications budgets tends to differ between companies.*

doing this varies from business to business. For some, corporate promotions will have its own budget, as will advertising, PR, internal communications, and the sales force, etc. If organisations put together the full amount spent on marketing communications, covering all the possible aspects described in this text, they would probably be shocked. The fact that the expenditure is the responsibility of different departments, possibly in different parts of the country or even the world, means that total expenditure is disaggregated and the full amount not always fully appreciated.

It is important to have financial controls on marketing communications just as in other areas of business. Financial controls are used to monitor and control expenditure and they are the basic language of business in assessing ultimate success or failure. Budgets are a fact of business life for all aspects of business, no less so for marketing communications. What makes the setting of budgets more difficult in this area are the longer-term implications and varied effects of marketing communications. Whereas a sales promotion activity may deliver immediate returns and so their cost versus returns may be easily assessed, in areas of advertising, corporate promotions, sponsorship and public relations their effects may not be so immediate or measurable. Allocating budgets to them becomes more of a leap of faith in which they are expected to be worthwhile activities (deliver a net contribution to the organisation) while recognising that their actual effects are difficult to measure. They represent a risk whose returns are difficult to quantify in terms of direct sales and profits even though other measures may be used.

Setting the budget

Setting budgets is an emotive topic. Finance is a limited resource. Any money spent on marketing has to come out of a finite pot and there are cash flow implications in that revenues follow expenditure. The saying that half the money spent on advertising is wasted, the problem is knowing which half, is attributed to the industrialist, Lord Leverhume. The implication behind this view (which has more than a grain of truth in it) is that when the effectiveness of advertising and other marketing communications are called into question, it is difficult to know what really works and, therefore, what marketing communications activities to finance and what size of budget to set. A further, and no less relevant, implication is that finances do indeed need to be allocated even if the extent of their effectiveness is unknown. The problem is not one of knowing if marketing communications work but, rather, knowing how well they work and if the budgets set are the right ones. The task of marketing communicators is to increase the efficiency of the marketing communication pound and make each pound work harder.

Top-down budgeting

System whereby budgets are set by senior management, disaggregated, and passed down to lower management.

Bottom-up budgeting

System whereby overall budgets are set by aggregating the individual budgets set by lower management and passed to senior management for approval.

Traditionally two processes (Exhibit 18.1) are involved in budget setting: **top-down** and **bottom-up**. The top-down process refers to the boardroom or senior executive (with possibly little or no direct connection or knowledge of the operating function) specifying how much will be available. The second process operates in exactly the opposite manner, by calling for the budget to be set by those working with it and sending it 'up' the company for approval and inclusion into the overall company budgets. Both processes have their pluses as well as minuses, and the compromise of using the two systems together is far more sensible. Without this, those constructing a budget in isolation at either end of the scale will fail to understand or take into account the needs of the other.

From the above, a pattern develops in the process of preparing a budget. In the formative stage there is a need to Communicate, then Construct, and finally having had

Exhibit 18.1 The top and bottom of budget setting

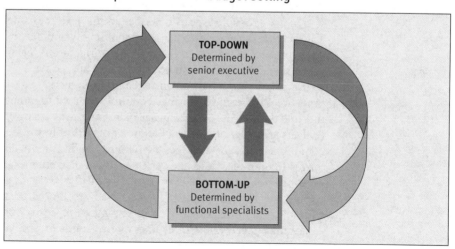

NEED TO KNOW

☑ *Budgets and the marketing communications activities they support should be evaluated for effectiveness and efficiency.*

the budget approved, Control the outcome. This process contains the three 'Cs' of budgeting. The purpose of budget setting ought to be to establish a realistic amount of money to allow marketing communications strategies to contribute fully to the success of the overall marketing plan.

In initiating a 'bid' for resources, marketing communications managers need to find a way of supporting the amounts required. In practice, this is usually a function of the persuasiveness of marketing and marketing communications managers in arguing their case, often based on little more than past experience, which may, or may not, be backed up with empirical evidence. If promotions in the past have been evaluated and shown to be effective, the chances of obtaining the desired budget is substantially increased. Indeed, if it can be shown that promotions have worked to the benefit of the organisation in the past, there is more of a case to be made to increase budgets. Evaluation of budgets and the marketing communications they support, are an important part of marketing communications management.

Using econometric modelling

In helping to determine budgets, economic analysis can be used with some effect. The models developed for this process are sometimes referred to as theoretical or academic models, quite simply because their use has been limited in practice, although this is not to imply they do not have a practical role to play. As methods, they can be used to help '**triangulate**' budget decisions. That is to say, it is worthwhile making use of a number of approaches and comparing results in order to arrive at a final decision, rather than putting too much emphasis on any single approach.

Triangulation of budget decisions

Means of determining final budgets by using a variety of methods and comparing the results from each before making a final decision.

Econometric modelling

The use of mathematical techniques to determine the effects of changes in marketing communications on sales and profits.

It may come as some relief to those readers who are less mathematically inclined that it is not the intention here to explore **econometric modelling** techniques. We would be remiss, however, if we failed to acknowledge their existence as an aid to budget determination and allocation and to point out the basic premise on which they are built.

Econometric techniques attempt to model the effects of changes in marketing communications expenditure on sales and profits. The presumption here is that measuring such a relationship is possible. But as has been pointed out previously, there are extreme difficulties in proving a direct relationship between marketing communications and sales effects; there are too many other variables at work to make this an easy task. Moreover, many marketing communications objectives are related to communications effects rather than sales effects. Certainly, it has not been possible to show the financial effects of producing integrated marketing communications – econometric studies have tended to focus on specific elements of the marketing communications mix, especially advertising. Nevertheless, they have confirmed what is perhaps intuitively obvious, that money spent on promotions creates a positive and growing effect on sales but only up to a point. This is shown in Exhibit 18.2 as an 'S' shaped curve and is briefly considered further, below.

One reason why econometric modelling is difficult is that it is unable to take account of different 'qualities' of promotions which we recognise as having a significant impact on marketing communications effectiveness. Models also have to account for a large number of extraneous variables not least of which is competitive activity which can affect the outcomes significantly. For those interested in exploring some of these econometric aspects further, the work of the PIMS study (Buzzell and Gale 1987) and of Arndt, Bass, Broadbent, Jones, and Simon should be consulted, examples of which are given in the selected further reading list at the end of this chapter.

Exhibit 18.2 The 'S' shaped response curve

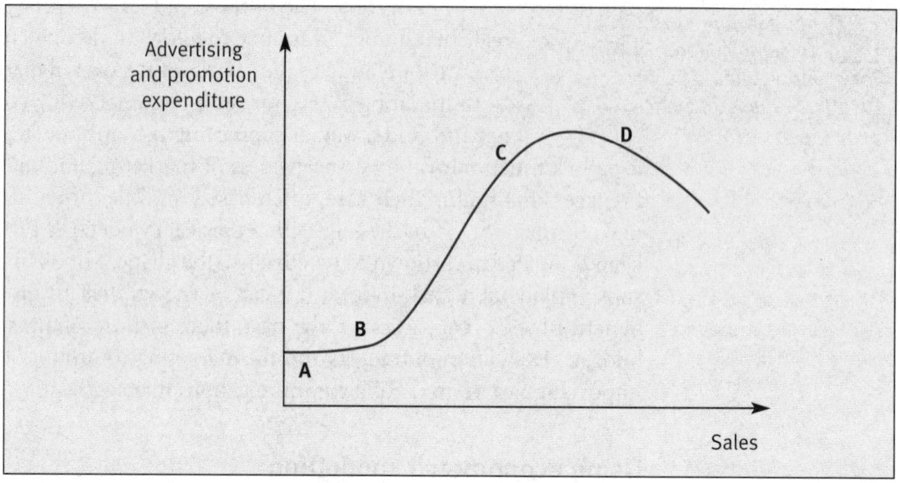

Marketing communications expenditure and sales effects

A benefit of the 'S' shaped response curve is that it allows a number of advertising and promotion effects to be explained, an appreciation of which not only helps in understanding budgeting issues but also in understanding evaluation issues (further described in Chapter 23). These effects are illustrated in Exhibit 18.2.

- *Minimum threshold effect (A).* The early part of the 'S' curve is shallow and almost a flat line because small amounts of expenditure are likely to have little impact on sales. As expenditure increases, so does the effect on sales.
- *Cumulative effect (B).* As more marketing communication activity is undertaken, the more opportunity there is for integration and synergy, one element of marketing communications building on another. As more money is spent, the more total effort is noticeable in the market. This cumulative effect creates a more rapidly rising response curve.
- *Diminishing returns effect (C).* The cumulative effects that give rise to a steeper response in the sales-to-marketing communication effort begin to wane as each successive promotional pound has a positive but reducing effect (a diminishing marginal return). The result is a diminishing return on increased effort. It is still worthwhile increasing the marketing communications budget but the benefits are becoming less and less in terms of sales results, although other communications benefits should also be taken into account. It is particularly at this point that marginal analysis is appropriate to ensure that there is a net contribution to the organisation, i.e. that benefits still outweigh the costs.
- *Negative returns effect (D).* Theoretically, it is possible to reach a turning point where spending more money has a negative effect and reduces sales. This might be because the target audiences have tired of the marketing communications and consider them to be annoying. Of course, in practice, rather than reducing expenditure, marketing communications messages are changed to ensure that this should not happen. Other reasons for negative returns include operating in a declining market where it may even be the case that market share is increasing but sales falling. If expenditure is reduced under these circumstances, sales may fall dramatically.

Budgeting in practice

Budgeting methods tend to be described in all major textbooks on marketing. They are suggested as methods of setting marketing budgets although the practice is better described as the setting of marketing communications budgets or advertising and promotion budgets (or A&P budgets as they are frequently called). The discrepancy, in part, is one of terminology. The term 'marketing budget', when it is used, is intended to refer to promotional activity only not marketing in its entirety. And within that, not to include the sales function which has a separate budget. Moreover, it will not include the staffing and management costs associated with marketing. The watchword is 'beware' when referring to budgets to ascertain precisely what costs they are intended to cover. Increasingly popular as a technique, **Activity Based Costing**, is being used to overcome some of the limitations of traditional costing and budgeting approaches.

One should also be aware that none of the methods of budget determination take into account the 'qualitative' aspects of marketing communications. By producing better marketing communications, it is possible to achieve excellent results on a limited budget that may not even be achieved by a competitor using a much larger budget. The content may be better, the use of media might be better, the choice, balance and integration of marketing mix elements might be better. Well-produced marketing communications allow the budget to be used more effectively and efficiently. In this way, companies can be said to gain a disproportionately better 'share of voice' (see Chapter 19).

(see Chapter 19)

WARNING

When comparing budgets, it is important to know exactly what they include.

Activity Based Costing

A costing approach which endeavours to include all factors in determining the total cost of any specific business activity. Unlike 'full costing' all costs are allocated to specific tasks rather than relying on allocations of overheads.

FOOD FOR THOUGHT

By producing 'better' marketing communications, smaller budgets can be used with greater effect than larger budgets.

Arbitrary method

Term given to the setting of budgets with little justification or obvious valid criteria.

Affordable method

Budgeting system whereby budgets are determined not on what needs to be done but on what the organisation believes it can afford at the time.

Competitive parity method

Budgeting system whereby budgets are set based on competitors' expenditures, which might be equalled or used to set at an appropriate proportion.

FOOD FOR THOUGHT

The percentage of sales approach is typically thought to be the most popular approach to setting budgets. However, most research is not done on the larger number of small businesses that probably use the arbitrary or affordable methods.

Five approaches to budgeting

Although other budgetary approaches are available, five of the more popular ones have been selected here for review:

- arbitrary method
- affordable method
- competitive parity method
- objective and task method
- percentage of sales method.

These methods should not be considered as distinctly different methods as they do overlap to some extent. The **arbitrary method**, for example, may use what the manager thinks can be afforded. The '**affordable method**' may determine what is affordable by using a percentage of the sales. '**Competitive parity**' may be determined from what competitors spend, not as a total amount, but on how much they allocate as a percentage of their sales. Other approaches are possible, for example those based on econometric modelling and return of investment. However, such methods should not be considered typical even if they are used by some organisations.

Budgeting methods vary in popularity with the 'percentage of sales' method reputed to be a favoured approach. However, given the sheer number of small businesses who are more likely to use 'arbitrary' or 'affordable' approaches (even if their total spends do not match those of the larger businesses), it is more probable that these methods are used in more numerous cases. In practice, no single method should be considered to be the best and, as suggested earlier, it may be better to come to a decision after 'triangulating' calculations by using more than one approach.

Exhibit 18.3 shows the results of one piece of research into budget setting methods in which percentage of sales was shown to be the preferred approach by a wide margin.

Exhibit 18.3 Budgeting methods used

Method	Companies using
Percentage of sales	44%
Affordability	21%
Objective and task	18%
Others	17%

Source: Adapted and reprinted from *The Marketing Book*, 1st Edition, Baker, M.J. (ed), Heinemann, '*Promotion*', by Crozier, K., Copyright © 1987, with permission from Elsevier.

Now let us look at each of the methods in turn.

Arbitrary method

The arbitrary method is not so much a method as an approach to arriving at a decision. As the term suggests, the budget is set by way of a judgement that seems right at the time. It is unlikely to be based on any significant criteria and is more likely to be based on 'gut feel' or intuition. This approach, however, may use underlying judgements about what has been spent previously and what may be needed for the future, given the future plans of the business.

Although this approach cannot be recommended, it should not always be presumed to be based on whim. Given the 'feel' that many managers have from years of experience in their businesses, budget allocations formulated through this arbitrary response can approximate budgets that could have been set by other means. The manager may merely have little way of articulating where the intuition has come from. As a method, though, it is somewhat 'hit and miss', and intuitions may be wrong.

Affordable method

This method is said to be product orientated rather than marketing orientated in that its calculations are not based on any market analysis. Organisations using this approach, like the arbitrary approach, are more likely to reflect a view that marketing communications are an expense rather than an investment. The affordable method requires that all costs are firstly calculated, an allowance made for what the organisation wishes to earn as a profit (or retain out of revenue in the case of not-for-profit organisations), and what is left over in the available pot of money is what can be afforded. The calculation requires some consideration of what is likely to be earned over the period for which the budget is being set (i.e. sales) and for this reason, shares some similarities with the percentage of sales method.

WARNING

When using the affordable method, extra care has to be exercised in particular situations such as when launching a new product or operating with declining sales.

A particular problem in the use of this approach is in the context of new product launches in which the marketing communications budget comes after other expenditure has been incurred in product development. There is an underlying danger that, having spent possibly large sums of money on development costs (even if the product is seen as an overall investment to the company), further spending on promotions is extending the risk too far. The consequence is that the company may choose to be over-cautious and not allocate sufficient funds to the product launch. The net result can be product failure.

Another difficulty arises when sales are not meeting target. This might be because of market changes (e.g. declining market) or as a result of particular competitive activity. At a time when higher budgets are needed, the affordable method may result in budget cuts.

Competitive parity method

Organisations operate in a competitive environment, even not-for-profit organisations like charities compete against other charities for revenue. It is, therefore, logical that note is taken of what competitors are doing. Competitive parity tries to equate budget allocation with those of competitors. Taken literally it means spending the same as competitors, although it would be unwise to view this method entirely in those terms. To use this method, it is first necessary to determine precisely who are the competitors. Second, recognition must be given to the relative sizes of competitors. A company's nearest competitor may be significantly bigger or significantly smaller than that company. Matching expenditure in this situation would not be sensible. The market position of the competition should also be considered. Marketing communications strategies for market leaders are likely to be different to the strategies adopted for market followers. Indeed, this is a particular finding of the PIMS study which has collected data on 'marketing' budgets and sales results for many years (Buzzell and Gale 1987) and still continues to do so. What is more sensible is to set proportional budgets based on the relative sizes and positions of competitors. Or adopt what is essentially a percentage of sales approach, in which data on the average industry advertising (or advertising and promotion) to sales ratios (A/S ratios or A&P/S ratios) are used to set budgets. These are available for many industries. If the industry average is 5% of sales, then one's own company budget can be set at 5% and, thus, achieve parity. One drawback of this is that while the average may be 5%, this may not reflect wide variations within the industry.

WARNING

⚠ *Industry average spends may hide significant and wide variations between specific competitors.*

As with the other methods described so far, this method cannot satisfactorily take account of sudden changes in competitive activity. Neither does it account for the differences between different competitors' marketing communications objectives. Nor does it account for the organisation's own objectives. It is based on historical evidence and, rather, assumes a generally static or stable existence. In more turbulent situations, this and the previous methods identified are extremely limited. What is significant about this method, though, is its emphasis on competitor intelligence – checking out what the competition is doing, and this has to be sensible. Using this method, alongside other methods, appears to be an advisable way to approach the budgeting task.

Share of voice

Concept that refers to how 'loud' one brand's marketing communications are compared with other competing brands. It may be measured in terms of marketing communications spends, or by subjective assessment of the relative attention created by competing marketing communications.

An alternative method to simple parity is to use a similar concept that seeks to assess 'share of voice'. In this, the organisation evaluates, on the basis of spends and/or research into levels of awareness, the organisation's position compared with those of competitors as perceived by the target market. The task would be to set budgets in line with the required share of voice wishing to be achieved. Again, care would have to be exercised to be realistic in terms of the relative size of the competitors. If they are very much larger, their share of voice is likely to be larger too. This basic concept has been used by Schroer (1990) and Jones (1990) to relate '**share of voice**' to 'share of market'; their work should be read for further details of this approach (see Chapter 19).

Objective and task method

The objective and task method is quite different from the other methods in that it seeks to arrive at a budget decision based on what marketing communications

IN VIEW 18.1

Seeing their way forward to a new competitive edge

After de-regulation of the optical trade, optician practices were allowed, for the first time, to undertake unrestricted marketing communications. The optical industry was initially characterised as a low-spend sector until the retail trade was revolutionised by the mass media approach of new entrants such as Vision Express. Moving the previously low-spend sector into new avenues of marketing communications, Vision Express experimented and succeeded with their TV campaigns and high promotional budgets.

A similar approach in the new homes market was adopted by Barretts, the builders. They re-positioned their media communications by adopting high-profile television commercials completely taking the building industry, and the market, by storm. Barrett Homes became instantly recognisable to all new home buyers, beating all other building firms in spontaneous awareness tests.

FOOD FOR THOUGHT

It is difficult to operationalise the objective and task method because it is not possible to guarantee that by undertaking a particular marketing communications task, or combination of tasks, a specified outcome will be achieved. Nor is it possible to know if the tasks were conducted in the most efficient way. There could be significant over-spending as a result of being over-cautious in using this method.

Percentage of sales method

Budgeting system whereby budgets are set by allocating a specified percentage of sales value. This method requires consideration of the means by which an appropriate percentage is determined and whether to base it upon past, current or future anticipated sales.

activities need to achieve. Its focus is on, first, determining objectives, and then deciding on the marketing communications tasks that are needed to achieve those objectives. By calculating the costs of those tasks, a budget can be set. In this way, the objective and task method is very much a bottom-up approach with each objective and task building on another to determine total costs.

Clearly, emphasis needs to be placed on deciding appropriate objectives in the first place and setting them in such a way as to facilitate the objective and task methodology. SMARRTT objectives, discussed in the next chapter, would fulfil this need. While emphasis on objective setting is an undoubted strength of this method in that attention is focused on what needs to be achieved, it is not always easy to set such objectives.

While some would say this method is the best, implementing it is very difficult indeed. The method makes a number of presumptions for it to be operationalised. Most important, it assumes that the relationship between objectives and tasks is well known and understood. And this is just not the case. If a sales objective or an awareness objective, for example, is set, there is no guarantee that a particular task or range of tasks will bring it to fruition. Yet unless the tasks are specified, it is not possible to complete the costing necessary to determine the budget. What has to be done in using this method, of course, is to use best estimates of the marketing communications tasks that are needed.

Another presumption is that the budget will be financed. The organisation may decide that too big a budget is being requested and this brings it back to an affordable approach albeit of a more sophisticated nature. Under these circumstances, alternative strategies and tactics have to be identified until an agreed budget is achieved.

Percentage of sales method

The **percentage of sales method** is a popular approach in which a fixed percentage of turnover is allocated to marketing communications. In other words, it links marketing communications expenditure directly to levels of sales. However, this still begs two related questions: what percentage and which turnover? To answer the first, it may be based on previous practice, on competitor allocations or on industry averages. Advertising and promotion to sales ratios may be used for this purpose. To answer the second, it could be based on historic sales – last year's sales or sales averaged over a number of years. It could be based on current sales levels, or it could be based on fore-

casted sales. If sales are falling, care has to be taken not to exacerbate the problem by simply allocating the same percentage level of budget to a decreasing revenue base. It may be at times like these that more needs to be spent to improve the sales position. This problem can be overcome by using forecasted sales instead of historic sales as the basis for the calcula-tion. Likewise, at times when sales are high, it may be necessary to 'peg' the budget. More promotions do not necessarily mean more sales will result, even at times of market growth. The 'S' curve described earlier shows how diminishing returns may result. By 'pegging' the budget, greater profits may be earned.

The percentage of sales method, in fact, incorporates a number of alternatives and in this way it may be seen to operate in ways similar to other approaches. By basing it on future sales, for example, it operates in a similar fashion to the objective and task method in that the budget allocated becomes one selected to achieve a sales objective. By choosing industry A&P/S norms, this is similar to competitive parity.

What percentage should be set?

In reviewing industry averages as a basis for determining the most appropriate per-centage to allocate, it is clearly evident that figures vary enormously from under 1% to over 25% of sales value. Manufacturers of games and toys might spend over 15%. Grocery products might vary between 3% and 7%. Soft drinks companies and car manufacturers are among the highest spenders of advertising money throughout the world, but their percentage of advertising to sales is modest, often below 5% (although they do also have significant expenditures on other promotional activities as well). But 5% of their huge sales revenues still accounts for an awful lot on money. In selecting a percentage, the way in which the company operates will also have an impact. If a com-pany relies entirely on selling through mail order, its budgets are going to be higher than if it operated through other channels of distribution. If it chooses to operate

through the Internet, this situation might be different again. Companies operating in industrial markets will allocate a different balance of budget with less going to advertising and more going to the sales force compared with consumer market companies.

To gain a feel of the sort of budgets that are allocated in practice, it is recommended that the trade press should be read regularly. In maga-zines such as *Campaign*, *Marketing*, *Marketing Week*, *Media Week* and *PR Week*, new campaigns and their budgets in all areas of marketing communications are reported weekly.

Organisational characteristics

A final, but by no means a minor, consideration in budget setting is the effect the cul-ture of the company has on the process. Not only does this affect the determination of the budget in the first place, organisational factors also play a key role in how promo-tional budgets are spent.

FOOD FOR THOUGHT

Various methods may be used for determining budgets, but agreeing budgets involves negotiation.

Budget setting is ultimately a human endeavour not a computational one, or at least one not solely based on computations. There is a high level of negotiation involved, particularly in larger organisations. These negotiations are affected by:

- custom and practice – what has seemed to work before – past behaviour, past performance;
- the power and politics within the company (especially between the senior executive, finance and marketing);
- the persuasiveness of marketing managers in obtaining/defending budgets;
- how traditionally 'expert' (external agencies) opinion has been utilised;
- what preferences and experience 'experts' bring to decision-making;
- the budget approval mechanism and channels of negotiation – who is involved, how many are involved, in what part of the process, and when;
- the pressures on managers to set optimal budgets;
- the pressures on managers to prove performance.

The cultural attitude of the management can seriously affect their use of external experts. This not only will have an impact on what agencies are selected but also whether their advice is accepted.

Summary

Budgets are both a resource and a constraint and increasing emphasis is being placed on being able to justify them in the light of marketing communications performance. In determining budgets it is important to clearly identify what they are to be used for because what is included and excluded from marketing (advertising and promotion) budgets seems to vary from company to company. While many managers may view marketing communications expenditure with suspicion, seeing it as an expense, it is more appropriate to view it as an investment in the brand and the organisation. Traditional accounting practices are changing to recognise brand assets and brand worth, which have grown out of sustained marketing communications effort. But marketing managers should not rest on their laurels. Budgets typically have to be fought for and won as part of a negotiation process. Expenditure has to be defended and this is made possible by evaluating marketing communications expenditure and showing its value to the organisation.

Setting budgets may be undertaken by either a top-down or a bottom-up approach or (preferably) by a combination of the two through 'communicating' with managers, 'constructing' an agreed budget, and 'controlling' the budget so that it can be shown to be utilised effectively and efficiently.

Five basic budgeting methods have been described and it is suggested that there is no single best method to use (although some methods can be shown to be better than others). It is recommended that methods are used in conjunction with each other in a process of 'triangulation' to determine the final allocation. Econometric analysis and modelling was alluded to briefly in recognition that it is an approach (or series of approaches to be more accurate) available to assist in budget setting. From the brief discussion, it is possible to identify four marketing communications effects.

Namely, 'minimum threshold effect', which suggests that budgets need to be set to a minimum amount to have any appreciable effect. 'Cumulative effect', which shows the power of synergy in marketing communications effort. 'Diminishing returns effect', which emphasises that after a point, the effectiveness of increases in expenditure experience diminishing returns. And 'negative returns effect' in which, even though budgets may be increased, sales decrease.

Self-review questions

1 Why are budgets said to be resources and constraints?

2 What aspects of the marketing communications mix tend to be excluded from the marketing communications budget?

3 Why is it important to assess the effectiveness of marketing communications from a budget setting point of view?

4 What is meant by top-down and bottom-up?

5 What does the 'S' shaped response curve measure?

6 What are the four marketing communication effects identified on the 'S' curve?

7 Identify the five budgeting methods and briefly describe each.

8 Why may the percentage of sales budgeting method be said to incorporate elements of the other methods?

9 Why is budget setting described as a negotiation process?

Project

Using past issues of trade magazines, identify examples of budget allocations referred to as part of the new campaigns reported, noting the type of products and industries to which they relate. Identify the range of activities included in the budget allocations.

Using BRAD and/or media rate cards (many are available on the Web), identify a list of costs for a selection of media.

References

Crosier, K. (1987), Promotion. In *The Marketing Book* (Baker, M., ed.). Heinemann.

Jones, J.P. (1990), Ad spending: maintaining market share. *Harvard Business Review*. January/February, 38–42.

Schroer, J. (1990), Ad spending: growing market share. *Harvard Business Review*, January/February, 44–48.

Selected further reading

Broadbent, S. (1997), *Accountable Advertising: A Handbook for Managers and Analysts.* Admap Publications.

Buzzell, R.D. and Gale, B.T. (1987), *The PIMS Principles: Linking Strategy to Performance.* The Free Press.

Jones, J.P. (1995), *When Ads Work: New Proof that Advertising Triggers Sales.* Simon and Schuster.

Chapter 19

Setting objectives, determining strategy and tactics

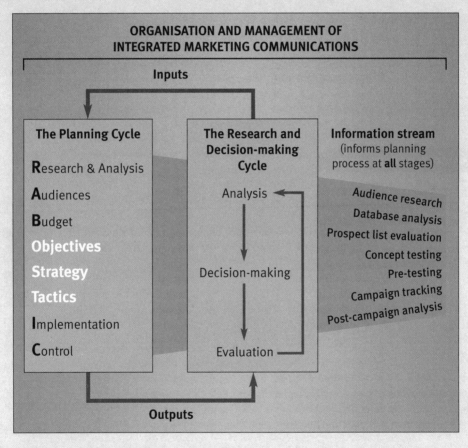

ORGANISATION AND MANAGEMENT OF INTEGRATED MARKETING COMMUNICATIONS

Inputs

The Planning Cycle

Research & Analysis
Audiences
Budget
Objectives
Strategy
Tactics
Implementation
Control

The Research and Decision-making Cycle

Analysis

Decision-making

Evaluation

Information stream
(informs planning process at **all** stages)

Audience research
Database analysis
Prospect list evaluation
Concept testing
Pre-testing
Campaign tracking
Post-campaign analysis

Outputs

The IMC RABOSTIC Planning Model

CD

To what extent do the objectives and subsequent strategy of the Fabia campaign in Case Study 2 address the brand image problems being faced by Škoda at that time? Would you have approached the problem differently? How important was the use of push and pull strategies to their total campaign?

Chapter outline

- The relationship between objectives, strategy and tactics
- Levels of objectives and strategies
- Setting objectives
- Determining strategy
- Strategic and tactical use of the marketing communications mix

Objectives

- To demonstrate the interrelationships between objectives, strategy and tactics
- To emphasise the importance and value of setting objectives
- To identify what makes good objectives
- To identify a range of strategic choices in marketing communications
- To outline the influences on the tactical choice of marketing communications mix elements

Professional perspective

Professor John Saunders Head of Aston Business School

It was a sad realisation. A broken old businessman once explained to me: 'You don't succeed by working hard. I worked hard all my life and failed.' He was right, although I do not think he ever understood why.

The old businessman never understood that success comes from understanding the difference between motion and direction. It is a sad feature of corporate life that businesses do not fail because of lack of activity. Most businesses fail while the people within them are highly active. What they fail to grasp is that activity does not mean action, action does not mean strategy and strategy does not mean success. There is a simple relationship between the four ideas: activity, action, strategy and success:

- **Activity** is motion, it is the exertion of energy in all directions.
- **Action** is the exertion of that energy in one direction,
- **Strategy** is about deciding what direction that motion should be in,
- **Success** comes from that direction being the right one.

Too often the creators of marketing communications confuse activity for strategy. More than that, many campaigns seek justification by following trends. In other words, 'doing what others are doing or what others have done'. That is easy and it saves managers having to do what marketers are really paid to do: creating wealth from ideas; value from vision. Often campaign budgets are based on 'what we spent last year' or 'what the competition is spending'. In other words: 'We don't know how much we should spend but someone did last year or the competition does'. Fortunately for many, the glamour and excitement of marketing communication hides that the proposed tactics are not based on objectives of strategy.

Dr Johnson had good reason to classify much advertising as puffery. Much of marketing communications is just that because it is not based on strategy or tactics to achieve the concrete marketing returns of awareness, attitude, preference, intention, trial or repeat, and the economics they bring.

The old man who worked hard and failed needed to understand: people do not succeed by looking busy. Success comes from working hard and smart.

J. Saunders

The relationship between objectives, strategy and tactics

Objectives

End results sought to be achieved.

Strategy

The general means by which objectives are intended to be achieved.

Tactics

Details of how strategies are intended to be achieved.

Chapter 13 presented a framework for the planning of marketing communication and outlined the key areas of objectives, strategy and tactics to be developed (Exhibit 19.1). This chapter discusses the in-depth development of **objectives**, **strategy** and **tactics** and the issues associated with this development.

So close is the relationship between the objectives, strategies and tactics of the marketing communication plan that most people become confused or use the terms very loosely. This confusion is entirely understandable and, frankly, should not be the cause of too much concern – as long as the decisions in each of these areas are clearly articulated.

Leslie Butterfield, one of the UK advertising industry's most respected strategists, and Chairman and Planning Director of Butterfield Day Davito Hockney (BDDH), identifies the distinction succinctly:

> An objective is the goal or aim or end result that one is seeking to achieve. A strategy is the means by which it is intended to achieve that goal or aim or end result. Thus, one should be able to state an objective in the absolute, to preface it with the word 'to'. A strategy therefore becomes the conditional element, prefaced by the word 'by' ... so an objective is where you want to be, a strategy is how you intend to get there.
>
> (Butterfield 1977, p. 85)

Exhibit 19.1 The eight planning questions

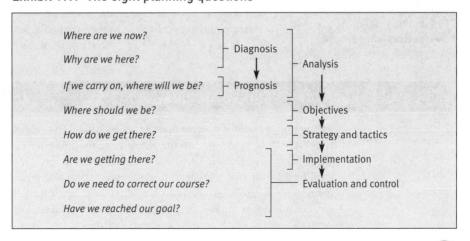

Where are we now?

Why are we here? — Diagnosis

If we carry on, where will we be? — Prognosis

— Analysis

Where should we be? — Objectives

How do we get there? — Strategy and tactics

Are we getting there? — Implementation

Do we need to correct our course? — Evaluation and control

Have we reached our goal?

On the matter of tactics, Paul Smith (1998) comments,

> **Tactics are the details of strategy. In marketing communications, tactics are the communications tools such as advertising, PR, direct mail, etc. The tactics in the marketing communications plan list what happens, when, and for how much.**

(p. 47)

Thus, objectives, prefaced by the word 'to', are statements about what we want to achieve. Strategies, prefaced by the word 'by', are broad statements about how we are to achieve the objectives. Tactics are about the 'fine' detail of the strategies showing how they can be *implemented*. They are most often associated with the individual elements of the marketing communications mix which, thus, become the implementational detail. Diagrammatically, objectives, strategies and tactics can be illustrated as in Exhibit 19.2. Strategy is the overall path between our present position and where we want to be at the end of our planning horizon. Tactical activities are illustrated as a zig-zag line along the strategic path because there will inevitably be movements on a day-to-day basis which have to be monitored and 'corrected'.

In most circumstances there is already a 'track record' of activity that has gone on in the past. The difference in position between where we want to be in the future (objectives) and where we would be if we simply carry on doing the same things is known as the '**strategic gap**' and this is what the strategy and tactics have to 'fill in' if the objectives are to be achieved.

Exhibit 19.3 is extracted from the excellent book by Schultz et al. (1994). It illustrates some very useful examples of what the authors refer to as strategies and tactics. Tactics are illustrated as implementational factors and are identified as marketing communications elements. The figure also illustrates the confusion that is frequently caused when addressing this subject area. Note how the authors' statements of strategy appear to be very much more like statements of objectives.

Although strategies have been described as broad statements of intent and tactics as the implementational detail associated with the elements of the marketing communications mix, the matter is further complicated by the fact that it is entirely reasonable to identify strategies for each of the mix elements themselves. The mix may be tactical in terms of the overall plan of campaign but each element has a strategic role. Thus, one talks of PR strategies, direct mail strategies, sponsorship strategies, advertising strategies, and so on. The reason for this is quite simple – there is a hierarchy of levels at which objectives and strategies exist. Just as marketing activities cannot be seen simply as the tactical expression of corporate strategies (marketing has a strategic and tactical role), so too marketing communications activities are not just tactical but have a strategic dimension.

Strategic gap

The difference in position between where an organisation wants to be at a specific point in time in the future (its objectives) and where it would anticipate being at that time if it simply carried on with its current activities.

WARNING

It is often difficult to separate objectives and strategy when compiling marketing communications plans. To avoid problems, ensure that objectives are prefaced with the word 'to' and describe the end-result you want to achieve. Strategies should be prefaced by the word 'by' and should include broad statements about how the objectives will be achieved.

Levels of objectives and strategies

Because organisations operate at different levels and in different functional areas, objectives have to be set related to the whole organisation's activities. From the objectives, strategies follow. Exhibit 19.4 illustrates the different levels at which they operate, each level feeding into each other to provide integration and synergy. Although the arrows connecting the different levels are uni-directional indicating that objectives and strategies cascade down the hierarchy, in practice, that actual setting of them is likely to be an iterative process which occurs top-down, bottom-up and from centre-outwards.

Exhibit 19.2 Relationship between objectives, strategy and tactics – the planning framework

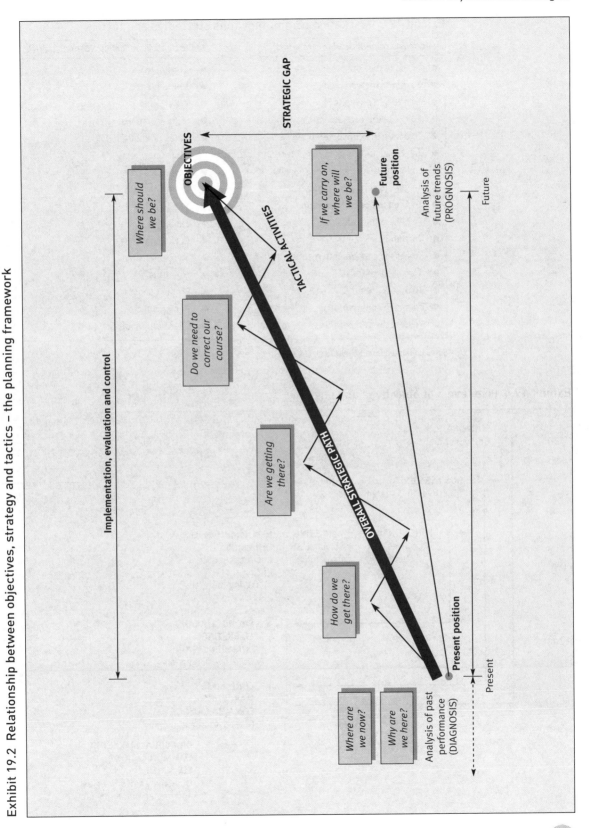

Exhibit 19.3 Marketing communications strategies and tactics

Marketing communication strategies	Implementation: communications tactics
● To make the consumer aware	● Corporate identity
● To inform the consumer	● Brand identity
● To educate the consumer	● Advertising
● To excite the consumer	● Public relations
● To action the consumer to buy	● Sales promotions
● To change the consumer's perception	● Direct marketing
● To improve the consumer's loyalty	● Personal selling
● To get the consumer to buy	● Word of mouth
● To keep the consumer happy	● Sponsorship
● To reward the consumer	● Exhibitions
● To stimulate	● Packaging
● To get the consumer to respond	● Merchandising
● To make a promise	● Literature
● To fulfil a promise	● Product design
● To match competition	● Pricing policies
● To beat the competition	● Distribution policies

Source: Adapted from Schultz et al. (1994)

Exhibit 19.4 Five levels of objectives and strategy

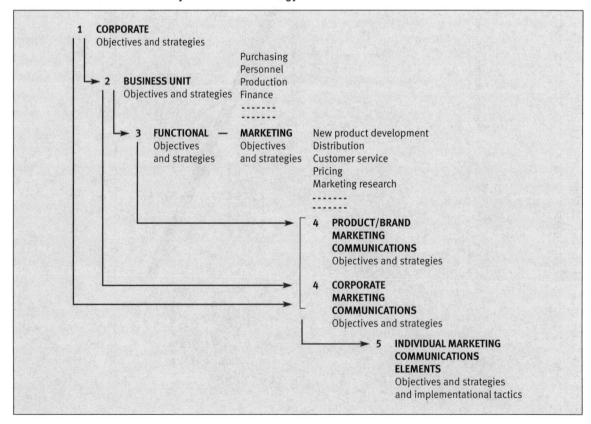

At level 5, the lowest level illustrated in Exhibit 19.4, it is vital that the objectives and strategies of all the individual marketing communications elements (and the tactics which follow from them) are integrated and contribute to the achievement of the total marketing communications objectives for individual products/brands, the corporate marketing communications at level 4 and the corporate objectives at levels 1 and 2. Integrated marketing communications represented in this way can be seen for what it really is, a composite of product and corporate marketing communications.

The interplay of objectives and strategies for individual products and the organisation as a whole can be seen in the branding strategies employed by different companies. Some choose their brands to stand independently, whereas others adopt a corporate 'umbrella' branding strategy. In the first instance, brand values are associated entirely (or almost entirely) with the individual product or product range. They have little or no communications relationship to the parent company. For example, Sara Lee, most notable for its cakes, also has brands such as Kiwi shoe cleaning products. It is obvious why Sara Lee avoid linking their name too heavily with shoe cleaning; there is no synergy between cleaning products and cakes. Indeed, there would be a negative association if they were both linked to the same Sara Lee corporate brand so one set of brand values is not allowed to carry over to the other set.

Mars, another huge corporation, is easily recognised for its 'Mars Bars', but Mars also has many other confectionery products in its portfolio that most people do not recognise as Mars company brands. Mars products are distinctly branded as separate entities. One of Mars' businesses is Pedigree Petfoods, a producer of animal feeds. While one of the leading brands of dog foods may be identified with the company, 'Pedigree Chum', most people would not recognise that the company also manufactures one of the leading brands of cat food, 'Whiskers'. This separation of brands is a quite deliberate corporate strategy employed by the company.

For companies such as BMW and BT, although each has distinct brands, the '**corporate brand**' is more significant than its 'product brands'. For the Virgin group, the corporate brand is everything. The Virgin name is used across all its varied product sectors. Companies that associate product and corporate **brand values** as a significant stance can use these values to the benefit of all their products; this can be especially helpful at times of new product launch. In the case of the Body Shop, ethical and 'green' brand values are communicated across their entire product range. This sort of **umbrella branding** strategy, however, is not a panacea for all situations. A poorly performing brand could have a detrimental effect on other brands linked with it.

Corporate brand

Term given to represent the organisation as a brand.

Brand values

The meaning or meanings that the brand generates in the minds of its target audiences.

Umbrella branding

Product branding in which the brands are closely related to other brands or the overall corporate brand.

IN VIEW 19.1

Cadbury gets smashed

One instance where umbrella branding was less successful was for Cadbury. Noted mainly for its confectionery products (chocolate, in particular), Cadbury extended its portfolio to include a ready prepared mashed potato product, which they named 'Cadbury Smash'. Despite some very memorable and effective advertising, which was applauded throughout the industry, 'Cadbury Smash' never achieved its sales objectives and the company's aspirations. The excellent Cadbury name provided no synergistic benefit to a product not perceived by the market to be part of the company's core confectionery activity.

Setting objectives

The importance of objectives

Objectives have a fundamental value in providing direction for an organisation if they are clearly stated, are compatible with each other and known, understood and followed. These ideals are frequently not met, but management tasks of coordinating and control are made much more difficult without the guiding force of objectives. As the saying goes, 'If you don't know where you're going, you won't know how to get there, or if you've arrived'.

Objective setting is not an easy task and objectives set in one functional area may well be at odds with those set in another functional area. This can be the root of many organisational conflicts. Producing objectives for the first time can be particularly difficult. In most instances, however, we are able to build on past experiences and on the analysis of previous objectives and the extent to which they were met. When new objectives are built on the old, what is realistic and what is achievable is much clearer.

Russell Colley (1961), in what was to become a landmark article, suggested several benefits of setting objectives:

- People work better when they have a clear idea of what they are trying to achieve. They know where they are aiming and have a better idea of the issues that have to be addressed.
- Promotions by nature are an ambiguous, subjective process. Any opportunity to introduce objectivity should be used.
- As the work of communications involves more specialists, it is necessary that they work to stated goals that are understood. Objectives reduce wasted effort and keep the team on target.
- Objectives allow measurement and a better allocation of resources. Organisations gain insight into future budget allocation through an understanding of past performance.

As Colley also emphasised, the use of objectives improves the client–agency relationship by improving communications between the two. Furthermore, they engender a better understanding between the personnel within each. By carefully identifying objectives and, importantly, putting them in writing and having them agreed, there is an increased specificity, clarity and objectivity in a field where subjectivity and vagueness could easily undermine productivity, efficiency and effectiveness.

Put simply, objectives are a vital part of the planning process and they enable strategy to be determined. They help give direction to all involved and provide a means by which performance can be assessed. Unfortunately, not all objectives are equally good.

SMARRTT objectives

An acronym that represents the level of detail that objectives should aim to achieve. It is a development from 'SMART' objectives that are referred to by some other authors. SMARRTT objectives are Specific, Measurable, Achievable, Realistic, Relevant, Targeted and Timed

SMARRTT objectives

Chapter 13 identified that objectives should be SMARRTT: specific, measurable, achievable, realistic, relevant, targeted and timed. **SMARRTT objectives** ensure a planner has clear and precise goals to build the strategy and against which to evaluate the campaign. The acronym SMARRTT usefully describes what makes a good objective (Exhibit 19.5).

Exhibit 19.5 SMARRTT objectives

Objectives	Why?
Specific	Objectives should be clear, precise and directional about what is to be achieved. Is it to generate awareness or some action, change perceptions or attitudes, etc. Objectives should relate to specific end results.
Measurable	Objectives should possess a quantified measurement statement (i.e. a percentage or absolute amount to be achieved) to enable precise evaluation of the campaign. For example, this could be 10,000 coupon returns, or £100,000 of editorial coverage or 60% prompted awareness.
Achievable	Objectives should be capable of being reached, in that the company/department/ suppliers have the resources to achieve the objectives set.
Realistic	Objectives set should be realistic. For example, large brand adoption percentages of a new product in short time scales are unrealistic. Unrealistic objectives are demoralising when the goals are not met and are subject to poor evaluation.
Relevant	Objectives should be appropriate for the task at hand. Once a problem or task is identified, the specific objectives should address that problem. They should have due regard to the marketing and corporate objectives and strategies and be capable of contributing towards them. If the essential task were to increase sales through direct marketing communications, setting objectives that would only improve levels of awareness would not meet the requirements of the campaign.
Targeted	All objectives should be related to the target audience(s) that are to be reached. If there is more than one target audience group in the campaign, objectives will be needed for each. For example, some objectives may be intended for target consumers, others for target customers, influencers, stakeholders, trade members, etc.
Timed	Objectives should have a clearly stated time frame to indicate by which time they are expected to be achieved. This enables the scheduling of the campaign to be monitored and indicates when the results can be evaluated.

Objectives and the hierarchy of effects

Hierarchy of effects models

Models that describe the stages individuals are said to progress through in moving from initial unawareness to final action such as purchase and consumption. A range of models or ways of describing the stages in the process exist.

DAGMAR model

In proposing DAGMAR (Define Advertising Goals for Measured Advertising Results), Russell Colley emphasised the importance of measuring advertising effectiveness against predetermined advertising objectives or goals. The same proposition is equally relevant for all forms of marketing communications.

Hierarchy of effects models describe the step-wise process through which individuals move when exposed to marketing communications; this includes the cognitive (thinking), affective (feeling) and conative (doing) steps. Hierarchy of effects models are referred to in various sections of this book. This is not to suggest that they are without criticism; Chapters 4 and 27, for example, identify some of their limitations. This book simply reflects their popularity in the literature and in practice.

Russell Colley (1961) popularised the use of the hierarchy of effects in developing his **DAGMAR model** (Define Advertising Goals for Measured Advertising Results). In this, he espoused the importance of setting objectives against each element within the hierarchy (or at least those that were relevant to the campaign being devised). Although his focus was upon advertising objectives, his propositions are equally appropriate for consideration across all marketing communications tools. Objectives are about achieving desired outcomes and these outcomes are most easily conceptualised around the hierarchy of effects (or similar models). This may be why they have been so enduring as a means of understanding the marketing communications process. Colley's particular hierarchy featured the need to set objectives (and subsequent strategies) in the areas shown in Exhibit 19.6.

Other researchers have developed their ideas from Colley and offered their own perspectives. Exhibit 19.7 is modified from Belch and Belch (1998), itself a development from Lavidge and Steiner (1961). It presents a complementary view of the transition

Exhibit 19.6 Colley's hierarchy of objectives (1961)

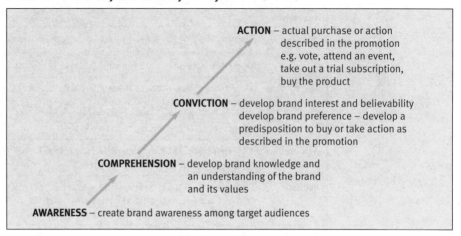

from awareness to purchase and the sort of objectives and promotions associated with the movement 'up' the hierarchy.

Debates about hierarchy of effects models frequently centre on whether or not behavioural response tends to be linear, that is to say, does people's behaviour always move from awareness through the stages to taking action (the 'think–feel–do' sequence)? Alternatively, is it possible for the sequence to be reversed, for example, by doing something first which generates feelings upon which thoughts are reflected? These issues remain largely unresolved with academics and practitioners alike failing to reach a consensus. The likely outcome is that there is no single behavioural model that can explain all types of buyer behaviour across all types of product and circumstance. Some further comments about this sequencing can be found in Chapter 27.

Sales versus communications objectives

Another raging debate concerns whether marketing communications should concentrate on sales outcomes rather than communications issues. This has given rise to what some refer to as two schools of thought, the Sales School and the Communications School (Rothschild 1987; Fill 1999).

The sales school

The sales school of thought strongly advocates that marketing communications are relatively valueless unless they achieve sales results. Any intervening changes that might occur in the target audience count for nothing unless sales or actions ensue. The only reasonable way to measure marketing communications effectiveness, therefore, has to be in demonstrable behaviour – especially purchase behaviour. Objectives should be set to achieve such behaviour.

The communications school

The communications school emphasises the communications variables that precede any sale. Unless a positive view is held about a brand (product or company), a sale is unlikely to result. The communications school recognises the stepwise movement leading to a sale and even beyond and that this can be affected beneficially by communications effort. This could be by generating awareness, inducing favourable attitudes,

Exhibit 19.7 The hierarchy of effects, objectives and promotional activity

Related attitudinal and behavioural dimensions	Movement towards purchase or other action	Example of types of objectives relevant to each stage of the hierarchy (12 month period)	Example of types of promotion relevant to objectives at each stage of the hierarchy
CONATIVE The realm of motives and actions **(doing)**	**Re-purchase Behaviour** ↑ **Purchase** ↑ **Trial**	To maintain regular use of brand among 5% of the target audience To achieve repeat purchase among 15% of the target audience To obtain trial among 20% of the target audience	Maintenance of brand building Reinforcement advertising Loyalty promotions Self-liquidating offers 2 for 1 Personal selling Branded packs Money-off couponing Price offers off next purchase Point of sale displays Trial size packaging Free samples Demonstrations Direct mail Cold call personal selling
AFFECTIVE The realm of emotions, feelings opinions and attitude formation **(feeling)**	↑ **Conviction** ↑ **Preference** ↑ **Liking**	To obtain intention to purchase among 25% of target audience within a 3-month period To gain inclusion of the brand into the repertoire sets of 30% of the target audience To create positive feelings and attitude about the brand among 50% of the target audience	Competitive and comparison advertising, argumentative copy, 'persuasive' argument Sampling Endorsement Demonstrations Exhibition stands Advertising PR, endorsement 'Image' copy Status or attractive appeals
COGNITIVE The realm of thoughts and associations **(thinking)**	↑ **Knowledge** ↑ **Awareness**	To create an understanding of brand values (the brand to be seen as ...) and interest in the brand among 70% of the target audience To create prompted recall of the brand and its advertising among 90% of the target audience	Advertising PR/editorial, announcements Slogans Jingles Teaser campaigns

Source: Reproduced from figure from Belch, G. and Belch, M.A. (1998), *Advertising and Promotion: an Integrated Marketing Communications Perspective, 4th Edition*, McGraw-Hill, reproduced with permission of The McGraw-Hill Companies.

encouraging trial, relieving post-purchase dissonance, or whatever. Advocates of communications objectives are also quick to point out that many factors, not just marketing communications, affect sales and, as such, sales are an inappropriate or inaccurate measure of effectiveness of marketing communications (see Chapter 23).

Both 'schools', of course, are right in their own way. The importance of the final outcome of action or sales cannot be ignored or underestimated. It has an important place in the total scheme of things. It may be entirely appropriate to include action/sales-related objectives within a campaign together with other marketing communications objectives such as awareness or preference building. It is equally possible

IN VIEW 19.2

Action oriented objectives

In setting objectives, 'doing' or 'action' words are commonly used to describe the desired effect. A brief checklist of some of the most common ones might be helpful.

Desired communication effect (hierarchy of effects terms)	Action associated with effect			
Awareness/Attention				
Brand (corporate/product)	Establish	Maintain	Increase	
Top of mind	Create		Raise	
Unprompted recall	Generate		Gain	
Prompted recall	Introduce		Build	
Recognition	Obtain		Change	
	Achieve		Develop	
	Inform		Stimulate	
	Announce			
Knowledge/Comprehension/ Understanding/Image	Establish	Maintain	Increase	
Brand values	Create		Raise	
Specific features/qualities	Generate		Gain	
Associations	Introduce		Build	
	Obtain		Change	
	Achieve		Develop	
			Stimulate	
Conviction/Interest/Desire/ Liking/Preference/ Believability	Establish	Maintain	Increase	Reinforce
Inclusion in repertoire set	Create		Raise	Enhance
	Generate		Gain	Improve
	Introduce		Build	Restore
	Obtain		Change	
	Achieve		Develop	
			Stimulate	
Attitude				
Positive	Establish	Maintain	Change	Reinforce
Favourable	Create		Convert	Enhance
Loyalty	Generate			Improve
Trust	Introduce			Restore
	Achieve			
Action				
Trial	Establish	Maintain	Change	Reinforce
Adoption	Create		Convert	Enhance
Purchase	Generate			Improve
Re-purchase	Introduce			Restore
	Obtain			
	Achieve			

for a specific campaign to only address part of the hierarchy of effects. A PR campaign may be run specifically, for example, to help build awareness or limit the damage caused by other bad publicity.

In selecting objectives, then, careful attention should be given to *both* communication and sales/action aspects for each promotional element and for the marketing communications mix as a whole with due regard for other marketing and corporate objectives in the context of an integrated marketing communications campaign.

John Rossiter and Larry Percy (1997) support the view of the importance of communications coupled with sales/action objectives. They have developed what they call the 'five communications effects'. Any form of marketing communications can influence these effects in whole, or in part. They describe the effects as,

> relatively enduring mental associations, connected to the brand, in the prospective buyer's mind (or in the minds of others), that are necessary to create the brand's position and predispose action ... It is helpful to regard the five communications effects as a series of five 'mental bins' which must be filled before the buyer will take action. (p. 109)

From their perspective, it is necessary to consider objectives related to *all* the areas of effect if marketing communications are to be successful. Exhibit 19.8 is based upon Rossiter and Percy's descriptions of each of the effects and a summary of the options of communications objectives options that need to be considered for each.

NEED TO KNOW

☑ *In selecting objectives, attention should be given to* both *communication and sales/action aspects for each promotional element and for the marketing communications mix as a whole with due regard for other marketing and corporate objectives in the context of an integrated marketing communications campaign.*

Exhibit 19.8 Rossiter and Percy's five communications effects defined and the objectives options available for each

Communication effect	Definition	Communications objectives options
1 Category need	Buyer's acceptance that the category (a good or a service e.g. music centre, security system) is necessary to remove or satisfy a perceived discrepancy between the current motivational state and the desired motivational state	● **Omit** reference to category need if it is already assumed to be present ● **Remind** if category need is latent ● **Sell** if new category users are targeted
2 Brand awareness	Buyer's ability to identify (recognise or recall) the brand within the category in sufficient detail to make a purchase	● **Brand recognition** if choice made at point of purchase ● **Brand recall** if choice made prior to purchase ● **Both** if justified
3 Brand attitude	Buyer's evaluation of the brand with respect to previous experiences and perceived ability to meet requirements	● **Create** brand attitude if unaware ● **Increase** if moderately favourable ● **Maintain** if maximally favourable ● **Modify** if moderate with no increase possible ● **Change** if negative
4 Brand purchase intention	Buyer's self-instruction to purchase the brand or to take purchase related action	● **Assume** no brand purchase intention in promoting for low-risk brand ● **Generate** in all other product promotion
5 Purchase facilitation	Buyer's response to other marketing and organisational activities to facilitate the purchase and that other factors will not hinder the purchase	● **Omit** purchase facilitation if there are no problems with other marketing mix activities ● **Incorporate** purchase facilitation in campaign if problems exist

Source: reproduced from table from Rossiter J. and Percy L. (1997) *Advertising Communications and Promotion Management, 2nd Edition*, McGraw-Hill, reproduced with permission of The McGraw-Hill Companies.

Determining strategy

Mintzberg's five strategy Ps (1995)

In studying the strategy process, Henry Mintzberg (1995) one of the most widely accepted authors on strategy, organisation and managerial issues, has identified five alternative perspectives. Each view of the strategy process has implications for the raison d'être behind developing marketing communications strategies and their focus of intent:

1 Strategy as *Plan*: Strategy is seen as a deliberate, planned and intended course of action with a set of guidelines to deal with a given situation (and contingencies where necessary). Implications are that strategies are comprehensive and integrated into a planning framework designed to meet organisational objectives.

2 Strategy as *Ploy*: Strategy is used as a specific competitive manoeuvre. This could be relatively short-lived or integrated into the organisation's long-term activities if it proves to be successful. For example, a product range may be extended to compete with lower priced competitor brands.

3 Strategy as *Pattern*: Strategy is developed out of a stream of actions. Strategy in this sense is not planned but evolves as a 'consistency in behaviour' whether or not it is intended.

4 Strategy as *Position*: Strategy is about the positioning of an organisation or its products in its (their) competitive and market environment(s). It might be as leader or follower or within a niche.

5 Strategy as *Perspective*: This is to do with the internal perspective developed consciously or unconsciously as a result of actions. It is about the viewpoint held and behaviour enacted by an organisation's employees and other stakeholders. Aston Martin car workers are likely to have more in common with TVR car workers in terms of the company perspectives held than they would with Ford, Nissan, Peugeot, Daewoo or Proton car workers. This reflects the sort of organisation, management and strategic stances each company adopts in its operations and its marketing effort.

'Strategy as pattern' is an emergent strategy that is likely to be less integrated. The marketing communications effort may well be less orchestrated. 'Strategy as perspective' may require marketing communications to focus on internal audiences. 'Strategy as position' will require very different marketing communications responses dependent on the position selected – market leaders are associated with relatively higher budgets. Based on PIMS (Profit Impact of Market Strategy) data, often over two-thirds of market leader promotional expenditure (not including sales force costs) is spent on advertising (Buzzell and Gale 1987). Market niches will need very careful targeting focus. 'Strategy as ploy' may require direct, head-on competitive marketing communications that could be switched and changed in reaction to competitor activities either reactively or pre-emptively. 'Strategy as plan' suggests greater need for analysis, more extensive integration and consistent planning.

What Mintzberg's insight has highlighted is that, in practice, organisations develop and utilise strategies in different ways that reflect their own management philosophies and operations.

Patti and Frazer creative strategy alternatives (1988)

Patti and Frazer (1988) have identified a range of seven strategic approaches that may be adopted in the development of marketing communications. Their strategies, particularly related to creative treatments, emphasise the message appeals that may be used as 'platforms' or 'themes' for campaign development. There is no reason to presuppose that the strategic choices they identify have to be adopted singly or used throughout all integrated elements of a campaign. It is better to consider the strategies as overlapping options in which there is the possibility of particular campaigns adopting hybrid combinations of the strategies Patti and Frazer propose. It would not be acceptable, however, to cause confusion with an ill-considered mix of approaches. Further aspects of creative decisions are considered in more detail in the next chapter (Chapter 20).

Generic strategy

A generic strategy is one in which there is no distinction made between brands. In terms of communication effects (Rossiter and Percy 1997), emphasis is placed upon category need rather than brand awareness. Promotions on behalf of industry groups might well fall into this strategic approach in which generic goods and services are promoted rather than individual companies and brands. Companies operating under monopolistic conditions, in powerful positions or undertaking joint industry promotions might also adopt a similar line of marketing communications to encourage greater use of the generic product. Market leaders might adopt this strategy as they would have the most to gain from any growth within a market sector or product category. Examples might include promotions for telephone communications, gas, sugar, milk, meat, soya bean substitutes, glass for packaging, radio as an advertising medium, etc.

Pre-emptive strategy

A pre-emptive strategy is one in which a generic claim is made but with some assertion that your brand is superior. This, Patti and Frazer (1988) contend, is then difficult for competitors to contest without simply being seen as imitators. They see this strategy as being most useful in growing or awakening a market where competitive promotions are generic or non-existent. Promotions for professional practices such as legal or accounting services could be an example of the use of this approach.

Unique selling proposition (USP) strategy

In this instance, the strategy emphasises the superiority of a brand based on a unique feature or benefit. In a highly competitive world, such features and benefits might be easily copied (unless protected by law e.g. patent) to eliminate or reduce competitive advantage. In practice, USPs are frequently based on more perceptual, rather than real, distinctions and a good creative strategy can be used to great effect in this context. Heineken lager has been promoted on the basis (it has used the creative theme) of 'refreshing the parts other beers cannot reach'. Heineken promotions have made the brand a leader based upon a humorous contention that has no grounding in fact, but the consuming population is fully aware of this and joins in the fun. Industrial companies may attempt to create a sense of uniqueness either through their core offerings or through their extended offerings such as expertise, delivery or service. These features may then be used in marketing communications to differentiate their products from competing products.

Brand image strategy

David Ogilvy, founding member of the worldwide advertising agency, Ogilvy and Mather, has long been associated with his views on the importance of brand image. This strategy relies on the development of mental or psychological associations through the use of semiotic devices (signs, symbols, images) and associations. Brands are differentiated not on physical characteristics or claims of uniqueness as such, but on the 'gestalt' or whole image formed in the minds of the public, especially target audience members.

It may be argued that where goods and services are largely homogeneous (which account for large proportions of consumer and industrial products), branding or brand imaging is particularly appropriate. In fact, it is difficult to think in terms of products and organisations not being branded in some way even if the branding is limited or not particularly well done. This may be through naming, use of logo, consistent use of colours or typefaces, packaging, etc. or fully blown branding strategies and tactics. Even commodity type products are frequently given brand identity through corporate branding activities.

Differentiation between products and companies and competitive advantage is achieved by 'winning hearts and minds'. As Al Ries and Jack Trout (1982) have commented, the battleground is not in the marketplace but in the minds of customers and consumers. So successful was Guinness in rejuvenating their brand by changing the perception of their beer through marketing communications efforts from an older, working man's drink to a younger man's, trendy drink that not only did they increase their sales, they also opened up the market for other similar Irish stout beers to follow.

Guinness's and Heineken's strategies both usefully highlight the fact that Patti and Frazer's strategy alternatives are not discrete or watertight strategic compartments. Both display a strong emphasis on brand image but Heineken's campaigns have been more clearly focused towards a USP approach whereas Guinness's, whether intended or not, have been more pre-emptive in nature, encouraging people to buy stout in general and the Guinness brand in particular.

Positioning strategy

Patti and Frazer (1988) see positioning as an attempt to build or occupy a mental niche in relation to identified competitors. They comment on this strategy as being particularly suitable for attacking a brand leader if sufficient resources are made available for aggressive efforts over a relatively long term. Ries and Trout (1982), however, warn of the dangers of directly attacking a brand leader as reprisals may follow. Positioning strategies are more fully explored in the next section.

Resonance strategy

A resonance strategy is one which attempts to 'strike a chord' by evoking meanings, experiences, thoughts, associations or aspirations that are relevant, meaningful and significant to target audiences. This may be very similar to brand imaging although, in this case, emphasis is put on marketing communications efforts that could feature aspirational and status-seeking themes or be 'a slice of life' in which, for example, viewers can relate the portrayed situations to themselves and their desires.

Affective strategy

An affective or emotional strategy attempts to invoke involvement and emotion. Not usually associated with a strong 'selling' emphasis, the message can nevertheless be extremely powerful. The Lynx (respect for animals) poster campaign, which featured a fur coat being dragged along the floor leaving behind a trail of blood, was an extremely emotive plea to stop animals being bred and slaughtered for their furs.

Informational strategy

This final category of strategic approach is not one identified by Patti and Frazer but is one that is worth its own heading. Here, the strategy is based on the view that an important element of the creative theme is to convey information. Huge amounts of classified advertising including recruitment advertising are based on this approach although it may be argued that this is less strategic and more tactical in nature. Campaigns where it is felt an educational role is necessary are likely to adopt an informational strategy and attempt to convey a lot of detailed information. This may not be undertaken in all forms of promotion under this strategy. Recent drug awareness campaigns, for example, have made use of radio advertising and sponsorship to encourage listeners to ring in and speak to specialist, confidential advisors for more information.

Positioning strategies

Positioning is most typically thought of in the context of competitive brand positioning; that is the brand's position in the 'minds' of the market in relation to competing brands. This is frequently 'mapped' using brand, conceptual or preference maps. Details of these are given in Chapter 16.

Strategic attempts to position a brand as distinct, even using non-rational, psychological propositions, are intended to create competitive differentiation and advantage while avoiding head-on competition. This perspective of positioning has been greatly expanded by David Aaker and Gary Shansby (1982) who have identified six different positioning strategies. In addition, a seventh one is identified here. It is only in the case of positioning with respect to a competitor that marketing communications comparisons with competitors are made (implicitly or explicitly). In other cases, it may be left up to the target audiences to determine, for themselves, the relationship between competing offerings.

Positioning by attribute, product characteristic or consumer benefit

The brand is perceived to be better than others in a particular way. Marketing communications emphasise these features. This is the basis of a USP strategy. Dyson vacuum cleaners clean better because they do not use a filter bag that can clog and reduce efficiency. RS Components provide an international service which they have built on the rapid ordering and delivery of an extensive range of electrical and electronic components.

Positioning by price/quality

This is a commonly pursued strategy and is sometimes over-used by competitors making the same claims. Positions can be sought in high price/high quality, prestige positions, in low price/poor quality positions or anywhere in between. Marketing communications attempt to convey a sense of value for money in whatever position is occupied. At the 'high end', promotions may be heavily based on image building and status. No mention may be made of price; it will be conveyed through imagery. At the 'low end', a 'no nonsense', down-to-earth approach may be featured clearly identifying 'low, low prices and sale discounts'.

Positioning by use or application

Segmentation and targeting can be carried out based on usage occasion; the same can be used for positioning. Industrial and domestic sealants are packaged for special uses. Small sized, ready mixed DIY products are packaged and promoted for small, one-off jobs. After Eight mints position themselves as after-dinner mints. Wash and Go is a shampoo and conditioner for people who have limited time to wash their hair. As the advertising extols, it is for people who want to 'wash and go'.

Positioning by product user

It is interesting that Aaker and Shansby should identify this as a distinct approach because marketing has always extolled the virtue of focusing on the requirements of target customers and consumers. It may be argued that marketing has always been about positioning by product user. However, in this instance, there is the implication of specific and increased focus, perhaps on a niche sector. In addition, although marketing activities may be targeted towards purchasers and users, this is not always highlighted in the marketing communications effort which organisations adopting this positioning strategy allow to shine through. High and Mighty stores promote themselves as clothing stores for larger men. Likewise, Long Tall Sally promotes clothing for larger women.

Positioning with respect to product category

Rather than overtly competing against another brand, a brand or product category might be positioned against, or as an alternative to, another product category. The competitive 'heat', therefore, is taken away from direct competitors and placed on to substitutes. Email is an alternative to postage. Rail haulage and transport is an alternative to road haulage and car travel. America's Amtrak rail company has positioned itself in part of its promotional effort against car and airline travel. Margarine brands have been promoted against butter brands and in Europe, cholesterol-reducing spreads are being positioned against margarines and butters.

Positioning against a competitor

Ries and Trout (1982) have been strong advocates of competitive positioning as a vital strategy. Their views, which have affected a whole generation of marketing strategists, emphasise the importance of customer and consumer perceptions of competing offerings. For this reason, brands must be promoted with a full understanding of their relative competitive position in the minds of target audience members.

This strategy might result in direct competitive comparisons or the positioning may be less direct. In highly competitive and relatively homogeneous markets such as cigarettes and soap powders, competitive positioning is of extreme importance not least because so few companies own so many different brands. The task is to position the brands to compete principally with the brands of the competitors rather than encouraging too much competitive rivalry between one's own brands.

Cultural positioning

A final positioning strategy, not actually included in Aaker and Shansby's (1982) list, is that of positioning by cultural reference. In this strategy, the brand is clearly associated with a particular culture, country, religion, ethnic group or sense of heritage or tradition. Harley-Davidson has positioned itself as 'Born in the USA'; Rolls Royce is clearly English; BMW, German; Citroen, French. Christian Bookshops position themselves by religion. The publishers Burke's Peerage leverage their aristocratic and heritage connections in promoting their range of publications.

Re-positioning

Before leaving the topic of positioning it is worth commenting upon the need to constantly review and assess a brand's position in the light of continually changing circumstances. A decision may be made to maintain its position, or having evaluated the situation, seek to move it to a new position. Brand mapping is a tool that can be particularly useful in this process. Not only may an assessment be made of a brand's proximity to other brands, but also areas can be identified that represent greater opportunities if the brand were to be moved closer to them. Three excellent, if commonly cited, examples of repositioning are Guinness, which was mentioned earlier, Johnson & Johnson Baby Shampoo which retained its original position and added a new position as a gentle shampoo for adults (subsequently they repeated this approach with other baby products), and Lucozade which was fully repositioned and rejuvenated when it moved from an energy drink for convalescents to a sports drink.

Push/pull strategies

Push promotional strategy

The focusing of promotional effort by manufacturers or suppliers of goods and services to encourage the trade channel members to stock, promote and sell products.

Pull promotional strategy

The focusing of promotional effort to encourage end customers and consumers to demand goods and services.

One of the most significant, yet basic strategic marketing communications decisions centres around the determination of push and pull strategies. These strategies are concerned with the marketing communications efforts focused towards trade/channel intermediaries (**push strategies**) and the final customers and consumers and the decision influencers that affect them (**pull strategies**). These strategies are also known as 'selling into the pipeline' and 'selling out of the pipeline', referring to push and pull strategies respectively – the 'pipeline' being the channels that facilitate the movement of goods and services through intermediaries (retailers, wholesalers, agents, brokers, etc.) to arrive at final use and consumption (industrial or consumer). Wherever intermediaries are involved, the rule of thumb is that *both* push and pull strategies should be used in an integrated fashion. To use one without the other (which is undertaken in certain circumstances with good effect) can result in higher risks of failure.

Push strategies encourage the trade to carry and promote products. They help to achieve distribution coverage, create trade goodwill and partnership. Pull strategies

IN VIEW 19.3

A truly great beer

Re-positioning is usually triggered by falling sales or the anticipation of faltering performance. Lowenbrau was a successful beer before attempts to re-position it caused it to falter. Originally positioned as 'a truly great German beer', it was exported out of Europe. When the brand was bought by the American company, Miller, from Philip Morris, the new owners decided that they would not be able to continue importing it quickly enough and started brewing it in the States. The position was changed to 'a truly great American beer' but this was at odds with the established perception. Miller spent millions of dollars creating a new position after losing a truly great position.

encourage products to be demanded. A combination of push and pull provides greater synergistic effect than can be achieved in the use of either strategy singly. Often joint promotions between channel members and manufacturers are undertaken to enhance trade partnership and 'pull' promotions.

It is interesting to note that distinctions are made between consumer and industrial/business-to-business companies as though they operate under significantly different circumstances. It is inappropriate for us to think this way in strategic marketing communications terms. While the balance of the mix may vary, there is more in common than there are differences. Among the biggest players in business-to-business marketing are the FMCG companies themselves. Although their products are targeted towards consumers, their marketing activities have to cover trade customers as well. In their marketing communications, push strategies feature strongly, even if these are not so widely known or so strongly reported. Likewise, industrial companies whose products may never be seen by the majority of consumers, can embark on elaborate pull strategies. In computing, Intel with its Pentium processor and in textiles, Dupont with its Lycra fabric are good examples. Both these companies have heavily branded their products, recognised in households throughout the world, yet they have never themselves sold a single product to consumers.

Push strategies and internal audiences

One area of push strategy that is typically taken for granted is the communication with internal audiences, most notably, employees. Employees need to be both informed and motivated to help push the product and the organisation forward. The obvious group of employees that need to be an integral part of the marketing communications effort is the sales force. Many organisations separate the sales force from other marketing functions; for this reason particular effort has to be made to ensure their full co-operation and involvement.

Although all customers are important, not all customers can be said to be equally important to a business. Paraphrasing George Orwell's *Animal Farm*, 'All customers may be equal, but some are more equal than others'. For this reason, some customers are singled out for preferential treatment. The sales force may be organised around a key account management structure to facilitate this. Chapter 31 gives more details about the role of the sales force.

But not only does the sales force have to be targeted as an internal 'push' audience, so do other employees and anybody else who is associated with the organisation who might have an impact on the organisation's performance. This is not to say that everybody becomes part of the target audience specification. It is a question of determining who needs to be identified when developing specific campaigns. This could include receptionists, telephonists and members of other functional departments – those who come into direct contact with customers or who might affect the relationship with customers.

Consider the Gas-Co. case given in In View 19.4. It illustrates the importance of marketing communications focused towards internal audiences and the strategic importance of all forms of customer contact management.

Share of voice, share of market

Share of voice (SOV) is an important concept that refers to how 'loud' an organisation's marketing communications are in the marketplace. There are other 'voices' competing to be heard in the marketplace and the strategic task is to be heard above

Share of voice

Concept that refers to how 'loud' one brand's marketing communications are compared with other competing brands. It may be measured in terms of marketing communications spends, or by subjective assessment of the relative attention created by competing marketing communications.

IN VIEW 19.4

Gas-Co. blows hot and cold over central heating

10 October

The marketing team met in good spirits. 'Well guys,' commented the Marketing Manager at the start of the meeting, 'It's actually all come together at long last. All that planning and hard work has paid off. I'm telling you, this feels just as it should. We're on our way to some major sales results this season.'

'The refurbishment of the retail showrooms is now complete and they are looking great,' stated Anne, one of the team responsible for the new retail designs. 'The lighting, the colour schemes, the signage – the whole scene is warm and inviting. Based on feedback from the retail staff everyone seems to think it's a real success. The sales staff have welcomed our new floor layouts. They really like our attempts to anticipate customer enquiries by splitting the showrooms into sales areas so that anybody walking through the door will be directed to an enquiry desk with a member of staff who is best able to answer their queries whether these be for account payment, showers, fires, cooking or central heating.'

'Staff training has made sure that enquiry handling and customer courtesy should go without a hitch,' commented Joe from Sales.

The Advertising Manager broke in, 'Talking about central heating, our new advertising will hit the streets next week and we'll start monitoring enquiries from then. The ads in the local press should really whet a few appetites. The timing is right and the price deal is a real winner.'

'Yes, this offer?' interrupted Jane, 'It may be a great deal, but who's it really aimed at? Surely it will only be suitable for a small number of our customers?'

'Yes, that's true, Jane, but we've got to start somewhere and the main aim of the ads is to generate enquiries. But there'll be no hard sell,' continued the Marketing Manager, 'We've gone all out for customer focus. Our research tells us that customers don't know what heating will be best for them so we've gone to a great deal of trouble to set up a way of giving them the best advice and service.'

'And there's nobody in a better position than us to help them,' chirped the Marketing Assistant, interrupting his boss in full flow.

'That's right, Alan, there's a lot of cowboys out there. If we channel customer enquiries to us we can be sure they're getting the right advice. We've been working hard with Engineering over the past year, they're key to our service. They reckon that there could be some demand for the system we're featuring in our ads, but that's not important because they also know that customers don't really understand the ins and outs of central heating. And that's where our sales staff come in. We've made special arrangements between Sales and Engineering so that when Sales get an enquiry, rather than trying to sell them the system featured in the ads, they will contact Engineering who will make an appointment to visit the customer – at a time convenient to the customer. And do a complete survey at no cost to them. The customer will be assured of getting the right system for them. The total emphasis is on helping the customer, giving advice and no pressure selling. You can't get more customer focused than that.'

The meeting went on as the coffee arrived. Everybody was in a good mood. The Marketing Manager had set the scene and they all agreed that the latest marketing efforts were sure to pay dividends. A lot of effort had gone into changing the stuffy image of Gas-Co. and their showrooms certainly reflected a change of policy towards a customer focus.

The retail staff had been put through customer training and product offers were being changed in the light of competitors' offers and to make them more customer-appealing. The stage was set for a new era for Gas-Co. The team had gone to great lengths to implement the customer-focused strategy that the Board had emphasised was vital to the continued success of the company.

25 October

I walked into the Gas-Co. showroom – it had a very pleasant decor. Cookers, fires, water heaters, showers, hanging signs and partitions broke the room into cosy, discrete areas each with its own desk and attendant. The showroom offered welcomed warmth from the cold, chill winds of the high street. I had entered for a purpose, but who was I to ask for help? Which desk? Which assistant?

'Excuse me, I saw your advertisement in the local paper, central heating at a special offer price.'

'What advertisement is that, sir?'

'It appeared in the local newspaper.'

'Oh, perhaps you had better ask at the desk straight ahead, Mrs Snow handles heating enquiries. I'm sure she will be back at her desk shortly.'

A cool reception, I thought. The cold shoulder.

I stood and waited … At last someone arrived, 'Would you like to take a seat, I shan't keep you a moment' … More waiting … 'Now, can I help you?'

'Yes, I hope so. I'm enquiring about central heating. Your advertisement says you can install a system for an excellent price.'

'Our advertisement?'

'Yes, in this week's local paper. You quote a price that …'

'Just a moment sir, I shall just go and ask the manager.' … 'Sorry to keep you waiting. The manager tells me that the system we advertised only includes a limited number of radiators and so on.'

'Could you give me some more details?'

'Well, we need to get our engineer to go and look at your house and he will explain what system you need. He can provide you with full details. I have very little information here and central heating can be somewhat complicated. It is better for someone to look at your property and see exactly what your requirements may be. Can we make arrangements for our engineer to call? He will have all the leaflets for the Glo-Worm System we advertised and he will be able to answer your questions.'

'Yes, all right.'

'Name? Address? Do you have a phone number where we can contact you? The engineer will ring and make an appointment.'

'I shall have to make special arrangements to be home, can't we arrange a date and time now?'

'No, the engineer makes his own appointments. We don't know his appointments schedule I'm afraid. He will ring you.'

I left the showroom a little hot under the collar with no further information and the assistant was not able to tell me when I might expect to hear from the engineer.

8 November

Two weeks had passed when I received a phone call at my office. I was out, but a message was left with a phone number to ring. I rang.

After a short delay during which the phone played some music (irritatingly, it was 'Greensleeves'. The third rendition of the chorus only succeeded in emphasising how long it took to answer the phone), someone answered, 'Gas-Co!'

'Could I speak to Mr Plumb, please?'

'Just connecting you.' More 'Greensleeves' …

A lady answered the phone. I repeated my request, 'Could I speak to Mr Plumb, please?'

'I'm sorry, Mr Plumb is out, may I help?'

'Yes, I'm returning his call as requested. I think he wanted to make arrangements to survey my house for central heating.'

'Do you have a reference number?'

'No, I'm sorry I don't. Would my name and address do?'

'I think you need to speak to Mr Plumb. He is normally in the office between 8.30am and 10.00am.'

'Shall I ring tomorrow?'

'That will be the best thing to do.'

That evening I arrived home. My mother-in-law told me that a 'Gas Man' had called. He was in the area and thought he would call on the off-chance and would call back in about an hour's time. Indeed he did and in half an hour had surveyed the house, taking notes and estimates of heights, lengths and widths of rooms.

'Yes, you will need an indirect cylinder and we shall have to put an expansion tank upstairs. We can put a wall-mounted, room-sealed, balanced-flue boiler in the kitchen and I should think a 35,000–40,000 BTU Fuelsaver would be adequate. I shall calculate your precise requirements and send you a quotation in the post. I shall need to take account of the room sizes and thermal coefficients you see.'

No, I didn't see. 'Can you explain what an indirect cylinder is, please?'

'Yes, certainly. Central heating works on a secondary, indirect, closed water system. We can either put in a new cylinder or convert your existing cylinder using a Yorkshire Sidewinder to prevent the central heating water and domestic water from mixing.'

I thought I had better change tack. 'Oh, how much do you think the whole central heating system will cost?'

'About £4200 I would think.'

'What about the system advertised in the paper?'

'That system is really only suitable for a small flat or for background heating or, perhaps, partial heating. Probably a maximum of 15,000 BTUs. I don't have any leaflets with me as the system isn't really any use for most people. I shall send you more information with the quote.'

I was little the wiser and my dinner was cold. I still didn't know what an indirect cylinder really was and was afraid to ask about balanced-flue boilers, BTUs and Yorkshire Sidewinders. I did know, however, that the system offered in the advertisement was not for me and if I wanted central heating I would have to pay considerably more than I had expected.

11 November

A few days later I received the quotation, £4290. No leaflets and no further information included.

10 December

One month later. I haven't heard any more from Gas-Co. and I still don't have central heating. Any offers?

the competitors and the rest of the noise. It is a relative term in that it is measured as a proportion of total marketing communications. Although, in principle it is measured using total marketing communication expenditure, in practice it is difficult to assess full expenditure on marketing communications. As a consequence, quantitatively, SOV tends to concentrate on advertising spends which are relatively easy to identify for one's own organisation, competitors and the market as a whole.

Researchers such as Jones (1990) and Shroer (1990) particularly emphasise the importance of relating SOV to **share of market** (SOM) to determine strategic budgets and resource allocation. In effect, SOV is measured in the same way that market share is measured but using marketing communication spends rather than sales value. If the total expenditure in the market is £10m and your organisation spends £1m, its SOV is 10%. Competitor shares are calculated in the same way and compared. While it would be unrealistic for a market follower to match the market leader's SOV (the market leader can afford a larger expenditure to maintain its market leadership), SOV analysis can be used to help determine whether an appropriate proportional level of marketing communications effort is being expended by considering the relationship between SOV and SOM. The basic argument being that a company should aim to achieve a share of voice equivalent to its share of market (SOV = SOM). In this situation, the promotional expenditure is directly proportional to the level of market share. If your market share is 5%, then your share of voice should be 5%. That is to say, it is reasonable to expect a company with 5% share of the market to be spending 5% of the market's promotional expenditure.

Equally, the following basic cases can be made:

- If SOV is less than SOM (SOV < SOM), more needs to be spent to reach equilibrium and achieve an appropriate level of marketing communications presence in the marketplace.
- If SOV is greater than SOM (SOV > SOM), more than necessary may be being spent to achieve greatest marketing communications efficiency. This is a point made by Jones (1990) and Buzzell et al. (1990) who suggest that some organisations' expenditures are too high with the consequence of wastage and lower profits.

Used in this way, SOV/SOM analysis can be very helpful in determining marketing communications strategies, at least in terms of budget calculations applied both to the total budget and to individual budget allocations between each of the promotional tools (if the data is available). But this level of analysis is relatively naïve. It could be made much more sophisticated by considering a range of other circumstances.

Product portfolio analysis, such as the **Boston Consulting Group Matrix**, allows us to recognise that marketing decisions have to be based on a fuller understanding of the roles of different products within a company's portfolio. 'Stars' require more marketing investment and 'Cash Cows' are used to generate higher returns to help support other products in the portfolio and new product development. Jones (1990) recognised this when he described that investment brands (Stars) need to have SOV > SOM, and profit-taking brands (Cash Cows) need to have SOV < SOM.

So far the description of share of voice has been directed towards its use in budgeting. Important though this is, there are other quantitative and qualitative implications of SOV. Rather than measuring expenditure, it is also possible to use the concept as a measure of coverage by actually counting numbers of advertisements, sales promotion activities, PR coverage, number of direct mail shots, number and types of sponsorships, number of exhibitions attended and stand space used, and so on, that competitors are undertaking at specific time periods and assessing one's own efforts

---

Share of market

Brand sales represented as a percentage of total market sales for all relevant competing brands.

Product portfolio analysis

Assessment of an organisation's range of products in relation to each other. A variety of approaches may be adopted, of which the Boston Consulting Group Matrix tends to be most widely reported.

Boston Consulting Group Matrix

Method of assessing an organisation's range or portfolio of products or SBU's in terms of their relative positions in a matrix or grid that plots each product's relative market share (as measured against the market leader, or if leader, nearest follower) against the market growth rate.

against these. It may be especially important, for example, to assess the extent of competitor coverage and use of specific media compared with one's own.

SOV can be used qualitatively. The analogy is that not only do you have to shout loud enough to be heard, but also clear enough to be understood. The 'quality' of marketing communications should, therefore, be assessed against competing activities, perhaps by comparing target audience perceptions. Robin Wight, senior strategist behind the marketing communications success of BMW cars, is very proud that BMW has achieved a significantly better share of market from their significantly lower share of voice expenditure. The quality of their promotions has made more effective and efficient use of their budgets (relative to competitors). Wight has made BMW's promotional pound work harder. While strategic decisions based purely on financial analysis will always be part of the story, the quality of marketing communications should also be part of the equation.

Strategic and tactical use of the marketing communications mix

A critical decision in developing marketing communications strategies is the selection of the appropriate balance of elements within the marketing communications mix. There can be no easy answer. The choice of mix activities and the balance between them will vary according to the circumstances and the preferences of the strategist. Type of product, specific objectives and competitive environment will always have their bearing upon the selection process too. The sections that follow are intended to provide a guide not a prescription to help understand some general factors affecting marketing communications mix choice.

Product life cycle, innovation diffusion and the marketing communications mix

During each stage of the product life cycle, a different balance or emphasis on particular promotional elements may be used and different target audiences focused upon. During the introduction of a new product, the focus may be on innovators, opinion leaders and early adopters (Exhibit 19.9). Then, subsequently, as the product extends to a mass market and moves through growth towards maturity, early and late majority may be targeted. Latterly, laggards may be the last group adopting the product as it

Exhibit 19.9 Distribution of product adoption categories

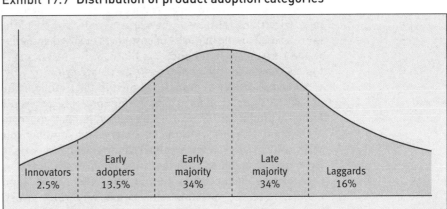

Exhibit 19.10 The product life cycle and examples of the strategic use of marketing communications

Introduction	Growth	Maturity/saturation	Decline
• Emphasis on awareness building especially among innovators and early adopters (pull strategies) • Emphasis on trade push strategies to obtain distribution acceptance • Emphasis on PR activities and advertising to generate awareness and image building and assist in positive attitude formation • Emphasis on sales promotions to induce trial and encouragement of inclusion in customers' repertoire sets • Strong sales force emphasis may be a feature for some products in, for example, industrial durable markets	• Emphasis continues on building awareness and adoption by new customers (early adopters, early majority) • Emphasis on trade push strategies to gain distribution penetration • Advertising and PR may be increased as increases in sales revenue permit larger expenditures • As product moves into mass market, wider audiences are included in target specification • Sales promotions may still be emphasised as new customers are encouraged but as demand increases, price offers may be used less • Promotions encouraging 'loyalty' may feature prominently • Efforts to encourage positive word of mouth	• More emphasis may be required on brand differentiation. If competitive environment requires it, re-positioning may be considered • Emphasis on keeping customers (loyalty promotions) and sales promotions to encourage brand switching from competing brands • Reminder advertising encouraging customers to keep brand within repertoire set • Sales promotions to encourage increased usage • Trade promotions used to maintain distribution penetration prominence	• Promotional effort may be reduced to harvest brand profits • Before decline, consideration will be given to rejuvenating brand or re-position brand to new users or attract lapsed users • 'New, improved' versions of the brand may appear and be promoted to extend the PLC

moves into its later maturity, saturation and subsequent decline phases. This pattern can be seen not only in mass consumer markets but also in smaller markets and industrial markets. Exhibit 19.10 offers a general guide to the use of marketing communications activities in relation to the product life cycle.

Types of product and the marketing communications mix

The nature of the product and the market it serves have a profound impact on the use of the marketing communications mix. The more a product fits into an industrial durable category, the more the emphasis is typically placed on personal selling as a primary activity. The more a product fits into a consumer convenience category, the more advertising is likely to play a primary role. The simple logic behind these distinctions is based on the numbers of customers involved and value of the product.

Industrial durable products are more likely to be of high value and have few customers compared with consumer convenience products which are likely to be of low value and may have customers counted in their millions. Interestingly, though, and not always appreciated from a marketing communications perspective, industrial convenience products (low relative value, used in quantity, 'consumed') may have more in common with their consumer counterparts (consumer convenience products) than other industrial products (industrial durables). Similarly, consumer durables may have more in common with industrial durables than products classified as consumer conveniences. Exhibit 19.11 illustrates how the relative emphasis placed on the levels of different promotional mix activities may vary with type of product.

Exhibit 19.11 Product categories and the marketing communications mix

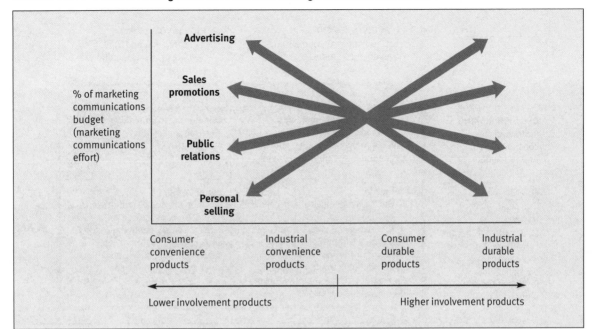

One implication of these different types of product, which is central to the use of the marketing communications mix, is the degree of **involvement** that customers and consumers have in product purchase and use (Broderick et al. 1998). Low involvement products are typified by low risk on the part of customers and consumers. They are more frequently purchased and are of lower value. They are insufficiently significant to cause the customer to make considered brand choice evaluations at least at a rational level. Brand emphasis is on brand image rather than on detailed or factual information. The lower the involvement the less customers make objectively considered decisions. The marketing communications mix is used to reflect this.

High involvement products are those associated with more major purchases, whether industrial or consumer, and are typified by higher risk on the part of the purchaser and user. They are less frequently purchased and are of higher relative value. There is greater need for more information and greater emphasis on brand evaluation. Because of these differences, the marketing communications mix for high involvement goods and services is necessarily quite different from that of low involvement goods and services.

Assael (1992) has proposed a typology of consumer decision-making based on decision-making and involvement (Exhibit 19.12). The vertical axis represents a continuum from *decision-making to habit*. The horizontal axis represents a continuum from high involvement to low involvement in the purchase and consumption process. Strategic and tactical marketing communications decisions can be based on each of the four boxes.

Involvement

Important concept, which recognises that customers' and consumers' interest and degree of involvement in product purchase and use vary with different types of product, from low involvement (best typified by frequently purchased, low-value goods) to high involvement (best typified by high-value, infrequently purchased products).

Hierarchy of effects and the marketing communications mix

As identified earlier, marketing communications, strategies and tactics are related to the hierarchy of effects process. This process is sometimes referred to as buyer

Exhibit 19.12 Low and high involvement decision-making

	LOW INVOLVEMENT E.g. consumer and industrial convenience products	**HIGH INVOLVEMENT** E.g. consumer and industrial durable products, capital purchases
DECISION-MAKING Information search, consideration and evaluation of brands	**Limited decision-making** Low risk, low interest. Requires little need to make cognitive effort. Limited information considered	**Complex decision-making** More rational evaluation of alternatives
HABIT Little or no information considered. Purchase and consumption made out of habit (habit formed out of previous repeated experiences)	**Inertia** Decision previously made even if not considered carefully. Brand selected may be one of a shortlist within the purchaser's repertoire set rather than a single brand. Same brand bought and used out of lack of motivation or interest to change	**Brand loyalty** Decision previously undertaken. Repeat purchase based on satisfaction with either decisions and experiences. Brand selected may be one of a shortlist within a purchaser's repertoire set

Source: From figure from *Consumer Behavior & Marketing Action*, South-Western College Publishing, (Assael, H. (1992), reproduced by kind permission of Professor Henry Assael.

readiness stages as it recognises a series of steps which are progressed through before a purchase or action is finally made. Marketing communications activities should be selected to best suit the purchaser's attitudinal or behavioural situation as typified by their stage of readiness or responsiveness. Mass advertising and public relations are both recognised as being useful tools in generating awareness and assisting in brand image building. They are accepted as being less good at encouraging actual purchase for which personal selling and direct response advertising are the strongest forms of promotion.

Summary

This chapter has outlined the interrelationships between objectives, strategy and tactics and identified the confusion often found when using these terms. To clearly differentiate between the terms, it is suggested that objectives are prefaced by the word 'to', and should be statements about *what* we want to achieve. Strategies, prefaced by the word 'by', are broad statements about *how* we are to achieve the objectives. Tactics detail how each of the strategies can be implemented.

The chapter has presented the key issues involved when setting objectives. The benefits of objectives are presented together with a framework for setting good objectives (although it is recognised that not all objectives can be couched in these terms). The SMARRTT framework outlines that objectives should be specific, measurable, realistic, relevant, targeted and timed. Distinctions are highlighted between sales and communications objectives. Alternative perspectives on strategy are described and the main strategic approaches to marketing communications are discussed.

The final section of the chapter identifies the general factors affecting tactical marketing communication mix choice, including:

● product life cycle
● innovation diffusion
● type of product
● involvement
● hierarchy of effects.

Self-review questions

1 What are the differences between objectives, strategy and tactics?

2 Describe how objectives and strategies can be viewed at different levels of the organisation.

3 What is an umbrella branding strategy?

4 Why is the setting of objectives important?

5 Explain what the SMARRTT framework stands for and why objectives should be SMARRTT.

6 What are the hierarchy of effects models?

7 Should objectives be sales or communications orientated? Explain your answer.

8 What are Mintzberg et al.'s five strategy Ps?

9 What are the main strategic approaches to marketing communications?

10 How do push and pull strategies differ?

11 What is share of voice?

Project

Select one example from the IPA's Advertising Works Series (Advertising Effectiveness Awards, NTC Business Publications). Identify the marketing communications objectives from one of the winning campaigns and evaluate them against the SMARRTT framework. Do the objectives meet the criteria? If not, is this a situation where the framework does not apply? Why?

References

Aaker, D. and Shansby, G. (1982), Positioning your product. *Business Horizons,* 25 (May/June), 56–62.

Assael, H. (1995), *Consumer Behaviour and Marketing Action.* South Western College Publishing.

Belch, G.E. and Belch, M.A. (1998), *Advertising and Promotion: An Integrated Marketing Communications Perspective* 4th edn, international edn. McGraw-Hill.

Broderick, A.J., Greenley, G.E. and Mueller, R.D. (1998), Utilising consumer involvement for international decision-making in the food retail market. *Proceedings of the EMAC Conference*, Stockholm, pp. 481–500.

Butterfield, L. (ed.) (1997), *Excellence in Advertising: The IPA Guide to Best Practice*. Butterworth-Heinemann.

Buzzell, R.D. and Gale, B.T. (1987), *The PIMS (Profit Impact of Market Strategy) Principles: Linking Strategy To Performance*. The Free Press.

Buzzell, R.D., Quelch, J.A. and Salmon, W.J. (1990), The costly bargain of sales promotion. *Harvard Business Review*, March/April, 141–149.

Colley, R. (1961), *Defining Advertising Goals for Measured Advertising Results*. New York: Association of National Advertisers.

Fill, C. (1999), *Marketing Communications: Contexts, Contents and Strategies* European 2nd edn. Prentice Hall.

Jones, J.P. (1990), Ad spending: maintaining market share. *Harvard Business Review*, January/February, 38–42.

Lavidge, R.J. and Steiner, G.A. (1961), A model for predictive measurements of advertising effectiveness. *Journal of Marketing*, 61 (October).

Mintzberg, H., Quinn, J.B. and Ghoshal, S. (1995), *The Strategy Process* European edn. Prentice Hall.

Patti, C.H. and Frazer, C.F. (1988), *Advertising: A Decision Making Approach*. Dryden Press.

Ries, A. and Trout, J. (1982), *Positioning: The Battle for Your Mind*. McGraw-Hill.

Rossiter, J.R. and Percy, L. (1997), *Advertising Communications and Promotion Management* 2nd edn. McGraw-Hill.

Rothschild, M.L. (1987), *Marketing Communications: from Fundamentals to Strategies*. DC Heath.

Schultz, D.E., Tannenbaum, S.I. and Lauterborn, R.F. (1994), *Integrated Marketing Communications: Pulling it Together and Making it Work*. NTC Business Books.

Shroer, J. (1990), Ad spending: growing market share. *Harvard Business Review*, January/February, 44–48.

Smith, P.R. (1998), *Marketing Communications: an Integrated Approach* 2nd edn. Kogan Page.

Selected further reading

IPA's Advertising Works Series – Advertising Effectiveness Awards, NTC Business Publications.

Kriegal, R.A. (1986), How to choose the right communications objectives. *Business Marketing*, April, 94–106.

Lambkin, M. and Day, G.S. (1989), Evolutionary processes in competitive markets: beyond the product life cycle. *Journal of Marketing*, July, 4–20.

Laskey, H.A., Day, E. and Crask, M.R. (1989), Typology of main message strategies for television commercials. *Journal of Advertising*, 18 (1), 36–41.

Chapter 20

Creative implementation

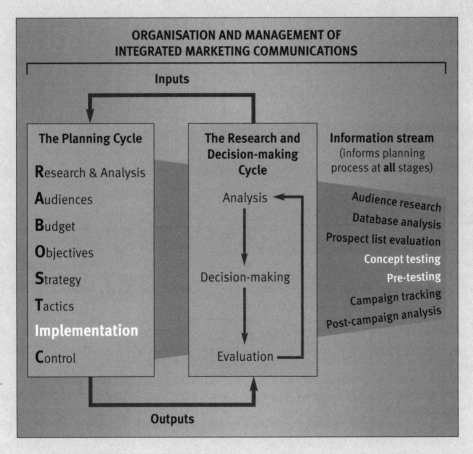

ORGANISATION AND MANAGEMENT OF INTEGRATED MARKETING COMMUNICATIONS

Inputs

The Planning Cycle

Research & Analysis

Audiences

Budget

Objectives

Strategy

Tactics

Implementation

Control

The Research and Decision-making Cycle

Analysis

Decision-making

Evaluation

Information stream
(informs planning process at **all** stages)

Audience research
Database analysis
Prospect list evaluation
Concept testing
Pre-testing
Campaign tracking
Post-campaign analysis

Outputs

The IMC RABOSTIC Planning Model

CD

What creative appeals did Škoda use in the Fabia campaign? Utilise Exhibit 20.5 to help with your answer. How were the creative appeals integrated across the campaign?

Chapter outline

- Creativity and integrated marketing communications
- Creative guidelines
- The role of creative briefs and briefing
- Developing ideas – the creative process
- Creative strategies – appeals and executions
- Creative tactics
- Assessing creative ideas

Objectives

- To consider what creativity is
- To present guidelines and describe techniques for improving creativity
- To discuss the role of briefs and briefing in the creative process
- To highlight common creative strategies, appeals and approaches adopted
- To explore creative elements used in marketing communications
- To identify what questions can be asked when assessing creative ideas and executions

Professional perspective

David Thomas Director, Thomas, Douglas Ltd

I've been involved in direct marketing communications for over 20 years now. It's a demanding discipline where you're literally as good as your last job. Results are everything. It all hinges on profitability and maximising return on investment.

In direct marketing communications we have certain advantages. We can *test* approaches. Indeed, we can test any number of variables. We can analyse results: make fine-tuned adjustments to improve our hit rate and continue to further refine our direct marketing campaigns over time.

Even though it may feature at the bottom of the direct marketing communications priority list (list, offer, creative) it is essential that the creative work does the job of exciting, inspiring, motivating, tantalising ... whatever it takes to achieve the desired response from individuals. The creative work must persuade them to send a cheque, reach for the telephone, ask for information, donate to charity, take that special magazine subscription or become a member of that very special golf club at only €10,000!

Sometimes the offers are blatant. Sometimes they are much more subtle.

The alchemy that forms the creative link between business strategists and people – like you and me is, in my view, still something magical.

Now the challenge is to connect and motivate in cyber space. The possibilities are limitless. This chapter provides a launch pad.

David Thomas

Creativity and integrated marketing communications

> Don't ask the centipede to work out with which foot he should start to walk, he wouldn't be able to move.

Like the centipede, if we try too hard to work out what makes creativity work, lost in contemplation, we would get nowhere. Creativity is hard to define. 'Like humour, it does not lend itself to dissection' (Nelson 1985, p. 23). Also, like humour, we enjoy some ideas, but we frown at others. Archimedes exclaimed 'Eureka', when he had his creative revelation while bathing, but good creative ideas cannot be relied upon to simply 'pop' into the mind. Most creatives agree that creativity requires discipline (Bill Bernbach 1971, founder member of Doyle Dane Bernbach): it is the reward of hard work. Creativity is the heart and soul of marketing communications. It is about the generation of new ideas, and new ideas are nothing more or less than a new combination of old elements (Rothschild 1987).

Creativity should not be seen as the preserve of the few, only for those who think they are creative and not for the rest who 'know' they are not. Creativity comes in many forms and most people have the ability to be creative in one form or another.

Creativity in integrated marketing communications should not be confined to creative ideas for 'ads'. All elements of the marketing communications mix require creativity and so does the rest of the management and planning process.

Message decisions clearly have to be creative in an industry that prides itself on creative communication. But *media* decisions also have to be creative. The creative use of the media can enhance the message appeal. Lack of creativity can destroy it. Press advertising for Boddingtons Beer for its national re-launch made creative use of the media by using the back outside covers of a variety of specialist magazines. When promoting a new range of squash rackets, 'Goudy Squash' needed to reach squash players, not squash enthusiasts. The typical monthly squash magazines were ruled out as not being read by the vast majority of players. The Target Group Index was used to identify new media options and men's magazines such as *Men Only* were selected for both their male and female readership.

NEED TO KNOW

☑ *Creativity can be applied to **all** aspects of marketing communications.*

IN VIEW 20.1

Have a break, have a Kit Kat

When we were working on the Kit Kat brief that became the Pandas ad, we realised that we had spent two days thinking too loose. We realised that we had to look at the structure, to think laterally about it. The traditional 'Have a break, have a Kit Kat' ads worked along the following lines: i) activity, ii) take a break, iii) activity with a spin. We looked at an alternative structure: no activity–activity–no activity, with the Kit Kat break taking place during the activity. The pandas came in when we thought about those 'nothing happens' news stories, such as the world's press around a zoo enclosure waiting for the Giant Pandas just sent from China to come out and mate, only they never do ... this is a story that everyone is familiar with. It's the familiar pantomime device of 'Look out, he's behind you', but given a fresh twist. And it gave Kit Kat yet another classic commercial in a campaign that has been running since 1934.

(Shelbourne and Baskin 1997, pp. 65–67)

Exhibit 20.1 Creativity is needed in all areas of the marketing communications process

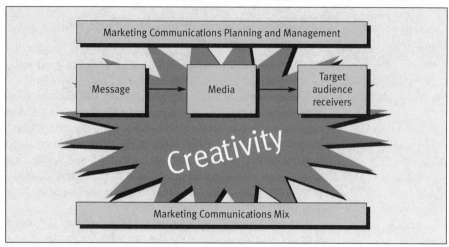

Target audience decisions have to be creative to satisfactorily define the target market customers and consumers and to look beyond them to identify audiences who influence the market – so much is dependent in marketing communications upon reaching the right people. If campaigns are targeted to international audiences, ideas have to be generated that will cross the boundaries.

Imaginative *planning and strategy* development are also important ingredients in selecting objectives and mix solutions to achieve successful creative campaigns. Exhibit 20.1 illustrates that creativity extends across the whole marketing communications process.

If defining creativity is difficult, working out what makes a creative idea and how it is created is even harder. As White (1993) observed, nobody can tell you how to create an advertisement.

> How do creative people create? Nobody really knows. Nobody really knows where ideas are born; where an unforgettable bar of music comes from; why a felicitous phrase pops into someone's head. No one really knows how some people can put words and pictures and sounds and ideas together in ways that can move millions of other people to think and feel and act.
>
> (Bert Manning 1987, Chairman and CEO of J. Walter Thompson USA, p. 233)

Some suggest that there are rules that can be applied. White (1993) starts by offering two:

Rule 1 There are no Rules

Rule 2 There may be exceptions to Rule 1

Copywriter Hank Sneiden (1977) comments,

> Rules ... stifle creativity, inspiration, initiative, and progress. The only hard and fast rule that I know of ... is that there are no rules. No formulas. No right way. Given the same problem, a dozen creative talents would solve it a dozen different ways.
>
> (p. 247)

Creative guidelines

If, then, rules should not be applied to creativity, perhaps the best that can be offered are some guidelines to be considered during the creative process. Exhibit 20.2 is an adaptation of suggestions made by Roderick White (1993), Planning Director of Lansdown Conquest. His proposals are related specifically to advertising, but with care, they can be used more broadly where appropriate.

When looking at Exhibit 20.2 it is easy to see why some creatives are so opposed to rules. While White offers some sound advice, for every suggestion there are examples of where the basic guideline is broken with good effect. The very fact that rules or conventions are broken is a creative trait in itself. Sometimes this is acceptable, sometimes not. The use of shocking and unusual images by Benetton's creative director (now ex-creative director), Oliviero Toscani, the man responsible for all of the company's controversial advertising, is an example of rule breaking. In so doing, he created memorable and very effective advertising. Rule breaking, being different, being original, can be dangerous, it can backfire, but when it works, it is what the marketing communications industry rewards with its top creative awards.

Steve Henry, creative director of the agency HHCL, has won many creative awards for his work, among them the Design and Art Directors 'Gold Pencil', the President's Award at the Creative Circle, and the Grand Prix at the Cannes Creative Awards. His advice is simple: 'If you want to make a difference, make it different' (Henry 1997, p. 173). Henry then offers his own suggestions for guidelines.

Find out what everybody else is doing in your marketplace. Then do something different.

Exhibit 20.2 Creative guidelines

General guidelines
- Every ad should embody a clear, straightforward proposition
- Say what you have to say in as few words as possible
- Use humour with caution
- Give the target audience credit for some intelligence
- Be original

Guidelines for film
- Music is critical
- Quick cuts are readily understood
- Get the brand name in early – and often
- The consumer likes to identify with the commercial
- TV is ideal for demonstration
- TV is extremely expensive
- Cinema commercials must entertain

Guidelines for print
- Put 'key' words in headlines
- Put the promise in the headline
- Keep the headline short
- Lay the ad out logically
- Reversed copy looks good – but beware of its use
- Double-page spreads look good – but beware of their use
- Only a single page will do – sometimes
- Photographs are better than illustrations: pictures are better than words

Guidelines for radio
- Remember it is not TV
- Radio means repetition

Henry (1997) offers the following example:

> Tony Hillier (our original Britvic [Tango] client) ... looked at a brand which was selling a million cans a day, and decided he could make a difference to this figure. (There's confidence for you.) Then he looked with us at the typical soft-drinks advertising of the time (which could be summed up in the visual image of boy meets girl on American street while sun shines and fire hydrant goes off) and decided to break the rules of the marketplace, and grab the high ground for his brand. Together, we created an advertising campaign that used street-credible, British humour for the first time in soft-drinks advertising. We also tried to avoid showing fire hydrants, whenever possible. We were rewarded by an increased sales figure of one-and-a-third million cans. A day. (p. 177)

Forget the logical proposition. And find the personality of the brand instead.

BMW, through agency WRVS, has designed creative treatments that let the personality of the brand shine through every piece of promotion. BMW has a personality that cares passionately about every detail of its engineering and design. It is what the HHCL agency call USP – **Unique Selling Persona** (instead of Unique Selling Proposition).

Unique selling persona

Uncommon term, used to describe a key element of a brand's personality.

Creatives sometimes like to re-present the product or brands as visual representations using drawings and photographs to illustrate their ideas of the 'essence' of the brand. The visuals might simply be a collage of material cut out from books and magazines. This avoids having to always find the right words to express what are essentially emotive issues. 'A picture paints a thousand words'. These visuals are pasted together to form what are frequently called '**mood boards**' or '**concept boards**'.

Mood boards/concept boards

Collection of visual materials (e.g. drawings, collage, montage) to replace or complement a written description that reflects the essence of a product or its customers/consumers.

Define the 'target market' so that you like and respect them.

Creatives, while working to traditional target market specifications, prefer to be closer to consumers or whomever the communication is targeted towards. The target audience statement can be 'personalised' with the use of mood board collages of images reflecting the audience member's lifestyle.

The role of creative briefs and briefing

Creative brief

Document that provides an outline of the creative task and the basis for creatives to develop their solutions.

Creative briefs and the process of briefing are used in the marketing communications industry as the mechanism for setting creatives on the task of developing ideas for a new campaign. Graham Bunting (1995), Creative Director at agency Primary Contact, makes a bold and unequivocal statement, that creativity itself 'starts with the brief' (p. 94). A creative brief is a written document that tries to encapsulate all the important points needed to develop creative ideas and ultimately a marketing communications campaign. It is short (only one, or maybe two pages if absolutely necessary), and is produced for the benefit of the creative team. (The creative team could be just one person, but in advertising agencies they frequently work in pairs – the copywriter and the art director – which helps the creative process; see Chapter 15, Agency operations.) As a document, it does not try to capture all the relevant market and marketing information – this will be consigned to other documentation (and is largely considered an encumbrance by creatives). Even though the brief may contain little information in itself, this is not to suggest that the creative process can best be undertaken in an 'information vacuum'. Having started with the brief, the creative process continues with making use of information to help develop ideas through greater understanding of the brand and the brand's market.

Research findings inform a great deal of creative decisions. Research is conducted to suggest to [art directors, designers], copywriters, layout artists, photographers and filmmakers what the most effective form and content of messages are.

(Brierley 1995, p. 142)

NEED TO KNOW

✓ *The creative brief is a short document that provides the basis of a more extensive verbal briefing with the creative and account team.*

The brief follows what Gary Duckworth (1997), Chairman of agency Duckworth Finn Grubb Waters, calls the 'relay race' in the marketing communications development process, in which it plays a pivotal role (Exhibit 20.3) between the first 'leg of the race', *strategic development*, and the third leg, *creative output*.

Contents of a brief

The briefing document attempts to provide only the essential information required by creatives to work on and develop their ideas. The *brief* is not the same as the *briefing*, although between them they should provide both direction and inspiration to the creative team (Duckworth 1997). When agencies are used, the task of writing briefs falls to account handlers and account planners (see Chapter 15). Charlie Robertson, founder member of Red Spider, an international network of account planners, has this to say about briefs,

A creative brief should be brief, but it does not have to be creative. However, a creative briefing should inspire. The distinction between the brief and the briefing is often overlooked ... Creative briefing is a process, not just the issuing of a document. The writing of a brief forces the author(s) through a discipline which answers questions that otherwise may be left vaguely defined, or be left so open in the briefing of creative people as to hinder their grasp of the task. Conversely, the briefing is an expansive task where it is desirable that creative people can see the different routes made possible by the briefing. (Robertson 1997, p. 48)

Exhibit 20.3 The marketing communications 'relay race'

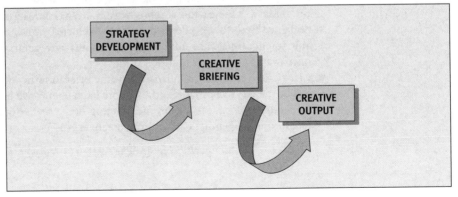

Robertson goes on to identify the general components of a brief which he comments are 'best tabled as questions to resolve' (1997, p. 53). The following list is a modification of suggestions made by Robertson (1997), Bunting (1995) and Duckworth (1997):

- Why are you promoting at all? What are the objectives? What are the roles of different elements of the mix?
- Who is the promotion aiming to influence? Who are we talking to? (Not just the demographics, but some idea of the psychographics/lifestyles.)
- What do you wish to communicate? What needs to be said? What is the 'proposition' – the 'main thought', the 'big idea', the '**copy platform**', the '**creative theme**'? (These are all terms to describe the same basic thing – what is the principal concept?) What brand identity? What values?
- Why do you think those aimed at will believe it?
- How do you wish to say it – what tone of voice?
- What do you think they will say having received this communication? Will they believe it?
- What are you not allowed to convey or what must be legally conveyed? Are there executional guidelines, things to avoid, things you must do?
- What are the special requirements (if any) – media requirements, timing?

Copy platform

The basic verbal or written message to be conveyed.

Creative theme/concept

The basic or fundamental creative idea to be conveyed.

Jaspar Shelbourne and Merry Baskin (1997), respectively Executive Creative Director and Director of Planning, J. Walter Thompson, have looked at the creative briefs and the briefing process from the creatives' perspective. Having asked the 40 creative teams working at JWT, 'What makes a good brief and briefing?', their findings highlight that they should have the following qualities.

- *Trigger words.* 'Words are like little bombs. The right ones can explode inside us, demanding an original and exciting solution instead of a mediocre, pedestrian one' (p. 69). **Trigger words** are words or phrases that can trigger an idea. It is a 'One-line-portable-take-away thought'. Examples include 'Persil "releases" clean', which led to a commercial that was centred around the metaphor of release and liberation, and 'Take Black Magic out of the kitchen and put it into the bedroom', which moved the chocolates away from ingredients-based promotions.
- *The correct amount of facts.* Limit the facts to those that are essential.
- *Relevance.* Relevance is about relevance to the product, relevance to the targets, and relevance to the time in which it is happening – the context. This makes the promotion up-to-date and reflects what is going on in the world and the social settings of the targets. 'One of the reasons why the OXO family have lasted so long and remained fresh for decades is because the vehicle (*the creative theme or concept*) was able to encompass the advent of such things as vegetarianism among teenagers, microwaves and empty nesting' (p. 74).
- *Clarity.* The clearer and more explicit the brief in terms of its thinking, the clearer will be the creative process and the more likely that it will be on target.
- *Open, not close, doors.* Briefs and briefing help create opportunities, not prevent them from happening. Quotes from creatives (p. 77) make the point well:

Trigger words

Words or phrases from which ideas most easily develop.

I don't like to find myself being straightjacketed by a brief rather than being released by it.

You mustn't be too prescriptive. Give us some air.

Be a Visionary. Show me a place I hadn't thought of.

Good planners act as gardeners, not gatekeepers.

Although the specific form of the brief will differ from agency to agency, and different emphases and information will be included depending upon the area of marketing communications being addressed, a pro-forma for a brief is offered in Appendix 20.1. The actual brief used by Duckworth Finn Grub Waters for the Daewoo account, which they handle, is shown in Appendix 20.2.

Developing ideas – the creative process

Creativity requires imagination and problem-solving skills and there are techniques available to assist in the creative process, many of which have been developed out of the socio-psychological sciences.

Juxtaposition

Creativity has been described as the ability to put together new combinations of thoughts (Young 1975). Seen in this way, creativity is about making relationships between ideas and thoughts. Juxtaposition is the putting together of ideas – ideas that, perhaps, were previously unrelated. The outcome is a new idea. The process of juxtaposition can be facilitated by a number of means, for example, putting relevant words or statements into a hat and randomly pulling them out in pairs or threes. The pop star, David Bowie, has been said to use this approach when writing lyrics for his songs.

Free association

In free association, a word, an image or a sound is considered and anything that comes to mind is recorded. Again, the approach basically involves the bringing ideas together in new relationships.

Convergent thinking and divergent thinking

Convergent thinking is associated with linear logic and the search for the 'correct' answer through a process of narrowing thoughts down. This form of thinking tends to be considered non-creative in that it is reductionist. While it may not be a generally recommended approach, it can lead to genuinely creative output.

Divergent thinking represents the opposite. It is free thinking seeking to open up ideas, to widen perspectives and ideas. It is the search for alternatives. Divergent thinking is more likely to lead to surprising, unusual and unexpected ideas. Whereas convergent thinking may be typified by concerted and concentrated effort and logical reasoning, divergent thinking is typified by letting things happen, letting the mind wander.

Lateral thinking

Pioneered by Edward de Bono, lateral thinking is about challenging our habitual thinking process to see things in a new light. Lateral thinking is a search for alternatives. The thinking process may involve inductive or deductive reasoning, convergent or divergent thinking, 'right and left brain' thinking. It involves the use of information, thoughts, intuition, feelings, emotion, judging, assessment, search for options, sequencing of ideas and evaluating their worth. Psychologists have identified that we all have our own predispositions and preferences about how we think. This has an effect on how we perceive our world and on our behaviour which in turn has a further effect on how we think and feel. Psychologists have classified people into types according to their thinking preferences and a number of classification systems have been developed. Lateral thinking encourages everyone to break their moulds. De Bono has constructed many thinking exercises to help.

Brainstorming

Probably the best-known creative thinking process is *brainstorming* which is carried out in groups. Brainstorming utilises free association as the principle behind the technique. It is given its 'force', however, through the multiplier effect of many people being involved. Everyone involved is valued for their ideas. Nobody's ideas are evaluated during the process. Nobody's ideas are rejected. And through the process of free association, one person's ideas may spark off another's. It is quantity of ideas, not judgement of ideas, that is wanted in brainstorming and one of the best ways of doing this is to have an informal meeting with a group of up to about ten people. The group, having been briefed on the topic, are allowed to give their suggestions so that everyone can hear them. A flip chart can be used to record the suggestions so that everyone can see them. The session is managed so that everyone can participate. It has been known for alcoholic drinks to be provided to reduce inhibitions.

This technique is favoured by brand name development companies who employ psychologists to run brainstorming focus groups, often using groups in many different countries throughout the world. Susannah Hart, a director of Interbrand, uses brainstorming extensively. 'In the course of a two- or three-hour creation session a group of six to eight people will create a mass of verbal raw material – perhaps five hundred names in total. Several such groups may be held' (Hart 1998).

Experimentation

This is not so much a technique as a frame of mind, the willingness to experiment with new ideas rather than being overly conservative.

Swipe files

'Every work of art is, in the final analysis, a compromise between tradition and revolt. It cannot be otherwise. For a composition that is wholly devoid of newness is dead; one that is wholly unconventional is incomprehensible.' So wrote Alexander Lindey on plagiarism and originality (1952). His comments are true of all 'new' ideas. The 'swipe file' is a collection of printed ideas that are collected to aid the development of creative ideas. It may be a collection of unrelated examples that represent work that the creatives have admired or have been impressed by over the years. Or it may be something collected especially for the purpose of the task in hand. There is nothing wrong with searching for inspiration outside of one's own head. New ideas lie all around, waiting for us to find them.

Progressing along the creative process

James Web Young, former creative vice-president of J. Walter Thompson's (USA), has developed what has become a popular approach to facilitating the creative process. For Young (1975),

> The production of ideas is just as definite a process as the production of Fords; the production of ideas, too, runs an assembly line; in this production the mind follows an operative technique which can be learned and controlled; and that its effective use is just as much a matter of practice in the technique as in the effective use of any tool. (p. 42)

Young has proposed a five-step 'production line' to aid the creative process.

- *Immersion* – information gathering and background research.
- *Digestion* – assimilation of the problem. Working with the information, playing with it in the mind.
- *Incubation* – putting the problems to one side. Allowing the subconscious to have an effect. 'Sleeping on the problem.'
- *Illumination* – seeing the light or solution. The birth of alternatives. Selection of the 'best' or 'best shortlist'.
- *Verification* – studying the idea(s) to make sure it fits the brief and solves the problem. Putting the idea(s) to others. Selection of the idea to 'polish' and develop into a practical solution.

Creativity such as this is invariably a team effort in which ideas are generated, evaluated and 'ditched' or 'worked up'. Before any idea appears as a final piece of marketing communication, it first has to be acceptable to colleagues. If the work is 'in-house' it will be colleagues within the company. If the work is in agency, the critics are other agency personnel before it is presented to the client who will then have to approve it or discard it.

In these early stages, creative ideas will be presented in a preliminary rough form. These could be:

- *Roughs or dummies* – hand drawings or computer graphics indicating what the finished artwork will look like for any printed medium, e.g. packaging, posters, and press advertisements.
- *A storyboard* – hand drawing of a series of images for a proposed moving sequence (TV, video, cinema, CD-ROM/DVD, Internet) indicating the progression of images, voice-over, and music proposed.
- *Photoboards and animatics* – these are alternatives to the storyboard using still photographs in the case of photoboards (Plate 16) and animated drawings or 'rough-cut' photographs in the case of animatics that will be shown on video.
- *Scripts and simple audio tapes* in the case of voice-overs, music and radio commercials.

Creative strategies – appeals and executions

In Chapter 19, seven creative strategy alternatives proposed by Patti and Frazer (1988) were described and an eighth option was added to their list. These were:

- Generic strategy
- Pre-emptive strategy
- Unique selling proposition strategy
- Brand image strategy
- Positioning strategy

- Resonance strategy
- Affective strategy
- Informational strategy.

These strategies can be used as a basis for the creative treatment of the marketing communications. Rather than repeating the descriptions of these strategies again here, you are recommended to review the material in Chapter 19.

Appeals and executions

An analysis of marketing communications, especially advertising, will reveal a range of commonly used creative themes and executions. These broadly fit into rational/emotional appeals, and product-oriented/consumer-oriented appeals. Exhibit 20.4 shows these as the axes of a matrix. The compartments should not be considered watertight. Marketing communications are not produced to fit only into one or the other box. But the matrix is a useful way of conceptualising the approaches available. Exhibit 20.4 also gives some examples of the sort of creative executions that could be used when making the various appeals. The Nescafé Gold Blend TV commercials, for example, made use of a 'slice of life' approach in the style of a 'TV soap' programme in which each advertisement revealed another episode of an ongoing story. The commercials traced the burgeoning romance of the two characters who met in the first episode. In so doing, they have adopted a consumer orientation/emotional appeal in promoting the product.

In Chapter 26, Exhibit 26.5 provides a checklist of 35 ways to gain attention in advertising. This list also serves as a reminder of the various appeals and executions that can be used in marketing communications generally, not just in advertising. Exhibit 20.5 is a representation of many of the details from that exhibit under the headings of appeals and creative executions.

Sean Brierley (1995), in his book *The Advertising Handbook*, provides an excellent summary of the use of creative approaches and this is reproduced in In View 20.2.

Exhibit 20.4 Categorising promotion appeals

	Product orientated	Consumer orientated
Rational	E.g. Factual Product comparison Expert spokesperson Hard sell	E.g. Factual Problem solution Celebrity
Emotional	E.g. Slice of life News sensation Celebrity Soft sell	E.g. Factual Product comparison Sex, glamour Music Humour

Exhibit 20.5 Approaches to appeals and creative executions

Appeals	Creative executions
● Product features	● Hard sell (e.g. buy now!)
● Lowest prices	● Soft sell (e.g. brand image)
● Greatest value	● Factual
● Product popularity (e.g. 'everybody wants this product', 'avoid disappointment buy now while stocks last')	● Informational
	● Rational/logical
	● Emotional
● Consumer self-enhancement (e.g. status)	● Price-based promotions and offers
● The 'Ah!' factor (e.g. use of animals –Andrex puppies)	● Guarantees
● Fear	● Competition-based promotions
● Humour	● Demonstration
● Sex	● Problem solution
● Sympathy	● Talking heads (i.e. close-up head and shoulders someone talking at you)
● Compassion (e.g. some charities)	
● Guilt (e.g. some charities)	● Testimonial
● Empathy	● Celebrity endorsement
● Nostalgia	● Spokesperson
● Escapism	● Slice of life
	● Drama
	● News style
	● Timeliness, prominence and proximity (i.e. of the moment, 'street' credible)
	● Advertising parody (i.e. one ad poking fun at another or at other sources,e.g. Fosters' humorous parody of the Häagen Dazs ice cream commercials
	● Teaser (i.e. promotions appear in partial instalments, only at the end is the full message understood, e.g. the launch of the Goldfish credit card whose promotions showed surreal images prior to launch and only made sense on the launch date
	● Animated characters (e.g. Smarties ads and packaging)
	● Character personality (e.g. Ronald McDonald)
	● Shock e.g. Lynx campaign against use of furs for clothing
	● Fantasy
	● Subliminal/symbolic embeds (i.e. hidden or embedded messages/images, e.g. French Connection f.c.u.k. advertisements)
	● Corporate identity/product balance Issue/cause related (e.g. linking promotions to 'worthy' causes)

IN VIEW 20.2

What creatives get up to

Creatives employ news-value criteria such as timeliness, prominence and proximity; they also use different or unusual images, distraction and presupposition to grab the consumer's attention. Once the attention is grabbed, creatives use other techniques to sustain interest, such as the use of suspense, mystery, fantasy and escape and nostalgia. Puzzles are often used, as well as traditional forms of story-telling. Creatives also try to undermine consumers' resistance and win their consent through personality endorsement, the use of stylish commercials, humour and, most recently, parody advertising ... Some ads contain direct exhortation to buy, others leave this as implicit ... many ads are constructed to aid memorability through the use of rhetorical techniques ... Creatives employ a number of stylistic techniques to grab the attention of the consumer: conventions of design and typography, adjectives, language games and rhetorical devices such as repetition and sameness to stand out and act as an aid to memory. Creatives also spend a great deal of time calculating the form, style and tone of the advertisements and use combinations of music, colour, typography, costume, voice, camera speed and lighting to evoke the right atmosphere. The sole purpose of such treatments is to produce the right kinds of reactions in the right target consumers.

(Brierley 1995, pp. 171 and 187)

Creative tactics

Having determined the basic strategies and ideas, the next task is to translate them into the finished output, the last leg in the relay race described earlier. Creatives make use of a variety of creative elements that are commonplace in all forms of promotions. They are the 'nuts and bolts' of advertisements, press releases, packaging, exhibition display, leaflets, etc. Some of the more obvious elements are identified here.

- *Headlines.* Headlines are the most striking element of the copy (the words). They may not be used at all in highly visual treatments. They may form the major feature where there is only typography. With the graphics, the headline works to gain attention and communicate the creative concept (the creative concept is also called the copy platform or creative theme). They are words in the leading position. In radio, they appear as the main element in the creative treatment. In packaging, the product name and company name will be the equivalent concept.
- *Display copy.* This is copy that appears in larger or bolder type than the main text (body copy) to attract attention and allow it to flow from the headline to the body copy.
- *Body copy.* Body copy is the term given for the main text. Usually, body copy is brief but some creative treatments require a lot of information to be disseminated. Body copy is always concise. It should be written in a style appropriate to the treatment and for the target audience.
- *Sub-heads.* Sub-heads are sectional headlines that break up the text and provide focus of attention on key points.
- *Captions.* Captions are short descriptions of text or visuals and further help to break up the body copy in layout terms.

- *Repetition.* One of the ironies in copywriting is that copy should be kept brief and to the point but repetition is widely used. Repetition is a vital element to many marketing communications but it should only be used to focus on the necessary points such as the core concept, the brand name or a telephone number in a radio commercial.
- *Slogans/strap lines/tag lines.* These terms essentially mean the same thing. Examples include 'BMW: The Ultimate Driving Machine', 'Mars: Helps You Work Rest and Play', or 'British Airways: The World's Favourite Airline'.
- *Calls to action.* Many promotions require that the target is encouraged to take some form of action, ring a free phone number, fill in a coupon, request more information, collect tokens, try a sample, buy a product, request a sales visit, etc. These are calls to action that should be facilitated within the promotion where they are applicable.
- *Pack shot.* The pack shot is a visual of the product being promoted.
- *Use of imagery and typography – words and pictures, layout.* The design of the promotion is, clearly, exceptionally important. The creative treatment will dictate the form the promotion will take and the balance between words and pictures. The typography selected has important visual impact, it is not only used to convey the words. Layout design affects the attractiveness of the promotion and should be produced recognising a variety of visual effects. Graphic designers are trained to produce designs that work. These issues are beyond the scope of this book but their importance and relevance should be recognised.
- *Use of signs.* In Chapter 3, Creating shared meaning in marketing communications, Exhibit 3.2 categorised the types of signs used in marketing communications. These signs and other symbols are 'shorthand' tools which can communicate very complex messages simply. Exhibit 3.3 identified other 'silent' communication methods that have similar implications. Creatives frequently adopt the use of such elements quite intuitively.

Assessing creative ideas

After implementation, creative ideas will be subject to evaluation as part of the overall assessment of marketing communications and Chapter 23 should be read for more details. Prior to this, creative ideas can be, and should be, assessed at a very early stage in their development. The questions that follow can be asked and assessment given throughout the creative development process.

- Is the creative approach consistent with the brand's marketing communications objectives (and previous campaigns)?
- Is the creative approach consistent with the creative strategy and objectives?
- Is the creative approach appropriate for the target audiences? Is it relevant?
- Does the creative approach lend itself to development and use in the future (do the ideas have 'legs')?
- Does the creative approach communicate a clear and convincing message?
- Does the creative execution overwhelm the message? Does the brand stand out?
- Is the creative approach appropriate for the media environment in which it will be seen?
- Will the creative execution grab attention? Is it persuasive? Will it be remembered?
- Does the creative execution meet regulatory constraints?

Wells et al. (1992) sum the issues into five areas: Relevance, Empathy, Originality, avoidance of Cliché, and Impact.

Summary

Creativity and how it works does not lend itself to close analysis. Setting rules for creativity tends to be difficult, but there are guidelines that can be set. Creativity is most often associated with the content and messages of marketing communications but it can apply to the entire marketing communications process.

This chapter has sought to provide some guidelines for creativity, identify the role and content of creative briefing, and offer suggestions on how creative ideas can be developed through a range of techniques. Common creative strategies, appeals and executions were highlighted and various component elements of promotions identified. Finally, the chapter noted the importance of evaluating creative ideas and a range of assessment questions were listed that should be used throughout the creative development process.

Self-review questions

1 In what ways might creative thinking be applied to media planning?

2 What two rules did White suggest can be applied to creativity?

3 What is the difference between creative briefs and creative briefing?

4 Who typically writes creative briefs within agencies?

5 What are 'trigger words'?

6 Describe the brainstorming technique.

7 Identify and describe the five-step process to creativity proposed by James Web Young.

8 Describe the eight creative strategies based on Patti and Fraser's proposals. When should creative ideas be assessed?

Project

Undertake an analysis of marketing communications materials – packaging, press advertisements, posters, direct mailings, exhibition stands, etc. – to assess the creative treatments used.

Identify the creative themes adopted and compare competitor approaches. Try to place the strategies adopted into one of the categories identified by Patti and Fraser. Compare the appeals and the creative executions used with those identified in this chapter.

Evaluate the layout and design – the use of typography, graphics, signs and symbols. Is the brand clearly identifiable and distinctive? Is a pack shot included? Are slogans used and how effective are elements such as headlines and body copy?

References

Bernbach, W. (1971), Bill Bernbach defines the four disciplines of creativity. *Advertising Age,* 5 July, 21–23.

Brierley, S. (1995), *The Advertising Handbook.* Routledge.

Bunting, G. (1995), Creativity. Chapter 6 in *The Practice of Advertising* (Hart, N., ed.), 4th edn. Butterworth-Heinemann.

Duckworth, G. (1997), Creative briefing. Chapter 7 in *Excellence in Advertising: The IPA Guide to Best Practice* (Butterfield, L., ed.). Butterworth-Heinemann.

Hart, S. (1998), Developing new brand names. Chapter 4 in *Brands: The New Wealth Creators* (Hart, S. and Murphy, J., eds). Macmillan Business.

Henry, S. (1997), Creative briefing: the creative perspective. Chapter 8 in *Excellence in Advertising: The IPA Guide to Best Practice* (Butterfield, L., ed.). Butterworth-Heinemann.

Lindey, A. (1952), *Plagiarism and Originality.* Harper and Brothers.

Manning, B. (1987), reported in M.L. Rothschild, *Marketing Communications: From Fundamentals to Strategies.* D.C. Heath.

Nelson, P.R. (1985), *The Design of Advertising* 5th edn. Wm. C. Brown Publishers.

Patti, C.H. and Frazer, C.F. (1988), *Advertising: A Decision Making Approach.* Dryden Press.

Robertson, C. (1997), Creative briefs and briefing. Chapter 4 in *How To Plan Advertising* (Cooper, A., ed.), 2nd edn. Cassell.

Rothschild, M.L. (1987), *Marketing Communications: From Fundamentals to Strategies.* D.C. Heath.

Shelbourne, J. and Baskin, M. (1997), The requirements for creativity: a creative director's perspective. Chapter 5 in *How To Plan Advertising* (Cooper, A., ed.), 2nd edn. Cassell.

Sneiden, H. (1977), Advertising pure and simple. Reported in G.E. Belch and M.A. Belch (1998), *Advertising and Promotion: An Integrated Marketing Communications Approach.* McGraw-Hill.

Wells, W., Burnett, J. and Moriarty, S. (1992), *Advertising: Principles and Practice* 2nd edn. Prentice Hall.

White, R. (1993), *Advertising: What It Is And How To Do It* 3rd edn. McGraw-Hill.

Young, J.W. (1975), *A Technique for Producing Ideas* 3rd edn. Crain Books.

Selected further reading

Butterfield, L. (ed.) (1997), *Excellence in Advertising: The IPA Guide to Best Practice.* Butterworth-Heinemann.

Cooper, A. (ed.) (1997), *How To Plan Advertising* 2nd edn. Cassell.

Appendix 20.1 Example brief pro-forma

CREATIVE BRIEF

Client .... Job No. ....

Product/Brand .... Date Issued ....

Project .... Due Date ....

Budget .... Campaign Start Date ....

What has happened so far? (*Background information*)

Why are we promoting the product in this instance?

Who are we talking to? (*Who are the target audiences, not just in demographic terms*?)

What do we want them to do?

What do we want them to think and feel? (*Desired response/attitudes*)

What tone of voice should we adopt?

What is the single most important thing we should convey? (*The main proposition, the big idea, the copy platform, the creative theme/concept*)

Why should they believe it?

What marketing communications tools will we be using?

Are there any constraints (*Restrictions – legal or otherwise, special requirements*?)

Account Director ....

Planning Director ....

Creative Director ....   Signature ....

Appendix 20.2 The Daewoo brief

As shown in Duckworth, G. (1997), Creative briefing. Chapter 7 in *Excellence in Advertising: The IPA Guide to Best Practice* (Butterfield, L., ed.), p. 163. Butterworth-Heinemann.

DUCKWORTH, FINN, GRUBB, WATERS
BRIEF

What is this brand called?　　Daewoo

Who do we want to buy it?
Broadly:　　　All motorists
Specifically:　Prospective buyers of saloons and hatchbacks costing £8–12k

They want a nice new car with the minimum of hassle. We need them to understand and be impressed by Daewoo's refreshingly different approach to selling cars.

Why should people buy this brand?

Daewoo is a different kind of car company because we're hassle-free.

Why should they believe us?

1. We have unique Daewoo showrooms, no dealerships
    - designed to help you relax and enjoy visit; café area, interactive displays. creche for kids, welcome to get in cars and poke around
    - staff who help if you want to and won't if you don't
    - long test drives arranged at your convenience

2. We agree a re-sale price when you buy the car so you can always sell it back to us without any risk
    - purchase prices are fixed, no haggling, so no-one gets a better deal than you

3. We give 4 years free serving, 4 years free AA membership, a 4-year mechanical warranty and an 8-year anti-corrosion guarantee with every new car (we can afford it because we have no middlemen)

4. When your car needs to be serviced we come to collect it and leave you with a new top spec courtesy car, free

5. On top of this we want to recognise the trust shown in us by our first UK customers, so everyone buying a Daewoo in our first three months will have their car replaced by an identical model, new, in August

---

Requirement:
TV for each area mentioned above
Press to add detail where needed
Outdoor likely to be wanted to add street presence

Signature	Date	Traffic	Date

Duckworth, Finn, Grubb, Waters Ltd, 41 Great Pulteney Street, London W1R 3DE. 0171 734 5888 Fax 0171 734 3716
Registered in England No. 2377231. Registered Office 41 Great Pulteney St. W1R 3DE.

Chapter 21

Media implementation

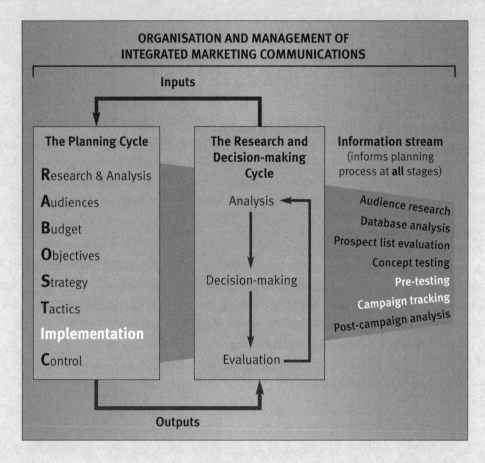

The IMC RABOSTIC Planning Model

CD

From the Case Study 2 material on the CD, identify the range of media used by Škoda across the Fabia campaign. Referring to Exhibit 21.1, evaluate the impact of each medium in terms of its reach, frequency and impact on each of the target audiences.

Objectives

- To complement and extend earlier chapters on media
- To emphasise the important media aspects of reach, frequency and impact, and examine how they are assessed
- To emphasise the importance of target audience identification
- To identify the need to see media decisions as part of the overall marketing communications process
- To present media planning and implementation as an interrelated, multi-staged cycle of activity
- To describe each of the stages of media planning and implementation
- To provide an understanding of selected media terms

Professional perspective

Harriet Frost Head of Communications Futures, OMP UK

Media implementation sounds a pretty functional process. It should be far from it.

Why? Because it involves a blend of two very powerful elements – vast money (usually) and vast choice (which increases by the day). Media planners and buyers aim to make the best of their clients' money through the choices they make. Many routes will be similar, but a few will deviate from the masses, whilst achieving the same goal.

Somewhat bizarrely it can be compared to the task of travelling from London to Scotland. You weigh up certain elements in your mind. Do you need to get there fast? How much can you afford? Would you prefer the scenic route? How important is comfort? How many of you are there? When do you need to arrive? What experience have you had travelling there before? There are now decisions and options at every turn – train, fly, car, boat, limousine, coach, hitchhike, cycle, charter a helicopter? All in one

➜

ts of short stages? Motorway or A roads? 1st or 2nd class? Heathrow or Gatwick? You could seek
ok at maps, read reviews, compare costs, compare with previous experience, look at timetables.
dia implementation is a bit like this – a navigation through a maze of options, with each one having the abil-
to be slightly different. We have immense ability to purchase mass communication and a huge number of
navigational and evaluation tools at our disposal. Much luckier than travellers to Scotland! These tools can be very
handy – when asked the equivalent of the 'so – which way did you come' question – a media practitioner can quote
CPT's, reach and frequency data, tracking studies, qualitative research, buying audits, awareness shifts … .

If only all communications objectives were as clear as 'I want to get to Scotland'. After all, the better the
brief, the better the trip.

Using marketing communications media

Reach

Also referred to as coverage or penetration. With frequency, impact and media cost it is one of the four most significant concepts in media planning. It is a measure of how many members of the target audience are reached by a medium or collection of media used in a campaign. Reach may be measured as a percentage or actual number. Reach is the number of target audience members exposed to the media/message at least once during a specified time period (e.g. duration of a campaign). Related terms are Exposure, GRPs, TVRs and Duplication.

Frequency

Although there is no universally accepted view of how many times a person should see or hear a marketing communications message for it to be effective, it is generally agreed that a single exposure is likely to be insufficient. Some argue that three impacts is a minimum. Frequency, then, is one of the four most significant concepts in media planning, along with reach, media cost and impact, in achieving marketing communications success. It is measured in terms of OTS/OTH, and is the number of times in a specified time period (e.g. duration of a campaign) that an average member of the target audience is exposed to the media/message.

Media play a central role in the marketing communications process by facilitating the movement of messages between senders and receivers. Media have been described earlier in Part 1, The Integrated Marketing Communications Process (specifically Chapter 5, Media – the Carriers of the Message, and Chapter 6, E-media), as all 'vehicles' or 'channels' that are capable of carrying or transmitting marketing communications messages. As such, they take very many different forms: not only is there press, TV and radio, but also word of mouth, leaflets, packaging, stationery, merchandise items, signage and even hot air balloons, park benches and bus tickets. This chapter extends Chapters 5 and 6 by considering the management of media from a planning and implementation perspective.

In all cases, the main aim of marketing communications media is to accurately convey messages determined by or on behalf of the marketing communicator. However, it is clear that some media are better able to do this than others, depending on the circumstances and the objectives to be achieved. Furthermore, from a management perspective, it is also important that the media are used within financial limitations. It is a relatively straightforward matter to ensure that a campaign is effective from the point of view of the message reaching its target audiences, but at what cost? There always have to be strict financial constraints.

Principal aims of marketing communications media

In using marketing communications media, the principal aims can be identified as:

- to contribute to the achievement of overall marketing communication objectives;
- to faithfully (without distortion) transmit messages;
- to reach specified target audiences and to do so with
  - most effect (effective),
  - least waste (efficient),
  - least cost (economic).

Exhibit 21.1 illustrates these aims diagrammatically and also identifies the three key concepts central to media planning – reach, frequency and impact. All these are discussed in detail later in this chapter.

Impact (1)

One of the four most significant concepts in media planning, the other three being reach, frequency and media cost. At a subjective level, 'impact' refers to the strength of impression made by a campaign or particular piece of marketing communication. It is a qualitative value. In part, 'impact' is achieved by the creative approach adopted, such as through the use of size, colour, typography, illustration and photography. But media selection and planning also play major parts through the right choice of media, positioning and repetition. For example, it is likely that a food advertisement would have a higher impact if it appeared in colour in *Good Housekeeping* than it would in black and white in the *Police Gazette*. This impact will be further increased by multiple insertions of the advertisement in the media to achieve effective reach.

Exhibit 21.1 Using the marketing communications media – principal aims

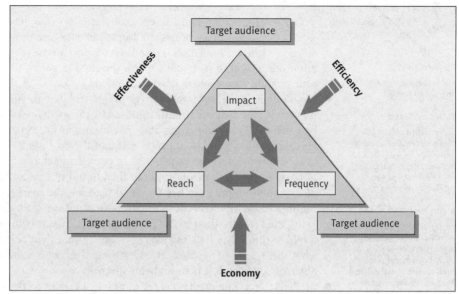

Media decisions, therefore, are ones of selecting the best media to achieve the principal aims described above. Of course, compromises have to be reached because there will always be competing factors. For example, cost will limit how many people can be reached with a piece of communication or it may prove difficult to ensure that enough people have received the marketing communication enough times to achieve the effect desired. 'Trade-offs' invariably have to be sought between efficiency, economy and effectiveness and between cost, reach, frequency and impact.

The media implementation cycle

Impact (2)

An impact is another way the term 'impact' is used, and represents the actual exposure of an item of marketing communication when an opportunity to see or hear has actually taken place. For example, 'commercial impact' is a term used in television to represent the viewing of any commercial by a single viewer. Two impacts would be equivalent to one person seeing the commercial twice or two people seeing the commercial once. The UK population is exposed to over 650 billion commercial impacts per year.

Media implementation – media decision-making, planning and buying – are complicated and skilled activities. Indeed, promotional agencies employ specialists to undertake the media function and over recent years there has been a massive growth in the use of media independents – organisations that specialise in media planning and buying. To simplify the process, it is possible to break media tasks down into a set of component parts. They may be considered to be stages in a cycle of activity. As illustrated in Exhibit 21.2, these parts are interrelated with each other (and with all other marketing communications activities). This should be borne in mind constantly to ensure the appropriate development of integrated marketing communications plans.

- *Marketing communications objectives and strategy.* Marketing communications objectives and strategy are determined before more detailed media plans can be developed. The setting of marketing communications objectives is an early part of the development of the marketing communications plan in which the media planner may be involved or, otherwise, the objectives would be 'handed down' to the media planner as the first part of the media plan. More details about marketing communications objectives are given in Chapter 19.
- *Target audiences.* Having set the marketing communications objectives, target audiences can be selected as focal points for the media plan. These are the individuals or groups of people to whom the marketing communications are directed and whom

Target market

Market segment selected for specific targeting.

Target audience

Those individuals or groups that are identified as having a direct or indirect effect on business performance, and are selected to receive marketing communications.

Media cost

Financial constraint is always an important element in media decision-making, as it is vital that media plans are both economic and efficient. Media objectives related to reach, frequency and impact have to be achieved within a media budget.

Media budget

This is the total amount of money available to the media buyer to purchase media time and space. The total media budget will be allocated to each of the mass media selected as part of the marketing communications plan. It is the task of the media buyer to purchase the media spots determined by the media planner at the best rates available, and to achieve cost savings wherever possible.

the media must reach. A word of warning! It is common practice to confuse target markets with target audiences. The **target market** is an expression of customers and consumers who, respectively, buy and use the product being promoted. **Target audiences** are these people *plus* many others who may *influence* the decision to buy and use the product. Marketing communications will be ineffective unless the right target audiences are selected. Target audiences are considered in Chapter 1 and in Chapter 17.

● *Media objectives.* Media objectives are set related to issues of *reach, frequency, impact* and the **cost** constraints imposed by the media budget. Consideration has to be given to how many target audience members are expected to receive the message, how often they should receive it and the role media will play in creating the most appropriate impression and impact. Impact is a subjective issue (but an important one) and media's role in this should not be underestimated. For example, when attempts were first made to broaden the market for wines in the UK, a number of distributors chose to advertise using small display ads in the press that 'whispered' rather than 'shouted' the product. It was believed that customers preferred to think they had 'discovered' a wine rather than being told what to buy. It is what some refer to as 'discreet advertising'. Impact is sometimes about being very obvious, sometimes it is about being discreet.

● *Media budget.* The **media budget** in practice relates to the use of mass media and will be set as part of the overall marketing communications budget. The total media budget will then be allocated to each of the main categories of media – press, TV, etc. As the media plan is implemented, some reallocation of funds may take place.

Exhibit 21.2 The media implementation cycle

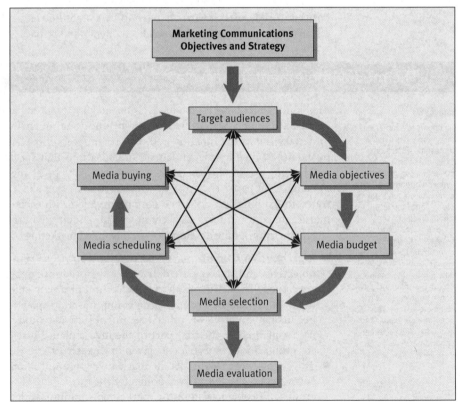

● *Media selection.* The setting of the media allocations are closely linked with the media selection process which also identifies the best individual media vehicles to meet the media objectives of *reach* and *impact*. The process, thus, involves choosing between the main media 'classes' (TV, press, radio, cinema, posters, direct mail and the Internet) and from within them choosing the specific media vehicles that will be used – Sky Sports TV, the Post Office, DRTV, Teletext, The European, Kompass Directory, Virgin Radio, a local cinema, Heathrow airport poster site, etc.

WARNING

⚠ *Principal areas of concern to media planners are reach, frequency and impact.*

● *Media scheduling.* Media scheduling is the process of determining the most appropriate times for the advertising to take place across all the media selected to achieve the media objective of *frequency*.

● *Media buying.* The media buying function is then the process of obtaining the best media deals for the media selected and scheduled.

● *Media evaluation.* As with other marketing communications activities, media implementation needs to be evaluated to ensure that its performance is as expected.

The sections below now discuss each of the principal areas of media implementation in greater detail.

Marketing communications objectives and strategy

Media plan

Document containing the detailed description of which media, at what cost, are to be used when in a campaign. Frequently, the terms media schedule and media plan are used interchangeably.

Overall marketing communications objectives and strategy provide the basis upon which media decisions are made, and they need to be determined before work on the **media plan** can commence. It may be said to be the first stage in the media implementation cycle, but one in which the media planner may have little or no involvement. Among the details will be a clear articulation of which target audience members have been selected for inclusion in the marketing communications effort. Without this, the marketing communications plan (and the media plan within it) cannot be successful. The clearer the marketing communications objectives and strategy, the easier it is to determine media objectives and allocate budgets among the media classes, to select the media and subsequently schedule and buy the media.

Target audience decisions

It is common practice in marketing to emphasise the importance of the target market, but this has to be taken further in marketing communications. Target markets are about *customers* – the people who buy goods and services. Better still, they are also about *consumers*. These are the people who literally use or consume the goods and services. Sometimes the customers and the consumers are the same people but often they are not. In family consumable purchases and industrial purchases, for example, the users of products are not necessarily the same as the buyers. It makes sense in marketing communications to consider communicating with both *buyers* and *users* if the communications effort is to be most successful. For example, in promoting toys, the marketing communications effort may be focused at parents *and* children.

WARNING

⚠ *Marketing communications objectives and strategy have to form the starting point to media planning.*

Influencers

Those people who exert an influence (positive or negative) on an organisation or its publics.

But we need to go still further! We need to go beyond the target market in determining our target audiences. We need to consider who else may be involved in the purchase decision or who else may influence it. If we are able to influence the **influencers** then there is greater likelihood that our communications will be more successful. For this

IN VIEW 21.1

Children's influence on consumer purchases

The table below shows the results of a survey of housewives who were asked if their children influenced the purchase of a range of family products. The percentage figures represent housewives who agree that their children exert an influence. The equivalent value represents the amount of family spending affected by children under the age of 15.

	Children's influence	Equivalent value (£)
Day-to-day meals	54%	£13bn
House	22%	£6.3bn
Holidays	44%	£3.3bn
Children's clothes	70%	£1.9bn
Car	17%	£1.6bn
Computers	33%	£1.6bn
Soft drinks	60%	£1.5bn
Restaurants	30%	£1.0bn
Toys	73%	£512m
Breakfast cereals	73%	£291m
TV/HiFi	22%	£58m
TOTAL		£31bn

Source: adapted from table on p. 6 from 'Children Decide', in *Hotline Virgin Trains Customer Magazine, Summer,* 1997, Virgin Trains. Reproduced with permission.

WARNING

Media planning requires that consideration is given to target audiences beyond the target market.

Publics

Term favoured by the public relations profession, referring to the many target audiences that communications may be focused towards.

Decision-Making Unit (DMU)

Also known as the Decision Making Group, the DMU concept recognises the involvement of a range of people in the decision-making process. The group may be formally organised, such as in a business-to-business purchase context, but more frequently is an unorganised group who influence the decision to buy. The DMU comprises a number of 'players' that may be described in slightly different terms by different authors, e.g. influencers, gatekeeper, specifier, decider, buyer and user.

reason, marketing communications target audiences can include members of the trade, opinion leaders, members of the media themselves, other members of the decision-making unit (DMU), employees, stakeholders, clubs and associations, aunts and uncles and anybody else who is relevant. In the public relations profession they refer to all these possible people as '**publics**'. This is not to say that everybody is actually selected as part of the target audience group. These people form our marketing communications 'segments' (just as in market segmentation) from which we must choose who to target.

Once the target audiences have been determined as part of an integrated marketing communications effort, it is then possible to make decisions about how each of the targets will be treated – and which media to use in reaching them.

The example given In View 21.2 illustrates imaginative marketing communications based on Chubb's sound understanding of the role performed by different members of the **decision-making unit**. The campaign featured the use of direct mail as this was the most cost-efficient and effective way of contacting Chubb's target audience. There would, of course, have been other elements involved in the total campaign, a campaign that proved to be very effective indeed because it did not rely just on a single player in the DMU, but *all* key players, and took advantage of a novel approach to create impact.

Other marketing communication mix elements available to Chubb include personal selling via the telephone and face-to-face, exhibition stands, leaflets, promotional giveaways, and advertising in business and industrial magazines. Industrial media may have been targeted with press releases to encourage editorial coverage. The trade may have been offered sales promotion incentives. Crime prevention officers and insurance companies may have been sent leaflets and information bulletins to generate a favourable impression of Chubb security systems. They may, in turn, have recommended the systems and offered lower insurance premiums to those companies that have them installed, and so on. All of these approaches are possible once a sound appreciation of target audiences and media options has been gained. In fact, this sort of understanding actually facilitates the creative process by opening up new creative possibilities. And this is what much of the marketing communications business is about.

IN VIEW 21.2

Chubb Security Systems

Chubb, an organisation noted for its locks and security systems, developed a security product particularly suited to manufacturing organisations based in small factory units. Market research identified the specific target market for the product and the buying behaviour of that target.

A campaign was developed which focused on the decision-making unit (DMU). The DMU concept recognises that buying decisions are often the result of decisions affected by many people and not just the purchaser. The DMU is the group of people (or players) who are most influential and involved in the purchase and use of the product. Four key players are commonly identified: the *Buyer*, the *User*, the *Specifier* and the *Decider*.

Research told Chubb that for their market there were, in fact, two key DMU players. One was the financial director who acted both in the capacity of decider and buyer. The other was the factory manager who acted in the capacity of specifier and user. In other words, the financial director would make the final decision about which security system to buy then actually be responsible for the purchase contract. The factory manager would influence the purchase by specifying the type of system required and be responsible for its use. The *combined* efforts of these two players would dictate whether a purchase would be made and, if so, which systems would be shortlisted and eventually purchased. Marketing communications targeted on only one or the other of the players would represent missed opportunities to maximise sales.

The industrial sales force has long known the value of identifying multiple points of contact within customer organisations. Users of the other elements of the marketing communications mix sometimes fail to do so. Chubb recognised the potential. They did not send a single, general communication to their potential organisation customers. Chubb's campaign focused on two people within each organisation. And it did so in an interesting and creative way. Small metal moneyboxes were purchased into which were put coins and information leaflets. Each moneybox had a lid, a lock and a key. A locked moneybox and covering letter was sent to the finance director of each of the potential customer organisations. At the same time, a letter with a key was sent to the factory manager of each organisation. In all cases, research had identified the names of each recipient so that the mailing was carefully targeted and personalised.

The covering letters, which gave no details of the product being promoted, requested that each finance director should contact the factory manager and that each factory manager should contact the finance director. In this novel way, members of the DMU were invited to get together to discuss what their mailings were about. Only after coming together were they able to discover the contents of the moneybox and the Chubb security system being offered. Why were coins put into the moneyboxes? Simply to ensure that the moneyboxes rattled. In this way they were more intriguing.

The campaign was a success – it was an award winner. To the delight of the company, sales targets were not only met, they were exceeded.

Media objectives

Media objectives

Objectives that are specifically focused on media tasks, and which define the role of the media in furthering the marketing communications objectives.

Media objectives are just one area of objectives in a long line of objectives that must be set to provide 'direction' for any organisation. Media objectives cannot be set satisfactorily without consideration of where the media task fits within the broader marketing communications function and, in turn, where this fits within marketing activities more generally. It is not for the media planner to set these other objectives but they will provide a context in which the media planner must operate. As Mary Oldfield, Strategic Planning Director, Leo Burnett, has said,

> **Media objectives are different from communications objectives. They should define the exact role media has in delivering brand objectives. The media planner must understand the brand, understand the consumer and use the media to build bridges between them.**
>
> Oldfield (1997)

To simplify the process of setting media objectives they can be reduced to three inter-related areas of primary concern to the media planner: reach, frequency and impact.

These concepts are significantly affected, in practice, by cost and time constraints and they are illustrated in Exhibit 21.3.

A useful checklist of questions can be asked to help with the objective setting and the general media planning process. The list below is adapted from Kaatz (1995).

Exhibit 21.3 Media objectives

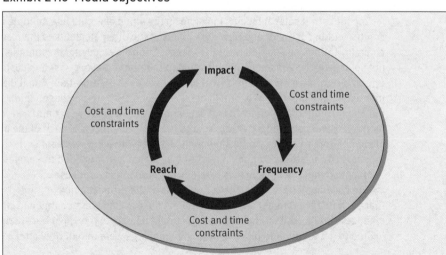

- Who do we want to reach?
- When do we want to reach them?
- Where do we want to reach them?
- How many do we need to reach?
- How frequently do we need to reach them?
- With what impact and effect?
- What media provide the best micro-environments and conditions for all the above?
- At what cost?
- Can we improve on it?

Reach

Coverage
Another term for reach.

Penetration
Another term for reach.

Exposure
Equivalent to opportunities to see or hear. An exposure is the placing of an item of marketing communication in a media vehicle that the target audience is *expected* to see or hear. It is therefore the *opportunity* to see or hear.

Insertions
Refers to the number of times an advertisement is placed in a medium. Discounts are available for multiple insertions.

Reach is the number of members of the target audience who are exposed at least once to the marketing communication during a specified period. The term can be used literally – it is the number *reached* by our communication. Sometimes the terms '**coverage**' or '**penetration**' are used as alternatives to 'reach'. Reach may be expressed in actual numbers but, often, it is expressed as a percentage of the total target audience group. A promotional campaign may result, for example, in 80% of the target audience being reached. However, there are some important things to consider when setting reach objectives.

First, being *exposed* to a message is not the same as being affected by it. The message could go completely unnoticed. This is where the issue of 'impact' comes in. There is also a difference between '**exposure** to the message' and 'exposure to the media vehicle' or what are called 'opportunities to see or hear'. A single advertisement may be placed in a magazine that is received by 30% of our target audience. The medium (i.e. the magazine) may be received by 30% but the actual advertisement may, in reality, be read by only 20% of our target audience. In practical terms we do not adjust for this discrepancy, but it should be noted that opportunities to see or hear marketing communications are more strictly opportunities to see or hear the medium through which our marketing message is transmitted.

Second, it is the members of our *target audience* who are important to us, not the population at large. There is little point in measuring reach in terms of everybody who might see or hear our message; this would represent wasted exposures.

Third, reach is only concerned with whether a member of the target audience has been exposed *at least once* to the message. It is not concerned with how many exposures have been achieved. This is an issue of 'frequency'.

As a rule, it is preferable to achieve a high level of reach and reach can be increased in a number of ways, by:

- increasing the media budget so that more **insertions** and exposures can be afforded;
- using multiple media classes rather than one, e.g. TV plus magazines (and also making use of non mass media). This is one reason why the use of primary and support media may be important;
- increasing the number and range of media vehicles, e.g. using three magazine titles rather than concentrating on one;
- creating diversity in the scheduling of the media, e.g. using different time spots on TV and radio, using weekend and weekday newspapers, using different seasonal issues of monthly magazines.

In each case, the task of increasing reach carries with it either, or both, cost and time constraints. It may not be affordable or desirable to increase reach above a point. Increasing reach may also increase the chances of greater wastage in that more non-target audience members may also be reached in the process and so the efficiency of the marketing communication may be reduced.

Measuring reach

Data used to measure reach is available from a variety of bodies and individual media owners. It is in the industry's best interests to ensure that such data is both widely available and as accurate as possible. It is on the basis of who reads, sees, watches or hears the media that media costs are determined. Those media that are able to reach more people and those that can reach popular target groups are in a position to charge higher prices. Thus, television is able to charge more than cinema and radio because its audiences are so much larger. TV charges are greater during peak viewing periods because more people are watching.

Examples of reach measures include **circulation** (press), mail-outs (direct mail), calls (telephone), **readership** (press), number of viewers (TV, video, cinema), number of listeners (radio), traffic–passers-by (posters), traffic–hits and page impressions (the Internet) and rating points (all media). Not only are the total numbers involved important to us but so are the breakdowns which give reader, listener, viewer and **traffic** profiles. Industry bodies such as **ABC//electronic**, JICNARS, JICPAR, RAJAR, BARB, MVR and CAA, and research reports such as TGI, ensure that a wealth of information exists, the aim of which is to create accurate audience measurement. Chapters 16 and 23 should be read for descriptions of these and other analysis and evaluation issues.

- *Circulation.* Circulation is a crude measure of reach although sometimes the limited availability of other information may require that this measure is used. It relates to the number of copies of an item of press – newspapers, magazines and directories – which have been distributed. A similar measure can be used for direct mail by measuring the number of letters/leaflets mailed out. Circulation should not be confused with print run. It is possible to have many copies printed but only a proportion of them circulated. In the case of press, the Audit Bureau of Circulation (ABC) audits newspaper and magazine media to ensure that published circulation figures are based on a calculation of copies dispatched less copies returned so that the final figures are literally those left in circulation. Verified free distribution (VFD) figures are produced in a similar way for newspapers and magazines that have no cover charge.

   BRAD (*British Rate and Data*) is a directory of mainly press publications that offer advertising space (although it also includes basic data for the other main media as well). This publication reports circulation figures and other relevant data on pretty much all recognised, regularly produced publications in the UK (and some that are international). Where an 'ABC' or 'VFD' appears next to the entry, the media planner can be sure that the circulation figures are audited and accurate.

- *Readership/viewers/listeners.* A better measure of reach is *readership*. In the case of TV, video and cinema, the measure is number of *viewers*, and for radio, it is the number of listeners. Outdoor posters have *passers-by*. Readership is determined by estimating the average number of people who read a publication and multiplying this figure by the circulation. Readership figures are greater than circulation figures because each copy of a publication is likely to be read by more than one person on average. Readership data is available through the National Readership Survey (NRS)

Circulation

The number of copies of a publication circulated in the market. Audited circulation figures are preferable as they are certified as accurate (see ABC), and represent the number of copies distributed less the number of copies returned to the publisher.

Readership (viewership/ listenership)

Estimate of the size of an audience determined through research. Each of the main media has bodies responsible for producing relevant data. Readership is produced by multiplying the circulation of a publication by the average number of readers per copy. (See BARB, CAA, JICNARS, JICPAR, MVR, RAJAR.)

Traffic (2)

Can refer to passers-by (as in poster measurement), or to the number of viewers of web pages (also called hits).

ABC//electronic

ABC, which was founded in 1931, has helped legitimise press as an advertising medium through the independent auditing of circulation. Established in 1996, ABC//electronic aims to do the same for the Internet by auditing Internet sites and traffic data using internationally agreed standards.

BRAD

British Rate and Data; monthly publication that presents cost, circulation and technical information on all significant publications that offer advertising space (and readership details of some of them). Brief details are also presented on the other mass media and media information of general interest. It is used as a major reference source within the industry. Other BRAD products include the BRAD Media Selector, BRAD Agencies and Advertisers, and BRAD Direct Marketing.

which covers much of the popular press but cannot cover everything. (It also covers some aspects of cinema viewing too.) The full survey can be purchased, but summary details are included for some publications in BRAD. For those publications that are not part of the NRS, the publishers themselves may have useful data.

By considering readership data, the media planner is in a much better position to assess reach not only in terms of total numbers of readers but, more importantly, in terms of readers within the target audience because data are available about the profile of readers. The data may not be presented in quite the terms required by the media planner, but an approximation may be used. For example, the target audience may be 20–25-year-olds but readership figures may be given for 18–25-year-olds.

Just as profiles are available for readership, so is audience measurement for all the main media, the more recent additions to which are the POSTAR measurements for poster audiences and ABC//electronic for the Internet. POSTAR, Poster Audience Research, replaced OSCAR, Outdoor Site Classification and Audience Research, in 1996. Importantly, POSTAR not only measures passer-by 'traffic' but also incorporates in its poster site classifications, an allowance for impact which it terms 'visibility adjusted impact'. This creates a much more valid and worthwhile measurement.

ABC//electronic, also established in 1996, has the aim of providing independent data on Internet traffic. Two other providers of this information are BPA International with their BPA Interactive, and Internet Profiles Corporation with their Nielsen I/PRO I/AUDIT. *Page impressions* (also referred to as page accesses and page requests), where specific information is requested, is becoming an international standard for measuring Internet audience traffic and is replacing the misleading *number of 'hits'* as a measurement commonly used in the past.

● *Rating points.* Another measure of reach is the rating point. It is used extensively in television viewing where it is called **TVRs** – television rating points or television ratings. Gross rating points (GRPs) is a measure that can be applied across all media. Rating points are measures that actually combine elements of both reach and frequency and for this reason they are discussed in more detail after the section below on frequency.

Frequency

Frequency is a measure of the number of times, on average, that a member of the target audience is *exposed* to a message (or more accurately, the media). It is generally presumed that if someone is exposed to the medium, she or he is exposed to the marketing communication message. Frequency is measured by Opportunities to See (OTS) or Opportunities to Hear (OTH). Strictly speaking, it is an average measure so although some members of the target audience may see an advertisement every time it is inserted, some may not see it at all and some may see it only some of the time.

The reason frequency is so important in media planning and implementation is because, as we all appreciate, if we see an advertisement once, and may have little impact on us, it may go relatively unnoticed. If we see an advertisement more times, the effect increases. Theoretically, if we see an advertisement too many times we may not only tire of it but may also learn to dislike it. This could create a negative attitude towards the product being advertised. Frequency, therefore, is important in achieving impact and, thus, effectiveness.

No one has agreed how many times it is necessary to receive marketing communications messages for them to be most effective. Given the range of variables that affect the outcome there cannot be a simple answer. It is generally agreed, however, that a frequency of 1 OTS would be ineffective. An exception to this has been in the use of ambient media described in Chapter 5 in which a single media event can result in generating a large amount of publicity. The projection on the Houses of Parliament of the Sega promotion is one such example. In advertising, some suggest 3 OTS should be the target. Krugman's ground-breaking work in the 1960s and 1970s (Krugman 1972) has given some insight into this issue but many have misinterpreted his findings because they failed to appreciate the distinction between exposures and impacts.

In integrated marketing communications terms what also needs to be recognised is the synergy achieved through the use of many media and marketing communications activities. For advertisers, say, to consider only the impact of advertising OTS would be to ignore the effect of other marketing communications activities. In practice, though, each activity within the marketing communications mix tends to be considered in isolation of the others because of the difficulty in measuring their collective impact. It is common, therefore, to consider issues of effectiveness in isolation or in terms of individual campaigns rather than as an integrated whole. Chapter 23 offers some suggestions whereby integration may be assessed.

Impact

Impact is about making the marketing communication noticed. Creating impact is vitally important to the whole of marketing communications activity and media implementation has its role to play in the process. It is fundamentally a qualitative concept although quantitative elements can be applied to it when rating points are used.

Qualitatively, impact refers to the quality of impression developed through marketing communications activity either related to an entire campaign or to one or more parts of it such as a single advertisement.

Impact can be created by the particular creative approach adopted – the visuals and the words. It is this sort of impact that many people think about when considering the impact of a piece of promotion or marketing communication. But impact can be further enhanced by the careful selection and scheduling of the media. Impact can be generated by the medium in which the marketing communication appears merely because of the type of medium it is. Choose the wrong medium, and a negative effect can be created. The media provides a '**micro-environment**' in which the marketing communication takes place which can either improve or reduce impact. The section on media selection considers this point in more detail.

Impact is also something that can be enhanced by increasing the chances of the communication being seen. This can be done either through increasing reach or increasing frequency or a combination of both. Seen in this way, impact is sometimes called '**media weight**', 'advertising weight' or 'promotional weight'. The heavier the weight, the greater the impact. But this can only be achieved at a cost!

The combination of reach and frequency in media is expressed as rating points and there are two types of rating points which particularly should be understood: television rating points and gross rating points.

NEED TO KNOW

☑ *Creating impact is vitally important to the whole of marketing communications activity and media implementation has a role to play in the process.*

Micro-environment

The marketing communications micro-environment is the immediate environment or surroundings in which marketing communications occur.

Media weight

Way of describing the relative impact created by particular media.

NEED TO KNOW

☑ *While creating impact is most usually thought of in connection with the quality of the creative treatment, media selection and use can have a powerful impact, too.*

Television rating points (or television ratings) – TVRs

TVRs are a measure of television audience and as such have become the 'unit of currency' by which television airtime is bought (see section on media buying below). The Broadcaster's Audience Research Board (BARB) is responsible for producing television audience data. A single TVR represents one per cent of the audience watching a programme. One hundred TVRs represent the total TV audience. For media planning purposes, having TVRs expressed in terms of the target audience is better than the television viewing audience at large. Fortunately, BARB data breaks viewing figures down by audience types which can assist target audience analyis. In this sense, TVRs represent reach.

Let us take an example. If there are 10 million people in the advertiser's target audience and a single advertisement reaches two million of them then the reach is 20% or 20 TVRs – two million viewers are 20% of the 10 million target audience. However, when planning a television campaign it is more likely that decisions are made to ensure that the viewers see the advertisement more than once. It may be planned for them to see the advertisement four times, for example. In this case, the media planner will aim for 400 TVRs, which is equivalent to the viewing audience of 100 TVRs (reach) seeing the ad four times (frequency) giving a total TVR measurement of $100 \times 4 = 400$ TVRs. This would *represent* a reach of 100% and a frequency of 4 OTS.

While this is true, in practice, the situation is typically a little more complicated. Over the period of the television campaign, the BARB data, which is collected continuously, may indicate that our target audience reach may not be 100% (indeed, this is unlikely). Remember that reach would be the percentage of the target audience that is exposed to the medium/message at least once. Some members of the target audience may not see the message at all during the time period. Reach is typically less that 100% except for extended or expensive campaigns. The figures may reveal that the audience reach is only 80%. If only 80% of our target audience has seen the advertisement four times, the TVRs would only be $80 \times 4 = 360$ TVRs. If 400 TVRs had actually been achieved with a reach of 80% (as identified through the BARB viewing figures), the resulting opportunities to see would have been 5 OTS ($80 \times 5 = 400$ TVRs).

Let us take another example. A media buyer has been set the task by the media planner to buy television advertising spots to achieve 70% reach of the target audience who have been identified as ABC1 adults aged 25–44 years old. The frequency objective is 4 OTS. How many TVRs does the buyer have to buy to meet these objectives? The calculation is, simply, 70% reach × 4 OTS frequency = 280 TVRs (of **ABC1** adults aged 25–44). This is the situation shown in the Lanson Champagne Media Schedule Summary example shown in Exhibit 21.4 where they used TV in the London region in the latter part of their total press and TV campaign. They actually achieved 275 TVRs which strictly gives a figure of 70% coverage (reach) at 3.93 OTS – they rounded this to 4 OTS. You will also see what appears to be another slight discrepancy. Although their target market was AB adults as indicated at the top of the schedule, the details presented as TVRs specify ABC1 adults. This is because the data provided by BARB does not completely match the target audience specification for Lanson Champagne. The advertiser simply had to use the closest match.

Although it is quite reasonable to think of all these calculations as a little complicated, they are nevertheless necessary and are used on a daily basis in the media industry.

ABC1

Popularly used market segment, measured by the socio-economic measure of occupation of the head of the household.

Gross rating points – GRPs

Having explained TVRs, gross rating points (GRPs) are now quite straightforward. They are calculated in just the same way as television rating points but are applied to any medium, not just television. It is the custom and practice of the television media business to use their own terminology.

Gross rating points are simply reach times frequency. They are a measure of weight (or media impact as we have called it). GRPs can be seen in Exhibit 21.4. The total 1105 GRPs are calculated by summing all the individual GRPs together. This figure is equivalent to all the target audience seeing the advertisements just over 11 times on average over the period of the campaign, which was a five-year period. We know, however, from the foregoing discussions that in reality some of the target audience members would have seen it more often; and some would have seen it less often; the figure of 11 is an average. It is also possible that a total reach of 100% may not have been achieved, but in this instance it is likely to have been a high coverage of the target audience given the duration of the campaign and the extent of media use.

In order to improve on the gross rating points measure, media planners can make use of '**weighted ratings points**'. If a range of media is used in a plan, it can be anticipated that some media will carry greater impact than others because of the characteristics of the media. Or it may be believed that the target audience members are reached more effectively. A qualitative value can be put on this so that it 'weights' the media such that those with higher impacts are favoured by being assigned 'weight' values that are higher.

Weighted ratings points

Rating points weighted to reflect the likely impact of a medium: the higher the weighting compared with other media, the greater the anticipated impact generated by the medium.

Exhibit 21.4 Media schedule summary for 5-year Lanson Champagne campaign

Medium	Period	Schedule (AB adults aged 25–44)	Gross rating points
Lifestyle magazines	Oct–Dec Year 1	30% reach at 1.5 OTS	45
Lifestyle magazines	June–Dec Year 2	35% reach at 4 OTS	140
Lifestyle magazines plus *The Times* (x%) and *Daily Mail* (x2)	Mar–Dec Year 3	50% reach at 3 OTS	150
Cinema (London/TVS)	May–Dec Year 3	25% reach at 2 OTS (within areas covered)	50
Lifestyle magazines plus *Independent* (x5) and *Daily Mail* (x3)	Mar–Dec Year 4	60% reach at 3.5 OTS	210
Cinema (London/TVS)	May–Jun/Oct–Dec Year 4	25% reach at 2 OTS (within areas covered)	100
Lifestyle magazines plus *Independent* (x1)	Feb–Dec Year 5	45% reach at 3 OTS	135
TV (London)	Jul–Dec Year 5	275 TVRs (ABC1 adults aged 25–44) giving 70% reach at 4 OTS	275
TOTAL			1105

$$GRPs = R \times F$$

$$\text{Weighted rating points} = R \times F \times I$$

where R = reach, F = frequency, I = impact.

It should be recognised that the reason why gross rating points are so called is because GRPs give a gross or *duplicated* audience measure. In the Lanson Champagne campaign some of the readers of the lifestyle magazines used in the campaign would be readers of *The Times* or *Independent* or *Daily Mail* which were also used. They might also have seen the cinema and TV ads. In other words, there would have been some **duplication** in the audience figures. Duplication is where the same member of the target audience sees the advertisement in more than one medium. *If* we were able to take away the duplication, the reach figure would be somewhat lower and a more realistic assessment of reach could be made. This would represent **net coverage/reach**.

The result of using GRPs that contain duplicated audience figures is that an 'over-estimate' of reach is created. On the other hand, because there is duplication, it means that to some extent there have been greater opportunities to see the advertisement for some people, i.e. those that would have seen the advertisement in more than one medium. These greater exposures may be helpful in creating greater impact. Duplication, in itself, is not a bad thing provided that its effect in implementation is recognised. Duplication reduces real reach but increases real frequency.

> **NEED TO KNOW**
>
> ☑ *Duplication in itself is not a bad thing. It can improve the opportunities to see, although it also reduces reach.*

Effective reach

Another feature in the use of gross rating points is the danger of interpreting them too simplistically. It would be inappropriate, for example, to presume that the campaign with the greatest GRPs would be the best.

Let us assume that a media planner is considering two alternative plans as shown below.

Media plan A	*Media plan B*
Reach = 50%	Reach = 90%
Frequency = 3 OTS	Frequency = 2 OTS
GRPs = 150	GRPs = 180

Exhibit 21.5 Duplicated target audience

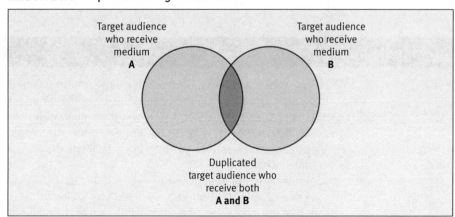

Effective reach

Refinement of the reach calculation. *Effective* reach is concerned with reaching target audience members with a minimum frequency, and thereby with impact. Only those target audience members who receive the marketing communication a specified number of times would be included in the effective reach measurement.

Dominance and share of voice

Relative concept in which it is possible to assess the impact being made by one competitor compared with another. The competitor with the greatest marketing communications impact would be seen to be the most dominant. It is similar to the notion of 'The one who shouts the loudest will be the one who is heard the best.' Although dominance or greatest 'share of voice' is often associated with the highest-spending competitor, dominance can be achieved by creating greater marketing communications impact through superior creativity and media choice. This is a kin to the notion 'The one who is heard the best is the one who is clearest'. Measures of dominance can include quantitative measures such as size of spend and GRPs, or qualitative assessments of impact.

One has a reach of 50% and a frequency of 3 OTS which give 150 GRPs. The second plan has a reach of 90% and a frequency of 2 OTS, giving 180 GRPs. Which is the better plan of the two? The answer, unfortunately, is 'it depends'. While the second has a better reach and better ratings, it has a lower frequency, i.e. opportunities to see. The media planner may decide that this will be insufficient to create effective impact. It may be more prudent to accept a lower reach but higher OTS as achieved in Plan A.

When making any decisions of this type the media planner has to consider reach, frequency and the relative costs of the plans before coming to a final decision. The planner may decide that plan B has too few OTS to be effective. Even if Plan A costs more to implement and even though reach is less than Plan B, it may be more effective in those it does reach. Plan B with higher reach and GRPs, if not effective, would simply represent a waste of money.

This illustrates the concept of **effective reach** which extends the idea of GRPs to recognise that it is necessary to ensure a minimum number of opportunities to see or hear a piece of marketing communication before it can be effective. Whether that minimum number is two, three, four or more is something upon which the industry is not agreed. Moreover, it is significantly affected by circumstances so that a generalised statement is probably not possible.

Dominance and share of voice

Hopefully, the intricacies of media planning have not been too confusing. Media buying is a business that results in many millions of pounds being spent every year. It is not surprising that great care has to be exercised in trying to achieve those three 'E's of economy, efficiency and effectiveness.

But there is one more issue that still needs to be addressed before leaving the subject of media objectives – **dominance and share of voice**. For organisations with small budgets operating in large markets, marketing communications dominance or 'high share of voice' is something they are not in a position to contemplate. For larger organisations or smaller organisations operating in niche markets, a degree of marketing communications dominance is a reasonable objective.

The argument is a straightforward one – it is better to be seen and heard as a major market player or, even, the market leader. In marketing communications terms, dominance is not about actually being leader, it is about creating the impression of leadership. Being the competitor with the largest marketing communications budget would help, but if not, clever creative treatment and media planning can overcome the problem. If you cannot shout the loudest, then shout the best.

Media budget

Having considered *media objectives*, it is now appropriate to move on to the next stage in the media implementation cycle, the issue of the *media budget*, which by its nature is a major constraining factor in media implementation. Availability of finance ultimately determines the range of options open. A small budget may preclude the use of TV or national press. A large budget may facilitate the achievement of high GRPs and extended scheduling.

While an overall budget will be set for the marketing communications effort in total (see Chapter 18, Budgets), the main task falling to the media planner is the allocation of the media part of the budget to each of the media activities. What is actually

When considering media plans and budgets, the situation can be quite complicated in deciding what should be included and what should be left out. The practice, quite simply, varies. Some choose to think about the media allocations broadly, others define it more narrowly and only consider the traditional mass media.

included in the media budget varies. Advertising media are most likely to be the mainstay of the media budget, other marketing communications activities being budgeted separately. However, some media budget allocations include items such as direct mail, some aspects of sales promotions, advertising and the Internet. Others include only some of the advertising media, and some may include some corporate promotions, public relations and internal communications. Still others may separate domestic marketing communications from international marketing communications. It is all about how the 'cake is sliced' and how the slices are handled.

While this may appear unnecessarily confusing, it merely reflects and emphasises the myriad approaches adopted by different managers and different organisations in how broadly they define and approach the media issue.

What needs to be borne in mind is that the media budget should be for just that, the media. Production costs, agency fees, etc. should not be included in this budget but will need to be accounted for elsewhere in the total budgeting process. If, for example, a total budget of £5 million has been allocated to advertising, the media budget can only account for part of this sum. If lavish television or cinema commercials are part of the marketing communications plan, these can cost up to and over £1 million to produce. If we presume that £4 million is available for the media budget, this amount can then be allocated to the different media. Exhibit 21.6 illustrates a hypothetical media budget allocation.

AC Nielsen-Meal

Source of information on competitor media use and expenditure.

A valuable source of information on media expenditure is **AC Nielsen-Meal**. This resource, previously MEAL (Media Expenditure Analysis Ltd) before being taken over by AC Nielsen, can be used to assess competitor and industry activity and spends, and help determine media budgets and selection. It is not at all uncommon for the media planner to wish for higher budgets than are usually allocated. Budgets in the order of £4 million as shown in the illustration are not always available. Financial resource is always limited, even for expensive campaigns, and the media planner has to be creative in terms of media selection and scheduling which are considered as the next two stages in the media implementation cycle.

Exhibit 21.6 Hypothetical media budget

Media budget allocations			Total budget £4,000,000
Primary medium		Secondary media	
	£		£
Television	2,000,000	Internet	25,000
		Consumer press	
		National dailies	250,000
		Sunday newspapers	175,000
		Consumer magazines	
		General interest	250,000
		Special interest	350,000
		Trade press	90,000
		Business magazines	150,000
		Cinema	100,000
		Consumer direct mail	450,000
		Trade direct mail	60,000
		Posters	100,000
Total	2,000,000	Total	2,000,000

Media selection

The overriding purpose of media selection is to reach the target audience, but in doing so, meet the objectives of the campaign within cost constraints.

Kotler (2000) has described media selection as the problem of finding the most cost-effective media to deliver the desired number of exposures to the target audience. In attempting to be more comprehensive, his description can be extended to include efficiency and economy as well as effectiveness. The media selection task, therefore, is one of achieving reach, frequency and impact within cost constraints.

The media selection decision can be broken down into four areas – inter-media, intra-media, primary medium, secondary (support) media – and these are described below.

Inter-media

Inter-media

Refers to the media planners' decision of which medium to use between the media classes, i.e. the selection between TV, radio, cinema, press and posters (outdoor and transport). Some planners also include direct mail and the Internet as main media classes. Inter-media decisions are media decisions at the broadest level.

The **inter-media** decision is one of choosing which main media (media classes) will be used in the media plan. Not only will the media objectives be paramount in this decision, so will the media budget which will put constraints on what is feasible.

There are other constraints. Legal and voluntary regulations may restrict or even prohibit the use of certain media for particular products or creative treatments. Cigarettes cannot be advertised on the television in the UK and all forms of cigarette advertising is restricted throughout the European Union. The use of children is heavily constrained. Some creative treatments can only be used after the 'watershed' time on television and this will affect scheduling.

Each of the media have their own characteristics which are described briefly in Chapter 5. These characteristics may suit particular creative approaches or they may dictate or limit certain choices. If it is decided that the product needs to be visually demonstrated as part of the creative treatment then radio becomes inappropriate. Posters have been used in recent years very effectively for teaser campaigns. Where the 'mass market' has to be reached and the task is one of generating brand awareness and image, television has proved popular.

NEED TO KNOW

☑ *Legal and voluntary regulations affect media decisions.*

Some years ago the Media Circle, a group of media professionals, developed a checklist of factors to be taken into account when making the inter-media decision (Wilmshurst 1985). The factors they identified (plus one additional factor, *media use*) were:

- Reach
- Creative scope

Creative scope

The extent of creative flexibility afforded by the medium.

Exhibit 21.7 **Key areas in the media selection process**

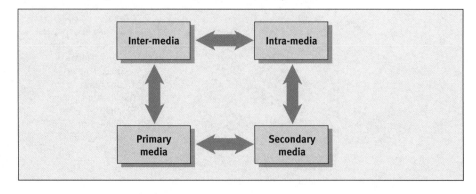

- Media use
- Sales history
- Marketing flexibility
- Trade reaction
- Competitors' use of media
- Size of budget
- Cost efficiency.
- *Reach.* Reach has already been discussed at length. If the media is incapable of reaching the target audience efficiently and effectively, it should be excluded from the media options being considered.
- *Creative scope.* This is about the quality of a medium to facilitate creative treatment. Does the medium permit the use of sound, moving picture, printed word, still picture, colour, flexibility of presentation, and so on?
- *Media use.* Media use is about the way in which target audience members use the media and the situation in which they used it. Is it read by an individual, is it seen by the family, is it heard on the way to work? Is it used in a social or work setting, etc.? Is it used for entertainment, as a reference for information, etc.?
- *Sales history.* Previous experience with the product being promoted and the medium being used should be considered. Records should always be kept of past performance and media should always be evaluated in order to build up a rich experience that can be used to inform new decisions and approaches.
- *Marketing flexibility.* What are the deadlines for submission of artwork or recordings to the media? What is the availability of the media? Are regional editions or broadcasts available? Does the medium reach an international audience? Can it be used to support localised initiatives such as product launches and test markets? Are backup services provided such as research and merchandising support?
- *Trade reaction.* What is the likely reaction of the trade to the medium being used? Sometimes TV advertising for major fast moving consumer goods is expected as a minimum. Where relevant, is the trade supportive?
- *Competitors' use of media.* There are two basic considerations here. Should the same media as the competitors are using be selected or should media that they are not using be selected? In a competitive situation, customers may expect to see a presence, a share of voice, by all key players. An absence may result in negative impressions. There are occasions, for example, where organisations feel they must attend certain exhibitions even if they doubt their effectiveness. An absence from them would be viewed by customers, competitors and the trade as a weakness. Using media not used by competitors may create the impression of greater share of voice.
- *Size of budget.* The amount available for use governs the type of media used and the extent of its use.
- *Cost efficiency.* This point is considered in greater length below under the heading of Media Buying. The media selected need to be effective and they need to limit any wastage.

These points, while identified by the Media Circle as relevant for *inter*-media decisions to select between the media classes, they are equally relevant for the *intra*-media decisions given below.

Intra-media

Intra-media

Refers to media decisions within a media class. It involves the selection of specific media vehicles.

Once the media classes have been chosen, the next task is one of selecting which specific media vehicles will be used to carry the message. While the inter-media decision is about choosing *between* the media classes, the **intra-media** decision is about choosing

BRAD

British Rate and Data; monthly publication that presents cost, circulation and technical information on all significant publications that offer advertising space (and readership details of some of them). Brief details are also presented on the other mass media and media information of general interest. It is used as a major reference source within the industry. Other BRAD products include the BRAD Media Selector, BRAD Agencies and Advertisers, and BRAD Direct Marketing.

within the media classes. Having selected press, for example, which press should be used – national daily newspapers, weekly or monthly magazines, general interest or special interest magazines, directories, trade press as well as consumer press and so on? Once these general decisions are made, which specific titles will be selected: *Yellow Pages, National Geographic, The Grocer, The Times*, etc.?

Information on the media is available from the media owners themselves through their rate cards and media packs as well as information provided through directories such as *British Rate and Data* (**BRAD**). Over the years, media planners build up a great deal of experience over which media vehicles have proven to be most effective. There is also the development of media planning software which can be used to assist the decision-making process.

There is a range of other, more detailed, factors that should be considered at this stage of the intra-media decision. What is important to recognise is that each media vehicle provides its own 'micro-environment' in which the marketing communication appears. This aspect was identified in greater detail in Chapter 7, The Changing Marketing Communications Environment. As has already been said, in selecting a medium, an assessment has to be made of its suitability not only based on reach, frequency and cost factors but also on its impact. The micro-environment provided by the medium can have a major effect on this impact because of the general 'atmosphere' it creates. To provide a 'flavour' of the task, Exhibit 21.8 gives some indication of the factors which should be taken into account when selecting a medium. Although the details are presented for a magazine, similar basic factors have to be considered for any medium. Appendix 21.1 provides details of selecting a radio station as a medium.

Primary medium and secondary (support) media

Primary medium

The medium that is singled out as being the most important or effective within a campaign. It is *likely* to be the one that accounts for the biggest spend, but not necessarily so.

Secondary media (support media)

Secondary media may also be referred to as support media. In an integrated campaign a range of media will be used, and although it is possible to use the media equally, it is more likely that emphasis will be placed on one medium – the primary medium. The other media will be used in a supporting or secondary capacity.

The media planner will typically use a range of media as part of the total media plan. In so doing, the planner has the option of equally weighting the media, or more likely, relying on one medium to be the main or **primary medium** with other media taking a *secondary* or support role. There is no general rule that can be used to determine the primary and secondary media; it really does depend on what is trying to be achieved based on the marketing communications objectives. **Secondary media**, however, should not be considered any less important. In supporting the primary medium they can add extra weight to a campaign and can achieve coverage that a primary medium cannot.

Media scheduling

Media scheduling is the process of 'timetabling' the media. Limited media funds will invariably prevent year-long advertising, although other marketing communications activities may well take place throughout the year. This means that decisions have to be made which will make best use of the media budget within the constraints of time and cost and which will still result in effective communications.

A useful way of conceptualising the task is to consider the problem in two parts. First, what will be the total *duration* of the campaign and second, how will the media be *spread* over that period? Campaigns are frequently considered over a one-year period because this can most easily be planned within an organisation's financial period. However, the period can be very much shorter or longer than this. A series of campaigns may be planned within the same year or one plan can be made to

NEED TO KNOW

☑ *Media scheduling can be thought of as problems of length of time covered by the plan (duration) and how the media will be used over that period (spread).*

Plate 11: The ASA's own newspaper and magazine advertisement promotes their purpose.
(The Advertising Standards Authority, p.203)

Plate 12: French Connection's advertising earns itself a place among ASA's top six examples of bad language.
(What are ethics? p.226) Plate 12 French Connection 'fcuk' advertisement reproduced by kind permission of French Connection Retail Ltd. and supplied by The Advertising Archive Ltd.

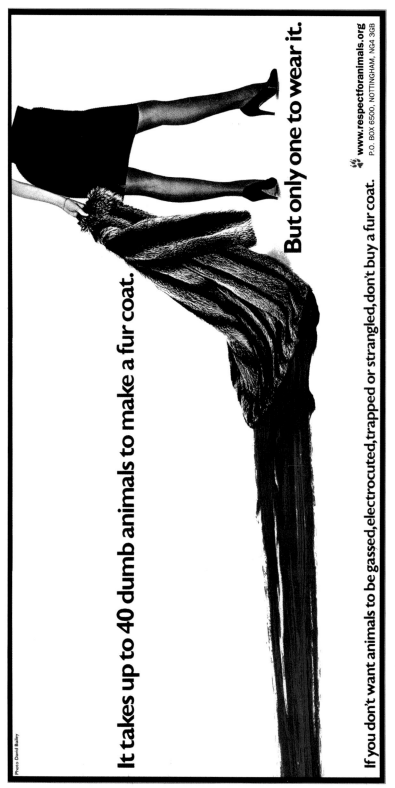

Plate 13: Like similar shocking advertising, this respect for animals poster grabs attention and receives a great deal of media publicity at no extra cost to the advertiser. (*What are ethics? p.226*)

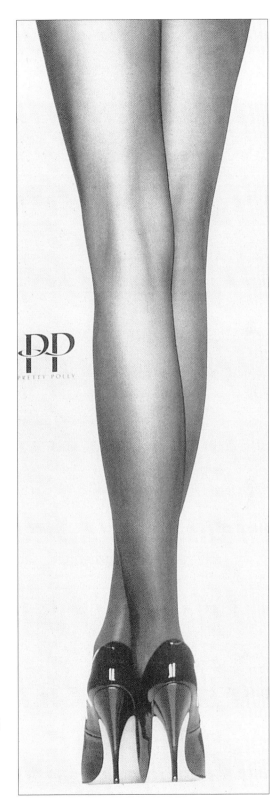

Plate 14: No one can doubt the added impact created by this extra large special build poster site constructed in London.
(In View 5.2, p.106)

Plate 15: The objective of Wonderbra's advertising is to gain attention. (*Objective setting, p.229*) So effectively have they met this objective that their posters generated as much as £50m extra publicity. (*Marketing public relations, p.555*)

Brooke Bond PG Tips 'Homework' 40 sec.

Kevin: Oh no!
Shirley: What's up, love?
Kevin: This project, I'm in real trouble if I don't finish it.

Geoff: What's it about, son?
Kevin: The ancient Egyptians.
Geoff: Well, it's all Greek to me, ha ha.

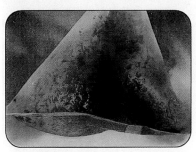

Geoff: Mind you, pyramids did inspire the new PG Tips bag.

Kevin: Eh?
Geoff: Just look at it, the eighth wonder of the world. Roomier, tastier and filled with treasure.
Shirley: Looks like you could do with a cup.

MVO: With PG's new pyramid bags tips never tasted so good, because they give more room to move than our flat bag ever could.

Shirley: How's your tea love?

Kevin: Mmmm, ten out of ten. But dad, how did they build the pyramids?

Geoff: Dunno, son. Ask your mummy, ha, ha, ha...

Plate 16: Example of a storyboard illustrating one of the famous PG Tips commercials. The use of such boards is referred to in *Chapters 20, 23* and *26* and they are especially useful in pre-testing tv and cinema commercials. Usually, for pre-testing purposes, the storyboard is hand-drawn and 'rough' rather than being this highly finished photoboard illustration. In this form, the board may be used as a stimulus for post-evaluation. Plate 16 from PG Tips commercials story boards reproduced by kind permission of Unilever Bestfoods UK (Van den Bergh Foods Ltd.).

Plate 17: Experian's MOSAIC (UK) groups the 1.6 million postcodes in the UK into one of 12 broad groups and S2 detailed types. Each group and type is described in terms of demographic, geographic and lifestyle characteristics. This example is a visual illustration of the Clever Capitalist type. (*Geodemographic products, p.387*)

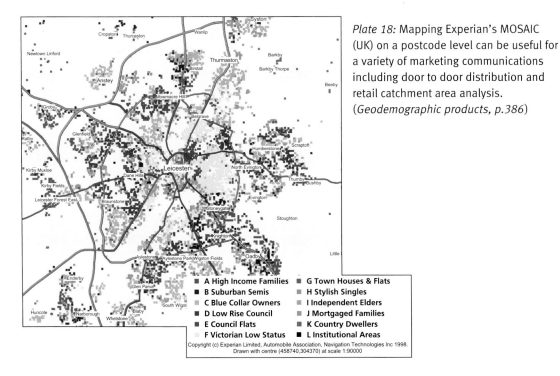

Plate 18: Mapping Experian's MOSAIC (UK) on a postcode level can be useful for a variety of marketing communications including door to door distribution and retail catchment area analysis.
(*Geodemographic products, p.386*)

■ A High Income Families	■ G Town Houses & Flats
■ B Suburban Semis	■ H Stylish Singles
■ C Blue Collar Owners	■ I Independent Elders
■ D Low Rise Council	■ J Mortgaged Families
■ E Council Flats	■ K Country Dwellers
■ F Victorian Low Status	■ L Institutional Areas

Copyright (c) Experian Limited, Automobile Association, Navigation Technologies Inc 1998.
Drawn with centre (458740,304370) at scale 1:90000

Plate 19: Creativity can be employed in the selection and use of the media as well as the choice of message. (*In View 5.3, p.106*)

Plate 20: BA have returned to the traditional Union Jack design after the launch of their new tail fin designs was unenthusiastically received in some quarters. *(p.555).*

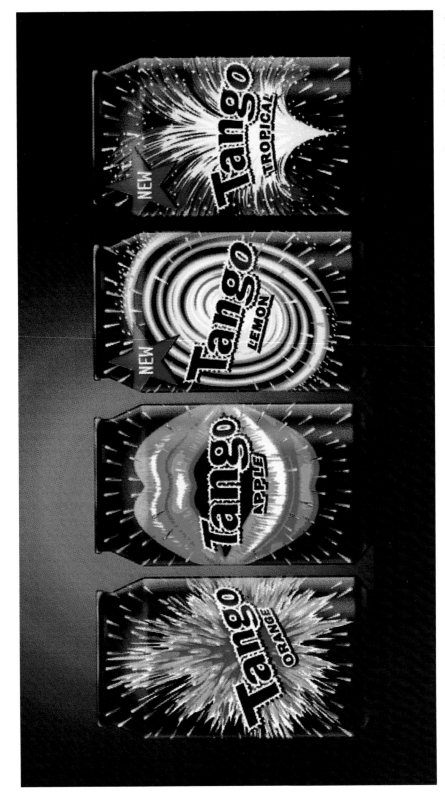

Plate 21: Tango used its innovative packaging concept as integral to the development of an 'anarchic, rebellious, masculine, funny and slapstick' brand image. (*In View 29.2, p.664*)

Exhibit 21.8 Selecting a magazine as an advertising medium

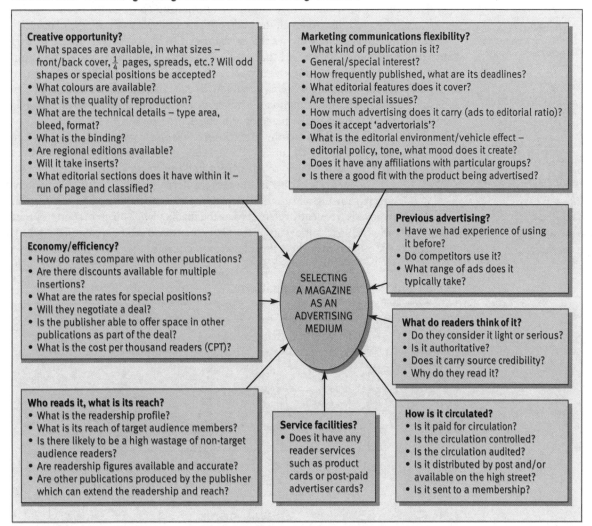

Creative opportunity?
- What spaces are available, in what sizes – front/back cover, $\frac{1}{4}$ pages, spreads, etc.? Will odd shapes or special positions be accepted?
- What colours are available?
- What is the quality of reproduction?
- What are the technical details – type area, bleed, format?
- What is the binding?
- Are regional editions available?
- Will it take inserts?
- What editorial sections does it have within it – run of page and classified?

Marketing communications flexibility?
- What kind of publication is it?
- General/special interest?
- How frequently published, what are its deadlines?
- What editorial features does it cover?
- Are there special issues?
- How much advertising does it carry (ads to editorial ratio)?
- Does it accept 'advertorials'?
- What is the editorial environment/vehicle effect – editorial policy, tone, what mood does it create?
- Does it have any affiliations with particular groups?
- Is there a good fit with the product being advertised?

Previous advertising?
- Have we had experience of using it before?
- Do competitors use it?
- What range of ads does it typically take?

Economy/efficiency?
- How do rates compare with other publications?
- Are there discounts available for multiple insertions?
- What are the rates for special positions?
- Will they negotiate a deal?
- Is the publisher able to offer space in other publications as part of the deal?
- What is the cost per thousand readers (CPT)?

SELECTING A MAGAZINE AS AN ADVERTISING MEDIUM

What do readers think of it?
- Do they consider it light or serious?
- Is it authoritative?
- Does it carry source credibility?
- Why do they read it?

Who reads it, what is its reach?
- What is the readership profile?
- What is its reach of target audience members?
- Is there likely to be a high wastage of non-target audience readers?
- Are readership figures available and accurate?
- Are other publications produced by the publisher which can extend the readership and reach?

Service facilities?
- Does it have any reader services such as product cards or post-paid advertiser cards?

How is it circulated?
- Is it paid for circulation?
- Is the circulation controlled?
- Is the circulation audited?
- Is it distributed by post and/or available on the high street?
- Is it sent to a membership?

Source: Adapted and reprinted from *The Fundamentals of Advertising*, 1st Edition, Wilmshurst, J., Butterworth-Heinemann, Copyright © 1985, with permission from Elsevier

NEED TO KNOW

☑ *A one-year period is a common time horizon for planning purposes although it could be shorter or longer.*

Drip

Media-scheduling approach in which expenditure is spread in relatively small amounts over the campaign period. The advantage can be to create presence over a longer period with a given budget.

cover a number of years. The Lanson Champagne campaign reported earlier actually ran over a five-year period.

The spread of activity can be planned to give either a drip or burst of activity or, to some extent, it can be a combination of both. Media specialists often talk of drip campaigns and burst campaigns or more generally, the 'pulsing' of media activity. The extent of the burst, or how slow, fast, light or heavy should be the 'drip', is entirely a matter of choice in achieving the marketing communications objectives and will be affected by what other marketing communications are being used as mutual support. Factors such as seasonal demand and competitor activity will also have their effect. Periods such as Christmas and other festivals are good examples of where promotional effort is significantly increased in many markets. The result is a pattern of media spending which can take one of a small number of general forms. Exhibit 21.9 illustrates these. As can be seen

Burst

Media-scheduling approach in which expenditure is concentrated into a relatively short period. The advantage can be to create a greater impact.

Pulsing

Term used to describe the media-scheduling pattern.

NEED TO KNOW

☑ *Media schedules and media plans placed on Gannt charts (diagrams showing the media activities against a time scale, i.e. showing what will be done and when) are very useful devices for summing up a campaign succinctly.*

---

from the figure, burst and drip activity can be plotted against media activity or media spend which can be level, rising, falling or alternating throughout the campaign period. Collectively, it illustrates all the basic options available to the media planner.

Intermittent drip pulsing allows the media spend to be spread very much further throughout the campaign period than could be justified on a continuous basis but care has to be taken to avoid losing impact. Adopting a rising or falling intermittent drip pulse can alleviate the problem. Burst activity has the potential advantage of creating a high level of immediate impact but is impractical to maintain over the life of a campaign. Burst activity takes place over a short time period but this can still be pulsed to some degree. It is worthwhile to note that these pattern formations can apply equally to the use of all marketing communication activity and not just that associated with advertising and the mass media.

The media schedule is an excellent device for clearly and comprehensively showing all significant elements of a media campaign and for this reason is frequently referred to as the media plan. This term is appropriate when all relevant details of the plan are presented. The term 'media schedule' is best used where the information is limited to schedule details only.

Exhibit 21.9 Media scheduling patterns

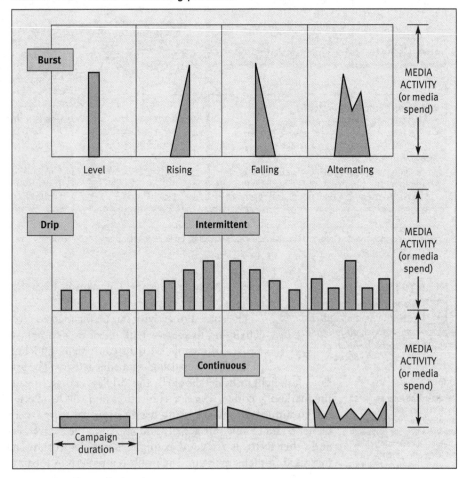

Source: Adapted from Kotler (2000)

Media buying – seeking economy, efficiency and effectiveness

Cost per thousand (CPT)

Measure of media efficiency; represents the cost of achieving a given coverage. Different media vehicles can be compared to determine which are likely to be best at reaching the target audience at least cost. Cost per thousand is an important measure, but the media decision may not always be based on the lowest-cost option, as other factors of effectiveness have to be considered. Valued impressions is a refinement of the cost per thousand calculation. VIPs are calculated by assigning 'weights' to the various components of the target audience. For example, all housewives might be included in the target audience. However, it may be decided that housewives with children are of greater interest. It would be possible to assign a weight of, say, 60 to housewives with children and, 40 to those without children to represent their relative importance. The housewives with children would then contribute more to the resulting cost per thousand calculation than those with no children.

WARNING

 Cost per thousand is a measure of cost efficiency not of effectiveness. It cannot be used to judge how well a message will be carried in the media.

NEED TO KNOW

☑ *CPT calculations should be based on **target audience** members, not the total audience.*

NEED TO KNOW

☑ *CPT and CPM are the same thing.*

One of the most important concepts in media buying is the concept of **cost per thousand (CPT)**. Cost per thousand is a measure of media *efficiency*. It allows different media to be compared on the basis of the amount it costs to reach each thousand members of a specified target audience.

CPT is referred to by some as a measure of cost 'effectiveness'. This can be misleading in that CPT measures cannot be used to suggest one medium is more effective than another in carrying marketing communication messages; other assessments have to be made to identify this. What CPT does is to give the media planner information to judge media only on the basis of cost as an efficiency measure and to do so in a fair and reasonable way.

Why CPT?

Because some media have larger audiences than others it would be unfair to compare the cost of one medium with another solely on the cost of placing an advertisement in each medium. Media with larger audiences charge higher rates than those with smaller audiences. If an assessment is made on the total cost alone, television would probably never be used – it is very expensive, but not unduly so when we consider that it reaches many millions of people. What is needed is a means to compare like with like. CPT is that measurement. It allows the media planner to compare the cost of reaching 1000 audience members of one medium with the cost of reaching 1000 members of another medium. The medium with the lower cost would be deemed the cheaper and more efficient.

While CPT may often be used to measure total audiences, this would not represent the best use of CPT (or any similar measure). As we have emphasised previously, it is not the audience of a medium *per se* which is important. What is important is how well it reaches the target audience. When using CPT, therefore, the calculation should be based on how much it costs to reach 1000 members of the target audience. Media can then be compared on an equitable basis.

CPT is also referred to as CPM. The 'M' in this case represents the Roman numeral for one thousand. And why measure per thousand? Simply because basing calculations on cost per individual would result in too many fractions of a penny or cent or whatever currency is being used. Usefully, CPT can be used as a measure for all types of media and marketing communications activities but care should be taken if using it to assess media classes.

Calculating CPT

The arithmetic is straightforward. The cost of an advertisement or item of marketing communication is divided by the number of target audience members reached.

$$CPT = \left(\frac{\text{Cost of advertisement (or cost of item of marketing communication)}}{\text{Number of members of the target audience reached}} \right) \times 1000$$

For example, if a direct mailing cost £50,000 and reached 200,000 target audience members:

$$CPT = \frac{50,000}{200,000} \times 1000 = £250$$

Exhibit 21.10 Example media evaluation using CPT

Imagine that as media planner you have been approached to recommend which press media would be most suitable for a client. The client wishes to advertise a private health insurance policy targeted towards ABC1 men and women aged between 35 and 54. A decision has already been made to use a black and white display advertisement in the national press. You are told the size of the advert and given a shortlist of daily press being considered which include *The Times*, *Financial Times*, *Daily Telegraph*, *Daily Mail* and *The Sun*.

   You are able to use this information to calculate what it would cost to place the advertisement in each of the papers and how many target audience members would be reached.

	A Total readership	B Target audience readership	C Cost of advertisement (per insertion) £	D CPT of total readership £	E CPT of target audience readership £
The Times	1,024,000	347,400	680	0.66	1.96
Financial Times	612,000	244,900	1,100	1.80	4.49
Daily Telegraph	2,347,000	673,600	1,440	0.61	2.14
Daily Mail	4,235,000	835,100	1,640	0.39	1.96
The Sun	9,891,000	652,800	2,360	0.02	3.62

The table shows some interesting results. By comparing the figures in column E we can see that both *The Times* and the *Daily Mail* have the lowest CPT figures and so they both represent the most cost-efficient media in this instance. If a single newspaper had to be selected, which one would you choose? One big advantage that the *Daily Mail* has is that it has more than twice the target audience reach compared with *The Times*, but the cost per insertion is also more than twice as much. It may be that the media environment of *The Times* is considered better than the *Daily Mail* and, therefore, is preferable. But then what about the other papers? Would they all be ruled out because they appear less cost efficient or are there other factors which come into the reckoning? Perhaps you would consider the media environment of the *Financial Times* to be the best for the product being promoted, but then it also has the largest CPT of the group.

   Of course, the problem can be alleviated to some extent by choosing more than one newspaper. It would also be wise to check on the effectiveness of the media by coding the advertisement. If it were a direct response advert, it would be easy to put a different code for each paper used on the reply coupon. Records would then show which was the best.

   What the example illustrates is that CPT can be a useful aid to decision-making but it is not the only factor to bear in mind. Other factors such as total cost, reach and impact come into play as has been identified earlier in this chapter. The table also illustrates how misleading it can be to use the figures in column D which are for total readership. In this instance, *The Sun* would appear extremely cost efficient because of its very high readership.

Media buying – factors affecting purchase

There are a variety of costs incurred when producing and placing advertisements and other forms of marketing communication in the media. Each of the media has a set of factors that affect the rates charged. Even the nature of the media has an effect on the costs of producing the items of communication needed. Television and cinema commercials can be expensive to produce (although this need not necessarily be the case). Producing artwork for a black and white or single colour (mono) A4 leaflet can be very cheap. Classified and some semi-display advertisements in the press can cost nothing to produce because the newspaper or magazine may set the advertisement free of charge.

But production costs are just one aspect of the total cost and are not the prime concern of the media buyer. When buying media, it is the media buyer's task to ensure that the best media is purchased to fulfil the requirements of the media plan, not least to buy the selected media at lowest cost. To do this, a good understanding of the media in all its various forms is necessary.

It is not the place of a book of this nature to cover production and media buying in detail (although Chapter 22 does provide an introduction to some aspects of production, particularly print production, with which the reader should be familiar). What are presented now are some brief details of factors that affect the rates charged by the media. These are given in Exhibit 21.11. To produce sound marketing communications plans these details need to be understood by all those participating in the process; the media buyer, the media planner, the creatives, the account handlers and planners and production specialists.

Exhibit 21.11 Media buying variables

Medium	Factors affecting rates and costs
Broadcast (analogue/digital) *TV (terrestrial, satellite, cable)* ● Local/regional/national/international	● Broadcast area ● Multi-channel ● Audience size – audience ratings ● Broadcast time – time of day ● Length of spot (seconds) ● Number of spots – volume and frequency ● How bought – audience ratings package, fixed time rates, run of week rates, pre-emptable rates, specific spot (non pre-emptable), negotiated deals
Radio ● Local/ regional/national/international	● Sponsorship package ● Production costs
Press *Newspapers* ● Local/regional/national/international ● Daily/weekly/weekday/weekend	● Type of ad – display, semi-display, linage, insert, advertorial ● Position of ad – run of paper, special position, classified, solus ● Style of ad – number of colours, photography/graphics/text only, bleed

→

Exhibit 21.11 continued

Medium	Factors affecting rates and costs
Magazines ● Local/regional/national/international ● Weekly/monthly/annually ● Consumer/business/trade ● General/special interest ● Men's/women's ● Association/club/company/'House' magazine ● Technical/professional/controlled circulation *Directories* ● Local/regional/national/international ● Periodically/annually/intermittent ● Consumer/business/trade	● Size of ad – double page spread (DPS), full page, part page, single column centimetres ● Number of insertions – volume and frequency ● Audience composition and size – readership/reach ● Availability of regional variations/editions ● Cost of publication and editorial/advertising ratio (affects rate charges) ● Print run, circulation, quality of production/ad income ● Production costs
Internet ● World Wide Web (www) web page ● Email	● Type – banner, bannerlink, sponsorship, logo ad, logo with link ● Size of ad – full banner, half banner ● Number of ads, sites ● Own site development ● Handling interactive responses
Posters *Outdoor – boards* ● Local/regional/national ● Roadside (billboards) ● Stations (rail, underground bus, ports, airports) ● Shopping areas ● Venues (e.g. sorts grounds) ● Specialised (e.g. aerial, benches, bins) *Outdoor – transport* ● Buses ● Taxis ● Poster vans *Inside* ● Shopping centres ● Buses ● Taxis ● Underground trains ● Public toilets	● Location ● Position ● Volume of traffic – passers-by (POSTAR ratings), passengers ● Quality of site (POSTAR ratings) ● Type of site ● Number of sites ● Size of ad – number of sheets ● Specials – e.g. 3D, illuminated, painted, semi-permanent ● Length of time ● Production costs
Cinema ● Local/regional/national	● Location ● Number of screens ● Length of spot ● Number of spots ● How bought – audience guarantee plan, film packages, film certificate, type of cinema ● Production costs
Direct mail ● Letters ● Catalogues/price lists ● Brochures/leaflets/booklets ● Circulars ● Newsletters ● Cards ● Samples ● Etc.	● Size of mail-out ● Cost of mailing list ● Cost of maintaining lists ● Sophistication of mailing ● Quantity of material in mailing ● Postage ● Production costs

From Exhibit 21.11, which only features elements of the mass media, it can be seen that many versions of media are available in each of the media classes. For each broad media class the main factors affecting rates and costs are presented. The actual rates charged can be found in publications like *British Rate and Data* and on rate cards that are available from the media owners themselves. An important task for the media buyer is to negotiate with the media owners to obtain discounts where they are available.

Media evaluation

It should be evident, given the importance placed on the role of media implementation, that it is essential for it to be evaluated as an activity. This means that its management as well as the performance of the media plan need to be considered. Questions to be asked include:

- Have the media objectives been achieved?
- Have we achieved the reach and frequency required –TVRs, GRPs, OTS?
- Did the media create the right impact?
- Has the media selected performed as expected?
- Were the best media selected?
- Was the media mix the best that could have been achieved?
- Was the balance of media allocations right?
- Did the secondary media fully support the primary medium?
- Have the media been bought well? Have cost savings been achieved?
- Have we stayed within budget?
- Has the media performed as an 'equal partner' within the total marketing communications effort? Was it properly integrated?
- Was the scheduling effective?
- What were the competitors doing?
- Were there any environmental factors influencing the outcomes?
- etc.

NEED TO KNOW

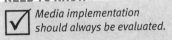
Media implementation should always be evaluated.

The evaluation process is an ongoing one with many of these questions needing to be posed at the planning stages and not just left until the campaign has finished. The answers will be both qualitative and quantitative.

Summary

The management of media – its analysis, planning, implementation and control – is fundamental to successful integrated marketing communications. The media are the carriers of messages to the target audience. The correct selection of media requires a sound understanding of the media and a sound appreciation of target audiences. Unless both are identified correctly, bridges cannot be built between the brand and the consumer, the organisation and its target audiences. Good media implementation is central to the role of marketing communications.

The principal task in using media is to reach the right people, the right number of times, with greatest effect, with the least waste, at least cost, without distorting the message. The watchwords in media are reach, frequency, impact, economy, efficiency and effectiveness.

Eight stages in the media implementation cycle have been identified and this chapter has taken each stage in turn and described its essential features. Marketing communications objectives and strategy, and target audience identification are the first two stages that are established. On the basis of these, media objectives and budget allocations can be determined prior to the tasks of media selection, scheduling and buying. The final stage identified was that of media evaluation.

A large number of 'technical' terms have been introduced in this chapter although they have been kept to a reasonable number. They are terms used extensively in the marketing communications industry and some understanding of them is advisable. Many of the terms are used in basic tasks undertaken by media professionals, or refer to resources and data available to assist media planners.

Self-review questions

1 Why is it so important to have a clear understanding of target audiences?

2 How would you describe the difference between target markets and target audiences?

3 Why is the concept of DMU important in media planning?

4 Name and define the three most essential considerations when setting media objectives.

5 Why is it important to recognise the difference between exposure to the medium and exposure to an advertisement?

6 What are TVRs, GRPs and OTS?

7 What is 'share of voice'?

8 What nine factors can be taken into consideration when selecting media?

9 What are drip and burst scheduling patterns?

10 How is CPT calculated? Why is it important to use target audience figures rather than total audience figures in the calculation?

11 Is it always the case that the medium with the lowest CPT will be the best to choose?

12 What range of factors affect the rates and costs when using poster sites as marketing communications media?

Project

You are faced with a similar situation to that shown in Exhibit 21.10. You are a media planner whose client wishes to sell private health insurance. The details of the target audience, size and type of advertisement are the same as those given in the exhibit. You are required to select five magazines as a shortlist of possible media and using BRAD or another source of published data (such as the rate cards and data produced by the magazine publishers), calculate the CPT values for each magazine. Which magazine has the lowest CPT? Would you recommend this magazine to the client – why or why not? Assuming that you could recommend more than one magazine, produce a media schedule for burst advertising and calculate the total costs.

References

Kaatz, R. (1995), *Advertising and Marketing Checklists* 2nd edn. NTC Business Books.

Kotler, P. (2000), *Marketing Management*. The Millennium Edition, 10th edn. Prentice Hall International.

Krugman, H. (1972), Why three exposures may be enough. *Journal of Advertising Research*, 12 (6), 11–14.

Oldfield, M. (1997), Presentation given to IPA Advertising and Academia Seminar, London, September.

Shimp, T.A. (1997), *Advertising, Promotion, and Supplemental Aspects of Integrated Marketing Communications*. The Dryden Press.

Wilmshurst, J. (1985), *The Fundamentals of Advertising*. Butterworth-Heinemann.

Hotline Virgin Trains Customer Magazine (1997) Children decide. Summer, p. 6.

Selected further reading

Davis, M.P. (1996), *The Effective Use of Advertising Media* 5th edn. Century Business.

Gensch, D.H. (1970), Media factors: a review article. *Journal of Marketing Research*, 7 (2).

Kent, R. (ed.) (1994), *Measuring Media Audiences*. Routledge.

Lancaster, K. and Katz, H. (1990), *Strategic Media Planning*. NTC Business Books.

McKeone, D. (1995), *Measuring Your Media Profile*. Gower.

McLuhan, M. (1964), *Understanding Media*. Routledge and Kegan Paul.

Murrey, G.B. and Jenkins, J.R.G. (1992), The concept of effective reach in advertising, *Journal of Advertising Research*, May/June, 34–42.

Priemer, A.B. (1989), *Effective Media Planning*. Lexington Books.

Russell, J.T. and Lane, W.R. (1996), *Kleppner's Advertising Procedure* 13th edn. Prentice Hall.

Sissors, J.A. and Bumba, L.J. (1991), *Advertising Media Planning* 5th edn. Crain Books.

Chapter 22

Production implementation

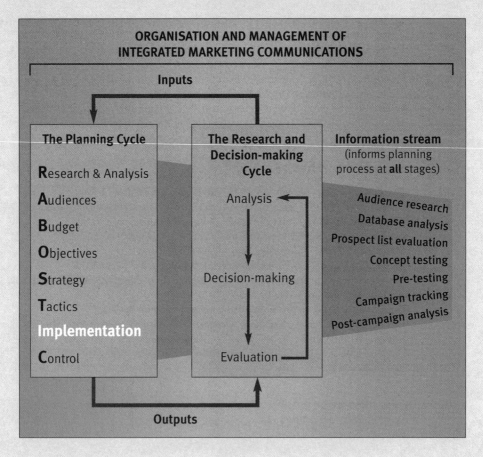

ORGANISATION AND MANAGEMENT OF
INTEGRATED MARKETING COMMUNICATIONS

Inputs

The Planning Cycle

Research & Analysis

Audiences

Budget

Objectives

Strategy

Tactics

Implementation

Control

The Research and Decision-making Cycle

Analysis

Decision-making

Evaluation

Information stream
(informs planning
process at **all** stages)

Audience research
Database analysis
Prospect list evaluation
Concept testing
Pre-testing
Campaign tracking
Post-campaign analysis

Outputs

The IMC RABOSTIC Planning Model

CD

Selecting one of the printed pieces of promotional material refered to in Case Study 2 on the CD, compile the printing brief that would have produced it. Follow the planning process outlined in Exhibit 22.2 to structure your brief.

Objectives

- To outline the rationale for a marketer's knowledge of production processes
- To present an overview of the print planning process
- To introduce the stages in the reproduction process
- To outline the major proofing methods
- To discuss the nature of colour and its impact on the reproduction process
- To introduce the main printing processes and related issues

Professional perspective

Paul Kilminster Systems Imaging Manager. Northcliffe Press Ltd

Having spent the last fifteen years working within the printing trade, from small instant print shops to large national newspapers, it is evident that the starting point for all printing is a clear understanding of customer requirements as it is often too late to make amendments when the product has been printed and this can prove very costly.

It is vitally important that time is taken in the initial stages of the design concept to discuss overall requirements with a printer, in order to eliminate any unforeseen problems. Many a time I have witnessed weird and wonderful designs that, when actually put to print, lose their impact.

Hence the need for a good working relationship between the printer and customer. Central to this is to 'speak the same language'. Printing is often perceived as a 'black art', with technical jargon used to confuse clients. This chapter aims to uncover this jargon, so when printers start talking about 'trannies, plates, offset lithography and negs' you are armed with sufficient knowledge to ensure an effective working relationship.

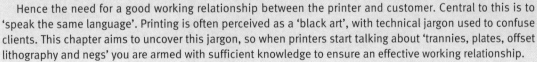

An introduction to broadcast and print production

Marketers often get involved in elements of the marketing communications production process. Production issues impact directly on the development and design of specific marketing communications. A basic understanding of these issues are, therefore, necessary to add to the marketer's toolkit. Even the marketing client whose communications are handled through an agency should be informed of basic production issues to encourage a good working relationship between all parties and to understand the rationale behind creative decisions. For the student of marketing communications, whose future career may lie in the client, the agency or the supplier side of the industry, an overview of production processes is vital.

We recognise that as media becomes ever more fragmented, the planning and scheduling of marketing communications campaigns become ever more complex (Exhibit 22.1). It would be impossible to provide a complete overview of production of every type of medium in one chapter. The planning of broadcast media has been detailed in Chapter 21. Additionally, it is unlikely that marketers will be involved in broadcast

NEED TO KNOW

☑ *Broadcast media production, though important, is less likely to be part of the general marketer's direct responsibility. Many marketers, however, have production management input into press, poster, magazine, direct mail and other print media.*

Exhibit 22.1 The fragmentation of the media

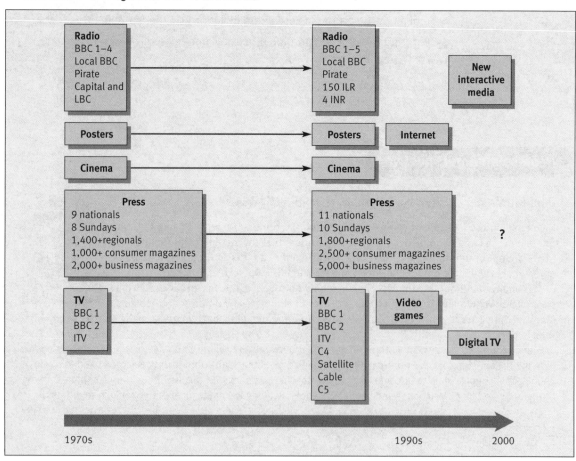

Source: From figure '*The fragmentation of the media*' from '*Below the Line Marketing*', in *Reuters' Business Insight* , Reuters (1998). Reproduced with permission.

production in any detail, unless they specialise in that area. Print production, however, is an area in which potentially all marketers can have planning responsibilities. It is pertinent, therefore, to detail relevant production issues that have a direct impact on the planning process.

Print planning and scheduling

Chapters 13 and 21 have outlined the importance of planning and scheduling media. The planning of a print job commences with the identification and evaluation of potential print suppliers. This is an important step in the planning process and suppliers should be evaluated on the services they provide, the equipment used and whether a good working relationship could be established. A site visit is strongly recommended to evaluate the process. Once the supplier has been chosen a print job plan can be developed, as outlined in Exhibit 22.2. A good working relationship with the supplier is crucial because you can use their detailed knowledge to help with the decision-making process.

Exhibit 22.2 Planning a print job

Planning stages	Questions	Examples
Background information	What do you want printed?	Brochure? catalogue? leaflet? letterhead? poster? magazine advertisement?
	What is the objective of this print job?	Increase company awareness? show products? Set out beforehand your objective for this print item. It will have a bearing on how it is designed as well as giving you something on which to measure its success.
	Who is your target audience?	New customers? small businesses? students? People respond differently to what they see and read. Their tastes and prejudices will affect the way in which they respond to your communication and this needs to be taken into consideration.
	How will you distribute it?	Handing out? using a mailing list? display rack? How you choose to distribute your print item will have an effect on the way it is designed. A mail shot, for example, must not be mistaken for junk mail or it will be thrown in the bin! A leaflet in a carousel will need to stand out from other leaflets.
	What will its finished size be?	A4? A5? 215mm x 303mm? Portrait/landscape?
	How many pages?	4 pages + cover? 1 page double sided? The number of pages should always be divisable by 4 – 4,8,12,16 etc. – unless you have a single-sided or a double-sided sheet or if you are having something wire/comb bound.
	What type of paper do you envisage it being on?	Cover: gloss/silk? Pages: matt/textured? There are many different types of paper available. Try to think about the 'feel' you are trying to create. Is it classy? Budget? Environmentally friendly? Arty? Try to select a paper that matches your objectives.
	What weight of paper do you envisage it being on?	Cover: 250 gsm? 300 gsm? Pages: 90 gsm? 120 gsm? The weight of paper that you will use depends on what you are going to use the document for. If it is going through the post, you will need to use a lighter paper, like 70–90gsm. If you go too light, however, the image on one side of the paper will show through to the other side.

Exhibit 22.2 continued

Planning stages	*Questions*	*Examples*
Budgeting and scheduling	What date do you need the job printed by?	Formulate a schedule working scheduling from this date.
	How much do you intend spending?	Design work? Printing? In total?
	How many do you want printing?	1,000? 2,000? 10,000? The more items you have printed the less cost per unit. If you have 1,000 leaflets printed it may cost 10p per item. If you increase the volume to 5,000, the unit cost may reduce to 6p. This is because the most expensive part of printing is in the setting up of the job.
Choosing the colours	What colours do you want to use?	Full colour? One colour? Two colour? Other?
	Do you have any corporate colours that should always be used?	Pantone reference? If your company has a corporate colour, usually found in the logo, your print item should feature this as a predominant colour. This helps create instant recognition in the minds of your audience.
	Are there any other colours you would like to use?	Light blue background? Red text? Colours often have certain associations with certain moods, symbolism, atmospheres etc. Can you use colour to enhance the effectiveness of your document?
Photographs and graphics	Will you be using photographs?	How many colour? How many black and white?
	How will you get the photographs?	I already possess them I'm taking them myself I need to arrange a photographer Design and Print to arrange
	How will you supply the photographs?	Print? 35mm slide? Transparency? Negative?
	Will you use illustrations? How will you supply them?	Maps? Diagrams? Logos? Design and Print to originate Design and Print to redraw from my roughs I'll supply on a disk I'll supply finished artwork I'll supply camera-ready artwork.
Wording and layout	How will you supply the wording?	Handwritten text Design and Print to copywrite based on my notes I'll supply a typed-up hardcopy I'll supply the text on disk.
	Have you proof-read the text?	
	Do you have a corporate typeface?	New Baskerville? Garamond? Some companies use a particular typeface or font all of the time which is part of their image. If the printer does not have the specific typeface required, they will be able to buy it for you. If you do have a corporate identity policy or house styles that need following make sure you let the printer know about them.
Folding, trimming, binding and finishing	How do you want the job bound?	Staples down spine? glued?
	Would you like a pocket?	None/Inside front/Inside back/With business card holder? What size of paper will it hold? How many sheets?
	Do you want to use special effects?	Die cut? Foil blocking? Spot UV? Lamination?
	How do you want the job folded?	A4 folded to 1/3 A4? A3 to A5?
Delivery and contact details	Ensure contact name is provided to the printer and the delivery date is agreed.	

Scheduling print

To avoid disappointment it is always advisable to work back from the distribution date to determine key production dates (Exhibit 22.3). It is a good idea to provide the printers with a lead time of at least two weeks in which the printer can get the proofs to you, output to film, make plates and print the job. So all text, photographs and artwork need to be sorted out before this. Press-time may be able to be booked in advance. The time-scale between these dates is dependent on the quantity to be produced and the complexity of the job.

Exhibit 22.3 Schedule key production dates

Days/ weeks	Days/ weeks	Days/ weeks	Days/ weeks	Days/ weeks	Days/ weeks	Days/ weeks
Submit camera-ready artwork and transparencies	Proof sign-off	Make-up final film and printing plates	Print	Finishing Enclosing	Delivery to you Mailing house Direct to post	Target launch date

The reproduction process

Printing processes, whatever their individual differences, follow the same initial stages of converting the original matter into an image carrier such as a plate, cylinder or stencil, which produces the finished printed form. It is important to understand each stage so that you understand when and where the marketing input is needed.

Artwork and film assembly

Traditional artwork

Traditional artwork takes the form of a pasted-down bromide onto a base board. A bromide is ordinary photographic paper. With few exceptions the artwork is the actual size of the job. A negative camera shot is taken of the bromide. Any transparencies of photographs are scanned and a negative film is output. Scanned film is placed into the artwork negative. Breakdowns are established for any spot colours and tints laid accordingly. Masks are created to crop the scanned images to the correct size and to expose the desired elements from the artwork negative. All these separate elements are then contacted onto one piece of film to create one colour separation. This is repeated for each colour. A proof is produced. When the job is passed by the client, machine plates are produced.

Digital reproduction

Digital printing is a technological breakthrough that compresses the printing process. Digital files go directly from the creator to the press through ISDN lines, eliminating colour separations, stripping, plate-making, press make-ready, and other stages. While digital printing can save time and money, its core benefit is its flexibility. The content can be changed, rearranged and updated until the operator sends the digital file to the press. This flexibility has great value in today's marketplace, where information

Exhibit 22.4 A sequence of events from originals to printing

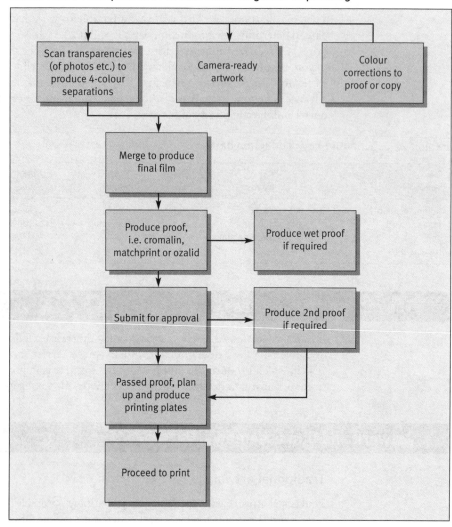

changes more rapidly than ever before. With the aid of special software, digital printing content can actually be varied during the press run. Personalised press runs of a publication, once only possible for low-end applications, such as direct mail, can now be produced with outstanding quality, in colour. This variable-data capability allows users to create customised materials designed to meet the needs of specific audiences.

Proofing systems and techniques

Proof

A draft representation of a printed product for the client to determine if the indicated result will be satisfactory. It becomes a 'contract' proof when the client and printer agree that it shows an acceptable quality of print.

A **proof** is a representation of a printed sheet. Proofs are produced at particular times in the printing cycle to allow the customer and the printer to judge at that stage if the indicated result is going to be satisfactory. In the initial stages of a job, proofs such as page and ozalid proofs are used for checking the accuracy and position of the printed elements on a page. At latter stages, it is the quality standards and colour registration which are being checked.

IN VIEW 22.1

Digital printing

The ultimate goal of direct marketing has always been to talk to segments of one, communicating to that individual on a personal basis. At best, however, direct mail has typically been mass segmented, offering perhaps a dozen variants on the same basic pack. A lot of the current use of digital print is to produce exactly that kind of output, with basic copy and one or two images varied according to the target segment. But digital printing is capable of so much more. In the US, General Motors runs a customer magazine programme for its 25 million drivers which has 23 million different versions of the magazine subject to each customer's interests. If a customer or prospect receives an item that both reflects the data the company holds on them, and appears to talk to them in a relevant way, then response rates, conversion rates and retention levels should all improve.

There are two key disadvantages to digital printing. The first, and most important, is cost. The unit cost of using digital print for recruitment mailing is relatively high. In practice, fulfilment packs are the key use of digital print. The second disadvantage is, if every item sent out to an enquirer is different, how do you sign off an approved piece of artwork? Stringent quality control to ensure the fit between pack and prospect is crucial.

Penetration of printing type in UK, based on top 500 corporate and public sector organisations

	1998	2003
Analogue	68%	39%
Digital	32%	61%

Source: Adapted from (Reed (1998)

With the advent of print on demand technology, the way print work is costed can be revised. Rather than printing hundreds of thousands, a four or five thousand print run is advised because of the high wastage. The risk of wastage is especially high in the financial services industry. If a leaflet is printed with a certain APR and the base rate goes up, all of that literature is out of date and will be thrown away. With digital printing, items can be run off within 24 hours of a response being received, incorporating the most up-to-date information. If storage and wastage costs are taken into account, digital print looks more reasonable. While a print run of 50,000 on conventional presses might cost just 10p per item, storage costs will add to this if items are held for some time, while wastage and spoilage will push up the true cost. Digital printing could turn out the same item as and when required for around 15p.

Non-colour proofing systems

Proofs of predominantly typematter are produced in the following ways:

- *Page proofs.* The typesetting is displayed on the computer terminal and needs to be thoroughly checked before it is made into pages. Page proofs are mainly used to ensure that the finished page format is correct in terms of the position and size of page elements – that is, type sizes, spacing, column widths, depth and graphics.

● *Bromide/ozalid proofs.* Using bromides and ozalids are the simplest methods of proofing a non-colour print job. A bromide is ordinary photographic paper exposed with the film. An ozalid or blueline is light-sensitive diazo paper cured with ammonia. This is usually reserved for corrections, text alterations or language variations where colour proofing is not required. It is a fast, inexpensive proofing system which can be pulled from any number of films within the job to check position, content and layout.

Colour proofs

Pre-production run colour proofs are produced to represent and equate as closely as possible to the finished printed result. A 'contract' proof refers to the buyer and the printer agreeing that the proof shows an acceptable quality of print. There are three main types of contract proof: digital, analogue and wet proof.

● *The wet proof.* These are generally regarded as the best method of proofing a job in that it produces a very accurate representation of the printed sheet. The major drawback is cost. A wet proof is produced on a flat-bed proofing press, using actual printing plates. These machines use ordinary ink and print on the paper and ink stock on which the job will be produced. The machine speed is very slow as the machine is hand-fed one sheet at a time.

Exhibit 22.5 An evaluation of wet proofing

CMYK inks

Cyan, magenta, yellow and black (key) are the primary inks used in printing. As these inks are used in wet proofing, it ensures a true representation of the colour to be delivered.

Advantages	Disadvantages
● Very accurate	● Costly (changes expensive)
● No size restriction	● Slow process
● Uses **CMYK inks**	
● Printed on paper	
● Multiple copies can be made	

● *The analogue proof.* This is a generic term for cromalin and matchprint, which use film to produce the proof. Cromalin is plastic material which is laminated with a photo-sensitive film. This is then exposed under the job film in the same manner as a printing plate. The exposure renders the image area on the laminate attractive to toner. Toner, in one of the four process colours, is evenly shaken over the laminate and the first colour is complete. The process is repeated four times to give the finished four-colour set. Matchprint proofs are similar to cromalin with one exception. Instead of using process coloured toner, the colour pigment is contained in the photo-sensitive film laminate itself. It is generally regarded that a matchprint is a more accurate reproduction. Advertising agencies generally favour analogue proofs such as cromalin and matchprint because of their speed of operation, generally cheaper price and more consistent results.

Exhibit 22.6 An evaluation of analogue proofing

Advantages	Disadvantages
● Accurate colour range	● Uses toner rather than ink
● Cost effective	● Many reprographic houses can not proof special colours
● Fast	● Colour range higher than is achievable on press
	● Normally, one copy only
	● Proof size limited to A3

● *The digital proof.* There are two types of digital proof: ink jet proof (Iris) and dye sublimation proof (digital cromalin). A dye sublimation proof is usually used as it is of higher quality.

Exhibit 22.7 An evaluation of digital proofing

Advantages	Disadvantages
● Quick to produce	● Uses CMYK substitute inks
● Corrections are easy	● Has limited range of substrates
● Has variable colour control	● Does not use film or plates
	● Colour range higher than achievable on press
	● Proof size limited to A3

The nature of colour and its role when evaluating proofs

Substrate

Any material which is used to print on to e.g. paper, card and plastic.

When evaluating proofs it is important to have an understanding of the relationship between the human eye and the image you are viewing on paper. Colour is light. Without light we see shapes without colour. The light source, therefore, has an effect on colour as do different substrates (light waves react with differing, reflective and absorptive qualities on paper). To reproduce colours, printers do not use the entire spectrum. They use three primary colours – red, green and blue. In various combinations these colours produce a reasonable representation of the colour spectrum. However, these primary colours cannot be used in the printing process because of their 'additive' qualities (increase to become brighter). Printing requires 'subtractive' qualities (to give a thin film of ink). The three primary colours when overlapping produce the subtractive yellow, cyan and magenta. This combination will produce most of the colour spectrum acceptable to the human eye, given the constraints of the printing process. When checking proofs, you need to be aware of:

● the colour of the light source,
● the intensity of the light source,
● the influence of unnatural and ambient light,
● the colour of surrounding area and paper quality.

A job may be printed in the process colours (cyan, magenta, yellow and black) or in spot colour. The best way to explain the difference is by using an example. Say you want to print a logo in red. You have two options: spot or process. If you choose spot colour then the logo will be printed in a specific red ink. If you choose process colour then a layer of magenta ink followed by a layer of yellow ink will be printed, i.e. the colour is made up on the paper using the four process inks. The result will be almost the same – but not always. Often, spot colours print more vividly than process colours, particularly oranges (which tend toward brown). Whether you use spot or process colours depends on what you are having printed. If you want a full colour brochure with photographs etc. then you need to use process colours. This is because a photograph is made up of innumerable colours. If you were printing each colour in a spot colour you would need to use a similar number of inks and that would be expensive and impractical. However, if you want to print one to four specific colours then probably spot colour would be the best option. But it really depends on the job. Speak to the printer, who should be pleased to advise you.

Care needs to be taken if passing a copy on a computer screen. The printed colours may not be accurately represented by what is on the screen. This is due to a number of reasons. First, the image on screen is made up of emitted light and an image printed in ink is seen via reflected light. Second, the image on your screen will look different from the same image on a different screen (or on paper). This is because screens are affected by all sorts of factors: room light and temperature, UV light, age of screen, how long it has been on, etc. As a rule of thumb, never trust the colours on a computer screen!

To decide on the right colours either consult a colour swatch system, such as Pantone, or consult a process colour guide which is a printed swatch of different combinations of inks in various percentages. For example it will show you what happens when 20% yellow is mixed with 40% cyan and 10% magenta. When you have seen the colour you like on paper enter this value into your software. The colour probably will not look the same on screen, but at least you will know what it is going to look like when printed.

The only sure way to guarantee an accurate representation of a contract's requirements is to pass the job on press on the paper to be used for the job. Once the job is passed to the printing press, however, changes are restricted. Moving elements of the job around at this stage is not an option. Once plates are on the press, only minor colour changes are possible without incurring costs for press 'downtime'. As outlined above, the human eye gives different interpretations of colour and under different lights will perceive colours differently. Altering the colour of one picture may dramatically alter the colour of another picture on the same inking/plate track. So even colour changes are limited on press. To ensure continuity between colour proofs and the printed sheet it is necessary to use colour bars or colour strips so that accurate and meaningful quality control comparisons can be made. Du Pont have produced a standard control strip based on the unified European offset colour scale. The Cromalin

IN VIEW 22.2

Guidelines for passing printer's proofs

1 Mark up in permanent ink everything which has appeared on the proof that you are not happy with, no matter how minor the fault may appear.

2 Write comments which are clear, unambiguous and that can be understood by a third party who knows nothing about the job.

3 Remember, proofs are 'sold as seen'. Allow yourself time to give them the attention they require.

4 Check the proof against a made-up dummy, and make sure the printer understands how the product folds.

5 Sign and date the proof.

6 Always retain a copy of the marked-up proof before returning it to the printers.

7 Ensure a second proof (if required) is created to check that your corrections have been made. Sign and date this proof or any further proofs that may be required.

8 Take your copy of the final approved and marked up proof if passing the job at the printers.

Eurostandard control strip contains the same elements as those used for checking the actual printed result. This means that values derived from the proof can be transferred to the actual print run where comparisons can then be made.

Printing processes

There are five major printing processes:

- Letterpress
- Offset lithography
- Gravure
- Flexography
- Screen.

The basic difference between them is how the printed image is created. The carrier of the printed image has two separate surfaces – an image or printing area and a non-image or non-printing area. The image area accepts the ink by mechanical or chemical means and the non-image area does not accept or retain ink. The inked image area is transferred to paper or other stocks usually by the application of pressure.

The most common printing process is lithography, although each process has its distinct strengths and weaknesses and is appropriate for different printing applications (Exhibit 22.8).

Letterpress

Letterpress is the oldest of the main printing processes and was the most widely used in the UK up until the early 1970s. Letterpress printing has almost died out as an economical production method today, but it is still considered to be by far the very best process for ultimate quality printing. Letterpress, together with flexography, is based on relief printing. In relief printing, the printing surface is raised above the non-printing area, and receives the ink which is transferred to the substrate when it is pressed against the printing surface. The ink rollers and the substrate only come into contact with the raised printing surface.

Exhibit 22.8 Comparing the five common printing processes

Lithography	Letterpress	Gravure	Flexography	Screen
Planographic printing	Relief printing	Intaglio printing	Relief printing	Stencil printing
Most common process	Little used	Specialised process	Not suitable for fine detail production	Relatively slow process
Limits on type and weight of substrate		Suited to cheaper grades of paper	Highly adaptable to a range of substrates	The most adaptable to range of substrates
Cost-effective				
Speed				

Lithography

Lithography, based on the planographic process, is the most widely used printing method today, due to its versatility, speed, quality and cost-effectiveness across a wide range of printed products. Planographic printing is based on the principle that water and ink do not mix. The image is transferred to paper (or other substrate) by allowing both ink and water to be applied to the image carrier (the printing plate). The plate is made of thin aluminium, coated with a light sensitive material. When exposed to UV light a molecular change occurs in areas that have allowed light to penetrate through the film. This produces two surfaces, one which accepts ink and one which rejects ink. The ink sticks to the image area of the plate while a water solution ensures the non-image area rejects the ink. The substrate (paper or board) is then pressed into contact with the whole surface of the printing plate. Nearly all lithography is offset, that is the image is first offset onto a rubber blanket from which it is transferred to paper.

The versatility of the process and the number of different types of machines allows the production of a very wide range of printed material. The small offset range of presses are ideal for producing stationery products such as letterheadings, business cards and forms. The range of work varies from mainly single colour and spot colour to four-colour process.

The larger sheet-fed presses cover paper sizes from above SRA3/B3 to above SRA0/B0 (based on the A and B series of international paper sizes).The range of work covers short magazine work, brochures, booklets to specialist work such as carton and tin printing. Sheet-fed presses are usually suitable for smaller quantities of print. However they are more flexible than web presses in terms of the paper thickness they can handle. They can print on a range of papers between 80 and 300 gsm at speeds between 8000 and 15,000 sheets per hour depending on ink coverage.

Web presses are neither as common nor as flexible as sheet-fed machines. The paper is a continuous ribbon fed from a roll or reel rather than individual sheets and can generally be printed on both sides of the sheet at the same time. The paper range on this type of machine is from 60 to 200 gsm and speeds of 50,000 impressions per hour can be achieved. Although the roll of paper is continuous, there is obviously a maximum and minimum printing image area. This area is referred to as the cut off. Within Europe, cut off sizes are based around the ISO A system of paper sizes. The conventional cut off is either 630 mm (16 pages A4) or 452 mm (8 pages A4). Web presses are used for longer runs and higher pagination than sheet-fed presses, mainly for newspaper and mass circulation magazines and catalogues.

Gravure

Gravure is based on the intaglio printing process and tends to be more specialised than relief or lithographic printing. The printing areas in intaglio printing are recessed – that is, an image is cut into the printing cylinder. The recesses are filled with ink and surplus ink is removed from the non-printing surface. The substrate is then pressed against the printing cylinder to transfer ink onto it. Intaglio printing produces a greater depth of ink than planographic printing which makes the colours appear richer to the eye. It is only relatively recently that the cylinders involved in printing the image onto the substrate have become cost-effective. This process is able to print at high speeds on non-absorbent materials with the use of solvent-based inks. It is best known for being capable of producing very high-quality colour printing on poorer-quality, cheaper grades of paper. The process is typically used by manufacturers of cartons and magazines (with print runs in the millions) and is also suitable for smooth textiles such as linen or silk.

Flexography

Flexography is the dominant relief printing process today and is an uncomplicated method of printing with normally a very simple ink system and is almost exclusively a web-fed process. It uses resilient rubber relief printing plates and fast-drying solvent or water-based inks. The plates are cheaper and faster to prepare than gravure cylinders, but tend to distort the image with fine detailed production. It is particularly suitable for long-run work and is highly adaptable to a range of substrates – from thin paper to heavy corrugated board, thin cellophane to thick flexible sheeting, vinyls and foils. The main applications include paper/plastic bags, plastic and fabric labels.

Screen printing

Screen printing is based on the stencil printing process which in effect stencils an image onto a substrate. A stencil is produced photographically and a fine mesh screen placed on top. Ink is spread across the mesh and passes through the stencil onto the substrate. The process is very slow but a wide range of substrates can be used.

Screen-process printing is best known for its ability to print a heavier ink film than any of the other processes. Screen printing can produce brilliant, sparkling solid colours or varied effects, such as lighter colours on a dark coloured substrate. The inks can be formulated to print opaque to block any matter underneath or transparent to make use of the colour combinations available by halftone screen printing. It is capable of very high-quality printing across a wide range of printed products including posters, T-shirts, printed plastic products and showcards.

Ink-jet printing

This utilises the 'spraying' of ink dots onto a required surface. In multiple array ink-jet printing, the ink-jet nozzle prints rows of dots onto a moving substrate, forming the printed image often from bitmapped images created from computer-generated graphics. Early application of ink-jet printing was in serial or code numbers on packaging products. Ink-jet has now expanded into a colour proofing method and is a major means of personalising print in direct mail and magazines.

Laser printing

This creates the printed image by the use of a controlled laser which is an acronym for Light Amplification by Stimulated Emission of Radiation. The original to be reproduced is exposed to light and scanned by a reading head which modulates a laser beam which scans across a photosensitive drum. Toner powder is attracted to the image areas on the drum and released onto the positively charged substrate as it passes the drum. The toner is heated which bonds it to the substrate. Instead of scanning in images, laser printers can also receive images in digital format produced from a computer. Laser technology is used for producing direct imaging-to-plate systems and for similar applications to those of ink-jet printing such as the personalisation of correspondence and computer listing from database files.

Print specifications

A description of any substrate (paper or board) should indicate the type of paper, colour and finish, size and grammage. Each of the different printing processes require certain characteristics to function effectively and to the price and/or quality standard required. For example, sheet-fed offset lithography requires an uncoated paper which has a firm surface and few loose fibres. Web-offset has an upper limit of paper grammage of 135 gsm when it is folded. Gravure is well suited to the cheaper grades of paper such as mechanicals. Screen printing can print on virtually any substrate including paper, board, plastic, glass, metal and fabric. Laser printing paper is required to be curl-free with a low moisture content and a weight of 60 gsm plus.

Paper sizes

There are three interelated standard ranges for paper and board: each range within the series being designated by an initial – A, B or C. Most printers are concerned only with the A range but, in between each of the sizes in the A range, come those of the B range, filling any gaps and intended primarily for poster work. The C range consists of the finished sizes of envelopes and folders which will contain A-sized items.

The basis of the international series of paper sizes is a rectangle having an area of one square metre. This basic size in each range is A0 (841 × 1189 mm), B0 or C0. If

Exhibit 22.9 **Selected types of paper**

Type of paper	*Qualities*
Newsprint	Used for newspapers. It is the cheapest paper to buy. A weight of 45–50 grams per square metre.
Mechanical SC print	A smooth gloss surface paper used extensively in gravure printing for products such as mass circulation magazines, colour supplements and catalogues. A weight of 54–80 grams per square metre.
Woodfree print	A clean, good colour sheet suitable for all types of general printing and stronger than mechanical printing. Used for a wide range of good quality commercial printing work including leaflets, booklets, reports and books. A weight of 60–135 grams per square metre.
Cartridge	A tough paper which may be rough, uncoated or coated. A weight of 60–170 grams per square metre and higher.
Offset print	Paper cheaper than cartridge, produced for litho printing and usually somewhat whiter than the rather creamy shade of traditional cartridge.
MG poster	Smooth surface on one side and rough finish on the other. Typically used for wrapping paper. A weight of 70–170 grams per square metre.
Coated	High coating weight, special pigments and a very smooth surface, usually with a high-gloss used for colourful glossy publications. Coated paper may be matt, satin, velvet or silk giving some indication as to the coating's smoothness. Coated papers are used for a wide range of high-quality commercial printing including reports, leaflets, booklets, folders and books. A weight of 60–200 grams per square metre.
Chromo	A high-grade coated paper, usually one-sided and having a thicker coating than art paper. Its main use is in label printing.

Exhibit 22.10 The area of the basic A0 is halved by halving the longer dimension

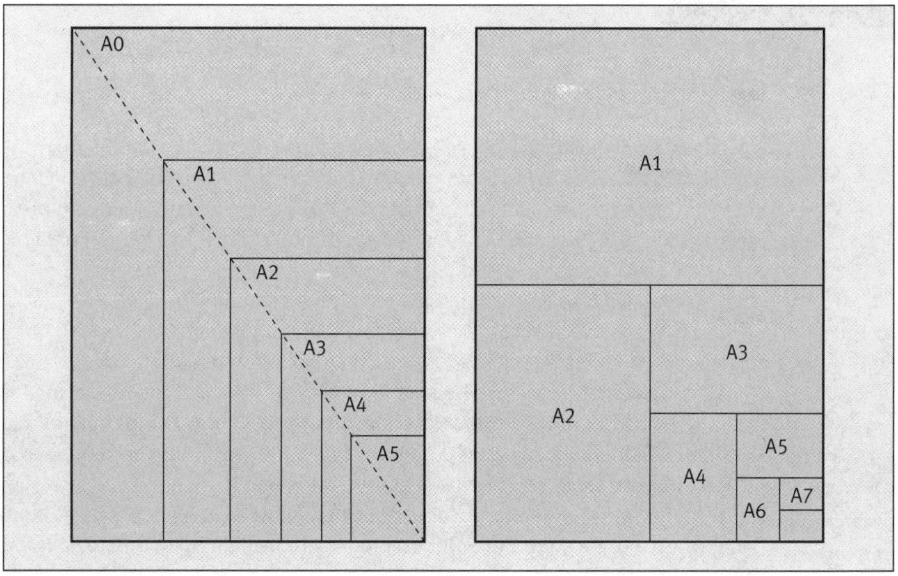

this is preceded by a figure, for example, 2A0, it indicates that the area of the basic A0 sheet has been doubled. If the letter designating the series is followed by a figure, for example A1, it indicates that the area of the basic A0 sheet has been halved. Similarly A2 is half A1, A3 is half A2, A4 is half A3 and so on. A4 is usual for business stationery, brochures and booklets, A5 for smaller printed items, A6 is the international postcard size, A7 for labels and compliment slips, A8 for business cards. While there are exceptions (such as books), A4 has become the usual size of the majority of printed reading matter. The major exception is in North America where the American version of quarto remains.

After printing, paper is trimmed at some stage of being finished. In order to keep to the A-size finished job, two untrimmed stock size ranges have been introduced – the RA primary and SRA supplementary ranges. In the RA range a normal trim is 3 mm. For example, an eight-page A5 upright booklet, trimmed size of 210×148 mm can be printed on a RA2 sheet (430×610 mm). If however, the work prints close to the edge of the sheet, a larger untrimmed sheet is necessary. The same job could be printed on an SRA2 sheet (450×640 mm).

Exhibit 22.11 ISO paper specifications

A range mm	B range mm	C range mm
2A0 1189 × 1682	2B0 1414 × 2000	
A0 841 × 1189	B0 1000 × 1414	
A1 594 × 841	B1 707 × 1000	
A2 420 × 594	B2 500 × 707	
A3 297 × 420	B3 353 × 500	
A4 210 × 297	B4 250 × 353	C4 229 × 324
A5 148 × 210	B5 176 × 250	C5 162 × 229
A6 105 × 148	B6 125 × 176	C6 114 × 162
A7 74 × 105	B7 88 × 125	C7 81 × 114
A8 52 × 74	B8 62 × 88	C8 57 × 81

Source: from ISO paper specification, permission to reproduce Table 22.11, ISO Paper Specifications is granted by BSI. ISO and British Standards can be obtained from BSI Customer Services, 389 Chiswick High Road, London W4 4AL, Tel: +44 (0) 20 8996 9001, email: cservices@bsi-global.com

IN VIEW 22.3

Envelope design

Envelope design is a dichotomy. A plain envelope personally addressed giving no clues as to what is inside may stand a better chance of being opened than an envelope which is branded. However, envelope design can also be intriguing enough to initiate opening, if the message is of relevance. Envelopes addressed to The Occupier arguably have little chance of being opened, let alone read. Even if it has a self-adhesive name and address label, it will have less appeal than if it were truly personalised. This has led to an array of creative designs, different size envelopes and unusual materials landing on our doorsteps as creatives strive to make the most visual impact and first impressions.

You do need to be careful with envelope design. Take the mail pack for Mercedes Benz created by Drayton Bird Partnership which was too big to go through letterboxes, for example. Despite being smaller than the Royal Mail's recommended dimensions, it still proved too large for many letterboxes. The 3D mailing was sent to 14,500 people and as the delivery was intended for a Saturday, when many people would be at home, it was felt that it would not be a problem. But due to a technical hitch, an unknown number of prospects received, instead, a notice to pick up an unknown parcel from their nearest delivery office, only to find a piece of unrequested mail!

Source: Farrow (1998)

Finishing

Finishing refers to the final operation in the production of the printed job. These operations include cutting and trimming, folding, collating and insetting, and binding. Basically there are two types of finishing systems:

- In-line finishing
- Off-line finishing.

In-line finishing

In-line finishing means that the techniques involved in producing the final format (the folding, binding etc.) are carried out immediately after printing has taken place on the same machine in one operation. Specialist in-line finishers have been available for a number of years to provide sophisticated direct response formats including personalisation. There are two main disadvantages to this system. First, if there are delays or problems with either the print or the finishing then one holds the other up. Second the paper roll has to run at a slightly slower speed for the finishing process than for printing, therefore, the printing takes longer than normal web production. The in-line system, being a web-fed process, is not really feasible for small quantities. This is due to the high set-up costs associated with this type of finishing.

Off-line finishing

Off-line finishing means that the printing process is separate from the finishing of a product. The off-line finishing is based mainly on cut sheet production. This does not necessarily mean that the print supplier is sheet-fed. If the quantity merits, the printing method could be web-offset and supplied as cut sheets to the finisher. Off-line finishing offers a far greater range of features, such as labels, multiple folds, stitching etc (Exhibit 12.12). The key advantage to this method is that quantities can be produced from around 5000 copies more competitively than with in-line finishing. This makes off-line finishing ideally suited for testing purposes in direct mail.

Folding methods

One of the most common yet most important of finishing operations is folding sheets of printed paper or board received from the pressroom. Folding may be perfomed by hand but is mostly done on a buckle or knife folder. A sheet of paper printed with a number of pages has to be folded so that the pages appear in correct sequence. Folding is a particularly important finishing operation because the final appearance of a job may be spoilt by inaccurate folds causing uneven margins which can not usually be rectified in subsequent operations. Exhibit 22.13 outlines a selection of complex folds.

Binding

Automated binding lines allow a fast throughput of bound-together work. Bound copies are produced either in saddlestitched, perfect-bound or thread-sewn form. Additionally reply cards and merchandise samples can be 'tipped on' by a card gluer, a shrink-wrap tunnel can wrap a thin film of protective plastic film around the block of finished copies, and a strapper unit secures string or plastic strapping around the shrink-wrapped bundles to aid handling.

The cheapest and fastest method of binding single sections is saddle-stitching. This is commonly used for magazines and booklets. Thread sewing is mainly used for better quality bookbinding and may also be used for some magazine work. For binding

Exhibit 22.12 Comparison of in- and off-line finishing

Finishing system	Advantages	Disadvantages
In-line	• One process production reduces lead times • Additional time for folding, trimming and personalisation are eliminated, reducing costs • All elements of a mailer can be produced in a single print run in full colour	• Normally only one type and weight of paper can be used on the format • Format restrictions due to inability to create cross-folded formats • Run lengths must be around 100,000 plus to be economically viable
Off-line	• Greater range of features • Better suited for small to medium quantity runs • Each component of a mailer can be produced on a different paper	• Costs can appear high due to the separate operations involved • Complex work can be very time-consuming • Not economical for run lengths above 750,000 copies on certain formats

Exhibit 22.13 Examples of complex folds

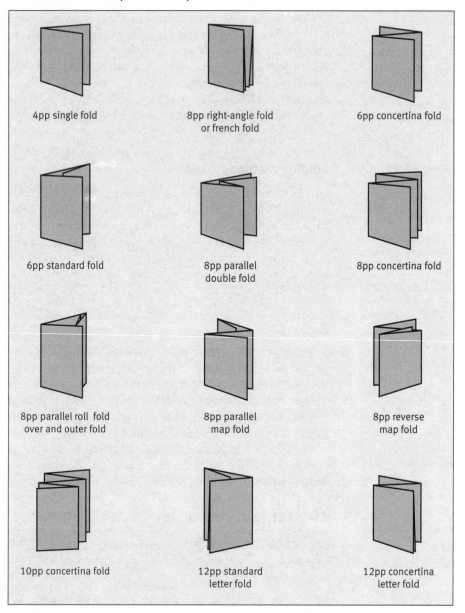

4pp single fold

8pp right-angle fold
or french fold

6pp concertina fold

6pp standard fold

8pp parallel
double fold

8pp concertina fold

8pp parallel roll fold
over and outer fold

8pp parallel
map fold

8pp reverse
map fold

10pp concertina fold

12pp standard
letter fold

12pp concertina
letter fold

Source: Speirs (1992). Reproduced by kind permission of H.M. Speirs, author of Introduction to Printing Technology, BPIF, London.

thick magazines, paperbacks and other bulky work for which saddle-stitching cannot cope and thread sewing is too slow and costly, perfect or adhesive binding is the preferred method. It is a practical method for binding thicker pagination magazines, directories and paperback books where economy is the prime consideration.

IN VIEW 22.4

Using fragrance in the finishing process

Today there are very few fragrances which cannot be bought from stock, ranging from roast chicken to apples and oranges! The fragrance 'slurry', as it is called, is mixed into glue and applied in the normal manner. There are two main methods of releasing the fragrance; scratch and sniff, and fragrance burst. Because the fragrance is contained within tiny spheres in the slurry, scratching or pulling the glue apart breaks the spheres and releases the scent.

Summary

This chapter has outlined the need for the marketer to possess a basic knowledge of the print production process. The planning of production is extremely important for the successful implementation of print media, and the planning process together with the reproduction stages have been detailed.

For the marketer, the production stages in which they will have most input are the brief and the proof. The main types of proofing systems have been outlined and the criteria to evaluate proofs have been discussed. Finally, different printing methods have been introduced, and the related paper, folding and binding issues outlined.

Self-review questions

1   What are the seven key planning stages in a print job?

2   What is digital printing?

3   Outline the five main types of non-colour and colour proofing systems available to a marketer.

4   What are the four factors you need to be aware of when evaluating a proof?

5   Why do you need to use process colours when printing a photograph?

6   What are the five main printing processes?

7   When would in-line finishing be used, and when would off-line finishing be appropriate?

Project

As a Marketing Assistant for a major high street bank, you are putting together a mailshot for a new credit card. Following the planning process in Exhibit 22.2, outline the complete brief for your printers.

References

AGFA (1997), *Chromapress and Intelistream: The Smart Approach to Digital Colour Printing.* Germany: AGFA.

Farrow, P. (1998), Creativity under wraps. *Precision Marketing*, 12 October, 29–30.

Reed, D. (1998), Variety is the spice you can add to your plate. *Precision Marketing*, 22 June, 16–20.

Reuters Business Insight (1998), *Below-the-line Marketing.* London: Reuters.

Speirs, H.M. (1992), *Introduction to Print Technology.* London: British Printing Industries Federation.

Selected further reading

Brewer, R. (1986), *Print Buying.* Newton Abbot: David and Charles.

Chapter 23

Evaluation and control of integrated marketing communications

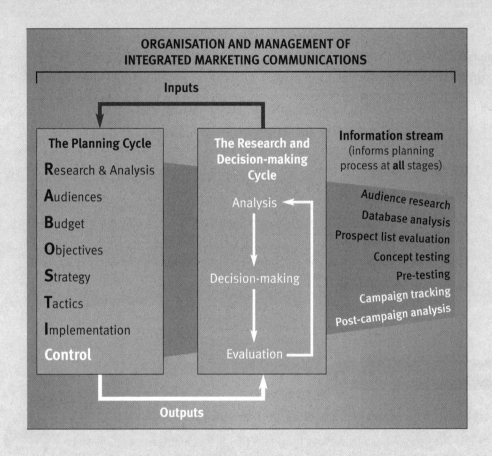

**ORGANISATION AND MANAGEMENT OF
INTEGRATED MARKETING COMMUNICATIONS**

Inputs

The Planning Cycle

Research & Analysis

Audiences

Budget

Objectives

Strategy

Tactics

Implementation

Control

**The Research and
Decision-making
Cycle**

Analysis

Decision-making

Evaluation

Information stream
(informs planning
process at **all** stages)

Audience research

Database analysis

Prospect list evaluation

Concept testing

Pre-testing

Campaign tracking

Post-campaign analysis

Outputs

The IMC RABOSTIC Planning Model

CD

Given the creative strategy adopted by Škoda in the Fabia campaign in Case
Study 2, how important was it to pretest the marketing communications
concepts? What examples of tracking studies can you identify from the case
study material on the CD? At the end of the campaign, what evaluation
measures were used to measure the success of the campaign? How well do
these relate to the original objectives set?

Chapter outline

- Why evaluate the marketing communications campaign?
- Evaluation issues for the marketing communications campaign
- Effectiveness, efficiency and economy
- Evaluation before, during and after the campaign
- Evaluation of specific campaign elements
- Evaluating marketing communications planning process
- Levels of integrated marketing communications
- Continuum of integrated marketing communications
- Dimensions of integrated marketing communications
- Marketing communications 'quality of integration' assessment profile

Objectives

- To identify the benefits of evaluating marketing communications campaigns
- To outline the evaluative issues at each stage of the marketing communications plan
- To present the criteria against which marketing communications campaigns are evaluated and the associated issues
- To review the process of pre-testing, post-testing and tracking marketing communications
- To introduce the concept of 'levels of integrated marketing communications' as a means of understanding the strategic and tactical implications of integration
- To provide an understanding of the various facets of integrated marketing communications and how these may be used to measure the extent integration has been achieved

Professional perspective

Robert Heath UK Group Managing Director, Icon Brand Navigation

Over twenty-five years in advertising have taught me that there are three main problems with marketing communication: 1) it's expensive, 2) it's a nightmare to get right, and 3) it's very hard to tell if it has worked.

Why is this so? Mainly because, unlike the readers of this book, the public at large are not very interested in brands. Consumers quickly discover that what one brand offers today is offered by every brand tomorrow, which means that the rewards resulting from trying to learn which brand is the best are frequently outweighed by the time and effort involved.

So when brands try to communicate with their consumers, they face an uphill task. No-one sits in front of their TV set, paper and pen in hand, waiting for the ad break! Consumers watch or listen to advertising at very low levels of attention, and spend very little time actively 'thinking' about what is being said. Instead they store what they see and hear just as it is received, as sensory associations. Over time, these associations come to define brands in our minds, and act to guide intuitive brand choice. Thus we buy toilet paper because of a Labrador puppy, insurance because of a red telephone, and cigarettes because of cowboys – and some of us even buy airline tickets because of a lilting piece of French operatic music!

This means that when we try to evaluate marketing communication we find ourselves floating in a sea of uncertainty. We find measures such as advertising awareness and recall go up and down, but do not correlate with movements in sales; we find that image grids, designed to enable consumers to tell us how brands compare, consistently overstate or understate the consumer's true opinions, and when we ask consumers to tell us what they will buy next time, we find their predictions differ from their behaviour.

What is the answer? Certainly it is to be wary of relying too heavily on measures such as ad awareness or recall, or questions such as consideration or purchase intention, when evaluating the effectiveness of communication. The true test of the effectiveness of marketing communication is what happens to the brand: if we can show convincingly that it has strengthened the brand, who really cares if anyone has seen it or can recall it?

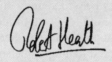

Chapter 16 demonstrated the interface between market research and marketing communications, and examined techniques for data collection and available data sources for understanding markets. This chapter outlines how these data sources can be applied in the evaluation of a marketing communications campaign and through that evaluation, control it.

Why evaluate the marketing communications campaign?

Marketing communications campaign

The performance and integration of all promotional marketing communications activities into a programme designed to achieve interrelated goals.

There are five benefits in evaluating the **marketing communications campaign**. These include:

1 *Improved decision-making* – based on the best available information that can be afforded.
2 *Risk reduction* – based on a greater understanding of the market and intended campaign.
3 *An improved campaign* – based on evaluating as many elements of the marketing communications plan as possible.
4 *Cost savings* – based on better effectiveness and efficiency.
5 *Accumulated wisdom* – based on the idea that learning about one campaign can help you with another.

In practice, it is unlikely that absolutely every aspect of any campaign can be evaluated. There might be constraints of time or money, or even 'political' obstacles inside the company. However, that does not stop it from being a desirable aim, or from it being worth attempting to optimise, as far as possible, the benefits mentioned above.

Also, none of the currently available evaluation procedures can be considered as perfect measures. However, it is far better to acknowledge their imperfections and use them to best effect to gain insight rather than not to evaluate at all. Indeed, the standard marketing communications agency position on this subject is that reliance on evaluation measures should never be to the extent that they replace executive judgement. They should aid it, but not act as a substitute for it.

Evaluation issues for the marketing communications campaign

Evaluating the campaign translates into evaluating different elements of the marketing communications plan. It also includes an eventual, retrospective taking stock of the way in which the marketing communications planning process was handled. In short, evaluation and control can be applied to all elements of the RABOSTIC model that is the basis for Part 2 of this book. To review, the key components include:

1 *Research and analysis* – this is an initial stage, and could involve using any of the data sources outlined in Chapter 16.

2 *Target audience profile* – this is likely to have been identified from sources such segmentation studies (Chapter 17), primary research surveys, TGI data and audit data (e.g. Nielsen). They help to identify dimensions such as brand awareness, patterns of consumption, brand loyalty, attitudes, media habits and psychographic lifestyle categories. These might then be further broken down by geographic factors such as regional analysis, and demographic/socio-economic factors, such as age, gender, income and social class. Prior qualitative research might also have investigated consumer perceptions and motivations, as well as the circumstances surrounding purchase and consumption.

3 *Budget* – it is likely to have been set in the light of information regarding competitor and market analysis, target audiences and company objectives (see Chapter 18). It should be broken down according to the required elements of the communications mix.

4 *Objectives* – specific promotional objectives will have been derived from the business and marketing objectives of the company, as well as from information gained at stages one and two above. These could include increasing brand awareness, increasing sales, increasing market share, building loyalty, reducing dissonance and an almost infinite range of other possibilities. However, they might be constrained by resource limitations, such as time and money. It is crucial to emphasise the importance of setting sound and realistic objectives, aided by the best available market information.

5 *Strategy and tactics* (*communications mix*) – the exact mix of different elements of marketing communications (e.g. advertising, public relations, personal selling, direct marketing, point-of-sale promotion and packaging) will depend on the information available about the product being promoted and its target consumers (stages one and two above). It will also depend on the objectives set, as at stage three above.

6 *Strategy and tactics* (*message/creative theme*) – the message content for directing at target consumers can be evaluated at every stage utilising market research. This can be before (pre-testing), during and after (post-testing) the implementation of the campaign. It might also involve 'tracking', which is the repeating over time of the same survey on identically composed samples. This can tell you on a comparative basis, for example, if marketing communications can be recalled, and if the level of product awareness and usage is increasing. A more detailed description of all these applications appears later in this chapter.

National Readership Survey (NRS)

Provides information about the readership of the main newspapers and magazines. A report is produced every six months covering a period of 12 months. The survey samples around 37,500 people, and uses computer-assisted personal interviewing methodology.

7 *Strategy and tactics (media)* – the choice of which media to utilise will also depend on the objectives set. However, it should be noted that prior evaluation is very likely to be guided, where appropriate, by data from such services as the **National Readership Survey** (NRS) and the **BARB** panel for TV audience ratings. These and other sources of media evaluation data were described in Chapter 16. Possible media include commercial TV, newspapers, periodicals, posters, cinema, commercial radio, the clothing worn by famous sporting personalities and even supermarket shopping trolleys! Such is the ingenuity of those involved, that new twists resulting in minor media opportunities are still occurring. The Internet must now also be increasingly considered as a serious contender in this context.

8 *Evaluation and control* – is an acknowledged part of the marketing communications planning process. As already indicated above, evaluation should be built into every stage of the plan, as well as reviewing the effectiveness and efficiency of the planning process retrospectively for any given campaign.

Effectiveness, efficiency and economy

BARB

Broadcasters' Audience Research Board. This body, established in 1980 and jointly owned by the BBC and ITV, is responsible for producing information on TV viewing activity and audience reaction. Electronic meters and diaries from over 4400 nationally representative households are used to record the information.

Each element within the marketing communications mix can be evaluated in terms of:

- Efficiency: doing things right
- Effectiveness: doing the right things
- Economy: doing things within a specified budget.

It is important to note that the marketing communications campaign should always be evaluated against the set of objectives set for it (Robinson et al. 1968). Typically, such objectives will require measures in three broad areas: media evaluation, message content (or communications effect), and sales effect. Media measurement has already been discussed in Chapter 16. However, there are a number of issues associated with evaluating message content and sales effect that can now be addressed. These are detailed overleaf.

Hierarchy of effects models and marketing communication evaluation

The apparent connection between message content and sales effect is often portrayed in the marketing communications literature as a number of linear, sequential models. These have been accused of being simplistic insofar as they assume relatively straightforward cause and effect. The consumer is seen as a sort of reactive sponge, without the capacity for being interactive or pro-active. It tends to appeal, though, to those of a pragmatic turn of mind, who might prefer conveniently to ignore possible difficulties in the quest for apparently rational explanations.

AIDA model

Marketing communications concept that models the stages through which marketing communications should move a potential customer: Awareness, Interest, Desire and Action. It is one of a number of hierarchy-of-effects models.

The **AIDA model** (Attention–Interest–Desire–Action), one of the hierarchy of effects models detailed in Chapter 4, is an example of this type of approach. It assumes that all consumers can be persuaded equally in what amounts to an almost automatic series of steps towards product purchase. This concept forms part of the marketing communications process model. Indeed, it is placed alongside another such linear model that is more sophisticated (Exposure – Reception – Cognitive Response – Attitude – Intention – Behaviour). However, you should also note that neither of these models stands alone, and both are placed in the context of a much more complex model that allows for the possibility of the consumer being proactive as well as reactive.

Attitude

A consistent, cognitive, affective or conative response to some form of internal or external stimulus.

The theory underpinning hierarchy of effects models is borrowed from the psychology of **attitudes**. Classically, attitudes are thought to have three components: the cognitive, affective and conative components. The cognitive component is that part of an attitude that can be approached on a rational level with information and persuasion. The affective component, on the other hand, is supposed to work on an emotional rather than a rational level. Some marketing communications attempt to appeal to one or other of these components, and some try and appeal to both simultaneously. The conative component is that relating to action and behaviour subsequent to or dependent upon the other two components. The theory is that if either or both of the cognitive and affective components can be influenced, then so can behaviour. However, different attitudes within a given individual might be held with differing levels of intensity. It also may not be necessary for attitude change to occur in an individual for behaviour to be influenced. If all or any of that is the case, then attitudes might be considerably more complex than classical theory suggests.

Evaluating sales effects

Sales effect is often sought in the evaluation of marketing communications. It is, however, extremely problematic to link a given unit of promotion with a given unit of sales, except in cases such as direct marketing communications (Chapter 27). Other exceptions include some sales promotion activities such as the sales of a product in a specific store before, during and after a period of in-store promotion for that product (all other variables remaining approximately the same). Sometimes surrogate measures such as intention to purchase are used instead of sales but there are many who criticise the validity of such measures. There are four key reasons why it is difficult to capture sales effects:

1 *The collective effect of variables in the marketing environment* – in the broadest possible scenario, all the variables in the marketing environment will have an effect on any receiver of marketing communications (in addition to the effect of the actual marketing communication). Such influences are potentially almost infinite in number, and will affect different individuals in different combinations, at different times and in different ways. They might include factors relating to the sender's

4Ps

Way of classifying the marketing mix into four categories: Product, Price, Promotion and Place.

product itself (i.e. the **4Ps** – especially price). They might also include factors relating to the general, external marketing environment, such as market trends, competitor activity, prevailing economic and social climates, technological innovation and regional and national laws and regulations. Indeed, these are all the variables that can be seen portrayed in almost any model of the consumer decision-making process.

2 *The uniqueness of individuals* – individual consumers/receivers of marketing communications constitute their own unique variables. They have their own unique personalities, their own unique value systems, their own unique sets of attitudes and their own unique collections of life experiences that will influence their decision-making process (Chapter 4).

3 *Lagged variables* – there is a time lag between the production of goods and the occurrence of retail sales. Thus, a batch of goods produced at the same factory at the same time will not all be sold at the retail level together. Depending on where they go and who buys them, they will all be sold on different occasions. This means that under no circumstances should production figures be used as an estimate of retail sales. They are entirely different entities.

It also follows that because goods produced together are most unlikely to be retailed together, any given unit of promotion (e.g. one exposure to a TV advertisement) cannot be identified as responsible for the retail sale of any particular unit of product. The item sold could have been in stock in the retail outlet for, say, one year, while the current promotion might have been running for only one month. It is also inevitable that the more intermediaries there are in a marketing channel (e.g. distributors, wholesalers, etc.), the longer is the minimum possible time lag before the product is retailed.

Another highly specific example of a time-lagged variable is the uptake of new technology. Some customers will purchase such a product (e.g. hand-held computers) much more quickly than others. They might be labelled as 'innovators' or 'early adopters' in marketing terminology, but, either way, they buy the product sooner rather than later. In some product areas (e.g. mobile telephones), certain customers might not buy until years after the first promotion has taken place. Then, they might be the so-called 'late majority', or even the 'laggards'. Who can say whether it was a specific exposure to one advertisement, a special offer or even a piece of free publicity that finally made the difference for any of these mobile 'phone purchasers? Put simply, there can be time delays (lagged effects) between marketing communications and subsequent purchase. This makes it difficult to confirm the direct relationship between cause (marketing communications) and effect (sales).

4 *Cumulative effects* – another point that should be noted relates to cumulative effects. Consider first the instance of a major consumer product being advertised on TV, such as canned beer. Though some viewers will see that TV commercial more times than others, most will probably see it several times at least. The point is that the more times a given individual sees that advertisement, the more likely it is that the advertisement and its message content will be recalled (though decreasing marginal returns tend to operate – implying some sort of optimum level of exposure for each individual). In other words, multiple exposures to a given promotional message almost certainly have some sort of cumulative effect. This, of course, will vary from individual to individual for any particular amount of exposure.

As a further consideration, if the product has also been promoted previously (i.e. it is not a new product), then there should also be some residual, cumulative effect from all past promotions (long-term effect). If the residual, cumulative effects of exposure to all promotion from all products of the same type (i.e. competitor activity, past and present) are also taken into account, then quite a complex picture begins to emerge. Add to that, for any given individual, the accumulated experience of all past and present purchases of all other types of goods during the whole of that person's life so far, and the picture is now complete. This is the background of cumulative effects against which (consciously or unconsciously) all current purchases are considered.

That, however, is not quite the whole story, as it is reasonable to suppose that the cumulative effects mentioned are also subject to progressive decay. That means that the effects of the earliest purchase experiences gradually wear off, followed progressively by all the rest. However, it is also reasonable to think of a customer's lifetime of purchases as a learning curve, with the lessons learned having a permanently modifying effect on purchase behaviour. In effect, this works as a feedback loop into all current purchases.

Other issues in capturing sales effects

There are other caveats for those seeking an increase in sales volume and value through marketing communications. For instance, the product's stage in its life cycle will have a significant impact. Many campaigns are for products that already show a downward trend in sales. In this case, even the best possible campaign may only slow the decline rather than reverse it. However, that is not to say that the marketing communications are not doing a good job.

Similarly, products in the mature stage of their life cycle might be profitably stable but show no growth. Yet it would never be suggested that such products should not be promoted. Indeed, not to promote a product would simply invite annihilation from competitors.

As regards a possible breakthrough in the area of measuring sales effect, computer modelling and single source, multi-task data perhaps offer the best hope. The former is intended to cope with multi-factorial situations, and the latter can combine TV viewing data (for the same respondents) with regularly recorded product purchases using home-based bar-code scanners. Even so, both these approaches are not beyond criticism. For instance, there is a definite limit to the number of variables that can be utilised in a practical computer model. That will cause it to fall short of a complete representation of real life, though key variables can be identified first using other techniques, such as AID (automatic interaction detection). As regards the respondents who participate in purchasing panels of any sort, the main concern is that they are likely to be self-selecting (in the sense that they want or agree to take part in the research) and therefore possibly atypical. Furthermore, 'multi-tasking', as it is called, is frowned upon in some quarters as being a dubious practice and a questionable methodology.

Evaluation before, during and after the campaign

The areas of media evaluation and consumer research that establishes attitudes, lifestyle and the subsequent segmentation of target consumers have both been discussed in Chapter 16. This section relates specifically to evaluating the message content of the campaign. This process might involve evaluation before (pre-testing), during and after the campaign has been launched (post-testing). Where multiple measures are taken over a period of time throughout the duration of a campaign, this is called 'tracking' and is discussed later.

Pre-testing

Pre-testing

Evaluation of marketing communications elements before their use at the start of a campaign.

This is sometimes referred to as 'copy testing', though this term seems unnecessarily limiting. The objectives of **pre-testing** include:

1 To evaluate if the message conveyed by the marketing communication in question is being perceived by target consumers as intended by those responsible for it. This can be in terms of the visual imagery, the copy and both together.
2 To provide information that will assist those responsible for such a marketing communication in achieving the optimum combination of visual imagery and copy for that product at a point in time.
3 By so doing, to reduce the risk of failure (sub-optimal combinations of the above), and the consequent waste of resources (e.g. time and money, especially).

Even when it has been stated that the point of pre-testing is to evaluate what is proposed, and thereby avoid mistakes, there are still quite a number of considerations. For instance, much pre-testing relates to advertising material, which might or might not be co-ordinated (themed) with other types of promotion (e.g. a poster site, a brochure for company representatives to leave with customers). Indeed, advertising material itself broadly divides into print advertisements and TV commercials. That is the familiar face of pre-testing, and one that will be expounded upon shortly. However, it should also be pointed out that a considerable amount of pre-testing is product related, as distinct from advertising related.

Concept testing, as it is called, frequently relates to new product development, and broadly defines the characteristics of the product at a point in time. At an early stage, it could be no more than a written description on half a side of A4. This might be submitted to a series of focus groups for consideration, which would be an appropriate, investigative methodology for such a situation (Chapter 16). Subsequently, the product concept would be refined and developed further, and could be re-tested on several occasions prior to launch. Then, price, product name and a possible pack might also be shown to respondents. Of course, in the case of new products, advertising themes are quite likely to have evolved originally from such work, and the advertising concept testing then dovetails in with other aspects of product development, to appear as one continuous process.

Looking at advertisement pre-testing in particular, this can be, of course, for a new or an existing product. Either way, some form of stimulus material illustrating the main idea of the advertisement is absolutely necessary for testing purposes. For print advertisements, such items of artwork are known as 'concepts', or sometimes 'roughs' or **'scamps'**. At this stage, there is simply no point in spending the money on producing a finished advertisement that might be only one of several possible ideas, and might also be radically changed or rejected after pre-testing. However, respondents have to be warned by the researcher not to judge the stage or even the standard of the artwork, but only the ideas portrayed in it.

The same point applies equally to stimulus material produced to represent TV advertisements. Unlike a print advertisement, movement is involved, and so a **storyboard** is produced (see In View 23.1 and Plate 16). Rather like the frames on the pages of a comic book, a series of still illustrations conveys the intended sequence of events and main characters. Each frame also has the appropriate piece of the proposed dialogue under it, so that this can also be considered. Alternatively, a series of still photographs known as **photomatics** could be used. This appears to give greater realism, but might in fact be more likely to mislead respondents as a result. Yet another alternative is a relatively cheaply produced animated sound cartoon, known as **animatics**. This time, realism is sacrificed to convey movement. So, there are a number of options, but the same principle applies about only judging the content and not the presentation.

Pre-testing marketing communications using qualitative research is very widespread, especially in the UK. There are a number of alternatives, which will be examined shortly. However, qualitative techniques (see Chapter 16) offer the capability and flexibility needed to investigate thoroughly all possible nuances of, say, an advertising concept. They also allow respondents to develop their own themes spontaneously, which can be very valuable. Group discussions (focus groups) are used most frequently, though depth interviews might be more productive with some types of hard to access respondents (e.g. managers in industry).

One of the criteria to be assessed is whether or not an advertising concept (or other item of marketing communications) has 'standout'. This term can broadly be

Scamps

Drafts or 'roughs' of creative ideas that are produced cheaply to be used for pre-testing and evaluation purposes.

Storyboard

Visual display of selected drawings illustrating the sequence of a TV, video or cinema commercial. Indications of sound and voice-over are also given.

Photomatics

Storyboard making use of still photographs rather than drawings.

Animatics

Animated version of the storyboard.

IN VIEW 23.1

Example of a storyboard

Volkswagon Polo 'Protection' 60 sec.

Music throughout.

Source: from Volkswagen Polo '*Protection*' *60 Sec*. story board reproduced by kind permission of DDB London

interpreted as meaning 'impact', though the implication is that this should have some positive effect on brand awareness. A linked issue is how many times respondents should be exposed to the stimulus material in the pretest situation in order to facilitate such an assessment. In real life, consumers probably see an advertisement at least several times, in an unrestricted manner. This is not possible in the test situation for obvious reasons. It is possible, though, to show a print advertisement concept in a focus group briefly to start with, cover it up during initial reactions, and then reveal it again for more prolonged viewing and debate. A moving stimulus for a TV commercial, such as animatics, could also be shown more than once.

It is not really reasonable to talk of the 'validity' of qualitative techniques, as is sometimes done. By definition, they do not attempt to measure anything except in broad, relative terms, and so they deliberately use small samples. Validity, or accuracy of data, is understandably a concern with quantitative research techniques. Yet qualitative techniques such as focus groups still rely wholly for their predictive power on the perceptions and experiences of a relatively small number of consumers to generate findings. This surely places a great deal of importance on the recruiting of genuine target consumers for such procedures. Of course, any prior segmentation studies should be helpful here.

Exhibit 23.1 Criteria for evaluating marketing communications concepts qualitatively

Criteria	Comments
Spontaneous reactions on first sight	A most useful indicator
Impact, or 'standout'	This can be negative as well as positive for a product
Main features	How appropriate and credible were the images, the characters portrayed, the storyline?
Visual impression	Was it pleasing aesthetically, and what about the colours?
Headlines, captions and other copy	Are they telling the same story as the visual images, and does it all gel as a cohesive whole?
Juxtaposition and relative importance of key elements	For example, company logo, brand name, pack shot etc. Is the branding strong enough, and does it add to brand identity (salience)?
Intended message	Important to check with respondents what they think the intended message is supposed to be. Advertisers could be in for a shock!
Ultimate preference (if appropriate), and any improvements	One of the great virtues of qualitative pre-testing is that respondents can be very helpful and constructive in making suggestions for amending or improving test material

The same, of course, is equally true of a number of other techniques that can be used to pretest marketing communications using small samples. These physiological techniques are not widely used but are of interest:

1 *The eye movement camera* – this is a technique for evaluating print advertisements, with one respondent at a time. The respondent is seated in the apparatus, and allowed only limited movement. The advertisement appears on a screen directly in front of the respondent's face, and the camera tracks the path of the eye over the

surface of the advertisement. The start point is noted, pauses on particular features are timed, and return visits to parts of the advertisement are counted. In theory, this process should be quite illuminating, but therein also lies the main problem, which is interpreting what it all means! For instance, does a relatively long pause on a particular feature or several return visits imply that the feature has interest, or does it just mean the respondent is struggling to comprehend it?

A short depth interview normally takes place after the exposure of each respondent to the stimulus material, but this is often too superficial to be much help. The results tend to be interpreted in terms of high or low impact, but as even high impact could actually be negative for the product in some instances, this might be quite misleading. Aggregating the results across even a small sample is also not easy, and so reliance on this as the only means of pre-testing could be dangerous.

2 *The tachistoscope* – this is a simpler device than the eye movement camera, and is based on a photographic slide projector. The speed of presentation and lighting conditions can be varied, which might be of particular relevance to poster sites. It relies on the respondent to note their recognition of various components of the stimulus material, and does seem to be helpful in assessing the rate at which an advertisement (print/static) conveys information.

3 *The psychogalvanometer* – this measures galvanic skin response, which is the electricity generated by chemical changes on the skin. A respondent is wired up to the machine, and then shown marketing communications in the form of stimulus material. There is no doubt that the device measures changes in the level of emotional arousal, but whether this is a positive or negative outcome in any specific instance would appear to be completely open to interpretation.

4 *The pupilometer* – this, too, can be used for TV commercials as well as print advertisements, and measures the extent to which the pupils in the eyes of the respondent dilate in response. Greater dilation is always interpreted as positive for the stimulus material.

5 *Voice-pitch analysis (VOPAN)* – this measures the extent to which a respondent's voice pitch differs from its own norm when viewing stimulus material. Here, the assumption is not made automatically that a higher voice pitch is positive for the product. That particular problem is solved by asking the respondent how they feel about the advertisement, and by making the assumption that this answer is always truthful and accurate. If there is both raised voice pitch and positive comment, then the reaction is taken to be favourable.

All of the above techniques have been befriended by certain agencies at various times, and advocated as being worthy of attention. However, a criticism of them is that they take place in a laboratory setting rather than as part of real life. By definition, therefore, they lack realism, and respondents are aware of the nature and purpose of the exercise. The same could also be said of pre-testing in focus groups and depth interviews. At least, though, they are more informal and conversational, and do not normally involve any strange equipment (unless video-recorded).

There is also one main quantitative approach to pre-testing. This approach is called a 'folder test' (portfolio test in the USA). It is not very widely used, though, as it requires just one virtually finished print advertisement. That, of course, would be more or less self-defeating in terms of the rationale for pre-testing as previously described. However, the test advertisement is placed in among carefully chosen others, either in some sort of folder, or as a mock-up magazine. It works by evaluating recognition and recall of the stimulus material after an appropriate viewing opportunity.

For pre-testing, this approach stands the danger of being somewhat superficial. However, it is more commonly used for post-testing, and so will be commented upon further in that context.

It is fair to state that quantitative approaches to pre-testing are more popular and have more credence in the USA than in Europe. Portfolio tests are used, and so is an approach called the 'consumer jury'. The latter involves about a hundred respondents giving their views on stimulus material using rating scales. Results from a consumer jury have been used with good effect by Škoda in their attempt to reposition their cars. Other quantitative approaches include inquiry tests and on-the-air tests. The former relates only to real-life print media, and counts the number of coupons returned for different versions of the advertisement. Different versions of the same advertisement in the same issue, but not in the same copy of the publication, are known as a 'split run'. On-the-air tests relate to radio and TV commercials, and again offer a real-life opportunity to evaluate different versions. Others, such as theatre tests and trailer tests, concentrate on the likely effect of the proposed advertising on product preference, and are akin to simulated test marketing. Some of these are undoubtedly applicable to the USA mainly on account of its large geographical size. Even so, it is worth mentioning that qualitative focus groups are still widely used in the USA for promotional pre-testing purposes.

Post-testing

Post-testing

The evaluation of marketing communications at the end of a campaign.

Having looked at pre-testing in some detail, it is necessary also to look at what sort of evaluation might be carried out after the campaign has been implemented. In the overall scheme of things, it is probably reasonable to suggest that **post-testing** is for many companies a lesser priority than pre-testing. Expenditure on the latter makes obvious sense, both in terms of 'getting it right' and as a form of insurance. However, once the money has been spent and the campaign launched, there are companies who in effect take a fatalistic view on the outcome. In so doing, they save a few pounds but deny themselves useful information.

In terms of what can be done, there are two areas that have already been covered in sufficient detail. One is media evaluation (Chapter 16 and Chapter 21), and the other is seeking to measure some sort of sales effect (earlier this chapter). While a definitive measure of the latter remains elusive, the media chosen for the campaign can be further evaluated at this stage for cost-effectiveness and audience reached.

Looking at other areas for post-testing, there are two that generally provide helpful feedback. The first of these is the message content and design of the marketing communication itself, and the second is the effect of that marketing communication on awareness, attitudes, purchase intention, claimed purchase behaviour and the like. Unlike pre-testing, the emphasis is not now on qualitative investigation, but on gathering hard evidence of performance on a quantitative basis (i.e. results in terms of survey based percentage figures, and not just illustrative quotes). Of course, it is possible to carry out qualitative post-testing, but it is less usual for the reasons stated.

Recognition

Evaluation of message content on the basis of an awareness of the marketing communication.

Recall

Evaluation of message content on the basis of aided (prompted) or unaided (unprompted) recollection of the stimulus material.

Message content and design

Concentrating firstly on message content and design, this is evaluated mostly on the basis of '**recognition**' and '**recall**' (Krugman 1985; Higie and Sewall 1991). As a term, 'recognition' equates with a basic awareness of the marketing communication on the part of the respondent. 'Recall' can be unaided or aided, and investigates the extent to which the respondent has a recollection of the stimulus material. With 'unaided recall', the respondent is initially not prompted or influenced in any way, and is asked only what advertisements they have seen recently, or maybe advertisements for a certain product category. If the advertiser's product is mentioned spontaneously, then the rest of the interview proceeds. If not, then 'aided recall' is resorted to by jogging the respondent's memory with the product name. Clearly, this all has to be carried out in the right sequence to avoid biasing the respondent. The underlying assumption here is that measuring recognition and/or recall can help predict brand purchase.

A number of agencies offer services based on these measures. The folder test is used for print advertisements, usually with a part of the interview taking place prior to looking at the stimulus material. This might be set in the context of a hall test or an in-home interview (Chapter 16). Other types of marketing communications (e.g. TV and radio commercials, and promotional literature) can also be evaluated in these settings and on the criteria above. Even telephone interviews can be used in certain circumstances, though any stimulus material must, of course, be sent in advance.

In the USA, there are a number of services that are worthy of note. For instance, the Starch Readership Service was developed by Daniel Starch in 1992, and looks only at recognition. Approximately 30,000 advertisements per year are surveyed in nearly 1000 publications using a non-random sample (see sampling in previous chapter), and so a good database exists for establishing so-called 'ad-norms'. With the magazine open, the respondent is asked to say whether he or she 'noted it', 'associated it with the brand', 'read-some' or 'read-most'. This allows useful comparisons to be made between advertisements. However, it also has been criticised for relying totally on claims made by respondents couched only in these terms. It would seem unlikely that views expressed in this way would always be completely accurate and truthful.

In contrast, the Bruzzone test in the USA (Bruzzone Research Company) tests consumer recognition of TV commercials by mailing a questionnaire that incorporates an especially prepared photographic storyboard to a true random sample of consumers. They are directed through the questionnaire by a series of instructions, and the results are again compared with established norms. Another test of TV commercials in the USA is the Burke Day-After Recall test (DAR). Telephone interviews (non-random) are conducted with a sample of 150 consumers, and recall is investigated once recognition has been established for that advertisement. However, this too has evoked criticism, on the grounds that it tests whether or not an advertisement has been received, but not whether its message has been accepted. Also, the whole area of recall is controversial, due to the decay that occurs naturally as time elapses after viewing an advertisement. Similar tests are conducted in other countries with many different research agencies offering their own specific services on a national or international basis.

Other areas for testing include those of attitudes, purchase intention, claimed purchase behaviour and related issues. These are frequently carried out by quantitative surveys using relatively large samples. U&A (usage and attitude) surveys fall into this category. A large sample is required because of the need to break the sample down quite extensively when analysing the results by different variables (e.g. age, income, product usage, etc.).

Such large-scale work is, of course, relatively costly and not all situations warrant such a dedicated expenditure. However, where the information requirement is simpler or less extensive, it is worth remembering the omnibus survey (Chapter 16). This can reach a relatively large sample most cost-effectively, and will solve this problem particularly for smaller companies, smaller sales and smaller enquiries generally.

Before leaving the subject, a few words need to be written about experimental designs in relation to quantitative post-testing. It was stated in Chapter 16 that because marketing problems tend to be multi-factorial, they do not lend themselves to true, controlled experiments (in the sense of the scientific method), and this is true. However, some researchers use what amounts to a quasi-experimental design for promotional post-testing. The term 'quasi-experimental' is used because the intervening variables in the test environment (other influences) cannot be rigorously and satisfactorily excluded, as would be the case in a true, controlled experiment.

In the 'before-and-after with control group' design this problem is addressed to some extent. There are two groups of respondents; the experimental group and a control group. The experimental group receives pre-measurement, exposure to the stimulus material (the marketing communications) and post-measurement on such issues as attitudes, preferences and intention to purchase. The control group receives only pre-measurement and post-measurement, but no exposure to the stimulus material.

Changes that would have occurred anyway, without exposure to the stimulus material, should be detected as a difference between the pre- and post-measurements in the control group. This is subtracted from that noted in the experimental group, with the net change supposedly being attributable to exposure to the stimulus material. A relatively large sample is necessary to gauge the crucial difference accurately in the control group, and even then, the act of pre-measurement can bias post-measurement with the same respondents.

A four-group version of this design tries to overcome this problem, but that too is fraught with yet more methodological difficulties, as well as escalating cost. It is difficult not to conclude that, realistically, there is little to be gained from such attempts over other methods already described.

Tracking studies

Tracking studies

The evaluation of marketing communications at various stages during their use. In this way, effects may be monitored throughout a campaign and modifications to the marketing communications plan introduced if necessary.

The concept of a **tracking study** is that it is not a 'one-off' at a point in time, but a repeat of a survey carried out previously. The more times it is repeated before, during and after the campaign is implemented, the more reference points will be obtained for purposes of comparison. As the key objective is to assess change as the campaign proceeds, more rather than fewer reference points can be useful. In terms of research design, this automatically means that all tracking studies are, by definition, of longitudinal design.

Very often, tracking studies concentrate on measures of brand awareness and image, recognition, recall and possibly impact, purchase intention and repeat purchase. Consequently, they can help minimise the risk of continuing to buy airtime for an advertisement that is failing to meet its objectives. However, a long-term view can also be taken, with tracking used to follow a product not just through a specific campaign, but all through its life cycle. Not too surprising, then, that tracking data is increasingly being used as input for computer modelling of the 'what if?' variety.

That apart, it is not the chosen criteria for measurement, or indeed the type of marketing communication being tested that are of most importance. Indeed, any of the quantitative approaches and techniques already described can be used. What is ultimately essential is that each time the survey is repeated, exactly the same questionnaire and stimulus material should be used, and it should always be with identically composed samples from the same population if the tracking is to be reliable (but in practice this is not always the case). The actual respondents do not have to be the same each time, as that in itself would raise methodological problems. They should, however, be chosen from one occasion to the next using exactly the same recruitment criteria (age, gender, social class, product usage, etc.). It follows from what has gone before that a tracking study can comprise a series of identical ad hoc surveys on behalf of a single client. Just as in post-testing (which is incorporated into the process of tracking), this can be expensive and even unnecessary. Consequently, omnibus surveys can again be used for the purpose as a cost-effective solution. Alternatively, a number of agencies offer various specialised tracking facilities. For instance, the agency BJM Research, part of the MBL group, provides advertising tracking services designed to meet the needs of individual clients. In contrast, NOP run TABS (Tracking Advertisement and Brand Strength), and over 2000 campaigns have been tracked since it commenced. A self-completion questionnaire is used, and normative data has been established. Different yet again is the more recent Scan*Pro range of services from Nielsen, which utilises the Scantrack and Homescan databases, and allows sales and promotions to be tracked over time.

Evaluation of specific campaign elements

While acknowledging the desirability of attempting to evaluate the whole campaign comprehensively, as mentioned earlier in this chapter, in fact this is not the norm. There might be all or any of a number of reasons for this situation. For instance, constraints of time and or finance might make it impossible or impractical to test all the components of a campaign in this way. For instance, pre-testing procedures, however reasonable and sensible, might be cut short by the need to meet deadlines in relation to pre-booked media scheduling commitments. Alternatively, the client company with the product might be convinced of the usefulness of pre-testing, but might be less inclined to spend yet more on post-testing.

Of course, this could also be at least partly because products differ markedly, and will not all have the same requirements. There is a massive difference between, for instance, a well-known brand of fast-moving consumer goods (e.g. a popular music CD) and a specialised business-to-business product in a niche market (e.g. a high-reach forklift truck for use in warehouses). The actual number of different types of promotion utilised for the former is likely to be greater than for the latter, and the need for them all to be evaluated and co-ordinated might also be greater. New products, of course, might require a greater concentration of resources in terms of evaluation prior to launch than existing products part-way through the product life cycle. Even then, a relaunch or repositioning exercise might necessitate great promotional expenditure on an existing product. Yet another important but fairly obvious difference in this context is between major products that are market leaders in valuable markets, and small, insignificant products that just do not justify much promotional expenditure in absolute terms.

So, all that explains some basic reasons why products might differ markedly in their campaign evaluation needs. In a sense, this is where well-intentioned generalisations cease to have relevance, as every real-life situation has to be examined on its own merits. That being the case, it probably does not matter that not all campaigns are evaluated in their entirety. Optimum evaluation requirements have to be matched with available resources.

So, for one product, a full programme of marketing research, covering qualitative pre-testing and quantitative post-testing and tracking studies, might be appropriate. For another product, though, the fact that the print advertisement is pretested in focus groups but not the direct mailing, might also be the optimum solution. Returning briefly to 'well-intentioned generalisations', it has to be said, however, that evaluating more rather than fewer elements in the communications mix is likely to be helpful as an aid to decision-making.

Evaluating the marketing communications planning process

This relates to the final part of the marketing communications plan outlined earlier in the chapter: control and evaluation. It comes right at the end, when all other parts of it have already been executed. What, then, is there left to evaluate? Well, for a start, it would be necessary to raise a question mark about the effectiveness of each of the stages of the plan itself. For instance, were the most appropriate objectives chosen? What expectations existed about how the elements of the promotions mix were expected to work? Were there enough measures used to evaluate the campaign, and were they the most appropriate and illuminating that could be obtained? What is being discussed here is a retrospective look at how the marketing communications planning process was actually applied in a particular circumstance. To have value, this should be a very practical exercise, and not at all theoretical or generalised.

Significantly, all the preceding discussion has covered evaluation of various aspects of marketing communications, now we need to turn our attention to the evaluation of the integration of marketing communications. The following sections of this chapter will address the different levels of IMC, a continuum of IMC and the dimensions of IMC in order to gain an appreciation of the issues involved. Using these concepts, the final section of the chapter will introduce a profile for assessing the quality of IMC.

Levels of integrated marketing communications

While it is argued that marketing communications should be integrated, the extent of integration can vary enormously. Marketing communications activities can vary from very small, 'one-off', discrete pieces of promotion (such as the mailing of an invitation to attend the opening of a new art gallery), to the development of a larger campaign which involves many promotional tools, and even to the development and co-ordination of multiple campaigns intended to achieve a greater goal possibly over an extended time period in many countries.

NEED TO KNOW

☑ *Levels of integration: The integration of marketing communications exists on multiple levels. These levels carry with them implications for both strategic and tactical decisions and executions.*

The need for integration and the scale of that integration becomes greater as the size and number of campaigns increase. It is necessary to determine just how important it is that all messages and images should be consistent or whether they can remain completely detached and, if so, what is the impact that this is likely to have on total effort. A military analogy may be drawn to help appreciate the concept. Military analogies are often used in marketing and business and even some of our terminology has been stolen from military application; 'strategy' and 'tactics', for example. In this instance, we can describe three levels of integration by reference to war, battles (campaigns) and skirmishes (Exhibit 23.2).

- *Level 1 – Skirmishes:* These are minor, short-lived military encounters of a more tactical nature. As individual activities they require little co-ordination and effort.
- *Level 2 – Battles or campaigns:* These involve many skirmishes that require a higher level of co-ordination and control to gain a more favourable outcome. They are both tactical and strategic in nature.
- *Level 3 – War:* A war involves many battles and is the most strategic level of engagement.

To achieve the objectives of the 'war', the management process as a whole is involved from the development of broadscale strategy (level 3) which maintains an overview of

IN VIEW 23.2

'More from the Mediterranean.' Integrating marketing communications at the Tunisian Tourist Board

The brief

A growing holiday destination in the 1980s, Tunisia has more recently found itself suffering from outdated perceptions and declining interest among UK tourists. Despite a fast-developing infrastructure, research in 1997 showed that people believed it to be a long-haul destination with poor hotels and little more than a few camels for entertainment. The Tunisian Tourist Board brought in Dynamo Promotional Marketing to update its image and drive up bookings.

The campaign

Dynamo simultaneously strove to create a new image for the country while convincing travel agents in the UK and Ireland that it was a competitive destination. The agency redesigned the Tunisian tourist logo and developed a new range of literature to convey a more modern feel than previous brochures. Dynamo devised the endline 'More from the Mediterranean' to reinforce the message that Tunisia is as close as many popular Mediterranean resorts. To bring the trade on board, the agency briefed operators on the campaign and ran a series of initiatives to stimulate interest. Its climax was sponsorship of the film premiere of 1997's blockbuster *The English Patient* which was filmed in Tunisia. To target consumers, Dynamo leafleted cinemas and ran a PR programme to highlight the appeal of Tunisia and its culture. In 1998, Dynamo created Tunisia's first TV advertising for a decade. Selected press and poster advertising was underpinned by a new Web site.

The result

The Tunisian Tourist Board was voted the best in the UK by travel agents in *Travel Weekly's* annual awards. The board's recent figures show bookings to Tunisia from the UK and Ireland up almost 30% year on year.

Source: *Marketing* (10 September 1998, p. 5)

all resources and their deployment, to the implementation of day-to-day operations (level 1) which can be planned to achieve greatest collective benefit (level 2). Skirmishes are managed to win the battle. Battles are managed to win the war. In the military, organisationally, personnel are managed in rigid hierarchical structures to facilitate the effective achievement of all three levels of integration and engagement. In commercial operations, such strict organisational structures do not exist. Managing integration, therefore, becomes very difficult. Chapter 14 addressed some of the organisational implications of integrated marketing communications.

Unless marketing communications are seen at the level 3, strategic 'war' level, then it is likely that many of the benefits of integration will be missed. Level 2 campaigns are often run in isolation from each other, but worse still, if level 1 skirmishes are always implemented as isolated incidents (e.g. if the promotional mix tools are not even integrated and consolidated into concerted action), it would be as if individual soldiers are not told what to do or how they should work together. Achievement of

Exhibit 23.2 Three levels of integration

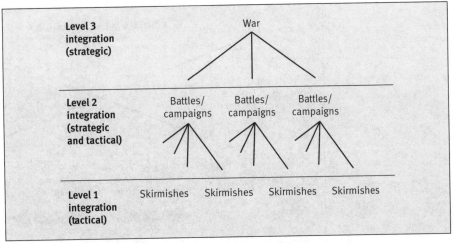

level 3 integration of marketing communications requires involvement of client and agency employees at all levels of the business from chief and senior executives to junior managers and non-management members of the workforce.

Is it possible to achieve integration without all three levels of integration? The answer is yes! And in practice this is what happens – to some extent. Some degree of integration is better than none. In many respects, much of the current interest in the benefits of integrated marketing communications has resulted in emphasis being placed at levels 1 and 2 so that at least campaigns become better co-ordinated with a greater interweaving of the elements of the promotional mix. The challenge for the future will be the development of marketing communications seen from its greatest strategic advantage.

Continuum of integrated marketing communications

Continuum of integrated marketing communications

This is a concept that emphasises that integration of marketing communications occurs to different degrees, and that greater benefits accrue from greater integration. The continuum also emphasises that separation between marketing communications elements can give rise to negative consequences.

Synergy

The effect of bringing together marketing communication elements in a mutually supportive and enhancing way so that the resulting whole is greater than the sum of its parts.

Exhibit 23.3 illustrates the value to be gained by integrating marketing communications activities. It is referred to as a '**continuum**' because it is rarely the case that such activities are either fully integrated or not. Rather, they are developed with varying degrees of integration at whatever level of integration or combination of levels. On the right-hand side of the exhibit, as a greater degree of integration is achieved, more positive benefits result. On the left-hand side of the exhibit, the opposite is true in which greater degrees of segregation result in increased negative effects.

Integration permits the opportunity for all marketing communications activities to build together to create a greater positive 'added value' than would otherwise be achieved by a loose collection of unconnected activities. The greater the degree of integration achieved, the greater the **synergy** and the greater the positive results. At the central point there is no integration of campaign elements but the lack of integration has only a neutral effect. Beyond this point and to the left there is an increased likelihood of each activity detracting from the others resulting in dysfunctional communications. The greater the degree of separation and dysfunction, the greater the negative value of the marketing communications effort. The development of marketing communications which lack integration, therefore, not only fail to add overall

Exhibit 23.3 Continuum of integrated marketing communications

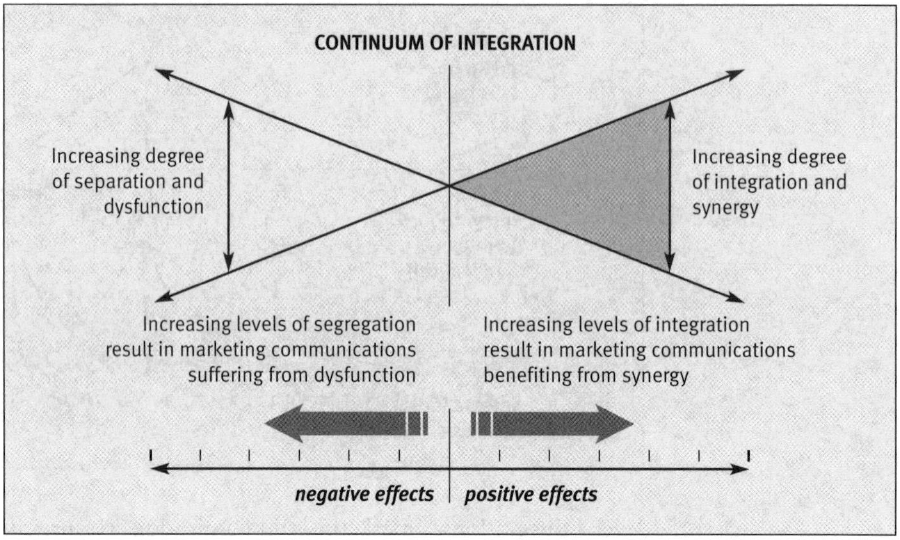

value through *synergistic effects* but they also run the risk of having a negative impact through dysfunctionality. Rather like the soldiers referred to above who receive no instruction, not only will they not complete their mission but they might well create more chaos in the process.

Dimensions of integrated marketing communications

Dimensions of integrated marketing communications

Many facets are involved in the integration of marketing communications. These different aspects are referred to here as the dimensions of integrated marketing communications.

The concept of '**dimensions of integrated marketing communications**' was introduced in Chapter 2 as one of the barriers that has to be overcome when trying to achieve integration. It may be described as a barrier insofar as it represents the numerous aspects of integration that may not be fully appreciated or addressed when trying to achieve integration.

The dimensions will be used as a basis for assessing the quality of integration later in this chapter and collectively they cover all the RABOSTIC planning model areas introduced at the start of Part 2 of this book. An indication of each relevant RABOSTIC area is given in bold in brackets at the end of each dimension which may be summarised in the following way:

Above-the-line communications

Term used to generally describe advertising promotions: that is, promotions that make use of commission-paying mass media – television, press, cinema, radio and posters. Also called above-the-line promotions and above-the-line advertising.

● *Promotional mix integration* – integration of the elements of the promotional mix. It is primarily in this context that the definition of integrated marketing communications used by the American Association of Advertising Agencies is focused. Integrated marketing communications, they say, is 'a concept of marketing communications planning that recognises the added value of a comprehensive plan that evaluates the strategic roles of a variety of communication disciplines, e.g. general advertising, direct response, sales promotion and public relations – and combines these disciplines to provide clarity, consistency, and maximum communications impact' (Duncan and Everett 1993). Implicit within this context is the need to integrate the objectives of each promotional mix element and *all* the media used. Media should be recognised as any medium used for the transmission of messages and not simply confined to the more traditional 'mass' or **above-the-line** advertising media. (RAB**OSTIC**)

● *Promotional mix with marketing mix integration* – integration of the elements of the promotional mix with those of the marketing mix. Not only is it necessary to seek integration between the promotional mix elements but, also, it is necessary to integrate the promotional mix with all the other elements of the marketing mix and to integrate the objectives of them all. It should be recognised that each marketing mix element has a potential communications value. For example, the price charged, or the nature of the distribution, or the materials used in the manufacture of the product all have something to say about the brand and all have a communications impact. True integration involves integration of all marketing mix and promotional mix elements. (RAB**OSTIC**)

● *Creative integration* – integration of creative themes, concepts and messages across the myriad marketing communications activities. Creative integration need not imply the development of a single theme and message although in many cases this is the preferred approach because of the advantages generated by having a single coherent message. There are occasions, however, where such an approach is not necessary, for example where there are clear distinctions between the audience groups targeted, or where there are distinctive and separate product offerings, or where there are distinctive corporate entities (**strategic business units, or SBUs**) even if they are part of a single conglomerate corporation. What is necessary is the recognition for the themes and messages to be planned together with an understanding of the impact they may have on each other. (RAB**OSTIC**)

● *Intra-organisation* – integration of all the relevant internal departments, individuals and activities *within* an organisation which generate and impact upon marketing communications. Such integration may be achieved through restructuring or otherwise ensuring that communications between all parties are facilitated and managed. This includes the interlinking and integration of relevant management and business objectives and the provision of resources and budgets to facilitate integrated marketing

Strategic business unit (SBU)

Strategically significant and identifiable part of a larger organisation. It may be a particular section of an organisation, or even a company within a larger group of companies.

FOOD FOR THOUGHT

To achieve integrated marketing communications, organisations may have to restructure and adopt new management practices.

Exhibit 23.4 Illustration of communication effects of all elements of the marketing mix

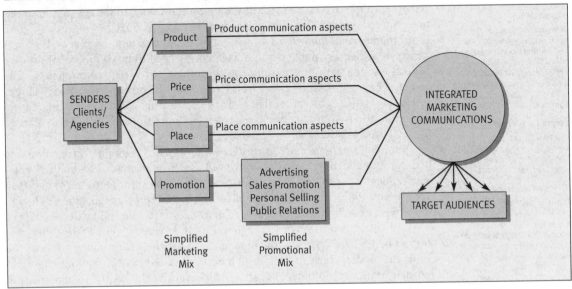

Source: Adapted from figure from *Marketing Communications Strategy*, BPP Publishing Ltd., (Betts, P., Huntington, S., Pulford, A., and Warnaby, G., 1995), Copyright © BPP Publishing Ltd. 1995

Below-the-line communications

Marketing communications that make use of the non-commission-paying media in all their forms, i.e. all forms of promotions other than advertising. Sometimes, incorrectly, it is referred to as below-the-line advertising. Although it remains a popular term, its usefulness is limited as it encompasses such a broad range of promotional activity.

Through-the-line communications

Marketing communications that span both above- and below-the-line activities.

Database management

The interactive management and maintenance of accurate customer and prospect customer information, competitor information, market information, and internal company information.

Target audience

Those individuals or groups that are identified as having a direct or indirect effect on business performance, and are selected to receive marketing communications.

Publics

Term favoured by the public relations profession, referring to the many target audiences that communications may be focused towards.

Stakeholders

Term used to describe the many and various groups of people who have an interest or involvement with an organisation. Stakeholders include suppliers, customers, consumers, investors, employees and distributors.

Corporate communications

Marketing and other business communications about the organisation to selected target audiences.

'Unitised' communications

This is an uncommon term, used here to distinguish between marketing communications that promote the organisation as a whole (corporate communications) and those that promote parts or 'units' of the organisation, such as its goods, services, brands, individuals or sections of the organisation.

communications. This might be described as the area of 'internal marketing'. Also included here is the *internal* management of all 'contacts' between stakeholder groups and the organisation. Many believe this is a fundamental and distinguishing part of integrated marketing communications that can play a major role in achieving and sustaining competitive advantage. (RAB**OST**IC)

- *Inter-organisational integration* – integration with and between all external organisations involved in marketing communications on behalf of an organisation. This includes all relevant companies within a corporate organisation, members of its distribution chains and the various agencies that work on their behalf, both above-the-line and **below-the-line.** By way of facilitating this, there has been, to some extent, a growth of agencies claiming to be 'through-the-line' providing a full range of marketing communications services 'under one roof'. There are arguments for and against such an approach. Chapters 14 and 15 considered some of the organisational implications of these issues. (RAB**OST**IC)

- *Information and database systems.* There is little dissent about the value of information and a well-managed database for integrated marketing communications. The role of **database management** is well recognised: 'As you integrate communications you must integrate marketing activities. To integrate marketing you must integrate sales and selling, and to integrate those functions, you must integrate the entire organisation ... The goal is to align the organisation to serve consumers and customers. Databases are rapidly becoming the primary management tool that drives the organisation's business strategy ...' (Schultz 1997). The foci of marketing communications are the company's stakeholders and target audiences among whom are the consumers and customers. The more that is known about them, the more effective the organisation's communications are likely to be. Today's databases are very much more than simple customer listings. Computing power has created the ability to store and cross-analyse vast amounts of data such as service and sales data, purchasing records, and attitudinal and behavioural data. There are many fields of data covering millions of transactions and relationships. Without this information it is unlikely that truly integrated marketing communications can exist. Databases are the foundation of sound Customer Relationship Management (CRM) systems and activities. In the context of IMC, this dimension includes all the relevant information required in the RABOSTIC planning model. (**RAB**OST**IC**)

- *Integration of communications targeted towards internal and external audiences.* A variety of **audiences**, 'publics' and 'stakeholders', need to be considered within the context of a marketing communications campaign or variety of campaigns. The audience members may be external and internal to the organisation. They will represent a variety of potentially disparate groups. Integrated marketing communications need to consider the roles and impact of each in order to manage the total process successfully. (RABOST**IC**)

- *Integration of corporate and 'unitised' communications.* **Corporate communications** (e.g. corporate identity) are often perceived as separate activities to '**unitised**' communications (e.g. product, brand, personality or trade communications) and they usually have different people responsible who act as '**corporate guardians**'. Despite the separation, organisations clearly recognise the strategic and tactical impact of corporate identity on all their other promotions. However, some achieve this integration better than others. Some organisations use their corporate identity as the 'umbrella' under which they place all their brands. Other organisations choose to let their brands stand independently. Whichever the choice, the total marketing communications process has to be carefully controlled to ensure integration, consistency and clarity across all its different forms. (RAB**OST**IC)

Corporate guardians

Means of describing those people who are responsible for ensuring consistency in corporate communications and the well-being of an organisation.

● *Geographical integration* – integration across national and international boundaries. Geographical integration is complicated through language, religious, cultural and regulatory variations. While it may be obvious that marketing communications take different forms in different countries, language, religious and cultural variations should also be recognised within national boundaries as well, sometimes within very small geographical areas. Belgium has the French and the Flemish; Spain has the Basques and the Catalans; Malaysia has the ethnic Chinese and the Malays; China has Manderin speakers and Cantonese speakers; America has ethnic groups of many different origins. The task of successful integration and national and global branding is made significantly more complex because of these features. (RAB<u>OSTIC</u>)

Marketing communications 'quality of integration' assessment profile

Process measures

Rather than measuring the effects of outcomes of activity (e.g. sales or awareness), an alternative approach is to assess or measure the activity or process itself.

Measuring integrated marketing communications is very difficult. First of all, there is no agreement on how (or whether it is even possible) to use output measures to assess the effectiveness of individual elements of marketing communications, let alone their combined effect. For this reason, it is suggested that it is preferable to use **process measures** (Pickton and Hartley 1998). As Duncan (1994) observes, there are two ways to measure and control most operations – through the use of *output* controls and *process* controls. 'Output controls evaluate the results of programs … Process controls evaluate how programs are developed … Up to now, however, process controls have seldom been used in marketing communications' (p. 26).

By combining the concepts of the 'continuum of integration' and the 'dimensions of integration' introduced earlier, it is possible to develop an instrument for assessing the 'quality of integration' of marketing communications.

NEED TO KNOW

☑ *Management improvement through the assessment of integrated marketing communications:*

The Quality of Integration Assessment Profile can be constructed through one or more management development exercises focused on reviewing marketing communications activities. The process of producing the profile itself helps to develop managers' understanding of marketing communications and the management development needs that are required to facilitate integration. It focuses attention on key marketing communications aspects and on areas of strengths and weaknesses.

Exhibit 23.5 illustrates such an approach to the assessment of integration. This is presented as an assessment profile. The profile provides the basis for evaluating the overall extent to which integration of marketing communications has been achieved. It does not represent an objective output measurement but is based on subjective appraisal of the various facets and process of integration.

The degree of integration may vary from being strongly dysfunctional to strongly synergistic and an assessment of these degrees can be made for each of the dimensions identified. A tick or a cross can be placed in the box considered most appropriate for each dimension of integration. The resulting assessment creates a 'profile' of the integration achieved. The further right that more crosses appear, the greater the overall quality of integration that has been achieved. If the profile is completed by a single individual, the results would be somewhat subjective but the approach can be adapted to involve a number of assessors who, through the activity of assessment, are more likely to produce an accurate and more objective profile. The very act of discussing the issues is, itself, of great benefit to the managers involved. In this way, the Quality of Integration Assessment Profile can be described as a management development tool.

Scores could be assigned to each level of integration for each dimension of integration. These scores could then be summed to provide a grand total score. While this is entirely feasible, it is not to be recommended. The allocation of scores would be some-

Exhibit 23.5 Quality of integration assessment profile

A profiling checklist for assessing the 'quality of integration' of marketing communications

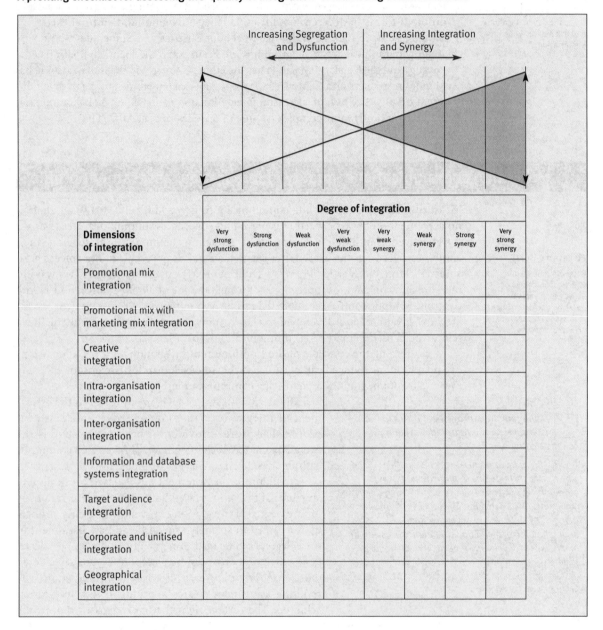

Dimensions of integration	Degree of integration							
	Very strong dysfunction	Strong dysfunction	Weak dysfunction	Very weak dysfunction	Very weak synergy	Weak synergy	Strong synergy	Very strong synergy
Promotional mix integration								
Promotional mix with marketing mix integration								
Creative integration								
Intra-organisation integration								
Inter-organisation integration								
Information and database systems integration								
Target audience integration								
Corporate and unitised integration								
Geographical integration								

what arbitrary and is exacerbated by the fact that the relative importance of each dimension is likely to vary. A simple, unweighted summation of scores would, therefore, not be particularly helpful. A profiling approach is favoured over a grand total score as it makes more obvious the principal areas of weakness.

Exhibit 23.6 illustrates a completed profile. The profile shows that there is room for improvement on all dimensions and this would not be a surprising result as the general quality of integration of marketing communications tends to be poor. What is relevant to note is that the weakest area and one that is most in need of improvement is that of 'intra-organisational integration'. This suggests that there are benefits to be gained by paying more attention to the ways in which the various parts of the organisation work together in the context of marketing communications. Together with the results for 'inter-organisational integration' and 'corporate and unitised integration' the profile indicates that significant improvements could result from a complete appraisal of the internal and external organisation and management of the marketing communications process.

NEED TO KNOW

Profiling is preferable to scoring: *Scoring schemes for the assessment of integration can be useful if applied only to each individual dimension. Summing individual scores to achieve a single rating only succeeds in obscuring the performance in specific dimensions and so reduces the effectiveness of the assessment process.*

This analysis is all the more significant when it is realised that the level of integration achieved for 'promotional mix integration' is relatively high. It is this single area which is most likely to be considered when attempting to achieve marketing communications integration, yet it is clear from the 'quality profile' that attention to this aspect alone would be totally inadequate. Assessment of a single dimension may lead to the inaccurate conclusion that a reasonable degree of integration was actually being achieved whereas the full picture indicates something quite different. Moreover, because of the interrelatedness of all the dimensions of integration it may only be possible to achieve further improvements in the area of 'promotional mix integration' through improvements in the other dimensions. In this instance, it is highly likely that improvements in the levels of 'inter-organisational' and 'corporate and unitised' integration would have a significant effect on the 'promotional mix integration'.

Exhibit 23.6 Quality of integration assessment profile

A completed marketing communications 'quality of integration' profile

	Degree of integration							
Dimensions of integration	Very strong dysfunction	Strong dysfunction	Weak dysfunction	Very weak dysfunction	Very weak synergy	Weak synergy	Strong synergy	Very strong synergy
Promotional mix integration							X	
Promotional mix with marketing mix integration				X				
Creative integration						X		
Intra-organisation integration		X						
Inter-organisation integration	X							
Information and database systems integration		X						
Target audience integration					X			
Corporate and unitised integration		X						
Geographical integration			X					

Summary

This chapter has examined the process of 'evaluating the campaign'. Evaluating the whole campaign is the ideal, and the rationale for this in terms of benefits, such as improved decision-making and risk reduction, was clear. This was followed by a review of what evaluation might possibly be achieved at each stage of the marketing communications planning process. The need for measures in three areas of effectiveness were highlighted and discussed, namely media evaluation, message content and design, and sales.

The difficulty of relating a given unit of promotional expenditure to a given unit of sales (i.e. measuring sales effect) was then critically assessed. A number of lagged and other intervening variables were identified as creating difficulties, as well as cumulative effects and differences in the perceptions of individuals.

Reasons for pre-testing were examined, such as evaluating whether the message perceived by consumers was the same as that intended by the advertisers. A distinction was drawn between concept testing for new products and for advertisements. Forms in which stimulus material might be presented were described, and a set of criteria for evaluating them provided. While rightly emphasising the importance of qualitative research for this purpose, a range of physiological techniques was also reviewed.

It was suggested that some companies might be less motivated to spend money on post-testing than pre-testing. This was not considered to be universal as it can provide valuable feedback. It was further suggested that in post-testing the emphasis tended to be on quantitative measures of performance, rather than on qualitative investigation. Recognition and recall tests are common for message content and design. Survey-based techniques, such as U&A studies, are the main approach for evaluating the effects of promotion on products.

Tracking studies comprise regularly repeated exercises to assess changes in the progress of the campaign. They concentrate upon topics such as brand awareness, recognition and recall. They could help prevent prolonged expenditure on a failing campaign. By definition, they are studies that should be repeated using the same questionnaire and stimulus material on identically composed samples from the same population. In practice, there might be reasons for a company evaluating only part of a campaign and not the whole. Scarcity of resources, such as time and money, might be important, and differences in status between products would play a part.

The final act of evaluation would be retrospective in terms of how the marketing communications planning process had worked in any specific instance. Questions would need to be asked about the appropriateness of objectives, how elements of the communications mix were expected to work and measures chosen to evaluate the campaign. In that way, useful lessons might be learned for the future.

The final parts of this chapter introduced and described a number of very important concepts related to integrated marketing communications. First, the concept of 'levels' of integrated marketing communications was identified to emphasise the strategic and tactical aspects of integration. From a planning perspective, integration requires that marketing communications are managed at the highest strategic level (level 3). Not untypically, much of what is currently considered as integrated marketing communications tends to be centred around the campaign planning level (level 2). Using a military analogy, level 1 integrated marketing communications was likened to skirmishes which are distinctly tactical in nature, short-lived and most likely to be implemented at relatively short notice (but ideally, within the context of an overall marketing communications campaign plan). Such level 1 marketing communications initiatives might be in response to unforeseen circumstances that necessitate some form of marketing communications action such as unexpected competitor activity or urgent pressures imposed by the trade in the distribution chain. In an extreme case, it might be in response to a crisis situation.

A second major concept introduced in the chapter was the notion of a 'continuum' of integration. Here, it was emphasised that integration can exist to varying degrees, both positively and negatively. Lack of integration was recognised as causing the potential for dysfunctional or counter-productive communications.

A third concept covered was that of 'dimensions' of integration. Through this concept an understanding can be developed of the various 'components' of integrated marketing communications. Integrated marketing communications requires that integration occurs within each dimension and between the dimensions.

By bringing together elements of the 'continuum of integration' and 'dimensions of integration' concepts, a fourth and final concept was developed – the quality of integration assessment profile. The profile was described both as a process measurement and as a management development tool that facilitates the evaluation of marketing communications integration throughout the organisation and its agencies and, in effect, covers all aspects of the RABOSTIC planning process.

Self-review questions

1 What are the five benefits of evaluating the campaign?

2 What types of evaluation are carried out at each stage of the marketing communications plan?

3 Identify the role played by lagged variables, cumulative effects, individual differences in perception and other intervening variables in evaluating a sales effect and a communications effect.

4 What are the main reasons for pre-testing marketing communications?

5 Compare and contrast qualitative, physiological and quantitative approaches to pre-testing marketing communications in the UK.

6 In quantitative post-testing, what is the difference between unaided and aided recall, and how do they both work in practice?

7 In your own words, describe what is meant by 'levels of integrated marketing communications'.

8 What factors make it difficult for total integrated marketing communications to be achieved?

9 The 'quality of integration assessment profile' proposes nine dimensions of integration. Identify and describe them.

10 The 'quality of integration assessment profile' is described as a process control rather than an output control. What is meant by this?

Project

You are a research executive, working closely with a marketing communications agency. The client company is about to embark on developing a chocolate bar that it hopes will be a major new product. Discuss with a colleague what sort of a marketing research programme for evaluating the product and all aspects of marketing communications you are going to recommend in a proposal.

References

Betts, P., Huntington, S., Pulford, A. and Warnaby, G. (1995), *Marketing Communications Strategy*. London: BPP.

Duncan, T.R. (1994), Is your marketing communications integrated? *Advertising Age*, 24 January, 64 (4), 26.

Duncan, T.R. and Everett, S.E. (1993), Client perceptions of integrated marketing communications. *Journal of Advertising Research*, May/June, 30–39.

Higie, R. and Sewall, M.A. (1991), Using recall and brand preference to evaluate advertising effectiveness. *Journal of Advertising Research*, 31 (April/May), 56–63.

Krugman, H.E. (1985), Point of view: measuring memory – an industry dilemma. *Journal of Advertising Research*, 25 (August/September), 49–51.

Marketing (1998), Intregrated Tunisia. 10 September, 5.

Pickton, D.W. and Hartley, R.A. (1998), Measuring integration: an assessment of the quality of integrated marketing communications. *International Journal of Advertising*, 17 (4), 447–465.

Robinson, P.J., Dalbey, H.M., Gross, I. and Wind, Y. (1968), *Advertising Measurement and Decision-Making*. Boston: Allyn and Bacon.

Schultz, D.E. (1997), Integrating information resources to develop strategies. *Marketing News*, 20 January, 31 (2), 10.

Selected further reading

Bearden, W.O. and Madden, C.S. (eds) (1996), Special issue: Integrated marketing communications. *Journal of Business Research*, 37 (3), November.

Brown, J. (1997), Impossible dream or inevitable revolution: an exploration of integrated marketing communications. *Journal of Communication Management*, 12 (1), 70–81.

Chisnall, P.M. (1997), *Marketing Research*. McGraw-Hill.

Crimp, M. and Wright, L.T. (1995), *The Marketing Research Process*. Prentice Hall.

Gonring, M.P. (1994), Putting integrated marketing communications to work today. *Public Relations Quarterly*, 39 (3), Fall, 45–48.

Massey, A. (1996), Integrating effectively. *New Perspectives*, 3 December.

Miller, D.A. and Rose, P.B. (1994), Integrated communications: a look at reality instead of theory. *Public Relations Quarterly*, Spring, 13–16.

Moriarty, S.E. (1994), PR and IMC: the benefits of integration. *Public Relations Quarterly*, 39 (3), 38–45.

Schultz, D.E., Tannenbaum, S.I. and Lauterborn, R.F. (1994), *Integrated Marketing Communications: Pulling it Together and Making it Work*. NTC Business Books.

Sykes, W. (1990), Validity and reliability in qualitative market research: a review of the literature. *Journal of the Market Research Society*, 32 (July), 289–328.

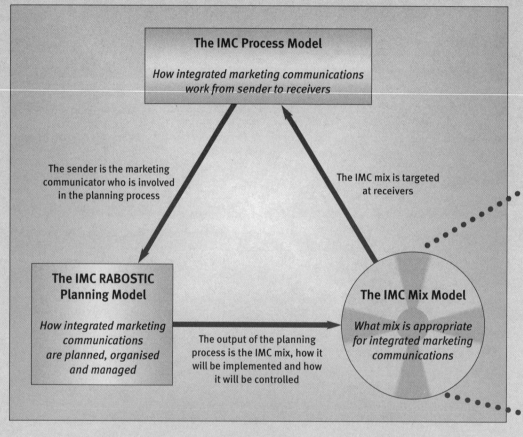

The IMC Process Model

How integrated marketing communications work from sender to receivers

The sender is the marketing communicator who is involved in the planning process

The IMC mix is targeted at receivers

The IMC RABOSTIC Planning Model

How integrated marketing communications are planned, organised and managed

The output of the planning process is the IMC mix, how it will be implemented and how it will be controlled

The IMC Mix Model

What mix is appropriate for integrated marketing communications

The Integrated Marketing Communications (IMC) Framework

Part 3

The Integrated Marketing Communications Mix

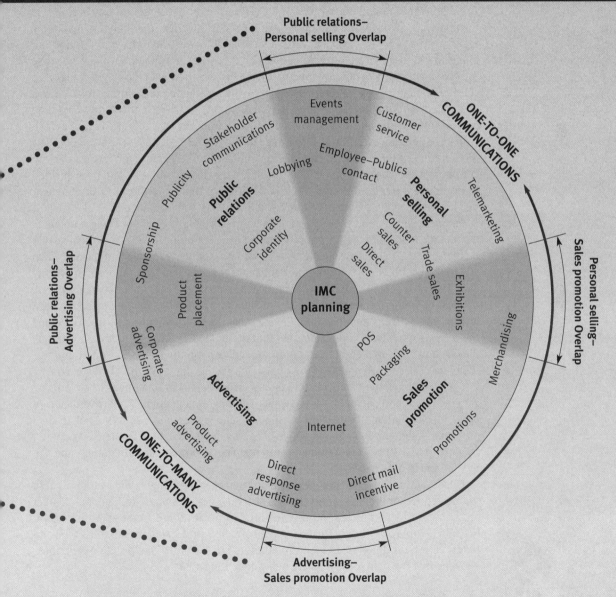

The Integrated Marketing Communications (IMC) Mix Model

Case Study 3

Pampers

The disposable nappy market in the UK is worth over £480 million per year and is dominated by two major competitors, Pampers and Huggies. The Pampers marketing team faced a number of critical issues, despite it having been the brand leader for many years. Huggies were perceived as the innovator in the marketplace because they were constantly creating new products. Huggies had also managed to develop close relationships with mothers using interactive marketing techniques. A less direct threat came from a growing independence among mothers, particularly first-time ones. Their use of widely available information from diverse sources to make decisions challenged traditional purchase patterns and reduced brand loyalty. The proliferation of information channels forced Pampers to explore a new approach to cut through the background noise to reach prospective customers. Pampers decided to introduce a one-to-one approach in addition to their traditional TV-driven campaigns. New channels were appropriated and existing ones enhanced.

Pampers decided to send a direct mail communication to mothers at eight points in the mother and baby's life: three pre-birth and five post-birth. Two CDs were also sent to mothers. One CD gives mothers an insight into how babies experience the world while still in the womb. A post-birth CD of baby massage was also sent. Appropriate nappy samples and discount coupons to encourage first purchase were included as well. Forty per cent of mothers are now online so the Internet could not be ignored as an opportunity for interactive communication. Pampers.com is built around three areas covering the aspects of childhood development that are of most interest to mothers: learning, playing and sharing. Parents can opt-in to receive a monthly newsletter that updates them about the development of their baby. Interactive digital TV (iDTV) was used as a bridge, combining the emotive strength and visual quality of traditional TV advertising with the depth and personalisation available through the Internet. Interactive digital TV offered the opportunity to develop consumer relations over time, using TV email to send profiled newsletters. The Internet and iDTV complement each other as there was only an overlap among 20 per cent of homes, and people use the services at different times of the day and in different ways.

Latest qualitative consumer research showed that there has been a turnaround in the perception of the brand and the way in which mothers relate to Pampers. Market share has risen and a clear market leadership position has been established. AC Nielson's *Top 100 Grocery Brands* survey showed that Pampers ranked 14th compared with rival Huggies at 34th. Consumers consistently give positive feedback, showing that the right messages are being communicated.

CD

More details of this case study can be found on the CD

Chapter 24

Public relations

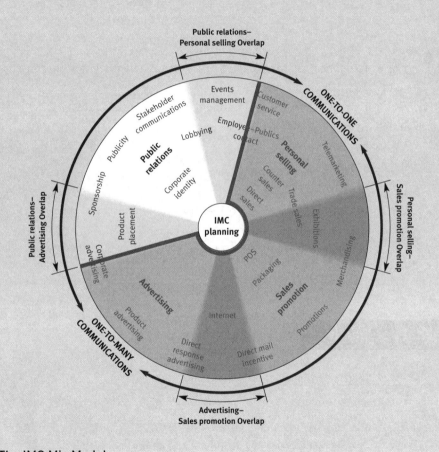

The IMC Mix Model

CD

Exhibit 24.4 details the marketing public relations (MPR) publics. Using the tools and activities of MPR identified in this chapter, outline how Pampers could target each of its relevant publics. Write a press release to one of these publics.

Chapter outline

- What is public relations?
- Defining public relations
- Public relations and marketing
- Marketing public relations (MPR)
- Scope of marketing public relations
- Marketing public relations audiences – the 'publics'
- Implementing marketing public relations
- Advantages and limitations of marketing public relations
- Measuring the effectiveness of marketing public relations

Objectives

- To define the broad realm of public relations and show its relationship to marketing
- To dispel the myth that publicity is 'free advertising'
- To define and focus on the area of marketing public relations
- To identify the scope and breadth of marketing public relations as a range of activities
- To describe each of the principal elements of marketing public relations
- To highlight the major advantages and limitations of marketing public relations
- To propose examples of how marketing public relations may be evaluated

Professional perspective

Bob Lawrence Head Warden, West Midland Safari & Leisure Park

The instinctive reaction of most people to media interest sees them on the defensive. Invariably perceived as intrusive, particularly during times of difficulty, the press are nevertheless simply doing their job; often grappling with a subject about which they know little or nothing. They also represent priceless exposure for your interests, free. But, it is important to get the facts right. The public's perception of events within your institution is largely shaped by how the media interprets the story.

The institutional reaction to crisis must be quick and accurate. If it's not you lose credibility. Once this has gone you've lost control. Bear two factors in mind. Firstly, it is not what a solicitor would necessarily advocate! Secondly, it is not always easy in a swift-moving media world requiring instant answers. We've all seen the instant analysis of the crash cause while the wreckage is still warm, from the bevy of hitherto unheard-of 'experts' who crawl from the woodwork on such occasions. Decide your version of events, adhere to them, supply the same information to everyone, but never ever lie. Summarise, but never lie. The truth will come out in the end and the instant someone smells 'cover up' you have got problems. Lying to cover up old lies comes next as you sink into a morass of confusion. 'Once you've got them by the balls their hearts and minds soon follow', said President Nixon of the people. The people's press turned the tables.

Come the crunch, nothing serves you better than knowing the media. You will know instinctively what they need, when and how. It forges a highly effective communication process and allows incisive reporting. Many a potential disaster which at best would be reported negatively has been turned about by having the confidence to allow media behind the scenes to see what happened and how. By using this media power to demonstrate the herculean attempts to redress a situation which you clearly are not going to win, you have the next best thing, heroic failure.

Though vilifying press reporting is a national pastime, it illustrates one of life's curious paradoxes. On the big screen, what does our detective hero do when he wants to discover what really occurred all those years ago? He turns up the press cuttings, of course; suddenly their contents are gospel! I've known many of our media people for 25 years, the reporters, the photographers and the camera operatives. Seldom then, if ever, have I turned on the TV, or opened a newspaper with any trepidation. Yes, the much maligned media have proved the best of bedfellows.

R. P. Lawrence

What is public relations?

Public relations

The planned and sustained effort to establish and maintain goodwill and mutual understanding between an organisation and its publics.

Publics

Term favoured by the public relations profession, referring to the many target audiences that communications may be focused towards.

For many years, the question of where **public relations** (PR) fits into the range of business activities in general, and its relationship to marketing in particular, has exercised the minds, pens and tongues of practitioners and academics alike. In our Integrated Marketing Communications Mix Model, it represents one of the four broad areas of marketing communications activities.

The problem faced is invariably one of definition in terms of the aims and activities that PR encompasses. These embrace many groups of people (target audiences, known in the PR world as '**publics**') and extend from:

- advice and counselling,
- relations with employees during redundancy and closure,
- relations with the local community and interest groups,
- lobbying,
- developing goodwill among all publics, and
- monitoring public opinion,

to:

- publicity,
- sponsorship and donations,
- dealing with negative publicity and 'crisis management' situations,
- the preparation of press releases and publications,
- helping to develop and maintain the corporate image,
- arranging events, and many more.

Some suggest that PR is a part of marketing, others that marketing is a part of PR. Many question whether it really matters, anyway. For PR practitioners it may be a

NEED TO KNOW

 PR programmes are frequently well-integrated campaigns.

matter of professional pride. Some do not wish to be too closely associated with marketing, seeing it solely as profit-focused when much PR activity has longer-term implications and fewer financial imperatives. They argue that PR is fundamentally about enhancing corporate reputation and generating and maintaining *goodwill* and that this should be separated from the sales functions.

FOOD FOR THOUGHT

PR events can make use of all elements of the marketing communications mix.

In practice, however, PR and marketing have much in common. It is becoming an invaluable additional discipline for those organisations looking outside themselves to consider a wider world. A world that is not bounded by the traditional concept of an organisation that solely works for its own benefit and keeps the outside world at bay. This situation has developed as a result of the ever-growing influence of an organisation's 'publics'. Those who clamour for organisations to accept wider social responsibilities are forcing change and PR has a major role to play in that change.

In keeping with the contentions of this book, PR (or at least those parts with which we are concerned) is seen primarily as a range of marketing communication tools that need to be integrated within the total marketing communications effort. In fact, PR programmes, themselves, are often composite marketing communications campaigns involving a wide range of integrated promotional activities focused at a range of target audience publics. PR events may be organised involving sales promotions, merchandise and exhibition activities. Personnel may be involved in hosting and in personal 'selling' capacities. Direct mail may be used for invitations. Publicity may accompany the events. Sponsorship may support them. Advertising may be used to announce them. For example, Philip Morris used advertising by taking out full-page advertisements as part of a PR campaign when it was forced to recall its Marlboro cigarettes after fears of contamination.

WARNING

Publicity should not be considered 'free advertising'.

Publicity, just one part of PR, is often confused with advertising and is sometimes called 'free advertising'. On two counts, this is incorrect. First, it is not 'advertising' and second, it is not 'free'. But it is understandable why this confusion occurs. Publicity uses mass media, as does advertising, but because it does not pay for the space it uses, it is presumed to be free. It should not be considered free, however, because there are costs associated with producing press releases and managing the PR activity. According to Chris Alder, Director of Coporate Communications, SAP:

NEED TO KNOW

Benefits of PR include relative low cost, high credibility and extensive visibility.

> **Free publicity is a fallacy, PR is not cheap. It involves costs and management time on top of agency fees.**   (Cobb 1998, p. 29)

Public relations activities can be very cost efficient but making them happen still requires substantial effort and resources.

There are numerous benefits associated with PR such as its relative low cost, the increased credibility that it can engender compared with other promotional tools and the extensive visibility it can create. These and other benefits render PR an invaluable contributor to the marketing communications mix. PR activities range far and wide, wider than the scope of our interest here. This chapter focuses primarily on an area that increasingly is described as 'marketing public relations' (MPR) – these are elements of PR that directly benefit marketing communications. They are an extremely powerful part of an organisation's communications mix that often, and regrettably, are under-valued and under-represented by marketing professionals.

FOOD FOR THOUGHT

MPR activities have the potential to be extremely powerful marketing communications, unfortunately, they are sometimes undervalued by marketing professionals.

Danny Moss (1990) has remarked that the term 'public relations' is often used in a negative way as a label that is attached to

> virtually any form of publicity or public statement issued by organisations almost irrespective of its purpose. In this sense, the term is often used in a pejorative sense, with the implication being that public relations involves some attempted 'sleight of hand' or merely an attempt to put a 'gloss' on the true facts, rather than being concerned to improve the presentation of the relevant information and facilitate an improved understanding of the issues in question.
>
> (Moss 1990, p. 1)

Like marketing, PR suffers from its cynics, perhaps with justification, as not all PR is undertaken out of pureness of spirit. However, this is true of all business and human activity. The public relations profession is at pains to stress its attitude towards honourable and professional practice. Commonly, public relations is associated with the identity an organisation projects towards its key target groups and its interrelationships with them. Corporate identity and community relations programmes are frequently thought of in this context. Roger Haywood (1984, 1991), a well-respected PR practitioner and author, has described PR as 'the projection of the personality of the organisation' and 'the management of corporate reputation'. In achieving this, it seeks to shape the attitudes and opinions of the interest and stakeholder groups with which it is involved. In this process, the organisation is beholden to its publics to keep them well informed if it is to be perceived in a favourable light over the long term. PR, then, is very much a *proactive*, not just a *reactive*, discipline.

Like marketing, there are many definitions of public relations. At its simplest, Hunt and Grunig (1994) define PR as:

> the management of communication between an organisation and its publics.
>
> (p. 6)

At the heart of this definition lies the basis of PR. It is about communications between one body, the organisation, and its many points of contact, its 'publics'. The choice of the word 'between' in the definition is significant. It recognises the growing acceptance of PR as a two-way communication so that the organisation both gives and receives information. Public relations is not only to do with disseminating information but also about collecting information which it uses to develop communication programmes and, where necessary, encourage change in organisational policy and behaviour.

Another definition of PR is that provided by the Institute of Public Relations. Their definition extends the earlier definition by emphasising the benign nature of PR communication in fostering *mutual understanding* and *goodwill*. These are commonly regarded features of public relations.

> Public relations practice is the planned and sustained effort to establish and maintain goodwill and mutual understanding between an organisation and its publics.
>
> (Institute of Public Relations)

Inherent in both definitions is that PR, like marketing, is a range of activities that have to be planned and managed. Both definitions appear to emphasise the role of PR at an organisational level, yet the practice of PR also embraces activities centred around individuals and products. Definitions of PR often fail to highlight this feature. This is of significance when PR is placed in the total marketing communications context. Public relations has a major role to play in product as well as corporate promotions. It is also used to promote individuals. In the world of politics, for example, individuals and the organisations they represent both fall under the PR spotlight. One thinks particularly of political leaders and cabinet members. In the commercial world, the role Richard Branson plays in the PR effort of the Virgin group is especially interesting. It is a symbiotic PR relationship from which he, as an individual, and Virgin, as an organisation, have both benefited. Another area frequently omitted in PR definitions and descriptions is specific reference to media relations, so often a significant part of public relations activities. It could be argued, though, that definitions implicitly include the media as one of the many groups of publics towards which PR activities are directed.

WARNING

Public relations should not only be thought of in the context of corporate promotions, it has a role in product promotions, too.

Two-way asymmetric communications

Communications from a sender to a receiver with little or delayed feedback, producing a non-direct dialogue.

Two-way symmetric communications

Direct dialogue between a sender and receiver of communications.

Hunt and Grunig (1994) have identified four typical ways in which PR is practised in organisations. These, they represent as four different PR perspectives; press agentry/publicity, public information, **two-way asymmetric** and **two-way symmetric**. Described as 'models', they are the philosophical basis on which PR is predicated, or frameworks on which it is built. These models represent different perspectives of PR held explicitly or implicitly through the PR actions undertaken by organisations. Exhibit 24.1 identifies the characteristics of each of these models.

Press agency/publicity perspective of PR

The unusual term 'press agentry' is used by Hunt and Grunig to cover press agents and press agencies. In this model, the role of PR is essentially one of propaganda. PR is seen as a flow of information *from* the organisation *to* its publics. The sole purpose is

Exhibit 24.1 Characteristic perspectives of PR

	One-way communications		Two-way communications	
Characteristic	**Press agentry/ publicity**	**Public information**	**Two-way asymmetric**	**Two-way symmetric**
Purpose	Propaganda	Dissemination of information	Scientific persuasion	Mutual understanding
Nature of communication	One-way Complete truth not essential	One-way Truth important	Two-way Unbalanced effects	Two-way Balanced effects
Communication model	Source...Receiver ⟶	Source...Receiver ⟶	Source...Receiver ⟶ ◄·········· Feedback	Group...Group ⟵ Feedback
Nature of research	Little 'Counting house'	Little Readability Readership	Formative evaluation of attitudes	Formative evaluation of attitudes
Typical uses	Sports, theatre, products, politicians, movie stars	Government, non-profit associations, business	Competitive business, agencies	Regulated business, agencies

Source: from figure from *Public Relations Techniques*, 1st Edition, Harcourt Brace (Wadsworth), (Hunt, T., and Grunig, J.E. 1994), reproduced by kind permission of Professor James E. Grunig.

PR launches a new career

The work of international publicists have rocketed Charlotte Church to stardom. In the space of less than a year, this schoolgirl became an international singing celebrity. Her rapid rise to fame and fortune has been accelerated by the media exposure, coverage and endorsement achieved by the efforts of the numerous publicists working on her, and her record company's, behalf. In 1999, her first American release went immediately into the No. 1 position of the American classics chart. She now appears as a celebrity on a variety of chat shows and programmes.

to obtain favourable editorial coverage through publicity. Little concern is shown for understanding the publics' points of view or for collecting information from the publics. It is an asymmetrical, one-way communication in which the organisation 'tells' its publics the information it wants them to know. Little concern may be shown for the truth although this need not typify all PR falling into this category. This approach represents a great deal of PR in practice. It is most notably used by publicists whose movie star, sports personality, celebrity and politician clients they promote.

Public information perspective of PR

This perspective is also asymmetrical and one-way with little or no attempt to gather information from publics to inform the organisation. Although less emphasis is placed on propaganda, there is nevertheless a bias towards disseminating only favourable information. Publicity activities are likely to be supported more strongly by newsletters, brochures and direct mail than in the case of press agentry. The public information model of PR is typified by government information promotions for such things as health, crime prevention and education. The public relations activities that surrounded the British Government's introduction of the Patient's Charter is an example of this type of one-way communications. At its extreme, emphasis is placed on objective, unbiased, factual reporting with little attempt to be persuasive where the role is seen as conveying information in an accurate, unemotional, unpersuasive, matter-of-fact fashion.

Two-way asymmetric perspective of PR

Although Hunt and Grunig describe this model as two-way communication, it remains asymmetrical because the information flow still remains unbalanced in favour of the organisation which believes that it is right and any change that is needed must come from the public not the organisation. As an approach it can be effective when there is little conflict between an organisation and its publics or where change in the target public is generally seen to be beneficial such as in cigarette and drugs awareness campaigns. Where conflict does exist, this approach can be ineffective. If the public information model is about 'telling', this model is about 'telling and selling'.

NEED TO KNOW

☑ *The two-way symmetrical model of communications is generally considered to represent the best model of communications.*

Two-way symmetric perspective of PR

The fourth approach to PR represents the most acceptable approach in that attempts are made to recognise publics as equal and vital partners to the organisation. Dialogue between the organisation and its publics is encouraged rather than the monologue of **one-way communication**. It is to this approach of PR that the Institute of Public Relations definition of PR given above is most attuned. It is claimed to be the most effective of the four models observed by Hunt and Grunig. It is a model of PR that is based on research to understand publics and the organisation's relationship to them. PR activities, while persuasive, will seek to foster mutual understanding between the organisation and its publics. As an approach, it recognises that the organisation may have to amend its attitudes, policies and behaviour in line with public opinion. For this reason, greater emphasis is placed on research and feedback activities making this a truly symmetrical communications process. When faced with public concern over genetically modified (GM) foods, supermarkets responded positively by launching PR campaigns emphasising their response in removing GM foods from their shelves.

In reviewing the descriptions of PR above, it is wise not to think of organisations adopting one or other approaches but, rather, that they have a predisposition to favour some approaches over others. Circumstances will tend to dictate which approach will be most appropriate at any given time. It is probably better to think of the models as alternatives available to the PR planner that may be selected based on what is most suitable for particular campaigns. It is perfectly feasible, therefore, for an organisation to adopt elements of all the models over a period of time although it is likely that the basic philosophy of the organisation will be revealed in the approach it tends to favour most. Two-way symmetric communications is very much the driving force behind direct marketing communications activities described in Chapter 27.

Public relations and marketing

PR and marketing are undeniably closely tied. To suggest that one is a part of the other, however, would be a too simplistic analysis.

Friend has had this to say about PR:

> **Working in support of marketing, PR has a primary function to promote. It also has to protect and project. This requires PR thinking across the full spectrum of an organisation's operations, or a series of irreconcilable differences and conflicts will invariably arise.**
>
> (Reported in Kitchen 1999, p. 346)

To help understand the relationship between marketing and PR, Kotler and Mindak (1978) have identified five different 'models'. The models represent a progressive sophistication in the relationship between marketing and PR with model 'E' arguably representing the most effective form from an integrated marketing communications perspective. Exhibit 24.2 is a development of Kotler and Mindak's original work in that it identifies two versions of model 'A' and all models illustrate PR's link to marketing through marketing communications.

NEED TO KNOW

☑ *Model 'E' represents the most effective form from an integrated marketing communications perspective.*

Model A(a) represents the least sophisticated arrangement of marketing and PR activities. In common with model A(b), there is no overlap whatsoever between marketing communications and PR. This is a traditional but changing view of how marketing and PR are handled within organisations. They are independent of each

Exhibit 24.2 Relationships between marketing and PR

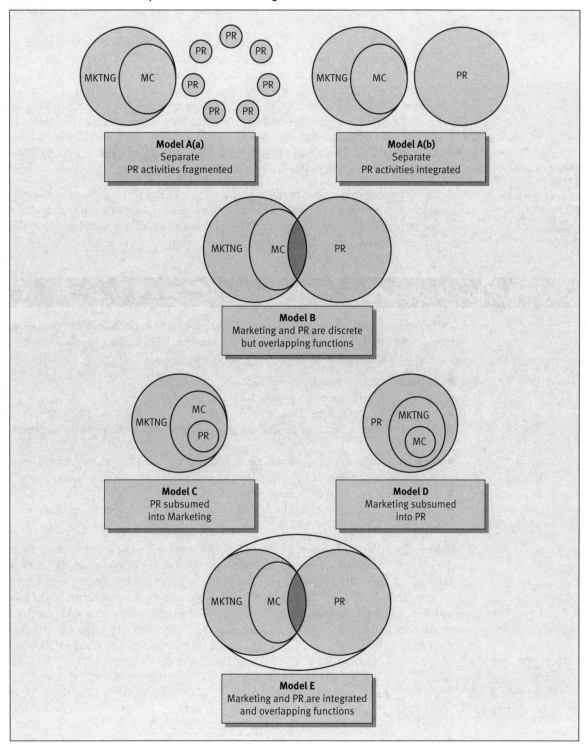

Model A(a)
Separate
PR activities fragmented

Model A(b)
Separate
PR activities integrated

Model B
Marketing and PR are discrete
but overlapping functions

Model C
PR subsumed
into Marketing

Model D
Marketing subsumed
into PR

Model E
Marketing and PR are integrated
and overlapping functions

Source: Adapted from Kotler and Mindak (1978)

other and perform different roles. The opportunity for integration and synergy between marketing and PR does not exist. Model A(a) also lacks any integration of the PR activities themselves.

Model B shows marketing and PR as equal partners with some overlap of roles. As functions, they remain largely independent. Model C shows PR entirely subsumed as a function of marketing, whereas model D shows a similar arrangement in reverse.

Model E represents a totally integrated approach towards marketing and PR that is supported in this book. It recognises each as separate but overlapping functions with their own roles but with inter-linked activities. They are mutually supportive in achieving marketing and PR objectives through orchestrated communications targeted at various marketing and PR audiences. The overlap area shown is the province of **marketing public relations (MPR)** which the authors describe as

Marketing public relations (MPR)

Those parts of public relations most focused towards marketing relevant activities.

> a healthy offspring of two parents: marketing and PR. MPR represents an opportunity for companies to regain a share of voice in a message-satiated society. MPR not only delivers a strong share of voice to win share of mind and heart; it also delivers a better, more effective voice in many cases. (p. 17)

Marketing public relations (MPR)

Definitions, models and approaches to PR give an insight to the breadth of the public relations function. Goodrich, Gildea and Cavanaugh (1979), in their article about PR's place in the marketing mix, identify it as involving:

- a planned effort or management function;
- the relationship between an organisation and its publics;
- evaluation of public attitudes and opinions;
- an organisation's policies, procedures and actions as they relate to the organisation's publics;
- steps taken to ensure that policies, procedures, and actions are in the public interest and are socially responsible;
- execution of an action or communication programme;
- development of rapport, goodwill, understanding and acceptance as the chief result sought.

Clearly, this reflects a broad-scale view of PR that needs focusing if it is to be of direct relevance to most marketing communications activities. This is particularly so when determining the marketing communications plans for individual brands rather than the corporate body as a whole. It is the overlap area between marketing and PR in which we are most interested here especially in the context of Kotler and Mindak's model E in Exhibit 24.2 above. This overlap area is increasingly being identified as marketing public relations (MPR) and which, over 20 years ago, Gage (1981) pre-

FOOD FOR THOUGHT

The majority of public relations activities fall under the remit of MPR.

dicted to be one of the fastest-growing segments of the PR field. Shandwick (1989), one of the world's largest international PR companies, has estimated that 20% of PR firms' fee income throughout the world is generated by PR for consumer products. Harris (1993) has reported that 70% of PR firms' business is marketing-related with the remaining 30% distributed among corporate, governmental, environmental and financial activities. There is little to suggest that this situation has changed in more recent years.

Shimp (2000) describes MPR as:

The marketing-oriented aspect of public relations, … the narrow aspect of public relations involving an organisation's interactions with consumers and other publics regarding marketing matters. (p. 608)

Perhaps, in view of Shandwick's and Harris's findings, Shimp's use of 'narrow' belies the full expanse of MPR activities. An award-winning example of the use of MPR integrated with other marketing communications is the Playtex Wonderbra campaign (Plate 15). It is estimated that as much as £50m of MPR media coverage was generated to complement the product's poster campaign (Barrett 1997).

Harris (1993) defines MPR as:

The process of planning, executing and evaluating programs that encourage purchase and consumer satisfaction through credible communications of information and impressions that identify companies and their products with the needs, wants, concerns and interests of consumers.

By focusing on consumers as the principal public, this definition usefully helps to distinguish MPR from PR in general. Unfortunately, it also *appears* to limit the range of publics that may be targeted as part of MPR activity. This is only a question of appearance. The definition should be viewed as including any and all publics that may be targeted for the fulfilment of MPR activities. Consumers are highlighted in the definition because they are the main 'end beneficiaries'. MPR can act on consumers or customers directly, or indirectly through targeting other publics such as the media, opinion leaders and other influencers. Furthermore, the definition does not preclude MPR from involvement in encouraging a whole range of actions on the part of one or more publics. The action encouraged by MPR does not have to lead directly to a purchase. It might attempt to affect attitudes and opinions which, ultimately, have a bearing on consumer satisfaction or in limiting unfavourable outcomes in the event of negative or crisis situations (Plate 20). Like advertising, PR activities can have a major use in reducing **dissonance** which, can be an important aspect in marketing communications.

Just as the corporate organisation as a whole is considered to be the province of PR (as reflected in definitions of PR), MPR tends to be associated with product or brand promotions. It is, in fact, inappropriate to think of MPR in this way. It is recognised that customers and consumers are influenced by branding activities at the corporate level as well as at the *product/brand* level. Many organisations rely very heavily on what some refer to as '**umbrella branding**' in which individual brands are closely associated with a larger brand range or the corporation as a whole. In FMCG confectionery markets, Cadbury is an example of a company that places all of its product brands under the Cadbury brand umbrella. These strategic considerations have been considered at greater length in Chapter 11.

Recognition that the marketing success of individual brands is strongly affected by corporate promotional activities carries with it a number of implications. Not least, it has to be accepted that MPR needs to be utilised not just at the product brand level but also at the corporate 'brand' level as well. However, if we are not careful, we shall only succeed in arguing a case that all PR activities fall under the remit of MPR. This is not the case being made in this chapter. PR is legitimately a wider discipline as illustrated in the opening remarks of the chapter.

Separating MPR from the wider field of PR has given rise to a distinction between marketing public relations and the rest. These other parts of PR are usually referred to

Dissonance

Term coined by Leon Festinger to describe a psychological state in which there is some incongruity (dissonance) between two or more thoughts. The resulting inconsistency encourages individuals to modify their thoughts to be more compatible or harmonious. Dissonance when recognised is an unstable state of mind.

Umbrella branding

Product branding in which the brands are closely related to other brands or the overall corporate brand.

Corporate public relations (CPR)

Those parts of public relations not directly concerned with a marketing or brand focus but take a broader corporate or whole business perspective.

Corporate marketing public relations/product marketing public relations

Two areas of marketing public relations focused towards the corporate and product brands respectively.

as **corporate public relations (CPR)**. In addressing the difference between the MPR and CPR, authors have tended to distinguish between them either by limiting MPR to a smaller range of PR activities or by limiting MPR to a smaller set of publics, namely customers, consumers and clients (e.g. Cutlip et al. 1995). Neither solution is satisfactory. MPR needs to have access to any relevant PR public and use any relevant PR tool to enhance marketing communications outcomes. Exhibit 24.3 illustrates the relationship between PR, MPR and CPR. Also shown are two sub-sets of MPR. These highlight the fact that MPR activities need to encompass the opportunity to promote products (individual brands) as well as organisations (the corporate brand). The terms 'corporate marketing public relations' and 'product marketing public relations' are used to identify these two different but connected strands of MPR.

Scope of marketing public relations

Marketing public relations can help support and achieve the full range of marketing communications objectives. MPR activities surrounding the use of pop stars Michael Jackson and Madonna increased Pepsi's awareness and interest levels by achieving millions of pounds worth of media exposure. A MPR campaign for Goodyear resulted in the sale of 150,000 Aquatred tyres even before other forms of promotion commenced. When the Adidas Predator football boot was developed, a MPR and sales promotion campaign was launched that resulted in retailers selling out of their stocks of the boot before the planned TV advertising campaign was even started.

MPR can raise awareness, inform, interest, excite, educate, generate understanding, build trust, encourage loyalty and even help generate sales – an outcome not often associated with PR activities. The manufacturer of Cobra golf clubs received enquiries from all over the world after Tiger Woods, a player with one of the longest tee drives among professional golfers, was seen using one of their clubs during the internationally televised US Open golf tournament. MPR can help to introduce new products and defend others at risk. It can create favourable impressions and limit the harm done by negative situations such as bad publicity or contamination scares as those faced by Perrier when traces of benzene were found in their bottled water. In particular, MPR can raise *visibility* and develop corporate and product *credibility* in ways that other promotional tools cannot.

FOOD FOR THOUGHT

MPR activities can have a direct effect on sales as well as the indirect effects that are more usually recognised.

Exhibit 24.3 The relationship of marketing public relations to the general fields of public relations and marketing

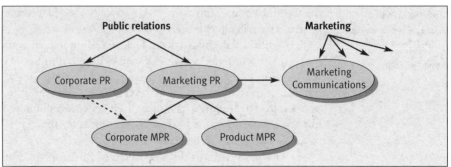

MPR should not be considered an afterthought to other elements in the marketing communications mix; it is an integral and important part of the mix. Many times, MPR is able to achieve marketing communications outcomes that could not be afforded through other promotional means.

The general areas with which MPR is most associated include:

- MPR planning and management
- Media relations
- Publicity
- Publications
- Corporate communications
- Public affairs and community relations
- Lobbying
- Sponsorship/donations
- Events management
- Crisis management
- Research and analysis.
- *MPR planning and management.* This area of MPR may be said to represent the overall management, organisation, planning and control of MPR. It involves identifying MPR tasks, setting objectives, defining publics, integrating MPR within the marketing communications mix, scheduling, managing the implementation of MPR, and assessing its effectiveness.
- *Media relations.* This is an important aspect of MPR and is linked to achieving publicity/editorial coverage. Media relations help to ensure good media coverage; encourage favourable, positive publicity; and discourage negative coverage. The development of personal relationships with editors and journalists is typically involved. This is an area that is very much the province of professional PR staff and media specialists.
- *Producing publicity.* Publicity production is a mainstay of MPR. It is most frequently associated with press and media releases and it involves disseminating positive information about the organisation and its products to achieve editorial coverage. Where necessary, it is also used to limit the negative effects of bad publicity.

  Publicity is frequently viewed as a particularly advantageous part of MPR because it is seen as being 'free' advertising. This fallacy has already been referred to earlier. However, publicity can be extremely effective and cost efficient. It has the potential to be very powerful communication that benefits from the credibility it creates by appearing as third-party, unbiased endorsement. That is to say, publicity creates the impression that it is produced by somebody not associated with the product, organisation, person or event being promoted and, as such, creates a higher degree of believability.

  But publicity should not be confused with advertising as it is a very different communications tool, created using a very different process. Editorial coverage cannot be controlled in the same way that an advertisement can. As with the rest of the marketing communications mix, publicity, to be most successful, needs to be managed. While organisations may take advantage of serendipitous publicity when it occurs by chance, to maximise its effect, it needs to be carefully produced and controlled.

- *Producing publications.* The production of publications is an important PR support function. A variety of publications may be produced from employee newsletters and financial reports to consumer magazines and media packs. They can be text, audio and video.

- *Corporate communications.* Corporate communications have an enormous range of possibilities, not all of which fall under the remit of MPR. Those that do, include corporate identity programmes, corporate image management, corporate advertising, some internal communications and some communications with other stakeholder groups.

- *Public affairs and community relations.* Building and maintaining local, national and international relations is what is involved in this aspect of MPR. It involves contact with the government and government agencies, special interest and professional groups as well as the local community.

- *Lobbying.* Lobbying is an approach associated with public affairs and media relations to build and maintain positive relations with, for example, group leaders, legislators, and officials. It involves persuasion and negotiation. Environmentalist groups lobby government to affect legislation affecting 'green' issues. Other special interest groups lobby to obtain or prevent action pertinent to their causes. Recently, lobbying has had a major effect on the control of genetically modified foods. A substantial amount of lobbying has taken place targeted at governments throughout the world on behalf of tobacco companies. These efforts have prevented or delayed action being taken to ban tobacco advertising and other promotions. Until recent years this has been very successful for the companies involved. However, in recent years, increasing amounts of legislation have been introduced that severely restrict what tobacco companies can do and say in their promotions.

- *Sponsorship and donations.* The giving of funds is a common practice among organisations but the sums donated vary significantly. Sponsorship while representing the giving of funds is in a very different league to simple donations. It may be on a small scale for some local activity or may involve many millions of pounds.

- *Events management.* Public relations activities frequently involve the staging of special events. They may be one-off events or conferences or something which occurs regularly. Internally, announcement meetings may be held to launch a new product or as part of managing company restructuring. Externally, events may be staged which intrinsically have a PR purpose or they may be 'stunts' intended to attract as much media coverage (publicity) as possible.

- *Crisis management.* Crisis management, sometimes referred to as 'damage limitation', is an important aspect of PR. It is the process of dealing with unforeseen negative events and circumstances that can range in degree of impact on an organisation from local concerns to full-scale disasters. It is argued that contingency plans should always be prepared so that procedures are in place for handling such occurrences. A significant example of a crisis management campaign was that following the Exxon Valdis oil spill disaster. Although an important area of PR, it is not a subject which is taken further here. More information on this topic can be found in most specialist public relations texts.

- *Research and analysis.* It should not be forgotten that a major part of any marketing communications activity, MPR included, involves the collection and analysis of information to aid the management, planning, implementation, evaluation and control process.

Marketing public relations audiences – the 'publics'

As with any other element of marketing communications, it is vital that all relevant MPR audiences are identified before any successful integrated campaign can be implemented. Obvious audience groups are customers and consumers. Clearly, however, these are only part of the total picture as it is necessary to also identify other publics who act as *influencers* on customers and consumers, the argument being to favourably influence the influencers so that they, in turn, might favourably influence customers and consumers.

The specific choice of publics to target is entirely dependent upon the nature of the task, the objectives of the MPR campaign and its role within the total marketing communications programme. Exhibit 24.4 provides a general list of potential audience groups.

NEED TO KNOW

☑ *Publics for specific campaigns should be carefully and appropriately targeted according to the needs dictated by the campaign objectives.*

Exhibit 24.4 List of MPR publics

- Consumers – past, present and potential
- Customers – past, present and potential
- Opinion leaders
- Influencers – specific publics identified that are situation specific and relevant to the MPR task
- The media – e.g. press, TV, radio
- Members of the general public
- The trade
- Employees
- Pressure groups
- Shareholders and investors
- Financial community – 'the City', advisors, etc.
- Civic and business organisations
- Professional and trade bodies/associations
- Local authority and government
- Suppliers
- Educators
- Community members

In specific cases, publics may be identified that are not shown here. This will be because they are peculiar to a particular market, business, location or industry. For example, if an educational toy is being promoted, not only may parents be targeted; schools, nurseries and playgroups may also be among the target audiences. In each case, the general rule of targeting applies – all audience groups should be defined as precisely as possible.

In developing any MPR campaign, it is useful to go through a checklist of publics to ensure that no particular group has been needlessly forgotten. As a rule of thumb, the media should always be considered for the role they play in leading opinion and in providing editorial coverage that may be received by many other target publics. As with other forms of marketing communications, having identified all the publics to be contacted, it is important to tailor MPR activities to match the interests of each if the greatest impact is to be achieved.

NEED TO KNOW

☑ *Targeted media should always be considered as part of the targeted publics when developing a campaign.*

Implementing marketing public relations

Given the wide-ranging scope of marketing public relations, it is not surprising there are many 'tools' involved in MPR campaigns. Exhibit 24.5 provides a useful checklist of the more popular ones. To achieve greatest effect their use should be co-ordinated and integrated not only between themselves but also with other marketing communications activities. In reality, this is not always easy. The personnel responsible for public relations activities may have only limited involvement with personnel responsible for other promotional activities. Advertising and promotions may fall under the remit of the marketing department. Sales force activities may be managed separately

NEED TO KNOW

☑ *Difficulties can arise in implementing MPR across organisational boundaries.*

from marketing. Trade marketing and channel management may be a separate function to consumer marketing. And public relations may report directly to the Chief Executive's office, bypassing all the other management hierarchy structures; the reason being that it is typically considered a corporate responsibility. As we have discussed earlier, however, marketing public relations have a significant role to play not only at the corporate level but also at the product level. As with all other aspects of management, functional boundaries are invariably necessary; the skill is in crossing them to achieve integrated campaigns.

Exhibit 24.5 Tools and activities of marketing public relations

- Media releases
- Media conferences
- Media contact and entertainment
- PR and publicity events and 'stunts'
- Lobbying
- Promotional materials (corporate and product) – videos, tapes, CDs
- MPR advertising
- Sponsorship and donations
- Product placement
- Advertorials
- Corporate identity materials
- Company website
- In-house magazines
- Customer magazines
- Exclusives
- Interviews and photo-calls
- Speeches, presentations and speech writing
- Corporate literature, e.g. financial reports
- Organisation events
- Facility visits

MPR activities may be managed internally or a PR agency may be used to complement internal staff in just the same way that advertising or sales promotions agencies may be employed to assist with other promotions. Chapter 15, Agency Operations, identified a variety of considerations to be borne in mind when appointing agencies but Exhibit 24.6 highlights some specific questions to be asked when appointing external PR professionals.

Media releases

Information passed to the media. This may take the form of press releases, video releases, media packs, and other documents and commentary.

- *Media releases.* The media is an important public in MPR and although uppermost in the minds of PR professionals, can be so easily forgotten by marketing managers. Principal media are the press, television and radio.

  Probably the most basic tool of MPR is the **media release** (often referred to as the press or news release see Exhibit 24.7). Its purpose is to be seen by editors and used

Exhibit 24.6 Selecting a PR agency – nine key questions

1 Do I need an agency or can the activities be handled internally?

2 Is the agency to be my 'arms and legs' and take on the responsibilities of an in-house press office?

3 Would the agency be required to write press releases and generate media coverage?

4 Should the agency provide high-level strategic counselling and planning? Do they have the skills to do so?

5 Should the agency be a young, bright and brash agency or one which would help project a more statesmanlike corporate personality?

6 Would the activity have the support of top management?

7 How much work would be generated?

8 What is the budget?

9 Can I work comfortably with the people?

Source: Adapted from Cobb (1998)

by them in preparing editorial for publication or production. A well-prepared release may be used without editorial change, this being more useful (and more likely to be used) than one requiring many changes. Editors and journalists receive huge numbers of releases. They will only shortlist ones that are well targeted and will be of interest to their readers, viewers or listeners. The skill in producing releases is to produce them in such a way that captures the main promotional points that need to be communicated. This should be done in such a way that will excite or be of specific interest to the targeted public. A number of releases may need to be prepared, each presented in the best way for each target public.

NEED TO KNOW

☑ *A general press or media release will not always be satisfactory even when considering only one news story. Multiple releases may need to be written to reflect the interests and perspectives of different media and their audiences.*

Media releases may be simple press releases, or may be much more elaborate media packs. They can include additional material such as information sheets, photographs, artwork, video and audio tapes, and CDs and DVDs. Video news releases (VNRs) and audio news releases (ANRs) can contain all the material needed for television and radio broadcast with no need for editors to capture their own footage. The Internet, web pages, bulletin boards and email are other ways of making releases available.

- *Media conferences.* Media conferences, events to which editors and journalists will be invited, may be organised when significant events occur. They are frequently used as a major communication tool by politicians but are not uncommon in the commercial world, too. New product launches or crisis events are times when a conference might be arranged. Pepsi hosted a media conference when it announced the end of its contract with Michael Jackson when he was accused of molesting children. When the pain-killer Tylenol was deliberately contaminated with a poison by an extortionist, Johnson & Johnson, the manufacturer, held a media conference as a means of maintaining confidence and quickly and effectively conveying how it was handling the situation. Despite potentially catastrophic consequences, the company was praised for its actions.

- *Media contact and entertainment.* This is very much part of developing favourable media relations on an ongoing basis. Publicists, PR agents, and PR and media specialists will maintain contact with editors and journalists as part of their day-to-day work.

Exhibit 24.7 Anatomy of a press release

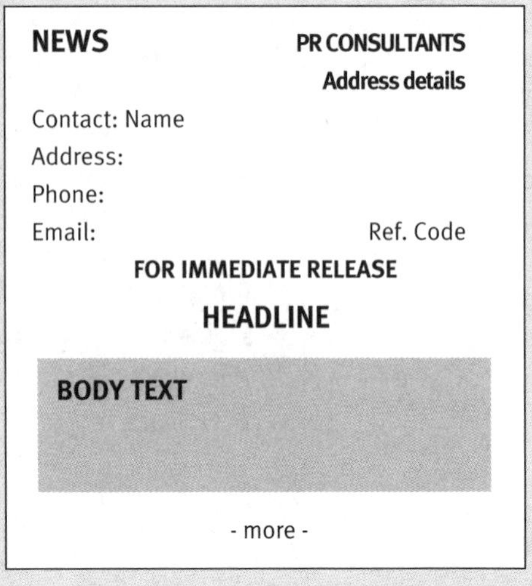

The purpose of press releases (or news releases – releases can be made available to media other than the press) is to attract editors' attention enough for them to want to include in their media. If well prepared, they will save editors a great deal of effort in having to rewrite them and increase the chances of them being accepted. More than one version of the release may have to be prepared to meet the needs of the editors of different media.

Press releases have common features designed to increase the chances of acceptance. First and foremost, the press release should be brief.

Paper

One side of plain white paper is recommended if at all possible. It is helpful for the editor to see all the information at a glance. If more than one sheet is used print only on one side. At the bottom of each page place the word 'MORE' to indicate following pages. Number the pages. At the end of the release, place the word 'End'. Coloured paper is sometimes used on the grounds that it should attract more attention. Generally, this is not to be recommended.

Typefaces

Use common, easy-to-read typefaces. 'Informal' typefaces should not be used. Make use of different sized fonts as appropriate for headings but keep font size changes to a minimum.

'News' flag

The words 'News', 'News Release' or 'Press Release' should appear in large type at the top of the press release to make it abundantly clear that the information is intended for news. Public relations agencies and companies issuing press releases on a regular basis will have their own specially designed Press Release blank letterheadings for this purpose.

Release date

Clearly identified at the top of the page will be the recommended release date for the information. It is best if the release is immediate (FOR IMMEDIATE RELEASE), but if not, an 'embargo' date should be identified EMBARGO: NOT FOR RELEASE UNTIL (date).

Contact person

The name, address and other contact details (e.g. phone number(s), email) of somebody who may be contacted for more information should be identified at the top of the page.

NEWS   **PR CONSULTANTS**
Address details

Contact: Name
Address:
Phone:
Email: Ref. Code

FOR IMMEDIATE RELEASE

HEADLINE

BODY TEXT

- more -

Identification number

Many organisations include a reference code number on each press release. Often the number will include a date reference and a file reference. This can be especially useful if large numbers of press releases are produced.

Headline

Should be short and simple. It should capture the reader's attention and summarise the information in the press release.

Body text

There is skill in preparing good headlines and main text if they are to be kept brief and focused while remaining interesting and informative. The first issue is to ask, 'Is it really news?' If it is not, it will fail to interest the editor. The opening statements should provide a summary lead into the rest of the article. It is advised that information is presented in order of importance with the most important points being raised first. Quotes are frequently used. Adopt a style appropriate for the media. If the media selected is diverse, it is possible to produce more than one version of the press release each of which puts a 'spin' on the details most suitable for the medium. Language and claims should not over-exaggerate or use unnecessary jargon.

Use of photographs or other visual material

Illustrative materials should be included as relevant with the press release to enhance its use. Details of the material should be explained e.g. name of people in the photograph could be given if relevant.

Source: Adapted from Hunt and Grunig (1994)

● *PR and publicity events and 'stunts'.* These may be one-off activities or ones that are regularly organised. Corporate events may be hosted annually to which customers, suppliers, media contacts, employees, etc. may be invited, usually for entertainment purposes. An organisation may hold corporate seats at a football stadium, racecourse, theatre or opera house, etc., which will be used for invited guests.

FOOD FOR THOUGHT

Lobbying is an activity that mostly goes on 'behind the scenes'. It can be extremely powerful even though most people may not always realise that it is taking place.

Other events may be staged specifically to generate publicity. At the launch of his autobiography, Chris Patten, ex-governor of Hong Kong, was available in bookshops in Hong Kong to sign his new book. When De Montfort University opened its new Engineering building, Her Majesty the Queen officiated at the opening ceremony. PR events are sometimes referred to as 'stunts' particularly if they are spectacular. Richard Branson's attempts to balloon around the world (with the Virgin logo prominently displayed) attracted a great deal of media attention and, while they are legitimate activities in their own right, they, and similar activities, have also ensured that the Virgin name has remained in the media spotlight over many years.

Lobbying

Approaches to influence such bodies as the government and other persuasive groups to favour the interests of the lobbyist.

● *Lobbying.* **Lobbying** is most closely associated with gaining favourable representation with members of the government. This might be either to encourage government action or to discourage it, depending upon the interests of the organisation. Cigarette companies lobby to dissuade legislation restricting their actions. Anti-smoking organisations lobby for the reverse. Companies producing health products not currently defined as pharmaceuticals, e.g. herbal preparations and health supplements, are currently lobbying European government to prevent a possible EU law requiring them to test and register their products as drugs. The companies say this will effectively put them out of business due to the costs and time delays in gaining registration. Lobbying for restricted use of genetically modified foods and changes in the package labelling of such foods has had a major impact on companies like Monsanto and has changed the behaviour of retailers such as Tesco and Sainsbury.

Lobbying need not be confined to government lobbying. It can be applied to any organisation or individual that might be identified as having a potential effect on the organisation doing the lobbying. Professional and trade bodies might be lobbied, or particular specialists, experts or celebrities. In the case of genetically modified foods, retailers were the target of lobbying activities to change their stocking and labelling policies.

● *Promotional materials.* Promotional materials of all descriptions may be used as part of MPR campaigns. Corporate videos and tapes, newsletters, magazines, brochures and direct mail can all be used.

● *MPR advertising.* Advertising for MPR purposes is used at the product and corporate level although it is usually thought of in the corporate advertising context. Whether an advertisement is intended for PR purposes or part of an advertising programme is likely to be an issue of who instigated the ad, the PR department or the advertising/marketing department, what its principal content is and who it is targeted towards.

● *Sponsorship and donations.* It is typical for sponsorship to be considered as part of the PR function. Like many MPR activities, sponsorship can be used to fulfil many different objectives, not necessarily PR ones. It is an important range of activities that are considered at length in Chapter 25. Donation giving is somewhat more altruistic and charitable in nature and may be done with little promotional benefit to the donor organisation (there may be tax benefits). It is common, though, for organisations to make it known that they do give to charitable and deserving causes and, in this way, seek to be seen as caring and concerned.

Product placement

The process of arranging for a company's products to be seen or referred to in the media, such as during television and radio programmes, videos, video games and cinema films.

- *Product placement.* **Product placement** is the process of arranging for a company's products and name to be seen or referred to in the media. This is most notable in film, and in TV and radio broadcasts, but it is equally valid in the print media. Benefits of placement are about products being seen and used, often with implied endorsement. Product placement is briefly referred to in Chapter 25 where the example of Rayban sunglasses is quoted. The sunglasses were worn by actor, Tom Cruise, throughout the film Top Gun with great effect on awareness, credibility and sales. A less successful example of product placement is for an electric drill. Black and Decker paid the producers of the 'Die Hard' films for their drill to be used by Bruce Willis during one of his exciting escape scenes. Although the Black and Decker drill was actually filmed being used, unfortunately, the scene was edited out of the final cut, Bruce Willis managing to escape without the aid of Black and Decker. Services can benefit, too, from product placement if they are mentioned or seen being used.

FOOD FOR THOUGHT

Product placement often has a subliminal effect. We see and hear it but do not consciously realise that it is there.

Advertorials

Advertisements that are designed to look as though they are editorial.

- *Advertorials.* **Advertorials** are advertisements, paid for in the usual way, but made to look like press editorial. They lack the 'glamour' and attractiveness of well-designed display advertisements but (and this is an important 'but'), they are designed to convey the credibility of third-party endorsement. They are designed to look as though they have been produced by somebody not associated with the product or company. Advertorials are required under the Advertising Standards Authority, Code of Advertising Practice, to carry a statement that it is an advertorial; often this is not very prominent. Although advertorials have been included in this section of MPR tools, when used, they are more likely to be initiated as part of an advertising campaign.

- *Corporate identity materials.* Corporate identity was described in Chapter 11, Image and Brand Management. It is an important part of the total marketing communications effort and covers all elements of company stationery and signage including the use of logos, symbols and company colours. Details of the corporate identity programme are usually kept in a company corporate identity manual which is used to provide the guidelines for all corporate identity work wherever it may appear – on letters and business cards, on company vehicles, offices and outlets, on company literature, packaging and advertising, etc.

- *Company website.* A growing area of promotional activity is the development and use by organisations of their own websites for MPR purposes. The growth in this area is quite phenomenal although the quality and functionality of websites are highly variable. Web pages for fan clubs have proliferated with official and unofficial sites being introduced daily, not only providing information but also using the sites to sell other promotional merchandise.

- *In-house magazines and customer magazines.* These are publications produced by or on behalf of an organisation targeted at customers or other publics such as employees, club members and shareholders. An in-house magazine could be in the form of a regular newsletter, a 'glossy' magazine or part of an intranet.

- *Exclusives.* MPR activities usually encourage wide coverage across the media but there may be occasions when it is better to give one medium sole or exclusive rights to a story. This is likely to increase the chance of acceptance and prominence of the story provided it is relevant to the medium's target audience.

- *Interviews, photo-calls, speeches, presentations and speech writing.* One of PR's functions is to provide spokespeople or arrange for representatives of the organisation to be available for interviews, comment, presentations and photo-opportunities. This helps ensure that the organisation's view over particular issues are conveyed in the most effective manner. There are many opportunities to arrange for photo-calls, give speeches and presentations to industry groups, business lunches, conferences, civic groups, etc. Speeches may be written by PR staff on behalf of presenters. Transcripts of speeches are often provided to the media as part of media releases.

- *Corporate literature.* Corporate publications may appear as magazines and corporate videos. These have been identified above. Other corporate literature might include that required by law such as company financial reports that are designed not only to fulfil legal obligations but also to act as promotional material in their own right.
- *Facility visits.* Tours around company offices, plant and facilities may be offered to the local community, general public, special interest groups and customers (actual and potential). Sellafield Nuclear Plant run by BNFL has a visitors' information centre. This plays an important central role as part of its promotional and PR activity. Vineyards, distilleries and brewers around the world offer hospitality visits as a normal part of their marketing communications activities.

It is a great temptation when undertaking MPR to deal with it in a fragmented fashion. Sending out press releases when there seems to be a need; arranging conferences and events when particular situations arise; reacting to competitor activities and market events; or boosting promotions when the promotional effort seems to be flagging, etc. Undoubtedly, MPR has a role to play in reacting to circumstances and events. Indeed, this is a strength of MPR. But it also has a *proactive* role to play as a much more co-ordinated and planned range of activities complementing all other forms of promotion.

When planning MPR campaigns, three sets of criteria can be used to select between the tools available. These criteria fall under the categories of *suitability*, *feasibility* and *acceptability*.

NEED TO KNOW

☑ *MPR activities can be effective when reacting to current, unplanned situations. They can also be effective when used proactively as part of a marketing communications plan.*

Suitability criteria

These criteria assess the appropriateness of the MPR activity to fit the task at hand. Typical criteria include:

- The extent to which the characteristics of the tool are suited to delivering the type of message the organisation wishes to communicate in terms of content, tone, and creative requirements of the message.
- The compatibility of the tool with other promotional and communication elements being employed and the overall image the organisation is seeking to achieve.
- The extent the tool allows particular strengths and opportunities to be exploited.
- The influence and credibility the tool is likely to have with particular publics being targeted.
- The extent to which use of the tool is likely to achieve the objectives set.

Feasibility criteria

These criteria assess how far the tool is capable of being successfully implemented given the resource constraints under which the organisation is operating. Typical criteria include:

- Whether the available budget is adequate for the tool to be used.
- Whether the organisation has the technology needed.
- Whether the organisation has the expertise needed to use the tool (or can hire it in).

- Whether there is sufficient time to make use of the tool.
- Whether the tool is a realistic approach to complete the task.

Acceptability criteria

These criteria assess how far the tool and its expected outcomes are acceptable to the organisation. Typical criteria include:

- Is the tool likely to achieve an acceptable level of coverage of target publics?
- Will the nature of the impact created meet the campaign's objectives?
- Will there be an acceptable level of control over the use of the tool?
- Is the risk of failure associated with the tool acceptable?
- Is the level of resources required to use the tool acceptable given the total resources available and the resources needed for other activities?

Advantages and limitations of marketing public relations

Marketing public relations activities are, without a doubt, important and valuable assets to the marketing communications mix. Within an integrated marketing communications plan, they complement other communications, sometimes performing roles that other marketing communications activities are unable to deliver at all or at least not as efficiently. They have the potential to provide high credibility and high visibility with cost efficiency. As Kitchen (1999) identifies:

> **Latterly, advertising, sales promotion, and personal selling have undergone difficulties in relation to achievement of cost-effective communication objectives … the emergence and application of MPR in the communications mix may be playing a significant complementary role in business organisations facing a more turbulent competitive environment.**   (p. 353)

NEED TO KNOW

☑ *MPR may be assessed in terms of their credibility, visibility and reach, cost and control abilities.*

Exhibit 24.8 summarises many of the advantages and limitations of MPR activities. They are grouped into four areas: credibility; visibility and reach; cost; and control.

Measuring the effectiveness of marketing public relations

As with all elements of marketing communications, any evaluation of their performance should be made in relation to the objectives set. If the intention is to generate sales leads, an evaluation of a public's attitudes will not be a sufficient assessment in itself, important though it may be. Objectives need to be set, be realistic and be matched against results. Frequently, a clippings book (**guard book**) is maintained either by the organisation or by its PR agency, in which publicity articles are collected. This can be facilitated by using one of a number of companies that offer media monitoring and news clipping services. This is one approach to maintaining a record of MPR activity, albeit the 'publicity' part of it. Many PR agencies have their own specific systems for evaluating their work. They do this not only to provide records of activity and measures of effectiveness, but also to emphasise the value of the work they carry out on the client's behalf.

Measures of effectiveness (and efficiency) fall into three broad categories: measures of the actual activities undertaken; measures of audience reception; and measures of

Guard book

Whenever the media refer to an organisation or its products, these may be collected and stored for reference in a guard book.

Exhibit 24.8 Advantages and limitations of marketing public relations

Credibility	● Received as third-party endorsement ● Perceived to be impartial ● Engenders trust, believability and confidence ● Not always overtly recognised as promotions ● Can be focused on product as well as corporate image and reputation ● Helps build brand awareness, knowledge and commitment ● Helps create and reinforce favourable opinions and limit or neutralise hostile or critical opinions ● Has positive benefit on sales and can help to generate sales leads
Visibility and reach	● Extends advertising reach ● Reaches audiences for some products that are not allowed to be advertised ● Reaches some audiences that advertising cannot reach as effectively or efficiently (reduces waste) ● Influences opinion leaders ● Formal opinion leaders by virtue of their position, e.g. MPs, editors, celebrities ● Informal opinion leaders by virtue of their personality or charisma ● Breaks through the advertising 'noise' and clutter by not being associated with advertising activities or being seen next to competitor advertising and other promotions
Cost	● Stretches advertising and promotional budgets by achieving extra editorial coverage for organisations, their products and even their advertising and promotions themselves (as achieved, for example, by Benetton, Club 18–30, Hoover and McDonald's) ● No purchase of airtime or media space needed in most instances ● Relative cost of MPR is low compared with other forms of promotion ● Available to small business and organisations, charity organisations and any organisations with low or very limited budget ● MPR is not free although the media coverage it generates is frequently referred to as such
Control	*Publicity* ● Low control over editorial coverage and editorial content, which can be altered from that intended. Media release can be used by editors to subvert the original positive messages to present them less positively or even emphasise negative aspects ● Accuracy of information presented in the media cannot be controlled ● Timing of appearance of releases cannot be controlled *Other MPR activities* ● Other MPR activities can be controlled in terms of their use, e.g. conferences, lobbying, sponsorship, etc., even if their effectiveness cannot be guaranteed

audience behaviour. The area of MPR evaluation that tends to be reported most is the area of publicity and editorial measurement. This forms a significant part of marketing public relations but assessment of other MPR activities should not be ignored. Exhibit 24.9 lists a range of measures as examples against these three categories. They should not be considered comprehensive.

It is very common practice to report on media coverage expressed in '**advertising equivalent** terms', for example, to say that a publicity campaign was worth £x of advertising. This is calculated by:

Advertising equivalent

Measure of public relations coverage whereby an estimate is made of what the coverage would have cost if it had been paid for at advertising rates.

1 calculating the amount of time given in TV and radio reports and the number of column centimetres given in editorial coverage;
2 estimating what it would cost if all this media coverage were paid for at advertising rates.

Thus, if a MPR campaign achieved five minutes of TV and radio news coverage and 200 column centimetres of press editorial and this was estimated to be equivalent to £150,000 at advertising rates, it could be said that the MPR campaign was worth £150,000 of advertising.

Exhibit 24.9 Measures of MPR effectiveness

		Assessment area	Examples
Measurement of actual MPR activity undertaken	*Coverage*	Evaluation of amount and type of editorial coverage achieved through publicity	Range and number of media Number of column centimetres or amount of time devoted to editorial Number of mentions Type of publication or broadcast Position in publication or broadcast
	Content	Content analysis of editorial coverage	Accuracy of editorial reflecting original media release Number of positive mentions, number of adverse mentions in all editorial Impact of editorial Use of content analysis software
		Evaluation of quality of MPR publications	Assessment of suitability of publications in communicating necessary information and creating favourable impressions
	Targeting	Evaluation of audiences reached	Total audience reach Target audience reach Audience wastage
	Actions	Response to events Efficiency of organisation of MPR activities Evaluation of contacts made	Speed of response in dealing with unplanned events Number of media contacts made, their positions in the media Number and 'quality' of lobbying contacts made
Measurement of audience reception		Surveys of levels of awareness and related attitudes	Tracking studies of awareness levels and attitude changes – pre-campaign, during and post-campaign
Measurement of audience behaviour		Measures associated with changes in behaviour	Attendance Sales

While this is common practice, it is not, on the whole, a valid way of measuring MPR effect. It tends to encourage misconceptions about the true cost and effect of publicity. It might be that the editorial was almost entirely negative or that it was seen by only a small proportion of the target audience. It might be that the level of awareness achieved, or impact created, was very much less than that which could have been achieved by £150,000 of well-designed and placed advertising.

Measuring the quantity of publicity is only part of the total evaluation process and it can misrepresent the actual effects achieved. Using quantitative measures alone might miss out on the more qualitative aspects of editorial coverage. Content analysis of editorial is always to be advised.

WARNING

! *Care should be exercised in placing too much reliance in using advertising equivalent measures when assessing MPR. The measures are frequently used but it is best to use them in conjunction with other assessments.*

To assist in this process, computer software is available which eases the task and avoids criticism of subjective assessment of content.

Summary

Public relations represents a wide spectrum of activities, many of which are particularly relevant to marketing communications; these fall within the remit of marketing public relations (MPR) which has been described as a 'healthy offspring' of the merging of marketing and public relations. MPR can be divided into corporate MPR and product MPR. At the corporate level, MPR is concerned with the organisation as a whole; at the product level, it is concerned with individual products and brands. All MPR activities should be considered in an integrative way.

In common with the theme adopted throughout this book, public relations practitioners have for a long time recognised the importance of focusing communications on a range of target audiences (publics) for whom particular communications are devised. This has perhaps led to a greater emphasis within the PR community of the importance of integration than has been evident elsewhere in the overall marketing communications field.

Hunt and Grunig (1994) have suggested that four public relations approaches predominate and that these are related to the extent to which PR is viewed as one-way or two-way communications. Their 'models' need not be confined to the field of PR but can, indeed, be considered relevant to all forms of marketing communications. Two-way, symmetric communication is generally to be encouraged and this, of course, is the driving force behind direct marketing communications which are featured in Chapter 27.

Various aspects (scope and tools) of MPR have featured prominently in this chapter and each one has been briefly described. The chapter has commented on how MPR effectiveness may be measured, and the main advantages and limitations of MPR, under the headings of credibility, visibility and reach, cost and control, have been identified. These four areas may be considered as critical areas of MPR. MPR offers particular advantages in terms of credibility, visibility and reach, and cost efficiency when compared to other fields of marketing communications but controlling MPR is not always straightforward, especially in the area of publicity.

Self-review questions

1 What is meant by the term 'publics'? Identify the major publics to any commercial organisation.

2 Why should publicity not be considered as free advertising?

3 Why is it difficult to control publicity?

4 What is meant by two-way asymmetrical communications?

5 What is the relationship between MPR and PR?

6 What are the eleven areas that have been identified within the scope of MPR?

7 What are the main components of a press release?

8 What is lobbying? How may it be used by an organisation?

9 Identify a range of advantages and limitations of MPR compared with other forms of marketing communications.

10 How might the effectiveness of publicity be measured?

Project

'There is no such thing as bad publicity'. Identify examples of negative publicity from the press and broadcast media and discuss the pros and cons of this statement.

For an organisation to which you have access, undertake an audit of their corporate promotional material. Assess the material in terms of its range and consistency. Does the organisation use a corporate identity manual as a rule book for corporate materials? Is the rule book followed?

References

Barrett, P. (1997), A marriage of PR and ads. *Marketing,* 30 October, 15.

Cobb, R. (1998), Pointing the way to PR. *Marketing,* 12 March, 29.

Cutlip, S., Center, A.H. and Broom, G.J. (1995), *Effective Public Relations.* Prentice Hall.

Gage, T.L. (1981), PR ripens role in marketing. *Advertising Age,* 5 (January), 10–11.

Goodrich, J.N., Gildea, R.L. and Cavanaugh, K. (1979), A place for public relations in the marketing mix. *MSU Business Topics,* 27 (Autumn), 53–57.

Harris, T. (1993), *The Marketer's Guide to PR: How Today's Companies Are Using the New Public Relations to Gain a Competitive Edge.* John Wiley and Sons.

Haywood, R. (1984), *All About PR.* McGraw-Hill.

Haywood, R. (1991), *All About Public Relations* 2nd edn. McGraw-Hill.

Hunt, T. and Grunig, J.E. (1994), *Public Relations Techniques.* Harcourt Brace.

Kitchen, P.J. (1993), Public relations: a rationale for its development and usage within UK fast-moving consumer goods firms. *European Journal of Marketing,* 27 (7), 367–384.

Kitchen, P.J. (1999), *Marketing Communications: Principles and Practice.* International Thompson Business Press.

Kotler, P. and Mindak, W. (1978), Marketing and public relations. *Journal of Marketing,* 42 (4), 13–20.

Moss, D. (1990), *Public Relations in Practice.* Routledge.

Shandwick plc (1989), *The Public Relations Consultancy Market Worldwide.* Shandwick plc.

Shimp, T.A. (2000), *Advertising, Promotion, and Supplemental Aspects of Integrated Marketing Communications* 5th edn. The Dryden Press.

Selected further reading

Harris, T. (1993), *The Marketer's Guide to PR: How Today's Companies Are Using the New Public Relations to Gain a Competitive Edge.* John Wiley and Sons.

Harrison, S. (1999), *Public Relations.* Thompson Business Press.

Howard, S. (1998), *Corporate Image Management: A Marketing Discipline for the 21st Century.* Butterworth-Heinemann.

Hunt, T. and Grunig, J.E. (1994), *Public Relations Techniques.* Harcourt Brace.

Moss, D. (1990), *Public Relations In Practice: A Casebook.* Routledge.

White, J. (1991), *How to Understand and Manage Public Relations.* Business Books.

Wragg, D. (1993), *Targeting Media Relations.* Kogan Page.

Chapter 25

Sponsorship

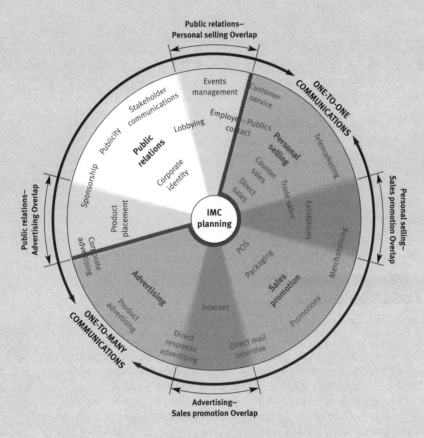

The Integrated Marketing Communications (IMC) Mix Model

CD

Using the CD material in Case Study 3 and your own research, identify which sponsorship strategies Pampers employ. Evaluate these strategies, as detailed in this chapter, in terms of: strategic fit, difficulty in imitation, tradeability of resource and limits to competition.

Objectives

- To identify factors that have contributed to the growth of sponsorship
- To explain different types of sponsorship and how these differ from charitable donations and patronage
- To identify benefits and risks associated with sponsorship
- To emphasise the need to think of sponsorship as a strategic activity that can create competitive advantage
- To discuss some of the problems and ethical issues currently faced by sponsorship managers

Professional perspective

Adrian Hitchen Executive Director, SRI

The way in which sport sponsorship is used as a marketing communications vehicle has changed markedly in recent years. Increasingly, companies are looking for more integrated ways to fit sponsorship into their overall marketing strategy or, in some cases, are now using it as a theme that runs throughout their marketing-communications mix. But whichever way you look at it, *integration* seems to be increasingly important, and not just in terms of using sponsorship to build 'traditional' marketing promotions, but also in terms of exploiting some of the more contemporary communications and technological developments.

The sponsorship market has evolved considerably from the late 1970s and early 1980s. In those days the general focus tended to be on creating awareness, putting the company or brand name in front of the largest possible audience. It was often seen as a relatively inexpensive form of advertising. It evolved, in my view, during the late 1980s and early 1990s to being treated as far more of a communication vehicle, where name awareness was clearly still necessary, but you couldn't possibly just leave it there and call it a day! Instead, sponsorship was increasingly seen as a platform from which to communicate a message to the consumer, and so greater emphasis was placed on creating and funding *proper* marketing support programs. We have now seen that evolve, I think, into a new era where companies are trying to build real interactivity into those sponsorship campaigns. It is no longer just a case of building a platform, standing on it and shouting to the crowd; it is now about trying to get some of that crowd to join you on the platform and to communicate with them in a one-to-one relationship. Sponsorship does allow you, in most contexts, to do that, because you are generally empathising with a fan of the sport or activity. So, bringing this up-to-date, the advent of new technology is addressing the perceived need for interactivity head on. I have no doubt whatsoever that as Internet usage grows and website marketing becomes a main item on more and more corporate marketing agendas, we will see sponsorship applications increasingly being constructed as one-to-one communications.

The same trend will be fuelled in the next five years or so, I believe, by digital television, especially as so many major media groups see sport as the mechanism through which to build their channel. With the acquisition of major sports rights by digital channels in the future (the terrain currently most occupied by the satellite and cable companies), I think we will see yet more applications of sponsorship on an individualised interactive basis. Furthermore, there is little doubt that both the sports organisations and, more especially, the sponsors are going to have to work harder at their communication. In the days ahead, the home viewer will also be his/her own television director, able to opt for any one of x different views of an arena or racetrack. In the case of Formula 1, for example, the viewer may even choose to be 'on board' with, say, Michael Schumacher for an entire race, if that is what s/he wants to do. It is clear that some of the traditional, simple, mechanisms for conveying the sponsorship message (a corporate logo on a race-car, for example) are going to be less and less effective, and will no longer enjoy the guaranteed exposure to a relatively passive viewing audience as in the past. But at the same time, the fact that viewers will still opt to watch a sporting event or access a sports website opens up many new and exciting opportunities to communicate in a much more dynamic manner. At present, I think we are seeing this more in the US than in Europe – as is so often the case, the US does lead – but I have no doubt that these new communications technologies, and consumer demand for interactive 'participation' will change sponsorship dramatically over the next ten years throughout the world.

Adrian Hitchin

IN VIEW 25.1

Owens-Corning and freestyle skiing: a perfect fit

In the mid-1980s, Owens-Corning was going through some changes. Diversification from insulation into other hardware supplies such as roofing shingles and window frames was accompanied by expansion into markets in Europe, Brazil and the Far East. Management at Owens-Corning wanted to portray an image both to these new markets and to investors on Wall Street that the company was fresh, exciting and worth investing in. After much research, it was decided to enter into a sponsorship agreement with the Canadian Freestyle Skiing team. The reason for this was given by the firm's Marketing Director, who suggested that 'sponsorship is a very inexpensive way, compared to traditional advertising, to get your message in programming'. And as for choosing freestyle skiing, he noted that:

> the sport is growing leaps and bounds, we're growing leaps and bounds, so it's great to piggyback on their growth; the sport is about innovation, people do things that other people are scared to death to do. Companies like ours want to be known for innovation. We're not just an insulation company any more, we're into other markets: roofing shingles, windows, lots of things, so what we're beginning to sell is innovation.

In addition, Owens-Corning's publicity material described the common link in values between the sport and the company: 'Freestyle is off the beaten path of tradition and the sport's unique qualities of panache, courage, and skill are directly transferable to the corporate style of Owens-Corning.' Recognising the resource that they had, the company was determined to hang on to it. It therefore set about developing the relationship into one that would prove beneficial for both parties. Owens-Corning first helped the sport gain Olympic status, then assisted with the development of a national training centre. It has also developed one of the best video libraries in the world on the sport and even helps train athletes to deal with life after retirement. The effort has worked. The two parties are in weekly contact, discussing new ideas that might be beneficial to one side or the other. As the Marketing Director told us, 'they give back to us everything we give to them; they love us as much as we love them'. The formal agreements between the two sides, which were first signed in 1986, have been renewed ever since, with little sign of any parting of the ways.

Source: J. Amis, N. PLant and T. Slack (1997), Achieving a sustainable competitive advantage: a resource-based view of sport sponsorship, *Journal of Sport Management*, 11(1), 80–96.

Sponsorship

Contribution to an activity by an organisation. Although sponsorship may be purely altruistic, it is normally undertaken with the expectation of achieving benefit for the sponsor, e.g. in achieving corporate or marketing-related objectives.

Sponsorship was described in the previous chapter as an aspect of public relations which is one of the four principal areas of the Integrated Marketing Communications Mix Model. It is a rapidly growing element of the marketing communications mix and yet, while it is one of the most widely used, it is also one of the least well understood. In 1996, the size of the global sponsorship market was estimated at US$16.6 billion, an increase of nearly US$9 billion from the 1990 figure, and a fifteen-fold increase from the US$1 billion spent in 1980. The two most lucrative markets are North America, which accounted for 36% of the 1996 expenditure, and Europe, which took up 33% (*Sponsorship News* 1997). Individual sponsorships ranged from a few hundred pounds for a local sports or cultural event to the US$40 million that companies like Eastman Kodak and Bausch & Lomb paid to sponsor the Atlanta Olympics. This growth pattern has continued into the new millennium throughout the world.

Reasons for the growth of sponsorship

The growth of sponsorship as a form of marketing communication can be attributed to a number of factors.

- *Concern over traditional promotional methods.* First, many corporations have become concerned about the value of traditional forms of marketing. Concomitantly, technological advancements have resulted in an explosion of marketing possibilities 'with the attendant problem of clutter and cost efficient access' (Meenaghan 1998, p. 4). As the number of commercial television and radio stations has risen, traditional advertising has produced a proliferation of messages within the medium. Sponsorship is seen as an alternative and often cheaper form of gaining exposure that avoids clutter and allows a sufficiently distinctive message to be seen and/or heard (Howard and Crompton 1995).
- *Creation of favourable associations.* Sponsorship has increasingly been viewed as a way in which to generate audience awareness while at the same time create an association between the values the sponsored entity exemplifies and the sponsoring

company (Meenaghan 1996). In View 25.1, for example, shows how an insulation company was able to create a sense of adventure and excitement about itself and its products by sponsoring freestyle skiing, one of the most thrilling of the Winter Olympic sports.

● *Overcomes linguistics/cultural barriers.* Sponsorship also has the ability to transcend cultural and linguistic barriers. It is no coincidence that sport, the arts and music are the areas that receive the most amount of sponsorship funding as these are activities with global appeal.

● *Wide/multiple target audience appeal.* Sponsorship as a marketing medium can be used to influence strategic partners, company staff, civic officials and government regulators, while at the same time appealing to customers and, as such, influence a company's 'bottom line'.

● *Overcomes legal barriers.* Sport sponsorship has also provided a vehicle to legitimate products such as alcohol and tobacco. While a number of countries ban or provide stringent regulations to govern the advertising of tobacco and alcohol products, sponsorship has provided a platform that has given these potentially harmful products an air of respectability. It also allows them access to television coverage and a youth market, nationally and internationally. In the past, tobacco companies have been particularly adept at using Formula 1 motor racing for this purpose. In Canada, concerns over tobacco sponsorship of sporting and cultural events has arisen and the federal government has given sponsored organisations a five-year period to find replacement funds. Similar restrictions are increasingly being applied throughout Europe.

● *Selective targeting.* Finally sponsorship has grown in popularity as a form of marketing communication because it provides an excellent means of targeting selected market segments. As Sleight (1989) pointed out,

> **sponsorship works because it fulfils the most important criterion of a communications medium – it allows a particular audience to be targeted with a particular message.** (p. 42)

Beefeater Gin's sponsorship of the Oxford–Cambridge boat race is a good example of such an association. Gin drinkers are mainly seen as a middle/upper-class set and these are the type of people who constitute the bulk of those who are interested in the boat race.

What is sponsorship?

There are a number of different definitions of sponsorship (e.g. Meenaghan 1983; Sleight 1989; Sandler and Shani 1993). In an attempt to provide a sufficiently broad definition to accommodate a wide range of sponsored activities, and the motives for such support, an adaptation to Berrett's (1993) definition is appropriate,

> **Sponsorship is a contribution to an activity by a commercial organisation in cash, or in kind, with the expectation of achieving corporate and marketing objectives.** (p. 325)

In the fulfilment of corporate objectives, sponsorship can be seen to have strategic recognition. Sponsorship may also be used for particular brand and marketing communications purposes and, as such, fulfil specific marketing objectives. It is important to distinguish sponsorship activity from charitable donations and patronage. Many companies make charitable donations or engage in patronage. Unlike sponsorship, these organisations rarely expect public recognition for this type of contribution. A sponsoring company will view its sponsorship as a business relationship from which it expects to gain a competitive advantage; philanthropy in the form of charitable donations and patronage carries no such direct expectation although there may be marketing public relations benefits that can be exploited. The section on cause-related marketing, later in the chapter, picks up this theme.

Forms and levels of sponsorship

There are many different forms of sponsorship such as sponsoring individuals, organisations, teams, events, and causes.

The sponsorship of individuals

The sponsorship of individuals, particularly sportsmen and women, has become an increasingly popular type of arrangement. Here, an individual performer is paid a fee to endorse a particular product or service, for example Gary Lineker's involvement with Walkers Crisps. Endorsements, because they involve individuals, are in some ways riskier than sponsoring a team or event. Following David Beckham's dismissal in the 1998 World Cup match against Argentina, an incident widely seen as leading to England's subsequent elimination from the tournament, Adidas immediately stopped screening the television advertisements that featured Beckham (Farrell 1998). This, of course, has not prevented Beckham becoming one of the highest paid personalities in 2003, commanding multi-million euro endorsement fees for his work. Similarly, Pepsi's sponsorship of Michael Jackson's World Tour was terminated when he came under police investigation for child abuse (Hitchen 1995). Endorsement by individual athletes can also lead to conflicts, such as occurred at the 1992 Olympics. Several members of the USA's basketball 'Dream Team' endorsed Nike products but Reebok was the official sponsor of the team and team tracksuits carried the Reebok logo. As a result, when they had to appear in their official tracksuits at the medal ceremony, those athletes who were Nike endorsers carried US flags to cover up the Reebok logo.

Levels of sponsorship

Sponsorship may also be provided at a number of different levels. The most visible example of this occurring is in the structure of the Olympic Games sponsorship programme. At the 1996 Games in Atlanta, there were three major categories of sponsor. At the highest level were TOP (The Olympic Programme) sponsors. These were the ten companies that were granted the right by the International Olympic Committee (IOC) to market themselves worldwide in association with the 1994 Winter and 1996 Summer Olympic Games. For the US$40 million that they paid for the privilege, these companies were able to make use of all Olympic marks and appropriate Olympic designations on their products. They were also given exclusive hospitality opportunities at the Games, granted preferential access to broadcast advertising, and had on-site concession and product sale/showcase opportunities (1994 Olympic Marketing Fact File). Below TOP sponsors were 'Centennial Olympic Games Partners': these companies, who included in their number Anheuser-Busch, AT&T and Delta Air Lines, were given marketing rights from the Atlanta Committee for the Olympic Games to associate themselves domestically (within the US) with the 1996 Games and the US Team. Below the 'Partners' were 'Centennial Olympic Games Sponsors' who had similar, but more narrowly defined, rights to the Partners (Rozin 1995). It is important to note that

not all of these agreements were in cash and some sponsors provided goods or services in lieu of cash. It is also worth pointing out that the money sponsors paid was just for attaining sponsorship rights. In addition to the US$40 million it provided to the IOC, Coca-Cola spent an additional US$200 million on leveraging its investment (Greising 1995). Also, many companies that were unwilling or unable to take on one of the major types of sponsorship were able to 'buy in' at a lower level by sponsoring a national Olympic Committee, for example the British Olympic Association, or supporting a national sport governing body, such as Basketball Canada. In this way, sponsors were able to associate with the Olympic Games at considerably less expense.

Official/title sponsorship

While the Olympic Games may be the pinnacle of sponsorship, similar tiers of support can be found in less grandiose events. Some sponsors are designated as 'official'. For example, for US$250,000 the Prudential Real Estate Affiliates assumed the title of 'Official Host' to the 1992 America's Cup. However, the organising committee also sold non-exclusive sponsorship packages to local businesses in the San Diego area where the race was to be held for only US$2500. This granted merchants the right to use the America's Cup logo on their stationery and have their name listed in the America's Cup directory (Catherwood and van Kirk 1992). Some companies buy what is referred to as 'title sponsorship'. For example Orange, the digital mobile phone company, created The Orange Prize for Fiction while companies such as Bass Brewery and Nationwide have had title sponsorship of the Premier Football League.

Other forms of sponsorship

Other opportunities that have been embraced by corporate sponsors include award ceremonies such as the ITV Barclaycard Champions of Sport event. Teams such as Manchester United (sponsored by Sharp and others) have also benefited, as have museums such as the London Science Museum, supported by Toshiba, and arts festivals such as the one in Belfast sponsored by Sainsburys. In the United States, where sponsorship is even more rampant than it is in Europe, sports facilities have become the most recent target for sponsors. The United Center, where the National Basketball Association's (NBA) Chicago Bulls and National Hockey League's (NHL) Chicago Blackhawks play, receives approximately US$875,000 from United Airlines. Continental Airlines Arena in East Rutherford, New Jersey, the home of the NBA's Nets and the NHL's Devils, receives an estimated US$2.2 million from the company. Similar arrangements exist with over 40 other major US sports stadia and arenas (Kirk 1997).

The ability to transcend national barriers and target a youth audience has made popular music another attractive sponsorship opportunity. Multi-national firms such as Coca-Cola, Pepsi and Philips have exploited the fact that Michael Jackson, Prince, Dire Straits and other artists can deliver a captive audience relatively cheaply (Meenaghan 1998). In fact, it has been estimated that 10% of all sponsorship expenditure in the United States in 1997 was on popular music (IEG 1997).

The benefits and risks of sponsorship

Why is it that companies are willing to spend such large amounts of money on the different forms of sponsorship highlighted above? What are the gains and potential losses that can emanate from this form of marketing activity? As was noted earlier, one of the benefits attributed to sponsorship is that it can be more efficient than other forms of marketing communication because it can generate both audience appeal and link the values of the sponsored entity to the sponsor. Sponsorship can also transcend cultural and geographical boundaries. It is effective at targeting different audiences, can help forge links with local business and political communities, and can be used to improve employee relations (Berrett 1993). While these characteristics have been widely cited as contributing to the rapid growth of sponsorship, they are not the only benefits. Others may include:

- *Community image building.* Sponsorship can be used to present the sponsoring company as a good corporate citizen, an organisation that gives back to the community. Slack and Bentz (1996), for example, showed how small business owners felt that they were able to build up an image as a socially responsible organisation with community politicians, the local media, and other non-consumer audiences because they sponsored local events. The goodwill that was established in this way could then be used when the manager needed help from one of these individuals or the organisations they represented.
- *Marketing leverage.* Sponsorship also appeals to corporations as a marketing communications medium because it can be tied to other marketing activities that are designed to influence both customers and strategic partners. Product trial opportunities which are often linked to sponsorships can, Howard and Crompton (1995) suggested, move a customer from the interest stage of the product adoption process to the desire stage, the stage which involves a serious evaluation about whether or not to purchase a product. They provided the example of the manufacturers of 'Ultra Fuel' high-carbohydrate drink that felt it could not compete with the advertising budget of Gatorade but wanted to get its drink into the hands of top-class athletes. It therefore sponsored a series of multi-sport and cycling events at which the product was available for sampling, thus achieving its objective at minimum expense.

> **NEED TO KNOW**
>
> ☑ *Sponsorship can facilitate movement along the hierarchy of effects. It is not only useful for heightening awareness, it can also encourage trial and use.*

- *Hospitality opportunities.* As well as influencing customers many companies want to create a good relationship with existing and/or potential partners, suppliers or distributors. One way to strengthen these business-to-business relationships is to tie sponsorship to hospitality opportunities. According to Meenaghan (1983):

> **hospitality refers to those opportunities whereby the company can make face-to-face contact with select publics in a prestigious social context, thereby strengthening and personalising relationships with decision makers, trade channels, and business associates.**
>
> (p. 37)

Corporate sponsorships of many art and cultural events, and sports spectacles like Wimbledon, are frequently used for this purpose.

- *Media leverage.* Because many of the events that receive sponsorship money are high profile, sponsors are often able to capitalise on the media attention that follows these types of activities. This coverage has also allowed some companies to circumvent regulations on their products which state that they are unable to advertise on television – alcohol and tobacco products being the most obvious examples.

Virginia Slims, for instance, gained considerable exposure for its support of women's tennis, something it would not be able to get through normal advertising channels. Even when there are restrictions on sponsorship, with the advent of satellite broadcasting local regulatory restrictions can be overcome by sponsoring activities known to gain international coverage.

Each of the benefits outlined above has been fairly well documented in the literature. However, work by Amis et al. (1997) and Slack and Bentz (1996), which has attempted to look at sponsorship using the strategic management literature as a framework for analysis, has suggested that there may be other more subtle benefits to this type of activity. Amis et al. (1997), for example, showed that sponsorship could be exploited just like any other resource to assist a firm to a position of competitive advantage. Slack and Bentz (1996) have suggested that one benefit that can accrue from sponsorship is that it can be used to counteract the strategic initiatives of competitors. Using data from a sample of small businesses involved in a variety of sponsorships, they showed how owner-managers become involved in similar sponsorships to competitors to negate any advantage the competitors may derive from their association with a team or event. This type of work, which takes its lead from the broader literature on strategic management and marketing, has considerable potential to increase our understanding of the benefits of sponsorship, but has as yet received only limited attention.

> **WARNING**
>
> ! It is important to choose the right sponsorship deals in the first place to ensure synergy between the sponsor and the sponsored. However, best-laid plans can go astray. Sponsorship deals, particularly with individuals, can go wrong through unforeseen and detrimental circumstances.

While there are many benefits that can be gained from sponsorship, it would be wrong to suggest that this type of activity does not come without risks:

- *Negative associations.* In some situations the image of the sponsored entity may have a negative impact on the company providing support. While this is most likely to be the case where an endorsement of an individual athlete is made, it can also involve a team or an event. For example, a sports team which does not perform well or a theatre production that flops is unlikely to provide its sponsor with the type of image they are expecting from the association.
- *Sponsorship clutter.* There is also the possibility that events may become 'overly sponsored'. Formula 1 cars, which carry a multitude of corporate names and logos, can present the type of clutter that companies try to escape by using sponsorship. Similar problems have been experienced by sponsors of soccer's World Cup Finals.
- *Over-commercialisation.* Excessive commercialisation can also turn off sponsors. John Hancock President David D'Alessandro was quoted as saying that at the 1996 Olympics many sponsors were insulted by the naked commercialism on the streets of Atlanta (*Business Week* 1998). Former Canadian ski coach, Currie Chapman, highlighted the impact that sponsorship can have on athletes when he suggested that it's not just the skiers going down the mountain but it's also a bank, a drugstore, a car parts chain as well.
- *Evaluation problems.* Sponsorship is also risky because, like other marketing communication tools, while it can have significant benefits these are extremely hard to assess empirically. There are a multitude of techniques used by marketing companies which range from surveying customers to see if they are influenced by sponsorships to evaluating the amount of media exposure a sponsored event receives. This latter approach was identified in Chapter 24, Public relations, as one of the methods used for assessing PR activities more generally, and publicity in particular. However, none of these provide a particularly valid form of evaluation and each can be confounded by factors such as the use of other marketing tools, carry-over

effects from previous campaigns, and uncontrollable environmental factors. In addition techniques such as ambush marketing (which are discussed in more detail later) can be effectively used to negate any advantage gained from sponsorship. Kinney and McDaniel (1996), for instance, found that at the 1992 Olympic Games, McDonald's and Visa were not recalled as being official sponsors at a significantly higher level than Wendy's and American Express which played an ambush role.

The strategic nature of sponsorship

In much of the literature, sponsorship has been described as a strategic activity. It is strategic because, as Slack and Bentz (1996) point out,

> it concerns decisions about the allocation of resources to achieve organisational objectives and also because it is used to align an organisation with the pressures and demands of its environment.
> (p. 177)

Sponsorship can be used strategically as part of an expansion strategy, in turnaround situations, or to create competitive advantage; like any other strategic initiative it also influences, and is influenced by, corporate culture, organisational structure and company leadership.

Much of the writing that has suggested that sponsorship is a strategic activity has focused on the way in which this type of activity can be used to attain corporate objectives. Abratt et al. (1987) produced a list of such objectives for sport sponsorship and suggested that potential television coverage, promoting corporate image, and the opportunity for media coverage were the most important reasons given by the 45 corporations who responded to their study. In a similar piece of work Witcher et al. (1991) surveyed 140 'large commercial organisations' and found the main objectives cited were the promotion of corporate image, television, radio, and press exposure, and the promotion of brand awareness. Marshall and Cook (1992) used companies from *The Times* list of the top 1000 companies and found building corporate image, appealing to a target audience, and having television and press coverage to be the highest objectives of these companies. While these types of studies have merit, they do not go far enough in enhancing our understanding of the strategic nature of sponsorship. Objectives, while useful at one level are, as Meenaghan (1983) has previously noted, often 'nothing more than post facto rationalizations of a particular sponsorship activity'.

In an attempt to go further than work which has merely identified the objectives of sponsorship initiatives, Amis et al. (1997) have utilised an approach known as the resource-based view of the firm (Grant 1991; Mosakowski 1993; Peteraf 1993). Their work has shown how sponsorship can be used strategically to establish and retain a position of competitive advantage. They argue that sponsorship needs to be seen as a resource in much the same way that a company sees its other physical or human resources.

Resources, such as sponsorship, can thus be a source of competitive advantage; however, to attain this position they must fulfil four criteria:

● *Strategic fit* – first, those companies that succeed in achieving competitive advantage through sponsorship do so by establishing a better 'fit' between themselves and the entity they sponsor than similar initiatives by other companies. Virginia Slims' link with women's tennis and Marlboro's support of Formula 1 and Indy Car racing represent such compatible images. Other cigarette companies have not been able to obtain such a fit and hence are trying to compete with an inferior resource. Similarly, In View 25.1 provides an example of how Owens-Corning built a strong relationship with the Canadian freestyle skiing team in an attempt to portray an image as an exciting, innovative company that set it apart from its competitors.

- *Difficult to imitate* – however, it is not simply enough for a company to have a superior sponsorship resource as any competitive advantage will be lost if that resource can be easily replicated. Therefore, the second criteria for a sponsorship to be a source of competitive advantage is that it must be difficult for a competitor to imitate. In order for this to occur the sponsorship undertaken must tie in 'with other facets of the [sponsoring] firm's image to produce a resource capable of discouraging industry competitors from directly competing with the resource' (Amis et al. 1997, p. 86). Owens-Corning worked hard to tie the excitement of freestyle skiing to their product but they also worked with the sports governing body to get freestyle skiing events into the Olympic Games. This enabled them to build up a strong rapport with the sport and, following the success of Canadian freestyle skiers at the 1994 Olympics, it meant that there was also a strong name association between the two entities. It would thus be very difficult for another company to easily duplicate the success of Owens-Corning with a similar sport, or persuade freestyle skiing to give up their sponsor in favour of a new arrangement. The signing of long-term contracts between the two organisations further strengthened this position of non-imitability.

- *Tradability of resource* – the Owens-Corning agreement also helped to fulfil the third criterion for competitive advantage sponsorship success, that the resource (in

---

IN VIEW 25.2

Japanese electronics company decides sponsorship is a waste of money

In the late 1980s, this consumer products company became established in Canada. It also became committed to a wide range of sport sponsorships. Money was invested in sponsoring Indy Car racing, golf tournaments, professional tennis, Canadian Olympic athletes, and a National Football League quarterback. The reasons for these outlays were explained by the company's Marketing Director as being:

because we had the dollars to do that and ... a vice-president who was very committed to sports. He loved sport, all kinds of sports, from car racing, to football, baseball, the whole wide range of stuff. So because of his personal interest we gave a lot more to sports than probably a lot of companies.

Athletes were used mainly at lavish product launches. However, there was no attempt to leverage their involvement across any other part of the marketing communications mix. There was almost a feeling that they were a luxury to be enjoyed during times of munificence, but not something that added real value. Therefore, when the company started to hit hard times, the sponsorship budget was virtually the first thing to be eliminated. From the early 1990s, no new sponsorship contracts were agreed, and existing deals were not renewed upon their expiration.

Source: J. Amis, N. PLant and T. Slack (1997), Achieving a sustainable competitive advantage: a resource-based view of sport sponsorship, *Journal of Sport Management*, 11(1), 80–96.

the form of the sponsorship) should be non-tradable or, if tradable, be of greater value in the firm that is currently employing it. Budweiser, for example, through its support of the Super Bowl and the creation of the well-known 'Budbowl', created a situation that protected its sponsorship resource from being traded to someone else by the Super Bowl organising committee. Owens-Corning did this by building up an association with freestyle skiing that was of more value within their company than with a rival. In addition to working with the sport to gain it Olympic recognition, the company also created a video library for the sport, had company staff help at domestic events, helped with the development of a national training centre, and worked with individual athletes to help prepare them for retirement.

● *Limits to competition* – the final factor that Amis et al. (1997) identified as a requirement for competitive advantage through sponsorship is the presence of *ex ante* limits to competition. That is to say, there must be risk and uncertainty surrounding the use of a resource to allow it to be secured at a rate below its true market value. Sponsorship presents this type of risk or uncertainty because there is always the possibility of an event, individual or team failing. Even a major event like the Olympic Games where preparations are painstakingly rehearsed can present a risk as IBM's experiences in 1996 clearly demonstrated. When Owens-Corning became involved with freestyle skiing, the sport was relatively new and did not have Olympic status. The firm was therefore able to build up a strong association cost-effectively, and thus gain maximum benefit from the sport's subsequent surge in popularity.

The work of Amis et al. (1997) shows just one way in which the strategic nature of sponsorship can be explored. This type of work is useful because sponsorship has largely moved from being pure philanthropy to being seen as an investment from which managers expect to receive a significant return. As such, decisions on what to sponsor and how much to spend have become inherently strategic in nature, and thus need to be considered in the light of what other marketing the firm is carrying out.

Integrating sponsorship into the marketing mix

Industry analysts are adamant that any sponsorship needs to be carefully integrated into the other components of the marketing communications mix. Nigel Geach (1998) of Sports Marketing Surveys, for example, has stated that the days of sponsoring a team or event because of personal interest are largely over. Successful sponsorship, he suggests, requires 'a total marketing package. It is not just a sticker on a car, a patch on a tennis player, you have to integrate it with all your other marketing activity.' This, of course, is a view endorsed throughout this text.

Too much sponsorship?

Even if sponsorship is well integrated into a company's marketing mix, there are signs that sponsorship investments are not producing the returns that they once did. The acknowledged worldwide leader in the sports marketing industry and a company that has built its reputation on securing high profile athletes to endorse its products, Nike, posted its first ever loss on 1 July 1998 (August and Cunningham 1998). While there are several reasons for this, not least the cyclical nature of the fashion industry on which Nike is dependent for the majority of its sales, it also suggests that the power of traditional sport sponsorship may be waning. Further evidence for this was provided by the 1998 soccer World Cup. According to a survey published in *Marketing Week*, almost 70% of the UK population believed that too many manufacturers were jumping on the World Cup bandwagon. Despite companies spending £20 million to be associated with the competition, and a similar amount on advertising, 66% of respondents could not name the tournament's 12 official sponsors. Even the sponsor cited most often, McDonald's, was only mentioned without prompting by 25% of those surveyed (Millar 1998).

A major reason for this apparent reduction in effectiveness is, paradoxically, the overall success of this form of marketing communications. This success has resulted in more firms wishing to get involved in sponsorship without a corresponding increase in the number of quality sponsorship opportunities. There has also been a realisation by property owners that they can maximise their incomes by differentiating between various levels of sponsorship opportunities. For example, in the case of the Olympic Games, a firm can become involved in TOP, or as an official sponsor of the Olympic Games Organising Committee, a National Olympic Committee, or a National Governing Body. This proliferation of sponsorship opportunities has led to clutter which, as we have seen in the case of the World Cup, has resulted in a decreased ability to influence consumers, while at the same time costs have continued to rise. According to Meenaghan (1998), this has devalued traditional sponsorship as a marketing communications tool. In order to differentiate one's firm in a cluttered market, sponsorship managers are looking at increasingly innovative ideas.

WARNING

! *Increasingly, popular sponsored activities are becoming overcrowded with marketing communications messages. In such a cluttered microenvironmental context (see Chapter 7), marketing communications may become much less effective.*

Sponsorship developments

Technological advancements have presented several new sponsorship opportunities, such as interactive games and the Internet. At the moment these are still relatively minor, but three areas that have grown markedly in recent years are **broadcast sponsorship**, **product placement** and **cause-related marketing** (Meenaghan 1998).

Broadcast sponsorship

Sponsorship of a particular TV or radio programme.

Product placement

The process of arranging for a company's products to be seen or referred to in the media, such as during television and radio programmes, videos, video games and cinema films.

Cause-related marketing

The process of associating an organisation with 'worthy' causes. Marketing communications benefits are gained by supporting and being seen to support worthwhile causes such as charities.

Broadcast sponsorship

A programme is deemed to be sponsored if any or part of its costs of production or transmission is met by an organisation or person, other than a broadcaster or producer, with a view to promoting its own or another's name, trademark, image, activities, products, or other direct or indirect commercial interests (Mintel 1997). The sponsorship of programme broadcasts began in earnest outside the US in the 1980s and has increased rapidly with the advent of satellite television, the liberalisation of broadcast regulations in the 1990 Broadcasting Act, and the harmonisation of European laws. As a result, this type of sponsorship has become more pronounced. This is exemplified by Texaco's three-year £12 million sponsorship of Formula 1 motor racing and Cadbury's £10 million sponsorship of Coronation Street. The Cadbury's–Coronation Street tie-up provides synergy between the two brands' positioning and target markets. All Cadbury's target groups are represented in the programme, from pensioners to young children, and the copy line used by Cadbury, 'the nation's favourite', appears to be a natural fit with Cadbury and Coronation Street being market leaders in their respective fields.

IN VIEW 25.3

Toyota launch New Year sponsorship deal with ITV

In December 1997 Toyota concluded a multi-year £18 million broadcast sponsorship deal with ITV. The sponsorship deal came in two parts. Firstly the car manufacturer sponsored up to 32 hours of programming on New Year's Eve and New Year's Day for five years up to the end of 2002. Additionally Toyota sponsored ITV's Movie Premiere series for three years.

Building awareness was seen as a key objective for the investment as confirmed by Neal Deeprose, Saatchi and Saatchi's media group director, the man responsible for putting the deal together. The sponsorship was used in the first year of the deal to launch the Avensis, Toyota's most important new car in years. With regard to the creative strategy the agency were careful with the executions to get the brand message across, i.e. 'It's a new year and this is a new car'. The deal was unique in the sense of making the sponsorship investment a central part of an important car launch.

Source: Cook (1997)

Exhibit 25.1 Eight options for programme sponsorship

Off-the-peg programme sponsorship

This is sponsorship of a programme that already exists. You pay your money and the programme is aired whenever the broadcaster wishes. The sponsorship could be of a particular programming feature such as Toyota's sponsorship of ITV's Movie Premiere series.

Made-to-measure programme sponsorship

The sponsor describes the sort of programme that is wanted and the broadcaster makes the programme or re-schedules an existing one that suits subject to not contravening national rules.

Pre-commissioned programme funding

This requires a producer or production company to be found who is willing to develop the sponsor's programme idea or one that presents an idea for funding to the potential sponsor. It is recommended that funding is withheld until there is a definite commission so that, as sponsor, you know that the programme will be aired. The producer maintains most of the control of the development.

Programme-led off-air promotion

This is where the sponsor exploits a programme through off-air promotions such as fact sheets, in-store promotions, use of the stars, etc. The sponsor is basically cashing in on the programme's popularity without necessarily being involved in sponsoring the programme itself.

Pre-sponsoring or pilot co-funding

The sponsor agrees to sponsor a programme before it is made or gives the producer development money to secure the right (either exclusive or joint) to sponsorship.

Invent own format, have a producer/broadcaster make it and sponsor it

The advantage of this route is that there is involvement in the process of production from the start. It requires the producer/broadcaster to like the idea enough to think it is worth producing. The programme is their's once made.

Speculative funding

In this instance, the sponsor himself arranges for a broadcaster to agree a commission. The sponsor makes her/his own programme and delivers it to the broadcaster once made. It is speculative in that there may be no guarantees that the programme will be commissioned. Once it is accepted, the sponsor owns the rights that can be sold on to others. As an alternative approach to limit the risk, if a broadcaster is willing to commission the programme idea before it is made, the sponsor can simply sell on the rights and have someone else make the programme. In reality, this is not really the area in which sponsors will tend to become involved.

Product placement

Product placement in TV programmes (not films) is highly limited in the UK but it is accepted that scripts require the use of, or mention of, products and services if they are to be believable. The use of products are, therefore, a natural programme requirement. It is possible to 'encourage' the use of a 'sponsor's' products in favour of other alternatives. The reality is that product placement occurs and that payment in cash or in kind is made for the privilege.

Source: Adapted from Armstrong (1996)

Broadcast sponsorship has been growing substantially both on TV and the radio. With the growth of commercial radio stations since 1990, radio sponsorship has seen a dramatic increase with the Radio Advertising Bureau estimating that, as an industry average, sponsorships and promotions accounted for 15%–20% of commercial radio revenues. One of the largest radio programme sponsorships is Pepsi's sponsorship of the Network Chart Show with the Association of Independent Radio Companies. Pepsi extended this sponsorship into television when they launched The Pepsi Chart Show on Channel 5 in 1997. This is an example of a new development in the area of programme sponsorship, outside the States, where the sponsor funds programme development, production and distribution. In the UK, television and radio programme sponsorship is regulated by the Independent Television Commission (ITC) and the Radio Authority (RA) respectively. The ITC Sponsorship Code was introduced in 1990 and updated in 1994, 1997 and 2000. There are various rules and regulations such as restrictions on sponsor product placement and influence over editorial content of the programmes. The regulations for radio sponsorship are not as stringent as those for television and may partly explain the greater use of this media by sponsors. The US and each of the European countries adopt their own codes for programme sponsorship and can vary significantly in their operation.

NEED TO KNOW

☑ *Television and radio sponsorship is subject to regulatory controls. In the UK, the bodies responsible are the ITC and the RA. The BBC and the independent television and radio broadcasters are also responsible for ensuring that the regulations are adhered to. Similar regulatory bodies exist in other countries throughout the world.*

Product placement

With sponsorship the audience knows what is on offer, with product placement it does not. Product placement is defined as the inclusion of, or reference to, a product or service within the programme in return for payment or other valuable consideration to the programme maker or ITC licensee. Strictly speaking, this is prohibited by the ITC and the BBC. However, both the ITC and the BBC are finding it increasingly difficult to control and hard to prove such cases given the proportion of programmes now made by independent programme makers. Because of this problem the ITC enforces the 'undue prominence rule' which considers whether a brand has been shown too prominently and whether the programme has gone beyond using a branded product or service to provide programme authenticity and realism. For example, the ITC fined Granada's *This Morning* programme £500,000 for the over-emphasis of a range of women's jewellery and a magazine competition.

NEED TO KNOW

☑ *Product placement is prohibited in the UK. But it still takes place.*

The same regulations, however, do not apply to films (made for cinema, TV, video or DVD) and with the growth of cinema, satellite/cable/digital and video/DVD over the last decade, they are seen as an increasingly viable media for companies. One of the most frequently cited examples is the placement of Ray-Ban sunglasses in the 1986 film *Top Gun*, which led to a turnaround in the company's fortunes. The film was a major success and the shades, Rayban Aviators, became synonymous with the star of the film, Tom Cruise. More recently in 1997, BMW supplied the makers of the James Bond film *Tomorrow Never Dies* with seventeen 750iL cars, each worth £75,000, in order to have their product associated with the James Bond character. Today, it would be hard to find any film without some element of product placement. Producers actively seek out and invite companies to participate as a means of partially funding production costs, together with tying in sponsorship and merchandising deals as part of the total film-making financial arrangements.

Cause-related marketing

Corporations have a long history of giving to charitable causes but in recent years they have become increasingly concerned about realising some commercial advantage for funds they give to these causes. As such, cause-related marketing has grown in popularity and in 1997 accounted for 9% of US sponsorship spending (IEG 1997). This type of sponsorship involves a firm aligning itself to a particular charitable cause or foundation, and supporting it either financially, or donating staff time and/or product. The sponsoring company, if providing a direct financial contribution, will often make this amount proportional to the sales generated by the promotion over a particular period of time (Meenaghan 1998). The United Way is a big beneficiary of this form of corporate giving in the US; the controversial Millennium Dome is a good example from the UK. Meenaghan (1998) suggests that cause-related marketing allows firms to portray themselves as 'caring, benevolent, community-oriented and humane' although he has cautioned that companies must be careful not to over-exploit the relationship and thus generate a negative reaction among the general public.

Ethical issues

WARNING

! *Ethical considerations should be borne in mind when choosing what to sponsor.*

The proliferation of sponsorship agreements has also led to a variety of tactics that have been morally questioned by some commentators including the exploitation of youth and the use of ambush marketing.

IN VIEW 25.4

Cause-related marketing pays dividends for American Express

When it became apparent that the Statue of Liberty required restoring, American Express (AMEX) jumped at the opportunity of becoming involved. However, this was not a gesture of pure philanthropy to the American people. The company had three specific objectives:

1 To increase credit card usage among its current card holders.
2 To encourage the acceptance of the card among merchants.
3 To increase the company's profile and derive image benefits that would lead to new members.

The scheme involved AMEX giving one cent to the restoration fund for each US-based transaction, and $1 for each new card issued. The project raised $1.7m for the project, while the company reported an increase in its credit card usage of 2.8% on the previous year, a greater acceptance of the card by merchants, and a public image of being more 'responsible, public-spirited and patriotic'.

Source: Meenaghan (1998)

Youth exploitation

As pressures on the public purse have increased, institutions such as schools and hospitals have become increasingly attracted to private sources of income. However, some have questioned whether it is appropriate for commercial enterprises to be allowed into these types of environment. A recent example that has provoked much comment in the media is a scheme in which the Tesco's supermarket chain is providing computers to various schools across the UK. The exposure of young, impressionable children to such a prominent marketing presence has drawn criticism from some politicians. Firms need to be aware that such negative publicity can be potentially harmful. A *Marketing Week* survey found that 58% of respondents felt that sponsors exploited children. Despite this, several companies are focusing aggressive campaigns on the youth market. Steve Martin, Marketing Manager at Adidas, has stated that his company looks for 'symbols that appeal to kids on and off the pitch'. Thus, he suggested, soccer star David Beckham with his good looks, love of fast cars, and pop-star wife, former Spice Girl Victoria Adams, is a perfect marketing image. In fact, as well as targeting children, Adidas is goes even further by sponsoring young athletes. Joe Cole, widely tipped as a future England soccer player, is among several youth players that Adidas has considered. According to Martin, 'all the big brands are fighting for [athletes] at that young age'. It is a practice that Nike have been carrying on for some time. Their sponsorship of the American Girl's High School Basketball Champions, Oregon City, has raised questions as to the ethics of exploiting a group of 15-year-olds to promote a product.

Ambush marketing

Ambush marketing

Organisation's intentional effort to weaken the effect of another's sponsorship.

Ambush or parasitic marketing involves a firm, often a competitor, attempting to deflect attention from another sponsor onto itself. McKelvey (1994) described **ambush marketing** as:

> a company's intentional effort to weaken or ambush its competitor's official sponsorship . . . by engaging in promotions or advertising . . . that seek to confuse the buying public as to which company really holds official sponsorship rights.
>
> (p. 20)

By so doing, ambush companies seek to gain the benefits of a particular sponsorship at a fraction of the cost. There are various ambush strategies that a firm can employ. The first is to sponsor the media coverage of the event but not the event itself. Second, a firm could sponsor a sub-category within a particular event, such as a National Governing Body of an Olympic sport, and then heavily market the association. Third, a company could sponsor an individual athlete, such as Gatorade's sponsorship of footballer Alan Shearer, and then run advertisements during the main event. Fourth, a firm might run a parallel advertising campaign in order to raise its own awareness with consumers at the same time that a competitor is trying to leverage its official sponsorship. Finally, a company could run an advertising campaign that features the type of activity being sponsored, but not the actual event. The last point is exemplified by Fosters' ambushing of Steinlager during the 1991 Rugby World Cup.

Ambush marketing can be very effective. Meenaghan (1996) cites the example of Wendy's advertising campaign that featured US figure skater Kristi Yamaguchi during the 1992 Winter Olympics. So effectively did Wendy's ambush official sponsor

NEED TO KNOW

☑ *There is no overarching regulation that controls sponsorship although it is still subject to professional codes of practice and the general law of the land.*

McDonald's that 57% of respondents to a Performance Research, Inc. survey incorrectly identified Wendy's as the official sponsor, while only 37% correctly identified McDonald's. In fact, the problems of ambush marketing has become so important that event owners such as the IOC, UEFA and FIFA have devised various sophisticated strategies to overcome them (Meenaghan 1998). These range from the packaging of broadcast rights with sponsorship agreements to the creation of 'hit squads' to enforce the rights of official sponsors and expose the ambushers.

Summary

This chapter has identified some of the issues that are involved in sponsorship agreements. While some emphasis has been placed on sporting examples, sponsorship can be related to a very wide range of activities and approaches. There is a need to understand that sponsorship has moved from being a purely philanthropic activity practised by firms with personal connections with a particular event or activity, to a resource that needs to be integrated into the firm's entire marketing communications mix. As such, it has been argued that potential sponsorship investments need to be considered at the strategic level in that they have the potential to assist the firm achieve a position of sustainable competitive advantage.

Sponsorship also involves a range of very effective tactical activities.

It is necessary to be aware of the clutter that has resulted in sponsorships becoming, potentially, less effective than they have previously been. Because of this, innovative ways have to be found that put the marketing communications message across to the target audience clearly and unambiguously. However, in attempting to do this, some firms have blurred the lines between morally acceptable and unacceptable behaviour. With no current wide-ranging legislation that covers the industry as a whole, each firm must decide where the limits lie between what is good marketing practice, and what is undesirable exploitation.

Self-review questions

1 What factors have contributed to the growth of sponsorship?

2 Why should sponsorship be considered a resource that can be exploited for competitive advantage?

3 What factors need to be present, according to Amis et al. (1997), in order for sponsorship to have the potential to lead to a position of competitive advantage?

4 In what ways can a firm engage in 'ambush' marketing? Is this unethical practice, or just effective marketing?

5 Given the ease with which ambush marketing can be implemented, does sponsorship represent good value for money?

6 Why does sponsorship's ability to transcend cultural and linguistic barriers make it a popular marketing communications tool? Which companies are likely to benefit most from this?

7 What is cause-related marketing and how does it differ from other aspects of sponsorship?

8 Do you think that companies should be allowed to market their products directly at children by sponsoring school activities and/or facilities?

Projects

Assume that you are the Marketing Communications Director of an alcoholic drinks company. Although the company has used sponsorship in the past, it has been on an ad hoc basis. You are considering the more strategic benefits of sponsorship for the first time. Your board has asked for some preliminary early suggestions as to what forms of sponsorship might be suitable for longer-term use as a part of the company's wider marketing communications plan. Identify the principal objectives that you would wish sponsorship to achieve, recommend what types of sponsorship the company should at first consider and indicate the synergistic benefits they might have with other elements of the marketing communications mix.

Look out for examples of programme sponsorship on TV and radio and product placement in the cinema, on television, radio, video and DVD. Identify how they are being used and how appropriate there use seems to be. How effective do you think your examples of programme sponsorship and product placement are and in what ways do you think the sponsors have benefited?

References

Abratt, R., Clayton, B.C. and Pitt, L.F. (1987), Corporate objectives in sports sponsorship. *International Journal of Advertising*, 6, 299–311.

Amis, J., Pant, N. and Slack, T. (1997), Achieving a sustainable competitive advantage: A resource-based view of sport sponsorship. *Journal of Sport Management*, 11, 80–96.

Armstrong, S. (1996), Advertiser TV: into uncharted territory. *Media Week*, 22 March, 21–23.

August, O. and Cunningham, S. (1998), Just do it, says Nike but teenagers say no thanks. *The Times*, 2 July, 1.

Berrett, T. (1993), The sponsorship of amateur sport – government, national sport organization, and corporate perspectives. *Society and Leisure*, 16, 323–346.

Business Week (1998), The risks and rewards of going for the gold. *Business Week*, 9 February, 64–65.

Catherwood, D.W. and van Kirk, R.L. (1992), *The Complete Guide to Special Event Management*. John Wiley & Sons.

Cook, R. (1997), Has sponsorship become a brand building tool? *Campaign*, 19 December, 10.

Farrell, S. (1998). Adidas gives red card to Beckham ads. *The Times*, 2 July, 5.

Geach, N. (1998), Sports marketing and sponsorship. Radio 5, 13 July.

Grant, R.M. (1991), The resource-based theory of competitive advantage: implications for strategy formulation. *California Management Review*, 33 (3), 114–135.

Greising, D. (1995), Let the hype begin. *Business Week,* 2 February, 117–118.

Hitchen, A. (1995), Sponsorship research – towards achieving and measuring sponsorship success. A paper presented at the International Conference on World Sport Management, Atlanta, 30 November.

Howard, D.R. and Crompton, J.L. (1995), *Financing Sport.* Morgantown, WV: Fitness Information Technology, Inc.

IEG (1997), *Annual Estimates of Sponsorship Expenditure.* Chicago, IL: International Event Group.

IOC (1994), *Olympic Marketing Fact File.* International Olympic Committee.

Kinney, L. and McDaniel, S.R. (1996), Strategic implications of attitude-towards-the-ad in leveraging event sponsorship. *Journal of Sport Management,* 10, 250–261.

Kirk, J. (1997), Arenas help airlines get in the game. *Chicago Tribune,* 4 June, 1.

Marshall, D.W. and Cook, G. (1992), The corporate (sports) sponsor. *International Journal of Advertising,* 10, 307–324.

McKelvey, S. (1994), Sans legal restraint, no stopping brash, creative ambush marketers. *Brandweek,* 18 April, 35.

Meenaghan, T. (1983), Commercial sponsorship. *European Journal of Marketing,* 7, 2–73.

Meenaghan, T. (1996), Ambush marketing – a threat to corporate sponsorship. *Sloan Management Review,* 38 (1), 103–113.

Meenaghan, T. (1998), Current developments and future directions in sponsorship. *International Journal of Advertising,* 17, 3–28.

Millar, S. (1998), Advertisers drain the cup dry. *The Guardian,* 10 July, 3.

Mintel (1997), *Annual Estimates of Sponsorship Market Values.* Mintel.

Mosakowski, E. (1993), A resource-based perspective on the dynamic strategy–performance relationship: an empirical examination of the focus and differentiation strategies in entrepreneurial firms. *Journal of Management,* 19, 819–839.

Peteraf, M.A. (1993), The cornerstones of competitive advantage: a resource-based view. *Strategic Management Journal,* 14, 179–191.

Rozin, S. (1995), Olympic partnership. *Sports Illustrated,* 24 July (special advertising section).

Sandler, D.M. and Shani, D. (1993), Sponsorship and the Olympic games: the consumer perspective. *Sport Marketing Quarterly,* 2, 38–43.

Slack, T. and Bentz, L. (1996), The involvement of small businesses in sport sponsorship. *Managing Leisure,* 1, 175–184.

Sleight, S. (1989), *Sponsorship: What Is It and How To Use It.* McGraw-Hill.

Sponsorship News (1997) July edition.

Witcher, B., Craigen, J.G., Culligan, D. and Harvey, A. (1991), The link between objectives and function in organizational sponsorship. *International Journal of Advertising,* 10, 13–33.

Selected further reading

European Journal of Marketing (1999), Sponsorship special edition, 33 (3 and 4).

International Journal of Advertising (1998), Sponsorship special edition, 17 (1).

Meenaghan, T. (1991), The role of sponsorship in the marketing communication mix. *International Journal of Advertising,* 10, 35–47

Chapter 26

Advertising

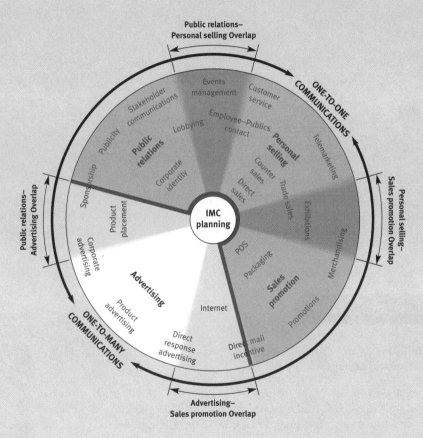

The Integrated Marketing Communications (IMC) Mix Model

CD

Select three different Pampers advertisements: a TV ad, a poster ad and a print ad. Using the checklist in Exhibit 26.6, evaluate the effectiveness of these advertisements. What are each of the advertisements objectives? How do they work in terms of strong and/or weak forces, salience and hierarchy of effects?

Chapter outline

- What is advertising? How does it differ from the other elements of the marketing communications mix?
- Benefits and role of advertising
- Does advertising work?
- Advertising – strong force or weak force?
- Salience and USP – survival of the fit enough, not the fittest
- Cognitive–affective–conative responses
- General theory of advertising versus situation-specific theory of advertising
- Types of advertisements
- Producing advertisements that work

Objectives

- To distinguish advertising from other elements of the marketing communications mix
- To emphasise advertising's use of the mass media
- To consider the main value of advertising
- To present arguments about how advertising is said to work
- To illustrate different types of advertisements
- To offer suggestions on how to produce effective advertisements

Professional perspective

Colin McDonald Principal Consultant, McDonald Research Editor of the *International Journal of Advertising*

In my book *How Advertising Works* (Advertising Association, 1992), I ended with a number of conclusions about the nature of advertising. I think these still hold true, and a brief restatement of some of them may be a good introduction to this chapter.

The sheer *variety* of advertising means that it will always be an art rather than a science and that generalisation is dangerous. It is worth keeping this in mind whenever we think about advertising. That said, advertising (as distinct from other marketing actions) does have some distinguishing features, which give it a special place.

First, advertising works within economics, not against it. It cannot swim against the tide of a market. In the West especially, there are many markets which have reached the limit of their development: advertising can do nothing to expand these. Individual consumers do not do things they do not otherwise want to do, purely as the result of advertising.

Within a market, advertising can be a powerful force in establishing and sustaining market share. It does this by investing the brand with its own 'equity', which in turn is maintained by various franchise-building activities (of which advertising is one) and, more importantly, by actual brand experience. A few brands attain positions which are hard for competition to assail: these top brands need less effort to stay ahead and may command premium prices. But advertising also helps the competition, and thus helps to keep prices down and to fuel the dynamic equilibrium between brands.

Advertising does not always work: a vital and difficult role for research is to ensure that it will. There is much evidence, especially now from single-source data and from the increasing corpus of IPA Effectiveness Awards, that effective advertising does quickly generate responses, including the bottom line (sales). But there is also wide agreement that short-term results from advertising are rarely if ever enough to pay back the cost: price promotions, in modern scanner data, often show much sharper results, which has led many companies to devote excessive amounts of budget below-the-line in spite of the proven cost and damage this can cause to the profitability and long-term health of the brand. Long-term effects are much harder to measure, because of the simultaneous occurrence and possible synergy of other variables which affect consumers over time. But they have to be the basis on which advertising budgets are justified, and the importance of measuring them is increasingly acknowledged. The good news is that data and methods of modelling it to identify longer-term effects are improving all the time. There is less excuse than there used to be for managements not to invest in the analytical techniques required to justify advertising budgets.

Colin McDonald

What is advertising? How does it differ from the other elements of the marketing communications mix?

Advertising

The use of paid mass media, by an identified sponsor, to deliver marketing communications to target audiences.

This first section of this chapter provides an understanding of **advertising** as just one element of the marketing communications mix and one of the four broad areas of marketing communications identified in our Integrated Marketing Communications Mix Model. It is important to recognise this as so many people prefer to use the word 'advertising' as though it describes all forms of promotional activity. It is not just the 'lay person' who confuses advertising in this way, there are many examples within the industry itself. Part of the reason for this is historic. Advertising is a term that has been popularised for the longest. We see bodies such as the Advertising Standards Authority, the Incorporated Society of British Advertisers and the European Advertising Standards Alliance who not only represent the interests of the advertising community but also embrace other promotional areas such as direct mail and sales promotion. Their names have been around for so long, they are unlikely to change them to better reflect their wider remits.

WARNING

! Many people confuse the meaning of advertising. It should be distinguished from other forms of marketing communications activity. Often it is used as a term to describe a wide range of different promotions well beyond the remit of advertising.

To complicate the matter, other terms are also used interchangeably with advertising. This ambiguity, of course, can and does cause quite a lot of confusion. As Crosier (1999) comments, 'Many business-to-business marketers use the term "publicity" to describe what a consumer-product brand manager would call advertising. Furthermore, the word for advertising in three major world languages – French, Portuguese and Spanish – is the direct equivalent of "publicity". To create still more confusion, commentators routinely describe publicity as "free advertising" and contrast it with "paid advertising"' (p. 266).

Advertising defined

The difficulty of defining what advertising is and what it is not is compounded by the fact that frequently it is combined with other promotional elements. Examples include sales promotion where a competition or a money-off offer is included in the advertisement, and direct marketing activities where a direct response coupon or telephone number is included.

As seems to be commonplace in the world of marketing, definitions abound. This is as true of advertising as it is of marketing itself. A reasonable definition of advertising should clearly distinguish it from other promotional elements (although at the end of the day some would argue 'does it really matter?'). It matters to the extent that confusion is avoided when talking and writing about it. If a manager asks for an advertising plan it should be just that and not a plan for the whole promotional mix.

In deference to the general usage of term 'advertising', Kotler et al. (1999) define it in a broad way as:

> **Any paid form of non-personal presentation and promotion of ideas, goods or services by an identified sponsor.** (p. 793)

Kotler, in previous works, has also identified that advertising uses the mass media. Advertising's use of mass media is considered here to be an important dimension of advertising although it begs the question of what, nowadays, to include as mass media. We suggest, as indicated in Chapter 5, Media – the carriers of the message, that it should include TV, radio, cinema, press, posters, direct mail and the Internet. Without some consideration of the media used for advertising, it could be confused with, say, an unmanned exhibition display which would meet the criteria of the above definition but would not generally be considered as a form of advertising.

Wells et al. (1992) give the following definition which includes reference to the mass media:

> **Advertising is paid non-personal communication from an identified sponsor using mass media to persuade or influence an audience.** (p. 10)

Crosier (1999) highlights the important components of advertising in his definition. Advertising is:

> **communication via a recognisable advertisement placed in a definable advertising medium, guaranteeing delivery of an unmodified message to a specified audience in return for an agreed rate for the space or time used.** (p. 266)

(The term 'agreed rate' has been used here to replace Crosier's term 'published rate' as there is often a difference between the rates published by the media and the eventual agreed rate which is actually paid by the advertiser after negotiation.)

The significance in Crosier's definition of *guaranteeing delivery* of an *unmodified message* in a *recognisable advertisement* for an *agreed rate* is the fundamental distinction between advertising and product placement and publicity. Product placement is the positioning of products in an editorial environment such as in a television programme or cinema film (or possibly, in somebody else's advertising). Publicity is not guaranteed to run in the media and may be subject to alteration of the original message by the media owners. This would not be the case for advertising. Advertising, furthermore, is required to be clearly identifiable as such. In situations where an advertisement is deliberately made to look like a publicity item (i.e. it is made to look like editorial), it is required to carry a statement that it is an advertisement feature. This requirement is imposed by the voluntary codes of practice adopted in many countries.

Coverage of advertising throughout this book

It is important to recognise that key elements of advertising include the determination of the best message in the most appropriate mass media to reach identified target audiences and to achieve stated objectives. These sorts of considerations are covered at length in many of the other chapters in this book. They are covered elsewhere because they are issues of relevance not only to advertising, but to all elements of the marketing communications mix. For this reason, the reader is advised that a substantial proportion of this book needs to be read in conjunction with this chapter if a full appreciation of advertising is to be reached. In particular, the following chapters are suggested for emphasis:

> **WARNING**
>
> ❗ *This chapter covers some aspects of advertising. It is important that other chapters are read in conjunction with this one if a fuller understanding of advertising is to be reached.*

- Chapters 1 and 2, which provide an overview of integrated marketing communications and advertising's place within it;
- Chapter 3, which covers issues related to the message;
- Chapters 5, 6 and 21 on media;
- Chapters 4 and 17, which provide an insight into buyer behaviour and an understanding of segmentation and targeting principles;
- Chapter 9 on regulation;
- Chapters 14, 15, and 18 on organisational, operational and budgeting issues;
- Chapters 13, 16, 19 and 23 on analysis, evaluation, planning, objective setting, strategy and tactics;
- Chapters 20 and 22, which cover creative and production issues.

Benefits and role of advertising

Advertising is often considered as the 'senior' element of marketing communications. This view is perhaps an historic one but is firmly entrenched in the minds of many. Those whose jobs are primarily focused on other elements of the promotional mix would, of course, challenge this with some justification. What is unequivocal is the fact that advertising accounts for huge proportions of promotional spends. Whether it is more important or less important than other elements should really not be an issue. Its relative importance is something that should be determined in each individual case as the marketing communication plan is developed.

> **NEED TO KNOW**
>
> ☑ *Advertising is inherently no more important than any other element of the marketing communications mix. Within the context of a particular campaign, it may be used more extensively than other elements or play a lead role. Alternatively, other elements may be given more weight and prominence. It depends upon what the campaign needs to achieve.*

Each promotional element, however, should be selected for those things that it is good at doing. And as has been identified previously, the elements should be placed together to achieve the benefits of integrative synergy (see Chapter 2, What is integrated marketing communications?).

Principal benefits of advertising are:

- it can reach mass audiences (large coverage),
- it, increasingly, is able to reach mass audiences selectively (i.e. better targeting),

- it has low unit cost (i.e. low cost per thousand),
- it is economical, efficient and effective at reaching large audiences,
- it is successful at brand maintenance (and many argue that it is successful in brand development).

However, how well an advertising campaign is planned and implemented will have a significant bearing on whether or not the above benefits are achieved.

Although anything from religious and political beliefs to government and charitable services can be advertised, the most money by far spent around the world is on corporate and brand advertising by such global giants as Procter & Gamble, Unilever, Nestlé, Philip Morris, General Motors, Nike, McDonald's and Coca-Cola to name but a few. The top five spenders alone account for worldwide billings of over US$20 billion.

What role advertising should play will be affected by the overall intentions of the advertising plan although it is generally agreed that advertising is better at achieving some things rather than others. It is considered, for example, to be capable of reaching large audiences and being effective and cost efficient at achieving high levels of awareness, creating brand differentiation, informing and reminding and, over the longer term, developing and maintaining brands. Some argue that once started, advertising should be a continuous activity. Although there may be a decay effect of advertising (i.e. if stopped, previous advertising will have a diminishing effect over a period of time), it is argued that advertising needs to be continuous if a market presence and share of voice is to be maintained. Because of the competitive nature of the marketplace, advertising should be used to maintain competitive advantage or, at least, maintain the brand in customers' brand repertoires or consideration sets. That is to say, encourage customers to include or maintain the brand as a possible purchase along with others that they usually buy.

Evidence from the PIMS study

FMCG

Fast-moving consumer goods – typified, for example, by such products as soap powders, cosmetics, sweets and crisps.

The PIMS (Profit Impact of Market Strategy) study, which for many years has collated and analysed FMCG marketing communications data from around the world, has led to a number of conclusions about how company profits are affected by (among other things) their use of marketing communications. For our purposes here, three conclusions are relevant and relate to (1) the proportion of spend as a function of market standing, (2) the proportion of spend as a function of market growth, and (3) the proportion of spend as a function of market fragmentation.

A&P budget

Allocation of expenditure on advertising and promotions.

1 For brand leaders, PIMS suggest that around 70% of the advertising and promotions (A&P) budget should be spent on advertising. The remaining 30% should be devoted to the other promotional tools in the marketing communications mix (not including personal selling which they considered, in line with industry practice, as a separately budgeted element). Number 2 and 3 brands should spend around 50–60% of their A&P budget on advertising.

2 In declining markets, the proportion of the A&P budget spent on advertising should increase. In growing markets, the proportion spent on other promotions should increase.

3 As markets concentrate, the proportion of advertising spend should reduce. In fragmented markets, the optimum profits were found when advertising was around 85% of the total marketing communications spend.

While the evidence for these conclusions is extensive, the conclusions themselves are not immutable; they are questioned by many marketing managers as to how widely the PIMS data may be applied and whether it is relevant in all situations. For example, questions may be raised over:

- applicability to non-FMCG product areas;
- long-term versus short-term effects;
- consistency and comprehensiveness of information – when submitting information on marketing communications budgets, how consistent and comprehensive were the companies data?
- applicability to different market situations, e.g. small markets, niche markets, operating with very small market shares;
- consideration of market growth – to what extent does zero growth or rates of growth/decline affect the situation?
- how should a concentrated or fragmented market be defined?

What is advertising used for?

NEED TO KNOW

☑ *Advertising is used extensively in industrial and business-to-business settings and not just for consumer promotions.*

Hierarchy of effects models

Models that describe the stages individuals are said to progress through in moving from initial unawareness to final action such as purchase and consumption. There exists a range of models or ways of describing the stages in the process.

Advertising is most frequently thought of in the context of consumer display advertising but this is inappropriate. It is also used widely for industrial and business-to-business products and for consumer and industrial classified advertisements. Although advertising can be seen as expensive in overall cost terms this has to be outweighed by the fact that many million members of target audiences can be reached. The cost to reach each member can, in fact, be very low indeed. With increasing fragmentation of media and the introduction of new media, the cost of advertising can be reduced through better targeting and the use of lower cost media such as the Internet.

A generalised view of the relative merits of each of the broad categories of the promotional mix is presented in Exhibit 26.1 in relation to the AIDA **hierarchy of effects** model that was discussed in more detail in Chapter 4. It should be emphasised that this is a simplistic perspective, but, nonetheless, it is a helpful one in developing an overview.

IN VIEW 26.1

Success of advertising

The Institute of Practitioners in Advertising reported on results from a study of data supplied by PIMS-Europe. The study examined the success of advertising and concluded that advertising has a positive effect on business success and contributes to corporate profitability. The report further commented that:

- Advertising impacts on customer value through its effect on perceived quality thus increasing profitability.
- It is how the money is spent that matters – not how much more is spent than competitors.
- The nature and content of advertisements really do matter – focusing on how product image or company reputation affects the customer's perception of quality and therefore value.

Source: IPA Report, Advalue 1 (1998)

Exhibit 26.1 The promotional mix mapped onto the AIDA hierarchy of effects model

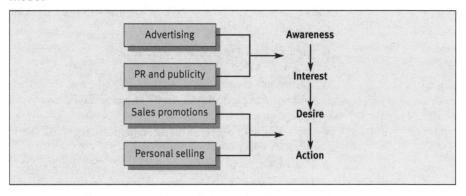

Advertising, like PR, is considered good at raising levels of awareness, generating interest and enhancing brand development. Typically, advertising is not considered to be a strong force in encouraging customers to take action (purchase). This view, however, is somewhat limiting and inaccurate. Advertising takes many forms, some that emphasise brand image and attributes, some that are very much 'hard sell'. Many of the discussions on how advertising works tend to be centred around FMCG consumer display advertising which is only a part of the total picture – important though it may be. **Classified advertising**, which accounts for a significant proportion of advertising spend (around one quarter of total advertising expenditure in the UK, for example), is a much ignored and maligned aspect of advertising. Significant levels of sales and actions result from classified advertising – from the purchase of secondhand products to sending in an application form for a new job in the case of recruitment advertising. By adding sales promotion offers within an advertisement it is possible to move customers through the hierarchy from generating awareness to taking action. Direct response advertisements expect action to be taken.

It is important to recognise that advertising is multi-faceted. All the more so as advertisements take advantage of improved technologies to move advertising away from 'tell-to-sell' approaches to encourage dialogue with customers and consumers. Increasingly, advertisements carry free-phone telephone numbers and web page addresses that can be used to provide more information and enhance the selling activity.

Classified advertising
Advertisements that appear in the classified sections of the mass media.

BARB
Broadcasters' Audience Research Board. This body, established in 1980 and jointly owned by the BBC and ITV, is responsible for producing information on TV viewing activity and audience reaction. Electronic meters and diaries from over 4400 nationally representative households are used to record the information.

Does advertising work?

The fact that so much resource is put behind advertising by so many organisations is testimony to the belief that advertising really does work. Millions of pounds are spent on researching advertising on an ongoing basis by organisations such as **BARB** and **JICNARS**, which are organisations responsible for commissioning research on television viewing and press readership respectively, as well as organisations such as AGB Taylor Nelson and Millward Brown, which regularly undertake awareness and attitudinal surveys (see Chapters 16 and 23 for more information). These activities all seek to confirm advertising's positive effects.

Yet it remains an unfortunate fact of life, despite all the research undertaken throughout this century and the billions of pounds spent on advertising worldwide, that little is actually *known* for certain about *how* advertising works. There are, of

JICNARS
Joint Industry Committee for National Readership Surveys. This body is responsible for producing the National Readership Survey.

course, many suggestions but no single view has predominated. Researchers have delved into the sociological, psychological and economic sciences to search for the answers. Their findings have relevance to all the marketing communications tools and not just advertising.

To the extent that advertising is seen to have a positive effect on awareness, attention, interests, perceptions, opinions, attitudes and sales, it is considered to be an exceptionally worthwhile promotional and communication tool. How it may actually achieve these results, however, remains something of a mystery.

NEED TO KNOW

☑ *Although the effects of advertising are frequently measured, how and why advertising works is little understood.*

Three ways of looking at advertising are given below to help us understand how it may work. The first considers the concepts of advertising as a strong force or a weak force. Even though it may be described as weak, the value of advertising is still considered to be invaluable. A second way of looking at advertising is to consider the concept of salience, which has to do both with the relevance of the product, as well as its advertising, to the audience. The third approach is based on studies of attitude and behaviour in which a hierarchy of cognitive, affective and conative responses are seen to predispose human behaviour. It is believed that advertising can affect these responses.

Advertising – strong force or weak force?

Over the last decade an argument has developed over how advertising works. The main protagonists have been J.P. Jones and A.S.C. Ehrenberg whose arguments centre on whether advertising has a strong or weak effect (see, for example, Jones 1990 and 1995, and Ehrenberg et al. 1999).

Advertising as a strong force

Strong force

Advertising seen as a strong force suggests that it has a direct and positive impact on sales.

Jones, who sees advertising as a **strong force**, would argue, along with many in the industry, that he has shown through some sophisticated sales analysis that advertising has a direct and positive impact on sales. This has confirmed intuitive views held over many years within the industry that advertising is a strong promotional element which works by:

- persuading people to buy,
- creating and building brands,
- differentiating between brands and
- increasing sales.

Weak force

Advertising seen as a weak force suggests that advertising works through a process of reinforcing and maintaining brand values and defending market share. Its effect on sales is therefore less direct.

Ehrenberg and colleagues by contrast, after completing extended studies across numerous product categories, question this interpretation. They argue, through empirical investigation, that advertising, while having a highly significant effect, does not work through the mechanisms of persuasion and brand differentiation so typically taken for granted. For them, advertising is called a **weak force**. While significant (they are not suggesting that advertising is in any way inferior or should be reduced), advertising works through a process of reinforcing values, maintaining brands and defending market share.

Whichever viewpoint may be right, both camps believe that advertising can be very effective, a fact confirmed over many years of the PIMS studies reported earlier which has collected marketing and advertising data from participating companies and shown a positive correlation between advertising expenditure and market performance. The strong/weak force arguments are ones about the mechanisms by which this works.

The strong force argument is both logical and intuitive and for many years, without empirical evidence to verify it, has been the basis for most of the advertising industry's contention for how advertising works and why large sums of money should be expended upon it. Jones's analysis has provided at least some extra ammunition for this view to be held. Advertising generates sales through increasing awareness without which the product could not be bought (even impulse purchases require an awareness of the product – most impulse buys are for products known about but not on the purchaser's original shopping list). Advertising, furthermore, presents persuasive arguments for product purchase and helps differentiate between competing brands. The 'proof of the pudding' for the strong force lobby is in sales results.

The weak force and queries over the hierarchy of effects

The weak force argument raises questions about the very presumptions laid down by the strong force protagonists. While recognising that advertising has a positive effect on sales, it questions the basis of the hierarchy of effects on which some of the strong force argument is based as the hierarchy presumes not only a specific sequence of effects but that these effects are achieved through a process of persuasion. The most quoted hierarchy of effects model is AIDA (see Chapter 4) which is attributed to Strong who introduced the concept as long ago as 1925. Significantly, it was originally introduced as a sales training model but, as its intuitive validity became widely accepted, it was adopted as a process applicable to marketing communications in general. (There are now numerous modified versions of the hierarchy of effects model.) The AIDA process suggests that the principal task is to move people from levels of unawareness to awareness, and through developing interest and desire, move them to take action – especially in the form of product purchase. (But there are other forms of action that are equally relevant such as requesting more information or a company catalogue.) Inherent in this model is the implication that advertising works through a process of persuading people to buy, that not only should they be aware of the product but that they should buy because advertising has convinced them that it is something they want. Advertising's role, therefore, is to make the market aware and provide sufficiently enticing and imaginative messages to generate interest and desire to purchase. Other promotional tools, of course, may be enlisted to further support the purchase outcome.

Under circumstances of heavy competition in mature markets a further advertising task would be to create brand differentiation in order to create preferences and desires for one brand in favour of another. Through brand differentiation, current purchasers are persuaded to continue buying their own brand and potential purchasers to switch from competing brands.

But the hierarchy of effects has been criticised by many as not being an accurate reflection of practice; that it is a too simplistic interpretation of complex behaviour; that people do not make their purchase decisions in the stated sequential way; and that advertising does not principally work by the hierarchy process in the majority of cases. In particular, it is noted that the largest proportion of advertising is undertaken by already well-known brands, so there should be no need to emphasise awareness building, even if awareness building is appropriate for new products and brands. For brands such as Coke, Pepsi, a host of soap powders, cars and foodstuffs, Microsoft,

NEED TO KNOW

☑ *The AIDA model of hierarchy of effects was the first model to be described. It was first used to assist in sales training but, subsequently, it was widely applied to promotions and marketing communications generally.*

FOOD FOR THOUGHT

The major world advertisers each spend millions of pounds worldwide. Their products are already widely known so that there can be little need to raise awareness levels. If this is so, what is the main purpose of advertising for such advertisers?

IBM and McDonald's, etc., awareness building or interest generation can hardly represent a major function for advertising for the majority of these big spenders.

On the issue of advertising as a persuader, the weak force lobby can make two points. First, studies do not generally reveal that people rush out to buy products after seeing advertisements (although there are occasions when the offer may be sufficiently enticing for this to happen). And second, as competing brands also advertise, if people were to be persuaded, they, presumably, would have stores of different brands of the same product. There is clearly, something more taking place which mediates the process. In studies of over 50 product categories, Ehrenberg and colleagues have shown that purchase propensities are mostly habitual, steady and predictable despite fluctuations that may occur week by week. They argue that this would not be the case if advertising were a strong force.

If the persuasive ability of advertising is brought into question, then so too is its ability to create brand differentiation – another feature of the strong force argument of advertising effects. The weak force lobby argues that brands are, in fact, poorly differentiated in advertising, the reason being the nature of competition. If a competitor finds a distinguishing feature that creates a brand advantage then, in practice, this is quickly copied to eliminate competitor advantage.

If physical distinctions cannot successfully be used to create differentiation, then it is suggested that differentiation can be achieved through brand positioning and 'emotional' appeals. Again, actual practice reveals difficulties here, at least in the manipulation of brand perceptions and attitudes. While attitudinal effects are best achieved during the introduction of new products, for established brands advertising appears to have little ability to shift attitudes and perceptions. And, of course, the majority of brands advertised are the established brands. New ones come and go with

IN VIEW 26.2

McDonald's and Hoover make you offers you cannot refuse

As McDonald's celebrated its anniversary, its free BigMac promotion led to some unexpected results. The offer, buy one get one free, was advertised extensively in the media but resulted in the food chain running out of its most basic ingredient, beef burgers. A public apology was announced, much to the embarrassment of the company, as demand exceeded supply. They did, however, receive lots of publicity.

Some years ago, Hoover, manufacturers of domestic appliances, advertised a special offer which gave Hoover purchasers free airline tickets. The demand could not be contained and led to the company refusing to honour their agreement until their parent company, Maytag, provided extra funds to bail them out. Again, a great deal of publicity ensued, but unlike the McDonald experience, most of it damaged the company significantly.

Both these examples demonstrate the power of promotional activity. In these instances, advertising's role was to make aware and inform – not of the brands, but to create awareness of the sales promotion offers. The demand generated is not an argument for the persuasive power of advertising but for the power of the sales promotion and the financial benefits that many purchasers found too good to miss.

few having the ability to succeed in the face of the fierce competition from those already in the market. If advertising were to have the power of persuasion it should possess the ability to create and re-create brand perceptions. But as Moran (1990) has noted,

> Researchers long have observed that attitude–perception shifts are easy to observe while tracking the introduction of a new brand, and devilishly difficult to observe with regard to established brands. It is ironic to note that repeat exposure to and total recall of such research findings has done little to change researchers' determination to stick with their old perception of the advertising process.

NEED TO KNOW

☑ *Advertising is said to develop attitudes towards, and perceptions about, products. While this may be true (especially for new products), advertising has limited ability to change attitudes towards established brands.*

Cognitive and post-purchase dissonance

Term coined by Leon Festinger to describe a psychological state in which there is some incongruity (dissonance) between two or more thoughts. The resulting inconsistency encourages individuals to modify their thoughts to be more compatible or harmonious. Dissonance when recognised is an unstable state of mind. Post-purchase dissonance may occur after purchase of a product.

This is not to suggest that advertising cannot shift perceptions but that it tends to do so with great difficulty and, perhaps, only after an extended period of time. Guinness is an example of a brand that had to generate a huge perceptual shift for its stout-based product. It succeeded in doing so but only after a number of unsuccessful attempts and over many years of concerted effort.

Ehrenberg's suggestion that advertising is a weak but effective force gives an alternative perspective on how advertising works. Rather than advertising being good at differentiating brands, persuading people to buy or creating sales growth, based on a series of studies, Ehrenberg maintains that advertising primarily reinforces customer/consumer decisions to buy and use brands. And this, he argues, is exactly what we see going on if we look at most of the advertising of established brands which accounts for such a large proportion of total advertising spend. Such advertising seeks to remind and reinforce past behaviours. Extra weight is given to this perspective by the work on **cognitive and post-purchase dissonance** which is described in Chapter 4.

It has generally been accepted for a long time that consumers are rarely loyal to a single brand. They tend to have a 'portfolio' of brands (also known as a repertoire or consideration set) to which they are loyal, switching between them as they desire. This applies even to brand leaders. Under these circumstances, the task of advertising becomes more one of maintaining a brand's position within consumers' consideration sets.

IN VIEW 26.3

Guinness moves its mark and opens up a market

Guinness, the most famous of the Irish stout-based beers, has been around for many years. Along with many other stouts, its popularity waned as more continental, lighter lager beers were favoured by younger drinkers throughout Europe. The problem facing Guinness was that its beer was perceived as an older man's drink and its market was literally dying out. This is hard to believe today after they have successfully repositioned their drink. But they did not achieve this easily or overnight.

Guinness had to shift consumer perceptions and re-target their beer towards 18–30-year-olds. The beer was fixed in people's minds as 'fuddy-duddy' and 'heavy', quite opposite to the image they wanted. After a number of years, a number of failed campaigns and a great deal of effort they finally succeeded.

With the new mindset and positioning in place, stout, now acceptable as a young drinker's beer, opened up new market opportunities which competitors soon took advantage of as they entered the growing market sector with beers such as Murphy's and Caffrey's, and opened up Irish-themed pubs such as Molly O'Grady's and O'Neills.

Salience and USP – survival of the fit enough, not the fittest

Salience

Term given to represent the degree of 'relevance' a brand may have to a customer/ consumer. The concept of salience recognises that it will vary between customers, and that brand values are not determined in terms of there being a single best brand.

Unique selling proposition (or point) (USP)

Term coined by Rosser Reeves to suggest that advertising strategy (and by implication other marketing communications) works best if there is a single, clear and unequivocal selling proposition.

To further help our understanding of the workings of advertising, Ehrenberg refers to the concept of '**salience**'. Salience has to do with customer/consumer relevance. It is the sum total of brand attributes (some of which are conferred via advertising), not any single element, that creates a positive attitude or predisposition towards the brand. It goes beyond simple aspects of awareness or levels of interest. Although to be salient a brand has to be distinctive, it does not have to appear to be better than all the others, let alone 'best'. Which is just as well because, in reality, in the vast majority of cases, brands are too alike. It is on this point that many misconceptions about advertising are founded. The phrase '**Unique Selling Point**' (**USP**) has been coined and is most frequently used to suggest that products literally should be 'unique'. This is patently not possible. It is a misunderstanding of the original USP concept that was proposed by Rosser Reeves many years ago. Competitive forces pretty much guarantee that brands are similar at least in most functional respects. If one competitor introduces a product improvement into the market, other competitors quickly follow to eliminate any avoidable competitive advantage.

The salience concept recognises that a brand only has to be considered sufficiently relevant to be included in consumer's consideration sets. The brand does not have to appear unique or best. As Ehrenberg et al. (1999) have put it, 'It is the survival of the fit enough, rather than of the fittest. The goal is not so much how well your brand is regarded, but how many consumers regard your brand well' (p. 226). In this way, brand shares are maintained. To increase sales and shares, advertising's effect has to increase the numbers of customers/consumers who believe the brand is salient, that it is a brand for them. To the extent that more are 'enlisted' as compared with those who have decided to drop the brand from their consideration set, there is more likely to be a net increase in sales. Other promotional activities will, typically, be used to further this outcome. The process of encouraging the adoption of a brand, Ehrenberg et al. (1999) refer to as '**nudging**'.

IN VIEW 26.4

Unique or not so unique?

The term 'Unique Selling Point' (USP) was coined by an American, Rosser Reeves. He used the term to represent his view that advertising works best when a single, differentiating proposition is stated – rather than confusing the advertisement with lots of propositions or ideas – and better still if that proposition is something different (unique) from what everybody else is saying. He never intended the concept of USP to represent a truly unique product. Indeed, he recognised that one of the biggest problems he faced in designing advertisements was the fact that brands were so alike. What he believed, and is followed by many others, is that advertising works best if you can find something new to say about the product. The concept of USP, then, does not rely on unique products, but rather is about a single, differentiating statement about a product. The USP concept is seen by some as being founded on advertising as a strong force. This need not be the case. To the extent that USPs help distinguish brands, they do not of themselves have to operate as strong forces, they can simply be used as reminders and reinforcers of customers' original decisions to buy.

When Bold washing powder was introduced into the market, television advertising featured the product being dissolved in water and a drop being placed into a bowl of water covered with a dark, oily film. The result was dramatic. Immediately, the dark film seemed to disappear. Bold was clearly and demonstrably very effective in removing oily stains. But was Bold actually any different from other washing powders in this regard? The answer is no. Any detergent or soap powder would have had the same effect under these conditions. It is a physical reaction. The advertisers, however, had managed to present what appeared as a USP because this sort of dramatic demonstration had not been seen before. The majority of viewers presumed that the effect was 'unique' to Bold. In this way, the advertising distinguished Bold from its competitors – at least in the short term.

But what of new brands or brands that are seeking to establish themselves? Although customers/consumers tend to be generally consistent in their buying and usage patterns, there is a degree of erosion of repeat-buying loyalty over time. There is a willingness to try new products. Ehrenberg and colleagues liken this to a somewhat leaky bucket. Even in a steady market, new brands will enter consumers' brand repertoires as old brands are discarded. A role of advertising, therefore, is to 'plug up the leaks'; to encourage the continuation of your brand within the portfolio; and to encourage loyalty. It is because advertising is relatively 'weak' that so much of it is required. And even though it may be described as 'weak', it is a very necessary part of the process. Other promotional tools may be used to fulfil other purposes such as promoting initial trial or assisting advertising in encouraging trial.

NEED TO KNOW

☑ *Although loyalty will exist towards the brands in the repertoire set, over time newer brands will replace older brands. The brand portfolio that makes up the repertoire, therefore, is not immutable. It will change over time as loyalties change over time.*

The model adopted by the weak force lobby is a modification to the hierarchy of effects model. They believe that consumers move through stages of Awareness (and, perhaps, some interest); Trial (which might initially be a very uncertain trial without any real commitment to the brand, this may be encouraged through sales promotional activities); Reinforcement (whereby use of the brand and support/reinforcement from promotional effort may result in liking, continued purchase, use and inclusion into the consideration set); and finally, Nudging (existing predispositions to buy the brand may at times be enhanced or decreased by, for example, competitors' nudging). This model is shown as:

$$A \rightarrow T \rightarrow R\,\&\,N$$

Cognitive–affective–conative responses

Having considered the roles of strong/weak forces, salience, consideration sets and the $A \rightarrow T \rightarrow R\,\&\,N$ process, a third area worthy of highlighting in the 'How does advertising work' debate is that of attitude development. Attitudes are closely linked to behaviour and are often considered precursors to it. If advertising (and other marketing communications) is to work, some consideration needs to be given to its effect on attitudes, particularly (but not exclusively) those of customers and consumers.

Studies of attitude (of which there have been many) frequently highlight a generic three-stage process in their development. The three stages, typically seen as sequential, involve thinking (cognitive), feeling (affective) and doing (conative) responses. We see a similar arrangement in all hierarchy of effects models. This might partially explain why they have been so enduring and why attitudes are relevant to an understanding of marketing communications. Exhibit 26.2 illustrates the relationship between the hierarchy of effects and attitude development.

Although widely accepted, criticism of hierarchy of effects models has been around as long as the models themselves. One criticism is that they are said to presume that the sequence of stages is linear – that they start with Awareness and finish with Action. Palda (1966) reported that there was no conclusive evidence of this sequence and questioned whether affective change had to precede conative change. Other authors have suggested that the sequence may vary depending upon the nature of the circumstances. Six variants of sequence are, therefore, possible based on the three stages:

Think–feel–do	Do–feel–think	Feel–think–do
Think–do–feel	Do–think–feel	Feel–do–think

In practice, Ray (1973) suggests that only three variants occur and these depend upon customer/consumer situations: think–feel–do ('learning'), think–do–feel ('low involvement'), and do–feel–think ('dissonance attribution').

FOOD FOR THOUGHT

Although there may be a hierarchy of effects, it should not be presumed that the sequence is always the same. What effect might this have on our behaviour and what are the implications for advertising?

The significance of these issues is that they raise questions about the role and use of advertising, and how it relates to the hierarchy of effects process. There has been the widely accepted presumption that for advertising to work, it must 'lead' prospects through a single think–feel–do process. Recognising human behaviour to be more complex than this allows us to appreciate that product adoption is likely to occur through a variety of different sequential processes. Advertising may have a different role and effect in each and can be focused on cognitive, affective and conative attributes as appropriate.

For example, in the do–feel–think model, a major role of advertising and why it can work so well is in dissonance reduction. In this situation, advertising works, not in trying to create awareness or interest, or in trying to persuade, or in trying to encourage action. It works by 'comforting' prospects by confirming that their previous actions, feelings and thoughts were the right ones. Having used or recommended the product, advertising supports prospects by reinforcing their decisions. In this way, it is said to relieve, reduce or avoid post-purchase dissonance. Consider for a moment the huge advertising campaigns of Coca-Cola. There is no awareness building necessary – the product is universally known. There is no strong sales pitch encouraging people to

Exhibit 26.2 The relationship between attitudes and the hierarchy of effects

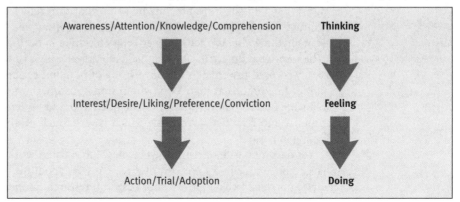

buy. The Coca-Cola message is of warm reassurance. Coca-Cola, 'It's the Real Thing' and 'Always Coca-Cola'.

If there is no single approach to how advertising is used and how it may work, we can begin to question the validity of a search for a general theory of how it works and, certainly, we can begin to recognise that the effects of advertising can legitimately vary. Perhaps it would be better to consider more 'situation-specific' explanations of advertising?

General theory of advertising versus situation-specific theory of advertising

It is clear that there is a lack of consensus about how advertising works and the task of understanding it is complicated by numerous interrelated factors which make it difficult to isolate advertising effects. Among them are:

- The cumulative effect of the use of many promotional activities over a single time frame.
- The impact of previous promotions and prevailing market perceptions.
- Competitive activity.
- Consumers/customers' own varied (idiosyncratic and inconsistent) behavioural responses to promotional activity.
- Time delays between promotional activity and subsequent behavioural responses.
- Non-controllable, exogenous variables occurring at the time of the promotional activity, for example, economic fluctuations, distributor activity, price variations, import and export behaviour.
- The difficulty in measuring individual promotional effects accurately and adequately.
- While measuring outcomes (*what* happened) may be possible, this does not explain *how* or *why* they happened.
- The role performed by advertising varies from one case to another. Advertising is likely to work differently if the aims of a campaign are to create favourable impressions compared with a campaign aimed at generating sales response.

Another way to look at the question of how advertising works is to take a different perspective. Perhaps it is not realistic to develop a general theory of advertising that can be applied to all products and circumstances? Perhaps each and every case has to be considered on its own merits? Perhaps the situational variables are so numerous that they prevent a general theory from applying? It can be imagined, for example, that the way advertising operates in a stable, mature market with strong competition and well-established brands may be somewhat different to that for an innovative product with little competition in a newly developing and growing market. Apart from anything else, the actual advertising objectives in both these situations are likely to be somewhat different. The arguments for advertising as a weak force do seem to be largely focused towards FMCG advertising of new and established consumer brands, and leading brands at that. What about non-consumer brands and the vast array of following brands – how can they be included in brand repertoires? What about direct response and classified advertising which is very much more than reminder or reinforcing in nature?

Yet despite a lack of consensus on how advertising works, advertising decisions have to be founded on some sort of theory or view about the way in which advertising affects purchase behaviour, whether based on research findings or on intuitive beliefs.

It would become impossible to plan advertising effectively if every case were different as there would be no foundation, background or experience upon which plans could be developed.

The reality of how advertising works is likely to lie somewhere between a grand, holistic or universal theory and one which argues that it is idiosyncratic and completely case specific. It is most likely that advertising functions in particular ways within particular parameters. Whereas it may be unwise to over-generalise about how advertising works in all circumstances, it is possible to hypothesise that advertising works in a reasonably consistent way in particular product and market situations. Unfortunately, little is known about the degrees of consistency or inconsistency of advertising effects under particular product and market conditions that could form the basis of a contingency theory of advertising. Although researchers have tended not to compare how advertising works within and between different product/market categories in any systematic way, it would be interesting to do so to assess the relative advertising effects under differing circumstances to determine the basis for a contingency model of advertising. Such categories, could include, for example, those shown in Exhibit 26.3 so that advertising effects could be measured across all relevant combinations of product and market types. For example, new brands entering mature mass markets could be contrasted with new brands entering growing niche markets. Rather than expecting advertising effects to be consistent across all types, they could be assessed within each category or combination of categories.

Exhibit 26.3 Example of categories that could be used when investigating advertising effects

Product types	*Market types*
● Fad products (e.g. cyber pets, Furbies)	● New markets
● 'Standard' products	● Mature markets
● New brands	● Declining markets
● Long established brands	● Growing markets
● Innovative products	● Mass markets
● 'Me-too' products	● Niche markets
● FMCGs	● Monopolistic/oligopolistic markets
● Consumer durable goods	● Markets with no dominant competitor
● Industrial/business-to-business products	● Fragmented markets
● High involvement/low involvement products	

Types of advertisements

When most people think about advertisements probably their thoughts first go to television ads, then to magazine advertisements or posters, and then to radio and cinema. What is probably not realised is that there are numerous varieties of advertisements many of which are taken for granted. For example, one of the most under-recognised areas is probably that of classified advertising which accounts for around 25% of all advertising expenditure in the UK. This is only slightly less than that being spent on television advertising. Although television advertising is often thought to be the most intrusive, the area that takes the lion's share of the advertising budget is press advertising, almost twice as much as TV.

What is important to recognise is that advertisements do not have to be major blockbusters; the *vast* majority of advertisements are not. They do not have to be 30-second or even 60-second TV ads; or full-page, full-colour magazine ads, or advertisements on huge poster sites. Effective advertising can be achieved through the use of creative and less intrusive approaches. These are best illustrated by reference to the numerous types of advertisements that appear in the press. A selection of these is described here.

Full-display ads

Full-display
advertisements

Advertisements that take advantage of the full creative opportunities afforded by the press media.

ROP

Run of paper – advertisements appearing in the non-classified sections of newspapers and magazines.

DPS

Double page spread – an advertisement that spans two pages across an open magazine or newspaper.

Solus positon

An advertisement appearing with no other advertisement around it.

Prime position

An advertisement appearing in a particularly advantageous position, such as front or back cover.

Semi-display
advertisements

Unlike full display, semi-display advertisements have creative restrictions placed on them, with limited or no graphics and limited typeface options.

Full-display advertisements appear in the printed media. They allow the greatest amount of creative freedom for the advertiser to design precisely what is wanted in the advertisement. Finished artwork is produced from which the final advertisement is printed. Full-display ads permit the use of colour, graphics, i.e. photos and drawings, and text. There is no creative limitation other than that dictated by the medium. The media charge a higher rate for full-display ads compared to semi-display and lineage. Full-display ads will typically, but not solely, be positioned **ROP** (run of paper), which means that they will appear in the main sections of newspapers or magazines. They do not need to be full page. They can be any size accepted by the media (measured by single column centimetres or proportions of a page) or can run over two (**DPS** – double page spread) or even more pages. They can be placed in **solus**, **prime** and special positions such as next to a particular feature or on the front or back page. An extra charge is usually levied for this. Some publications will even negotiate special position arrangements if the creative treatment requires it. For example, the German kitchen and white goods manufacturer Bauchnecht ran a series of quarter-page, full-colour advertisements in one issue of *Cosmopolitan* in a checkerboard effect interspersed with editorial.

Semi-display ads

Semi-display ads are similar to full-display but have limitations placed on their design. They may contain no graphics at all or only limited graphic options. Type faces used for text would also be limited. The publication may set a semi-display ad rather than requiring artwork to be produced. A semi-display insertion costs less than a full-display.

Exhibit 26.4 Advertising expenditure by medium (UK)

Advertising medium	Expenditure (1996 £ million)	Expenditure (1996%)	Expenditure (2000 £ million)	Expenditure (2000%)
Total press	6413	53.1	8609	50.6
Television	3379	28.0	4646	27.3
Posters (outdoor and transport)	466	3.9	823	4.8
Radio	344	2.8	595	3.5
Cinema	73	0.6	128	0.8
Direct Mail	1404	11.6	2094	12.1
Internet	–	–	155	0.9
TOTAL	**12080**	**100.0**	**17006**	**100.0**
Display advertising	9312	77.1	13077	76.9
Classified advertising	2768	22.9	3929	23.1
TOTAL	**12080**	**100.0**	**17006**	**100.0**

Source: The Advertising Association's *Advertising Statistics Year Book 2001*, published by World Advertising Research Center, www.warc.com. Reproduced with permission.

Classified advertising – lineage/wordage ads

Classified sections in the press are those sections, typically towards the end of the publication, in which advertising and notices are printed under specific headings or classifications. Classified sections include births, deaths and marriages, public notices, personal, television, entertainment, holidays, travel, accommodation, property, situations vacant, motor vehicles, home and garden, finance, business-to-business, for sale, under a tenner, and many more. The print is very tightly set.

Classified sections are not designed for their overall appearance other than typically to look cluttered. Display and semi-display advertisements are often accepted but frequently space is bought by the line or by the word. This is known as **lineage** and **wordage**. The back pages of local papers are usually awash with closely packed classified lineage advertisements set by the newspapers.

An important question arises here. If advertisements are supposed to be designed to be attractive and to stand out in order to gain attention, how then can classified advertising be effective? Classified advertisements by their nature tend to be very similar and packed together. The significant and important point to remember with classified advertisements is that they are actively 'searched' by viewers. Unlike much ROP display advertising, classified advertisements attract attention through the classifications under which they appear. As such, the advertisement does not have to compete with other text for attention. The viewer will consciously look for the advertisement details.

Lineage
Advertising space that is bought by the line and presented in classified sections of the press.

Wordage
Advertising space that is bought by the word and presented in classified sections of the press.

FOOD FOR THOUGHT

Classified ads are usually tightly packed with limited opportunity for individual ads to create impact. If this is so, how can they be effective?

Advertorials

Advertorials are press advertisements that are made to look like editorial. Many advertising codes of practice in Europe and elsewhere require a heading to be included in advertorials identifying them as advertising features. It is believed that advertisements appearing in this form may convey a greater sense of credibility.

Advertorials
Advertisements that are designed to look as though they are editorial.

Infomercials

Infomercials are the TV equivalent to advertorials in the press. There are, in effect, long commercials usually containing more information than normal commercials.

Infomercials
Television commercials designed to convey large amounts of information.

Direct response ads

Direct response advertisements contain some 'call-to-action' or response within the advertisement. The ad may contain a coupon return, for example, or telephone number, postal address or website address.

Direct response advertisements
Advertisements that contain the means by which a direct response may be made by the reader, viewer or listener: e.g. an email address, a coupon, or a telephone/fax number.

Web page/home page

Web or home pages are pages of information placed within websites on the Internet. They can contain colour, graphics, text, audio, video and animation. RealAudio and Real-Time Video accessed directly from the Internet eliminates the time-consuming need to download information making web pages and websites much more flexible. Although listed here as a type of advertisement because they are commonly referred to as such, it is preferable not to refer to web pages as advertising as they are more akin to a brochure or leaflet in electronic form. In the strict sense of advertising that we are

Web/home page
A web page is like a file available through the World Wide Web, typically containing text, images and links to other pages. An organisation's website is likely to contain a collection of web pages, each with its own file reference (html address). A home page is an organisation's starting page.

trying to encourage here (and one that is reflected in the Advertising Association's reporting of Internet advertising expenditure in Exhibit 26.4), it is better to consider websites and pages as marketing communications approaches more generally rather than as a form of advertising. Of course, they frequently carry advertising in the form of banner ads, etc.

Banner advertisement

Type of advertisement often appearing as a banner across the whole or part of the width of a web page.

Banner ads and banner links

These are advertisement 'banners' which may contain the advertiser's name, a graphic and a brief message. They can be moving, flashing or static, often extend across a full web page and are carried on other people's web pages usually for a fee. The banner is likely to contain a hypertext link to the advertiser's website. Clicking on the banner with a computer mouse activates this.

Hypertext link

Link (a web address or graphic) on a web page, a simple computer mouse click on which moves the viewer to a new web page.

Intermercial

This is the Internet equivalent to a television commercial. Like a commercial break between TV programmes, intermercials appear between content on a website. Using Real-Time Video eliminates the need for excessive delays in downloading information. They are considered by many to be unnecessarily intrusive and unwelcome.

Intermercial

The Internet version of a television commercial, which appears between viewing of web pages.

FOOD FOR THOUGHT

Screen saver: Not strictly meeting the definition as a form of advertising, screen savers have become a popular form of promotion.

Screen savers

Screen savers have been used successfully by companies to encourage the downloading of their promotional material. A notable and extremely successful example is the Guinness screen saver which featured video footage from one of their advertising campaigns.

Producing advertisements that work

Many authors have offered advice on how to produce advertising that works. This advice tends to concentrate on the specific mechanics of producing an individual advertisement rather than considering its role within the wider context of a campaign or integrated marketing communications plan. Much of this advice is based on the many years of experience of copywriters and art directors (see Chapter 15, Agency operations). Exhibits 26.5 and 26.6 summarise a lot of their suggestions for improving the quality of the advertisement content.

Exhibit 26.5 Thirty-five ways to gain attention in advertisements

1	Humour	13	News	25	Exaggeration
2	Real-life dramatisations	14	Emotion	26	Glamour
3	Slices of life	15	Cartoons	27	Personalities
4	Testimonials	16	Animation	28	Spokespersons
5	Guarantees	17	Charts	29	Free phone numbers
6	Comparisons	18	Computer graphics	30	The product alone
7	Problem solving	19	Claymation	31	The product in use
8	Characters	20	Music	32	Different uses of the product
9	Talking heads	21	Symbols	33	Effects of not using the product
10	Recommendations	22	Animals	34	Before and after
11	Reasons why	23	Contests and sweepstakes	35	The package as the star
12	Facts	24	Offers		

Source: Adapted from Kaatz (1995)

Exhibit 26.6 Checklist for effective advertisements

Copywriting

1 Does the copy offer a big benefit?

2 Is the copy easy to see and read?

3 Is it written in the audience's language? Is it easy for them to identify with the copy, to be involved?

4 Does the copy attract the audience?

5 Is the copy believable?

6 Has the copy stressed what is unique or different?

7 Think about the copy in relation to other visuals and to the campaign and the brand as a whole.

Source: Adapted from Burton and Purvis (1993)

Print ads

1 Is the message clear at a glance? Can you quickly tell what the ad is all about?

2 Is there a benefit in the headline?

3 Does the illustration support the headline?

4 Does the first line of copy support or explain the copy or illustration?

5 Is there a USP?

6 Is the ad easy to read and to follow?

7 Is the type large and legible?

8 Is the advertiser/product clearly identified?

9 Have all excess words, phrases, or ideas been deleted?

10 If there is a coupon or clip-out, is it large enough to easily complete, is it easy to remove or obtain, does it contain an ad reference number for subsequent evaluation?

11 If there is a 'call-to-action', have all the relevant information/contact points been provided?

12 Does the ad link to previous marketing communications activities? Does it support the wider campaign?

13 Are appropriate 'identifiers' present, e.g. logo, slogan?

Source: Adapted from Schultz and Barnes (1995)

Posters

1 Is it easy to read at high speed?

2 Is the typeface simple and bold?

3 Does it require the viewer to squint or strain?

4 Are the visuals striking and 'grabbing'?

9 Does it trigger an action response; provoke a laugh, answer a question, invite a 'call to action'?

10 Is the total effect a poster that stands out from its surroundings?

Exhibit 26.6 continued

5 Do the background colours blur into words and pictures?	11 Does it take advantage of opportunities received previously or through other media?
6 Do all the visual elements reinforce one another, are they instantly memorable?	12 Does it very succinctly convey (in seven words or less) at a glance everything it needs to say?
7 Are the product, packaging and related icons easy to recognise?	13 Does the message convey a USP? If not, does it matter?
8 Where appropriate, does it make use of a unique or unusual size or shape?	*Source*: Adapted from Kaatz (1995)

Radio

1 Is the commercial written conversationally for the ear so that it is *visually* and *conceptually* clear through words and sounds?	10 Has overwriting and crowding the commercial with too much copy been avoided?
2 Is the listener involved and captured, has her/his imagination been excited?	11 Is the appeal made clear?
3 Is there one, strong, central idea? Is it a USP?	12 If the message is news, has it been made to sound important?
4 Has the prospect been singled out as though writing to just her or him?	13 Is a friendly tone and feeling maintained throughout? If not, are the feelings engendered the ones you want the prospect to have?
5 Does the commercial sound the way the prospect speaks?	14 If the commercial is supposed to be humorous, is it really funny?
6 Is the mood for the product based upon how you want the listener to hear and react?	15 Is material used in other media used or enhanced through the radio commercial?
7 Have you remembered mnemonics – those words, music and effects that can register well in the prospect's mind?	16 Is there a 'call-to-action'? Is it sufficiently compelling?
8 Has attention been quickly established?	17 Once is not enough, is everything important repeated that the listener might not get the first time around?
9 Is the brand clearly identified? Will the product's name be quickly and easily registered in the prospect's mind?	18 Is there synergy with other elements of the campaign and the advertiser's image?
	Source: Adapted from Book et al. (1984)

Television and cinema

1 Is there a single central message or idea? Is it your strongest, most provocative idea?	18 Are the pictures explicit, simple and single-minded?
2 Is the message a USP, i.e. how does it relate to competitive offerings?	19 Do the words reinforce the pictures or are they merely redundant? Is the copy structured to maximise the impact of the visuals?
3 Is the message clearly and explicitly stated?	20 Because television and cinema are primarily visual media, have you avoided wasting words?
4 Can the actions you want be communicated in the desired atmosphere within the time available?	21 Have you kept the commercial simple and avoided cramming your spot with too many scenes, too much action, or too many effects?
5 Have you matched the format, structure and style of your commercial so they are all compatible with each other and with your product or service?	22 Are the words clear and meaningful *in themselves* and will they be understood by the target audience viewers?
6 How does the commercial relate to previous treatments, your other brands and other marketing communications elements?	23 Are the words clear and meaningful at each point in the story, or do they depend for their meaning or impact on something that has not yet occurred in the story?
7 Does the commercial contain appropriate 'identifiers' such as logo and slogan?	24 Have you written clearly and conversationally?

Exhibit 26.6 continued

8 Have you clearly identified your product and implanted the brand name strongly in the viewer's mind?

9 Are you on track with the strategy statement and marketing objectives?

10 Are the benefits of the product clearly demonstrated?

11 Does the opening shot set the stage and convey only what is essential to the understanding of what follows?

12 Do the opening seconds attract the viewer in a way that is relevant to the viewer and the product? Is attention quickly gained? Does the viewer understand, 'What's in it for me?'

13 Is involvement created?

14 Does the product enter at the *right moment* and not just the first moment?

15 Do the shots progress in a logical order (or 'illogically logical' order), and does each successive shot advance the story and add to the viewer's knowledge of what is going on?

16 Is a deliberately 'teasing' approach adopted to gain interest?

17 Are the video and the audio elements matched so as not to confuse the viewer?

25 Could the viewer repeat the story of the commercial without mentioning the product? Does the product seem irrelevant to the commercial?

26 If it is a 60-second commercial could it be cut to a 30-second commercial (or a 30-second to a 15-second commercial)? Does the extra time really add to the idea, impact or effectiveness?

27 Is the story believable or, if exaggerated, acceptable? Is the selling message believable within an unbelievable or exaggerated story?

28 Has the commercial been timed to make sure it is not so fast that it loses its dramatic appeal or leaves the viewer behind?

29 Have ideas or important points been repeated to help register your selling idea?

30 Are you prepared to revise the commercial? Will free rein be given to the producer/director to make the commercial even better?

Source: Adapted from Baldwin (1982), and Book et al. (1984)

Summary

Advertising is a specific and unique part of the marketing communications mix. Unfortunately, many people think of advertising in a much broader sense even to the extreme of being used to describe any and all forms of promotion. This causes much confusion. Advertising has been described here as a form of promotion that uses the *mass* media paid for by a *clearly identified advertiser*.

Advertising has particular benefits over other promotional tools and accounts for a large part of all promotional activity undertaken. Despite the fact that there is no clear and undisputed understanding of how it actually works, huge sums of money are spent on it each year. Many people do not question how advertising works. They simply assume that it does work, and the money spent on it merely give testimony to its efficacy.

In general, advertising is believed to be particularly good at generating awareness and in helping to develop and maintain brands. In simple terms, it is said to work through developing brand 'salience' so that consumers can believe it to be a brand for them. The brand, therefore, has to be distinctive to differentiate it from competing brands, but not necessarily better. For new brands, an emphasis has to be placed on generating awareness and trial and this can be strongly supported by the use of other promotional tools. Thereafter, and for established brands, the principal task has to be in maintaining salience if the brand is to continue to be included in customers'/consumers' consideration sets.

Advertising can lead consumers to try a brand when new, it can reassure consumers, reinforce trials, and perhaps 'nudge' more of an established brand to be used. Advertising is something that occurs in many forms that can be used to progress buyers along the hierarchical chain to the final purchase; this may particularly be so if the advertising contains sales promotional elements and 'calls-to-action'. Some concern was expressed over the sequencing of the hierarchy of effects models and it was suggested that advertising may work in a different way such as through post-purchase dissonance reduction.

In considering how advertising works, details have been presented of:

- advertising as both a strong and a weak force,
- the importance of relevance (salience),
- consideration of the meaning of USP (unique selling point),
- advertising's relationship to the hierarchy of effects,
- the roles of trial and reinforcement, and
- the need to consider attitudinal/behavioural responses.

It has been suggested that while it may be difficult to determine a general theory of how advertising works because there are, simply, too many variables that affect the outcome, it may be better to consider more contingency-based explanations.

Towards the end of this chapter, different types of advertisement were identified and it was pointed out that although advertising is most often thought of with regard to its more flamboyant manifestations, it also exists in more modest forms including the humble, but prolific, classified advertisement. Finally, checklists were provided that may be used when considering the content of good advertisements.

Self-review questions

1 What are the main distinguishing features of advertising?

2 What are the main benefits of advertising?

3 The PIMS study has suggested that advertising expenditure as a proportion of A&P budgets should either increase or decrease under certain conditions. What are these conditions?

4 What questions have been raised about the general application of the PIMS findings?

5 What is advertising said to be particularly effective in achieving?

6 What is meant by the weak and strong forces of advertising? Do you think it is possible for advertising to exhibit both weak *and* strong forces in different circumstances?

7 What is 'salience' and why is it an important concept in understanding the way in which advertising may work?

8 What is USP? Why is it important to recognise that this does not mean that products have to be unique?

9 What is meant by cognitive, affective and conative responses to advertising? How do they relate to the hierarchy of effects?

10 What role would advertising play if it were trying to relieve post-purchase dissonance?

11 Do you think there could ever be a general theory of the way in which advertising works?

12 What is meant by 'full-display', 'semi-display' and lineage advertisements? What is the difference between classified and ROP advertisements?

13 How is it possible for classified advertising to be effective if classified advertisements are often poorly designed and fail to stand out to attract the viewer's attention?

14 What are some of the main considerations to be borne in mind when producing advertising copy?

Project

Contrast a small selection of display advertisements for perfumes and luxury cars with direct response display advertisements. Assess the styles adopted and the content of each. What do they tell you about the objectives the advertisers are trying to achieve, their views about how they think advertising works and the components of what they think makes a good advertisement?

References

Advertising Association (2001), *Advertising Statistics Yearbook*. Advertising Association.

Baldwin, H. (1982), *Creating Effective TV Commercials*. NTC Business Books.

Book, A.C., Cary, N.D. and Tannenbaum, S.I. (1984), *The Radio and Television Commercial*. NTC Business Books.

Burton, P.W. and Purvis, J. (1993), *Which Ad Pulled Best*. NTC Publishing.

Crosier, K. (1999), Advertising. In P.J. Kitchen, *Marketing Communications: Principles and Practice*. International Thomson Business Press.

Ehrenberg, A.S.C., Scriven, J.A. and Bernard, N.R. (2000), Advertising established brands: an international dimension. In S. Moyne, *The Handbook of International Marketing Communications*. Blackwell.

Jones, J.P. (1990), Advertising: strong or weak force? Two views an ocean apart. *International Journal of Advertising*, 9 (3), 233–246.

Jones, J.P. (1995), *When Ads Work: New Proof That Advertising Triggers Sales*. Simon and Schuster.

Kaatz, R. (1995), *Advertising and Marketing Checklists* 2nd edn. NTC Business Books.

Kotler, P., Armstrong, G., Saunders, J. and Wong, V. (1999), *Principles of Marketing* 2nd European edn. Prentice Hall Europe.

Moran, W.T. (1990), Brand presence and the perceptual frame. *Journal of Advertising Research*, October/November, 9–16.

NTC (2001), *The European Marketing Pocket Book*. NTC Publications Limited.

Palda, K.S. (1966), The hypothesis of a hierarchy of effects: a partial evaluation. *Journal of Marketing Research* 3 (February), 13–24.

Ray, M.L. (1973) Marketing communication and the hierarchy of effects. In *New Models for Mass Communication Research* (P. Clarke, ed.). Sage Annual Review of Communication Research, Vol. 2, Sage Publications, pp. 147–176.

Schultz, D.E. and Barnes, B.E. (1995), *Strategic Advertising Campaigns*. NTC Business Books.

Strong, E.K. (1925), *The Psychology of Selling*. McGraw-Hill.

Wells, W., Burnett, J. and Moriarty, S. (1992), *Advertising Principles and Practice*. Prentice Hall.

Selected further reading

Advertising Works (1980 onwards), Bi-annual series of publications. NTC Business Books.

Barry, T. and Howard, D.J. (1990), A review and critique of the hierarchy of effects in advertising. *International Journal of Advertising*, 9, 121–135.

Brierly, S. (1995), *The Advertising Handbook*. Routledge.

Broadbent, S. (1997), *Accountable Advertising: A Handbook for Managers and Analysts*. Admap Publications.

Franzen, G. (1994), *Advertising Effectiveness*. NTC Business Books.

Hart, N. (ed.) (1995), *The Practice of Advertising* 4th edn. Butterworth-Heinemann.

The Marketing Pocket Book (annual) NTC Business Books

McDonald, C. (1992), *How Advertising Works*. NTC Business Books.

White, R. (1993), *Advertising: What It Is and How To Do It* 3rd edn. McGraw-Hill.

Williamson, J. (1978), *Decoding Advertisements*. Marion Boyars Publishers.

Appendix 26.1 International advertising

Tables from *The Marketing Pocket Book 2001* and *The European Marketing Pocket Book, 2001*, published by World Advertising Research Center, www.warc.com. and reproduced by permission.

Distribution of advertising expenditure

Country	Total value 2000 (US $m) (rounded)	Total %	Press %	TV %	Radio %	Cinema %	Posters outdoor/ transport %
Austria	2000	100	62.8	22.4	8.0	0.4	6.4
Belgium	2000	100	46.4	37.1	8.4	1.3	6.8
Denmark	1400	100	75.9	18.8	2.0	0.5	2.8
Finland	1200	100	74.1	19.7	3.1	0.2	2.9
France	9600	100	50.5	29.6	7.1	0.8	12.0
Germany	20 000	100	65.4	25.5	4.1	1.0	4.0
Greece	1200	100	50.2	45.9	3.9	–	–
Ireland	610	100	62.9	23.1	6.7	0.7	6.6
Italy	7000	100	39.4	54.1	4.1	–	2.4
Netherlands	3600	100	72.8	18.3	5.2	0.4	3.3
Norway	1100	100	72.9	20.3	4.3	0.8	1.7
Portugal	1000	100	35.1	47.0	6.1	0.5	11.3
Spain	5300	100	44.2	41.9	8.7	0.8	4.4
Sweden	2000	100	69.7	21.8	3.5	0.5	4.5
Switzerland	2600	100	72.2	11.2	2.7	1.1	12.8
UK	18 000	100	57.4	33.2	4.2	0.9	4.3
USA	132 000	100	48.0	38.9	12.9	–	0.03

[These figures should be taken as indicative as the proportions spent in each medium will vary from year to year to a small extent.]

Advertising as a percentage of gross domestic product (GDP)

Country	%
United Kingdom	1.24
Switzerland	1.01
Austria	0.97
Portugal	0.95
Greece	0.95
Germany	0.95
Netherlands	0.91
Finland	0.90
Spain	0.89
Ireland	0.83
Sweden	0.80
Belgium	0.80
Denmark	0.79
Norway	0.73
France	0.67
Italy	0.61

Source: Adapted from NTC (2001)

20 top advertising agency networks in Europe

1	McCann–Erickson
2	BBDO Group
3	Young & Rubicam
4	Ogilvy & Mather
5	Euro RSCG
6	Publicis
7	DDB Needham
8	Grey
9	Lowe Lintas
10	J. Walter Thompson
11	Bates
12	TBWA
13	D'Arcy
14	Leo Burnett Co.
15	Saatchi & Saatchi Advertising
16	FCB
17	Draft
18	Rapp Collins
19	Campus
20	Carlson

Source: Adapted from NTC (2001).

14 top media agency networks in Europe

1	Carat
2	OMD
3	Media Planning
4	Mediacom
5	The Media Edge
6	CIA Media
7	Universal McCann
8	Initiative/Western
9	Optimedia
10	Mindshare
11	Mediavest
12	Starcom
13	Zenith
14	TN Media

Source: Adapted from NTC (2001).

Chapter 27

Direct marketing communications

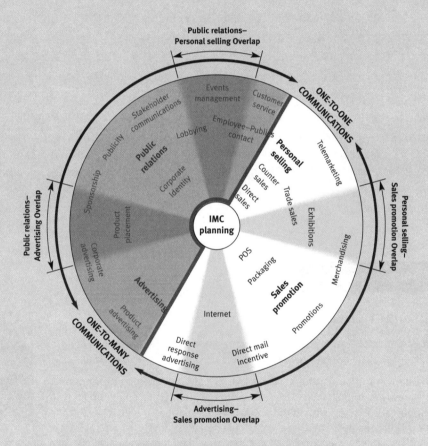

The Integrated Marketing Communications (IMC) Mix Model

CD

Using the AIMRITE framework detailed in this chapter, assess the direct marketing media used by Pampers in their campaign.

Chapter outline

- What is direct marketing communications?
- Offers and incentives in direct marketing communications
- Media in direct marketing communications
- Creative approaches to direct marketing communications
- Testing and measurement in direct marketing communications

Objectives

- To identify the role direct marketing communications plays in the integrated marketing communications mix
- To outline the direct marketing communications planning process
- To introduce the use of offers and incentives in direct marketing communications
- To summarise the media choices available in direct marketing communications
- To identify the key creative approaches used in direct marketing communications
- To demonstrate the uses of measurement and testing in direct marketing communications

Professional perspective

Graeme McCorkell Chairman, The Institute of Direct Marketing

- Meaning*less* terms: *relationship marketing, loyalty marketing, integrated marketing*.
- Meaning*ful* terms: *direct marketing, database marketing, one-to-one marketing*.

Authors and suppliers of marketing services like to coin new words and phrases to emphasise the newness of their ideas. Thus, in marketing, new terms spring up fairly frequently. Most often, these are used to put a new spin on old ideas. A good test of their meaningfulness is to consider if they have a feasible opposite.

Relationship marketing sounds desirable but, in reality, the term is meaningless. All marketing, all selling implies a relationship between the marketer and the customer. The relationship may be close or distant, direct or indirect, robust or fragile. But it must exist. There is no such thing as a non-relationship marketing. Therefore, relationship marketing is simply a fine sounding phrase, empty of true meaning. The same applies to loyalty marketing, a term that has come to stand for little more than card-based customer reward programmes, a direct marketing tactic.

Marketers and their suppliers sometimes seek to emphasise their ability as all-rounders by referring to 'integrated marketing'. But who would advocate *dis*integrated marketing? Surely, that would be a contradiction in terms, being no more than poorly planned or executed marketing.

On the other hand, most long-established companies have practised *indirect* marketing for the majority of their history. Direct marketing is genuinely descriptive. So is database marketing and more narrowly so. No company can practise database marketing to the exclusion of seeking business from outside. So ex-database marketing not only exists but is essential.

Likewise, one-to-one marketing describes a particular process in which the individuality of the customer is recognised. There must be many companies who would find it impracticable to recognise the individuality of every one of their customers.

Furthermore, while it is certainly possible to tailor communications on a one-to-one basis and is often possible to tailor terms of business and even the product, no company can devise a strategy for every customer. Marketing planning is concerned with market segments of sufficient size to pay back an investment. Therefore, one-to-one marketing can describe no more than a part of the whole marketing process. In practice, database marketing and one-to-one marketing each form a part of direct marketing.

The term 'direct marketing' was actually introduced by Lester Wunderman (founder of one of the world's first and largest direct marketing agencies) in a speech to the Hundred Million Club in New York, in 1961. It answered the need for a new term to describe a broader range of activities and responses than could be summed up as 'mail order' and it has withstood the test of changing times.

G. McCorkell

What is direct marketing communications?

What is direct marketing communications?

The utility of direct marketing is now well established in marketing communications and beyond. Fundamentally, direct marketing communications use an array of marketing communications activities from around the Integrated Marketing Communications Mix Model which are targeted at end customers and users. In this way they are not confined to any one area of the model and do not represent a discrete set of activities or approaches. Direct marketing communications can include personal selling such as face-to-face sales and telemarketing, as well as direct response advertising and direct mail, all of which frequently make use of sales promotions along the way. Readers may want to pay particular attention to Chapters 1, 2, 12, 13, 23 and 31 in connection with this chapter.

Mailshot

Promotional material sent through the post.

In modern businesses, direct marketing is far more than merely a few tactical **mailshots** or a door-to-door leaflet drop to back up an advertising campaign. Thanks to the analytical power of a marketing database, companies if they so wish can use direct marketing as a complete system, or framework of marketing that can replace general marketing components like retail outlets, market research, and even the salesforce. Take First Direct, the telephone-based bank. It has no retail outlets. It recruits its customers using direct response press advertising. Its operations (24-hour banking facilities) are delivered through a direct system – the telephone and a customer database. The database is used to trigger any marketing initiatives to its customers. And it works: 94% of First Direct's new custom is now attracted through word of mouth from delighted existing customers.

Today, direct marketing is a marketing system based on individual customer records held on a database. These records are the basis for marketing analysis, planning, implementation of programmes, and control of all this activity. Compared to

Database

Collection of data, usually on computer, stored to provide useful, convenient and interactive access to information.

traditional brand marketing, the advantage of the direct marketing approach is that the use of the **database** forces a natural focus on customers rather than products. Modern direct marketing thinking (for example, Peppers and Rogers 1993), holds that it is better to understand one's customers as individuals in more detail, than to build up product brands. Direct marketing also encourages us to think in terms of customer relationships with the company – are we talking to 'new prospects' or 'loyal, established customers'? In this respect, there is a natural alignment between direct marketing and 'relationship marketing' (Tapp 1998; O'Malley et al. 1999).

As the First Direct example above demonstrates, the key to modern direct marketing is the capture of individual customer details at the first sale, so that the marketer can begin a relationship with that customer, subsequently treating them differently over time in order to generate repeat business. As Tapp (1998) has pointed out, the recording of individual data and direct contact allowing a dialogue are key elements in operationalising a relationship marketing strategy.

Relationship marketing

View that emphasises the importance of the relationships developed between an organisation and other parties including customers, partners, suppliers and the trade.

One of the best examples of **relationship marketing** is that practised by salespeople. Direct marketing seeks to emulate the sales/customer relationship as far as possible, by gathering personal details, communicating individually, and wherever possible adjusting offers to individual taste.

This focus on *existing customers* rather than attracting sales from anyone has long been a strength of direct marketing. This was reported by Reichheld (1996) as strongly linked to better profitability across a wide range of sectors, and has been a major theme of marketing strategy throughout the 1990s and now into the new millennium.

Direct mail and the telephone have become synonymous with direct marketing. However, direct mail does *not* equal direct marketing. It is merely one of the media used within a direct marketing system which revolves around the database. Direct mail and the telephone are both media which get us directly to our customers, and which they can use to respond directly to us, potentially bypassing any retail middleman. While these are the two key media used by direct marketers at present, in fact most media can be used for direct response activity of one type or another. Significantly, the Internet is increasingly being used for this purpose.

> **WARNING**
>
> ❗ *Direct marketing communications is* not *restricted to direct mail. Potentially all media can utilise a direct function, e.g. direct response TV advertising, direct response radio advertising, Internet communications, telephone communications.*

Chapter 13 has outlined the integrated marketing communications RABOSTIC planning process. A direct marketing communications plan follows the same process but there are specific planning requirements to the offers and incentives, media and creative approaches, and testing and measurement (Exhibit 27.1). The rest of the chapter covers these areas in detail.

Offers and incentives in direct marketing communications

Offers

Propositions made to customers indicating what they will receive and what they will have to give.

Incentives

Inducements to encourage customers to take up offers.

The **offer** is the proposition you make to the customer: the totality of what we are offering to the customer, and what we expect back for it. **Incentives** are a part of the offer, are the specific inducements or stimuli used to help turn consumer desire into action at the point of sale. Part of the direct marketing process is the need to stimulate a response (i.e. 'action'). Thus direct marketers may use simple incentives like free gifts in return for quick response, or complex mechanics like 'loyalty schemes', involving smart cards capturing customer transaction data. Incentives can also be described as **sales promotions** (see Chapter 28 for complete review of sales promotions) as they

Sales promotion

Widely used term covering a myriad of promotional activities, excluding advertising, PR and personal selling. Sales promotion is associated with free offers, price deals, premium offers, and other promotions including merchandising, point-of-sale displays, leaflets and product literature.

Exhibit 27.1 A direct marketing communications plan

The market (Research and Audiences)

1 Segment (based on existing customers if possible – customer profiling).

2 Decide on final target markets.

Resources and desired outcomes (Budgets and Objectives)

3 Identify available budgets.

4 Set objectives.

The offer (Strategies)

5 Decide product/price proposition.

6 Decide incentive approach.

Communication (Strategies, Tactics and Implementation)

7 Decide media and contact over time.

8 Decide timing issues.

9 Develop creative platforms.

10 Design a detailed test programme.

11 Roll out.

Monitor (Control)

12 Evaluate the programme.

are 'the art and science of making something happen' (Rapp and Collins 1987). Peattie and Peattie (1993) established the following three key objectives for sales promotions:

- to attract new customers to 'trial';
- to reward loyal customers;
- to grow sales among existing customers.

The problem with retail-based sales promotion is that much of the 'give-away' is wasted as most of the purchases are made by customers who would have bought anyway, and deal-conscious compulsive brand switchers. Therefore relatively few takers of the promotion are genuine trialists. Indeed, Kotler (1995) noted extensive evidence of an apparent lack of any lasting change in consumer behaviour after the promotion has finished.

Rapp and Collins (1987) point out that direct marketers can take a different approach to sales promotions. The direct marketing system allows different customer categories to be identified, split and treated separately (In View 27.1). The use of offers and incentives targeted at existing customers and new prospects are outlined below.

Offers and incentives to existing customers

Carelines

Mechanisms, usually telephone but could be other facilities such as fax and email, to help facilitate easy communications between an organisation and its customers.

Direct marketers use communication programmes targeted at existing customers to help retain customers, and tactics which are designed to maximise the profitability of existing customers through extra sales. Direct marketing is used to provide information sheets, newsletters, product catalogues, and other vehicles which deliver help, news, information and ways of making the product more valuable to consumers. Driven by the need to make it easy for customers to respond to the organisation, **carelines** have grown considerably in importance throughout Europe.

IN VIEW 27.1

The advantages of incentives through direct marketing: a wine direct operation vs a retailer

Let us compare a wine retailer with a database-driven 'wine direct' operation. We can take a typical promotion, say, a free bottle of new Romanian wine on any purchase of a box of 12.

1 Retailer

Possible new entrant into market	Loyal to competitor	Brand switcher	Loyal to company
activate?	no effect?	activate	waste

2 Wine Direct

Possible new entrant into market	Loyal to competitor	Brand switcher	Loyal to company
increase offer	increase offer	activate	do not promote

Wine Direct uses sales promotion in a superior manner in the following ways:

1 It adjusts the promotion to its own loyal customers thereby avoiding wastage.
2 It increases the offer to audiences that are tougher to incentivise.

Of particular importance in communication programmes are loyalty magazines. These provide high-quality added-value communications to existing customers, in an effort to create extra value and hence provide another reason to stay with that supplier. Another important device for improving dialogue with customers is the use of clubs. Clubs can create value for customers when:

● customers have high involvement with the product, e.g. Walt Disney's children's club;
● membership bestows an element of status, e.g. the BMW club;
● customers would value the association with other members, e.g. Harley-Davidson's Harley Owners Group.

Up-selling

Selling related products such as upgrades to customers who have purchased the product previously.

Cross-selling

Selling other products to existing customers.

Loyalty schemes

Sales promotions intended to encourage customers to continue purchasing a particular product or purchasing from a particular supplier. Such 'loyalty' is most often achieved through economic incentives.

Reichheld (1996) made the point that direct marketers have known for years: a firm's loyal customers are far more likely to buy its products than new prospects. If customers are satisfied with the product they first bought, they will be favourably inclined to purchase more of it, or to purchase an upgrade. Computer software consumers who enjoyed the basic product of a computer game are likely to be hot prospects for a higher priced upgrade. This is up-selling. As customers get used to your company and learn more about your offerings, the logical next step is to cross-sell. Thus a bank may interest a current account customer in a credit card or loan (Exhibit 27.2).

Loyalty schemes

There can scarcely be a soul left among us who has not encountered a loyalty scheme somewhere. Loyalty schemes are systems which persuade customers to prefer one

Exhibit 27.2 **Contact life cycle to increase revenue from loyal customers**

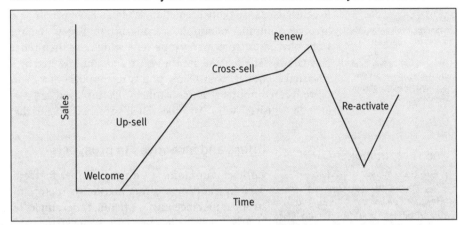

supplier to another through 'spending-related rewards' and related marketing activities. The core mechanic to all schemes is essentially quite simple: customers accrue 'points' or some other measured unit of value, in return for spend with that company or brand. At some point, these points may be redeemable by the customer for something of value, be it money-off future purchase, gifts, cash back, or privileged services.

These schemes do not engender loyalty by themselves; they must be part of a retention strategy in order to work. By themselves, they are only sales promotions – incentives for a particular purchase. When used properly these schemes become an integral part of the direct marketing system – they act as the vehicle through which customer transaction data is collected.

IN VIEW 27.2

The Tesco Clubcard loyalty scheme

Until recently, as a result of its Clubcard scheme, Tesco sent out targeted magazines to five segments of its database, based on lifestage. These magazines, which were sent with the regular quarterly customer statements to six million of the nine million members, have now been dropped, with no negative effect on sales.

Tesco continues to send out tightly targeted offers and direct mail to its customers. These are based on their buying patterns, as shown by use of the Clubcard, which records every item purchased by its members. Tracking is thus made virtually foolproof. This knowledge of buying patterns ensures that, for example, over-sixties are not sent vouchers for nappies. Clubcard membership has now grown to over eleven million.

Tesco also runs four clubs: - 'Baby & Toddler', 'Kids', 'Healthy Living' and 'Wine Club', which are also used to deliver targeted offers to their members.

Source: Tesco Clubcard image reproduced by kind permission of Tesco Stores Ltd.

Cross-category promotion scheme

Form of joint loyalty promotion involving organisations from different product categories. Frequently, customers earn points from a variety of suppliers, which are added together for later redemption.

Cross-category promotion schemes (co-branded cards)

Recently **cross-category promotion schemes** have become popular. Here the scheme involves a number of suppliers from different sectors. Consumers can earn points from purchases from many suppliers, which are then redeemed for rewards in the normal way. The scheme may be set up and administered by an independent company who makes money from selling points to suppliers at a higher rate than their payout on redeemed points from consumers. Examples of cross-category loyalty schemes include British Airways' Air Miles, Shell's Smart Card and the Nectar card.

Offers and incentives to prospects

FOOD FOR THOUGHT

*Book/music/wine clubs frequently make use of a 'Monthly Special' which is sent to you automatically. How often do you get round to sending it back if you do not want it? Lack of time, disinclination to exert oneself, leads to **inertia**: the simple maintenance of the status quo. 'Opt-out' schemes capitalise on this!*

Contact communication programmes to acquire customers have been used in traditional direct marketing sectors for a long time. Usually a strong initial incentive is offered, for example 'three books for a pound' – clearly a loss leader, but with some strings attached in which the customer is directed to buy further products at full price over a period of time. The mechanics are termed either 'opt in' or 'opt out'. With opt out, the company sends products at regular intervals to the customer; if they do not want these, they must act by sending back the product. The success of this technique is due to customer inertia. The alternative is opt in. Here the customer has to act if they do want the product. This is usually aligned with some condition such as 'the customer buys a further six albums of choice at the regular price within the next two years'.

Other techniques used by direct marketers to attract new customers include free trial, and member-get-member (incentives to current customers in return for recommending someone they believe will be interested in the company's products).

Media in direct marketing communications

While most media can be used for direct communications, Exhibit 27.3 outlines the main media choices open to direct marketers. The most important media for direct marketers were traditionally direct mail, the telephone and press, and these are still prime choices. However, to these can be added the growing use of direct response TV, door drops and the most significant development for direct marketing, the Internet. In the next section the main factors to consider before choosing media are introduced together with an overview of the key media.

Exhibit 27.3 The range of media used in direct marketing communications

- Direct response national press
- Classified adverts in press
- Direct response local press
- Direct mail
- Telephone
- Direct response TV
- Direct response radio
- Posters
- Inserts
- Door to door
- Magazines
- Internet
- Statement stuffers
- Take ones

Factors affecting media choice in direct marketing communications

Direct marketing authors (e.g. Nash 1995; Stone 1996) and marketing communications writers (e.g. Smith and Taylor 2002) have discussed various ways of assessing media. These have been brought together into a framework, termed **AIMRITE**, to aid in making consistent media choices:

Audience: does the media reach the desired target audience?

Impact: does the media have sufficient impact to ensure the message has a chance of getting through the clutter?

Message: does it help ensure the message is clearly communicated? Does it add to the message?

Response: does it make responding easy?

Internal management: does it enhance the efficient management of the campaign?

The End result: what are the costs and projected likely revenues? Taking all the above into account and looking at typical response rates for your media, how likely are you to hit target for the campaign?

Experience has shown that it is necessary to go through the disciplined approach of AIMRITE to make the right decisions. This is because no one medium has stood out as clearly superior in fetching the highest response at lowest cost. In fact, it is a general rule that those media which elicit a higher response also tend to be the most expensive. For example, although telephone responses are potentially the highest of any media, the costs are also the highest.

An overview of direct media

Direct mail

Such is the historical importance of this medium, direct mail is often mistakenly seen as synonymous with direct marketing. Although it is no longer the biggest direct marketing media in many countries (for example, in the US and UK, more marketing budget is now spent on the telephone), direct mail remains extremely important, even if its public perception with consumers is of 'junk mail'.

Compared to other media, there is no doubting the impact value of direct mail. As something with the customer's address on it, coming through the door in the morning, it is hard to ignore. However, one downside to direct mail's impact is the poor public image that the media is saddled with. Commonly known as 'junk mail', this term has become popular jargon, along with a set of preconceptions that the industry has great difficulty in shifting.

WARNING

Be wary of 'average response rates'. Response rates vary widely by industry sector, mailing list, creative and offer.

When used in acquisition of new customers, direct mail requires a list of target prospects. These lists come in many forms, and are available to the marketer for a fee or, increasingly, are generated through the firm's own database. A key strength of direct mail is its ability to use lasered letters to carry a different message to each recipient. Potentially millions of different messages could be sent, according to each prospect or customer's situation. Overall, direct mail is a success story. Average response rates (a dangerous concept – rates can vary dramatically) can be 1–2% for mailers to prospects, and much higher than this to existing customers.

Exhibit 27.4 Summary of strengths and weaknesses of direct mail

Strengths	Weaknesses
● Highly targetable	● But you need a suitable list or database
● Responsive	● But expensive
● Payback can be outstanding	● But internal management is committing
● Creative medium	● But regarded as downmarket
● Good for detail	● But can be intrusive

Telemarketing

Outbound telemarketing

Telephone calls *to* customers.

Inbound telemarketing

Receiving telephone calls *from* customers.

The telephone in direct marketing is used in two ways. One is to make outbound calls to customers and prospects, known as **outbound telemarketing**, and the other is to use the telephone to take calls from customers, known as **inbound telemarketing**.

All the signs are that the growth of outbound telemarketing will continue as we move further into this new millennium. This may be because in addition to its tactical role as a way of making a sale, it also has an increasingly strategic role as a major part of many companies' relationship marketing strategies. The link between the phone and relationship marketing is evident because of the key role of the telephone in providing service.

The telephone is probably the most powerful of all media in terms of its impact on the customer, the potential for response, and the potential for getting it disastrously wrong. The main problems arise when a company calls people 'cold' with no reason for calling other than a crude attempt to sell something. This is not seen as sound business practice by many blue chip companies yet it is frequently used.

In terms of its ability to get messages through clutter, and in terms of the receiver's reaction to it as a medium, the telephone probably has the greatest impact of all media. It is very difficult to filter out telephone marketing in the way people filter out other marketing communications. However, compared to media like direct mail or inserts, the telephone can only be used for relatively straightforward messages. People can only take on board limited information aurally.

At its best, results with telemarketing can be astounding. Used appropriately, with a well thought-out offer, well targeted at one's own customers, positive responses well in excess of other media can be achieved. One telecommunications company achieved 60% take-up to an offer of telephone-related services. However, at a cost of about £6 per contact on average, high responses are needed just to break even. Even at 10% response, a gross margin of £60 would then be needed on the sale in order to break

IN VIEW 27.3

Telemarketing response rates

A mobile communications company makes 100 outbound telemarketing calls to prospects at £6 per contact. Each mobile phone the company sells costs £30 plus £2.50 post and packaging. The gross profit on each phone is £15. In order to break even, a 40% response rate is needed (40 customers @ £15 gross margin = £600). To achieve a 10% increase in returns (i.e. £660 in gross profit), a response rate of 44% is needed. The telemarketing operators are in for a tough time to meet this target – we hope the contact list is good!

Exhibit 27.5 Summary of strengths and weaknesses of outbound telemarketing

Strengths	Weaknesses
● Highly specific in its targeting	● But the most expensive medium
● Very powerful in getting response	● But potentially viewed as intrusive
● Intimate	● But needs close management
● Immediate response	● But message must be kept simple

even. As a result, telemarketing outbound is best used for high margin goods, or customers with high lifetime values which companies are increasingly using as part of their customer analysis and as part of the process of determining integrated marketing communications programmes. As the cost of telephoning decreases, the break-even point is lowered. Many companies have set up efficient call centres, many of which are based overseas, India being a particularly popular choice, as there is no reason to locate such centres in the country of origin if costs are lower elsewhere.

The use of inbound telephone is now widespread in most developed countries, in particular for response handling for direct marketing campaigns. One outstanding feature of inbound telemarketing is that it is one of the few of what might be termed 'pure direct marketing' media that the public actually likes! Unlike outbound telephone promotion, which is viewed with heavy suspicion and hostility, inbound is perceived positively by most consumers.

Customer recruitment media

While the telephone and mail are the two key retention media, a number of options are available when attracting new customers for the first time, specifically press, magazines, TV and the Internet.

National and *local press* are extensively used by direct marketers. More than half of all press advertising is direct response, with financial services, automobile, mail order and retail all big players. If you are looking for high volumes of exposure, with a broadly defined or as yet unknown audience, then the press could be your answer. Note that a press advert may only generate 0.01–0.05% response to a typical advert. However, the media costs are low in terms of cost per thousand reached, often at well under £10 per thousand, and so press is as competitive as other media in terms of cost per response.

Exhibit 27.6 Summary of strengths and weaknesses of customer recruitment media

	Strengths	Weaknesses
Press	Awareness as well as response	Low creative options
Magazines	Segment audience by interest	But long lead times
DRTV	High powers of persuasion and credibility	But messages must be simple
Radio	Can be considered as similar to TV	But less impact than TV and messages must be simple
Internet	Expanding in use, it is low cost and high coverage	Requires the customer to visit the site to respond (site may be missed)
Inserts	More impactful than press	But seen as 'junk'

Whereas local press tends to target according to geography, *magazines* tend to split consumers out according to their interests. If you need to segment your audience by lifestyle therefore, magazines are a useful channel to think about. Everything from *Army Quarterly and Defence Journal* to *Audiophile with HiFi Answers* through to *Potholing Weekly* and back to *True Romances* are out there. Magazines offer more impact on your audience than will press. This is for two reasons: the magazine brand itself may be relevant to the product you are selling, and you may gain from association with the media brand values. Second, magazine production values are higher than press, with higher quality paper and full colour.

According to Merit Direct, '*Direct Response TV* is an idea whose time has come'. When we come to compare media, quite simply, TV is different. As Nash (1995) has said, nothing else permits the advertiser to demonstrate, prove and, crucially, to *dramatise* as well as TV does (how many mailers can you remember? Contrast this against TV adverts you recall). Most TV advertising till recently has been dedicated to brand building, but recently there has been a rapid rise in direct response TV or mixing both: brand response TV, which combines both brand building and response. This growth can be attributed to issues like channel fragmentation, the increased use of the telephone to purchase goods, and the need to make TV advertising more accountable.

TV offers direct marketers massive audience coverage, low costs per thousand reached, and superb creative opportunities. Against this, it remains difficult for the audience to respond (they must remember the telephone number or website) and calls tend to come in at the same time to the company and are therefore difficult to manage. Although typically considered to offer less impact, radio can likewise be an effective medium.

Inserts are leaflets carried by many papers, supplements and magazines. These carry a coupon or telephone response number. Disliked by consumers because they fall out of their Sunday supplements, this is also exactly the reason why they get noticed and hence attract a higher response than press adverts. However, the client must pay both media and production costs.

The one medium which threatens to rewrite the rules is the Internet. Direct response transactions over the Internet have been taking place in measurable volumes since 1996, and are set to grow considerably. This is because of the very low costs of advertising (a website can be established for a few hundred pounds), low costs of access (local rates for worldwide access); and the genuine international nature of the medium. It is very easy to make a purchase using a credit card, and the initial security fears are fast being eroded. In the long term, the Internet looks set to break the economic structure of direct response media by being considerably cheaper in terms of cost/response than its rivals. Against these advantages, however, it is important to note that:

- the telephone has more interactivity than the Internet;
- at present, DRTV can facilitate a more creative approach;
- media such as TV and press create a 'public' awareness which the Internet cannot replicate.

Creative approaches to direct marketing communications

... I have to invent a Big Idea for an advertising campaign before Tuesday. Creativity strikes me as a high-falutin word for the work I have to do between now and Tuesday. (David Ogilvy, *Ogilvy on Advertising*)

Bird (1989) has described the creative contribution as the 'moment of truth' for direct marketing communications. He referred to the moment when prospects or customers engage with the advert. However, Bird would have been the first to agree that compared to other campaign elements – the targeting, the media, offer and incentive, and the timing – creativity assumes *lower* importance in direct marketing communications. This has been demonstrated many times in market tests. Nevertheless, in an industry where the creation of ideas is so important, it is churlish for textbooks to ignore the contribution of creativity to the direct marketing business.

Direct marketing creativity has traditionally been dominated by the 'unique selling proposition' approach, which focuses on *selling* by leading the prospect through a series of reasoned, logical arguments. This contrasts with advertisers' need to create atmosphere and produce entertainment as part of their mission to create emotional liking for their products. With the growth of direct marketing into sectors previously dominated by general marketing techniques has come suggestions that direct marketing needs to embrace a wider creative influence. The car industry is a classic example of this need, requiring as it does both brand building and direct response from its messages to prospects.

Direct marketing's precision and control in testing allows even small changes in creativity to be accurately related to behaviour changes by consumers. Chapter 4 has detailed the **hierarchy of effects models**. Direct response is primarily about getting the prospect from awareness through to action (response), *all within the one advert* (**AIDA**).

Hierarchy of effects models

Models that describe the stages individuals are said to progress through in moving from initial unawareness to final action such as purchase and consumption. A range of models or ways of describing the stages in the process exist.

AIDA model

Marketing communications concept that models the stages through which marketing communications should move a potential customer: Awareness, Interest, Desire and Action. It is one of a number of hierarchy-of-effects models.

The two key tools used to attract *attention* in all written direct marketing media are the headline and the picture. Research conducted using cameras to follow readers' eye movements has shown that the eye is attracted to an advert by these two main elements. Halsey (1992), in a review of creativity in direct marketing, outlined self-interest, news and curiosity as the three core platforms for headline writing.

At the *interest* stage the prospects are looking at your advert, with their curiosity aroused. They are looking for something of interest. The next requirement of the advert is to foster that interest by building on the primary benefit you presented in the headline or picture. At the interest stage, the prospect is still hedging his bets. The frame of mind is one of appraisal, which tends to be made on a logical, calculating basis.

Desire is different. Here, your prospect has started to have some *emotional feeling* for the product or service. He starts to *imagine* what it is like to own or experience what you are selling; he pictures himself doing this. With desire, emotion takes over from logic and the powerful motivations leading towards a sale are in place. The point of good creative technique is that it triggers and then fosters these emotional feelings. Emotional benefits are linked with the product – looking good, arousing envy in your friends, being successful, having control, and so on.

Finally, there are two creative strands to generating *action*. One is to emphasise the need to act straightaway. The other is to minimise the effort required. Direct marketers use various creative techniques which maximise the sense that time is short. For example: 'Limited edition product', 'Free gift if you reply in 10 days', 'Act now to avoid paying/discomfort/loss later'.

Testing and measurement in direct marketing communications

Managers undertaking general marketing communications have distinct problems in measuring the worth of their activities. This is due to the lack of precision in relating spend to revenue (see Chapters 18 and 23). In contrast, an advantage of direct marketing communications lies with its ability to precisely connect any marketing communications spend to corresponding customer revenues. Direct marketers can focus on an identified group of customers on their database, and track exactly how much is spent on them over the year, and how much revenue they generate for the company.

Market test

Trial in the marketplace before full launch.

Roll-out

The incremental process of launching a marketing initiative into the market area by area until full market coverage is achieved.

This close control also allows direct marketers to carefully **test market** their new initiatives before embarking on expensive **roll-outs**. This particularly applies to activities aimed at existing customers, and also when private media (mail and telephone) are used to attract new customers. Private media, to existing or new customers, allows us to know precisely who we are targeting, when we launch the initiative, and crucially, to know that any responses are due to that initiative and not to something else. If we send a mailer offering cases of wine to prospects, we can ask them to quote a code on response which we record. This ties that response to the precise mailing offer.

Direct marketers can test different variations of the elements of their campaigns against standard control approaches. For example, a wine merchant can test a 'buy a case and get one bottle free' incentive against a control offer which has no incentive. She would mail say 10,000 randomly chosen customers with the test, and compare with another 10,000 customers acting as the control. By keeping all the other elements the same, she can pin down any rise in response to the incentive. The key elements to test are customer type, media type, product, incentive, timing and creative approach, in diminishing order of importance.

Summary

This chapter has investigated the increasingly important role that direct marketing communications has to play in the integrated marketing communications mix. The strategic importance of databases to companies and their central role as an integrator of much communications activity has been highlighted. This chapter develops the role the database plays in direct marketing and outlines the core components of direct marketing offers and incentives, media, creative approaches, and testing and measurement.

Self-review questions

1 What is direct marketing communications?

2 What are the three key objectives for sales promotion?

3 How does direct marketing communications incentives differ from retail-based sales promotion?

4 When would a club be used in a communications programme?

5 How is the AIMRITE framework used to help with media choices?

6 What are the advantages and disadvantages of direct mail, telemarketing and customer recruitment media?

7 What are the differences between customer recruitment and customer retention media?

8 What are the two creative approaches to generate action?

Collect a direct response press or magazine advertisement or a piece of direct mail. Using the AIMRITE framework, critically appraise the media choice made. Identify how the communication could be improved.

References

Bird, D. (1989), *Commonsense Direct Marketing*. Kogan Page.

DMA (1996), *Direct Marketing Association Census*. London: DMA Records Centre.

Halsey, B. (ed.) (1992), *The Practitioner's Guide to Direct Marketing*. The Institute of Direct Marketing.

Kotler, P. (1995), *Marketing Management, Analysis, Planning, Implementation and Control* 7th edn. Englewood Cliffs, NJ: Prentice Hall.

Marketing Technique (1997), *Stores get sold on glossies*. Redwood Publishing, 4 September, 6–8.

Nash, E. (1995), *Direct Marketing, Strategy, Planning, Execution* 3rd edn. McGraw-Hill.

NDL Limited (1996), Promotional material.

O'Malley, L., Patterson, M. and Evans, M. (1999), *Exploring Direct Marketing*. London: International Thomson Business Press.

Peattie, K. and Peattie, S. (1993), Sales promotion, playing to win. *Journal of Marketing Management*, 9, 255–269.

Peppers, D. and Rogers, M. (1993), *The One–One Future*. Piatkus.

Rapp, S. and Collins, T. (1987), *Maximarketing*. McGraw-Hill.

Reichheld, F.F. (1996), *The Loyalty Effect*. Bain and Company.

Roncorroni, S. (1992), Using the telephone for profit. *The Practitioner's Guide to Direct Marketing*, (B. Halsey, ed.). The Institute of Direct Marketing.

Smith, P.R. and Taylor, J. (2002), *Marketing Communications, An Integrated Approach*. Kogan Page.

Stone, B. (1996), *Successful Direct Marketing Methods* 5th edn. NTC Business Books.

Tapp, A. (1998), *Principles of Direct and Database Marketing*. London: Financial Times Management Pitman.

Selected further reading

Jones, S.K. (1995), *Creative Strategy in Direct Marketing*. NTC Business Books.

McCorkell, G. (1997), *Direct and Database Marketing*. Kogan Page.

Wilmhurst, J. (1993), *Below-the-Line Promotion*. Butterworth-Heinemann.

Chapter 28

Sales promotion, merchandising and point of sale

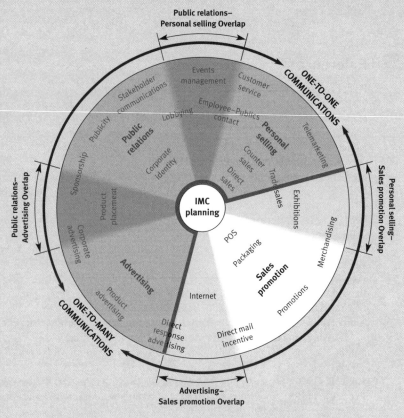

The Integrated Marketing Communications (IMC) Mix Model

CD

Using the CD material in Case Study 3 and your own research, collect examples of different Pampers sales promotions. How can each of these sales promotions be evaluated? Does Pampers integrate sales promotions, merchandising and point of sale with other communication activities? Can you recommend improvements to their strategy?

Objectives

- To emphasise the relevance and importance of sales promotions within the marketing communications mix
- To indicate the relationship between sales promotions, merchandising and point of sale
- To describe the range of sales promotions activities
- To emphasise sales promotion's role in trade, business-to-business and employee push and pull marketing communications strategies
- To recognise the short-term tactical nature of sales promotions and their longer-term strategic value
- To emphasise sales promotion's ability to encourage action and complement other marketing communications activities
- To highlight the areas where sales promotions are particularly effective and illustrate their use
- To emphasise the need to evaluate sales promotions effectiveness

Professional perspective

Barry Clarke Chairman and Chief Executive, Clarke Hooper

Most sales promotion doesn't work. It does not promote sales nor does it achieve any of the wide-ranging business objectives which are often assigned to promotion campaigns by those who commission them. Most promotions are poorly conceived, inadequately funded, burdened with conflicting objectives and bereft of management attention.

This may seem a sad reflection on the business in which I have worked for the past 38 years, particularly since promotion marketing has relentlessly seized a growing share of all marketing expenditures across those four decades.

At its best, promotion marketing can help attract new users, build customer loyalty and contribute to the long-term development of brands. At its best, it can shape a market, decisively influence success in the launch or re-launch of brands and offer an outstanding return on investment.

→

Truly successful sales promotion campaigns are clearly targeted, fresh and original, true to the spirit of the brand and brilliantly communicated. Success is based on a heady blend of scientific precision and creative inspiration. I love this business because it combines flair and imagination with objectivity, accountability and honed organisational skills.

Great sales promotion campaigns come from companies that take promotion seriously. They come when top management treats its promotions as seriously as its advertising. They come in businesses that are able to measure success and evaluate performance.

You can see those characteristics in the promotions of Procter & Gamble, Unilever, Shell and Esso in the 60s and 70s; Sony, Guinness, Cadbury and Heinz in the 70s and 80s; *The Sun, The Daily Mail*, Walkers and Tesco in the 90s and 2000s. And in the work of McDonald's consistently and globally for more than 30 years.

They have all learned from experience, built success on success. They have encouraged creativity and insisted on impeccable delivery. They have built great brands.

B. Clarke

Growth and importance of sales promotions

Below-the-line communications

Marketing communications that make use of the non-commission-paying media in all their forms, i.e. all forms of promotions other than advertising. Sometimes, incorrectly, it is referred to as below-the-line advertising. Although it remains a popular term, its usefulness is limited as it encompasses such a broad range of promotional activity.

Sales promotions are a growth area within the marketing communications mix. In its broadest sense, as one of the four areas of the Integrated Marketing Communications Mix Model, it embraces a wide range of marketing communications and typifies much of what is thought of as below-the-line promotions, even though **below-the-line** promotions actually applies to an even wider group of marketing communications activities.

Sales promotion's importance to the marketing communications mix should not be underestimated as it adds an extensive range of effective tools to the marketing communications armoury. As Crosier and Bureau (1990) note, sales promotions is

a highly elastic term, embracing a host of marketing tactics. … A fundamental distinction can now be proposed between economic-incentive sales promotions, such as free samples, premium offers money-off deals …; and communication-initiative sales promotions, such as product literature. (p. 227)

NEED TO KNOW

☑ *Sales promotions fall under the classifications of 'economic incentives' and 'communication initiatives'.*

WARNING

❗ *It is difficult to assess the full extent of the sales promotions industry because it is difficult to decide precisely what to include and difficult to obtain accurate data.*

In determining the growth of sales promotions, measures of sales promotion spends always present difficulties of what to include and what not to include in the calculation. This is compounded by the difficulty of actually obtaining the data itself. This is unlike the situation with advertising where mechanisms have long been established for working out its expenditure. In 1988, the Advertising Association and the Institute of Sales Promotion (ISP) conducted an initial survey to identify the criteria for measurement of sales promotion. This was not completed and has not been followed up since (Cummins 1998). In 1997, the ISP estimated a sales promotion expenditure of £7.5 billion in the UK, a figure comparable with advertising spends (more recent estimates have suggested that it even exceeds advertising). Around a decade ago it was estimated that the advertising to sales promotion expenditure ratio was 60:40. In 1997, this was more like 30:70 in favour of sales promotions, at least for many consumer goods companies (Kotler 1997) who are known, traditionally, to be the big advertising spenders.

Reasons for growth

FOOD FOR THOUGHT

The advertising to sales promotion ratio suggests that more money is spent on sales promotion activities than on all forms of advertising.

A number of reasons have been suggested for the growth of sales promotions.

- *Changing locus of power from manufacturers to retailers.* Retailers have become larger and more powerful, often dictating terms to manufacturers. They favour sales promotions, and associated merchandising and point-of-sale promotions. Strong sales promotions to the trade have become necessary elements of marketing communications as part of manufacturers 'push' promotional strategies.

- *Customer demand and expectations.* Sales promotions have proliferated in consumer markets. Increasingly, customers have come to expect sales promotional offers and activities as part of the marketing communications effort, and have become increasingly responsive to these activities making sales promotions an effective range of marketing communications tools.

- *Emphasis on short-term results.* Sales promotions are noted for their ability to generate immediate and short-term effects. As increased emphasis has been placed on short-term results (rightly or wrongly), sales promotions have become favoured activities, not least because measuring their effects and effectiveness are typically much easier than for advertising and public relations. Sales promotions have a more direct and immediate effect on the bottom-line sales and profits.

Brand parity

Situation where brands are seen as being equivalent.

Price sensitivity

The more customers are price sensitive, the more they are affected by small changes in price.

- *Increased brand parity and price sensitivity.* There are fewer distinctions between brands so that there is less reason to favour one over another. At the same time, customers have become more price aware and price sensitive so that sales promotions featuring economic (price) incentives have a greater role to play.

- *Reduced brand loyalty.* Customers display brand-switching behaviour and are not typically loyal to a single brand, one reason being because of the similarity between brands. Chapter 4 introduced the concept whereby consumers have a 'portfolio' of brands from which they select their preferred choice depending upon the prevailing circumstances at the time. Sales promotions are effective in encouraging switching behaviour *from* competitors' brands and discouraging switching to competing brands.

FOOD FOR THOUGHT

The fragmentation of markets (and changes in the media) has resulted in sales promotions often being able to target marketing communications audiences better than traditional forms of advertising.

- *Market fragmentation.* The fragmentation of markets has reduced the effectiveness of the traditional mass media in reaching specifically defined audiences as emphasised in Alan Toop's quote in In View 28.1. Sales promotions have proven to be an effective alternative.

IN VIEW 28.1

'Demassification' of markets leads to changes in marketing communications

This 'demassification' of markets and media thus reduces those economies of scale on which all modern marketing has been based, and at the same time reduces manufacturers' ability to communicate with large numbers of consumers frequently and cheaply through advertising.   (Toop 1994)

● *Synergy.* Research findings indicate that the sales effects of marketing communications are greater when advertising and sales promotions are carried out simultaneously (hence the value of integration). One finding involving 21 different brands in eight different consumer goods markets (Roberts 1996) suggests that the sales effects can be between two and seven times greater. This finding should not come as a surprise to anyone who believes in the value of integrated marketing communications because advertising and sales promotions are highly complementary activities in moving customers through the hierarchy of effects from awareness to action/trial (see Chapter 4, Marketing communications psychology, and Chapter 26, Advertising). Moreover, a lot of advertising actually uses sales promotional offers such as, for example, an announcement of a sale or reduced prices, special deals and competitions.

FOOD FOR THOUGHT

When sales and advertising are integrated as combined activities, their joint effect can significantly increase sales compared with using them singly.

Defining sales promotions, merchandising and point of sale

Sales promotions, merchandising and point of sale are not discrete areas of marketing communications. It is best to think of sales promotions as an over-arching range of activities of which merchandising and point of sale form a part. Shimp (2000) provides two definitions of sales promotion, one in the main body of his text and one in his glossary of terms. On the one hand, he uses sales promotion to mean

NEED TO KNOW

Sales promotions are best viewed as the overarching range of activities of which merchandising and point of sale are a part.

The use of any *incentive* by a manufacturer or service provider to induce the *trade* (wholesalers or retailers) and/or *consumers* to buy a brand and to encourage the *salesforce* to aggressively sell it. The incentive is *additional to the basic benefits* provided by the brand and *temporarily changes its perceived price or value.* (p.442)

WARNING

Definitions of sales promotions tend to emphasise its financial incentive elements but ignore other marketing communications aspects.

This definition has a number of admirable qualities. It also has some significant failings. On the plus side, it emphasises the role sales promotions have in trade as well as consumer (end-customer) promotions and, thereby, their use in both *push* and *pull* marketing communications strategies (see Chapter 19, setting objectives, determining strategy and tactics). It also emphasises another key audience group, the salesforce, who can also be targeted with sales promotion incentives. On the minus side, it over-emphasises the use of incentives as the sole focus of **sales promotion** activity. Important though incentives are in representing a significant proportion of sales promotion activity, this singular emphasis is to the detriment of other aspects of sales promotions. In Crosier and Bureau's (1990) terms, it captures the economic-incentive element of sales promotions but ignores the communication-initiative dimension which is so much a part of the work involved in **merchandising** and point of sale. Surprisingly, the definition seems to suggest that sales promotion is something undertaken by manufacturers and service providers to encourage the trade and consumers, but appears to exclude reference to the huge amount of sales promotion activity undertaken by the trade itself (the retailers and wholesalers) and sales promotions focused on business-to-business customers who can also be considered as part of trade marketing.

The definition below, favoured here, is based on Shimp's (2000) second definition and as can be seen, proposes a broader perspective to sales promotions. This permits incentivised and non-incentivised sales promotions, and the opportunity for sales

Sales promotion

Widely used term covering a myriad of promotional activities, excluding advertising, PR and personal selling. Sales promotion is associated with free offers, price deals, premium offers, and other promotions including merchandising, point-of-sale displays, leaflets and product literature.

Merchandising

Range of sales promotions activities intended to ensure that products are easily available, and prominently and attractively displayed at point of sale.

promotions to be undertaken by anybody. Although encouraging action is an important part of sales promotions, the definition allows that action to take the form of purchase behaviour or other acceptable outcomes. Such outcomes may be requesting more information, attendance at an event or becoming a member of a club, for example (the intended action would be specified as part of the sales promotion objectives). The perceived value of the product being promoted, frequently, but not exclusively, may be through offering extra benefits such as money-off vouchers or the chance of winning a prize, but may otherwise be through improved merchandising activities at the point of sale, such as through a change of shelf display, or affecting the atmosphere at the point of sale.

> **Sales promotions are marketing communications activities used to encourage the trade and/or end customers to purchase or take other relevant action by affecting the perceived value of the product being promoted or to otherwise motivate action to be taken.**

In the case of sales promotions targeted internally towards an organisation's own staff, the promotions may be used to encourage sales staff to 'push' the products harder and this may be achieved by providing incentives or extra promotional material to assist their task. In this way, the product is perceived to be more worthwhile to sell. Other internal sales promotions may be used less as incentives and more to communicate or to motivate.

Merchandising as one element of sales promotions may be described as:

> **Activities intended to ensure that products are easily available, and prominently and attractively displayed at point of sale.**

It is also used to describe the activity of making promotional products available such as those associated with new film releases. Merchandising, in this context, originally played a supportive role. It is now a multi-billion pound business in its own right. Merchandising is most likely to be at a point of sale (but this is not necessarily so). Many organisations even employ 'merchandisers' whose task it is to develop displays and check that their products are subsequently displayed appropriately displayed in retail outlets, particularly important when competing products are also available close

IN VIEW 28.2

Motivating the Halifax

When Halifax was converting from a building society to a bank, many staff faced higher workloads and it was essential to maintain motivation and morale. Four weeks before the conversion, all staff received a promotion pack featuring a Strike It Rich gamecard. This was divided into nine grid references covered in latex. Twice weekly, specially filmed programmes – 'The X Marks The Spot Prize Draw' – ran on branch TV. In the programmes, a flying helicopter landed on a grid and staff had to watch, scratch off the latex and if their reference number matched that on the TV, ring the agency hotline in order to claim a cash prize. The value of the prizes rose with every programme until, on the final day, two lucky players each won a Ford Escort. Over 38,000 employees took part, enjoying the fun it added to their jobs at a time when motivation was crucial to a smooth conversion.

Planograms

Diagrams or plans showing store and shelf layout.

by. Some organisations (most notably retailers) use '**planograms**' to assist in shelf display and layout. These are diagrams of exactly how shelving and display units should be laid out and how products should be displayed upon those units. They are especially important if retailers wish to ensure consistency of display in all of their stores, the planogram being issued by head office to each individual outlet. The designs will take account of latest offers and deals in which agreements are made to allocate particular shelf space and locations. Manufacturer merchandisers would be responsible for checking that allocations are made correctly, that stores maintain displays correctly and that adequate stocks are held. Increasingly, with modern technology, the task of maintaining stocks and ordering of more supplies is an automatic one.

'Merchandiser' is also a term given to a display unit itself and 'merchandise' is often used to mean the products offered for sale. 'Merchandise manager' is a term favoured by some distributors for a person responsible for sourcing and selecting ranges of products, and maintaining and displaying them at the point of sale. It is even used as a title by some organisations in preference to brand or marketing manager.

FOOD FOR THOUGHT

Merchandising at point of sale appeals to all senses and affects the total customer experience.

Point of sale (POS)

Marketing communications activities that take place where products are bought and sold.

Point of sale (POS) merely describes what it says and refers to sales promotion activities placed at the point where products are bought and sold. In North America, the term used is 'point of purchase' (POP), and given the proliferation of American texts, this term is now gaining in popularity throughout Europe and the rest of the world. Point of sale is literally the point at which the sale is made, the cash point or checkout desk, but is usually extended to refer to the store in general. Merchandising activities take place at the POS and, as well as involving visual display, also involve 'atmospherics' which have to do with the overall purchase sensory experience. This includes space between aisles, lighting, signage, music/sounds and smells. Supermarkets frequently have bakeries attached or otherwise fabricate pleasant smells such as those of bread or coffee aromas.

NEED TO KNOW

Point of purchase (POP) is another term for point of sale (POS) and is favoured by the Americans.

Strategic and tactical use of sales promotions

Sales promotions are highly tactical in nature and can effectively be used as a response to competitor activity or simply as a response to improve sales that are not meeting targets. The fact that sales promotions are intended to encourage quick action means that they are ideally suited to tactical manoeuvring.

But sales promotions need not only be reactive and they need not be solely tactical in nature. The sales promotion industry is at pains to emphasise the more strategic values of sales promotions. 'Sales promotion is strategic if it enhances the firm's distinctive capabilities, increases competitive advantages and builds long-term relationships' (Cummins 1998). Sales promotions become more strategic in nature when they are not used for a 'quick fix' but, rather, are planned in advance with one activity building on the previous one to establish continuity of marketing communications. In this way, they are used to impact on longer-term values and not just to impose temporary effects, which would be a more tactical approach. However, the argument of whether sales promotions are tactical or strategic is a tenuous one. Some would simply say that when used in conjunction, this is merely the forward planning of a series of tactical activities rather than something that is truly strategic. What is probably more important to recognise is the flexibility of sales promotions, that they can be:

NEED TO KNOW

Sales promotions are said to be tactical and strategic.

NEED TO KNOW

Sales promotions are highly flexible and can be used both reactively and proactively.

- *reactive* to specific situations and implemented as one-off quick responses;
- *proactive* – planned as part of a larger pre-planned campaign and sustained marketing communications effort, integrated with a range of sales promotions and other marketing communications activities.

Sales promotion objectives

Chapter 19 outlined the characteristics of good objectives and this applies as much to sales promotions as it does to any element of marketing communications. Chapter 19 should be read for further details. Areas of objectives pertinent to sales promotions include: increasing volume, encouraging trial, increasing repeat purchase, increasing frequency or amount of use, widening use, increasing loyalty, extending usage, creating awareness and interest, gaining intermediary support, deflecting attention from price, emphasising price, discriminating among users, and supporting database enhancements.

In setting objectives it is useful to know what sales promotions are particularly good at doing; for this purpose, a list is provided below. The list is broken into three sections, each of which identifies the major target groups that sales promotions can be focused on. Having identified what objectives need to be fulfilled, the most appropriate sales promotion activities can be selected.

Consumer sales promotions

- Improve sales of existing products
- Encourage repeat purchase by current users
- Encourage trial by new customers of existing products
- Help introduce new products
- Encourage trial of new products
- Pre-empt competitive marketing communications, i.e. before competitive action
- Counteract competitive marketing communications, i.e. after competitive action
- Increase product usage
- Encourage brand 'loyalty'/discourage brand switching
- Facilitate collection of customer database information
- Complement other marketing communications 'pull' activities.

Trade sales promotions

- Help introduce new products to the trade
- Encourage distribution penetration
- Increase allocation of shelf space
- Improve shelf display positioning
- Encourage use of special display or display features (on or off shelf)
- Provide extra incentives over competing products
- Help stimulate trade salesforce motivation
- Help overcome over-stocking problems or slow moving lines
- Help achieve short-term sales targets, i.e. encourage early ordering
- Help in the management of customer payments, e.g. early or prompt payment
- Help 'lock-in' trade buyers to own products in favour of competing products
- Facilitate collection of customer database information
- Complement other marketing communications 'push' activities.

Employee sales promotions

- Stimulate sales force motivation for new, improved or existing products
- Provide extra 'assistance' for sales staff, e.g. create extra sales promotion materials for their use
- Encourage the meeting of sales targets
- Help in the management of customer debt, e.g. reduction of overdue debts
- Encourage sales staff to generate leads
- Improve the quality of leads/qualified leads
- Encourage non-sales staff to generate leads
- Encourage all staff to improve customer contact and relations
- Complement other marketing communications 'push' activities.

Sales promotion activities

WARNING

Sales promotions should be developed as an integrated part of the marketing communications package and not just considered as isolated elements.

There is a vast array of possible activities that can be classified as sales promotions. The majority are most closely associated with providing direct incentives, usually financial or financially related. Other activities are communications related and involve providing information or display. A range of activities is briefly described below under the same principal target groups as above. In practice, a number of techniques may be used across two or all three areas. The range identified below should not be considered comprehensive, although it is intended to be representative of the more common activities.

Sales promotion activities will often be used in conjunction with one another and with other marketing communication tools. Their design should be complementary to the product being promoted and should be developed with due regard to the impact they may have on brand image.

NEED TO KNOW

There are many legal restrictions and voluntary regulatory codes of practice imposed on sales promotions.

There are both legal and self-regulations imposed by the industry that control the use of sales promotions and many aspects are best left to specialist sales promotion agencies – not just to come up with good ideas and be effective in implementing them, but to do so within the regulatory system that governs their use. Chapter 9, Regulation and legal controls, gives details of some of the regulations that surround sales promotions.

Consumer focused sales promotion activities

Consumer sales promotions (along with other consumer-targeted marketing communications) are pull promotional activities designed to encourage demand by end-customers that will 'pull' products through the distribution chain. As indicated above, many of the same activities described here can be used equally well (although with some modifications) as trade and business-to-business sales promotions.

Sampling

Standard or trial-sized samples of the brand are provided free or at a reduced price to encourage trial. They may be available from retailers, on-pack, through the mail, attached to, or within, magazines and newspapers, or delivered door-to-door.

IN VIEW 28.3

Spillers Little Rascal

Spillers Petfoods felt there was a gap in the market for cat treats and the best opportunity to plug it would be to target Felix cat food buyers, who had been involved in promotional activities in the past. They knew that the direct mail pack had to be very 'Felixy' and include some play value if it was to appeal. The pack, sent out to a mailing list of 241,000, emphasised the theme; 'Does Your Rascal Deserve a Reward?' It contained product samples, such as Felix Meaty Sticks, postcards, a 'Daily Rascal' newspaper, a Felix sticker, a play ball, feeding information, a coupon and a direct response questionnaire. 40,000 sent back the questionnaire, 15,000 redeemed the coupon.

Couponing

Coupons are extensively used in a variety of forms and are associated with other elements of sales promotions such as money-off offers and contests. They can appear:

- on-pack, in-pack and near-pack
- in advertisements
- in direct mail and door-to-door leaflets
- at point of sale – printed and on display, computer printed (see In View 28.3).

Redemption rates for coupons can vary enormously and can be as low as 5% or less. One advantage of couponing is that an attractive offer can be made to entice an initial sale in the knowledge that only a small proportion of people will actually trade in the coupon later. Where coupons require completion with name and address (many do not have this requirement), the data can be used to add to a database. Care has to be exercised in forecasting redemption rates, as miscalculations can prove catastrophic. Coupons or vouchers are often used for money-off offers.

Premiums

Self-liquidating offer

Sales promotion that pays for itself.

Premiums are merchandise items or services. They include free goods and services such as a free extra item of the product being purchased (two for one premium, or BOGOF – 'buy one get one free'), a free item of some other product or a free service such as entry into a leisure park. Or the premium might be money off another purchase. This would typically require proof of purchase of the original product or coupons. **Self-liquidating premiums** are offers where consumers are given the opportunity to buy a promotional item at an attractive price, usually accompanied with one or more proofs of purchase. For example, Kellogg's have offered 'Sunshine' breakfast bowls for sale and Nescafé have offered branded coffee cups to purchasers of their products. The principal advantage of self-liquidating offers is that they are cost free to the company, the costs are recovered in the price charged for the offer – hence they are self-liquidating. At the same time, in the case of these two and similar examples, the company has the added advantage of customers owning another piece of their promotional material (having paid for the privilege). Self-liquidating offers can also involve joint, tie-in promotions with other owned brands or tie-ins with other companies.

IN VIEW 28.4

Reebok

A Reebok promotion featured exclusively in Allsports stores, with a variety of POS aids. Purchasers of selected Reebok products received a free and exclusive limited edition video, concentrating on Reebok-sponsored international footballer, Ryan Giggs. With the video was included a competition entry form, with a prize of a VIP trip to see a Premier League match. The target market was 14–24-year-olds, with an interest in sport, particularly football.

IN VIEW 28.5

Trebor Bassett put their Maynards brand in the shade

Motorists visiting BP, Shell and Esso garages were targeted in a 'Maynards Wine Gums Free Car Shade' promotion. It aimed to improve sales of wine gums, in a sector where they already had good distribution but needed more trial and display. In particular, Trebor Bassett wanted drivers to pick up big bags, so it temptingly offered a free car shade with every three family bags of Maynards products. The car shades were placed with the sweets at aisle ends, with bright clear POS material, to catch attention. More than 100 petrol forecourts took up the promotion. Over 100,000 car shades were claimed during the month-long promotional period.

WARNING

It is imperative to carefully calculate the expected financial impact on an organisation of proposed sales promotion activities.

Not all premium offers work out successfully even if they have a positive impact on sales. This can occur if the promoter has not accurately anticipated the effect on stocks of the product or on the effect on bottom-line profits. McDonald's Big Mac 'buy one and get a second one free' promotion commenced with anticipatory TV and press advertisements. When the sales promotion actually started, McDonald's soon ran out of burgers. They could not fill demand and were forced to publicly apologise in an attempt to assuage the bad publicity. They had not appreciated how successful the promotion was going to be and, unfortunately, had not forecast sufficient quantity of product.

Money-off

Money-off offers are the most recognised use of sales promotions. Immediate price reductions should, however, be carefully controlled as they have a full and immediate impact on sales value and profits. A sale is an example of a store-wide sales promotion held at key times such as spring, autumn, Christmas and January, or for a purpose such as closing down, refurbishing, etc. Otherwise money-off offers are made in relation to specific products and may be made in a variety of ways, such as:

- on pack, immediate price reduction
- money-off voucher, immediate price reduction
- money-off voucher for next purchase

IN VIEW 28.6

Hoover's big dust up

Hoover, who gave away free flights to various destinations around the world with purchases of their products worth £100 or more, saw their sales rise significantly as the promotion attracted customers to rush out and buy Hoover products before the promotion deadline. Dealers reported that people were buying two vacuum cleaners at a time to take advantage of the offer. Unfortunately, Hoover was unable to honour the deal. The travel agency handling the promotion reported 100,000 responses within months of the start of the promotion, twice what they had expected. Lots of bad publicity ensued and Maytag, the parent company, had to come to the rescue to bail Hoover out.

WARNING

! *Unlike other promotions, immediate price reductions have an instantaneous effect on sales revenue. Price reductions can trigger off 'price wars'.*

- money-off voucher for other products
- computer-generated immediate price reduction
- computer-generated vouchers (current purchases and future purchases).

Money-off offers are usually designed as short-term expedients but some brands appear to run one price reduction after another, creating a clear impression and expectation in people's minds. They are easy to imitate and do have the danger of encouraging a 'price war'.

IN VIEW 28.7

Computer tells you how much

It was soon realised that computerised tills and scanners, first developed to speed up the checkout process at point of sale, could be used as inventory and sales tracking devices. By logging out all purchases, stores have an instant and continuous computer record of all transactions. These were used to check against stock levels and automatically trigger new order requests. It was later realised that such systems could also be used to catalogue customer purchases as they go through the checkout, and create coupons and price rewards for the purchases made. Put this together with customer loyalty swipe cards and you have the ability to track individual customer transactions over time.

The systems associated with these activities are a young and growing field with three system types dominating the field today.

- *Purchase-activated incentives information* – electronically generated paper coupons, promotional messages, product information and other incentives dispensed at the checkout, based on scanner-read actual purchases.
- *Frequent-shopper programmes* – campaigns where customers receive added value based on product and/or retailer loyalty, e.g. based on shopper reward points accumulated over time.
- *Electronic discounts* – credits that are earned and money-off automatically deducted from the customers' shopping transactions.

➜

'Catalina' is one example of these systems in operation. It monitors product barcodes as they are scanned in at the checkout. The retailer or manufacturer has already identified specific products, pack sizes or customer groups in advance to trigger an immediate response. Whenever the triggers appear, the Catalina printer produces a coupon with a message/voucher, which is handed to the customer along with the receipt. Each coupon is individually generated and will be directly relevant to the shopper; it is, therefore, more likely to influence the customer's behaviour. Research indicates that this is the case and is able to be so in a far more cost-efficient way than other approaches. The Catalina system is able to interact with the store's database, can read loyalty cards and can produce appropriate coupon incentives. Unlike mass marketing and direct mail, this approach is able to bypass completely the 'irrelevant' customers who don't buy a particular type of item, no matter what the brand, and concentrate instead on instantly recognising and rewarding customers that matter.

Source: Adapted from Maguire (1997).

Bonus packs

Bonus packs include an extra quantity of the product in the pack for no extra price increase. The perceived added value is a reduction in price without having to actually reduce price. One benefit of bonus, and banded packs below, is that they discourage brand switching – the consumer is enticed by the added value and, simply, has more of the product to use.

Banded packs

These are multi-packs of the same product, or more than one product, 'banded' together for an inclusive price. It might be two or three packs of the same item, or a free film with a camera, for example.

Contests

Competitions of a variety of forms are a popular sales promotional tool. Specific legal rules have to be adhered to when using competitions. They often involve the use of an element of skill and tie-breakers, in the case of possible joint winners. Prizes vary in value from very small items to a trip around the world. Where there is no element of skill and winners are determined purely by chance, no purchase of the product itself is likely to be necessary. Scratch cards, which the holder has to rub away the surface to reveal a prize, are frequently used. These offer immediate feedback to customers on whether they have won or not and while there may be chances of winning large prizes, this can be controlled by the promoter to restrict winning cards.

Tie-in sales promotions

Tie-ins are where multiple products are involved in sales promotions. The products may be from the same company (intra-company tie-ins) or from different companies (Inter-company tie-ins). A useful illustration of an inter-company tie-in is a McDonald's place mat which was given out with every meal eaten instore and featured McDonald's, Mattel, Toys'Я'Us, Disney and Pixar Studios. The place mat promoted Disney's *A Bug's Life* film and merchandise associated with the film. Sales promotion offers included a family holiday in San Francisco (including a visit to Pixar Studios, joint makers of the film), a contest to win Mattell 'Talkin' and Movin' Flik' figures and *A Bug's Life* yo-yos, a price reduction offer when *A Bug's Life* action figures were bought from Toys'R'Us, and free entry prize draw coupon requiring name and address details. With so many offers up for grabs, McDonald's hoped to sell more burgers.

IN VIEW 28.8

Pepsi's unlucky number

One contest proved to be extremely costly for Pepsi-Co. In the Philippines, a sales promotion was run in which cash prizes were awarded to holders of Pepsi bottle tops bearing the number 349. A computer error resulted in 500,000 bottle tops being printed with this number. The prize money would have cost Pepsi-Co around $18 million if it had to be paid out. Although a great deal of resentment was caused, the payouts were reduced costing Pepsi-Co about $10 million, still a very substantial sum. To Pepsi-Co's relief, the Philippines justice department dismissed thousands of lawsuits and discharged the company from criminal liability.

Source: Adapted from Shrimp (1997).

Cause-related sales promotions

These are sales promotions in which benefits are provided to a worthy cause as part of the promotion. For example, the European Scuba-Diving School in Turkey sells T-shirts featuring their name, logo, and a picture of dolphins. The T-shirts are sold with the guarantee that for each sale, 1,500,000 Turkish lira will be donated to the 'Save the Dolphin' fund. Other examples include joint promotions between clubs, associations and societies, and credit card and insurance companies. In return for allowing their members to be targeted, members receive discount benefits and the societies receive a donation for every card or policy taken.

Merchandising/point-of-sale displays/demonstrations

These promotions are anything that entices customers to buy or take action through display and atmospherics as described earlier in this chapter. It includes window displays, shelf and aisle displays, the use of video, and other appeals to any of the five senses. Air conditioning systems can be used to duct bad odours such as fish smells out of the store, while smells of fresh bread from the store bakery can be distributed throughout the store. These and the use of background music can be used to create a favourable ambience to encourage sales and further visits to the store.

IN VIEW 28.9

Honda demonstrate how to do it

Honda launched their CR-V (Compact Recreational Vehicle), a four-wheel drive car, with a refrigerator, a picnic table, and to which a shower could be attached. The target market was considered to be drivers in their late 20s or early 30s, who might otherwise be customers for sports convertibles or off-roaders. Prospects were sent four successive mailings: an ice-cube mould, a salt and pepper pot, a sponge and, finally a Ray-Ban sunglasses case with the news that, if they turned up at a showroom to test drive the CR-V, they could collect a pair of Ray-Bans afterwards. It was supported with press advertising, posters and advertorials in a variety of magazines; 4000 prospects and 2000 customers were mailed and this generated 1021 test drives – a 17% response.

Demonstrations can be in-store, at exhibitions and in-home, in person or on video/CD-ROM/DVD. The intention is to show the use of products and they are particularly useful for complex items or services such as holidays, which can easily be featured on video. Test driving a car at a local car showroom would be another example of demonstration.

Interactive kiosks are a relatively new development in which customers can interact with a computer rather than simply watch a demonstration or they can be used to seek information instead of asking a sales person. An example is given in In View 28.10.

IN VIEW 28.10

Red Kite kick Puma into new media age

To promote Puma's range of products, Red Kite, a new media agency, produced a highly interactive visually engaging in-store touch screen kiosk that featured Puma's current catalogue of sports footwear. Digital video sequences of classic moments in soccer history together with emotive music and sound effects emphasise Puma's sporting heritage. New media techniques such as QuickTime VR enhanced the customer's experience with virtual 3D objects and environments. These enabled viewers to see the footwear from any angle and receive information on how the boot/shoe was constructed for optimal comfort and efficiency. A 'shoe-selector' allowed users to intelligently choose footwear according to their individual criteria.

Source: Adapted from Red Kite (1999).

FOOD FOR THOUGHT

The release of merchandise items to coincide with film releases has resulted in a multi-billion pound industry.

A phenomenal growth area in merchandising has been that associated with new film releases. It is said the film producers make more money from the intellectual property rights and licensing agreements of the characters in the films than they do from the films themselves. The Disney Company are 'masters' of this activity and have extensive ranges of merchandise available from each of their recent and older films. They even have their own stores throughout the world, which concentrate on selling these merchandise items. Good examples of films taking advantage of merchandising include *Teenage Mutant Ninja Turtles*, the *Star Wars* series, *The Lion King* and *The X Men* among many, many others. Merchandising of this type has now developed into complete business ventures in their own right and has to be recognised as more than simple sales promotions. Films like Times Warner's *Space Jam* are little more than 90-minute advertisements for the licensed merchandise they promote. As Times Warner's chief Gerald Warner boasted in *The New York Times*, 'This isn't a movie, it's a marketing event.' Many of them involve joint promotion opportunities and tie-ins such as Kentucky Fried Chicken's massive promotions campaign built around its joint promotions with the Star Wars film, *The Phantom Menace*.

Information leaflets/packs and catalogues

This area of sales promotions often overlaps with marketing public relations. Leaflets, packs and catalogues come in all shapes and sizes and are made available through direct mail, at retail outlets, in- and on-pack, in public places such as libraries, and so on. They can include printed, audio and visual material. Leaflets very often contain money-off vouchers as well as product and company information. Disney, for exam-

FOOD FOR THOUGHT

The Internet as a medium can be used for marketing communications activities in numerous ways, including for sales promotion purposes.

ple, advertises the availability of a video it produces of its holiday resorts, which is sent to anyone who requests it. Direct marketing company, Neways, sends out audio tapes of their products as part of their sales promotion. Many companies make use of information telephone lines. Catalogues, produced by direct mail houses and catalogue high street retailers, are fundamental to their business. The Internet is used heavily as a sales promotional tool.

IN VIEW 28.11

Go ahead for McVities

McVities, producers of 'Go Ahead', a range of low fat biscuits and other low fat snack foods, wished to increase the rate of trial. Leaflets and money-off coupons were sent to names selected from databases and also inserted in slimming magazines. The recipients were encouraged to fill in coupons and return them by being offered the chance to win a Caribbean holiday in a free prize draw. The company increased awareness of the product range and its benefits and obtained the names and addresses that could be targeted in later promotions.

IN VIEW 28.12

K'NEX connects on the Web

K'NEX International set up a website to enhance its ability to compete with the construction toy rival, Lego, which also uses the Internet. The website is a good illustration of the immense amount of material and variety that electronic publishing offers. The K'NEX website promotional offers have included an online treasure hunt, a monthly free prize draw; free downloadable software, a catalogue, and a special game, all targeted to appeal to their 8–12-year-old target consumers.

'Loyalty' schemes

Loyalty schemes are much-favoured sales promotion activities although there is some debate as to the extent of 'loyalty' that is actually engendered with many customers owning loyalty cards from different competing retailers. What loyalty schemes do is to encourage customers to purchase more items from, or make more use of, the organisation of which they are 'members'. The 'badge' of the loyalty scheme is the 'loyalty card', which will be carried around, typically with a number of others, by the customer. The fact that customers belong to so many competing schemes does reduce some of the impact. They are, however, undoubtedly effective and are used extensively by the large multiple outlet retailers. Loyalty schemes offer the

NEED TO KNOW

Loyalty schemes are popular as a marketing tool. However, the term 'loyalty' may frequently be misapplied. Most loyalty schemes operate by offering incentives to buy; this may be seen less as 'loyalty' and more as 'inducement'.

opportunity to such retailers to be creative in their sales promotions, which they can increasingly target to specific customer groups. This significantly improves the chances of developing effective and pertinent offers.

Behind the loyalty schemes lie impressive computing power. Each time a loyalty card is used, purchases and purchasers are tracked. A history of personal buying behaviour is developed. Through this process, a wealth of detail is stored which can be used as a basis for selecting and targeting further promotions. These are virtually guaranteed to be of relevance to the customer. A natural development has been the increase in the use of loyalty schemes for joint promotions. This is where two or more organisations offer inter-company tie-in promotions such as those described above. The Shell Smart card, for example, has involved participation with John Menzies newsagents, Victoria Wine off-licences, Dixon and Curries electrical stores, the RAC motoring services, HMV record shops, Air Miles, UCI cinemas and Hilton Hotels. The Nectar card is another example.

> **NEED TO KNOW**
>
> ☑ *Loyalty schemes require the collection and control of large amounts of data. Computing power has made it possible for loyalty schemes to run effectively and with high degrees of sophistication.*

Trade focused sales promotion activities

This section describes those sales promotions that can be targeted towards trade customers. Trade customers might be members of the manufacturer's (or service provider's) channel of distribution (e.g. wholesalers and retailers), or might be business-to-business customers. When using intermediaries, trade sales promotions (along with other marketing communications) help to 'push' products through the distribution chain by encouraging channel members to stock and sell them to end-customers. It should be remembered when embarking on trade promotions to intermediaries that not only do the managers of the trade organisations have to be considered, so do their sales staff for whom specific sales promotions may be designed.

> **NEED TO KNOW**
>
> ☑ *When considering trade sales promotions, business-to-business customers, channel members and the sales staff working for the trade companies should all be considered.*

Consumer promotions

A feature often overlooked is the fact that consumer promotions themselves are very attractive as an incentive to channel customers. The simple reason for this is that anything that is likely to encourage end-customers to buy is in the best interests of the channel. It is common practice, therefore, to ensure that details of consumer promotions are featured in channel promotions.

Allowances

Allowances to the trade come in many different forms and include:

- discounts/price reductions
- additional free products
- special terms
- target pay-backs.

Discounts and price reductions may be given, for example, to favoured customers, as part of a special promotional push or for purchase of large quantities. *Additional free products* are useful incentives in that they are only a marginal extra cost to the manufacturer and can be sold by dealers at full price. The value of this form of sales promotion to the trade, therefore, is greater than the cost of providing it by the manufacturer. *Special terms* may be arranged by negotiation and may be price or payment related (e.g. an extension to the payment period), or may feature some other marketing aspect such as special delivery arrangements or special packaging. *Target pay-backs* are an interesting feature which many of the large multiple retailers now demand of their suppliers. This is a performance-related allowance where the manufacturer or service provider agrees a refund of money if certain targets are met. Prices per unit are agreed for different quantities, the price being lower the higher the quantity bought, but the customer does not guarantee how much they will buy over a given period. The retailer or wholesaler will purchase the product as needed at the price agreed for the quantity they estimate they will require over that period. If they are able to purchase more than first anticipated which brings them down to the lower price point, the supplier has to refund the over-payment. This can amount to millions of pounds per annum for some fast-moving consumer goods companies.

Contests and incentives

These are trade contests and incentive programmes to encourage better performance from trade management and their sales staff. They may take the form of competitions or performance-related incentives for achieving targets, for which financial rewards or prizes will be given. Incentives may also be given to simply encourage participation in supplier driven sales promotions. These might be in-store promotions designed by a supplier or they might be in the form of payment for every item sold. This will be to encourage sales of one company's products over those of competitor products. Payments or prizes will be available not only to the dealership, but also to individual qualifying managers and sales staff.

Point-of-sale materials and merchandising

Point-of-sale and merchandising material will be made available to channel members either free of charge or at reduced cost. This benefits the trade in that they are in a position to obtain display material at limited or no cost to themselves. They are, thus, more likely to push the supplier's products in favour of competing products. They may be relatively small items such as shelf stickers and 'tent' cards, or major free-standing displays. As one example of this, ice-cream companies provide refrigerated display cabinets to retailers. They require, however, that only their products should be sold out of the cabinets. This is a practice that has gone on for many years and it effectively locks-in retailers to specific manufacturers. But so extensive is this practice that it is now being looked at as a restrictive trade practice which may be banned or otherwise limited.

Another example is the Puma interactive kiosk featured in In View 28.10. The kiosk was first made available for sale to the trade at Puma's International World Meeting. Seeing the customer potential, retailers were keen to adopt them in their stores, which resulted in sales of the kiosks to outlets throughout Europe and other parts of the world. Additionally, a CD-ROM version has helped maximise the promotion's potential by running on any standard desktop or notebook computer. Puma are now developing ten foreign language versions.

Demonstration equipment and demonstration personnel are other areas that can be considered under the heading of merchandising. Video/CD-ROM/DVD players and monitors may be provided to show pre-recording tapes and disks or, in the case of live demonstrations, personnel may be provided. Manufacturers will also make available merchandising staff to assist with retailer in-store displays.

Sampling

Samples are made available to channel members as a means of helping them encourage sales. They are also extensively offered to business-to-business customers.

Gifts and free merchandise

It is very common practice to provide free gifts to trade customers. In fact, the merchandise used for such gifts is a muti-million pound industry in itself. Many merchandise items carry the company logo as an extra part of the sales promotion. The gifts can vary from pens, calendars and diaries to very much more expensive merchandise like cars and other luxury goods. Holidays, hospitality, and tickets to theatres and sports events are also other common gifts. Professional bodies such as the Chartered Institute of Purchasing and Supply frown on the practice of gift giving and some companies ban or restrict the acceptance of gifts for fear that they unduly influence purchase decisions towards personal gain rather than in the best interests of company.

WARNING

! *Offering free gifts as incentives should be done sensitively.*

Information leaflets/packs and catalogues

The primary purpose of these trade items is to be informative in explaining the range of products available, and give pricing and ordering procedures. Such materials may also be supplied to channel members subsequently to be used in consumer promotions.

Joint promotions

Joint or cooperative promotions between the manufacturer/service provider and channel members can be a cost-effective partnership in which the costs and effort are shared between the parties involved. This area is not restricted to the production of sales promotion items but can involve a full array of marketing communications activities. Joint promotions may be initiated by the trade or the supplier. At one extreme, a joint promotion may be where a dealer receives a contribution towards the cost of local advertising. At another extreme, it may involve a number of partners in an international multi-promotional campaign such as the McDonald's tie-in consumer sales promotion described earlier.

Employee focused sales promotion activities

It is always worthwhile remembering that sales promotions offer excellent marketing communications opportunities to target internal sales and non-sales staff.

IN VIEW 28.13

Ariston keep the sales staff informed

Merloni Domestic Appliances launched the Ariston Dialogic washing machine. Its features included determining what level of water, soap powder and spin speed were needed for each load. Clearly there was a need to ensure that retail store staff had a good understanding of the machine before selling it to consumers. A promotion to educate all levels of selling staff was put into action with a Dialogic presentation pack. Store owners/managers received detailed briefing notes, a video cassette, which they could play to staff and a reference booklet. Floor staff received a more detailed audio cassette, with a pocket guide that summarised the essential features. A prize message was placed on one of the cassettes to make floor staff listen to the entire cassette. A phone-in competition was created to check their understanding.

The tools available have already been outlined in the sections above, information leaflets/packs, incentives and competitions all commonly being used. Their principal purpose would be to help improve performance, but can also be used to inform and motivate. The section above on sales promotion objectives gives extra suggestions of some of the other areas where sales promotions can be effective and the Halifax (In View 28.2) and Ariston (In View 28.13). In Views give brief examples of their use.

Evaluating sales promotions

There are many different sales promotion possibilities to achieve numerous sales promotion objectives. Evaluation of the activities is important and many of them lend themselves well to direct evaluation because of the way they are expected to lead to short-term action-related results.

Coupon returns can be measured easily. Take-up rates of particular offers, likewise. Sales increases in value and volume terms can also be measured, although these might be the result of other factors as well. Qualitative research can be conducted to assess people's views of the nature of the sales promotion and, as is clearly identified in Chapter 23, it is always wise to carry out evaluative research in the forms of pre-testing, post-testing and tracking studies. The problems identified in In View 28.6 may well have been avoided if appropriate pre-testing had been undertaken. The use of demonstrations and interactive kiosks can be assessed quantitatively and qualitatively. Evaluation of other forms of sales promotions may not be so straightforward. The effects of point-of-sale merchandising may not have an explicit and direct effect on sales although their quality is unquestionably important.

In common with the evaluation of all marketing communications, it is recommended that sales promotions should be assessed against the objectives set for them. This will only be possible provided clear objectives are stated at the outset. Post-campaign evaluation should be used to check the extent to which the objectives have actually been met, but an assessment of the probability of achievement can be made before implementation. Schultz and Robinson (1986) have proposed five key questions to be asked *prior* to the start of any sales promotion during its development stage.

NEED TO KNOW

✓ *Pre-testing, post-testing and tracking should all be part of the evaluation process. This applies to all elements of the marketing communications mix. Part of the evaluation procedure should be to make an assessment against the objectives set.*

- *How good is the general idea?* The idea should first be assessed against the sales promotion objectives to ensure that the most appropriate sales promotion technique is being used in a creative way.

- *Will the sales promotion appeal to the target audience?* The idea should be assessed against the appeal it will have to the target audience. Making a particular premium offer may be a good idea but if the premium being offered is of little interest or value to the target customer, the sales promotion is not likely to succeed. Conversely, if the offer is seen to be exceptionally good, great care must be taken in evaluating the likely cost of the promotion and whether it will result in a net contribution to the organisation or a net loss if it was implemented.

WARNING

❗ *Sales promotions should be distinctive, simple, easy to follow, easy to use and their appeal should be directed towards specific target audiences. Any offers made should result in net contribution to the organisation.*

- *Is the idea unique or is the competition doing something similar?* Creativity is as important to sales promotions as it is to advertising. Truly unique sales promotion ideas are few and far between and most are variations on the same themes. This does not prevent them, however, from being creative, interesting and appealing. These are qualities that should be sought. Knowing what the competitors are

WARNING

> ❗ *Sales promotions require careful planning to assess their possible effects, not only on anticipated sales but also on the resource implications that they will have for the organisation.*

offering both to the trade and consumers is important. Matching or exceeding competitive offerings may not be necessary as long as the sales promotion stands out by appearing to be different.

● *Is the sales promotion presented clearly so that it can be noticed, understood and responded to?* The guideline is simple: sales promotions should be easy to follow and use. They should stand out, be easily understood and responding to them should be straightforward. This means that the promotion itself should meet these criteria *and* the organisational back-up should be put into place to ensure that difficulties do not arise. This requires, for example, that whoever is handling the promotion (in-house or through an agency) has the staff and systems to cope.

● *How cost efficient and effective is the sales promotion?* Can the promotion be managed efficiently and within budget allocations? Has the whole promotion been fully costed to estimate the likely returns? Are anticipated redemption rates (if relevant) realistic? Do forecasts suggest that the sales promotion will result in a net contribution to the organisation, i.e. will it be worthwhile?

IN VIEW 28.14

Volkswagen Financial Services spring into action

In early 2002, Volkswagen Financial Services (VWFS) identified the need to re-launch its Personal Contract Plan (Solutions) across the VW Group retailer network (Audi, Volkswagen, SEAT and SkodaAuto). Sales of Solutions were flagging. Critically, retailer perception was low, as was motivation to sell the product (which is basically a car finance deal). The goal was to motivate retailer agents to achieve a targeted 50% increase in sales. The finance product was restructured, made more flexible and renamed *New Solutions* as the company did not want to lose the connections with the existing product offering.

Devised by the McCann-Erickson agency, *New Solutions* was launched on 6 June 2002 targeted at the 5,000 employees across the VW Group retailer network and their customers. The 'Slinky' (the popular flexible metal spring toy) was used successfully as a metaphor representing the flexibility of the product and was used by retailers to explain the benefits of the *New Solutions* finance deals. Packaged in a branded *New Solutions* tube and distinctively coloured to match each of the four brands (VW, Audi, SEAT and Skoda), the Slinky was sent to sales staff at all retailer outlets in preparation for the full launch to end-customers. Not only did it create a striking visual image, but it quickly became immensely popular with sales people. It was a perfect training and selling tool showing how customers might stretch their payments over a variety of flexible contract periods. Reinforcing this message, the image of the Slinky was featured in distinctive POS display material that included special paint jobs on showroom cars, posters and swing tickets, among many other things. It was featured on leaflets, and in retailer and training packs. Even springy pens were used as giveaways to emphasise the flexible, springy theme. The promotional materials were quickly snapped up as collectable items. Clearly, the campaign was focused both internally towards VW Group retailers and their staff as well as externally towards the end-customers who came into their showrooms. Retailer training by VW employees, face-to-face meetings with VW Development Managers and communication through the VWFS newsletter augmented the total promotional effort.

Sales tracking and mystery shopping were used to measure effectiveness since the launch date. VW Business Development Managers conducted research audits and issued staff questionnaires. Group discussions were held to obtain feedback. The results – sales represented on average 6% of live finance agreements prior to launch. Four weeks after launch, this had already increased to 14%. Sales of the standard *New Solutions* product increased by over 60% in the same period. New product derivatives also gained incremental sales. Employees reported excellent response levels and motivation towards the product. The *New Solutions* campaign was given a Marketing Effectiveness Award by the Financial Services Forum. The judges were particularly impressed with how the campaign had recognised the importance of internal marketing communications audiences.

Summary

Sales promotions, merchandising and point of sale represent a wide choice of below-the-line marketing communications activities. They are growing in relative importance within the marketing communications mix if expenditure on them is considered a measure of worth. They are certainly highly flexible activities and complement other marketing communications well.

They are most associated with incentives, price deals and competitions but their remit is much wider. They can be applied with great effect to trade, business-to-business, employee and consumer promotions. The emphasis tends to be on tactical applications because they can be so effective in encouraging action. Sales promotion offers are frequently used as part of advertising activities in which they help move customers from awareness to actual purchase.

Merchandising is seen as a part of sales promotions and itself takes many forms even though it is most often thought of in the context of point-of-sale displays. 'Merchandise' is a term also used instead of 'product' and is, therefore, related to many forms of product presentation. Point of sale is anywhere that products are made available for sale.

Although largely tactical in nature, sales promotions have strategic implications, especially when they are used as a part of integrated marketing communications seeking to achieve longer-term marketing communications goals. They are used to facilitate both push and pull promotional strategies.

This chapter has presented examples of those areas where sales promotions are seen to be most effective and has described an array of sales promotion activities in order to give a sense of the promotional opportunities available. These range from price- and value-related promotions (economic incentives) to information- and display-related promotions (communications initiatives). Many sales promotions feature tie-ins and joint/cooperative promotions. Loyalty schemes are a relatively recent development that have grown enormously in use, especially with the large consumer goods retailers. Such schemes have the added bonus of delivering customer information that can be collected in databases and used to improve the design and targeting of subsequent promotions.

Finally, this chapter has emphasised the importance of evaluating sales promotions before they are implemented as part of their design stage (pre-testing), while they are running, and after they have finished (tracking and post-evaluation).

Self-review questions

1 Sales promotions are examples of below-the-line promotions; what does this mean?

2 According to Crosier and Bureau, sales promotions broadly fit into two categories of activities. One is economic incentives, what is the other?

3 This chapter suggests seven reasons for the growth of sales promotions. What are they?

4 How would you describe what sales promotions are?

5 What broad target groups can be reached with sales promotions?

6 Identify a range of marketing objectives that sales promotions are good at helping to achieve.

7 What are tie-in sales promotions?

8 What are loyalty schemes and why are they so popular?

9 What is a target pay-back?

10 What five questions should be asked as part of the pre-launch evaluation of a sales promotion campaign?

Project

Visit a local supermarket and identify the range of sales promotion, merchandising and point-of-sale promotional activities being used. (Is the supermarket using computer-generated promotions at the till?) Separate the promotions into manufacturer and retailer/store-initiated promotions. Consider a selection of these and evaluate, in your opinion, their effectiveness. What do you think about the total effect that all the sales promotions are having on customers?

References

Crosier, K. and Bureau, J.R. (1990), Definition of sales promotion. In M.J. Baker, *Dictionary of Marketing and Advertising* 2nd edn. Macmillan.

Cummins, J. (1998), *Sales Promotion: How to Create and Implement Campaigns that Really Work* 2nd edn. Kogan Page.

Kotler, P. (1997), *Marketing Management: Analysis, Planning, Implementation and Control.* Prentice Hall.

Maguire, S. (1997) Retailers, check out in-store tools. *Marketing Week*, 3 July, 36–37.

Mitchell, A. (1997), Hey! That's my right. 20:20, Virgin Customer Magazine.

Red Kite (1999), Puma AG www.kite.co.uk.

Roberts, A. (1996), What do we know about advertising's short-term effects? *Admap*, February, 42–45.

Schultz, D.E. and Robinson, W.A. (1986), *Sales Promotion Management.* NTC Business Books.

Shimp, T.A. (2000), *Advertising, Promotion, and Supplemental Aspects of Integrated Marketing Communications* 5th edn. Dryden Press.

Shrimp, T.A. (1997) *Advertising, Promotion and Supplemental Aspects of Integrated Marketing Communications.* 4th edn. Dryden Press.

Toop, A. (1994), *The Marketing Society Review.*

Selected further reading

Brown, C. (1996), *ISP Handbook of Sales Promotion.* Kogan Page.

Dowling, G.R. and Uncles, M. (1997), Do customer loyalty programmes really work? *Sloan Management Review*, Summer, 72–82.

Nielsen, A.C. (1993), Sales promotion and the information revolution. *Admap*, January, 80–85.

O'Malley, L. (1998), Can loyalty schemes really build loyalty? *Marketing Intelligence and Planning*, 16 (1), 255–269.

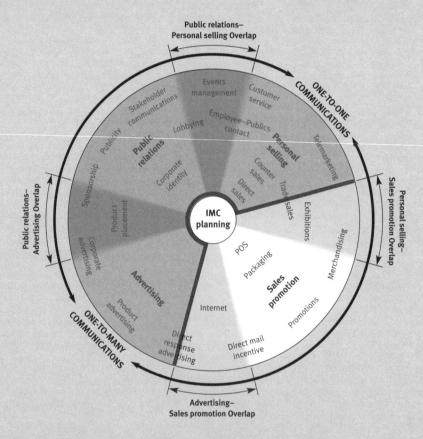

The Integrated Marketing Communications (IMC) Mix Model

CD

Identify the main competitors of Pampers. Using the CD material in Case Study 3 and your own research, collect samples of different packaging. Compare and contrast the packaging of the main brands on the basis of attractiveness, recognition and differentiation. Using the packaging features in Exhibit 29.2, evaluate how Pampers packaging enhances its brand image.

- The visual identity of the brand
- The components of a package
- Utilising packaging as a competitive advantage
- Packaging in the integrated marketing communications mix
- Packaging design

Objectives
- To introduce the importance of packaging in the integrated marketing communications mix
- To outline the functional and emotional benefits of packaging
- To detail the key components of a package
- To demonstrate what impact packaging has on brand image, consumer perception and the point of sale
- To outline the key elements in a packaging design brief

Professional perspective

Peter McKenna Smurfit Communications

A small package, wrapped in black with a delicate gold trim and the barely perceptible brand of Tiffany's. You know it is expensive, thoughtful and requires an emotive decision. Inside the black box reveals the diamond solitaire and, again, the Tiffany's logo, which is slightly hidden in the ruffled white silk adorning the top. It's Christmas and you're right, packaging is not important. It's essential.

Packaging is understated. It is undervalued. It is that part of the marketing communication with the greatest impact. Sensuous, its tacit impact and visual longevity is regretfully often under exploited.

From the simple but ingenious corrugated box – where the intrinsic design offers extraordinary strength, product protection, foldability, print versatility and most importantly recyclability – expressed in world-class designs like those developed by the Jefferson Smurfit Group for Waterford Crystal or Baileys Cream Liquor, creativity at its best, to the omnipotent Tetrapack, an industry standard in packaging perishable liquids.

Introduce colour and shape to the standard computer and iMac becomes a fashion icon. Preserve the original shape of the bottle and Coca-Cola achieves annual multiplicity of mind share. Perfumeries have long recognised the emotive connection, from the elegant classicism of Chanel No 5 to the conical modernism of Issey Miyake. Olive oil in slender square glass, mineral water in deep blue, Grolsch beer with the intriguing stopper, easy pour milk, squeezable ketchup, resealable bacon, swan-necked disinfectant, the six pack ... packaging is not integral, it is the marketing message.

But packaging is simple to conceive, a mundane exercise, a brief for the design junior. Really – I challenge you to build a structure stronger than the honeycomb or the spider's web; to develop preservative qualities more efficient than the nutshell or the banana skin. All beautiful, all natural, and all impossible to reproduce synthetically.

A well-designed package is a masterpiece of creativity. It will deliver the essentials, prescribed ingredients, sell-by dates and lend brand reinforcement. The choice of colour, substrate, disposability, product protection, ease of handling and integration into the manufacturing process are all elements that require careful consideration and an intimate knowledge of the medium.

Next Christmas, before you make up your mind, open it. Packaging: you have it in a nutshell.

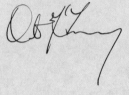

The visual identity of the brand

Packaging

The 'clothing' the product appears in. It combines functional protection with a medium (the pack) for graphic design and product information.

Brand values

The meaning or meanings that the brand generates in the minds of its target audiences.

Packaging is widely thought of as the visual identity of the brand (e.g. Danton de Rouffignac 1990). It both embodies **brand values** and differentiates one brand from others. Cowley (1991) states:

> ... where I would look to make the biggest difference for the least amount of money is in packaging. Packaging is where brand marketing began. The pack shape and surface is as much a medium for projecting brand values as the television commercial, and it has the bonus of being virtually free. (p. 14)

Packaging is a marketing tool that combines graphic design with marketing concepts to create an identity for the brand. An ideal package is one which brings to the customer's mind the essence of what the brand is all about whenever and wherever it is seen (Lewis 1991). It can be effectively used to influence customer choice at the point of sale in terms of reducing the uncertainty and risk inherent in product choice, and it acts as a concrete reminder at the point of sale and at home. Most importantly, its appeal plays an important role in attracting consumers' attention. As a result, packaging can make a major contribution to the success of the brand as a whole.

Packaging is often, however, a relatively neglected area in marketing. Milton (1991), in recognising this issue, states that:

> In the average brand manager's day, very little time is actively devoted to design management. Packaging design is often the neglected ingredient in the marketing mix, even though the brand's recognition is fundamental to its success and critical to its promotion. (p. 3)

Packaging comprises a number of physical or functional benefits including the storage of the product, the extension of the product's shelf life, the facilitation of physical storage, the protection of the product during distribution, the communication of usage information, and the assurance of consistent quality. Packaging, however, is capable of a great deal more than these functional benefits (Danton de Rouffignac 1990; Milton 1991; Southgate 1994; Hine 1995). Empirical research conducted at

Exhibit 29.1 The emotional (and psychological) benefits of packaging

1   To be a communications tool for the marketers to express and convey the brand values and images.

2   To be aesthetically pleasing.

3   To have a strong visual impact — to stand out, to be eye-catching, to differentiate itself from the other brands, to attract the eyes of the consumers and to gain attention on the shelf.

4   To be a living expression of what the brand stands for.

5   To add value in the eyes of the consumers.

6   To act as a reminder for the brand at the point of sale and at home.

7   To provide cues to the consumers to express their loyalty to the brand.

8   To create an emotional link with the right kind of target audience.

Source: Adapted from Chareonlarp (1997)

Aston Business School summarises the key emotional and psychological benefits of packaging, as expressed by a cross-section of brand managers in key industry sectors. Exhibit 29.1 summarises these benefits.

Three major aspects of the visual impact of packaging can be drawn from the characteristics identified:

- attractiveness
- recognition
- differentiation.

If a package fails to perform one of these three functions, it is likely to fail as a package.

This chapter presents packaging as an important communication tool that can be strategically utilised to project the brand's images and values and be employed as an emotional benefit that intrinsically differentiates one brand from another.

The components of a package

To achieve visual impact, packaging should command the eye through colour and design, establish its identity, be aesthetically pleasing, invite handling and purchase and fulfil its protective role (Danger 1968). Exhibit 29.2 summarises the most important features of packaging.

As long ago as the early 1970s, Briston and Neill (1972) suggested five packaging components that designers need to address. The same five components are as relevant today:

1   *Appearance*: this is dependent on two main elements – shape and surface decoration.
2   *Protection*: varies enormously with the nature of the product, the final destination, the distribution system and the total time that protection is required.
3   *Function*: this is dependent on two main factors – those concerned with its end use and those concerned with its behaviour on the packaging/filling line.
4   *Cost*: should be at a minimum overall cost.
5   *Disposability*: this is concerned with the solid waste management and the environment.

Exhibit 29.2 Packaging features

Packaging features	Descriptions
1 Colour	Has powerful emotional signals; acts as symbolic metaphors for elements; e.g. Cadbury's purple packaging has associations with luxury and quality.
2 Typography	Communicates product worth; e.g. ornate script on wine labels suggests elegance, sophistication and quality.
3 Logo	Signifies the brand's individuality and unique image; e.g. white Coca-Cola script on red background and bright red script signature of Kellogg's Cornflakes.
4 Type/material	Depends largely on types of products and purpose of use; can be recyclable, biodegradable, and environmentally friendly; e.g. boxes (paper or tin), cartons (Tetrapack), bags (paper, film or plastic), bottles (glass, plastic, aerosol or squeezable), tubes, cans, jars, etc.
5 Shape and structure	Effectively grabs attention; e.g. Coke's contour bottle, Jif's yellow, lemon-shaped package, etc.
6 Label or mark	Varies with types and materials of packages; can be printed on the package itself or other materials; e.g. letterpress, gravure, flexography, lithography, silkscreen, hot die stamping or gold blocking (see Chapter 22).
7 Size	Encourages product usage; e.g. 1 pint, 500 ml, 1 litre of milk package.

Utilising packaging as a competitive advantage

Brand image

Brand image

The perception of the brand held by the market.

A brand is likely to have a set of intangible values accumulated over time (refer to Chapter 11). This set of values equates to the brand's image. **Brand image** is the total set of expectations and intangible values which are created in the customer's mind by all marketing communications and other points of company/product contact a customer is exposed to. Image can derive from the brand's attributes, benefits, advertising campaigns, packaging, slogan and so on. Brand image can simply be defined as the 'perception' that the consumers have of a brand. Brand image is generally synonymous with the brand's strategic personality (Upshaw 1995). **Brand personality** is the outward face of the brand, the characteristics most closely associated with human traits. Brands can be perceived as friendly, sophisticated, prestigious, traditional, classic, stylistic, and so on.

Brand personality

The fundamental essence of the brand.

Brand image is frequently confused with **brand identity** (Diefenbach 1992). They are related but distinct concepts. Brand identity is the objective reality of a brand while brand image exists in consumers' minds. This means that brand image, which derives from the subjective views of consumers, is an interpretation of the objective marketing stimuli transmitted by marketers. Marketers' ultimate goal is, therefore, to create congruence between brand image and brand identity, i.e. to provide the consumers with the information required to derive with an accurate image of the brand.

Brand identity

The cues used to convey the brand personality to create the brand image.

For a brand's image to be defined, it must possess an array of associations of physical properties and attributes (packaging, slogans, logos, symbols, advertising campaigns, advertising presenters, etc.) as well as the emotional benefits and feelings (the intangible components associated with a brand) that come from product consumption (Engel et al. 1995).

IN VIEW 29.1

Coca-Cola uses packaging to create distinctiveness

Coke wants a distinctive can to help it stand out in the increasingly crowded cola market. Pepsi now markets itself in blue, but Coke is still fighting off copycat brands across the world. 'This is a significant point of differentiation for us. There is only one contour shape and it belongs to Coca-Cola,' said a spokeswoman. A contoured steel can is already on test in Germany. It is popular, but Coke says the production process is too costly. Now UK can-makers have been briefed to develop a cheaper aluminium version, enabling Coke to start rolling out the can and trade mark the shape.

Source: Marshall (1996)

Type of packaging in the soft drinks market	Functions, benefits and limitations
1 PET plastic bottle	Better clarity than PVC; can be variably coloured; light; completely resealable; particularly suitable for carbonated soft drinks; cheap; convenient; unbreakable (500ml – safe and great size for kids); easy to open; rigid structure for graphics; varies in sizes; appropriate for long-life drinks; recyclable.
2 PVC plastic bottle	More opaque than PET; can have a handle on it; light; completely resealable; particularly suitable for still soft drinks; convenient; cheap; unbreakable; easy to open.
3 Glass bottle	Indicates high-quality, premium products; not safe for kids; resealable to a certain extent; both returnable and non-returnable depending on the point-of-sale; recyclable.
4 Aluminium-mix can	Particularly suitable and functional for carbonated soft drinks; unresealable (single-serve); effective structure for graphics; generally cheap but higher price than steel due to the world shortage; opened easily (aluminium lid allowing stay-on ring pull); recyclable.
5 Steel-mix can	Particularly suitable and functional for carbonated soft drinks; cheaper than aluminium; unresealable (single-serve); opened easily (aluminium lid allowing stay-on ring pull); recyclable; effective structure for graphics.
6 Tetra-pack carton	Ideal for kids; particularly suitable for still soft drinks; comes in various sizes; cheap; unresealable (single-serve); appropriate for long-life drinks; recyclable; provides valuable fuel for 'energy from waste' schemes.

Source: Adapted from the promotional materials of Britvic Soft Drinks Ltd and Coca-Cola & Schweppes Beverages Ltd (1997)

IN VIEW 29.2

Tango's brand image

The brand image of the carbonated soft drink, Tango, is described as anarchic, rebellious, British, masculine, innovative, funny and slapstick (Plate 21). Each of the four flavours add to the central brand image with their own complementary values – the 'hit of orange', the 'seduction of apple', the 'euphoria of lemon' and the 'charge of black-currant'. To communicate the brand's image, marketing activities have included a famous advertisement called the 'Slap Ad', the Tango black can which indicates masculinity and the dare-to-be-different attitude, and a 10-metre green tongue built during the sampling tour to represent the seductive sensation of Apple Tango.

Consumer perception

In the fast moving consumer goods market alone, thousands of products and brands are available for consumers to purchase. Due to the nature of human cognitive processes, consumers are automatically prevented from sensory overload through highly selective perceptual filters, i.e. only selected items are perceived. A crucial task for the marketer is, therefore, to try in every way they can to initiate brand awareness in the consumer's mind and to prevent their brands from being filtered out before the purchase decision.

Perception

The process of synthesising information to make sense of the world. People's perceptions of the same stimuli can vary.

As detailed in Chapter 4, **perception** is the process of recognising, selecting, organising and interpreting stimuli in order to make sense of the world around us (Harrell 1986). The perception of a brand can be considered from two aspects: first, what the marketer wants a consumer to perceive of the brand, and second, what the consumer actually perceives. Perceptions of products or brands mainly derive from various marketing efforts. These stimuli are summarised in Exhibit 29.3 (Woodruffe 1995).

Exhibit 29.3 Influences on consumer perception

Product	quality, styling, packaging design (colour, logo, typography, shape, etc.), brand name, guarantees and other features.
Price	discount pricing, extended credit, list price and payment period.
Promotion	advertising, personal selling, sales promotions (premium, coupons, sweepstakes, etc.) and public relations.
Place	distribution channels/coverage and geographical location.

Source: Woodruffe (1995).

Self-image

The personal perception or image of oneself.

Packaging has an impact on the consumers' perceptual processes in two ways. First, the consumers tend to associate their **self-image** with the created image of the brand which is symbolised by the packages that they own or use. That is, they will choose to purchase only those brands which enhance their own self-image. A brand with a positive image is capable of attracting and retaining consumers who normally prefer to identify their own self-image with the image of the brands they choose to purchase.

Aesthetics
Attractive appearance.

Aspirational self-image
Self-image as one would like to be.

Second, the **aesthetics** of packaging initiates consumer interest and captures attention which can lead to a purchase decision (Lubliner 1996).

Consumers tend to choose products or brands which appear to be consistent with the perceptions of themselves and reject those that are incongruous with them. Creating a brand image in line with the target customer group's self-image or **aspirational self-image** is an effective way of retaining the brand in the consumer's mind. De Chernatony and McDonald (1992) describe the relationship between the consumers' self-image and brand's image as:

> ... consumers' personalities can be inferred from the brands they use, from their attitudes towards different brands and from the meanings brands have for them. Consumers have a perception of themselves and they make brand decisions on the basis of whether owning or using a particular brand, which has a particular image, is consistent with their own self-image. They consider whether the ownership of certain brands communicates the right sort of image about themselves. Brands are only bought if they enhance the conception that consumers have of themselves, or if they believe the brand's image to be similar to that which they have of themselves.

(pp. 144–145)

Advertising has been considered as the main brand image builder. Consumers initially become aware of particular brands through advertising media. They then begin to form an image about the brands from the information offered in the advertising. Repeated exposures to the advertising enhance the likelihood that an image in the consumers' minds will be stronger. Brand image can be strongly enhanced by developing the brand's psychological, rather than physical, differentiation in advertising. That is, brand image is created by associating the brand with particular symbols. In imbuing a brand with an image, advertisers choose the preferred meaning, i.e. symbols, and transfer that meaning to the brand. As a result, that image will become the brand's distinct personality and will be automatically associated with the brand by the consumers.

While advertising is crucial in building brand image, packaging also has a significant role to play. Packaging reminds consumers of the brand and represents the brand's image at the point of sale where the purchase decision is actually made (Milton 1991; Bond 1996). Packaging features such as shape, logo, typography, colour, materials, etc., are designed to signify the image of the brand. For example, the purple colour of Cadbury's chocolate communicates quality, Jif's lemon-shaped package clearly portrays the freshness of lemon juice and the logo of St Michael from Marks & Spencer represents the long-established reputation of the brand. Southgate (1994) emphasises the significance of packaging:

> Marketing people spend a great deal of their time, and by far the greatest part of their budgets, on advertising. Marketers, in focusing so intently on advertising, are often missing an enormous trick. If they spent a corresponding amount of time and energy on their packaging design, they could achieve even better sales results – and at a fraction of the cost. So the pack can have an even more crucial role than advertising in creating and sustaining brand values, because the pack (unlike the ad) is there at the times when it really matters – at the moment of decision to buy, and at the moment when the product is being experienced in use.

(pp. 11–12)

Packaging can act as an image enhancer for the brand. It is only recently that marketers have discovered a commercial advantage to be gained from packaging. Rather than simply reminding people that 'I'm here', the pack works harder by projecting the brand's personality, influencing emotional links, attracting attention, sustaining loyalty and actively persuading people to 'buy me' (Lewis 1991). Packaging must intrigue, inform, involve, entertain and persuade. Effective packages, therefore, must be those which are capable of engaging the consumers at the point of sale for a few valuable moments as each consumer will only allow a limited period of time for each brand to make a sale. In the consumer choice process, the sensory features of a package such as design, colour and typography emphasises and communicates the image a brand possesses.

Using packaging to communicate brand image can become a real consumer benefit by transforming the pack into an emotional value or psychological visual cue which acts as an iconic sign for the brand and, thus, facilitates the consumers in the choice process. This is because emotional benefits can be offered as an added value over the competitive brands to the consumers who are looking for a differentiated product. The totality of structure, pictures, words, colours, graphics and logo of a package can say a lot about what the brand stands for. This means that the package can inspire the consumers to identify themselves with, or to express their loyalty to, the brand.

> There are no ads at point-of-sale, where it really matters. Only packs. There are no ads at home in the cupboard to reinforce brand values every time we use a product. Only packs. There are no ads on display in the bathroom or in the drinks cabinet saying who we are (because we are what we buy), only packs.
>
> (Southgate 1994, p. 11)

The physical package, therefore, must be designed to convey the image inherent in the brand to the consumers because the pack as an iconic sign of the image can say a lot about a brand before a buyer even picks it up (O'Kane 1996). It is true that all packages, over time, will automatically absorb the image of the brand. But it can work more quickly and effectively if it is designed to actively communicate the brand image, not merely to be a passive receptacle (Southgate 1994).

Consumers can emotionally benefit from a package which projects appealing, distinctive and non-imitatable values with which they can associate themselves and with which no other brands can compete. This is because, in today's marketplace, the competition is so drastic that making a purchase decision solely on product performance is increasingly difficult (Milton 1991). The emotional values delivered by packaging, therefore, boost the importance of a particular brand in the consumers' minds. Milton further elaborates on the important role of packaging in the competitive marketplace:

> Packaging can strengthen the brand and create loyalties between the customer and the retailer or manufacturer, a factor that is often overlooked. Whilst retaining the visual sum of the brand proposition, packaging must reassure through its identification and convince through its imagery. Furthermore, the visual signals and codes that attract the consumer and effect an actual purchase must continue working in the home environment. In essence, … established. Design can add value to a brand as well as encourage emotional responses. This is crucial to building consumer loyalty, and helpful when justifying premium brand prices.
>
> (pp. 67–68)

The point of sale

The point of sale is normally designed and lit to allow all products to be displayed attractively. These products, however, will not be equally attractive. On the shelf where the products are positioned, 'standout' is what needs to be achieved. Because

IN VIEW 29.3

Pepsi goes blue

One type of visual cue used to express brand values and images on packaging is *colour communication coding* – using different colours to convey different messages. One of the world's most controversial marketing strategies of the carbonated soft drinks industry ever to take place in the 1990s was the Pepsi 'Going Blue' project. Pepsi's re-branding exercise aimed to differentiate the brand from other brands in the market: to create a greater distinction between Pepsi and Coca-Cola's red can and as a defence against the wave of new cola launches, including Virgin and own-label brands, which have used red livery. In addition, according to the theory of psychological effects on colour perception, 'blue' has been strongly associated with coolness (Danger 1968). Pepsi's old design was dominated by red, white and blue which had no connection with the refreshing and thirst-quenching values. The 'Going Blue' project aims to achieve consistency between Pepsi's values and its packaging. Furthermore, it is believed that Coca-Cola, being the market leader, has set 'red' as a colour trend for the cola category since it first existed in 1886. Virgin Cola and other own-label cola brands take this category cue into account and are continuously following this trend. Pepsi, appearing to be too powerful to follow the trend, breaks the rule of the category. It has moved away by going blue to differentiate itself from the crowd. Colour trends have also been set in other categories of carbonated soft drinks. For example, lemonade normally comes in clear bottles or green cans to indicate the values of clarity and refreshment, as green connotes coolness, freshness and lemon or lime.

Source: Adapted from Marshall (1996)

there are so many different brands dressed in different packages clustered nearby, a particular pack must be sufficiently appealing to grab the consumers' attention immediately. The pack works hardest at the point of sale since this is where it is actually chosen by the consumers, where the purchase is going to be made. At the moment a consumer is standing in front of the shelf, the pack that stands out from the crowd and effectively describes its image wins the game. Hine (1995) illustrates this phenomenon:

> In the average half-hour trip to the supermarket, 30,000 products vie for shopper's attention, and those that get noticed have only a sixth of a second to make their sales pitch. Today's marketers know they have to trigger desire instantly – and they do so, visually, by creating packages that make exactly the right promises.

(p. 1)

Although shopping trips are planned by consumers, there is clear evidence that around 50% of purchases are unplanned or impulse decisions, including substitutions (e.g. Danton de Rouffignac 1990). This is accounted for, in part, by the attractiveness of packaging at the point of sale. Engel et al. (1995) have noted that impulse buying is characterised by a state of psychological dis-equilibrium in which a person can feel temporarily out of control. The consumer will experience a sudden, often powerful and persistent urge to buy something immediately. Packaging is an important marketing tool used to initiate the consumers' out-of-control state.

Retailing power

Large retailers, such as Tesco, Sainsbury and Safeway in the UK and Aldi and Lidl and Swartz in Germany, have the ability to command almost total on-shelf space, so that acquiring these spaces is highly challenging between manufacturers (Halverson 1996). Furthermore, these giant retailers are increasingly threatening the manufacturers of branded products by launching a wide variety of 'own-label brands' to be sold side by side with the manufacturers' brands. This practice is growing very rapidly and successfully, especially in the UK's retail food markets. Retailers' own brands are often priced well below the manufacturers' brands but with comparable quality, thus placing a considerable threat to market share. One of the key goals of brand managers is to ensure 'sufficient shelf space' at the point of sale.

The growing power of these strong retailers has led to a derivation of a modern sales strategy called 'trade marketing' (Southgate 1994). This is the development of a real partnership between marketers and the key retailers. These retailers will be consulted with regards to various aspects of brand management – for example, the match between the packaging design and the display shelves. This minimises the risks borne by brand marketers of their brands being rejected by the retailers (because they no longer take whatever is given to them) or having insufficient shelf space (because there is immense competition between powerful brands).

Packaging in the integrated marketing communications mix

No one marketing communication activity can exist on its own. Bringing together all marketing communications, where each of the media being used in a campaign are co-ordinated in time, message and graphics, produces a synergistic overall effect (Hart 1996).

Advertising

Packaging can work hand-in-hand with advertising in delivering brand messages, values and images to consumers. A large difference between a brand's advertising image and its physical on-shelf appearance can create discontinuity in the mind of the consumers (Milton 1991). This is because people look for some visible link between what they have seen and believed and what they actually buy. A correctly designed package should be an effective marketing communications medium in its own right (Briston and Neill 1972). The packaging of a particular brand, therefore, must be congruous with other marketing communications in order to form a consistent brand image in the consumer's mind. A package must represent and communicate the product's promises by acting as a reinforcement of the image created by advertising (Lubliner 1996) and all other marketing communications efforts.

Sales promotion

Packaging is normally used with sales promotions in the special or non-routine events when a brand is receiving a boost. These events could be seasonal occasions, sale events or premium given-away events. Seven types of promotional packages are described in Exhibit 29.4.

Exhibit 29.4 Using packaging in sales promotion

Types of promotional package	Characteristics
1 **Money-off pack**	Printing the announced flash on the package.
2 **Bonus size package**	Retaining the standard pack's price with an increase in pack's size.
3 **Coupon pack**	Coupon, bearing a stated value, being redeemable against the purchase of the product; coupon being packed into the container of the same or another product; building up brand loyalty.
4 **Pack-on premium**	Attaching a premium on to the standard package by adding new outer case or shrink wrapping; premium visibility enhancing appeal; having high risk of pilferage.
5 **Pack-in premium**	Placing a premium inside the standard package; premium normally bearing some relation to the product or its use.
6 **Premium package**	Having re-use value after the use of original contents; making a constant brand reminder during re-use period.
7 **Self-liquidator**	Allowing the consumers to buy the promotional products at a reduced price by sending in, in addition to the money, a certain number of labels, tokens, or other evidence to prove the purchase of the promoted package. Where the costs of the extra promotion are met by the money received for the promotional offer, this is said to be self-liquidating i.e. the promoter covers costs.

Source: Adapted from Briston and Neill (1972)

Packaging design

Packaging design is the process which not only requires competent brand marketers, but also the competencies of creative design consultants. Part of what influences the ability of the design consultant to create a well-designed package depends upon the 'design brief' carried out by the marketing team prior to the actual implementation of the pack design process. A whole set of information, particularly the brand values and images, is synthesised to arrive at the core concepts or ideas to be developed into a real pack design. It is, therefore, beneficial to discuss the most pertinent aspects that the marketing team have to take into consideration when formulating a brief for a design consultant in the packaging design process.

- What are the short-term and long-term marketing objectives for the brand?
- How are we going to effectively deal with the design management? How strategic and complicated is the design project? Should we hire an external design consultant or should we use our own in-house consultancy?
- Have we ourselves truly understood our brand in order to present a complete design brief to the consultant? If not, to which particular aspects do we need to give more attention before meeting the consultant?
- Have we fully recognised the concept of the representation of brand image through packaging? If so, how can our brand's image be represented visually on the package?
- Is our brand characterised by a clear image or personality well known as well as well liked by its target audience in order to be communicated through packaging? These images and values of the brand are central in the pack design process and must be presented to the design consultant in the first brief.

- Can we provide additional significant information, such as (1) the history and background information of the brand and its market, (2) aims and objectives of the brand and the design, (3) a brief of the strategy to be implemented, (4) the type of packaging design (a design for a newly-launched brand or a redesign for an existing brand), (5) problem definition which the packaging design has to solve, and (6) the time-scale and budget for the project?
- If it is a packaging redesign, what has our current packaging design accomplished? Is it consistent with the advertising? If it is a design for a newly-launched brand, the messages being communicated must be consistent with the advertising.
- In the case of a redesign, do we want to retain some of the existing elements of the package and develop from that heritage or do we want to create a new design from scratch?
- Have we taken into consideration such variables as cultural and societal cues, its shelf impacts, the threats of imitating brands, and so on?

Being able to answer all the questions listed above, it is very likely that the marketing team will present a complete design brief to the design consultant from which an effective packaging design process can be developed. The core concept is simple: marketers must be able to encourage their design consultant to understand the brand as much as they do.

Summary

This chapter has explained how packaging can be used strategically both to project brand image and values, and to differentiate one brand from another. Historically packaging is a rather neglected area in marketing, yet it is a crucial component in the integrated marketing communications mix. The specific functional and emotional benefits of packaging are outlined in the chapter.

The chapter also demonstrates how competitive advantage can be created by packaging through:

- the enhancement of brand image and providing synergy with other marketing communications, particularly advertising and sales promotion;
- attention/awareness generation in consumer perception in general and particularly at the point of sale.

Self-review questions

1 Summarise the functional and emotional benefits of packaging.

2 What are the five components of packaging that designers need to address?

3 How can packaging be used to enhance a brand's image?

4 Explain how packaging can impact on a consumer's perceptual process.

5 What is the relationship between a consumer's self-image and a brand's image?

6 What impact does packaging have at the point of sale?

7 How can packaging be used in integrated marketing communications?

8 What are the main questions a brand manager should address when preparing a packaging design brief?

Project Select a fast moving consumer good package and associated press advertisement. Do the packaging components reflect/enhance the brand's image? If so, how? Present your findings in a 1000-word report. Include copies of the materials you have used.

References

Bond, C. (1996), Here's looking at you kid. *Marketing*, April, 23.

Briston, J.H. and Neill, T.J. (1972), *Packaging Management*. Essex: Gower Press.

Chareonlarp, S. (1997), An investigation of the representation of brand image through packaging. MSc Marketing Management Dissertation, Aston Business School, Aston University, Birmingham.

Cowley, D. (ed.) (1991), *Understanding Brands: By 10 People Who Do*. London: Kogan Page.

Danger, E.P. (1968), *Using Colour to Sell*. London: Gower Press.

Danton de Rouffignac, P. (1990), *Packaging in the Marketing Mix*. Oxford: Butterworth-Heinemann.

De Chernatony, L. and McDonald, M.H.B. (1992), *Creating Powerful Brands*. Oxford: Butterworth-Heinemann.

Engel, J.F., Blackwell, R.D. and Miniard, P.W. (1995), *Consumer Behaviour*. Florida: The Dryden Press.

Halverson, R. (1996), Juicing up the beverage market. *Discount Store News*, October, 35 (19), F55.

Hart, N.A. (1996), *The CIM Marketing Dictionary*. Oxford: Butterworth-Heinemann.

Hine, T. (1995), *The Total Package*. Boston, MA: Little, Brown and Co.

Lewis, M. (1991), *Brand packaging*. In *Understanding Brands: By 10 People Who Do* (D. Cowley, ed.). London: Kogan Page.

Lubliner, M. (1996), Sell by design. *Beverage World*, 115 (July), 46–50.

Marshall, S. (1996), Coke can get in shape to battle copycat brands. *Marketing*, August, 1.

Milton, H. (1991), *Packaging Design*. London: The Design Council.

O'Kane, B. (1996), Good things come in good packaging. *Nation's Business*, 84 (10), 6.

Southgate, P. (1994), *Total Branding by Design*. London: Kogan Page.

Upshaw, L.B. (1995), *Building Brand Identity: A Strategy for Success in a Hostile Marketplace*. New York: John Wiley and Sons.

Woodruffe, H. (1995), *Services Marketing*. London: Pitman Publishing.

Selected further reading

Booth-Clibbon, E. (ed.) (1996), *Design Groups Index: British Packaging Design for Today's Consumer Interface*. London: Internos Books.

Emberson, S.T. (1997), Copy cat killers. *In-Store Marketing*, April, 14–17.

Gander, P. (1996), Identity parade. *Marketing Week*, 19 (26), September, 47–50.

Paine, F.A. and Paine, H.Y. (1983), *A Handbook of Food Packaging*. Glasgow: Leonard Hill.

Chapter 30

Exhibitions and trade shows

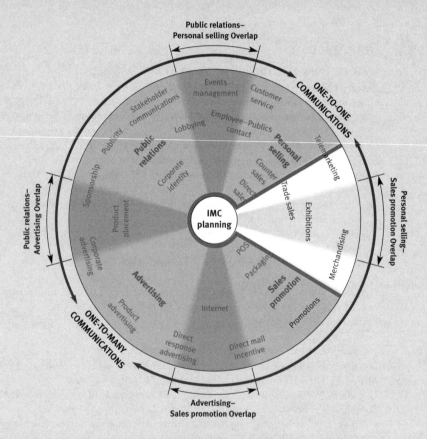

The Integrated Marketing Communications (IMC) Mix Model

CD

What role could exhibitions and trade shows have in the Pampers integrated marketing communications campaign? Exhibits 30.1–30.3, detailing reasons to exhibit, may help you to structure your answer. How could Pampers evaluate whether an exhibition or trade show has been successful?

Objectives

- To explain the role of exhibitions and trade shows in the marketing communications mix
- To describe ways of assessing the effectiveness of exhibition activity
- To outline a planning sequence for exhibitions
- To identify the strengths and weaknesses of exhibiting
- To explain which marketing objectives are best addressed by exhibitions

Professional perspective

Barry Cleverdon Chief Executive, The NEC Group

The art of marketing communications is becoming ever more sophisticated, as more and more companies discover the value of the live experience that exhibitions create.

A brand is now so much more than simply the product or service itself. Brands must be able to come alive, to excite, to communicate a feeling or association that shouts much more than just its ability to perform a given task.

And increasingly, marketers are recognising that the best way to bring that brand to life is through live event marketing. The growth in exhibitions, roadshows, product-sampling, interactive experiences is borne directly out of the realisation that nothing beats the 'touch-and-feel' of the live experience.

Far from replacing the need for people to meet face-to-face, technological advance has proved a catalyst to its increasing popularity. While we are able to make instant contact, in words and pictures, with any location in the world, people also still want to meet.

Today's successful organisations know how to combine technology with live experience. They realise that the choice is not between technology and face-to-face communications, but rather how best to combine these two essential tools.

Live events enable suppliers to talk directly to consumers. Targeting of communication – and therefore marketing spend – increases value-for-money.

There has to be value in any activity, a fact that is driving forward the quality of face-to-face communications. All exhibitions at the NEC now embrace some form of interactive participation. No longer can an exhibition be simply a series of stands and exhibits – exhibitors today are increasingly creative, as exhibitions have come alive to meet the increasing demands of consumers.

Face-to-face communications has come of age – a dynamic environment delivering real results for go-ahead companies.

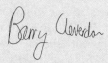

IN VIEW 30.1

Expo Inter

Each year, around August, the Brazilian city of Porto Alegre hosts the biggest agricultural show in South America. Ranchers and breeders from Brazil, Argentina, Chile, Uruguay and Paraguay come to show their prize animals and to see the latest offerings from equipment manufacturers.

The world's major manufacturers of tractors and machinery are there: John Deere, Massey-Ferguson, David Brown, Caterpillar. The world's leading producers of fertilisers and pesticides exhibit there, too: ICI, Belgo-Mineira, DuPont. For the manufacturers, it is an opportunity to show their products to potential customers from a wide range of countries who are all in one place for this one occasion. It reduces travelling time for salespeople in a part of the world where roads are not always good and where distances are vast (Brazil alone is as large as Australia or the USA). In some cases, the ranchers themselves are coming from remote parts of the Andes or the Amazon forest, where the main access to the outside world is either by light aircraft or by boat.

For the gauchos who accompany the ranchers, Expo Inter provides an opportunity to travel and see the big city; for these traditional cowboys, the open plains of the pampas are their usual home, and many of them rarely sleep inside a building, let alone see a city the size of Porto Alegre. The show gives them the opportunity to meet old friends from other parts of the country, to swap stories, and to take part in the competitions and games which form part of the event.

For the ranchers, the show offers a chance to meet the manufacturers, to discuss the merits of the latest equipment and chemical products, and to meet other ranchers from other countries and exchange ideas and techniques. Above all, the show enables people who otherwise rarely see each other to interact and refresh their thinking about agricultural issues.

All those who attend Expo Inter agree that it is irreplaceable; in no other way could all their objectives be met given the distances involved and the infrastructure problems in South America. The future of this vast showcase for South American farming is thus assured for years to come.

Exhibitions in the marketing communications mix

Exhibitions and trade shows

Temporary events for the purpose of displaying and/or selling products; usually based around a particular theme, product category or customer grouping. They are principally designed to bring together potential buyers and sellers under one roof.

Exhibitions and trade shows provide a temporary forum for sellers of a product category to exhibit and demonstrate their products to prospective buyers. Agricultural shows fulfil a similar function, but are usually biased more towards competitions among livestock breeders and other types of farmer rather than being purely about promoting products.

Some exhibitions exist as marketplaces where buyers and sellers meet; these are called selling exhibitions. Others (such as The Motor Show) exist purely as promotional vehicles, with no actual buying and selling taking place at the exhibition (non-selling exhibitions). Some exhibitions are open to the public, while others are business-to-business vehicles. Exhibitions and trade shows/events can take many forms from humble in-store special displays, to conferences, to very large international trade and consumer shows like the International Spring Fair at the NEC, the UK's biggest show.

While this chapter tends to emphasise the largest exhibitions and trade shows, readers should not ignore the value of much smaller activities and simple displays that may consist of little more than a few display boards. It is common to see, for example, small temporary displays in shopping centres and malls, in company reception areas, and in public places such as libraries. The place of exhibitions and shows has been indicated in our Integrated Marketing Communications Mix Model as lying in a broad overlap area between two of our main marketing communications areas – sales promotions and personal selling. To make them successful, however, all areas of the mix are typically utilised. So, for example, an exhibition or a show may be advertised and PR activities may be used to gain media coverage of the event.

Considerable controversy exists as to whether exhibitions are cost-effective and which promotional objectives they best address; the area is considerably under-researched by academics, and much of the existing research has been conducted by parties with vested interests who may or may not be entirely unbiased in their findings. Nonetheless, exhibitions are used by many firms at one time or another and, therefore, merit at least as much consideration and preparation as any other communication tool.

FOOD FOR THOUGHT

Exhibitions and trade shows are often less-considered areas of marketing communications. Yet they account for huge amounts of expenditure and are undertaken in one form or another by virtually all organisations, whether this be part of a major event or as a small display area within a store or public area.

IN VIEW 30.2

Award winning exhibition

Having scooped the 'Organisers' and 'Effectiveness' Gold Awards and top award for best trade exhibition, the International Spring Fair is the UK's biggest and most important annual focus for the consumer goods retail industry. It attracts 4000 exhibitors and 80,000 retail buyers from the UK and overseas. Recognised by the Department of Trade and Industry as a major source of export business, it generates an estimated £1.6bn at trade prices annually. The number of overseas visitors has doubled since the Fair started and now account for 15% of the total. Exhibitors find the event a particular bonus in that they obtain extra business from specialist retailers who are not their core buyers, the exhibition proving to be an exceptionally cost-efficient way of reaching them.

The organisers are at pains to ensure a favourable exhibition experience. Products and stands are categorised into clearly identifiable sections making life easier for visitors. There is early opening, breakfast clubs and business clinics, buyers' clubs, exhibitor lounges, VIP clubs and hospitality suites, dedicated entrances for overseas visitors, free interpreter services and playcare centres. The Fair has its own radio station with news, music and exhibition information from parking arrangements, to Fair events and PR for exhibitors. With heightened attention to customer service, temporary staff taken on specially for the event by the organisers all receive training to ensure that all representatives have sufficient knowledge to answer exhibitor and visitor enquiries in a friendly manner.

In promoting the Fair itself, along with the usual exhibition catalogue and printed materials, direct mail, PR and advertising are undertaken in a variety of different languages. Special travel packages are arranged to make overseas attendance as efficient as possible. Publicity plays a major role, and travel agents and chambers of commerce, along with the retail buyers themselves, are considered to be particular marketing communications target audiences for a host of promotional activities. A 24-hour fax information and pre-registration service ensures rapid response times. The International Spring Fair truly is an exhibition success story.

Source: Adapted from *Marketing* (1996).

Exhibitions and trade fairs are widely regarded as a powerful way for firms to reach a large number of potential customers face-to-face at a cost far below that of calls by salespeople. Exhibitions do, indeed, bring together buyers and sellers under one roof in a way that is unique; it is probably the closest thing most modern businesses have to the medieval marketplace, which is so often held up as an example of ideal marketing practice.

Substantial sums of money are devoted to exhibitions: during 1995, £750m was spent on trade, consumer and agricultural shows in the UK, which was double the amount spent on outdoor and transport advertising (£378m) and more than the advertising spend in consumer magazines (£533m) or business directories (£639m). If private events are included (£266m), the spend approaches that of the advertising spend on national newspaper advertising (AA 1997). On average, around 8% of UK firms' promotional budgets are spent on exhibiting (Campaign 1992). In the USA, over 9000 trade shows are held annually, with firms taking part allocating approximately 22% of their marketing budgets to the activity (Trade Show Bureau 1992). While these figures change year-on-year, it is still clear that exhibitions and trade shows account for a substantial part of marketing communications budgets. For some firms they may be the most important elements of their promotional activities. As a general statement, the level of importance of this area of marketing communications is likely to be greater for industrial and b2b companies although the actual role it plays in a marketing communications plan needs to be considered against other promotional opportunities.

Despite the widespread use of exhibitions as promotional tools (for exhibitors) and as sources of up-to-date information about the latest developments (for visitors), relatively little research has been conducted into them. This may be due to the difficulties of obtaining a definitive answer as to whether exhibitions are really an effective way to promote; it may be due to the difficulty of reconciling the aims of exhibitors with the aims of the visitors; or it may be due to entrenched attitudes on the part of exhibitors, non-exhibitors and exhibition managers. One of the areas in which conflict occurs is in the split between activities which directly relate to personal selling (lead generation, appointment-making, and closing of sales) and activities which relate to other marketing functions such as public relations, promotion and new-product launches, and marketing research.

Certainly attitudes among exhibitors and non-exhibitors can be extremely polarised. There are firms that have little other promotional activity than exhibitions, so strong is their belief in the efficacy of the medium; equally there are marketers who do not believe that exhibitions serve any useful purpose whatever as a promotional tool.

Exhibitions and trade fairs are concerned with two main areas of marketing communications: activities directly related to making sales, and areas which relate to more general promotion activities. Some exhibitions are intended primarily as selling events, where the visitors to the exhibition would expect to be able to buy goods directly from the exhibitors, while other exhibitions (called non-selling exhibitions) exist primarily to show the latest developments in the industry.

Reasons for exhibiting

Most research into managers' perceptions of trade shows and exhibitions confirms the view that managers see exhibitions in terms of making sales. This is true of both US and European research; even when the managers do not expect to take orders at the

NEED TO KNOW

☑ One important role of exhibitions and trade shows is to increase sales either directly on the stand or through follow-up activity.

shows, they still tend to expect to obtain leads, qualify prospects, and open sales at shows. This is particularly apparent in the staffing of stands; managers predominantly staff the stands with sales people, even though there is evidence to suggest that visitors do not like this (Tanner and Chonko 1995).

In an international survey, Shipley et al. (1993) identified 13 reasons for exhibiting, of which seven were directly related to selling, with six representing non-selling activities. Exhibit 30.1 shows the exhibitors' ranking of reasons for exhibiting. This research showed that taking sales orders ranked low on the list (although, of course, this depends on the nature of the exhibition itself). This is despite the fact that much of the strategy-orientated research into exhibitions has focused on the level of resources committed to participation (Bonoma 1983; Herbig et al. 1994), with the decision being made according to the number of sales leads the show is likely to generate (Cavanaugh 1976; Kijewski et al. 1992).

Trade fairs and exhibitions tend to be regarded as selling opportunities in much of the literature, particularly in the practitioner textbooks, with an emphasis on the low cost per contact made, as compared with cold calling in the field.

NEED TO KNOW

☑ Prospects made via exhibitions are generally recognised to be less expensive than field contacts.

Sharland and Balogh (1996), for example, define effectiveness as the number of sales leads generated, followed up and successfully closed, and efficiency is the comparison between the cost of trade show participation versus other sales and promotion activity.

Exhibit 30.1 Reasons for exhibiting

Objective	UK companies Rank	Overseas companies Rank
Meet new customers	1	1
Enhance company image	2	2
Interact with customers	3	4
Promote existing products	4	3
Launch new products	5	5
Get competitor intelligence	6	6
Get edge on non-exhibitors	7	9
Keep up with competitors	8	8
Enhance personnel morale	9	13
Interact with distributors	10	7
General market research	11	11
Take sales orders	12	12
Meet new distributors	13	10

Source: Adapted from figure from '*Dimensions of trade show exhibiting management*', in '*Journal of Marketing Management*', Vol. 9, No. 1, 1993, Westburn Publishers, (Shipley, D., Egan, C., and Wong, K.S., 1993), reprinted with permission of Westburn Publishers Ltd.

NEED TO KNOW

☑ Research has indicated that whereas some managers believe that the primary purpose of exhibitions is related to selling activities, others believe that their non-selling related activities are more important.

This view of exhibitions as selling opportunities is certainly borne out by other research. Exhibit 30.2 summarises the views of exhibitors based on interviews with managers of firms who spend a very high proportion of their marketing budgets on exhibiting (Blythe and Rayner 1996).

For the most part, the managers quoted above (in common with others) regarded selling as being the primary function of exhibitions. In fact, some managers expressed surprise that there could be any other

Exhibit 30.2 Representative statements regarding reasons for exhibiting

Percentage of budget spent on exhibitions	Statements about objectives
80%	We aim to see 200–300 people, to sell, and to reach into the market to launch new products.
80%	In the main to sell and launch new machines, but also to sell existing products and to contact and meet existing customers.
70–75%	Nothing in the precise sense. To meet as many new customers as possible.
100%	To try to sell.
95%	Not really, because it is viewed as a PR job, not an order-taking exercise. However the main aim of the exercise is to get a reaction to next season's lines.

Source: 'The evaluation of non-selling activities at British trade exhibitions', in Marketing Intelligence and Planning, Vol. 14, No. 5, 1996, Emerald Group Publishing Limited, (Blythe, J. and Rayner, T., 1996). Reproduced by permission.

reason for exhibiting. Having said that, Kerin and Cron (1987) found that non-selling activities are considered by some exhibitors to be more important than selling activities. Indeed, their research contrasts strongly with other research and shows selling to be much lower on the list of important factors. Many firms view exhibitions as an opportunity to enhance the company image, for example, or to carry out some general marketing research – to find out what the competition are offering, for instance. Although it can be argued that the purpose of all marketing activity is, ultimately, to make sales, not all activities relate directly to the personal selling function. Although the received wisdom (and the prevailing view) is that exhibitions are tools for personal selling, not all exhibitors agree.

> **NEED TO KNOW**
>
> ☑ Enhancing the corporate image is seen as one of the most important non-selling roles of exhibitions and trade shows.

It is, therefore, entirely possible that non-selling aims are more important (or at least more realistic) in exhibiting. The main non-selling activity that firms do report as an aim is enhancing the corporate image; for some this is the most important aim (see Exhibit 30.3). Shipley et al. (1993) (Exhibit 30.1) found that it ranked second for both domestic and overseas exhibitors, and 25% of respondents in a US survey reported 'establishing a presence' as their primary goal in exhibiting (Tanner and Chonko 1995).

Exhibit 30.3 Relative importance of exhibition and trade show aims

Aim	Rank	Mean score (out of 10)
Enhancing corporate image	1	5.32
Introduce new products	2	5.14
Identify new prospect	3	5.08
Getting competitive information	4	4.94
Servicing current customers	5	4.69
Enhancing corporate morale	6	3.75
Selling at the show	7	2.79
New product testing	8	2.17

Source: Adapted from Kerin and Cron (1987)

IN VIEW 30.3

Award winning exhibitor

Ford, Belgium received the title, 'Exhibition Champion', Exhibitors' Gold Award and top award for 'Best Use of Exhibition Techniques' for their stand at the Brussels Motor Show. The stand was designed by 'Imagination', a company specialising in design and exhibition display.

Ford dedicated a 4000 square-metre hall to its stand and was the only manufacturer not actively selling at the Show. Instead, emphasis was placed on a thematic approach, 'The Nature of Safety', with the stand being designed partly as a vehicle display and partly as a calm, relaxed 'walk-through' experience with no pressure selling. Visitors entered the stand via one of three short tunnels where videos continually played presentations of natural earth settings and sound effects. Entering the vehicle display, people were drawn to the 'experience' by a large 'pro-cube' television wall providing colour and movement, where they encountered three vivid natural environments in succession; a tropical rainforest, a hostile desert, and cool oceans. Soundscapes, lighting and 3-D effects, textured floors, projection and video were all employed to develop the sensory experience. The final area was a dark, theatrically-lit rotunda displaying the Ford vehicle range. Visitors left the rotunda to view the outer exhibition laid out in a traditional autoshow manner with renewed interest. Almost 8000 people a day passed through The Nature of Safety experience on weekdays and 16,000 a day at weekends. The Belgian Automobile Journalists Association named it 'Most Informative Stand' and it gained widespread press and TV coverage in the Benelux countries.

Source: Adapted from Marketing (1996)

This background of dissent about the true value of exhibitions naturally leads some exhibitors to question whether there is a value at all, and of course some exhibitors move away from exhibitions and towards road shows or other means of promotion or lead generation. Equally, there is dissent among academics as to the value of exhibitions; Sashi and Perretty (1992) express doubts about the overall usefulness of trade shows, Bonoma (1983) is critical of them, yet Gopalakrishna et al. (1995) are of the opinion that trade shows are effective. Not unnaturally, the exhibition industry itself reports that exhibitions are very effective in generating sales leads and other benefits. The point not always addressed in such debates is the role of exhibitions and shows as an integrated part of wider marketing communications. It is in this wider context that their true value may be better assessed.

Visitors' views of exhibitions

Those who question the selling role of exhibitions and trade shows may well be right to do so. For example, there is a conflict between the exhibitors' view of exhibitions and the visitors' view. Many visitors do not have any role in purchasing (Gramann 1993), and in fact the majority have no direct role. Some are students on visits from their universities and colleges, some are competitors who are not themselves exhibiting, some are consultants or others who are trying to make contact with exhibitors in order to sell their own services. They are therefore unlikely to become qualified leads (although they might well be 'useful contacts').

Some researchers report visitors complaining of 'too much sales pitch' (Chonko et al. 1994); many visitors are on information-gathering expeditions rather than intending to specifically purchase anything. Trade shows may be most useful to purchasers in the information-gathering and vendor selection stages of the decision-making process. Given this conflict between visitor expectations and exhibitor expectations, it is presumably up to market-orientated exhibitors to adapt their approaches on the stand (Tanner 1994). Exhibitors really need to ask themselves why the visitors come and in most cases will find that they did not come to be sold to. But this is not to undermine their importance in fulfilling other marketing communications objectives.

Planning and evaluating exhibitions

Although exhibitions are expensive activities, many firms do not put sufficient time and effort into planning. In some cases this is because the management believe that the exhibition is merely a flag-waving exercise and do not expect to get anything tangible from it; in other cases the exhibition is a one-off or infrequent activity, and thus imposes an extra burden on the marketing team which disrupts their usual routine.

In fact, a properly planned and executed exhibition is likely to take up six months or more in total, both in the preparation beforehand and in the follow-up activities afterwards. Exhibit 30.4 identifies the recommended stages to follow in the exhibition and trade show planning process.

Exhibit 30.4 Stages in planning an exhibition or trade show

Stage 1	Set objectives
Stage 2	Select which exhibition/trade show to attend
Stage 3	Plan for staffing the stand
Stage 4	Plan support promotions
Stage 5	Decide stand layout and contents – design stand
Stage 6	Plan follow-up activities
Stage 7	Plan the 'project' – logistics
Stage 8	Evaluate and follow-up

Stage 1

The first stage is to decide what the objectives of the exhibition are; this goes beyond merely deciding what the reasons are for exhibiting. The objectives need to be realistic (bearing in mind the visitor profile of the exhibition), they need to be achievable (within the context of the firm's resources) and they need to be quantifiable (and mechanisms must be in place to monitor their achievement). See Chapter 13, Marketing communications planning and plans, and Chapter 19, Setting objectives, determining strategy and tactics, for more information on the use of SMARRTT objectives in the planning process.

Formal objective-setting appears to be influenced by a combination of importance of the activity and the ease or difficulty of assessment. Most exhibitors state that personal selling is the main aim of exhibiting, or

NEED TO KNOW

☑ *Objectives for exhibition and trade show events should be set to orchestrate with other marketing communications and they should be set to meet SMARRTT criteria.*

WARNING

! *Many organisations do not set clear objectives for their exhibitions. This cannot be considered good practice.*

indeed the only aim; most are able to set formal objectives for taking sales orders, but the majority (more than two-thirds) are unable or unwilling to set objectives for interacting with existing customers. If most firms do not set objectives for this activity, clearly even fewer would set objectives for non-selling activities such as enhancing the company image (Blythe 1997). Objectives should be set in conjunction with the overall marketing communications objectives, with a view to integrating exhibition promotions with other marketing communications activities.

Stage 2

The second stage of the planning process is to decide which exhibition to attend. This decision will rest on the following factors:

- The number of available exhibitions to choose from. In some industries there are only one or two suitable exhibitions each year.
- The visitor profile of the exhibition. Most exhibition organisers will provide this information based on the previous year's attendance. Obviously information from this source will need to be treated with some circumspection; exhibition organisers are unlikely to give a negative picture.
- The cost of exhibiting.
- The availability of suitable space in a good location.
- The timing of the exhibition relative to the firm's business cycle and other communication projects.
- The profile of exhibitors (i.e. which competitors will be exhibiting and which will not).
- The profile of visitors and their role in the decision-making unit.
- The prestige level of the exhibition. It would be hard to imagine any major car manufacturer not exhibiting at the London, Brussels and Frankfurt Motor Shows, for example.

IN VIEW 30.4

The Sound and Vision Exhibition

The annual Sound and Vision Exhibition is organised by *What HiFi?* magazine, the leading journal for HiFi enthusiasts. Firms exhibiting at the show range from one-man businesses selling components and peripherals, through to multinationals such as Panasonic and JVC exhibiting their latest models.

Strangely, research has shown that most of the firms exhibiting do not set objectives for the exhibition, yet the reasons given vary from firm to firm. The giant firms do not set objectives because the exhibition is only a tiny part of their overall promotional budget; it is almost beneath their notice. The tiny firms don't set objectives because they don't really know how to. The medium-sized firms don't set objectives because they can't afford to evaluate the outcomes.

In fact, the only people who appear to be clear about their objectives for the exhibition are the visitors, who are going to see (and hear) the very latest in HiFi equipment.

Stage 3

The third stage is to plan the staffing of the exhibition stand. Most managers tend to use the salesforce to man the stands, but this has the disadvantage of taking salespeople off the road. Also, research evidence shows that most visitors are not actually in a position to buy, but are probably engaged in the information search stage of the buying process. Unless the show is primarily a selling show, therefore, it is more productive to man the stand with technical people, with perhaps one salesperson to handle buyers and collect leads. Some exhibitors employ temporary staff for the exhibition period; this has the advantage of freeing up the firm's permanent staff and avoiding the disruption of routine that exhibitions often cause, but can mean that the stand is staffed with people who have no long-term commitment to the firm and its success. A way round this is to use the temporary staff for leaflet distribution around the exhibition to encourage visitors to visit the firm's stand. To gain more attraction on the stand, models and hosts/hostesses are frequently employed. A number of firms within the marketing communications industry specialise in providing staff for these sorts of purposes.

IN VIEW 30.5

Making an announcement

As an example of a pre-exhibition promotion, HYDRATIGHT^{TM}, an engineering company, sent out a novel mailing announcing its stand at a forthcoming 'Offshore Europe' trade show.

The company's announcement took the form of a small leaflet which when opened to reveal its contents, actually played a fanfare of trumpets – sure to attract attention. This was achieved by a small electronic device inserted into the leaflet, which was triggered by simply opening up the leaflet, in just the same way that musical birthday cards are activated by opening up the card. The fanfare certainly ensured an interested reader and the contents announced the details of the exhibition and which stand HYDRATIGHT^{TM} would be on.

Stage 4

The fourth stage is to plan the support promotions before, during and after the exhibition. These may include direct mailshots to potential visitors and advertising campaigns in advance of the exhibition (often including the use of promotional media and database addresses held by the exhibition organisers); press releases in the trade or consumer press as appropriate; and extra activity by the salesforce both before the exhibition (inviting existing customers to visit the stand) and afterwards (following up new enquiries). Joint promotions and sponsorship with the exhibition/show organisers is a common marketing communications practice.

FOOD FOR THOUGHT

Exhibitions and trade shows are good places to launch new products.

Stage 5

The fifth stage is to decide on the layout of the stand, the stand contents and its design. Exhibition specialists would often be used for this purpose. Since visitors are usually information gathering, the stand needs to be eye-catching and attractive, but also should convey solid information. Exhibitions and trade shows are often good places to launch new products, so the firm's latest offerings need to be on the stand. It is often useful to have an area that is away from the public view so that potential customers can discuss their needs with the salesperson in private. Some refreshments can be available, and the quiet area can also serve as a rest area for stand staff.

Stage 6

The sixth stage of planning is to plan for follow-up activities after the exhibition. A surprising number of exhibitors fail to do this, with the result that the salesforce are unable to follow up on leads generated (Blythe and Rayner 1996). The main problem with delaying the follow-ups is that the prospects will undoubtedly have contacted the firm's competitors as well (since they will almost certainly be at the same exhibition). This may mean that a delay allows the competition to get the business, so the salesforce should clear their appointment books for about a month after the exhibition in order to have time to do follow-up visits.

Stage 7

The seventh stage of planning is to arrange the logistics of the exercise. This means ensuring that the equipment, furnishings, promotional material and the staff are all transported to the exhibition at the right time and arrive in good condition to make the exhibition a success. Exhibition specialists can be invaluable in making these arrangements.

Stage 8

Finally, once the exhibition is over, two activities need to be carried out. First, there should be follow-up sales and promotional activities. Second, the success of the show should be evaluated. This can be carried out by formal market research, or by counting the number of leads generated, or the number of visitors to the stand, or whatever other means are appropriate to the objectives decided upon. Evaluation *should be* planned for in just the same way as the rest of the exhibition is planned and not left as an afterthought. Many exhibitors do not have systems in place for evaluating their activities; the following quotes illustrate this (Blythe and Raynor 1996):

> The costs of exhibiting are readily identifiable but not the benefits.
>
> It's impossible to say how much effect the exhibition had, any attempt to quantify the benefits of exhibiting has been avoided.
>
> Exhibitions are a necessity, but good value for money is a very difficult thing to quantify.
>
> We do evaluate on a costs v. sales basis to a certain extent.
>
> We intended to create a database ... so far we haven't had the time.
>
> We attempted to ... track sales leads arising from new contacts at the show but abandoned this when the administration became too cumbersome.

It transpired that few companies had any formal evaluation systems in place, even for selling activities; still fewer had systems for tracking non-selling activities. The reasons given for this were as follows:

The variables are too vague.

The variables are too intangible.

Very non-quantifiable.

Any attempt would be unscientific.

The benefits are too hard to identify.

The lead time causes a tracking problem.

It would take up too much time.

It would be too expensive.

Intangible objectives are hard to formulate and thus achievements are hard to measure.

Undoubtedly these difficulties are perfectly valid, and of course for an individual firm in the field, it may well be more expensive to find out the answers than it is to live with the problem.

More research is needed into the reasons why firms do not evaluate, but some possible reasons include:

1 The firm doesn't have the resources to carry out the evaluation.
2 The activity is not important enough to warrant evaluation.
3 The evaluation would be too difficult or expensive.
4 The firm is owner-managed and therefore the owner feels able to estimate the effectiveness of the exhibition without formal evaluation (Blythe and Raynor 1996).

Non-evaluation of such an expensive, time-consuming and (often) disruptive activity would seem to be perverse, to say the least. It would be hard to imagine a firm conducting, for example, a nationwide poster campaign without evaluating the results, yet exhibiting represents (nationally) significantly more expenditure than outdoor poster advertising.

Summary

This chapter has been about exhibitions and trade shows. While most agree that exhibitions are a powerful communications tool, since no other activity brings so many buyers and sellers together under one roof, there is controversy and dissent about their use and effectiveness.

Much of this dissent arises from the problem of deciding what should be the criteria for considering an exhibition to have been successful or not. An organisation which sets unrealistic objectives (for example, setting sales objectives for a non-selling exhibition), or which fails to plan properly for following up the enquiries generated, is likely to blame the exhibition when the fault lies with them. Equally, many managers believe blindly in exhibitions while not actually having any mechanisms in place for evaluating the activity.

Exhibitions require a considerable degree of commitment, not just for the week or so of the exhibition but for the months preceding and following the event. As an activity, it is too expensive and too high-profile to be left to chance. Exhibitions and shows can vary significantly in size and purpose and include even the humble exhibition display in company reception areas and public libraries. Whatever the situation, they should be planned and be recognised as an important part of the wider marketing communications mix of activities with which they should be carefully integrated.

Self-review questions

1 What are the main aims of exhibitions?

2 What estimated average percentage of firms' promotional budgets is spent on exhibitions?

3 Why would it be more appropriate for some stands to be staffed by engineers rather than by salespeople?

4 Why should leads be followed up as quickly as possible?

5 What are the eight stages in the planning and evaluation process?

6 If exhibitions are such a powerful marketing communications activity, why is there an increasing trend to use roadshows and other promotional means instead?

Project

Visit one or more exhibitions. Carefully observe and evaluate all the activities that are going on. Consider the organisation of the exhibition as a whole; the number of stands, layout, visitor attendance, exhibitor attendance, promotional/ informational materials, atmosphere, all the supporting services. Consider the whole event from a visitor's perspective.

Evaluate the event(s) from exhibitors' perspectives. Consider stand designs and competitive activities. What do you think makes a good stand design? How are the stands staffed? Do staff appear to be 'selling' or 'information giving'. How active and enthusiastic do they appear to be? What do you think are the objectives of the exhibitors; do you think they are all the same? Consider the full range of marketing communication tools that are used at exhibitions. How many different types can be identified? Think about the examples given in the In View sections above to provide ideas.

References

Advertising Association (1997), *Marketing Pocket Book.* NTC Publications.

Bonoma, T.V. (1983), Get more out of your trade shows. *Harvard Business Review,* 61, 75–83.

Blythe, J. (1997), Does size matter? Objectives and measures at UK trade exhibitions. *Journal of Marketing Communications,* 3 (1).

Blythe, J. and Rayner, T. (1996), The evaluation of non-selling activities at British trade exhibitions – an exploratory study. *Marketing Intelligence and Planning,* 14 (5).

Campaign (1992), *The Campaign Report.* Haymarket.

Cavanaugh, S. (1976), Setting of objectives and evaluating the effectiveness of trade show exhibits. *Journal of Marketing*, 40 (October), 100–103.

Chonko, L.B., Tanner, J.F. and McKee, J. (1994), Matching trade show staff to prospects. *Marketing Management*, 3, 40–43.

Gopalakrishna, S., Lilien, G.L., Williams, J.D. and Sequeira, I.K. (1995), Do trade shows pay off? *Journal of Marketing*, 59, 75–83.

Gramann, J. (1993), *Independent Market Research. Centre Exhibitions,* National Exhibition Centre.

Herbig, P., O'Hara, B. and Palumbo, F. (1994), Measuring trade show effectiveness: an effective exercise? *Industrial Marketing Management*, 23, 165–170.

Kerin, R.A. and Cron, W.L. (1987), Assessing trade show functions and performance: an exploratory study. *Journal of Marketing*, 51, 87–94.

Kijewski, V., Yoon, E. and Young, G. (1992), *Trade Shows: How Managers Pick Their Winners.* Institute for the Study of Business Markets.

Marketing (1996), *The Marketing Exhibition Effectiveness Awards.* Haymarket.

Sashi, C.M. and Perretty, J. (1992), Do trade shows provide value? *Industrial Marketing Management*, 21, 249–255.

Sharland, A. and Balogh, P. (1996), The value of non-selling activities at international trade shows. *Industrial Marketing Management*, 25, 59–66.

Shipley, D., Egan, C. and Wong, K.S. (1993), Dimensions of trade show exhibiting management. *Journal of Marketing Management*, 9 (1).

Tanner, J.F. (1994), Adaptive selling at trade shows. *Journal of Personal Selling and Sales Management*, 13, 15–24.

Tanner, J.F. and Chonko, L.B. (1995), Trade show objectives, management and staffing practices. *Industrial Marketing Management*, 24, 257–264.

Trade Show Bureau (1992), *Ten by Ten.* Trade Show Bureau.

Chapter 31

Personal selling and sales management

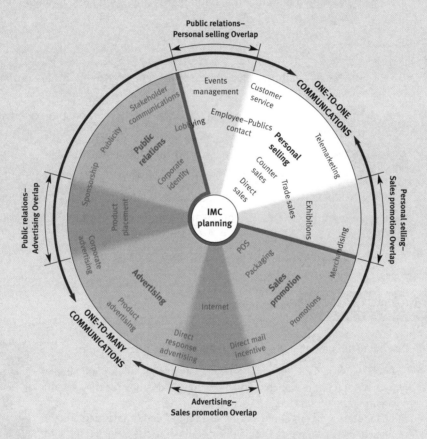

The Integrated Marketing Communications (IMC) Mix Model

CD

Select two business customers of Pampers e.g. supermarket, other retail outlet. Using Exhibit 31.6, Defining/Selecting Key Accounts, evaluate the account attractiveness of your selection against Pampers' business strengths. What sales strategies would you recommend Pampers to pursue with the two accounts?

Chapter outline

- Importance of personal selling within integrated marketing communications
- The changing role of personal selling and sales management
- Salesforce structures
- Selling and negotiation
- Key account management
- Agent and distributor sales management
- Selling by telephone
- Salesforce motivation – the negative role of commission
- Sales strategy
- Marketing communications and increasing points of customer contact

Objectives

- To stress the importance of personal selling as an integral part of marketing communications
- To emphasise the move from transactional to relationship-based selling approaches
- To identify common approaches to salesforce structures
- To provide an overview of personal selling and sales management activities
- To demonstrate a strategic approach to integrated sales management
- To identify key issues facing sales management today

Professional perspective

Keith Slater Director of International Development, Ingersoll Rand

My involvement over the years in salesforce development has been to advise and support salesforce leadership in the pharmaceutical and engineering industries, as they seek to strengthen their marketplace performance.

There is much anecdotal comment about what makes an effective salesperson, and there are many consultancies promoting their selling skills models. Sales leadership, faced with this, increasingly need to focus on facts and evidence, such as the findings of Huthwaite International's substantial research programmes. These, and other research evidence, have caused businesses to review not only traditional approaches to selling, but also personal sales leadership and managerial styles. Too many times, I have seen the temptation, as a 'quick fix', to jump straight into a professional selling skills model and the programmes to deliver it – sometimes without enough real research into what actually works with customers.

My experience is that if not enough attention is paid first to the professional and leadership qualities and competencies required, then all the sales training in the world cannot compensate for ineffective leadership.

Decisions on how the organisation wants to approach the market and customers set the framework for maximising customer satisfaction and profitability. Sales leadership needs to agree on a selling skills model which supports these decisions and understand it deeply themselves, so they can recruit, coach, assess and improve performance – not only for their own direct sales team but to equip distributors to be able to do the same (where the channel to market is through distribution).

This chapter explores many of these issues. As you work through it, I would ask that you are careful to distinguish between the usage of 'sales management', referring to the management of sales, and 'sales management' referring to the management of sales people. The two meanings are inextricably linked but distinct.

Importance of personal selling within integrated marketing communications

Personal selling, and the management of the activities of personal selling, is one of the principal areas identified in most descriptions of the promotional mix. It is one of the four areas that has been identified in the Integrated Marketing Communications Mix Model. Yet for most marketing communications practitioners it is an area that is frequently ignored, not through lack of respect for its importance but simply because, within the typical organisational management structure, it is a very separate function. But not only is the salesforce an important part of external marketing communications (one of the most powerful and flexible), the salesforce is also an important target group for internal marketing communications to ensure that its members are fully briefed to undertake the marketing communications and selling task they do.

NEED TO KNOW

☑ *Not only does the salesforce act in the capacity of salespeople, in an indirect way so do other employees.*

Not only should the salesforce be thought of as personal sellers for an organisation. All employees have a marketing communications role to play in their discourse with the external public, whether or not they have a formal selling role to play. Therefore, they too, should be considered in the wider sense of a 'salesforce'.

In a book that purports to extol the virtues of integrated marketing communications, personal selling is clearly an area that cannot be ignored, although it is accepted that it has not featured strongly so far in this book. This chapter seeks to remedy that situation.

The changing role of personal selling and sales management

NEED TO KNOW

☑ *Probably the most significant change in thinking over the recent years is the move to recognising importance of developing longer-term customer relations and improving customer retention. The emphasis has moved away from transactional selling.*

Selling and sales management in the late 1990s and the new millennium is very different from, say, 20 or 30 years ago. Selling has at long last gained respectability as a profession having previously had a somewhat dubious reputation. Indeed, the Institute of Professional Sales, formed in 1997 by the Chartered Institute of Marketing, is testimony to this fact, receiving support from major organisations such as IBM and Parcelforce.

Wilson (1993) refers to some of the varied roles that salespeople now have to perform as part of their daily activities, rather than just selling. These new roles are identified as:

- Customer partner
- Buyer/seller team coordinator
- Customer service provider
- Buyer behaviour expert
- Information gatherer

- Market analyst and planner
- Sales forecaster
- Market cost analyser
- Technologist.

The focus of attention in the best organisations has shifted from salespeople concentrating on seeking new customers, to retaining existing ones and building relationships. It is now widely accepted that customer retention is a far more profitable strategy than customer acquisition. This move represents one of the most significant changes in marketing thinking from simple **transactional selling** to **relationship marketing**.

Sales training courses used to heavily feature techniques of *objection handling* and *closing* when making sales presentations to customers. Many of these techniques, however, do more harm than good as buyers do not like to be pressurised into making decisions. There tends to be much less emphasis on these today particularly when considering major versus low-value sales. This is an issue that is specifically highlighted later in In View 31.3. The SPIN © questioning model (Huthwaite Research Group 1998), which is also discussed later, is a far more effective tool to use when making sales presentations to uncover customers' explicit needs.

Different authors classify sales roles in different ways. Chonko et al. (1992) classify sales jobs into two broad categories: 'service selling', which concentrates on getting sales from the existing customer base, and 'developmental selling' which aims to convert prospects into customers. Anderson (1995) refers to three basic roles, namely, 'order taking', 'order supporting' and 'order getting'. Similarly, Lancaster and Jobber (1997) split the selling function into three subsets: 'order-takers', 'order-creators' and 'order-getters'. Donaldson (1998) has developed what he refers to as a 'modern classification' of selling types. He identifies the following:

- *Consumer direct* – salespeople who deal directly with the general public and are primarily order getters. This is the area of retailing. The products may be cosmetics, vitamins or white goods such as washing machines and dishwashers.
- *Industrial direct* – salespeople focused on obtaining orders. These are often of a much higher value and good negotiation skills may be required to complete the sale. Products include components, ships and engineering tools.
- *Government/institutional direct* – selling to these customers is often through an invitation to tender.
- *Consumer indirect* – salespeople may be employed by fast moving consumer goods companies selling repeat business to retail outlets.
- *Industrial indirect* – salespeople are likely to be involved in selling to and supporting distributors. A salesperson employed by a company manufacturing roofing tiles is likely to spend a lot of time working with builders' merchants.
- *'Specifier' sales* – Donaldson states, 'this is a difficult form of selling where the sale is to have the product or service specified by a major influencer in the purchase decision, not the user of the product.' Donaldson actually refers to this role as 'missionary sales' but this term tends to conflict with other uses where it signifies a 'missionary' salesperson as one who makes first contact.

Transactional selling

Selling where the emphasis is simply placed on achieving the sale and following the steps proposed to a successful sale.

Relationship marketing

View that emphasises the importance of the relationships developed between an organisation and other parties including customers, partners, suppliers and the trade.

WARNING

Techniques of 'objective handling' and 'closing' need to be dealt with in different ways for low value and high value sales. Their use may be contrasted in the context of transactional selling and relationship selling.

Key accounts

Usually taken to mean a major customer, but can best apply to any customer that the organisation has determined to be significant for whatever reasons.

- *Key account sales* – **key account** customers are those of strategic importance to the selling company, serviced by appointed managers trained to meet that customer's specific needs. This is fully explained later in this chapter.
- *Food brokers* – salespeople may represent a number of producers selling to large retail outlets.
- *Telesales* – a subset of telemarketing, telesales may be used for a variety of pre- and post-selling activities as well as selling the company's products. This is fully explained later in this chapter.
- *Systems selling/team selling* – several people from different functions may work together as part of the 'team'.
- *Franchise selling* – can cover a wide range of products and has become increasingly popular.
- *International selling* – concentrating solely on domestic sales for many businesses is no longer an option. As with other selling activities, it is important that international sales are integrated within the overall marketing planning framework.

It should not be assumed, therefore, that all forms of selling are the same. Sales roles are reflected in Exhibit 31.1. Different products involve different levels of complexity from simple low value sales through to complex high value sales. Similarly, some sales roles require relatively simple communication and relationship-building skills, whereas skills for key or global account managers will have to be highly developed. Successful organisations ensure a good match between the skills exhibited by the salesperson and those needed for the role.

In this chapter, the importance of moving away from simply focusing on customer acquisition to a focus on customer retention is stressed. The way organisations interact with their customers is a key influencing factor in increased business profitability. Decisions need to be made regarding, say, the frequency of customer visits and how customers want to interact with the company in conjunction with the resources (time, money, people) available to the organisation. For example, do customers prefer to communicate via the Internet, over the telephone, by fax or face-to-face with the salesperson? It is important to recognise that Western approaches to selling may not

Exhibit 31.1 Sales roles

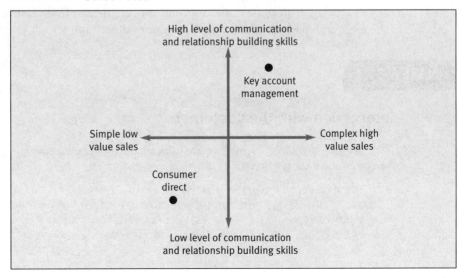

WARNING

> Approaches to selling are not identical throughout the world. Different cultures, customs and norms require that sales approaches are re-appraised to suit the customer's own culture. This is particularly important in the context of business-to-business selling.

successfully transfer to other cultures, or, indeed, to all cultures within Western Europe – that old maxim still applies 'think globally, act locally!' Procedures and customs adopted in China are very different to those adopted in the UK. This should be borne in mind whenever dealing with customers from other countries, whether the business is being transacted at home or abroad.

Salesforce structures

The salesforce is obviously the 'front line' when it comes to customer contact. When seeking to improve customer contact and marketing communications with customers, they, and other employees throughout the organisation, need to be considered and appropriate organisational structures developed. As part of overall restructuring, companies are increasingly reassessing the structure of their salesforces to best serve those customers that are key to the business, some even contracting out their selling activities to specialists. Companies are recognising that even if *all* customers are important, some are more important than others!

Lancaster and Jobber (1997) suggest salesforce structures may be based on geographic coverage, products, or customers – including market, account size and account type structures.

Geographic coverage structure

Traditional methods of salesforce organisation have primarily been developed to maximise geographic coverage of the market. Obvious advantages with this approach include its simplicity, with each salesperson having a sales territory or area in which they have exclusive responsibility for selling the company's products and services. Such a structure enables the salesperson to develop strong personal relationships with customers, which is now considered highly desirable. Disadvantages arise, however, when the company's product range becomes diversified, requiring the salesperson to learn the intimate details of a wide product range. The inevitable result is the risk of limited knowledge of certain products or the development of 'favourites' which typically tend to be those to whom the salesperson finds easiest to sell. A geographic approach may be localised to regions of a country, such as specific counties, states,

IN VIEW 31.1

Interaction with the customer

Hilary Scarlett, Director of Smythe Dorward Lambert, the UK's leading communications management consultancy says:

> Reputation is determined not by what is promised but by what is actually delivered. In assessing this, the customer is mostly influenced by the behaviour and attitude of the staff with whom they interact – not just in sales and customer support, but in other areas too. Employees are the brand ambassadors for the organisation.

Tactical management of territory

The design and organisation of sales territory is not a simple activity. Particularly in global markets it is tempting to simply allocate staff to a geography based on language and the cost efficiencies offered by less travelling. However, as more and more companies are recognising that geography may not be an effective basis for segmentation and global companies find their customer base is also made up of global players, so vertical marketing segments which cross geographic boundaries are more and more common. Balancing the tension between efficiency of a locally based sales activity with the effectiveness of an industry or segment expert sales person is not easy. Careful assessment of the cost versus the added customer value must be made and resources allocated flexibly.

Source: Hatton (1998)

provinces, departments, and television regions, or, in the case of multi-national and global companies, split into world areas such as Europe, Asia/Pacific Rim, America, etc. The approach is entirely dependent upon the selling company's selling and distribution capabilities.

Product structure

Another common approach to salesforce organisation places the *product* at the centre of the structure – an approach which is widely used, not least because decision-makers in customer companies tend to be organised along product lines. Typically, the structure is borne out of necessity to organise the company's selling activities to promote an extensive range of products. The advantage of this is that the salesperson has intimate knowledge of the products sold; however, a significant disadvantage arises when the customer sees several different salespeople from the same company. This results in duplicated sales effort or, more probably, customer annoyance from too frequent visits. Such a situation needs very careful management.

Customer-based structures

Modern approaches to salesforce organisation put the *customer at the centre* of the structure. There are a number of different structures used: market- or industry-based; account size-based; new or existing account-based.

- *Market- or industry-based* – market- or industry-based structures consider the types of customers the company serves, for example, a company selling computer systems may organise itself to serve banks, manufacturers and retailers, all of whom have different requirements from their suppliers in terms of frequency of purchase, support, warranty, invoicing, etc. It is obvious the successful selling organisation will be that which has intimate knowledge of the requirements of each type of business. This type of organisation is also able to spot trends in the separate industries in which it operates.
- *Size of account-based* – salesforce structures which consider size of account are now increasing since the recognition of key accounts requires focus on those customers which generate the most profitable business for the company. Use of a salesforce is

extremely expensive and it is now common to see a telesales operation where once the salesforce was dominant. It is typical to see tiers of account management which includes at its highest level national or key accounts. The salesforce is commonly used to serve medium-sized customers and telesales operations are used to serve small customers or provide back-up to other tiers within the structure.

● *Type of account-based* – the structural approach of using two different salesforces for *new accounts* and *existing accounts* is also common practice. This is because salespeople handling new customers require different personal attributes and qualities to be successful – for example, new account generation requires good prospecting skills and the ability to handle rejection. A slight variation of this is typical in industrial selling situations where 'development' teams are used to promote new products and 'maintenance' teams existing products. One reason new products fail is product ignorance, whereby it is not introduced properly to the customer. The risk of failure may be reduced by addressing training issues.

> **NEED TO KNOW**
>
> ☑ *Many organisations adopt more complex, multiple sales structures in favour of a single form of sales structure.*

There are no hard and fast rules with salesforce structures and many organisations combine approaches ending up with a complex organisational structure which meets the needs of their customers and the market as well as maximising their own strengths in terms of distribution, selling skills and other marketing skills. It is important to recognise that the issues above not only have an impact on the structure itself but also influence the total marketing communications approach with some customers being favoured with greater sales staff contact and others where other forms of marketing communications are emphasised (such as telesales).

Selling and negotiation

Selling and negotiation are terms often used interchangeably – comments such as 'negotiation is selling, it's just discussing what the customer requires'; 'some sales take longer and involve more work'; or 'selling is negotiation, negotiation is selling' are not uncommon. However, the two terms should not be considered synonymous. Huthwaite Research Group (1998, incorporating the work of Rackham 1995) states that if the terms of agreement cannot be varied, then you are selling, or persuading, not negotiating (see Exhibit 31.2), furthermore, the size of sale is irrelevant. They define negotiation as

> **NEED TO KNOW**
>
> ☑ *Selling and negotiating are similar and related terms but they represent different aspects of the sales task. Negotiation exists when both parties are willing to 'give' and 'take' in the sales process. If the terms are fixed, no negotiation is possible.*

An attempt by two or more parties to reach an agreement where (i) both parties can vary the terms; (ii) resource is scarce; (iii) agreement and conflict exist simultaneously.

Selling

Selling is most often described as a personal selling process that consists of a number of sequential elements. This approach is described by Donaldson (1990) as the traditional model of personal selling. Some stages of the *traditional model* do not, however, take adequate account of customers' needs and so are inappropriate when selling to key accounts – an increasingly significant element of the sales function within organisations. This section reviews the traditional model, highlights the stages where particular care has to be exercised in key accounts, and offers an alternative and preferred approach.

Exhibit 31.2 Negotiating agreement

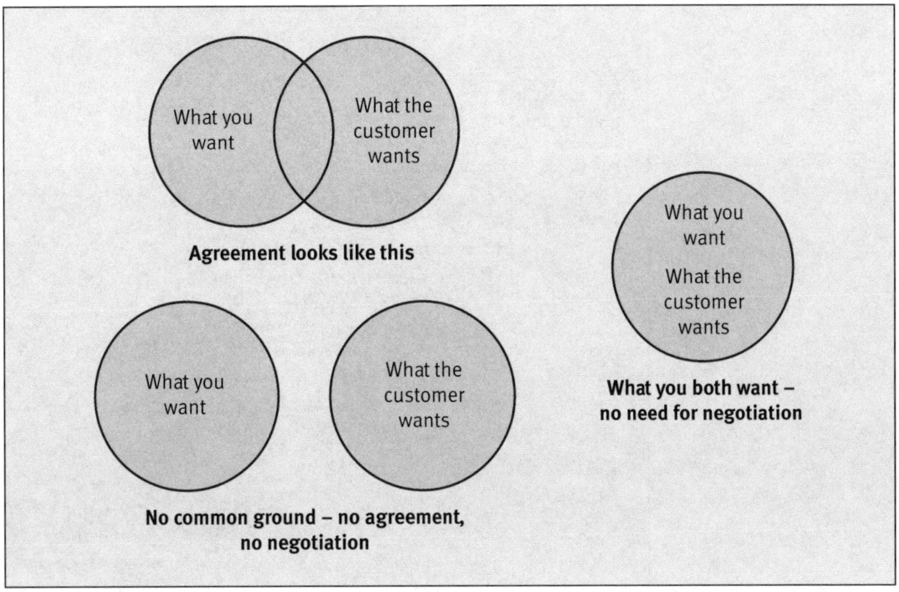

Source: Copyright © 1998 Huthwaite Research Group Limited.

- *Stage 1 – Prospecting and evaluating.* The salesperson prospects to maintain and build up the customer database. Prospects can be found from a variety of sources, e.g. trade shows, exhibitions, trade directories, the Internet, lapsed customers, purchased lists, direct marketing efforts, etc. A list of potential names is, however, of little value without their being evaluated as to the prospects' ability to buy, including their means and willingness. Once this process has been completed, they can be categorised as *qualified prospects.*
- *Stage 2 – Preparing.* Before the salesperson makes a visit to a potential customer it is essential that thorough preparation is carried out. All too often salespeople carry out inadequate preparation.
- *Stage 3 – Approaching the customer.* The initial approach to a customer may follow a previous sales call, a referral, or be just a *cold call.*
- *Stage 4 – Making the presentation.* During the presentation the salesperson will endeavour to discover the customer's needs. This will then enable the salesperson to fit his own products or services to meet the customer's requirements, explaining various features and benefits. During the course of the presentation, however, the customer is likely to raise some objections – for example, the price is too high; the product specification is wrong, the product availability is too slow, etc. The more objections a customer raises, the less likely he is to buy. This is the first stage which should be addressed in selling to key accounts.
- *Stage 5 – Overcoming objections.* Objections raised by the customer are handled in the most appropriate way by the salesperson (these techniques are not discussed in this book). This is highly inappropriate for key accounts. Often key account managers are professional purchasers, who find objection-handling techniques irritating and condescending – the likely result will be lost business. This is not to suggest that objection handling is unnecessary in key accounts, it simply means that the way it is handled may be different.

Exhibit 31.3 Traditional stages of selling

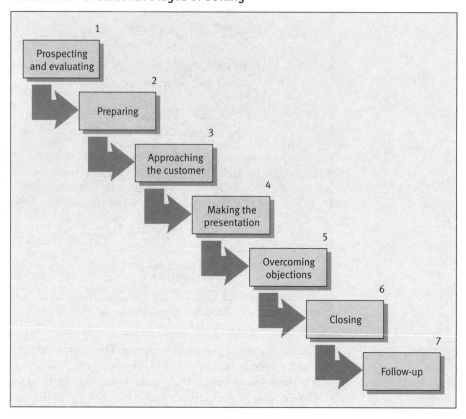

- *Stage 6 – Closing.* The salesperson uses any one of a number of closing techniques which may unduly pressurise the customer to make the decision to purchase. Closing has to be handled appropriately for key accounts: sales are complex, completed over several sales calls and probably the result of some negotiation between different levels of management in both the selling company and the customer company.
- *Stage 7 – Follow-up.* After an order is delivered it is essential the salesperson follows up with the customer to ensure everything is satisfactory. The salesperson may be able to rectify any mistakes and, more importantly, avoid repetition of errors. Salespeople may be reluctant to follow up because they fear negative feedback; however, this stage is crucial for repeat business, particularly in key accounts, where management of the relationship between the selling company and the customer paves the way for future business.

Rackham (1995) has defined four outcomes in the case of larger sales calls. These are *order, no sale, continuation* and *advance*. He has proposed that an 'advance' consists of an event taking place, either in the call or after it, which moves the sale forwards towards a decision, while a 'continuation' is where the sale will continue but no specific action has been agreed with the customer to move it forward. The traditional model of selling does not explicitly consider these two outcomes, often seen in key account management.

IN VIEW 31.3

Different techniques are needed for major sales

Commercial sales training companies and marketing textbooks pursuing the traditional approach to personal selling have identified key parts of the process as *objection handling* and *closing* (see Kotler and Armstrong 1991; McCarthy and Perrault 1990; Adcock et al. 1995). However, caution has to be exercised in applying techniques associated with these aspects, particularly for major sales. There is overwhelming evidence that the use of these techniques can be counterproductive in major sales and may result in lost business.

Huthwaite Research Group conducted research involving 35,000 sales calls over 12 years in 23 different countries and found skills being taught for low-value or single call sales are wholly inappropriate for selling in major sales. For example, traditional approaches to selling and sales training are based on assumptions which suggest a sale can be concluded in one visit; objections can be easily handled; forced closing techniques have no long-term impact on buyer feelings; and the more presentations a salesperson can squeeze into the day, the higher will be the sales revenue.

SPIN® selling

The SPIN® questioning model, developed by Rackham (see Exhibit 31.4), draws out the customer's explicit needs through a process of investigation. The first stage, preliminaries, replaces stage 4 of the traditional model, SPIN® is then used at stage 5, following which the salesperson demonstrates capability in meeting the customer's requirements and only then obtains commitment, i.e. stage 6. The significance of Huthwaite Research Group's work, published by Rackham (1990) is now recognised by several writers (e.g. Donaldson 1990; Wilson 1993; Winkler 1993), while others such as Hannon (1995), refer to *consultative selling*.

Negotiation

Negotiation is entered into by parties who are willing to 'give' and 'take' on points within the negotiation and are able to reach a mutual agreement. The parties negotiate on the division of issues of common interest although, on entering the negotiation, there may be conflict on these issues. Examples of issues are price, delivery terms, service support, etc. Agreement is reached through a process of bargaining – an exchange of detailed information on the issues at stake which also incorporates the parties' beliefs and expectations. The techniques used often combine both argument and persuasion.

In selling to key accounts, negotiation also comprises internal and external relations, i.e. internal to the organisation with other managers and levels of management, such as production, quality control and service specialists; and external with the customer. It is often the key phase in developing long-term relationships between the companies (Carlisle and Parker 1989).

There are, however, two approaches to sales negotiations, 'distributive or competitive negotiation' and 'integrative or collaborative/problem-solving negotiation'. The competitive model of selling typically involves negotiation where there is perceived to

Exhibit 31.4 The Spin® model of selling

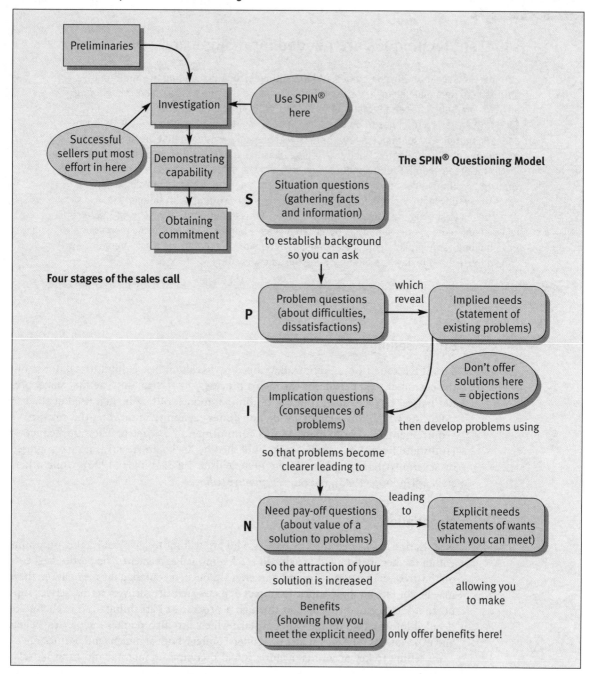

Source: Adapted from Rackham (1990). Copyright © 1990 Huthwaite Research Group Limited, SPIN® is a registered trademark of Huthwaite Research Group Limited

Exhibit 31.5 Ranges in negotiations

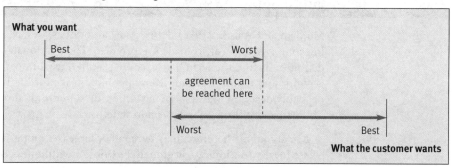

be one 'winner' – the 'win/lose' scenario; or where bargaining on issues is positional, i.e. consists primarily of concession making; and where the relationship between the individuals is unfriendly or adversarial. In contrast, integrative negotiations aspire to joint gains, where there are 'win/win' agreements; where the bargaining process is based on interests, i.e. involves both concession making and a search for mutually profitable alternatives; and where the relationship is friendly. Murrey (1986) offers stereotypical characterisations of these two types of negotiators:

> The competitive negotiator is a zealous advocate: tough, clever, thorough, articulate, unemotional, demanding, aggressive and unapproachable – a Sylvester Stallone 'Rambo' type who achieves victory by defeating the opponent. [While the collaborative negotiator is] thorough and articulate, but in addition: personable, cooperative, firm, principled, concerned about the other side's interests, and committed to fairness and efficiency – a Jimmy Stewart 'Mr Smith Goes to Washington' approach to resolving disputes amicably.

Although this implies a clear distinction between the two approaches, it is, however, more of a continuum, as suggested by Andes (1992). Thus, negotiations may involve a mix of both competitive and collaborative moves, depending on the amount of trust between the companies and individuals; their propensity for risk-taking; their power and flexibility; as well as the negotiating skill of the individuals involved in the process. In selling to and negotiating with key accounts, as the relationship evolves, the less tangible issues of trust and flexibility play an increasingly important role.

There are no definitive guidelines for sales negotiations. However, Huthwaite Research Group in their original research found skilled negotiators (i.e. those who were deemed to be effective by both parties) had a track record of success, a low implementation failure rate, an ability to prepare and plan their negotiation strategy, could think of issues in terms of ranges (see Exhibit 31.5) and more frequently tested their understanding of agreements. Conversely, unskilled negotiators tend to think in terms of 'fixed point' objectives.

The salesperson is often the most visible and the most flexible marketing communication medium in the selling company, particularly in a business-to-business environment. It is, therefore, essential he communicates efficiently and effectively with the customer in order to achieve long-term competitive advantage. Clearly, then, organisations that focus on customer needs, trust and co-operation are more likely to be survivors. Those looking for short-term gain at the expense of their customers are less likely to survive.

Key account management

Millman and Wilson (1995) define a key account as: 'A customer identified by a selling company to be of strategic importance'. Their rationale for putting forward this definition is that the term 'key account' is often used interchangeably with national account and major account. Many people, if asked to define a key account would probably describe it as a large customer, or something along those lines; however, Millman and Wilson (1995) go on to state,

> Key accounts, therefore, may be small or large by comparison with the seller; operate locally, nationally or globally; exhibit a willingness to forge close long-term relationships with sellers, or operate at arm's length and be brutally optimistic in their dealings. What is critical in classifying customers as key accounts is that they are considered by the seller to be of strategic importance.

Pareto principle

Also known as the 80:20 rule, it appears to apply to many situations. For example, it is frequently observed that the majority of sales (80%) come from a minority of customers (20%).

Customers that are of strategic importance to an organisation need to be looked after. Losing such an important customer can have a serious negative affect on cash flow and profitability since they are likely to account for significant sales revenue. In determining which accounts are key, a **Pareto analysis** is a useful exercise. Pareto suggests approximately 80% of revenue comes from 20% of customers – it is surprising just how often this proves to be the case, and can be used to identify the most important accounts to your business. Just because a customer is large, does not automatically mean a company will want to give it the special attention associated with key accounts – not all customers are profitable and any decision to give a customer key account status must make sound commercial sense. Indeed, Millman and Wilson (1995) propose aligning the organisation's strengths with customer account attractiveness (see Exhibit 31.6). These authors also discuss Shapiro et al.'s (1987) classification of customers according to their profitability, both financial and relational, while acknowledging the operational difficulty in accurately measuring relationships.

NEED TO KNOW

☑ It is important for organisations to determine just who are the key customers (accounts). However this may be determined, key accounts are those customers who are important to the organisation, and for whom special arrangements should be considered in line with the potential returns from such customers.

Millman and Wilson (1995) have devised a six-stage key account management (KAM) relational development model (see Exhibit 31.7), which they see as providing a useful tool for examining sources of competitive advantage and characterising managerial behaviour.

- *Pre-KAM* – management needs to determine which customers or potential customers are candidates for key account status. It is pointless trying to develop a customer into a key account if that customer is either not interested in building a relationship or is unlikely to be profitable.
- *Early-KAM* – involves identifying potential opportunities to develop the business. Millman and Wilson (1995) state:

> at this stage, tentative adaptations will be made to the seller's offer in order to more closely match buyer requirements. The focus of the sales effort will be on building trust through consistent performance and open communications.

The main contact will be between the key account manager in the selling company and the main contact in the buying company.
- *Mid-KAM* – trust begins to develop between both buyer and seller. The salesperson is likely to take a less important role as other contacts between different functions begin to develop between both organisations. Some relationships may only develop as far as that of preferred supplier (McDonald et al. 1996).

Exhibit 31.6 Defining/selecting key accounts

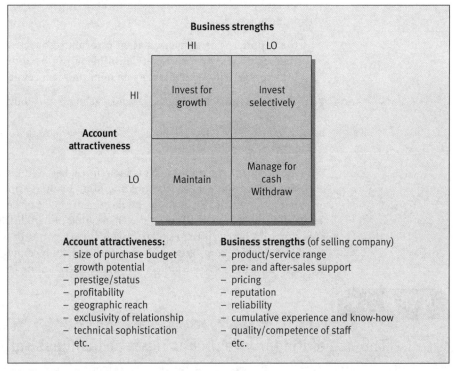

Account attractiveness:
- size of purchase budget
- growth potential
- prestige/status
- profitability
- geographic reach
- exclusivity of relationship
- technical sophistication
  etc.

Business strengths (of selling company)
- product/service range
- pre- and after-sales support
- pricing
- reputation
- reliability
- cumulative experience and know-how
- quality/competence of staff
  etc.

Source: Millman and Wilson (1995)

Exhibit 31.7 KAM relational development model

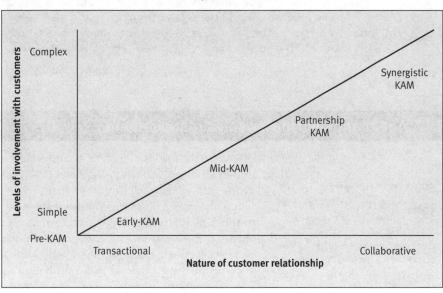

Source: Millman and Wilson (1995)

- *Partnership-KAM* – this is the mature stage of KAM. Close communications develops between corresponding parts of each organisation. Millman and Wilson describe how

  > the supplier is often viewed as an external resource of the customer and the sharing of sensitive commercial information becomes commonplace as the principal activity is increasingly on joint problem resolution.

- *Synergistic-KAM* – KAM goes beyond partnership as both organisations operate almost as one.
- *Uncoupling-KAM* – few relationships last forever and there may be a natural end to a partnership or a split-up.

With the decline of the traditional field salesforce, key account management is becoming much more important. Various methods of marketing communications are increasingly used in key account management, e.g. Starkey (1997a) reports, 'An increasing application of the use of telemarketing in handling key accounts in a support function between the regular calls by key account executives or key account managers'. Indeed, some argue that face-to-face sales meetings are essential, but there are exceptions and some customers prefer unassisted selling (see In View 31.4).

IN VIEW 31.4

The use of the Internet in business-to-business sales

A report on the use of the Internet prepared by the Hewson Group states,

> the 'automated transparent sales office' of the future is precisely what many customers are starting to demand. After all, for how long will customers continue to pay for account managers and telephone operators to interpret computer screen data on product availability, price and delivery? It is the customer who pays for account managers to add their own spin on information – almost as they see fit; 'letting customers down gently' when the information is not good and building up 'brownie points' when the news is good?

Agent and distributor sales management

FOOD FOR THOUGHT

Employing sales staff is very expensive. It makes sense to consider other means of communicating and selling to the market particularly when those other means can be very effective.

Keeping a salesforce on the road is expensive. According to a report entitled 'Balancing the Selling Equation: Revisited' (Abberton Associates 1997), there are more than 470,000 people employed in selling functions in the UK at an annual cost of £19 billion. The average cost of employing a salesperson is quoted at £49,400 and of this 57% is absorbed by indirect expenses. Clearly, these figures will change year-on-year but the message remains the same – a salesforce may be very effective but it is also very costly. Companies constantly have to appraise their cost efficiency and contribution against alternative marketing communications approaches. An alternative to employing a direct salesforce is to contract out to either an agent or a distributor. Effectively, wholesalers and retailers represent an extended salesforce to manufacturers.

The use of agents and distributors becomes a particularly attractive proposition as an organisation moves into areas further away from its home base. Using an agent or

Push promotional strategy

The focusing of promotional effort by manufacturers or suppliers of goods and services to encourage the trade channel members to stock, promote and sell products.

Pull promotional strategy

The focusing of promotional effort to encourage end-customers and consumers to demand goods and services.

distributor does, however, mean sacrificing some control over the selling operation. It is because of this feature that the **'push' strategies** identified in Chapter 19, Setting objectives, determining strategy and tactics, become so important. Not only is it necessary to devise marketing communications targeted towards end-customers (**'pull' strategies**), it is also vital to devise marketing communications targeted at the 'salesforce', especially if this 'salesforce' is external and independent. Integrated marketing communications are unlikely to be successful without combined push/pull efforts.

There are many different types of agent, manufacturer's representative and distributor. The terminology used may be country or industry dependent. Generally, the differences are recognised as follows.

Comer (1991) uses Don Coleman's definition of an agent (also known as a manufacturer's representative) as

An independent proprietor, partnership or company that represents two or more manufacturers or service organisations within a given territory on a commission basis handling related but usually non-competitive products.

The principal, or supplying organisation, is most likely to have contact with the final customer via direct delivery of product and invoicing of the customer (the agent's commission being paid separately). In other words, the agent's role is to introduce buyer and seller and facilitate the sale. There are instances in some countries or product categories, however, where an agent may stock the product or invoice the customer. The customer could be an end-customer or a distributor.

A distributor is defined as an independent proprietor, partnership or company that usually takes title to the goods, carries stock and sells on its own account. Income is earned from the margin, i.e. the difference between the purchase and sales price. They may sell goods over the counter and/or employ their own field salesforce. For a comparison of agents and distributors see Exhibit 31.8.

An organisation wishing to appoint a third party needs to consider the amount of control it wishes to retain over its products or services, and choose accordingly. Clearly, distributors have greater freedom to act independently, which may cause problems if not carefully monitored and managed. It is essential to consider the inclusion of agents and distributors in the organisation's marketing communications strategy, giving consideration to cooperative advertising and promotional campaigns as well as incentives to distributors and agents. The following discussion highlights

Exhibit 31.8 Proximity to selling companies of agents and distributors

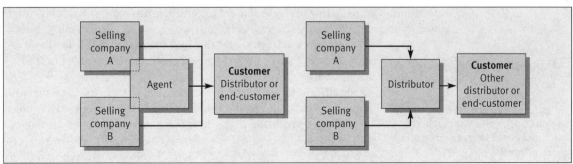

some of the factors that need to be considered as a minimum when selecting agents and distributors.

- *Geographic cover.* A company looking for an agent or distributor needs to determine which particular geographical market it wants to move into then try and find an organisation which can adequately cover this area without being too stretched.
- *Other product lines.* Consideration needs to be given to other product lines the agent or distributor is already handling (or is committed to handle in the future). For instance, a policy decision may be taken not to appoint an agent or distributor that is handling a direct competitor's products. Alternatively, it may be an advantage to be associated with a specialist firm carrying a number of similar products. Care needs to be taken to ensure the range of products handled by an agent or distributor is compatible with one's own.
- *Training and support.* A prospective agent or distributor must be able to demonstrate its provision of adequate training and support for its own salesforce in sales skills and product knowledge. Any weaknesses in this area may reflect badly on the supplier.
- *Technical ability.* Particularly for complex products, technical ability will be of great importance and careful attention will need to be paid to assessing the overall technical skills of the salesforce. It is essential to ensure the agent's or distributor's salesforce has an equal level of technical knowledge as the home salesforce.
- *Honesty and ability.* It goes without saying you should be able to trust implicitly agents or distributors you appoint – they must have absolute commercial integrity and competence to fulfil any reasonable tasks you ask.
- *Reputation.* Some effort should be made to determine the overall reputation of a potential agent or distributor by making various trade enquiries. It may be particularly helpful to enquire from other organisations using them to sell products or services.
- *Number and quality of sales representatives.* It is essential the agent or distributor has sufficient sales representatives to cover the required territory and that these are of the right calibre and quality.
- *Financial strength.* Many organisations when dealing with new customers fail to make adequate enquiries about their financial strength. This is no less important when appointing agents or distributors, and particularly so when dealing with overseas organisations.
- *Personalities.* The 'right chemistry' between the individuals in both organisations helps enormously.

Selling by telephone

Selling by telephone is generally referred to as 'telesales' which are part of the overall 'telemarketing' process which also highlights the use of call centres for telemarketing operations. Telemarketing and telesales are terms often used interchangeably but, as noted by Starkey (1997a), there are in fact four main aspects to telemarketing, namely, lead generation, telesales, building and maintaining the database, and customer care (customer carelines and crisis management) of which telesales is but one.

A significant factor in the growth of telesales, particularly for more complex products and services such as finance, is customer acceptance. This is at least partly due to the customer's increasing sophistication as a result of marketing efforts. Customers are no longer prepared to accept poor service over the telephone. The Henley Centre report (1996),

WARNING

! *Telesales and telemarketing are terms that are frequently confused. It is best to think of telesales as just one aspect of a broader range of activities that are included under the heading of telemarketing.*

NEED TO KNOW

☑ *Telesales are a cost-efficient way of communicating with customers and can support other approaches effectively. They are particularly useful for the more numerous lower value accounts.*

Teleculture 2000, states that if a single telephone call is badly handled a customer would prefer not to buy from that organisation again.

Customers can be sold to by two methods: either by calling prospective customers (outbound telesales) or by selling to customers when they call into either the company or call centre (inbound telesales). One of the earliest applications for telesales was for selling advertising space in local and regional newspapers, both for classified and display advertisements. Now virtually all newspapers and magazines use telesales for selling advertising space. Telesales has also been used for many years within the food distribution industry as it provides a cheap and cost-effective way of keeping in contact with trade customers on a regular basis. Customer contact management software provides telesales operatives instantly with full details of customer histories including what products the customer purchased most recently and the price paid.

With the increasing cost of keeping a salesforce on the road, telesales is proving to be a far more cost-effective and efficient way of keeping in contact and selling to lower value accounts. Depending on the territory and the business, a sales representative may be able to call on between five and ten customers a day, sometimes very much less. The same salesperson could make contact with far more people using the telephone. Some organisations are practising what they refer to as *telephone account management.* The Royal Mail is now using the telephone to serve some 300,000 medium-sized business customers where the turnover is less than £40,000 per year. While it is easy to justify using the telephone for low-value accounts, some organisations are now using the telephone for providing a support function to key accounts between visits by either key account executives or the key account manager.

Planning the telesales call

Planning is essential so the agent can stay in control of the telephone call. This can be achieved by providing a framework for both:

- *structure* – what to talk about,
- *process* – how to go about talking to customers.

There are two principal types of framework that can be used. *Scripts* may be the most appropriate framework for inexperienced telesales agents when dealing with basic products or taking payment details over the telephone. In the case of payment details it is most important that everything is recorded correctly and not omitted. If the agent is not careful, however, the script can appear rather 'wooden' and can easily irritate the customer at the other end of the telephone line. *Prompts,* on the other hand,

IN VIEW 31.5

Viking Direct

Viking Direct, an office supplies and stationery company, arrived in the UK from the USA in the early 1990s. From their head office and call centre in Leicester, they are able to distribute anywhere the next day within the UK mainland. Viking mail out catalogues to customers on a regular basis. Customers are then able to telephone in (inbound telesales) to place orders quoting reference numbers from the catalogues. Their telesales operations have been augmented with the use of the Internet as a 'shop window' and ordering process.

provide a much greater degree of flexibility although they should only be used by experienced telesales agents and may be more suitable when selling complex products or services. Two common types of *prompts* are:

- product planners
- bubblegrams.

Product planner prompts

Prompts or cues provided in the form of a table as guidelines to telesales operators.

Bubblegram prompts

Prompts or cues provided in the form of a picture or map as guidelines to telesales operators. So called because the prompts are shown as interlinking 'bubbles' of ideas, statements or questions.

The **product planner** provides information for the telesales agent in table format. Care must be taken, however, not to just read information from the table just as if it were a list. The **bubblegram**, on the other hand, provides information for the telesales agent in pictorial format and can be regarded as a map or flow chart with no particular starting point. Exhibit 31.9 shows an example bubblegram for selling a portable printer. The printer is in the bubble at the centre of the diagram and is linked to other bubbles which contain possible upgrades or facts that may be relevant to the potential purchaser.

Exhibit 31.9 Bubblegram for a portable printer and options

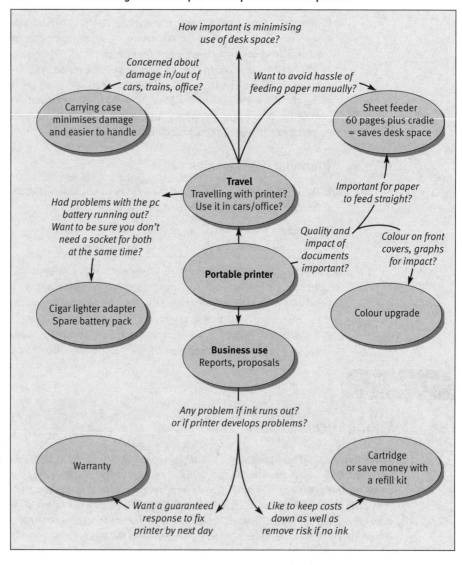

In-house, buy in or both?

Most telemarketing and telesales operations are carried out in-house; however, there is a trend towards a greater use of bureaux as they may be able to offer similar or better service levels. There are four basic development operations that can be considered (Starkey 1997a):

- set up an in-house operation to handle inbound and outbound calls;
- buy in all activities from a third party bureau;
- use a bureau to set up and test the operation and when running smoothly, move it in-house;
- use a bureau to set up and test the operation before moving it in-house but still retain the bureau for specific tasks.

Ethical issues

Telesales has in the past had a poor reputation. Steps have now been taken to clean up the industry image. For instance, there is now the Telephone Preference Service where customers can register if they do not want to receive unsolicited telephone calls. The Direct Marketing Association has also produced clear guidelines regarding use of the telephone and these are reproduced in Exhibit 31.10.

Exhibit 31.10 DMA guidelines for selling by telephone

1	The name of the organisation on whose behalf a sales, marketing or service call is made or received shall be voluntarily and promptly disclosed.
2	The purpose of the call shall be clearly stated early in the conversation.
3	Telephone marketers shall not evade the truth or deliberately mislead.
4	Sales, marketing or service calls shall not be executed in the guise of research or a survey.
5	Calls should normally be made between the hours of 8.00am and 9.00pm.
6	Telephone marketers shall avoid the use of high pressure tactics which could be construed as harassment.

Salesforce motivation – the negative role of commission

Rackham et al. (1991) argue that in traditional sales management great emphasis is placed on the importance of motivating the salesforce. In interviews with successful major account managers, caution over the subject is evident. The authors state,

> In general, most motivation tools such as incentive payments, prizes, or motivational speakers do a much better job of helping people work harder than helping them work smarter. We might, for example, persuade you to put in an additional hour a day, or to make five more sales calls per month, by offering you double your present salary. By using money in this way as a motivational tool, we can probably motivate you to work harder. But whether we double your salary or quadruple it, we're unlikely to cause you to work smarter.   (Rackham et al. 1991)

Paying people commission or increasing their commission might persuade people to work harder but it is not necessarily able to persuade them to work smarter. In addition, paying people by commission communicates a certain message to customers, namely, we are rewarding our salespeople on the basis of how much they can sell to you, not whether what they sell to you is what you actually need or want.

Customers in the past have been suspicious of salespeople because they fear being oversold to or sold the wrong products. Removing this cause of suspicion should, therefore, help in building relationships between suppliers and their customers. This would also assist in changing the image of a firm being 'sales driven' to 'customer focused'. Paying salespeople purely on a commission basis is ineffective if a company wants long-term high performance coupled with quality business. If they have to resort to *heavy duty 'carrots'* then they may have the wrong product, have not considered customers' real needs or they are too focused on short-term results.

IN VIEW 31.6

The pensions mis-selling scandal

The pensions mis-selling scandal is clear proof that commission selling pays no regard to customer requirements. An article in *The Financial Times* of 20 March 1997 stated,

> *The debacle has arisen because commission hungry salesmen persuaded thousands of people to leave generous occupational schemes for personal pensions in the late 1980s and early 1990s.*

The managing director of a pensions advisory firm (fee charging) is quoted in *The Sunday Times* of 9 March as saying,

> *In any job you have to demonstrate your worth to the client and a consumer can never be comfortable with the quality of advice if the guy giving the advice only gets paid if he makes the sale.*

The rationale for commission selling can be traced back to F.W. Taylor's 'Principles of Scientific Management' and B.F. Skinner's work on behaviourism. Taylor believed that people should be carefully monitored and motivated with a variety of carrots and sticks. Skinner did his research with rats and pigeons and then applied most of his theories to people. Douglas McGregor proposed two contrasting theories of management: Theory X states the assumption is that people are lazy and will try and get away with doing as little as possible unless you extrinsically motivate them to care about the job they are doing; Theory Y states that no one goes to work to do a bad job and that people try to do the best they are capable of doing. Organisations talk about people being the most important assets, yet many still continue to manage, motivate and reward them based on an old-fashioned Theory X style of management. Highly respected psychologist Alfie Kohn (1997) says:

> **You can make a person do something – that's what rewards and punishment are good at for a while, but you can't make them want to do something, which is what motivation means.**

Advocates of commission selling fail to understand the difference between intrinsic motivation and extrinsic motivation. Intrinsic motivation means you like what you do for its own sake. Extrinsic motivation means you do one thing in order that another will happen. According to Kohn, intrinsic and extrinsic motivation tend to be related inversely and not additively and the more you use rewards such as commission (extrinsic motivator), the more intrinsic motivation tends to decline, so you have to keep rewarding because the intrinsic motivation has virtually gone.

IN VIEW 31.7

Marshall Industries transforms

Marshall Industries is the fourth largest distributor of electronic components in the USA and was once a typical 'sales driven' organisation with managers' rewards based on sales revenue. The result was no co-operation between districts, as one would not help another with inventory in order to close a sale and district managers would invade each other's territory.

A few years ago CEO Rob Rodin attended a four-day seminar with Dr W. Edwards Deming on Management Transformation. The company then became managed as a 'system'. Employees went onto a salary, sales went up, co-operation increased and there was a switch from focus on sales to focus on the customer.

Marshall pioneered sales via the Internet and is a leader in salesforce automation. Companies who come to Marshall to benchmark their organisation believing their own problem is a technological one, soon find out their real problem is frequently rooted in the traditional way they compensate their salespeople.

For many traditional sales-driven organisations, commission is part of the company culture. Remunerating and motivating salespeople by commission tends to be deeply ingrained. *The Sunday Times* (9 March 1997) quotes Bob Gill, Director of Corporate Affairs, Allied Dunbar,

> We have examined commission from all points of view and it is a central part of our culture. Commission is something we are wedded to. Various pilot schemes, where we have tried to do it differently, have not worked for us. Our culture promotes successful sales people and commission is the purest form of performance-related pay.

IN VIEW 31.8

Zytec Corporation switches

Zytec Corporation is a $250m turnover company in the OEM electronics business and the 1991 winner of the Malcolm Baldridge National Quality Award. They switched over to paying a straight salary in 1990. John Steel, Vice President of Sales, says the benefits of the changes to Zytec today are:

● complex quota setting and incentive compensation delivery systems are gone;
● accounts/customers can be assigned to optimise time and territory for all;
● fear, uncertainty, doubt and suspicion that surrounded incentive compensation are eliminated;
● we know we cannot 'manipulate' sales reps' behaviour by 'tuning and tweaking' the incentive compensation plan.

Nearly a year later, the Prudential, employer of the largest salesforce in the UK, changed tack from the rest of the industry and scrapped commission payments to its insurance salesforce. Caroline Merrell, writing in *The Times* (26 February 1998), reported,

> Sir Peter Davis, group chief executive, yesterday admitted that his review of the company's UK operation launched last year had revealed a change was needed to the way Prudential's 4,500 salesmen sold products. He said: 'We are changing the culture of the direct salesforce from hunters to farmers.'

Sales strategy

An integrated marketing communications approach requires that all forms of marketing communications are considered part of the overall picture, whether the communication is through personal selling, direct mail, the Internet or telemarketing. As identified earlier, the Henley Centre's *Teleculture 2000* report warned that if a single telephone call is badly handled customers would prefer not to buy from that organisation again. Other means of communication with customers such as a badly written mailshot, a 'user unfriendly' website or a poorly conducted sales call are likely to have similar repercussions or consequences. In implementing sales strategies, organisations must be aware of, and consider, whether their mode of communication is acceptable to the receivers.

Sales strategies should link to other functional strategies and be designed to meet overall corporate objectives and strategies. Wilson (1997) reports how three American academics, Strahle, Spiro and Acito, suggest sales strategies may be based upon the product portfolio analysis marketing technique of building, holding, harvesting and divesting. A number of potential sales strategies and sales activities considered to support these marketing strategies are summarised in Exhibit 31.11.

- *Build.* Building sales volume can be achieved in a number of different ways. Particular activities to existing customers might involve cross-selling and upselling or increasing contact frequency (e.g. sales visits, telesales calls, direct mail etc.) while new customer activity will involve acquisition techniques. Database building will be a key feature since the salesforce is able to provide much useful information. A major priority is customer retention – as Reichheld and Sasser (1990) remind us, cutting the customer defection rate by 5% can increase profits from between 25% to 85% depending on the industry. Acquiring new customers is comparatively expensive, taking a number of years to pay back the investment. As trust in the relationship builds between the customer and supplier, therefore, so does the opportunity to sell more or different products and services.
- *Hold.* Maintaining sales volume can be achieved by ensuring the contact frequency with customers is maintained at existing levels and by focusing on customer retention.
- *Harvest and divest.* Sales strategies for harvest and divest involve reducing selling costs by cutting inventory levels and customer contact frequency, although this may damage the customer–supplier relationship. Inventory level reduction, however, is the norm for particularly manufacturing organisations involved in just-in-time operations.

Exhibit 31.11 Sales strategies

Marketing strategy	Sales strategy	Sales activities
Build	● Build sales volume ● Increase sales volume ● Obtain premium price from 'value added' sales	● Provide high service levels, particularly in presale service ● Product market feedback ● Cross sell/upsell to existing accounts ● Target new accounts and potential accounts (lead generation and database building) ● Increase contact frequency with existing accounts ● Focus on customer retention and acquisition
Hold	● Maintain existing sales volume	● Increase support and service levels to current accounts ● Cross sell/upsell to existing accounts ● Maintain contact frequency with existing accounts ● Focus on customer retention
Harvest	● Reduce selling costs ● Selectively maintain sales volume in key accounts	● Reduce service levels ● Maintain service levels ● Eliminate unprofitable accounts ● Reduce contact frequency with existing accounts
Divest	● Clear out inventory ● Reduce selling costs	● Inventory dumping ● Eliminate service

Source: Adapted and reprinted from *CIM Handbook of Selling and Sales Strategy*, 1st Edition, Jobber, D. (ed), Butterworth-Heinemann, '*Strategic sales planning*', by Wilson, K.J., Copyright © 1997, with permission from Elsevier

Marketing communications and increasing points of customer contact

The advent of new technologies for selling and sales activities has had the effect of increasing the number of points of customer contact. Sales strategies employed by organisations now taking account of these additional distribution channels and routes to market. As Friedman and Goodrich (1998) comment,

NEED TO KNOW

☑ *Multi-channel marketing communications and sales strategies are invariably more effective and suited to customer needs than any single approach. This merely re-emphasises the significance of integrated marketing communications.*

Good products and a skilled salesforce used to be a winning formula. Today that approach seems to be more expensive, less efficient, and market-limiting than an ever-growing variety of alternative approaches, including direct mail, telemarketing, the Internet, resellers, and business partners of every conceivable variety.

Indeed, companies using the array of distribution channels to supplement direct sales are able to achieve significantly lower marketing and selling costs and yet increase their revenue growth and market coverage. The skill lies in selecting the use of multi-channels with best effect to meet customer and organisational needs. Friedman and Goodrich (1998) have identified the benefits of multi-channel strategies as cost reduction, market coverage and customer alignment. Cost reductions can be achieved by 're-segmenting' the customer base for selling purposes by the most efficient and effective channel contact, e.g. telesales can be used for lead generation and pre-selling. Market coverage can be improved by re-grouping a fragmented market of small or widely dispersed customers through the use of call centres, the Internet and distributor networks. Improved customer alignment can be achieved by allowing customers to choose the channels of communication and transaction they prefer, so enhancing their self-control – not all customers wish to be contacted more frequently by the salesforce. Banks are facilitating this type of customer alignment by encouraging contact through the post, phone, email, the Internet, cash points (their own and others), and through their network of branches.

Summary

Selling and sales management is at last evolving in line with the marketing concept. The salesforce is the main interface between organisations and their customers and the personal selling function is now receiving a higher profile with increasing emphasis on key skills such as negotiation. Indeed, a vast array of titles are now given to the sales role, according to levels of communication with the customer and complexity of sale. Furthermore, many organisations are undergoing significant changes of salesforce structure to meet their customers' needs, integrating activities such as selling by telephone with key account management and incorporating new technologies such as the use of call centres and the Internet to reflect their sales strategies, in line with their overall marketing communications plans.

Factors influencing this change emanate from both the needs of customers, who now have greater say in how they are sold to, and the selling organisation. Costs involved in running a salesforce are significant. With the adoption of new technologies coupled with the focus on retention rather than acquisition, many organisations have successfully cut the number of salespeople they employ to a minimum or strategically re-deployed them. Benefits of changes are seen, not surprisingly, by the organisation whose increased returns are the result of more effective sales management, and customers whose needs are met to their expectations. Despite the obvious advantages of an integrated approach to personal selling and sales management, barriers to change remain. Motivation of the salesforce is a significant bone of contention with all but a few notable exceptions realising that a change in emphasis away from incentivising high sales will result in stronger and longer relationships with customers.

Self-review questions

1 What has been the *major* shift in the role of the sales function in recent years?

2 Donaldson has classified 12 different selling situations. What are they?

3 In what ways can salesforces be structured?

4 Identify the seven different stages in traditional selling.

5 How does SPIN® differ from the traditional model of selling? Why is this better?

6 Describe each of the development stages in key account management.

7 Why is it increasingly popular for organisations to sell by telephone? What are the advantages and disadvantages?

8 How might abolishing financial incentives for the salesforce be of benefit to the organisation?

9 What are the selling activities associated with the four main marketing strategies of Build, Hold, Harvest and Divest outlined in this chapter?

Project

Using an organisation with which you are familiar, chart how it structures and organises itself for the sales function. Consider the range of agents, distributors and customers it has and how it defines and groups these. Evaluate the different selling and marketing communications methods it uses and how it focuses these on the different groupings. How well integrated does the whole activity appear to be? Does the organisation use a database to facilitate its sales activities? Assess how well the organisation's selling activities are integrated with its other marketing communications. What advice would you give to the organisation for improvement?

References

Abberton Associates (1997), *Balancing the Selling Equation: Revisited.* Abberton Associates.

Adcock, D., Bradfield, R., Halborg, A.I. and Ross, C. (1995), *Marketing Principles and Practice* 2nd edn. Pitman Publishing.

Anderson, R. (1995), *Essentials of Personal Selling.* Prentice Hall.

Andes, R.H. (1992), Message dimensions of negotiation. *Negotiation Journal,* 8 (2), 125–130.

Carlisle, J.A. and Parker, R.C. (1989), *Beyond Negotiation: Redeeming Customer–Supplier Relationships.* John Wiley and Sons, pp. 35–36.

Chonko, L., Enis, B.M. and Tanner, J.F. (1992), *Managing Salespeople.* Allyn and Bacon.

Comer, J.M. (1991), Selling and Sales Management. Allyn and Bacon.

Donaldson, B. (1990), *Sales Management: Theory and Practice.* Macmillan.

Donaldson, B. (1998), *Sales Management: Theory and Practice* 2nd edn. Macmillan.

Friedman, L.G. and Goodrich, G. (1998), Sales strategy in a multiple channel environment. *Journal of Selling and Major Account Management,* 1 (1).

Hannon, M. (1995), *Consultative Selling™: The Hanan Formula for High Margin Selling at High Levels* 5th edn. AMACOM.

Hatton, A. (1998), *Marketing Success: Tactical Management.* Chartered Institute of Marketing.

The Henley Centre (1996), *Teleculture 2000.* The Henley Centre Report.

Huthwaite Research Group (1998), *Negotiation Skills Trainer Manual.* Huthwaite Research Group (unpublished).

Kohn, A. (1997), Why performance based pay cannot work. *Proceedings of the 10th Annual Conference of British Deming Association,* National Motorcycle Museum, Birmingham, 14 May.

Kotler, P. and Armstrong, G. (1991), *Principles of Marketing* 5th edn. Prentice Hall.

Lancaster, G. and Jobber, D. (1997), *Selling and Sales Management* 4th edn. Pitman Publishing.

McCarthy, E.J. and Perrault, W.D. (1990), *Basic Marketing* 10th edn. Irwin.

McDonald, M., Millman, T. and Rogers, B. (1996), *Key Account Management – Learning From Supplier and Customer Perspectives.* Cranfield School of Management.

McGregor, D. (1960), *Human Side of Enterprise*. McGraw-Hill.

Millman, T. and Wilson, K.J. (1995), From key account selling to key account management. *Journal of Marketing Practice Applied Marketing Science,* 1, 9–21.

Millman, T. and Wilson, K.J. (1997), Defining key account attractiveness in business-to-business markets. Paper presented at the 33rd Annual Conference of National Account Managers Association, Fort Lauderdale, Florida, April.

Murrey, J.S. (1986), Understanding competing theories of negotiation. *Negotiation Journal,* 2 (April), 179–186.

Rackham, N. (1990), *Making Major Sales*. Gower.

Rackham, N. (1995), *SPIN Selling*. Gower.

Rackham, N., Friedman, L. and Ruff, R. (1991), *Getting Partnering Right: How Market Leaders Are Creating Long-Term Competitive Advantage*. McGraw-Hill.

Reichheld, E.F. and Sasser, W.E. (1990), *Zero Defections Quality Comes to Services. Harvard Business Review*, Sept/Oct.

Shapiro, B.P., Rangon, K., Moriarty, R.T. and Ross, E.B. (1987). In Millman, T. and Wilson, K. (1997), Defining key account attractiveness in business-to-business markets. Paper presented at the 33rd Annual Conference of National Account Managers Association, Fort Lauderdale, Florida, April.

Starkey, M.W. (1997a), Telemarketing. In *CIM Handbook of Selling and Sales Strategy* (Jobber, D., ed.). Butterworth-Heinemann.

Starkey, M.W. (1997b), Moving away from commission based remuneration for sales people. *Institute of Directors Conference,* 19 June, London.

Starkey, M.W. (1997c), Out of Commission. *Salesforce,* 22 September.

Wilson, K.J. (1993), Managing the industrial salesforce of the 1990s. *Journal of Marketing Management,* 9, 123–139.

Wilson, K.J. (1997), Strategic sales planning. In *CIM Handbook of Selling and Sales Strategy* (Jobber, D., ed.). Butterworth-Heinemann.

Winkler, J. (1993), *Winning Sales and Marketing Tactics*. Butterworth-Heinemann.

 ## Selected further reading

Jobber, D. (ed.) (1997), *CIM Handbook of Selling and Sales Strategy*. Butterworth-Heinemann.

A la carte/specialist agency Agency offering limited, specialist services in a specific area of marketing communications.

A&P budget Allocation of expenditure on advertising and promotions.

ABC See Audit Bureau of Circulation.

ABC//electronic ABC, which was founded in 1931, has helped legitimise press as an advertising medium through the independent auditing of circulation. Established in 1996, ABC//electronic aims to do the same for the Internet by auditing Internet sites and traffic data using internationally agreed standards.

ABC1 Popularly used market segment, measured by the socio-economic measure of occupation of the head of the household. (Also see Socio-economic segmentation.)

Above-the-line communications Term used to generally describe advertising promotions: that is, promotions that make use of commission-paying mass media – television, press, cinema, radio and posters. Also called above-the-line promotions and above-the-line advertising.

AC Nielsen-Meal Source of information on competitor media use and expenditure.

Account managers Also called account handlers, account executives and account directors. People who work within agencies and whose primary role is to interface between the client and the agency.

Account planners Agency people responsible for developing a clear understanding of the market situation in which marketing communications will take place. Involves research and knowledge of the market, relevant buying processes and the client's position. Account planners will use this knowledge to assist in planning for marketing communications.

ACORN ACORN stands for 'A Classification Of Residential Neighbourhoods'. It is a commercially available geodemographic system. A range of ACORN systems are available that cover different groupings.

Activity based costing A costing approach which endeavours to include all factors in determining the total cost of any specific business activity. Unlike 'full costing' all costs are allocated to specific tasks rather than relying on allocations of overheads.

Adaptation The process of acclimatisation to messages in which changes in the perceptual filtering process take place over time.

Adaptation strategy Marketing communications messages and media that are changed from country to country to better suit the particular requirements of individual markets.

Advertising The use of paid mass media, by an identified sponsor, to deliver marketing communications to target audiences.

Advertising Effectiveness Awards These awards are given as recognition of those campaigns judged to have proven their effectiveness. They represent examples of excellent marketing communications practice.

Advertising equivalent Measure of public relations coverage whereby an estimate is made of what the coverage would have cost if it had been paid for at advertising rates.

Advertorials Advertisements that are designed to look as though they are editorial.

Ad-wearout The impact of an advertisement (or as may apply to any other form of marketing communications) as it declines when it is repeated.

Aesthetics Attractive appearance.

Affordable method Budgeting system whereby budgets are determined not on what needs to be done but on what the organisation believes it can afford at the time.

Agency group Network of agencies working together.

Agency pitch Short for agency sales pitch, the pitch is an opportunity for an agency to present itself, its ideas and proposed solutions to a client's brief, usually in competition with other shortlisted agencies for the chance of winning the client's business.

Agents Term used here to describe all individuals and organisations involved in the marketing communications process within and external to the organisation.

AIDA model Marketing communications concept that models the stages through which marketing communications should move a potential customer: Awareness, Interest, Desire and Action. It is one of a number of hierarchy-of-effects models. (Also see Hierarchy of effects.)

AILA information processing framework See Hierarchy of effects.

AIMRITE Acronym used to assist the evaluation and selection of media for direct marketing communications, referring to Audience, Impact, Message, Response, Internal management, and The End result.

AIO inventory Collection of Attitudes, Interests and Opinion statements used to assess respondents' views.

Allegory Message that is used to symbolise a deeper meaning.

AMBA model Media planning process model that includes Audience, Media, Buying and Assessment.

Ambient advertising and media According to Concord – the specialist outdoor agency that claims to have first defined the terms – ambient advertising is any non-traditional, out-of-home advertising which by definition utilises less usual external media, such as laser projections, or the use of fields into which messages are cut.

Ambush marketing Organisation's intentional effort to weaken the effect of another's sponsorship.

Analysis and evaluation cycle Part of the process of using the stream of information in the RABOSTIC planning model.

Animatics Animated version of the storyboard.

Arbitrary method Term given to the setting of budgets with little justification or obvious valid criteria.

Art directors Those responsible for producing creative ideas and visual designs. Typically work in partnership with copywriters.

Artwork Traditionally artwork takes the form of a pasted-down bromide onto a base board. It is the final preparation before conversion into the final printed material. Digital processes can now be used to replace traditional finished artwork.

Aspirational self-image Self-image as one would like to be.

ATMs Automated Telling Machines: cash point machines.

ATR model Three-stage process of behaviour involving the movement from Awareness to Trial to Repeat behaviour. (Also see Hierarchy of effects.)

Attitude (1) Comprising three components: Cognitive-Affective-Conative (thinking-feeling-doing), an attitude is considered to be relatively enduring and results in a consistent response to given internal or external stimuli.

Attitude (2) Katz four functions for attitudes Utilitarian function, value expressive function, knowledge function, ego-defence function.

Audit Bureau of Circulation (ABC) Organisation that certifies audited net sales of publications. ABC figures, which are reported in BRAD, indicate the actual number of copies of a publication in circulation. Basically, the circulation figure is calculated by deducting returned copies from the number originally distributed. Audited circulation can be considered a fair reflection of the number of copies actually being read.

Automated call distributor Electronic system by which telephone calls can be routed to appropriate departments or contacts without the need for direct human contact.

Awareness set A proportion of possible choices in a decision.

Banded pack Pack of products strapped or banded together.

Banner advertisement Type of advertisement often appearing as a banner across the whole or part of the width of a web page.

BARB Broadcasters' Audience Research Board. This body, established in 1980 and jointly owned by the BBC and ITV, is responsible for producing information on TV viewing activity and audience reaction. Electronic meters and diaries from over 4400 nationally representative households are used to record the information.

BCG Matrix See Boston Consulting Group Matrix.

Behavioural paradigm of buyer behaviour Proponents of this paradigm generally believe that to find out what is going on in the mind of an individual is not achievable. The behaviourist approach suggests that buyer behaviour is a function of past learned experiences (behaviour) and stimuli that are predominantly found in the environment. Behavioural theorists believe that marketing communications activity should be focused on creating the correct environmental cues for the individual and on monitoring the responses to these cues as a guide to future activity.

Behavioural segmentation Segmentation based on behavioural characteristics towards particular goods or service categories.

Below-the-line communications Marketing communications that make use of the non-commission-paying media in all their forms, i.e. all forms of promotions other than advertising. Sometimes, incorrectly, it is referred to as below-the-line advertising. Although it remains a popular term, its usefulness is limited as it encompasses such a broad range of promotional activity.

Body copy Body copy is the term given for the main text or words. Usually, body copy is brief but some creative treatments require a lot of information to be disseminated. (Also see Headlines.)

BOGOF Buy One Get One Free.

Bonus pack Special offer pack containing something extra either in or on pack.

Boston Consulting Group (BCG) Matrix Method of assessing an organisation's range or portfolio of products or SBU's in terms of their relative positions in a matrix or grid that plots each product's relative market share (as measured against the market leader, or if leader, nearest follower) against the market growth rate. First developed by the Boston Consulting Group.

Bottom-up budgeting System whereby overall budgets are set by aggregating the individual budgets set by lower management and passed to senior management for approval.

BRAD *British Rate and Data*; monthly publication that presents cost, circulation and technical information on all significant publications that offer advertising space (and readership details of some of them). Brief details are also presented on the other mass media and media information of general interest. It is used as a major reference source within the industry. Other BRAD products include the BRAD Media Selector, BRAD Agencies and Advertisers, and BRAD Direct Marketing.

Brand The totality of what the consumer takes into consideration before making a purchase decision.

Brand equity The value of the brand's name, symbols, associations and reputation to all target audiences who interact with it.

Brand identity The cues used to convey the brand personality to create the brand image.

Brand image The perception of the brand held by the market.

Brand loyalty The degree of loyalty a customer has towards a brand in favouring it over other alternatives. It is something that companies endeavour to encourage but given the competitive environment frequently find that customers are not so loyal to a single brand.

Brand map A graphical representation of competing brands in relation to one another based on people's perceptions. Also called position maps and perceptual maps.

Brand parity Situation where brands are seen as being equivalent.

Brand personality The fundamental essence of the brand.

Brand value The financial expression of brand equity.

Brand values The meaning or meanings that the brand generates in the minds of its target audiences.

Branding Strategy to differentiate products and companies, and to build economic value for both the consumer and the brand owner.

Branding strategies Typically four main branding strategies are identified: corporate umbrella branding, family umbrella branding, range branding and individual branding.

Broadcast Widely and publicly available radio and television transmissions.

Broadcast sponsorship Sponsorship of a particular TV or radio programme.

Bromide Photographic production of original artwork used as a basis in the subsequent print production process.

Bubblegram prompts Prompts or cues provided in the form of a picture or map as guidelines to telesales operators. So called because the prompts are shown as interlinking 'bubbles' of ideas, statements or questions.

Burst Media-scheduling approach in which expenditure is concentrated into a relatively short period. The advantage can be to create a greater impact.

CAA Cinema Advertising Association; responsible for much of the data on cinema audiences. Information on cinema-going is also collected as part of the NRS data.

Call centre Central resource that groups personnel together for telemarketing, both outbound (sales calls to customers and potential customers, or relationship marketing activities) and inbound (customers, responding to direct response advertising, customers requiring service).

Calls to action Many promotions require that the target is encouraged to take some form of action; ring a freephone number, fill in a coupon, request more information, collect tokens, try a sample, buy a product, request a sales visit, etc. These are calls to action that should be facilitated within the promotion where they are applicable.

Capacity model of attention Model developed by Kahneman that recognises only limited attention can be given to all the stimuli available in the environment. People have only limited information processing resources. For this reason, emphasis tends to be placed on the need for marketing communications to attract attention.

CAPI Computer Assisted Personal Interviewing.

Captions Captions are short descriptions of text or visuals and help to break up the body copy in layout terms.

Captious cues The ambiguous, misleading or deceptive use of country of origin product identifiers (cues).

Carelines Mechanisms, usually telephone but could be other facilities such as fax and email, to help facilitate easy communications between an organisation and its customers.

CATI Computer Assisted Telephone Interviewing.

Cause-related marketing A commercial activity by which businesses and charities or caused form a partnership with each other to market an image, product or service for mutual benefit.

Cause-related sales promotions Sales promotions linked to a worthy cause.

CD-ROM and DVD Compact Disc Read-Only Memory and Digital Video Disk. These are laser-read disks containing huge quantities of digital information.

Celebrity endorsement The use of a well-known person to promote a company or product brand. (Also see Ohanian's celebrity endorser credibility scale.)

Centrifugal forces Country-level forces external to an organisation 'pushing' it to adapt marketing programmes.

Centripetal forces Internal organisational forces (e.g. policy, structure, culture, economies of scale) 'pulling' an organisation to standardise marketing programmes.

Circulation The number of copies of a publication circulated in the market. Audited circulation figures are preferable as they are certified as accurate (see ABC), and represent the number of copies distributed less the number of copies returned to the publisher.

Classified advertising Advertisements that appear in the classified sections of the mass media.

Client brief Usually a written document, but could be presented verbally, outlining relevant background information and the principal marketing communications task to be undertaken.

CMYK inks Cyan, magenta, yellow and black (key) are the primary inks used in printing. As these inks are used in wet proofing, it ensures a true representation of the colour to be delivered.

Cognitive dissonance Term coined by Leon Festinger to describe a psychological state in which there is some incongruity (dissonance) between two or more thoughts. The resulting inconsistency encourages individuals to modify their thoughts to be more compatible or harmonious. Dissonance when recognised is an unstable state of mind.

Cognitive learning Learning by thinking through a problem or task.

Cognitive paradigm of buyer behaviour Focuses on the individual's thought processes when making purchasing decisions. The cognitive paradigm sees consumer choice as a problem-solving and decision-making sequence of activities, the outcome of which is determined principally by the buyer's intellectual functioning, and rational, goal-directed processing of information.

Commission rebating Arrangement between a client and its advertising agency (or media independent) whereby some of the media commission the agency receives is passed on to the client by way of a discount on media costs.

Commission-earning system System of payment in which advertising agencies are paid commission for booking media on behalf of clients.

Communication Transactional process between two or more parties whereby meaning is exchanged through the intentional use of signs and symbols.

Communications loop The two-way nature of communications from sender to receiver and back again.

Comparative advertising Advertising in which competing products are compared.

Competitive parity method Budgeting system whereby budgets are set based on competitors' expenditures, which might be equalled or used to set at an appropriate proportion.

Competitive positioning The communication of how a brand is different from the competition in terms of key consumer choice criteria.

Computer-aided sales support The electronic systems for direct access to customer and product data by the sales team.

Concept boards (Also known as mood boards.) Collection of visual materials (e.g. drawings, collage, montage) to replace or complement a written description that reflects the essence of a product or its customers/consumers.

Connotative meaning A meaning that is not shared.

Consumer ethnocentrism Consumer beliefs about the appropriateness and morality of buying foreign products.

Consumer involvement The degree to which consumers involve themselves in the whole consumption process. Although it is commonly referred to as 'consumer' involvement, it is best thought of as 'customer' involvement, and relates to the level of involvement with which the customer engages in the purchase decision. Involvement can vary significantly, depending upon product category and the customer's level of interest or predisposition. Levels of involvement can vary from high (e.g. purchase of a car) to low (e.g. purchase of a chocolate bar).

Contacts Any personal or non-personal communication between selected target audience members and the organisation.

Continuum of integrated marketing communications Concept that emphasises that integration of marketing communications occurs to different degrees, and that greater benefits accrue from greater integration. The continuum also emphasises that separation between marketing communications elements can give rise to negative consequences.

Contract proof Proof that print buyer and printer agree shows an acceptable quality of print.

Cooper's creative planning cycle Consists of six stages: Familiarise, Hypothesise, Synthesise and inspire, Optimise, Evaluate, and Review.

Copy platform The basic verbal or written message to be conveyed.

Copywriters Those responsible for producing creative ideas and marketing communications text or 'copy'. Typically work in partnership with art directors.

Corporate brand Term given to represent the organisation as a brand.

Corporate communications Marketing and other business communications about the organisation to selected target audiences.

Corporate guardians Means of describing those people who are responsible for ensuring consistency in corporate communications and the well-being of an organisation.

Corporate identity The basis upon which the organisation is known and understood, and the means by which corporate personality is expressed.

Corporate image The impression of an organisation, created by the corporate identity, as perceived by the target audiences.

Corporate marketing public relations/product marketing public relations Two areas of marketing public relations focused towards the corporate and product brands respectively.

Corporate personality The composite organisational traits, characteristics and spirit.

Corporate public relations (CPR) Those parts of public relations not directly concerned with a marketing or brand focus but take a broader corporate or whole business perspective.

Corporate social responsibility A business philosophy that recognises the social, cultural and environmental consequences of business practices and subsequently demonstrates actions that appear to further some social good, beyond the interests of the firm and that which is required by law.

Corporate umbrella branding The organisation and all its products are branded under the same corporate name, for example Heinz.

Corrective advertising The requirement for advertisers to produce promotional material to correct any previous advertising considered to be misleading or incorrect.

Cost per thousand (CPT) Measure of media efficiency; represents the cost of achieving a given coverage. Different media vehicles can be compared to determine which are likely to be best at reaching the target audience at least cost. Cost per thousand is an important measure, but the media decision may not always be based on the lowest-cost option, as other factors of effectiveness have to be considered. Valued impressions is a refinement of the cost per thousand calculation. VIPs are calculated by assigning 'weights' to the various components of the target audience. For example, all housewives might be included in the target audience. However, it may be decided that housewives with children are of greater interest. It would be possible to assign a weight of, say, 60 to housewives with children and 40 to those without children to represent their relative importance. The housewives with children would then contribute more to the resulting cost per thousand calculation than those with no children.

Country of origin image The sum of beliefs, ideas and impressions that a person holds of products of a specific country.

Coverage Another term for reach.

Creative brief Document that provides an outline of the creative task and the basis for creatives to develop their solutions.

Creative hot shops Agencies specialising in creative ideas and solutions, other aspects of campaigns being handled by other agencies.

Creative methods Creatives make use of a variety of techniques to aid the creative process; these include juxtaposition, free association, convergent thinking, divergent thinking, lateral thinking, brainstorming, experimentation, and the use of swipe files.

Creative scope The extent of creative flexibility afforded by the medium.

Creative theme/concept The basic or fundamental creative idea to be conveyed.

Creatives General term for art directors, designers and copywriters. Responsible for developing creative and design solutions.

Credentials presentation An opportunity for selected agencies to present details of their backgrounds, history and achievements in order to convince a potential client to include them on its agency selection shortlist.

Credibility The degree to which communications are believed.

Crisis management The planned management response to potentially damaging circumstances.

Cross-category promotion scheme Form of joint loyalty promotion involving organisations from different product categories. Frequently, customers earn points from a variety of suppliers, which are added together for later redemption.

Cross-selling Selling other products to existing customers.

Culture Hollensen has defined culture as the accumulation of shared meanings, rituals, norms and traditions among the members of an organisation or society. It is what defines a human community, its individuals, its social organisations as well as its economic and political system. It includes both abstract ideas such as values and ethics, as well as material objects and services such as clothing, food, art and sports that are produced or valued by a group of people.

Cumulative effect Describes the situation where increasing marketing communications activity builds up the effects it creates: the greater the marketing communications, the greater the effect (at least up to a point).

Customer contact management The strategic and tactical tasks involved in the management of positive, 'personal' communication between an organisation and its customers; recognising this should be complementary to image and brand management.

Customer information and service The systems in place to allow customers to contact the organisation quickly and easily.

Customer lifetime value The total estimated revenue that a customer is expected to be worth to a company usually expressed as Net Present Value (NPV) i.e. after discounting for inflation.

Customer loyalty This concept is usually taken to mean the degree of loyalty a customer has towards a brand or an organisation. It is something that companies endeavour to encourage but given the competitive environment frequently find that customers are not so loyal to a single brand or organisation. An alternative perspective is to reverse the consideration and think about the degree of loyalty a company has towards its customers. (Also see Brand loyalty.)

Customer relationship management (CRM) Also known as customer relationship marketing although some authors attempt to draw some distinctions between the two. It is a view that emphasises the importance of the relationships developed between an organisation and its customers. It involves the strategic and tactical management tasks to achieve positive communications and long-term customer relationships. (Also see Customer/audience relationship management and Relationship marketing.)

Customer/audience relationship management (CARM) This extends the CRM concept to a wider range of audience groups than just customers that integrated marketing communications need to address. It involves the strategic and tactical management tasks to achieve positive ongoing communications and long-term relationships between an organisation and its audiences. (Also see Customer relationship management.)

Customisation strategy The development of individual marketing communications specifically designed for each country.

Cybermarketing Term used to describe marketing activities using e-media.

DAGMAR model In proposing DAGMAR (Define Advertising Goals for Measured Advertising Results), Russell Colley emphasised the importance of measuring advertising effectiveness against predetermined advertising objectives or goals. The same proposition is equally relevant for all forms of marketing communications. (Also see Hierarchy of effects.)

Database Collection of data, usually on computer, stored to provide useful, convenient and interactive access to information.

Database management The interactive management and maintenance of accurate customer and prospect customer information, competitor information, market information, and internal company information.

Database marketing The use of accurate customer and prospect customer information, competitor information, market information and internal company information stored on a computer database to focus marketing activities towards targets.

Database technology The use of accurate customer and prospect customer information, competitor information, market information and internal company information stored on a computer database to focus marketing activities towards targets.

Deal loyalists Customers who purchase a brand only when it is on special promotion, and switch between brands to purchase those on 'deal'.

Decision-making The process the decision-maker goes through in arriving at a final decision. Decision-making can involve the use of thoughts and feelings, and can be affected by others and previous behaviour.

Decision-Making Unit (DMU) Also known as the Decision Making Group, the DMU concept recognises the involvement of a range of people in the decision-making process. The group may be formally organised, such as in a business-to-business purchase context, but more frequently is an unorganised group that influences the decision to buy. The DMU comprises a number of 'players' that may have an effect on the purchase outcome e.g. influencers, gatekeeper, specifier, decider, buyer and user.

Decoding The process of converting a message into meaning.

Demographic changes – Changes in basic population characteristics such as occur over time in social class constitution and age ranges.

Demographic segmentation Segmentation based on general population characteristics.

Denotative meaning A meaning that is the same for everybody.

Deontology The idea that there are absolute moral rights and wrongs.

Diffusion of innovation See Innovation diffusion.

Digital printing Process in which digital computer files are sent directly to the printing press, eliminating the need for intermediate stages of production.

Dimensions of integrated marketing communications Many facets are involved in the integration of marketing communications. These different aspects are referred to here as the dimensions of integrated marketing communications.

Diminishing returns effect Describes the situation where increases in marketing communications activities have a positive but reducing effect with each successive extra effort or increase spend.

Direct mail The use of postal services to deliver marketing communications materials. It may be considered an aspect of advertising in that it is used as a mass medium even though it can be used for individually targeted messages. It should not be confused with direct marketing, which is a much broader concept.

Direct response advertisements Advertisements that contain the means by which a direct response may be made by the reader, viewer or listener: e.g. an email address, a coupon, or a telephone/fax number.

Direct response marketing Marketing system based on individual customer records held on a database. These records are the basis for marketing analysis, planning, implementation of programmes, and control of all this activity. This system ensures a focus on marketing to customers rather than on the marketing of products.

Display copy These are the words that appear in larger or bolder type than the main text (body copy) to attract attention and allow it to flow from the headline to the body copy.

Disposable and discretionary incomes The sums of money available to people to spend after other committed expenditure (e.g. mortgage and tax payments) has been paid.

Dissonance See Cognitive dissonance.

Distribution date Final date by which finished printed material has to be complete and available for distribution.

Dominance and share of voice Relative concept in which it is possible to assess the impact being made by one competitor compared with another. The competitor with the greatest marketing communications impact would be seen to be the most dominant. It is similar to the notion of 'The one who shouts the loudest will be the one who is heard the best'. Although dominance or greatest 'share of voice' is often associated with the highest-spending competitor, dominance can be achieved by creating greater marketing communications impact through superior creativity and media choice. This is akin to the notion 'The one who is heard the best is the one who is clearest'. Measures of dominance can

include quantitative measures such as size of spend and GRPs, or qualitative assessments of impact.

DPS Double page spread – an advertisement that spans two pages across an open magazine or newspaper.

Drip Media-scheduling approach in which expenditure is spread in relatively small amounts over the campaign period. The advantage can be to create presence over a longer period with a given budget.

Duplication When using a range of media, it is likely that two or more media will be seen or heard by the same person. This is known as duplication. This has the advantage of increasing the OTS/OTH and thereby increasing frequency (the number of times a marketing communication message may be received) but also has the effect of reducing the net reach.

Econometric modelling The use of mathematical techniques to determine the effects of changes in marketing communications on sales and profits.

Economy When undertaking any marketing communications activity, this has to be done within resource constraints. Greatest effect is sought even within a limited budget. (Also see Efficiency and Effectiveness.)

Effective reach Refinement of the reach calculation. *Effective* reach is concerned with reaching target audience members with a minimum frequency, and thereby with impact. Only those target audience members who receive the marketing communication a specified number of times would be included in the effective reach measurement.

Effectiveness It is important to be effective integrated marketing communications. This may be simply described as 'doing the right things'. (Also see Efficiency.)

Efficiency It is important to achieve efficiency in integrated marketing communications. This may be simply described as 'doing things right'. (Also see Effectiveness.)

Elaboration Likelihood Model Proposed by Petty and Cacioppo, the Elaboration Likelihood Model recognises that individuals are sometimes willing to think very carefully about a piece of marketing communication and sometimes hardly think about it at all. The degree of amount of thoughtful consideration in these circumstances is called *elaboration*. It represents the amount of effort the recipients are willing to put in for themselves and, in this way, add to the communication by bringing in their own thoughts, attitudes, feelings and experiences. The nature and amount of elaboration will have an impact on the persuasiveness of the communication.

Electronic data interchange (EDI) Method of transferring data from computer to computer.

Electronic inks and electronic paper Mechanism of producing text and images by using small electronic impulses on special 'paper' that changes colour in response to electrical charges.

Electronic marketing The utilisation of the Internet to transact business; also known as e-commerce.

E-media Any digital, interactive or online communication platform such as the Internet, interactive TV and electronic multimedia.

Encoding The process of creating intended meaning in a message.

Enumeration districts Small collections of households or properties based on census data collection.

EPOS Electronic Point of Sale.

Ethnocentrism The practice of assuming that others think and believe as we do.

Evoked set Limited selection of choices brought to mind and from among which a final selection may be made.

Exhibitions and trade shows Temporary events for the purpose of displaying and/or selling products; usually based around a particular theme, product category or customer grouping. They are principally designed to bring together potential buyers and sellers under one roof.

Experiential appeals The brand's appeals to the consumers' desire for sensory pleasure, variety and cognitive stimulation.

Experiential learning Learning through behaviour and experience. Learning by doing.

Exposure Equivalent to opportunities to see or hear. An exposure is the placing of an item of marketing communication in a media vehicle that the target audience is *expected* to see or hear. It is therefore the *opportunity* to see or hear.

Extensive problem-solving Part of the decision-making process in which the decision is extended owing to the perceived complexity of the final decision.

Extranet Application of an intranet that permits access to specific users outside an organisation's normal intranet while still preventing access by the general public.

Eye movement camera Equipment used for evaluating advertisements in print. A special camera is used to track a respondent's eye movement as an advertisement is scanned. A line tracks all movement and in this way a clear indication is given as to which parts of the advertisement are looked at and by how much.

Family Life Cycle Consists of stages as the partnership and family develop including: Batchelor stage, Newly weds, Full nest 1, Full nest 2, Full nest 3, Empty nest 1, Empty nest 2, Solitary survivor (working), Solitary survivor (retired). With the increasing incidence of single parents, separations and divorces, new categories to represent these situations could be considered.

Family umbrella branding The organisation has a corporate brand and a separate brand for its products, for example Marks & Spencer's St Michael brand.

Fee-based remuneration A method of charging a client for work rendered based on a set agreed sum of money (a fee).

Feedback This occurs when there is two-way communication, so that communications flow between sender and audience and back again.

Film Where used, part of the print production process involving photographic reproduction.

FMCG Fast-moving consumer goods – typified, for example, by such products as soap powders, cosmetics, sweets and crisps.

4Cs It is proposed that integrated marketing communications should have Coherence, Consistency, and Continuity and should be Complementary.

4Es It is proposed that integrated marketing communications should be Enhancing, Economical, Efficient and Effective.

4Ps Way of classifying the marketing mix into four categories: Product, Price, Promotion and Place.

Frequency Measure of the number of times, on average, that a member of the target audience is *exposed* to a message (or more accurately, the media). It is generally presumed that if someone is exposed to the medium, she or he is exposed to the marketing communication message. Frequency is one of the four most significant concepts in media planning, along with reach, media cost and impact, in achieving marketing communications success. Frequency is measured by Opportunities to See (OTS) or Opportunities to Hear (OTH).

Full service agency Term used to describe agencies that claim to offer complete marketing communications solutions. Through-the-line and one-stop shop agencies are associated terms.

Full-display advertisements Advertisements that take advantage of the full creative opportunities afforded by the press media.

Functional appeals The communication of the brand's specific attributes or benefits capable of solving consumers' current consumption-related problems.

Functional silos The barriers erected between functions and departments that tend to cause separation between functional groups.

Geodemographic segmentation Method of segmenting the market based on the classification of small geographic areas (enumeration districts) according to the characteristics of their inhabitants – principally house types and house locations.

Geographic segmentation Segmentation based on location measures.

Global niche strategy Strategy for standardised marketing communications that focus on similar niche groups across countries.

Global strategy Strategy that is based on taking advantage of cultural similarities to produce standardised, global marketing communications.

Global village Term coined by Marshall McLuhan to describe the way in which communications appear to be making the world seem smaller and interactions more immediate.

Gross domestic product (GDP) Measure of a nation's output and wealth.

Gross national product (GNP) Measure of a nation's output and wealth.

Gross Rating Points (GRPs) Determined by multiplying reach by frequency. They may be applied to any medium. The term used in the television industry is TVRs. (Also see TVRs.)

Guard book Whenever the media refer to an organisation or its products, these may be collected and stored for reference in a guard book.

Headlines Headlines are the most striking element of the copy (the words). They are words shown in the leading position. The headline works to gain attention and communicate the creative concept (the creative concept is also called the copy platform or creative theme). In radio, they appear as the main element in the creative treatment. In packaging, the product name and company name will be the equivalent concept.

Heuristics Problem-solving rules.

Hierarchy of effects models Models that describe the stages individuals are said to progress through in moving from initial unawareness to final action such as purchase and consumption. A range of models or ways of describing the stages in the process exist. One of the earliest models for the management of marketing communications is the Awareness–Interest–Desire–Action (AIDA) structure proposed in the nineteenth century by Elmo Lewis. Lewis's model proposes that buyers move from one state to the next on the way to consumption. It is the sequence of states that gives this type of model its form and many later models have adopted the idea of a sequence of states. They largely vary in the number of states and their description of those states. For example, Lavidge and Steiner suggested that the sequence should be Awareness–Knowledge–Liking–Preference–Conviction–Purchase. The link to Lewis's model is obvious. In all of the sequential models there are difficulties in researching the levels of awareness needed to proceed to the next stage, whatever its label, and it is a well-established fact that positive preferences do not automatically lead to consumption. Colley provided an alternative sequential model by relating it to the objective to be achieved. Colley's model has four stages which are essentially similar to those in the traditional sequential models (Awareness–Comprehension–Conviction–Action). The difference between Colley's approach and that of the sequential models is that Colley suggests that any stage could provide the objective for marketing communications independent of the rest. This model is usually known by the acronym DAGMAR (Defining Advertising Goals for Measured Advertising Results). By associating the sequence with management objectives and an indication that results could be measured, Colley took a step forward in the application of marketing communications theory. Information processing models help us to understand some of the cognitive functioning of these models. McGuire's hierarchy of information processing model proposes four stages that may be gone through when receiving and processing information, Exposure–Attention–Comprehension–Acceptance–Retention. A similar model is AILA,

Attention–Interpretation–Learning–Attitudes. Ehrenberg's Awareness–Trial–Reinforcement (ATR) model approaches the question of communications effects from a behaviourist perspective. Unlike the sequential models, Ehrenberg argues that buyers are generally very aware of the range of alternative products and brands available. He argues that buyers have considerable buying experience and that they follow relatively stable buying patterns. The communications emphasis is thus shifted to the reinforcement of benefits gained from previous consumption. This focus addresses the learning process with the aim of improving the prospects for the development of brand loyalty and future consumption.

High-context communications Most of the information of the communication relies on factors external to the communication itself; it relies on contextual cues to give it meaning. It requires a high level of interpretation by the receiver.

Hit rate Term used to describe the number of times a web page or site is visited.

Hypertext link Link (a web address or graphic) on a web page, a simple computer mouse click on which moves the viewer to a new web page.

Image and brand management The strategic and tactical tasks involved in the management of positive, 'non-personal' communication between an organisation and its audiences; recognising this should be complementary to customer/audience relationship management.

IMC Mix Model This is one of the three main models used throughout this book. It is the basis for Part 3. It identifies and categorises the range of marketing communications 'tools'.

IMC Process Model This is one of the three main models used throughout this book. It is the basis for Part 1. It describes the integrated marketing communications process from senders to receivers.

Impact (1) One of the four most significant concepts in media planning, the other three being reach, frequency and media cost. At a subjective level, 'impact' refers to the strength of impression made by a campaign or particular piece of marketing communication. It is a qualitative value. In part, 'impact' is achieved by the creative approach adopted, such as through the use of size, colour, typography, illustration and photography. But media selection and planning also play major parts through the right choice of media, positioning and repetition. For example, it is likely that a food advertisement would have a higher impact if it appeared in colour in *Good Housekeeping* than it would in black and white in the *Police Gazette*. This impact will be further increased by multiple insertions of the advertisement in the media to achieve effective reach.

Impact (2) An impact is another way the term 'impact' is used, and represents the actual exposure of an item of marketing communication when an opportunity to see or hear has actually taken place. For example, 'commercial impact' is a term used in television to represent the viewing of any commercial by a single viewer. Two impacts would be equivalent to one person seeing the commercial twice or two people seeing the commercial once. The UK population is exposed to over 650 billion commercial impacts per year.

Inbound telemarketing Receiving telephone calls *from* customers.

Incentives Inducements to encourage customers to take up offers.

Influencers Those people who exert an influence (positive or negative) on an organisation or its publics.

Infomercials Television commercials designed to convey large amounts of information.

Information processing The stages of thought that the individual goes through to convert incoming stimuli into useful knowledge.

Information stream The flow of information used in the integrated marketing communications planning process as part of the RABOSTIC planning model.

Innovation diffusion Term given to the process whereby a new product enters and is subsequently adopted by the market. Most frequently associated with the work of Carl Rogers who has proposed that diffusion and adoption is characterised by customers falling into a range of 'types'; innovators, early adopters, early majority, late majority and laggards.

Insertions Refers to the number of times an advertisement is placed in a medium. Discounts are available for multiple insertions.

Institute of Practitioners in Advertising One of a number of professional advertising industry bodies based in the UK.

Integrated marketing communications mix In its simplest form, the process of integrating all elements of the marketing communications mix across all customer contact points to achieve greater brand coherence.

Interference Like noise, interference creates message distortion. A distinction can be made between the two by suggesting that interference is deliberately generated noise.

Inter-media Refers to the media planners' decision of which medium to use between the media classes, i.e. the selection between TV, radio, cinema, press and posters (outdoor and transport). Some planners also include direct mail and the Internet as main media classes. Inter-media decisions are media decisions at the broadest level.

Inter-media decisions Choices made between media classes.

Intermercial The Internet version of a television commercial, which appears between viewing of web pages.

Internet Collection of globally interrelated computer networks that facilitate computer communications.

Intra-media Refers to media decisions within a media class. It involves the selection of specific media vehicles.

Intra-media decisions Choices made between different media vehicles.

Intranet Closed or private network on the Internet to which only specific users, internal to an organisation can gain access.

Involvement Important concept, which recognises that customers and consumers interest and degree of involvement in product purchase and use vary with different types of product, from low involvement (best typified by frequently purchased, low-value goods) to high involvement (best typified by high-value, infrequently purchased products).

ISO paper system Internationally agreed system of standard paper sizes.

ISPs Internet service providers – organisations that provide access to the Internet.

JICNARS Joint Industry Committee for National Readership Surveys. This body is responsible for producing the National Readership Survey.

JICPAR Joint Industry Committee for Poster Audience Research. This body is now responsible for taking forward the new initiatives in poster audience research. OSCAR (Outdoor Site Classification and Audience Research) has been used in the industry for some years to classify poster sites on the basis of passers-by. This presumed that passers-by had an opportunity to see, and sites were classified according to number of passers-by. POSTAR (Poster Audience Research) which came into force in February 1996, has now replaced OSCAR as a preferred measurement system. It covers 73,000 poster panels – the majority of all sites in the UK. It uses a measure of likelihood to see a poster panel and not just pass by it. What is now termed visibility-adjusted impact replaces the simple opportunity-to-see approach adopted by OSCAR. Transport advertising and tube advertising research are handled by other bodies such as TDI with their BAD (Bus Audience Data) and Trac (Tube Research and Audience Classification).

Joined-up thinking Term used by the Institute of Practitioners in Advertising to suggest evidence of a common thread or consistency seen running throughout a marketing communications campaign.

Joint or cooperative promotions Promotions undertaken jointly by two or more organisations for mutual benefit e.g. two or more manufacturers or service providers or manufacturer and trade intermediaries.

Key account management (KAM) The process and procedures for managing key accounts. (Also see Key accounts.)

Key accounts Usually taken to mean a major customer, but can best apply to any customer that the organisation has determined to be significant for whatever reason.

Knocking copy Text that offers negative or disparaging comments about someone or something else.

Lagged effect Describes the situation when there may be a time delay before there is a noticeable audience response to a piece of marketing communications.

Lead time Time required prior to the distribution date to ensure all print work is completed.

Levels of IMC Integration of marketing communications can be seen to occur on three levels which have been related to a military analogy; the level of a war (i.e. marketing communications throughout the whole of an organisation, the level of a campaign (i.e. as in a marketing communications campaign, and the level of skirmishes (i.e. little integration but short-term reactions to the market within the overall plan of campaign).

Lifestage Segmentation based on the different stages of life that people go through, incorporating such factors as age, marital status and family size. The Family Life Cycle (FLC) is an example of lifestage segmentation.

Lineage Advertising space that is bought by the line and presented in classified sections of the press.

Listenership (readership/viewership) Estimate of the size of an audience determined through research. Each of the main media has bodies responsible for producing relevant data. Readership is produced by multiplying the circulation of a publication by the average number of readers per copy. (Also see BARB, CAA, JICNARS, JICPAR, MVR, RAJAR.)

Lobbying Approaches to influence such bodies as the government and other persuasive groups to favour the interests of the lobbyist.

Locus of power The place where most power in a structure or system resides.

Low-context communications The communication is largely self-contained, and does not rely on contextual cues to convey its meaning.

Loyalty marketing Marketing activities intended to encourage customers to continue purchasing a particular product or purchasing from a particular supplier.

Loyalty schemes Sales promotions intended to encourage customers to continue purchasing a particular product or purchasing from a particular supplier. Such 'loyalty' is most often achieved through economic incentives.

Macro-environment (of marketing communications) The marketing communications macro-environment is the wider environment in which the organisation operates. It includes both internal *and* external factors that affect the organisation. In the marketing communications context, it incorporates the economists' ideas of macro *and* micro environments as well as internal organisational factors. (Also see Micro-environment, PEST and PRESTCOM.)

Mailshot Promotional material sent through the post.

Manufacturers consumer advertising (MCA) Advertising targeted at end-customers by the manufacturers themselves.

Market mavens These are people who know where to shop, who know all about different products and brands, and what are the latest promotions. Their views are valued and they receive prestige and satisfaction from supplying information to friends and others. They are sought after as major sources of advice. They are shapers and formers, they are market opinion leaders whose word of mouth can play a significant role in buyer and consumer behaviour.

Market research brief Document or verbal instruction outlining the market research problem and task.

Market research proposal Document outlining proposals designed to fulfil the research brief.

Market segmentation The process of dividing a market into homogeneous segments using one or a range of possible alternative segmentation methods, each segment being composed of customers or consumers sharing similar characteristics. (Also see Segmentation bases and Target marketing approaches.)

Market test Trial in the marketplace before full launch.

Marketing budget A frequently misleading term which usually refers to the advertising and promotions budget and not, as it implies, to the marketing expenditure allocated for all marketing activities.

Marketing communications Communications with target audiences on all matters that affect marketing performance.

Marketing communications campaign The performance and integration of all promotional marketing communications activities into a programme designed to achieve interrelated goals.

Marketing communications context The macro and micro environment in which marketing communications take place.

Marketing communications media In its widest sense, *anything* that is capable of carrying or transmitting marketing communications messages.

Marketing communications mix The range of activities/tools available to an organisation to communicate with its target audiences on all matters that affect marketing performance.

Marketing communications plan Document that summarises the main issues and details of marketing communications activities, including relevant background information and marketing communications decisions.

Marketing communications process model Description of the principal elements involved in the process of communication between sender and receiver.

Marketing database technology The use of accurate customer and prospect customer information, competitor information, market information and internal company information stored on a computer database to focus marketing activities towards targets.

Marketing ethics The systematic consideration of marketing and marketing morality related to 4P issues (product, price, place, promotion).

Marketing mix Range of marketing activities/tools that an organisation combines and implements to generate a response from the target audience.

Marketing public relations (MPR) Those parts of public relations most focused towards marketing relevant activities.

Marketing/market research The information-gathering and analysis part of the marketing function that provides relevant information on which marketing decisions may be based and evaluated. Market research is that part of marketing research directed towards market information.

Mark-up Percentage or actual sum of money added to the fee charged to an agency by a supplier (e.g. printer). The marked-up total is then charged to the client.

MCA See Manufacturers consumer advertising.

McCracken's meaning transfer model States that distinctions of class, status, gender, age, personality and lifestyle types are all part of what a celebrity endorser transfers to the brand.

McGuire's hierarchy of information processing Exposure–Attention–Comprehension–Acceptance–Retention.

McKinsey's 7S approach to management Structure, Strategy, Skills, Staffing, Style, Systems and Shared Values.

Media budget This is the total amount of money available to the media buyer to purchase media time and space. The total media budget will be allocated to each of the mass media selected as part of the marketing communications plan. It is the task of the media buyer to purchase the media spots determined by the media planner at the best rates available, and to achieve cost savings wherever possible.

Media buyers Those responsible for buying media time and space in the mass media.

Media class Refers to the media as a main category, such as television, radio, cinema, posters, press, direct mail, the Internet, etc.

Media commission The financial commission given to advertising agencies and media independents by media owners when they buy advertising space or time.

Media cost Financial constraint is always an important element in media decision-making, as it is vital that media plans are both economic and efficient. Media objectives related to reach, frequency and impact have to be achieved within a media budget.

Media coup The ability to attract extensive media coverage (publicity) through a staged event, activity or news story.

Media independents Companies specialising in planning and buying media. They buy space and time (e.g. time spots on television) from media owners, and sell to agencies and advertisers. They, themselves, are not media owners.

Media inflation The rise in media prices year on year.

Media neutral planning Planners recognise the value of all media within a campaign and do not seek to presume a bias of one medium over another – each is chosen as the best fit for the job.

Media objectives Objectives that are specifically focused on media tasks, and which define the role of the media in furthering the marketing communications objectives.

Media plan Document containing the detailed description of which media, at what cost, are to be used when in a campaign. Frequently, the terms media schedule and media plan are used interchangeably.

Media planners Usually best applied to those responsible for planning the selection, scheduling and use of marketing communications mass media in advertising agencies and media independents.

Media releases Information passed to the media. This may take the form of press releases, video releases, media packs, and other documents and commentary.

Media research Part of marketing research focused on researching media selection and use.

Media schedule List of media vehicles with dates of insertions. Media schedules usually have accompanying data, such as sizes of ads, airtime, costs, TVRs/GRPs, and coverage. Sometimes schedules are referred to as media plans, because they contain most of the relevant information that would be included in a media plan.

Media vehicles The actual media within a media class. For example, *The Times, Cosmopolitan, Time* magazine, *Readers Digest* and so on are media within the 'Press' media class.

Media weight Way of describing the relative impact created by particular media.

Merchandising Range of sales promotions activities intended to ensure that products are easily available, and prominently and attractively displayed at point of sale.

Message research Part of marketing research focused on testing all aspects of creative messages.

Metaphor Association of one thing with another suggesting that the two are the same: e.g. 'He was a lion in battle.'

Micro-environment (of marketing communications) The marketing communications micro-environment is the immediate environment or surroundings in which marketing communications occur. This should not be confused with economists' views of the micro-environment. (Also see Macro-environment.)

Mind-set Particular way of thinking or view held.

Minimum threshold effect Describes the situation where a 'minimum' has to be spent before any discernible marketing communications effect can be noticed.

Mintzberg's 5 strategy Ps Mintzberg has proposed that there are five key marketing strategies that companies can adopt: Plan strategy, Ploy strategy, Pattern strategy, Position strategy and Perspective strategy.

Modelling Attempt to realistically represent the processes involved in marketing communications.

Monochrome Single colour or black and white.

Mood boards (Also known as concept boards). Collection of visual materials (e.g. drawings, collage, montage) to replace or complement a written description that reflects the essence of a product or its customers/consumers.

MOSAIC A commercially available geodemographic system which is obtainable for 16 countries and GlobalMOSAIC can analyse consumers across national markets to support the development of international strategies. In the UK there are 12 broad MOSAIC groups subdivided into 52 detailed types.

Multi- or full-service agency In contrast to an 'à la carte' agency, the full-service agency offers a complete and integrated range of marketing communications services. One-stop shop and though-the-line agency are associated terms.

Multimedia The use of many media forms; usually most associated with electronic media.

Multimedia stations Free-standing kiosks where computer access is facilitated either using CD-ROMs/DVDs or linked to other computers. These may be kiosks provided in retail stores, for example.

Multinational strategy Strategy recognising cultural diversity to develop marketing communications adapted to suit different countries.

MVR (Media Vision Research) In conjunction with BARB, MVR tracks, analyses and reports in-home video viewing. As the BARB panel of respondents are used, this provides single-source data, which allow video and TV viewing habits to be determined and cross-referenced.

Narrowcast Restricted radio, television, video and audio transmission.

National Readership Survey (NRS) Provides information about the readership of the main newspapers and magazines. A report is produced every six months covering a period of 12 months. The survey samples around 37,500 people, and uses computer-assisted personal interviewing methodology.

Negative returns effect Describes the situation where, although marketing budgets may be increased and more effort expended, the actual effect created is negative, not positive, and further effort is counter-productive unless significant changes are made.

Negative synergy Term used to represent the negative effects of not achieving synergy between integrated marketing communications elements. Lack of integration may not merely result in no synergistic benefits, but may actually result in detrimental consequences that could be caused through confusion, lack of effectiveness and efficiency, or misunderstanding.

Negotiation Attempt by two or more parties to reach an agreement where: (i) the parties can vary the terms; (ii) resource is scarce; (iii) agreement and conflict exist simultaneously.

Neighbourhood RISC Is a commercially available system that combines psychographics and geo-demographics to provide an insight into why particular brands are attractive to particular consumer groups and how best to design promotional campaigns that appeal to prospective purchasers. Customers or prospects are targeted by socio-cultural type rather than by demographics – it targets by attitudes rather than behaviour. Neighbourhood RISC subdivides consumers based on three key motivational types – from self-focused to socially conscious, from conservative to explorative, from locally focused to globally aware. This results is ten socio-cultural types; Explorers, Pleasure Seekers, Mobile Networkers, Avid Consumers, Social Climbers, Care Givers, Moral Guides, Traditionalists, Guardians and Survivors.

Net coverage/reach Total reach less allowance for duplication.

New media Usually most associated with new electronic media such as the Internet, interactive TV and electronic multimedia.

Noise Distortions created in the encoding or decoding process that can result in inaccurate interpretation of meaning.

Non-personal communications One-way communication (at a distance) with prospects and customers.

Non-probability sampling Sampling methods in which elements of a given population do not have an equal chance of being selected.

Non-sampling error Errors or inaccuracy caused through the research process that can be attributed to factors other than sampling errors.

Objective and task method Budgeting system whereby budgets are set based on a determination of the objectives to be achieved and the means by which they are expected to be achieved.

Objectives End results sought to be achieved.

Offers Propositions made to customers indicating what they will receive and what they will have to give.

Offline Use of an e-medium/computer disconnected from a modem.

Ohanian's celebrity endorser credibility scale Consists of Attractiveness–Trustworthiness– Expertise.

One-stop shop Term used to describe agencies that claim to offer complete marketing communications solutions. Through-the-line and full service agencies are associated terms.

One-way communications Communications from a sender to a receiver with no feedback or dialogue.

Online Use of a computer while linked via telephone modem to other computers.

Opportunities to see/hear (OTS/OTH) A measure of frequency. It is the number of times in a specified time period (e.g. the duration of a campaign) that an average member of the target audience is exposed to the media/message. One OTS or OTH is the opportunity for a target audience member to see or hear an item of marketing communication once. It represents the *potential* to see or hear. It is not a guarantee of the marketing communication's being seen or heard. (Also see Impact 2.)

Orchestration Graphic way of referring to the process of integrating marketing communications.

OTH See Opportunities to see/hear.

OTS See Opportunities to see/hear.

Outbound telemarketing Telephone calls *to* customers.

Outside-in approach to integrated marketing communications Way of looking at marketing communications by adopting a perspective that starts by first looking outside the organisation for direction and understanding of the task required, and then determines marketing communications by secondly considering the organisation itself. It is a perspective determined by playing the role of an outsider looking into the organisation.

Own-label brand Product that carries the name of the resellers – wholesalers or retailers – rather than the manufacturers, and is sold exclusively through the resellers' outlets.

Pack shot The pack shot is a visual of the product being promoted.

Packaging The 'clothing' the product appears in. It combines functional protection with a medium (the pack) for graphic design and product information.

Page impressions Improvement on 'hits' to measure Internet traffic. Page impressions require that the web page is used.

Pantone colours One of a number of colour-matching systems. Each colour on a colour swatch is made up of known combinations of process colours, and each is given its own unique reference number for easy identification.

Pareto principle Also known as the 80:20 rule, it appears to apply to many situations. For example, it is frequently observed that the majority of sales (80%) come from a minority of customers (20%).

Patti and Frazer's Creative Strategy Patti and Frazer have proposed seven alternative creative strategies that can be adopted in marketing communications (to their seven, an extra strategy has been included at the end; generic strategy, pre-emptive strategy, USP strategy, brand image strategy, positioning strategy, resonance strategy, affective strategy, and informational strategy.

Penetration Another term for reach.

Percentage of sales method Budgeting system whereby budgets are set by allocating a specified percentage of sales value. This method requires consideration of the means by which an appropriate percentage is determined and whether to base it upon past, current or future anticipated sales.

Perception The process of synthesising information to make sense of the world. People's perceptions of the same stimuli can vary.

Perceptual filter The means by which an individual reduces the multitude of stimuli to those to which attention can be paid. This is a largely involuntary action.

Perceptual map See Brand map.

Performance-related payment by results System whereby agency remuneration is linked to agreed performance criteria.

Permission marketing Narrowly, email promotions that offer opt-in or opt-out opportunities to recipients so that further marketing communications are only received by those who wish to receive future emails. More broadly, it relates to any marketing communications (e.g. direct mail) that offer opt-in and opt-out options.

Personal communications Two-way dialogue (face-to-face or at a distance) with prospects and customers.

PEST Environmental analysis framework representing the Political environment, the Economic environment, the Social environment, and the Technological environment. (Also see PRESTCOM.)

Photoboards and animatics these are alternatives to the storyboard using still photographs in the case of photoboards and animated drawings or 'rough-cut' photographs in the case of animatics that will be shown on video.

Photomatics Storyboard making use of still photographs rather than drawings.

Planning and decision-making process The sequence of decisions and activities involved in putting together a marketing communications plan.

Planning cycle The sequence of decisions and activities involved in putting together a marketing communications plan.

Planograms Diagrams or plans showing store and shelf layout.

Plates Where used, part of the print production process in which the image is transferred onto a metal plate ready for printing.

Point of purchase (POP) Term meaning the same as point of sale; favoured in the US.

Point of sale (POS) Marketing communications activities that take place where products are bought and sold.

Position Map See Brand map.

Positioning The relative perceptual position of one brand usually compared with competing brands although a range of positioning approaches are possible to achieve this. (Also see Positioning strategies.)

Positioning strategies Although it is typical to consider positioning in relation of one brand to another, there are a range of positioning strategies available to ultimately achieve this; by attribute, product characteristic or consumer benefit; by price/quality by use or application; by product user; with respect to product category; against a competitor; and cultural positioning.

POSTAR Poster Audience Research. See JICPAR.

Post-purchase dissonance Term coined by Leon Festinger to describe a psychological state in which there is some incongruity (dissonance) between two or more thoughts. The resulting inconsistency encourages the individual to modify their thoughts to be more compatible or harmonious. Dissonance when recognised is an unstable state of mind. Dissonance can occur at any time. Post-purchase dissonance occurs after the purchase has been made.

Post-testing The evaluation of marketing communications at the end of a campaign.

Premiums Range of sales promotion incentives in which customers are given something extra.

PRESTCOM An extended environmental and organisational analysis framework representing the Political environment, the Regulatory environment, the Economic environment, the Social environment, the Technological environment, the Competitive environment, the Organisational environment, and the Market environment.

Pre-testing Evaluation of marketing communications elements before their use at the start of a campaign.

Pre-vetting The process of checking and approving advertisements before they are released.

Price sensitivity The more customers are price sensitive, the more they are affected by small changes in price.

Primary medium The medium that is singled out as being the most important or effective within a campaign. It is *likely* to be the one that accounts for the biggest spend, but not necessarily so.

Primary research Primary research is always gathered first hand. It is customised to suit the research problem. It can be exploratory in nature, or it may have conclusive measurement of some sort as the deliberate aim. (Also see Qualitative and Quantitative research.)

Prime position An advertisement appearing in a particularly advantageous position, such as front or back cover.

Print production The physical process involved in producing finished printed marketing communications.

Printing Processes There are a range of printing processes generally available: Letterpress, Offset lithography, Gravure, Flexography, Screen, Ink-jet, Laser. They vary in quality and speed of output.

Probability sampling Sampling methods in which all elements of a given population have an equal chance of being selected.

Process colours Particular colours of printing ink (cyan, magenta, yellow and black) that when combined in printing produce full colour prints. (Also see CMYK inks.)

Process measures Rather than measuring the effects of outcomes of activity (e.g. sales or awareness), an alternative approach is to assess or measure the activity or process itself.

Product Refers to brands, goods, services and any specific object of promotion, and can include, for example, events and personalities.

Product life cycle Sales of products are said to display their own life cycle over a period of time. The life cycle has a series of stages that include introduction, growth, maturity, saturation, and decline. Different marketing communications efforts are more or less appropriate in the different life cycle stages

Product marketing public relations/Corporate marketing public relations Two areas of marketing public relations focused towards the corporate and product brands respectively.

Product match-up hypothesis Hypothesis stating that a celebrity endorser's image should match as closely as possible to a product's characteristics if the promotion is to be credible.

Product placement The process of arranging for a company's products to be seen or referred to in the media such as during television and radio programmes, videos, video games and cinema films.

Product planner prompts Prompts or cues provided in the form of a table as guidelines to telesales operators.

Product portfolio analysis Assessment of an organisation's range of products in relation to each other. A variety of approaches may be adopted, of which the Boston Consulting Group Matrix tends to be most widely reported.

Production The department or agency section responsible for arranging for all work to be produced based on original concepts provided by the creatives.

Project-by-project billing System whereby the agency charges the client for each individual project it undertakes.

Promotions Term used interchangeably with marketing communications. Traditionally identified as one of the four key components of marketing.

Proof A draft representation of a printed product, for the client to determine if the indicated result will be satisfactory. It becomes a 'contract' proof when the client and printer agree that it shows an acceptable quality of print.

Psychogalvanometer A device that measures galvanic skin response, which is the electricity generated by chemical changes on the skin. It is like a 'lie-detector'. A respondent is 'wired' up to the machine, and then shown marketing communications in the form of stimulus material. There is no doubt that the device measures changes in the level of emotional arousal, but whether this is a positive or negative outcome in any specific instance appears to be open to interpretation.

Psychographic segmentation Segmentation based on psychological dimensions such as values, lifestyles, attitudes, interests and opinions.

Public relations (PR) The planned and sustained effort to establish and maintain goodwill and mutual understanding between an organisation and its publics.

Publics Term favoured by the public relations profession, referring to the many target audiences that communications may be focused towards.

Pull promotional strategy The focusing of promotional effort to encourage end-customers and consumers to demand goods and services.

Pulsing Term used to describe the media-scheduling pattern.

Pupilometer A device used to assess commercials as well as print advertisements, and measures the extent to which the pupils in the eyes of the respondent dilate in response. It relies on natural human responses to pleasant stimuli. Greater dilation (pupils become bigger) suggests a positive response to the stimulus material.

Push promotional strategy The focusing of promotional effort by manufacturers or suppliers of goods and services to encourage the trade channel members to stock, promote and sell products.

Qualitative research Qualitative research is an in-depth, investigative approach with an discretion on the part of the interviewer to 'dig and delve' into the interviewees' responses as necessary. There are four methods of data collection commonly employed in qualitative research: Depth interviews, Duos' interviews, Focus groups and Case histories. The aim of qualitative research is to find out what 'relevant others' think (e.g. target consumers about aspects of a possible TV advertisement), and to uncover whatever issues are important in the situation. Such an approach is only feasible on a relatively small sample, and there is deliberately no intention to measure anything, except in broad, relative terms. So, findings from such research are illustrated with 'flavoursome' quotes, rather than percentages. While the samples used may be deemed to be representative of the target market/audience, this does not mean representative in a statistical sense.

Quality of Integration Assessment Profile An approach to be used to assess the extent to which marketing communications are integrated across a range of dimensions. (Also see Continuum of integrated marketing communications and Dimensions of integrated marketing communications.)

Quantitative research Quantitative research is designed to explain what is happening and the frequency of occurrence. It is an approach that has measurement as its main aim, and reported findings are usually illustrated with percentages. Of necessity, samples are relatively large in size, with the intention of creating statistical validity.

RABOSTIC planning model This is one of the three main models used throughout this book. It is the basis for Part 2. It is an acronym for: Research and analysis, Audience, Budget, Objectives, Strategy, Tactics, Implementation, Control. These elements are part of the Research and Decision-making Cycle. The model also includes an Information Stream, a Planning Cycle and the Organisation and Management of IMC.

RAJAR Radio Joint Audience Research. This body is jointly owned by the BBC and the Commercial Radio Companies Association. It is responsible for conducting national and local surveys for the radio industry as a whole on a quarterly basis.

Reach Also referred to as coverage or penetration. With frequency, impact and media cost it is one of the four most significant concepts in media planning. It is a measure of how many members of the target audience are reached by a medium or collection of media used in a campaign. Reach may be measured as a percentage or actual number. Reach is the number of target audience members exposed to the media/message *at least once* during a specified time period (e.g. duration of a campaign). Related terms are exposure, GRPs, TVRs and Duplication.

Readership (viewership/listenership) Estimate of the size of an audience determined through research. Each of the main media has bodies responsible for producing relevant data. Readership is produced by multiplying the circulation of a publication by the average number of readers per copy. (Also see BARB, CAA, JICNARS, JICPAR, MVR, RAJAR.)

Recall Evaluation of message content on the basis of aided (prompted) or unaided (unprompted) recollection of the stimulus material.

Recognition Evaluation of message content on the basis of an awareness of the marketing communication.

Reference group Group of people to whom an individual relates such that her/his behaviour is potentially influenced by that of others in the group. There are many possible groups that may act as a reference group: family, peers, work colleagues, professional bodies, social groups, etc.

Relationship marketing View that emphasises the importance of the relationships developed between an organisation and other parties including customers, partners, suppliers and the trade.

Repetition One of the ironies in copywriting is that copy should be kept brief and to the point but repetition is widely used to good effect and to create emphasis and memorability.

Re-positioning Process of encouraging changed perceptions of a brand in the marketplace in comparison with competing brands.

Research and decision-making cycle The circular process of analysing, deciding and evaluating marketing communication plans and actions.

Retainer Fee paid by the client to its agency, usually on a regular basis, to retain the services of the agency. The fee is calculated to recompense the agency fairly for work it anticipates carrying out.

Roll-out The incremental process of launching a marketing initiative into the market area by area until full market coverage is achieved.

ROP Run of paper – advertisements appearing in the non-classified sections of newspapers and magazines.

Rossiter and Percy's five communications effects Category Need, Brand Awareness, Brand Attitude, Brand Purchase Intention, Purchase Facilitation.

Roughs or dummies Drawings or computer graphics indicating what the finished artwork will look like for any printed medium, e.g. packaging, posters, and press advertisements.

Routine problem-solving Characterised by habit, this form of decision-making involves little consideration of alternatives.

Sales promotion Widely used term covering a myriad promotional activities, excluding advertising, PR and personal selling. Sales promotion is associated with free offers, price deals, premium offers, and other promotions including merchandising, point-of-sale displays, leaflets and product literature.

Salience Term given to represent the degree of 'relevance' a brand may have to a customer/consumer. The concept of salience recognises that it will vary between customers, and that brand values are not determined in terms of there being a single best brand.

Sampling error Inaccuracy caused through selecting a sample rather than the population as a whole.

Scamps Drafts or 'roughs' of creative ideas that are produced cheaply to be used for pre-testing and evaluation purposes.

Schemas Foundations of understanding. Schemas are remembrances of experiences that allow us to make sense of our environment and determine suitable courses of action, by recognising linkages and similarities with previous experience.

Schramm's communications process Schramm identified the communications process as consisting of four elements: sender, message, media and receivers. The IMC Process Model is a more sophisticated development from this simple model.

Screen saver Not strictly meeting the definition as a form of advertising, screen savers have become a popular form of promotion.

Script (1) Repetition of previous behaviour.

Script (2) Written description of sound and motion advertisements/promotions giving the dialogue to be used and outline of what the advertisement is to be.

Search engine Website that maintains an index of other web pages and sites that may be searched using keywords. Access to other sites is facilitated by hypertext links – links that may be simply clicked on to move from one web page to another.

Secondary media (support media) Secondary media may also be referred to as support media. In an integrated campaign a range of media will be used, and although it is possible to use the media equally, it is more likely that emphasis will be placed on one medium – the primary medium. The other media will be used in a supporting or secondary capacity. (Also see Primary medium.)

Secondary research Secondary research is often known as 'desk research'. A key characteristic is that it is always gathered from existing, published sources (i.e. 'second-hand' or secondary material).

Segment Group of individuals who are expected to respond in a similar way to an organisation's marketing activity.

Segmentation bases Demographics, Geographics, Geodemographics, Psychographics (lifestyle and personality), Behavioural.

Self-image The personal perception or image of oneself.

Self-liquidating offer Sales promotion that pays for itself.

Self-regulation Voluntary control of acceptable marketing communications agreed by the marketing communications industry itself.

Semi-display advertisements Unlike full display, semi-display advertisements have creative restrictions placed on them, with limited or no graphics and limited typeface options.

Semiotics The scientific discipline of studying the meanings associated with signs, symbols and brands.

7 stages of personal selling (traditional) Prospecting and evaluating, Preparing, Approaching the customer, Making the presentation, Overcoming objections, Closing, Follow-up.

7Ps Way of classifying the marketing mix into seven categories: Product, Price, Promotion, Place, People, Process and Physical evidence.

Share of market Brand sales represented as a percentage of total market sales for all relevant competing brands.

Share of voice Concept that refers to how 'loud' one brand's marketing communications are compared with other competing brands. It may be measured in terms of marketing communications spends, or by subjective assessment of the relative attention created by competing marketing communications.

Sign A sign is anything that signifies something.

Simile Comparison of one thing with another using the words 'like' or 'as': e.g. 'He fought like a lion in battle.'

Slogans Also called strap lines and tag lines. These terms essentially mean the same thing. Examples include 'BMW: The Ultimate Driving Machine', 'Mars: Helps You Work Rest and Play'.

SMARRTT objectives An acronym that represents the level of detail that objectives should aim to achieve. It is a development from 'SMART' objectives that are referred to by some other authors. SMARRTT objectives are Specific, Measurable, Achievable, Realistic, Relevant, Targeted and Timed.

Socio-economic segmentation The classification of consumers on the basis of education, income and occupation.

Solus position An advertisement appearing with no other advertisement around it.

Spam emails Emails containing general information sent to a wider audience who have not requested the email (typically based on an email list, perhaps bought from a list broker or another company).

SPIN® selling Developed by Rackham, SPIN®, selling is designed to draw out the customer's explicit needs through a process of investigation involving the use of Situation questions, Problem questions, Implication questions, and Need pay-off questions.

Split-run Different versions of the same advertisement are published in the same issue, but not in the same copy of the publication. It is an approach that can be used to test advertisements.

Sponsorship Contribution to an activity by an organisation. Although sponsorship may be purely altruistic, it is normally undertaken with the expectation of achieving benefit for the sponsor, e.g. in achieving corporate or marketing-related objectives.

Spot colour Area of single or solid colour.

Stakeholders Term used to describe the many and various groups of people who have an interest or involvement with an organisation. Stakeholders include suppliers, customers, consumers, investors, employees and distributors.

Standardisation strategy The use of similar or identical marketing communications across countries.

Storyboard A series of images for a proposed moving sequence (TV, video, cinema, CD-ROM/DVD, Internet) indicating the progression of images, voice-over, and music proposed.

Strap lines See slogans.

Strategic business unit (SBU) Strategically significant and identifiable part of a larger organisation. It may be a particular section of an organisation, or even a company within a larger group of companies.

Strategic gap The difference in position between where an organisation wants to be at a specific point in time in the future (its objectives) and where it would anticipate being at that time if it simply carried on with its current activities.

Strategy The general means by which objectives are intended to be achieved.

Strong force Advertising seen as a strong force suggests that it has a direct and positive impact on sales.

Sub-culture Subdivision of a main culture with its own set of behavioural norms. A distinct cultural group that exists as an identifiable segment within a larger, more complex society. (Also see Culture.)

Sub-headings Sub-heads are sectional headlines that break up the text and provide focus of attention on key points.

Substrate Any material which is used to print on to e.g. paper, card and plastic.

Support media See Secondary media.

SWOT Organisational analysis framework representing organisational Strengths, Weaknesses, Opportunities and Threats.

Symbolic appeals The brand communications' appeal to consumers' desire for self-enhancement, group membership, affiliation and belongingness.

Symbols Things that represent, stand for, or are associated with something else.

Synergy The effect of bringing together marketing communication elements in a mutually supportive and enhancing way so that the resulting whole is greater than the sum of its parts.

Tachistoscope This is a simple device based on a photographic slide projector. Images are presented quickly and respondents are asked to report what they remember. The procedure gives an indication of the impact and quality of an advertisement or point-of-sale display.

Tactics Details of how strategies are intended to be achieved.

Tag lines See slogans.

Target audience Those individuals or groups that are identified as having a direct or indirect effect on business performance, and are selected to receive marketing communications.

Target market Market segment selected for specific targeting.

Target marketing approaches Undifferentiated marketing (mass marketing), Differentiated marketing, Concentrated marketing, Niche marketing, and Mass customisation marketing. Additionally, in international contexts, Global marketing and Global Niche marketing. (Also see Market segmentation and Segmentation bases.)

Targeting The selection of one or more market segments.

Teleology The idea that morally right actions benefit the greatest number of people.

Television Rating Points (TVRs) Said to be the main currency in television advertising. TVRs are an estimate of the audience for a TV advertisement, and are determined through BARB data. They are in effect index numbers that represent the proportion of the potential viewing audience.

Test market This is the use of a representative small geographical area of the total target market to facilitate a controlled experiment in which one or more proposed marketing actions are trialed. Test marketing assesses the viability of a new product, new market or new marketing communications before embarking on a full launch.

TGI Target Group Index; one of the largest continuous pieces of consumer research conducted in the UK. It involves around 24,000 respondents annually, and is produced by the British Market Research Bureau. It is an example of one of a number of surveys conducted by a variety of research companies that provide consumer data. TGI provides information about buying habits across thousands of branded products (some 2500), and includes data about the media habits, attitudes and opinions of respondents. It is an extremely valuable source of consumer and media information.

3Ms model Summary of the resource requirement for campaign management including Men (personnel requirements), Money (financial requirements), and Minutes (timing requirements).

Through-the-line agency Term used to describe agencies that claim to offer complete marketing communications solutions. Full service and one-stop shop agencies are associated terms.

Through-the-line communications Marketing communications that span both above- and below-the-line activities.

Tie-ins Multiple products involved in a single sales promotion.

Tint Process of breaking a solid colour into a series of dots or lines. Through this process, tones or tints of a colour are achieved by varying the amount or size of dots or lines for printing: the lower the concentration, the lighter the tint appears.

Top-down budgeting System whereby budgets are set by senior management, disaggregated, and passed down to lower management.

Total set The complete set of alternative choices in a decision.

Tracking studies The evaluation of marketing communications at various stages during their use. In this way, effects may be monitored throughout a campaign and modifications to the marketing communications plan introduced if necessary.

Trade allowances Incentives provided to trade buyers in the form of extra allowances such as special purchase terms.

Traffic (1) Describes the function that ensures that the development and production of agency work is completed to deadline through all the various stages from initial brief, through creative solutions, to final production. It is a crucial part of agency operations.

Traffic (2) Can refer to passers-by (as in poster measurement), or to the number of viewers of web pages (also called hits).

Transactional marketing Marketing in which the emphasis is placed on each individual purchase situation in contrast to relationship marketing. The increased focus placed on developing long-term customer relationships in today's marketing is considered to be a major shift in marketing philosophy. (Also see Relationship marketing.)

Transactional selling Selling where the emphasis is simply placed on achieving the sale and following the steps proposed to a successful sale.

Triangulation of budget decisions Means of determining final budgets by using a variety of methods and comparing the results from each before making a final decision.

Trigger words Words or phrases from which ideas most easily develop.

Turf battles Discussions and disagreements between groups of employees from different parts of an organisation, each favouring their own points of view. This is associated with power struggles within organisations between individuals and sections.

Two-way asymmetric communications Communications from a sender to a receiver with little or delayed feedback, producing a non-direct dialogue.

Two-way symmetric communications Direct dialogue between a sender and receiver of communications.

Umbrella branding Product branding in which the brands are closely related to other brands or the overall corporate brand.

Unique selling persona Uncommon term, used to describe a key element of a brand's personality.

Unique selling proposition (or point) (USP) Term coined by Rosser Reeves to suggest that advertising strategy (and by implication other marketing communications) works best if there is a single, clear and unequivocal selling proposition.

Up-selling Selling related products such as upgrades to customers who have purchased the product previously.

'Unitised' communications This is an uncommon term, used here to distinguish between marketing communications that promote the organisation as a whole (corporate communications) and those that promote parts or 'units' of the organisation, such as its goods, services, brands, individuals or sections of the organisation.

VALS Values and Lifestyles is a psychographic segmentation approach developed by SRI in which individuals are classified based on enduring personality traits and purchase behaviour. VALS places western consumers into one of eight segments, the main dimensions of which are primary motivation (horizontal dimension) and resources (vertical dimension). VALS recognises three primary motivations which people have a tendency to pursue, these being *ideals, achievement* and *self-expression.* The extent to which their wishes may be turned into reality is restricted by their resources. These eight types are Innovators, Thinkers, Believers, Achievers, Strivers, Experiencers, Makers and Survivors. The Japanese version of VALS, by contrast, divides society on the basis of two key consumer attributes: life orientation and attitudes to social change. Japan-VALS identifies four primary life orientations: *traditional ways, occupations, innovation,* and *self-expression.* Based on these the system identifies ten segments that lie at the core of most Japanese consumer markets; Integrators, Self-Innovators, Self-Adapters, Ryoshiki Innovators, Ryoshiki Adapters, Tradition Innovators, Tradition Adapters, High Pragmatics, Low Pragmatics and Sustainers.

Verified Free Distribution (VFD) Certification given to circulation figures of free distribution press when their circulation figures have been independently audited. (See ABC.)

Vertical communications Internal communications between different hierarchical levels of employees, e.g. between managers and their subordinates.

Vicarious learning Learning from the experiences of others, not by one's own direct experience.

Viewership (readership/listenership) Estimate of the size of an audience determined through research. Each of the main media has bodies responsible for producing relevant data. Readership is produced by multiplying the circulation of a publication by the average number of readers per copy. (Also see BARB, CAA, JICNARS, JICPAR, MVR, RAJAR.)

Viral marketing Email promotion that encourages recipients to pass on what they have received to others who they think will be interested.

Virtual agencies Term used to describe the selection of specialist individuals from different agencies or from within an agency group to work together as though they were members of the same agency.

Voice-pitch analysis (VOPAN) This measures the extent to which a respondent's voice pitch differs from its own norm when asked questions while viewing stimulus material.

Watershed The time up to which television advertising and programming are rigorously restricted. After the watershed, more adult material is considered acceptable.

Weak force Advertising seen as a weak force suggests that advertising works through a process of reinforcing and maintaining brand values and defending market share. Its effect on sales is therefore less direct.

Web/home page A web page is like a file available through the World Wide Web, typically containing text, images and links to other pages. An organisation's web site is likely to contain a collection of web pages, each with its own file reference (html address). A home page is an organisation's starting page.

Weighted ratings points Rating points weighted to reflect the likely impact of a medium: the higher the weighting compared with other media, the greater the anticipated impact generated by the medium.

WOM See Word of mouth communications.

Wordage Advertising space that is bought by the word and presented in classified sections of the press.

Word-of-mouth communications Literally, verbal communication between individuals. Word-of-mouth is typically a part of the total process of marketing communications in which messages are transmitted from the sender to many receivers. Word-of-mouth communications are the conversations held between the receivers, whether or not all members received the original marketing communication. Opinion leaders and other reference group members may have a strong influence on the effectiveness of the original intended message.

World Wide Web Huge collection of documents and files available through the Internet.

Xenophilia An affinity or liking for things foreign.

Young's five-step creative process Young's sequential process for developing creative ideas involves immersion, digestion, incubation, illumination, and verification.

Index

Notes
1. Page numbers in **bold** indicate **definitions** in glossary and **highlighted** terms in text
2. Most references are to the United Kingdom, unless otherwise indicated
3. First names in brackets indicate the name is that of a firm

IMPORTANT: READ CAREFULLY

WARNING: BY OPENING THE PACKAGE YOU AGREE TO BE BOUND BY THE TERMS OF THE LICENCE AGREEMENT BELOW.

This is a legally binding agreement between You (the user or purchaser) and Pearson Education Limited. By retaining this licence, any software media or accompanying written materials or carrying out any of the permitted activities You agree to be bound by the terms of the licence agreement below.

If You do not agree to these terms then promptly return the entire publication (this licence and all software, written materials, packaging and any other components received with it) with Your sales receipt to Your supplier for a full refund.

SINGLE USER LICENCE AGREEMENT

❐ YOU ARE PERMITTED TO:

- Use (load into temporary memory or permanent storage) a single copy of the software on only one computer at a time. If this computer is linked to a network then the software may only be installed in a manner such that it is not accessible to other machines on the network.

- Make one copy of the software solely for backup purposes or copy it to a single hard disk, provided you keep the original solely for back up purposes.

- Transfer the software from one computer to another provided that you only use it on one computer at a time.

❐ YOU MAY NOT:

- Rent or lease the software or any part of the publication.

- Copy any part of the documentation, except where specifically indicated otherwise.

- Make copies of the software, other than for backup purposes.

- Reverse engineer, decompile or disassemble the software.

- Use the software on more than one computer at a time.

- Install the software on any networked computer in a way that could allow access to it from more than one machine on the network.

- Use the software in any way not specified above without the prior written consent of Pearson Education Limited.

ONE COPY ONLY

This licence is for a single user copy of the software
PEARSON EDUCATION LIMITED RESERVES THE RIGHT TO TERMINATE THIS LICENCE BY WRITTEN NOTICE AND TO TAKE ACTION TO RECOVER ANY DAMAGES SUFFERED BY PEARSON EDUCATION LIMITED IF YOU BREACH ANY PROVISION OF THIS AGREEMENT.

Pearson Education Limited owns the software You only own the disk on which the software is supplied.

LIMITED WARRANTY

Pearson Education Limited warrants that the diskette, CD rom or DVD on which the software is supplied are free from defects in materials and workmanship under normal use for ninety (90) days from the date You receive them. This warranty is limited to You and is not transferable. Pearson Education Limited does not warrant that the functions of the software meet Your requirements or that the media is compatible with any computer system on which it is used or that the operation of the software will be unlimited or error free.

You assume responsibility for selecting the software to achieve Your intended results and for the installation of, the use of and the results obtained from the software. The entire liability of Pearson Education Limited and its suppliers and your only remedy shall be replacement of the components that do not meet this warranty free of charge.

This limited warranty is void if any damage has resulted from accident, abuse, misapplication, service or modification by someone other than Pearson Education Limited. In no event shall Pearson Education Limited or its suppliers be liable for any damages whatsoever arising out of installation of the software, even if advised of the possibility of such damages. Pearson Education Limited will not be liable for any loss or damage of any nature suffered by any party as a result of reliance upon or reproduction of or any errors in the content of the publication.

Pearson Education Limited does not limit its liability for death or personal injury caused by its negligence.

This licence agreement shall be governed by and interpreted and construed in accordance with English law.